A PROPERTY LAW READER

CASES, QUESTIONS & COMMENTARY

Bruce Ziff

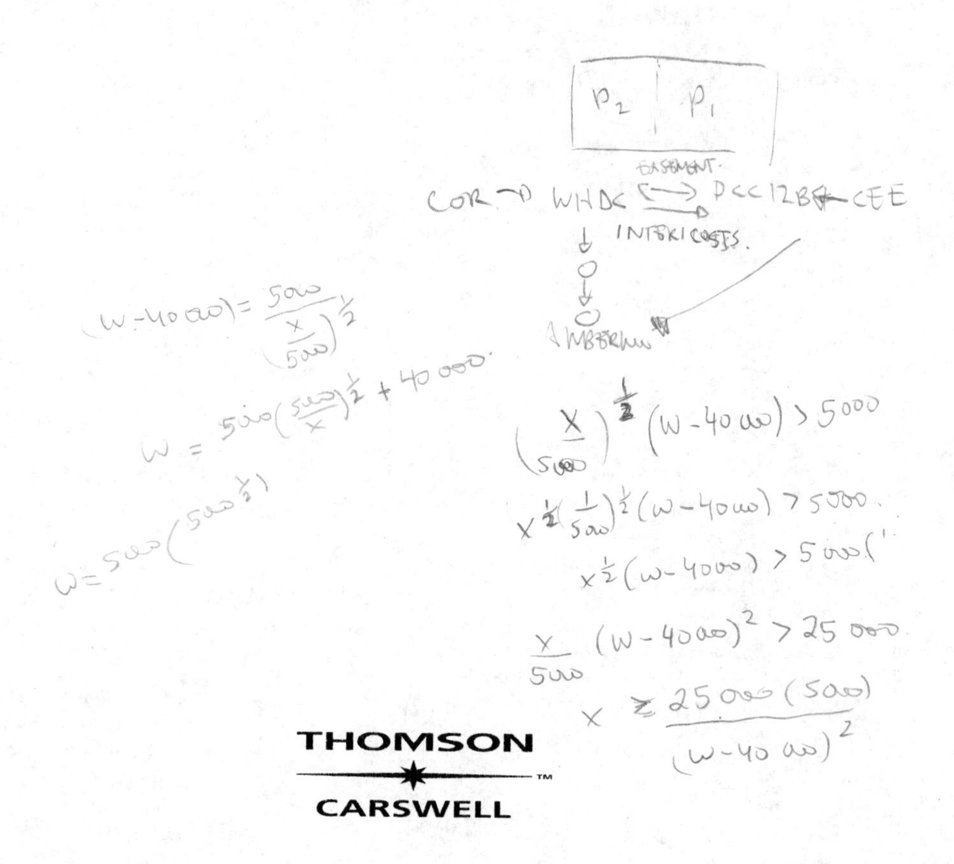

THOMSON
CARSWELL

National Library of Canada Cataloguing in Publication

Ziff, Bruce H
A property law reader : cases, questions and commentary / Bruce Ziff.

Includes index.
ISBN 0-459-24121-4

1. Property—Canada. I. Title.

KE618.A7Z53 2004 346.7104 C2004-901376-9
KF560.Z53

One Corporate Plaza
2075 Kennedy Road
Toronto, Ontario
M1T 3V4

Customer Relations:
Toronto 1-416-609-3800
Elsewhere in Canada/U.S. 1-800-387-5164
Fax 1-416-298-5094
www.carswell.com
carswell.orders@thomson.com

PREFACE

This collection of readings is designed for use in property law courses in Canada. Generally speaking, the topics track the contents of *Principles of Property Law*, and these materials have been designed to be used either with that textbook or as a standalone reader.

My goal is to provide a contemporary and contextual treatment of the law of property in the common law jurisdictions. The primary operating assumption is that property is taught in first year in Canadian law schools because it provides a foundation for an extensive array of upper-year courses and, later on, a grounding for a broad range of areas of practice. These basic subjects include Aboriginal law, intellectual property, environmental law, real estate conveyancing, municipal planning, poverty law, wills and trusts, family law, natural resources law, commercial transactions, taxation; the list could go on. The coverage found here reflects that function. A second premise is that fundamental principles and policies should be examined and critiqued. Such an approach is commonly adopted in legal education, but it is especially appropriate in the study of property. There is a great deal of provincial variation, prompting one to concentrate on the overarching principles. And a critical perspective is valuable because contentious issues abound. Property law is, after all, about the allocation of scarce resources; and that is the essence of politics.

I appreciate that there is a great deal of material in this book; probably too much for a single course. I am also aware of the very different treatments and orderings found among Canadian property course offerings. Time is limited; choices have to be made. What should be included? What should be stressed? My aim here is to provide as much breadth of substantive coverage as possible. At the same time, there are only about 100 principal cases contained within the 12 chapters; a modest number as these things go. The cases that are included, some of which are lengthy, are supposed to supply the depth. Many have been chosen because they contain useful expositions of law and policy.

Other touchstones have guided the selection process. I have looked far and wide for appropriate learning resources. In consequence, materials from a host of sources, disciplines, and jurisdictions have been included. Currency was another guiding factor. Property courses can sometimes take on the feel of a jaunt through English legal history. The law studied sometimes seems like a preface to the real law, which will eventually be studied in some other course. The imprint of ancient (sometimes very ancient) English doctrines on Canadian property law is undeniable; in some areas it is virtually indelible. Still, it is when arcane rules resurface in current controversies that their relevance to an understanding of property law is most apparent.

This project could not have been completed without the assistance of many people. I am grateful to have been granted permission to reproduce a number of published works; these have been listed elsewhere in the opening pages. The Faculty of Law at the University of Alberta provided funding for research assistance at various stages. Melodie Hope and Tracie Scott undertook the work; they were excellent. Tracie Scott also prepared two essays, both of which appear in Chapter 2. Todd Pinsky, Jackie Gervais-Jones and Michael Hodge provided production assistance at Carswell. I am appreciative of the support that I have received over the years from both my students, as well as my property-teaching colleagues at the University of Alberta – Cathy Bell, Rob Chambers and Moe Litman. And, as ever, thanks also to my loving family, Barb, Hannah and Eli.

My general cut-off date for the law is September 1, 2003.

Bruce Ziff
February 20, 2004

ACKNOWLEDGMENTS

We are grateful to the following individuals and publishers for permission to reproduce materials drawn from the following sources:

J.B. Baron, "Gifts, Bargains, and Form" 64 Ind.L.J. 155 (1989). Copyright 1989 by the Trustees of Indiana University. Reprinted by permission.

R.L. Barsh, "How Do You Patent a Landscape? The Perils of Dichotomizing Cultural and Intellectual Property" (1999) 8 I. J. C. P. 14.

B.J. Barton, *Canadian Law of Mining* (Calgary: Canadian Institute of Resources Law, 1993).

R.W. Bauman, "Property Rights in the Canadian Constitutional Context" (1992) 8 S.A.J.H.R. 344.

V.L. Been & Joel Beauvais, "The Global Fifth Amendment? NAFTA's Investment Protections and the Misguided Quest for an International 'Regulatory Takings' Doctrine", 78 N.Y.U.L.Rev. 30 (2003).

P. Butt, *Land Law*, 4th ed. (Sydney: Lawbook Co., 2001). Reproduced with permission by the Lawbook Co., part of Thompson Legal & Regulatory Limited.

R. Chambers, *An Introduction to Property Law in Australia* (Sydney: Lawbook Co., 2001). Reproduced with permission by the Lawbook Co., part of Thompson Legal & Regulatory Limited.

M. Conway, "Equity's Darling?" in S. Scott-Hunt & H. Lim, eds., *Feminist Perspectives on Equity and Trusts* (London: Cavendish, 2001).

N. Crago, "Bequests of Tangible Chattels in Succession" (1999) 28 U.W.A. L. Rev. 199.

J. Cribbett & C.W. Johnson, *Principles of the Law of Property* (Westbury, N.Y.: Foundation Pr., 1989).

R.C. Ellickson, "Property in Land", 102 Yale L.J. 1315 (1993).

R.A. Epstein, "Holdouts, Externalities, and the Single Owner: One More Salute to Ronald Coase", 36 J. of L. & Econ. 553 (1993).

A.J. Esau, "The Judicial Resolution of Church Property Disputes: Canadian and American Models" (2003) 40 Alta. L. Rev. 767.

P. Filion, *The Impact of Restrictive Covenants on Affordable Housing and Non-Single Family Use of Homes: A Waterloo Region Case Study* (1993).

M.A. Flagg, "Star Crazy: Keeping the Right of Publicity Out of Canadian Law" (1999) 13 I.P.J. 179.

T. Flanagan, *First Nations? Second Thoughts* (Montreal & Kingston: McGill-Queen's U.P., 2000).

J.W. Lem, "Annotation: *Unisys Canada Inc.* v. *York Three Associates Inc.*" (2002) 44 R.P.R. (3d) 140.

J. Lem, "Annotation" (2002) 50 R.P.R. (3d) 4.

J.W. Lem & B.G. Clark, "Annotation" (2002) 5 R.P.R. (4th) 2.

S. Levmore, "Variety and Uniformity in the Treatment of the Good-Faith Purchaser" 16 J. Legal Stud. 43 (1987).

C. Lewis, "The Right to Private Property in a New Political Dispensation in South Africa" (1992) 8 S.A.J.H.R. 389.

U. Mattei, *Basic Principles of Property Law: A Comparative Legal and Economic Introduction* (Westport Conn: Greenwood Pr., 2000). Reproduced with permission of Greenwood Publishing Group, Inc., Westport, CT.

L.A. McCrimmon, "Understanding the Rule Against Perpetuities: Adopting a Five-Step Approach to a Perpetuities Problem" (1997) 5 Aust. Prop. L.J. 130.

T.J. Micelli & F. Sirmans, "Partition of Real Estate; Or, Breaking Up is (Not) Hard to Do", 29 J. Legal Stud. 783 (2000).

L.A. McCrimmon, "Understanding the Rule Against Perpetuities: Adopting a Five-Step Approach to a Perpetuities Problem" (1997) 5 Aust. Prop. L.J. 130.

T. W. Merrill, "Property and the Right to Exclude", 77 Neb.L.Rev. 730 (1998).

P.A. O'Connor, "Security of Property Rights and Land Title Registration Systems" Ph.D. Thesis,Monash University (2003).

Ontario Law Reform Commission, *Report on Basic Principles of Land Law* (Toronto: A.G. (Ont.), 1996).

J.V. Orth, "Does the Fee Tail Exist in North Carolina?", 23 Wake Forest L. Rev. 767 (1988).

P.M. Perell, "A Commentary on *Amberwood Investments Ltd. v. Durham Condominium Corp. No. 123*" (2002) 50 R.P.R. (3d) 52.

W. Renke, "Homestead Legislation in the Four Western Provinces" in J.G. McLeod & M. Mamo, eds., *Matrimonial Property Law in Canada* (Toronto: Carswell, 1995).

T. Rotenberg, "The False Fiduciary" (2001) 41 R.P.R. (3d) 130.

D. Schneiderman, "NAFTA's Takings Rule: American Constitutionalism Comes to Canada" (1996) 46 U.T.L.J. 499. Reprinted by permission of University of Toronto Press Incorporated (www.utpjournals.com).

L.D. Smith, "Bailment With Authority to Mix and Substitute" (1995) 111 L.Q.R. 10.

E. Spring, *Law, Land, & Family: Aristocratic Inheritance in England, 1300-1800* (Chapel Hill: U.N.C. Pr., 1993). Copyright 1993 by the University of North Carolina Press.

D. Sugarman & R. Warrington, "Land law, citizenship, and the invention of 'Englishness': Thestrange world of the equity of redemption" in J. Brewer & S. Staves, eds., *Early Modern Conceptions of Property* (London: Routledge, 1995).

C.R. Vernon, "Life Lease Housing: An Ownership Alternative for Ontario Seniors" (2001) 37 R.P.R. (3d) 40.

P. J. Weiser, "The Internet, Innovation and Intellectual Property",103 Colum. L. Rev. 534 (2003).

T.G. Youdan, "The Length of a Title Search in Ontario" (1986) 64 Can. Bar Rev. 507.

J.s. Youngblood Henderson, "Mikmaw Tenure in Atlantic Canada" (1995) 18 Dal. L.J. 196.

B. Ziff, *Unforeseen Legacies: Reuben Wells Leonard and the Leonard Foundation Trust*(Toronto: Osgoode Society & U.T.P., 2000).

B. Ziff, "Restrictive Covenants: The Basic Ingredients" in *Special Lectures of the Law Society ofUpper Canada 2002, Real Property Law: Conquering the Complexities* (Toronto: Irwin Law, 2003).

B. Ziff, "Title Insurance: The Big Print Giveth, But Does the Small Print Taketh Away?" in D.Grinlinton, ed., *Torrens in the Twenty-first Century* (Wellington N.Z.: LexisNexis, 2003)

TABLE OF CONTENTS

CHAPTER 12: PRIORITIES AND REGISTRATION

TABLE OF CASES

CHAPTER 1
THE NATURE OF PROPERTY

1. INTRODUCTION

Two short vignettes help to explain the goals of this introductory chapter.

The first relates to the photograph. I came across that peculiar sign at a for-profit health clinic in Scotland some years ago. It is easy to understand in an intuitive way the sense in which the phrase "strictly private" is being used here. But what does the idea of *private* property mean? The question is raised because the audacious message carries with it a veiled threat. A failure to obey can produce legal consequences: one might suffer the humiliation of being carted off the property by the police and perhaps charged criminally, or be sued in a court of law. There is a distinct *public* dimension to the edict, for the state may be called upon to take action. Therefore, the protected interest here is not, strictly, private at all. Moreover, one can think about the relevant "property" as comprising the building and grounds of the clinic. However, the critical aspect about this situation is that the rights asserted serve to frame a relationship among *people* — in this instance as between the owner of the property and any would-be entrant.

The second story is drawn from the largely unremarkable case of *Bowen Estate v. Bowen* 2001 CarswellOnt 3149, 42 E.T.R. (2d) 1 (S.C.J.). There, a court was called upon to determine the validity of a clause of a will under which the deceased (the testator) had directed the trustees of his estate to draw the name of one of six persons and to award a platinum diamond ring to the person selected by this lottery. The clause was found to be valid. The case is interesting because it prompts one to think in general about the manner in which we allocate goods. As *Bowen* illustrates, in a world of scarce resources it is perfectly acceptable for a person to be entitled to a valuable object through the combined forces of affection, whimsy and luck.

This chapter, then, explores the meaning of property in law, especially private property, and compares that form of entitlement with other conceptions of ownership. It also considers how we seek to justify the rules for the distribution of goods that currently exist under law.

At the beginning of one's legal education it is tempting to seek the comfort that certainty seems to offer. However, one learns that the image of law as a science with bright-line concepts and cut-and-dried answers is a mirage. In fact, indeterminancy abounds. Nowhere is that more apparent than when confronting the meaning of property in law and the arguments used to justify the forms that property rights take.

2. THE "PROPERTIES" OF PROPERTY

C. Lewis, "The Right to Private Property in a New Political Dispensation in South Africa" (1992) 8 S.A.J.H.R. 389, at 393-5 [footnotes omitted]

What is meant by "Property"? . . .

In Anglo-American jurisprudence . . . there is much debate over the meaning of the term "property", and as to its coherence as a legal concept. . . . C.B. MacPherson, for example, has argued that the use of the term to designate things, or to designate exclusive individual rights to private property, is inappropriate. Property, he maintains, is a right, not a thing, and we must distinguish between different kinds of property, namely common property, private property and state property. "As soon as any society," says MacPherson "by custom or convention or law, makes a distinction between property and mere physical possession it has in effect defined property as a right . . . Property is a claim that will be enforced by society or the state, by custom or convention or law."

Jeremy Waldron, however, makes clear the distinction between rights and objects, stating:

> The concept of property is the concept of a system of rules governing access to and control of material resources. Something is to be regarded as a material resource if it is a material object capable of satisfying some human need or want. In all times and places with which we are familiar, material resources are scarce relative to the human demands that are made on them. (Some, of course, are scarcer than others.) Scarcity, as philosophers from Hume to Rawls have pointed out, is a presupposition of all sensible talk about property. If this assumption were ever to fail (as Marx believed it some day would) then the traditional problem of the nature and justification of rival types of property system would probably disappear.

On the other hand, Thomas C. Grey takes the view that the manifold use of the term property is an indication that property no longer exists as a meaningful legal concept. He discusses several senses of "property" to support his thesis that property is no longer a coherent category in legal thinking. The Law of Property is, for law teachers and students, the body of law concerned with the use of land, of real estate. Lawyers and economists, by contrast, identify property rights with rights in rem as distinguished from rights in personam . . .

A third meaning of "property" arises from the purposive account of it given by some economists who include among property rights all the entitlements whose purpose is to "advance allocative efficiency by allowing individuals to reap the benefits and requiring them to bear the costs generated by their activities." Such an account would also include personality rights, but would exclude welfare and social security entitlements. A fourth, and contrasting, meaning would, on the basis that the purpose of private property is to protect security and independence, include what Charles Reich called the "new property" — public law entitlements to welfare and social security.

Yet another view is possible on an interpretation of the provisions of the American constitution prohibiting expropriation ("taking for a public purpose") without compensation: the property that can be taken, says Grey, has been "reified" into "things" or "pieces of property". Thus a deprivation of the right to use airspace has not been regarded as a "taking" because it is not "sufficiently thing-like to be subject to the just compensation requirement."

A sixth usage distinguishes between property and liability rules according to the nature of the sanctions imposed on violation. Property rules are enforced by injunction . . . or criminal sanctions, whereas liability rules are enforced by the award of money damages. But, as Grey points out, this conception differs widely from common usage, since ownership, for example, is protected by both property and liability rules . . .

T. W. Merrill, "Property and the Right to Exclude" 77 Neb.L.Rev. 730 (1998) at 730-9 [footnotes omitted]

I. Introduction

The Supreme Court is fond of saying that "the right to exclude others" is "one of the most essential sticks in the bundle of rights that are commonly characterized as property." I shall argue in this Essay that the right to exclude others is more than just "one of the most essential" constituents of property — it is the *sine qua non*. Give someone the right to exclude others from a valued resource, i.e., a resource that is scarce relative to the human demand for it, and you give them property. Deny someone the exclusion right and they do not have property.

Of course, those who are given the right to exclude others from a valued resource typically also are given other rights with respect to the resource — such as the rights to consume it, to transfigure it, to transfer it, to bequeath or devise it, to pledge it as collateral, to subdivide it into smaller interests, and so forth. These other rights are obviously valuable and important, and it is not improper to speak of them as part of the standard package of legal rights enjoyed by property owners in most contexts. My claim is simply that in demarcating the line between "property" and "nonproperty" — or "unowned things" (like the air in the upper atmosphere or the resources of the ocean beyond a certain distance from shore) — the right to exclude others is a necessary and sufficient condition of identifying the existence of property. Whatever other sticks may exist in a property owner's bundle of rights in any given context, these other rights are purely contingent in terms of whether we speak of the bundle as property. The right to exclude is in this sense fundamental to the concept of property . . .

II. The Right to Exclude and the Concept of Property

Within the existing literature about the institution of property, there is a broad consensus about several propositions. This consensus does not extend, however, to the precise role that the right to exclude plays in defining that institution. I will briefly enumerate the principal points of consensus, and then turn to the disagreement over how to characterize the role of the right to exclude.

A. Points of Consensus

First, nearly everyone agrees that the institution of property is not concerned with scarce resources themselves ("things"), but rather with the rights of persons with respect to such resources. A copy of Tom Wolfe's latest novel sitting in a bookshop is a scarce resource. But considered solely as an object, it is not property. The book can be characterized as property only by invoking certain rights that persons have with respect to it. For example, the book might be said to be the property of the bookshop, meaning that the bookshop has certain rights with respect to the control and disposition of it. Or the book might be said to be the property of a customer who has purchased it from the bookshop, in which case the customer would have certain rights with respect to the control and disposition of it.

Similarly, there is a consensus that the concept of property includes the rights of persons with respect to both tangible and intangible resources. Most people understand, at least in some dim fashion, that Tom Wolfe has something called a "copyright" in the contents of the book he has written, and that this copyright is Wolfe's property. They understand this to mean that Wolfe has certain rights with respect to reproduction of the book, and that these rights are separate and distinct from the rights that exist with respect to particular physical copies of the book.

There is also a consensus that property means something different than mere possession. In both lay and legal understanding, to speak of possession of scarce resources is to make a statement of fact about which persons are in control of particular resources. Property, in contrast, refers not to a statement of fact but to a norm (or norms). Thus, if I pick up a copy of Tom Wolfe's book in the bookstore and start to read it, I can be said to be in possession of the book. But I cannot be said to own it; it is the property of the bookshop until I pay for it. Moreover, it is understood that property rights generally trump possessory rights. After reading the Tom Wolfe novel in the bookshop for 15 minutes, the shopkeeper may ask me either to buy it or put it down. The shopkeeper is entitled to make this demand, since the bookshop has a property right in the book superior to my possession of it.

Given that property is a norm, there is also a consensus that property cannot exist without some institutional structure that stands ready to enforce it. The usual assumption is that this institution is the state. But it is also possible that it is meaningful to speak of property rights in contexts governed by less formal enforcement mechanisms, such as social ostracism. Thus, it may be possible to speak of property rights in library carrels, or in particular bedrooms in homes, where it is understood that certain persons have normative claims to these scarce resources and that these claims will be enforced by the common consent of those who participate in a particular social unit. With respect to most controversies of concern to lawyers, however, property rights "are created and their dimensions are defined by existing rules or understandings that stem from an independent source such as state law — rules or understandings that secure certain benefits and that support claims of entitlement to those benefits."

Finally, there is a consensus that the concept of property is not limited to private property, but includes also what may be called common property and public property. Private property may be said to exist where one person or a small number of persons (including corporations and not-for-profit organizations) have certain rights with respect to valuable resources. Common property may be said to exist where all qualified members of a particular group or community have equal rights to valuable resources. An example would be a common pasture open to all members of a particular village for the grazing of livestock. Public property may be said to exist where governmental entities have certain rights with respect to valuable resources, analogous to the rights of private property owners. An example would be a municipal airport.

In sum, there is a general consensus that property refers to particular rights of persons or entities with respect to scarce tangible and intangible resources; that property is distinct from and superior to the mere possession of resources; that the rights associated with property require some institutional structure that stands ready to enforce these rights; and that property may be private, common, or public.

B. Three Schools of Thought Regarding the Right to Exclude

There is, however, much less consensus regarding the nature and content of the particular rights that persons have when they are said to have property. In particular, although it is widely agreed that someone who has property in a resource typically will have at least some right to exclude others from using or interfering with that resource, there is disagreement about how central this right is to the understanding of property. Generally speaking, it is possible to identify three different intellectual traditions regarding the role of the right to exclude. These may be called "single-variable essentialism," "multiple-variable essentialism," and "nominalism."

Probably the oldest continuing tradition in attempts to define property is essentialism — the search for the critical element or elements that make up the irreducible core of property in all its manifestations. The patron saint of property essentialism is William Blackstone, the first full-time law professor at an English-speaking university. In fact, Blackstone endorsed not one but two essentialist definitions of property, corresponding to what I call the single-variable and the multiple-variable versions.

The first or single-variable version of essentialism posits that the right to exclude others is the irreducible core attribute of property. Thus, Blackstone I:

> There is nothing which so generally strikes the imagination, and engages the affections of mankind, as the right of property; or that sole and despotic dominion which one man claims and exercises over the external things of the world, in total exclusion of the right of any other individual in the universe.

Under this conception, the right to exclude ("sole and despotic dominion") is both a necessary and sufficient condition of property. Many other scholars in succeeding generations, including Jeremy Bentham, have also appeared to endorse some such notion. Perhaps the best-known exposition of this perspective was provided by the philosopher and New Deal lawyer Felix Cohen. His posthumously-published Socratic dialogue on the nature of private property considers a number of attributes commonly associated with property, and through the positing of examples and counterexamples concludes that only the right to exclude is invariably connected with all forms of property. Cohen vividly summarizes his discussion in a manner suitable for memorialization on the blackboard:

> That is property to which the following label can be attached:
> To the world: Keep off X unless you have my permission, which I may grant or withhold.
> Signed: Private citizen
>
> Endorsed: The state.

Single-variable essentialism also finds extensive if somewhat qualified support in the decisions of the contemporary U.S. Supreme Court. The Court has said of the right to exclude that it is "universally held to be a fundamental element of the property right;" that it is "one of the most essential rights" of property; and that it is "one of the most treasured" rights of property. Although all these statements imply that the right to exclude is not the only right associated with property, no other right has been singled out for such extravagant endorsement by the Court. Moreover, the Court's decisions suggest that governmental interference with the right to exclude is more likely to be considered a taking of property without compensation under the Fifth Amendment than are interferences with other traditional elements of property.

The second version of essentialism, also found in Blackstone, posits that the essence of property lies not just in the right to exclude others, but in a larger set of attributes or incidents, of which the right to exclude is just one. Thus, Blackstone II: "The third absolute right, inherent in every Englishman, is that of property: which consists in the free use, enjoyment, and disposal of all his acquisitions, without any control or diminution, save only by the laws of the land." This version of essentialism holds that property is defined by multiple attributes or incidents. Blackstone describes these multiple attributes as the rights of "free use, enjoyment, and disposal." Curiously, the right to exclude others — which as we have seen is elsewhere deemed by Blackstone to be the defining element of property — fails to make an appearance on this list. Moreover, it would seem that the rights of "free use" and "enjoyment" are arguably redundant, or at least largely overlapping. But these anomalies have been overlooked in subsequent accounts, which have translated the Blackstonian trilogy as the rights of "possession, use, and disposition," or alternatively, the rights to exclude, to use or enjoy, and to transfer.

Under the multiple-variable version of essentialism, the right to exclude is a necessary but not a sufficient condition of property. Without the right to exclude, there is no property. But more than the right to exclude is needed in order to create a package of rights sufficiently impressive to be called property.

This multiple-variable essentialism has also been defended by later generations of commentators. The most elaborate of these efforts is that of Tony Honore, an Oxford legal scholar, who sought to identify the "standard incidents of ownership" that are present when an individual is the "full owner" in a mature, liberal legal system. He concluded that there are eleven such incidents: (1) the right to possess; (2) the right to use; (3) the right to manage; (4) the right to the income of the thing; (5) the right to the capital; (6) the right to security; (7) the incident of transmissibility; (8) the incident of absence of term; (9) the duty to prevent harm; (10) liability to execution; and (11) the incident of residuarity. Honore conceded that not all of these incidents are present in all cases in which we speak of property. But they represent the paradigm of full ownership, against which various types of incomplete or partial ownership must be understood.

Multiple-variable essentialism also finds some support in the Supreme Court's decisions. On several occasions, the Court has stated that "property rights in a physical thing have been described as the rights 'to possess, use and dispose of it.'" This of course is the modern variant on Blackstone's original trilogy of rights.

The third school, which I call nominalism, views property as a purely conventional concept with no fixed meaning — an empty vessel that can be filled by each legal system in accordance with its peculiar values and beliefs. On this view, the right to exclude is neither a sufficient nor a necessary condition of property. It may be a feature commonly associated with property, but its presence is not essential; it is entirely optional. A legal system can label as property anything it wants to.

Although traces of the nominalist conception can be found in the Nineteenth Century, it is basically a product of the Legal Realist movement of the Twentieth. For the Realists, property was not defined by a single right or definitive trilogy of rights. Rather it is a "bundle of rights." Moreover, this bundle has no fixed core or constituent elements. It is susceptible of an infinite number of variations, as different "sticks" or "strands" are expanded or diminished, added to or removed from the bundle altogether. Thus, the Realists understood that the universe of things called property is purely a matter of social convention. Perhaps the most influential figure in the development of the nominalist perspective was Wesley Hohfeld. Although Hohfeld apparently never used the bundle of rights metaphor, his analysis of legal concepts as a series of bipolar "jural relations" laid the ground work for a conception of property as a collection of socially-contingent entitlements.

Subsequent Legal Realist scholars took Hohfeld's jural relations and derived from it an extreme form of nominalism. As one Realist writer, Walter Hamilton, stated in an entry on "Property" in the 1937 edition of the *Encyclopedia of the Social Sciences*, property is nothing more than "a euphonious collection of letters which serves as a general term for the miscellany of equities that persons hold in the commonwealth." The American Law Institute's *Restatement of Property*, published in 1936, adopted a similarly open-ended definition of property.

This sort of extreme nominalism continues to be found in contemporary writing about property. For example, in an influential essay, Thomas Grey has argued that the concept of property has so many variations and specialized uses that its meaning has "disintegrated." He concludes, in keeping with the sceptical position of the Realists, that "the specialists who design and manipulate the legal structures of the advanced capitalist economies could easily do without using the term "property" at all."

Today, the nominalist conception is more-or-less the orthodox understanding of property within the American legal community. Law students have been instructed for years that the bundle of rights metaphor accurately captures the nature of the institution of property. The Supreme Court has also jumped on the nominalist bandwagon, and has on many occasions itself described property in terms of the bundle of rights metaphor (albeit often in a context where the Court also says that the right to exclude is "among the most essential" of the bundled rights).

These three schools of thought — single-variable essentialism, multiple-variable essentialism, and nominalism — do not exhaust the possibilities with respect to understanding of the nature of property. One of the most sophisticated modern expositions of property by a philosopher is that of Jeremy Waldron. Borrowing a distinction developed by Ronald Dworkin, Waldron argues that private property is best understood as a general "concept," of which the various incidents or elements catalogued by Honore and others embody different "conceptions." He defines the general concept of private property as the understanding that, "in the case of each object, the individual person whose name is attached to that object is to determine how the object shall be used and by whom. His decision is to be upheld by the society as final." This general concept, Waldron argues, takes on different conceptions in different contexts, depending on the type of resource involved, the traditions of the legal system, whether ownership is unified or divided, and so forth. For example, agricultural land may be subject to different types of restrictions on use than is personal property.

From the vantage point of this essay, Waldron's account can be seen as a combination of single-variable essentialism and nominalism. His definition of the core concept of private property — giving a named individual "final" authority to determine how resources "shall be used and by whom" — bears a strong family resemblance to Blackstone's sole and despotic right to exclude. Waldron would not define property solely in terms of this feature, however, but depicts property as morphing into a variety of conceptions in a manner consistent with the bundle of rights metaphor associated with nominalism. For example, he argues that the right of inheritance is entirely contingent and that one could have a system of private property with or without inheritance, without affecting the conclusion that the system was still one of private property . . .

QUESTIONS

1. What implications flow from the absence of a full consensus about the core meaning of the term property?

2. As Professor Merrill notes, private property is often contrasted with common or public (state) property. Consider first the idea of common property. Merrill gives as an example of this form, "a common pasture open to all members of a given village for the grazing of livestock." Some economists distinguish between two forms of common property. One is described as open access. Here, as the name implies, there are no restrictions on the right of access. Everyone is entitled; no one can be excluded lawfully. By contrast, the common pasture described by Merrill is sometimes referred to by economists as communal property. In what way, if at all, does the idea that everyone has a right to open access goods differ from the idea that for such goods no property rights exist? In what ways, if at all, does communal property differ from private property?

3. Property is described as "public" when the right of exclusion is reposed in a governmental authority. In what way, if at all, do or should the rules associated with public property differ from those applicable to private ownership?

Yanner v. Eaton
(1999) 166 A.L.R. 258 (Australia H.C.) [footnotes omitted]

[Murrandoo Yanner, a member of the Gangalidda tribe of Aboriginal Australians, used a traditional harpoon to kill two juvenile estruarine crocodiles. The meat and skins were used for non-commercial purposes. Yanner was charged with taking fauna without legal authority under Queensland's *Fauna Conservation Act 1974* (the "*Fauna Act*"). Under paragragh 54(1)(a) of that Act "a person shall not take, keep, or attempt to take or keep fauna of any kind unless [that person] is the holder of a licence, permit, certificate or other authority granted and issued under this Act."

Yanner asserted that he was exercising his native title right to hunt as protected by the *Native Title Act 1993(Cth.)*. Section 211 of that Act allows native title holders to exercise and enjoy such rights for personal, domestic or non-commercial communal needs, even where a general law prohibits the activity. The classes of activities protected include hunting, fishing, gathering and cultural or spiritual activities.

At trial, Murrandoo Yanner's clan was held to have had a pre-colonization connection within the area from which the crocodile had been taken, and that the hunting of juvenile estuarine crocodiles has a cultural and spiritual significance to the Gangalidda tribe. However, it was submitted that even if there had once been a native title right to hunt estuarine crocodiles, the *Fauna Act* had extinguished that right in 1974 when estuarine crocodiles were declared to be protected fauna. Critical to this argument was section 7 of the *Fauna Act*, which states as follows:

> All fauna, save fauna taken or kept during an open season with respect to that fauna, is the property of the Crown and under the control of the Fauna Authority.

(Section 7 was amended in 1984. The words "otherwise than in contravention of this Act" were inserted after the phrase "taken or kept". "Nothing turns on this amendment": Judgment of Gummow J. at n. 108.)

According to Australian native title case law (see especially *Mabo v. Queensland (No.2)* (1992) 175 C.L.R. 1 (Australia H.C.)), a pre-existing native title right will be extinguished by the granting of an inconsistent right. Thus, it was argued that section 7 of the *Fauna Act* extinguished this native title right in 1974, could not be revived by the *Native Title Act,1993*. So, the case turned on the interpretation of section 7 of the *Fauna Act* that made fauna "property" of the Crown. If the High Court interpreted this section so as to give the Crown absolute or full beneficial ownership of fauna, Yanner's right to hunt estuarine crocodiles would have been extinguished in 1974, and therefore it it would afford no defence to the charge under the *Fauna Act*. If, however, this Act gave the Crown less than full beneficial ownership, Yanner's right to hunt would be protected by the *Native Title Act*, and he would be exempt from the licencing requirement.]

Gleeson C.J., Gaudron, Kirby, and Hayne JJ.: . . .

"Property"

The word "property" is often used to refer to something that belongs to another. But in the Fauna Act, as elsewhere in the law, "property" does not refer to a thing; it is a description of a legal relationship with a thing. It refers to a degree of power that is recognised in law as power permissibly exercised over the thing. The concept of "property" may be elusive. Usually it is treated as a "bundle of rights". But even this may have its limits as an analytical tool or accurate description, and it may be, as Professor Gray has said, that "the ultimate fact about property is that it does not really exist: it is mere illusion". Considering whether, or to what extent, there can be property in knowledge or information or property in human tissue may illustrate some of the difficulties in deciding what is meant by "property" in a subject matter. So too, identifying the apparent circularity of reasoning from the availability of specific performance in protection of property rights in a chattel to the conclusion that the rights protected are proprietary may illustrate some of the limits to the use of "property" as an analytical tool. No doubt the examples could be multiplied.

Nevertheless, as Professor Gray also says, "An extensive frame of reference is created by the notion that 'property' consists primarily in control over access. Much of our false thinking about property stems from the residual perception that 'property' is itself a thing or resource rather than a legally endorsed concentration of power over things and resources."

"Property" is a term that can be, and is, applied to many different kinds of relationship with a subject matter. It is not "a monolithic notion of standard content and invariable intensity". That is why, in the context of a testator's will, "property" has been said to be "the most comprehensive of all the terms which can be used, inasmuch as it is indicative and descriptive of every possible interest which the party can have".

Because "property" is a comprehensive term it can be used to describe all or any of very many different kinds of relationship between a person and a subject matter. To say that person A has property in item B invites the question what is the interest that A has in B? The statement that A has property in B will usually provoke further questions of classification. Is the interest real or personal? Is the item tangible or intangible? Is the interest legal or equitable? For present purposes, however, the important question is what interest in fauna was vested in the Crown when the *Fauna Act* provided that some fauna was "the property of the Crown and under the control of the Fauna Authority"?

The respondent's submission (which the Commonwealth supported) was that s. 7(1) of the *Fauna Act* gave full beneficial, or absolute, ownership of the fauna to the Crown. In part this submission was founded on the dictum noted earlier, that "property" is "the most comprehensive of all the terms which can be used". But the very fact that the word is so comprehensive presents the problem, not the answer to it. "Property" comprehends a wide variety of different forms of interests; its use in the Act does not, without more, signify what form of interest is created.

There are several reasons to conclude that the "property" conferred on the Crown is not accurately described as "full beneficial, or absolute, ownership". First, there is the difficulty in identifying what fauna is owned by the Crown. Is the *Fauna Act* to be read as purporting to deal with the ownership of all fauna that is located within the territorial boundaries of the State but only for so long as the fauna is within those boundaries, or does it deal with all fauna that has at any time been located within those boundaries? That is, does the *Fauna Act* purport to give the Crown ownership of migratory birds only as they pass through Queensland, or does it purport to give ownership to the Crown of every bird that has ever crossed the Queensland border?

Secondly, assuming that the subject matter of the asserted ownership could be identified or some suitable criterion of identification could be determined, what exactly is meant by saying that the Crown has full beneficial, or absolute, ownership of a wild bird or animal? The respondent (and the Commonwealth) sought to equate the Crown's property in fauna with an individual's ownership of a domestic animal. That is, it was sought to attribute to the Crown what Pollock called "the entirety of the powers of use and disposal allowed by law".

At common law, wild animals were the subject of only the most limited property rights. At common law there could be no "absolute property", but only "qualified property" in fire, light, air, water and wild animals. An action for trespass or conversion would lie against a person taking wild animals that had been tamed, or a person taking young wild animals born on the land and not yet old enough to fly or run away, and a land owner had the exclusive right to hunt, take and kill wild animals on his own land. Otherwise no person had property in a wild animal.

"Ownership" connotes a legal right to have and to dispose of possession and enjoyment of the subject matter. But the subject matter dealt with by the *Fauna Act* is, with very limited exceptions, intended by that Act always to remain outside the possession of, and beyond disposition by, humans. As Holmes J. said in *Missouri v. Holland*: "Wild birds are not in the possession of anyone; and possession is the beginning of ownership."

Thirdly, there are several aspects of the *Fauna Act* which tend to suggest that the property in fauna conferred on the Crown may not easily be equated with the property an individual may have in a domestic animal. The property rights of the Crown would come and go according to the operation of the exception contained in s. 7(1) of fauna taken or kept "otherwise than in contravention of this Act during an open season with respect to that fauna". As open seasons were declared and fauna taken, what otherwise was the property of the Crown, ceased to be. Next there are the references in ss. 71(2) and 83(3) to forfeiture of fauna to the Crown. Even accepting that s. 84 says that these sections shall not prejudice or affect the rights of the Crown conferred by s. 7, why were ss. 71(2) and 83(3) necessary if the Crown owned the fauna? Then there are the provisions of s. 7(2) that "[l]iability at law shall not attach to the Crown by reason only of the vesting of fauna in the Crown pursuant to this section". The Crown's property is property with no responsibility. None of these aspects of the *Fauna Act* concludes the question what is meant by "property of the Crown", but each tends to suggest that it is an unusual kind of property and is less than full beneficial, or absolute, ownership.

Fourthly, it is necessary to consider why property in some fauna is vested in the Crown. Provisions vesting property in fauna in the Crown were introduced into Queensland legislation at the same time as provisions imposing a royalty on the skins of animals or birds taken or killed in Queensland. A "royalty" is a fee exacted by someone having property in a resource from someone who exploits that resource. As was pointed out in *Stanton v. Federal Commissioner of Taxation*:

> . . . the modern applications of the term [royalty] seem to fall under two heads, namely the payments which the grantees of monopolies such as patents and copyrights receive under licences and payments which the owner of the soil obtains in respect of the taking of some special thing forming part of it or attached to it which he suffers to be taken.

That being so, the drafter of the early Queensland fauna legislation may well have seen it as desirable (if not positively essential) to provide for the vesting of some property in fauna in the Crown as a necessary step in creating a royalty system. Further, the statutory vesting of property in fauna in the Crown may also owe much to a perceived need to differentiate the levy imposed by the successive Queensland fauna statutes from an excise. For that reason it may well have been thought important to make the levy as similar as possible not only to traditional royalties recognised in Australia and imposed by a proprietor for taking minerals or timber from land, but also to some other rights (such as warren and piscary) which never made the journey from England to Australia.

In light of all these considerations, the statutory vesting of "property" in the Crown by the successive Queensland fauna Acts can be seen to be nothing more than "a fiction expressive in legal shorthand of the importance to its people that a State have power to preserve and regulate the exploitation of an important resource". So much was acknowledged in the second reading speech on the Bill which first vested property in fauna in the Crown. The Minister said:

> It [the fur industry] is an industry that really belongs to the people, and although the Bill, amongst other things, makes it quite clear that the native animals of the State belong to the people of the State, I do not think there is any doubt in the minds of any one regarding that question already. The native animals belong to the people in just the same way as the timber and the minerals belong to the people, and they cannot be sold without permission.

Roscoe Pound explained why wild animals and other things not the subject of private ownership are spoken of as being publicly owned. He said:

> We are also tending to limit the idea of discovery and occupation by making res nullius (eg, wild game) into res publicae and to justify a more stringent regulation of individual use of res communes (eg, of the use of running water for irrigation or for power) by declaring that they are the property of the state or are "owned by the state in trust for the people." It should be said, however, that while in form our courts and legislatures seem thus to have reduced everything but the air and the high seas to ownership, in fact the so-called state ownership of res communes and res nullius is only a sort of guardianship for social purposes. It is imperium, not dominium. The state as a corporation does not own a river as it owns the furniture in the state house. *It does not own wild game as it owns the cash in the vaults of the treasury.* What is meant is that conservation of important social resources requires regulation of the use of res communes to eliminate friction and prevent waste, and requires limitation of the times when, places where, and persons by whom res nullius may be acquired in order to prevent their extermination. *Our modern way of putting it is only an incident of the nineteenth-century dogma that everything must be owned.*

The "property" which the *Fauna Act* and its predecessors vested in the Crown was therefore no more than the aggregate of the various rights of control by the Executive that the legislation created. So far as now relevant those were rights to limit what fauna might be taken and how it might be taken, rights to possession of fauna that had been reduced to possession, and rights to receive royalty in respect of fauna that was taken, (all coupled with, or supported by, a prohibition against taking or keeping fauna except in accordance with the Act 1975). Those rights are less than the rights of full beneficial, or absolute, ownership. Taken as a whole the effect of the *Fauna Act* was to establish a regime forbidding the taking or keeping of fauna except pursuant to licence granted by or under the Act . . .

The appeal should be allowed, the orders of the Court of Appeal of Queensland set aside and in lieu it should be ordered that the order *nisi* be discharged.

McHugh J. (dissenting): . . .

In its natural and ordinary meaning, s. 7 vests in the Crown, and takes away from everyone else, the right to deal with fauna as defined by the Act. Other provisions of the Act give a right to apply for a licence to take fauna. But s. 7 destroyed all existing rights to take fauna. At common law, the only right of property in wild animals was "the exclusive right to catch, kill and appropriate such animals which is sometimes called by the law a reduction of them into possession." That right arose from the possession of land on which the animals happened to be or from a Crown grant to enter another's land for the purpose of catching, killing or appropriating wild game. No doubt in Australia, the existence of common law native title rights meant that Aboriginals had similar rights over fauna.

Section 7 of the Act reverses the common law rules and vests all rights of catching, killing and appropriating fauna in Queensland in the Crown. It therefore gives to the Crown the sole right of catching, killing and appropriating fauna in Queensland together with the right to exclude every other person from catching, killing and appropriating that fauna. If the term "property" has any recognisable meaning in the Act, it must at least have conferred those rights on the Crown and taken them away from every other person once the Act was proclaimed . . .

Undoubtedly, s. 7 does more than give to the Crown the exclusive right to kill, take or appropriate fauna and to take away from others any pre-existing right to do those things. The section gives to the Crown every right, power, privilege and benefit that does or will exist in respect of fauna together with the right, subject to the Act, to exclude every other person from enjoying those rights, powers, privileges and benefits. That is the ordinary meaning of property, although, of course, the term can have a more limited meaning depending upon the terms of the instrument which creates it. Whatever else property may mean in a particular context, it describes a relationship between owner and object by reference to the power of the owner to deal with the object to the exclusion of all others, except a joint owner.

The appellant would have it that s. 7 has a more limited meaning than that set out in the previous paragraph. His argument suggests that the property in fauna in Queensland vests in the Crown only upon other persons taking or dealing with the fauna. Another version of the argument is that the Act has effectively created a new, negative form of property — that property in s. 7 is no more than a label which describes what the Crown notionally has after the Act has identified the circumstances in which others may take, possess and pay royalties to the Crown in respect of fauna.

If "property" in s. 7 meant no more than the residue of other people's rights or the measure of the Crown's entitlement to royalties, it would seem to serve little purpose, if indeed it serves any purpose at all. I see no indication in the Act that "property" in s. 7 has such a limited function or meaning. Words in legislative instruments should not be read as if they were buildings on a movie set — structures with the appearance of reality but having no substance behind them. When the Queensland legislature declared that the property in fauna is vested in the Crown, it should be taken to have meant what it said. That being so, the ordinary meaning of property should not be ignored. "Property" in s. 7 should not be taken as meaning no more than the residue of control over fauna which the Crown has after others have carved out their entitlements to take and keep fauna pursuant to a licence granted by or under the Act. That is to turn the Act on its head. The content of s. 7 is the starting point for, not the result of, determining the Crown's power over fauna in Queensland.

The short answer to the appellant's arguments is that s. 7 says that all fauna *is* the property of the Crown. Acts of Parliament speak from their enactment. Consequently, the ordinary and natural meaning of s. 7 is that, after the commencement of the Act, the property in fauna is and always remains in the Crown until it disposes of it or a person, acting in accordance with the Act, puts an end to the Crown's property in particular fauna. Moreover, the fauna is and remains "under the control of the Fauna Authority." To the absolute rule that property in fauna in Queensland is in the Crown, s. 7(1) contains an exception — when fauna is taken in open season in accordance with the Act, the property in the fauna passes to the person who has taken it. However, I cannot see how that exception provides any ground for thinking that the nature of the property that the Crown has in the fauna is less than every right, power, privilege and benefit that does or will exist in respect of the fauna or that from the commencement of the Act the Crown did not have the right to exclude every other person from enjoying those rights, powers, privileges and benefits. To contend that the Crown obtains no property in fauna until it is taken, killed or appropriated is to deny the plain words of s. 7(1).

It is also to deny the assumption on which s. 7(2) of the Act is based. That assumption is that, but for s. 7(2), the Crown's ownership of the fauna might make it liable for the damage or harm that particular birds or mammals might cause while at large.

Consider also some of the consequences of upholding the appellant's arguments. The Crown would obtain property in fauna only when a bird, mammal or declared animal was killed, taken, or otherwise appropriated by a third party. Presumably, the Crown would lose its property as soon as the third party gave up possession of it — at all events if that party set the bird or mammal free. The arguments of the appellant must also mean that "the control of the Fauna Authority" only commences when a third party has killed, taken or appropriated fauna. Presumably, the hapless officers of the Authority, seeing an unlicensed person about to kill or otherwise take or deal with fauna, would have no statutory authority to act until the unlicensed person takes action. Until death, taking or appropriation had occurred, the officers would have no more legal authority to act to protect the bird or mammal than any other citizen.

The appellant contended that it would be absurd for the legislature to have intended that the Crown should have property in wild animals before they were caught. Illustrations were given during argument — the migratory bird flying through Queensland being one example. Once it is perceived that the purpose of the Act is to put an end to arguments about who has the property in or the right to hunt fauna as defined, I see nothing absurd in the legislature of Queensland giving to the Crown the property in all fauna in Queensland — even migratory birds. In any event, it leads to no more absurd results than the opposing contention which would vest property in the Crown when a young boy trapped a migratory bird but would divest it when he let it go, making property in fauna in Queensland depend upon a kind of statutory version of what old system conveyancers called springing and shifting uses.

Nor is there anything unusual in a person having property in an object of which he or she is unaware. The common law has long recognised that a person may have property in an object although he or she was unaware of its existence. Thus in *R. v. Rowe*, an indictment for larceny charged the accused with stealing a piece of iron from the bed of a canal and laid the property in the iron in the canal owner who apparently did not know of its existence. The Court of Crown Cases Reserved held that the indictment was good.

By declaring (s. 7) that the property in fauna in Queensland is vested in the Crown and then in subsequent sections defining the circumstances in which others may take that property, the Act proclaimed upon its commencement that henceforth no one, land owner, Aboriginal or holder of a grant from the Crown, had any right to kill, take or appropriate fauna as defined. That being so, the appellant had no right which the *Native Title Act* protected when it came into force . . .

The appeal must be dismissed.

NOTE

The concurring opinion of Gummow J. has been omitted, as has the dissenting opinion of Callinan J.

QUESTIONS AND COMMENTS

1. How did the majority define property within the meaning of the *Fauna Act*? What was Justice McHugh's definition? Which do you prefer?

2. Categorize the definitions of "property" found in *Yanner* using the labels proposed by Professor Merrill.

3. Although one often sees property described as a bundle of rights, it is also commonplace to emphasize that property involves duties/responsibilities/obligations. It is certainly the case that few, if any, property rights are not constrained in some way under law. The use of a parcel of land in a Canadian urban centre is likely to be controlled by dozens of rules emanating from the municipal, provincial and federal levels of government. Is it sensible to regard these as inherent features of ownership?

In *Backhouse v. Judd* [1925] S.A.S.R. 16 (S.C.) the idea that duty is integral to ownership arose in the context of an allegation of cruelty to animals. There, the owner of certain horses was convicted of negligently failing to provide proper and sufficient food contrary to the *Prevention of Cruelty to Animals Act 1908*. Liability for this omission could be found only if there was a duty to provide proper care. Napier J. held (at 20-1) that the duty arose from ownership of the animals:

> When a penalty is imposed for failure to supply, it presupposes a public duty to supply. In default of any duty otherwise expressed or defined in the Act itself, and in default of any pre-existing duty to which the intent may reasonably be referred, this imposition of the penalty must be understood to create the duty, leaving the Courts to define it as best they may, and to evolve their own answers to the questions which necessarily arise — On whom is the duty imposed? when does it arise? and how may it be discharged? Having regard to the scope of the Act, it is impossible to suppose that the subsection is referable to the pre-existing legal duties which I have mentioned. The only possible meaning is that here, as in other respects, the Statute is intended to give legal force and efficacy to obligations which are already accepted as social duties, and as binding, in conscience, upon civilized people. The Statute presupposes the existence of some such moral duty, and provides for its enforcement. It assumes that the Courts will be able to ascertain and define the proper scope and limits within which this duty ought to be enforced. This method of legislation simplifies the task of the draftsman; but the Courts have no authority to do more than expound the intention expressed by Parliament, and it might have been more satisfactory if the Legislature had been able to indicate its intentions more definitely.
>
> In my view . . . the scope of the penalty is to be confined in cases of which it can be said that they fall quite clearly within the moral duty, as it is accepted (or, to speak more accurately, as the Courts may think that it must be accepted) by every reasonable member of this community. If this is so, I think that it must be restricted to people who have in some way accepted the responsibility for the care and keeping of the animal. If the duty had been voluntarily undertaken by contract, or in any other case, where it already exists as a legal obligation due to the owner, I see no reason why the section should not apply to punish the omission as a violation of the public right. Apart from cases of this sort, it seems to me that the only satisfactory basis for the duty is that of ownership. There is nothing novel in the idea that property is a responsibility as well as a privilege. The law which confers and protects the right of property in any animal may well throw the burden of the responsibility for its care upon the owner as a public duty incidental to the ownership. In this form, and subject to the limitations implied by the language of the sub-section, I think that the general sense of the community must certainly recognize the moral obligation. I think, therefore, that the proper view of the section is that the owner of the animal is the person who is primarily charged with the duty of supplying it with proper and sufficient food and water. He may relieve himself of that burden by procuring it to be undertaken, or by taking proper and sufficient steps to have it discharged, by

someone else. If he has done so, there may be a failure to supply, but the failure is not due to his act or neglect, and does not fall within the scope of the penalty. But in every case the obligation must be so restricted as to exclude a failure which is unavoidable owing to the necessities of the case, or to circumstances which could not have been foreseen by reasonable diligence. This, again, is implicit in the words of the subsection — "wantonly or negligently."

4. Among the elements found within the bundle, does there exist a basic right to destroy one's own property? That question arose in the case of *Re Wishart Estate* 1992 CarswellNB 69 (Q.B.), which involved the will of one Clive Wishart. At the time of his death, Wishart had owned four horses. His will directed the executors to "have my horses shot by the Royal Canadian Mounted Police and then buried". The executors applied to the court for directions as to whether this provision was valid.

The case received press coverage in Canada and the United States; petitions were signed, and letters were sent to the courthouse. One, written by a young girl, was reproduced in the judgment. It read: "DEAR JUDGE, PLEASE DON'T LET ANYONE KILL THE HORSES. I LOVE HORSES BUT MY DAD WON'T LET ME HAVE ONE. I WILL BE SAD IF THEY GET KILLED. FROM JENNIFER."

The evidence was that Wishart treated these animals as pets and was devoted to them. His direction was motivated, it was concluded, by the desire to ensure that they would not be mistreated after his death. At the hearing, the New Brunswick S.P.C.A. undertook to supervise the care of the animals. Accordingly, Justice Riordan held that "[t]his should satisfy what I see, from what I have heard, as the real intention and desire of Clive Wishart, that the horses not be abused and be properly cared for". Yet it was added that, if this construction of the will was in error, the clause would be contrary to public policy and hence void. (The doctrine of "public policy," which can be invoked to invalidate property dispositions, is addressed in Chapter 7.) Riordon J. said:

> Obviously public policy is a very general term, difficult to define and a determination of what is against public policy can of course be subjective. In my opinion, the destruction of four healthy animals for no useful purpose should not be upheld and should not be approved. To destroy the horses would benefit no one and would be a waste of resources and estate assets even if done humanely. It is my conclusion that to destroy Barney, Bill, Jack and King as directed in the Will would be contrary to public policy. The direction in the Will is therefore void.

What if Wishart had decided to put the horses down during his lifetime? Indeed, what if he decided to take all of his hard-earned property and destroy it in a bonfire. Should he (we) be permitted to do so?

5. In *Eyerman v. Mercantile Trust Co. N.A. et al.* 524 S.W.2d 210 (Mo. C.A., 1975), which was cited in *Re Wishart*, an attempt was made to distinguish between the rights of owners while alive, and the will-making power:

> While living, a person may manage, use or dispose of his money or property with fewer restraints than a decedent by will. One is generally restrained from wasteful expenditure

or destructive inclinations by the natural desire to enjoy his property or to accumulate it during his lifetime. Such considerations however have not tempered the extravagance or eccentricity of the testamentary disposition here on which there is no check except the courts.

In the early English case of *Egerton v. Brownlow*, 10 Eng. Rep. 359, 417 (H.L.C. 1853), it is stated: "The owner of an estate may himself do many things which he could not (by a condition) compel his successor to do. One example is sufficient. He may leave his land uncultivated, but he cannot by a condition compel his successor to do so. The law does not interfere with the owner and compel him to cultivate his land (though it may be for the public good that land should be cultivated) so far the law respects ownership; but when, by a condition, he attempts to compel his successor to do what is against the public good, the law steps in and pronounces the condition void and allows the devisee to enjoy the estate free from the condition."

Is this distinction cogent?

6. Comment on the validity of the following testamentary provision (i.e., one made by will): "I direct my executor to demolish my house at 923 Washington Street and charge the cost to my estate within one year of my death and offer the property to the City of Buffalo which by agreement has a right to purchase it for one hundred dollars ($100) and to pay the expense of closing." See *In re Estate of Beck* 676 N.Y.S.2d 838 (Surr. Ct., 1998).

7. The law may not recognize a right as one of property for all purposes. For example, in *R. v. Stewart* [1988] 1 S.C.R. 963, 1988 CarswellOnt 960, 1988 CarswellOnt 110, a question arose as to whether the stealing of confidential information was theft for the purposes of the generic theft provisions of the *Criminal Code*, R.S.C. 1970, c. C-34, sub. 283(1) [now sub. 322(1)]. In that case, Stewart endeavoured to gain access to documents containing confidential employee information. Lamer C.J. said (at para. 25):

> Even if confidential information were to be considered as property under civil law, it does not, however, automatically follow that it qualifies as property for the purpose of the criminal law. Conversely, the fact that something is not property under the civil law is likewise not conclusive for the purpose of the criminal law. Whether or not confidential information is property under the *Criminal Code* should be decided in the perspective of the criminal law.

Owing largely to the complex political issues associated with a decision to criminalize theft of confidential information (not to mention a host of difficult definitional problems), the Court held that any such determination should be left to Parliament. *Cf. Carpenter et al. v. U.S.* 484 U.S. 19 (S.C., 1987).

3. THE CASE FOR PRIVATE PROPERTY

It should be apparent that Canadian law recognizes forms of private, common and public property. However, it is equally patent that the blend of regimes is not in equal parts: private property dominates. Why should that be so?

C. Lewis, "The Right to Private Property in a New Political Dispensation in South Africa" (1992) 8 S.A.J.H.R. 389, at 411-9 [footnotes omitted]

I shall sketch briefly, and in rudimentary terms, the traditional theories advanced in favour of the institution of private property, and the difficulties associated with the justifications. One of the oldest justifications is based on the right of the discoverer of property to take control of it, and to dispose of it . . . As the American jurist Morris Cohen said:

> Few accumulations of great wealth were ever simply found. Rather were they acquired by the labour of many, by conquest, by business manipulation, and by other means. It is obvious that today at any rate few economic goods can be acquired by discovery and first occupancy.

And even if we concede that the first occupier may retain control over a thing, this does not mean that she should be able to use it arbitrarily, or dispose of it in any way she deems fit. The theory of occupancy does not account for acquisition by transfer or by inheritance.

The labour theory holds that every one is entitled to the produce of her labour. The difficulties inherent in this justification are obvious: very few things are produced by the labour of one person alone; the theory does not take account of need on the part of others, and, like the occupancy theory, does not account for inheritance and transfer. But labour as a justification for private property holding cannot be discounted altogether, and, as we will see, is often considered as a factor to be taken into account in mixed justificatory theories.

Some philosophers have tried to deduce the right to property from the individual's right to act as a free person, for the ability to be free is dependent on the opportunities made possible by private property. The inherent flaw in this theory is that, while it accounts for rights in personal items, even in land held for private occupation, it does not justify private property in resources required by the public. One of the chief exponents of the personality justification of property was Hegel, whose arguments are traversed in detail by Waldron, and will be referred to below.

The economic theory in favour of private property claims that maximum productivity is promoted by it: the person who makes the greatest profit is the person who has the greatest power to foresee demand. Cohen asserts (and recent events in Eastern Europe, and the collapse of the Soviet Union appear to bear him out, although the debate has not been conclusively finished) that the history of agriculture and industry show that there is a strong *prima facie* case for the view that greater productivity prevails under individual ownership. Again, however, there are flaws in the approach. Many things, including land, are not increased in number by making them private property. There are inherent sources of waste in a regime of private enterprise, for as Cohen points out, the success of the "economically fittest" is likely to result in the failures of those less fit — which results in loss to the community.

And, most importantly, private property in industry may be argued to sacrifice the interests of society to commercial profit.

Utilitarian theories have also played an important role. These maintain that the total, or average, happiness of society will be greater if resources, particularly the means of production, are owned and controlled by individuals (an argument closely allied with the economic argument sketched above). Waldron maintains that Aristotle's views on property are utilitarian, in that he considers that social disharmony will be avoided if each person has his own land on which to work, and more will be produced when each person applies himself to what is his own property. Aristotle none the less argued in favour of the communal uses of resources: he differed from Plato, however, in maintaining that the sharing of wealth should be the result of virtue rather than legal compulsion.

The principal difficulties with utilitarian arguments are that they take human interests and desires as given, assuming that the fulfilment of a desire has a positive value and that they are quantifiable. Further, the arguments take no heed of the problem of distribution. Waldron argues that a utilitarian who is concerned to maximize the happiness or satisfaction in a community is incapable of taking into account the deprivation or poverty of a few. Thus equality and justice, on a pure utilitarian theory, are not important considerations.

Waldron takes an entirely different approach to the question whether the right to property can be justified. His is a rights-based approach. Waldron's definition of a rights-based argument is "one showing that an individual interest considered in itself is sufficiently important from a moral point of view to justify holding people to be under a duty to promote it". His aim is to consider what individual interests are served by the existence of private property (as opposed to some other form of property regime, such as a socialist or communist regime), and whether these interests are so important from a moral perspective that they justify their enforcement and protection by government.

In determining the meaning of "interest", Waldron distinguishes between preferences and objectively determined interests which a person might prefer not to have promoted. As with rights, there are different conceptions of the concept, and he prefers to leave open the question of the particular conception of interest which is envisaged in a particular theory of rights.

To achieve his aim, Waldron analyses two lines of rights-based argument: the one is associated with Locke and the libertarian philosopher Robert Nozick; the other with Hegel. Waldron suggests that both approaches hold that individuals have an interest in owning things which is sufficiently important to command respect and to restrain governmental action. The Hegelian line argues that this is a basic human interest which everyone has, while on the Lockean approach, the interest is one which people have only because of what they have done, or have acquired from someone else. The Lockean right to property is a "special right", whereas the Hegelian right is "general". A special right is one arising from a transaction between individuals, or from a particular relationship, and the corresponding obligation is limited to the other party to the transaction or relationship. A general right, on the other hand, is a moral right which avails against everyone in the sense that it is protected against interference by others.

Waldron argues that the core of John Locke's theory of property is a special-right-based argument for private property. His central thesis is that by labouring on material resources in a state of nature, a person acquires an interest in them which is important enough, from a moral point of view, to support the principle that other people, and governments, have a duty not to deprive him of the resources without his consent. But people generally have no right to acquire such an interest. On the Lockean approach, there is no general right to appropriate, or to be given the opportunity to do so. However, Locke acknowledged a general right to subsistence where an individual could not appropriate resources for himself. The right to subsistence, together with special rights arising from appropriation, would lead, argued Locke, to a prosperous society, albeit an unequal one.

Locke's arguments in justification of an entitlement over a resource created by mixing one's labour with it were that private appropriation was the only way to meet human needs; and that the mixing of one's labour in itself gives rise to entitlement. Waldron points out that the latter argument is incoherent, and that the former is not true. Locke's justification of the institution of private property thus fails.

In order to demonstrate that no special-right-based theory of property can succeed, Waldron also looks at the theory of historical entitlement, exemplified by the writing of Robert Nozick. Waldron claims the following for Nozick's thesis (a thesis which amounts to no more than the "bare bones of a theory"). Nobody has any right to hold resources as private property unless rights have been acquired by particular people over particular resources by particular actions or transactions. A system of positive law would determine which actions or transactions were able to give rise to rights of use and control. Nozick concedes no other rights, not even one to subsistence. Nor does he attempt any moral, social or economic justification for the right of property that arises in this way. Waldron argues that a theory which makes no allowance for subsistence, and protects only those rights acquired in accordance with "a principle of justice" is not tenable.

Justice will be achieved, on the Nozick account, if a distribution is made only to those who are entitled to hold. The specification of just procedures is to be found in an inductive definition of "entitlement": a person who acquires a holding in accordance with the principle of justice in acquisition is entitled to that holding; one who acquires from him in accordance with the principle of justice in transfer is entitled to the holding. No one is entitled to a holding except through repeated applications of these steps. Nozick does not elaborate on what amounts to justice in acquisition. And original acquisition is, as we have seen, no longer of any practical significance. Thus the principle of justice in acquisition is, although crucial to any theory of historical entitlement, elusive. Waldron asks:

> What were conditions like when resources were first taken into ownership? How well developed was moral consciousness? Were those to whom the principle was supposed

> to apply capable of implementing it properly? Could it conceivably have been a principle which they held and abided by explicitly? Or in any way? If we turn from ancient to modern capabilities, how can *we* make sense *now* of principles whose only direct application was hundreds or perhaps thousands of years ago? If we cannot, does that not deprive such a principle of any right to be regarded as the generating basis of a system of entitlements that is to continue to constrain us today?

The theory of historical entitlement must thus also fail.

Would a general-right-based argument fare any better? A general justification of private property (right-based or otherwise) is, according to Waldron, "one which shows why private ownership is important, i.e., why it is important in general that individuals should have rights of this sort. It does not base this account on the importance of the particular relations which particular individuals might enter into with particular things." A general theory of private property allows us to say what is important about private property systems without having to refer to specific individuals or things. It also does not presuppose any particular economic or political dispensation.

Waldron asserts that many of the general justifications of private property are based on, or closely connected with, the rights of freedom and liberty. Arguments of this nature take different forms, such as the argument that the liberties associated with private property (the liberty to make decisions about the use of a resource without being constrained by, or interfering with others, the liberty to take refuge in a private place, freedom to alienate one's property and so on) are important for people in general; or the argument that such liberties are important for establishing oneself as a free person. Freedom, in this context, is not simply negative — the absence of impediments to action — it is positive in the sense that it is a moral status attained through one's own efforts, or with the help of others. Waldron sketches several arguments for private property based on the notion of positive liberty.

Private property offers security and independence. A free person must have sufficient economic security not to have to depend on others. It allows for self-assertion and recognition — a free person must be able to assert himself as free and independent. A natural resource has no purpose unless given one by an individual: by investing a natural resource with a purpose, an individual becomes aware of the importance of will and rationality. The freedom of self-assertion justifies the claim that everyone should be eligible to hold private property.

Freedom from coercion, and autonomy, are also promoted by private property, in the sense that "being a free man positively requires some degree of material security, since without it one would never have the opportunity to exercise the reflection, restraint and control that constitutes an autonomous life". But Waldron concedes that at most this is an argument for the provision of pressing material needs. When combined with the need for moral, political and economic independence, however, this freedom generates a strong argument for a "property-owning democracy in which material security is guaranteed to all on the basis of resources or sources of income that they *own*".

The argument that private property supports freedom and moral duty is a complex one. In crude terms, it is that the restriction of an owner's activities amounts to a restriction on liberty. In the context of land ownership, one would argue that the morally worthy actions of cultivating land and taming natural resources should not be limited. But the right to use one's resources would have to be limited by the constraint of reasonableness in order to avoid the metamorphosis of the liberty to licence.

The most powerful argument for private property based on positive liberty is that it promotes stability, discipline and responsibility in the exercise of free will. Subsistence depends on the management of resources, and thus control over resources will teach foresight and prudence. Similarly, it will enhance productivity in that it allows individuals to work productively on their own resources, and on their own initiative. (This is not an argument in support of a special-right to property, merely an indication of the relationship between property and responsibility.)

These are but some of the aspects of positive liberty that favour the institution of property. The question that must be faced, however, is whether they are sufficiently compelling to justify private property. There are many who would argue that positive liberty could be promoted equally well by a system of collective or common property. But as Waldron points out, the purpose of a right-based argument is to justify a system of private property of a general type, and not existing systems of Western capitalist societies.

The particular general-right-based argument justifying private property analysed by Waldron is that of Hegel, although, as Waldron observes, Hegel was not purporting to provide such a justification, nor is his argument, without interpolation, clearly right-based. Waldron's analysis of Hegel's views on property (in very broad terms) is that property is needed by everyone for the development of freedom and personality. People cannot be free unless their basic physical needs are met. These needs can be satisfied by possession rather than ownership, and so they are insufficient in themselves to justify property. But the development of personality does require private property in order to sustain and develop the qualities that define an individual's status.

Ethical development involves a transition from the inner subjective world of the individual to the external objective world. The world of material objects is the appropriate realm for the initial excursion of free will to take place. In appropriating the natural resources of the world people display their natural superiority over nature. Through owning and controlling property, an individual can embody his will in external objects, thus transcending the subjectivity of his existence. Property is thus essential to human development, and poverty of great concern. Poverty is not, however, a problem to which Hegel offers a solution.

The principal difficulty with any argument for private property based upon liberty or freedom is encountered in the famous Proudhon strategy. In answer to the argument that property ensures the inviolability of the person, Proudhon said:

> [I]f the liberty of man is sacred, it is equally sacred in all individuals; . . . if it needs property for its objective action, that is, for its life, the appropriation of material is equally necessary for all. . . . I will only prove, by all the arguments [by which the right of property is justified] the principle of equality which kills it. . . . Every argument which has been invented in behalf of property, *whatever it may be*, always and of necessity leads to equality; that is to the negation of property.

It is difficult to counter such a strategy. If property is required for the exercise and protection of one person's liberty, then it is required equally for all others' liberty. For one without property, the existence of a general right to it is useless. Waldron says:

> Though arguments based on a general right to liberty may be used by those who have private property to rebut attempts to expropriate them or to take the resources that they own into collective ownership, consistency requires that the same arguments be deployed with equal fervour on behalf of those who have no private property to rebut attempts to perpetuate their propertylessness or to perpetuate the situation in which they have to rely either on collective provision or on the goodwill of property-owners for their material well-being. In each case the moral concern is the same: people need private property for the development and exercise of their liberty; that is why it is wrong to take all of a person's private property away from him, and that is why it is wrong that some individuals should have had no private property at all.

If one accepts that everyone has a right to property (in the sense that there must in fact be property for all) then the Proudhon scepticism is somewhat diminished. However, the issue of distribution then becomes crucial, as does the question of equality, which Proudhon considered necessary. Is it sufficient that each person has enough to ensure her liberty, or must surplus resources be redistributed in order to achieve equality? The answer to this will of course depend on the economic system adopted by a particular society . . .

Waldron argues that it is not enough to give all people in a society the opportunity to have property. If opportunity were all that was meant by the right to property, then it would be a strange and "asymmetrical" right — one that would allow for radical inequality, such that wealth would be concentrated in the hands of a few, and the bulk of society would have no chance of a decent life. This issue is central to the problems facing the framers of the South African constitution. The proposed bill of rights does nothing other than address eligibility to acquire property, and protect those who already have it. If the right to property is based on the positive liberty of the individual, then the majority of people in the country will be deprived not only of shelter and the resources necessary to lead a decent life, but also of that liberty. "Freedom requires private property, and freedom for all requires private property for all. Nothing less will do."

Apart from the difficulty of implementing a general right to property, there are notional obstacles in its path. One very real difficulty is that the principle of justice requiring property for all would be frustrated by the very exercise of the right of property itself. If property were distributed in order to ensure liberty, or ethical development, the exercise of the property holder's freedom to dispose of the property would defeat the achievement of the liberty allowed for by property.

The second major problem was given expression by Karl Marx: it is inherent in the notion of private property that there be inequality. The distribution of the means of production will inevitably lead to the concentration of private property rights in the hands of a few.

Waldron does not offer a solution to these problems (although he does show how different conceptions of property might address them to some extent), nor does he adopt any particular justification of private property, save in so far as he insists upon provision in any system for meeting basic needs. His use of certain analytical apparatus in considering the justificatory theories advanced by others is, however, illuminating, particularly in demonstrating that the right to positive freedom requires property for all.

Munzer, on the other hand, does propose a solution to the problems of private property. His theory is pluralist in that it "contains several irreducible principles that sometimes conflict: when conflicts occur, priority rules can resolve some, but not all, conflicts". The basic principles upon which the theory rests are utility and efficiency, justice and equality, and a principle of desert based on labour. In broad terms, the theory is based on the argument that a satisfactory theory of property should include a principle recognizing the factors affecting peoples' happiness, welfare and preference satisfaction: a principle allowing for the achievement of the maximum utility and efficiency in the use, possession and transfer of resources: a principle ensuring justice in the distribution of resources by providing the minimum required for anyone to lead a fully human life in society, and reducing inequality between people: and, although of least importance, a principle of desert for one's actions. His theory results in a justification of some private property limited by "sensible government regulation".

The principle of utility and efficiency assumes that people have equal moral worth. It is not utilitarian in that it does not regard utility (whatever that may be — pleasure, happiness, welfare and so on) as the sole standard of right and wrong. Rather, the principle has two parts: the first, a version of utility, requires the maximization of utility in the use and possession of resources. The second part, the aspect of efficiency, requires maximizing the welfare of all in so far as use, possession and transfer are concerned . . .

QUESTIONS AND COMMENTS

1. Which of the justifications described by Carole Lewis do you think ring true for Canadian society?

2. To what extent are the justifications for private property premised on a certain image of human nature?

3. In what ways does private property advance or subvert democracy?

4. Do you believe that there is an innate, genetic, or primordial need for property? If so, what type of property regime would be most appropriate?

5. The debate about the virtues of private property must of course be assessed against the backdrop of the available options. As we have seen, in general terms, it is helpful to think of a triad of possibilities (private, public, common) or a spectrum of blended variations. See further M.A. Heller, "The Dynamic Analytics of Property Law", 2 Theoretical Inquiries in Law 79 (2001). Hence, Neil Komesar acknowledges that private property regimes are functionally superior in complex societies:

> If, in the unkempt world of high numbers and complexity, private property is superior to the other property systems, it is not because private property improves in its performance as numbers and complexity increase. The case for private property must lie in the fact that, as numbers and complexity increase, its ability to function — its ability to establish the correct incentives and produce the correct level of participation — disintegrates more slowly than the ability of alternate systems of property.

N.K. Komesar, *Law's Limits* (New York: C.U.P., 2001) at 135.

In a famous article entitled "The Tragedy of the Commons" (1968) 162 Science 1243, Garrett Hardin sought to demonstrate that common ownership led to the overcomsumption and hence ruination of common property. He posited a situation in which a common pasture was used for the grazing of cattle. An owner of livestock using the pasture would derive all of the profits from his or her cattle, but the cost to that owner in terms of the degradation of the pasture was borne by all users. Owing to this disequilibrium, the logical result would be from that farmer to graze as many cattle on the commons as possible. However, all of the farmers might well adopt the same logic. The result would be the rapid ruination of the pasture. Now, if the commons were privatized, some argue, the self-interested farmers would not act so rashly. To overstock one's own pasture would lead to direct and full personal loss. In other words, once the land is privatized, the landowners reap the full benefits, but must absorb the entire burden resulting from grazing. Benefits and burdens are internalized.

What lessons does the tragedy hold for environmental control laws? Do you think that the tragedy would arise if both the livestock and the cattle were held in common? Would it be possible to regulate the commons to prevent overuse? Does private property require state regulation?

6. The ancient common law rules governing grazing were recently discussed by the House of Lords in *Bettison v. Langton* [2002] 1 A.C. 27 (H.L.) at 30-1 (*per* Lord Nicholls of Birkenhead):

> Despite the continuing growth of towns and cities, ancient common lands still cover about 1.4 m acres, over 4% of the total area of England and Wales. Some commons, such as Clapham Common, are now within built up areas. But the great bulk of common

> lands are in the countryside, notably the extensive hill commons in the north and south west of England and in Wales.
>
> For centuries many farmers whose lands adjoin the local common have enjoyed the right to put out their sheep and cattle to graze on the common. The animals wintered on the farms, but in the summer months they were let out to graze on the open common. . . . These rights have feudal origins, but this should not be allowed to obscure their continuing importance. What happens on the commons is of importance to the local farmers. What happens on the commons is also of wider importance. Commons have considerable amenity value. Increasingly, what happens on the commons is a matter of general public concern. They are the last reserve of uncommitted land in England and Wales. They are an important national resource.
>
> Traditionally grazing rights are an adjunct of the lands of the farmers who own the rights. The rights had their origin in actual or presumed grant, usually the latter. The law assumes that long continued use must have had a lawful origin. The number of animals that a farmer was entitled to depasture on the common was limited to the animals his land could support through the winter. The language was picturesque: the right was limited to the number of beasts "levant and couchant" ("getting up and lying down") on the farmer's holding in the winter months. These rights could be passed on or sold, but only with the farm to which they were appurtenant. They were to be enjoyed by the occupier for the time being. They could not be sold separately, or "severed ", from the farm.
>
> Most grazing rights were governed by the principle of levancy and couchancy, but not always. Sometimes a grazing right might be for a fixed number of animals. Then the right, known as a right in gross, could be sold separately. Historically, grazing rights in gross are rare.

Why haven't the remaining common pastures suffered the tragic fate predicted by Hardin? Does the above passage provide clues?

7. Following the publication of Hardin's paper, a significant body of empirical evidence has been gathered about the workings of common property, both open access and communal. Recently, Louis De Alessi surveyed the literature on point: L. De Alessi, "Gains from Private Property" in T.L. Anderson & F.S. McChesney, eds., *Property Rights: Cooperation, Conflict and Law* (Princeton: Princeton U.P., 2003) at 90. The studies cover a wide range of activities (such as Atlantic whale hunting, the fur trade in Canada, fisheries, elephant conservation practices in Zimbabwe, state regulation of alligator hunting in Florida, land settlement, even antarctic explorations, where it was shown that private exploitations were more efficient and safer than those that were publicly funded). De Alessi concluded (at 108):

> Private property rights provide workable rules for solving a society's increasingly complex economic problems. . . . The evidence . . . suggests that individual or communal private property rights promote investment in maintaining and improving resources, development of new institutions and technologies, and faster, fuller response to changes in circumstances. Outputs and incomes are larger than under alternative arrangements.
>
> Relative to open access, government regulation can establish more secure property rights, increasing the incentive to maintain or improve a resource . . . Regulatory constraints and uncertainty about regulators' behavior, however, limit the gains.

8. Compare, however, the analysis offered by Daniel Cole in D.E. Cole, *Pollution and Property: Comparing Ownership Institutions for Environmental Protection* (Cambridge: Cambridge U.P., 2002). While recognizing the limits of pure open access systems, Cole questions (at 16) Hardin's assumption that private owners would not "knowingly overexploit their resources":

> This assumption is empirically and theoretically dubious. Empirically, individual private owners have often done exactly what Hardin assumes they would not do. Daniel Bromley (1991, p. 171) reminds us of the dust bowls that resulted when supposedly "'omniscient' private entrepreneurs" plowed up the American prairie against the advice of agricultural experts. More recently, in the 1990s private timber owners in the American Pacific northwest increased harvesting to unsustainable levels either to avert or to pay for junk bond financed hostile takeovers (see Power 196, p. 138). According to economic theory, meanwhile, it is entirely rational for resource users to extinguish rather than conserve resources in some circumstances (see Gordon 1958). Colin Clark (1973a, pp. 950-1) has shown, for example, that the "extermination of an entire [animal] population may appear as the most attractive policy, even to an individual resource owner," when "(a) the discount (or time preference) rate sufficiently exceeds the maximum reproductive potential of the population, and (b) an immediate profit can be made from harvesting the lat remaining animals." The outcome may not be socially optimal, but private property owners make decisions to maximize private, not social, benefits (see Clark 1973b; Larson and Bromley 1990; Schlager and Ostrom 1992).

See also *ibid.* at 95*ff.*

Likewise, James Boyle notes that "while earlier scholarship extolled enclosure's beneficial effects, some more recent empirical research has indicated that it had few, if any, effects in increasing agricultural production. The tragedies predicted in articles such as Hardin's Tragedy of the Commons did not occur": J. Boyle, "The Second Enclosure Movement and the Construction of the Public Domain", 66-SPG Law & Contemp. Probs. 33 (2003) at 36. See also the references cited at note 9 of his paper.

9. What if private property rights are too fragmented, that is, individual entitlements are held so diffusely that significant co-operation among private owners is required to carry out complex commercial activity? In recent years, this type of situation has been referred to as the tragedy of the "anticommons":

> Anticommons property can best be understood as the mirror image of commons property. A resource is prone to overuse in a tragedy of the commons when too many owners each have a privilege to use a given resource and no one has a right to exclude another. By contrast, a resource is prone to underuse in a "tragedy of the anticommons" when multiple owners each have a right to exclude others from a scarce resource and no one has an effective privilege of use. In theory, in a world of costless transactions, people could always avoid commons or anticommons tragedies by trading their rights. In practice, however, avoiding tragedy requires overcoming transaction costs, strategic behaviors, and cognitive biases of participants, with success more likely within close-knit communities than among hostile strangers. Once an anticommons emerges, collecting rights into usable private property is often brutal and slow.

M.A. Heller & R.S. Eisenberg, "Can Patents Deter Innovation? The Anticommons in Biomedical Research", 280 Science 698 (1998) at 698 (footnotes omitted). See also M.A. Heller, "The Tragedy of the Anticommons: Property in the Transition from Marx to Markets", 111 Harv.L.Rev. 621 (1998); F. Parisi *et al.*, "Simultaneous and Sequential Anticommons", online: <http://ssrn.com/abstract__id=388880>.

For example, the anticommons problem can arise in relation to intellectual property rights (such as patents) especially in the burgeoning field of biotechnology. As Carl Shapiro explains:

> [T]houghtful observers are increasingly expressing concerns that our patent (and copyright) system is in fact creating a *patent thicket*, a dense web of overlapping intellectual property rights that a company must hack its way through in order to actually commercialize new technology. With cumulative innovation and multiple blocking patents, stronger patent rights can have the perverse effect of stifling, not encouraging, innovation.

C. Shapiro, "Navigating the Patent Thicket: Cross Licenses, Patent Pools, and Standard-Setting", online: <http://repositories.cdlib.org/iber/cpc/CPC00-011>.

How might such problems be overcome?

10. Richard Posner suggests that economically effective property laws should strive to do three main things. First, the promotion of "exclusivity" is essential. By this is meant that the law should allocate rights of property to defined individuals and should provide appropriate means to recognize, enforce and protect those rights. Theft and free-riding should be minimized. The law should protect individual entitlements and inhibit others from deriving benefits from the property entitlements of others. Second, universality should be promoted; as many goods should be available for exchange by as many potential holders as possible. Third, the law should facilitate transferability of entitlements. By encouraging and assisting exchange, goods can gravitate to those most willing to acquire them. See R.A. Posner, *Economic Analysis of Law*, 5th ed. (New York: Aspen Law & Business, 1998) at 38.

The importance of these elements — and principally the idea of protected exclusivity — can be seen in the highly influential work of economist Hernando de Soto. In *The Mystery of Capital* (New York: Basic Books, 2000), de Soto tackles the question of why capitalism has succeeded in western nations while failing to achieve comparable success elsewhere in the world. The answer, he argues, does not lie in the absence of wealth in third world nations. His empirical findings suggest that most of the poorer nations already have the assets needed to develop strong economies. Taking Egypt as one example, he claims that the value of the property held in that country is considerable: 55 times as much as the total foreign aid received by that nation.

The problem he identifies is that much of this wealth exists on the margins of the *de jure* (i.e., legal) property system. Goods are exchanged in black markets, homes have been built on lands for which no title is held, and so forth. The absence of stable property holdings is of particular importance, since the inability to demonstrate a valid title effectively prevents the use of land as security for loans. By contrast, in Western nations,

> every parcel of land, every building, every piece of equipment, or store of inventories is represented in a property document that is the visible sign of a vast hidden process that connects all these assets to the rest of the economy. Thanks to this representational process, assets can lead an invisible, parallel life alongside their material existence. They can be used as collateral for credit. The single most important source of funds for new businesses in the United States is a mortgage on the entrepreneur's house. These assets can also provide a link to the owner's credit history, an accountable address for the collection of debts and taxes, the basis for the creation of reliable and universal public utilities, and a foundation for the creation of securities (like mortgage-backed bonds) that can then be rediscounted and sold in secondary markets. By this process the West injects life into assets and makes them generate capital . . .

Hence, the failure of market economies in emerging nations arises in large measure from the inability to release the capital potential locked into the existing assets:

> The poor inhabitants of these nations — five-sixths of humanity — do have things, but they lack the process to represent their property and create capital. They have houses but not titles; crops but not deeds; businesses but not statues of incorporation. It is the unavailability of these essential representations that explains why people who have adapted every other Western invention, from the paper clip to the nuclear reactor, have not been able to produce sufficient capital to make their domestic capitalism work.

As de Soto observed, the emergence of extra-legal ownership land claims arose in frontier settlements in the United States, where squatters appropriated lands beyond the state-sanctioned borders. In time, and out of necessity, these titles were confirmed. This pattern occurred elsewhere, including in Australia, and to a lesser extent in Canada: see J.C. Weaver, *The Great Land Rush and the Making of the Modern World, 1650-1900* (Montreal & Kingston: McGill-Queen's U.P., 2003) at ch. 7, *passim.* For instance, in Edmonton in the 1880s, a string of river lots located just outside the Hudson's Bay Reserve lands were appropriated by squatters before the lands had been surveyed. The Edmonton *Bulletin* contains this account of the situation in the townsite at the time:

> While Winnipeg, in common with other Manitoba towns, has been enjoying an unprecedented boom in real estate, and prices have been soaring in the skies, Edmonton has been modestly following suit. Last summer's emigration made the commencement of a town imperative, and as the vicinity of the H.B. Co. Fort had been from time immemorial the business centre of the Upper Saskatchewan country that locality was, of course, selected as the site. But as the H.B. Co. have a reserve of 3,000 acres around the Fort, which was not then open for sale, the adjacent claims were taken, and lots 50 x 100, purchased from the original settlers, went as high as $90, *although not a line was surveyed or the remotest prospect of a deed ever being given or received was in view.* Notwithstanding this about $8,000 worth of buildings were erected in the fall. *But as the original settlers held no titles they were afraid to sell lest their rights to the balance of their claims should be prejudiced and buyers were, of course, afraid to invest in more than they actually needed for present use.*

> This was the state of affairs when the sale of lots on the H.B. Co. property was opened. The survey had been made — just finished — the location suited, the site was high and dry, a title could be got without any difficulty, the price was low and the terms easy. The consequence was the moment the sale opened there was a rush for lots that would have surprised even a Winnipeg auctioneer, and in three or four days $12,000 worth or about 400 lots, were sold subject to building conditions. The sale was then closed, from what reason can only be surmised . . .

"The Boom" Edmonton *Bulletin*, February 4, 1882, at 3 (emphasis added).

In short, protected exclusivity of ownership is a hallmark of an efficient property regime.

11. In Canada, there is no limit on wealth accumulation, nor on the amount of property that can be given away by an owner on death. Given the rationales of private property considered by Carole Lewis, how can one justify an unlimited freedom to dispose of property by will or gift?

12. Does the "labour" theory of ownership contain more than a reiteration of the economic efficiency argument?

13. Consider this observation:

> Property is a paradox. It aims at security and stability. Yet the stability can be achieved only by making property rights responsible to each person's need to have some measure of the same security. This requires making property rights contingent on their effects in the world and especially on their effects on those excluded from the world of property.

Joseph William Singer, *The Edges of the Field* (Boston: Beacon Pr., 2000) at 76.

What is the relationship between property and freedom? In what way can property diminish freedom?

14. In Mark Ascher's "Curtailing Inherited Wealth", 89 Mich.L.Rev. 69 (1990) at 73-4, the following reforms are advanced, which if adopted would reduce the ability of owners to confer property entitlements through inheritance:

> My proposal views inheritance as something we should tolerate only when necessary — not something we should always protect. My major premise is that all property owned at death, after payment of debts and administration expenses, should be sold and the proceeds paid to the United States government. There would be six exceptions. A marital exemption, potentially unlimited, would accrue over the life of a marriage. Thus, spouses could continue to provide for each other after death. Decedents would also be allowed to provide for dependent lineal descendants. The amount available to any given descendant would, however, depend on the descendant's age and would drop to zero at any age of presumed independence. A separate exemption would allow generous provision for disabled lineal descendants of any age. Inheritance by lineal ascendants (parents, grandparents, etc.) would be unlimited. A universal exemption would allow a moderate amount

of property either to pass outside the exemptions or to augment amounts passing under them. Thus, every decedent would be able to leave something to persons of his or her choice, regardless whether another exemption was available. Up to a fixed fraction of an estate could pass to charity. In addition, to prevent circumvention by lifetime giving, the gift tax would increase substantially.

Would this regime make good law? See Professor Ascher's article for the arguments for and against his proposals.

4. NOVEL CLAIMS

Even if one can be convinced that the arguments in favour of privatizing ownership are sound (and you may not be), at least two further questions need to be addressed. One concerns the proper scope of private ownership — what things should be amenable to private ownership? The second deals with the basis upon which these entitlements should be allocated — how should private property rights be distributed? In studying the cases included in this section, consider the extent to which the rationales for privatization of resources find their way into the analysis of property claims. Consider also what other values hold sway.

The first two cases — *International News Service v. Associated Press*, and *Victoria Park Racing and Recreation Grounds Ltd. v. Taylor* — form an analytical couplet, and should be read together.

International News Service v. Associated Press
248 U.S. 215 (1918)

Pitney J.:

The parties are competitors in the gathering and distribution of news and its publication for profit in newspapers throughout the United States. The Associated Press, which was complainant in the District Court, is a co-operative organization, incorporated under the Membership Corporations Law of the state of New York, its members being individuals who are either proprietors or representatives of about 950 daily newspapers published in all parts of the United States . . . Complainant gathers in all parts of the world, by means of various instrumentalities of its own, by exchange with its members, and by other appropriate means, news and intelligence of current and recent events of interest to newspaper readers and distributes it daily to its members for publication in their newspapers. The cost of the service, amounting approximately to $3,500,000 per annum, is assessed upon the members and becomes a part of their costs of operation, to be recouped, presumably with profit, through the publication of their several newspapers. Under complainant's by-laws each member agrees upon assuming membership that news received through complainant's service is received exclusively for publication in a particular newspaper, language, and place specified in the certificate of membership, that no other use of it shall be permitted, and that no member shall furnish or permit any one in his employ or connected with his newspaper to furnish any of complainant's news in advance of publication to any person not a member. And each member is required to gather the local news of his district and supply it to the Associated Press and to no one else.

Defendant is a corporation organized under the laws of the state of New Jersey, whose business is the gathering and selling of news to its customers and clients, consisting of newspapers published throughout the United States, under contracts by which they pay certain amounts at stated times for defendant's service. It has widespread news-gathering agencies; the cost of its operations amounts, it is said, to more than $2,000,000 per annum; and it serves about 400 newspapers located in the various cities of the United States and abroad, a few of which are represented, also, in the membership of the Associated Press.

The parties are in the keenest competition between themselves in the distribution of news throughout the United States; and so, as a rule, are the newspapers that they serve, in their several districts. Complainant in its bill, defendant in its answer, have set forth in almost identical terms the rather obvious circumstances and conditions under which their business is conducted. The value of the service, and of the news furnished, depends upon the promptness of transmission, as well as upon the accuracy and impartiality of the news; it being essential that the news be transmitted to members or subscribers as early or earlier than similar information can be furnished to competing newspapers by other news services, and that the news furnished by each agency shall not be furnished to newspapers which do not contribute to the expense of gathering it . . .

The bill was filed to restrain the pirating of complainant's news by defendant in three ways: First, by bribing employees of newspapers published by complainant's members to furnish Associated Press news to defendant before publication, for transmission by telegraph and telephone to defendant's clients for publication by them; second, by inducing Associated Press members to violate its by-laws and permit defendant to obtain news before publication; and, third, by copying news from bulletin boards and from early editions of complainant's newspapers and selling this, either bodily or after rewriting it, to defendant's customers.

The District Court, upon consideration of the bill and answer, with voluminous affidavits on both sides, granted a preliminary injunction under the first and second heads, but refused at that stage to restrain the systematic practice admittedly pursued by defendant, of taking news bodily from the bulletin boards and early editions of complainant's newspapers and selling it as its own. The court expressed itself as satisfied that this practice amounted to unfair trade, but as the legal question was one of first impression it considered that the allowance of an injunction should await the outcome of an appeal. 240 Fed. 983, 996. Both parties having appealed, the Circuit Court of Appeals sustained the injunction order so far as it went, and upon complainant's appeal modified it and remanded the cause, with directions to issue an injunction also against any bodily taking of the words or substance of complainant's news until its commercial value as news had passed away . . .

The only matter that has been argued before us is whether defendant may lawfully be restrained from appropriating news taken from bulletins issued by complainant or any of its members, or from newspapers published by them, for the purpose of selling it to defendant's clients. Complainant asserts that defendant's admitted course of conduct in this regard both violates complainant's property right in the news and constitutes unfair competition in business. And notwithstanding the case has proceeded only to the stage of a preliminary injunction, we have deemed it proper to consider the underlying questions, since they go to the very merits of the action and are presented upon facts that are not in dispute. As presented in argument, these questions are: (1) Whether there is any property in news; (2) Whether, if there be property in news collected for the purpose of being published, it survives the instant of its publication in the first newspaper to which it is communicated by the news-gatherer; and (3) whether defendant's admitted course of conduct in appropriating for commercial use matter taken from bulletins or early editions of Associated Press publications constitutes unfair competition in trade.

. . . Complainant's news matter is not copyrighted. It is said that it could not, in practice, be copyrighted, because of the large number of dispatches that are sent daily; and, according to complainant's contention, news is not within the operation of the copyright act. Defendant, while apparently conceding this, nevertheless invokes the analogies of the law of literary property and copyright, insisting as its principal contention that, assuming complainant has a right of property in its news, it can be maintained (unless the copyright act by complied with) only by being kept secret and confidential, and that upon the publication with complainant's consent of uncopyrighted news of any of complainant's members in a newspaper or upon a bulletin board, the right of property is lost, and the subsequent use of the news by the public or by defendant for any purpose whatever becomes lawful . . .

In considering the general question of property in news matter, it is necessary to recognize its dual character, distinguishing between the substance of the information and the particular form or collocation of words in which the writer has communicated it.

No doubt news articles often possess a literary quality, and are the subject of literary property at the common law; nor do we question that such an article, as a literary production, is the subject of copyright by the terms of the act as it now stands . . .

But the news element — the information respecting current events contained in the literary production — is not the creation of the writer, but is a report of matters that ordinarily are *publici juris*; it is the history of the day. It is not to be supposed that the framers of the Constitution, when they empowered Congress "to promote the progress of science and useful arts, by securing for limited times to authors and inventors the exclusive right to their respective writings and discoveries" (Const. art. 1, §8, par. 8), intended to confer upon one who might happen to be the first to report a historic event the exclusive right for any period to spread the knowledge of it.

. . . The peculiar value of news is in the spreading of it while it is fresh; and it is evident that a valuable property interest in the news, as news, cannot be maintained by keeping it secret. Besides, except for matters improperly disclosed, or published in breach of trust or confidence, or in violation of law, none of which is involved in this branch of the case, the news of current events may be regarded as common property. What we are concerned with is the business of making it known to the world, in which both parties to the present suit are engaged. That business consists in maintaining a prompt, sure, steady, and reliable service designed to place the daily events of the world at the breakfast table of the millions at a price that, while of trifling moment to each reader, is sufficient in the aggregate to afford compensation for the cost of gathering and distributing it, with the added profit so necessary as an incentive to effective action in the commercial world. The service thus performed for newspaper readers is not only innocent but extremely useful in itself, and indubitably constitutes a legitimate business. The parties are competitors in this field; and, on fundamental principles, applicable here as elsewhere, when the rights or privileges of the one are liable to conflict with those of the other, each party is under a duty so to conduct its own business as not unnecessarily or unfairly to injure that of the other . . .

Obviously, the question of what is unfair competition in business must be determined with particular reference to the character and circumstances of the business. The question here is not so much the rights of either party as against the public but their rights as between themselves. See *Morison v. Moat*, 9 Hare, 241, 258. And, although we may and do assume that neither party has any remaining property interest as against the public in uncopyrighted news matter after the moment of its first publication, it by no means follows that there is no remaining property interest in it as between themselves. For, to both of them alike, news matter, however little susceptible of ownership or dominion in the absolute sense, is stock in trade, to be gathered at the cost of enterprise, organization, skill, labor, and money, and to be distributed and sold to those who will pay money for it, as for any other merchandise. Regarding the news, therefore, as but the material out of which both parties are seeking to make profits at the same time and in the same field, we hardly can fail to recognize that for this purpose, and as between them, it must be regarded as quasi property, irrespective of the rights of either as against the public.

In order to sustain the jurisdiction of equity over the controversy, we need not affirm any general and absolute property in the news as such. The rule that a court of equity concerns itself only in the protection of property rights treats any civil right of a pecuniary nature as a property right (*In re Sawyer*, 124 U. S. 200, 210, 8 Sup. Ct. 482, 31 L. Ed. 402; *In re Debs*, 158 U. S. 564, 593, 15 Sup. Ct. 900, 39 L. Ed. 1092); and the right to acquire property by honest labor or the conduct of a lawful business is as much entitled to protection as the right to guard property already acquired . . . It is this right that furnishes the basis of the jurisdiction in the ordinary case of unfair competition . . .

Not only do the acquisition and transmission of news require elaborate organization and a large expenditure of money, skill, and effort; not only has it an exchange value to the gatherer, dependent chiefly upon its novelty and freshness, the regularity of the service, its reputed reliability and thoroughness, and its adaptability to the public needs; but also, as is evident, the news has an exchange value to one who can misappropriate it.

The peculiar features of the case arise from the fact that, while novelty and freshness form so important an element in the success of the business, the very processes of distribution and publication necessarily occupy a good deal of time. Complainant's service, as well as defendant's, is a daily service to daily newspapers; most of the foreign news reaches this country at the Atlantic seaboard, principally at the city of New York, and because of this, and of time differentials due to the earth's rotation, the distribution of news matter throughout the country is principally from east to west; and, since in speed the telegraph and telephone easily outstrip the rotation of the earth, it is a simple matter for defendant to take complainant's news from bulletins or early editions of complainant's members in the eastern cities and at the mere cost of telegraphic transmission cause it to be published in western papers issued at least as early as those served by complainant. Besides this, and irrespective of time differentials, irregularities in telegraphic transmission on different lines, and the normal consumption of time in printing and distributing the newspaper, result in permitting pirated news to be placed in the hands of defendant's readers sometimes simultaneously with the service of competing Associated Press papers, occasionally even earlier.

Defendant insists that when, with the sanction and approval of complainant, and as the result of the use of its news for the very purpose for which it is distributed, a portion of complainant's members communicate it to the general public by posting it upon bulletin boards so that all may read, or by issuing it to newspapers and distributing it indiscriminately, complainant no longer has the right to control the use to be made of it; that when it thus reaches the light of day it becomes the common possession of all to whom it is accessible; and that any purchaser of a newspaper has the right to communicate the intelligence which it contains to anybody and for any purpose, even for the purpose of selling it for profit to newspapers published for profit in competition with complainant's members.

The fault in the reasoning lies in applying as a test the right of the complainant as against the public, instead of considering the rights of complainant and defendant, competitors in business, as between themselves. The right of the purchaser of a single newspaper to spread knowledge of its contents gratuitously, for any legitimate purpose not unreasonably interfering with complainant's right to make merchandise of it, may be admitted; but to transmit that news for commercial use, in competition with complainant — which is what defendant has done and seeks to justify — is a very different matter. In doing this defendant, by its very act, admits that it is taking material that has been acquired by complainant as the result of organization and the expenditure of labor, skill, and money, and which is salable by complainant for money, and that defendant in appropriating it and selling it as its own is endeavoring to reap where it has not sown, and by disposing of it to newspapers that are competitors of complainant's members is appropriating to itself the harvest of those who have sown. Stripped of all disguises, the process amounts to an unauthorized interference with the normal operation of complainant's legitimate business precisely at the point where the profit is to be reaped, in order to divert a material portion of the profit from those who have earned it to those who have not; with special advantage to defendant in the competition because of the fact that it is not burdened with any part of the expense of gathering the news. The transaction speaks for itself and a court of equity ought not to hesitate long in characterizing it as unfair competition in business.

The underlying principle is much the same as that which lies at the base of the equitable theory of consideration in the law of trusts — that he who has fairly paid the price should have the beneficial use of the property. Pom. Eq. Jur. §981. It is no answer to say that complainant spends its money for that which is too fugitive or evanescent to be the subject of property. That might, and for the purposes of the discussion we are assuming that it would furnish an answer in a common-law controversy. But in a court of equity, where the question is one of unfair competition, if that which complainant has acquired fairly at substantial cost may be sold fairly at substantial profit, a competitor who is misappropriating it for the purpose of disposing of it to his own profit and to the disadvantage of complainant cannot be heard to say that it is too fugitive or evanescent to be regarded as property. It has all the attributes of property necessary for determining that a misappropriation of it by a competitor is unfair competition because contrary to good conscience.

The contention that the news is abandoned to the public for all purposes when published in the first newspaper is untenable. Abandonment is a question of intent, and the entire organization of the Associated Press negatives such a purpose. The cost of the service would be prohibited if the reward were to be so limited. No single newspaper, no small group of newspapers, could sustain the expenditure. Indeed, it is one of the most obvious results of defendant's theory that, by permitting indiscriminate publication by anybody and everybody for purposes of profit in competition with the news-gatherer, it would render publication profitless, or so little profitable as in effect to cut off the service by rendering the cost prohibitive in comparison with the return. The practical needs and requirements of the business are reflected in complainant's by-laws which have been referred to. Their effect is that publication by each member must be deemed not by any means an abandonment of the news to the world for any and all purposes, but a publication for limited purposes; for the benefit of the readers of the bulletin or the newspaper as such; not for the purpose of making merchandise of it as news, with the result of depriving complainant's other members of their reasonable opportunity to obtain just returns for their expenditures.

It is to be observed that the view we adopt does not result in giving to complainant the right to monopolize either the gathering or the distribution of the news, or, without complying with the copyright act, to prevent the reproduction of its news articles, but only postpones participation by complainant's competitor in the processes of distribution and reproduction of news that it has not gathered, and only to the extent necessary to prevent that competitor from reaping the fruits of complainant's efforts and expenditure, to the partial exclusion of complainant . . .

Brandeis, J. (dissenting): . . .

The knowledge for which protection is sought in the case at bar is not of a kind upon which the law has heretofore conferred the attributes of property; nor is the manner of its acquisition or use now the purpose to which it is applied, such as has heretofore been recognized as entitling a plaintiff to relief . . .

Courts are ill-equipped to make the investigations which should precede a determination of the limitations which should be set upon any property right in news or of the circumstances under which news gathered by a private agency should be deemed affected with a public interest. Courts would be powerless to prescribe the detailed regulations essential to full enjoyment of the rights conferred or to introduce the machinery required for enforcement of such regulations. Considerations such as these should lead us to decline to establish a new rule of law in the effort to redress a newly-disclosed wrong, although the propriety of some remedy appears to be clear.

NOTE

The dissenting opinion of Holmes J., with which McKenna J. concurred, is omitted.

QUESTIONS

1. What is *quasi*-property? Is it possible to describe the right arising out of this case as one of property (and not, therefore, *quasi*-property)?

2. What values underlie the majority and minority positions?

3. The embargo on the defendant ordered in the *I.N.S.* case was designed to last only for a few hours. Why should the defendant be able to use the information after that period elapses? Wouldn't it still be reaping what others have sown?

4. The plaintiff was reporting on events of the day. Isn't it reaping what others have sown, those "others" being the subjects of the stories?

5. Imagine what might have transpired had the defendant (I.N.S.) prevailed in this case. Pitney J. suggests an answer. He offered that news collection would be rendered "profitless, or so little profitable as in effect to cut off the service by rendering the cost prohibitive in comparison with the return." What evidence is marshalled to support this view? Is that result inevitable? Would I.N.S. benefit from such an outcome, given the manner in which it conducted its business?

6. Is it significant that *I.N.S. v. A.P.* involved news and not some other form of information? In *Archibold v. C.F.A.O.* [1966] Ghana L.R. 79 (H.C.), 12 songs written by the plaintiff had been recorded and sold by the defendant company. However, the music had never been reduced to writing or fixed in any way, so no copyright

could be claimed. Could an action be maintained for the wrongful appropriation? Drawing on *I.N.S. v. A.P.*, Hayfron-Benajmin J. (at 85-6) said that it could:

> In *International News Service v. Associated Press* due to modern publicity and problems of mass communication and industrial methods, the United States Supreme Court went as far as to restrain a press service from "pirating" news items from the bulletin boards or early editions of the papers of the plaintiff's service: that is, from rapidly transmitting the news for reproduction to the defendant's own client's newspapers throughout the country. And yet there can scarcely be copyright in the news item of a daily paper as such. The majority said that while vis-à-vis the public there was no property in news after publication there was such as between the parties:
>
> > . . . at the same time and in the same field, we hardly can fail to recognise that for this purpose and as between them, it must be regarded as quasi-property.
>
> I am not unmindful of the famous statement by Cheshire and Fifoot in their *Law of Contract* (3rd ed.), p. 517 that:
>
> > The prefix "quasi" is commonly used by lawyers when they wish to extenuate, if not to justify, a classification which, though convenient in practice or hallowed by tradition, is not supported by logic.
>
> But as Holmes said in his *Common Law*, p. 1,
>
> > The life of the law has not been logic: it has been experience. The felt necessities of the time, the prevalent moral and political theories, intuitions of public policy, avowed or unconscious, even the prejudices which judges share with their fellow-men, have had a good deal more to do than the syllogism in determining the rules by which men should be governed.
>
> In Ghana as in many parts of Africa, the advent of industrialisation is economically extending the nature of property. The once overwhelming importance of landed property is gradually being eclipsed by the growth of new forms of wealth, not least is what is called in some circles "intellectual" property. With the advent of broadcasting, television and other mass media of communication, the person with an ability and skill to compose musical works has a valuable source of wealth. It this to be restricted to only the literate among the population? I think not. I therefore hold that this action is maintainable, ...

7. Compare *National Basketball Association v. Motorola*, Inc. 105 F.3d 841 (2nd Cir., 1997). In that case, the N.B.A. sued the manufacturer and promoter of a hand-held device that provided real-time data concerning N.B.A. games (Motorola). A suit was also launched against an online service provider. It was claimed argued that the defendants had engaged in copyright infringement, false advertising, the false designation of origin, contravention of the *Communications Act*, and — of prime significance here — commercial misappropriation *à la* the *I.N.S.* case.

At first instance, an injunction was granted based only on this latter ground. That decision was reversed on appeal. The appellate court decision rests principally on the pre-emption provisions of the *Copyright Act* of 1976, which limit the scope of causes of action that overlap with the Act. It was held that only a narrow "hot news" claim is not pre-empted by the statute. Hot news claims were described as containing five elements: It must be shown that (i) the plaintiff generates or collects information at some cost or expense; (ii) the value of the information is highly time-sensitive; (iii) the defendant's use of the information amounts to free-riding; (iv) the defendant's use of the information is in direct conflict with a good or service offered by the plaintiff; and (v) permitting free-riding would so reduce the financial incentive of the plaintiff so that the existence or quality of the plaintiff's labours would be substantially threatened.

Applying these elements, Circuit Judge Winter, for the Court, wrote:

> We conclude that Motorola and STATS have not engaged in unlawful misappropriation under the "hot-news" test set out above. To be sure, some of the elements of a "hot-news" *INS* claim are met. The information transmitted to SportsTrax is not precisely contemporaneous, but it is nevertheless time-sensitive. Also, the NBA does provide, or will shortly do so, information like that available through SportsTrax. It now offers a service called "Gamestats" that provides official play-by-play game sheets and half-time and final box scores within each arena. It also provides such information to the media in each arena. In the future, the NBA plans to enhance Gamestats so that it will be networked between the various arenas and will support a pager product analogous to SportsTrax. SportsTrax will of course directly compete with an enhanced Gamestats.
>
> However, there are critical elements missing in the NBA's attempt to assert a "hot-news" *INS*-type claim. As framed by the NBA, their claim compresses and confuses three different informational products. The first product is generating the information by playing the games; the second product is transmitting live, full descriptions of those games; and the third product is collecting and retransmitting strictly factual information about the games. The first and second products are the NBA's primary business: producing basketball games for live attendance and licensing copyrighted broadcasts of those games. The collection and retransmission of strictly factual material about the games is a different product: e.g., box-scores in newspapers, summaries of statistics on television sports news, and real-time facts to be transmitted to pagers. In our view, the NBA has failed to show any competitive effect whatsoever from SportsTrax on the first and second products and a lack of any free-riding by SportsTrax on the third.
>
> With regard to the NBA's primary products — producing basketball games with live attendance and licensing copyrighted broadcasts of those games — there is no evidence that anyone regards SportsTrax or the AOL site as a substitute for attending NBA games or watching them on television. In fact, Motorola markets SportsTrax as being designed "for those times when you cannot be at the arena, watch the game on TV, or listen to the radio . . . "
>
> The NBA argues that the pager market is also relevant to a "hot-news" *INS*-type claim and that SportsTrax's future competition with Gamestats satisfies any missing element. We agree that there is a separate market for the real-time transmission of factual information to pagers or similar devices, such as STATS's AOL site. However, we disagree that SportsTrax is in any sense free-riding off Gamestats.
>
> An indispensable element of an INS "hot-news" claim is free riding by a defendant on a plaintiff's product, enabling the defendant to produce a directly competitive product for less money because it has lower costs. SportsTrax is not such a product. The use of

pagers to transmit real-time information about NBA games requires: (i) the collecting of facts about the games; (ii) the transmission of these facts on a network; (iii) the assembling of them by the particular service; and (iv) the transmission of them to pagers or an on-line computer site. Appellants are in no way free- riding on Gamestats. Motorola and STATS expend their own resources to collect purely factual information generated in NBA games to transmit to SportsTrax pagers. They have their own network and assemble and transmit data themselves.

To be sure, if appellants in the future were to collect facts from an enhanced Gamestats pager to retransmit them to SportsTrax pagers, that would constitute free-riding and might well cause Gamestats to be unprofitable because it had to bear costs to collect facts that SportsTrax did not. If the appropriation of facts from one pager to another pager service were allowed, transmission of current information on NBA games to pagers or similar devices would be substantially deterred because any potential transmitter would know that the first entrant would quickly encounter a lower cost competitor free-riding on the originator's transmissions.

However, that is not the case in the instant matter. SportsTrax and Gamestats are each bearing their own costs of collecting factual information on NBA games, and, if one produces a product that is cheaper or otherwise superior to the other, that producer will prevail in the marketplace. This is obviously not the situation against which *INS* was intended to prevent: the potential lack of any such product or service because of the anticipation of free-riding.

For the foregoing reasons, the NBA has not shown any damage to any of its products based on free-riding by Motorola and STATS, and the NBA's misappropriation claim based on New York law is pre-empted.

8. In *Morris Communications Corp. v. P.G.A. Tour, Inc.* 235 F.Supp.2d 1269 (M.D. Fla., 2002), an issue arose as to whether the PGA Tour, Inc. had a property right in real-time golf scores. PGA sought to restrict Morris Communications from attending PGA golf tournaments unless Morris first agreed not to transmit, via the internet, real-time golf scores obtained from the media centres located at the tournaments. At PGA tournaments, scores are collected by the PGA from all 18 holes and relayed to a media centre by a system referred to below as RTSS.

Morris alleged that the PGA Tour was exercising an unlawful monopoly power over access to its golf tournaments, and was using that power unfairly by seeking to stifle competition in market for syndicated real-time golf scores. The gist of this allegation, therefore, was that PGA was in violation of anti-trust law. In response, PGA sought to show that the restriction it imposed on use of RTSS was a legitimate business practice. Hence, the PGA Tour asserted that it held a property right to RTSS, and that its restrictions on the use of RTSS was a reasonable means of safeguarding against free riding on this collected information.

The Court found in favour of PGA. But what of the *Motorola* case? Here is what Schlesinger D.J. said (at 1279-82):

. . . In *Motorola*, the court found that Motorola did not free-ride when it created a network that disseminated scores from NBA basketball games. *See Motorola*, 105 F.3d at 854.

Three distinctions between Motorola and the instant case make Morris's claim untenable. First, the *Motorola* court used a very high standard for free-riding that is applicable only in cases with the hot-news exception, which will be discussed in greater detail below. More importantly, the information that Motorola used to create its product was in the public domain, having been broadcast on television or radio. *See id.* at 843. Specifically, Motorola-paid reporters, who had heard the radio or television broadcast scores, reported the information to a central location and merely relayed what had been known to the world. *See id.* at 844. Golf, unlike basketball, precludes a single person gathering all the information occurring on all 18 holes. So when television and radio cover a basketball game, the score is presented to the public through those media outlets, allowing Motorola to obtain the information and republish it. If Morris were able to gather scores from all 18 holes through a television or radio broadcast, Morris could then republish that information, absent a hot-news exception. However, golf's atypical format prevents any single television or radio broadcast from providing results from all 18 holes live. The PGA Tour does publish the scores in the media center, but the media cannot disseminate that information except as the PGA Tour's press credentials allow them to do. As a result, the scores, which are not protected by copyright, remain outside the public domain and within the PGA Tour's control, because the PGA Tour provides access with certain restrictions. Finally, Motorola benefitted from the NBA's costs in producing and marketing the games and from the radio and television stations who paid for broadcast rights: that is Motorola capitalized on the NBA' s positive externalities. However, the NBA and the broadcast stations had already reaped the profits of their investment, and the information was in the public domain at the moment of broadcasting. Additionally, once in the public domain, Motorola "expend[ed] their own resources to collect purely factual information generated in NBA games." *Id.* at 854. While here, Morris does not expend its own resources in gathering information, which is not in the public domain, but instead free-rides on the PGA Tour's compilation of scores. . . .

Morris additionally argues that even if there is free-riding, it must reach the level that would justify a "hot news" property right. However, the Court finds that to be a business justification free-riding does not have to reach the level that the *Motorola* court held necessary for a hot news exception. The *Motorola* court required the free-riding to be so pervasive that all incentives to undertake an activity would be lost. See *Motorola*, 105 F.3d at 853. However, to be a valid business reason, a much lower level of free riding will justify excluding competitors. *See Areeda*, Antitrust Law, Vol. III, ¶ 658(f) ("once a proffered business purpose has been accepted as asserted in good faith and not as pretense, the defense does not require 'balancing' of social gains against competitive harms . . .").

Property Right in the Scores

The PGA Tour claims that the restrictions have a valid business justification, because they are necessary to protect a property right in the scores that it compiled by use of RTSS. Morris argues that the PGA Tour lacks a property right in the score, thus negating the claimed business justification. For the following reasons, the Court finds that the PGA Tour does have a property right in the scores compiled by the use of RTSS, but that property right vanishes when the scores are in the public domain.

The PGA Tour's property right does not come from copyright law, as copyright law does not protect factual information, like golf scores. . . . However, the PGA Tour controls the right of access to that information and can place restrictions on those attending the private event, giving the PGA Tour a property right that the Court will protect.

In the early half of the 20th Century, the Supreme Court dealt with a similar issue in several cases, known as the "ticker cases". In *Board of Trade of the City of Chicago v. Christie Grain and Stock Company*, 198 U.S. 236, 25 S.Ct. 637, 49 L.Ed. 1031 (1905), the appellee sought an injunction preventing the use and distribution of "continuous quotations of prices on sales of grain." *See id.* at 245, 25 S.Ct. 637. There the Supreme Court held, "plaintiff's collection of quotations is entitled to the protection of the law. It stands like a trade secret. The plaintiff has the right to keep the work which it has done, or paid for doing, to itself. . . . The plaintiff does not lose its rights by communicating the result to persons, even if many, in confidential relations to itself, under a contract not to make it public." *Id.* at 250, 25 S.Ct. 637. The Supreme Court further stated, "[t]ime is of the essence in matters like this . . . if the contracts with the plaintiff are kept, the information will not become public property until the plaintiff has gained its reward. A priority of a few minutes probably is enough." *Id.* at 251, 25 S.Ct. 637.

In *Moore v. New York Cotton Exchange*, 270 U.S. 593, 46 S.Ct. 367, 70 L.Ed. 750 (1926), plaintiff sought an injunction forcing defendant to furnish plaintiff with a ticker and a declaration that defendant was a monopolist. *See id.* at 603, 46 S.Ct. 367. The Supreme Court held that the allegations did not support a claim under the Sherman Act and refused to grant the injunction. *See id.* at 603-05, 46 S.Ct. 367. The Supreme Court reiterated the holding of the *Christie* Court that the exchange had a property right in the information "which relates solely to its own business upon its own property." *Id.* at 606-07, 46 S.Ct. 367. Further, the exchange was able to determine to whom it will sell: "the ordinary right of a private vendor of news or other property." *Id.* at 605, 46 S.Ct. 367. Accordingly, the Court found that the exchange's actions were appropriate and legitimate to protect and to further its business. *See id.* at 606, 46 S.Ct. 367.

Like the "ticker cases", the instant case deals with facts that are not subject to copyright protection. The compiler of the information in both cases collects information, which it created, at a cost. Also the events occur on private property to which the general public does not have unfettered access, and the creator of the event can place restrictions upon those who enter the private property. The vastly increased speed that the Internet makes available does not change the calculus or the underlying property right. Accordingly, the PGA Tour, like the exchanges in the ticker cases, has a property right in the compilation of scores, but that property right disappears when the underlying information is in the public domain. . . . [footnotes omitted]

Victoria Park Racing and Recreation Grounds Ltd. v. Taylor (1937) 58 C.L.R. 479 (Australia H.C.)

Latham C.J.: . . .

The plaintiff company carries on the business of racing upon a racecourse known as Victoria Park. The defendant Taylor is the owner of land near the racecourse. He has placed an elevated platform on his land from which it is possible to see what takes place on the racecourse and to read the information which appears on notice boards on the course as to the starters, scratchings, &c., and the winners of the races. The defendant Angles stands on the platform and through a telephone comments upon and describes the races in a particularly vivid manner and announces the names of the winning horses. The defendant the Commonwealth Broadcasting Corporation holds a broadcasting licence under the regulations made under the *Wireless Telegraphy Act* 1905-1936 and carries on the business of broadcasting from station 2 UW. This station broadcasts the commentaries and descriptions given by Angles. The plaintiff wants to have the broadcasting stopped because it prevents people from going to the races and paying for admission. The evidence shows that some people prefer hearing about the races as seen by Angles to seeing the races for themselves. The plaintiff contends that the damage which it thus suffers gives, in all the circumstances, a case of action . . .

I am unable to see that any right of the plaintiff has been violated or any wrong done to him. Any person is entitled to look over the plaintiff's fences and to see what goes on in the plaintiff's land. If the plaintiff desires to prevent this, the plaintiff can erect a higher fence. Further, if the plaintiff desires to prevent its notice boards being seen by people from outside the enclosure, it can place them in such a position that they are not visible to such people. At sports grounds and other places of entertainment it is the lawful, natural and common practice to put up fences and other structures to prevent people who are not prepared to pay for admission from getting the benefit of the entertainment. In my opinion, the law cannot by an injunction in effect erect fences which the plaintiff is not prepared to provide. The defendant does no wrong to the plaintiff by looking at what takes place on the plaintiff's land. Further, he does no wrong to the plaintiff by describing to other persons, to as wide an audience as he can obtain, what takes place on the plaintiff's ground. The court has not been referred to any principle of law which prevents any man from describing anything which he sees anywhere if he does not make defamatory statements, infringe the law as to offensive language, etc., break a contract, or wrongfully reveal confidential information. The defendants did not infringe the law in any of these respects . . .

It has been argued that by the expenditure of money the plaintiff has created a spectacle and that it therefore has what is described as a quasi-property in the spectacle which the law will protect. The vagueness of this proposition is apparent upon its face. What it really means is that there is some principle (apart from contract or confidential relationship) which prevents people in some circumstances from opening their eyes and seeing something and then describing what they see. The court has not been referred to any authority in English law which supports the general contention that if a person chooses to organize an entertainment or to do anything else which other persons are able to see he has a right to obtain from a court an order that they shall not describe to anybody what they see. If the claim depends upon interference with a proprietary right it is difficult to see how it can be material to consider whether the interference is large or small — whether the description is communicated to many persons by broadcasting or by a newspaper report, or only to a few persons in conversation or correspondence. Further, as I have already said, the mere fact that damage results to a plaintiff from such a description cannot be relied upon as a cause of action.

I find difficulty in attaching any precise meaning to the phrase "property in a spectacle." A "spectacle" cannot be "owned" in any ordinary sense of that word. Even if there were any legal principle which prevented one person from gaining an advantage for himself or causing damage to another by describing a spectacle produced by that other person, the rights of the latter person could be described as property only in a metaphorical sense. Any appropriateness in the metaphor would depend upon the existence of the legal principle. The principle cannot itself be based upon such a metaphor . . .

Rich J. (dissenting): . . .

A man has no absolute right "within the ambit of his own land" to act as he pleases. His right is qualified and such of his acts as invade his neighbour's property are lawful only in so far as they are reasonable having regard to his own circumstances and those of his neighbour (*Law Quarterly Review*, vol. 52, p. 460; vol. 53, p. 3). The plaintiff's case must, I am prepared to concede, rest on what is called nuisance. But it must not be overlooked that this means no more than that he must complain of some impairment of the rights flowing from occupation and ownership of land. One of the prime purposes of occupation of land is the pursuit of profitable enterprises for which the exclusion of others is necessary either totally or except upon conditions which may include payment. In the present case in virtue of its occupation and ownership the plaintiff carries on the business of admitting to the land for payment patrons of racing. There it entertains them by a spectacle, by a competition in the comparative merits of racehorses, and it attempts by all reasonable means to give to those whom it admits the exclusive right of witnessing the spectacle, the competition and of using the collated information in betting while that is possible on its various events. This use of its rights as occupier is usual, reasonable and profitable. So much no one can dispute. If it be true that an adjacent owner has an unqualified and absolute right to overlook an occupier whatever may be the enterprise he is carrying on and to make any profitable use to which what he sees can be put, whether in his capacity of adjacent owner or otherwise, then to that extent the right of the occupier carrying on the enterprise must be modified and treated in law as less extensive and ample than perhaps is usually understood. But can the adjacent owner by virtue of his occupation and ownership use his land in such an unusual way as the erection of a platform involves, bring mechanical appliances into connection with that use, i.e., the microphone and the land line to the studio, and then by combining regularity of observation with dissemination for gain of the information so obtained give the potential patrons a mental picture of the spectacle, an account of the competition between the horses and of the collated information needed for getting, for all of which they would otherwise have recourse to the racecourse and pay? To admit that the adjacent owner may overlook does not answer this question affirmatively . . .

There can be no right to extend the normal use of his land by the adjoining owner indefinitely. He may within limits make fires, create smoke and use vibratory machinery. He may consume all the water he finds on his land, but he has no absolute right to dirty it. Defendants' rights are related to plaintiff's rights and each owner's rights may be limited by the rights of the other.

Indeed the prospects of television make our present decision a very important one, and I venture to think that the advance of that art may force the courts to recognize that protection against the complete exposure of the doings of the individual may be a right indispensable to the enjoyment of life. For these reasons I am of opinion that the plaintiff's grievance, although of an unprecedented character, falls within the settled principles upon which the action for nuisance depends. Holding this opinion it is unnecessary for me to discuss the question of copyright raised in the case.

I think that the appeal should be allowed . . .

Dixon J.: . . .

The plaintiff's counsel relied in the first instance upon an action on the case in the nature of nuisance. The premises of the plaintiff are occupied by it for the purpose of a racecourse. They have the natural advantage of not being overlooked by any surrounding heights or raised ground. They have been furnished with all the equipment of a racecourse and so enclosed as to prevent any unauthorised ingress or, unless by some such exceptional devices as the defendants have adopted, any unauthorised view of the spectacle. The plaintiff can thus exclude the public who do not pay and can exclude them not only from the presence at, but also from knowledge of, the proceedings upon the course. It is upon the ability to do this that the profitable character of the enterprise ultimately depends. The position of and the improvements to the land thus fit in for a racecourse and give its occupation a particular value. The defendants then proceed by an unusual use of their premises to deprive the plaintiff's land of this value, to strip it of its exclusiveness. By the tower placed where the race will be fully visible and equipped with microphone and line, they enable Angles to see the spectacle and convey its substance by broadcast. The effect is, the plaintiff says, just as if they supplied the plaintiff's customers with elevated vantage points round the course from which they could witness all that otherwise would attract them and induce them to pay the price of admission to the course. The feature in which the plaintiff finds the wrong of nuisance is the impairment or deprivation of the advantages possessed by the plaintiff's land as a racecourse by means of a non-natural and unusual use of the defendant's land.

This treatment of the case will not, I think, hold water. It may be conceded that interferences of a physical nature, as by fumes, smell and noise, are not the only means of committing a private nuisance. But the essence of the wrong is the detraction from the occupier's enjoyment of the natural rights belonging to, or in the case of easements, of the acquired rights annexed to, the occupation of land. The law fixes those rights. Diversion of custom from a business carried on upon the land may be brought about by noise, fumes, obstruction of the frontage or any other interference with the enjoyment of recognised rights arising from the occupation of property and, if so, it forms a legitimate head of damage recoverable for the wrong; but it is not the wrong itself. The existence or the use of a microphone upon neighbouring land, is, of course, no nuisance. If one, who could not see the spectacle, took upon himself to broadcast a fictitious account of the races he might conceivably render himself liable in a form of action in which his falsehood played apart, but he would commit no nuisance. It is the obtaining a view of the premises which is the foundation of the allegation. But English law is, rightly or wrongly, clear that the natural rights of an occupier do not include freedom from the view and inspection of neighbouring occupiers and of other persons who enable themselves to overlook the premises. An occupier of land is at liberty to exclude his neighbour's view by any physical means he can adopt. But while it is no wrongful act on his part to block the prospect from adjacent land, it is no wrongful act on the part of any person on such land to avail himself of what prospect exists or can be obtained. Not only is it lawful on the part of those occupying premises in the vicinity to overlook the land from any natural vantage point, but artificial erections may be made which destroy the privacy existing under natural conditions. In *Chandler v. Thompson* (1811) 3 Camp 80 at 82; 170 ER 1312 at 1313, Le Blanc J. said that, although an action for opening a window to disturb the plaintiff's privacy was to be read of in the books, he had never known such an action maintained, and when he was in the common pleas he had heard it laid down by Eyre L.C.J. that such an action did not lie and that the only remedy was to build on the adjoining land opposite to the offensive window. After that date there is, I think, no trace in the authorities of any doctrine to the contrary. In *Johnson v. Wyatt* (1863) 2 DeG J & S 18 at 27; 46 ER 281 at 284, Turner L.J. said: "That the windows of the house may be overlooked, and its comparative privacy destroyed, and its value thus diminished by the proposed erection . . . are matters with which, as I apprehend, we have nothing to do", that is, they afford no ground for an injunction . . . This principle formed one of the subsidiary reasons upon which the decision of the House of Lords was based in *Tapling v. Jones* (1865) 11 HLC 290 at 317; 11 ER 1344 at 1355. Lord Chelmsford said:

> . . . the owner of a house has a right at all times . . . to open as many windows in his own house as he pleases. By the exercise of the right he may materially interfere with the comfort and enjoyment of his neighbour; but of this species of injury the law takes no cognisance. It leaves everyone to his self-defence against an annoyance of this description; and the only remedy in the power of adjoining owner is to build on his own ground, and so to shut out the offensive windows.

When this principle is applied to the plaintiff's case it means, I think, that the essential element upon which it depends is lacking. So far as freedom from view or inspection is a natural or acquired physical characteristic of the site, giving it value for the purpose of the business or pursuit which the plaintiff conducts, it is a characteristic which is not a legally protected interest. It is not a natural right for breach of which a legal remedy is given, either by an action in the nature of nuisance or otherwise. The fact is that the substance of the plaintiff's complaint goes to interference, not with its enjoyment of the land, but with the profitable conduct of its business. If English law had followed the course of development that has recently taken place in the United States, the "broadcasting rights" in respect of the races might have been protected as part of the quasi-property created by the enterprise, organisation and labour of the plaintiff in establishing and equipping a racecourse and doing all that is necessary to conduct race meetings. But courts of equity have not in British jurisdictions thrown the protection of an injunction around all the intangible elements of value, that is, value in exchange, which may flow from the exercise by an individual of his powers or resources whether in the organisation of a business or undertaking or the use of ingenuity, knowledge, skill or labour. This is sufficiently evidenced by the history of the law of copyright and by fact that exclusive right to invention, trade marks, designs, trade name and reputation are dealt with in English law as special heads of protected interests and not under a wide generalisation.

In dissenting from a judgment of the Supreme Court of the United States by which the organized collection of news by a news service was held to give it in equity a quasi-property protected against appropriation by rival news agencies, Brandeis J. gave reasons which substantially represent the English view and he supported his opinion by a citation of much English authority (*International News Service v. Associated Press*). His judgment appears to me to contain an adequate answer both upon principle and authority to the suggestion that the defendants are misappropriating or abstracting something which the plaintiff has created and alone is entitled to turn to value. Briefly, the answer is that it is not because the individual has by his efforts put himself in a position to obtain value for what he can give that his right to give it becomes protected by law and so assumes the exclusiveness of property, but because the intangible or incorporeal right he claims falls within a recognized category to which legal or equitable protection attaches.

In my opinion the right to exclude the defendants from broadcasting a description of the occurrences they can see upon the plaintiff's land is not given by law. It is not an interest falling within any category which is protected at law or in equity. I have had the advantage of reading the judgment of Rich J., but I am unable to regard the considerations which are there set out as justifying what I consider amounts not simply to a new application of settle principle but to the introduction into the law of new doctrine . . .

Appeal dismissed.

NOTE

McTiernan J. agreed with Latham C.J. and Dixon J.; Evatt J. dissented.

QUESTIONS

1. What significance did the law of nuisance play in the reasoning of this case? How does the nuisance-based analysis differ from the argument based on property in a "spectacle"?

2. In what way, if at all, can *Victoria Park* be distinguished from *I.N.S.*? Consider these two assessments. In "The Concept of Property: Property in Intangibles" (1978) 94 L.Q.R. 103, at 106, D.F. Libling offered this position:

> In the author's view, in the *Victoria Park* case, reasoning, analogous to that used in the *Associated Press* case, should have been applied. It should have been recognised that Taylor had a right to build (subject to building laws) whatever he liked on his land and

that he had a right to admit whomever he liked on his land. Angles had a right to look around and describe what he saw. But it should have also been recognised that they had no right to so contrive their activities that they appropriated the profits that could be made out of a spectacle that the plaintiff brought into being by expenditure of labour and money and for the purpose of profit making.

In *Pittsburgh Athletic Co. v. KQV Broadcasting Co.* 24 F. Supp. 490 (Pa. Dist.Ct., 1938) A had been granted the exclusive rights to broadcast play-by-play accounts of the Pittsburgh Pirates baseball games. An action was brought against B, a rival broadcaster who was providing coverage of the games derived from accounts of paid observers stationed outside of the stadium. In the course of deciding in favour of the plaintiff, Judge Schoonmaker referred (at 492, 493) to both the *I.N.S.* case and *Victoria Park*, which had been decided just beforehand:

On the unfair competition feature of the case, we rest our opinion on the case of *International News Service v. Associated Press* . . . In that case the court enjoined the International News Service from copying news from bulletin boards and early editions of the Associated Press newspapers, and selling such news so long as it had commercial value to the Associated Press. . . .

Defendant seeks to justify its action on the ground that the information it receives from its observers stationed on its own property without trespassing on plaintiff's property, may be lawfully broadcast by it. We cannot follow defendants's contention. . . . The cases cited by them we have carefully studied and are unable to accept as authority. In the Australian case, *Victoria Park Racing, etc. v. Taylor* . . . where the information broadcast was obtained from a tower adjoining a race track, the court refused an injunction, because there was neither a trespass on plaintiff's race track, or a nuisance created by defendant.

The doctrine of unfair competition is not recognized under English Common Law. Therefore this decision is not an authority.

3. Review the modern approach to "hot news" cases, as outlined in the *Motorola* decision. Apply the reasoning found there to the facts of *Victoria Park*.

4. What should Canadian law be?

Moore v. The Regents of the University of California 793 P.2d 479 (Cal. S.C., 1990) [footnotes omitted]

I. Introduction

Panelli J.:

We granted review in this case to determine whether plaintiff has stated a cause of action against his physician and other defendants for using his cells in potentially lucrative medical research without his permission. Plaintiff alleges that his physician failed to disclose preexisting research and economic interests in the cells before obtaining consent to the medical procedures by which they were extracted. The superior court sustained all defendants' demurrers to the third amended complaint, and the Court of Appeal reversed. We hold that the complaint states a cause of action for breach of the physician's disclosure obligations, but not for conversion.

II. Facts . . .

The plaintiff is John Moore (Moore), who underwent treatment for hairy-cell leukemia at the Medical Center of the University of California at Los Angeles (UCLA Medical Center) . . .

Moore first visited UCLA Medical Center on October 5, 1976, shortly after he learned that he had hairy-cell leukemia. After hospitalizing Moore and "withdr[awing] extensive amounts of blood, bone marrow aspirate, and other bodily substances," Golde [FN1] confirmed that diagnosis. At this time all defendants, including Golde, were aware that "certain blood products and blood components were of great value in a number of commercial and scientific efforts" and that access to a patient whose blood contained these substances would provide "competitive, commercial, and scientific advantages."

On October 8, 1976, Golde recommended that Moore's spleen be removed. Golde informed Moore "that he had reason to fear for his life, and that the proposed splenectomy operation . . . was necessary to slow down the progress of his disease." Based upon Golde's representations, Moore signed a written consent form authorizing the splenectomy.

Before the operation, Golde and Quan "formed the intent and made arrangements to obtain portions of [Moore's] spleen following its removal" and to take them to a separate research unit. Golde gave written instructions to this effect on October 18 and 19, 1976. These research activities "were not intended to have . . . any relation to [Moore's] medical . . . care." However, neither Golde nor Quan informed Moore of their plans to conduct this research or requested his permission. Surgeons at UCLA Medical Center, whom the complaint does not name as defendants, removed Moore's spleen on October 20, 1976.

Moore returned to the UCLA Medical Center several times between November 1976 and September 1983. He did so at Golde's direction and based upon representations "that such visits were necessary and required for his health and well-being, and based upon the trust inherent in and by virtue of the physician-patient relationship . . ." On each of these visits Golde withdrew additional samples of "blood, blood serum, skin, bone marrow aspirate, and sperm." On each occasion Moore travelled to the UCLA Medical Center from his home in Seattle because he had been told that the procedures were to be performed only there and only under Golde's direction.

"In fact, [however,] throughout the period of time that [Moore] was under [Golde's] care and treatment, . . . the defendants were actively involved in a number of activities which they concealed from [Moore] . . ." Specifically, defendants were conducting research on Moore's cells and planned to "benefit financially and competitively . . . [by exploiting the cells] and [their] exclusive access to [the cells] by virtue of [Golde's] on-going physician-patient relationship . . ."

Sometime before August 1979, Golde established a cell line from Moore's T-lymphocytes. On January 30, 1981, the Regents applied for a patent on the cell line, listing Golde and Quan as inventors. "[B]y virtue of an established policy . . ., [the] Regents, Golde, and Quan would share in any royalties or profits . . . arising out of [the] patent." The patent issued on March 20, 1984, naming Golde and Quan as the inventors of the cell line and the Regents as the assignee of the patent. (U.S. Patent No. 4,438,032 (Mar. 20, 1984)) . . .

III. Discussion . . .

[Pannelli J. first discussed the law of breach of fiduciary duty and lack of informed consent, finding that the facts alleged by Moore could found a cause of action on these grounds.]

B. Conversion

Moore also attempts to characterize the invasion of his rights as a conversion — a tort that protects against interference with possessory and ownership interests in personal property. He theorizes that he continued to own his cells following their removal from his body, at least for the purpose of directing their use, and that he never consented to their use in potentially lucrative medical research. Thus, to complete Moore's argument, defendants' unauthorized use of his cells constitutes a conversion. As a result of the alleged conversion, Moore claims a proprietary interest in each of the products that any of the defendants might ever create from his cells or the patented cell line . . .

1. Moore's Claim Under Existing Law

To establish a conversion, plaintiff must establish an actual interference with his *ownership or right of possession* . . . Where plaintiff neither has title to the property alleged to have been converted, nor possession thereof, he cannot maintain an action for conversion." (*Del E. Webb Corp. v. Structural Materials Co.* (1981) 123 Cal.App.3d 593, 610-611, 176 Cal.Rptr. 824, emphasis added. See also *General Motors A. Corp. v. Dallas* (1926) 198 Cal. 365, 370, 245 P. 184.)

Since Moore clearly did not expect to retain possession of his cells following their removal, to sue for their conversion he must have retained an ownership interest in them. But there are several reasons to doubt that he did retain any such interest. First, no reported judicial decision supports Moore's claim, either directly or by close analogy. Second, California statutory law drastically limits any continuing interest of a patient in excised cells. Third, the subject matters of the Regents' patent — the patented cell line and the products derived from it — cannot be Moore's property.

Neither the Court of Appeal's opinion, the parties' briefs, nor our research discloses a case holding that a person retains a sufficient interest in excised cells to support a cause of action for conversion . . .

Lacking direct authority for importing the law of conversion into this context, Moore relies, as did the Court of Appeal, primarily on decisions addressing privacy rights. One line of cases involves unwanted publicity . . .

Not only are the wrongful-publicity cases irrelevant to the issue of conversion, but the analogy to them seriously misconceives the nature of the genetic materials and research involved in this case. Moore, adopting the analogy originally advanced by the Court of Appeal, argues that "[i]f the courts have found a sufficient proprietary interest in one's persona, how could one not have a right in one's own genetic material, something far more profoundly the essence of one's human uniqueness than a name or a face?" However, as the defendants' patent makes clear — and the complaint, too, if read with an understanding of the scientific terms which it has borrowed from the patent — the goal and result of defendants' efforts has been to manufacture lymphokines. Lymphokines, unlike a name or a face, have the same molecular structure in every human being and the same, important functions in every human being's immune system. Moreover, the particular genetic material which is responsible for the natural production of lymphokines, and which defendants use to manufacture lymphokines in the laboratory, is also the same in every person; it is no more unique to Moore than the number of vertebrae in the spine or the chemical formula of hemoglobin . . .

The next consideration that makes Moore's claim of ownership problematic is California statutory law, which drastically limits a patient's control over excised cells. Pursuant to Health and Safety Code section 7054.4, "[n]otwithstanding any other provision of law, recognizable anatomical parts, human tissues, anatomical human remains, or infectious waste following conclusion of scientific use shall be disposed of by interment, incineration, or any other method determined by the state department [of health services] to protect the public health and safety." Clearly the Legislature did not specifically intend this statute to resolve the question of whether a patient is entitled to compensation for the nonconsensual use of excised cells. A primary object of the statute is to ensure the safe handling of potentially hazardous biological waste materials. Yet one cannot escape the conclusion that the statute's practical effect is to limit, drastically, a patient's control over excised cells. By restricting how excised cells may be used and requiring their eventual destruction, the statute eliminates so many of the rights ordinarily attached to property that one cannot simply assume that what is left amounts to "property" or "ownership" for purposes of conversion law . . .

Finally, the subject matter of the Regents' patent — the patented cell line and the products derived from it — cannot be Moore's property. This is because the patented cell line is both factually and legally distinct from the cells taken from Moore's body. Federal law permits the patenting of organisms that represent the product of "human ingenuity," but not naturally occurring organisms. (*Diamond v. Chakrabarty* (1980) 447 U.S. 303, 309-310, 100 S.Ct. 2204, 2208, 65 L.Ed.2d 144.)

Human cell lines are patentable because "[l]ong-term adaptation and growth of human tissues and cells in culture is difficult — often considered an art . . .," and the probability of success is low. (U.S. Congress, Office of Technology Assessment, New Developments in Biotechnology: Ownership of Human Tissues and Cells (1987) at p. 33 (hereafter OTA Rep.)). It is this *inventive effort* that patent law rewards, not the discovery of naturally occurring raw materials. Thus, Moore's allegations that he owns the cell line and the products derived from it are inconsistent with the patent, which constitutes an authoritative determination that the cell line is the product of invention. Since such allegations are nothing more than arguments or conclusions of law, they of course do not bind us. (*Daar v. Yellow Cab Co.* (1967) 67 Cal. 2d 695 at p. 713, 713 Cal.Rptr. 724, 433 P.2d 732.)

2. Should Conversion Liability Be Extended?

As we have discussed, Moore's novel claim to own the biological materials at issue in this case is problematic, at best. Accordingly, his attempt to apply the theory of conversion within this context must frankly be recognized as a request to extend that theory. While we do not purport to hold that excised cells can never be property for any purpose whatsoever, the novelty of Moore's claim demands express consideration of the policies to be served by extending liability . . . rather than blind deference to a complaint alleging as a legal conclusion the existence of a cause of action.

There are three reasons why it is inappropriate to impose liability for conversion based upon the allegations of Moore's complaint. First, a fair balancing of the relevant policy considerations counsels against extending the tort. Second, problems in this area are better suited to legislative resolution. Third, the tort of conversion is not necessary to protect patients' rights. For these reasons, we conclude that the use of excised human cells in medical research does not amount to a conversion.

Of the relevant policy considerations, two are of overriding importance. The first is protection of a competent patient's right to make autonomous medical decisions. That right, as already discussed, is grounded in well-recognized and long-standing principles of fiduciary duty and informed consent. (See, e.g., *Cobbs v. Grant* [(1972) 8 Cal.3d 229] at pp. 242-246, 104 Cal.Rptr. 505, 502 P.2d 1; *Bowman v. McPheeters* [(1947) 77 Cal.App.2d 795] at p. 800, 176 P.2d 745.) This policy weighs in favor of providing a remedy to patients when physicians act with undisclosed motives that may affect their professional judgment. The second important policy consideration is that we not threaten with disabling civil liability innocent parties who are engaged in socially useful activities, such as researchers who have no reason to believe that their use of a particular cell sample is, or may be, against a donor's wishes.

To reach an appropriate balance of these policy considerations is extremely important. In its report to Congress (see fn. 2, *ante*), the Office of Technology Assessment emphasized that "[u]ncertainty about how courts will resolve disputes between specimen sources and specimen users could be detrimental to both academic researchers and the infant biotechnology industry, particularly when the rights are asserted long after the specimen was obtained. The assertion of rights by sources would affect not only the researcher who obtained the original specimen, but perhaps other researchers as well.

> Biological materials are routinely distributed to other researchers for experimental purposes, and scientists who obtain cell lines or other specimen-derived products, such as gene clones, from the original researcher could also be sued under certain legal theories [such as conversion]. Furthermore, the uncertainty could affect product developments as well as research. Since inventions containing human tissues and cells may be patented and licensed for commercial use, companies are unlikely to invest heavily in developing, manufacturing, or marketing a product when uncertainty about clear title exists. (OTA Rep., *supra*, at p. 27.)

Indeed, so significant is the potential obstacle to research stemming from uncertainty about legal title to biological materials that the Office of Technology Assessment reached this striking conclusion: "[R]egardless of the merit of claims by the different interested parties, resolving the current uncertainty may be more important to the future of biotechnology than resolving it in any particular way." (OTA Rep., *supra*, at p. 27.)

We need not, however, make an arbitrary choice between liability and nonliability. Instead, an examination of the relevant policy considerations suggests an appropriate balance: Liability based upon existing disclosure obligations, rather than an unprecedented extension of the conversion theory, protects patients' rights of privacy and autonomy without unnecessarily hindering research.

To be sure, the threat of liability for conversion might help to enforce patients' rights indirectly. This is because physicians might be able to avoid liability by obtaining patients' consent, in the broadest possible terms, to any conceivable subsequent research use of excised cells. Unfortunately, to extend the conversion theory would utterly sacrifice the other goal of protecting innocent parties. Since conversion is a strict liability tort, it would impose liability on all those into whose hands the cells come, whether or not the particular defendant participated in, or knew of, the inadequate disclosures that violated the patient's right to make an informed decision. In contrast to the conversion theory, the fiduciary-duty and informed-consent theories protect the patient directly, without punishing innocent parties or creating disincentives to the conduct of socially beneficial research.

Research on human cells plays a critical role in medical research. This is so because researchers are increasingly able to isolate naturally occurring, medically useful biological substances and to produce useful quantities of such substances through genetic engineering. These efforts are beginning to bear fruit. Products developed through biotechnology that have already been approved for marketing in this country include treatments and tests for leukemia, cancer, diabetes, dwarfism, hepatitis-B, kidney transplant rejection, emphysema, osteoporosis, ulcers, anemia, infertility, and gynecological tumors, to name but a few. (Note: *Source Compensation for Tissues and Cells Used in Biotechnical Research: Why a Source Shouldn't*

Share in the Profits (1989) 64 Notre Dame L.Rev. 628 & fn. 1 (hereafter Note, Source Compensation); see also OTA Rep., *supra*, at pp. 58-59.)

The extension of conversion law into this area will hinder research by restricting access to the necessary raw materials. Thousands of human cell lines already exist in tissue repositories, such as the American Type Culture Collection and those operated by the National Institutes of Health and the American Cancer Society. These repositories respond to tens of thousands of requests for samples annually. Since the patent office requires the holders of patents on cell lines to make samples available to anyone, many patent holders place their cell lines in repositories to avoid the administrative burden of responding to requests. (OTA Rep., *supra*, at p. 53.) At present, human cell lines are routinely copied and distributed to other researchers for experimental purposes, usually free of charge. This exchange of scientific materials, which still is relatively free and efficient, will surely be compromised if each cell sample becomes the potential subject matter of a lawsuit. (OTA Rep., *supra*, at p. 52.)

To expand liability by extending conversion law into this area would have a broad impact. The House Committee on Science and Technology of the United States Congress found that "49 percent of the researchers at medical institutions surveyed used human tissues or cells in their research." Many receive grants from the National Institute of Health for this work. (OTA Rep., *supra*, at p. 52.) In addition, "there are nearly 350 commercial biotechnology firms in the United States actively engaged in biotechnology research and commercial product development and approximately 25 to 30 percent appear to be engaged in research to develop a human therapeutic or diagnostic reagent . . . Most, but not all, of the human therapeutic products are derived from human tissues and cells, or human cell lines or cloned genes." (*Id.*, at p. 56.)

In deciding whether to create new tort duties we have in the past considered the impact that expanded liability would have on activities that are important to society, such as research. For example, in *Brown v. Superior Court, supra*, 44 Cal.3d 1049, 245 Cal.Rptr. 412, 751 P.2d 470, the fear that strict product liability would frustrate pharmaceutical research led us to hold that a drug manufacturer's liability should not be measured by those standards. We wrote that, "[i]f drug manufacturers were subject to strict liability, they might be reluctant to undertake research programs to develop some pharmaceuticals that would prove beneficial or to distribute others that are available to be marketed, because of the fear of large adverse monetary judgments." (*Id.*, at p. 1063, 245 Cal.Rptr. 412, 751 P.2d 470.

As in *Brown*, the theory of liability that Moore urges us to endorse threatens to destroy the economic incentive to conduct important medical research. If the use of cells in research is a conversion, then with every cell sample a researcher purchases a ticket in a litigation lottery. Because liability for conversion is predicated on a continuing ownership interest, "companies are unlikely to invest heavily in developing, manufacturing, or marketing a product when uncertainty about clear title exists." (OTA Rep., *supra*, at p. 27.) In our view, borrowing again from *Brown*, "[i]t is not unreasonable to conclude in these circumstances that the imposition of a harsher test for liability would not further the public interest in the development and availability of these important products." (*Brown v. Superior Court, supra*, 44 Cal.3d at p. 1065, 245 Cal.Rptr. 412, 751 P.2d 470.)

Indeed, this is a far more compelling case for limiting the expansion of tort liability than *Brown*. In *Brown*, eliminating strict liability made it more difficult for plaintiffs to recover actual damages for serious physical injuries resulting from their mothers' prenatal use of the drug diethylstilbestrol (DES). (*Brown v. Superior Court, supra*, 44 Cal.3d at pp. 1054-1055, 245 Cal.Rptr. 412, 751 P.2d 470.) In this case, by comparison, limiting the expansion of liability under a conversion theory will only make it more difficult for Moore to recover a highly theoretical windfall. Any injury to his right to make an informed decision remains actionable through the fiduciary-duty and informed-consent theories.

If the scientific users of human cells are to be held liable for failing to investigate the consensual pedigree of their raw materials, we believe the Legislature should make that decision. Complex policy choices affecting all society are involved, and "[l]egislatures, in making such policy decisions, have the ability to gather empirical evidence, solicit the advice of experts, and hold hearings at which all interested parties present evidence and express their views. . . ." (*Foley v. Interactive Data Corp.*, 47 Cal.3d at p. 694, fn. 31, 254 Cal.Rptr. 211, 765 P.2d 373.) Legislative competence to act in this area is demonstrated by the existing statutes governing the use and disposition of human biological materials. Legislative interest is demonstrated by the extensive study recently commissioned by the United States Congress. (OTA Rep., *supra*.) Commentators are also recommending legislative solutions. (See Danforth, *Cells, Sales, and Royalties: The Patient's Right to a Portion of the Profits* (1988) 6 Yale L. & Pol'y Rev. 179, 198-201; Note, Source Compensation, *supra*, 64 Notre Dame L.Rev. at pp. 643- 645.)

Finally, there is no pressing need to impose a judicially created rule of strict liability, since enforcement of physicians' disclosure obligations will protect patients against the very type of harm with which Moore was threatened. So long as a physician discloses research and economic interests that may affect his judgment, the patient is protected from conflicts of interest. Aware of any conflicts, the patient can make an informed decision to consent to treatment, or to withhold consent and look elsewhere for medical assistance. As already discussed, enforcement of physicians' disclosure obligations protects patients directly, without hindering the socially useful activities of innocent researchers.

For these reasons, we hold that the allegations of Moore's third amended complaint state a cause of action for breach of fiduciary duty or lack of informed consent, but not conversion . . .

Mosk J.:

I dissent.

Contrary to the principal holding of the Court of Appeal, the majority conclude that the complaint does not—in fact cannot—state a cause of action for conversion. I disagree with this conclusion for all the reasons stated by the Court of Appeal, and for additional reasons that I shall explain. For convenience I shall discuss the six premises of the majority's conclusion in the order in which they appear.

1. The majority first take the position that Moore has no cause of action for conversion under existing law because he retained no "ownership interest" in his cells after they were removed from his body. (Maj. opn., *ante*, p. 156 of Cal.Rptr., p. 489 of 793 P.2d.) To state a conversion cause of action a plaintiff must allege his "ownership or right to possession of the property at the time of the conversion" (*Baldwin v. Marina City Properties, Inc.* (1978) 79 Cal.App.3d 393, 410, 145 Cal.Rptr. 406). Here the complaint defines Moore's "Blood and Bodily Substances" to include *inter alia* his blood, his bodily tissues, his cells, and the cell lines derived therefrom. Moore thereafter alleges that "he is the owner of his Blood and Bodily Substances and of the by-products produced therefrom . . ." And he further alleges that such blood and bodily substances "are his tangible personal property, and the activities of the defendants as set forth herein constitute a substantial interference with plaintiff's possession or right thereto, as well as defendants' wrongful exercise of dominion over plaintiff's personal property rights in his Blood and Bodily Substances."

The majority impliedly hold these allegations insufficient as a matter of law, finding three "reasons to doubt" that Moore retained a sufficient ownership interest in his cells, after their excision, to support a conversion cause of action. (Maj. opn., *ante*, p. 156 of 271 Cal.Rptr., p. 489 of 793 P.2d.) In my view the majority's three reasons, taken singly or together, are inadequate to the task.

The majority's first reason is that "no reported judicial decision supports Moore's claim, either directly or by close analogy." (Maj. opn., *ante* , p. 156 of 271 Cal.Rptr., p. 489 of 793 P.2d.) Neither, however, is there any reported decision rejecting such a claim. The issue is as new as its source — the recent explosive growth in the commercialization of biotechnology.

The majority next cite several statutes regulating aspects of the commerce in or disposition of certain parts of the human body, and conclude in effect that in the present case we should also "look for guidance" to the Legislature rather than to the law of conversion. (*Id.* at p. 156 of 271 Cal.Rptr., at p. 489 of 793 P.2d.) Surely this argument is out of place in an opinion of the highest court of this state. As the majority acknowledge, the law of conversion is a creature of the common law. " 'The inherent capacity of the common law for growth and change is its most significant feature. Its development has been determined by the social needs of the community which it serves. It is constantly expanding and developing in keeping with advancing civilization and the new conditions and progress of society, and adapting itself to the gradual change of trade, commerce, arts, inventions, and the needs of the country.' In short, as the United States Supreme Court has aptly said, 'This flexibility and capacity for growth and adaptation is the peculiar boast and excellence of the common law.' . . . Although the Legislature may of course speak to the subject, in the common law system the primary instruments of this evolution are the courts, adjudicating on a regular basis the rich variety of individual cases brought before them." (*Rodriguez v. Bethlehem Steel Corp.* (1974) 12 Cal.3d 382, 394, 115 Cal.Rptr. 765, 525 P.2d 669.)

. . . My point is that if the cause of action for conversion is otherwise an appropriate remedy on these facts, we should not refrain from fashioning it simply because another court has not yet so held or because the Legislature has not yet addressed the question. We need not wait on either event, because neither is a precondition to an exercise of our long-standing "power to insure the just and rational development of the common law in our state" (*Rodriguez v. Bethlehem Steel Corp., supra*, 12 Cal.3d 382, 394, 115 Cal.Rptr. 765, 525 P.2d 669).

2. The majority's second reason for doubting that Moore retained an ownership interest in his cells after their excision is that "California statutory law . . . drastically limits a patient's control over excised cells." (Maj. opn., *ante*, p. 158 of 271 Cal.Rptr., p. 491 of 793 P.2d.) For this proposition the majority rely on Health and Safety Code section 7054.4 (hereafter section 7054.4), set forth in the margin. The majority concede that the statute was not meant to directly resolve the question whether a person in Moore's position has a cause of action for conversion, but reason that it indirectly resolves the question by limiting the patient's control over the fate of his excised cells: "By restricting how excised cells may be used and requiring their eventual destruction, the statute eliminates so many of the rights ordinarily attached to property that one cannot simply assume that what is left amounts to 'property' or 'ownership' for purposes of conversion law." (Maj. opn., *ante*, pp. 158-159 of 271 Cal.Rptr., pp. 491-492 of 793 P.2d.) As will appear, I do not believe section 7054.4 supports the just quoted conclusion of the majority . . .

Secondly, even if section 7054.4 does permit defendants' commercial exploitation of Moore's tissue under the guise of "scientific use," it does not follow that — as the majority conclude — the statute "eliminates so many of the rights ordinarily attached to property" that what remains does not amount to "property" or "ownership" for purposes of the law of conversion. (Maj. opn., *ante*, p. 159 of 271 Cal.Rptr., p. 492 of 793 P.2d.)

The concepts of property and ownership in our law are extremely broad. (See Civ.Code, §§654, 655.) A leading decision of this court approved the following definition: "The term 'property' is sufficiently comprehensive to include every species of estate, real and personal, and everything which one person can own and transfer to another. It extends to every species of right and interest capable of being enjoyed as such upon which it is practicable to place a money value." (*Yuba River Power Co. v. Nevada Irr. Dist.* (1929) 207 Cal. 521, 523, 279 P. 128.)

Being broad, the concept of property is also abstract: rather than referring directly to a material object such as a parcel of land or the tractor that cultivates it, the concept of property is often said to refer to a "bundle of rights" that may be exercised with respect to that object—principally the rights to possess the property, to use the property, to exclude others from the property, and to dispose of the property by sale or by gift. "Ownership is not a single concrete entity but a bundle of rights and privileges as well as of obligations." (*Union Oil Co. v. State Bd. of Equal.* (1963) 60 Cal.2d 441, 447, 34 Cal.Rptr. 872, 386 P.2d 496.) But the same bundle of rights does not attach to all forms of property. For a variety of policy reasons, the law limits or even forbids the exercise of certain rights over certain forms of property. For example, both law and contract may limit the right of an owner of real property to use his parcel as he sees fit. Owners of various forms of personal property may likewise be subject to restrictions on the time, place, and manner of their use. Limitations on the disposition of real property, while less common, may also be imposed. Finally, some types of personal property may be sold but not given away, while others may be given away but not sold, and still others may neither be given away nor sold.

In each of the foregoing instances, the limitation or prohibition diminishes the bundle of rights that would otherwise attach to the property, yet what remains is still deemed in law to be a protectible property interest. "Since property or title is a complex bundle of rights, duties, powers and immunities, the pruning away of some or a great many of these elements does not entirely destroy the title . . ." (*People v. Walker* (1939) 33 Cal.App.2d 18, 20, 90 P.2d 854 [even the possessor of contraband has certain property rights in it against anyone other than the state].) The same rule applies to Moore's interest in his own body tissue: even if we assume that section 7054.4 limited the use and disposition of his excised tissue in the manner claimed by the majority, Moore nevertheless retained valuable rights in that tissue. Above all, at the time of its excision he at least had *the right to do with his own tissue whatever the defendants did with it*: i.e., he could have contracted with researchers and pharmaceutical companies to develop and exploit the vast commercial potential of his tissue and its products. Defendants certainly believe that *their* right to do the foregoing is not barred by section 7054.4 and is a significant property right, as they have demonstrated by their deliberate concealment from Moore of the true value of his tissue, their efforts to obtain a patent on the Mo cell line, their contractual agreements to exploit this material, their exclusion of Moore from any participation in the profits, and their vigorous defense of this lawsuit . . .

3. The majority's third and last reason for their conclusion that Moore has no cause of action for conversion under existing law is that "the subject matter of the Regents' patent — the patented cell line and the products derived from it — cannot be Moore's property." (Maj. opn., *ante*, p. 159 of 271 Cal.Rptr., p. 492 of 793 P.2d.) The majority then offer a dual explanation: "This is because the patented cell line is factually and legally distinct from the cells taken from Moore's body." (*Ibid.*, italics added.) Neither branch of the explanation withstands analysis.

First, in support of their statement that the Mo cell line is "factually distinct" from Moore's cells, the majority assert that "Cells change while being developed into a cell line and continue to change over time," and in particular may acquire an abnormal number of chromosomes. (Maj. opn., *ante*, p. 159, fn. 35 of 271 Cal.Rptr., p. 492, fn. 35 of 793 P.2d.) No one disputes these assertions, but they are nonetheless irrelevant. For present purposes no distinction can be drawn between Moore's cells and the Mo cell line. It appears that the principal reason for establishing a cell line is not to "improve" the quality of the parent cells but simply to extend their life indefinitely, in order to permit long-term study and/or exploitation of the qualities already present in such cells. The complaint alleges that Moore's cells naturally produced certain valuable proteins in larger than normal quantities; indeed, that was why defendants were eager to culture them in the first place. Defendants do not claim that the cells of the Mo cell line are in any degree more productive of such proteins than were Moore's own cells. Even if the cells of the Mo cell line in fact have an abnormal number of chromosomes, at the present stage of this case we do not know if that fact has any bearing whatever on their capacity to produce proteins; yet it is in the commercial exploitation of that capacity — not simply in their number of chromosomes — that Moore seeks to assert an interest. For all that appears, therefore, the emphasized fact is a distinction without a difference.

Second, the majority assert in effect that Moore cannot have an ownership interest in the Mo cell line because defendants patented it. The majority's point wholly fails to meet Moore's claim that he is entitled to compensation for defendants' unauthorized use of his bodily tissues *before* defendants patented the Mo cell line: defendants undertook such use immediately after the splenectomy on October 20, 1976, and continued to extract and use Moore's cells and tissue at least until September 20, 1983; the patent, however, did not issue until March 20, 1984, more than seven years after the unauthorized use began. Whatever the legal consequences of that event, it did not operate retroactively to immunize defendants from accountability for conduct occurring long before the patent was granted.

Nor did the issuance of the patent in 1984 necessarily have the drastic effect that the majority contend. To be sure, the patent granted defendants the exclusive right to make, use, or sell the invention for a period of 17 years. (35 U.S.C. §154.) But Moore does not assert any such right for himself. Rather, he seeks to show that he is entitled, in fairness and equity, to some share in the profits that defendants have made and will make from their commercial exploitation of the Mo cell line. I do not question that the cell line is primarily the product of defendants' inventive effort. Yet likewise no one can question Moore's crucial contribution to the invention—an invention named, ironically, after him: but for the cells of Moore's body taken by defendants, *there would have been no Mo cell line*. Thus the complaint alleges that Moore's "Blood and Bodily Substances were absolutely essential to defendants' research and commercial activities with regard to his cells, cell lines, [and] the Mo cell-line, . . . and that defendants could not have applied for and had issued to them the Mo cell-line patent and other patents described herein without obtaining and culturing specimens of plaintiff's Blood and Bodily Substances." Defendants admit this allegation by their demurrers, as well they should: for all their expertise, defendants do not claim they could have extracted the Mo cell line out of thin air.

Nevertheless the majority conclude that the patent somehow cut off all Moore's rights—past, present, and future—to share in the proceeds of defendants' commercial exploitation of the cell line derived from his own body tissue. The majority cite no authority for this unfair result, and I cannot believe it is compelled by the general law of patents: a patent is not a license to defraud. Perhaps the answer lies in an analogy to the concept of "joint inventor." I am aware that "patients and research subjects who contribute cells to research will not be considered inventors." (OTA Rep., *supra,* at p. 71.) Nor is such a person strictly speaking a "joint inventor" within the meaning of the term in federal law. (35 U.S.C. §116.) But he does fall within the spirit of that law: "The joint invention provision guarantees that all who contribute in a substantial way to a product's development benefit from the reward that the product brings. Thus, the protection of joint inventors encourages scientists to cooperate with each other and ensures that each contributor is rewarded fairly.

> Although a patient who donates cells does not fit squarely within the definition of a joint inventor, the policy reasons that inform joint inventor patents should also apply to cell donors. Neither John Moore nor any other patient whose cells become the basis for a patentable cell line qualifies as a 'joint inventor' because he or she did not further the development of the product in any intellectual or conceptual sense. Nor does the status of patients as sole owners of a component part make them deserving of joint inventorship status. What the patients did do, knowingly or unknowingly, is collaborate with the researchers by donating their body tissue
>
> . . . By providing the researchers with unique raw materials, without which the resulting product could not exist, the donors become necessary contributors to the product. Concededly, the patent is not granted for the cell as it is found in nature, but for the modified biogenetic product. However, the uniqueness of the product that gives rise to its patentability stems from the uniqueness of the original cell. *A patient's claim to share in the profits flowing from a patent would be analogous to that of an inventor whose collaboration was essential to the success of a resulting product. The patient was not a coequal, but was a necessary contributor to the cell line.* (Danforth, *Cells, Sales, & Royalties: The Patient's Right to a Portion of the Profits* (1988) 6 Yale L. & Pol'y Rev. 179, 197, fns. omitted, italics added (hereafter Danforth).)

Under this reasoning, which I find persuasive, the law of patents would not be a bar to Moore's assertion of an ownership interest in his cells and their products sufficient to warrant his sharing in the proceeds of their commercial exploitation.

4. Having concluded — mistakenly, in my view — that Moore has no cause of action for conversion under existing law, the majority next consider whether to "extend" the conversion cause of action to this context. Again the majority find three reasons not to do so, and again I respectfully disagree with each.

The majority's first reason is that a balancing of the "relevant policy considerations" counsels against recognizing a conversion cause of action in these circumstances. (Maj. opn., *ante*, p. 160 of 271 Cal.Rptr., p. 493 of 793 P.2d.) The memo identifies two such policies, but concedes that one of them — "protection of a competent patient's right to make autonomous medical decisions" (*id.* at p. 160 of 271 Cal.Rptr., p. 493 of 793 P.2d) — would in fact be promoted, even though "indirectly," by recognizing a conversion cause of action. (*Id.* at p. 160 of 271 Cal.Rptr., at p. 493 of 793 P.2d.)

The majority focus instead on a second policy consideration, i.e., their concern "that we not threaten with disabling civil liability innocent parties who are engaged in socially useful activities, such as researchers who have no reason to believe that their use of a particular cell sample is, or may be, against a donor's wishes." (Maj. opn., *ante*, p. 160 of 271 Cal.Rptr., p. 493 of 793 P.2d.) As will appear, in my view this concern is both overstated and outweighed by contrary considerations.

The majority begin their analysis by stressing the obvious facts that research on human cells plays an increasingly important role in the progress of medicine, and that the manipulation of those cells by the methods of biotechnology has resulted in numerous beneficial products and treatments. Yet it does not necessarily follow that, as the majority claim, application of the law of conversion to this area "will hinder research by restricting access to the necessary raw materials," i.e., to cells, cell cultures, and cell lines. (Maj. opn., *ante*, p. 161 of 271 Cal.Rptr., p. 494 of 793 P.2d.) The majority observe that many researchers obtain their tissue samples, routinely and at little or no cost, from cell-culture repositories. The majority then speculate that "This exchange of scientific materials, which still is relatively free and efficient, will surely be compromised if each cell sample becomes the potential subject matter of a lawsuit." (Maj. opn., *ante*, p. 162 of 271 Cal.Rptr., p. 495 of 793 P.2d.) There are two grounds to doubt that this prophecy will be fulfilled.

To begin with, if the relevant exchange of scientific materials was ever "free and efficient," it is much less so today. Since biological products of genetic engineering became patentable in 1980 (*Diamond v. Chakrabarty* (1980) 447 U.S. 303, 100 S.Ct. 2204, 65 L.Ed.2d 144), human cell lines have been amenable to patent protection and, as the Court of Appeal observed in its opinion below, "The rush to patent for exclusive use has been rampant." Among those who have taken advantage of this development, of course, are the defendants herein: as we have seen, defendants Golde and Quan obtained a patent on the Mo cell line in 1984 and assigned it to defendant Regents. With such patentability has come a drastic reduction in the formerly free access of researchers to new cell lines and their products: the "novelty" requirement for patentability prohibits public disclosure of the invention at all times up to one year before the filing of the patent application. (35 U.S.C. §102(b).) Thus defendants herein recited in their patent specification, "At no time has the Mo cell line been available to other than the investigators involved with its initial discovery and only the conditioned medium from the cell line has been made available to a limited number of investigators for collaborative work with the original discoverers of the Mo cell line."

An even greater force for restricting the free exchange of new cell lines and their products has been the rise of the biotechnology industry and the increasing involvement of academic researchers in that industry. When scientists became entrepreneurs and negotiated with biotechnological and pharmaceutical companies to develop and exploit the commercial potential of their discoveries — as did defendants in the case at bar — layers of contractual restrictions were added to the protections of the patent law.

In their turn, the biotechnological and pharmaceutical companies demanded and received exclusive rights in the scientists' discoveries, and frequently placed those discoveries under trade secret protection. Trade secret protection is popular among biotechnology companies because, among other reasons, the invention need not meet the strict standards of patentability and the protection is both quickly acquired and unlimited in duration. (Note, *Patent and Trade Secret Protection in University-Industry Research Relationships in Biotechnology* (1987) 24 Harv.J. on Legis. 191, 218-219.) Secrecy as a normal business practice is also taking hold in university research laboratories, often because of industry pressure (*id.* at pp. 204-208): "One of the most serious fears associated with university-industry cooperative research concerns keeping work private and not disclosing it to the researcher's peers . . . Economic arrangements between industry and universities inhibit open communication between researchers, especially for those who are financially tied to smaller biotechnology firms." (Howard, [*Biotechnology, Patients' Rights, and the Moore Case* (1989) 44 Food Drug Cosm.L.J. (hereafter Howard)] at p. 339, fn. 72.)

Secondly, to the extent that cell cultures and cell lines may still be "freely exchanged," e.g., for purely research purposes, it does not follow that the researcher who obtains such material must necessarily remain ignorant of any limitations on its use: by means of appropriate record-keeping, the researcher can be assured that the source of the material has consented to his proposed use of it, and hence that such use is not a conversion. To achieve this end the originator of the tissue sample first determines the extent of the source's informed consent to its use — e.g., for research only, or for public but academic use, or for specific or general commercial purposes; he then enters this information in the record of the tissue sample, and the record accompanies the sample into the hands of any researcher who thereafter undertakes to work with it. "Record keeping would not be overly burdensome because researchers generally keep accurate records of tissue sources for other reasons: to trace anomalies to the medical history of the patient, to maintain title for other researchers and for themselves, and to insure reproducibility of the experiment." ([*Toward the Right of Commerciality: Recognizing Property Rights in the Commercial Value of Human Tissue* (1986) 34 UCLA L.Rev. 207] at p. 241 [hereafter Toward the Right of Commercialty]). As the Court of Appeal correctly observed, any claim to the contrary "is dubious in light of the meticulous care and planning necessary in serious modern medical research."

. . . The majority claim that a conversion cause of action threatens to "destroy the economic incentive" to conduct the type of research here in issue (maj. opn., *ante*, p. 162 of 271 Cal.Rptr., p. 495 of 793 P.2d), but it is difficult to take this hyperbole seriously. First, the majority reason that with every cell sample a researcher "purchases a ticket in a litigation lottery." (*Id.* at p. 162-163 of 271 Cal.Rptr., at p. 495-496 of 793 P.2d.) This is a colorful image, but it does not necessarily reflect reality: as explained above, with proper record-keeping the researcher acquires not a litigation-lottery ticket but the information he needs precisely in order to avoid litigation. In contrast to *Brown*, therefore, here the harm is by no means "unavoidable." Second, the risk at hand is not of a multiplicity of actions: in *Brown* the harm would be suffered by many members of the public — the users of the end product of the process of developing the new drug — while here it can be suffered by only one person — the original source of the research material that began that process. Third, the harm to the latter will be primarily economic, rather than . . . potentially grave physical injuries . . .

In any event, in my view whatever merit the majority's single policy consideration may have is outweighed by two contrary considerations, i.e., policies that are promoted by recognizing that every individual has a legally protectible property interest in his own body and its products. First, our society acknowledges a profound ethical imperative to respect the human body as the physical and temporal expression of the unique human persona. One manifestation of that respect is our prohibition against direct abuse of the body by torture or other forms of cruel or unusual punishment. Another is our prohibition against indirect abuse of the body by its economic exploitation for the sole benefit of another person. The most abhorrent form of such exploitation, of course, was the institution of slavery. Lesser forms, such as indentured servitude or even debtor's prison, have also disappeared. Yet their specter haunts the laboratories and boardrooms of today's biotechnological research-industrial complex. It arises wherever scientists or industrialists claim, as defendants claim here, the right to appropriate and exploit a patient's tissue for their sole economic benefit — the right, in other words, to freely mine or harvest valuable physical properties of the patient's body: "Research with human cells that results in significant economic gain for the researcher and no gain for the patient offends the traditional mores of our society in a manner impossible to quantify. Such research tends to treat the human body as a commodity — a means to a profitable end. The dignity and sanctity with which we regard the human whole, body as well as mind and soul, are absent when we allow researchers to further their own interests without the patient's participation by using a patient's cells as the basis for a marketable product." (Danforth, *supra*, 6 Yale L. & Pol'y Rev. at p. 190, fn. omitted.)

A second policy consideration adds notions of equity to those of ethics. Our society values fundamental fairness in dealings between its members, and condemns the unjust enrichment of any member at the expense of another. This is particularly true when, as here, the parties are not in equal bargaining positions. We are repeatedly told that the commercial products of the biotechnological revolution "hold the promise of tremendous profit." (*Toward the Right of Commerciality, supra,* 34 UCLA L.Rev. at p. 211.) In the case at bar, for example, the complaint alleges that the market for the kinds of proteins produced by the Mo cell line was predicted to exceed $3 billion by 1990. These profits are currently shared exclusively between the biotechnology industry and the universities that support that industry. The profits are shared in a wide variety of ways, including "direct entrepreneurial ties to genetic-engineering firms" and "an equity interest in fledgling biotechnology firms" (Howard, *supra*, 44 Food Drug Cosm.L.J. at p. 338). Thus the complaint alleges that because of his development of the Mo cell line defendant Golde became a paid consultant of defendant Genetics Institute and acquired the rights to 75,000 shares of that firm's stock at a cost of 1 cent each; that Genetics Institute further contracted to pay Golde and the Regents at least $330,000 over three years, including a *pro rata* share of Golde's salary and fringe benefits; and that defendant Sandoz Pharmaceuticals Corporation subsequently contracted to increase that compensation by a further $110,000.

There is, however, a third party to the biotechnology enterprise — the patient who is the source of the blood or tissue from which all these profits are derived. While he may be a silent partner, his contribution to the venture is absolutely crucial: as pointed out above (pt. 3, *ante*), but for the cells of Moore's body taken by defendants there would have been no Mo cell line at all. Yet defendants deny that Moore is entitled to any share whatever in the proceeds of this cell line. This is both inequitable and immoral. As Dr. Thomas H. Murray, a respected professor of ethics and public policy, testified before Congress, "the person [who furnishes the tissue] should be justly compensated . . . If biotechnologists fail to make provision for a just sharing of profits with the person whose gift made it possible, the public's sense of justice will be offended and no one will be the winner." (Murray, *Who Owns the Body? On the Ethics of Using Human Tissue for Commercial Purposes* (Jan.-Feb.1986) IRB: A Review of Human Subjects Research, at p. 5.)

There will be such equitable sharing if the courts recognize that the patient has a legally protected property interest in his own body and its products: "property rights in one's own tissue would provide a morally acceptable result by giving effect to notions of fairness and preventing unjust enrichment . . . Societal notions of equity and fairness demand recognition of property rights. There are bountiful benefits, monetary and otherwise, to be derived from human biologics. To deny the person contributing the raw material a fair share of these ample benefits is both unfair and morally wrong." (*Toward the Right of Commerciality, supra,* 34 UCLA L.Rev. at p. 229.) "Recognizing a donor's property rights would prevent unjust enrichment by giving monetary rewards to the donor and researcher proportionate to the value of their respective contributions. Biotechnology depends upon the contributions of both patients and researchers. If not for the patient's contribution of cells with unique attributes, the medical value of the bioengineered cells would be negligible. But for the physician's contribution of knowledge and skill in developing the cell product, the commercial value of the patient's cells would also be negligible. Failing to compensate the patient unjustly enriches the researcher because only the researcher's contribution is recognized." (*Id.* at p. 230.) In short, as the Court of Appeal succinctly put it, "If this science has become science for profit, then we fail to see any justification for excluding the patient from participation in those profits."

5. The majority's second reason for declining to extend the conversion cause of action to the present context is that "the Legislature should make that decision." (Maj. opn., *ante,* p. 163 of 271 Cal.Rptr., p. 496 of 793 P.2d.) I do not doubt that the Legislature is competent to act on this topic. The fact that the Legislature may intervene if and when it chooses, however, does not in the meanwhile relieve the courts of their duty of enforcing — or if need be, fashioning — an effective judicial remedy for the wrong here alleged. As I observed above (pt. 1, *ante*), if a conversion cause of action is otherwise an appropriate remedy on these facts we should not refrain from recognizing it merely because the Legislature has not yet addressed the question. To do so would be to abdicate *pro tanto* our responsibility over a body of

law — torts — that is particularly a creature of the common law. And such reluctance to act would be especially unfortunate at the present time, when the rapid expansion of biotechnological science and industry makes resolution of these issues an increasingly pressing need . . .

6. The majority's final reason for refusing to recognize a conversion cause of action on these facts is that "there is no pressing need" to do so because the complaint also states another cause of action that is assertedly adequate to the task (maj. opn., *ante*, p. 163 of 271 Cal.Rptr., p. 496 of 793 P.2d); that cause of action is "the breach of a fiduciary duty to disclose facts material to the patient's consent or, alternatively, . . . the performance of medical procedures without first having obtained the patient's informed consent" (*id.* at p. 150 of 271 Cal.Rptr., at p. 483 of 793 P.2d). Although last, this reason is not the majority's least; in fact, it underlies much of the opinion's discussion of the conversion cause of action, recurring like a leitmotiv throughout that discussion.

The majority hold that a physician who intends to treat a patient in whom he has either a research interest or an economic interest is under a fiduciary duty to disclose such interest to the patient before treatment; that his failure to do so may give rise to a nondisclosure cause of action; and that the complaint herein states such a cause of action at least against defendant Golde. I agree with that holding as far as it goes.

I disagree, however, with the majority's further conclusion that in the present context a nondisclosure cause of action is an adequate — in fact, a superior — substitute for a conversion cause of action. In my view the nondisclosure cause of action falls short on at least three grounds . . . [T]he nondisclosure cause of action (1) is unlikely to be successful in most cases, (2) fails to protect patients' rights to share in the proceeds of the commercial exploitation of their tissue, and (3) may allow the true exploiters to escape liability. It is thus not an adequate substitute, in my view, for the conversion cause of action . . .

NOTE

Lucas C.J., Eagleson and Kennard JJ. concurred with Panelli J. The concurring decision of Arabian J. has been omitted, as has the decision of Broussard J., dissenting in part and concurring in part.

QUESTIONS

1. The Court decided that there was no action in conversion but that Moore could base a claim on breach of a fiduciary duty and lack of informed consent. Why, if at all, does it matter which kind of claim is brought?

2. What were the main bases of Panelli J.'s holding that conversion would not lie? How were these reasons critiqued in the minority opinion of Mosk J.?

3. According to the majority ruling, what effect would finding that Moore held property rights in his cells have on the economics of medical research? Compare this reasoning with that used by the majority in *I.N.S.* What similarities and differences do you see?

4. Does the outcome of the case mean that if the patient's genetic material had been stolen from a lab, the researchers would not be able to sue in conversion? See *United States v. Arora* 860 F. Supp. 1091 (U.S. Dist. Ct. Maryland, 1994).

5. Assume that the majority ruling in *Moore* represents Canadian law. Assume also that a Canadian patient in the position of John Moore becomes aware of the special properties of his/her cells. Can that person enter into a bargain with biomedical researchers for the use of his or her cells? If so, does it matter whether or not one can be said to have property in one's cells?

6. If Moore had succeeded in establishing a property right in this case, how might the medical research industry respond?

7. What do these two opinions say about the morality of commodifying body parts?

8. In *Newman v. Sathyavaglswaran* 287 F.3d 786 (C.A. 9th Cir., 2002) an action was brought against the Los Angeles County Coroner's office by parents whose deceased children's corneas had been removed without parental consent. The gist of the claim was that the parent's property had been taken without due process of law. The United States Circuit Court of Appeal reviewed the existing American and English case law on the property rights in dead bodies, and concluded (by a 2:1 majority) that the parents had a cause of action. For the majority, Circuit Judge Fisher said (at 798):

> At bottom, "property rights serve human values. They are recognized to that end, and are limited by it." *State v. Shack*, 58 N.J. 297, 277 A.2d 369, 372 (N.J. 1971). The property rights that California affords to next of kin to the body of their deceased relatives serve the premium value our society has historically placed on protecting the dignity of the human body in its final disposition. California infringed the dignity of the bodies of the children when it extracted the corneas from those bodies without the consent of the parents. The process of law was due the parents for this deprivation of their rights.

Is this ruling consistent with that in *Moore*?

Gould Estate v. Stoddart Publishing Co.
30 O.R. (3d) 520, 1996 CarswellOnt 3537 (Gen. Div.)

Lederman J.:

Background

In 1956, Glenn Gould ("Gould"), then a young concert pianist, was interviewed by Jock Carroll ("Carroll") for an article in Weekend Magazine. They talked on a variety of occasions and in numerous venues, including Carroll accompanying Gould on a vacation to the Bahamas. During this time, Carroll took approximately 400 photographs of Gould and copious notes, including some tape recordings, of their conversations. Certain of these photographs and comments of Gould were used in the magazine article. Nearly 40 years later, in 1995, Carroll published through Stoddart Publishing Co. Limited a book entitled "Glenn Gould: Some Portraits of the Artist as a Young Man". Gould had died in 1982 and Gould's Estate did not authorize its publication or receive royalties from the book.

The book makes use of over 70 of the original 400 photographs and draws very extensively on the conversations that Carroll recorded back in 1956. The text of the book is largely comprised of extracts from these conversations. It is undisputed that Carroll is the owner of the copyright in the photographs. Gould's Estate, however, in these two actions, seeks damages claiming, (i) that use of the photographs amounts to the tort of appropriation of personality, the cause of action for which may be asserted by the Estate; and (ii) that copyright in the oral conversations recorded by Carroll rests with Gould (now his Estate) and as such the conversations may not be used without the permission of the Estate.

The Photograph Action

Apart from using the photographs for a story in Weekend Magazine, there was no discussion among Carroll, Gould or Gould's agent, Walter Homburger ("Homburger"), as to their further unrestricted use.

In 1956, Homburger invited Carroll to take pictures of, and do a story on, Gould and it was apparent to Carroll that Gould and his agent were anxious to generate exposure for this up and coming young artist. The photos and interview took place one year after Gould's major U.S. concert debut, less than one year after his first U.S. record release, and the same year as a major North American concert tour. Given the number of photographs taken, Carroll was of the view that Gould would have been delighted if Carroll used them in subsequent publications so as to create further publicity for him. At no time during his life, did Gould or anyone on his behalf ever take the position that he had the right to restrict or control the use of these photographs. On this basis, the defendants say that Carroll was free to use the photographs in any manner he saw fit.

On the other hand, the Gould Estate argued that it was well known that Gould was an intensely private individual who guarded his privacy. He took great care with the management of his personal image and reputation, and was scrupulously careful about the quality of materials which were released under his name, or projects in which he participated. He has been referred to as "Canada's own Greta Garbo". Homburger, in his affidavit, stated that Gould had a keen business sense and a well developed ability, even as early as 1956, to manage his own reputation and image. It is argued that the court should infer that, apart from the Weekend Magazine article, Gould would not have given a general licence to Carroll to publish the photographs and his sayings at some future time without first obtaining Gould's approval.

If Gould has a proprietary right to his personality, then the onus is on the defendants to show that Carroll had permission to appropriate that right by publishing the photographs of Gould. The onus should not be on the holder of the right to prove that he had placed restrictions on the exploitation of his own property.

The first question should then be: Did Gould in fact have any proprietary rights in his image, likeness or personality which have been appropriated by the publication of the photographs in the book?

i) The Tort of Appropriation of Personality

In Ontario, the common law tort of misappropriation of personality was first articulated by Estey J.A. in the Court of Appeal in *Krouse v. Chrysler Canada Ltd.* (1974), 40 D.L.R. (3d) 15 (Ont. C.A.). While no formal definition of the tort was offered, he stated at pp. 301:

> . . . there may well be circumstances in which the Courts would be justified in holding a defendant liable in damages for appropriation of a plaintiff's personality, amounting to an invasion of his right to exploit his personality by the use of his image, voice, or otherwise with damage to the plaintiff. . . .

In *Athans v. Canadian Adventure Camps Ltd.* (1977), 17 O.R. (2d) 425 (H.C.), Henry J., citing Krouse, *supra*, stated at p. 434:

> . . . it is clear that Mr. Athans has a proprietary right in the exclusive marketing for gain of his personality, image and name, and that the law entitles him to protect that right, if it is invaded.

In *Joseph v. Daniels* (1986), 11 C.P.R. (3d) 544 (B.C. S.C.), Wallace J. also gave recognition to this fact, stating at p. 549:

> . . . The cause of action is proprietary in nature and the interest protected is that of the individual in the exclusive use of his own identity in so far as it is represented by his name, reputation, likeness or other value.

The same type of tort, usually under the name "right of publicity", is also well recognized in the United States. First coined in *Haelan Laboratories Inc. v. Topps Chewing Gum Inc.*, 202 F.2d 866, 868 (U.S. 2nd Cir. 1953), "right of publicity":

> has since come to signify the right of an individual, especially a public figure or a celebrity, to control the commercial value and exploitation of his name and picture or likeness and to prevent others from unfairly appropriating this value for their commercial benefit. (see *Presley v. Russen*, 513 F.Supp, 1339 (U.S. Ct. D.N.J. 1981)).

The Gould Estate submits that the book in question is a compilation of photographs of Gould and the act of selling the book constitutes commercial exploitation. Accordingly, it argues that this amounts to unlawful appropriation of Gould's personality.

The few Canadian cases dealing with this tort have generally involved situations in which the name or image of an individual enjoying some celebrity status has been used in the advertising or promotion of the defendant's business or products. (Note that *Joseph*, *supra*, was decided on slightly different grounds. There it was held that since it was not possible for the viewer to identify the person in the photograph, as only his torso was depicted, there could be no appropriation of personality.)

Generally then, there has been an implication that the celebrity is endorsing the activity of the defendant. This contextual factor seems to have been an important underlying consideration in the courts' reasoning. In *Krouse*, *supra*, for example, Estey J.A. pointed out, at p. 29:

> . . . Here the photograph was not used in such a way as to associate the respondent with the commercial enterprise or production of the Spotter [the name of a product], a fact which is not without legal significance.

Similarly, in *Athans*, Henry J. was concerned with whether the material in question had "the effect of establishing any connection in the minds of the relevant public between Mr. Athans and the [summer] camp" (p. 436). It should be pointed out that in *Athans*, *supra*, damages were ultimately awarded despite the judge's finding that people viewing the material in question would not conclude that the plaintiff was actually endorsing the defendant's waterskiing school. Instead, the plaintiff recovered on the basis that:

> . . . [t]he commercial use of his representational image by the defendants without his consent constituted an invasion and *pro tanto* an impairment of his exclusive right to market his personality and this, in my opinion, constitutes an aspect of the tort of appropriation of personality. [p. 437]

While at first glance this decision may seem to support the present defendants' broad interpretation of commercialization, the decision is consistent with the endorsement context. *Athans* was a situation where an identifiable "representational image" was utilized by a waterskiing school in the school's promotional brochure. Therefore, on the basis of these Canadian authorities it would seem open to the court to conclude, on a contextual basis, that the tort of appropriation of personality is restricted to endorsement type situations.

More broadly, it also seems clear that in articulating this tort the court must be mindful of the public interest. In *Krouse*, *supra*, the Ontario Court of Appeal explicitly stated at p. 30:

> Progress in the law is not served by the recognition of a right which, while helpful to some persons or classes of persons, turns out to be unreasonable disruption to the community at large and to the conduct of its commerce.

While not explicitly offering any principles that ought to guide the development of this tort, the Court at p. 30 did warn:

> The danger of extending the law of torts to cover every such exposure in public not expressly authorized is obvious.

The U.S. courts have similarly recognized the necessity of limits on the right of personality. These limits are usually discussed in terms of First Amendment considerations: "the scope of the right of publicity should be measured or balanced against societal interests in free expression" (*Presley, supra*, p. 1356). In *Presley, supra*, the United States District Court (Brotman D.J.) stated at p. 1356:

> Thus, the purpose of the portrayal in question must be examined to determine if it predominantly serves a social function valued by the protection of free speech. If the portrayal merely serves the purpose of contributing information, which is not false or defamatory, to the public debate of political or social issues or of providing the free expression of creative talent which contributes to society's cultural enrichment, then the portrayal generally will be immune from liability. If, however, the portrayal functions primarily as a means of commercial exploitation, then such immunity will not be granted.

Accordingly, the right of publicity has not been successfully invoked in cases where the activity in question consists of thoughts, ideas, newsworthy events or matters of public interest. In this regard, it is important to note that:

> . . . the scope of the subject matter which falls within the protected area of the "newsworthy" or of "public interest" extends far beyond the dissemination of news in the sense of current events and includes all types of factual, educational and historical data, or even entertainment and amusement. (*Current Audio Inc. v. RCA Corp.*, 337 N.Y.S. 2d 949 (U.S. Sup. Ct. 1972) at 95456)).

Conversely, the right of publicity has been upheld in situations where famous names or likeness are used "predominately in connection with the sale of consumer merchandise or solely for purposes of trade — e.g., merely to attract attention" (*Presley*, p. 1358). As a result, Elvis Presley posters, pewter replicas of a statue of Elvis Presley, a "Howard Hughes" game which included Hughes' name and other biographical information, and a board game utilizing the names and biographies of famous golfers, have all been found to infringe the right of publicity (see *Presley, supra*, p. 1358 fn 19). All were found to be commercial products which were not vehicles through which ideas and opinions are regularly disseminated.

While Canada does not have a constitutional provision akin to the First Amendment which is applicable to the private law, no principled argument has been advanced to suggest that freedom of expression considerations should not animate Canadian courts in identifying the public interest and placing limits on the tort of appropriation of personality. Indeed, freedom of expression would seem to be a compelling and reasonably coherent basis for defining the "obvious" need for limits noted by Estey J.A. in *Krouse, supra*.

In the end then, and perhaps at the risk of oversimplifying, it seems that the courts have drawn a "sales vs. subject" distinction. Sales constitute commercial exploitation and invoke the tort of appropriation of personality. The identity of the celebrity is merely being used in some fashion. The activity cannot be said to be about the celebrity. This is in contrast to situations in which the celebrity is the actual subject of the work or enterprise, with biographies perhaps being the clearest example. These activities would not be within the ambit of the tort. To take a more concrete example, in endorsement situations, posters and board games, the essence of the activity is not the celebrity. It is the use of some attributes of the celebrity for another purpose. Biographies, other books, plays, and satirical skits are by their nature different. The subject of the activity is the celebrity and the work is an attempt to provide some insights about that celebrity.

Adopted to the present case, the book in question contains 26 pages of text by Carroll together with photographs depicting Gould in posed and spontaneous moments at the beginning of his concert career. I agree with the comment on the overleaf:

> They capture the passion and brilliance of Gould as pianist, the solitude of Gould as artist and the boyish nature of Gould as a young man.

Although it is primarily through Gould's own images and words, this book provides insight to anyone interested in Gould, the man and his music. The author added his own creativity in recounting his time spent with Gould and in making decisions about which photographs and text to use and how they should be arranged to provide this glimpse into Gould's solitary life. There is a public interest in knowing more about one of Canada's musical geniuses. Because of this public interest, the book therefore falls into the protected category and there cannot be said to be any right of personality in Gould which has been unlawfully appropriated by the defendants.

ii) Survivability of the Right of Publicity

Although not necessary to the decision in view of the above finding, the issue had arisen as to whether the tort of appropriation of personality survives the death of the individual and I am impelled to make some comments about this. Of those U.S. jurisdictions which have considered the matter, the substantial majority recognize that the right of publicity is devisable and descendible. It also seems clear that the modern trend is toward this recognition (see *Jim Henson Productions v. John T. Brady & Assoc.,* 867 F.Supp. 175 (U.S. S.D.N.Y. 1994), particularly at p. 189).

The defendants place some reliance on the fact that in the three provincial Privacy Acts which provide for a cause of action for the appropriation of personality (Newfoundland, Saskatchewan and British Columbia), the right of action is extinguished by the death of the individual whose rights are alleged to have been violated. However, this factor is not persuasive in the case at bar. In creating a statutory right of action, the legislature may obviously impose statutory restrictions on that cause of action. Here though, the case is grounded in a common law cause of action. As such it is not constrained by the restrictions which apply to the statutory right of action.

A more theoretical approach to distinguishing the Privacy Acts can be found in U.S. law. There, several cases have recognized a distinction between the right of privacy and the right of publicity (see *Henson, supra*, p. 188). The former is considered a personal tort and is designed to protect an individual's interest in dignity and peace of mind. The right of publicity, on the other hand, protects the commercial value of a person's celebrity status. As such, it is a form of intangible property, akin to copyright or patent, that is descendable. Given that the Canadian statutory rights of action are found in Privacy Acts, it would certainly seem that, following the U.S. reasoning, whatever statutory restrictions there may be on the rights of action for privacy violations and unauthorized use of personality, they should not be applied to the common law tort of appropriation of personality.

The right of publicity, being a form of intangible property under Ontario law akin to copyright, should descend to the celebrity's heirs. Reputation and fame can be a capital asset that one nurtures and may choose to exploit and it may have a value much greater than any tangible property. There is no reason why such an asset should not be devisable to heirs under s. 2 of the *Succession Law Reform Act*, R.S.O. 1990, c. S.26.

As a final comment on this topic, the U.S. cases on both sides of the right of publicity debate have expressed concern over whether there should be a durational limit on the right of publicity after it is inherited (see *Presley*, *supra*, 1355 fn. 10, and *Lugosi v. Universal Pictures*, 603 P. 2d 425 (U.S. Sup. Ct. 1979) at p. 430). For the present purposes though, suffice it to say that Gould passed away in 1982, and it seems reasonable to conclude that whatever the durational limit, if any, it is unlikely to be less than 14 years. The protection granted by other intangible property rights such as patents and copyrights is longer. So, too, any durational limit on Gould's right of publicity would not yet have expired . . .

Disposition

There is no basis in law for the plaintiff's actions. Accordingly, there will be summary judgment dismissing both actions. If parties agree, I will fix costs of the actions including these motions after receiving written submissions.

NOTE

The Ontario Court of Appeal dismissed an appeal from this ruling: (1998) 39 O.R. (3d) 545, 1998 CarswellOnt 1901 (C.A.), treating the question as a matter of basic copyright law. Finlayson J.A., for the Court of Appeal said (at para. 27):

> I am not persuaded that I should analyze the facts of this case in the context of a claim for misappropriation of personality. I am satisfied that it can be disposed of on conven-

tional copyright lines and there is no necessity to explore any balance between privacy rights and the public's interest in a prominent Canadian.

An application by the executors of the Gould Estate for leave to appeal to the Supreme Court of Canada was dismissed on January 7, 1999: (1999) 236 N.R. 396 (note) (S.C.C.).

QUESTIONS AND COMMENTS

1. What policy considerations justify a legally enforceable right of publicity?

2. In "An Exclusive Right to Evoke", 44 B.C.L.Rev. 291(2003) at 308, Stacey Dogan summarized the current American law on the right of publicity:

> As it stands, . . . the right of publicity extends to any commercial, unauthorized use of a device or symbol — including but not limited to an individual's name, likeness, or voice — that brings to mind a celebrity. Although theoretically the use must also commercially benefit the defendant, courts generally assume that if the celebrity link is made, such a benefit exists. The defendant need not use any particular attribute of the celebrity or deceive the public into thinking that it has. Evocation, alone, is enough.

In M.A. Flagg, "Star Crazy: Keeping the Right of Publicity Out of Canadian Law" (1999) 13 I.P.J. 179, at 235-6, it is suggested that an adoption of the American jurisprudence on the appropriation of personality should be resisted:

> Canadian courts have recently been moving towards adopting common law doctrines akin to the "right of publicity" in the United States. Doing so, however, is problematic because our two systems of law have characterized the policy framework that underlies this right in different ways. While American law is a patchwork that recognizes personal privacy rights *and* proprietary interests in a person's identity, the Canadian common law has not separated the rights conceptually. Rather, the catch-all appropriation action has developed without a clear conceptual basis to guide it. Given that fact, our courts ought to begin again the process of analyzing the appropriation tort, and recognizing it as the violation of a personal right giving rise to damages for psychic or emotional distress. The adoption of a broad property right over commercial uses made by others of an individual's identity would lead directly to the situation that now exists in the United States — a judicial licensing scheme for celebrities in performance and advertising interests. That approach has been criticized because it tends to favour the rights of successful and well-known individuals over the rights of the public to depict, use, parody, or honour many of the cultural icons of our time. It can only be through a broad and generous definition of the public interest in creating and interpreting popular culture that Canadian law will avoid the conceptual and constitutional difficulties that plague the law in this area in the United States. This will be evident if our courts view the appropriation tort through the prism of statutory intellectual property law, which seeks to balance creators' and users' rights, and through the prism of the *Charter*, which seeks equality and does not place property rights on a pedestal.

Do you agree?

3. Although the cases considered in the latter part of this chapter have concerned the development of new property rights, the focus on novel claims can be somewhat misleading. It is true that the law of property is dynamic. To take a clear example, patent rights are constantly being conferred for new inventions. At the same time, woven into the basic fabric of property law in the common law tradition can be found the notion new forms of property should not be readily recognised by the courts. This is especially apparent in relation to land law. Borrowing from the language of civil legal systems, it is sometimes said that a principle of *numerus clausus* applies. In other words, property rights are confined to a closed (or almost closed) set.

Within the English jurisprudence, the best-known expression of this position can be found in the case of *Keppell v. Bailey* (1834) 2 My. & K. 517, 39 E.R. 1042 (Ch.) at 1049 [E.R.], where Brougham L.C. stated:

> [I]t must not therefore be supposed that incidents of a novel land can be devised and attached to property at the fancy or caprice of any owner. It is clearly inconvenient both to the science of the law and to the public weal that such a latitude should be given. There can be no harm in allowing the fullest latitude to men [sic] in binding themselves and their representatives, that is, their assets real and personal, to answer in damages for breach of their obligations. This tends to no mischief, and is a reasonable liberty to bestow; but great detriment would arise and much confusion of rights if parties were allowed to invent new modes of holding and enjoying real property, and to impress upon their lands and tenements a peculiar character, which should follow them into all hands, however remote. Every close, every messuage, might thus be held in a several fashion; and it would hardly be possible to know what rights the acquisition of any parcel conferred, or what obligations it imposed. The right of way or of common is of a public as well as of a simple nature, and no one who sees the premises can be ignorant of what all the vicinage knows. But if one man may bind his message and land to take lime from a particular kiln, another may bind his to take coals from a certain pit, while a third may load his property with further obligations to employ one blacksmith's forge, or the members of one corporate body, in various operations upon the premises, besides many other restraints as infinite in variety as the imagination can conceive. . . .

This idea is not treated as out-moded. In *Amberwood Investments Ltd. v. Durham Condominium Corporation No. 123* 50 R.P.R. (3d) 1, 2002 CarswellOnt 850 (C.A.) (to be studied in Chapter 10) at 21*ff.*, the Ontario Court of Appeal stressed the limits that should be imposed on judicial activism in relation to the law of real property.

4. What function does *numerus clausus* serve? In T.W. Merrill & H.E. Smith, "Optimal Standardization in the Law of Property: The *Numerus Clausus* Principle", 110 Yale L.J. 1 (2000) the authors focus on the economic impact of restricting the number of fancy interests permitted under law. They conclude (at 69):

> *Numerus clausus* makes sense from an economic perspective. By permitting a significant number of different forms of property but forbidding courts to recognize new ones, the *numerus clausus* strikes a balance between the proliferation of property forms, on the one hand, and excessive rigidity on the other. Proliferation is a problem because third parties must ascertain the legal dimensions of property rights in order to avoid violating the rights of others and to assess whether to acquire the rights of others. Permitting the

> free customization of new forms of property would impose significant external costs on third parties in the form of higher measurement costs. On the other hand, insisting on a "one size fits all" system of property rights would frustrate those legitimate objectives that can be achieved only by using different property rights that fall short of full ownership. Optimal standardization is the solution, and the *numerus clausus* moves the legal system closer to the optimum, although we do not claim it generates a perfect mix of forms.
>
> By insisting that courts respect the status quo in terms of the menu of property rights, the *numerus clausus* also channels legal change in property rights to the legislature. This institutional choice dimension . . . reinforces the information cost minimization features of the doctrine, because legislated changes communicate information about the legal dimensions of property more effectively than judicially mandated changes.

Compare this explanation for the emergence of *numerus clausus*:

> The attachment of promises to land creates user rights in a property resource, and as such, may be regarded as a partitioning of property rights. By treating land-related promises as enforceable contracts that bind the contracting parties rather than real rights that run with the land in perpetuity, doctrines such as . . . *numerus clausus* . . . in civil law, have served as instruments to limit the cases of dysfunctional fragmentation.

F. Parisi et al., "Simultaneous and Sequential Anticommons" online: <http://ssrn.com/abstract_id=388880>

REVIEW QUESTIONS

1. In "Dialogue on Private Property", 9 Rutgers L.Rev. 357 (1954) at 365, Felix Cohen sets out a simple hypothetical situation designed to assist in understanding how rules for allocating ownership rights might be constructed. Imagine that somewhere, on a warm summer's day, under the shade of a tree, a young foal is born. To whom, if anyone, should the law allocate ownership of this newly created being? Consider all of the possible ownership rules that might be invoked. If you were called upon to rank these possible rules, what criteria would be germane to such an ordering?

2. In the past few years much has been written in the popular press about an issue that is sometimes referred to as "cultural appropriation". That term has been defined as "the taking — from a culture that is not one's own — of intellectual property, cultural expressions or artifacts, history and ways of knowledge". Consider the following illustrations:

> Example 1: At the beginning nineteenth century, sculpted marble friezes were taken from the Parthenon on orders from Lord Elgin (at one time the British Ambassador to the Ottoman Empire). These so-called Elgin Marbles were sold to the British Museum in 1916, where they remain on display.
>
> Example 2: A folk singer from the United States recorded an ancient Senegalese folk song, the writer of which is unknown.

Example 3: A muscle relaxant, known as d-turbocurarine, is patented by a pharmaceutical company. It was derived from an Amazonian arrow poison.

Example 4: A non-native writer published stories learned from members of a west coast Native band. According to the customs and traditions of that band, the stories can only be retold by select elders.

Example 5: A non-native artist paints works based on images of Native cultures of North America. Patterns and symbols, found on carpets, earthware, blankets and clothing are used. Images of the peoples of the region, dressed in traditional attire, are also created.

Example 6: The Nahua peoples of Mexico, under the hegemonic control of Spain, adopt the colonial discourses of this imperial presence, assimilating the cultural practices of this (European) Other.

Example 7: W.P. Kinsella published a series of stories set on the Hobbema reserve in Alberta. The stories are all fictional, as are the characters, though some of those characters are given names of people living on the reserve.

Example 8: Jazz, blues, soul, rap, and other musical forms emanating out of the black musical experience in America are adopted by non-black musicians and audiences as part of a mainstream musical tradition.

See B. Ziff & P.V. Rao, eds., *Borrowed Power: Essays on Cultural Appropriation* (New Brunswick, N.J.: Rutgers U.P., 1997).

Are questions of cultural appropriation amenable to a property law analysis? If so, in what way are the values affected by the process of cultural appropriation comparable to those that touch the law of property generally?

None of the examples of appropriation described above constitutes infringements of current Canadian law. Should that change?

The Model Act reproduced below was prepared under the auspices of WIPO and UNESCO in the early 1980s. In what way does the Model Act endeavour to respond to questions of cultural appropriation? Does it deal with all of the values implicated by the concept of appropriation?

Model Provisions for National Laws on the Protection of Expressions of Folklore Against Illicit Exploitation and Other Prejudicial Actions

Considering that folklore represents an important part of the living cultural heritage of the nation, developed and maintained by the communities within the nation, or by individuals reflecting the expectations of those communities;

Considering that the dissemination of various expressions of folklore may lead to improper exploitation of the cultural heritage of the nation;

Considering that any abuse of commercial or other nature or any distortion of expressions of folklore are prejudicial to the cultural and economic interests of the nation;

Considering that expressions of folklore constituting manifestations of intellectual creativity deserve to be protected in a manner inspired by the protection provided for intellectual productions;

Considering that such a protection of expressions of folklore has become indispensable as a means of promoting further development, maintenance and dissemination of those expressions, both within and outside the country, without prejudice to related legitimate interests;

The following provisions shall be given effect:

Principle of Protection

1. Expressions of folklore developed and maintained in [insert the name of the country] shall be protected by this [law] against illicit exploitation and other prejudicial actions as defined in this [law].

Protected Expressions of Folklore

2. For the purposes of this [law], "expressions of folklore" means productions consisting of characteristic elements of the traditional artistic heritage developed and maintained by a community of [name of the country] or by individuals reflecting the traditional artistic expectations of such a community, in particular:

(i) verbal expressions, such as folk tales, folk poetry and riddles;

(ii) musical expressions, such as folk songs and instrumental music;

(iii) expressions by action, such as folk dances, plays and artistic forms or rituals;

whether or not reduced to a material form; and

(iv) tangible expressions, such as:

(a) productions of folk art, in particular, drawings, paintings, carvings, sculptures, pottery, terracotta, mosaic, woodwork, metalware, jewellery, basket weaving, needlework, textiles, carpets, costumes;

(b) musical instruments;

(c) architectural forms.

Utilizations Subject to Authorization

3. Subject to the provisions of Section 4, the following utilizations of the expressions of folklore are subject to authorization by the [competent authority mentioned in Section 9, paragraph 1,] [community concerned] when they are made both with gainful intent and outside their traditional or customary context:

(i) any publication, reproduction and any distribution of copies of expressions of folklore;

(ii) any public recitation or performance, any transmission by wireless means or by wire, and any other form of communication to the public, of expressions of folklore.

Exceptions

4.(1) The provisions of Section 3 shall not apply in the following cases:

(i) utilization for purposes of education;

(ii) utilization by way of illustration in the original work of an author or authors, provided that the extent of such utilization is compatible with fair practice;

(iii) borrowing of expressions of folklore for creating an original work of an author orauthors;

(2) The provisions of Section 3 shall not apply also where the utilization of the expressions of folklore is incidental. Incidental utilization includes, in particular:

(i) utilization of any expression of folklore that can be seen or heard in the course of a current event for the purposes of reporting on that current event by means of photography, broadcasting or sound or visual recording, provided that the extent of such utilization is justified by the informatory purpose;

(ii) utilization of objects containing the expressions of folklore which are permanently located in a place where they can be viewed by the public, if the utilization consists in including their image in a photograph, in a film or in a television broadcast.

Acknowledgement of Source

5.(1) In all printed publications, and in connection with any communications to the public, of any identifiable expression of folklore, its source shall be indicated in an appropriate manner, by mentioning the community and/or geographic place from where the expression utilized has been derived.

(2) The provisions of paragraph 1 shall not apply to utilizations referred to in Section 4, paragraphs 1(iii) and 2.

Offences

6.(1) Any person who willfully [or negligently] does not comply with the provisions of Section 5, paragraph 1, shall be liable to. . .

(2) Any person who, without the authorization of the [competent authority referred to in Section 9, paragraph l,] [community concerned] willfully [or negligently] utilizes an expression of folklore in violation of the provisions of Section 3, shall be liable to . . .

(3) Any person willfully deceiving others in respect of the source of artifacts or subject matters of performances or recitations made available to the public by him in any direct or indirect manner, presenting such artifacts or subject matters as expressions of folklore of a certain community, from where, in fact, they have not been derived, shall be punishable by . . .

(4) Any person who publicly uses, in any direct or indirect manner, expressions of folklore willfully distorting the same in a way prejudicial to the cultural interests of the community concerned, shall be punishable by . . .

Seizure or Other Actions

7. Any object which was made in violation of this [law] and any receipts of the person violating it and corresponding to such violations, shall be subject to [seizure] [applicable actions and remedies].

Civil Remedies

8. The sanctions provided for in [Section 6] [Sections 6 and 7] shall be applied without prejudice to damages or other civil remedies as the case may be . . .

Authorization

10.(1) Applications for individual or blanket authorization of any utilization of expressions of folklore subject to authorization under this [law] shall be made [in writing] to the [competent authority] [community concerned].

(2) Where the [competent authority] [community concerned] grants authorization, it may fix the amount of and collect fees [corresponding to a tariff [established]

[approved] by the supervisory authority.] The fees collected shall be used for the purpose of promoting or safeguarding national [culture] [folklore].

(3) Appeals against the decisions of the competent authority may be made by the person applying for the authorization and/or the representative of the [interested community.] . . .

Relation to Other Forms of Protection

12. This [law] shall in no way limit or prejudice any protection applicable to expressions of folklore under the copyright law, the law protecting performers, producers of phonograms and broadcasting organizations, the laws protecting industrial property, or any other law or international treaty to which the country is party; nor shall it in any way prejudice other forms of protection provided for the safeguard and preservation of folklore.

Interpretation

13. The protection granted under this [law] shall in no way be interpreted in a manner which could hinder the normal use and development of expressions of folklore.

Protection of Expression of Folklore of Foreign Countries

14. Expressions of folklore developed and maintained in a foreign country are protected under this [law]

(i) subject to reciprocity, or

(ii) on the basis of international treaties or other agreements.

CHAPTER 2
PROPERTY IN PERSPECTIVE

1. INTRODUCTION

This chapter will provide a contextual basis for the current law of property in Canada.

The first matter to be considered is the origins of the law. It is conventionally understood that property law in the common law provinces of Canada derives its foundations from the law of England. When the territories of what is now Canada came under English rule, the law of England was transported through the invocation of rules governing the reception of that law into colonial holdings. Territories that were conquered or ceded from other imperial powers retained the pre-existing legal regimes until these were altered. Settler colonies were subject to a different rule, even though they too were effectively conquered or ceded — from Aboriginal nations. For so-called settled colonies, the laws of England were regarded as received into the new territories in so far as the laws were considered appropriate to the new lands. (With regard to Aboriginal property, it will be seen in Chapter 5 that establishing British sovereignty did not thereby extinguish various entitlements, including land rights.) It is argued below that in those instances when a question arose as to whether or an existing law was received (i.e., was the law applicable to circumstances in Canada or not), it was most often decided that the law in question should be taken to have been adopted. In short, the initial impact of English law in Canada was significant. And it is still very much in evidence.

It is only through a consideration of the history of property law that sense can be made of the ways in which property rights are categorized. The ways in which interests are aggregated forms the second contextual element considered in this chapter.

One can study property law in the abstract, that is, without concern about how the rules affect, and are affected by, the distribution of ownership in a given society and other considerations. Studying property doctrine in isolation does have value: it allows for an assessment of whether ownership rules possess internal coherence; it is useful to certain styles of algebraic or theoretical critique. However, it should already be apparent that cases are not resolved in this kind of societal vacuum. When, for example, in *Moore v. Regents of U.C.* (studied in Chapter 1), a California court rejected the property claim (based on conversion), its holding was influenced by the potential effect that allowing such a claim could have on medical research. More generally, rules of ownership are applied in a world where rights have already been distributed, and where a small elite have plenty, others enough, and some very little. Life is not like the game of Monopoly, where we all start at Go, with the same wealth and with an equal chance to acquire Boardwalk. Many people live on Baltic Avenue and can never realistically aspire to more than a small green house on Marvin

Gardens. The nature of wealth and poverty in Canada — which is no more than a tally of property rights — is addressed below.

Property law also has a constitutional dimension. Under Canada's federal system of governance, jurisdiction over property is divided. Moreover, the law contains various built-in protections for property holders — restraints on government action. These protections are considered in the final part of this chapter.

2. THE SOURCES OF CANADIAN PROPERTY LAW

J. Cribbet & C.W. Johnson, *Principles of the Law of Property* (Westbury, N.Y.: Foundation Pr., 1989) 28-38 [footnotes omitted]

SECTION 1. THE RISE OF FEUDALISM

Feudalism grew out of the chaos of the Dark Ages, the period from the fifth to the tenth centuries A.D. It is difficult for us to visualize the total collapse of Western civilization which followed the decline of the Roman Empire. It was not just the fall of a single state but the disintegration of all law and order. Even the habit of or feeling for a stable society gradually disappeared. It became once again, as in the dawn of history, a world of disorganized individuals who looked to their own might for the minimum essentials of life . . .

The need for security and some sense of stability survived the collapse of the Roman peace. Since it could not be found in the state, the individual turned to the strongest of his fellows and put his fate in hands which appeared to be more capable than his own. Thus arose the practice of *commendation* by which a weaker man became the vassal of a stronger man, the lord, through a ceremony of homage which promised mutual duties of support and protection. The vassal needed protection for more than just his family and himself; he needed security for his property which consisted almost solely of land. The land was his means of livelihood and if he lost it to marauders he might as well lose life itself. Feudalism, from the start, was both a system of government and a method of holding property. The lord was, in effect, given the land which he must then protect. The vassal no longer owned what had been his land, he "held" the land "of" the lord as if he were a tenant. This method of landholding had little in common with the modern law of landlord and tenant, except the name, and should not be confused with it. The land which the vassal now held was called his "fief", "feudum," or "feud" and has become the "fee" of our modern law.

This system of feudal tenure did not end with a simple relationship between one lord and one vassal but became, by the process of "subinfeudation," a lengthening chain between the top feudal lord and the actual possessor of the land. There was no theoretical limit to subinfeudation and as many as five or six mesne lords might be involved, each serving as a link between the lord above and the vassal below. As the central state began to reassert its strength, the king became the lord at the top of the heap and the only one who was always a lord and never a vassal. Even this last statement needs modification, for William the Conqueror was himself a vassal of the King of France. The pattern was much as follows:

CROWN

■

Tenant in chief (*in capite*)

■

Mesne lords (both lord and vassal)

■

Tenant in demesne (the vassal in possession of the land)

This feudalistic system was general over all of western Europe but it never became the sole method of land ownership on the Continent. There were isolated pockets that held out, where the landowners did not become tenants of some powerful noble. This land was called *allodial* as opposed to tenurial and it was subject to various fates. Some of it developed into petty kingdoms and other tracts were linked to the kings of France or Germany by non-feudal ties. In England, on the other hand, all of the land was subjected to feudalistic tenure by William the Conqueror and *allodial* lands were eventually unknown. This point is significant because the universality of feudalism in England led to the consolidation of the law into a systematic whole, while no such result followed on the Continent since the "law of the feuds" could not be applied to the *allodial* land.

English land law begins, for all practical purposes, with 1066 and the Battle of Hastings. The Anglo-Saxon England which existed before the Norman conquest had its own system of law, undoubtedly influenced by the feudalism of the Continent, but within a generation it had been absorbed into the new Norman scheme. How this happened is a fascinating story in its own right, but the key factor is that one powerful noble, William the Bastard, stood at the top of the landholding pyramid and all of the land in England was "held" of him. This complete feudalisation of England is eloquently evidenced by the Domesday Book, a register of landholders compiled by William for tax purposes. The pages of the book reveal the substitution of the formula, "*A* holds of *B*; *B* holds of the King," for any prior conception of land ownership.

What was this law of the feuds? How was the relationship of tenure controlled between the king, the lords, and the vassals? The first question requires a look at the incidents of feudal tenures; the second a survey of the courts and remedies of twelfth century England. Tenures must, at the outset, be classified as free and unfree. Feudalism was an aristocratic concept and you can be sure that no overlord would be found plowing in the field . . . The free tenures stopped just short of the actual tillers of the soil, the *villeins* who were bound to the land by an unfree tenure. We will first discuss free tenures and then turn briefly to the unfree type, followed by a quick look at the court structure which enforced them both.

SECTION 2. FREE TENURES

There were four types of free tenure, each of them designed to fulfill a particular need. The principal need was for *security* and the typical tenure therefore was *knight service*. The name fairly well describes the tenure. In return for his feud (fee), the tenant agreed to furnish forty days of armed service to the lord per year. At first this probably was done by the tenant himself but later he hired men to serve in his stead and as the need for a private army diminished, with the growth of the central government, a money payment (scutage) was substituted for the original personal service.

A second need was for *splendor*, for the full panoply of pomp and circumstance which went with a medieval aristocracy. Since there was no money economy, the lord bought these things with land and *serjeantry* tenure was the result. Serjeantry was subdivided into grand and petty; the former being restricted to tenants in chief who performed ceremonial services for the king and the latter covering the less august types of service. Examples of serjeantry tenure included: butlers, cooks, sword bearers, suppliers of military transport and weapons, and such improbable duties as "holding the head of our Lord the King between Dover and Whitsand as often as he should happen to pass over sea between those ports."

A third need was for things of the *spirit*. In those rough times the days on this earth were none too pleasant at best . . . How better make sure of the joy to come than by giving lands for that express purpose? *Frankalmoin* tenure resulted and while it took many forms the tenant was always a priest or a religious body.

The fourth and final need of the times was for *subsistence*, for the crops and products of the soil without which life could not continue. Out of this great need arose *socage* tenure. Actually, it was a kind of residual tenure and Professor Hargreaves suggests that the only accurate way of defining it is to say that it compromised any free tenure which did not fall within the other three types. However, it frequently included labor services on the demesne land of the lord and hence is thought of as the subsistence tenure. It should not, however, be confused with the unfree tenures which will be discussed later and which also related to tilling the soil. Socage tenure was less aristocratic than the other three, in fact it had aspects of the non-feudal, and this had interesting consequences in the development of the law.

In each of the four free tenures certain characteristic services were due from the tenant to the lord, but there were also other rights and obligations involved called the incidents of tenure. These incidents fell into two general classes, first, those which arose during the lifetime of the parties and which involved the personal relationship of the lord and tenant and, second, those which arose on the death of the tenant and hence might be called feudal problems of inheritance. The first class included homage, fealty, and the aids. The second was composed of escheat, relief, wardship, and marriage.

Homage was the ceremony by which the tenant became the lord's man. Fealty was the oath taken by the tenant in which he promised to be loyal to the lord. The duty of the tenant to supply financial support to the lord on specific occasions was called an aid and eventually there came, in England, at least, to be three such aids. They were the ransoming of the lord, the knighting of his eldest son, and the marriage of his eldest daughter.

The second class of incidents requires a bit more discussion. What happened to the feud when the tenant died? If he died without an heir there was no problem. The land was originally the lord's, "held" of him by the tenant. Remove the tenant by death without an heir and the land simply returned to him who "owned" it before. This incident was called escheat and is the name still given to the similar process by which the state succeeds to the property of a man who dies intestate without heirs. In feudal times the land also would revert to the lord if the tenant committed a felony. This *forfeiture* of the feud was said to occur because the felon's blood was attained or corrupted.

Suppose the tenant had an heir who had attained his majority and was ready and able to succeed to the feud? The tenurial relationship was a highly personal one and just because the lord was willing to be served by the father was no reason that he should have to accept the son. The lord might want the land back so that he could give it to an entirely different person as a tenant. It was finally settled, however, that the land should pass to the heir but that he must pay a sum of money, called a relief, to his lord for this privilege. This may not have been the origin of the modern estate and inheritance taxes but at least it was a feudal incident that had the same effect as our "death duties." . . .

SECTION 3. UNFREE TENURES

In spite of these variations, all of the free tenures had much in common and represented a generally coherent scheme of land distribution — a scheme which served the needs of a feudal society quite as efficiently as the present law serves our twentieth century society. But the feudal pattern did not stop with the free tenures, it included another important type of land holding — copyhold tenure, which grew out of the old custom of villeinage. Copyhold was an unfree tenure and was reserved for those who actually tilled the soil. It can be understood best by a brief glance at the medieval manor.

The manor was the basic unit on which English feudalism was built. The typical manor consisted of: "(a) the land belonging to the lord, which was called his demesne, (b) the land held of the lord by free tenants whether in socage or knight service, (c) the land held of the lord by persons called villein tenants, (d) rights of jurisdiction exercisable by the lord over the free tenants in the Court Baron, and over the villeins in the Court Customary, and (e) waste land on which the tenants were entitled to pasture their cattle." As we have pointed out previously, the free tenures were essentially aristocratic (especially knight service, serjeantry, and frankalmoin) so it was left to the villeins to do the backbreaking work of medieval farming. They were not free men but serfs who belonged to the manor and thus to the lord. It is true that some socage tenants also farmed the land but they held their feud according to the established incidents and were free men.

The position of the villein was not quite so precarious as it might seem and he was entitled to certain protection in the customary court of the manor. But he did not have any access to the king's court because he was thought of as a creature of the lord over whom the king had no direct control. With the passage of the centuries, the role of the villein changed and he was freed from the soil . . . Suffice it to say that the individual became a free man but that the tenure itself continued to be classified as unfree and the nomenclature changed from villeinage to copyhold tenure. The term copyhold arose as follows: "The copyhold tenant, like his predecessor the villein, held at the will of the lord, but yet at the same time he held on the conditions which had become fixed by the customs of his particular manor. The lord's will could not be exercised capriciously, but only in conformity with custom. He still held a court, and that court kept records of all transactions affecting the lands. These records were called the rolls of the court. When, for instance, a tenant sold his interest to a third party, the circumstances of the sale would be recorded, and the buyer would receive a copy of the court rolls in so far as they affected his holding. Inasmuch as he held his estate by copy of the court roll, he came to be called a copyholder."

SECTION 4. COURTS, LEGISLATION, AND THE DECLINE OF FEUDALISM

This, then, was the law of the feuds. Of course, it was not written down in the form of legislation and much of it was more accurately custom than law. It was enforced, when need be, by the courts of the period and they worked out the details of the feudal structure. Originally, the local courts of the lord handled most of the problems of the manor and there was no law common to all of England. But the king too had a court and from the early days of the Conquest the tenants-in-chief had access to the jurisdiction of the Crown when their land was in dispute. The developing writ system gave them a *praecipe in capite*, a species of the Writs of Right for the recovery of land. Since the writ was so ancient it was dilatory, cumbersome, and subject to the defect of trial by battle. The evolution by which this archaic remedy was ultimately replaced by writs of entry and, finally, by the action of ejectment makes a complicated story. The history of these early forms of action is really the history of the law of land, for within the mystic language of the wrist was worked out the full significance of possession, seisin, and the relativity of title. Beginning in 1154, with the accession of the great lawgiver Henry II, the royal courts gradually took over most of the controversies involving the land held by free tenure and eventually even the copyhold tenant found justice in the king's court.

By the early years of the thirteen century the feudalistic system of tenures was firmly rooted in England. The later history of tenures is a tale of steady disintegration under the inexorable pressures of a changing society. The first departure of major significance came in 1290 with the statute of *Quia Emptores*, one of the most important pieces of legislation in the history of land . . . Simply put, it abolished subinfeudation and provided that all future alienations of land must be by substitution. For various reasons it was to the interest of the great lords to prevent a further lengthening of the feudal chain and this could be done only by ending subinfeudation. As a result, when a mesne lord conveyed his feud to a stranger the latter stepped into the conveyor's shoes (was substituted for him) instead of becoming a tenant of the conveyor. Since 1290, it has been legally impossible to alienate a fee simple absolute so that there shall be tenure between grantor and grantee; the grantee holds the land as tenant of the grantor's lord. It should be noted that *Quia Emptroes* also provided that no more tenures in frankalmoin could be created.

It was impossible to devise land until 1540, with the passage of the Statute of Wills. This meant that prior to that time the land frequently escheated to the overlord for want of an heir. Treason was a common offense, since the landholder was likely to choose the wrong side in the continuous struggle with the king. This meant forfeiture of the land because of the tainted blood. Both escheat and forfeiture gradually reduced the length of the feudal chain and, since *Quia Emptores* had put an end to further subinfeudation, more and more land came to be held directly of the king.

Other forces were also at work, reducing the significance of the various obligations of tenure. Even in the twelfth century the money payment of scutage had taken the place of military service and by the sixteenth century most of the services due in socage tenure had been commuted to a fixed money rent. With the inflation resulting from the discovery of the wealth of the New World these fixed rents ceased to be valuable and indeed were hardly worth the trouble of collecting . . . In 1660, the Statute of Tenures marked the end of the strictly feudal period of English land law. It turned knight service and serjeantry into socage tenure, destroying all incidents of value except escheat. The honorary services of grand serjeantry were retained but this had no real significance to land law. The aids were abolished and this ended the last burdensome incident of socage tenure. Frankalmoin was not affected by the Act of 1660 and, in theory, it may still exist if created prior to *Quia Emptores* (1290), but the tenure has no practical modern significance.

The Statute of Tenures applied only to freeholds; copyhold tenure continued in England until the twentieth century. However, the special incidents of copyhold, which included the rights of the lord to the mines and timber of the tenant, could be sold to the copyholder and the great proportion of copyhold land had become freehold by the end of the nineteenth century. The last vestiges of the old distinctions were finally swept away in England on January 1, 1926, when a series of Acts, known collectively as "The Property Legislation of 1925" came into effect. All copyholds were automatically converted into socage tenure. Escheat was abolished, even for those cases where an intervening lord could be discovered, and when a tenant dies intestate without any heirs his estate now goes directly to the Crown as *bona vacantia* (property without an owner).

Professor Hargreaves sums up the present law of England: "It follows that for practical purposes all land is now held directly of the Kings by socage tenure, though the services and incidents have no disappeared, and that consequently the existence of tenure no longer has any direct effects. Its indirect effects, however, still remain, for they are the basis of the modern doctrine of estates . . ."

B. Ziff, "Warm Reception in a Cold Climate: English Property Law and the Suppression of the Canadian Legal Identity" [revised; footnotes omitted]

. . . [T]here are different reception rules affecting colonial holdings, depending on whether the colony was established by conquest (including cession) and settlement. In brief, in the case of conquered or ceded colonies, the starting point was that the pre-existing local law would remain in force until altered by the new sovereign. For settled colonies . . . the general rule is that the laws of England form part of the laws of the colony in so far as these are applicable to conditions in the colony. The crucible of *applicability* is, of course, of considerable value . . . How Canadian courts treat the question of suitability should tell us something about the extent to which Canada was perceived as distinct from England. Which *property* laws, designed initially for application in England, were regarded as sufficiently suitable to the circumstances, physical, economic and social, in this part of the Empire?

The short answer is: most English laws, it seems. It has been suggested that the applicability doctrine was widely used in Upper Canada as a means of rejecting English theory and practice until the latter decades of the 19th century. However, the case law, at least that governing the adoption of English land law statutes, does not display such an overall pattern. In Canada, in cases in which reception questions were raised, the applicability requirement was almost always met. Hence, the *Statute of Uses*, *Quia Emptores*, the *Statute of Elizabeth* governing fraudulent conveyances, the *Statute of Anne* concerning accounting in co-ownership, as well as partition, wills, intestacy, and settled estate statutes, were all found to have been received. In British Columbia, a host of English legislative measures dealing with property matters were expressly incorporated into the statutes of the Province, including *Quia Emptores* and the *Statute of Uses*. Something important was being said about how a proper juridical foundation ought to be constructed.

There are only a few outliers. For example, the *Statute of Enrolments* was found not to form part of the law of Nova Scotia; and a statute allowing Crown liens against the land of select public officers was held to be inapplicable in that colony. Likewise, a number of cases held that English mortmain laws were not part of Canadian law. It seemed, of course, pointless, to impose restrictions on corporate landholding, and this was the view taken elsewhere in the Empire when the question arose. However, these outcomes are exceptional.

Common law doctrines are subject to the same standard of applicability. Jean Côté has suggested that "courts rarely question the suitability of common-law rules, while English statutes are thought a rather novel and exotic intrusion." This conclusion echoes the view found in an important mid-nineteenth century Nova Scotia decision, *Uniacke v. Dickson*, in which it is suggested also that the colonists themselves drew this distinction between common law and statute. Even so, I have not found that the suggested pattern emerges, even on reviewing Côté's own carefully compiled table of reception cases, at least as far as property law is concerned.

Canadian judges seem, if anything, more willing to depart from past judge-made doctrines. Flexibility and growth is, after all, integral to the common law.

It is predictably the case that when the courts have resisted the imposition of a common law rule, social and economic conditions of Canadian life have been important. Geographic factors have likewise figured in the analysis. This is true, for instance, with regard to several fundamental rules governing water. In some provinces it was decided that the rules concerning the title to beds did not follow the English law to the letter, with its stress on whether the body was tidal or not. Such an approach was not suitable to the "great rivers" of North America, and as a result it became the law in most of common law Canada that navigability was the true test. Likewise, in an Alberta case it was suggested that the so-called common law rule governing surface water was "wholly inapplicable to a country bounded upon one entire side by mountains and having within its limits large tracts of land broken by hills, valleys, ravines, swales and sloughs [etc.]" . . .

The most marked departure from principles of English property doctrine is to be found in the Newfoundland case law. In the earliest reported decisions one sees the emergence of indigenous property rules, largely shaped by the judgments of Chief Justice Francis Forbes. The fashioning of this unique body of principles was dictated for the most part by the island's colonial raison d'être, namely, the fishery. It was conceived of as a fishing station and a training ground; a nursery for seamen. Indeed, permanent settlement in Newfoundland was not encouraged, and so until the second decade of the 19th century British colonial policy was against the granting of titles on the island.

In 1831, Chief Justice Richard Tucker felt that "it may be safely asserted that, up to the present hour, Newfoundland is considered by the Imperial Parliament as deriving her chief value from being the seat of the first fishing-establishment in the universe . . . [I]f there be one object connected with this island, *to which all considerations must yield and give place*, the fishery must undoubtedly be that precise object." Accordingly, it was held that fishermen (but only fishermen) were — "by the custom of the island" — entitled to a stay of execution in a civil actions, for it was a matter of "national policy" that fishermen be allowed to prosecute their business until the end of the season. Likewise, if a contract called for the "usual credit", custom dictated that payment was not due until the fall of the year. A landlord was accorded the traditional battery of remedies available under English law, including the right to levy distress, unless the property involved was a fishing plantation, in which case distraint was not tenable. Also, special rules of possession developed concerning the first occupancy of positions in fishing waters, and ownership of seals killed on the ice floes.

The resort to custom was also affected by other local circumstances. In the aftermath of a devastating fire in St. John's, a series of cases held that where leased premises were destroyed by fire it was an accepted custom in the town of St. John's (though not part of English law) that the tenant was entitled, but not obliged, to surrender the premises to the landlord. Although the wisdom of that rule was later doubted (would it not encourage arson?), and the existence of the underlying custom called into question, in 1893 it was held that the principle had become so well entrenched as to require legislative intervention to displace it.

Judicial creativity in Newfoundland was robust. Overall, however, I am not sure that Canadian courts were eager to stray too far from the path beaten by the English common law. Consider all of the English principles governing leases, future interests, easements, and so forth, that have been accepted without ado. And deference to English law continues to manifest itself in curious ways. In 1984, the ancient rule in *Purefoy v. Rogers* (circa 1671) was applied to an Ontario will, with the result that an otherwise valid remainder interest was struck down. Nobody today sees the rule as anything other than out-dated and capricious; yet it was applied. The question of whether *Purefoy* had ever formed part of Ontario law, or in any event was now dead, was not addressed. Likewise, in a 1980 decision, the Ontario Court of Appeal was called upon to consider whether *Shelley*'s case (*circa* 1583) applied. On the facts, the rule was not triggered. It is true that there is authority holding that the rule in *Shelley's* case was not part of the law of the Northwest Territories. However, whether or not *Shelley* was received into Ontario was not discussed by the Court of Appeal; nor was it considered whether the rule should now be jettisoned. Nor, for that matter, was any of this argued . . .

Let me suggest two reasons why this pattern of adherence exists . . . The first explanation is instrumental in nature. Prudence points to the reception of a given rule when the absence of adoption creates uncertainty. It is also convenient: it would often be pointless to re-invent the wheel. In addition, most property law statutes were designed only to rectify the common law; to reject such a statute might mean that the unreformed common law would govern. More important, property law is like a gossamer cloth. Unravel it at your peril. By the 1830s tenure served little more than a descriptive function even in English land law. By the time that the *Statute of Tenures* was enacted in 1660, the economic functions of feudal tenures in England had been rendered obsolete. What remained was a basic infrastructure no more (or less) suitable to England than Canada. Even so, the report of the (English) Real Property Commissioners in 1832 recommended against abolishing the concept on the ground that it was "an innovation too dangerous to be prudently hazarded". One sees this same attitude adopted in the 1992 Australian native title case of *Mabo*, where it is observed that "[i]f the slate were clean, there would be something to be said for the view that the English system of land law was not, in 1788, appropriate for application to the circumstances of a British penal colony . . .". Still, it was acknowledged that it was not now possible to revisit that matter.

The common law, even the apparently ossified features of feudal land law, was malleable enough to adapt to new environs, whether economic, social or geographic. Commercial realities were changing in England in the 19th century, as they were in British North America, and many common law doctrines continued to serve current needs because of a capacity for reinvention. As R.C.B. Risk has observed, the private law conferred "blank powers", and "[t]he power of the fee simple did not differentiate between use of land in Sussex and the use of land in western Ontario".

There would, of course, be nothing within legal education or the practice of law, wedded in these early years to English models, that might serve to unsettle the juridical penchant to adopt English doctrine with little ado. Likewise, the superintendence of the Judicial Committee of the Privy Council and the canonical stature of works such as Blackstone's *Commentaries* served to bolster an already entrenched posture of judicial conservatism. And for lawyers, change is risky. The devil you know if always preferable to the one you don't; that is a cardinal principle among obsessively cautious real estate practitioners. This surely explains why the *Statute of Uses* was treated as received, and, in British Columbia and Ontario, incorporated into provincial legislation. It was safer to dance around the Act than to pretend or assume that it did not exist.

A second reason is normative. It strains credulity to suggest that the morass of rules that form the body of English land law might be seen as representing anything approaching the apotheosis of justice. Yet, one finds within imperial discourse of this period a resolute confidence in the superiority of English political institutions, and this is manifested in part in a belief in the right-headedness of English justice. The common law was viewed as encoding principles of universal justice, "having its foundations in those general and immutable principles of justice which should regulate the intercourse of men with men, wherever they may reside". For Blackstone, the general reception of English law into settler colonies was "the birthright of every subject". The common law was seen as a repository of centuries of collected wisdom. It was as much a symbol of progress and the development of civilization as any to which one might point. These types of claims, advanced also as part of the case for nineteenth-century imperialism, are wholly consistent with the outcome of most Canadian reception cases. To discard the received learning of the common law always carried with it the potential cost of somehow taking a backwards step, and not of forging ahead.

It is possible to overstate this point. For one thing, it will be recalled that the rules for the adoption of English law for ceded and conquered territories called for the retention of existing local laws. As with the approach for settled colonies, a critical value was continuity. In addition, recall that the idea of inapplicability is built into the idea of reception. Diversity is contemplated. Blackstone's account of the applicability proviso had to do with concerns that some English laws, such as the "artificial refinements and distinctions incident to the property of a great and commercial people" were unnecessary and inconvenient. Lord Denning, in his inimitable style, while asserting that English common law contained "many principles of manifest justice and good sense with advantage to peoples of every race and colour all the world over", recognised that there were many refinements and technicalities that might not be suitable elsewhere, and that in "these far-off lands" the laws must be such that people will both understand and respect them. In short, the universal application of the common law, however excellent it might be, was not pursued at all cost.

I am not sure the views about the lack of suitability of some received law (discussed just above) explains or describes the Canadian experience. Some English rules were rejected because they ceased to have a useful function, even in England.

At other times, the English law was not adopted or replaced because it was, euphemistically speaking, awful, or peculiar, or utterly ill-suited to the circumstances in North America.

In these cases, few as they are, a faint image is being projected of a new land, without the social or physical limitations, or the legal baggage, of England. Apart from the experience in Newfoundland, the most forceful articulation of a sense of colonial independence of this type is perhaps that found in the 1848 Nova Scotia decision in *Uniacke v. Dickson*, referred to briefly above. There it was said that,

> In the early settlement of a colony, when the local legislature has just been called into existence, and has its attention engrossed by the immediate wants of the members of the infant community in their new situation[,] the courts . . . would naturally look for guidance . . . to the general laws of the mother country; and would exercise greater latitude, in their adoption of them than they would be entitled to do as their local legislature . . . assumed its proper position. *Every year should render the courts more cautious in the adoption of law that had never been previously introduced into the colony.* [Emphasis dded.]

However, as I have observed above, the pattern of development advocated in this passage did not emerge . . .

3. BASIC DIVISIONS IN THE LAW OF PROPERTY

R. Chambers, *An Introduction to Property Law in Australia* (Sydney: LBC, 2001) at 37-41

There are a number of ways to organize the law of property. Distinctions can be drawn according to the nature of things subject to property rights or according to the nature of the property rights to which things can be subject. These are the traditional methods of classifying property rights, but they suffer from two limitations: obsolescence and isolation. The first limitation is the product of a long history. Many of the categories into which property rights are divided were created centuries ago. Changes in law and society have rendered some of those categories obsolete and yet they persist as potential sources of confusion.

Secondly, the traditional categories of property law tend to isolate it from other areas of law. Categories based on the nature of the thing or the nature of the right have no counterparts outside the law of property. Since personal rights do not depend on the existence of a thing and differ from property rights by nature, it is difficult to make meaningful comparisons between property and other laws . . .

Land/Goods

The most important division in the law of property may be that which is drawn between land and other things. Most things other than land are referred to as goods (and less commonly as chattels). There are many things which are neither land nor goods, such as money, shares in a corporation, or copyright in a song. Goods are those things, other than land, which are tangible, such as a car, a dog, or a loaf of bread. The distinction between land and goods is a natural starting point. It is easy to understand why the law makes this distinction. Generally speaking, land is both permanent and stationary. It remains relatively constant while the people who use the land come and go. Most other things are transitory. Animals die, clothes wear out, and food gets eaten. Also, goods can be moved from one place to another. A parcel of land will always be subject to whatever laws apply to that location, while a car made in one state may become subject to the laws of several different states and territories as it is moved from place to place.

Roman law classified things as either movable (*res mobiles*) or immovable (*res immobiles*): Barry Nicholas, *An Introduction to Roman Law* (1962) p. 105. Countries with civil codes, like France, Germany, and Japan, adopted this classification. Countries like Australia, which adopted the British common law, use a different system under which property is either real or personal (sometimes called realty and personalty). This corresponds roughly with the civilian categories of immovable or movable and our popular notions of the distinction between land and goods. However, it is important to know that the categories of goods/land, personal/real, and movable/immovable do not correspond to one another with precision.

Real/Personal

The distinctions between land and goods and between immovables and movables are based on the nature of the thing. In contrast, the distinction between real and personal property is based on the nature of the right. It is derived from the forms of legal actions used in 13th and 14th century England: Williams, "The Terms Real and Personal in English Law" (1888) 4 *Law Quarterly Review* 394. Certain property rights to land were classified as real property because the holder of the right could bring a real action to recover the land from someone who was wrongly in possession of it. Other property rights were classified as personal property because there was no real action available to recover the thing itself. Instead, the holder of a personal property right had a personal action to be compensated for the loss caused by the person who wrongly interfered with that right.

The categories of real and personal property continue to be used and are commonly associated with the categories of land and goods. This is because all real property rights are rights to land, while most personal property rights are not. However, the similarity is misleading because there are property rights to land which, strictly speaking, are not real property. A lease of land . . . was considered not to be real property because there was no real action which would allow a dispossessed tenant to recover the leased land itself. In the 15th century, another form of action, called ejectment, was developed to allow tenants to recover possession of leased land. Since ejectment was not a real action, leases of land were not reclassified as real property, but are sometimes found under the strange heading, chattels real: Simpson, *A History of the Land Law* (2nd ed, 1986) pp. 74-76. Ironically, ejectment proved to be a more efficient remedy than the real actions and soon displaced them as the means of protecting real property rights: Megarry & Wade, *The Law of Real Property* (5th ed, 1984) pp. 1155-1159.

The end of the real actions removed the original basis for the distinction between real and personal property. The right to recover the thing itself is no longer limited to real property. In addition to leases of land, the law allows the holders of property rights to goods which are difficult or impossible to replace (such as family heirlooms, original paintings, or made-to-order machine parts) to recover those goods from others wrongly in possession of them. So, the categories of realty and personalty no longer indicate with accuracy whether a property right entitles the holder to recover the thing itself or merely to receive compensation for its loss.

The distinction between real and personal property should not be confused with the distinction between rights *in rem* and rights *in personam*: Hohfeld, "Fundamental Legal Conceptions as Applied to Judicial Reasoning" (1917) 26 *Yale Law Journal* 710 at 752-753. Personal property rights are not personal rights. They are property rights because they relate to external things and are enforceable generally against other members of society. However, they are normally enforced by means of personal rights. For example, a thief who steals your car commits an actionable wrong (the tort of conversion . . .) and is liable to compensate you for your loss. Your right to your car is a property right, while your right to be compensated is a personal right against the specific person who wrongly interfered with your property right.

Legal/Equitable

Property rights can also be divided into legal and equitable rights. Like real and personal property, these categories are based on the nature of the right and were created by legal conditions which have since ceased to exist. Prior to 1875, the common law of England was administered by common law courts, such as the courts of King's Bench and Common Pleas. Rights which could be enforced in those courts are called legal rights. A separate body of law, called equity, was administered by the court of Chancery. Rights which could be enforced in the Chancery, but not in the common law courts, are called equitable rights.

A statute called the *Judicature Act 1873* merged those courts into a single High Court of Justice, which continued to administer common law and equity as separate bodies of law. This process was copied in Australia. In each state and territory, the courts of common law and equity have been merged into a single superior court empowered to administer both law and equity: see Meagher, Gummow & Lehane, *Equity Doctrines and Remedies* (3rd ed, 1992) pp. 37-44. So, the separate categories of legal and equitable property rights continue to exist even though the court structure which created them does not. As F.W. Maitland said, in *Equity*, (rev. ed, 1936) p. 1:

> We have no longer any courts which are merely courts of equity. Thus we are driven to say that Equity now is that body of rules administered by our . . . courts of justice which, were it not for the operation of the *Judicature Acts*, would be administered only by those courts which would be known as Courts of Equity.

Although the body of law known as equity can be defined only historically, by reference to conditions which have ceased to exit, it continues to be a vital part of the law. The rules of equity were created to fill gaps in the common law and correct perceived injustices. Many of those rules were patterned after the common law and, therefore, most legal property rights have an equitable counterpart (and vice versa). For example, a lease of land can be either legal or equitable depending on whether that lease would have been recognized in a court of common law or only in a court of equity.

The nature of equitable property rights will be discussed in more detail in Chapter [6]. It is sufficient at this stage to note that there are still important practical differences between legal and equitable property rights. Two main differences are the manner of their creation and their durability. First, . . . most equitable property rights can be created with less formality than the comparable legal property rights. Secondly, . . . they tend to be less durable than legal property rights and are more easily extinguished by competing property rights to the same thing.

Tangible/Intangible

Property rights are sometimes classified according to whether they are tangible or intangible. Other terms for these categories are corporeal and incorporeal: see Butt, *Land Law* (3rd ed, 1996) pp. 400-401. All property rights are intangible in the sense that they are rights enforceable against other persons, regardless of the nature of the thing to which those rights relate. The distinction depends on whether the property right entitles the holder to possession of the thing involved. Tangible (corporeal) property rights include the right to possession of some thing, while intangible (incorporeal) property rights do not . . .

Personal property is often classified as tangible or intangible. A right to possession of goods is called a chose in possession (using the French word for thing) and a personal property right to an intangible thing is called a chose in action. The latter term is also used to refer to purely personal rights, such as a bank account or other rights to receive the payment of money. When used in that sense, the chose (thing) is the obligation to which the personal right corresponds . . .

Property Creating Events

Another way to organize property rights is according to the events that create them. Peter Birks has identified four main categories ("Equity in the Modern Law: An Exercise in Taxonomy" (1996) 26 *UWA Law Review* 1 at 8): "The Rights which people bear, whether in personam or in rem, derive from the following events: wrongs, consent, unjust enrichment, and others." The origins of these categories can be found in Roman law.

Most property rights are created by consent, such as a sale of goods, a bequest in a will, or a grant of a mortgage. Property rights can also be created by wrongdoing. For example, an employer may have a property right to any bribes received by her or his employees. There are property rights created by unjust enrichment, such as the right to recover land or goods transferred by mistake. The miscellany of other events includes the creation (and destruction) of property rights brought about by physical changes to things.

This taxonomy of property rights is useful because it brings together and invites comparisons between different rights which tend to be studied and applied as discrete compartments of property law. For example, mortgages are often relegated to separate chapters near the end of property law textbooks (and law school subjects) and never related to, say, gifts of chattels. The same types of events create property rights regardless of whether those rights are real or personal, legal or equitable, and tangible or intangible . . .

QUESTIONS

1. Slot the following items, using the categories described by Rob Chambers: a book; an IOU; flax growing on a farm (see *Hoegy v. General Accident Assurance Co. of Canada* 75 D.L.R. (3d) 44, 1977 CarswellOnt 776 (Co. Ct.); a contract under which A agrees to provide banjo lessons to B; electricity supplied to a home by a utility company: see *Brown v. The Queen in Right of British Columbia* 20 B.C.L.R. 64, 1979 CarswellBC 797 (C.A.).

2. Section 2 of the *Chattels Real Act*, R.S.N.L. 1990, c. 11, declares:

> All lands . . . which by the common law are regarded as real estate shall . . . be held to be "chattels real", and shall go to the executor or administrator of any person or persons dying seized or possessed thereof as any other personal estate passes to the personal representatives, any law, custom or usage to the contrary notwithstanding.

This enigmatic provision was enacted in 1834, and there remains a debate as to its meaning. One view is that the section serves a limited function: it merely abolishes the ancient rules governing the devolution of real property on death. As with the resort to the reliance on the custom of the island in the shaping of a unique set of common law principles, this legislative measure was seen as designed for a society that conceived of itself as a simple fishing settlement in which the complexities of English succession laws were quite superfluous. On this narrow reading, the Act is merely an early version of a reform measure that was eventually adopted throughout the common law world.

The alternative view is that by virtue of this statute there is no such thing as real property in Newfoundland! What that means to conveyancing practice is somewhat difficult to fathom. In the 1860 decision in *Evans v. Doyle* (1860) 4 Nfld. L.R. 432 (Full Ct.) at 436, Robinson J. could not find authority that "lands in this colony have ever been adjudged realty"; *cf. Walbank v. Ellis* (1853) 3 Nfld. L.R. 400 (S.C.). Accordingly, in the *Evans* case it was said that the 1834 Act was intended to confirm the law as understood in the colony. The premise behind this larger reading is, I think, captured in a 1952 decision, left unreported until 1994, in which the scope of the Act was discussed in these terms:

> I need not decide the old controversy as to whether this Act reduces land to the chattel level of all purposes or only for purposes of devolution; beyond observing that as the feudal characteristics of land were of necessity inapplicable to the conditions of settlements in the wilderness of North America, it would not be unfair to regard these chattels real acts (for similar acts were to be found elsewhere) as finishing, rather than beginning, the alteration of the land laws. It is true that we still recognise estates in land; but is not that a function of its immovability and permanence, rather than an inheritance of legal doctrine?

Cahill v. Caines 120 Nfld. & P.E.I.R. 84, 1952 CarswellNfld 9 (S.C.) at 87 (*per* Dunfield J.). See further A.C. McEwen, *Newfoundland Law of Real Property — The Origin and Development of Land Ownership* (Ph.D. Thesis, University of London, 1979) at ch. 9, *passim*; R. Gushue, "The Law of Real Property in Newfoundland" (1926) 4 Can. Bar Rev. 310.

COMMENTS

1. As Rob Chambers observes in the extract above, there are a variety of ways to disaggregate property rights. Most of the analysis presented in this Casebook focuses on private law rights; little mention is made of the criminal law of theft, fraud and so forth. Other forms of public law regulation, such as that governing municipal planning (such as zoning) are addressed only in passing. Dr. Chambers identifies the penchant within the process of categorization to isolate property conceptions artificially, when in fact a strong interrelationship often exists. The law of theft depends to some extent (although not universally) on private law notions of property. Certainly, the rationale for criminal protections relates to the goals of private ownership canvassed in Chapter 1.

2. One thing that should be obvious is that the categories used in Canadian law are not of universal application, to be found in non-common law property regimes. The distinction between real property and personalty is a product of history; treating a lease as a chattel real can best be understood in that peculiar light. In Chapter 5 of this Casebook we will examine the basic legal principles governing the recognition of Aboriginal title and related matters. At that point it will be seen that Canadian law regards Aboriginal entitlements as *sui generis* (unique). What that means is that basic common law rules may not necessarily be applied to Aboriginal rights. Moreover, the idiosyncratic and isolating divisions in Canadian property law stand in marked contrast to the ways in which other cultures conceive of the idea of property. The description offered by Russell Barsh below seeks to describe one contrasting view.

R.L. Barsh, "How Do You Patent a Landscape? The Perils of Dichotomizing Cultural and Intellectual Property" (1999) 8 I. J. C. P. 14, at 14-22 [footnotes omitted]

For a variety of conceptual, historical, and political reasons, contemporary international law distinguishes between "natural" land forms, cultural monuments, movable cultural property, the performing arts, and scientific knowledge. Indigenous peoples do not make these distinctions. Rather, they tend to regard landscapes as inherently cultural products in which artworks, literature, performances, and scientific knowledge systems are inextricably embedded. Scientific knowledge must periodically be rehearsed within the landscape in recitations and performances that remember the historical process by which people and their nonhuman kinfolk constructed the landscape. Detaching specific cultural or scientific "objects" from the landscape and commodifying them, as is contemplated by most current proposals for protecting indigenous peoples' rights, will undermine the indigenous institutions and procedures necessary for perpetuating the quality and validity of local knowledge . . .

No state contends that indigenous peoples should be denied rights to their unexploited funds of useful knowledge, or to the diversity of cultures within which they have maintained their knowledge. Agreement on the precise legal form such rights should take has been impossible, however, because of fundamental differences of interests among states and between states and indigenous peoples. Indigenous peoples insist that scientific knowledge is an inalienable part of their cultures and territories. Developing countries want preferential access to all of the indigenous knowledge within their borders, hoping to stimulate the development of more exportable commodities. Industrialized countries want immediate access to indigenous peoples' knowledge under the least restrictive conditions — preferably conventional intellectual property mechanisms such as patents — so that they can develop new commodities to sell back to developing countries.

In the rush to reach a political consensus on indigenous science, an important conceptual problem has been overlooked. The path of least resistance for indigenous peoples seeking state protection is to accept a separation of land, culture, and science into separate legal categories, to be protected under separate international instruments and through separate intergovernmental mechanisms. If this separation is implemented, indigenous cultures may gain a reprieve, but the price will be a distortion of the very nature of indigenous cultures, and of the relationship between indigenous peoples and their lands . . .

Indigenous peoples conceive of landscapes as socially constructed moral spaces, fashioned out of relationships among coexisting species that have developed over a very long time through marriages, treaties, and shared endeavors. The ecosystem is a dynamic network of kinship, trade, and diplomacy, of which human societies are only one part and in which alignments of power and cooperation continue to shift and change with little warning. In order to survive, humans must understand and respect their commitments to other species, exercise caution whenever they intervene in other species' affairs, and watch the ecosystem very carefully for signs of impending changes. A seasonal cycle of travel, visiting landmarks, medicine gathering, and performances constitutes an annual "reading" of the ecosystem and of the history of interspecies relationships embedded within key features of the landscape. By reading the landscape and performing it, people teach, rehearse, and exercise their responsibilities, renewing the land.

The significance of journeys and performances must be understood in the context of the fact that most ecosystems are anthropogenic. In other words, the physical and biological landscape is a human product. Human activity has modified landforms, altered the abundance of plants and animals, changed water flows and soil chemistry. Agriculture is a familiar example: even before the steel plow and internal-combustion engine, farmers created distinctive landscapes of fields, ditches, and terraces that altered pre-existing ecosystems and create new ecological niches, such as the hedgerows of Celtic Britain and the carp ponds of Tang China. Shifting cultivation in tropical forests creates a distinctive patchiness in forest architecture by altering processes of succession. Nonagricultural peoples are also active ecological engineers, notably through the periodic use of fire to restructure plant communities, and thereby create and maintain unnatural landscapes, such as Australia's eucalyptus forests and North America's sweeping tall-grass prairies . . .

From an indigenous perspective, then, an ancestral landscape is a book of human history and ecological science. It can be read through the performance of stories and ceremonies associated with landmarks, which serve as the chapter headings and index. Each generation adds to the text (as in all good empirical science) through patient observation of changes in the ecosystems which each landmark anchors in mental space. Oceanscapes and skyscapes are embedded by seafaring peoples with history and science in the same way. I refer to this textual quality of a long-travelled and extensively co-adapted landscape as "embeddedness," emphasizing the layers of linguistic, social, spiritual, and ecological knowledge and meaning that rest beneath the visible panorama.

Embeddedness can be found in "engineered landscapes," such as the elaborately terraced mountain farms and lowland irrigation networks of southeast Asia or the Andes, as well as in landscapes that have simply been traveled, foraged, and observed. Indigenous ecological models may traditionally be recorded and communicated in media that Europeans regard, moreover, as "artistic" and emotive rather than empirical, such as song and movement. Honeybees have long been known to communicate spatial models to one another through dance, so it should come as no surprise that human dances can be used to demonstrate animal behavior, trophic webs, or ecological principles. My Blackfoot and Cree students have been exploring the reasons why certain species figure prominently as inspirations for Prairie Indian dances: some were useful to people (for example, bison) while others played key ecological roles (wolves and beaver), or served as indicators of ecological productivity (eagles and prairie chickens).

Many indigenous peoples make two-dimensional maps but usually do not respect the Western convention of using rectilinear coordinates to represent terrestrial orientation and physical distance. They tend to focus on time rather than space, often representing the elapse of time as a spiral rather than a straight line. Time maps depict the journey and stops along the way to hunt, conduct ceremonies, and tell stories. The earliest European maps also used courses, stations, and elapsed time rather than rectilinear coordinates, which were developed by Roman surveyors preoccupied with ownership of the earth's surface — and thus with measurable geometric boundaries.

Within the indigenous paradigm, then, the landscape is not merely a storage place for various kinds of things, some of which are useful. It is a library of local history and possibilities, and the appearance, behavior, and spatial distribution of landforms and species is a text that can be read in prescribed sequences. The landscape is also a laboratory in which new knowledge is continually being created, as humans and other species switch strategies and adapt to one another anew. Since people are as much a part of the co-adaptive mechanism as birds or trees, the removal of the people or the termination of their way of interacting with the landscape necessarily results in a cascade of responsive ecological adjustments. As a Kalahari San elder explained to me, if the people are removed "the land will die."

Removing the knowledge of the people — their specific protocol for reading the scientific text embedded in their landscape — will have the same effect. All species have co-adapted with human activity; change the human activity and "the land will die," by gradually evolving into a different landscape. Grasslands revert to scrub, and quilted biodiverse forests become oligarchic forests with the cessation of human burning, hunting, herding, and horticulture.

The embedding of landscapes is not unique to indigenous or tribal peoples as we classify them today. European landscapes were embedded with Gallic, Teutonic, and Celtic stories centered on sacred springs and groves, like the grove that Caesar Augustus ordered his engineers to destroy during the seige of Marseilles. The *Volkerwanderung* that followed the collapse of centralized Roman administration resulted in a massive redistribution of ethnic groups (e.g., the Germanic Lombards and Franks to Gallic northern Italy and France), but migrating groups eventually invested their new landscapes with fresh layers of stories and sacred meaning. Europeans migrating to the Americas, especially those who lived for generations close to the land, also invested the landscape with sacred meanings and localized knowledge. In the words of one Mennonite farmer with whom I exchanged observations about prairie dynamics, "every field is a little different from the others." . . .

There is considerable diversity in the ways indigenous societies distribute the responsibility for maintaining knowledge. Authority and expertise may nominally reside with individuals for a lifetime (e.g., Northwest Coast and Mi'kmaw), or with groups in rotation (Blackfoot). In either case, however, the underlying function of customary law is keeping knowledge systems intact and continuously accessible within a specific kin group or community. Even where entrusted to individual specialists in whose reputations the community must trust (much the same as within Western science, engineering, and medicine), knowledge remains firmly anchored in ecological space and cannot be detached and moved . . .

If I am correct in this generalization, knowledge is an intrinsic part of a single social process that mediates land use and knowledge. Breaking knowledge into fragments and separating those fragments from the land truncate its scientific value, distort its social meaning, and undermine the balance of power within indigenous societies . . .

4. PROPERTY, CLASS, AND POVERTY

T. Scott, "Poverty in Canada: An Analytical Overview"

> Property rights are, by nature, social rights; they embody how we, as a society, have chosen to reward the claims of some to finite and critical goods, and to deny the claims to the same goods by others. Try as we might to separate this right from choice, conflict and vexing social questions, it cannot be done.
>
> Laura Underkuffler-Freund[1]

Introduction

Poverty is, at its core, the lack of an adequate amount of property; and thus is a manifestation of the social choices and conflicts that are embedded in our system of property distribution and protection. In exploring the definitions, measures, causes, effects, and solutions posited in the literature on poverty one sees vastly disparate opinions. In this article I will explore some of the differing views on the issue in connection with the social and economic belief systems from which they surface.

In doing so, I will predominantly draw from the literature that lies at opposite ends of the ideological spectrum. The work of Christopher Sarlo of the Fraser Institute represents a free market perspective. The Fraser Institute's mandate is "the redirection of public attention to the role of the competitive markets in providing for the well-being of Canadians."[2] Organizations such as the Canadian Council on Social Development ("CCSD"), the National Anti-Poverty Organization, and the National Council on Welfare present a welfarist perspective. This literature reflects the belief that markets create unacceptable levels of inequality in society, especially in certain identifiable groups.

Poverty, By Definition is . . .

There is no universally accepted, or government-sanctioned definition of poverty in Canada.[3] Christopher Sarlo argues that a definition of poverty must correspond to what he calls "commonly held notions of poverty."[4] He argues that one such notion is that one lives in poverty "if [one] lacks any item required to maintain long-term physical well-being."[5] By contrast, social welfare community advocates main-

---

1 L. Underkuffler-Freund, "Property: A Special Right", 71 Notre Dame L. Rev. 1033 (1996) at 1046.

2 Online: Fraser Institute Homepage <http://www.fraserinstitute.ca/> (date of access: June 29, 2003).

3 For a good discussion on the debate about poverty lines in Canada see National Council on Welfare, *A New Poverty Line Yes or No* (Ottawa: National Council on Welfare, 1999). See also Canadian Council on Social Development, "Defining and Redefining Poverty: A CCSD Perspective" online: <http://www.ccsd.ca/pubs/2001/poverty/pp.htm> (date of access: June 30, 2003).

4 C.A. Sarlo, *Measuring Poverty in Canada* (Vancouver: Fraser Institute, 2001) at 11.

5 *Ibid.*

tain that "any definition of poverty must take into account social and psychological as well as physical well-being."[6] Thus, it is reasoned, a definition of poverty should reflect the level of income at which people experience marginalization. The justification for this approach is the catalogue of negative social, psychological, and physical effects that are experienced by people living at low-income levels. In addition, this type of definition recognizes the detrimental impact on society as a whole that results from the existence of poverty among some.

These approaches obviously identify different badges of poverty. Sarlo proposes a Basic Needs Measure determined by calculating the "cost of a list of necessities of life that would be required for physical maintenance and good health on an ongoing basis. This list includes the four basic necessities of food, shelter, clothing and health care".[7] The following table sets out Sarlo's Basic Needs Poverty lines for 2000.[8]

Size of Household	Basic Needs Poverty Lines (CDN$)
1 Person	8875
2 Persons	13926
3 Persons	16926
4 Persons	19962
5 Persons	22206
6 Persons	24602

A social welfarist poverty line would look quite different. It would focus not only on the number of Canadians whose physical survival is threatened, but also those Canadians who are unable to develop to their full human potential due to economic hardship. Thus the CCSD, and many other organizations have predominantly used the Statistics Canada Low Income Cut-Off Measure ("LICO") as an indicator of poverty. The LICOs are not an officially sanctioned poverty line,[9] but have been used as the indicator of "straitened circumstances" for some 25 years.[10]

6 D.P. Ross, K.J. Scott, & P.J. Smith, *Canadian Fact Book on Poverty* (Ottawa: Canadian Council on Social Development, 2000) at 6.

7 *Supra*, note 4 at 17.

8 C.A. Sarlo, "Measuring Poverty in Canada" online: Fraser Institute Critical Issues <http://oldfraser.lexi.net/publications/critical_issues/2001/poverty/section_02.html> (date of access: June 20, 2002).

9 I.P. Fellangi, *On Poverty and Low Income*, online: Statistics Canada <http://www.statcan.ca/enEilish/concepts/poverty/pauv.htm> (date of access: June 20, 2002).

10 A. Kazemipur & S.S. Halli, *The New Poverty in Canada: Ethnic Groups and Ghetto Neighbourhoods* (Toronto: Thomson Educational Pub., 2000) at 18.

These cut-offs are developed by conducting a family expenditure survey, then "estimating the percentage of gross income spent by the average Canadian family on food, clothing and shelter. It then somewhat arbitrarily marks this percentage up by 20 percentage points. The final percentage corresponds on average to a given household income level, and this becomes the low income cut-off for that year".[11] While highly criticized by organizations like the Fraser Institute as being inflated and arbitrary, LICOs are still the most commonly used measures of poverty.[12] The following table shows the LICOs for 2002.[13]

Statistics Canada's Low Income Cutoffs

	Size of Community				
Size of Family	**>500,000**	**100,000 - 499,999**	**30,000 - 99,999**	**<30,000**	**Rural Areas**
1	$19,261	$16,521	$16,407	$15,267	$13,311
2	$24,077	$20,651	$20,508	$19,083	$16,639
3	$29,944	$25,684	$25,505	$23,732	$20,694
4	$36,247	$31,090	$30,875	$28,729	$25,050
5	$40,518	$34,754	$34,521	$32,133	$28,002
6	$44,789	$38,418	$38,150	$35,498	$30,954
7	$49,060	$42,080	$41,788	$38,882	$33,907

Federal and territorial governments have also added another absolute measure of poverty which, it is hoped "might achieve greater consensus and serve as a more efficient tool than the existing measures."[14] These poverty lines are determined by deciding on a "basket of necessities", and then pricing the basket according to location".[15] The following table is the Low Income Cut-Off Levels compared to the Market Basket Measure for a family of two adults and two children.[16]

11 *Supra*, note 6 at 15.

12 *Supra*, note 3.

13 Online: Canadian Council on Social Development <http://www.ccsd/factsheets/fs_lic02.htm> (date of access: June 29, 2003).

14 See Human Resources and Development Canada, *The Market Basket Measure — Constructing a New Measure of Poverty*, online: Human Resources and Development <http://www.hrdc-drhc.ca/sp-ps/arb-dgra/publications/bulletin/vol4n2/e/v4n2_01e.html> (date of access: June 29, 2003).

15 *Supra*, note 6 at 22.

16 *Supra*, note 14.

Low Income Cutoff Levels and Market Basket Measure Thresholds For Families of Two Adults and Two Children by Province and Community Size

Population:	over 500,000	100,000 - 499,000	30,000 - 99,000	under 30,000	Rural Communities
Low Income Cutoff Levels (LICOs)	$32,238	$27,651	$27,459	$25,551	$22,279
Newfoundland	N/A	$21,234	N/A	$19,986	$18,714
Prince Edward Island	N/A	N/A	$21,310	$20,074	$20,074
Nova Scotia	N/A	$21,291	$19,899	$21,447	$19,635
New Brunswick	N/A	$19,230	$20,742	$18,474	$17,982
Quebec	$19,953	$19,077	$18,825	$18,657	$17,889
Ontario	$25,194	$23,202	$22,722	$22,362	$20,370
Manitoba	$21,746	N/A	$21,086	$19,970	$19,730
Saskatchewan	N/A	$20,582	$19,190	$20,162	$19,226
Alberta	$19,930	N/A	$19,486	$19,750	$17,626
British Columbia	$25,196	$24,128	$22,712	$22,136	$20,516

Note: N/A indicates that there are no communities of this size in the province

While the Canadian Ministry of Human Resources Development Canada sees this new measure as a compromise between absolute and relative poverty lines, there has been criticism of this measure as well, especially in relation to what counts as necessaries.[17]

As the preceding discussion demonstrates, we are far from a consensus on what poverty means in Canada. The differences reflect divergent political positions. Sarlo's poverty lines reflect an acceptance of the social inequality that is inevitably generated by the marketplace. He stresses the importance of choice. Hence, homelessness is seen as a result of the homeless' lack of exploiting existing social programs because of "[m]istrust of 'the system', personal pride, the excitement and spontaneity of street life, the perception that they would be pressured to find employment, and expected loss of freedom".[18] In explaining the continuing problem of poverty, he writes:

> Lowering the poverty rate further is going to be much more difficult because those still poor today have a much different range of problems keeping them in poverty. They may lack self-esteem, making it difficult for them to imagine themselves achieving self-sufficiency. They may have motivational or attitudinal problems that limit their labour-market attainments. They may also have problems with addiction or mental illness, or engage in anti-social or criminal activities that impede their progress. Add to this the increasing generosity of our social programs after the mid-1970's, which creates for

17 Canadian Council on Social Development, "Defining and Redefining Poverty: A CCSD Perspective" online: <http://www.ccsd.ca/pubs/2001/poverty/pp.htm> (date of access: June 30, 2003).

18 *Supra*, note 4 at 184.

some at the low end of the income disincentive to work, and we have a possible explanation for stubbornness and "downward stickiness" of the poverty rate.[19]

This brand of "poor-bashing"[20] focuses on perceived individual deficiencies. However, as Leslie Regelous writes: "people who need income assistance are not criminals, cultural subversives or lazy. They are unemployed or unemployable. Both can happen to any of us at anytime."[21] Social welfarists argue that the correlation between low income and social maladies actually justifies a higher poverty line: "To integrate these people into society requires a special effort. To facilitate a permanent escape from poverty, such an effort must include special services to assist people in overcoming or adapting to some of their problems."[22] The disturbing correlation between mental, physical and social problems among low-income individuals can either be seen as the justification for their plight, or the product of the social isolation of poverty.

The differences in the measurement and definition of poverty led Sarlo to conclude in 1996 that "poverty is not a major problem in Canada".[23] In 2001 he questioned his 1996 estimate of an 8% poverty rate: due to the possibility of the "under-reporting income, in-kind gifts, part-year families, student loans, and business losses"[24] he thought the figure might have been too high. According to the CCSD, however, using the Low Income Cut-Offs the number of Canadians living in straitened circumstances has increased. The overall poverty rate in Canada increased approximately 4% to 17.5% between 1989 and 1997. This figure means that 5.2 million Canadians lived on family incomes below the LICO.[25] Families had a 14% incidence of poverty; unattached individuals a 39.6% incidence.[26] The following table produced by the CCSD demonstrates the total number of Canadians in poverty in 1971, 1981, 1989 and 1997.[27]

---

19 *Supra*, note 4 at 36.

20 J. Swanson, Poor-Bashing: *The Politics of Exclusion* (Toronto: Between the Lines, 2001) at 3.

21 L. Regelous "We Want it to Stop", online Edmonton Social Planning Council <http://www.edmsvc.com/Edmonton%20Facts/edmfacts_November1999.htm#wewant> (date of access: June 20, 2002)

22 *Supra*, note 4 at 58.

23 C.A. Sarlo, *Poverty in Canada*, 2nd ed. (Vancouver: Fraser Institute, 1996) at 193.

24 *Supra*, note 4 at 58.

25 *Supra*, note 6 at 46.

26 *Supra*, note 6 at 47.

27 *Ibid.*

POVERTY RATES AND TOTAL NUMBERS IN POVERTY, 1973, 1982, 1989 AND 1997

	1973		1981		1989		1997	
	Number (thousands)	Rate (%) *	Number (thousands)	Rate (%) **	Number (thousands)	Rate (%) ***	Number (thousands)	Rate (%) ****
Families	701	13.4%	721	11.3%	786	11.0%	1,175	14.0%
Unattached Individuals	767	40.2%	940	37.5%	1,101	34.4%	1,633	39.6%
All Households	1,468	20.6%	1,661	18.7%	1,887	18.3%	2,808	22.4%
65+	506	41.0%	533	33.8%	531	26.6%	609	24.8%
<65 years	962	16.3%	1,129	15.5%	1,356	16.3%	2,199	21.8%
Total Persons	3,269	16.2%	3,339	14.0%	3,489	13.5%	5,222	17.5%

Notes: *1969 base; ** 1978 base; ***1986 base; ****1992 base. Numbers may not sum due to rounding.
Source: Tabulations by authors based on Statistics Canada's Survey of Consumer Finance Microdata.

Who are the poor?

Studies by the Canadian Council on Social Development and the Centre for Social Justice, suggest that the dynamics of poverty in Canada have also changed. Despite a recovering economy in the late 1990's, the economic welfare of middle and lower income Canadians has not improved.[28] According to Ross "the rate and depth of poverty among working-age households has increased. This phenomenon is documented in Armine Yalnizyan's book *Canada's Great Divide: The Politics of The Growing Gap Between Rich and Poor in the 1990's*.[29] She reports that a growing number of middle-class families are sliding down the income-earning ladder. Between 1989 and 1997, for example, the number of families that had an after tax income of under $35,038 grew from 30% to 37%. In *The Growing Gap: A Report on Growing Inequality Between Rich and Poor in Canada*, Yalnizyan reports that the number of families that reported a middle-range income (between $30,169 and $69,929) fell from 60% of the population to 40% of the population.[30]

Even the employed are vulnerable to poverty, as the minimum wages across the provinces are substantially lower than the LICOs. The following table documents the disparity between the minimum wage and the Low Income Cut-Offs in 1995.[31]

---

28 *Ibid.*

29 A. Yalnizyan, *Canada's Great Divide: The Politics of the Growing Gap in Canada Between Rich and Poor* (Toronto: Centre for Social Justice, 2000) at 6.

30 A Yalnizyan, *The Growing Gap: A report on growing inequality between rich and poor in Canada* (Toronto: Centre for Social Justice, 1998), online: Centre for Social Development <http://www.socialjustice.org/issues/gap/a2.jpg> (date of access: July 7, 2003).

31 G. Schellenberg & D.P. Ross, *Left Poor By the Markets* (Ottawa: Canadian Council on Social Development, 1997) at 43.

	Lone Parent (One Earner) with One Child		**One-earner Couple with Two Children**	
	Difference between minimum-wage income & LICO	**Minimum-wage Income as % of LICO**	**Difference between minimum-wage income & LICO***	**Annual Minimum wage Income as % of LICO**
Newfoundland	- 8,211	55	- 17,355	36
PEI	- 8,085	55	- 17,166	37
Nova Scotia	- 7,379	59	- 16,523	39
New Brunswick	- 7,639	57	- 16,835	38
Quebec	- 5,611	69	- 14,755	46
Ontario	- 3,843	79	- 12,987	52
Manitoba	- 6,859	62	- 16,003	41
Saskatchewan	- 6,963	62	- 16,107	41
Alberta	- 7,691	57	- 16,835	38
BC	- 3,531	80	- 12,675	53

*This difference is calculated as the low income cut-off minus the total income of workers employed 40 hours per week, 52 weeks per year at the minimum wage in each province. Poverty lines are for urban centres with a population of 100,000 to 499,999 (1992 base), except in PEI where poverty lines are for urban centres with populations of 30,000 to 99,999. Source: Prepared by the Centre for International Statistics at the CCSD using Labour Canada's fact sheet "Minimum Wage Rates for Experiences Adult Workers" (March 1996) and Statistics Canada's Income Distribution by Size in Canada, 1994.

Even Sarlo admits that the minimum wage is not an adequate wage.[32]

Women suffer higher incidences of poverty than men at all ages, and in all family types.[33] Lochhead and Scott confirm that not only do women have a higher chance of experiencing poverty, but also are more likely to be "persistantly poor."[34] They report that in the years of 1994-95 one of four women versus one in six men experienced at least one year of poverty.[35] The most important factor Lochhead and Scott found which contributed to women's poverty was family structure. While all single adult households have a higher incidence of poverty "the incidence of poverty among this group is greatest for women regardless of their age or status as a parent."[36] In fact, a full 44.7% of unattached women, and 44.8% of lone parent women expe-

32 *Supra*, note 23 at 181. Despite his admission of the inadequacy of minimum wage he still however advocates its elimination.

33 See C. Lochhead & K. Scott, *The Dynamics of Women's Poverty in Canada* (Ottawa: Status of Women Canada, 2000) at 10.

34 *Ibid*, at 51.

35 *Ibid.*

36 *Ibid*, at 51.

rienced poverty in the years of the study.[37] Some would contest that the feminization of poverty is a serious issue,[38] but the disadvantage of women in Canada seems well-established.[39]

Women thus face dire economic consequences for the roles they play in our society, and many Canadian children are facing the consequences. On November 24th,1989 the House of Commons made a unanimous all party resolution "to achieve the goal of eliminating poverty amongst Canadian children by the year 2000".[40] Despite this promise, based upon LICO's an estimated 21% more children live in poverty in Canada than in 1989.[41] The following table demonstrates the child poverty rates from 1990 to 1996.[42]

37 *Ibid*, at 14.

38 *Supra*, note 23 at 181.

39 *Supra*, note 10 at 25.

40 Cited online: Campaign 2000: End Child Poverty in Canada <http://www.campaign2000.ca> (date of access: June 29, 2003).

41 *Ibid.*

42 Online: Canadian Council for Social Development "Poverty Statistics" <http://www.ccsd.ca/factsheets/fscphis2.htm> (last updated 2002).

Child Poverty Rates by Province, Canada, 1990-1996

Incidence (%)							
	1990	1991	1992	1993	1994	1995	1996
Atlantic Provinces	18.3	19.9	19.9	20.6	20.1	23.1	21.2
Newfoundland	20.8	20.6	26.8	21.8	23.4	26.2	20.2
PEI	14.0	15.6	12.7	11.4	13.3	14.2	18.5
Nova Scotia	16.8	20.6	19.4	23.4	20.5	21.5	23.5
New Brunswick	18.6	19.2	15.9	18.0	18.3	24.4	19.8
Quebec	19.5	20.4	19.3	21.4	19.8	22.6	22.0
Ontario	14.8	17.3	16.3	20.8	18.1	19.1	20.3
Prairie Provinces	21.1	22.4	24.3	22.7	20.4	22.1	22.3
Manitoba	24.0	30.9	24.2	26.1	22.8	23.2	26.6
Saskatchewan	21.8	22.4	24.0	24.8	22.9	21.8	22.3
Alberta	19.8	19.2	24.5	20.6	18.5	21.7	20.7
British Columbia	17.6	14.4	19.3	21.5	21.2	20.8	20.2
CANADA	17.8	18.9	19.2	21.3	19.5	21.0	21.1
Notes: Children under 18 years of age. Based on Statistics Canada's Low-income Cut-offs, 1992 base.							
Source: Prepared by the Canadian Council on Social Development, using data from Statistics Canada, Cat. 13-569-XPB.							

While the term "child poverty" is still used to refer to children living in straitened circumstances, it is universally recognized that child poverty is a result of family poverty. Analysts of the phenomenon of child poverty have been exploring the effects of Canadian social policies on families with children on child poverty rates. While the Fraser Institute endorses the view that child poverty is a manifestation of parental irresponsibility,[43] the National Council on Welfare assert that

> Both child poverty and women's economic vulnerability reflect the lack of support for parenthood, the undervaluing of children and the ambivalence about women's roles. Both are symptoms of a labour market which has failed to protect family incomes during hard economic times.[44]

---

43 C. Freiler & J. Cerny, *Benefitting Canada's Children: Perspectives on Gender and Social Responsibility* (Ottawa: Status of Women Canada, 1998) at 17.

44 National Council on Welfare, *Child Poverty Profile 1998* (Ottawa: National Council on Welfare, 2001) at 1.

This is not to say that only children of single mothers live in poverty. The poverty rate for single parent mothers in 1998 was high at 52.9%, but for two-parent families with children under 7 the poverty rate was still 10.4%.[45] These depressing statistics led the National Council on Welfare to conclude that only an integrated approach that addresses "labour, income support, employment, equity and education policies in tandem with child care and early childhood education"[46] could adequately address the issue of child poverty.[47]

While the feminization of poverty is a long recognized phenomenon in Canada, the racialization of poverty has been largely ignored. In *The New Poverty in Canada: Ethnic Groups and Ghetto Neighbourhoods*, Kazemipur and Halli explore the concentration of poverty in certain neighborhoods or "ghettos". They argue that:

> The rise of poverty, the hardening of racial and ethnic cleavages, and the rise of the influence of neighbourhoods — gave the new poverty another unique feature: poverty has become spatially concentrated in certain neighbourhoods, known as "ghettos", "inner city" and "poverty zones", and they have become the habitats mostly of minority groups.[48]

The table below demonstrates that the bottom segment — visible minorities — are two to four times more likely to live in poverty than those of European origin.[49]

---

45 *Ibid*, at 55.
46 *Ibid.*
47 *Ibid.*
48 *Supra*, note 10 at 12.
49 *Ibid*, at 100.

Poverty Rate of Ethnic Groups, 1991

Ethnic	Poverty Rate
Dutch (Netherlands)	10.4
Canadian	11.6
Italian	11.9
German	12.5
British	13.8
Jewish	13.9
Balkan origins	14.1
Portuguese	15.1
Ukrainian	15.2
French origins	16.6
South Asian	18.6
Hungarian (Magyar)	18.7
Polish	20.5
Filipino	20.8
Greek	21.1
Chinese	23.5
Black/Carribean	32.7
Vietnamese	35.1
Spanish	38.5
Arab origins	39.4
Aboriginal	39.1
West Asian origins	41
Latin, Central and South American	41.1

Kazemipur and Halli also posit that the concentration of poor minorities in "ghetto" neighbourhoods causes social isolation, the creation of a "culture of poverty"[50] and ultimately propagates poverty in these neighbourhoods:

> The concentration of poverty of poor in certain neighbourhoods means that their contacts to the lifestyles and life approaches of the non-poor, and a lack of awareness of their own existential situation in contrast to the non-poor. This lack of knowledge of other possible alternatives leads to a belief that their situation is inevitable and unavoidable, the only one they can have.[51]

Aboriginal peoples in Canada have a distinct plight. In the 1998 report on the state of Economic, Social and Cultural Rights prepared by the United Nations Committee on Economic, Social and Cultural Rights reported that

> There has been little or no progress in the alleviation of social and economic deprivation among Aboriginal people. In particular, the Committee is deeply concerned at the shortage of adequate housing, the endemic mass unemployment and the high rate of suicide, especially among youth in the Aboriginal communities. Another concern is the failure to provide safe and adequate drinking water to Aboriginal communities on reserves. The delegation of the State Party conceded that almost a quarter of Aboriginal household dwellings require major repairs for lack of basic amenities.[52]

These depressing poverty statistics for Aboriginals are not even reflected in the overall poverty rate, as Aboriginals on reserves are not counted.[53]

The disabled also face a higher rate of poverty. Sarlo states "there is no firm evidence regarding the adequacy of assistance to severely disabled persons in Canada."[54] Yet, the Canadian Council on Social Development reports that

> The poverty rate among all persons with disabilities was 30.8 per cent, compared to 18.4 percent for individuals with no disabilities. Women with disabilities tend to have a higher rate of poverty than do men: 33.1 per cent compared to 28.2 per cent. Among the working-age population (those aged 16 to 64 years), their poverty rate (35.1 per cent) was about five percentage points higher for all individuals with disabilities.[55]

While admittedly the poverty rate may not describe the adequacy of the support disabled people receive, this suggests that the disabled have a far higher risk of living in straitened circumstances.

---

50 See *ibid*, at 33, for a detailed discussion of the concept of a "culture of poverty".

51 *Ibid*, at 36-7.

52 Committee on Economic, Social and Cultural Rights, *Report on the 18th & 19th Sess.*, UN ESC, 1998, Supp. No. 2, UN Doc. E/C.12/1998/26. Para. 392.

53 *Supra*, note 6 at 10.

54 *Supra*, note 25 at 167.

55 *Supra*, note 6 at 76.

Conclusion

Poverty is ultimately about choice. Not the type of choice however that Sarlo implies in his work, but the choice of what Canadian society views as a tolerable or desirable level of inequality. While Sarlo openly accepts that there will be inevitable inequality in the polity, the social welfare community sees these inequalities as intolerable and unnecessary. The prevalence of poverty in single mothers, the disabled and ethnic minorities strongly suggest that characteristics like gender, ethnicity and disability all have substantial negative effects on economic status. It is thus not a remote conclusion that the discrimination and devaluation suffered by these groups is related to their fragile economic circumstances.

J. Waldron, "Homelessness and the Issue of Freedom" 39 U.C.L.Rev. 295 (1991) at 296-7, 300-2 [footnotes omitted]

Everything that is done has to be done somewhere. No one is free to perform an action unless there is somewhere he is free to perform it. Since we are embodied beings, we always have a location. Moreover, though everyone has to be somewhere, a person cannot always choose any location he likes. Some locations are physically inaccessible. And, physical inaccessibility aside, there are some places one is simply not allowed to be.

One of the functions of property rules, particularly as far as land is concerned, is to provide a basis for determining who is allowed to be where. For the purposes of these rules, a country is divided up into spatially defined regions or, as we usually say, places. The rules of property give us a way of determining, in the case of each place, who is allowed to be in that place and who is not. For example, if a place is governed by a private property rule, then there is a way of identifying an individual whose determination is final on the question of who is and who is not allowed to be in that place. Sometimes that individual is the owner of the land in question, and sometimes (as in a landlord-tenant relationship) the owner gives another person the power to make that determination (indeed to make it, for the time being, even as against the owner). Either way, it is characteristic of a private ownership arrangement that some individual (or some other particular legal person) has this power to determine who is allowed to be on the property . . .

The concept of being *allowed* to be in a place is fairly straightforward. We can define it negatively. An individual who is in a place where he is not allowed to be may be removed, and he may be subject to civil or criminal sanctions for trespass or some other similar offense. No doubt people are sometimes physically removed from places where they are allowed to be. But if a person is in a place where he is not allowed to be, not only may he be physically removed, but there is a social rule to the effect that his removal may be facilitated and aided by the forces of the state. In short, the police may be called and he may be dragged away . . .

For the most part the homeless are excluded from all of the places governed by private property rules, whereas the rest of us are, in the same sense, excluded from all but one (or maybe all but a few) of those places. That is another way of saying that each of us has at least one place to be in a country composed of private places, whereas the homeless person has none.

Some libertarians fantasize about the possibility that all the land in a society might be held as private property ("Sell the streets!"). This would be catastrophic for the homeless. Since most private proprietors are already disposed to exclude him from their property, the homeless person might discover in such a libertarian paradise that there was literally nowhere he was allowed to be. Wherever he went he would be liable to penalties for trespass and he would be liable to eviction, to being thrown out by an owner or dragged away by the police. Moving from one place to another would involve nothing more liberating than moving from one trespass liability to another. Since land is finite in any society, there is only a limited number of places where a person can (physically) be, and such a person would find that he was legally excluded from all of them. (It would not be entirely mischievous to add that since, in order to exist, a person has to be somewhere, such a person would not be permitted to exist.)

Our society saves the homeless from this catastrophe only by virtue of the fact that some of its territory is held as collective property and made available for common use. The homeless are allowed to be — provided they are on the streets, in the parks, or under the bridges. Some of them are allowed to crowd together into publicly provided "shelters" after dark (though these are dangerous places and there are not nearly enough shelters for all of them). But in the daytime and, for many of them, all through the night, wandering in public places is their only option. When all else is privately owned, the sidewalks are their salvation. They are allowed to be in our society only to the extent that our society is communist.

This is one of the reasons why most defenders of private property are uncomfortable with the libertarian proposal, and why that proposal remains sheer fantasy. But there is a modified form of the libertarian catastrophe in prospect with which moderate and even liberal defenders of ownership seem much more comfortable. This is the increasing regulation of the streets, subways, parks, and other public places to restrict the activities that can be performed there. What is emerging — and it is not just a matter of fantasy — is a state of affairs in which a million or more citizens have no place to perform elementary human activities like urinating, washing, sleeping, cooking, eating, and standing around. Legislators voted for by people who own private places in which they can do all these things are increasingly deciding to make public places available only for activities other than these primal human tasks. The streets and subways, they say, are for commuting from home to office. They are not for sleeping; sleeping is something one does at home. The parks are for recreations like walking and informal ball-games, things for which one's own yard is a little too confined. Parks are not for cooking or urinating; again, these are things one does at home. Since the public and the private are complementary, the activities performed in public are to be the complement of those appropriately performed in private. This complementarity works fine for those who have the benefit of both sorts of places. However, it is disastrous for those who must live their whole lives on common land. If I am right about this, it is one of the most callous and tyrannical exercises of power in modern times by a (comparatively) rich and complacent majority against a minority of their less fortunate fellow human beings . . .

At the outset I recited the truism that anything a person does has to be done somewhere. To that extent, all actions involve a spatial component (just as many actions involve, in addition, a material component like the use of tools, implements, or raw materials). It should be fairly obvious that, if one is not free to be in a certain place, one is not free to do anything at that place. If I am not allowed to be in your garden (because you have forbidden me) then I am not allowed to eat my lunch, make a speech, or turn a somersault in your garden. Though I may be free to do these things somewhere else, I am not free to do them there. It follows, strikingly, that a person who is not free to be in any place is not free to do anything; such a person is comprehensively unfree. In the libertarian paradise we imagined in the previous section, this would be the plight of the homeless. They would be simply without freedom (or, more accurately, any freedom they had would depend utterly on the forbearance of those who owned the places that made up the territory of the society in question).

Fortunately, our society is not such a libertarian paradise. There are places where the homeless may be and, by virtue of that, there are actions they may perform; they are free to perform actions on the streets, in the parks, and under the bridges. Their freedom depends on common property in a way that ours does not. Once again, the homeless have freedom in our society only to the extent that our society is communist.

That conclusion may sound glib and provocative. But it is meant as a reflection on the cold and awful reality of the experience of men, women, and children who are homeless in America. For them the rules of private property are a series of fences that stand between them and somewhere to be, somewhere to act. The only hope they have so far as freedom is concerned lies in the streets, parks, and public shelters, and in the fact that those are collectivized resources made available openly to all.

It is sometimes said that freedom means little or nothing to a cold and hungry person. We should focus on the material predicament of the homeless, it is said, not on this abstract liberal concern about freedom. That may be an appropriate response to someone who is talking high-mindedly and fatuously about securing freedom of speech or freedom of religion for people who lack the elementary necessities of human life. But the contrast between liberty and the satisfaction of material needs must not be drawn too sharply, as though the latter had no relation at all to what one is free or unfree to do. I am focusing on freedoms that are intimately connected with food, shelter, clothing, and the satisfaction of basic needs. When a person is needy, he does not cease to be preoccupied with freedom; rather, his preoccupation tends to focus on freedom to perform certain actions in particular. The freedom that means most to a person who is cold and wet is the freedom that consists in staying under whatever shelter he has found. The freedom that means most to someone who is exhausted is the freedom not to be prodded with a nightstick as he tries to catch a few hours sleep on a subway bench.

There is a general point here about the rather passive image of the poor held by those who say we should concern ourselves with their needs, not their freedom. People remain agents, with ideas and initiatives of their own, even when they are poor. Indeed, since they are on their own, in a situation of danger, without any place of safety, they must often be more resourceful, spend more time working out how to live, thinking things through much more carefully, taking much less for granted, than the comfortable autonomous agent that we imagine in a family with a house and a job in an office or university. And — when they are allowed to — the poor do find ways of using their initiative to rise to these challenges. They have to; if they do not, they die.

Even the most desperately needy are not always paralyzed by want. There are certain things they are physically capable of doing for themselves. Sometimes they find shelter by occupying an empty house or sleeping in a sheltered spot. They gather food from various places, they light a fire to cook it, and they sit down in a park to eat. They may urinate behind bushes, and wash their clothes in a fountain. Their physical condition is certainly not comfortable, but they are capable of acting in ways that make things a little more bearable for themselves. Now one question we face as a society — a broad question of justice and social policy — is whether we are willing to tolerate an economic system in which large numbers of people are homeless. Since the answer is evidently, "Yes," the question that remains is whether we are willing to allow those who are in this predicament to act as free agents, looking after their own needs, in public places — the only space available to them. It is a deeply frightening fact about the modern United States that those who have homes and jobs are willing to answer "Yes" to the first question and "No" to the second . . .

QUESTIONS

1. How would you answer the questions posed by Jeremy Waldron at the end of this passage?

2. Professor Waldron has identified the interplay between homelessness, property, and freedom. Having regard only to the other justifications for private property discussed in Chapter 1, how would you describe the implications of homelessness?

3. What are the other consequences of homelessness?

R. v. Clarke
1998 CarswellOnt 4854, 23 C.R. (5th) 329 (Prov. Div.)

[*R. v. Clarke* raised this question: "Is a genuine intention to dramatize the plight of the homeless by publicly attempting to break into an empty building to establish a 'squat' a defence to a charge of mischief?" (*per* Cole Prov. J. at 331).

The case involved a charge of minor damage to properties in downtown Toronto. Two buildings on Carlton St. containing bachelor apartments had become occupied (squatted) during the mid-1990s. It is estimated that about 20 people were living there, though the premises had neither electricity nor running water. In 1995 a property manager was hired to ensure that no additional squatting took place and steps were taken accordingly.

The accused, Clarke and Heroux, were organizers for the Ontario Coalition Against Poverty (OCAP). In early March 5, 1997, they were among a group of over 20 people who had entered both buildings in an attempt to establish a squat. The plan was to clean up the premises and stay there for a day in order to "(a) dramatize politically the need for concerted action to deal with the problems of the homeless, and (b) perhaps negotiate — he was not entirely clear with whom — to remain there for a longer period, during which a more permanent squat might be established." (*Ibid.* at 332.) However, the police evacuated the premises.

OCAP decided to hold a more public demonstration in April. A rally at Allan Gardens was advertized, which was to be followed by a march to, and occupation of, the Carlton St. properties. OCAP also prepared a proposal for a "Use it or Lose it Bylaw". Copies of that document were distributed during the speeches in Allan Gardens.

The rally and march took place and Clarke and Leroux announced that they were going to occupy the buildings for a 24-hour period. After various attempts were made to pry off plywood from a ground floor window, the police, in attendance throughout, arrested the accused. A charge of mischief was laid.

Several defences were advanced. Under subsection 429(2) of the *Criminal Code*, a conviction for mischief cannot be sustained where the accused act on the basis of colour of right, justification or excuse. Were these elements present?]

Cole Prov. J.: . . .

I consider it important to keep in mind throughout that there is no evidence that these particular accused were homeless on April 19, 1997. As mentioned in the accused's factum, no doubt some of the others who attempted to, or who actually did, enter the buildings during that demonstration were homeless, including possibly some of those whose charges were dismissed at the conclusion of the Crown's case. However, the two accused whose cases I am currently considering were not homeless in any way that condition has been described in these proceedings. Nor can it be said that these accused were under any legal obligation to assist any homeless person on April 19, 1997. It is clear from the record that, while they were genuinely attempting to act to assist both those homeless persons in attendance at the demonstration and to dramatize the plight of so many others, at law they were under no duty to do so. In my judgment these two factors make a considerable difference in the way these accused should, in law, be regarded.

(a) Colour of Right:

. . . On their own evidence the accused here did not assert that they felt that the buildings had been abandoned by their owner, thereby possibly giving them a right to enter and occupy them (as shrewdly noted by Crown counsel in his submission, had this been the case, it might have afforded the accused a defence to the charges). Nor did they seek to justify their entry on the basis of any legal claim of adverse possession. Indeed, both Exhibit 2 and the accused's testimony make it entirely clear that they knew these properties were owned by a developer, despite which they intended to enter and occupy them. The fact that they had been charged with trespass on a recent previous occasion for entering the same buildings and the large-scale police presence on April 19, make this even clearer.

In my judgment all of this indicates that the accused had no "legal" colour of right when they entered these buildings . . .

(b) Justification and Excuse:

The accused expressly eschewed reliance on the defence of "necessity" articulated by the Supreme Court of Canada in *Perka v. R.* (1984), 14 C.C.C. (3d) 385 (S.C.C.). This they were surely right to do, as the severe limitations placed on that defence by the court mean that it would likely have failed in this case. On the factual record before me, there is no conceivable way in which the accused could be said to have acted in a situation "so emergent and the peril so pressing that normal human instincts cry out for action and make a counsel of patience unreasonable" (at 400; emphasis added). Furthermore, unlike the international drug smugglers in that case whose disabled boat grounded on a Canadian beach in deteriorating weather conditions, the accused in this case do not assert that they needed to break into these buildings for their own self-preservation. As I have already stated, it is clear from the record that these two accused make no claim that what they did was motivated by their own state of homelessness; rather, they did the acts complained of in order (a) to make a political statement, and (b) potentially to provide housing for others.

Despite counsel's stipulation that they were not seeking to raise a defence of necessity, *Perka* is important for its analysis of the oft-confused terms "justification" and "excuse". After quite a lengthy historical analysis of the emergence of the defence in philosophy and at law, Dickson J. (as he then was) noted:

> Criminal theory recognizes a distinction between "justifications" and "excuses". A "justification" challenges the wrongfulness of an action which technically constitutes a crime. The police officer who shoots the hostage-taker, the innocent object of an assault who uses force to defend himself against his assailant, the good Samaritan who commandeers a car and breaks the speed laws to rush an accident victim to hospital, these are all actors whose actions we consider rightful, not wrongful. For such actions people are often praised, as motivated by some great or noble object. The concept of punishment often seems incompatible with the social approval bestowed on the doer.
>
> In contrast, an "excuse" concedes the wrongfulness of the action but asserts that the circumstances under which it was done are such that it ought not to be attributed to the

> actor. The perpetrator who is incapable, owing to a disease of the mind, of appreciating the nature and consequences of his acts, the person who labours under a mistake of fact, the drunkard, the sleepwalker: these are all actors of whose "criminal" actions we disapprove intensely, but whom, in appropriate circumstances, our law will not punish. (at 396-7) . . .

Despite the fact that s. 490(2) leaves both "justification" and "excuse" available as potential defences to a charge of mischief, in my opinion these quotations make it clear that what the accused must claim here as a matter of law is not that their actions were justified in law, but that their conduct should nevertheless be excused from criminal legal sanction because "it is not politic to punish it" . . .

As previously noted, the accused do not claim that they participated in attempting to break into the buildings to preserve themselves from immediate harm. Nor do they claim that they were leading others into the buildings to protect them from imminent danger. They do not and cannot claim, as was said in *Morgentaler* (1975), 20 C.C.C. (2d) 449 (S.C.C.) that their "wrongful act was truly the only realistic action open or whether [they were] making what in fairness could be called a choice". At best they can only claim that they were committing these acts so that others would be able to move in to the squat which they hoped to create. While I have heard in this trial ample and disturbing evidence about the debilitating medium and long term effects of homelessness, I reiterate that I have no evidence before me which goes any way to establishing that what the accused did in these circumstances was necessary for the protection either of themselves or of some identified person legally under their care from immediate harm or danger.

What flows from this is that, as meritorious as the accused's intentions might have been, from a legal perspective it becomes much more difficult to say that their acts may be said to fit into the quite circumscribed category of excuses recognized by our criminal law.

Thus, I do not consider that the accused's acts can be said to fall within the definition of an "excuse" as characterized by the majority in *Perka* . As it is clear that as they were making a choice their "wrongful act cannot have been involuntary in the relevant sense" (*Perka* at 400):

> to be involuntary the act must be inevitable, unavoidable and afford no reasonable opportunity for an alternative course of action that does not involve a breach of the law. (at 406)

I next consider whether the accused can derive any defence from the concurring reasons of Wilson J. in *Perka*. In thinking this through I note that, while she generally accepted the analysis of Dickson J., Her Ladyship insisted on leaving open some types of justification on which a defence of necessity might be premised. Accepting, as seems obvious from the record in this case, that the accused's motivations were genuinely altruistic, can it not be said that, even though as a matter of law they cannot be "excused", perhaps they acted with legal justification?

Despite leaving the door somewhat open, it is quite clear in my judgment that Wilson J. did not intend that any defence of justification would arise from the kinds of facts which exist in the case at bar. First, it is entirely clear that Her Ladyship was not including "excuse" cases among those in which a defence of "justification" might arise; as with Dickson J. she was clear that "the nature of an excuse is to personalize the plea so that, while justification looks to the rightness of the act, excuse speaks to the compassion of the court for the actor." (at 414) Thus, while the layperson might view the altruism of acts such as those being considered as being "justified" by the epidemic of homelessness that unfortunately disgraces this city and others throughout the so-called "developed" world, as a matter of law, any defence must lie, if at all, in "excuse".

Second, as Dickson J. had done in his judgment, Wilson J. reiterated the caveat expressed by Dickson J. in his earlier judgment in *R. v. Morgentaler (No. 5), supra*, that:

> [n]o system of positive law can recognize any principle which would entitle a person to violate the law because on his view the law conflicted with some higher social value. (at 497)

She went on to say that

> This statement, in my view, is clearly correct if the "higher social value" to which the accused points is one which is not reflected in the legal system in the form of a duty. That is to say, *pursuit of a purely ethical "duty" such as, for example, the duty to give to charity, may represent an ethically good or virtuous act but is not within the realm of legal obligations and cannot therefore validly be invoked as a basis on which to violate the essential proposition that although "a morally motivated act contrary to law may be ethically justified. . . the actor must accept the [legal] penalty for his action"*: *United States v. Moylan* (1969) 417 F. 2d 1002 at p. 1008 (4th Cir.). (at 417; emphasis added)

Wilson J. spoke with approval of the English Court of Appeal's refusal to accept a defence of necessity in relation to a charge of trespass (*Southwark London Borough Council*), *supra*. She wrote:

> . . . not only can the system of positive law not tolerate an individual opting to act in accordance with the dictates of his conscience in the event of a conflict with legal duties, but it cannot permit acts in violation of legal obligation to be justified on the grounds that social utility is thereby increased. (at 418)

I thus conclude that there is nothing in the separate reasoning of Wilson J. which can be of any assistance to the accused here. Their acts may well, from a political perspective, have been "the right thing to do". As a matter of law, however, their culpability cannot be "excused". As Her Ladyship noted, the relief, if any, of actors such as these is to be restricted to the matter of sentence . . .

It must be remembered that this is a criminal trial, in which the accused are obliged to raise only such defences as are allowed by our law. Although the law must be ever vigilant that it not foreclose potential defences (as Wilson J. was careful to stress in the various passages I have cited), in my judgment these accused cannot raise as their defence to the specific charge which they face any general "entitlement" of others to adequate housing, nor the fact that Canada has apparently refused to live up as fully as it has committed to do to its treaty obligations under the International Covenant on Economic, Social and Cultural Rights.

Accused convicted.

QUESTIONS

1. Given the reasoning of Judge Cole, would a homeless person, totally broke and seeking shelter, be able to raise successfully a defence of necessity to a charge of mischief in (otherwise) like circumstances?

2 In what way can the law work to effect change on behalf of homeless people? See further J. L. Hafetz, "Homelessness Legal Advocacy: New Challenges and Directions for the Future", 30 Fordham Urban L.J. 1215 (2003).

5. PROPERTY AND THE CONSTITUTION

(a) introduction

The constitutional dimensions of property law involve two matters. One concerns the legislative authority over property as between the federal and provincial levels of government. Stepping back from constitutional technicalities for a moment, it can be seen that many legislative powers, at both levels, affect property rights in major ways. In the following note prepared by Tracie Scott some of the key constitutional heads of power are reviewed.

The second matter concerns the extent to which property rights receive constitutional protection from state action. As will be seen, unlike the American *Bill of Rights*, the *Canadian Charter of Rights and Freedoms, 1982* does not contain an explicit, thick protection of the right to private property. Such a right is in fact conspicuous by its absence. However, as will be seen, that is not the end of the inquiry. In this section various entrenched and non-entrenched property protections are also outlined.

(b) property and federalism

T. Scott, "Legislative Jurisdiction Over Property Under the Canadian Constitution"

Introduction

A legal positivist treats property as being solely a construction of law. As Bentham wrote "[p]roperty and law were born and die together. Before laws were made there was no property; take away laws and property ceases".[1] In a federal system of government, such as that found in Canada, the question then becomes this: from which level of government does property emanate?

The basic answer to that question is to be found in the *Constitution Act, 1867*, which delineates the division of legislative powers between the federal and provincial governments. Within the *Constitution Act*, sections 91 (defining federal powers) and section 92 (the provincial counterpart) are the most important (but not the only) provisions. Speaking in general terms, it will be seen below that provincial authority over matters of property is extensive. Consequently, many of the principles discussed in this Casebook fall within the provincial domain. (And because there is a great deal of diversity across the country, many of the basic rules discussed in this book are subject provincial variation.) Even so, it will also become evident in the brief review that follows that to treat property as simple a matter of provincial concern would be an error.

The inter-relationship between federal and provincial powers is complex. This is because almost any object of legislative concern can, seemingly, have both provincial and federal dimensions. Moreover, the manner in which this inevitable duality has affected the reading of the constitution has evolved over time. As Bruce Ryder explains, there has been a shift in constitutional interpretation in the last century: a "modern paradigm has replaced the classical paradigm as the dominant approach to the judicial interpretation of the division of powers".[2] The classical paradigm is one in which,

> Each level of government must act within its hermetically sealed boxes of jurisdiction, or "watertight compartments" ("compartiments etanches"). Any spillover effects on the other level of government's jurisdiction will not be tolerated. Such legislative spillover must be contained, either by ruling such laws ultra vires, or by "reading them down" so that they remain strictly within the enacting legislature's jurisdiction.[3]

The modern paradigm, however,

> Simply prohibits each level of government from enacting laws whose dominant characteristics ('pith and substance') is the regulation of a subject matter within the other level of government's jurisdiction. Exclusivity, on this approach, means the exclusive ability to pass laws that deal predominantly with a subject matter within the enacting government's catalogue of powers. If a law is in pith and substance within the enacting legislature's jurisdiction, it will be upheld notwithstanding that it might have spillover effects on the other level of government's jurisdiction.[4]

In short, the modern interpretive approach allows for considerable overlap.

---

1 J. Bentham, *Theory of Legislation* (New York: Oceana, 1975) at 68.

2 B. Ryder, "The Demise and Rise of the Classical Paradigm in Canadian Federalism: Promoting autonomy for the Provinces and First Nations" (1991) 36 McGill L.J. 309 at 309.

3 *Ibid*, at 312.

4 *Ibid.*

Provincial Jurisdiction over Property

Under section 92(13) of the *Constitution Act, 1867*, the provinces are given legislative competence over "property and civil rights in the province". Patrick Monahan has summarized the scope of the expansive power conferred on the provinces by virtue of this section:

> Since virtually all provincial laws regulate "rights' in some way, virtually all provincial laws could be said to be in the scope of section 92(13). In fact, section 92(13) is so sweeping that there are usually only two ways in which a provincial law regulating rights could be found to be unconstitutional. The first possibility is that the provincial legislation deals directly with a particular matter that falls squarely within one of the classes of subjects enumerated in section 91. The second possibility is that the provincial law deals directly with rights of individuals or entities outside the province and, for this reason, the provincial law does not deal with matters "within the province".[5]

In consequence, one can see that as a general matter, a provincial act affecting property is likely to be seen as valid under section 92(13) so long as it (i) does not invade an exclusive federal area of jurisdiction such as the criminal law, and (ii) is directed at property or transactions within the province. In both of these situations, the contours are not rigid, and the reasoning of the courts is often nuanced and sometimes obscure.

Take for example the problem of determining whether a provincial prohibition amounts to a proper exercise of section 92(13) or an invalid (*ultra vires*) attempt to impose a criminal sanction (a federal power under section 91(27)). *Westendorp v. The Queen*[6] concerned a challenge to a Calgary by-law that prohibited persons being present on public streets for the purpose of prostitution. The Supreme Court of Canada found that the by-law was directed at an activity that had been traditionally controlled by the criminal law; hence, it was unconstitutional. However, in *R. v. Banks*[7] an Ontario court upheld a provincial statute that imposed penalties for aggressive panhandling and squeegeeing. The accused argued that the law, in effect, criminalized panhandling. The Court however found that the law was a valid exercise of section 92(13).

The question of whether provincial law concerns property and civil rights "in the province" can be equally difficult. Consider these two examples. In *Carnation Co. v. Quebec (Agricultural Marketing Board)*[8] the Supreme Court of Canada upheld a provincial regulatory scheme that set the price of milk in Quebec, despite the fact that most of the milk affected by the scheme was exported to other provinces. By contrast, in *Manitoba (A.G.) v. Manitoba Egg & Poultry Assn.*,[9] a provincial egg marketing scheme was found to be unconstitutional because it regulated all eggs in

---

5 P.J. Monahan, *Constitutional Law* (Concord: Irwin Law, 1997) at 101.

6 [1983] 1 S.C.R. 43, 1983 CarswellAlta 1, 1983 CarswellAlta 316.

7 55 O.R. (3d) 374, 2001 CarswellOnt 2757 (C.J.).

8 [1968] S.C.R. 238, 1968 CarswellQue 36.

9 [1971] S.C.R. 689, 1971 CarswellMan 46, 1971 CarswellMan 86.

Manitoba, including imported eggs. The Supreme Court held that "[t]he proposed scheme has a direct object the regulation of the importation of eggs, and it is not saved by the fact that the local market is under the same regime".[10]

Natural Resources: Section 109, Section 92(5), and 92A

In 1867, the four original provinces, Nova Scotia, New Brunswick, Ontario, and Quebec, were given constitutional authority rights over "all lands, mines, minerals and royalties" (s. 109). In 1930, Manitoba, Alberta, Saskatchewan, and British Columbia were later put in the same position. In addition, the provinces have power over "the management and sale of the public lands belonging to the provinces and the timber and the wood thereon" (s. 92(5)). Some older case law suggests that in relation to these Crown-held lands, s. 92(5) gave the provinces broader powers than those found in section 92. In *Smylie v. The Queen*,[11] the Ontario Court of Appeal upheld a provincial condition imposed on timber cut on provincial Crown lands that specified that such timber had to be processed in Canada. As William Moull has said:

> What [*Smylie v. The Queen* suggest[s]] . . . is that in the absence of contradictory legislation at the federal level, the exercise of provincial proprietary rights can extend into areas otherwise exclusively reserved to the Parliament under Section 91. If what is meant by this suggestion is that provincial legislation enacted under section 92(5) can intrude upon areas of federal legislative jurisdiction, so long as no actual federal legislation puts a stop to that intrusion, then section 92(5) would have a much broader scope than any other head of provincial legislative power under section 92.[12]

The increased importance of natural resource revenue however precipitated a series of court battles in the 1970s over the validity of provincial mineral royalty schemes. The encompassing reading of provincial jurisdiction under 92(5) did not survive this spate of litigation. In one leading case, *Canadian Industrial Gas & Oil Ltd. v. Saskatchewan*[13] (*CIGOL*), the Supreme Court struck down the province's mineral tax and royalty provisions because it constituted an "indirect tax", which is an exclusively federal head under section 91(3). The provinces have the legislative power to impose *direct* (not indirect) taxes under section 92(2).

These disputes prompted the entrenchment of section 92A in 1982. This provision gives the federal and provincial governments concurrent powers over the exploration, development, and conservation of non-renewable natural resources, forestry resources, and electrical energy. Section 92A(2) also gives the provinces the power to "make laws in relation to the export from the province to another part of Canada" as long as this does not give rise to discriminatory pricing systems.

---

10 *Ibid*, at 717 (*per* Laskin J.).

11 (1900) 27 O.A.R. 172 (C.A.).

12 W.D. Moull, "Natural Resources: Provincial Proprietary Rights, The Supreme Court of Canada, and the Resource Amendments to the Constitution", (1983) 21 Alta. L.Rev. 472 at 476.

13 [1978] 2 S.C.R. 545, 1977 CarswellSask 109, 1977 CarswellSask 140.

Section 92A(4) confers on the provinces the power to "make laws in relation to the raising of money by any mode or system of taxation" in respect to natural resources, solving the problem that arose in *CIGOL*.

Other Relevant Provincial Powers

While the provinces' authority over property and civil rights together with the power granted over natural resources comprise the dominant authority for provincial legislation over property, several other enumerated heads are also germane. The provinces have authority to legislate in relation to the incorporation of companies with provincial objects (92(11)); hospitals, asylums, and charitable institutions (92(7)); the issuance of licenses to raise of revenue for local purposes (s. 92(9); and local works and undertakings (92(10)). Provinces can also punish by fine for violation of any provincial law (s 92(15)) and pass laws concerning "all matters of a merely local or private nature in the Province" (s. 92(16)).

Federal Jurisdiction over Property

The provincial power over property and civil rights is, patently, quite sweeping. However, bearing in mind the modern paradigm as described by Ryder, there remains ample room for federal jurisdiction over property matters even though such measures incidentally invade the provincial domain. So, in the 1882 Privy Council decision in *Russell v. The Queen*,[14] a question arose as to whether the federal power over "peace, order and good government" could be validly exercised in a way that affected property rights. As Sir Montague Smith reasoned in that decision:

> Few, if any laws, could be made by Parliament for the peace, order and good government of Canada which did not in some incidental way affect property and civil rights; and it could not have been intended, when assuring to the provinces exclusive legislative authority on the subject of property and civil rights, to exclude the Parliament from the exercise of this general power whenever any such incidental interference would result from it. The true nature and character of the legislation in the particular instance under discussion must always be determined, in order to ascertain the class of subjects to which it really belongs.[15]

Trade and Commerce: Section 91(2)

Under Section 91(2) the federal government has the "legislative authority to regulate international and inter-provincial trade — the regulation of goods, persons, capital, or services crossing provincial or Canadian borders for a commercial purpose".[16] The courts have been fairly consistent in limiting the scope of section 91(2) in so far as local *intra*-provincial trade is concerned.[17] Nevertheless, regulatory

14 (1881-82) LR 7 App. Cas. 829 (Canada P.C.).

15 *Ibid*, at 839.

16 Monahan, *supra*, note 5 at 249.

17 See *British Columbia (A.G.) v. Canada (A.G.)* [1937] A.C. 377, 1937 CarswellNat 5 (Canada P.C.); *Labatt Breweries of Canada Ltd. v. Canada (A.G.)* [1980] 1 S.C.R. 914, 1979 CarswellNat 7, 1979 CarswellNat 631.

schemes under federal constitutional authority to provide for the general regulation of trade affecting the whole dominion have passed constitutional muster with ease.[18] For example, in *General Motors of Canada Ltd. v. City National Leasing*[19] the validity of a section in the federal *Combines Investigation Act*[20] that created a civil action for infringing certain provisions of the act was unsuccessfully challenged. Although the creation of civil actions falls squarely under provincial jurisdiction, the Supreme Court upheld the legislation because it was part of a general regulatory scheme within the federal trade and commerce power.

The Federal government has the "plenary authority to negotiate and enter into international agreements on Canada's behalf",[21] an increasingly important power. In addition, section 92A(3) provides that provincial jurisdiction to legislate in relation to the export of natural resources to other provinces does not derogate from the federal power in relation to trade and commerce. Note however, that the authority to implement treaties is shared by the federal and provincial governments in accordance with their respective jurisdictions.

Other Enumerated Property Powers of the Federal Government

Section 91 gives other powers to the federal government that affect property. Principal among these are: the power to raise tax revenue by any means (s. 91(3)); sea coast and inland fisheries (s. 91(12)); currency, coinage, banking, bills of exchange, interest and legal tender (ss. 91(14)-(16), (18)-(20)); bankruptcy (s. 91(21)) and patent, trademarks, and copyrights (ss. 91(22)(23)); and criminal law — including of course property crimes (s. 91(27)). The federal government also has the power to legislate over interprovincial and international transportation systems (these are exceptions to provincial power carved out of s. 92(10).

In addition, section 91(24) provides for federal jurisdiction over "Indians, and Lands reserved for the Indians". It has been settled in *Delgamuukw v. British Columbia*[22] that this includes any land subject to an aboriginal interest, however acquired. In *Delgamuukw*, a case that appears in Chapter 5 of this Casebook, the Province of British Columbia argued that section 109 of the *Constitution Act* transferred ownership of Indian land to the provinces, and with it the power to extinguish aboriginal title. The Supreme Court disagreed. The federal Crown retains legislative jurisdiction over native lands including the power to extinguish aboriginal title. Indeed, while provincial legislation might validly regulate or infringe the exercise of aboriginal rights, provincial legislation that purported to affect the core elements of "Indianness" would be *ultra vires*. Hence, any attempt by a provincial government to extinguish aboriginal title would be ineffective.

---

18 Monahan, *supra*, note 5 at 258-64.

19 [1989] 1 S.C.R. 641, 1989 CarswellOnt 956, 1989 CarswellOnt 125.

20 R.S.C. 1970, c. C-23, s. 31.1. See now *Competition Act*, R.S.C. 1985, c. C-34.

21 Monahan, *supra*, note 5 at 275.

22 [1997] 3 S.C.R. 1010, 1997 CarswellBC 2358, 1997 CarswellBC 2359.

The federal government also holds an important residual power that arises by virtue of the opening words of section 91, which speak of federal authority "to make laws for the peace, order and good government of Canada" (POGG). This broad language has been interpreted to confer powers to legislate in areas not expressly contemplated by the enumerated heads, pass laws of national concern, and respond to emergencies.[23]

Concurrency and Collision

Property may be understood as a creation of law, and in Canada those laws may be created under either provincial or federal authority. With regard to some matters (such as natural resources) it can be seen that there is explicit recognition of concurrent powers.

With regard to other areas, overlap is implicitly possible. As argued above, this situation is the natural and predictable outflow of the modern approach Canadian constitutional interpretation.[i] For example, consider the array of laws directed at environmental protection. Jurisdiction over the environment is not expressly allocated in the constitution. Here, both levels of government can assert jurisdiction; indeed both have been active in this field. Provincial competency derives from its power over property and civil rights, and its proprietary rights under section 109. Federal jurisdiction over the environment emanates from various federal powers, including POGG. In *R. v. Crown Zellerbach Canada Ltd.*[24] the Supreme Court upheld provisions of the *Ocean Dumping Control Act*[25] that prohibited the dumping of substances at sea without a permit. It had been alleged that the federal government was not empowered to enact prohibitions that affected internal waters of Canada. A majority of the Court held that such regulation was a matter of national concern, and so was within the POGG power. Monahan has said that

> [The *Crown Zellerbach*] definition of POGG would appear to grant Parliament much of the power it would need to fulfill its international obligations with respect to environmental protection as they evolve. It would also grant the Parliament jurisdiction to deal effectively with domestic persons, activities, or transactions where those matters have environmental effects beyond the province in which they originate; or are single and distinct.

Where otherwise valid provincial and federal legislation conflict, such that compliance with one necessitates breach of the other, the doctrine of paramountcy provides that the provincial law is rendered in operative to the extent of the conflict.[26]

---

23 See generally P. Hogg, *Constitutional Law of Canada*, Student ed. (Toronto: Carswell, 2001) at 421-52.

24 [1988] 1 S.C.R. 401, 1988 CarswellBC 755, 1988 CarswellBC 137.

25 R.S.C. 1974-75-76, c. 55.

26 *Multiple Access v. McCutcheon* [1982] 2 S.C.R. 161, 1982 CarswellOnt 128, 1982 CarswellOnt 738.

(c) constitutional, non-constitutional, and quasi-constitutional protections of property

R.W. Bauman, "Property Rights in the Canadian Constitutional Context"
(1992) 8 S.A.J.H.R. 344, at 344-5, 348-55, 359-61 [footnotes omitted]

Introduction

. . . [O]ne of the remarkable features of the *Canadian Charter of Rights and Freedoms* is that it does not include an explicit right to property among the categories of protected legal rights. This was not an oversight. Legislators and commentators debated the inclusion of property rights on repeated occasions leading up to the enactment of the *Charter* in 1982, but ultimately such rights were rejected . . .

Why did Canadians take this apparently anomalous step of excluding property rights from the *Charter*? This deletion seems unusual because many of the liberally-inspired constitutions of Western democracies include property rights as a fundamental category of protected rights. The reasons underlying this public policy choice that I will suggest and explore include the following. First, Canadian legislators and lawyers remain generally uncomfortable about the range of rights that might eventually be constitutionally sheltered by the concept of "property". Second, there had been successful attempts before 1982 to protect the "enjoyment of property rights" in the Canadian constitution. The experience of that form of protection created little pressure for entrenchment of equivalent provisions in the *Charter*. Third, some rights that relate to the traditional concept of property, including "life, liberty, and security of the person", *were* explicitly included in the *Charter*, and this was thought to cover many of the vital interests that an entrenched property right would otherwise protect. Fourth, several provincial governments were opposed to the specific inclusion of property rights for fear that these might curtail substantially the ability of those administrations to make legislation that was necessary to solve peculiar provincial problems. Fifth, it continues to be a matter of intense controversy whether property is such a fundamental value that it should be ranked alongside such other legal rights as the right "to be secure against unreasonable search or seizure" or the right "not to be subjected to any cruel or unusual treatment or punishment" . . .

Existing Constitutional Protection of Property in Canada

For nearly a century after the enactment of the *Constitution Act, 1867*, Canadians had no explicit constitutional bulwark against the deprivation of property rights by government. There were significant legislative measures that directly or indirectly impaired the ownership or enjoyment of property. Challenges to legislation that created this effect had to be modulated through questions about whether the particular province had the relevant jurisdiction under the scheme of distribution of powers established in the *Constitution Act, 1867*.

In the late nineteenth century, the province of British Columbia passed regulations that excluded various classes of workers, specifically children under twelve years of age and adult males who were Chinese, from employment in that province's mines. When a corporation operating a colliery sought to hire workers who were immigrants from China, a shareholder of that corporation challenged the company's decision, alleging that it violated the B.C. law. The legislation, like child labour laws in the U.S. that were challenged around the same time, arguably invaded the mineowner's right to property and its liberty of contract. The Privy Council struck down the law in question, reasoning that the province had, through this law, encroached on the federal government's jurisdiction over "naturalization and aliens".

In the 1960s, in response to concerns about the consolidation of large landholdings by Hutterite colonies in Alberta, that province imposed maximum limits on the size of communal holdings and required prior governmental approval for additional acquisitions by colonies. One of the Hutterites objected on constitutional grounds to this set of regulations. The ground on which the courts eventually settled the validity of the regulations was not, however, the fundamental value of private property. Instead, the legislation was declared valid as relating to land use, a proper use of provincial legislative power, despite its incidental effect of restricting the property rights of the Hutterites and despite the discrimination thus evidenced on the basis of religion.

A further Canadian historical instance that should be mentioned was the forced relocation and internment of Japanese-Canadians and the deprivation of their property during the Second World War. There was an irrational fear that such citizens would operate as a fifth column on Canada's west coast. Several thousand Japanese-Canadians and their families were forced to evacuate their residences and were sent either to the interior of British Columbia or to other provinces. Individuals who resisted were placed in a concentration camp in Ontario. Unlike in the US, where in such cases as *Korematsu v. U.S.*, arguments could be raised under the equal protection clause or other parts of the Fifth Amendment, there was in Canada no constitutional protection that could avail the individuals who suffered under this extraordinarily harsh policy. Only within the past year has the Canadian government offered to establish a trust fund worth several million dollars to benefit the surviving Japanese-Canadian victims and their families. As might be expected, the potential claimants under this gratuitous policy maintain that the amount offered fall short of a fair settlement for the deprivation of land, homes, personal property and freedom that took place in the 1940s.

It was against this background that the *Canadian Bill of Rights*, an ordinary statute, was enacted by the federal Parliament in 1960. It remains in effect and contains specific protection for property and for equality. It provides in s. 1(a) a right to the "enjoyment of property" and the right not to be deprived of it "except by due process of law". This measure closely resembles the due process clauses contained in the Fifth and the Fourteenth Amendments of the U.S. Constitution.

A provision similar to s. 1(a) was not carried forward into the *Charter* in 1982, despite the repeated efforts of Prime Minister Pierre Trudeau to see this legal right entrenched. The matter was vigorously contested and, owing at least in part to the opposition of the New Democratic Party and of some provincial governments, particularly those of Saskatchewan and Prince Edward Island, the right to property was omitted from the *Charter*. The government of Prince Edward Island was apparently worried that provincial laws restricting foreign ownership of land in that province would be subject to constitutional attack . . . In Saskatchewan, the primary reason to fear the constitutional protection of property rights was the limit this might place on the ruling New Democrats' plans to nationalize key industries. Even in Alberta, long a bastion of free market enterprise ideology, the provincial government lined up against the proposal to include property rights in the *Charter*. The objection in this case related to the ability of an Alberta administration to regulate the exploration, refining, and distribution of petroleum and natural gas, particularly as carried out by large multinational corporations.

Subsequent attempts to introduce an entrenched right to property, initiated by resolutions in the British Columbia, New Brunswick, and Ontario legislatures, as well as in the House of Commons, failed to attract the requisite support before they expired. The minimum number of provinces required to adopt this kind of constitutional amendment was never achieved. The outside date for garnering provincial support was May, 1991. That date passed without significant public comment in the Canadian media.

The explicit protection in the *Bill of Rights* of a right to property remains in force today. Several features make this a relatively feeble and underemployed right. First, the right provided by the *Bill of Rights* has not been as solicitously guarded as many of the legal rights contained in the *Charter*: courts have been extremely reluctant to invalidate laws that infringe this right to property. Second, s. l(a) of the *Bill of Rights* applies only to laws made by the federal Parliament and the right itself can be changed by Parliament acting alone. Third, s. 1 of the *Bill of Rights* refers only to "the right of the individual." This appears to exclude as claimants all non-natural persons, such as corporations. As the first decade of litigation under the *Charter* has shown, the pursuit through the courts of the vindication of rights and freedoms has frequently been led by corporate claimants.

There have been few cases interpreting s. 1(a). It remains unclear, for example, whether the due process exception in the *Bill of Rights* should be interpreted as requiring simply a fair procedure to be followed by the government, or whether it actually guarantees compensation for owners of property who have been deprived of it. Nor is it obvious that the Supreme Court of Canada, in interpreting s. 1(a), would invariably treat the right to property as subject to a "procedural", but not a "substantive", form of due process. There have been hints in this direction, but the courts have not conclusively settled whether s. 1(a) entitles them to review an impugned law only for the propriety of the procedures leading up to its adoption, or whether they can judge the contents of the law against a standard of justice. Issues such as this would become acutely relevant if a right to property were eventually added to the *Charter*.

Property rights are also specifically protected in various provincial bills of rights. For example, the *Alberta Bill of Rights*, first enacted in 1972 as an ordinary statute by the province, recognizes every person's right to the enjoyment of property.

Although a right to property was omitted from the *Charter*, this does not mean that a person's property is perennially at risk to being taken away by governmental action. The jurisdiction of each province over "property and civil rights" underpins the ability of provincial governments to expropriate private property from its owners. In every Canadian jurisdiction procedural guarantees exist to ensure that the owner receives timely notice and a fair hearing before the expropriation can be carried out. The owner whose land is affected must be notified and advised of rights provided in the expropriation statute, including the right to object to the taking and the right to obtain appraisal advice. In addition, an exercise of the power of expropriation usually is accompanied by payment of adequate compensation for the property affected. How compensation is measured in such jurisdictions as Alberta has been changed in the past two decades. Where, under the former common law rules, a basic principle of compensation was "value to the owner", the modern regime adopts the principle of "market value" plus specifically enumerated heads of compensation (including, e.g., disturbance damages).The modern statutes allow for the establishment of special tribunals with the necessary expertise to conduct hearings and assess the appropriate compensation.

Expropriation and land use regulation are among the more visible instances of an individual property-owner confronting the awesome power of the state. It should not, however, be forgotten that many of the principles developed at common law provide considerable protection of settled expectations in relation to property rights. Whether the law provides protection in the form of property rules or liability rules, the point is that state action is often devoted to securing reliance interests, facilitating transfer of forms of private property, and resolving disputes over ownership and use. Despite the lack of specific constitutional guarantees, owners of property arc protected in myriad ways under Canadian law.

Why Does a Right to Property Require Charter Protection?

A common starting place for justifying the inclusion of property rights in the *Charter* is the matter of Anglo-Canadian constitutional history. The *Magna Carta*, signed by King John in 1215, referred specifically to restraints on the power of the monarch to usurp the property rights of his subjects. The *Constitution Act, 1867* similarly presents an image of political legitimacy and stability that is built on the continuity and respectability of propertied legislators. To include property rights in the *Charter* would only extend a time-honoured tradition.

A second source of support for entrenching property rights is the existence of similar guarantees in major international agreements, many of which Canada has signed. For example, the Universal Declaration of Human Rights includes a right not to be arbitrarily deprived of one's property. The European Convention for the Protection of Human Rights and Fundamental Freedoms, which served as one model for the *Charter*, protects property rights in Art. 1.

A third, more powerful line of argument in favour of constitutionalizing property rights derives from those political and legal theorists who have treated property as a core idea of modern liberal government. According to John Locke in the seventeenth century, the foundation of political societies can be traced to the need to protect established property interests. The just acquisition of property by an individual is a primary activity that Locke thinks governments must respect, even if it took place in a pre-political era. Without settled entitlements, government would be neither desirable nor possible. On this view, property rights, largely based on appropriation in a pre-market setting, become the paradigm of all legal rights in a society. The *Charter*, as we have it today, is devoted to the ideal that individuals should be autonomous moral creatures. Their zone of personal space, involving freedom of belief and mobility, should not suffer unwarranted government intrusion. Without the protection of constitutional guarantees, individuals and their private interests are placed at the mercy of an overweening state power that will invariably invoke the justification of a "public" use or purpose in overriding settled interests. This may be done arbitrarily or without adequate compensation. A guarantee of property rights is one means to require governments to act fairly towards its citizens.

Those who, before 1982, favoured the inclusion of a constitutionally guaranteed right to property might have assuaged their disappointment by the argument that this kind of right was implicitly contained in s. 7. From the *Charter* jurisprudence that has developed, it is now clear that the Supreme Court of Canada has rejected the idea that s. 7 of the *Charter* includes many of the economic rights traditionally associated with property. This is perhaps a major reason that the debate over the need for an explicit *Charter* guarantee has been revived.

The extension of legal rights under the *Charter* to include the right to property can also be viewed as part of the ideological tilt that is evident in other aspects of the federal government's proposals. The economic philosophy that underlies the proposal for a more efficient, market-based economic union, with constitutional protection for business against legislative intervention, is strikingly libertarian.

What Might Be the Impact of Entrenching Property Rights?

From the perspective of those who advocate including property rights in the *Charter*, the main advantage to be gained is the added assurance that governments will be restrained from taking property without serious safeguards. The courts in Canada will be empowered to act as sentinels, always vigilant to decry state action that directly or indirectly diminishes or terminates the social or economic rights attached to a person's property. Courts are already practised in this area. According to some legal theorists, most common law adjudication, including the development of property doctrines, can best be analysed as economic decision making concerning the distribution of resources within a society.

Though the federal proposals of the past year do not mention how property rights would interplay with the rest of the *Charter*, it should be kept in mind that those rights would likely be subject to the limitations imposed on private ownership by the presence of s. 1 in the *Charter*. This saving provision, which allows the government to justify a law that otherwise infringes a legal right, would permit the courts to assess whether the infringement is "demonstrably justified in a free and democratic society." It is not clear whether a proposed property guarantee would also be subject to s. 33. This would permit a government to declare, for a limited period, that a law operates notwithstanding the guarantees contained in the *Charter*.

Adding property as a protected legal right in the *Charter*, in or about s. 7, could create severe interpretive difficulties in respect of, for example, aboriginal and treaty rights. The courts in Canada are still reluctant to characterize aboriginal rights as ownership of the land in question. The entrenchment of property rights would create a further constitutional barrier for establishing aboriginal title. The property rights of intervening parties would be constitutionally protected against any aboriginal claim.

The opponents of a *Charter* property right have contended that many desirable types of legislation will be dangerously exposed to constitutional attack. In particular, they draw our attention to the interpretation of the due process clauses by the U.S. Supreme Court in one of its "reactionary phases". For over a generation, the approach of the majority of that Court was to interpret the due process clauses as more than simply procedural limits on the deprivation of life, liberty or property. Instead, the Court deployed a concept of "substantive" due process and succeeded in striking down state laws providing for minimum wages, for maximum hours of work, and for sanctions against anti-union activities. These measures were characterized as state interference with the right to contract and the right to use one's own property. This trend was not reversed until 1937. From time to time, there have been alarms sounded in the U.S. that the Supreme Court could relapse into a *Lochner* approach.

The opponents of entrenching property rights fear that the Supreme Court of Canada will ultimately adopt an approach involving a review of the substantive content of legislation. Among the programmes and policies that might be at risk under an entrenched property right are the following:

(a) rent control legislation;
(b) minimum wage and pay equity plans;
(c) occupational health and safety regulation;
(d) matrimonial property regimes that provide for the division of property on separation or divorce;
(e) environmental controls; and
(f) natural resource management schemes . . .

Conclusion

This modest discussion is intended to provide some guidance on the ambit and effect of an entrenched right to property, using the Canadian situation as illustrative. Much more investigation and debate is required before one can fully understand both the advantages and the costs, from a public policy perspective, of awarding property some form of explicit constitutional protection. As this discussion has sought to demonstrate, it is useful to peer into the nature and range of the interests and parties that might benefit from constitutional recognition. Protecting property rights per se will inevitably protect the interests of those persons (both individual and corporate) who already own property. This type of protection will not help those who lack property. We can be sure that rights associated with property are in constant evolution. They will reflect the contingent, particular background political morality on which legislators and judges base their work. Placing property rights under the protection of a Charter or Bill of Rights will require judges and lawyers to construct tests to determine when there has been a deprivation of property that breaches the procedural or substantive requirements contained in the constitutional document. The activity of developing and applying different kinds of tests or standards has given rise to a considerable body of constitutional doctrine in the U.S. It has also stimulated academic controversy whether the resulting body of doctrine is coherent or principled.

Finally, it should be recognized that, on a theoretical level, constitutional entrenchment of property rights can be used to achieve contrasting purposes. Some theorists would argue that this form of constitutional protection should be used to shield the holders of entitlements against a patterned redistribution that is meant to achieve a projected form of social justice. One of the most eloquent defenders of property rights against such efforts to use the law to promote a desirable end-state pattern of property ownership is Robert Nozick. He questions, for example, the legitimacy of taxation measures, which he characterizes as "on a par with forced labor".

In another direction, it has been argued that the constitutional interpretation of the idea of property permits lawmakers to reconsider the justifications for and limitations on private property. Under this political and moral theory, constitutional construction of a right to property should be guided by a triad of principles. These include the principle of efficiency and utility, the principle of desert based on labour, and the principle of justice and equality? This avowedly "pluralist" theory of property would both shape, and be constrained by, any constitutional doctrine that has already emerged or that would follow from a constitutional guarantee of the right to property.

The discussion here is cautionary. There are dangers on all sides once a nation adopts a constitutional guarantee of property rights. The consequences are unpredictable, incalculable, and difficult to reverse. Proposals to entrench a right to property are an invitation to serious rethinking — from a political as well as from a legal perspective — about the relevant principles and the role of courts. In Canada, where revising our constitutional arrangements has become something of a national neurosis, we do not seem capable of finally disposing of the issue of property rights in relation to the *Charter*. While a property guarantee is not included in that document, this has not entailed that Canadians, in the decade since the *Charter* was enacted, have suffered widespread expropriation without procedural or compensatory guidelines. While our federal and provincial governments remain equivocal on this issue, there is widespread scepticism about making the right to property a separate and articulate constitutional value. In this one aspect at least, it cannot be said that property *per se* is part of the bedrock of our polity.

QUESTIONS AND COMMENTS

1. As Richard Bauman notes, despite the absence of an explicit *Charter* guarantee, property is not left completely unprotected. Take the obvious example of section 8, which provides that "[e]veryone has the right to be secure against unreasonable search and seizure". Section 8 is designed to serve privacy interests, and can work to limit the ability of the state to enter one's home: see further *R. v. Feeney* [1997] 2 S.C.R. 13, 1997 CarswellBC 1015, 1997 CarswellBC 1016, reconsideration granted 1997 CarswellBC 3179, 1997 CarswellBC 3180 (S.C.C.). The guarantee of freedom of expression in paragraph 2(b) has been used to prevent regulation of commercial advertizing: see *e.g.*, *R.J.R.-MacDonald v. Canada* [1995] S.C.R. 199, 1995 CarswellQue 119, 1995 CarswellQue 119F. The right to freedom of religion has been used to attack Sunday trading prohibitions: see, *e.g.*, *R. v. Big M. Drug Mart* [1985] 1 S.C.R. 295, 1985 CarswellAlta 316, 1985 CarswellAlta 609. In brief, *Charter* rights have been effective in protecting a range of commercial interests and activities: see further R.W. Bauman, "Business, Economic Rights, and the Charter" in D. Schneiderman & K. Sutherland, eds., *Charting the Consequences: The Impact of Charter Rights on Canadian Law and Politics* (Toronto: U.T.P., 1997) at 58.

There is more: Section 15 provides for equality under law and may be used to attack discriminatory property entitlements. A contravention of the *Charter* can be saved under section 1, provided that it can be shown that the contravention represents "a reasonable limit prescribed by law [that] can be demonstrably justified in a free and democratic society". The need to protect defined property interests can be marshalled as a justification under section 1. Moreover, section 35 of the *Constitution Act, 1982* provides protection for Aboriginal rights, including, pre-eminently, land rights: see *Delgamuukw v. British Columbia* [1997] 3 S.C.R. 1010, 1997 CarswellBC 2358, 1997 CarswellBC 2359 (covered in Chapter 5). And, as will be seen in Chapter 10, the *Charter* affects rights associated with *public* property. The right of exclusion over public property, as wielded by the state, must sometimes yield in the name of *Charter* guarantees to freedom of expression and assembly. In other words, the use of the *Charter* to curb the state's exclusionary powers over its property produces various private rights of access over state-owned lands.

2. Some attempts to invoke the *Charter* to protect other forms of economic/proprietary interests have fared less well. In *Gosselin c. Québec (Procureur général)* 221 D.L.R. (4th) 257, 2002 CarswellQue 2706, 2002 CarswellQue 2707 (S.C.C.), a bold argument was advanced. It was maintained that section 7 of the *Charter*, which guarantees the right to "life, liberty and the security of the person", places a positive duty on the state to ensure adequate levels of subsistence.

The case involved a challenge to Quebec regulations concerning social assistance which provided that recipients under 30 years of age would receive less in aid than recipients over that age. The rules also provided that recipients under 30 could increase their level of benefit if they participated in specified government programs. Louise Gosselin challenged these rules, asserting among other things that the law violated sections 7 and 15 of the *Charter*. The equality argument under section 15 succeeded; the section 7 argument was rejected by a 3:2 majority. McLachlin C.J., while unconvinced that section 7 was triggered, nevertheless left open the possibility that the section might someday be read as conferring positive rights:

> Section 7 states that "[e]veryone has the right to life, liberty and security of the person" and "the right not to be deprived" of these "except in accordance with the principles of fundamental justice". The appellant argues that the s. 7 right to security of the person includes the right to receive a particular level of social assistance from the state adequate to meet basic needs. She argues that the state deprived her of this right by providing inadequate welfare benefits, in a way that violated the principles of fundamental justice. There are three elements to this claim: (1) that the legislation affects an interest protected by the right to life, liberty and security of the person within the meaning of s. 7; (2) that providing inadequate benefits constitutes a "deprivation" by the state; and (3) that, if deprivation of a right protected by s. 7 is established, this was not in accordance with the principles of fundamental justice. The factual record is insufficient to support this claim. Nevertheless, I will examine these three elements.
>
> Can s. 7 apply to protect rights or interests wholly unconnected to the administration of justice? The question remains unanswered. In *R. v. Morgentaler*, [1988] 1 S.C.R. 30 (S.C.C.), at p. 56, Dickson C.J., for himself and Lamer J. entertained (without deciding on) the possibility that the right to security of the person extends "to protect either interests central to personal autonomy, such as a right to privacy". Similarly, in *Irwin Toy Ltd. c. Québec (Procureur général)*, [1989] 1 S.C.R. 927 . . . at p. 1003, Dickson C.J., for the majority, left open the question of whether s. 7 could operate to protect "economic rights fundamental to human . . . survival". . . .
>
> Even if s. 7 could be read to encompass economic rights, a further hurdle emerges. Section 7 speaks of the right *not to be deprived* of life, liberty and security of the person, except in accordance with the principles of fundamental justice. Nothing in the jurisprudence thus far suggests that s. 7 places a positive obligation on the state to ensure that each person enjoys life, liberty or security of the person. Rather, s. 7 has been interpreted as restricting the state's ability to *deprive* people of these. Such a deprivation does not exist in the case at bar.
>
> One day s. 7 may be interpreted to include positive obligations. To evoke Lord Sankey's celebrated phrase in *Edwards v. Canada (Attorney General)* (1929), [1930] A.C. 124 (Canada P.C.), the *Canadian* must be viewed as "living tree capable of growth and expansion within its natural limits": see *Reference re Provincial Electoral Boundaries*, [1991] 2 S.C.R. 158 (S.C.C.), at p. 180, *per* McLachlin J. It would be a mistake to regard s. 7 as frozen, or its content as having been exhaustively defined in previous cases . . .
>
> The question therefore is not whether s. 7 has ever been or will ever be recognized as creating positive rights. Rather, the question is whether the present circumstances warrant a novel application of s. 7 as the basis for a positive state obligation to guarantee adequate living standards.
>
> I conclude that they do not. With due respect for the views of my colleague Arbour J., I do not believe that there is sufficient evidence in this case to support the proposed interpretation of s. 7. I leave open the possibility that a positive obligation to sustain life, liberty, or security of person may be made out in special circumstances. However, this is not such a case. The impugned program contained compensatory "workfare" provisions and the evidence of actual hardship is wanting. The frail platform provided by the

facts of this case cannot support the weight of a positive state obligation of citizen support. . . .

(Compare the incandescent dissenting opinion of Arbour J.).

3. As Dr. Bauman notes, the *Canadian Bill of Rights*, S.C. 1960, c. 44, which is still in force, contains non-entrenched protections, and is applicable to federal legislation. Section 1 provides in part:

> 1. It is hereby recognized and declared that in Canada there have existed and shall continue to exist without discrimination by reason of race, national origin, colour, religion or sex, the following human rights and fundamental freedoms, namely,
>
> (a) the right of the individual to life, liberty, security of the person and enjoyment of property, and the right not to be derived thereof except by due process of law . . .

As with much of the *Bill of Rights*, this protection has been given a narrow reading. Hence, legislation that bars war veterans from suing the federal government for breach of fiduciary duty in the handling of pension and disability benefits has been held *not* to violate section 1(a): *Authorson (Litigation Guardian of) v. Canada (Attorney General)* 2003 CarswellOnt 2773, 2003 CarswellOnt 2774 (S.C.C.).

In some provinces, a functional counterpart exists. For example, section 1 of the *Alberta Bill of Rights*, R.S.A. 2000, c. A-14, contains a virtually identical protection:

> It is hereby recognized and declared that in Alberta there exist without discrimination by reason of race, national origin, colour, religion or sex, the following human rights and fundamental freedoms, namely: (a) the right of the individual to liberty, security of the person and enjoyment of property, and the right not to be deprived thereof except by due process of law . . .

Moreover, the *Alberta Personal Property Bill of Rights*, R.S.A. 2000, A-31, enacted in 1999, states:

> 2. . . . where (a) personal property is owned by a person other than the Crown, and (b) a provincial enactment contains provisions that authorize the acquiring of permanent title to that personal property by the Crown, those provisions are of no force or effect unless a process is in place for the determination and payment of compensation for the acquiring of that title. . . .
>
> 4. . . . every provincial enactment, whether enacted before or after the coming into force of this Act, shall be construed and applied so as not to abrogate, abridge or infringe on, and so as not to authorize the abrogation or abridgment of or infringement on, any of the rights or benefits provided for under this Act unless an Act of the Legislature expressly declares that that enactment operates notwithstanding the Alberta Personal Property Bill of Rights.
>
> 5. The Lieutenant Governor in Council may make regulations exempting any matter, provincial enactment or provision of a provincial enactment from the application of section 2.

(Section 1 defines "personal property" as "only tangible personal property that is capable of being physically touched, seen or moved." Section 3 contains various exemptions, including one for taxing legislation.)

The common law also protects vested property rights. In *Manitoba Fisheries Ltd. v. The Queen* [1979] 1 S.C.R. 101, 1978 CarswellNat 146, 1978 CarswellNat 565, the Supreme Court endorsed the view that unless the words of statute clearly demand otherwise, legislation is not to be construed so as to take away the property without compensation. (See further R. Sullivan, *Sullivan and Driedger on the Construction of Statutes*, 4th ed. (Toronto: Butterworths, 2002) at 400*ff.*)

Consider also Article 1110 of the *North American Free Trade Agreement* (NAFTA):

> Article 1110: Expropriation and Compensation
>
> 1. No Party shall directly or indirectly nationalize or expropriate an investment of an investor of another Party in its territory or take a measure tantamount to nationalization or expropriation of such an investment ("expropriation"), except:
>
> (a) for a public purpose;
> (b) on a non-discriminatory basis;
> (c) in accordance with due process of law and the general principles of treatment provided in Article 1105; and
> (d) upon payment of compensation in accordance with paragraphs 2 to 6.
>
> 2. Compensation shall be equivalent to the fair market value of the expropriated investment immediately before the expropriation took place ("date of expropriation"), and shall not reflect any change in value occurring because the intended expropriation had become known earlier. Valuation criteria shall include going concern value, asset value (including declared tax value of tangible property) and other criteria, as appropriate to determine fair market value.
>
> 3. Compensation shall be paid without delay and be fully realizable. . . .

In D. Schneiderman, "NAFTA's Takings Rule: American Constitutionalism Comes to Canada" (1996) 46 U.T.L.J. 499, at 501, 512-4, the gist of these provisions is described:

> NAFTA provides an exceptional remedy for investors resident within the other member states. If their investments have been directly or indirectly expropriated or nationalized, or subject to measures tantamount to expropriation, NAFTA entitles these investors to sue before an international trade tribunal. The tribunal's awards are enforceable within the domestic courts of each of the state parties. The expropriation provisions are unique in that all other provisions of NAFTA require that a state-party to the agreement, rather than a private actor, initiate mechanisms for compliance. The expropriation provisions also are distinctive in that they incorporate the American constitutional principles of "due process" and the prohibition against "takings" of private property without compensation and valid public purpose. . . .

The NAFTA chapter on investment forbids the parties to "directly or indirectly" nationalize or expropriate investments in which investors resident in the other party-states have an interest, or to take measures "tantamount to" nationalization or expropriation. The definition of "investment" is expansive: it includes almost any form of business interest, including interests arising from securities held in, loans made to, or anticipated contracts arising from, an investor's enterprise. Measures which amount to the taking of investments are prohibited under NAFTA unless they meet four criteria. Takings must be:(a) for a public purpose; (b) on a non-discriminatory basis; (c) in accordance with due process of law and Article 1105(1); and (d) on payment of compensation in accordance with paragraphs 2 through 6.

Paragraphs 2 through 6 require that compensation be equivalent to the fair market value of the investment, and that it be "paid without delay" and be "fully realizable" and "transferable."

In addition, NAFTA provides an exceptional remedy for private investors. Should a party breach these investment rules, an investor resident in one of the other party-states, rather than simply the party-state itself, can seek to enforce NAFTA obligations before an arbitration tribunal. The tribunal's decisions are "binding" and the parties are obliged to ensure that these awards are enforceable within their territories. Federal and provincial laws provide, at present, for the enforcement of such international arbitration awards before domestic courts. NAFTA provisions which benefit the rights of investors ultimately, then, are enforceable within domestic courts of law and are binding in the same way as are other constitutional commitments. This is unlike FTA and GATT, which to do not entitle individuals and corporations resident within the party-states to seek enforcement directly.

Moreover, it is axiomatic that NAFTA cannot be unilaterally amended by a party-state. Plus, under Article 2205 a party-state may not withdraw from NAFTA unless six-months notice is given.

Provincial and federal laws provide for compensation in the event of a governmental expropriation of property: see generally E.C.E. Todd, *The Law of Expropriation and Compensation in Canada*, 2nd ed. (Toronto: Carswell, 1992). The nature of this right to compensation, set in contrast with the American law of "takings", is analyzed in the case of *Mariner Real Estate Ltd. v. Nova Scotia (Attorney General)* 68 L.C.R. 1, 1999 CarswellNS 254 (C.A.), which is reproduced below.

Mariner Real Estate Ltd. v. Nova Scotia (Attorney General) 68 L.C.R. 1, 1999 CarswellNS 254 (C.A.)

[In order to preserve the beach and dune system as "an environmental and recreational resource", the Province of Nova Scotia enacted the *Beaches Act*, R.S.N.S. 1989, c. 32. The legislation regulates the use of public and private beaches. Any development — a path, trail, road, building, or other structure not indigenous to the beach — is prohibited unless authorization from the designated Minister is obtained.

The respondents applied for authorization from the Minister to construct single family dwelling units on Kingsburg Beach. That permission was denied. A study, solicited by the Minister to evaluate the effects of development on the area, concluded that it was in the best interests of both the public and the property owners that no construction be permitted on the dunes, owing to (i) the sensitive nature of the land forms, and (ii) the consequences that the breakdown of the dune systems might have on the structures.

The respondents sought a declaration that their lands had been *de facto* expropriated by virtue of the decisions made under the *Beaches Act*. The trial judge held that the respondents had been deprived of land within the meaning of the *Expropriation Act*, R.S.N.S. 1989, c. 156, and hence were entitled to be compensated. The province appealed.]

Cromwell J.A.: . . .

III. Analysis:

(a) De facto Expropriation:

The respondents" claim that what was, in form, a designation of their land under the *Beaches Act* is, in fact, a taking of their land by a statutory authority within the meaning of the *Expropriation Act*. This claim of *de facto* expropriation, or as it is known in United States constitutional law, regulatory taking, does not have a long history or clearly articulated basis in Canadian law. We were referred to only three Canadian cases in which such a claim was made successfully, only two of which dealt with the expropriation of land.

The scope of claims of *de facto* expropriation is very limited in Canadian law. They are constrained by two governing principles. The first is that valid legislation (primary or subordinate) or action taken lawfully with legislative authority may very significantly restrict an owner's enjoyment of private land. The second is that the Courts may order compensation for such restriction only where authorized to do so by legislation. In other words, the only questions the Court is entitled to consider are whether the regulatory action was lawful and whether the *Expropriation Act* entitles the owner to compensation for the resulting restrictions.

De facto expropriation is conceptually difficult given the narrow parameters of the Court's authority which I have just outlined. While *de facto* expropriation is concerned with whether the "rights" of ownership have been taken away, those rights are defined only by reference to lawful uses of land which may, by law, be severely restricted. In short, the bundle of rights associated with ownership carries with it the possibility of stringent land use regulation.

I dwell on this point because there is a rich line of constitutional jurisprudence on regulatory takings in both the United States and Australia which is sometimes referred to in the English and Canadian cases dealing with *de facto* expropriation:

see for example *Belfast Corp. v. O.D. Cars Ltd.*, [1960] A.C. 490 (H.L. (N.I.)). The Fifth Amendment to the United States Constitution (which also applies to the States through the Fourteenth Amendment) provides that private property shall not be taken for public use without just compensation. In the Australian Constitution, section 51(xxxi) prohibits the acquisition of property except upon just terms. While these abundant sources of case law may be of assistance in developing the Canadian law of *de facto* expropriation, it is vital to recognize that the question posed in the constitutional cases is fundamentally different.

These U.S. and Australian constitutional cases concern constitutional limits on legislative power in relation to private property. As O'Connor, J. said in the United States Supreme Court case of *Eastern Enterprises v. Apfel* (1998), 118 S. Ct. 2131, the purpose of the U.S. constitutional provision (referred to as the "takings clause") is to prevent the government from " . . . forcing some people alone to bear public burdens which, in all fairness and justice, should be borne by the public as a whole." Canadian courts have no similar broad mandate to review and vary legislative judgments about the appropriate distribution of burdens and benefits flowing from environmental or other land use controls. In Canada, the courts" task is to determine whether the regulation in question entitles the respondents to compensation under the *Expropriation Act*, not to pass judgment on the way the Legislature apportions the burdens flowing from land use regulation.

In this country, extensive and restrictive land use regulation is the norm. Such regulation has, almost without exception, been found not to constitute compensable expropriation. It is settled law, for example, that the regulation of land use which has the effect of decreasing the value of the land is not an expropriation. As expressed in Ian MacF Rogers, *Canadian Law of Planning and Zoning* (Toronto: Carswell, 1999 (looseleaf) at s. 5.14, "The law permits the appropriation of prospective development rights for the good of the community but allows the property owner nothing in return." Numerous cases support this proposition including *Belfast Corporation v. O.D. Cars* (*supra*) and *Hartel Holdings Co. Ltd. v. Calgary*, [1984] 1 S.C.R. 337. Many others are reviewed by Marceau, J. in *Alberta v. Nilsson*, 1999 CarswellAlta 499 at para 35*ff*. I would refer, as well, to the following from E.C.E. Todd, *The Law of Expropriation in Canada*, (2nd, 1992) at pp. 22-23:

> Traditionally the property concept is thought of as a bundle of rights of which one of the most important is that of user. At common law this right was virtually unlimited and subject only to the restraints imposed by the law of public and private nuisance. At a later stage in the evolution of property law the use of land might be limited by the terms of restrictive covenants.
>
> Today the principal restrictions on land use arise from the planning and zoning provisions of public authorities.•*By the imposition, removal or alteration of land use controls a public authority may dramatically increase, or decrease, the value of land by changing the permitted uses which may be made of it. In such a case, in the absence of express statutory provision to the contrary an owner is not entitled to compensation or any other remedy notwithstanding that subdivision approval or rezoning is refused or development is blocked or frozen pursuant to statutory planning powers*•in order, for example, to facilitate the future acquisition of the land for public purposes. "Ordinarily, in this

> country, the United States and the United Kingdom, compensation does not follow zoning either up or down . . . (but) a taker may not, through the device of zoning, depress the value of property as a prelude to compulsory taking of the property for a public purpose. . . . (emphasis added)

In light of this long tradition of vigorous land use regulation, the test that has developed for applying the *Expropriation Act* to land use restrictions is exacting and, of course, the respondents on appeal as the plaintiffs at trial, had the burden of proving that they met it. In each of the three Canadian cases which have found compensation payable for *de facto* expropriations, the result of the governmental action went beyond drastically limiting use or reducing the value of the owner's property. In *The Queen in Right of British Columbia v. Tener et al.*, [1985] 1 S.C.R. 533, the denial of the permit meant that access to the respondents" mineral rights was completely negated, or as Wilson, J. put it at p. 552, amounted to total denial of that interest. In *Casamiro Resource Corp. v. British Columbia* (1991), 80 D.L.R. (4th) 1 (B.C.C.A.), which closely parallels *Tener*, the private rights had become "meaningless". In *Manitoba Fisheries v. The Queen*, [1979] 1 S.C.R. 101, the legislation absolutely prohibited the claimant from carrying on its business.

In reviewing the *de facto* expropriation cases, R.J. Bauman concluded, and I agree, that to constitute a *de facto* expropriation, there must be a confiscation of ". . . all *reasonable* private uses of the lands in question.": R.J. Bauman, "*Exotic Expropriations: Government Action and Compensation*", (1994) 52 The Advocate 561 at 574. While there is no magic formula for determining (or describing) the point at which regulation ends and taking begins, I think that Marceau, J.'s formulation in *Nilsson* is helpful. The question is whether the regulation is of "sufficient severity to remove virtually all of the rights associated with the property holder's interest." (at para 48).

Considerations of a claim of *de facto* expropriation must recognize that the effect of the particular regulation must be compared with reasonable use of the lands in modern Canada, not with their use as if they were in some imaginary state of nature unconstrained by regulation. In modern Canada, extensive land use regulation is the norm and it should not be assumed that ownership carries with it any exemption from such regulation. As stated in *Belfast*, there is a distinction between the numerous "rights" (or the "bundle of rights") associated with ownership and ownership itself. The "rights" of ownership and the concept of reasonable use of the land include regulation in the public interest falling short of what the Australian cases have called deprivation of the reality of proprietorship: see e.g., *Newcrest Mining (W.A.) Ltd. v. The Commonwealth of Australia*, [1996-1997] 190 C.L.R. 513 at p. 633. In other words, what is, in form, regulation will be held to be expropriation only when virtually all of the aggregated incidents of ownership have been taken away. The extent of this bundle of rights of ownership must be assessed, not only in relation to the land's potential highest and best use, but having regard to the nature of the land and the range of reasonable uses to which it has actually been put. It seems to me there is a significant difference in this regard between, for example, environmentally fragile dune land which, by its nature, is not particularly well-suited for residential development and which has long been used for primarily recreational purposes and a lot in a residential subdivision for which the most reasonable use is for residential construction . . .

(b) The Effects of Regulation:

In my opinion, where a regulatory regime is imposed on land, its *actual application* in the specific case must be examined, not the potential, but as yet unexploited, range of possible regulation which is authorized. This point is demonstrated by the *Tener* case. The Court was clear in that case that the taking occurred as a result of the denial of the permit, not by the designation under the *Park Act* which required the permit to be obtained.

The American constitutional cases have recognized the importance of looking at the actual application of the regulatory scheme as opposed simply to its potential for interference with the owner's activities. The U.S. Supreme Court requires in regulatory takings cases that there be a final decision regarding the application of the challenged regulations to the property: see *Suitum v. Tahoe Regional Planning Agency* (1997), 117 S. Ct. 1659 at 1664-5. This rule is based on the common sense proposition that a ". . . Court cannot determine whether a regulation has gone "too far" unless it knows how far the regulation goes": see *MacDonald, Sommer & Frates v. Yolo County* (1986), 106 S. Ct. 2561. In my view, the same principle applies to claims of *de facto* expropriation in Canada.

The declaration sought and granted by the trial judge in this case was that the designation of the lands pursuant to the *Beaches Act* constituted an expropriation within the meaning of the *Expropriation Act*. In my opinion, this was an error. While the act of designation imposes on the respondents" lands a regulatory regime, that does not, of itself, constitute an expropriation. One of the respondents" main complaints is that they were refused permission to build dwellings on the lands. That refusal was not an inevitable consequence of the designation of the lands as a beach, but flowed from the refusal by the Minister of permission required to develop the lands pursuant to s. 6 of the Regulations. If permission to build had been granted, would the designation have effected a *de facto* expropriation? The answer, I think, is self-evidently no. It was not, therefore, the designation alone that was crucial, but the designation in combination with the refusal of permission to develop the lands by building dwellings.

My determination that the trial judge erred in this way does not resolve the appeal. The broader question of whether the designation, *together with* the decisions made under the regulatory regime it imposed, constitute an expropriation was argued at trial and in this Court. That broader question is, therefore, properly before us.

(c) Is loss of economic value loss of land under the Expropriation Act?

The trial judge found that the respondents had been deprived of land. His main conclusion appears to have been that the loss of "virtually all economic value" constituted the loss of an interest in land. He also found, however, that the ". . . fee simple in the [respondents'] lands has been stripped of its whole bundle of rights." Both aspects of his holding are before us in this appeal and, in my respectful view, both are in error . . .

The judge further found that the loss of virtually all economic value was the loss of land within the meaning of the *Expropriation Act*. This holding contains two key elements: that the loss of all economic value is the loss of land within the meaning of the *Act*, and further, that the loss of virtually all economic value is a taking of land as those phrases appear in the *Expropriation Act*.

I will address in this part of my reasons the first of these holdings. Does the loss of economic value of land constitute the loss of land within the meaning of the *Expropriation Act*?

The *Expropriation Act* does not define land exhaustively, but states that land *includes "any estate, term, easement, right or interest in*, to, over or affecting land": section 3(1)(i) . . .

The authorities generally take an expansive view of what may constitute land for the purposes of expropriation legislation . . .

While the term "land" must be given a broad and liberal interpretation, the interpretation must also respect the legislative context and purpose. As I will develop below, the *Expropriation Act* draws a line, on policy grounds, between the sorts of interference with the ownership of land that are compensable under the *Act* and those which are not. That line, in general, is drawn where land is taken. In interpreting where this line falls, the Court must give the term a meaning which is both consistent with the *Act's* remedial nature but also with appropriate regard to the legal context in which the term was adopted. It is not the Court's function, as it would be if applying a constitutional guarantee of rights of private property, to evaluate the legality or fairness of where the legislature has drawn that line, but to interpret and apply it . . .

The loss of interests in land and the loss of the value of land have been treated distinctly by both the common law and the *Expropriation Act*. In my view, this distinct treatment supports the conclusion that decline in value of land, even when drastic, is not the loss of an interest in land. To understand this point, it is necessary to consider briefly compensation for "injurious affection", that is, injury to lands retained by the owner which results from the taking.

Section 26 of the *Expropriation Act* sets out the main heads of compensation payable upon expropriation:

26. The due compensation payable to the owner for lands expropriated shall be the aggregate of

(a) *the market value of the land* or a family home for a family home determined as hereinafter set forth.

(b) the reasonable costs, expenses and losses arising out of or incidental to *the owner's disturbance* determined as hereinafter set forth;

(c) damages for injurious affection as hereinafter set forth; and

(d) *the value to the owner of any special economic advantage* to him arising out of or incidental to his actual occupation of the land, to the extent that no other provision is made therefor in due compensation. (emphasis added)

Pursuant to s. 30(1), compensation is payable to the owner of land for loss or damage caused by injurious affection; this is a defined term under the Act:

3. (1) In this Act, . . .

(h) "injurious affection" means . . .

(ii) where the statutory authority does not acquire part of the land of an owner,

(A) such reduction in the market value of the land of the owner, and

(B) *such personal and business damages, resulting from the construction and not the use of the works by the statutory authority, as the statutory authority would be liable for if the construction were not under the authority of a statute,* . . . (emphasis added)

Pursuant to ss. 26(c) and 30(1) and 3(1)(h), the *Act* provides for compensation to the owner of land where there has been no taking of that owner's land. The important points are first, that compensation for injurious affection as defined in the *Act* is *the only instance in which compensation is provided for the loss of value of land absent the taking of an interest in land.* Second, the legislative scheme for compensation draws a sharp dividing line between loss resulting *from a taking of land* and the loss of value of land caused by other governmental activities. In short, a sharp, and in a sense, arbitrary division is made for the purposes of compensation between takings and losses caused in other ways . . .

The important point is this. While the distinction between the value of land and interests in land is, in one sense highly technical, it is, nonetheless, deeply imbedded in the scheme of compensation provided for under the *Expropriation Act.* It is fundamental to the entitlement to compensation under the *Act* claimed by the respondents. This is so because the distinction defines the line between cases in which governmental interference with the enjoyment of land is compensable under the *Act* and cases in which it is not. An impressive argument may be made supporting a broader approach to compensation for governmental interference with the enjoyment of land. The logic of drawing the line based on whether an interest in land has been lost may, as noted by Wilson, J. above, be seriously questioned. Nonetheless, the *Expropriation Act* draws the line in this way. It is, therefore, necessary to give the legislation an interpretation consistent with the words employed and the underlying policy decision which they reflect.

I conclude, therefore, that the learned trial judge erred in holding that the loss of virtually all economic value of the respondents" land, was the loss of an interest in land within the meaning of the *Expropriation Act*.

(d) Loss of the "bundle of rights"

That brings me to the trial judge's holding that the effect of the designation and the way it was applied here was to strip the fee simple of its whole bundle of rights. The cases have long recognized that at a certain point, regulation is, in effect, confiscation. The law insists that the substance of the situation, not simply its form, be examined. As noted in *Nilsson*, restrictions on the use of land may be so stringent and all-encompassing that they have the effect of depriving the owner of his or her interest in the land, although leaving paper title undisturbed.

While the decline in economic value of land is not the loss of an interest in land, it may be *evidence* of the loss of an interest in land. As the respondents" appraiser, Mr. Hardy, stated in his report, the value of land is a reflection of several factors, including the scope of the incidents of ownership attached to the lands in question:

> Our consideration of the legal basis and economic factors of value in land valuation concluded that it is the rights of ownership that give land value and it is these rights that are the subject of valuation. When the rights of ownership are excessively restricted or removed, it is logical that the value of the land is diminished, destroyed or made idle.

It follows that, where the effect of land use regulation is to eliminate virtually all the normal incidents of ownership, this will be reflected in the market value of the land. It is not, however, the decline in market value that constitutes the loss of an interest in land, but the taking away of the incidents of ownership reflected in that decline.

We have been referred to only three Canadian cases in which compensation has been ordered where governmental regulatory action has been held to be a *de facto* expropriation: *Tener*, *Casamiro* and *Manitoba Fisheries* . . . Judging by these cases, *de facto* expropriations are very rare in Canada and they require proof of virtual extinction of an identifiable interest in land (or, in *Manitoba Fisheries*, of an interest in property).

The respondents submit that the *Beaches Act* and the Regulations, coupled with the refusal of Ministerial permission for development, prohibit virtually all activities normally associated with the ownership of land. The trial judge accepted this submission.

Preclusion of residential development, as proposed by the respondents, particularly on lands of this environmental sensitivity, is not, of itself, the extinguishment of virtually all rights associated with ownership. For example, Mariner and 20102660 N.S. Limited proposed to build using standard concrete basements. In considering these applications, the Minister had before him the Jacques Whitford report which opined that standard concrete foundations would cause serious damage to the dune systems. Furthermore, it was clear on the evidence that the building of residences on two of the Moshers" lots (i.e., the cemetery and garden lots) would not be permitted, quite apart from the *Beaches Act*. Yet it is not submitted that the requirements dealing with lot size and septic requirements constitute expropriation because they, in effect, prevent building residences on these lots.

With respect, the trial judge erred in finding that the *Beaches Act* designation and ensuing regulation resulted in the expropriation of these two of the Moshers" properties. Residences could not be built on them prior to the designation, and there is no evidence that permission for other uses has been refused.

What of the properties for which permission to build single family dwellings was refused? The trial judge found that virtually all incidents of ownership had been removed through that refusal and the other restrictions applied to the land. With great respect to the trial judge, I disagree.

Many of the restricted activities may be authorized by permit. These include most of the traditional recreational uses described by Mrs. Mosher in her evidence. However, there is no evidence that a permit has been sought for any of these kinds of activities, much less refused. That being so, it is hard to follow the respondents" argument that all of these things are prohibited. As noted earlier, it is not the requirement to obtain a permit that constrains the enjoyment of the land, but its refusal. When, as here, the claim is that the impact of a regulatory scheme has, in effect, taken away *all* rights of ownership, it is not the existence of the regulatory authority that is significant, but its *actual application* to the lands. As stated in *MacDonald, supra*, the Court cannot determine whether regulation has gone too far unless it knows how far the regulation goes.

The respondents in this case proved at trial that they would not be allowed to build the proposed single family residences. With respect to three of the Mosher's lots, there was not even an application to build; as mentioned, residential development on two of those lots was probably impossible quite apart from the designation. Some reasonable or traditional uses of this dune property may be allowed by permit. Aside from the applications to build fences, no applications for permits relating to these other uses have been made, let alone refused. The respondents had the burden of proving that virtually all incidents of ownership (having regard to reasonable uses of the land in question) have, in effect, been taken away. Neither the respondents nor the Province appear to have explored the possibility that development specifically designed in a way consistent with protection of the dunes might occur. The respondents, while asserting that all reasonable uses of the land are precluded by the operation of the *Act* and Regulations, have not shown that they would be denied the required permits with respect to such other reasonable or traditional uses of the lands.

In short, there is an absence of evidence relating to environmentally appropriate development plans on the land in question, and an absence of evidence of refusal of permission for the respondents to engage in other reasonable or traditional uses. These, in combination, result, in my opinion, in the respondents having failed to establish that virtually all incidents of ownership have, by the effect of the *Act* and Regulations, been taken away.

I would conclude, therefore, that the respondents failed to establish that they had been deprived of land within the meaning of the *Expropriation Act*.

(e) Acquisition of Land

As noted, there must not only be a taking away of land from the owner but also the acquisition of land by the expropriating authority for there to be an expropriation within the meaning of the *Act*.

There is no suggestion here that the Province acquired legal title or any aspect of it. The land remains private property although subject to the regulatory regime established by the *Beaches Act*. The argument is that the effect of the regulatory scheme is, for practical purposes, the acquisition of an interest in land.

The respondents submit (and the trial judge held) that *Tener* stands for the proposition that where regulation enhances the value of public land, the regulation constitutes the acquisition of an interest in land. I disagree.

In my respectful view, *Tener*, is, at best, equivocal on this point. When the judgments in *Tener* are read in their entirety and in light of the facts of the case, there is no support for the proposition on which the respondents rely. It is clear in the judgments of both Estey, J. and Wilson, J. in *Tener* that what was, in effect, acquired in that case was the reversion of the mineral interests which had been granted by the Crown. Estey, J. stated that "[e]xpropriation . . . occurs if the Crown . . . acquires from the owner an interest in property." He added that the acquisition of the "outstanding interest" of the respondents was a step in the establishment of the Park. He concluded that "[t]he denial of access to these lands occurred under the *Park Act* and *amounts to a recovery by the Crown of a part of the right granted to the respondents in 1937*." In other words, the effect of the regulatory scheme was not only to *extinguish* the mineral rights of the respondents, but to re-vest them in the Crown. Similarly, Wilson, J. held that the effect of the denial of access was to remove an encumbrance from the Crown's land. She stated that ". . . what in effect has happened here is *the derogation by the Crown from its grant of the mineral claims to the respondents" predecessors in title* . . . it is nonetheless a derogation of the most radical kind one which . . . amounts to a total denial of that interest".

The respondents place great weight on comments of Estey, J. in *Tener* to the effect that the action taken by the government was to enhance the value of the park. These comments, while on their face supportive of the respondents" position, must be read in the context of Estey, J.'s statements in the case that an expropriation necessarily involves the acquisition of land and that the extinguishment of the Teners" mineral rights constituted, in effect, the re-acquisition of such rights by the Crown. I do not think, with respect, that his statements to the effect that the re-acquisition enhanced the value of the park takes away from his holding that the Crown re-acquired in fact, though not in law, the mineral rights which constituted land under the applicable definition . . .

I conclude that for there to be a taking, there must be, in effect, as Estey, J. said in *Tener*, an acquisition of an interest in land and that enhanced value is not such an interest.

The respondents further submit that their lands have been effectively pressed into public service and that this is sufficient to constitute an acquisition of land. The judgment of the United States Supreme Court in *Lucas v. South Carolina Coastal Council* (1992), 112 S.Ct. 2886 is relied on. I do not think that case assists us here.

The U.S. constitutional law has, on this issue, taken a fundamentally different path than has Canadian law concerning the interpretation of expropriation legislation. In U.S. constitutional law, regulation which has the effect of denying the owner all economically beneficial or productive use of land constitutes a taking of property for which compensation must be paid. Under Canadian expropriation law, deprivation of economic value is not a taking of land, for the reasons I have set out at length earlier. It follows that U.S. constitutional law cases cannot be relied on as accurately stating Canadian law on this point. Moreover, in U.S. constitutional law, as I understand it, deprivation of property through regulation for public purposes is sufficient to bring a case within the constitutional protection against taking for "public use", unlike the situation under the *Expropriation Act* which requires the taking of land. It is not, as I understand it, necessary in U.S. constitutional law to show that the state acquires any title or interest in the land regulated. For these reasons, I conclude that the U.S. takings clause cases are not of assistance in determining whether there has been an acquisition of land within the meaning of the Nova Scotia *Expropriation Act* . . .

Returning to the respondents" submissions in this case, in my opinion, the freezing of development and strict regulation of the designated lands did not, of itself, confer any interest in land on the Province or any other instrumentality of government. I am reinforced in this opinion by many cases dealing with zoning and other forms of land use regulation. Estey, J., in *Tener* , notes that ordinarily compensation does not follow zoning either up or down. The Supreme Court of Canada in [*Toronto Area Transit Operating Authority v. Dell Holdings*, [1992] 1 S.C.R. 32] accepted the general proposition that, under our law, owners caught up in the zoning or planning process, but not expropriated, must simply accept the loss (provided, of course, that the regulatory actions are otherwise lawful). Development freezes have consistently been held not to give rise to rights of compensation: for a review of the authorities, see *Nilsson, supra*. One of the bases of these decisions is that the restriction of development generally does not result in the acquisition of an interest in land by the regulating authority.

There was no evidence that the economic value of the Crown's land was enhanced. Even if its value could be considered to be enhanced in some other sense, such enhancement, in my view, is not an acquisition of land for the purposes of the *Expropriation Act*.

I conclude that the trial judge erred on this aspect of the case. In my respectful view, regulation enhancing the value of public property, if established, is not an acquisition of "land" within the meaning of the *Expropriation Act* . . .

Appeal allowed.

NOTE

Glube C.J.N.S. concurred. Hallett J.A. wrote a short judgment, concurring in the result.

QUESTIONS AND COMMENTS

1. In the *Mariner* case, Cromwell J.A. referred to the American case of *Lucas v. South Carolina Coastal Council* 112 S.Ct. 2886 (1992). It too dealt with the protection of ecologically sensitive seacoast property. Two residential coastal lots in South Carolina were purchased in 1986 by David Lucas for development purposes. In 1988 the state government passed the *Beachfront Management Act*, under which a local council can designate lands as being unavailable for development. Unlike the Nova Scotia *Beaches Act*, the legislation provided for no exceptions to this prohibition, so that the statutory scheme once applied to the locale "had the direct effect of barring [Lucas] from erecting any permanent structures on his two parcels": *ibid*, at 2889 (*per* Scalia J.). A majority of the United States Supreme Court found that the legislative measure was a taking. For the majority, Scalia J. outlined the governing principles:

> Prior to Justice Holmes's exposition in *Pennsylvania Coal Co. v. Mahon*, 260 U.S. 393, 43 S.Ct. 158, 67 L.Ed. 322 (1922), it was generally thought that the Takings Clause reached only a "direct appropriation" of property . . . or the functional equivalent of a "practical ouster of [the owner's] possession," . . . Justice Holmes recognized in *Mahon*, however, that if the protection against physical appropriations of private property was to be meaningfully enforced, the government's power to redefine the range of interests included in the ownership of property was necessarily constrained by constitutional limits. 260 U.S., at 414-415, 43 S.Ct., at 160. If, instead, the uses of private property were subject to unbridled, uncompensated qualification under the police power, "the natural tendency of human nature [would be] to extend the qualification more and more until at last private property disappear[ed]." *Id.*, at 415, 43 S.Ct., at 160. These considerations gave birth in that case to the oft-cited maxim that, "while property may be regulated to a certain extent, if regulation goes too far it will be recognized as a taking." *Ibid.* Nevertheless, our decision in *Mahon* offered little insight into when, and under what circumstances, a given regulation would be seen as going "too far" for purposes of the Fifth Amendment. In 70-odd years of succeeding "regulatory takings" jurisprudence, we have generally eschewed any "set formula" for determining how far is too far, preferring to "engag[e] in . . . essentially ad hoc, factual inquiries." *Penn Central Transportation Co. v. New York City*, 438 U.S. 104, 124, 98 S.Ct. 2646, 2659, 57 L.Ed.2d 631 (1978). . . . We have, however, described at least two discrete categories of regulatory

action as compensable without case-specific inquiry into the public interest advanced in support of the restraint. The first encompasses regulations that compel the property owner to suffer a physical "invasion" of his property. In general (at least with regard to permanent invasions), no matter how minute the intrusion, and no matter how weighty the public purpose behind it, we have required compensation. . . .

The second situation in which we have found categorical treatment appropriate is where regulation denies all economically beneficial or productive use of land. . . . As we have said on numerous occasions, the Fifth Amendment is violated when land-use regulation "does not substantially advance legitimate state interests *or denies an owner economically viable use of his land.*"

We have never set forth the justification for this rule. Perhaps it is simply, as Justice Brennan suggested, that total deprivation of beneficial use is, from the landowner's point of view, the equivalent of a physical appropriation. . . . Surely, at least, in the extraordinary circumstance when *no* productive or economically beneficial use of land is permitted, it is less realistic to indulge our usual assumption that the legislature is simply "adjusting the benefits and burdens of economic life," *Penn Central Transportation Co.*, 438 1018 U.S., at 124, 98 S.Ct., at 2659, in a manner that secures an "average reciprocity of advantage" to everyone concerned, *Pennsylvania Coal Co. v. Mahon*, 260 U.S., at 415, 43 S.Ct., at 160. And the *functional* basis for permitting the government, by regulation, to affect property values without compensation — that "Government hardly could go on if to some extent values incident to property could not be diminished without paying for every such change in the general law," *id.*, at 413, 43 S.Ct., at 159 — does not apply to the relatively rare situations where the government has deprived a landowner of all economically beneficial uses. On the other side of the balance, affirmatively supporting a compensation requirement, is the fact that regulations that leave the owner of land without economically beneficial or productive options for its use — typically, as here, by requiring land to be left substantially in its natural state — carry with them a heightened risk that private property is being pressed into some form of public service under the guise of mitigating serious public harm. . . .

We think, in short, that there are good reasons for our frequently expressed belief that when the owner of real property has been called upon to sacrifice *all* economically beneficial uses in the name of the common good, that is, to leave his property economically idle, he has suffered a taking. . . .

Where the State seeks to sustain regulation that deprives land of all economically beneficial use, we think it may resist compensation only if the logically antecedent inquiry into the nature of the owner's estate shows that the proscribed use interests were not part of his title to begin with. This accords, we think, with our "takings" jurisprudence, which has traditionally been guided by the understandings of our citizens regarding the content of, and the State's power over, the "bundle of rights" that they acquire when they obtain title to property. It seems to us that the property owner necessarily expects the uses of his property to be restricted, from time to time, by various measures newly enacted by the State in legitimate exercise of its police powers; "[a]s long recognized, some values are enjoyed under an implied limitation and must yield to the police power." *Pennsylvania Coal Co. v. Mahon*, 260 U.S., at 413, 43 S.Ct., at 159. And in the case of personal property, by reason of the State's traditionally high degree of control over commercial dealings, he ought to be aware of the possibility that new regulation might even render his property economically worthless (at least if the property's only economically productive use is sale or manufacture for sale). See *Andrus v. Allard*, 444 U.S. 51, 66-67,

> 100 S.Ct. 318, 327, 62 L.Ed.2d 210 (1979) (prohibition on sale of eagle feathers). In the case of land, however, we think the notion pressed by the Council that title is somehow held subject to the "implied limitation" that the State may subsequently eliminate all economically valuable use is inconsistent with the historical compact recorded in the Takings Clause that has become part of our constitutional culture.
>
> Where "permanent physical occupation" of land is concerned, we have refused to allow the government to decree it anew (without compensation), no matter how weighty the asserted "public interests" involved, *Loretto v. Teleprompter Manhattan CATV Corp.*, 458 U.S., at 426, 102 S.Ct., at 3171— though we assuredly *would* permit the government to assert a permanent easement that was a pre-existing limitation upon the landowner's title. . . . We believe similar treatment must be accorded confiscatory regulations, *i.e.*, regulations that prohibit all economically beneficial use of land: Any limitation so severe cannot be newly legislated or decreed (without compensation), but must inhere in the title itself, in the restrictions that background principles of the State's law of property and nuisance already place upon land ownership. A law or decree with such an effect must, in other words, do no more than duplicate the result that could have been achieved in the courts — by adjacent landowners (or other uniquely affected persons) under the State's law of private nuisance, or by the State under its complementary power to abate nuisances that affect the public generally, or otherwise.

2. In *Mariner*, Cromwell J.A. contrasted the constitutional mandate given to American courts to review takings with the role accorded to Canadian courts under expropriation legislation. He wrote:

> Canadian courts have no similar broad mandate to review and vary legislative judgments about the appropriate distribution of burdens and benefits flowing from environmental or other land use controls. In Canada, the courts" task is to determine whether the regulation in question entitles the respondents to compensation under the *Expropriation Act*, not to pass judgment on the way the Legislature apportions the burdens flowing from land use regulation.

Do you agree with Cromwell J.A.'s view that the policies that inform the American constitutional protections differ from those applicable under a non-entrenched regime such as that found in the Nova Scotia *Expropriation Act*?

3. In what other ways does Cromwell J.A. distinguish American takings law from the legislative scheme for expropriation of land in Nova Scotia?

4. Of all of the protections of property rights in Canada described above, which would you regard as the most extensive?

In my opinion, it is NAFTA; far and away. Indeed, because of the built-in constraints on unilateral amendment, NAFTA has been described as a form of constitutional instrument: see D. Schneiderman (1996) 46 U.T.L.J. 499, at 500, n. 8 and the authorities cited there. Furthermore, following an extensive review of American takings jurisprudence, together with the terms of NAFTA and the existing arbitral awards under that treaty, Vicki Been and Joel Beauvais conclude that "NAFTA's Article 1110 and similar provisions do not merely "internationalize" the Takings Clause of the Fifth Amendment of the U.S. Constitution, but rather extend the scope of potential regulatory takings claims in significant respects.": V.L. Been & Joel Beauvais, "The Global Fifth Amendment? NAFTA's Investment Protections and the Misguided Quest for an International "Regulatory Takings" Doctrine", 78 N.Y.U.L.Rev. 30 (2003) at 143. The issue is, incidentally, not confined to NAFTA: comparable provisions can be found in many bilateral investment treaties (B.I.T.s) worldwide: *ibid*, at 34.

5. What effect might NAFTA ultimately have on Canadian public policy? Again, Been and Beauvais (at 132-4) are instructive:

> [A] common charge of Article 1110's critics is that the provision will deter beneficial social and environmental regulation because regulators may soften or abandon proposed regulatory changes (or discontinue existing regulatory programs) rather than incur the cost of defending against takings claims, and/or paying a compensation award. Indeed, foreign investors clearly have used NAFTA claims or the threat of such claims in several instances as a "sword" in opposing regulation, with mixed success.
>
> Most notably, in April 1997, Ethyl Corporation, a U.S. manufacturer of the gasoline additive MMT, brought a US $200 million claim against Canada, alleging that a Canadian ban on the importation of MMT violated Article 1110 and several other Chapter 11 disciplines. Canada settled the claim before the NAFTA tribunal reached the merits, agreeing to rescind the ban, issue a public statement conceding that the government had no evidence that MMT causes harm, and paying Ethyl approximately $13 million. More recently, a task force established by several major American pesticide manufacturers threatened to bring a Chapter 11 claim in response to a proposed Canadian ban on twenty-eight pesticides; Canada's Environment Minister, André Boisclair, for now has refused to back down on the regulations.
>
> In 1994, R.J. Reynolds and other U.S. tobacco companies threatened a Chapter 11 claim for "hundreds of millions of dollars" against the Canadian government if Canada adopted plain-packaging legislation to discourage teen smoking. The tobacco lobby argued that the plain-packaging requirement would expropriate the value of their trademarks. The NAFTA issue was made moot when the Canadian Supreme Court struck down the regulation as violative of constitutional free speech requirements, but recent events make clear that the tobacco industry continues to see the threat of NAFTA litigation under Article 1110 as a useful lobbying tool. In 2001, Philip Morris has used similar tactics to oppose a proposed ban on the use of the words "light" and "mild" on cigarette packaging in Canada. The company argued that the terms are an integral part of registered trademarks and that the ban would violate Article 1110 by expropriating these trademarks and associated goodwill.
>
> Whether and to what extent such tactics continue to be effective will be affected by the way in which NAFTA tribunals address future expropriation claims. At present, however, the uncertainty over how far NAFTA can be pushed to provide protection for property owners, coupled with federal, state and local regulators" unfamiliarity with NAFTA and its ISDM procedures, and regulators" concerns about both the expense of defending against NAFTA claims and about their potential liability for compensation awards, at the very least make NAFTA a useful threat for those who oppose environmental and land use regulation.

6. Assume that the landowner in the *Mariner* case was an American investor. Apply Article 1110 of NAFTA.

7. Do you think that the *Canadian Charter of Rights and Freedoms* should be amended to include a takings rule?

CHAPTER 3
THE PHYSICAL DIMENSIONS OF PROPERTY

1. INTRODUCTION

Property, on one persuasive account, is about the power to exclude. For such an entitlement to have practical meaning, the line between "what is mine" and what is not must be ascertained. This chapter is devoted to an analysis of the lines that separate entitlements — boundaries, loosely defined.

The physical entity called land has, of course, three dimensions. That being so, boundary questions can concern both the lateral extent of ownership (the area on the surface) as well as the entitlements on the vertical axis (rights above and below the surface). The first part of the chapter considers how these rights are determined, and how they are recorded in documents of title. Boundaries, as will be seen, are rather more permeable and less crystal-clear than one might first think.

As noted in the introductory chapter, economic efficiency and a faith in the market underscore one line of argument in support of private property. In fact, efficiency is *the* dominant justificatory theory relied on in contemporary debates about property systems. With that in mind, this chapter draws on economic analysis as a means of assessing the rules governing the spatial dimensions of ownership. This form of inquiry can of course be carried through to other issues covered in this Casebook.

In Chapter 2, the distinction between real and personal property was outlined. In this chapter we return to that dichotomy by considering issues relating to the physical "border" between the two categories. So, for example, a shrub purchased at a greenhouse is obviously personal property; it is a chattel, a chose in possession, a good. But once it is planted in the garden of Blackacre its legal characterization is (in all probability) transformed. It becomes part of the land, along with the soil, the grass, the garage and so forth. The law of fixtures regulates this transformation.

The same metamorphosis can occur when chattels are combined, such as when liquids or widgets belonging to two or more persons are intermixed, or where goods become fused together, or where some item (corn) is so completely altered (say, into whiskey) by another person, that ownership of the finished product is at issue.

In sum, this chapter explores the spatial dimension of the mine/thine divide.

2. LAND: AIRSPACE AND SUBSURFACE RIGHTS

(a) introduction

A transfer of land will recite in some way (to be discussed later in this chapter) the dimensions of the property to be sold. Rarely is mention made of the buildings on the land; certainly the buildings are not referred to in the abstract or certificate of title. It is also uncommon for the transfer document to specify the rights to the space above the land (the airspace). As to the subsurface, a deed may indicate whether or not mineral rights are included, but everything else is left unstated. In the absence of an express term, what rules govern?

(b) above the surface

Didow v. Alberta Power Ltd.
60 Alta. L.R. (2d) 212, 1988 CarswellAlta 109 (C.A.)

Haddad J.A.:

The single issue in this appeal is to determine, on the particular facts which follow, whether the respondent has trespassed the air space above the appellants' land.

The material facts are not in dispute. The respondent, an electrical utility company, constructed a power line on the municipal road allowance along the east side of the appellants' land. The distance between the centre of the base of four power poles, each approximately 50 feet in height, to the boundary of the appellants' land is two feet. The cross-arms conductors and attaching wires at the top of each pole (collectively called "the cross-arms") protrude six feet into the air space above the appellants' land.

The appellants in these proceedings, commenced by originating notice of motion, seek a declaration that the cross-arms amount to a trespass. The following paragraph from the affidavit of the appellant, Kenneth W. Didow, sets forth the appellants' concerns:

> There is an old farm yard with a residence on the land. The power line overhangs the east side of the farm yard and we consider it to be unsightly. Since Alberta Power Limited cut down the existing trees under the overhang, we would be reluctant to plant trees in any other area of the overhang. We are also concerned about the danger associated with the lines and the location and operation of tall machinery and equipment such as steel augers or metal granaries under the overhang. In addition, the overhang will restrict the use of aerial spraying and seeding on the land.

The learned chambers judge considered a series of authorities and concluded that the protrusion did not interfere with the appellants' possession of the air space or its right to possession [45 Alta. L.R. (2d) 116, 37 C.C.L.T. 90, 36 L.C.R. 139, 70 A.R. 199]. He applied the following test [pp. 123-24]:

> Clearly the question is, is it an interference with possession or even the right to possession?
>
> Here the applicants do not claim any diminution in their right to full enjoyment of their property. Indeed, the facts are that they are not making use of the air space occupied by the cross-arms and wires and they have no intention of doing so.

With respect, that statement does not take into account the problems, actual or potential, referred to in Kenneth W. Didow's affidavit. Moreover, I have read the relevant authorities and applying the principles and tests I extract therefrom I arrive at a conclusion contrary to that reached by the learned chambers judge. Accordingly, I would allow the appeal.

The character of a trespass was not put in controversy. In essence, it is an unjustifiable interference with possession. The appellants are the registered owners of the land below the air space and their status to bring this action is not in dispute.

A resolution of the issue before the court turns on the extent of the rights acquired by the appellants to the column of air above and within the boundaries of the land.

The jurisprudence in this area of the law has developed from early English cases, before the advent of air traffic, where decisions were influenced by the maxim *cujus est solum, ejus est usque ad coelum et ad inferos* (referred to hereafter as "the Latin maxim") which in simple language means that the owner of a piece of land owns everything above and below it to an indefinite extent.

The authorities cited can, generally speaking, be divided into two groups:

1. Cases involving permanent structural projections into the air space above another's land;

2. Cases involving a transient invasion into the air space above another's land at a height not likely to interfere with the land owner.

With respect to cases in the first group, the weight of authority favours the view that a direct invasion by a permanent artificial projection constitutes a trespass.

The appellants, as have all claimants to air space, rely in the main on the Latin maxim. This maxim has been the subject of constant attack in air space litigation over the years and if not discredited has been qualified in its application. Some of the older cases cited by the respondent were aimed at establishing that an overhanging encroachment will have nuisance value only and is therefore not actionable in trespass. This theory is no longer viable, according to recent authority, at least insofar as it applies to structures of a permanent nature.

The first of the early decisions cited is *Baten's Case* (1610), 9 Co. Rep. 53b, 77 E.R. 810, where a portion of the defendant's new home was found to overhang part of the plaintiff's home. Notwithstanding reference to the foregoing maxim the court characterized the overhang as a nuisance. Today, by the application of modern concepts, the overhang, in my view, would be treated as a trespass.

In *Pickering v. Rudd* (1815), 4 Camp. 219, 171 E.R. 70, and *Fay v. Prentice* (1845), 1 C.B. 828, 135 E.R. 769, it was said that the appropriate remedy in each case was an action in nuisance. Each dealt with projections over an adjoining property.

In *Pickering*, the alleged overhang consisted of a board and Lord Ellenborough did not "think it a trespass to interfere with the air superincumbent on the close". Caution led him to reject trespass by reasoning that to hold otherwise "an aeronaut is liable to an action in trespass *quare clausum fregit*, at the suit of the occupier of every field over which his balloon passes in the course of his voyage." Subsequent judicial pronouncements and existing laws regulating aircraft have now removed Lord Ellenborough's concern. His decision has been supplanted by more recent authority. (See *Kelsen v. Imp. Tobacco Co. (of Great Britain & Ireland)*, [1957] 2 Q.B. 334, [1957] 2 W.L.R. 1007, [1957] 2 All E.R. 343.) . . .

The authorities . . . establish that the right to use land includes the right to use and enjoy the air space above the land. These cases cautiously fall short of saying that ownership of land includes ownership of all air space above the land. In any event, they serve to make clear that intrusion by an artificial or permanent structure into the air space of another is forbidden as a trespass.

Cases which fall into the second group involve transient invasion of air space at a height unlikely to affect the landowner. The cases in this group to which the respondent is attracted deal with airplanes. Predicated on sound logic and common sense both case law and statute law now decree that a landowner cannot object to air traffic which does not interfere with the use and enjoyment of his property.

The respondent's strongest submission is that actionable trespass only occurs when the intrusion into air space actually interferes with a landowner's use and enjoyment of that space. Its submissions follow the statements leading to the decision reached by the chambers judge. The argument is directed to convince the court that a landowner cannot object to an intrusion into air space over his land which he is not actually occupying and using for the time being. Counsel points to public policy principles developed by the courts to permit the use of aircraft in air space and then argues that analogous public policy considerations apply to air space intrusion by overhead electrical installations. As an extension of that argument he says that tens of thousands of miles of transmission lines across Alberta occupy private property.

The analogy is hardly appropriate. Aircraft, which are transient and invade space at a height beyond the contemplation of reasonable and ordinary use by the landowner, cannot be equated with a low level intrusion of a permanent nature. I agree with the opinion stated of Griffiths J. in *Lord Bernstein of Leigh v. Skyviews & Gen.*

Ltd., [1978] A.C. 479, [1977] 3 W.L.R. 136, [1977] 2 All E.R. 902, that low flying aircraft might very well commit a trespass.

Moreover, if there are many miles of transmission lines already trespassing the air space above private property without any leave or licence, they will not transform an unlawful practice into a lawful one.

The respondent cited *Lacroix v. R.*, [1954] Ex. C.R. 69, [1954] 4 D.L.R. 470, to advance the proposition that the landowner's rights to the air space over his property were limited to what he could possess or occupy. This case arose out of a claim for compensation for an easement to provide lighting for the purposes of aerial navigation of aircraft using the Dorval Airport as well as a claim for damages. It was alleged that the air space over the claimant's land was used by aircraft as a flightway to and from the airport. Fournier J. referred to the Latin maxim as a maxim not suited to meet the development and invention of today's world. In its application, its interpretation in his view, has to be restricted without depriving the landowner of full enjoyment of his property — a principle which he endorsed. That portion of his judgment which lends support to the respondent's position is to be found at pp. 76-77 where he said:

> It seems to me that the owner of land has a limited right in the air space over his property; it is limited by what he can possess or occupy for the use and enjoyment of his land. By putting up buildings or other constructions the owner does not take possession of the air but unites or incorporates something to the surface of his land. This which is annexed or incorporated to his land becomes part and parcel of the property . . .
>
> I need go only so far as to say that the owner of land is not and cannot be the owner of the unlimited air space over his land, because air and space fall in the cateogry of *res omnium communis*. For these reasons the suppliant's claim for damages by reason of the so-called establishment of a flightway over his land fails.

The second case which gives the respondent comfort is *Air Can. v. R.*, [1978] 2 W.W.R. 694, 86 D.L.R. (3d) 631, (sub nom. *Min. of Fin. (Man.) v. Air Can.*) [1978] C.T.C. 812 (C.A.), cited to expound the proposition that ownership of air space cannot be claimed by anyone as it falls under the category of *omnium communis*. This case is distinguishable on the facts as the claim to jurisdiction to air space is made by the province of Manitoba. It unsuccessfully asserted its right to levy a sales tax against Air Canada in respect of goods and services provided by it while occupying air space over the province. Moreover, the case is not founded in trespass. However, the comments of Monnin J.A. (now C.J.M.) are relevant and of some significance. After accepting a statement made by the trial judge, which is of no account here, he said at p. 697:

> . . . I would rather rest the case on the basis that air and airspace are not the subject of ownership by anyone, either state or individual, but fall in the category of *res omnium communis*.

Later in his reasons, Mr. Justice Monnin (at p. 699) quoted an extract from the judgment delivered in *Lord Bernstein of Leigh v. Skyviews & Gen. Ltd.*, *supra*, at p.

907 — in which Griffiths J. qualified the application of the Latin maxim by suggesting "a balance" in compromising the rights of landowners against the general public. Monnin J.A. then added these remarks:

> The maxim cannot go further than to direct the owner or occupier of land in his enjoyment of the land and also to prevent anyone else from acquiring any title or exclusive right to the space above such land so as to limit a person to whatever proper use he can make of his land.

After giving due consideration to the judgment in *Bernstein* I find the reasoning of Griffiths J. most persuasive. He reviewed the earlier decisions which found favour with the Latin maxim and the circumstance in each instance in which it was applied. At p. 905 of his reasons, he said:

> The plaintiff claims that as owner of the land he is also owner of the air space above the land, or at least has the right to exclude any entry into the air space above his land. He relies on the old Latin maxim, *cujus est solum ejus est usque ad coelum et ad inferos*, a colourful phrase often on the lips of lawyers since it was first coined by Accursius in Bologna in the 13th century. There are a number of cases in which the maxim has been used by English judges but an examination of those cases shows that they have all been concerned with structures attached to the adjoining land, such as overhanging buildings, signs or telegraph wires, and for their solution it has not been necessary for the judge to cast his eyes towards the heavens; he has been concerned with the rights of the owner in the air space immediately adjacent to the surface of the land.
>
> That an owner has certain rights in the air space above his land is well established by authority.

Following a reference to *Gifford v. Dent* Mr. Justice Griffiths discussed the judgment of McNair J. in *Kelsen.* He quoted the words used by McNair J. in reaching his final conclusion and then made this assessment relevant to that decision at p. 906:

> I very much doubt if in that passage McNair J was intending to hold that the plaintiff's rights in the air space continued to an unlimited height or "ad coelum" as counsel for the plaintiff submits. The point that the judge was considering was whether the sign was a trespass or a nuisance at the very low level at which it projected. This to my mind is clearly indicated by his reference to Winfield on Tort in which the text reads: ". . . it is submitted that trespass will be committed by [aircraft] to the air-space if they fly so low as to come within the area of ordinary user." The author in that passage is careful to limit the trespass to the height at which it is contemplated an owner might be expected to make use of the air space as a natural incident of the user of his land. If, however, the learned judge was by his reference to the Civil Aviation Act 1949, and his disapproval of the views of Lord Ellenborough in *Pickering v. Rudd*, indicating the opinion that the flight of an aircraft at whatever height constituted a trespass at common law, I must respectfully disagree.
>
> I do not wish to cast any doubts on the correctness of the decision on its own particular facts. It may be a sound and practical rule to regard any incursion into the air space at a height which may interfere with the ordinary user of the land as a trespass rather than a

> nuisance. Adjoining owners then know where they stand; they have no right to erect structures overhanging or passing over their neighbours' land and there is no room for argument whether they are thereby causing damage or annoyance to their neighbours about which there may be much room for argument and uncertainty. But wholly different considerations arise when considering the passage of aircraft at a height which in no way affects the user of the land.

Griffiths J. makes a valid distinction between permanent structures which interfere with air space and transient invasions by aircraft to demonstrate that differing considerations apply. At the same time, his remarks convey approval of the decision reached by McNair J. in *Kelsen*. In my view the approach he pursues is both reasonable and practical. Lord Wilberforce took the opportunity to trace the Latin maxim's origin and to attack its literal application in *Commr. for Ry. v. Valuer-General*, [1974] A.C. 328, [1973] 2 W.L.R. 1021, [1973] 3 All E.R. 268, [1972-73] A.L.R. 1209, [1973] 1 N.S.W.L.R. 1 (sub nom. *Commr. for Ry. (N.S.W.) v. Wynyard Hldg. Ltd.)* (Aus.). The maxim found its way into a dispute regarding the valuation of land for rating purposes. At pp. 351-52 (A.C.) Lord Wilberforce described the maxim as:

> so sweeping, unscientific and unpractical a doctrine is unlikely to appeal to the common law mind. At most the maxim is used as a statement, imprecise enough, of the extent of the rights, prima facie, of owners of land . . .

The criticism levelled at the Latin maxim by Lord Wilberforce and others no doubt influenced the reasoning of Griffiths J. in *Bernstein v. Skyviews*. Recognizing that the maxim must be given limited application, Griffiths J. conceived the idea of striking a "balance".

The quotation from the *Bernstein* case at p. 907, which appears in the reasons delivered by Monnin J.A. in *Air Can.* provides a reasonable test in determining the rights of a landlord to the air space above his land. He said:

> The problem is to balance the rights of an owner to enjoy the use of his land against the rights of the general public to take advantage of all that science now offers in the use of air space. This balance is in my judgment best struck in our present society by restricting the rights of an owner in the air space above his land to such height as is necessary for the ordinary use and enjoyment of his land and the structures on it, and declaring that above that height he has no greater rights in the air space than any other member of the public.

Fournier J. in *Lacroix* limited the landowner's rights to what he could possess and occupy. Griffiths J. in *Skyviews* took a broader view by recognizing the landowner's right to enjoy the use of air space above his land without limitation except as to height. Beyond the height necessary for the landowner's use, the air space becomes public domain.

The Supreme Court of the United States has also considered the landowner's rights in air space in *U.S. v. Causby*, 328 U.S. 256, 90 L. Ed. 1206, 66 S. Ct. 1062 (1946). While rejecting the Latin maxim as having no place in the modern world —

it preserved the landowner's rights to this extent at pp. 264-65 which, in my view, is consistent with the views of Griffiths J. in *Bernstein v. Skyviews*:

> The landowner owns at least as much of the space above the ground as he can occupy or use in connection with the land . . . The fact that he does not occupy it in any physical sense — by the erection of buildings and the like — is not material . . . While the owner does not in physical manner occupy that stratum of airspace or make use of it in the conventional sense, he does use it in somewhat the same sense that space left between buildings for the purpose of light and air is used. The superadjacent airspace at this low altitude is so close to the land that continuous invasions of it affect the use of the surface of the land itself. We think that the landowner, as an incident to his ownership, has a claim to it and that invasions of it are in the same category as invasions of the surface.

The two concepts which become apparent are firstly, that the courts will not give literal effect to the Latin maxim and secondly, the proper remedy for interference with a landowner's air space with a permanent fixture is in trespass as opposed to nuisance.

In my opinion, the balancing criterion formulated by Griffiths J. is a logical compromise to the rights of the landowner and the general public. It is a test I adopt. I view this test as saying a landowner is entitled to freedom from permanent structures which in any way impinge upon the actual or potential use and enjoyment of his land. The cross-arms constitute a low level intrusion which interferes with the appellant's potential, if not actual, use and enjoyment. This amounts to trespass.

For the sole purpose of comment I refer to the cases of *Woollerton & Wilson Ltd. v. Richard Costain Ltd.*, [1970] 1 W.L.R. 411, [1970] 1 All E.R. 483, and *Lewvest Ltd. v. Scotia Towers Ltd.* (1981), 19 R.P.R. 192, 10 C.E.L.R. 139, 126 D.L.R. 239 (Nfld. T.D.), where, in each instance, it was held that an overhanging crane used in the construction of a building trespassed a landowner's air space, notwithstanding that the cranes were not permanent intrusions. In light of the distinction now recognized in encroachment cases between nuisance and trespass my inclination would be to characterize the overhanging cranes as a nuisance.

I would allow the appeal and grant the appellants the declaratory relief sought by them. The appellant are entitled to costs throughout.

NOTES

1. Leave to appeal to the Supreme Court of Canada was refused: (1989) 94 A.R. 320 (note) (S.C.C.).

2. There is a surprise ending to this case. Following the dismissal of the application for leave to appeal, the Province of Alberta amended the *Hydro and Electric Energy Act*, R.S.A. 2000, C. H-16, subs. 37(3), (4). The Act now permits permit the type of airspace intrusions that were in issue in *Didow* and provides that no compensation or any other remedy is available to landowners. For the spirited legislative debate

surrounding this move, see *Alberta Hansard*, 2nd Sess., 22nd Leg. 414*ff*, and 1467*ff* (1990).

QUESTIONS

1. What rule governs the delimitation of a landowner's airspace rights according to *Didow*? What is the rationale of that rule?

2. What remedy did the plaintiff seek in this case? What would the effect of awarding damages have on the property rights of the parties?

3. In the factum filed by the respondent (Alberta Power Ltd.) the following is asserted:

> The Land Use By-Law for the Municipal District of Spirit River, within the which municipality the lands are located, provides for a minimum setback for buildings and structures of at least 134 feet from a municipal road. And a building is defined by the by-law as including "anything constructed or *placed* on, in, over or under land." Trees, hedges, shrubs, shelterbeds or closed fences must, according to the by-law, be located no closer than 50 feet from the right of way of a municipal road. [Emphasis in original at page 3, para 5; Appeal No. 86030788AC]

Should this by-law matter in determining the outcome of the case?

4. Watson owns a beach property. For the past year, he has been plagued by gliders who descend from the top of the escarpment and land on the beach, near or directly in front of his lot. He is quite concerned that some may land in his back yard (where his children frequently play). Many of the gliders do pass over his property and he is aware of at least one occasion in which one person did land in his backyard. What recourse, if any, would you recommend? What additional facts, if any, would you need to know?

(c) below the surface

Edwards v. Sims
24 S.W.2d 619 (Kentucky C.A., 1929)

[This celebrated case concerns the ownership of part of the Great Onyx Cave, which is (now) part of Mammoth Cave National Park in Kentucky. The Great Onyx cave was developed as a tourist attraction by one Edwards, on whose land the cave's mouth was located. However, part of the cave, approximately one-third, was directly below the lands of one Lee. The cave was several hundred feet below Lee's lands, and was inaccessible to him.

An action was commenced by Lee against Edwards for trespass. A preliminary issue arose as to whether a survey of the cave could be ordered. Could Edwards be compelled to allow entry onto his property so that a survey could be undertaken?]

Stanley J.:

. . . *Cujus est solum, ejus est usque ad coelum ad infer[ ]os* (to whomsoever the soil belongs, he owns also to the sky and to the depths), is an old maxim and rule. It is that the owner of realty, unless there has been a division of the estate, is entitled to the free and unfettered control of his own land above, upon and beneath the surface. So whatever is in a direct line between the surface of the land and the center of the earth belongs to the owner of the surface. Ordinarily that ownership cannot be interfered with or infringed by third persons . . . There are, however, certain limitations on the right of enjoyment of possession of all property, such as its use to the detriment or interference with a neighbor and burdens which it must bear in common with property of a like kind . . .

With this doctrine of ownership in mind, we approach the question as to whether a court of equity has a transcendent power to invade that right through its agents for the purpose of ascertaining the truth of a matter before it, which fact thus disclosed will determine certainly whether or not the owner is trespassing upon his neighbor's property. Our attention has not been called to any domestic case, nor have we found one, in which the question was determined either directly or by analogy. It seems to the court, however, that there can be little differentiation, so far as the matter now before us is concerned, between caves and mines. And as declared in 40 C. J. 947:

> A court of equity, however, has the inherent power, independent of statute, to compel a mine owner to permit an inspection of his works at the suit of a party who can show reasonable ground for suspicion that his lands are being trespassed upon through them, and may issue an injunction to permit such inspection.

There is some limitation upon this inherent power, such as that the person applying for such an inspection must show a *bona fide* claim and allege facts showing a necessity for the inspection and examination of the adverse party's property; and, of course, the party whose property is to be inspected must have had an opportunity to be heard in relation thereto. In the instant case it appears that these conditions were met . . .

We can see no difference in principle between the invasion of a mine on adjoining property to ascertain whether or not the minerals are being extracted from under the applicant's property and an inspection of this respondent's property through his cave to ascertain whether or not he is trespassing under this applicant's property . . .

Logan, J. (dissenting):

The majority opinion allows that to be done which will prove of incalculable injury to Edwards without benefiting Lee, who is asking that this injury be done. I must dissent from the majority opinion, confessing that I may not be able to show, by any legal precedent, that the opinion is wrong, yet having an abiding faith in my own judgment that it is wrong.

It deprives Edwards of rights which are valuable, and perhaps destroys the value of his property, upon the motion of one who may have no interest in that which it takes away, and who could not subject it to his dominion or make any use of it, if he should establish that which he seeks to establish in the suit wherein the survey is sought.

It sounds well in the majority opinion to tritely say that he who owns the surface of real estate, without reservation, owns from the center of the earth to the outmost sentinel of the solar system. The age-old statement, adhered to in the majority opinion as the law, in truth and fact, is not true now and never has been. I can subscribe to no doctrine which makes the owner of the surface also the owner of the atmosphere filling illimitable space. Neither can I subscribe to the doctrine that he who owns the surface is also the owner of the vacant spaces in the bowels of the earth.

The rule should be that he who owns the surface is the owner of everything that may be taken from the earth and used for his profit or happiness. Anything which he may take is thereby subjected to his dominion, and it may be well said that it belongs to him. I concede the soundness of that rule, which is supported by the cases cited in the majority opinion; but they have no application to the question before the court in this case. They relate mainly to mining rights; that is, to substances under the surface which the owner may subject to his dominion. But no man can bring up from the depths of the earth the Stygian darkness and make it serve his purposes; neither can he subject to his dominion the bottom of the ways in the caves on which visitors tread, and for these reasons the owner of the surface has no right in such a cave which the law should, or can, protect because he has nothing of value therein, unless, perchance, he owns an entrance into it and has subjected the subterranean passages to his dominion.

A cave or cavern should belong absolutely to him who owns its entrance, and this ownership should extend even to its utmost reaches if he has explored and connected these reaches with the entrance. When the surface owner has discovered a cave and prepared it for purposes of exhibition, no one ought to be allowed to disturb him in his dominion over that which he has conquered and subjected to his uses.

It is well enough to hang to our theories and ideas, but when there is an effort to apply old principles to present-day conditions, and they will not fit, then it becomes necessary for a readjustment, and principles and facts as they exist in this age must be made conformable. For these reasons the old sophistry that the owner of the surface of land is the owner of everything from zenith to nadir must be reformed, and the reason why a reformation is necessary is because the theory was never true in the past, but no occasion arose that required the testing of it. Man had no dominion over the air until recently, and, prior to his conquering the air, no one had any occasion to question the claim of the surface owner that the air above him was subject to his dominion. Naturally the air above him should be subject to his dominion in so far as the use of the space is necessary for his proper enjoyment of the surface, but further than that he has no right in it separate from that of the public at large. The true principle should be announced to the effect that a man who owns the surface, without reservation, owns not only the land itself, but everything upon, above, or under it which he may use for his profit or pleasure, and which he may subject to his dominion and control. But further than this his ownership cannot extend. It should not be held that he owns that which he cannot use and which is of no benefit to him, and which may be of benefit to others.

Shall a man be allowed to stop airplanes flying above his land because he owns the surface? He cannot subject the atmosphere through which they fly to his profit or pleasure; therefore, so long as airplanes do not injure him or interfere with the use of his property, he should be helpless to prevent their flying above his dominion. Should the waves that transmit intelligible sound through the atmosphere be allowed to pass over the lands of surface-owners? If they take nothing from him and in no way interfere with his profit or pleasure, he should be powerless to prevent their passage?

If it be a trespass to enter on the premises of the landowner, ownership meaning what the majority opinion holds that it means, the aviator who flies over the land of one who owns the surface, without his consent, is guilty of trespass as defined by the common law and is subject to fine or imprisonment, or both, in the discretion of a jury.

If he who owns the surface does not own and control the atmosphere above him, he does not own and control vacuity beneath the surface. He owns everything beneath the surface that he can subject to his profit or pleasure, but he owns nothing more. Therefore, let it be written that a man who owns land does, in truth and in fact, own everything from zenith to nadir, but only for the use that he can make of it for his profit or pleasure. He owns nothing which he cannot subject to his dominion.

In the light of these unannounced principles which ought to be the law in this modern age, let us give thought to the petitioner Edwards, his rights and his predicament, if that is done to him which the circuit judge has directed to be done. Edwards owns this cave through right of discovery, exploration, development, advertising, exhibition, and conquest. Men fought their way through the eternal darkness, into the mysterious and abysmal depths of the bowels of a groaning world to discover the theretofore unseen splendors of unknown natural scenic wonders. They were conquerors of fear, although now and then one of them, as did Floyd Collins, paid with his life, for his hardihood in adventuring into the regions where Charon with his boat had never before seen any but the spirits of the departed. They let themselves down by flimsy ropes into pits that seemed bottomless; they clung to scanty hand-holds as they skirted the brinks of precipices while the flickering flare of their flaming flambeaux disclosed no bottom to the yawning gulf beneath them; they waded through rushing torrents, not knowing what awaited them on the farther side; they climbed slippery steeps to find other levels; they wounded their bodies on stalagmites and stalactites and other curious and weird formations; they found chambers, star-studded and filled with scintillating light reflected by a phantasmagoria revealing fancied phantoms, and tapestry woven by the toiling gods in the dominion of Erebus; hunger and thirst, danger and deprivation could not stop them. Through days, weeks, months, and years — ever linking chamber with chamber, disclosing an underground land of enchantment, they continued their explorations; through the years they toiled connecting these wonders with the outside world through the entrance on the land of Edwards which he had discovered; through the years they toiled finding safe ways for those who might come to view what they had found and placed their seal upon. They knew nothing, and cared less, of who owned the surface above; they were in another world where no law forbade their footsteps. They created an underground kingdom where Gulliver's people may have lived or where Ayesha may have found the revolving column of fire in which to bathe meant eternal youth.

When the wonders were unfolded and the ways were made safe, then Edwards patiently, and again through the years, commenced the advertisement of his cave. First came one to see, then another, then two together, then small groups, then small crowds, then large crowds, and then the multitude. Edwards had seen his faith justified. The cave was his because he had made it what it was, and without what he had done it was nothing of value. The value is not in the black vacuum that the uninitiated call a cave. That which Edwards owns is something intangible and indefinable. It is his vision translated into a reality.

Then came the horse leach's daughters crying: "Give me," "give me." Then came the "surface men" crying, "I think this cave may run under my lands." They do not know they only "guess," but they seek to discover the secrets of Edwards so that they may harass him and take from him that which he has made his own. They have come to a court of equity and have asked that Edwards be forced to open his doors and his ways to them so that they may go in and despoil him; that they may lay his secrets bare so that others may follow their example and dig into the wonders which Edwards has made his own. What may be the result if they stop his ways? They destroy the cave, because those who visit it are they who give it value, and none will visit it when the ways are barred so that it may not be exhibited as a whole.

It may be that the law is as stated in the majority opinion of the court, but equity, according to my judgment, should not destroy that which belongs to one man when he at whose behest the destruction is visited, although with some legal right, is not benefited thereby. Any ruling by a court which brings great and irreparable injury to a party is erroneous.

For these reasons I dissent from the majority opinion.

Appeal dismissed.

QUESTIONS

1. According to the majority in *Edwards v. Sims*, what rule governs the ownership of the subsurface?

2. What set of rules are argued for in the dissenting opinion? What underlying justifications are advanced by Logan J.?

3. Does it make sense to adopt different rules for ownership of airspace and subsurface rights?

(d) an economic perspective

Private property is supposed to be consonant with economically efficient resource allocation. The pursuit of efficiency can thus be used as a measure of the efficacy of property rules. Are the rules governing airspace and subsurface rights efficient?

Over the last 50 years or so, considerable attention has been paid to the interplay between law and economics. There is now a wealth of writing on this subject and congeries of thought on the subject. Neil Duxbury warns that,

> Today, law and economics is a subject over which controversy and confusion reigns. Defining the subject is like trying to eat spaghetti with a spoon. Law and economics can be positive, normative, neoclassical, institutional, Austrian — quite simply the subject is weighed down by a multitude of competing methodologies and perspectives which are not always easily distinguishable.

N. Duxbury, *Patterns of American Jurisprudence* (New York: O.U.P., 1995) at 314. See generally N. Mercuro and S.G. Medema, *Economics and the Law: From Posner to Post-Modernism* (Princeton: Princeton U.P., 1997).

Law and economics can provide useful tools for the assessment of property law, as this section of the casebook will endeavour to demonstrate. However, a problem that has sometimes attended this kind of interdisciplinary analysis concerns the different conceptions of property used by economists and lawyers. As Cole and Grossman explain:

> There are few, if any, concepts in economics more fundamental than "property rights." Most elementary economics texts make the point, often early in the book, that a system of property rights "forms the basis for all market exchange" and that the allocation of property rights in society affects the efficiency of resource use.
>
> More generally, assumptions of well-defined property rights underlie all theoretical and empirical research about functioning markets. The literature further assumes that when rights are not clearly defined, market failures result. The meaning of property rights is, thus, fundamental to the language of economics.
>
> Given the importance of property "rights" in economics, it might be expected that there would be some consensus in economic theory about what property "rights" *are*. But no such consensus appears to exist. In fact, property "rights" are defined variously and inconsistently in the economics literature. Moreover, the definitions offered by economists sometimes are distinctly at odds with the conventional understandings of legal scholars and the legal profession.

Cole & Grossman, "The Meaning of Property 'Rights': Law vs. Economics", 78 Land Econ. 317 (2002) at 317.

Arguably the most influential economist in this field is Ronald Coase. In a celebrated article, "The Problem of Social Cost", 3 J. of L. and Econ. 1 (1960) (reputed to be the most cited American law review article of all time), Professor Coase described what later became known as the Coase theorem. The theorem is designed to show that efficient resource use can occur regardless of how the law initially determines ownership rights. It is, in essence, a liberal or libertarian perspective: as long as smooth bargaining processes are in place, any state allocation of entitlements will be adjusted by private parties to produce an economically efficient allotment. The proviso that frictionless bargaining occur is an important one, and will be discussed later on. For now, let us focus on the central feature of the theorem.

I refer to the term "efficiency" here to mean the result of an allocation — whether non-consensual or through an agreed exchange — from A to B, the result of which is to benefit B to a greater extent than a detriment is suffered by A. The type of cost-benefit approach is commonly referred to as a Kaldor-Hicks measure of efficiency. For a more detailed, yet highly accessible explanation of Kaldor-Hicks and other conceptions of efficiency, see F.H. Stephen, *The Economics of the Law* (Ames, Ia: Iowa State U.P., 1989) at 57-62.

Many articulations of the theorem exist: I have offered a very general one above. Bottomley and Parker describe the theorem in these terms:

> At its simplest, the Coase theorem maintains that, in the absence of transaction costs, an efficient allocation of resources will result, irrespective of legal rules; that is, irrespective of which party is assigned the property right in a situation of conflicting uses.

S. Bottomley and S. Parker, *Law in Context,* 2nd ed. (Annandale, N.S.W.: Federation Pr., 1997) at 300. For an introduction to the fundamentals of law and economics and its relevance to the study of law, see *ibid.* at ch. 11, *passim.*

Here is Richard Posner's definition:

> [I]f transactions are costless, the initial assignment of a property right will not affect the ultimate use of the property.

R.A. Posner, *Economic Analysis of Law*, 5th ed. (New York: Aspen Law & Business,1998) at 8.

At first glance, Coase's point seems banal. What he appears to be saying is that property will wind up in the hands of the party that values it most. Big deal: this is merely the backbone concept of welfare economics. However, an example may help to show the explanatory potential of the Coase theorem.

In the English case of *Sturges v. Bridgman* (1879) 11 Ch. D. 852 (C.A.) an action in nuisance was brought by a doctor against a confectioner, whose business was adjacent to the medical office. In short, it was complained that the noise caused by the confectioner's machines seriously interfered with the use of the doctor's consultation room.

In the end, the doctor won. However, as Coase observed, the doctor could have been induced to forego this court-awarded entitlement for a fee. If the confectioner would be better off by paying enough to cover the doctor's losses, the confectioner would be wise to make such an offer. If the confectioner had won the case, and the relative values remained the same (i.e., the confectioner valued the right to make noise more than the doctor valued that particular quiet space), then a court outcome that favoured the confectioner would not likely be altered by agreement. Likewise, on the reverse set of facts, and assuming smooth bargaining, the doctor would either retain the right to use the consultation room as is (if he won) or would buy that right (if he had lost the case).

In brief, while one might initially think that it was for the courts to decide which activity is to be allowed and which must stop, the Coase theorem claims that in a perfect bargaining environment that is not the end of the matter: the parties will find the efficient outcome no matter what the court decides.

Let us now return to the proviso recognised by the theorem, but pushed to the side so far in this discussion — the assumption of easy bargaining or zero transaction costs. If transaction costs are non-existent or low, the theorem works. The term transaction costs was initially used to refer to costs associated with striking bargains. To know just how much to pay for a commodity typically requires research. If you have had the misfortune to enter into the used car market, you may be aware of the time, energy and money that must be expended to avoid being ripped off. In complex transactions there will usually be conveyancing and legal fees. Where the right to a commodity is in dispute, clearing up uncertainty produces an additional financial burden.

More generally, not all bargains that seem sensible on paper will come to fruition. For one thing, a sufficiently constituted market must exist. That element was probably not present in *Edwards v. Sims*. There, Edwards could bargain with Lee and no one else. (This is referred to as a bilateral monopoly.) What if their personal enmity was so great that it obstructed the forming of a mutually satisfactory bargain? (See generally P.H. Huang, "Reasons With Passions: Emotions and Intentions in Property Rights", 79 Or.L.Rev. 435 (2000).) Conversely, there may be too many parties: suppose for example, that a power company emits pollutants that adversely affect an entire town. Assume also that local residents might well be in a position to sue the company and could perhaps obtain an injunction preventing continued contamination. It might be more valuable to the power company to continue production, even if this meant buying out all of the potential claimants. However, what if one resident decides to hold out? (For a situation where, miraculously, a bargain was struck on these facts, see G. Parchomovsky & P. Siegelman, "Selling Maybury: Communities and Individuals in Law and Economics": online: <http://ssrn.com/abstract_id=405081>.)

Since Coase's breakthrough work, attention has increasingly turned to the types of factors that interfere with deal-making. Allusion has already been made to the problems of hold-outs, and bilateral monopolies; these are not the only impediments. For instance, it is assumed in the theorem that the initial allocation is itself a neutral event. In other words, apart from the obvious fact that the party given the entitlement is better off as a result, the likelihood of a subsequent bargain being struck is not otherwise affected. However, empirical studies into the economic behaviour of owners suggest the presence of what is referred to as the "endowment effect" (sometimes called the ask/offer problem) that can affect subsequent strategic conduct. The premise here is that the monetary value placed on a given object by a person is affected by whether or not one currently owns that object. The theory of the endowment effect posits that a party is likely to ask more for an item if currently held, than one would be willing to pay to acquire that same item.

Consider the study undertaken by Jack Knetsch several years ago: J.L. Knetsch, "The Endowment Effect and Evidence of Nonreversible Indifference Curves", 79 Am. Econ. Rev. 1277 (1989). Subjects were divided into three groups: they were given either (i) a candy bar, (ii) a mug, or (iii) no initial allocation. The candy people were then asked if they wished to swap for the mug; the mug people were likewise given a chance to exchange. Those with no initial entitlement were simply asked to select one or the other of the items. Here are the results:

	Proportion Favoring (in Percent)		
Group	Mug over Candy	Candy Over Mug	N
1. Give up mug to obtain candy	89	11	76
2. Give up candy to obtain mug	10	90	87
3. No initial entitlement	56	44	55

It is sometimes thought that the endowment effect is no more than the manifestation of the desire of people to make a good bargain. "By cheap and sell dear" is an age-old expression. However, the study described above suggests that something more subtle is also involved. The test subjects were not asked to bargain, only to accept an exchange or not. Both the candy and the mug groups wished to maintain the *status quo*. See also R. Korobkin, "The Endowment and Legal Analysis" online: <http://ssrn.com/abstract_id=326360>. In sum, the initial court allocation is not neutral; it can influence subsequent bargaining conduct.

Let us now return to the two cases presented on spatial dimensions: *Didow* and *Edwards v. Sims* to see what a Coasean analysis can tell us about efficiency. According to Coase, assuming nil transaction costs, it should not matter who won these court cases: the judicial resolution is just the starting point for negotiations, and will not dictate who winds up with the disputed property right.

To test the theorem in relation to airspace disputes, we need to insert some financial information. In *Didow,* the problem was that power poles had been placed too closely to private property, with the result that they arguably invaded private airspace. Assume that the least costly response of the power company, acting on its own, is to dig up and move all the posts along the farm's perimeter, at a total cost of $32,000. (Or that it could bury the wires for the same cost.) Assume also that the airspace is essentially of little value to the farmer. What happens if the power company wins? What happens if the farmer wins?

Assume now that the farmer wishes to protect against the effects that the proximate exposure of electricity may have on his/her livestock. Accordingly, the farmer is willing to pay $40,000 to install appropriate insulation, but no more. Again, what if the farmer wins? What if the power company wins?

These examples assume that the problem affects only the two parties engaged in the lawsuit. However, we know from the case report that "tens of thousands of transmission lines across Alberta occupy private property." Does that affect the applicability of the Coase theorem? Is the only difference that the monetary values will be much higher?

Consider these hypothetical facts: the lowest cost of abating all of these thousands of airspace trespasses is $3 million. The total value to all of the affected farmers is minimal (say, $100,000). We should probably also know the extent of the power companies available resources. Let us say that, all things considered, they could pay $1 million to effect the necessary changes. Its preference as to what it can do is therefore constrained by this ceiling. Will the theorem still hold (i.e., will the ultimate usage be the same regardless of the legal outcome)? (The same exercise can be carried out by supplementing the facts of *Edwards v. Sims* with hypothetical values: see B. Ziff, *Principles of Property Law*, 3rd ed. (Toronto: Carswell, 2000) at 91*ff*.)

Finally, assume that bargaining proves fruitless; no deal is struck. Where that is the outcome, the initial allocation becomes the final one. In other words, in instances where bargaining is not frictionless, the judicial resolution becomes rather important. What should that be? That question is addressed in the following extract, with reference to the case of *Edwards v. Sims*.

R.A. Epstein, "Holdouts, Externalities, and the Single Owner: One More Salute to Ronald Coase"
36 J. of L. & Econ. 553 (1993) at 563-7 [footnotes omitted]

... [D]oes the ownership of the surface carry with it the ownership of the land beneath and the sky above? Both of these issues have been subject to extensive debate in the common law, for if the surface owner has not taken possession of the underground minerals and space, why then should he be given ownership of it? The correct answer is that the single ownership of surface and minerals minimizes the holdout and externality problems that would otherwise exist. If the two estates were separate in their initial conception, then holdout problems would arise because the owner of the mineral estate would have to bargain with the owner of the surface in order to gain access to what existed below. At the same time, externality problems would arise because the working of the minerals could easily lead to subsidence of the soil above. The rule that starts both estates under the hands of the surface owner facilitates the voluntary transactions that permit the extraction of minerals and the creation of the necessary easements for the mining to go forward, even when (as is usually the case) the owner of the surface interest is not the party best able to exploit the minerals below ground.

Yet even here there are reasons to be cautious. One of the best illustrations of this problem arises with the well-known cases on the ownership of caves. On this point Ronald Coase, in a famous passage from his article on the Federal Communications Commission, showed great insight into the nature of the basic problem but then (oddly enough) understated the importance of transactions costs economics in working it to a final solution. Thus Coase writes,

> Whether a newly discovered cave belongs to the man who discovered it, the man on whose land the entrance to the cave is located, or the man who owns the surface under which the cave is situated is no doubt dependent on the law of property. But the law merely determines the person with whom it is necessary to make a contact to obtain the use of the cave. Whether the cave is used for storing bank records, as a natural gas reservoir, or for growing mushrooms depends, not on the law of property, but on whether the bank, the natural gas corporation, or the mushroom concern will pay the most in order to be able to use the cave.

Coase did not include tourist attractions on his list, and that omission is not insignificant. There are close substitutes for keeping records, storing natural gas, or growing mushrooms. But tourists have little interest in visiting bank vaults, gas tanks, or mushroom farms. But they do want to see the wonders of the caves. Ironically, the difficulty with this passage stems from Coase's failure to take into account the serious transactions costs problem that can creep into cases where two persons stand in a stark bilateral monopoly relationship to each other, as is the case with tourism.

To see why the problem of use is sensitive to the nature of the use, consider the three possibilities set out by Coase himself. One of these is to assign the interest in the cave to the surface owner. Frequently, however, the cave in question will lie beneath the land of two or more surface owners, while its entrance lies under the land of only one: indeed, for any problem to arise, such has to be the case, for otherwise the owner of the cave's mouth and the cave's interior would be the same person.

The fears of divided ownership under the rule that assigns the cave to the surface owner are confirmed in *Edwards v. Sims*, a case that involved a bitter dispute over the ownership of the Great Onyx Cave. The court took the conventional view and assigned (or recognized, depending on your jurisprudence) ownership rights to a cave so that each owned that portion of the cave that lay beneath his portion of the surface. The upshot was a fierce, protracted, and unresolvable holdout problem over the division of the spoils from the possible use of Lee's land, to which access could be gained only through Edwards' entryway. (Sims was the judge against whom *mandamus* was sought.) To make matters worse, prior to the suit, Edwards had conducted guided tours over the entire cave, including Lee's portion. Once it was decided after the fact that Lee owned this portion of the cave, the court had to struggle with a formula for determining the division of the tour proceeds previously earned, taking into account not only the respective value of the two portions of the cave but also the other inputs (advertising and cave improvements, for example) that helped generate the gross revenues. The lawsuit dragged on for about a dozen years, to the edification of no one.

One could envision a similar set of unfortunate disputes happening under the second of Coase's rules where the cave is awarded to the nonowner who discovers its mouth. The holdout arises if the landowner may block the cave owner from reaching the cave, with an outcome that would doubtless parallel that in the original case.

Given the enormous holdout problems that arise with two of Coase's three proposed solutions, it is no wonder that strong support has coalesced for the third of Coase's solutions—that which assigns the complete ownership and the use of the cave to the landowner who owns the mouth of the cave, regardless of where the cave lies or who has discovered it. Now the full cave is subject to a single owner, so there is no need to forge that single (but unattainable) transaction that allows the efficient exploitation of the underground space. As an added bonus, the entire restitution action that took place with the Great Onyx Cave could have been averted as well because single ownership ends the apportionment problem.

Ironically, the permutations in ownership are not exhausted by these three alternatives. A fourth possibility is to treat the cave as the subject to joint ownership. As with the first arrangement, the percentage interest of each surface owner is measured by the extent of the cave underneath his land, perhaps some allowance might be made for the location of the mouth of the cave. But the scheme differs from the first in that each party has an proportionate share of the whole cave instead of exclusive ownership of the fraction that lies beneath his land. This fourth solution overcomes the holdout problem by allowing the party with control over the cave mouth to use the whole cave without the consent of the other owner, who (by a bit of stretch) is then given a *pro rata* share of the net profits. The holdout problem is thus replaced by a serious accounting problem in setting the share of the gain. Indeed, since the owner of the interior space has no control over the utilization of the cave, a simple rental arrangement seems preferable to a share of the profits, based on the maxim that residual claims should follow effective control.

A fifth solution is, of course, to allow one party to take over the land of another, on payment of some compensation — which seems clearly preferable if the original allocation of rights takes either of the two forms just mentioned. In the end, the sixth solution did happen, which is that the state took by condemnation the interest of both Edwards and Lee, in order to operate the cave itself. But the case for the reallocation of property rights, with or without compensation, is not made on *a priori* grounds. In line with the central thesis of this article, the solution *eminent domain* makes sense only because the externality risk is small: the surface owner who cannot reach his land loses nothing but the possibility of holdout from the exchange, while the owner of the cave mouth loses the relatively small use value that the land has if the access value to the cave is not taken into account.

In the end, the presence of transactions costs appears to give us the clearest justification for the deviation from the traditional *ad inferos* rule that Edwards urged in supporting his claim to the cave. It minimizes transactions costs by avoiding a horrendous holdout problem that existed in the case or the complex accounting problems that arise with a system of forced joint ownership. But again, the preferred solution comes only at a positive cost. Thus, if the other surface owner wishes to mine out his own land, thereby destroying the integrity of the cave below, a serious externality problem would arise that could have been averted if the *ad inferos* rule continued to govern ownership of the cave. The superiority of assigning ownership of the cave to the owner of its (single) mouth thus rests on an empirical judgment that it is worth trading in a huge holdout problem for a far smaller externality problem. The concern with transactions costs, which best explains the *ad inferos* rule, also explains the desired exception to it. The assignment of rights in caves is far more critical to a successful outcome than Coase's analysis, which assumed low transactions costs, suggests . . .

QUESTIONS

1. In terms of economic efficiency, alone, which solution do you prefer?

2. In what ways, if at all, does the recognition of labour and occupancy claims collide with efficiency claims in a case such as *Edwards v. Sims*?

3. What allocational rule would be most conducive to the protection of the cave as a natural treasure?

4. Margaret Davies writes:

> The Coase theorem has been taken up in a fairly major way by the law and economics theorists at the University of Chicago (and their followers elsewhere). In general terms it is used as an argument against government regulation — this only adds to transaction costs and makes it more difficult to achieve the effective solution."

M. Davies, *Asking the Law Question*, 2nd ed. (Prymont, N.S.W.: L.B.C., 2002) at 163-4.

Indeed, this was at the heart of Coase's political agenda:

> Coase's policy prescription differs from the hitherto economic approach derived from Pigou, *The Economics of Welfare* (4th ed. 1932), which assumed that externalities could be corrected by imposing a tax on the externality creating activity equal to [its] cost. A first principle to be derived from the Coase paper ["The Problem of Social Cost"] is that, on the assumption that transactions between the affected parties are costless, allocative efficiency will be reached without government intervention and, indeed, whether or not the imposition of the externality is permitted under *private* law."

A.I. Ogus & C.G. Veljanovski, *Readings in the Economics of Law and Regulation* (Oxford: Clarendon Pr., 1984) at 83.

Does the Coase theorem, as qualified by the proviso and related matters, prove what Coase sought to prove?

REVIEW QUESTION

Given the Coase theorem, it really does not matter who won in the *Victoria Park Raceway* case. After all, either way the defendants or the plaintiff would have acquired a private property interest (in particular, a chose in action) to a "spectacle", which could then be transferred to the party that valued it most. Do you agree?

(e) mines and minerals

B.J. Barton, *Canadian Law of Mining* (Calgary: Canadian Institute of Resources Law, 1993) at 28, 40, 42-7, 65 [footnotes omitted]

The basic common law rule is that minerals except gold and silver are part of the land itself and belong *prima facie* to the owner of the soil, the owner of the land. More strictly, it is presumed that the land of which a proprietor of an estate has *seisin* includes the minerals in the land. Useful and accurate though this rule is, one must stress that it is a *prima facie* rule, not an absolute one. Indeed, exceptions to the rule are so frequent that the rule simply does not provide an accurate description of mineral ownership anywhere in Canada, except perhaps for the case of the Crown.

. . .

The policy of reserving or excepting minerals to the Crown on the occasion of a Crown grant or patent of land has been a major force in keeping minerals in public ownership in most parts of Canada. It has had enormous significance in shaping the political and legal environment for the development of mineral resources. It has ensured that there is relatively free access to minerals, on terms that the government has set. The policy has been supported by mineral land taxes aimed at returning private minerals to public ownership. Another supporting policy has been that of removing the right to a fee simple patent or Crown grant of mineral rights or mineral lands from the mining legislation. Lands and minerals are no longer completely alienated from the Crown. Instead, the mining lease is now the longest and most secure form of disposition of mineral rights that the mining legislation offers.

One might look for the origins of the policy of Crown reservation of minerals in the recognition by the common law of the royal prerogative to gold and silver, but its real crystallization, in most provinces and in the territories, occurred in the last decades of the nineteenth century and the first of the twentieth. (Ontario took a different path and did not implement a full reservation of minerals.) It is interesting to note that, at the same time, the same thing was happening elsewhere. In the United States, the move towards the reservation of minerals from patents made out of the public domain occurred in a piecemeal fashion at a later date, and did not become as widespread as in Canada until 1976. In Australia, the first general requirement for a reservation of minerals was enacted in 1884, and, by 1909, the requirement had spread to all states . . .

There is an enormous body of case law on the meaning of "mines" and "minerals." . . .

The most useful way to describe the modern law in a summary fashion is to propose the main rules and then to mention several secondary points. The three main principles are the vernacular test, the purposes and intentions test, and the exceptional circumstances test.

The Vernacular Test. In deciding whether in a particular case a substance is a "mineral," the true test is whether it was so regarded in the vernacular of miners, commercial people, and landowners at the time when the severance took place. This test has been accepted in every Canadian case but one, and it has prevailed on occasions where the other two main rules, below, have not been applied. The test has been invoked to prefer the vernacular meaning at the time of the transaction was the same as at the present, unless sufficient grounds to the contrary are given . . .

The Purposes and Intentions Test. In construing a reservation of mines and minerals, regard must be had not only to the words employed to describe the things reserved, but also to the leading purpose or object that the deed or statute embodies. "Mines" and "minerals" are not definite terms; they are susceptible to limitation or expansion according to the intention with which they are used. Evidence of such circumstances varies the *prima facie* meaning of the word "minerals." Circumstances including purposes of intentions of this kind have included the granting of land for agricultural purposes with the grantee covenanting to cultivate and the taking of land to build a railroad.

The Exceptional Occurrences Test. From this second rule derives a third, that the word "minerals" in a reservation does not include the ordinary rock of the district, but rather exceptional or rare substances, that is, exceptional in use, character, value, or occurrence. An interpretation that gives the common rock or subsoil to the mineral owner will usually defeat the purposes of the severance of ownership of surface and minerals . . .

In distinguishing "minerals" from ordinary rock, the courts avoid the geological meaning of the word and, in so doing, lean towards preservation of the surface. This tendency recurs in the context of the right of support. The "exceptional occurrence" test is on the decline and is perhaps best taken as an offshoot of the "purposes and intentions" test. Nevertheless, it has good authority behind it and it has not fallen into disuse . . .

The cases have also made the following secondary points:

1. The question of what is meant by "mineral" is a question of fact. The evidence taken is most important because the term is not definite and must be understood from the vernacular.

2. The same principles of construction are to be applied equally to deeds, other instruments, Crown grants, and a variety of different Acts.

3. The onus of establishing that a substance is within a reservation of minerals is always on the person alleging it to be within the reservation.

4. Whether a substance can be worked for the purpose of a profit can still be relevant to the meaning of "minerals." The purpose of profit may have a bearing upon the question of whether certain substances have been recognized as included in the term "minerals," but does not necessarily determine that they have been ordinarily understood to be so included.

   . . .

   It is doubtful whether the economics of working should absolutely control the question. The "profit" test is linked with the "exceptional occurrence" test and, like it, is best taken as a offshoot of the "purposes and intentions" test.

5. The meaning of "minerals" is not restricted by the fact that the substance cannot be worked except by destroying the surface and that there is no right to work in that manner. This need not contradict the "exceptional occurrence" test. Equally, the reservation of working rights appropriate to one kind of minerals does not prevent the word "minerals" from including other minerals.

6. If no limitations are imposed in the severance, "minerals" is to be construed in its widest sense. However, the cases are not consistent in deciding whether this *prima facie* wide sense is varied or narrowed by the addition of other specific substances. In some cases the *ejusdem generis* rule may apply. For example, "minerals'' in its very widest sense may include all things not animal or vegetable, but if it is used with "metals" or "springs of oil," it has been given a narrower interpretation. The phrase "all mines, minerals, petroleum, gas, coal and valuable stone" has been held to show that "minerals" is not used in its

> widest sense, but means exceptional substances only, and does not include sand and gravel. Similarly, the particular words "all mines and minerals, coal or valuable stone" have bene held to narrow the meaning of the word "minerals." On the other hand, "mines" has been held not to restrict "minerals" in the phrase "mines and minerals." The general words "all coal and other minerals" could not be construed *ejusdem generis* with coal without rendering them meaningless; it would be impossible to single out a genus of minerals to which the general words could be confined. Finally, the word minerals in "minerals, precious or base (other than coal)" was free from ambiguity and not restricted to metallic substances.

The principles of interpretation of reservations reviewed here are generally congruent with normal principles of construction of instruments. Although the means to the end have varied from time to time, the basic object of the leading cases seems always to have been to ascertain the intention of the parties by giving ordinary meanings to the words that they have used. While this general congruence with ordinary principles of construction prevails, the interpretation often words "mines and minerals" has led to the growth of special rules as well.

3. LATERAL BOUNDARIES

A boundary is an imaginary line drawn to mark the perimeter of a property. Naturally enough, the location of a plot of land has to be described in a conveyancing document. That delineation is called the legal description.

Where large tracts of land have been mapped, and a large cadastral image of the area has been created, land can be identified by reference to its placement within that cadastre. A township system of mapping under which land is parcelled into squares is the predominant method used in Canada. As John Weaver has noted, "[i]n North America, the grid prevailed; however, exact characteristics diverged." J.C. Weaver, *The Great Land Rush and the Making of the Modern World, 1650-1900* (Montreal & Kingston: McGill-Queen's U.P., 2003) at 232. Fortunately, many of the problems associated with the use of a grid system had been ironed out once it was time to undertake the township survey in the west:

> On the relatively flat Canadian prairies — that enormous latecomer to the great land rush — the township grids, fitted into a grand design of evenly spaced meridians and baselines, was unrolled at one pronouncement for the entire region." *Ibid.*

Under this system, a series of major vertical reference points called meridians are established. Three such meridians — numbered 4, 5 and 6 in the grand dominion land survey of the Prairies — are located in Alberta. A series of vertical lines run parallel to the meridians creating vertical zones called ranges. Horizontal "township lines" intersect the range lines. The boxes that result from these intersections are called townships. Each township is further divided into 36 sections. These sections can be further divided into quarter-sections and other legal subdivisions (or LSDs). So, for example, in the celebrated land registration case of *Turta v. C.P.R.* [1954]

S.C.R. 427, 1954 CarswellAlta 24, the land in dispute was described as: "The northwest quarter of section 17, Township 50, range 26, west of the fourth meridian".

When land is subdivided in irregular ways, locating a precise tract of land by reference to a basic grid is not easy. A survey plan may be created to allow, among other things, for ease of identification and description. For example, a residential property in Calgary may be situated on what is a small part of a township section. Once a plan is registered, that land may be described by reference to a numbered lot, found on a numbered block of land, as described on a numbered plan. Here is such a description:

Plan 2449JK
Block 7
The westerly 36 feet of Lot 14
Excepting thereout all mines and minerals

Another method is to describe the land in terms of metes and bounds. In short, this means to delineate the location of the perimeter from a known reference point. Consider for example these two legal descriptions:

Example 1:

All that tract, piece, or parcel of Land, situate, lying and being on Lot or Township Number Thirty Seven (37) bounded as follows, that is to say: — Commencing at the centre of the Bridge on MacDonald's Brook on the road leading in from the Hillsborough to Savage Harbour, thence running West thirty nine chains to the western boundary of Abraham VanGuelder Wiggins' land thence South along said boundary ten chains. Thence East sixty chains thence North to MacDonald's brook aforesaid, thence following said brook Westwardly to the place beginning. Containing Sixty Acres of land a little more or less. Also one half of the Marsh situated on the aforesaid Lot or Township Number Thirty Seven Formerly occupied by the late Donald MacDonald. Containing six Acres a little more or less.

See *Doyle v. MacDonald* 1999 CarswellPEI 66, [1999] 2 P.E.I.R. 195 (T.D.), affirmed 2001 CarswellPEI 99, 614 A.P.R. 125 (C.A.), leave to appeal to the S.C.C. refused 221 Nfld. & P.E.I.R. 361 (note), 2002 CarswellPEI 98, 2002 CarswellPEI 99 (S.C.C.).

Example 2:

ALL THAT CERTAIN lot, piece or parcel of land situate at Brookfield, in the County of Colchester and Province of Nova Scotia more particularly bounded and described as follows:

BEGINNING at a point on the western side of the Mountain or New Road, so-called, at a point where the norther boundary of land hereby conveyed intersects same;

> THENCE southerly along the western <boundary> of the said highway a distance of one hundred and twenty-one (121) rods to an iron pin set in said highway <boundary>;
>
> THENCE westerly to a stone drain, seventy-six (76) rods;
>
> THENCE northerly a distance of eighty-seven (87) rods to an iron pin in the Kennedy line;
>
> THENCE easterly along said Kennedy line a distance of eighty-four (84) rods to the western boundary of the first-mentioned highway and point of beginning.
>
> CONTAINING fifty-two (52) acres, more or less.

See *Metlin v. Kolstee* 2002 CarswellNS 252, 649 A.P.R. 27 (C.A.), leave to appeal to the S.C.C. dismissed 2003 CarswellNS 64, 2003 CarswellNS 65 (S.C.C.).

No matter what method of description is used, there is room for error. First of all, the legal description is not always controlling: it might not actually describe the property to be transferred. The description in a deed is one piece of evidence used to determine if it should be taken as an accurate reflection of the intention of the parties to the transfer. Extrinsic evidence, including the manner in which the parties occupied the land, may also be probative.

In addition, the legal description may itself be ambiguous; i.e., there is no internal coherence. Again, extrinsic evidence may aid in determining what was meant. Where the intention remains unclear, it can be resolved by favouring one descriptive element over another:

> . . . The general rule to find the intent where there is any ambiguity in the grant, is to give most effect to those things about which men are least liable to mistake. . . . On this principle the things usually called for in a grant, that is, the things by which the land granted is described, have been thus marshalled: *First*, the highest regard had to natural boundaries; *Secondly*, to lines actually run *and corners actually marked* at the time of the grant; *Thirdly*, if the lines and courses of an adjoining tract are called for, the lines will be extended to them, if they are sufficiently established; *Fourthly*, to courses and distances, giving preference to the one or the other according to circumstances . . .

McPherson et al. v. Cameron (1868) 7 N.S.R. 208 (C.A.), at 212 (*per* Dodd J.), cited with approval in *Metlin v. Kolstee* 2002 CarswellNS 252, 649 A.P.R. 27 (C.A.), leave to appeal to the S.C.C. dismissed 2003 CarswellNS 64, 2003 CarswellNS 65 (S.C.C.).

So, for example, consider a grant that describes a line between an adjacent property (the old Simpson place) and a natural monument (the willow tree east of the stream) as comprising 47 feet. In fact the distance is 52 feet. Presumptively, the ambiguity (is the line at the tree, or at 52 feet?) is resolved by disregarding the statement of distance. The natural monument is regarded as being more reliable.

As mentioned, a legal description needs a starting reference point. In Example 1 above, one must first locate Lot or township number 37 and then proceed to the centre of the bridge. A purpose-built monument may be laid into the ground, as is the norm when land is surveyed and a plan developed. Problems can arise, however, if the original monument cannot be located. There is also the danger that it might have been intentionally and wrongfully repositioned. Or a monument may be have been placed in error at the time of survey. For instance, in *Kristiansen v. Silverson* [1929] 3 W.W.R. 322 (Sask. C.A.), the Hudson's Bay Co. sold the north-west quarter of a section of land to A; shortly afterwards HBC sold the northeast quarter to B. Each grant referred to the appropriate township survey description, and also stated that the purchased land contained 160 acres more or less. The township plan referred to both quarters as containing 160, as did the surveyor's notes. However, the monument on the ground that marked the boundary between the two quarters had been improperly placed from the outset. As a result, the northwest quarter was enlarged by almost 20 acres. It was held, in accordance with established principle, that it is the placement of the monument on the ground that governs the size of the parcels.

When neighbours are unable to determine their boundary, a boundary can be agreed upon under the conventional line doctrine. The guiding principles were discussed by Nation J. in *Robertson v. Wallace* 33 R.P.R. (3d) 264, 2000 CarswellAlta 437 (Q.B.), which is reproduced below.

Of course, the proper location of the boundary line is only one problem that may affect neighbourly relations. A host of other grievances can arise. The rights of neighbours are to some extent policed by the law of torts. Prominent here is the tort of private nuisance, which regulates conflicting uses among nearby landowners. In general, nuisance law tries to strike a balance between the otherwise legitimate activities of nearby property owners, such as where the right of a confectioner to operate machinery clashes with the need of a neighbouring physician for peace and quiet: see *Sturges v. Bridgman* (1879) 11 Ch. D. 852 (C.A.), discussed above in relation to the Coase theorem. See further A.M. Linden, *Canadian Tort Law*, 7th ed. (Toronto: Butterworths, 2001) at 525*ff.*

In this section, several other features of the law governing neighbours are canvassed. These concern: trees growing on more than one property; fences, improvements accidentally made on adjoining land, and the right of support from adjacent and subjacent land. In Chapter 4 we will see that under the law of adverse possession the wrongful occupation of land can over time give rise to title to that property good against even the original paper-title holder.

(a) land bounded by land

Robertson v. Wallace
33 R.P.R. (3d) 264, 2000 CarswellAlta 437 (Q.B.)

Nation J.:

Introduction

In 1890, a Dominion Land Surveyor James MacMillan surveyed the West bank of the High River in s. 7-19-28-W4M. As he stood in the Prairie sun, he could hardly have anticipated what a keen interest would be shown more than one hundred years later in his field notes and his work. His survey was incorporated into the Township Plan of 1893. The West bank of the river was used in the N.E. 1/4 of s. 7 as the natural boundary to divide land owned by the Wallace family to the north and west, and the Robertson family to the south east. A dispute arose over the true boundary between the lands, as the river changed its course.

In 1994 Mr. Mintz surveyed the boundaries of the Wallace lands. The Registrar filed his plan and issued a new title to Mrs. Wallace, which on its face increased her lands by over 20 acres, and created overlapping titles to some lands. Mrs. Wallace sold her interest in s. 7 to the Matwychuk-Goodmans. When Mrs. Robertson's use of some land in section 7 was challenged by those purchasers in 1997, she brought this lawsuit. It deals with issues of accretion, avulsion, riparian rights and the true boundary between the lands . . .

Conventional Boundary Issues

a. Background

The law relating to conventional boundaries is enunciated by Ritchie, C.J. in *Grasett v. Carter* (1884), 10 S.C.R. 105 (S.C.C.) at p. 110 as follows:

> I think it is clear law, well established at any rate in the Lower Provinces where I came from, and I believe it must be established everywhere, that where there may be a doubt as to the exact true dividing line of two lots, and the parties meet together and then and there determine and agree on a line as being the dividing line of the two lots, and, upon the strength of that agreement and determination, and fixing of a conventional boundary, one of the parties builds to that line, the other party is estopped from denying that is the true dividing line between the two properties.

This principle has been enunciated and approved in several other cases: *Kaneen v. Mellish* (1922), 70 D.L.R. 327 (P.E.I. S.C.); *Piers v. Whiting*, [1923] 3 D.L.R. 879 (C.A.); *Phillips v. Montgomery* (1915), 43 N.B.R. 229 (C.A.); and *Flello v. Baird* an April 20, 1999 decision of the B.C.C.A. in action CA 024227 in Vancouver [reported (1999), 172 D.L.R. (4th) 741 (B.C. C.A.)]. The principles set out in these cases illustrate that the necessary elements to prove a conventional boundary are: there must be adjoining land owners, they must have a dispute or uncertainly about the location of the dividing line between the properties, they must agree on a division line, and then recognise it as a common boundary.

Conventional lines are discussed in some detail by N. Siebrasse, in an article entitled "The Doctrine of Conventional Lines" (1995), 44 University of New Brunswick Law Journal 229. The policy aim is to reduce the expense of determining boundaries and grew out of the historical reality of the Maritime provinces, where surveyors were not readily available, and few of the early descriptions of properties where based on actual surveys. It carries over today in these circumstances, and also where the doctrine of estoppel would operate, when parties have agreed on a boundary, and one party has relied on that agreement to build, or take steps, and it would be unfair to now insist on a proper or other determination of the boundary.

The recognition of the line can be oral, or in writing or by conduct, but the evidence to support the conventional line must be clear and definite. The onus of proof is on the party claiming ownership by virtue of the conventional line.

b. The Evidence

Both Mrs. Wallace and Mrs. Robertson testified that they gathered there was a dispute in their families about the location of the boundary between their respective parcels in the quarter. Mrs. Robertson was on the ranch periodically from the mid-1950s. She moved onto the ranch in 1957 with her first husband. She always had the understanding that the land east of the injunction fence was the Robertsons'. She has no direct knowledge of when the fence was built or by whom, but the Robertsons, since the 1950s, had grazed their cattle for a few months a year on the lands across the river from their other land holdings. She was aware of instances when the injunction fence was repaired by both the Wallaces and the Robertsons. The fence was used to divide the cattle: cattle of the Wallaces if found on the east side of the fence were pushed back, just as Robertson cattle that got on the west side of the fence were pushed back. Mrs. Robertson felt that around the time her husband passed away, the Wallaces intentionally placed cattle on the east side of the injunction fence, for periods from 1969 to 1973. The evidence of Catherine Robertson and Mr. Dale Pope, both related to Mrs. Robertson, confirmed Mrs. Robertson's understandings.

Mrs. Wallace testified that as a child she would cross the injunction fence to pick berries, swim in the river, and access a gravel pit through the disputed lands on the east side of the injunction fence. She lived on the ranch until 1954. She always understood the fence separated the cattle, and confirmed it was in her personal knowledge that members of her family and the Robertson family would at times fix the fence. She acknowledged an understanding of a dispute between her father and Mrs. Robertson's father about the boundary between the lands. She knew the Robertsons claimed land on the "Wallace" side of the river, but she did not know how much or the basis for their claim. She acknowledged her brother ran cattle to the west of the injunction fence from the 1950s to 1989, and she was aware he felt the

Robertson family owned the lands to the east of the fence. Mrs. Wallace did not reside on the quarter, and took title from her brother in 1989, when her mother's estate was settled. She was aware a surveyor did some work on the boundary in 1984 as her mother was upset about the Robertson cattle being on the disputed land. Mrs. Wallace testified her mother was in poor health and chose not to pursue boundary issues then.When she and her brother had appraisals of the quarter done in 1988, both acknowledged there was an issue about the boundary with the Robertsons. After 1989, Mrs. Wallace rented her land out to others who pastured their cattle there.

It is clear from the evidence that Mrs. Wallace and Mrs. Robertson never discussed with each other the fence or the boundary of their lands from the 1950s up to this lawsuit. It is also clear that the location of the injunction fence does not follow the course of the river as it was in 1890 or any subsequent time for its whole distance, it is conveniently placed to keep the Wallace cattle on the highland and away from the river, and the Robertson cattle on the lowland. It is also clear from the evidence that the flooding of the Highwood River means that fences closer to the river or in the flood plain will not last.

There is evidence to suggest a disagreement about the boundary. There is no direct evidence of an express agreement as to the boundary, if made it was not written, and no admissible oral evidence about it is available. The conduct of the parties may allow the court to infer an earlier agreement, however, the conduct must be clear to show the parties intended and implicitly agreed the fence should be the boundary.

The Plaintiff, Mrs. Robertson, bears the onus of proof. Without direct evidence of an agreement, I must carefully look at the evidence of conduct. The establishment of the fence, its maintenance, and use allows the Robertson cattle to use the east side of the fence. From that one can certainly infer an agreement on the use of the fence to separate the cattle in a geographically feasible way. However, on the evidence, I am not able to say this conduct and use of the land infers an agreement that the fence was to be the actual boundary between the lands. The acquiescence or conduct must be sufficient to establish the line was meant to be the boundary between the lands. I am left having heard all the evidence with the perception of an uneasy truce about the use of the lands, but I do not consider that evidence to prove on the balance of probabilities that there was an agreement to the boundary or ownership of lands . . .

QUESTION

In *Bea v. Robinson* 1977 CarswellOnt 435, 18 O.R. (2d) 12 (H.C.) Boland J. held that where the parties cannot determine the location of their boundary line because they have made no inquiries or other attempts to discover it, the boundary is not truly uncertain, and hence it cannot be set by agreement. Moreover, a conventional line boundary cannot be presumed to be the true line if there exists a registered instrument — such as a deed or plan — that contradicts the agreement. Consequently, a parole agreement entered into under these circumstances is an unenforceable attempt to convey land without the formal requirements of writing and registration.

In "The Doctrine of Conventional Lines" (1995) 44 U.N.B.L.J. 229, Norm Siebrasse takes issue with this holding, noting that it is contrary to established authority. The author states (at 262) that Boland J.'s ruling is "astounding, but it in no way reflects the law". As a matter of policy is the conclusion in *Bea v. Robinson* sound?

Koenig v. Goebel
[1998] 6 W.W.R. 56, 1998 CarswellSask 13 (Q.B.)

Klebuc J.: . . .

Facts

The appellants and the respondent own and live on adjoining residential properties. The subject of this appeal is a 30-40-year-old Manitoba Maple (the "Tree") which straddled the common boundary of their properties. Both owners claimed sole ownership of the Tree although neither produced any evidence as to whom, if anyone, had planted it, nor the basis on which it was allowed to grow. However, the evidence confirms that the appellants had looked after the Tree for years before and after the respondent had purchased her property.

In August of 1995, a large branch of the Tree broke during a windstorm thereby causing the appellants concern about the Tree's health. They had it inspected by Gilbert Schmidt, an arborist, who concluded that the Tree was unhealthy and required immediate removal for safety reasons. Without consulting the respondent, the appellants had the Tree removed by the firm which employed Mr. Schmidt. The respondent, in response, commenced an action in trespass for damages which resulted in the judgment under appeal.

At trial the respondent and her daughter testified that the Tree was healthy, but during cross-examination each admitted that she had not carefully inspected the Tree before its removal. Their evidence was supported in part by the evidence of Rick VanDuyvendyk, a person the trial judge declared to be an expert on trees. Mr. VanDuyvendyk testified that he had examined photographs of the Tree taken two or three years before the trial and the stump of the Tree which exhibited a lot of solid wood. Based on such examination, he concluded the Tree was healthy and did not constitute a hazard. He appraised the value of the Tree within a range of $9,400 and $14,000. In doing so, he relied on the *Guide for Plant Appraisal* published by the International Society of Arboriculture, 8th ed., 1992, a publication commonly used in appraising the value of trees.

The appellants and Mr. Schmidt testified that the Tree was unhealthy and needed to be removed. Mr. Wagner, also an arborist, supported their evidence. The learned trial judge clearly preferred the evidence of Mr. VanDuyvendyk and of the respondent and gave judgment for the $5,000 plus costs and interest.

The Law

The incidence of legal actions for the destruction of boundary trees (often termed "tree trespass") has increased with urbanization and the redevelopment of mature urban properties. Conflict and uncertainty as to the legal rights and obligations of adjoining property owners regarding boundary trees has impeded the resolution of such actions. Governing legislation is limited to *The Land Titles Act*, R.S.S. 1978, c. L-5. Beyond s. 2(k) thereof defining land to include trees and timber unless otherwise specifically excepted, the Act is silent on whether an owner has any rights over those portions of a boundary tree that stand on the adjoining property. Nor does it impose limitations on what an owner may do with those portions of a boundary tree that stand on his or her land. Therefore, guidance must be sought in the common law. The conflicting opinions expressed in the authorities and the increasing significance of "tree trespass," mandates a broader review of the governing principles than might otherwise be necessary to decide the issues in the appeal.

The precise location of a boundary tree subjected to "tree trespass" has influenced the decisions reached in many authorities. For ease of discussion, I have grouped boundary trees into three main categories solely on the criteria of location. The "Border Tree" category encompasses trees whose trunks are solely on one property at ground level, but whose roots encroach into an adjoining property, or whose canopy of branches invades the air space above an adjoining property. The "Straddle Tree" category includes trees whose trunks straddle the common boundary between adjoining properties at ground level. Included therein are three sub-categories: the first includes only those trees planted along a common boundary with the consent of the adjoining owners, or their predecessors in title ("Consensual Trees"). The second encompasses those trees planted on one property but whose trunks have expanded over a common boundary onto the adjoining property ("Straying Trees"). The third includes trees whose origins are unknown ("Voluntary Trees").

Border Trees

There is clear authority for the proposition that a property owner is legally entitled without notice to cut those branches and roots of a neighbour's Border Tree which extend onto his property or air space although such action may kill the tree. See *Graham v. Da Silva* (1984), 34 R.P.R. 264 (Ont. Co. Ct.); *British Columbia (Attorney General) v. Saanich Corp.*, [1921] 1 W.W.R. 471, 56 D.L.R. 482 (B.C. C.A.); *Anderson v. Skender* (1993), [1994] 1 W.W.R. 186 (B.C. C.A.); *Centrum Land Corp. v. Institute of Chartered Accountants of Ontario* (1988), 64 O.R. (2d) 289 (H.C.). However, the British Columbia Court of Appeal in *Anderson* at p. 188 made the following cautionary observation:

> . . . The view that a landholder has an absolute right to destroy a neighbour's border trees, by needless infliction of mortal injury on those portions which extend into the former's property, will perhaps be decided in another case after more complete argument, and I will for now say no more than that I think this view of the law ought not in the meantime to receive gratuitous support or encouragement.

None of these authorities, save the trial judge's decision in *Anderson*, suggest that the presence of roots or branches in or over a property gives its registered owner a proprietary interest in the neighbour's Border Tree. To the contrary, *Halsbury's Laws of England* (4th, Reissue) Vol. 4(1) (Butterworths: London, 1992) at para. 946 notes that the right to abate a nuisance does not entitle a property owner to "appropriate severed branches or fruit growing on overhanging branches" of his neighbour's tree. Nor is such owner entitled to injunctive relief absent damage to his property. See *Halsbury's,* para. 974.

Straddle Trees

The law concerning Straddle Trees (Consensual, Straying or Voluntary) is far from clear. One line of authority provides that such trees are the common property of the adjoining owners and neither owner may unilaterally remove the same beyond trimming back its branches and roots. The other line provides that location of a Straddle Tree does not create a common property interest, save for Consensual Straddle Trees. It posits that ownership of the tree is governed by who planted it and not its location. Further, any proprietary interest that may arise because of a tree's location produces no special right or obligation restricting an adjoining owner from removing any portion of a tree that encroaches on her or his property.

(i) Proprietary Interest Position

Authority for the proprietary interest position may be found in *British Columbia (Attorney General) v. Saanich Corp.,* and *Halsbury's Laws of England, supra.* In *Saanich*, Martin J.A. at p. 474 stated the governing principles as follows:

> . . . as it is admitted that the trunk stands partly upon each property then the two landowners are tenants in common of the tree, and it was held in *Waterman v. Soper* (1698), 1 Ld. Rayd. 737:
>
> > Two tenants in common of a tree, and one cuts the whole tree; though the other cannot have an action for the tree, yet he may have an action for the special damage by this cutting; as where one tenant in common destroys the whole flight of pigeons. . . .

In *Anderson v. Skender*, the trial judge made two findings of note: first, that the defendants had a 25 percent interest in the plaintiff's Border Trees because a major part of their root system encroached on their lands; secondly, the right of self help in abating a nuisance did not extend to materially injuring a neighbour's tree. The British Columbia Court of Appeal confirmed its decision in *Saanich* but rejected the trial judge's finding of a proprietary interest based on the location of roots and branches and his limitation on the right of self help. Regarding the latter, Taylor J.A. made the following observations at pp. 190 and 191:

> The law of nuisance is clear that an owner of land is entitled to cut branches or roots of a neighbour's trees which extend over the property line: *Lemmon v. Webb,* [1894] 3 Ch.

1 (C.A.); *Butler v. Standard Telephones & Cables Ltd.; McCarthy v. Standard Telephones & Cables Ltd.*, [1940] 1 K.B. 399; *McCombe v. Read*, [1955] 2 Q.B. 429; *Davey v. Harrow Corp.*, [1958] 1 Q.B. 60 (C.A.); *Morgan v. Khyatt*, [1964] 1 W.L.R. 475 (P.C.).

Mr. Justice McKenzie was of the view that this right of self-help does not extend to a cutting of stems, but we were referred to no authority on this point. The case of *Loverock v. Webb* (1921), 30 B.C.R. 327 (C.A.), does not support that view. As I have said, we need not decide whether the right of self-help extends to a cutting likely to prove fatal to a border tree where, with the application of proper arboricultural technique, the tree could have been saved. The point is an important one, and I mention it again, because if the law were such that a landholder is entitled to destroy a neighbour's border trees at will by assaulting any wood or root projecting over the line, many such trees could be killed with impunity by neighbours seeking to improve their light or view, or for any other reason to be rid of them, and much of the remaining border screening in residential areas might in this way be destroyed. . . .

Since the Skenders did not restrict their assault on the trees to that which could be sanctioned on any view of the law of nuisance - because they went over the property line in severing two - their liability in trespass is undeniable. It is only in respect to the third tree that they did not trespass.

In summary, these authorities conclude that only Straddle Trees lead to a proprietary interest of a kind that prohibits an adjoining property owner from cutting down any portion of their trunks without the consent of the adjoining property owner. Theoretically the authorities impose a unilateral, unregistered easement over the adjoining properties. Otherwise, the right to self help in abating a nuisance is unrestricted provided the self help is accomplished without trespassing on the adjoining property.

(ii) Non-Proprietary Position

Authority for the position that a Straddle Tree is not the common property of the adjoining property owners (unless it is a Consensual Straddle Tree) is to be found in *Centrum Land Corp. v. Institute of Chartered Accountants of Ontario et al., supra*; *Graham v. Da Silva, supra*; and *Bottan v. Richmond Hill (Town)*, (May 25, 1995), Doc. Toronto 910CQ-2502 (Ont. Gen. Div.).

The facts in *Centrum* are similar to those before me. There the plaintiff Centrum and the defendant (the "Institute") owned adjoining properties. Along the common boundary line grew trees that had not been planted by mutual consent of the adjoining owners or their predecessors in title. The Institute intended to remove completely several trees and to cut back the roots and branches of others that encroached onto its property to the extent that some of them would die. Centrum applied for a permanent injunction restraining the Institute from taking such steps on the basis that it had a proprietary interest in the subject trees of a nature which prohibited the Institute from damaging the same. The Ontario High Court of Justice rejected Centrum's claim of a proprietary interest in the trees sufficient to restrain the Institute from damaging or removing them. It dismissed the application. The court refused to follow *Peters v. Dodge* (1910), 45 N.S.R. 33 (C.A.).

At p. 296, Arbour J. made the following observations:

Although there is a dearth of authorities on the proprietary rights of landowners with respect to trees growing on boundary lines, the respective rights of adjacent landowners are fairly well established in so far as trees growing on their respective properties are concerned. It would seem to me to be a fair analysis of the problem in this case to examine the situation that the Institute would be in if the trees which will be affected by its construction project were entirely on Centrum's land. *To put it another way, I would have thought that Centrum could have no greater right in the trees on the boundary line than it would have if the trees were completely on its land.* (Emphasis added.)

If this were the case, the Institute would clearly be entitled, in my opinion, to remove any branches or roots of such trees which interfere with the peaceful enjoyment of its property, including the right to build on it within an inch of the boundary line: see 4 Hals., 4th ed., pp. 381-3, paras. 873-874. If the tree is so close to the boundary line that the cutting back of the offending branches or roots is likely to jeopardize the ability of the tree to survive the cut, I was referred to no authority which suggests that the adjacent owner must then suffer the nuisance. I agree with the disposition of *Graham v. Da Silva* which imposed no such limitations in similar circumstances.

It goes without saying that if the trees in this case were located entirely on the Institute's land, they could be removed by the Institute despite their shade and ornamental value to the plaintiff's tenant. If the trees were located entirely on Centrum's land, the Institute could remove any part of them which would interfere with its construction plans. Absent the provisions of the *Trees Act*, which clearly do not apply in this case, I cannot see how the situation can be different merely because the trees happen to grow on the boundary line. . . .

The Saskatchewan Position . . .

The authors in *Halsbury's Laws of England*, *supra*, at p. 425, para. 945 conclude that the ownership of a tree growing on a boundary is a question of fact to be determined on the facts of each case and that ownership is *prima facie* with the property owner who planted the tree. While they concede that Straddle Trees have been held to be the common property of the adjoining landowners, they suggest the "better view is that such a tree remains in the ownership of the land on which it was planted, even when the trunk, roots and branches extend into the adjoining property." I agree.

For the appeal, I conclude the applicable law is as follows:

(1) Where the identity of the owner who planted the tree is discernible by direct evidence, or by inference, ownership of the tree is *prima facie* in that owner and his or her successors and assigns. Otherwise s. 2(k) of *The Land Titles Act* applies.

(2) A Straddle Tree planted with the agreement of adjoining property owners is owned in common by them and each has a proprietary interest in the whole of the tree that may be protected by registration of a caveat. Where it is not determinable which owner planted the tree or permitted it to grow initially on his or her property, ownership in common will not be implied.

(3) If the branches or roots of a tree on A's land encroach onto B's land, B may cut back the offending branches or roots, even if the ability of the tree to survive is jeopardized.

(4) A tree located on A's land that encroaches onto B's land constitutes a nuisance which B may abate by cutting any part of the tree (roots or branches) that encroach on B's land. This right of self help does not entitle B to trespass on A's land.

Neither party raised the issue of whether an adjoining property owner owes a duty of care to the other owner regarding a boundary tree that is sufficient to found an action in negligence. Therefore, I will not deal with the issue . . .

Analysis

There is some evidence which supports the trial judge's finding that the Tree "was in full foliage, healthy, and not in any sense dangerous." I must accept his finding.

The trial judge found the Tree to be the property of the respondent. The evidence is insufficient evidence to support his conclusion. Nor did he apply the law correctly to the limited facts he found. However, whether the respondent solely or partially owned the Tree is immaterial because her claim is for damages based on the appellants' trespass. I therefore will not dwell on the issue.

The evidence clearly establishes that a substantial portion of the Tree's trunk, roots and branches encroached on the appellants' property and air space. Since there is no evidence of the Tree being a Consensual Straddle Tree, the applicants had the right to remove those portions that stood on or over their land on two grounds, even though such action might kill the Tree. First, they were the legal owners of such parts by virtue of s. 2(k) of *The Land Titles Act* and therefore entitled to deal with the same. Secondly, such parts comprised a nuisance (to the extent the respondent had any interest therein) which they were entitled to abate. However, either right did not entitle them or their agents to enter upon the respondent's property without her consent and remove the entire Tree. By doing so they committed the tort of trespass and became liable for consequential damages . . .

But for the written request by the parties that I re-assess damages should I conclude that the learned trial judge's assessment is not sustainable, I would have referred the matter to the Provincial Court. To avoid the significant cost and inconvenience associated with a new trial over a small amount, I have complied with their request despite the apparent difficulties. The evidence strongly suggests that the Tree could not have survived had the appellants restricted their activities to their property. Consequently, it is difficult to assess damages for the loss of the benefit of shade, the aesthetic joy provided by the Tree or the loss in the market value of the respondent's property, if any. In my opinion, the respondent is entitled to restorative costs of $642 associated with planting a small replacement tree plus $900 for the loss of the benefit of shade, aesthetic joy, diminution of property value and the cost of removing the stump. No punitive damages are awarded because the appellants' behaviour was not so reprehensible that it deserved punishment.

In summary, the judgment of the trial judge is set aside and an award of damages in favour of the respondent for the sum of $1,542 substituted therefor. No costs are awarded to either party.

QUESTIONS AND COMMENTS

1. In many jurisdictions, legislation regulates fences shared by neighbours. In Ontario, for example, sections 3 and 4 of the *Line Fences Act*, R.S.O. 1990, c. L.17, provides:

> 3. An owner of land may construct and maintain a fence to mark the boundary between the owner's land and adjoining lands.
>
> 4. (1) Where the owner of any land desires to have a fence constructed to mark the boundary between the owner's land and the land of an adjoining owner, or where such a fence exists, to have it repaired or reconstructed and where the owner has not entered into a written agreement with the adjoining owner for sharing the costs of the construction, reconstruction or repair, as the case may be, of such fence, the owner may notify in the prescribed form the clerk of the local municipality in which the land is situate that the owner desires fence-viewers to view and arbitrate as to what portion of the fence each owner shall construct, reconstruct or repair and maintain and keep up.

The Ontario Act contains elaborate procedures for arbitration and review. Compare the keystone provisions of the Alberta *Line Fence Act*, R.S.A. 2000, c. L-13:

> 2.(1) When 2 owners or occupiers of adjoining parcels of land desire to erect a line or boundary fence between the adjoining parcels for the common advantage of both of them they shall bear the expense of the erection, maintenance and repair of the fence in equal shares.
>
> (2) If the owner or occupier of a parcel of land erects a line or boundary fence between the land and an adjoining parcel of land the owner or occupier of the adjoining parcel of land shall, as soon as that owner or occupier receives any benefit or advantage from the line or boundary fence by the enclosure of that owner's or occupier's land or any portion of it or otherwise, pay to the first mentioned owner or occupier a just proportion of the then value of the line or boundary fence and afterwards the expense of maintaining and repairing the fence shall be borne by the adjoining owners or occupiers in equal shares.
>
> 3.(1) If adjoining owners or occupiers of land disagree as to

(a) the quality of the fence that has been or that is to be erected,

(b) the proportion of the value of the fence to be borne by the parties to the dispute,

(c) the amount of the expense incurred in erecting, maintaining or repairing the fence,

(d) the proper location of a proposed or existing line or boundary fence,

(e) the just proportion of a line fence that each owner or occupier should make or put in repair, or

(f) the amount that an owner or occupier should pay as compensation to the other for making or keeping in repair any fence, they shall each appoint an arbitrator to determine the matter in dispute.

(2) The arbitrators shall, after first giving the parties reasonable notice of the time and place where they intend to meet for the purpose of hearing and determining the matter in dispute, attend at the time and place and hear the parties and their witnesses and make their award in respect of all matters in dispute.

(3) If either of the parties refuses or omits to appoint an arbitrator within 48 hours after a demand is made in writing on the party to do so by the other party, that other party may apply to a justice of the peace who, on being satisfied by the oath of a credible witness that the demand has been made and not complied with, may appoint an arbitrator for the person refusing or omitting to appoint, and the arbitrator appointed shall proceed and act and all steps shall be taken as provided in this section as if the arbitrator had been appointed by the person refusing or omitting to appoint.

(4) When the arbitrators are unable to agree, they shall appoint an umpire who shall make an award as to the matter in dispute.

Which approach is preferable?

2. Subsection 37(1) of the *Conveyancing and Law of Property Act*, R.S.O. 1990, c. C.34 provides:

Where a person makes lasting improvements on land under the belief that it is the person's own, the person or the person's assigns are entitled to a lien upon it to the extent of the amount by which its value is enhanced by the improvements, or are entitled or may be required to retain the land if the Ontario Court (General Division) is of opinion or requires that this should be done, according as may under all circumstances of the case be most just, making compensation for the land, if retained, as the court directs.

It has been held that the Ontario provision encompasses mistakes arising from an error in the title, as well as where the physical location of the boundary is erroneously determined: see further the review of authorities in *Re Worthington et al.* 24 O.R. (2d) 646, 1979 CarswellOnt 1368 (Co. Ct.).

3. Under general principles of tort, the wrongful entry onto the land of another is a trespass, and it matters not that the defendant believed he or she was entitled to enter.

In other words a mistake, however honest and reasonable it might be, is no defence to an action. That being so, why does the above provision allow the wrongdoer to recover against the land owner?

4. Consider this comparative analysis found in U. Mattei, *Basic Principles of Property Law: A Comparative Legal and Economic Introduction* (Westport Conn: Greenwood Pr., 2000) at 134-5:

> A direct consequence of the owner's sovereignty over his or her property should be that in case someone builds or encroaches in any other way across the boundaries of the owner's land, the latter has a choice between keeping the encroachment (in case he or she values it) or forcing the former to remove the encroachment. This logical and strict application of the right to exclude others is, however, severely limited by the need to consider the rights of the good-faith possessor as well as the need to avoid the unjustified enrichment of the owner against the builder.
>
> The Napoleonic Code, in principle (Article 555), grants the owner the power to make the choice. As usual, this followed by a number of legal systems, including the Italian (Article 936). In both the French and the Italian systems, if the owner opts to retain the building, he or she will owe the builder an indemnity which is calculated as the lower sum between the cost of the building and the increase in value of the land. If, however, the builder acted in good faith or the owner had knowledge of the building, both legal systems do not allow the owner to force the removal (in technical terms, they deny the *Ius tollendi*).
>
> In Germany, paragraph 946 of the BGB extends the owner's right onto whatever is "essentially incorporated" to the soil. Paragraph 94 considers buildings essential parts of the land. Paragraph 951 affords the builder an action of unjust enrichment when the owner retains the building. If, however, the owner makes use of Paragraph 1004 to protect the integrity of his or her land and to force the builder to remove the encroachment, nothing is due to the latter. Paragraph 1004 is not available against the good-faith possessor. In sum, German law reaches, albeit through a somewhat complex path, the same results as the Franco-Italian model.
>
> In common law, the property of the building is acquired by the owner of land, and there is no action of unjustified enrichment available in these cases. The doctrine of promissory estoppel, however, which protects reliance, may allow the remedy of reimbursement for the value of the building. In a number of American jurisdictions, moreover, special "improver statutes" may offer the good-faith builder an action of unjust enrichment.
>
> This brief description shows how we can observe a common core of Western law as far as the problem of the ownership of buildings on someone else's land is concerned. Through a regime that parties are completely free to negotiate away (default rules), legal systems tend to grant the right to the owner of land and at the same time to limit economic imbalance through a system of compensation to the builder. This is captured by the Latin expression *superficies solo caedit*. When it is correctly interpreted as a general principle, it is efficient because it clearly describes property rights and because it encourages the solution of any possible conflicts by means of direct negotiation. The default nature of such a regime introduces another important power of the land owner. He or she can transfer to someone else the right to keep constructions on his or her soil.

Blewman v. Wilkinson [1979] 2 N.Z.L.R. 208 (C.A.)

Cooke J.:

It has long been accepted that a landowner has a right to enjoy his own land in its natural state, unaffected by any act done by way of excavation on the adjacent or subjacent land. If and when an excavation which has interfered with the support of land by land causes damage by subsidence, the landowner for the time being has a right of action against the original excavator. Liability is strict in that negligence need not be proved. The leading New Zealand case is the Court of Appeal decision in *Byrne v. Judd* (1908) 27 N.Z.L.R. 1106 . . .

The present appeal from Jeffries J. raises the question whether the principle applies if the person excavating owned all the land at the date of the excavation but has since subdivided it. Can the owner for the time being of one of the lots in the subdivision sue the original excavator if the lot now subsides in consequence of the excavation?

The facts of the present case are not complicated. In 1964 the defendant subdivided some five acres of land owned by him at Paremata. The lot with which the case is concerned, lot 7, slopes down from the south to the north. To give access to rear sections the defendant had a right of way cut immediately below lot 7, so that the northern boundary of lot 7 was a bank about 9 to 12 fee high at its highest point. The subdivision was intended to be of good standard and in some respects the current local body requirements were exceeded. The defendant himself has his home there. He had competent professional advice, the subdivision being carried out for him by a well-known firm of consulting engineers and surveyors. The earthmoving contractors cut the bank at a batter of 1:2 (according to the Judge's finding) which at that time was considered a reasonable standard for the district. The bottom third of the bank was greywacke or at least some form of sandstone and has remained substantially stable as cut. Above that was clay with some sand in it, while the surface was a light layer of loam. According to expert evidence of the plaintiffs, this clay material is very susceptible to wind and rain erosion unless there is a good cover. It is important to emphasise that the case for the plaintiffs has not been based on any allegation of negligence in the design or construction of the subdivision or otherwise. It is interference with the natural right of support on which they rely.

After the earthworks and other necessary works had been carried out the subdivision was legally completed and lots were sold at auction in November 1964. The original purchaser of lot 7 held it until 1972 without building on it and then sold it to the plaintiffs. He was hardly ever at the property and apparently took little interest in it. During his ownership neighbours experienced quite a constant problem from the upper part of the bank falling away and blocking their drive. When the plaintiffs bought, the bank had still not been planted or given any form of artificial protection. In the cross-examination of the plaintiff Mr. Blewman there is the following passage:

What I want to put to you is that the bank line when you bought the property was in a state where it needed a crib wall as much then as it does now? — No doubt.

And indeed that was your view when you purchased? — It was expressed between the land agent and myself but it did not have to be done straight away.

At the time of the purchase it would have been possible to simply trim the bank up with a bit of shovel work to give an even bank and planted shrubs? — You could have done that, I guess.

Because of the state of the bank the plaintiffs decided not to construct a driveway on the top of the bank as they had once contemplated. Their house has been sited on a bench cut on the section to the south. At the date of the trial the plaintiffs had done nothing to retain or plant the bank but had watched it gradually erode until at least certain steps on the northern side of the house were in some jeopardy. Whether any action short of building a retaining wall would have been an effective long-term remedy is in dispute. Since the trial, so we were told from the Bar, the plaintiffs have had a retaining wall constructed. There is no doubt that, in the Judge's words, the top of the batter had eroded quite badly in a southern direction. It is not suggested that the weight of the house contributed to this result.

The Judge held that the plaintiffs had no cause of action, and they appeal. The immediately striking feature of the case is that from the time of its subdivision as a separate property this parcel of land has never enjoyed support from the soil removed in the cutting of the right of way. That has been patent for all to see. No previous case of similar facts has been discovered, but Mr. Gray relies on some observations of Lord Blackburn in *Dalton v. Angus* (1881) 6 App Cas 740, 808-809:

It is; I think, conclusively settled by the decision in this House in *Backhouse v. Bonami* 9 HLC 503 that the owner of land has a right to support from the adjoining soil; not a right to have the adjoining soil remain in its natural state (which right, if it existed, would be infringed as soon as any excavation was made in it); but a right to have the benefit of support, which is infringed as soon, and not till, damage is sustained in consequence of the withdrawal of that support.

This right is, I think, more properly described as a right of property, which the owner of the adjoining land is bound to respect, than as an easement, or a servitude *ne facias,* putting a restriction on the mode in which the neighbour is to use his land; but whether it is to be called by one name or the other is, I think, more a question as to words than as to things. And this is a right which, in the case of land, is given as of common right; it is not necessary either in pleading to allege, or in evidence to prove, any special origin for it; the burthen, both in pleading and in proof, is on those who deny its existence in the particular case. No doubt the right is suspended, or rather perhaps cannot be infringed, whilst the adjoining properties are in the lands of the same owner. He may dig pits on his own land, and suffer his own adjoining land to fall into those pits just as he pleases. When he severs the ownership and conveys a part of the land to another, he gives the person to whom it is conveyed (unless the contrary is expressed) not a right to complain of what has been already done, but a right to have the support in future. It is, I think, now settled that the conveyance may be on much terms as to prevent any such right arising (see *Rowbotham v. Wilson* 8 HLC 348; *Smith v. Darby* LR 7 QB 716; *Eadon v Jefcock* LR 7 Ex 379; *Aspden v. Seddon* LR 10 Ch 394).

The four cases cited by Lord Blackburn relate to such matters as the reservation on a conveyance of land of a right to work mines and let down the surface. They do not directly touch this case. As to the example of a man digging pits on his own land, Mr. Gray may possibly be right in his submission that Lord Blackburn meant that after severance a purchaser could sue for fresh subsidence caused by the old digging, but it is far from certain. Whatever the meaning of this perhaps rather oracular statement, it was an *obiter dictum* by Lord Blackburn. It has to be remembered also that even as to principles on one view more directly involved in the speeches in *Dalton v. Angus,* that case was not followed by our predecessor s in this Court in *Bognuda's* case. In the latter case it was held that a person excavating on his own land may owe a duty of care in respect of buildings on the adjacent land. The action was in fact against a contractor, but the judgments identified him with the adjoining owner by whom he was employed.

In *Petrofina Canada Ltd. v. Moneta Porcupine Mines Ltd.* (1969) 9 D.L.R. (3d) 225, 229, Laskin J.A., delivering the judgment of the Ontario Court of Appeal, appears to have thought that if a landowner mines on his own land and subsequently sells the surface only, the owner of the surface for the time being can recover for fresh subsidences caused by the old mine workings. Decisions of that Judge are entitled to great respect. But that judgment proceeded on the footing that the plaintiff knew nothing of the mines at the time of purchase. Nor was the Court called on to make any full investigation of the law, because the action failed for other reasons: namely that the weight of the plaintiffs plant and buses may well have caused the collapse and the heads of damages claimed were irrecoverable in any event . . .

On the main point, Mr. Gray's argument is not without some force. Presumably, in a typical *Byrne v. Judd* type of case if a neighbour was excavated, a purchaser may buy land manifestly threatened by the excavation (making whatever use he can of that risk in his negotiations with the vendor) and then sue the excavator when a subsidence occurs — subject only to the plaintiff's duty to act reasonably to mitigate his damages. From the purchaser's point of view it can be urged that it should be immaterial whether or not the excavation happens to have occurred before or after the initial severance of title. Such a situation has not arisen in any case cited to us from any jurisdiction. But my brother Somers has found some judicial dicta, to be mentioned in his judgment, which tend against the argument for the appellants.

While this Court is no doubt free to extend the *Byrne v. Judd* principle to such a situation, I think that two factors tell against doing so. First, New Zealand conditions. A great many urban subdivisions have taken place in steep or slopping terrain, with extensive earthworks. The idea of imposing strict liability on a subdividing owner when a subsidence occurs perhaps many years later, and not withstanding that he acted on proper professional advice at the time, is unattractive. Unless he or his agents can be shown to have been at fault it seems to me more just to leave the loss lying where it falls. Hillside subdivisions and the like are so typical in this country and slips and other subsidences such commonplace hazards that, unless fault can be demonstrated, a purchaser can fairly be expected to accept the risk. Insurance (if any) should be his concern.

Secondly it is important to stress the related point that when strict liability for depriving land of natural support by excavation on neighbouring land was established the law of negligence was in its infancy. In the era of such cases as *Dalton v. Angus* and *Byrne v. Judd* the general concept of duties of care was hardly known. The law regarding land use was expressed rather in terms of defined proprietary rights. Now the pervading tort of negligence extends to this field also, as witness the *Bognuda* and *Bowen* cases. In my opinion a subdividing owner *prima facie* owes to subsequent owners of the lots a duty of reasonable care in respect of the planning and construction of his subdivision. Often this will require him to engage appropriately skilled advisers and contractors. In turn the professional advisers and contractors concerned will likewise have duties of care to subsequent owners. It may be that the subdividing owner will be liable for negligence by his agents, but that point does not arise in this case. Nor do we have to rule on the significance in a negligence action of knowledge of the problem on the part of a subsequent owner before his purchase. It is enough to say that such knowledge could well have been a formidable difficulty in the way of the plaintiffs in this case if they had sued in negligence. What is clear is that in general the owners of the lots will have such remedies as the modern flexible law of negligence gives. I am not satisfied that it would be just to give them any are greater protection against either the original subdivider or his agents.

For these reasons I would hold that, at any rate where it is manifest that sections in a subdivision have been created by excavation, the subdividing owner is not under a strict non-contractual duty to a subsequent owner of a section on which subsidence occurs because of the excavation, but that the principles of the law of negligence will apply. That is enough to dispose of the present case. It is better not to try to dispose of hypothetical cases of different facts.

The Court being unanimous, the appeal is dismissed.

NOTE

The concurring judgments of Richardson and Somers JJ. have been omitted.

QUESTIONS AND COMMENTS

1. The right of support applies to land in its natural state, and does not extend to the support of buildings on that land. By the same token, if the withdrawal of support causes subsidence, and if it can be established that it is not the result of the weight of buildings, the loss of support is actionable. Moreover, compensation may be awarded for any consequential damage to structures that occurs.

2. Conversely, the mere withdrawal of support does not give rise to a cause of action. It is only when damage to the land occurs that compensation can be sought: see

Bullock Holdings Ltd. v. Jerema 1998 CarswellBC 141, 15 R.P.R. (3d) 185 (S.C. [Chambers]), where these principles and the early English authorities are set out. Why is there a different rule for land and buildings? Should it be necessary for the properties to be contiguous?

3. A right of vertical of support also exists. Hence, where A owns the surface, and B the mines and minerals, mineral exploration leading to subsidence is actionable. A sufficient causal connection is presumed in the absence of evidence to the contrary.

4. The right of support may be waived by agreement. The existence of such a term can be of great importance in claims arising from mining operations. In *Fuller v. Garneau* 61 S.C.R. 450, 1921 CarswellAlta 92, the Supreme Court of Canada dealt with the key interpretive issues. What language is sufficient to find that the right to support has been released? Anglin J. said this (at 458-60):

> The question to be determined on this appeal is whether a reservation of mines and minerals *simpliciter* in a grant of land carries with it all the rights and privileges, actual and potential, which the reservation of mines and minerals with full power to work the same, and for this purpose to enter upon and use or occupy the . . . lands or so much thereof or to such an extent as may be necessary for the effectual working of the said minerals or the mines, pits, seams and veins containing the same found in the grant of the land here in question from the Crown, may confer. For the appellant it is contended that there is a substantial difference in regard to the right to destroy or cause subsidence of the surface and certain other rights.
>
> The implication in the mere reservation of them in a grant of land of the right to win, get and take away the minerals is recognized by a long series of authorities. . . .
>
> But that the right so implied is always subject to the condition that its exercise shall not prejudice the surface owner's natural right to support is conclusively established by many authorities in English courts . . . The surface cannot be destroyed however necessary it may be to do so for the practical working of the mines. . . .
>
> As Lord Macnaghten said in *Butterknowle Colliery Co. v. Bishop Auckland Industrial Co-operative Society*, [1906] A.C. 305, at p. 313 . . . :
>
>> The result seems to be that in all cases where there has been a severance in title and the upper and the lower strata are in different hands, the surface owner is entitled of common right to support for his property in its natural position and in its natural condition without interference or disturbance by or in consequence of mining operations, unless such interference or disturbance is authorized by the instrument of severance either in express terms or by necessary implication.This presumption in favour of one of the ordinary and most necessary rights of property holds good whether the instrument of severance is a lease, or a deed of grant or reservation, or an inclosure Act or award. To exclude the presumption it is not enough that the mining rights have been reserved or granted in the largest terms imaginable, or that powers and privileges usually found in mining grants are conferred without stint, or that compensation is provided in measure adequate or more than adequate to cover any damage likely to be occasioned by the exercise of those powers and privileges.

> But where it is established that the mines cannot be worked or the minerals extracted without entailing such consequences, an express order to work the mines and get the minerals necessarily implies the right to cause subsidence and destruction of the surface. This is the result of the decisions in *Butterley Co.* v. *New Hucknall Colliery Co.*, [1910] A.C. 381, 79 L.J. Ch. 411 . . .

Duff and Mignault JJ. delivered separate concurring opinions; Davies C.J. and Idinton J. dissented.

5. Should the question of whether a loss of support is a *necessary* result of the right to work the minerals be determined by reference to circumstances, including the state of mining technology, as at the time of the grant, or when the excavation occurs?

6. Consider a situation in which A owns mineral rights under Blackacre and works the minerals. As a result — but at some later time — the surface owned by B subsides. At the time that this damage occurs the mineral estate is in the hands of C. Is C liable? See *Stellarton v. Acadia Coal Co.* 31 N.S.R. 261, 1898 CarswellNS 59 (C.A.), holding no; accord *Vecchio v. Pinkus* 833 S.W.2d 300 (Tex.App., 1992). See *contra* the dissenting opinion of Weaver C.J. in *Vecchio* at 302:

> I would hold that the duty of lateral support from adjoining land runs with the ownership of that land. A purchaser of land certainly has the right to inspect the same for defects before acquiring it and should assume the risk of such defects.

(b) water boundaries

R. v. Nikal
[1996] 1 S.C.R. 1013, 1996 CarswellBC 950, 1996 CarswellBC 950F

Cory J.:

The appellant is a Wet'suwet'en Indian of the Moricetown Band. He lives in the village of Moricetown which is within the boundaries of Moricetown Reserve No. 1. The reserve comprises lands on both sides of the Bulkley River. On July 20 and 23 1986, officers of the Department of Fisheries and Oceans watched the appellant gaff salmon in the Bulkley River at Moricetown. When he was asked for his licence he stated that he did not have one. He was then charged with fishing without a licence contrary to s. 4(1) of the *British Columbia Fishery (General) Regulations,* SOR/84-248. The Regulations provided that Indian people were entitled to a free permit to fish for salmon in the manner they preferred.

The appellant took the position that the *Fisheries Act*, R.S.C., 1985, c. F-14 (formerly R.S.C. 1970, c. F-14), and Regulations did not apply to him as the licensing scheme infringed his aboriginal rights as provided in s. 35(1) of the *Constitution Act, 1982* . . .

The appellant further contended that the Bulkley River is, at this point, part of the Moricetown Reserve and that as a result he was bound solely by the band by-law as it pertains to fishing in the river . . .

[After an extensive review of relevant general policies and the evidence related to the instant dispute, Cory J. concluded (at para. 62) that "there was never any intention on the part of the Crown to allot an exclusive fishery for the Moricetown Band." The Court then considered whether under general principles concerning water boundaries, the Bulkley River formed part of the Reserve, and as such was subject only to reserve by-laws governing fishing.]

The Application of the Ad Medium Filum Aquae *Presumption*

The appellant argued that the intention of the Crown to allot fishery rights to the band as part of the reserve was to a large extent irrelevant in this case. The basis for the argument is that the Crown only intended to reserve the fishery in navigable waters, and that in non-navigable waters, which the appellant contends includes the Bulkley River at the reserve, the presumption *ad medium filum aquae* applies, and accordingly the river surrounded, as it is on both sides by the reserve, would be presumptively part of the reserve.

Assuming without deciding that the doctrine of *ad medium filum aquae* should apply to Indian Reserves, it is not applicable in this case for three reasons. First, it must be remembered that the doctrine is only applicable in cases where the river forming the boundary is not navigable. The Bulkley River is navigable above and below the Moricetown gorge and should be considered a navigable river. This in itself is a sufficient basis for determining that the river did not form part of the reserve and that the presumption of ownership to the middle of the river cannot arise. Secondly, at the time the reserve was created the English common law provided that the fishery was a right which was severable from the title to the river bed itself. Thus, even if the presumption *ad medium filum aquae* were to apply to pass title to the bed of the river to the band, the presumption has no effect on the fishery as the Crown specifically refused to allot an exclusive fishery to the band. It was the clear intention of the Crown to reserve all of the fishery to itself. It follows that any by-law with respect to fishing would therefore be beyond the band's authority as control of this riparian right remained with the Crown. Thirdly, if the presumption could possibly be said to apply it was rebutted in light of the evidence that the Crown never intended to grant nor did it grant the bed of the river to the band. It will be necessary to say a little more with regard to each of these aspects.

When Does the Ad Medium Filum Aquae *Presumption Apply?*

In British Columbia, the civil and criminal laws of England were adopted as at November 19, 1858 "so far as the same [were] not by local circumstances inapplicable": *The English Law Ordinance*, 1867, S.B.C. 1867, No. 70, s. 2 (now *Law and Equity Act*, R.S.B.C. 1979, c. 224, s. 2). Similar language also introduced the common law of England into Manitoba and Alberta, although in other provinces, such as Ontario, no allowance was made for "local circumstances".

As La Forest explained in his book *Water Law in Canada — The Atlantic Provinces* [Ottawa: Information Canada, 1973] at pp. 241-42, the English rule was that:

> the owner of land through which a non-tidal stream flows owns the bed of the stream unless it has been expressly or impliedly reserved; and if the stream forms the boundary between lands owned by different persons, each proprietor owns the bed of the river *ad medium filum aquae* — to the centre thread of the stream.

While this rule expressed the common law as it existed in England, the courts in western Canada have not applied this rule to navigable rivers. Thus in the case of *Re Iverson and Greater Winnipeg Water District* (1921), 57 D.L.R. 184 (Man. C.A.), Dennistoun J.A. wrote, at pp. 202-3:

> These references to the common law of England indicate clearly to my mind that they are not and never were applicable to conditions in this Province. Here the public right in navigable waters whether under the Hudson's Bay tenure or since 1869 under the title vested in the Crown, was prior to, and superseded all private rights acquired by grant or settlement, upon the banks of a navigable stream. In a country occupied from the earliest days by hunters, trappers, fishers and traders whose main and almost exclusive highways were the rivers and streams, such laws were contrary to the requirements and necessities of the whole community.
>
> The applicability of the common law of England to navigable rivers in respect to the *ad medium* rule may be doubted when it is remembered that the importance of public rights in non-tidal navigable waters was not recognised in England when title to land upon their banks was acquired.
>
> In this country the public right of navigation and of fishery in all navigable waters has always existed and been recognised.

Similarly, in the same year the Alberta Court of Appeal in the case of *Flewelling v. Johnston* (1921), 59 D.L.R. 419, held that the English common law presumption did not apply in the very different circumstances which existed in Canada. In short, the "local circumstances" which existed in Canada rendered the common law inapplicable with respect to navigable rivers . . .

I am in complete agreement with the reasoning and conclusions of the Manitoba and Alberta Courts of Appeal. The wording of the Manitoba, Alberta, and British Columbia statutes leads inexorably to the conclusion that the decisions of the Manitoba and Alberta Courts of Appeal are correct and applicable to British Columbia.

This conclusion is further supported by the statements of La Forest J. in *Friends of the Oldman River Society v. Canada (Minister of Transport),* [1992] 1 S.C.R. 3, at p. 54, where he said:

The common law of England has long been that the public has a right to navigate in tidal waters, but though non-tidal waters may be navigable in fact the public has no right to navigate in them, subject to certain exceptions not material here. Except in the Atlantic provinces, where different considerations may well apply, in Canada the distinction between tidal and non-tidal waters was abandoned long ago; see *In Re Provincial Fisheries* (1896), 26 S.C.R. 444; for a summary of the cases, see my book on *Water Law in Canada* (1973), at pp. 178-80. Instead the rule is that if waters are navigable in fact, whether or not the waters are tidal or non-tidal, the public right of navigation exists. That is the case in Alberta where the Appellate Division of the Supreme Court, applying the *North-West Territories Act*, R.S.C. 1886, c. 50, rightly held in *Flewelling v. Johnston* (1921), 59 D.L.R. 419, that the English rule was not suitable to the conditions of the province. There is no issue between the parties that the Oldman River is in fact navigable.

What is the Correct Test for Navigability, and Is the Bulkley River a Navigable River?

It is clear that the *ad medium filum aquae* presumption has no application to navigable rivers in British Columbia. From the earliest times the Courts and legislatures of this country have refused to accept the application of a rule developed in England which is singularly unsuited to the vast non-tidal bodies of water in this country. It is therefore necessary to determine whether the Bulkley River can properly be considered to be a navigable river.

To assess navigability, the entire length of the river from its mouth to the point where its navigability terminates must be considered. On this issue I am in agreement with the reasoning and conclusions of Wallace J.A. in the Court of Appeal. In particular I would adopt the statements of Anglin J. (as he then was) in the case of *Keewatin Power Co. v. Kenora (Town)* (1906), 13 O.L.R. 237 (H.C.). There the navigability of the Winnipeg River was in question. It was a river not unlike the Bulkley River in that various falls and rapids necessitated numerous portages between stretches of good water. Anglin J. wrote at p. 263:

But it is argued that in any event the *ad medium* rule should apply to such parts of navigable rivers as are in their natural state non-navigable owing to impediments such as falls or rapids. Such is not my opinion. Once the navigable character of the river is established, up to the point at which navigability entirely ceases the stream must be deemed a public highway, though above that point it is private property: *The Queen v. Robertson*, 6 S.C.R. 52.

The inconvenience which would ensue were the soil of the bed of the same river in alternate stretches vested in the Crown, *juris publici* , and in the riparian owners, *juris privati*, affords strong ground for the belief that the law is not in a condition which would produce such results. Then again, though navigation at the falls in the east branch of the Winnipeg river is presently impossible, the engineers say that a canal to overcome the natural obstacle which the falls present is quite possible. Is not the stream even at this point navigable *in posse*? I think it is.

There is judicial authority for the proposition that a natural interruption of navigation in a river, in its general character navigable, does not change its legal characteristics in that

> respect at the point of interruption, and that riparian owners are not at such point presumed to own the bed *ad medium filum*: *Re State Reservation at Niagara Falls* (1884), 16 Abbott's N. C. (N.Y.) 159, 187; 37 Hun 507, 547-8. [Emphasis added.]

Similarly, Henry J. in *Re Coleman and Attorney-General for Ontario* (1983), 143 D.L.R. (3d) 608 (Ont. H.C.), at p. 614 (cited with approval by Wallace J.A. at the Court of Appeal) found that:

> Interruptions to navigation such as rapids on an otherwise navigable stream which may, by improvements such as canals be readily circumvented, do not render the river or stream non-navigable in law at those points. . . .

Finally, La Forest in his book *Water Law in Canada — The Atlantic Provinces*, *supra*, states at p. 181:

> Thus the whole of a river or lake may be regarded as navigable even though at some point navigation may be impossible or possible only for small craft by reason of rapids or shoals.

The Bulkley River is navigable both above and below the Moricetown Canyon and should be considered a navigable river. The fact that it is not navigable at the Moricetown gorge cannot alter that conclusion. Since the *ad medium filum aquae* presumption has no application to navigable rivers in British Columbia, it has no application to the Bulkley River in its passage through the Moricetown Reserve. On this basis alone it can be concluded that reserve does not include the river.

The Fishery is Separate from Ownership of the Bed

The appellant contends that the *ad medium filum aquae* presumption became applicable in British Columbia on November 18, 1858, when the common law of England was explicitly adopted as the law except to the extent that it was inapplicable. Accordingly, it is argued that when the Crown granted land to the Indians it implicitly included the title to the river *ad medium filum aquae*. Where, as in this case, the river is bordered on both sides by the reserve, the principle would act to give title to the entire river bed to the reserve. Accordingly, the river would be "on the reserve", subject only to the Crown's ability to demonstrate that such a grant was not intended. I cannot accept that position.

To understand why the presumption does not apply requires a review of the common law rules concerning water. H. J. W. Coulson and Urquhart A. Forbes in *The Law relating to Waters* (2nd ed. 1902), at p. 100, explain the application of the *ad medium filum aquae* presumption in the following terms:

> When the lands of two conterminous proprietors are separated from each other by a running non-tidal stream of water, each proprietor is *primâ facie* owner of the soil of the *alveus*, or bed of the river, *ad medium filum aquae*. The soil of the *alveus* is not the common property of the two proprietors, but the share of each belongs to him in severalty. . . . Where the same person is the proprietor of the ground on both sides of the stream, he is *primâ facie* the proprietor of the whole of the channel. . . .

> The presumption that, by a conveyance describing the land thereby conveyed as bounded by a river, it is intended that the bed of the river, usque ad medium filum, should pass, may be rebutted by proof of surrounding circumstances in relation to the property in question, which negative the possibility of such having been the intention.

One of the rights that flow from this possession of the bed is the right to the fishery. This is explained by the authors, at p. 104, in the following terms:

> The right of fishery being a right of property, the presumption is that each owner of land abutting on a non-tidal stream has the right of fishing in front of his land, *usque ad medium filum aquae*; and where a man possesses land on both sides of the water, he has the sole right of fishing.

However, the authors go on to explain that this right of fishery is severable from the title, with the result that the right can be granted to another, or reserved from a grant . . .

Clearly the fishery, even where the *ad medium filum aquae* presumption otherwise applies, can be severed from the ownership of the river bed. The evidence presented clearly establishes that there was no intent on the part of the Crown to grant an exclusive fishery. As a result, any grants of title to land adjacent to rivers, navigable or otherwise, must be taken as excluding the fishery, even if it was accepted that the *ad medium filum aquae* presumption was otherwise applicable. The consequence for this appellant is obvious. Even if the *ad medium filum aquae* should make the soil of the river bed part of the reserve, the explicit reservation of the fishery from the grant makes any by-law with respect to the fishery *ultra vires* the band's authority.

The Presumption is Rebutted

Any intent to grant the bed of the river has been conclusively rebutted. It will be remembered that the acreage of the reservation indicates an intention to exclude the river. In addition, the retention of the fishery by the Crown leads to the presumption that the bed of the river was retained by the Crown . . .

As a result, it would appear that the common law as it existed at the time the reserve was allotted would lead to the conclusion that the presumption that the title to the bed of the river would pass with the allotment of the shore had been rebutted. There is no doubt that the Crown intended to keep the fishery in its own possession. Accordingly, the allotment of the shore cannot be presumed to have included the title to the bed of the river *ad medium filum aquae*. To the contrary, the presumption is that with the title to the fishery goes the title to the bed of the river. The appellant has failed to demonstrate any intention or action on the part of the Crown to rebut this presumption.

It may now be helpful to summarize what I consider to be the relevant evidence and the applicable principles of law which determine the first issue.

1. The Crown in all of its manifestations was consistently clear in its statements that no exclusive fishery should be granted to Indian bands in British Columbia. This is consistent with the fact that the Crown had no power to grant an exclusive fishery, and that after Confederation this would involve the grant of provincial property.

2. The correct test for an assessment of navigability is to consider the entire length of the river. A section of the river which is non-navigable in fact does not necessarily render either the river as a whole or that section non-navigable in law if it is found to be substantially navigable throughout. The Bulkley River is navigable both above and below the Moricetown Canyon, and is therefore a navigable river.

3. The presumption *ad medium filum aquae* does not apply on the facts of this case because:

a. Correctly considered the river is navigable, and the application of *ad medium filum aquae* to navigable rivers was not adopted into the common law of British Columbia since it was unsuited to local conditions.

b. Fishing as a right can be the subject of a separate grant or reservation. On the facts of this case it is clear that the fishery was reserved from the allotment.

It follows that the band by-law does not apply to the Bulkley River . . .

[Cory J. next considered whether the licencing provisions contravened section 35 of the *Constitution Act, 1982*, which protects Aboriginal rights. A contravention was found.]

Accordingly, the appellant must be acquitted of the charge of fishing without a licence contrary to section 4(1) since the licence condition infringed his aboriginal rights and the licence was therefore unconstitutional . . .

The order of the Court of Appeal of British Columbia convicting the appellant must be set aside and his acquittal restored . . .

NOTE

Lamer C.J. and LaForest, Sopinka, Gonthier, Iacobucci and Major JJ. concurred. McLachlin J. (as she then was) with L'Heureux-Dubé J. concurring, delivered a dissenting judgment.

QUESTIONS

1. According to this judgment: (i) What is the English law on the ownership of abutting water courses? (ii) What principles apply in British Columbia? and (iii) What principles apply in Atlantic Canada?

2. What effect does section 3 of *Public Lands Act*, R.S.A. 2000, c. P-40, s. 3 have on the rules governing the ownership of beds and shores:

> 3.(1) Subject to subsection (2) but notwithstanding any other law, the title to the beds and shores of (a) all permanent and naturally occurring bodies of water, and (b) all naturally occurring rivers, streams, watercourses and lakes, is vested in the Crown in right of Alberta and a grant or certificate of title made or issued before, on or after May 31, 1984 does not convey title to those beds or shores.
>
> (2) Subsection (1) does not operate (a) to affect a grant referred to in subsection (1) that specifically conveys by express description a bed or shore referred to in subsection (1) or a certificate of title founded on that grant, (b) to affect the rights of a grantee from the Crown or of a person claiming under the grantee, when those rights have been determined by a court before June 18, 1931, or (c) to affect the title to land belonging to the Crown in right of Canada.

3. In view of the above provision, describe the boundaries of the following property: "To A . . . the north-east quarter of Section thirty-three (33) in Township Forty-Five (45) Range Twenty (20) West of the 4th Meridian . . ." Assume that nine acres of this parcel are covered by a lake and that the lake is wholly situated within the quarter section. See *Milk River v. McCombs* [1978] 4 W.W.R. 614, 1978 CarswellAlta 247 (C.A.) especially at 630 W.W.R.

4. When land is bounded by water, it is inevitable that changes to the shoreline, great or small, will occur. The land mass may be reduced by erosion or flooding. Conversely, accretions to the land or the recession of the water may be augment the size of the parcel. When that occurs the law of accretion governs the effect of these changes on title.

In *Nastajus v. North Alberta (Land Registration District)* 49 Alta. L.R. (2d) 206, 1987 CarswellAlta 1 (Q.B.), reversed on other grounds 64 Alta. L.R. (2d) 300, 1989 CarswellAlta 9 (C.A.), Miller A.C.J. outlined the general principles:

> Accretion may occur either by the gradual deposit of soil or sand or by the permanent recession of the water (*Clarke v. Edmonton*, [1930] S.C.R. 137 at 144, [1929] 4 D.L.R. 1010 [Alta.]). The rationale for the doctrine of accretion is set out by Lord Wilberforce in *Southern Centre of Theosophy Inc. v. State of South Australia*, [1982] A.C. 706, [1982] 2 W.L.R. 544, [1982] 1 All E.R. 283 (P.C.), at pp. 287-88:
>
>> This is a doctrine which gives recognition to the fact that where land is bounded by water, the forces of nature are likely to cause changes in the boundary between the land and the water. Where these changes are gradual and imperceptible (a phrase considered further below), the law considers the title to the land as applicable to the land as it may be so changed from time to time. This may be said to be based on grounds of convenience and fairness. Except in cases where a substantial and recognisable change in boundary has suddenly taken place (to which the doctrine of accretion does not apply), it is manifestly convenient to continue to regard the boundary between land and water as being where it is from day to day or year to year. To do so is also fair. If part of an owner's land is taken from him by erosion, or diluvion (ie advance of the water) it would be most inconvenient to regard the

boundary as extending into the water; the landowner is treated as losing a portion of his land. So, if an addition is made to the land from what was previously water, it is only fair that the landowner's title should extend to it. The doctrine of accretion, in other words, is one which arises from the nature of land ownership from, in fact, the long-term ownership of property inherently subject to gradual processes of change. When land is conveyed, it is conveyed subject to and with the benefit of such subtractions and additions (within the limits of the doctrine) as maybe take place over the years. It may of course be excluded in any particular case, if such is the intention of the parties. But if a rule so firmly founded in justice and convenience is to be excluded, it is to be expected that the intention to do so should be plainly shown.

The authorities have given recognition to this principle. They have firmly laid down that where land is granted with a water boundary, the title of the grantee extends to that land as added to or detracted from by accretion, or diluvion, and that this is so whether or not the grant is accompanied by a map showing the boundary, or contains a parcels clause stating the area of the land, and whether or not the original boundary can be identified.

The process of accretion must be gradual and imperceptible. The increase should not be observable from moment to moment or hour to hour. That the result of the process is perceptible is of no consequence, so long as the process is gradual (*Clarke, supra*, at p. 144). Whether or not the process in a given case is gradual and imperceptible is a question of fact to be answered by the trial judge.

In the case of the recession of water, the newly exposed land must be connected to the riparian (water-bounded) land in order to support a claim for accretion.

A newly formed island will belong to the owner of the lakebed (*Water Law in Canada*, by Gerard V. La Forest, p. 229). By virtue of s. 3 of the *Public Lands Act,* R.S.A. 1980, c. P-30, as amended, the owner of the lakebed will generally be the provincial or federal Crown. With respect to lands under provincial jurisdiction, the only exceptions occur where the original grant specifically conveyed the lakebed by express description or the ownership of the lakebed was determined by a court prior to 18th June 1931. The riparian right of accretion does not, however, depend upon ownership of the lakebed and the doctrine of accretion applies even if the Crown owns the lakebed (*Clarke, supra*, at pp. 150-51).

The right to accreted land does depend upon whether the property runs to the shoreline. If, for example, the Crown reserves a narrow strip between the shore and the property line, any accretion would enure to the benefit of the Crown (*Monashee Ent. Ltd. v. Min. of Recreation & Conservation (B.C.)* (1981), 28 B.C.L.R. 260, 21 R.P.R. 184, 23 L.C.R. 19, 124 D.L.R. (3d) 372 (C.A.)). "The test is whether the land in fact comes to the water's edge under the grant and not upon the manner of land description within the grant", per Dickson J.A. (*Chuckry v. R.*, [1972] 3 W.W.R. 561 at 575, 27 D.L.R. (3d) 164, 2 L.C.R. 249; affirmed [1973] S.C.R. 694, [1973] 5 W.W.R. 339, 35 D.L.R. (3d) 607, 4 L.C.R. 61 [Man.]). . . .

5. Why insist that the accretion be gradual and imperceptible? In *Southern Centre of Theosophy v. South Australia* (1981) [1982] A.C. 706 (Australia P.C.) at 721, Lord Wilberforce addressed the rationale of this requirement:

> One naturally searches for a reason or rationale for the requirement that the process be gradual and imperceptible, but this proves elusive. *Blackstone's Commentaries*, 4th ed. (1770), vol. 2, p. 262, puts it on the ground "de minimis non curat lex" a theory exposed to the objection that the result may turn out to be far from minimal but a contribution has been made by the idea that an addition to land may be too minute and valueless to appear worthy of legal dispute or separate ownership: . . . Alderson B. in *In re Hull and Selby Railway* (1839) 5 M. & W. 327, 333 gave as the reason: "That which cannot be perceived in its progress is taken to be as if it never had existed at all," an explanation which may appeal to the amateur of legal fictions; it was preferred to Blackstone's by Lord Chelmsford in *Attorney-General v. Chambers*, 4 De G. & J. 55, 68. Another, and perhaps more realistic, explanation is (as already suggested) that the rule is one required for the permanent protection of property and is in recognition of the fact that a riparian property owner may lose as well as gain from changes in the water boundary or level. But whatever is the true explanation of the rule — and there may well be more than one reason for it — what is certain is that it requires a distinction to be made between such progression as may justly be considered to belong to the riparian owner, and such large changes or avulsions as should more properly be allocated to his neighbour. Since there is a logical, and practical, gap or "grey area" between what is imperceptible and what is to be considered as "avulsion," the issue of imperceptibility or otherwise was always considered to be a jury question. . . .

Are you persuaded by this explanation?

6. What if the accretion is *not* gradual and imperceptible? The case of *Robertson v. Wallace* 33 R.P.R. (3d) 264, 2000 CarswellAlta 437 (Q.B.), discussed above in relation to the conventional line doctrine, also involved a failed claimed of accretion, and it illustrates the implications that such a finding can have for the state of title.

At around the turn of the twentieth century, two adjacent properties were conveyed to the predecessors in title of the litigants in the case. The Robertson title read "All that portion of section X that lies to the east and south of the west bank of Highwood River. . .". The Wallace title read: "All that portion of section X that lies west and north of the west bank of the Highwood River".

Some years after the initial grants, but still many years ago, two events occurred: (i) an oxbow in the river-course broke, which added to the land constituting the west bank, and (ii) an island in existence at the time of the grants become part of the west bank. The river now ran east of these places. Wallace claimed these areas (about 20 acres in all) because they were now west of the west bank, i.e., they were west of the river flow.

The Wallace claim failed. On the evidence it was shown that the change had been rapid (an avulsion). Therefore, the original location of river — not its current location — still defined the boundary, even though the descriptions quoted above uses the river as a reference point. Nation J. said this (at 302):

> In so far as the Highwood River is still the boundary in some places, riparian rights . . . will continue to operate to change the location of the boundary as the river changes course. In between stations five and ten . . . the boundary is no longer the river and therefore is not subject to change by virtue of riparian rights.

Accordingly, the parties' certificates of title were ordered to be amended to reflect that holding.

7. Very similar facts occurred in *Cox v. F-S Prestress, Inc.* 797 So. 2d 839 (Miss. S.C., 2001). There, the disputed lands were

> approximately 17 acres of land situated on the Bouie River in Forrest County. The disputed land was once part of a peninsula which jutted into a westerly bend of the river. The river flowed around the peninsula and formed its western boundary. This formation of land and river resembled the typical "horseshoe" or "ox-bow" bend of a river meander. The disputed land was attached by the narrow neck of the peninsula to a larger tract of land to the east. This neck of land was known as the "falls," and water flowed over it in times of high water on the river. . . .
>
> Until the events described below, the peninsula containing the disputed land lay east of the river, collared in the ox-bow. . . .
>
> At some point in time, about 1960 according to the chancellor's findings of fact, the river created a cut-off, a new main channel running through the falls area in the neck of the ox-bow. The disputed land was now situated west of the river channel, with the waters of the "new" main channel of the river completely separating it from formerly contiguous lands to the east. On the west margin of the disputed land lay the remnant of the "old" channel, now reduced to a slough. This slough is under water in places and dry in places. Although the disputed land is sometimes referred to as an "island," it appears that this "island" is completely surrounded by water only in times of high water, at which times the slough completely fills with water.

For the Supreme Court of Mississippi, Banks P.J. wrote (at paras. 18-23) that the critical change was avulsive in nature:

> The law of accretion and avulsion is based on public policy. Perhaps the most practical reason offered for the rule of accretion, which changes boundaries, is to give a riparian owner the benefit of access to water. . . . It has been said that the rationale for the law of avulsion is to mitigate the hardship of a change in title resulting from a sudden movement of a river. . . .
>
> [T]he chancellor found that over an eighteen year period the river created a cut-off by gradually eroding the neck of the peninsula. An island was thus created, as the disputed parcel was separated from the larger tract to the east by the new main channel of the river. The chancellor found that the change in the river was caused by accretion and that the boundaries of the properties changed as a result.
>
> The instant case presented the chancellor with a somewhat novel factual situation, at least insofar as cases decided by this Court. This case presents some facts which are characteristic of accretion, but other facts which are characteristic of avulsion.
>
> Undoubtably, accretion was involved to some degree in this process. The soil in the neck of the peninsula was lost to the adjacent lands by laws of accretion as the neck was eroded and washed into the river to be deposited elsewhere. This alluvium was distributed to the banks of the river by process of accretion. This is not in dispute.

> Notwithstanding the chancellor's finding that the disputed parcel was detached over time, we disagree with his ultimate conclusion that the boundaries of the disputed land were changed under the law of precedents applied to these facts. By careful analysis of the applicable body of common law, we conclude that the Bouie River changed its position relative to the disputed land by an act of avulsion.
>
> If the speed of the entire process was the only factor to consider, we would be compelled to hold that the Bouie River changed its course in relation to the disputed land by process of accretion. Accretion occurs gradually and imperceptibly. . . . But . . . it is the change in the thalweg of a stream which effects a change in boundaries under the law of accretion. The testimony here was that the new main channel, the thalweg, formed very rapidly after this land was cutoff by the river, whether or not this may have happened in time of flood. These facts suggest that an avulsion occurred. . . .

Given the reasoning in *Wallace v. Robertson* and *Cox v. F-S Prestress, Inc.*, is the rupture of an oxbow virtually always to be treated as avulsive? If so, is that good law?

REVIEW QUESTIONS

1. Section 2 of *The Water Rights Act*, C.C.S.M. c. W80, states:

> Except as otherwise provided in this Act, all property in, and all rights to the use, diversion or control of, all water in the province, insofar as the legislative jurisdiction of the Legislature extends thereto, are vested in the Crown in right of Manitoba.

Does this mean that, apart from whatever rights are conferred in the Act, no one other than the Crown can actually own water in Manitoba?

2. A owns property described as follows:

> All that portion of the North West Quarter of Section Thirty-Five (35) Township Forty-Five (45) Range Twenty-Three (23) West of the Fourth Meridian in the said Province [of Alberta] not covered by any of the waters of a certain surveyed lake as shown on a plan of survey of the said Township signed at Ottawa on the 22nd day of February, A.D. 1895 containing One Hundred and Forty-Six (146) acres more or less.
>
> Reserving thereout all coal.

Assume, alternatively, the following, and advise A accordingly:

(a) it is discovered that the initial acreage was 156 acres not 146.

(b) the body of water referred to in the legal description has receded, so that the dry area is now 159 acres. A wishes to drill for petroleum on the area that was once under water. See *Eliason v. Alberta (Registrar, North Alberta Land Registration District)* 1980 CarswellAlta 268, 115 D.L.R. (3d) 360 (Q.B.).

(c) A discovers coalbed methane gas (CBM) underneath a substantial portion of the northwest quarter. An expert on the subject advises A of the nature of this gas in the following opinion letter:

> The coalification process generates methane and other gases. . . . Because coal is porous, some of that gas is retained in the coal. CBM gas exists in the coal in three basic states: as free gas; as gas dissolved in the water in coal; and as gas "adsorped" on the solid surface of the coal, that is, held to the surface by weak forces called van der Waals forces. . . . These are the same three states or conditions in which gas is stored in other rock formations. Because of the large surface area of coal pores, however, a much higher proportion of the gas is adsorped on the surface of coal than is adsorped in other rock. . . . When pressure on the coalbed is decreased, the gas in the coal formation escapes. As a result, CBM gas is released from coal as the coal is mined and brought to the surface.

Amoco Production Co. v. Southern Ute Indian Tribe 119 S.Ct. 1719 (1999) at 1724 (*per* Kennedy J.).

In the course of answering these questions, identify any additional information that you would need to know to provide a complete opinion.

4. FIXTURES

When a chattel becomes a fixture, it ceases to be personal property and the title to that item is subsumed into that of the realty. The first case reproduced below, *La Salle Recreations*, demonstrates how Canadian courts determine whether an item has been transformed into a fixture. The second, *Diamond Neon*, illustrates some of the consequences of that designation.

LaSalle Recreations Ltd. v. Canadian Camdex Investments Ltd. 68 W.W.R. 339, 1969 CarswellBC 55 (C.A.)

[This case involved a dispute between secured creditors over the right to repossess wall-to-wall carpeting. The carpeting had been purchased under a conditional sales agreement, under which the carpet vendor retains title as security until the full purchase price is paid. The building within which the carpet was installed was itself subject to a mortgage.

The mortgage was duly registered in the land titles office, and the conditional sales agreement was registered in the companies register. By virtue of the combined effect of sections 12 and 15, the *Conditional Sales Act, 1961* (since replaced), where goods become affixed to the land, the security interest created under a conditional sales agreement is not binding against a subsequent mortgagee of land unless the agreement was also properly registered in the appropriate land registry office. That step was not taken. Priority over the carpets thus turned on whether or not the carpets had become fixtures. If so, the mortgagee of the land obtained priority over the conditional vendor of the carpets.]

McFarlane, J.A.: . . .

In their arguments counsel referred to and analysed carefully a large number of authorities. It is probably an understatement to say that it would be very difficult to reconcile many decisions relating to this subject. It is really, I think, a matter of applying well-established principles to the particular circumstances of each case. I do not find the United States cases to which counsel referred of much assistance. They not only conflict with each other but appear to be based, in some instances at least, upon principles somewhat different from those which have evolved in our jurisprudence. I have considered all of the English and Canadian cases discussed by counsel and in particular *Hellawell v. Eastwood* (1851) 6 Exch. 295, 20 L.J. Ex. 154, 155 E.R. 554; *Holland v. Hodgson* (1872) L.R. 7 C.P. 328, 41 L.J.C.P. 146; *Hobson v. Gorringe*, [1897] 1 Ch. 182, 66 L.J. Ch. 114; *Re De Falbe; Ward v. Taylor*, [1901] 1 Ch. 523, 70 L.J. Ch. 286, affirmed (*sub nom. Leigh v. Taylor*) [1902] A.C. 157, 71 L.J. Ch. 272; *Reynolds v. Ashby*, [1904] A.C. 466, 73 L.J.K.B. 946.

A study of these and other authorities has led me to the conclusion that the principles to be applied are stated accurately by Meredith, C.J. speaking for a divisional court in *Stack v. Eaton* (1902) 4 O.L.R. 335 at 338, as follows:

> I take it to be settled law:
>
> (1) That articles not otherwise attached to the land than by their own weight are not to be considered as part of the land, unless the circumstances are such as shew that they were intended to be part of the land.
>
> (2) That articles affixed to the land even slightly are to be considered part of the land unless the circumstances are such as to shew that they were intended to continue chattels.
>
> (3) That the circumstances necessary to be shewn to alter the *prima facie* character of the articles are circumstances which shew the degree of annexation and object of such annexation, which are patent to all to see.
>
> (4) That the intention of the person affixing the article to the soil is material only so far as it can be presumed from the degree and object of the annexation.

Haggert v. Brampton (Town) (1897) 28 S.C.R. 174, was a dispute between mortgagor and mortgagee where the mortgage charged "all the real estate of them the mortgagors, including all the machinery there was or might thereafter be annexed to the freehold, and which should be known in law as part of the freehold." Delivering the judgment of the Supreme Court of Canada King, J. after referring to certain authorities, commented on the object of annexation as follows at p. 182:

> In passing upon the object of the annexation, the purposes to which the premises are applied may be regarded; and if the object of setting up the articles is to enhance the value of the premises or improve its usefulness for the purposes for which it is used, and if they are affixed to the freehold even in a slight way, but such as is appropriate to the use of the articles, and showing an intention not of occasional but of permanent affixing,

> then, both as to the degree of annexation and as to the object of it, it may very well be concluded that the articles are become part of the realty, at least in questions as between mortgagor and mortgagee.

Special attention must be given to the use of the word "permanent" in this context. I note the word is used in contra-distinction to "occasional." When used with reference to affixing or annexing chattels to realty I cannot believe that "permanent," a relative term, means remaining in the same state and place forever or even for an indefinitely long period of time. Especially must this be so where the chattels being considered are subject to wear and tear through use. Moreover, I think regard must be had to the fact that the use is in a modern hotel where changes from time to time in colour schemes and decor may become important for the purpose of efficient commercial operation of the hotel as a hotel. In my opinion the word "permanent," as used by King, J., should be interpreted for the purposes of this appeal as indicating the object of having the carpeting remain where it is so long as it serves its purpose. I think the permanency of the original affixing, in this sense, is not affected by the consideration that it might well be intended to replace the carpeting if it should later become worn or stained or be of a colour or pattern then thought unpleasant or undesirable for the purpose of the hotel operation.

I proceed to apply these principles to the facts admitted and proved in this case.

As to the degree of annexation, it is not necessary to give a detailed description. A method known as Robert's smooth-edge was used. A narrow lath was nailed to the floors around the perimeters of the areas to be carpeted. These laths have short nails or pins protruding upwards and at an angle toward the walls. Rubber undermatting was then placed inside the lath stripping and stapled to the unfinished plywood floor by comparatively small staples placed about nine inches apart. The warp of the carpeting was then pressed onto the nails or pins, the carpeting being stretched into position with the assistance of an instrument known as a "knee kicker." The result is that the carpeting is held smoothly and firmly in position. Both the carpeting and the rubber matting are, however, removable with little difficulty and without causing more than trifling damage to either. The smooth-edge itself can also be removed without causing real damage to floor or walls although the lath, nails and pins would probably be of no further use.

In some portions of the hotel floors, subject to very heavy usage, ribbed rubber matting was firmly glued down. A comparatively small quantity of carpeting was fixed to stairs in a different manner. These coverings could not be so readily removed, but they account for such a trifling part of the whole that I think they should be disregarded.

Considering the facts just summarized I think the degree of annexation should be described as slight.

Turning to the object of annexation, the question is whether the goods were affixed to the building, though slightly, for the better use of the goods as goods, or for the better use of the building as a hotel building. Counsel for the respondent pointed out quite correctly, that the question is not whether carpeting is useful or necessary to a hotel, but whether the annexation of the carpets was for the better use and enjoyment of the carpets as such or for the better use of the building as a hotel building. The factors in this case, in addition to others already mentioned, bearing on this question appear to me to be:

(1) The unfinished plywood flooring was entirely unsuitable and could not be expected to be used as a floor in a hotel with the character of the Villa Motor Hotel.

(2) The undermatting and carpeting, if left resting on the plywood by their own weight, would not provide proper floors in such a hotel for reasons of both appearance and utility.

(3) The annexation was reasonably required for the completion of the floors as such, having regard to the character and intended use of the areas involved.

(4) The evidence shows that in comparable hotels carpeting is quite commonly replaced at intervals of three to five years.

(5) It is also established that a ready market exists for used carpeting after its removal.

Weighing all these circumstances, I am of the opinion that the object of the annexation was the better and more effectual use of the building as a hotel and not the better use of the goods as goods. It follows that, in my opinion, the carpeting and accessories were annexed to the land in such a manner and under such circumstances as to constitute fixtures . . .

QUESTIONS

1. What test(s) did the Court apply to determine whether the carpeting was a fixture or a chattel?

2. In *LaSalle Recreations* the Court listed five factors that were to be taken into account in this case. In what way are those considerations of assistance?

3. Draft an agreement to sell the classroom in which property is taught. None of the chattels are to pass as part of this transaction.

4. Certain fixtures that are installed by tenants are subject to special rules. The basic principles governing such "tenants' fixtures", as they are called, are set out by Saunders J. in *Frank Georges Island Investments Ltd. v. Ocean Farmers Ltd.* 563 A.P.R. 201, 2000 CarswellNS 74 (S.C. [Chambers]) at para. 42:

> "Tenant fixtures" were described in *Stack v. T. Eaton Co.*, [(1902), 4 O.L.R. 335 (C.A.)] as a . . . principle or rule which applied uniquely to fixtures attached by tenants to the leased property. Meredith, C.J. described this category of fixtures as follows:

> That, even in the case of tenants' fixtures put in for the purposes of trade, they form part of the freehold, with the right, however, to the tenant, as between him and his landlord, to bring them back to the state of chattels again by severing from the soil, and that they pass by a conveyance of the land as part of it, subject to this right of the tenant. (at p. 338)

Williams & Rhodes, *Canadian Law of Landlord and Tenant* (6th ed.), vol. 2 describes this unique right of tenants, in certain circumstances, to remove fixtures:

> Fixtures of a chattel nature erected or placed by tenant upon the leased premises, for the purposes of carrying on a trade, for ornament or as a domestic convenience become part of the freehold but may nevertheless be severed. If so severed, they cease to be "fixtures" and resume their character as chattels. They may be removed by the tenant or his assigns, provided that such removal may be effected without serious injury to the freehold. (at pp. 13-17)
>
> Not every fixture affixed to the land may be removed prior to the end of the lease term simply because it is attached by a tenant. The article must be either:
>
> > (a) for the purpose of carrying on a trade; or
> >
> > (b) ornamental in nature or for the purpose of domestic convenience. (Williams & Rhodes, *supra.*, Vol. 2, pp. 13-17)
>
> This particular sub-category of tenants' fixtures has come to be described as "trade fixtures". "Trade fixtures" are defined as:
>
> > Things which a tenant has fixed to the freehold for the purposes of trade or manufacture may be taken away by him during the term whenever the removal is not contrary to any express or implied stipulation in his lease. But the items must be capable of being removed without causing material injury to the estate: *Cartwright v. Herring* (1904), O.W.R. 511 (Ont. H.C.); or "irreparable damage": *Spyer v. Phillipson*, [1931] 2 Ch. 183 (C.A.); *Can. Credit Men's Trust Association (Campbell River Mills Ltd.) v. Ingham*, [1933] 1 W.W.R. 8, 4 B.C.R. 300 (S.C.); affirmed [1933] 3 W.W.R. 305, 47 B.C.R. 358, [1933] 4 D.L.R. 626 C.A.; *Liscombe Falls Gold Mining Co. v. Bishop* (1904), 35 S.C.R. 539; and without being entirely demolished or losing their essential character or value: *Hughes v. Towers* (1866), 16 U.C.C.P. 287 (C.A.). (Williams & Rhodes, *supra.*, Vol. 2, p. 13-20.1) . . .

In *Carabin v. Offman* (1998), 222 A.P.R. 407 87 N.S.R. (2d) 407 (C.A.), the Nova Scotia Court of Appeal confirmed that a tenant's right to remove leasehold improvements must be exercised before the term expires. Hart, J.A. wrote:

> . . . The law is clear and the tenant must have understood that his only right was to make use of those improvements during the term of the lease and remove them before the end of that term if he wished to have any further benefit from them. They would otherwise forfeit to the landlord who may or may not receive any benefit from them. . . .

What is the rationale for the principle that a leaseholder (i.e., a tenant) can affix goods that become part of the realty and enure to the benefit of the freeholder? Why confer a right of removal, and how do we account for the limitations on that right?

5. It is possible for the parties to agree to alter the basic rules governing the removal of tenants' fixtures. In *Levesque v. J. Clark & Son Ltd.* 1972 CarswellNB 232, 7 N.B.R. (2d) 478 (Q.B.), Dickson J. offered that "in the course of a long commercial tenancy various fixtures may be added and alterations made by a tenant with the permission of his landlord. When such additions or alterations complement the use to which premises are normally put, as here in the case for instance of the sign holder on the roof, the foundation for the sign post in the yard, and the tire rack, I do not think the parties could be considered as necessarily having contemplated their removal on termination of the lease." What factors should inform the determination of whether the right to remove tenants' fixtures at the expiry of the term has been waived?

6. Most agricultural fixtures are excluded from the common law definition of tenants' fixtures: *Elwes v. Maw* (1802) 3 East 37, 102 E.R. 510 (K.B.). In England, the common law was altered by the *Landlord and Tenant Act, 1851* (Imp.) c. 25. In *Carscallen v. Leeson* 1927 CarswellAlta 23, [1927] 4 D.L.R. 797 (C.A.), it appears to have been assumed that this Act was received into the Northwest Territories (including Alberta). *Cf. Cherry v. Bredin* 1927 CarswellSask 40, [1927] 3 D.L.R. 326 (C.A.).

Diamond Neon (Manufacturing) Ltd. v. Toronto-Dominion Realty Co. [1976] 4 W.W.R. 664, 1976 CarswellBC 198 (C.A.)

Robertson J.A.:

This appeal turns upon whether, at the time when the defendant purchased a parcel of land (a) a metal pole fastened to a block of concrete embedded in the soil, (b) a large (14 feet by 12 feet) sign hanging from the pole, and (c) a large (2 1/2 feet by 21 feet) sign attached firmly to a shack on the land were fixtures. If they were not, their later sale by the defendant was a conversion of chattels belonging to the plaintiff; if they were, the plaintiff can lay no claim to them and its action for conversion must fail. The manufacture and installation of the pole and signs by the plaintiff was done pursuant to a contract between the plaintiff and Uptown Motors Ltd. ("Uptown"), which was a dealer in used cars. One sign read "Drive in. We buy cars. Uptown Motors" and the other sign read "Drive in. We buy cars". Each sign had stuck to it a plastic plate or decal (about 1 1/2 inches by 10 1/2 inches in size) with the word "Diamond" (part of the plaintiff's name) on it. The contract, in which the plaintiff was called "the Owner", provided:

> (i) REMOVAL OF DISPLAY: The display shall remain the property of the Owner and shall not by reason of attachment to any realty be deemed a fixture. Upon the termination of this lease the Owner may remove the display.

By another provision in the contract the plaintiff "leased" the things to Uptown for a term (which was later renewed) at a monthly rental. The land belonged to Western Canadian Properties Ltd., of which Uptown was a tenant. Later Dueck on Broadway Ltd. ("Dueck") became tenant of the land and Uptown assigned its rights under the contract to Dueck. The contract expired and the plaintiff leased the things to Dueck (then tenant of the land) for a term that expired. Dueck vacated the land and the things were allowed to remain there, the plaintiff expecting that it might be able to lease them to another used car dealer. Western Canadian Properties Ltd. sold the land to the defendant. At this time the defendant had no knowledge of any contract relating to the things. Subsequently the defendant sold the things to Nettie Holdings Ltd. It is this sale that the plaintiff says was a wrongful conversion of its chattels.

[Robertson J.A. then referred to the analysis in the *LaSalle Recreations* case.]

In my opinion both the degree of annexation and the object of the annexation force the conclusion that the things had become part of the realty before the defendant bought the land.

It is elementary that the defendant could not be affected by the contracts for leasing the things, when it had no knowledge of them when it bought the land.

At the trial the plaintiff sought to establish that, some six months after the defendant bought the land and before it sold the things to Nettie Holdings Ltd., the defendant had notice of the plaintiff's claim to be the owner of the things and thereupon became bound by the contract or contracts of leasing. The learned trial Judge found against the plaintiff on the question of fact and on appeal the plaintiff sought to reverse that finding. I would not interfere with the trial Judge's finding in this matter, he having heard the witnesses and formed his conclusion upon a consideration of the evidence. Even, however, if the defendant did have notice of a claim by the plaintiff some six months after buying the land, such notice could not affect the character of these articles, title to which had already passed to the defendant in the nature they possessed at the date of sale.

For the plaintiff it was argued that, when the defendant was negotiating the purchase of the land and saw the things affixed to it, the defendant came under an obligation to make inquiries to ascertain whether the things were really part of the land and not chattels owned by some third person. I see no merit in this submission.

The learned trial Judge held that the defendant acquired title to the signs and pole when it bought the land and accordingly that it did not convert them when it severed and sold them, and he dismissed the action. In my respectful opinion he was right, and I would dismiss the plaintiff's appeal.

Carrothers J.A. (dissenting):

Having had the advantage of reading the reasons for judgment of my brother Robertson, I find myself in complete agreement with his recitation of the facts (including his affirmation of the finding of fact by the trial Judge that the respondent had neither notice of the sign rental contract nor subsequent telephoned advice as to the appellant's ownership of the signs in question) and his statements of the main issue and the principles of law applicable to that issue. However, I am respectfully at variance with him on the application of that law in this particular case in view of the uniqueness of the objects involved.

It seems to me that a sign, by its very wording, has a unique ability to speak for itself on the matter of the intention or purpose of the tenant and the owner of the real property in question as to whether that sign was intended to become part of the land or intended to continue as a chattel. To use the phraseology of Meredith C.J. cited with approval by McFarlane J.A. in *La Salle Recreations Ltd. v. Can. Camdex Investments Ltd.* (1969), 68 W.W.R. 339, 4 D.L.R. (3d) 549 (B.C. C.A.), to my mind the wording of a sign is capable of constituting circumstances [p. 344] "to shew that they [articles affixed to the land] were intended to continue chattels" and to [p. 344] "shew the degree of annexation and object of such annexation, which are patent to all to see".

I draw the analogy of two identically fabricated (though not objects of art) brass plates securely fastened with the same degree of affixation to either side of an entrance doorway, with no contractual or declaratory evidence of ownership. One plate bears the civic address of the premises, being permanent information relative to the land, enhancing the value of the premises and improving its usefulness for any and all purposes for which it might be used. The other plate bears the name, professional qualifications and office hours of, say, a doctor, lawyer, or chartered accountant occupying the premises as a tenant for the purposes of carrying on his profession, being information relative to the particular occupation of the particular occupant and being as transitory as his tenancy. Applying the established principles of law, I would think that a purchaser of the premises would be entitled to assume that the address plate was intended to be a fixture forming part of the realty but suggest that, in the absence of evidence of abandonment, the name plate was intended to remain a chattel belonging personally to the tenant.

Applying these principles in this way to the case at bar, I am inclined to the view that a sign bearing the name and stating the business of a former tenant, in the absence of evidence of abandonment, is not necessarily conclusive of the intention of the landlord and the tenant as to whether or not the sign was installed as a removable chattel but it ought to have put the purchaser on enquiry as to whether these signs were to be included in the conveyance of the realty. The fact that the purchaser subsequently severed the signs from the realty and sold them as chattels is confirmatory of the expectation that they might have been viewed as chattels at the time of the sale and purchase of the realty.

For these reasons I would allow the appeal.

QUESTIONS

1. Which position do you prefer?

2. When was the magic moment at which the title to the sign was lost by Diamond Neon?

3. Would the outcome of the *Diamond Neon* case have been different had a plaque been placed at the foot of the sign — patent for all to see — that read as follows: "This display shall remain the property of the Owner, Diamond Neon, and shall not by reason of attachment to any realty be deemed a fixture"?

4. One can understand the predicament of companies such as Diamond Neon, and the carpet vendor in *LaSalle Recreations*. Both sought to retain an interest in goods for valid commercial purposes, only to be thwarted by the operation of the law of fixtures.

A response to this kind of dilemma is to create a legislative regime designed to mitigate the operation of the common law rules as to fixtures. It will be recalled that the carpet vendor in *LaSalle Recreations* would have retained its priority over the carpets had its security interest been registered in the appropriate land registry office. The failure to take that step proved its ruination.

Describe and assess the following provisions, found in the *Personal Property Security Act*, R.S.O. 1990, c. P.10:

> 1.(1) "security interest" means an interest in personal property that secures payment or performance of an obligation, and includes, whether or not the interest secures payment or performance of an obligation, the interest of a transferee of an account or chattel paper . . .
>
> 34.(1) A security interest in goods that attached,
>
> > (a) before the goods became a fixture, has priority as to the fixture over the claim of any person who has an interest in the real property; or
> >
> > (b) after the goods became a fixture, has priority as to the fixture over the claim of any person who subsequently acquired an interest in the real property, but not over any person who had a registered interest in the real property at the time the security interest in the goods attached and who has not consented in writing to the security interest or disclaimed an interest in the fixture.
>
> (2) A security interest mentioned in subsection (1) is subordinate to the interest of,
>
> > (a) a subsequent purchaser for value of an interest in the real property; or
> >
> > (b) a creditor with a prior encumbrance of record on the real property to the extent that the creditor makes subsequent advances,

> if the subsequent purchase or subsequent advance under a prior encumbrance of record is made or contracted for without knowledge of the security interest and before notice of it is registered in [the proper land registry] . . .

(3) If a secured party has an interest in a fixture that has priority over the claim of a person having an interest in the real property, the secured party may, on default and subject to the provisions of this Act respecting default, remove the fixture from the real property if, unless otherwise agreed, the secured party reimburses any encumbrancer or owner of the real property who is not the debtor for the cost of repairing any physical injury but excluding diminution in the value of the real property caused by the absence of the fixture or by the necessity for replacement.

(4) A person entitled to reimbursement under subsection (3) may refuse permission to remove the fixture until the secured party has given adequate security for the reimbursement . . .

(7) A person having an interest in real property that is subordinate to a security interest in a fixture may, before the fixture has been removed from the real property by the secured party in accordance with subsection (3), retain the fixture upon payment to the secured party of the amount owing in respect of the security interest having priority over the person's interest.

5. What is the effect of section 35 of *The Law of Property Act*, C.C.S.M., c. L90?

35. Notwithstanding anything in any agreement for sale of land or in any mortgage of land whenever made or given, or in any agreement renewing or extending it, or in any agreement collateral thereto, or any other agreement, no erection, machinery, plant, building, improvement or other chattel erected, placed or put upon farm land sold or mortgaged shall, by reason only of a declaration, agreement or covenant in the agreement of sale or mortgage or in any agreement collateral thereto or any other agreement, become or be deemed to be a part of the realty.

5. THE TRANSFORMATION OF CHATTEL OWNERSHIP

As we have seen, the law of fixtures concerns the joining of chattels to realty. A comparable result can occur when chattels belonging to more or more persons become somehow "connected". This might occur where, for example, fungible goods such as apples belonging to A become combined with those of B. Such an event is called variously, confusion, intermixture, admixture or commingling. Or, items that are initially quite distinguishable from one another can become inextricably fused. This might occur where A extensively rebuilds the engine and body of a car, only to discover later that the parts were stolen and belong B (or that the car actually belongs to B). This is known as an accession. Also, a chattel might be fundamentally transformed, such as where A's iron poles are crafted into an elaborate wrought-iron gate and fence. This event is sometimes referred to as an alteration. Roman law called this *specificatio*.

Taking someone else's goods, even innocently, can amount to a wrong (such as the tort of conversion). However, there is a separate legal question: who owns the object under dispute? The following cases deal with that question.

Glencore International A.G. et al. v. Metro Trading International Inc. [2001] 1 Lloyd's L.R. 284 (Q.B. (Comm. Ct.))

[Metro Trading International (MTI) was in the business of buying, mixing, and selling oil. Glencore, Caltex, Mobil, Texaco and Arexco had contracts for the storage of oil in MTI's facility in Fujairah (in the United Arab Emirates). The oil was not stored separately, but commingled with oil of similar quality. Metro Oil, a company associated with MTI, had entered into a refining contract with the Texaco. Under its terms, Texaco provided MTI with crude oil to be refined by Metro in exchange for quantities of the refined oil. Thus not only was the ownership of the commingled oil in question, but also the ownership of oil that had been transformed into a new product.

In 1998 MTI went into bankruptcy, at which time there was only 750,000 tonnes of oil held in their Fujairah facility. According to the oil companies, there should have been 2.5 million tonnes in storage.

This decision is a result of preliminary proceedings to determine what system of law governed the transactions in question. Justice Moore-Bick held that the law of Fujairah should govern. The United Arab Emirates Civil Code however seeks to fulfill the intentions of the parties in contractual matters. English law was treated as relevant to the issue of intention.]

Moore-Bick J.: . . .

Authorized commingling and blending

It is trite law that delivery of goods to a bailee for storage has no effect on the general property in the goods which remains at all times with the bailor. The bailee's duty is to redeliver the goods to the bailor in accordance with the terms of the bailment. So long as the goods retain their original identity no difficulties arise, but questions of property do arise once the original identity is lost, and one way in which that may occur is by the storage of goods in a mixed bulk. Until recently this question had received relatively little attention in English law, although it had been considered in a number of cases in the United States where grain is often stored in common silos. Where several people deliver goods of the same kind to a warehouse keeper to be stored in a mixed bulk the storage agreement may all be in the same standard terms and may indicate clearly where property lies. If that is the case, then in addition to the individual contracts between each bailor and the warehouse keeper, it may be possible to find that a separate contract of the kind which in *Clarke v. Dunraven*, [1897] A.C. 59 was held to have come into existence between all the bailors and the warehouse keeper which regulates their property rights in the bulk.

If the goods have been delivered to the warehouse keeper simply for the purpose of storage, the depositor is unlikely to have intended that the property should pass to the warehouse keeper. In these circumstances in the absence of any agreement to the contrary the mixed bulk will be owned in common by those whose goods have contributed to it, each depositor becoming an owner in proportion to the amount of his contribution. As goods are added to or drawn from the bulk the interest of the contributors will vary to reflect the quantity of goods still held to their order. These principles which were developed in the American cases, in particular *Sexton v. Abbot & Graham*, (1880) 44 Iowa 181, *Nelson v. Brown, Doty & Co.*, (1880) 44 Iowa 555 and *Savage v. Salem Mills Co.*, (1906) 85 Pac. 69, were approved by the House of Lords in *Mercer v. Craven Grain Storage Ltd.*, [1994] C.L.C. 328. In these circumstances since no property passes to the warehouse keeper it is appropriate to describe him as a bailee, even though his obligation is to redeliver to each depositor not the identical goods deposited with him but the same quantity of goods of the same description drawn from the mixed bulk of which they formed part.

The same principles apply whether the mixed bulk is composed entirely of goods owned by individual bailors or includes goods owner by the warehouse keeper himself, provided there is no intention to pass property or dominion over the goods to him. However, if the warehouse keeper is entitled to treat the goods as his own, the contract will be regarded as one of sale and property will pass on delivery, subject to any agreement to the contrary. Thus in *South Australian Insurance Co. v. Randell,* (1869) L.R. 3 P.C. 101 farmers delivered wheat to millers who stored it in common as part of their current stock from which they would draw either for sale or for grinding in their mill. The terms on which the farmers delivered wheat gave them the right to demand the return of an equivalent quantity of wheat of the same quality, or the market price, and gave the millers the option of delivering wheat or paying the market price. The transaction therefore amounted to a contract for sale because it gave the miller the right to dispose of the gods entirely as they chose.

The essential distinction between blending and commingling is that where blending has taken place the resultant product is different in nature from both its original constituents. This creates certain conceptual difficulties in the case of unauthorized blending to which I shall return, but should not ordinarily create difficulties where the blending is carried out pursuant to a contract . . .

Unauthorized commingling and blending

The effect on proprietary interests of the unauthorized commingling of one persons's goods with those of another was considered by Mr. Justice Staughton in the case of *Indian Oil Corporation Ltd. v. Greenstone Shipping S.A. (Panama)*, [1987] 2 Lloyd's Rep. 286; [1988] 1 QB. 345 following a detailed review of the earlier authorities. The case concerned the mixing on board a vessel of a cargo of crude oil with a quantity of crude oil belonging to the shipowners which represented the residues of cargoes carried on previous voyages. The receivers made a claim for short delivery of cargo on the grounds that they were entitled to receive all the pumpable cargo on board, including previous cargo residues. When the cargo was loaded the residues were distributed among a number of cargo tanks and this raised the question whether the shippers had consented to the mixing taking place. There was some uncertainty about that, but in the end Mr. Justice Staughton approached the matter on the assumption that there had been no such consent. Having considered the authorities on mixing from *Stock v. Stock*, (1594) Poph 37 to *Jones v. De Marchant*, (1916) 28 D.L.R. 561 Mr. Justice Staughton expressed his conclusion as follows:

> Seeing that none of the authorities is binding on me, although many are certainly persuasive, I consider that I am free to apply the rule which justice requires. This is that, where B wrongfully mixes the goods of A with goods of his own, which are substantially of the same nature and quality, and they cannot in practice be separated, the mixture is held in common and A is entitled to receive out of it a quantity equal to that of his goods which went into the mixture, any doubt as to that quantity being resolved in favour of A. He is also entitled to claim damages from B in respect of any loss he may have suffered, in respect of quality or otherwise, by reason of the admixture.
>
> Whether the same rule would apply when the goods of A and B are substantially of the same nature and quality must be left to another case. It does not arise here. The claim based on a rule of law that the mixture became the property of the receivers fails.

This solution to the problem of wrongful mixing of goods of the same kind seems to me, with respect, to be correct both as a matter of justice and principle. None of the parties before me sought to suggest that I should not follow it and I have no hesitation in accepting it as a correct statement of the law.

This brings me to the question which was left open in *Indian Oil v. Greenstone*, namely, the effect on proprietary interests of the wrongful and irreversible mixing of goods of different kinds. Mr. Schaff submitted that the leading cases on mixing do not draw any distinction between mixing goods of the same kind and mixing goods of different kinds. He therefore argued that in this case also the contributors must at worst become owners in common of the mixture in proportion to their contributions and that if for some reason that were not possible, the innocent contributor would acquire sole title to the mixture. Mr. Smith, however, submitted that the effect of the blending is to produce a new commodity different in kind from either of its constituents. The original goods cease to exist altogether and new goods are created in their place, title to which vests in the person who produced them. It is at this point that the rules relating to mixing and the rules relating to the creation of new commodities come into contact.

The authorities considered by Mr. Justice Staughton in *Indian Oil v. Greenstone* all concern the effect of mixing goods of similar kinds. They all deal with the consequences of the plaintiff's inability to identify his own property, but none of them considers the effect of a change in the essential nature of the goods for the simple reason that it was unnecessary to do so. The old authorities tended to favour the view that even in the case of mixture of similar goods property in the mixture vests entirely in the innocent party; in those cases, therefore, there was no need for a debate of the kind which one sees in *South Australian v. Randall* about the effect of loss of identity consequent on mixing similar and dissimilar goods, but it is also true to say that they do not directly consider the implications of creating a new commodity . . .

In *Jones v. De Marchant*, (1916) 28 D.L.R. 561 the plaintiff's husband took 18 beaver skins which she owned and, together with four additional skins which he himself provided, had them made up into a coat which he gave to his mistress, the defendant. The plaintiff sought to recover the coat from the defendant on the grounds that it was her property. Richards, J.A. considered the case to be governed by the principles of accession and held that the coat as a whole belonged to the plaintiff. In discussing the principle of accession, however, the Judge referred to a line of authority which suggests that where goods are wrongfully used to create a new commodity English law is more concerned with the origin of the new commodity than with the fact that a new commodity has come into existence. In the first edition of his work on the law on torts Sir John Salmond stated that the true principle of English law is that property in chattels is not lost simply because they are processed into another form, for example, if corn is ground into flour, or trees cut down and sawn into timber, even though one would ordinarily say that flour is essentially different from corn and sawn timber different from standing trees. Certainly there is old authority for this view, as one can see from the *Case of Leather*, Y.B. 5 Hen. VII fol.15, referred to by Richards, J.A. in *Jones v. De Marchant*, in which leather had been wrongfully taken and turned into shoes, and *In Re Oatway*, [1903] 2 Ch. 356 Mr. Justice Joyce said

> It is a principle settled as far back as the time of the Year Books that, whatever alteration of form any property may undergo, the true owner is entitled to seize it in its new shape if he can prove the identity of the original material: see Blackstone, vol. ii. p. 405, and *Lupton v. White*. But this rule is carried no farther than necessity requires, and is applied only to cases where the compound is such as to render it impossible to apportion the respective shares of the parties. . . .

One of the more extreme examples of this principle in operation is to be found in the American case of *Silsbury & Calkins v. McCoon & Sherman*, (1850) 3 N.Y. 379 which is also referred to in *Jones v. De Marchant*. In that case corn was taken from its owner and turned into whisky. Despite such a radical alternation in the characteristics of the original goods, the majority held that the whisky belonged to the owner of the corn. The case is very interesting for a number of reasons. It appears from the report of the argument that the Court was treated to a careful analysis of the Roman law principles of *specificatio* and *accessio* as well as having its attention drawn to many of the early English authorities and commentators. It is also interesting in that it suggests a distinction is to be drawn between an innocent wrongdoer and a wilful wrongdoer, although, as the Court accepted, that is not one which has been recognized in any of the English authorities. The case is also notable for the quality of the dissenting judgment which draws attention to the dangers inherent in being too ready to ignore changes in the essential nature of the goods . . .

"Mixing" and "mixture" are ordinary words, not terms of art. They are apt to describe a range of different operations from the addition of a small quantity of one type of material to a large bulk in order to make a slight adjustment to one of its characteristics without changing its essential nature (e.g., the addition of sugar to tea or anti-knock compounds to petrol) to the blending of substantial quantities of different materials in order to produce something which in commercial terms, and perhaps also in terms of its structure and chemical composition, is different from the original ingredients (e.g., flour, eggs, milk, etc. to make a cake, or resin, glues and woodchips to form chipboard). This part of the phase 1 issues is concerned with the latter type of mixing, that is the deliberate blending of two or more oils of different grades or specifications in order to produce oil of a grade or specification commercially different from any of its ingredients.

Mr. Smith's submission was essentially a simple one: if goods have ceased to exist because they have been turned into something completely new, the person who made that new thing automatically acquires title to it by virtue of the fact that he made it, is in possession of it and can exercise dominion over it. There is much to be said for that proposition and the doctrine of *specificatio* is well established in Scots law: see *International Banking Corporation v. Ferguson, Shaw & Sons*. However, it is less clear that it forms parts of English law, at any rate in its full rigour. The principle for which Mr. Smith contended would, I think, offend many people's sense of justice in a case where the original materials belonged entirely to someone other than the maker of the new commodity, even if he were unaware of the fact; it is even more likely to do so in a case where the maker of the new commodity knew that he had no right to take and use them. It was for this reason that from early times English law allowed the original owner to recover his goods even though in one sense they had been turned into something new, for example, leather into shoes (*Case of Leather*, Y.B. 5 Hen. VII fol.15) or standing trees into sawn timber (*Anon.* Moore 20, 72 E.R. 411). These cases, which were followed and applied in the American cases of *Betts and Church v. Lee*, 5 Johns. 348 (timber wrongfully cut down and turned into shingles), *Curtis v. Groat* 6 Johns. 169 (timber cut down and turned into charcoal) and *Silsbury v. McCoon* itself, are reflected in the passage from judgment of Mr. Justice Royce in *Re Oatway* to which I referred earlier. The Courts did recognize, however, that there would come a point at which the original matters could not be sufficiently identified in the new article to permit recovery by the owner. None of the examples I have given are cases involving mixing, of course, but they do show that it is necessary to approach the proposition that a new commodity automatically belongs to its manufacturer with some care. The old authorities support the conclusion that merely working the original materials to produce a new article is not enough to vest title in the manufacturer if he is a wrongdoer; nor, in the light of *Jones v. De Marchant* and *Silsbury v. McCoon*, is the mere addition of other materials belonging to the manufacturer himself.

The cases to which I have referred proceed on the principle that the owner of goods which are wrongfully taken and used to make a new commodity can recover them from the wrongdoer, even in their altered form, if he can identify them in that new commodity and show that it is wholly or substantially composed of them. In such cases the work carried out on the goods by the wrongdoer, as well as additions of small amounts of his own materials, are treated as attaching to the goods by accession. This appears most clearly from the judgment in *Jones v. De Marchant*. Under this approach title depends not on the creation of a new commodity, but on the ability of the original owner to identify his goods in the new commodity. Viewed in that way it is difficult to see why the owner of the leather should be able to recover the shoes, or the owner of the trees the boards, but the owner of the stolen ingredients should not be entitled to recover the cake into which they have been wrongfully been made, even if their physical presence is less obvious. There are, of course, limits to the extent to which it is possible to identify the original materials in the new commodity, but in any view that is essentially a matter of fact in each case. The examples of the cattle cake and the fuel oil canvassed in *Borden* can, I think, properly be treated as cases where the goods can no longer be regarded as remaining in existence as a substantial component of the product with the result that property in them must be considered to have passed to the farmer or the steelmaker, as the case may be, by accession. Historically English law has not considered that a wrongdoer who has improved the goods by his labour or by providing additional materials of a relatively minor nature, such as the thread used to turn leather into shoes, should be entitled to property in the new commodity or compensation for his labour or materials. The position would probably be different, however, if the new commodity substantially represented work or materials provided by the wrongdoer . . .

I can now return to the case of wrongful blending of oil products. Two cases call for consideration: the first is where a wrongdoer takes oil belonging to two or more persons which he then blends for his own purposes. In such a case I have no doubt that the two contributors become owners in common of the blended bulk. Each can identify his own oil as a constituent of the bulk and as a wrongdoer of the blender cannot acquire title as against the previous owners . . . This does not, I think, mean that in cases of mixed goods the contributors are always entitled to equal interests in the bulk, simply that there must be equality of treatment. In my view that would require the Court to take account not only of the quantity of goods which each had contributed but also the value of those goods.

The second case is where a wrongdoer takes oil belonging to another which he then blends with his own oil. Again, the innocent contributor is able to identify his oil as a substantial constituent of the bulk and as a wrongdoer the blender is unable to override his property. The position is very similar to that of *Jones v. De Marchant*, with this exception, that, unlike the coat in that case, the blended bulk is capable of division . . .

The authorities on mixing do not in my view point to any different conclusion. They start from the proposition that where one person wrongfully mixes his goods with those of another so that they cannot be separated, the innocent party is entitled to recover the whole of the mixture. Thus in *Spence v. Union Marine Insurance Co. Ltd.*, (1868) L.R. 3 C.P. 427 Bovill, C.J. said at pp. 437-438

> It has long been settled in our law, that, where goods are mixed so as to become undistinguishable, by the wrongful act or default of one owner, he cannot recover, and will not be entitled to his proportion, or any part of the property, from the other owner.

Similarly, in *Sandeman & Sons v. Tyzack and Branfoot Steamship Co. Ltd.*, [1913] A.C. 680 Lord Moulton said at pp. 694-695

> My Lords, if we proceed upon the principles of English law, I do not think it a matter of difficulty to define the legal consequences of the goods of "A." becoming indistinguishably and inseparably mixed with the goods of "B.", "A." can claim the goods. He is guilty of no wrongful act, and therefore the possession by him of his own goods cannot be interfered with, and if by the wrongful act of "B." that possession necessarily implies the possession of the intruding goods of "B.", he is entitled to it (2 *Kent's Commentaries*, 10th ed., 465).

It is not clear that Lord Moulton had in mind the case where the mixture had produced an entirely new thing, but the approach is the same, namely, that the interests and the proprietary rights of the wrongdoer are subordinated to those of the innocent party. At the same time he recognized that the law in this area could not be regarded as settled and might need to be developed to meet the requirements of substantial justice in other types of cases. Similarly, in *Re Oatway* Mr. Justice Joyce recognized that the "settled principle" that the innocent party in an altered form might have to give away where the nature of the goods permitted a fair distribution between the wrongdoer and the innocent party. In the passage in his judgment which follows that which I cited earlier he said at p. 359:

> But this rule is carried no further than necessity requires, and is applied only to cases where the compound is such as to render it impossible to apportion the respective shares of the parties. Thus, if the quality of the articles that are mixed be uniform, and the original qualities known, as in the case of so many pounds of trust money mixed with so many pounds of the trustee's own money, the person by whose act the confusion took place is still entitled to claim his proper quantity, but subject to the quantity of the other proprietor being first made good out of the whole mass: 2 *Stephen's Commentaries* (13th ed.), 20.

In *Indian Oil v. Greenstone* Mr. Justice Staughton considered that justice required that in a case of wrongful mixing of similar goods the mixture should be held in common and that each party should be entitled to receive out of the bulk a quantity equal to that of his goods which went into the mixture, any doubt as to that quantity being resolved in favour of the innocent party. He reached that conclusion on the grounds that the proprietary interest of the innocent party could thereby be adequately protected without overriding the proprietary interests of the wrongdoer to a greater extent than was necessary in order to do so . . . In my judgment it applies with equal force in the case where the wrongdoer mixes or combines two or more commodities to produce something new, provided that the new thing is a fungible which is capable of being shared between the contributors pro rata without destroying its identity. In some cases, of course, a *pro rata* division will not be possible: the coat in *Jones v. De Marchant* is one example. In such cases the Court may need to resort to other principles in order to do substantial justice, as Lord Moulton recognized in *Sandeman v. Tyzack*.

In the light of the authorities I have therefore reached the conclusion that when one person wrongfully blends his own oil with oil of a different grade or specification belonging to another person with the result that a new product is produced, that new product is owned by them in common. In my view justice also requires in a case of this kind that the proportions in which the contributors own the new blend should reflect both the quantity and the value of the oil which each has contributed. As in other cases of mixing, any doubts about the quantity or value of the oil contributed by the innocent party should be resolved against the wrongdoer. The innocent party is also entitled to recover damages from the wrongdoer in respect of any loss which he has suffered as a result of the wrongful use of his oil . . .

McKeown v. Cavalier Yachts Pty. Ltd. (1988) 13 N.S.W.L.R. 303 (S.C., Eq. Div.)

[The case involved competing claims to the ownership of a yacht referred to in the judgment as the Cavalier 30/10. The plaintiff owned a laminated hull which was to be turned into the finished product. An agreement was entered into between the plaintiff and Cavalier Yachts (the first defendant) and several other parties to complete the work. In return, the plaintiff provided, *inter alia*, a trade-in yacht (the GAC), and a down payment of $2,000. That was in June 1987.

In September 1987, Cavalier agreed to sell its fixed assets, stock, works-in-progress and existing leases to Spartech (the second defendant). Whether that agreement was ever fully completed was in doubt, although it was clear that there were no assignments of the contracts between Cavalier and its customers (such as the plaintiff).

The plaintiff was unaware of this change in ownership, and in October 1987 he entered into a new agreement with Cavalier under which Cavalier was to oversee the construction of the yacht. Despite written terms to the contrary, the Court accepted a reading between the lines of this contract that called for the plaintiff to pay an additional $20,000 (which seems to have been satisfied by providing the GAC yacht as earlier promised). The work undertaken thereafter — by Spartech — had a value of $24,409. The value of the plaintiff's hull prior to that work being undertaken was $1,777.

Spartech claimed that it had not received payment for its work on the yacht. Having no contractual rights against McKeown, Spartech instead asserted ownership of the yacht. The basis of this claim was that McKeown's hull (initially worth $1,777) had become an accession to the work performed by Spartech (worth $24,409). McKeown, who had fulfilled all of the terms of his agreement with Cavalier, claimed to be entitled to the yacht, and so sought an order for its return (an order for "specific restitution").]

Young J.: . . .

The effect of the *Common Law Procedure Act, 1854* (U.K.) was to permit courts at common law to give specific restitution at the election of the plaintiff in a proper case so that the defendant would be bound to deliver up the chattel rather than just pay damages. However, it was held in *Whitely Ltd. v. Hilt* [1918] 2 K.B. 808, and affirmed in other cases, that our *Supreme Court Act, 1970*, s. 93, and its predecessors, only gave the court a discretion to order return *in specie* in lieu of damages and that ordinarily the court would not exercise that discretion in favour of the plaintiff where the chattel had no special value or interest and damages would fully compensate . . .

There are not very many examples in the decided cases exemplifying when an order for specific restitution should be made in detinue. The principle would appear to be that such cases at least extend to cover the area where in equity orders for specific restitution would have been made before 1854. In *General Motors Acceptance Corporation of Australia v. Davis*, [1971] V.R. 734, an order was made that the plaintiff have a writ of delivery with respect to a motor vehicle. As to this, Trindade and Cane in their *Law of Torts in Australia* (1985) at 137, aptly remark: ". . . It is not clear from the report of the case why it was not regarded as an ordinary article in commerce or why specific restitution of the motor car was ordered."

In the instant case, the reason why the second defendant says I should not in my discretion order specific restitution even if the plaintiff may by virtue of the technical operation of the doctrine of accession own the whole chattel is that it would be unfair for the plaintiff to take the value of the defendant's work without paying for it. As to this, of course, the plaintiff replies that by virtue of the trade-in he virtually has paid for the balance owing on the boat and it is only because of the secret dealings between the defendants that there is any doubt about the matter. However, leaving this to one side for the present, is it appropriate to decline to make an order in detinue for specific recovery where it might be "unjust" to do so, or would give to the plaintiff some benefit more than he was entitled to or perhaps deserved?

Fleming on Torts, 7th ed. (1987) at 67-68 says of the court's power to order return of the actual chattel in an action in detinue:

> . . . This remedy, however, is still discretionary and not a matter of right. It will not be granted, for example in case of unreasonable delay or if the chattel is an ordinary article of commerce and of no special value generally or to the plaintiff. Again, in case the defendant added to its value, an unconditional order for redelivery would be the more unfair as, in assessing damages, he would be entitled to credit for it; hence if anxious for its return *in specie*, the plaintiff must be prepared to make a fair allowance for the improvements. *Greenwood v. Bennett* [1973] Q.B. 195. . . .

In matters such as the present, if the minor chattel can be physically detached, an order may be made for its return, or refused subject to compensation or damages in the case of its loss. If it cannot be conveniently detached then compensation may be imposed as a term of repossession or detention . . .

It is now necessary to turn to an examination of the law of accession. Such an examination usually commences with a quotation from a passage from *Halsbury's Laws of England* which in the 4th edition is found in vol. 35, par. 1138 at 634:

> If any corporeal substance receives an accession by natural or artificial means, as by the growth of vegetables, the pregnancy of animals or the embroidery of cloth, the original owner is entitled by his right of possession to the property in its improved state. Similarly, when the goods of one person are affixed to the land or chattel, for example a ship, of

another, they may become part of it and so accrue to the owner of the principal thing. . . .

[The Court then referred to a number of earlier authorities, including especially *Silsbury v. McCoon* 3 N.Y. 379 (1850), discussed in the case of *Glencore International A.G. et al. v. Metro Trading International Inc.*, above.]

[In] *Thomas v. Robinson*, Speight J. discussed the authorities and Professor Guest's article and held that it was an extremely relevant factor as to whether an innocent third party had added to someone else's chattel without any actual or constructive notice of another's ownership and cases where there was such knowledge. In the end he came to a practical result and held at 392:

> In matters such as the present, if the minor chattel can be physically detached, an order may be made for its return, or refused subject to compensation or damages in the case of its loss. If it cannot be conveniently detached then compensation may be imposed as a term of repossession or detention.

In the instant case, there is no doubt at all in my mind, on the facts, that the present article, namely, a yacht that is almost ready to be sailed, is a chattel that would be injuriously affected if the accretions added by the second defendant were removed from it. The article as it now exists has gradually been formed by building upon the laminated hull piece by piece until it has taken its current form. To remove the accretions would just be to destroy the current article. Accordingly, in my view, the doctrine of accession appears to apply.

One problem with applying the doctrine is that, in the instant case, the laminated hull was only worth $1,777, whereas the accretions are worth $24,409. Counsel for the defendant points to these figures and says that the accretions accordingly are the major chattel, and the laminated hull the minor chattel, so that the doctrine of accession operates that the property in the laminated hull has now acceded to the later accretions rather than the other way around. Although the authorities speak in terms of principal chattel and minor chattel, there are none, as far as I am aware, which have ever defined these terms. Whilst it may be that in some cases one can deal with such distinction by way of comparing the respective values of the things involved, in the instant case counsel for the plaintiff, I believe, put up a complete answer to the proposition. He submitted that it was quite incorrect to compare the total of the work done to the laminated hull with the value of the hull. Quite clearly the work was done gradually and the true position was that some work was done to the laminated hull making it more valuable, at that stage that work acceded to the laminated hull, and the whole of the product belonged to the plaintiff. A little further work was done, and that little further work acceded to the hull and again the hull became the plaintiff's property, and this was the result as each extra bit of work was gradually done to the hull. In my view, that is the correct way of looking at the case.

Counsel for the second defendant then says that his client must be taken to be an innocent bystander who thinks that he owns a chattel and does work on it believing that it is his own. The second defendant's counsel submits that the second defendant had bought Cavalier Yachts' work in progress and might reasonably have assumed that the boat Cavalier 30/10 in its yard was its property. I cannot accept this submission. First, there is the problem for the second defendant that there is no reliable evidence to show that its purchase of Cavalier Yachts business was ever completed. Secondly, it left Arrowsmith in charge as manager and was in a position to find out what the correct position was. Thirdly, the standard form of contract used by Cavalier Yachts would appear to pass property in the yacht under construction to the person for whom the yacht was being built and it would seem that the proprietors of the second defendant had knowledge of that and fourthly, it is straining credulity to think that the second defendant would have done work on Cavalier 30/10 other than believing that it was a yacht with which Cavalier Yachts had some contractual rights and obligations over. If it did work without making any inquiry as to what those rights or obligations were, then it hardly seems to me that it can be placed in the category of a person who buys a chattel not knowing about a defect in title.

In my view, the work done by the second defendant forms part of the laminated hull and the whole of the current product is the property of the plaintiff . . .

The plaintiff's claim really is in detinue or else for specific restitution of goods. So far as detinue is concerned, as has been seen, it is discretionary as to whether the Court will order return of the goods in specie or leave the plaintiff to damages. One of the factors that the Court bears in mind when making this decision is whether the chattel is sufficiently unique as to make damages inappropriate. In my view, in Australia in 1988, a person's yacht has sufficient individuality to fall into the class of a special or unique chattel.

Accordingly, the case is one where I should order specific return of the yacht which, as I have held, is the property of the plaintiff, but the question then is what compensation should be given to the defendant, if any, for the improvements?

The cases do not seem to give a court any guidance as to how it goes about assessing compensation. The court is expected to make a "fair and just allowance": *Peruvian Guano Ltd. v. Dreyfus Brothers & Co.* (at 176).

The most authoritative treatment of this problem that I have been able to find is in Professor Birks' *An Introduction to the Law of Restitution* (1985) at 122 and following. It appears clear that if the plaintiff sues for damages in respect of a chattel, and the defendant has improved the chattel, the defendant is entitled to compensation for the extent to which at the time at which the goods fall to be valued, the value of the goods is attributable to the improvement. However, where the plaintiff does not claim damages and where the added value of the chattel has not been realised by it being sold, one must ask oneself why the plaintiff should give compensation to the defendant for the enhanced value of his chattel. If it can be said that the plaintiff has given full and free acceptance to the work done by the second defendant then it is appropriate that the second defendant be compensated for its work. At first blush this looks like a case of free acceptance because the plaintiff knew that the work was going on and what happened to his laminated hull was what he wanted to happen to it, that is, the hull to be built into a yacht. The problem, however, is that the financial deal between the plaintiff and Cavalier Yachts meant that the work could be done without further payment by the plaintiff except perhaps for sales tax. It is to be noted that it would appear that had the second defendant sued the plaintiff for the value of the work, it almost certainly would have failed: see *Boulton v. Jones* (1857) 2 H&N 564; 157 E.R. 232.

It would seen that in a case where the plaintiff expects X to do work on his chattel which will not mean any moneys having to be paid out of that person's purse and as things turn out, Y does the work, even though the work done is what the plaintiff expected, the acceptance of the work is "not free enough to make the enrichment 'unjust'": cf. Birks, op. cit. at 116. Accordingly, it seems to me that the test for compensation in this class of case is whether the work done conferred on the plaintiff an incontrovertible benefit. If it did, the plaintiff must pay compensation as a prerequisite to obtaining an order for specific recovery of the chattel and the measure of that compensation is the amount of incontrovertible benefit.

Applying such a test to the instant case, one runs into the problem of the $20,000 trade-in. It seems to me that in this area of the law, one looks at the transaction as a whole. The plaintiff parted with his hull and the GAC trade-in. That is what the plaintiff lost less perhaps any amount that can be recovered from Cavalier Yachts. However, in this situation, because the only compensation which the second defendant can obtain is the amount of the incontrovertible benefit the position appears to be that the plaintiff should transfer to the second defendant any claim that it has against the first defendant rather than it be sent to the master to value the amount of such a claim.

On this basis, if one took the cost value of the work done (which is not the appropriate figure ordinarily) then the plaintiff would, upon indemnifying the second defendant in respect of sales tax, and upon assigning to the second defendant any claim he has against the first defendant, and upon paying to the second defendant the sum of $4,409, be entitled to an order that the yacht be delivered to him.

The debatable figure in the quotation that I have just set out is the $4,409. This is the cost price of the work. What needs to be considered by the master is the increased value in the yacht as a result of the second defendant's work rather than the cost of providing such work which cost presumably includes profit margins.

In all the circumstances, it seems to me appropriate that I merely publish these reasons and stand the proceedings over for short minutes of order to be brought in. It may be that the plaintiff just cannot afford to pay the sales tax and compensation in which case the parties may agree on the property being sold and some other order being made with respect to the proceeds. It may be that the parties can agree on figures to avoid an enquiry before the master.

So far as costs are concerned, the plaintiff has substantially but not entirely succeeded. I will hear counsel on costs when the short minutes are brought in, but it may well be that this is a case where the plaintiff should recover say two-third of his costs.

Order accordingly.

QUESTIONS AND COMMENTS

1. In *Thomas v. Robinson* [1977] N.Z.L.R. 385 (S.C.), referred to in *Cavalier Yachts*, Speight J. outlined (at 389-90) four tests one might employ to determine whether an accession has occurred:

> First is the case of injurious removal, namely, where the added chattels cannot be separated from the principal without destroying or seriously damaging it. Such cases could involve welding metal or similar irreversible process, as contrasted with cases of those mechanical constructions which can be separated into their integral parts. Given sufficient skill and patience even a motorcar engine can be removed leaving a non-functioning but undamaged remainder. According to Professor Guest's first suggestion, if the part can be removed without damaging the remaining principal chattel then there would be no accession even though the removed part is of vital functional importance. This test was adopted in several cases relating to tyres, in particular . . . in Canada in *Goodrich Silvertown Stores v. McGuire Motors Ltd.* [1936] 4 DLR 519.
>
> The second test which is suggested is even more stringent against the interests of the owner of the principal chattel and the inquiry is as to "separate existence". . . . On this approach accession would only arise if there has been complete incorporation to the point of extinction of identity such as a brick in a house or a plank in a ship. No authority I have found would question that that at least is a case of accession, but need the incorporation be as final as that?
>
> The third test and one which on first sight, makes most appeal in modern conditions from the point of commercial common sense, is that of destruction of utility. The question would be: even though the article can be removed without damage to the principal chattel, would that nevertheless destroy its usefulness as such. To this effect was a Canadian case, *Regina Chevrolet Sales Ltd. v. Riddell* [1942] 3 DLR 159, which has for reasons of common sense appealed to the learned magistrate. The judgment of Macdonald JA is based upon the concept that an article, such as a motor vehicle, is looked on in ordinary terms as a functioning unit and not as a collection of separate parts, and the intention of him who makes the substitution or addition is that the parts should blend with the principal chattel for the purpose for which it is in existence. With respect, I suggest that no compelling authority was cited to support the learned judge's statement of broad principle.
>
> A fourth test is suggested by Professor Guest — one of his own devising — namely, the degree and purpose of annexation. He suggests that the court's approach should be flexible and empirical so that articles intended to be permanent parts of the chattel would pass on accession but others could be treated as mere accessories depending in each case on the facts of the case including the degree of annexation, the nature of the chattel and the intention of the parties. . . .

See also *Frank Dunn Trailer Sales Ltd. v. Paziuk* 1994 CarswellSask 486, (sub nom. *Paziuk v. Frank Dunn Trailer Sales Ltd.*) 127 Sask. R. 303 (Q.B.).

Which test was applied in *Cavalier Yachts*? Is it necessary that the law adopt a single test of accession for all circumstances?

2. On what basis is the "principal chattel" determined for the purposes of the law of accession? What are the implications of that determination? Do you agree with the Court's finding as to which item formed the principal chattel?

3. Do you agree that McKeown should be required to compensate Spartech? If compensation is warranted, how should it be calculated?

4. Principles under the rubric of accession determine ownership of newborn animals. The general rule is that the owner of the mother owns the offspring. An exception has been carved out for swans: here the cygnets are divided equally between the owner of the cock and hen: *Case of Swans* (1592) 7 Co. Rep. 15b, 77 E.R. 435.

Assume that A loans two mares to B. The mares give birth during the course of the loan. Who is entitled to the offspring? See *Dillaree v. Doyle* 43 U.C.Q.B. 442, 1878 CarswellOnt 205 (Q.B.). Compare *Tucker v. Farm & General Investment Trust Ltd.* [1966] 2 Q.B. 421 (C.A.).

Gidney v. Shank
1995 CarswellMan 446, [1996] 2 W.W.R. 383 (C.A.)

Huband J.A.:

The case centres on a claim for restitution as a remedy for unjust enrichment. The claim was allowed in part by Beard J. of the Court of Queen's Bench on a motion by the plaintiff for summary judgment [[1995] 5 W.W.R. 385, (sub nom. *Gidney v. Feuerstein*) 101 Man. R. (2d) 197]. The amount of the judgment was $806.25, plus costs, and the defendant Feuerstein appealed.

Feuerstein was the owner of a freighter canoe which was stolen from him on some unidentified date prior to May of 1983. The record does not reveal the condition of the canoe at the time it was stolen.

In May of 1983, the plaintiff Gidney purchased a canoe from a third party, Darrell Hedman, for $100. At that time it was in a dilapidated condition. Gidney proceeded to repair it, investing one hundred hours of his own labour plus out-of-pocket expenses which cost $806.25.

In November of 1983, the police attended at Gidney's residence and the canoe was removed by the police as part of a criminal investigation. Ultimately, one Cam Walker was charged with and convicted of stealing the canoe from Feuerstein.

At the conclusion of the trial the authorities had a 21-foot freighter canoe on their hands, and both Gidney and Feuerstein laid claim to it. The canoe was returned to Feuerstein and on November 23, 1984 Gidney instituted a legal action in the Court of Queen's Bench. Besides Feuerstein, the statement of claim named several other defendants, namely, two police officers, a Crown attorney, and the Attorney-General of Saskatchewan. It asserted that those defendants were collectively responsible for the initial seizure of the canoe and the subsequent decision to return it to Feuerstein.

The statement of claim demands the return of the canoe and, in the alternative, a money judgment of $1,906.25 being the estimated value of the canoe at that time, plus compensation for loss of enjoyment, and damages for the unreasonable seizure of the canoe by the co-defendants.

At some stage a settlement was arrived at between Gidney and the other co-defendants, under which Gidney received $2,000.

Not much happened with respect to the claim against Feuerstein until the spring of 1993 when Gidney moved for summary judgment.

When the matter finally came on for argument before the motions judge, Gidney was represented by counsel but Feuerstein did not appear and was unrepresented.

The case was argued on the basis of restitution and unjust enrichment. Beard J. wrote a lengthy judgment in which she makes a masterful review of the authorities. Ultimately, she concluded that this was a case of unjust enrichment for which the remedy should be a monetary award. Taking into account the settlement which had taken place with the co-defendants, the motions judge concluded that the amount should be $806.25, being Gidney's out-of-pocket expenses in making the repairs.

The motions judge refers to the criteria for determining that there has been unjust enrichment, as expressed in the reasons for decision of Dickson J., first in *Rathwell v. Rathwell*, [1978] 2 S.C.R. 436 [[1978] 2 W.W.R. 101], and subsequently in *Becker v. Pettkus*, [1980] 2 S.C.R. 834 at 848:

> . . . there are three requirements to be satisfied before an unjust enrichment can be said to exist: an enrichment, a corresponding deprivation and absence of any juristic reason for the enrichment. This approach, it seems to me, is supported by general principles of equity that have been fashioned by the courts for centuries . . .

Beard J. held that, the canoe having been returned to Feuerstein in an improved condition, there was an enrichment. She also concluded that there was a corresponding deprivation to Gidney who lost the benefit of his labour and expenditures. With these conclusions I am in full accord.

But the learned motions judge also found that there was no juristic reason for the enrichment, and on that point I am unable to agree. While the reasons for decision are lengthy, that portion dealing with the existence, or otherwise, of juristic reason for the enrichment are quite brief (at p. 210):

The third element proposed in *Rathwell*, that of a lack of juristic reason for the enrichment, is met in this case by the plaintiff's evidence that it was his mistaken belief of ownership which caused him to undertake the repairs to the canoe. In *Rathwell*, Dickson J. qualified the requirement for a lack of juristic reason with the words "such as a contract or other disposition of law" (at p. 306). Maddaugh and McCamus ["The Law of Restitution" (Aurora: Canada Law Books Inc., 1990)] state that the "other disposition of law" would include such things as a valid gift or a law, such as a taxation law, requiring payment (at p. 46). In this case, the uncontradicted evidence is that the benefit resulted from a mistake of fact, being the plaintiff's belief that he was the owner of the canoe, and there is no evidence that there is any juristic reason which would entitle the defendant to retain the benefit.

With respect, I think that "juristic reason" was given too narrow an interpretation. In my view there was a juristic reason for the enrichment, namely, that there was no relationship between Gidney and Feuerstein, and consequently Feuerstein had no knowledge that Gidney was investing time and money in the canoe. Feuerstein neither consented nor acquiesced to that investment. In the case of *Fibrosa Spolka Akcyjna v. Fairbairn Lawson Combe Barbour Ltd.*, [1943] A.C. 32 (H.L.), Lord Wright made this comment (at p. 61):

It is clear that any civilized system of law is bound to provide remedies for cases of what has been called unjust enrichment or unjust benefit, that is to prevent a man from retaining the money of or some benefit derived from another which it is against conscience that he should keep.

The reference to conscience is germane. In the cases where unjust enrichment is found to exist, and where a remedy is provided, it would be inequitable for the defendant to retain the benefit. But that is because the defendant knew, or should have known, of the plaintiff's efforts and either consented or acquiesced to what the defendant was doing. Where that is so it is against conscience for the defendant to retain the benefit without compensation. But in the present case there is nothing to bind the conscience of Feuerstein.

In *Hill Estate v. Chevron Standard Ltd.* (1992), 83 Man. R. (2d) 58 [[1993] 2 W.W.R. 545], this Court considered the issue of unjust enrichment in a dispute regarding an oil lease. One William Jennings Hill owned certain mineral rights. Chevron Standard Ltd. acquired a lease of those mineral rights, but it turned out to be void. Nevertheless, after the death of Mr. Hill Chevron proceeded to successfully drill for oil. The question arose whether Chevron could maintain a claim against the Hill estate for unjust enrichment. No doubt the Hill estate was enriched, and there was a corresponding deprivation to Chevron. But this court held that there was indeed a juristic reason for the enrichment (at pp. 70-71):

Where the Chevron case fails is that there is indeed a "juristic reason" for the enrichment, namely, that, functioning without a valid lease, Chevron was a trespasser in drilling for and extracting oil belonging to the William Jennings Hill estate.

Decided cases are of little assistance in determining what is meant by "juristic reason." It simply comes down to this: if there is an explanation based upon law for the enrichment of one at the detriment of another, then the enrichment will not be considered unjust and no remedy, whether by constructive trust or otherwise, will be available. For example, there might be a contract between the parties under the terms of which an enrichment by one at the expense of the other is contemplated or justified.

In the present case, had Chevron been a licensee invited onto the property to drill for petroleum, equity might have come to its assistance, as was the case in *Inwards and others v. Baker*, [1965] 1 All E.R. 446. In that case a father induced his son to build a bungalow on the father's land. The son did so, and invested some moneys in the project in the expectation of being allowed to live in the dwelling. Upon the father's death, the trustees of the father's estate attempted to dispossess the son and take over the property, but the court, on equitable grounds, upheld the right of the son to remain.

It is understandable that equity would protect a licensee, but I cannot see how equity will afford protection to a trespasser. Chevron's lease was void, and Chevron had been so warned by the letter of December 8, 1982 from [the estate's solicitor].

But the matter rests not on the warning given, but rather on the fact that, from beginning to end, Chevron had no leave or license from William Jennings Hill to deal with his mineral holdings. Neither William Jennings Hill in his lifetime nor the administratrix of his estate after his death, authorized Chevron to trespass upon their property. In proceeding without valid legal authority Chevron provided the juristic reason for the enrichment, and it cannot be regarded as unjust.

The "explanation based on law" in the present case is the absence of any relationship between the parties, coupled with the ownership of the canoe by Feuerstein. The absence of a relationship necessarily meant that Feuerstein had no knowledge and that he neither consented nor acquiesced to the betterment of his canoe.

I should make it clear that we would confront an entirely different situation if the canoe had remained in Gidney's possession and the legal action had been commenced by Feuerstein in an attempt to reclaim the property. There is case law to the effect that in an action for detinue the Court has a discretion to exercise as to whether it will order restitution or give damages in lieu thereof: *Mayne v. Kidd* (1951), 1 W.W.R. (N.S.) 833 (Sask. C.A.). I make no comment as to what might have been appropriate in that very different factual situation.

Feuerstein is entitled to costs in this Court. Because he was unrepresented at the time, Feuerstein is not entitled to costs in the Court of Queen's Bench but the order of costs against him in that Court is also set aside.

Appeal allowed.

QUESTIONS AND COMMENTS

1. Contrast the analysis in *Gidney v. Shank* with that in *McKeown v. Cavalier Yachts*.

2. In 1996, Adam bought an antique bugle in an antique shop for $300. He had the bugle gold-plated, a process that was completed in two days. The total cost of the

plating was $700. (Adam's intention was to sell the bugle.) The bugle, it is discovered, belongs to Joan Pusey, who sues for its return. How would you resolve the dispute?

3. Z finds a Dave Keon hockey card from 1966-67. Its original value was about 10 cents. A huge fan of Keon, Z has the card encased in a thick plastic lamination with a wooden base, at a cost of $35. Later it is established that the card belongs to A. And estimates are that the card is now worth $100. Who is entitled to the card? In answering that question, identify uncertainty on the facts and in the law.

4. In what ways, if at all, do the principles discussed in these cases resemble the law governing improvements mistakenly made on the land of another (such as section 37 of the *Conveyancing and Law of Property Act*, R.S.O. 1990, c. C.34)?

5. The problems that arise in relation to the combining of choses in possession (oil, yachts, canoes, and so on) can occur in relation to choses in action. For example, it is well established that a trustee must not commingle trust funds with other monies. Imagine that a trustee withdraws money from a trust account and deposits it in his or her personal account. So long as the money remains there no particular difficulty arises. Assume, however, that money is withdrawn and used to purchase some asset. Whose money are we to assume has been used? Should it matter if the money is squandered on a bad investment, or used to acquire an asset that appreciates in value? What policies should guide the law? See further L.D. Smith, *The Law of Tracing* (Oxford: Clarendon Pr., 1997) for a detailed consideration of this complex area. See also *Foskett v. McKeown* (2000) [2001] 1 A.C. 102 (H.L.).

6. Consider also subsection 4(2) of Ontario's *Family Law Act*, R.S.O. 1990, c. F.3. Under Part I of that Act, a court is empowered to divide marital property on marriage breakdown or the death of a spouse. Some holdings are exempt from division, such as pre-marriage property. Once the parties are married, if the exempt property is used to acquire other type of property, the original exemption is, in effect, "traced" to the new property:

> 4.(2) The value of the following property that a spouse owns on the valuation date does not form part of the spouse's net family property:
>
> > 1. Property, other than a matrimonial home, that was acquired by gift or inheritance from a third person after the date of the marriage.
> >
> > 2. Income from property referred to in paragraph 1, if the donor or testator has expressly stated that it is to be excluded from the spouse's net family property.
> >
> > 3. Damages or a right to damages for personal injuries, nervous shock, mental distress or loss of guidance, care and companionship, or the part of a settlement that represents those damages.
> >
> > 4. Proceeds or a right to proceeds of a policy of life insurance, as defined in the *Insurance Act*, that are payable on the death of the life insured.

> 5. *Property, other than a matrimonial home, into which property referred to in paragraphs 1 to 4 can be traced.* [Emphasis added.]

Assume, for instance, that at the time of marriage W had $3,000 in a savings account. Shortly after the marriage W deposited additional money, and there are withdrawals and deposits on an ongoing basis. Some of the money is used for groceries, some for consumer durables. How does one calculate the extent of the remaining exemptions? Should the same principles that regulate trustees be applied here? See further B. Ziff, "The Tracing of Matrimonial Property: A Preliminary Analysis" in M.E. Hughes & E.D. Pask, eds., *National Themes in Family Law* (Toronto: Carswell, 1988) at 55.

7. Finally, consider an illustration drawn from the law of intellectual property. First, assume that A prints 10,000 copies of a manuscript, the copyright to which is owned by its author, B. The breach of copyright having been detected, B now lays claim to the books. In effect, B's copyright has become intermixed with A's paper and ink. Section 38 of the *Copyright Act*, R.S.C. 1985, c. C-42, contemplates such a situation:

> Subject to subsection (2), the owner of the copyright in a work or other subject-matter may
>
> > (a) recover possession of all infringing copies of the work or other subject-matter, and of all plates used or intended to be used for the production of infringing copies, and
> >
> > (b) take proceedings for seizure of those copies or plates before judgment if, under the law of Canada or of the province in which those proceedings are taken, a person is entitled to take such proceedings, as if those copies or plates were the property of the copyright owner.
>
> (2) On application by
>
> > (a) a person from whom the copyright owner has recovered possession of copies or plates referred to in subsection (1),
> >
> > (b) a person against whom proceedings for seizure before judgment of copies or plates referred to in subsection (1) have been taken, or
> >
> > (c) any other person who has an interest in those copies or plates a court may order that those copies or plates be destroyed, or may make any other order that it considers appropriate in the circumstances. . . .
>
> (4) In making an order under subsection (2), the court shall have regard to all the circumstances, including
>
> > (a) the proportion, importance and value of the infringing copy or plate, as compared to the substrate or carrier embodying it; and
> >
> > (b) the extent to which the infringing copy or plate is severable from, or a distinct part of, the substrate or carrier embodying it.

To what extent, if at all, do these provisions differ from the common law principles discussed above?

CHAPTER 4
THE CONCEPT OF POSSESSION

1. INTRODUCTION

Possession is a concept of considerable importance in the law. Yet it is also a term that possesses great flexibility. Its core meaning accords with our intuitive understanding of the term, but at the margins there is considerable scope for definitional uncertainty.

Chapter 1 examined the idea that first occupancy is sometimes invoked to justify property claims. It remains one use of the idea of possession in law. The topics considered here are designed to demonstrate the roles that possession plays in *ordering*, *proving*, and *perfecting* property claims. This analysis reveals a great deal about the relative nature of title in Canadian law, and the place of certainty and repose in advancing efficiency and fairness.

To begin, we examine the meaning(s) and legal significance of the age-old idea of possession as the basis of title by reference to a twenty-first century decision about a very valuable baseball.

2. SOME BASIC DEFINITIONS

Popov v. Hayashi
2002 WL 31833731 (Cal. S.C.) [footnotes omitted]

McCarthy J.:

Facts:

In 1927, Babe Ruth hit sixty home runs. That record stood for thirty-four years until Roger Maris broke it in 1961 with sixty-one home runs. Mark McGwire hit seventy in 1998. On October 7, 2001, at PacBell Park in San Francisco, Barry Bonds hit number seventy-three. That accomplishment set a record which, in all probability, will remain unbroken for years into the future.

The event was widely anticipated and received a great deal of attention.

The ball that found itself at the receiving end of Mr. Bond's bat garnered some of that attention. Baseball fans in general, and especially people at the game, understood the importance of the ball. It was worth a great deal of money and whoever caught it would bask, for a brief period of time, in the reflected fame of Mr. Bonds.

With that in mind, many people who attended the game came prepared for the possibility that a record setting ball would be hit in their direction. Among this group were plaintiff Alex Popov and defendant Patrick Hayashi. They were unacquainted at the time. Both men brought baseball gloves, which they anticipated using if the ball came within their reach.

They, along with a number of others, positioned themselves in the arcade section of the ballpark. This is a standing room only area located near right field. It is in this general area that Barry Bonds hits the greatest number of home runs. The area was crowded with people on October 7, 2001 and access was restricted to those who held tickets for that section.

Barry Bonds came to bat in the first inning. With nobody on base and a full count, Bonds swung at a slow knuckleball. He connected. The ball sailed over the right-field fence and into the arcade . . .

When the seventy-third home run ball went into the arcade, it landed in the upper portion of the webbing of a softball glove worn by Alex Popov. While the glove stopped the trajectory of the ball, it is not at all clear that the ball was secure. Popov had to reach for the ball and in doing so, may have lost his balance.

Even as the ball was going into his glove, a crowd of people began to engulf Mr. Popov. He was tackled and thrown to the ground while still in the process of attempting to complete the catch. Some people intentionally descended on him for the purpose of taking the ball away, while others were involuntarily forced to the ground by the momentum of the crowd.

Eventually, Mr. Popov was buried face down on the ground under several layers of people. At one point he had trouble breathing. Mr. Popov was grabbed, hit and kicked. People reached underneath him in the area of his glove. Neither the tape nor the testimony is sufficient to establish which individual members of the crowd were responsible for the assaults on Mr. Popov. The videotape clearly establishes that this was an out of control mob, engaged in violent, illegal behavior. Although some witnesses testified in a manner inconsistent with this finding, their testimony is specifically rejected as being false on a material point.

Mr. Popov intended at all times to establish and maintain possession of the ball. At some point the ball left his glove and ended up on the ground. It is impossible to establish the exact point in time that this occurred or what caused it to occur.

Mr. Hayashi was standing near Mr. Popov when the ball came into the stands. He, like Mr. Popov, was involuntarily forced to the ground. He committed no wrongful act. While on the ground he saw the loose ball. He picked it up, rose to his feet and put it in his pocket . . .

Mr. Popov eventually got up from the ground. He made several statements while he was on the ground and shortly after he got up which are consistent with his claim that he had achieved some level of control over the ball and that he intended to keep it. Those statements can be heard on the audio portion of the tape. When he saw that Mr. Hayashi had the ball he expressed relief and grabbed for it. Mr. Hayashi pulled the ball away. Security guards then took Mr. Hayashi to a secure area of the stadium.

It is important to point out what the evidence did not and could not show. Neither the camera nor the percipient witnesses were able to establish whether Mr. Popov retained control of the ball as he descended into the crowd. Mr. Popov's testimony on this question is inconsistent on several important points, ambiguous on others and, on the whole, unconvincing. We do not know when or how Mr. Popov lost the ball.

Perhaps the most critical factual finding of all is one that cannot be made. We will never know if Mr. Popov would have been able to retain control of the ball had the crowd not interfered with his efforts to do so. Resolution of that question is the work of a psychic, not a judge.

Legal Analysis:

Plaintiff has pled causes of actions for conversion, trespass to chattel, injunctive relief and constructive trust.

Conversion is the wrongful exercise of dominion over the personal property of another. There must be actual interference with the plaintiff's dominion. Wrongful withholding of property can constitute actual interference even where the defendant lawfully acquired the property. If a person entitled to possession of personal property demands its return, the unjustified refusal to give the property back is conversion.

The act constituting conversion must be intentionally done. There is no requirement, however, that the defendant know that the property belongs to another or that the defendant intends to dispossess the true owner of its use and enjoyment. Wrongful purpose is not a component of conversion . . .

Conversion does not exist, however, unless the baseball rightfully belongs to Mr. Popov. One who has neither title nor possession, nor any right to possession, cannot sue for conversion. The deciding question in this case then, is whether Mr. Popov achieved possession or the right to possession as he attempted to catch and hold on to the ball.

The parties have agreed to a starting point for the legal analysis. Prior to the time the ball was hit, it was possessed and owned by Major League Baseball. At the time it was hit it became intentionally abandoned property. The first person who came in possession of the ball became its new owner.

The parties fundamentally disagree about the definition of possession. In order to assist the court in resolving this disagreement, four distinguished law professors participated in a forum to discuss the legal definition of possession. The professors also disagreed.

[They are Professor Brian E. Gray, University of California, Hastings College of the Law; Professor Roger Bernhardt, Golden Gate University School of Law; Professor Paul Finkelman, The Chapman Distinguished Professor of Law, The University of Tulsa School of Law; and Professor Jan Stiglitz, California Western School of Law. The discussion was held during an official session of the court convened at The University of California, Hastings College of the Law. The session was attended by a number of students and professors including one first year property law class which used this case as vehicle to understand the law of possession: footnote 17]

The disagreement is understandable. Although the term possession appears repeatedly throughout the law, its definition varies depending on the context in which it is used. Various courts have condemned the term as vague and meaningless.

This level of criticism is probably unwarranted.

While there is a degree of ambiguity built into the term possession, that ambiguity exists for a purpose. Courts are often called upon to resolve conflicting claims of possession in the context of commercial disputes. A stable economic environment requires rules of conduct which are understandable and consistent with the fundamental customs and practices of the industry they regulate. Without that, rules will be difficult to enforce and economic instability will result. Because each industry has different customs and practices, a single definition of possession cannot be applied to different industries without creating havoc.

This does not mean that there are no central principles governing the law of possession. It is possible to identify certain fundamental concepts that are common to every definition of possession.

Professor Roger Bernhardt has recognized that "[p]ossession requires both physical control over the item and an intent to control it or exclude others from it. But these generalizations function more as guidelines than as direct determinants of possession issues. Possession is a blurred question of law and fact."

Professor Brown argues that "[t]he orthodox view of possession regards it as a union of the two elements of the physical relation of the possessor to the thing, and of intent. This physical relation is the actual power over the thing in question, the ability to hold and make use of it. But a mere physical relation of the possessor to the thing in question is not enough. There must also be manifested an intent to control it."

The task of this court is to use these principles as a starting point to craft a definition of possession that applies to the unique circumstances of this case.

We start with the observation that possession is a process which culminates in an event. The event is the moment in time that possession is achieved. The process includes the acts and thoughts of the would be possessor which lead up to the moment of possession.

The focus of the analysis in this case is not on the thoughts or intent of the actor. Mr. Popov has clearly evidenced an intent to possess the baseball and has communicated that intent to the world. The question is whether he did enough to reduce the ball to his exclusive dominion and control. Were his acts sufficient to create a legally cognizable interest in the ball?

Mr. Hayashi argues that possession does not occur until the fan has complete control of the ball. Professor Brian Gray, suggests the following definition "A person who catches a baseball that enters the stands is its owner. A ball is caught if the person has achieved complete control of the ball at the point in time that the momentum of the ball and the momentum of the fan while attempting to catch the ball ceases. A baseball, which is dislodged by incidental contact with an inanimate object or another person, before momentum has ceased, is not possessed. Incidental contact with another person is contact that is not intended by the other person. The first person to pick up a loose ball and secure it becomes its possessor."

Mr. Popov argues that this definition requires that a person seeking to establish possession must show unequivocal dominion and control, a standard rejected by several leading cases. Instead, he offers the perspectives of Professor Bernhardt and Professor Paul Finkelman who suggest that possession occurs when an individual intends to take control of a ball and manifests that intent by stopping the forward momentum of the ball whether or not complete control is achieved.

Professors Finkelman and Bernhardt have correctly pointed out that some cases recognize possession even before absolute dominion and control is achieved. Those cases require the actor to be actively and ably engaged in efforts to establish complete control. Moreover, such efforts must be significant and they must be reasonably calculated to result in unequivocal dominion and control at some point in the near future.

This rule is applied in cases involving the hunting or fishing of wild animals or the salvage of sunken vessels. The hunting and fishing cases recognize that a mortally wounded animal may run for a distance before falling. The hunter acquires possession upon the act of wounding the animal not the eventual capture. Similarly, whalers acquire possession by landing a harpoon, not by subduing the animal.

In the salvage cases, an individual may take possession of a wreck by exerting as much control "as its nature and situation permit". Inadequate efforts, however, will not support a claim of possession. Thus, a "sailor cannot assert a claim merely by boarding a vessel and publishing a notice, unless such acts are coupled with a then present intention of conducting salvage operations, and he immediately thereafter proceeds with activity in the form of constructive steps to aid the distressed party."

These rules are contextual in nature. The are crafted in response to the unique nature of the conduct they seek to regulate. Moreover, they are influenced by the custom and practice of each industry. The reason that absolute dominion and control is not required to establish possession in the cases cited by Mr. Popov is that such a rule would be unworkable and unreasonable. The "nature and situation" of the property at issue does not immediately lend itself to unequivocal dominion and control. It is impossible to wrap ones arms around a whale, a fleeing fox or a sunken ship.

The opposite is true of a baseball hit into the stands of a stadium. Not only is it physically possible for a person to acquire unequivocal dominion and control of an abandoned baseball, but fans generally expect a claimant to have accomplished as much. The custom and practice of the stands creates a reasonable expectation that a person will achieve full control of a ball before claiming possession. There is no reason for the legal rule to be inconsistent with that expectation. Therefore Gray's Rule is adopted as the definition of possession in this case.

The central tenet of Gray's Rule is that the actor must retain control of the ball after incidental contact with people and things. Mr. Popov has not established by a preponderance of the evidence that he would have retained control of the ball after all momentum ceased and after any incidental contact with people or objects. Consequently, he did not achieve full possession.

That finding, however, does not resolve the case. The reason we do not know whether Mr. Popov would have retained control of the ball is not because of incidental contact. It is because he was attacked. His efforts to establish possession were interrupted by the collective assault of a band of wrongdoers.

A decision which ignored that fact would endorse the actions of the crowd by not repudiating them. Judicial rulings, particularly in cases that receive media attention, affect the way people conduct themselves. This case demands vindication of an important principle. We are a nation governed by law, not by brute force.

As a matter of fundamental fairness, Mr. Popov should have had the opportunity to try to complete his catch unimpeded by unlawful activity. To hold otherwise would be to allow the result in this case to be dictated by violence. That will not happen.

For these reasons, the analysis cannot stop with the valid observation that Mr. Popov has not proved full possession.

The legal question presented at this point is whether an action for conversion can proceed where the plaintiff has failed to establish possession or title. It can. An action for conversion may be brought where the plaintiff has title, possession or the right to possession.

Here Mr. Popov seeks, in effect, a declaratory judgment that he has either possession or the right to possession. In addition he seeks the remedies of injunctive relief and a constructive trust. These are all actions in equity. A court sitting in equity has the authority to fashion rules and remedies designed to achieve fundamental fairness.

Consistent with this principle, the court adopts the following rule. Where an actor undertakes significant but incomplete steps to achieve possession of a piece of abandoned personal property and the effort is interrupted by the unlawful acts of others, the actor has a legally cognizable pre-possessory interest in the property. That pre-possessory interest constitutes a qualified right to possession which can support a cause of action for conversion.

Possession can be likened to a journey down a path. Mr. Popov began his journey unimpeded. He was fast approaching a fork in the road. A turn in one direction would lead to possession of the ball — he would complete the catch. A turn in the other direction would result in a failure to achieve possession — he would drop the ball. Our problem is that before Mr. Popov got to the point where the road forked, he was set upon by a gang of bandits, who dislodged the ball from his grasp.

Recognition of a legally protected pre-possessory interest, vests Mr. Popov with a qualified right to possession and enables him to advance a legitimate claim to the baseball based on a conversion theory. Moreover it addresses the harm done by the unlawful actions of the crowd.

It does not, however, address the interests of Mr. Hayashi. The court is required to balance the interests of all parties.

Mr. Hayashi was not a wrongdoer. He was a victim of the same bandits that attacked Mr. Popov. The difference is that he was able to extract himself from their assault and move to the side of the road. It was there that he discovered the loose ball. When he picked up and put it in his pocket he attained unequivocal dominion and control.

If Mr. Popov had achieved complete possession before Mr. Hayashi got the ball, those actions would not have divested Mr. Popov of any rights, nor would they have created any rights to which Mr. Hayashi could lay claim. Mr. Popov, however, was able to establish only a qualified pre-possessory interest in the ball. That interest does not establish a full right to possession that is protected from a subsequent legitimate claim.

On the other hand, while Mr. Hayashi appears on the surface to have done everything necessary to claim full possession of the ball, the ball itself is encumbered by the qualified pre-possessory interest of Mr. Popov. At the time Mr. Hayashi came into possession of the ball, it had, in effect, a cloud on its title.

An award of the ball to Mr. Popov would be unfair to Mr. Hayashi. It would be premised on the assumption that Mr. Popov would have caught the ball. That assumption is not supported by the facts. An award of the ball to Mr. Hayashi would unfairly penalize Mr. Popov. It would be based on the assumption that Mr. Popov would have dropped the ball. That conclusion is also unsupported by the facts.

Both men have a superior claim to the ball as against all the world. Each man has a claim of equal dignity as to the other. We are, therefore, left with something of a dilemma.

Thankfully, there is a middle ground.

The concept of equitable division was fully explored in a law review article authored by Professor R.H. Helmholz in the December 1983 edition of the Fordham Law Review. Professor Helmholz addressed the problems associated with rules governing finders of lost and mislaid property. For a variety of reasons not directly relevant to the issues raised in this case, Helmholz suggested employing the equitable remedy of division to resolve competing claims between finders of lost or mislaid property and the owners of land on which the property was found.

There is no reason, however, that the same remedy cannot be applied in a case such as this, where issues of property, tort and equity intersect.

The concept of equitable division has its roots in ancient Roman law. As Helmholz points out, it is useful in that it "provides an equitable way to resolve competing claims which are equally strong." Moreover, "[i]t comports with what one instinctively feels to be fair".

Although there is no California case directly on point, *Arnold v. Producers Fruit Company* (1900) 128 Cal. 637 provides some insight. There, a number of different prune growers contracted with Producer's Fruit Company to dry and market their product. Producers did a bad job. They mixed fruit from many different growers together in a single bin and much of the fruit rotted because it was improperly treated.

When one of the plaintiffs offered proof that the fruit in general was rotten, Producers objected on the theory that the plaintiff could not prove that the prunes he contributed to the mix were the same prunes that rotted. The court concluded that it did not matter. After the mixing was done, each grower had an undivided interest in the whole, in proportion to the amount of fruit each had originally contributed.

The principle at work here is that where more than one party has a valid claim to a single piece of property, the court will recognize an undivided interest in the property in proportion to the strength of the claim.

Application of the principle of equitable division is illustrated in the case of *Keron v. Cashman* (1896) 33 A. 1055. In that case, five boys were walking home along a railroad track in the city of Elizabeth New Jersey. The youngest of the boys came upon an old sock that was tied shut and contained something heavy. He picked it up and swung it. The oldest boy took it away from him and beat the others with it. The sock passes from boy to boy. Each controlled it for a short time. At some point in the course of play, the sock broke open and out spilled $775 as well as some rags, cloths and ribbons.

The court noted that possession requires both physical control and the intent to reduce the property to one's possession. Control and intent must be concurrent. None of the boys intended to take possession until it became apparent that the sock contained money. Each boy had physical control of the sock at some point before that discovery was made.

Because none could present a superior claim of concurrent control and intent, the court held that each boy was entitled to an equal share of the money. Their legal claims to the property were of equal quality, therefore their entitlement to the property was also equal.

Here, the issue is not intent, or concurrence. Both men intended to possess the ball at the time they were in physical contact with it. The issue, instead, is the legal quality of the claim. With respect to that, neither can present a superior argument as against the other.

Mr. Hayashi's claim is compromised by Mr. Popov's pre-possessory interest. Mr. Popov cannot demonstrate full control. Albeit for different reasons, they stand before the court in exactly the same legal position as did the five boys. Their legal claims are of equal quality and they are equally entitled to the ball.

The court therefore declares that both plaintiff and defendant have an equal and undivided interest in the ball. Plaintiff's cause of action for conversion is sustained only as to his equal and undivided interest. In order to effectuate this ruling, the ball must be sold and the proceeds divided equally between the parties.

The parties are ordered to meet and confer forthwith before Judge Richard Kramer to come to an agreement as to how to implement this decision. If no decision is made by December 30, 2002, the parties are directed to appear before this court on that date at 9:00 am.

The court retains jurisdiction to issue orders consistent with this decision. The ball is to remain in the custody of the court until further order.

NOTE

On June 25, 2003, the Bonds baseball was sold at auction to Todd McFarlane (formerly of Calgary, and the creator of the Spawn comic), for US$450,000. Several years earlier McFarlane had paid US$3.2 million for Mark McGwire's 70th home run ball.

In accordance with the ruling of McCarthy J., the proceeds were split between Popov and Hayashi. The San Jose Mercury News reported that Hayashi believed that his share would essentially cover his legal expenses, but little more. "'I'm pretty certain it will be a wash for me,' he said, noting that his legal bills were in the range of $200,000. But nevertheless the former Cisco employee seemed relieved that the ordeal was over": L. Arantani, "Bonds' 73rd homer sells for $450,000", San Jose

Mercury News, June 25, 2003, online: <www.mercurynews.com/mld/mercurynews/sports/6176766.htm>. Popov's bill was much higher: $473,500.

QUESTIONS AND COMMENTS

1. What elements are necessary to constitute possession in law? Based on the facts outlined in the judgment, in your opinion was Popov in possession?

2. The rules of baseball applied in the major leagues provide the following description of a "catch":

> A CATCH is the act of a fielder in getting secure possession in his hand or glove of a ball in flight and firmly holding it; providing he does not use his cap, protector, pocket or any other part of his uniform in getting possession. It is not a catch, however, if simultaneously or immediately following his contact with the ball, he collides with a player, or with a wall, or if he falls down, and as a result of such collision or falling, drops the ball. It is not a catch if a fielder touches a fly ball which then hits a member of the offensive team or an umpire and then is caught by another defensive player. If the fielder has made the catch and drops the ball while in the act of making a throw following the catch, the ball shall be adjudged to have been caught. In establishing the validity of the catch, the fielder shall hold the ball long enough to prove that he has complete control of the ball and that his release of the ball is voluntary and intentional. A catch is legal if the ball is finally held by any fielder, even though juggled, or held by another fielder before it touches the ground. Runners may leave their bases the instant the first fielder touches the ball. A fielder may reach over a fence, railing, rope or other line of demarcation to make a catch. He may jump on top of a railing, or canvas that may be in foul ground. No interference should be allowed when a fielder reaches over a fence, railing, rope or into a stand to catch a ball. He does so at his own risk. If a fielder, attempting a catch at the edge of the dugout, is "held up" and kept from an apparent fall by a player or players of either team and the catch is made, it shall be allowed.

This definition was not referred to in the judgment. Would it be relevant?

3. According to McCarthy J., what is required to create a pre-possessory interest? Do you agree with the Court's resolution of the case?

4. What function is served by the basic rule requiring the interference with possession (or the right to possession) as the foundation of an action in conversion?

5. As alluded to in *Popov v. Hayashi*, the law of possession has been central to the common law rules governing the ownership of wild animals. In the Australian decision of *Yanner v. Eaton* (1999) 166 A.L.R. 258 (Australia H.C.), reproduced in Chapter 1, the basic common law rules concerning the acquisition of title to wild animals were summarized by Gleeson J. (at 265-6):

> At common law, wild animals were the subject of only the most limited property rights. At common law, there could be no "absolute property" but only "qualified property" in fire, light, air, water and wild animals. An action for trespass or conversion would lie against a person taking wild animals that had been tamed, or a person taking young wild

animals born on the land and not yet old enough to fly or run away, and a landowner had the exclusive right to hunt, take and kill wild animals on his [or her] own land [*per ratione soli*]. Otherwise no person had property in a wild animal.

Ownership is described as being "qualified" and not absolute because title is lost if the animal escapes. What is the rationale for conferring only a qualified property right over wild animals?

6. What should count as sufficient possession so as to give rise to a right to property in wild animals? That question arose in the famous case of *Pierson v. Post* 3 Caines 175 (S.C.N.Y., 1805). There, as Post was pursuing a fox, Pierson intervened, killing the fox and taking possession of it. An action for trespass was initiated by Post against Pierson. After a review of the ancient learning on the subject of possession, Tompkins J., for the majority, held for Pierson:

> . . . *Pufendorf*, lib. 4. c. 6. s. 2. and 10. defines occupancy of beasts *ferae naturae*, to be the actual corporal possession of them, and *Bynkershoek* is cited as coinciding in this definition. It is indeed with hesitation that Pufendorf affirms that a wild beast mortally wounded, or greatly maimed, cannot be fairly intercepted by another, whilst the pursuit of the person inflicting the wound continues. The foregoing authorities are decisive to show that mere pursuit gave Post no legal right to the fox, but that he became the property of Pierson, who intercepted and killed him.
>
> It therefore only remains to inquire whether there are any contrary principles, or authorities, to be found in other books, which ought to induce a different decision. . . .
>
> Barbeyrac, in his notes on *Pufendorf*, does not accede to the definition of occupancy by the latter, but, on the contrary, affirms, that actual bodily seizure is not, in all cases, necessary to constitute possession of wild animals. He does not, however, *describe* the acts which, according to his ideas, will amount to an appropriation of such animals to private use, so as to exclude the claims of all other persons, by title of occupancy, to the same animals; and he is far from averring that pursuit alone is sufficient for that purpose. To a certain extent, and as far as Barbeyrac appears to me to go, his objections to Pufendorf's definition of occupancy are reasonable and correct. That is to say, that actual bodily seizure is not indispensable to acquire right to, or possession of, wild beasts; but that, on the contrary, the mortal wounding of such beasts, by one not abandoning his pursuit, may, with the utmost propriety, be deemed possession of him; since, thereby, the pursuer manifests an unequivocal intention of appropriating the animal to his individual use, has deprived him of his natural liberty, and brought him within his certain control. So also, encompassing and securing such animals with nets and toils, or otherwise intercepting them in such a manner as to deprive them of their natural liberty, and render escape impossible, may justly be deemed to give possession of them to those persons who, by their industry and labour, have used such means of apprehending them . . . .
>
> The case now under consideration is one of mere pursuit, and presents no circumstances or acts which can bring it within the definition of occupancy by Pufendorf, . . . or the ideas of Barbeyrac upon that subject. . . .
>
> We are the more readily inclined to confine possession or occupancy of beasts *ferae naturae*, within the limits prescribed by the learned authors above cited, for the sake of

certainty, and preserving peace and order in society. If the first seeing, starting, or pursuing such animals, without having so wounded, circumvented or ensnared them, so as to deprive them of their natural liberty, and subject them to the control of their pursuer, should afford the basis of actions against others for intercepting and killing them, it would prove a fertile source of quarrels and litigation.

Livingston J. delivered a firey dissenting opinion. He suggested that the case "should have been submitted to the arbitration of sportsmen, without poring over Justinian, Fleta, Bracton, Pufendorf, Locke, Barbeyrac, or Blackstone". Moreover,

> [b]y the pleadings it is admitted that a fox is a "wild and noxious beast." Both parties have regarded him, as the law of nations does a pirate. . . . His depredations on farmers and on barn yards, have not been forgotten; and to put him to death wherever found, is allowed to be meritorious, and of public benefit. Hence it follows, that our decision should have in view the greatest possible encouragement to the destruction of an animal, so cunning and ruthless in his career. But who would keep a pack of hounds; or what gentleman, at the sound of the horn, and at peep of day, would mount his steed, and for hours together, "*sub jove frigido*," or a vertical sun, pursue the windings of this wily quadruped, if, just as night came on, and his stratagems and strength were nearly exhausted, a saucy intruder, who had not shared in the honours or labours of the chase, were permitted to come in at the death, and bear away in triumph the object of pursuit? . . .
>
> Now, as we are without any municipal regulations of our own, and the pursuit here, for aught that appears on the case, being with dogs and hounds of imperial stature, we are at liberty to adopt one of the provisions just cited, which comports also with the learned conclusion of Barbeyrac, that property in animals *ferae naturae* may be acquired without bodily touch or manucaption, provided the pursuer be within reach, or have a *reasonable* prospect (which certainly existed here) of taking, what he has *thus* discovered an intention of converting to his own use.

7. In what way, if at all, are economic and labour-based arguments used in the majority judgment in *Pierson v. Post*? In what way, if at all, does this line of reasoning differ from the focus of the dissenting opinion? Which of the two approaches found in *Pierson v. Post* generates the greatest enforcement costs? Which approach would produce the greatest cost to third parties (i.e., those affected by the presence or absence of foxes)? Which kinds of costs are likely to be greater? See further, D. Dharmapala & R. Pitchford, "An Economic Analysis of "Riding to Hounds": Pierson v. Post Revisited", 18 J. of L. Econ. & Org. 39 (2002).

8. Returning to *Popov v. Hayashi*, Patrick Stoklas has maintained that "Judge McCarthy's decision does not meet either of the concerns expressed in *Pierson v. Post*; it does not establish certainty, nor does it reduce conflict": P. Stoklas , "*Popov v. Hayashi*, A Modern Day *Pierson v. Post*: A Comment on What the Court Should Have Done with the Seventy-Third Home Run Baseball Hit By Barry Bonds", 34 Loy. U. Chicago L.J. 902 (2003) at 904-5. Is the winner-take-all approach found in *Pierson v. Post* to be preferred?

9. Compare *Pierson v. Post* with the Newfoundland case of *Doyle v. Bartlett* (1872) 5 Nfld. R. 445 (S.C.). In that case, members of a schooner called Native Lass,

commanded by Doyle, took possession of seal carcasses found piled and marked on the ice floes. The seals, some 800 in all, had been killed about 15 days earlier by the crew of the steamship Nimrod. White, the master of the Nimrod, had purported to gift the seals to Bartlett, master of the steamship Panther. (A gift requires a transfer of possession.) When the Panther reached the place where the carcasses had been deposited, the crews of the Native Lass and the Panther rushed to stow the carcasses. Who was entitled to the seals? Robinson J. held (at 450-2) as follows:

> The first question that was raised in the argument was, whether the verbal gift of the seals by White to Bartlett passed any property whatever to the donee, and upon that point there are conflicting authorities and the law is unsettled; but, according to my view, no necessity arises to determine that question, because it seems to me that White had not perfected his ownership of these seals, and, not having any right in himself, could not convey to another by any mode or instrument what he did possess.
>
> The grounds upon which I rest this opinion were fully stated by me in *Clift vs. Kane*, determined in March, 1870.
>
> I held, in that case, conformably as I believed with the established law of the land, that to enable anyone to acquire private property of animals *ferae naturae*, he must either actually have secured them in complete possession or have been (when interrupted by a wrong-doer) in a position to reduce them under his complete control, and that such control could not be said to have been completed so long as they continued floating about beyond his power to recover.
>
> The facts in the present case seem to me singularly illustrative of the reasonableness, if not absolute necessity of such a doctrine.
>
> It appears that in the latter end of March Captain White spread his numerous crew over a circuit of eight miles of ice, killing seals in all directions, leaving them where they were killed, and hoisting flags until at one time he had thirty-two ensigns flying over that vast area. Several thousands of these seals he appears never again to have reached or even to have seen, and, practically, he was as incapable of appropriating them to his own use as if he had never left port. Now, with great respect for those who entertain a different opinion, I cannot bring myself to believe that a man can consistently with law establish any claim whatsoever to wild animals which he had failed to capture, or can prevent others engaged in the same adventure from appropriating to their own use dead seals after the killer of them had left them adrift upon the ocean and demonstrated his inability to reclaim them. Still, in the absence of legislative enactment differences of opinion may and do arise in courts of justice upon the subject, for the seal-fishery is an enterprise peculiar in many of its features and in which circumstances are likely to occur wherein it is difficult to apply strict legal principles. The very element upon which it is carried on has no parallel as the scene of any other trade or business. It is conducted upon ice-fields that partake of the solidity of land and of the mobility of water, and the dominion which a hunter acquires over a wild animal by the mere act of killing it upon land is by no means as surely acquired over a seal on the ice, which is often as difficult to secure when dead as when living; it behoves, therefore, all engaged in such an adventure to act in a spirit of mutual concession, and, in pursuing their own interests, not to ignore the fair claims of *fellow-laborers*.

> In my opinion it may safely be affirmed that so long as the killer of seals has the "*animus revertendi*," combined with the *potentia recuperandi*, no one has a legal right to interfere with him, but the moment he abandons the pursuit of the dead animals, either from inability to reach them or incapacity to stow them, that moment they revert to the common stock and again become the prize of the first finder who can secure them.
>
> In this case Doyle was the first finder of the seals White had killed, but before he could secure them by manual possession Bartlett appeared upon the scene; thenceforth it became a race between the two crews as to which of them should take most, and each of them became the owners of just as many as and no more than they respectively secured by manual possession; the principle of constructive possession of the whole by reason of the possession of a part does not, in my opinion, apply to the case of seals situated as these were in relation to mere finders who were not killers.

In what ways, if at all, does *Doyle v. Bartlett* differ from *Pierson v. Post*? In establishing ownership rules for wild animals, should efficiency be the trumping value?

10. In *Popov v. Hayashi*, it was accepted that possession requires two elements: physical control and an intention to possess. However, as one can see from the rules discussed in *Pierson v. Post*, manual control (manucaption) is not always demanded. Sometimes "constructive possession" will suffice. In contemporary legal parlance, constructive possession refers to a form of possession in which the mandated elements of control and/or intention have been relaxed. An owner does not have to be constantly in contact with land to be in possession of it. Likewise, one might be considered to have the intention to possess items on one's property even though the presence of those items is unknown. These ideas are explored further in the discussion of adverse possession and finders law, below. For now, a simple example can be drawn from the law of animals.

Although the title to wild animals is normally lost once an animal escapes control, this rule is not applied if it can be demonstrated that the animal possesses *animus revertendi* (the intention or habit of returning). In other words, where a wild animal, say, a falcon, has been trained to return to its owner, the title is not lost even though it is no longer in the immediate control of the owner. How can this sub-rule be explained?

11. The general rule governing wild animals — the principle of first occupancy — is found throughout the law of property. One prominent application concerns the staking of claims to minerals under what is termed the system of free entry. See generally G. Barton, *Canadian Law of Mining* (Calgary: Canadian Institute of Resources Law, 1993) at ch. 5, *passim*. Its North American structure arose from the adaptation of English custom to the circumstances of the great gold rushes. Here, in its purest form, it allowed the staking of minerals claims on public lands on a first discovery basis. (As to the development of claim rules during the California gold rush, see A.G. McDowell, "From Commons to Claims: Property Rights in the California Gold Rush," 14 Yale J. of Law & Humanities 1 (2002)). The current mining regime in Ontario derives from those sources:

Except where otherwise provided, the holder of a prospector's licence may prospect for minerals and stake out a mining claim on any,

(a) Crown lands, surveyed or unsurveyed;

(b) lands, the mines, minerals or mining rights whereof have been reserved by the Crown in the location, sale, patent or lease of such lands where they have been located, sold, patented or leased after the 6th day of May, 1913,

not at the time,

(c) on record as a mining claim that has not lapsed or been abandoned, cancelled or forfeited; or

(d) withdrawn by any Act, order in council, or other competent authority from prospecting, location or sale, or declared by any such authority to be not open to prospecting, staking out or sale as mining claims.

A licensee may stake out a mining claim on any land open for prospecting and, subject to the other provisions of this Act, may work such claim and transfer his or her interest therein to another person, but, where the surface rights in the land have been granted, sold, leased or located by the Crown, compensation must be made . . . (*Mining Act*, R.S.O. 1990, c. M.14, ss. 27-8)

For the rules as to how to stake a claim properly, see O.Reg. 7/96.

12. A modern adaptation of the principle of first occupancy occurs daily in cyberspace. The practice of gaining first registration of a domain name in the hope of reselling at a profit is a common form of what is often referred to as "cybersquatting" (or name-napping). See generally B.B. Cotton, "Prospecting or Cybersquatting: Registering Your Name Before Someone Else Does", 35 J. Marshall L.Rev. 287 (2002), where three types of cybersquatters are described: "ransom grabbers" (as described above); "warehousers", who wait for the owner of the trademark to seek out a transfer; and "competitor grabbers" who intentionally register domain names containing typographical errors but which approximate famous names.

A controversy concerning cybersquatting arose in *Black v. Molson Canada* 2002 CarswellOnt 2414 (S.C.J.). There, Black acquired the domain name "Canadian.biz", through an application auction and lottery process. Later, Molson sought an order that Black transfer the domain name to the beer manufacturer. The dispute fell to be resolved under a protocol called the STOP policy, to which a party registering a domain name agrees to be bound. Under that protocol, an initial allocation of a domain name can be challenged and reallocated where there elements are found to be present: (1) the domain name is identical to a trademark or service mark in which the complainant has rights; (2) the respondent has no rights or legitimate interests in respect of the domain name; and (3) the domain name has been registered or is being used in bad faith. Ultimately, it was held that Black's plan to use the site as a clearinghouse for Canadian business opportunities was legitimate. In fact, Molson's challenge failed on all three criteria.

In these early days of cyber-jurisprudence, it is generally accepted that the acquisition of a domain name solely for the purpose of reselling it to someone else is not a legitimate use. Indeed the American *Anticyberquatting Consumer Protection Act*, which came into effect in 1999, provides that a civil action may be brought against a person who registers the name of another living person, or a name which is substantially and confusingly the same, "with the specific intent to profit from such a name by selling the domain name for financial gain to that person or any third party": 15 U.S.C. § 1129(1)(a). See also *Saskatoon Star Phoenix Group Inc. v. Noton* [2001] 9 W.W.R. 63, 2001 CarswellSask 325 (Q.B.). Why should that be so? Does such a rule contradict the proposition that first in time is first in right? Is cybersquatting inefficient? Would the application of the Coase theorem shine light on the issues here?

13. In "The New, New Property" 81 Texas L.Rev. 715 (2003) at 720, Anupam Chandler observes that:

> Like the fox in *Pierson v. Post*, domain names are now generally subject to the rule of first possession, with domain names handed out for a nominal sum on a first-come, first-served basis. By [a]warding domain names to those technologically adept and wealthy enough to grab available domain names . . . our current system replicates real-world inequalities in cyberspace.

What other allocation rules might be established in place of first occupancy? See K. Manheim & L. Solum, "An Economic Analysis of Domain Name Policy" online: <http://ssrn.com/abstract=410640>.

3. ACQUISITION OF TITLE BY POSSESSION: SQUATTERS

(a) land

In the summer of 2000, Mr. Zaoqi Guo discovered that his fence encroached onto the property of his next-door neighbour, Mrs. Dominica Carrozzi. It was a minor encroachment: about 1.6 feet at the front of their lots, and only .6 feet at the rear. It was Mrs. Carrozzi's recollection that the fence was there when she bought her land in 1986. Mr. Guo had purchased his lot in 1992 from the Vietnamese Canadian Buddhist Association; the association had owned that land since 1982.

Once the mistaken placement was uncovered, relations between the two property owners soured, and the matter wound up in court. Mr. Guo prevailed: an Ontario Superior Court held that although the fence was wrongly placed, Mr. Guo and his predecessors in title had been in adverse possession of the strip for a period of more than 10 years. Mrs. Carrozzi's title to the strip was extinguished: *Carrozzi v. Guo* 3 R.P.R. (4th) 203, 2002 CarswellOnt 3162 (S.C.J.).

There is nothing particularly remarkable about these facts or the outcome. Nor is the law of adverse possession confined to erroneous encroachments on small strips of property. The result in the case flows from the application of general principles governing the centuries-old law of adverse possession. How does the doctrine work? Why is adverse possession part of the law of property?

Keefer v. Arillotta
72 D.L.R. (3d) 182, 1976 CarswellOnt 853 (C.A.)

Wilson J.A.:

This is an appeal from an order of His Honour Judge Nicholls holding that the respondents had acquired a possessory title to a portion of the appellants' land subject to an easement remaining in the appellants.

The facts are more fully set out in the reasons for judgment of the learned trial judge but the more significant ones for purposes of this appeal may be summarized under the following headings:

1. the nature and location of the land in issue;

2. the chain of title;

3. the conduct of the owners.

The Nature and Location of the Land in Issue:

It is unnecessary to describe the land by its metes and bounds description. Suffice it to say that it is a narrow strip of land 8 feet wide by 105 feet deep running between the residential property of the respondents to the south and the business premises of the appellants to the north. The most easterly 41 feet of the strip running back from the street line is a stone drive-way. Extending westward from the drive-way is a grassy area running up to a frame garage owned by the respondents and located at the rear of the strip. A concrete walk-way adjacent to the appellants' store runs up the side of the store alongside the stone drive-way to a set of steps which lead up to a concrete landing giving access to an apartment located over the store. To the west of the steps and concrete landing is an entrance door to an addition which was built on to the rear of the store in 1949 by the appellants' predecessors in title.

The Chain of Title:

The appellants' and the respondents' properties were initially owned by one Martin Cloy. In 1918 Mr. Cloy conveyed the property now owned by the respondents to one Elzear Lynch together with a right-of-way of ingress and egress over a portion of his own property, the strip of land in issue on this appeal. In each subsequent conveyance of that property, including the conveyance made in July of 1957 to the respondents, the right-of-way over the appellants' land was granted.

When Mr. Cloy died in July of 1921 the land he had retained, now owned by the appellants, passed to his widow Maude Cloy who was also his executrix. As executrix she conveyed it to herself as devisee under the will but inadvertently included in the conveyance the lands already conveyed by her husband to Mr. Lynch. To rectify this error Mrs. Cloy made a new deed to Mrs. Lynch, who had acquired the land on her husband's death, and this deed made in April of 1926 included the grant of right-of-way over the strip of Mrs. Cloy's land. In November of 1952 Mrs. Cloy transferred her land to her son Douglas Cloy and again through inadvertence omitted to make that conveyance subject to the right-of-way in favour of Mrs. Lynch. Douglas Cloy remedied this in March of 1958 by a quit claim deed in favour of the respondents who by that time had become the owners of the adjoining land. In August of 1972, when Douglas Cloy sold his property to the appellants' predecessors in title, he made the grant subject to the respondents' right-of-way and, when they in turn sold it to the appellants in February 1973, they likewise made their grant subject to the respondents' right-of-way.

It is accordingly clear, so far as the chain of title to the respective properties is concerned, that the respondents took their property in 1973 subject to the right-of-way of the appellants over the strip of land in issue on this appeal and the appellants obtained their right-of-way down through the chain of title to their own property but also by express grant in Douglas Cloy's quit claim deed made in March of 1958.

The Conduct of the Owners:

The learned trial judge made a number of important findings with respect to the use of the strip of land made over the years by the owners of the two adjoining properties.

(a) The respondents and their predecessors in title:

Since the respondents' property has always been used as a dwelling house, the main use of the strip made by the owners of that property has been as a drive-way. Up until about 1956 the respondents' car was kept in the garage but since that time the garage has been used as a storage shed and the car has been left on the drive-way at night. Although the respondent Mr. Keefer uses the car to go back and forth to work, it is also sometimes parked in the drive-way during the day and so occasionally are the cars belonging to the respondents' friends when they come to visit. The trial judge found that in the 1960's a disabled car was left at the rear of the drive-way for some four years.

The trial judge found also that the Keefers on several occasions had put gravel on the drive-way at their own expense. They also kept it free of snow in the winter-time. This may not be significant since they have a right-of-way over it and the Cloys closed down the store every winter and went to Florida.

As far as the grassy area to the west of the stone drive-way is concerned, the evidence disclosed that the grass had for many years been tended by the owners of the respondents' property, including the respondents themselves, and that the respondents occasionally held barbecues and picnics on it with no objection from the Cloys. The evidence that the Keefers made a skating rink of part of the grassy area on three winters does not appear to be significant since it was when the Cloys were wintering in Florida. The evidence, however, that no objection was made by Mr. Cloy when in 1952 Mr. Keefer moved the garage located at the rear of his property over onto the rear of the strip in order to line it up with the drive-way is clearly significant.

(b) The appellants and their predecessors in title:

The appellants' premises have always been used for business purposes, first in Martin Cloy's time as a grocery store and later by Douglas Cloy as a marine supply store for vessels plying up and down the Welland Canal. Since 1972, when Douglas Cloy sold the property to the respondents' predecessors in title, it has been used as a general variety store. Douglas Cloy was assisting his father in the business prior to the conveyance to Elzear Lynch and gave evidence on behalf of the appellants as to the use made by his parents and himself of the property from 1918 to 1972. The Cloys never lived on this property.

The strip of land was used by the Cloys in the early days to give access to an ice house at the rear of the store. The ice house was filled in the winter with blocks of ice cut from the Welland Canal. Deliveries were made from it originally by means of a horse and wagon and later by truck. In 1949 the ice house was removed and a one-storey addition was built on to the rear of the store. The addition was used partly as an office and partly for the storage of soft drinks. Access to the addition was through a door to the west of the stone steps and landing which provided access to the apartment over the store. Soft drinks were delivered by truck to the store room. If there was a car parked in the drive-way, the soft drinks would be taken by a small hand-cart; if the drive-way was clear, the truck would drive up to the entrance door to make its deliveries.

Mr. Cloy testified that he never parked his car in the drive-way but that trucks parked there occasionally when unloading supplies if the drive-way was clear. Mr. Cloy's customers also sometimes parked in the drive-way for short periods of time when making purchases.

The tenants of the apartment above the store entered from the street by the concrete walk-way running alongside the drive-way, but the one tenant who owned a car did not leave his car in the drive-way. Moving trucks used the drive-way and, when tenants were moving in or out, the Keefers always moved their car if it happened to be in the drive-way at the time. The owners used the walk-way to visit the apartment. They also used a portion of the grassy area to get to and from the side entrance to the storage and office premises built on to the rear of the store in 1949.

Mr. Cloy testified that both he and his father had put gravel on the drive-way over the years, but he acknowledged that the last time he had put gravel on was probably in 1956. Because of the store's being closed in the winters from December to March every year when he and his family went to Florida, no trucks or customers' cars would be parked in the drive-way during the winter months. His evidence was that they had been wintering in Florida for the past eighteen years.

The Issue:

His Honour Judge Nicholls, after reviewing the evidence of user by both owners over the years, stated:

> The possession (of the plaintiffs and their predecessors in title) was not consistent with the rights accruing from the specific grant of right-of-way but far exceeded them. Counsel for the plaintiff expressed the opinion that the grant of right-of-way matured into a possessory title.

He also stated:

> The possession of the plaintiffs and their predecessors in title was open, visible and continuous for far more than the requisite number of years, but the question arises as to whether there was exclusive possession.

With all due respect to the learned trial judge, I believe that the crucial question in this case is whether the respondents' possession challenged in any way the right of the legal owner to make the use of the property he wished to make of it. This is not a case where the Keefers could be viewed as trespassers on their neighbours' property so that any act of theirs on the property was a challenge to the constructive possession of the owners. Possession is not adverse to the extent it is referable to a lawful title; *Thomas v. Thomas* (1855), 2 K. & J. 79 per Page-Wood V.C. at p.83. The Keefers were on their neighbours' property pursuant to their grant of right-of-way and, even if they exceeded the rights they had by virtue of the right-of-way, this would not necessarily mean that their right-of-way matured into a possessory title.

The use an owner wants to make of his property may be a limited use and an intermittent or sporadic use. A possessory title cannot, however, be acquired against him by depriving him of uses of his property that he never intended or desired to make of it. The "*animus possidendi*" which a person claiming a possessory title must have is an intention to exclude the owner from such uses as the owner wants to make of his property.

Viewed in this light the evidence that the Cloys never parked their car or truck on the strip of land, far from being helpful to the respondents' case, is harmful to it. It shows that the Cloys never intended or wanted to use the strip for parking. Indeed, this is clear from the fact that they gave the owner of the adjoining property a right of ingress and egress over it. Similarly, the fact that the respondents created a skating rink on the grassy area in the winter-time when the appellants were in Florida has in my view no real significance in terms of the ouster of the true owner. The true owner was probably quite content to give the Keefers full rein on the property while the store was not in operation. The trial judge was obviously correct in his finding that, even when the appellants were operating the store, the respondents were using the strip for more than a means of ingress and egress to their property. I do not believe, however, that this is the test for the acquisition of possessory title. The test is not the respondents exceeded their rights under the right of way but whether they precluded the owner from making the use of the property that he wanted to make of it: *Re St. Clair Beach Estates Ltd. v. MacDonald et. al.* (1974) 5 O.R. (2d) 482, 50 D.L.R. (3d) 650. Acts relied on as dispossessing the true owner must be inconsistent with the form of enjoyment of the property intended by the true owner. This has been held to be the test for adverse possession since the leading case of *Leigh v. Jack* (1879) 5 Ex. D. 264.

The onus of establishing title by possession is on the claimant and it is harder for a claimant to discharge this onus when he is on the property pursuant to a grant from the owner. It was held in *Littledale v. Liverpool College*, [1900] 1 Ch. 19, that acts done on another's land may be attributed to the exercise of an easement, rather than to adverse possession of the fee.

In *Pflug and Pflug v. Collins*, [1952] O.R. 519 at p. 527, [1952] 3 D.L.R. 681 at p. 689 [affirmed [1953] O.W.N. 140, [1953] 1 D.L.R. 841], Mr. Justice Wells (as he then was) made it clear that a person claiming a possessory title must establish (1) actual possession for the statutory period by themselves and those through whom they claim; (2) that such possession was with the intention of excluding from possession the owner or persons entitled to possession; and (3) discontinuance of possession for the statutory period by the owner and all others, if any, entitled to possession. If he fails in any one of these respects, his claim fails.

In my view the respondents fail in both (2) and (3) above. I do not believe that while the Cloys owned the strip of property in issue the Keefers ever intended to oust them from the limited use they wanted to make of it. The evidence discloses that the relationship between the Cloys and Keefers was excellent and that there was never any trouble with the respondents when delivery trucks occasionally used the driveway for unloading supplies, when customers parked for short periods on the driveway when making purchases at the store, when tenants were moved in and out of the upstairs apartment and when they came and went to the apartment. Nor did Douglas Cloy take any exception to the Keefers parking their car in the driveway. Why would he, even if it were an excessive use of the right of way, if it did not impede him in the use he wanted to make of the property? His whole posture appears to have been that of an accommodating neighbour anxious to avoid any trouble. This is clear from the one contentious incident disclosed by the evidence, i.e., the incident when one of Mr. Cloy's tenants in the upstairs apartment left his car in the driveway and had a "run-in" with Mr. Keefer. When his tenant reported this to him, Mr. Cloy told him to park somewhere else because "I don't want to fight with my neighbours."

The evidence of Mr. Keefer was "I never had ant problems with Doug (Mr. Cloy) as far as the driveway was concerned." He testified on one occasion Mr. Cloy left his car in the driveway overnight so that he was unable to get his car out in the morning. He therefore pushed Mr. Cloy's car onto the road and Mr. Cloy apparently made no objection to his having done that. I cannot attach great significance to this as evidencing the assertion of possessory title by the Keefers since the Cloys, having given the Keefers a right of ingress and egress, had no right to block Mr. Keefer's egress. Mr. Keefer was perfectly entitled to do what he did. I cannot find on the evidence that the Keefer's possession was with the intention of excluding the Cloys from the limited use they wanted to make of the property. I think that the issue of possessory title is something that has arisen since the Cloy's property changed hands and the hitherto amicable relations between the adjoining owners disintegrated.

As far as proof of the discontinuance of possession by the owner is concerned, I do not believe that the Cloy's did discontinue their possession of any part of the strip of land other than the portion at the rear occupied by the respondent's garage. I think that with respect to that portion the constructive possession of the owners was displaced by the actual possession of the Keefers for more than the statutory period. However, as far as the balance of the strip is concerned, I think the owners made such use as they wanted. It was used as an access to the apartment above the store and to the entrance of the addition at the rear of the store. It is true that the Cloys may not have used the full width of the strip for this purpose, but the authorities make it clear that the constructive possession which a legal owner has of the whole property is not ousted simply because he is not in actual possession of the whole. Possession of part is possession of the whole if the possessor is the legal owner: *Great Western R. Co. v. Lutz* (1881), 32 U.C.C.P. 166. I find, therefore, that the respondents have not discharged the onus of proving discontinuance of possession of the strip (other than the portion occupied by their garage) by the owners for the statutory period.

I would allow the appeal and hold the respondents entitled to a declaration that the appellants' title has been extinguished only with respect to that part of the land occupied by the respondent's garage.

The appellants should have their costs of the appeal.

NOTE

The dissenting opinion of MacKinnon J.A. has been omitted.

QUESTIONS AND COMMENTS

1. What are the requisite elements of adverse possession? What must the paper title holder do within that period to prevent the full running of the clock?

2. Why does the law allow for the acquisition of title by adverse possession? What is the general purpose of a statute of limitations?

3. At common law, it is well established that a person acquiring a legal interest in land is bound by all pre-existing legal interests affecting that land. The fact that the second interest was purchased without knowledge of the prior entitlement is of no consequence. The second legal title holder is bound. This rule (first in time is first

in right) arose prior to the introduction of land recording systems. In a sale transaction, the vendor would be called upon to demonstrate a good root of title going back to a specified period (say, 40 or 60 years). However, to repeat, even if a diligent search was undertaken and no problems were detected, this provided no guarantee that a prior claimant could not later come forward. Can this context provide an explanation of the emergence of the law of adverse possession?

4. Does the concept of adverse possession conflict with the idea of first occupancy?

5. Does the concept of adverse possession encourage the productive use of land? Does it encourage trespassing?

6. Is the concept of adverse possession economically efficient?

7. Is the law of adverse possession consistent with the goals of environmental protection?

8. Should the law state that a squatter who succeeds in an adverse possession claim be required to compensate the original owner?

9. B occupies land owned by A. Some years later, B purports to transfer her interest in this land to C. What, if anything, does C acquire? Can C bring an action against D, a newcomer, in the event that D seeks to take possession of the premises from C?

In answering these questions, consider the judgment in *Jewett v. Bil* 1999 CarswellNB 100, 536 A.P.R. 280 (C.A.), reproduced here in full:

> The Court (Orally):
>
> There were three 100-acre blocks of land for which there was no apparent chain of title in the Parish of Kingsclear, New Brunswick.
>
> The parties together with a third person conveyed the properties into one another in an attempt to acquire a paper chain of title. As a result, one of the 100-acre properties (Lot 12) was conveyed by the appellant to the respondent.
>
> The trial Judge found as a fact that the respondent paid taxes on Lot 12 since 1978 and had harvested wood on it and inspected it occasionally. She concluded the respondent had a "bare possessory title but the [appellant] had no title to this lot."
>
> In this appeal, the appellant raises only one ground, namely: the trial Judge committed an error when she concluded that the respondent had sufficient possession of the land, Lot 12, to maintain an action in trespass.
>
> The jurisprudence on this issue is summarized in [John] Fleming's, *The Law of Torts*, 7th ed. ([Toronto]: Carswell, 1987) in this way:
>
>> Possession of land may be in a person who has no legal title to it and is himself in wrongful occupation as regards another. A disseisor is nonetheless a possessor

> although, as between himself and the rightful owner, he has no *right* to possession until his adverse possession has ripened into ownership by lapse of time. But, just as legal title to land without possession does not support an action of trespass against third parties, so possession without legal title thereto is sufficient. Hence, a defendant in an action of trespass cannot set up the right of the true owner in order to justify his infringement of the plaintiff's de facto possession: he cannot plead the so-called jus tertii, that is, assert that another has a better right to possession than the plaintiff, unless he committed the entry by his authority. The reason is that it is more conducive to the maintenance of order to protect de facto and even wrongful possession against disturbance by all and sundry than to deny legal aid to a disseisor merely because of the flaw in his title.

We are of the view that the trial Judge did not make any error on the facts and the law when she concluded that the respondent had sufficient possession of the land as against the appellant to maintain an action for trespass. The appeal is dismissed with costs in accordance with the Tariff of the *Rules of Court*.

Appeal dismissed.

The concept of *jus tertii* (the right of a third person) reflects an important precept of the law of property: title is a relative concept. Hence, in an action between X and Y, it is irrelevant that Z may in fact have a right that trumps both of theirs. As the quotation from John Fleming points out, that holds true so long as neither A nor B were acting on the authority of Z.

It is sometimes said that when a plaintiff is claiming a wrong based not on possession *per se*, but on an interference with the *right* to gain possession, he or she must be prepared to meet the defence of *jus tertii*. In principle, this should mean no more than that the right to possession must be proven to reside in the plaintiff, and not some other party.

10. In the *Keefer* case, why did the claim to the roadway fail? Why did the claim to the area where the garage was placed succeed?

Teis v. Ancaster (Town)
(1997) 152 D.L.R. (4th) 304, 1997 CarswellOnt 2970 (C.A.)

Laskin J.A.:

John and Elsie Teis claimed possessory title to two strips of land — the "ploughed strip" and the "laneway" — located on the western edge of Jerseyville Park, a public park owned by the Town of Ancaster and used mainly to play baseball. For more than 10 years, both the Teis and the Town mistakenly believed that the Teis owned these two strips of land. In a judgment dated January 18, 1994, Lazier J. declared that the Teis were owners by adverse possession of the ploughed strip and the laneway but that the public was entitled to travel over part of the laneway by car and all of the laneway by foot. The Town appeals and asks that the Teis' action be dismissed. The Teis cross-appeal and ask to delete that part of the judgment granting the public a right-of-way over the laneway.

The main issue on the appeal is whether a person claiming possessory title must show "inconsistent use" when both the claimant and the paper title holder mistakenly believe that the claimant owns the land in dispute. Inconsistent use means that a claimant's use of the land is inconsistent with the true owner's intended use of the land. The other issue on the appeal is whether the trial judge made a "palpable and overriding error" in holding that the Teis had "actual possession" of the disputed strips for the ten-year period prescribed by the *Limitations Act*, R.S.O. 1980, c. L.15.

In my opinion, the test of inconsistent use does not apply to a case of mutual mistake and the trial judge did not err in finding actual possession. Accordingly, I would dismiss the appeal. I would also dismiss the cross-appeal because of the findings of fact made by the trial judge.

Background Facts

Before 1968, a man named Alexander Hunter owned all of the land in the area in question. In December, 1968, Hunter conveyed to the Town a 66-foot strip of land called the Maple Street extension. At the same time, Hunter also conveyed to the Town a parcel of land north of the Maple Street extension. In 1971, the Town converted this parcel into a public park, which it called Jerseyville Park. Hunter died in March 1969. In August of that year, his estate conveyed to the Teis the land south of the Maple Street extension. In July, 1971, the Hunter estate conveyed to the Teis the land north of the Maple Street extension and directly west of Jerseyville Park (the "north field"). In September, 1970, before closing the purchase of the north field, the Teis went into possession of it, took out the trees and weeds, and ploughed it. The Teis have farmed the north field continuously from 1970 onward.

The two disputed strips of land are legally owned by the Town. They lie along the western edge of Jerseyville Park and each ranges in width from roughly ten to fifteen feet. The Teis have considered the ploughed strip part of the north field and therefore have farmed it since 1970. The Teis created the laneway to move their ploughs and other farm equipment. Members of the public have also used the laneway for recreational walking and for parking their cars when little league baseball was being played in Jerseyville Park. The Teis have never fenced their land.

Before 1989 the Town did not challenge the Teis' use of the ploughed field or the laneway. In 1989, however, the Town built a clubhouse in the northwest corner of Jerseyville Park. The clubhouse eliminated part of an existing park area and caused the Town to look for other short-term parking for users of the park. On August 1, 1989, the Town's Chief Administrative Officer sent the following memorandum to the Town's Director of Culture and Recreation, Paul Harrison:

> As per our discussions yesterday and today, could we please inform the farmer who is occupying 5 metres of our property on the west side of the Jerseyville Park and also some land on the south side, to stop using the public land as soon as his crop is off.

> I am afraid that if this man can get 10 years of unobjected occupancy from the Town, he might be in a position where we could not actually get him off our property and he has acquired our land simply through our failure to notify him to vacate the land.

Despite this memorandum, Harrison apparently never told the Teis to stop using the ploughed strip or the laneway. Still, after the clubhouse was built, the public began to interfere significantly with the Teis' use of these two strips of land. In 1991, the Teis sued for possessory title.

The Appeal

Under ss. 4 and 15 of the *Limitations Act* the interest of the true owner of land may be extinguished by a person who has been in adverse possession of that land for ten years. Sections 4 and 15 provide:

> 4. No person shall make an entry or distress, or bring an action to recover any land or rent, but within ten years next after the time at which the right to make such entry or distress, or to bring such action, first accrued to some person through whom the person making or bringing it claims, or if the right did not accrue to any person through whom that person claims, then within ten years next after the time at which the right to make such entry or distress, or to bring such action, first accrued to the person making or bringing it. . . .
>
> 15. At the determination of the period limited by this Act to any person for making an entry or distress or bringing any action, the right and title of such person to the land or rent, for the recovery whereof such entry, distress or action, respectively, might have been made or brought within such period, is extinguished.

At the end of the ten year period these provisions bar the remedy and extinguish the title of the true owner.

The requirements a claimant must satisfy to establish possessory title were set out by Wells J. in *Pflug v. Collins*, [1952] O.R. 519 (Ont. H.C.), a case relied on by Lazier J. and referred to with approval by Wilson J.A. in the following passage of her majority judgment in *Keefer v. Arillotta* (1976), 13 O.R. (2d) 680 at 692 (Ont. C.A.):

> In *Pflug and Pflug v. Collins*, [1952] O.R. 519 at p.527, [1952] 3 D.L.R. 681 at p.689 [affirmed [1953] O.W.N. 140, [1953] 1 D.L.R. 841], Mr. Justice Wells (as he then was) made it clear that a person claiming a possessory title must establish (1) actual possession for the statutory period by themselves and those through whom they claim; (2) that such possession was with the intention of excluding from possession the owner or persons entitled to possession; and (3) discontinuance of possession for the statutory period by the owner and all others, if any, entitled to possession. If he fails in any one of these respects, his claim fails. . . .

(a) Actual Possession

The first requirement is actual possession for the ten-year period. To succeed, the acts of possession must be open, notorious, peaceful, adverse, exclusive, actual and continuous. If any one of these elements is missing at any time during the statutory period, the claim for possessory title will fail. The trial judge found that all of these elements had been met for more than ten years. This finding is a finding of fact, which cannot be set aside on appeal unless the trial judge made a "palpable and overriding error." In my view, the Town has failed to demonstrate such an error.

Possession must be open and notorious, not clandestine, for two reasons. First, open possession shows that the claimant is using the property as an owner might. Second, open possession puts the true owner on notice that the statutory period has begun to run. Because the doctrine of adverse possession is based on the true owner's failure to take action within the limitation period, time should not run unless the delay can fairly be held against the owner. Ziff, *Principles of Property Law*, 2nd ed. (Carswell, 1996) at pp. 118-126.

The Town does not contest the trial judge's finding that the Teis' possession of the ploughed strip and the laneway was open and notorious. Equally, the Town does not contest the trial judge's finding that the Teis had actual, peaceful, and exclusive possession of these two strips for the statutory period. The Town does challenge the trial judge's finding that the Teis' possession was adverse and continuous.

The element of adversity means that the claimant is in possession without the permission of the owner. If the claimant acknowledges the right of the true owner then the possession is not adverse. To show the absence of adversity, the Town relies on Harrison's evidence of a meeting with Mr. Teis in 1978 or 1979. According to Harrison, at the meeting, Teis admitted that he was using the Town's lands and Harrison told him "that it was alright for him to use the laneway." Teis denied that such a meeting ever took place. The trial judge, as he was entitled to do, rejected Harrison's evidence. He therefore did not err in holding that the element of adversity had been met.

The Town also argues that the Teis' possession was seasonal or intermittent and not continuous. The nature of the acts needed to establish possession depends on the type of property. For some types of property, even intermittent use will satisfy the element of continuity. As Gale C.J.H.C. said in *Walker v. Russell*, [1966] 1 O.R. 197 (Ont. H.C.), at 210:

> The sufficiency and character of the possession necessary to pass title must be considered and tested in the light of the circumstances which surround each particular case. Acts which amount to possession in one case may be wholly inadequate to establish it in another. Matters such as the nature of the property, the appropriate and natural uses to which it can be put, the course of conduct which the owner might reasonably be expected to adopt with a due regard to his own interests, are all matters to be considered in evaluating the adverse possession which has been proved to have been exercised by a trespasser or successive trespassers. . . .

I agree with the trial judge that the Teis showed ongoing or continuous use. I would not give effect to this ground of appeal.

(b) Inconsistent Use

The appellant's main ground of appeal is that the trial judge erred by not giving effect to the test of inconsistent use. The Town acknowledges that the Teis intended to exclude the Town from possession of the disputed strips for more than ten years and that the Town was effectively dispossessed for the statutory period. But the appellant submits that the Teis' possession of the disputed strips was not inconsistent with the use the Town intended to make of them. The appellant argues that, because the Town did not need the ploughed strip or the laneway for Jerseyville Park before 1989, the Teis' previous use was not inconsistent with the Town's intended use and therefore the limitation period did not begin to run until 1989 at the earliest. The trial judge did not advert to the test of inconsistent use in his reasons.

This test appears to have originated with the English case of *Leigh v. Jack* (1879), 5 Ex. D. 264 (Eng. C.A.) in which Bramwell L.J. said at 273:

> I do not think that there was any dispossession of the plaintiff by the acts of the defendant: acts of user are not enough to take the soil out of the plaintiff and her predecessors in title and to vest it in the defendant; in order to defeat a title by dispossessing the former owner, acts must be done which are inconsistent with his enjoyment of the soil for the purposes for which he intended to use it: that is not the case here, where the intention of the plaintiff and her predecessors in title was not either to build upon or to cultivate the land, but to devote it at some future time to public purposes. The plaintiff has not been dispossessed, nor has she discontinued possession, her title has not been taken away, and she is entitled to our judgment.

Wilson J.A. imported this test into Ontario case law in her judgment in *Keefer v. Arillotta, supra.* She viewed it as relevant to the claimant's obligation to demonstrate an intention to possess, the second requirement set out in *Pflug, supra* . . . She reiterated this proposition in *Fletcher v. Storoschuk* (1981), 35 O.R. (2d) 722 (Ont. C.A.).

In the subsequent case of *Masidon Investments Ltd. v. Ham* [(1984), 45 O.R. (2d) 563], Blair J.A. also applied the test of inconsistent use but he viewed it as relevant to the claimant's obligation to demonstrate discontinuance of possession by the true owner for the statutory period, the third requirement set out in *Pflug, supra.* In Blair J.A.'s view, the notion of "adversity" in the phrase adverse possession is reflected in the test of inconsistent use . . .

In all three cases — *Keefer, Fletcher* and *Masidon* — the person claiming a possessory title had knowingly trespassed on the owner's land. The claimant had used the land knowing that it belonged to someone else. In *Wood v. Gateway of Uxbridge Properties Inc.* (1990), 75 O.R. (2d) 769 (Gen. Div.), Moldaver J. held that the test of inconsistent use did not apply to a case of mutual mistake about title. I agree with Moldaver J. I am also of the opinion that the trial judge treated the case under appeal as a case of mutual mistake. He found that, for the statutory period, both the Teis and the Town mistakenly believed that the Teis owned the two disputed strips. This finding is reasonably supported by the evidence. Therefore, in my view, the test of inconsistent use cannot defeat the Teis' claim to a possessory title.

The test of inconsistent use focuses on the intention of the owner or paper title holder, not on the intention of the claimant. It is a controversial element of an adverse possession claim even when the claimant knowingly trespasses on the owner's land. See *Ziff, supra* at pp.124-126 and Bucknall, "Two Roads Diverged: Recent Decisions on Possessory Title" (1984), 22 Osgoode Hall L.J. 375. Taken at face value, its application could unduly limit successful adverse possession claims, especially when land is left vacant. A paper title holder could always claim an intention to develop or sell the land, or could maintain that a person in possession cannot hold adversely to someone who does not care what is happening on the land.

Even accepting, however, that the test applies to cases of knowing trespass, it cannot apply to cases of mutual mistake. If it did apply, every adverse possession claim in which the parties were mistaken about title would fail. Inconsistent use means that the claimant's use of the land is inconsistent with the true owner's intended use. If the true owner mistakenly believes that the claimant owns the disputed land, then the owner can have no intended use for the land and, correspondingly, the claimant's use cannot be inconsistent with the owner's intended use. As Moldaver J. wrote in *Wood, supra* at 778:

> I must confess some difficulty applying this 'test' to the case at bar. I say this because the true owners did not know that they were the rightful owners of the two-acre parcel during the requisite time frame. How then is it possible to determine what use they intended for the property when they at no time even contemplated its use? And if they had no intended use for the property, how can one compare the use of the applicants to find consistency or lack thereof with a non-existent intended use?

Therefore, if a claimant were required to show inconsistent use when both parties were honestly mistaken about the true boundary line, the claimant could never make out a case of adverse possession. Such a result would offend established jurisprudence, logic and sound policy.

The law reports contain many cases in which an adverse possession claim has succeeded though the parties were mistaken about who owned the disputed land. These cases are cited by Anderson J. in *Beaudoin v. Aubin* (1981), 33 O.R. (2d) 604 (H.C.) and by Moldaver J. in *Woods, supra*. None of these cases even refer to the test of inconsistent use.

It makes no sense to apply the test of inconsistent use when both the paper title holder and the claimant are mistaken about their respective rights. The application of the test would defeat adverse possession claims in cases of mutual mistake, yet permit such claims to succeed in cases of knowing trespass. Thus applied, the test would reward the deliberate squatter and punish the innocent trespasser. Policy considerations support a contrary conclusion. The law should protect good faith reliance on boundary errors or at least the settled expectations of innocent adverse possessors who have acted on the assumption that their occupation will not be disturbed. Conversely, the law has always been less generous when a knowing trespasser seeks its aid to dispossess the rightful owner. Blair J. discussed this policy in *Masidon, supra*, at p. 574:

> The policy underlying the *Limitations Act* was stated by Burton J.A. in *Harris v. Mudie* (1883), 7 O.A.R. 414, as follows at p. 421:
>
>> The rule, as I understand it, has always been to construe the *Statutes of Limitations* in the very strictest manner where it is shewn that the person invoking their aid is a mere trespasser . . . and such a construction commends itself to one's sense of right. They were never in fact intended as a means of acquiring title, or as an encouragement to dishonest people to enter on the land of others with a view to deprive them of it.
>
> Robins J.A. speaking for this court in *Giouroukos* case [*Giouroukos v. Cadillac Fairview Corp.* (1982), 37 O.R. (2d) 364] reiterated this policy when he said at pp. 187-8:
>
>> When all is said and done. this is a case of a businessman seeking to expand significantly the size of his commercial land holdings by grabbing a valuable piece of his neighbour's vacant property. The words of Mr. Justice Middleton used in denying the claim of an adverse possessor to enclosed land in *Campeau v. May* (1911), 19 O.W.R. 751 at p.752, are apposite:
>>
>>> It may be said that this makes it very hard to acquire a possessory title. I think the rule would be quite different if the statute was being invoked in aid of a defective title, but I can see nothing in the policy of the law, which demands that it should be made easy to steal land or any hardship which requires an exception to the general rule that the way of the transgressor is hard.

The test of inconsistent use furthers this policy by strengthening the hand of the true owner in the face of an adverse possession claim by a knowing trespasser. Applying the test to claims by persons who honestly, though mistakenly, use land not their own, defeats this policy. I therefore conclude, as Moldaver J. did in *Wood*, that the test does not apply to cases of mutual mistake about ownership.

Before considering the facts of this case in the light of this conclusion, I wish to address two related points. First, in *Masidon, supra*, Blair J.A. held that the test of inconsistent use captured the notion of "adversity" in the phrase "adverse possession." Of course, the phrase does not appear in the *Limitations Act*. Nonetheless, it conveniently describes claims for possessory title under the statute. If "adversity" is required, I would hold that, at least in a case like the one under appeal, adversity simply means being in possession without the authorization of the paper title holder. See *Beaudoin v. Aubin, supra* at pp. 612-614.

Second, in cases of mutual mistake, even requiring the claimant to show an intention to exclude the owner from possession — the second requirement in *Pflug* — is problematic. It might be asked: "How could the applicants' intend to dispossess the true owner when they believed . . . that they were the true owners?" *Per* Moldaver J. in *Woods*, *supra* at 778. The answer is provided by Blair J.A. in *Masidon* at p. 575:

> The appellant's occupancy of the land was not justified by any suggestion of colour of right or mistake as to title or boundaries. Occupation under colour of right or mistake might justify an inference that the trespasser occupied the lands with the intention of excluding all others which would, of course, include the true owners.

In other words, in cases of mutual mistake the court may reasonably infer, as indeed I infer in this case, that the claimants, the Teis, intended to exclude all others, including the paper title holder, the Town.

I now return to the evidence and the trial judge's findings of fact. Although the trial judge did not expressly state that this was a case of mutual mistake, he effectively found that, throughout the ten year statutory period, both the Teis and the Town mistakenly believed that the Teis owned the disputed strips . . .

Because the parties mistakenly believed that Teis owned the disputed strips for more than ten years, the test of inconsistent use does not apply. Therefore, in my view, this ground of appeal must fail, as must the Town's appeal.

The Cross-Appeal

The Teis submit that the trial judge erred in declaring that the public had a right-of-way over the laneway. A possessory title may be subject to a right-of-way. See *Ziff*, *supra*, at p. 119. The trial judge granted a right-of-way because he found that:

> This particular lane has not been in the exclusive domain of the plaintiffs. Members of the public have traversed these lands on foot and at times when the lands to the east were being used for recreation, including Little League Baseball, vehicles were parked on part of the [laneway] from time to time.

This finding was supported by the evidence of Town residents and Mr. Teis. I would not interfere with it. Accordingly, in my view the cross-appeal must fail.

Adverse Possession of Municipal Park Land

Most adverse possession claims involve disputes between private property owners. In this case, the Teis claim adverse possession of municipally owned land. I have some discomfort in upholding a possessory title to land that the Town would otherwise use to extend its public park for the benefit of its residents. Still, the Town did not suggest that municipally owned park land cannot be extinguished by adverse possession or even that different, more stringent requirements must be met when the land in dispute is owned by a municipality and would be used for a public park. This case was argued before the trial judge and in this court on the footing that the ordinary principles of adverse possession law applied. The application of those principles to the evidence and the trial judge's findings of fact justify extinguishing the Town's title to the ploughed strip and the laneway.

Several American states have legislation that prevents a limitation period from running against "municipal property devoted to public use." See 3 Am. Jur. (2d) § 271. Even at common law, some American courts have decided that municipally owned land used for a public purpose, such as a park, cannot be acquired by adverse possession. See, for example, *Meshberg v. Bridgeport City Trust Co.,* 429 A.2d 865 (U.S. Conn. S.C. 1980) and *Schmitt v. Carbondale* (City), 101 A. 755 (U.S. Penn. S.C. 1917).

In Canada, Alberta is the only province with legislation protecting all municipally owned land against claims of adverse possession. *Municipal Government Act*, S.A. 1994, c. M-26.1, s. 609. In Ontario, streets, highways, and road allowances have been protected from adverse possession or encroachment claims. In *Household Realty Corp. v. Hilltop Mobile Home Sales Ltd.* (1982), 37 O.R. (2d) 508 at 515 (C.A.), Thorson J.A. cited with approval the following passage from Rogers, *Law of Canadian Municipal Corporations*, 2nd ed., vol. 2 (Toronto: Carswell, 1971) at 1096:

> The right of ownership in real property, such as a highway, a market or a public wharf, held by a municipality for the common benefit or use of its inhabitants and of the Queen's subjects in general, is of such a public character that it cannot, as a general rule, be lost by adverse possession over the prescriptive period. It is expressly declared by the statute that road allowances cannot be extinguished by adverse possession.

Whether, short of statutory reform, the protection against adverse possession afforded to municipal streets and highways should be extended to municipal land used for public parks, I leave to a case where the parties squarely raise the issue.

Conclusion

I would dismiss both the appeal and the cross-appeal with costs.

QUESTIONS AND COMMENTS

1. What policy arguments were advanced in support of the Court of Appeal's holding that the test of inconsistent use did not apply?

2. Assume that the Teis family had discovered the error nine years after the fence was wrongly placed. Should the test of inconsistent use apply?

3. In *J.A. Pye (Oxford) Ltd. v. Graham* [2003] 1 A.C. 419 (H.L.), the House of Lords repudiated (or at the very least seriously confined the scope of) the test of inconsistent use in Engand. There, the land had been leased to one Michael Graham by the paper title holder. The lease arrangement expired, though Graham remained in possession. On the facts, it was determined that Graham had been in possession without permis-

sion from 1984 until proceedings were launched by the paper title holders in 1999. The relevant limitation period was 12 years. The House of Lord held, unanimously, in favour of the squatter. As to the test of inconsistent user, Lord Browne-Wilkinson wrote (at paras. 36, 45):

> The question is simply is whether the defendant squatter has dispossessed the paper owner by going into ordinary possession of the land for the requisite period without the consent of the owner . . .
>
> The suggestion that the sufficiency of possession can depend on the intention not of the squatter but of the true owner is heretical and wrong. If reflects an attempt to revive the pre-1833 concept of adverse possession requiring inconsistent user. . . . The highest it can be put is that, if the squatter is aware of a special purpose for which the paper owner uses or intends to use the land and the use made by the squatter does not conflict with that use, that may provide some support for a finding as a question of fact that the squatter had no intention to possess the land in the ordinary sense but only an intention to occupy it until needed by the paper owner. For myself I think there will be few occasions in which such an inference could be properly drawn in cases where the true owner has been physically excluded from the land. But it remains a possible, if improbable, inference in some cases.

Is this view preferable to the current law in Ontario?

4. It has been suggested that adverse possession will not lie if the squatter acknowledges the title of the paper owner. An offer by the squatter to purchase or lease the land can serve as one form of acknowledgment. In *Pye*, that idea was constricted, if not rejected outright (at para. 46):

> In a number of cases (such as the present case) squatters have given evidence that if they had been asked by the paper owner to pay for their occupation of the disputed land or to take a lease they would have been prepared to do so. . . . Once it is accepted that the necessary intent is an intent to possess not to own and an intention to exclude the paper owner only so far as is reasonably possible, there is no inconsistency between the squatter being willing to pay the paper owner if asked and his being in the meantime in possession. An admission of title by the squatter is not inconsistent with the squatter being in possession in the meantime.

5. As a general rule, a squatter must be in actual possession of the disputed land. However, where the claimant enters the land under colour of title (such as where the legal description in the deed erroneously includes the land in issue), actual possession of part of the land will count as possession of the entire property. These principles were described by Sedgewick J. in *Bentley v. Peppard* 33 S.C.R. 444, 1903 CarswellNS 77, at 445-6:

> As the decision of the case mainly depends upon the question whether or not the rights of the parties are to be determined by the provisions of the Statute of Limitations, it may be well to state certain fundamental propositions, the proper application of which to the facts in controversy must settle this appeal.

1. According to the English law the word "possession", as applied to real estate, has a purely technical meaning. The word "occupancy" is not a word of legal import apart from its popular acceptation. Occupancy may as a matter of fact negative possession in its legal sense, but possession in the same sense is consistent with non-occupancy. In other words, all land in the dominions of the Crown must be in the possession of some one, whether that "some one" be the Crown itself or a natural or artificial entity. "Vacant" land — "abandoned" land, (where title is involved) is an impossibility. Possession must be somewhere — in somebody — and he who has the title is presumed to have the possession unless the actual dominion and occupancy is elsewhere.

2. Where the owner (also a non-technical word) — the person having a present legal estate, whether by word of mouth or by a written instrument — lets blackacre, the tenant accepting and entering by virtue thereof has possession of every foot of ground comprised in blackacre, although he may possess himself of but one foot of it only.

3. Where a person without title and without right (in Canada we call him a "squatter") enters upon land, his possession in a legal sense is limited to the ground which he [sic] actually occupies, cultivates and encloses; it is a *possessio pedis* — nothing more.

4. But where a person in good faith under a written instrument from one purporting to be the proprietor, enters into blackacre — a definite territorial area — his actual occupancy of a part — no matter how small — in the absence of actual adverse occupancy by another, gives him a constructive possession of blackacre as a whole. He has it, as the phrase is, under " colour of title ."

See also *Re Matchless Group Inc.* 2002 CarswellNfld 258, 4 R.P.R. (4th) 202 (C.A.).

Describe what it means to have actual possession of land.

6. The rules for adverse possession of Crown land typically differ from those applied to private holders. For example, in Alberta, adverse possession of Crown land has been abolished: *Public Lands Act*, R.S.A. 2000, c. P-40, s. 4. In Nova Scotia, the general limitation period for actions to recover land is 20 years; for Crown land the period is 40 years: *Limitation of Actions Act*, R.S.N.S. 1989, c. 258, ss. 10, 21.

(b) chattels

Barberree v. Bilo
84 Alta. L.R. (2d) 216, 1991 CarswellAlta 225 (Q.B.)

Feehan J.: . . .

The matter concerns the ownership and right to possession of a Gold Wing motorcycle bought by Barberree in 1985. There is no disagreement that Barberree owned the motorcycle. Her husband, Aslin, removed it from her possession at the time of the couple's separation on October 19, 1985. Barberree demanded a return of the motorcycle from Aslin but the demand was refused.

Aslin, representing the motorcycle to be his, sold it to the defendant Bilo on July 26, 1990 for $5,200. Bilo became aware, prior to taking possession of the chattel, that Barberree was the registered owner. In a conversation with Barberree, Bilo undertook to stop payment on his cheque to Aslin but was unable to and now takes the position that title (ownership) and possession lie in him.

The matter was heard before Master Breitkreuz and was disposed of in his reasons for decision dated July 12, 1991. At p. 4, the learned master held that because of his reading of the Limitation of Actions Act, R.S.A. 1980, c. L15: "the plaintiff [Barberree] has lost her rights of recovery against the third party seller, and that he can transfer title free and clear of the plaintiff's claim."

The learned master then went on to deal with the matter in two additional ways. The first addressed whether the existence of an action under the *Matrimonial Property Act*, R.S.A. 1980, c. M9, preserved Barberree's claim against the chattel. He found that it did not. The second was the extent of Barberree's obligation to register her rights in the motorcycle under the Central Registry system. The master held Barberree did have a responsibility to so register and the failure to do so rendered her claim against the *bona fide* purchaser for value an incurable defect.

The matter was heard before me on November 8, 1991, and I have had the opportunity to consider the arguments of both parties and the materials submitted.

What I am faced with is the long extant problem of the conflict of two important principles of law. In the words of Lord Denning (*Bishopgate Motor Finance Corp. v. Transport Brakes Ltd.*, [1949] 1 K.B. 322, [1949] 1 All E.R. 37 at 46 (C.A.)):

> In the development of our law, two principles have striven for mastery. The first is the protection of property. No one can give a better title than he himself possesses. The second is the protection of commercial transactions. The person who takes in good faith and for value without notice should get a good title.

It is the collision of these same two principles that gives rise to the action in the matter before me. Counsel for Bilo submits that the concept of adverse possession can be applied to the case at bar. He suggests that with the effluxion of time, that is, with the expiry of the two-year limitation period within which an action in conversion can be launched, Barberree loses not only her cause of action but also her title in the chattel of which she has been dispossessed. When this happens, the possessor of the chattel, the husband Aslin in this case, acquires "prescriptive" title to the goods. In support of this line of argument, counsel for Bilo puts forward the article by Mr. J.E. Côté (as he then was), "Prescription of Title to Chattels" (1969), 7 Alta. L. Rev. 93, and *Phillips v. Murray,* [1929] 2 W.W.R. 314, [1929] 3 D.L.R. 770 (Sask. C.A.).

Counsel for Barberree, on the other hand, submits Bilo's interpretation would result in a thief being allowed "to keep his booty" because of passage of time. Counsel for Barberree submits Barberree has not lost her right of ownership and is entitled to sue Bilo in conversion as she is entitled to another two-year limitation of action period against this new defendant when he refused her demand for the return of the motorcycle.

The position put forward by the counsel for Bilo reflects the law in England and the United States, and at least in one province in Canada, notably Manitoba. In these jurisdictions, it is the statute which sets out the extinguishment of title. For example, in Manitoba, similar to the English position, the *Limitation of Actions Act*, R.S.M. 1987, c. L150 (also C.C.S.M., c. L150), s. 54(2), reads as follows:

> Where any such cause of action has accrued to any person, and the period prescribed for bringing that action and for bringing any action in respect of such a further conversion or wrongful detention as aforesaid has expired, and he has not during that period recovered possession of the chattel, the title of that person to the chattel is extinguished.

It should be noted that there is a six year limitation period under this Act.

In Alberta, however, there exists no such statutory provision. While recommendations to adopt this approach have been put forward in the Côté article, and by the Alberta Law Reform Institute in its report "Limitations" (1989), the law remains as it has always been. The doctrine of adverse possession does not apply to personal property. Title (or ownership) in the motorcycle has not passed to Aslin and remains in Barberree.

Having decided that title remains in Barberree, this leads me to two further conclusions. The first is that the principle of "nemo dat quod non habet" applies to this situation: "no one can give that which he does not have." Aslin's rights were of possession only. Thus when Bilo purchased the motorcycle from Aslin, Bilo's rights were no more than the seller's, that being one of possession only. Since Aslin did not have title to the motorcycle, he was unable, in the absence of the consent of the rightful owner, Barberree, to transfer any more than his own rights of possession.

Meanwhile, the doctrine of simple possession continues to apply to this matter: a possessor of goods can assert ownership over those goods as against all the world except for the rightful owner. In this case, Barberree continues to be the rightful owner with a right to immediate possession.

These findings lead me to the conclusion that Barberree's action against Bilo is founded in law and should proceed.

Counsel for Bilo also posits that Barberree's right of action against Aslin has expired under s. 51(*g*) of the *Limitation of Actions Act*. The limitation period for commencing an action in conversion begins to run from the time a demand to turn over the chattel is made and refused: see *Davis v. Henry Birk & Sons Ltd.*, [1981] 5 W.W.R. 559, affirmed [1983] 1 W.W.R. 754, 41 B.C.L.R. 137, 142 D.L.R. (3d) 356 (C.A.). The period runs for two years from the date of the refusal. Hence, the two-year limitation period in which an action can be launched against Aslin appears to have expired. However, once the property passed to Bilo, the limitation for an action against him begins to run anew since he now has committed a fresh conversion.

Barberree can found a cause of action against him within two years from the time of her demand to Bilo and his refusal: see *Miller v. Dell*, [1891] 1 Q.B. 468, [1891] 60 L.J.Q.B. 404 (C.A.). Thus Barberree's action against Bilo is timely. It is within the two-year limitation period as far as Bilo is concerned. I find the learned master erred in deciding otherwise and his reasons for decision are overturned . . .

In conclusion, the learned master's decision is overturned and Barberree is entitled to an order of replevin for the delivery of the subject motorcycle.

O'Keeffe v. Snyder
416 A.2d 862 (N.J.S.C., 1980)

Pollock J.:

This is an appeal from an order of the Appellate Division granting summary judgment to plaintiff, Georgia O'Keeffe, against defendant, Barry Snyder, d/b/a Princeton Gallery of Fine Art, for replevin of three small pictures painted by O'Keeffe . . . In her complaint, filed in March, 1976, O'Keeffe alleged she was the owner of the paintings and that they were stolen from a New York art gallery in 1946. Snyder asserted he was a purchaser for value of the paintings, he had title by adverse possession, and O'Keeffe's action was barred by the expiration of the six-year period of limitations provided by N.J.S.A. 2A:14-1 pertaining to an action in replevin. Snyder impleaded third party defendant, Ulrich A. Frank, from whom Snyder purchased the paintings in 1975 for $35,000.

The trial court granted summary judgment for Snyder on the ground that O'Keeffe's action was barred because it was not commenced within six years of the alleged theft. The Appellate Division reversed and entered judgment for O'Keeffe. O'Keeffe, supra, 170 N.J.Super. at 92, 405 A.2d 840. A majority of that court concluded that the paintings were stolen, the defenses of expiration of the statute of limitations and title by adverse possession were identical, and Snyder had not proved the elements of adverse possession. Consequently, the majority ruled that O'Keeffe could still enforce her right to possession of the paintings . . .

The record, limited to pleadings, affidavits, answers to interrogatories, and depositions, is fraught with factual conflict. Apart from the creation of the paintings by O'Keeffe and their discovery in Snyder's gallery in 1976, the parties agree on little else.

O'Keeffe contended the paintings were stolen in 1946 from a gallery, An American Place. The gallery was operated by her late husband, the famous photographer Alfred Stieglitz . . .

In September, 1975, O'Keeffe learned that the paintings were in the Andrew Crispo Gallery in New York on consignment from Bernard Danenberg Galleries. On February 11, 1976, O'Keeffe discovered that Ulrich A. Frank had sold the paintings to Barry Snyder, d/b/a Princeton Gallery of Fine Art. She demanded their return and, following Snyder's refusal, instituted this action for replevin . . .

Frank claims continuous possession of the paintings through his father for over thirty years and admits selling the paintings to Snyder. Snyder and Frank do not trace their provenance, or history of possession of the paintings, back to O'Keeffe.

As indicated, Snyder moved for summary judgment on the theory that O'Keeffe's action was barred by the statute of limitations and title had vested in Frank by adverse possession. For purposes of his motion, Snyder conceded that the paintings had been stolen. On her cross motion, O'Keeffe urged that the paintings were stolen, the statute of limitations had not run, and title to the paintings remained in her . . .

Our decision begins with the principle that, generally speaking, if the paintings were stolen, the thief acquired no title and could not transfer good title to others regardless of their good faith and ignorance of the theft . . . Proof of theft would advance O'Keeffe's right to possession of the paintings absent other considerations such as expiration of the statute of limitations . . .

The trial court found that O'Keeffe's cause of action accrued on the date of the alleged theft, March, 1946, and concluded that her action was barred. The Appellate Division found that an action might have accrued more than six years before the date of suit if possession by the defendant or his predecessors satisfied the elements of adverse possession. As indicated, the Appellate Division concluded that Snyder had not established those elements and that the O'Keeffe action was not barred by the statute of limitations.

The purpose of a statute of limitations is to "stimulate to activity and punish negligence" and "promote repose by giving security and stability to human affairs". *Wood v. Carpenter*, 101 U.S. 135, 139, 25 L.Ed. 807, 808 (1879) . . . A statute of limitations achieves those purposes by barring a cause of action after the statutory period. In certain instances, this Court has ruled that the literal language of a statute of limitations should yield to other considerations . . .

To avoid harsh results from the mechanical application of the statute, the courts have developed a concept known as the discovery rule . . . The discovery rule provides that, in an appropriate case, a cause of action will not accrue until the injured party discovers, or by exercise of reasonable diligence and intelligence should have discovered, facts which form the basis of a cause of action . . . The rule is essentially a principle of equity, the purpose of which is to mitigate unjust results that otherwise might flow from strict adherence to a rule of law . . .

[W]e conclude that the discovery rule applies to an action for replevin of a painting . . . O'Keeffe's cause of action accrued when she first knew, or reasonably should have known through the exercise of due diligence, of the cause of action, including the identity of the possessor of the paintings . . .

In determining whether O'Keeffe is entitled to the benefit of the discovery rule, the trial court should consider, among others, the following issues: (1) whether O'Keeffe used due diligence to recover the paintings at the time of the alleged theft and thereafter; (2) whether at the time of the alleged theft there was an effective method, other than talking to her colleagues, for O'Keeffe to alert the art world; and (3) whether registering paintings with the Art Dealers Association of America, Inc. or any other organization would put a reasonably prudent purchaser of art on constructive notice that someone other than the possessor was the true owner.

The acquisition of title to real and personal property by adverse possession is based on the expiration of a statute of limitations. R. Brown, *The Law of Personal Property* (3d ed. 1975), s. 4.1 at 33 (Brown). Adverse possession does not create title by prescription apart from the statute of limitations . . . To establish title by adverse possession to chattels, the rule of law has been that the possession must be hostile, actual, visible, exclusive, and continuous. *Redmond v. New Jersey Historical Society*, 132 N.J.Eq. 464, 474, 28A.2d 189 (E. & A. 1942) . . .

[T]here is an inherent problem with many kinds of personal property that will raise questions whether their possession has been open, visible, and notorious . . .

Other problems with the requirement of visible, open, and notorious possession readily come to mind. For example, if jewelry is stolen from a municipality in one county in New Jersey, it is unlikely that the owner would learn that someone is openly wearing that jewelry in another county or even in the same municipality. Open and visible possession of personal property, such as jewelry, may not be sufficient to put the original owner on actual or constructive notice of the identity of the possessor.

The problem is even more acute with works of art. Like many kinds of personal property, works of art are readily moved and easily concealed. O'Keeffe argues that nothing short of public display should be sufficient to alert the true owner and start the statute running. Although there is merit in that contention from the perspective of the original owner, the effect is to impose a heavy burden on the purchasers of paintings who wish to enjoy the paintings in the privacy of their homes . . .

The problem is serious. According to an affidavit submitted in this matter by the president of the International Foundation for Art Research, there has been an "explosion in art thefts" and there is a "worldwide phenomenon of art theft which has reached epidemic proportions".

The limited record before us provides a brief glimpse into the arcane world of sales of art, where paintings worth vast sums of money sometimes are bought without inquiry about their provenance. There does not appear to be a reasonably available method for an owner of art to record the ownership or theft of paintings. Similarly, there are no reasonable means readily available to a purchaser to ascertain the provenance of a painting. It may be time for the art world to establish a means by which a good faith purchaser may reasonably obtain the provenance of a painting. An efficient registry of original works of art might better serve the interests of artists, owners of art, and bona fide purchasers than the law of adverse possession with all of its uncertainties . . . Although we cannot mandate the initiation of a registration system, we can develop a rule for the commencement and running of the statute of limitations that is more responsive to the needs of the art world than the doctrine of adverse possession.

We are persuaded that the introduction of equitable considerations through the discovery rule provides a more satisfactory response than the doctrine of adverse possession. The discovery rule shifts the emphasis from the conduct of the possessor to the conduct of the owner. The focus of the inquiry will no longer be whether the possessor has met the tests of adverse possession, but whether the owner has acted with due diligence in pursuing his or her personal property.

For example, under the discovery rule, if an artist diligently seeks the recovery of a lost or stolen painting, but cannot find it or discover the identity of the possessor, the statute of limitations will not begin to run. The rule permits an artist who uses reasonable efforts to report, investigate, and recover a painting to preserve the rights of title and possession.

Properly interpreted, the discovery rule becomes a vehicle for transporting equitable considerations into the statute of limitations for replevin . . .

It is consistent also with the law of replevin as it has developed apart from the discovery rule. In an action for replevin, the period of limitations ordinarily will run against the owner of lost or stolen property from the time of the wrongful taking, absent fraud or concealment. Where the chattel is fraudulently concealed, the general rule is that the statute is tolled . . .

The discovery rule will fulfill the purposes of a statute of limitations and accord greater protection to the innocent owner of personal property whose goods are lost or stolen . . .

By diligently pursuing their goods, owners may prevent the statute of limitations from running. The meaning of due diligence will vary with the facts of each case, including the nature and value of the personal property. For example, with respect to jewelry of moderate value, it may be sufficient if the owner reports the theft to the police. With respect to art work of greater value, it may be reasonable to expect an owner to do more. In practice, our ruling should contribute to more careful practices concerning the purchase of art.

The considerations are different with real estate, and there is no reason to disturb the application of the doctrine of adverse possession to real estate. Real estate is fixed and cannot be moved or concealed. The owner of real property knows or should know where his property is located and reasonably can be expected to be aware of open, notorious, visible, hostile, continuous acts of possession on it.

Our ruling not only changes the requirements for acquiring title to personal property after an alleged unlawful taking, but also shifts the burden of proof at trial.

Under the doctrine of adverse possession, the burden is on the possessor to prove the elements of adverse possession . . . Under the discovery rule, the burden is on the owner as the one seeking the benefit of the rule to establish facts that would justify deferring the beginning of the period of limitations. [. . .]

Read literally, the effect of the expiration of the statute of limitations . . . is to bar an action such as replevin. The statute does not speak of divesting the original owner of title. By its terms the statute cuts off the remedy, but not the right of title. Nonetheless, the effect of the expiration of the statute of limitations, albeit on the theory of adverse possession, has been not only to bar an action for possession, but also to vest title in the possessor. There is no reason to change that result although the discovery rule has replaced adverse possession . . .

Before the expiration of the statute, the possessor has both the chattel and the right to keep it except as against the true owner. The only imperfection in the possessor's right to retain the chattel is the original owner's right to repossess it. Once that imperfection is removed, the possessor should have good title for all purposes . . .

To summarize, the operative fact that divests the original owner of title to either personal or real property is the expiration of the period of limitations. In the past, adverse possession has described the nature of the conduct that will vest title of a chattel at the end of the statutory period. Our adoption of the discovery rule does not change the conclusion that at the end of the statutory period title will vest in the possessor.

We next consider the effect of transfers of a chattel from one possessor to another during the period of limitation under the discovery rule. Under the discovery rule, the statute of limitations on an action for replevin begins to run when the owner knows or reasonably should know of his cause of action and the identity of the possessor of the chattel. Subsequent transfers of the chattel are part of the continuous dispossession of the chattel from the original owner. The important point is not that there has been a substitution of possessors, but that there has been a continuous dispossession of the former owner . . .

For the purpose of evaluating the due diligence of an owner, the dispossession of his chattel is a continuum not susceptible to separation into distinct acts. Nonetheless, subsequent transfers of the chattel may affect the degree of difficulty encountered by a diligent owner seeking to recover his goods. To that extent, subsequent transfers and their potential for frustrating diligence are relevant in applying the discovery rule. An owner who diligently seeks his chattel should be entitled to the benefit of the discovery rule although it may have passed through many hands. Conversely an owner who sleeps on his rights may be denied the benefit of the discovery rule although the chattel may have been possessed by only one person.

We reject the alternative of treating subsequent transfers of a chattel as separate acts of conversion that would start the statute of limitations running anew. At common law, apart from the statute of limitations, a subsequent transfer of a converted chattel was considered to be a separate act of conversion . . . Adoption of that alternative would tend to undermine the purpose of the statute in quieting titles and protecting against stale claims . . .

The majority and better view is to permit tacking, the accumulation of consecutive periods of possession by parties in privity with each other . . .

As explained by Professor Walsh:

> The doctrine of tacking applies as in corresponding cases of successive adverse possessions of land where privity exists between such possessors. Uncertainty is created by cases which hold that each successive purchaser is subject to a new cause of action against which the statute begins to run from that time, in this way indefinitely extending the time when the title will be quieted by operation of the statute. It should be entirely clear that the purposes of statutes of limitation are the same whether they relate to land or chattels, and therefore the same reasons exist for tacking successive possessions as the prevailing cases hold. Nevertheless, under the cases, new actions in conversion arise against successive purchases of the converted property, and there is strong reason back of the argument that the statute runs anew against each succeeding cause of action. No doubt the prevailing rule recognizing privity in these cases may be based upon the argument that the possessory title is transferred on each successive sale of the converted chattel, subject to the owner's action to recover the property, and the action of replevin which is his proprietory action, continues in effect against succeeding possessors so that the statute bars the action after the successive possessions amount to the statutory period. (Walsh, *supra* at 83-84.)

In New Jersey tacking is firmly embedded in the law of real property . . . The rule has been applied also to personal property . . .

The decisions in the case of chattels are few. As a matter of principle, it is submitted this rule of tacking is as applicable to chattels as to land. A denial of the right to tack would, furthermore, lead to this result. If a converter were to sell the chattel, five years after its conversion, to one ignorant of the seller's tort, the disposed owner's right to recover the chattel from the purchaser would continue five years longer than his right to recover from the converter would have lasted if there had been no sale. In other words, an innocent purchaser from a wrong-doer would be in a worse position than the wrong-doer himself, a conclusion as shocking in point of justice as it would be anomalous in law . . .

It is more sensible to recognize that on expiration of the period of limitations, title passes from the former owner by operation of the statute. Needless uncertainty would result from starting the statute running anew merely because of a subsequent transfer . . . It is not necessary to strain equitable principles, as suggested by the dissent, to arrive at a just and reasonable determination of the rights of the parties. The discovery rule permits an equitable accommodation of the rights of the parties without establishing a rule of law fraught with uncertainty . . .

We reverse the judgment of the Appellate Division in favor of O'Keeffe and remand the matter for trial in accordance with this opinion.

NOTES

1. The dissenting opinions of Sullivan and Handler JJ. have been omitted.

2. In J. Dukeminier & J.E. Krier, Eds., *Property*, 4th ed. (New York: Aspen Law & Business, 1998) at 165, it is reported that this dispute was settled before trial: "O'Keeffe took 'Seaweed', Snyder took another painting, and the third was sold at auction at Southeby's to pay lawyers' bills."

QUESTIONS

1. In *Solomon R. Guggenheim Foundation v. Lubell* 569 N.E.2d 426 (N.Y.C.A., 1991), the approach in *O'Keeffe* was rejected. In *Lubell*, a museum sought the return of a stolen work of art that had been acquired by an innocent purchaser. The purchaser/defendant argued that the limitation period had run and therefore the plaintiff was statute-barred. This argument was rejected by the New York Court of Appeals. Wachtler C.J., for the Court, held (at 429-31):

> New York case law has long protected the right of the owner whose property has been stolen to recover that property, even if it is in the possession of a good-faith purchaser for value . . . There is a three-year Statute of Limitations for recovery of a chattel. The rule in this State is that a cause of action for replevin against the good-faith purchaser of a stolen chattel accrues when the true owner makes demand for return of the chattel and the person in possession of the chattel refuses to return it . . . Until demand is made and refused, possession of the stolen property by the good-faith purchaser for value is not considered wrongful . . . Although seemingly anomalous, a different rule applies when the stolen object is in the possession of the thief. In that situation, the Statute of Limitations runs from the time of the theft, even if the property owner was unaware of the theft . . . at the time that it occurred . . .
>
> We have re-examined the relevant New York case law and we conclude that the Second Circuit should not have imposed a duty of reasonable diligence on the owners of stolen art work for purposes of the Statute of Limitations.
>
> While the demand and refusal rule is not the only possible method of measuring the accrual of replevin claims, it does appear to be the rule that affords the most protection to the true owners of stolen property. Less protective measures would include running the three-year statutory period from the time of the theft even where a good-faith purchaser is in possession of the stolen chattel, or, alternatively, calculating the statutory period from the time that the good-faith purchaser obtains possession of the chattel . . . Other States that have considered this issue have applied a discovery rule to these cases, with the Statute of Limitations running from the time that the owner discovered or reasonably should have discovered the whereabouts of the work of art that had been stolen . . .
>
> [O]ur decision today is in part influenced by our recognition that New York enjoys a worldwide reputation as a pre-eminent cultural centre. To place the burden of locating stolen artwork on the true owner and to foreclose the rights of that owner to recover its property if the burden is not met would, we believe, encourage illicit trafficking in stolen art. Three years after the theft, any purchaser, good faith or not, would be able to hold

> onto stolen art work unless the true owner was able to establish that it had undertaken a reasonable search for the missing art. This shifting of the burden onto the wronged owner is inappropriate. In our opinion, the better rule gives the owner relatively greater protection and places the burden of investigating the provenance of a work of art on the potential purchaser.

2. Compare and contrast the approaches taken in these cases. Which do you prefer?

3. In *Barbarree v. Bilo* reference was made to s. 54(2) of the *Limitation of Actions Act*, C.C.S.M, c. L150. In addition, s. 54(1) provides as follows:

> Where any cause of action in respect of the conversion or wrongful detention of a chattel has accrued to any person, and before he recovers possession of the chattel, a further conversion or wrongful detention takes place, no action shall be brought in respect of the further conversion or detention after the expiration of six years from the accrual of the cause of action in respect of the original conversion or detention.

In what way, if at all, does this provision alter the law of adverse possession of chattels?

4. THE RELATIVE NATURE OF TITLE: FINDERS

Trachuk v. Olinek
[1996] 4 W.W.R. 137, 1995 CarswellAlta 802 (Q.B.)

Gallant J.:

The plaintiff, Trachuk, and the four defendants, Olinek, Fulkerth, Austin and Muntz (the "four defendants"), each claim the right to possession of and title to $75,960 (the "money") which was uncovered from under the surface of a quarter section of farmland near Two Hills, Alberta, namely, under SW7-53-12-W4 (the "quarter section"), on May 6, 1992 by the four defendants. After the defendants discovered the money they notified the police and delivered the money to the police. In due course an interpleader order was granted resulting in this action to determine which of the two sets of claimants are entitled to possession of the money and any interest from investment thereof.

The remaining defendants, Michael Wandzilak, who had temporarily claimed to be the true owner of the money, Signalta Resources Ltd. ("Signalta"), the grantee under one of the easements that are hereinafter described, and Her Majesty the Queen in Right of Alberta, which had claimed under the doctrine of treasure trove, have withdrawn their claims.

Counsel for the four defendants indicated to the Court in argument that the defendants claim jointly, as a unit. In other words, it will not be necessary for the Court to decide whether any of the four defendants has a superior claim to any of the other four defendants.

Trachuk bases his claim on being an occupier of the quarter section, and being in possession of the money by virtue of being in *de facto* possession of the lands which contained it, and by virtue of having been granted the right to possession of those lands. The four defendants base their claim on the basis that they are finders of the money and that the fortunate finders of lost property are entitled to it as against all the world except the real owner.

A prior owner of the quarter section, Canadian Pacific Railway Company ("CPR") had granted a surface lease dated September 8, 1959 (the "surface lease"), to Hudson's Bay Oil & Gas Company Limited with respect to a 4.44-acre portion of the quarter section, for an oil or gas well site (the "well site premises") and an access road thereto. The lessee's interest in the surface lease was assigned to Amoco Canada Resources Ltd. ("Amoco"). At trial both counsel agreed that, at all relevant times, Amoco was the holder of the lessee's interest in the surface lease. The surface lease was, at all relevant times, registered against the title to the quarter section.

There was a provision in the surface lease that after the expiration of the initial 21-year term on September 8, 1980, the lease would automatically renew for a further period of 21 years, which would extend the lease until September 8, 2001.

Marathon Realty Company Limited ("Marathon"), successor in title from CPR, was registered owner of the quarter section at all times relevant to this action.

Marathon had granted three easements on the quarter section: the first dated November 4, 1970 in favour of Voyager Petroleums Ltd.; the second dated February 12, 1975 in favour of Sulpetro of Canada Ltd.; and the third dated April 15, 1980 in favour of Signalta. Under each of the three easements rights-of-way were granted to the grantee for the purpose, inter alia, of installation, servicing, use and removal of pipelines and apparatus relating to the oil and gas industry, and thereunder was granted the right of ingress and egress for all purposes incidental to the grant. The easements were registered against the title to the quarter section. The rights-of-way for the easements were from about 50 to 60 feet wide and ran in several directions from the gas well in the well site premises and not only appear to overlap each other to some extent there, but also overlap with the well site premises.

In 1992 Signalta owned a pipeline that connected the gas well at the well site premises to another well north of the quarter section, through one of the easements. Olinek was an independent contractor, contracting for the operation and maintenance of gas wells. Signalta contracted with Olinek to disconnect its pipeline from the gas well. In order to effect the work in question, Olinek hired, as subcontractors, Austin as a supplier and operator of a backhoe, Fulkerth as a welder, and Muntz as a labourer.

On May 6, 1992, the four defendants attended at the well site premises. On Olinek's instruction part of the fence that Trachuk had constructed on the well site premises was removed from around a shed which covered the gas well. A pipe protruded through the south wall of the shed. At the end of that pipe was a valve. A metal pipe, called a "riser," ran downwards from that valve, down to a pipeline below the surface of the land which ran easterly away from the shed, connecting below ground with the Signalta pipeline in its right-of-way running from that well. Olinek was to disconnect the riser from the valve and cut it off below the surface of the ground, about 40 inches down.

After the riser was disconnected, Austin, operating the backhoe, began to remove the soil that covered the pipeline under the valve. When he had dug down about 12 inches to 18 inches below the surface, the backhoe uncovered and ripped open a plastic bag, about 6 inches cubed in size, wrapped with duct tape. The bag contained Canadian paper currency in $100, $50 and $20 denominations, bound in sub-lots of $1,000 each, ten of which sub-lots were bound together into larger lots except for one large lot, totalling in all $75,960. Some of the paper money was dated in 1991. The location where the money was found was about 18 to 24 inches southeasterly from the riser and about 18 to 24 inches southerly from the shed. On that southerly side of the shed, Trachuk's fence was located about 4 feet away from and parallel to that side of the shed. The entirety of the money was found on the shed side of that fence. During argument, counsel for Trachuk conceded that Trachuk's fence was entirely on the well site premises.

Trachuk is a farmer who resided at all relevant times on lands adjacent to the quarter section. He leased the quarter section from Marathon under three successive leases (the "agricultural use leases"), for cultivation thereof and for grazing of his cattle. The terms of the leases ran respectively from January 1, 1989 until December 31, 1989; from March 1, 1990 until October 31, 1990; and from April 1, 1991 until October 31, 1991. In each of the agricultural use leases the well site premises were specifically excepted out.

In the spring of 1989, after the first agricultural use lease of the quarter section was signed by Trachuk and Marathon, Trachuk intended to pasture cattle on the quarter section. He was concerned about the presence of a methanol tank and a natural gas well on the well site premises as well as the pipes and valve protruding outside the wooden shed which enclosed the well. He was concerned that his cattle would rub against the valve and damage it or cause it to release liquids dangerous to the cattle. He said that he had initially discussed with Marathon the need for fencing around the shed. A representative from Marathon told him to build it himself. He asked Amoco to fence the well site but Amoco, by its representative, refused and indicated that he could construct the fence himself and that Amoco would pay him for his labour. He built the fence and Amoco reimbursed him for his labour. The perimeter of the fence was in the shape of a square or rectangle, with the sides approximately parallel to the well site premises. As I stated, the entirety of the fence was located on the well site premises. He constructed a gate in the fence which enabled him to pass as a pedestrian through the fence to the side where the shed was located. Occasionally Trachuk's calves would enter the enclosure under the barbed wire fence and Trachuk would have to enter the enclosure to take the calves out. It appears that he seldom entered the enclosure.

No one directed to Trachuk if he did construct a fence, where it should be located.

Trachuk indicated that in building the fence he was not attempting to restrict access of the oil company personnel to the well site, that they had a right to be there, that the surface lease road was for the benefit of the oil company, and that the shed was the oil company's responsibility. With respect to the 2.81 acres more or less around the well on the well site premises, he did not plant any grass or crops inside the fenced area. Nor did he spray any chemicals to control vegetation within the fenced area. He saw oil company personnel on the access road occasionally. He saw operators walking in and out of the shack and he never told them to go away, or told them what work to do or how to do it.

In the summer of 1991 Trachuk and his wife observed a patch of moist dirt on the ground between the well site fence and the shed. The soil appeared to be freshly turned. It appears that that probably was the area where the money was later discovered.

Steven Schuppler, farmlands property manager for Marathon, testified on behalf of Trachuk. Schuppler said that Marathon did not require any fencing on the quarter section and that it would be extremely unusual to have the surface lease lands separately fenced.

Schuppler stated that it was Marathon's policy to let a tenant have the use of all of the land in a leased quarter section, including as much of surface lease lands as possible, in order to keep the weeds under control. Marathon's lessees were encouraged by Marathon to pasture all those lands, or cultivate them, right up to the access road and other improvements on the surface lease premises.

It was Schuppler's intention to keep the quarter section continually occupied until it was sold, and to cause it to be sold after the expiration of the lease to Trachuk on October 31, 1991.

In the late part of 1991 Schuppler told Trachuk that Trachuk could use the quarter section until the spring of 1992; that Trachuk would have the first right of refusal to purchase the quarter section if a third party wished to purchase it, and the right to further lease the quarter section if Marathon did not sell it by the spring of 1992. He gave Trachuk the right to use the quarter section until any sale or other leasing of the quarter section. Trachuk was to continue with the property as if he had a lease of the property.

Schuppler indicated that in the spring of 1992, prior to April 23, Schuppler met with Trachuk at Trachuk's farm. At that meeting Schuppler and Trachuk agreed that Marathon would lease the quarter section to Trachuk from April 1, 1992 to November 2, 1992, for the sum of $1 on the basis that Trachuk would pay the realty taxes of $408 when due. No formal lease document for that term was prepared. Under their arrangement Trachuk was to continue in occupation of the quarter section, and he did continue in occupation.

On April 23, 1992, Marathon gave a letter to Trachuk enclosing a draft offer to purchase the quarter section. Trachuk was to sign it and send it to Marathon together with the required deposit by May 4, 1992. The letter states that the sale is subject to the approval by Marathon. Trachuk signed the offer and sent his cheque for the required deposit within the required time. The offer to purchase is dated April 28, 1992. The offer to purchase recites, among other things, the existence of the surface lease and provides that Marathon retains all right, title and interest in and to the surface lease for a period of 25 years commencing from the adjustment date and retains all right, title and interest in and to the surface rights affected by the surface lease during the 25-year period, with a provision for earlier termination at Marathon's option. The offer further provides that Trachuk shall have bare legal title to the lands with respect to which the surface lease was granted.

On May 2 or May 3, 1992, Trachuk placed his cattle on the quarter section pursuant to the occupancy arrangement above described.

Marathon issued its receipt for Trachuk's deposit on May 4, 1992, executed its acceptance to the offer on May 19, 1992 and, thereafter, sent a copy of the accepted offer to Trachuk.

Therefore, at the time that the monies were uncovered, Trachuk was lessee under the oral arrangement made with Schuppler and was not yet owner of the quarter section.

The claims of the parties revolve around the rights of persons who claim to be in possession or enjoy rights to possession — as I stated, this is a contest between the four defendants who uncovered and possess chattels of an unknown person, as against a party who claims to be in possession of the lands (or to have the right of such possession), under the surface of which those chattels had been secreted and then recovered. The Court is not being asked to rule on the rights of the true owner of the money as against the claims of the two sets of claimants in this case. There is no evidence as to who the true owner of the money is.

Marathon, the registered owner of the quarter section at the time that the money was uncovered, has not advanced any claim even though it is clear that Marathon, through Schuppler, was aware of the full particulars of the uncovering of the money. The lessee under the surface lease and the grantees under the easements are not present claimants.

The questions for determination by the Court are whether the plaintiff or four defendants have the right to possession of the money, and if both do, which of the two has the superior right. The claimants ask for a declaration of entitlement, but it is clear that the most either could be granted is a possessory title — a right to exclusive possession of the money except as against one who is able to prove a superior claim.

The four defendants rely on the old saying, "Finders keepers, losers weepers." That old saw does not state the law. A better old maxim would be, "Possession is nine-tenths of the law."

Persons who discover money and assume control of it under the circumstances of the four defendants in this case assume the position of a quasi-bailee of the money. Bailment is generally defined as the rightful possession of goods by one who is not the owner, by mutual consent. A finder holds the position of a special kind of gratuitous bailee because, unlike the consensual bailee, he may refuse to hand over the thing found until he has had a reasonable opportunity to satisfy himself that the claimant is the person entitled to it. A person in the position of a bailee has responsibilities to the true owner to care for the chattel in possession. In this case, each of the parties claiming is apparently desirous of assuming those duties.

The finder of a lost chattel, while not acquiring any absolute property or ownership in the chattel, acquires a right to keep it against all but the true owner or those in a position to claim through the true owner, or one who can assert a prior right to keep the chattel which right was subsisting at the time when the finder took the chattel into his care and control. *Armory v. Delamirie* (1722), 1 Stra. 505 (A chimney sweep's boy who found a jewel succeeded against a jeweller to whom he had offered it for sale, who refused to pay a price acceptable to the boy or to return it); *Bridges v. Hawksworth* (1851), 21 L.J.Q.B. 75 (A finder was entitled as against an occupier to a packet of bank notes found on the floor of a shop); *Parker v. British Airways Board,* [1982] 1 Q.B. 1004, [1982] 1 All E.R. 834 (C.A.) (A passenger was held entitled to a gold bracelet found by him in an executive lounge at Heathrow.)

The reported cases show that a distinction is to be drawn between circumstances where a lost chattel has been found on privately owned land as compared to the uncovering of a chattel which was intentionally placed on or under privately owned land. The former are, in the reported cases and relevant texts, called "true finder cases." No apparent nomenclature has been given to the latter, but perhaps they might appropriately be called "recovery cases."

One must consider in this case whether the money had been lost or deliberately left. To lose something is not to place something carefully and voluntarily in the place one intends, whether or not one then forgets it. When you lose something you casually and involuntarily part with possession of it. The thing is usually found in a place or under circumstances which show to the finder that the owner's will was not employed in placing it there. No one could reasonably say that the money, which contained bills dated in 1991, being located about 18 inches below the surface of the land, had been parted with casually and involuntarily and that the will of the person who placed it there was not employed in placing it.

It cannot be reasonably said that the package of money was abandoned so that the true owner is deemed to have relinquished all title or claim to it as if he had thrown it away so that it would become owned by the person who discovered it and took it into possession. Evidence would be required to show abandonment on a balance of probabilities, and there is no such evidence.

When one considers the recent date of some of the bills, the method in which the money was packaged, the value of the money, and the fact that the money was discovered about 18 inches below the surface of the soil, one must conclude that it was probably deliberately secreted there. I find that the four defendants were persons in possession of the money, which money had been deliberately hidden under the surface of the quarter section. Because the money had been deliberately hidden under privately owned land, the general rule, that the finder of lost property is entitled to it as against all the world except the real owner, does not apply.

A recoverer is able to acquire a possessory title to a recovered chattel only subject to the rights of the owner or occupier of privately owned land when the chattels are under the land or attached thereto. As a general principle, where a person has possession of a house or land, with a manifest intention to exercise control over it and the things which may be upon or in it, then, if something is found on or under that land, whether by an employee of the owner or by a stranger, the presumption is that the possession of that thing is in the owner of the location in question. *Parker v. British Airways Board, supra*; *South Staffordshire Water Co. v. Sharman*, [1896] 2 Q.B. 44; *City of London Corp. v. Appleyard*, [1963] 2 All E.R. 834, [1963] 1 W.L.R. 982 (Q.B.); *Grafstein v. Holme* (1958), 12 D.L.R. (2d) 727 (Ont. C.A.). Questions of intention to exclude, custody, control, and the like, are questions of fact. *Bridges v. Hawksworth* shows that the occupier of land does not in all cases possess an unattached thing on his land even though the true owner has lost possession of it. In *Kowal v. Ellis* (1977), 76 D.L.R. (3d) 546 [[1977] 2 W.W.R. 761] (Man. C.A.), the finder of a pump which had been lying on open land occupied by a defendant was entitled to retain it against him because the defendant's occupancy alone endowed him with no prior possession as a bailee.

It is necessary to consider the question of whether Trachuk had the *de facto* occupancy or possession of the lands where the money was uncovered, or whether he had been granted such a right.

Central to this case are the concepts of occupancy and possession and it may be appropriate to consider the philosophic rationale for possessory title. O.W. Holmes stated in "The Common Law," (and I quote from *Cases and Readings on Personal Property*, E. Fraser, 3rd Ed., 1954):

> Possession is a conception which is only less important than contract . . . Why is possession protected by the law, when the possessor is not also the owner? . . . Law, being a practical thing, must found itself on actual forces. It is quite enough, therefore, that man, by an instinct which he shares with the domestic dog . . . will not allow himself to be dispossessed, either by force or fraud, of what he holds, without trying to get it back again. Philosophy may find a hundred reasons to justify the instinct, but it would be totally immaterial if it should condemn it and bid us surrender without a murmur. As long as the instinct remains, it will be more comfortable for the law to satisfy it in an orderly manner, than to leave people to themselves. If it should do otherwise, it would become a matter for pedagogues, wholly devoid of reality . . .
>
> To gain possession . . . a man must stand in a certain physical relation to the object and the rest of the world, and must have a certain intent. These relations and this intent are the facts of which we are in search.

"Possess" is defined in Black's Law Dictionary, 5th edition, as follows:

> To occupy in person; to have in one's actual and physical control; to have the exclusive detention and control of; to have and hold as property; to have a just right to; to be master of; to own or be entitled to.

In *Towers & Co. v. Gray*, [1961] 2 Q.B. 351 at 361, Lord Parker C.J. stated: "The term 'possession' is always giving rise to trouble."

Earl Jowitt said in United States of *America v. Dollfus Mieg et Cie. S.A.*, [1952] A.C. 582 at 605:

> The person having the right to immediate possession is, however, frequently referred to in English law as being the "possessor" — in truth the English law has never worked out a completely logical and exhaustive definition of "possession."
>
> For my part, I approach this case on the basis that the meaning of "possession" depends on the context in which it is used . . .

In *Halsbury's Laws of England*, 4th edition, vol. 35, para. 1211, the authors deal with the meanings of "possession," in part, as follows:

> 1211. Physical and Legal Possession Distinguished.
>
> "Possession" is a word of ambiguous meaning, and its legal senses do not coincide with the popular sense. Its meaning depends upon the context in which it is used. In English law it may be treated not merely as a physical condition protected by ownership, but as a right in itself. The word "possession" may mean effective, physical or manual control, or occupation, evidenced by some outward act, sometimes called de facto possession or detention as distinct from a legal right to possession. This is a question of fact rather than of law.
>
> "Possession" may mean legal possession: that possession which is recognized and protected as such by law. The elements normally characteristic of legal possession are an intention of possessing together with that amount of occupation or control of the entire subject matter of which it is practically capable and which is sufficient for practical purposes to exclude strangers from interfering. Thus, legal possession is ordinarily associated with *de facto* possession; but legal possession may exist without *de facto* possession, and *de facto* possession is not always regarded as possession in law. A person who, although having no *de facto* possession, is deemed to have possession in law is sometimes said to have constructive possession.

Legal possession differs from *de facto* possession: it relates to the right to possession. For the purposes of this case *de facto* possession by Trachuk means occupation by him. Occupation is a matter of fact and exists only where there is a sufficient measure of control to prevent strangers from interfering. *Newcastle City Council v. Royal Newcastle Hospital*, [1959] A.C. 248 at 255, [1959] 1 All E.R. 734 at 735, 736 (P.C.) . . .

As I stated, for the purposes of this case, we can assume that occupancy and actual possession are synonymous. But it is clear that either term, in the context of this case, requires the intent and ability to control the use of land and exclude others from it and particularly requires the intention to exclude visitors from articles situate on or under the land; *Goodhart* (1928), 3 C.L.J. 195 at 199ff.

What is the evidence of the *de facto* possession or the right of possession of Trachuk to the precise area of the lands where the money was recovered? Did he have the intention to exclude or the ability to exclude persons from those lands? Did he have control over those lands?

The evidence does not support Trachuk's contention that he was in *de facto* control of that portion of the lands. Trachuk erected the fence around the well site premises with the intention of excluding his livestock from that enclosure. He appears to have seldom entered the fenced enclosure. His purpose in any such entry was to remove his calves which had entered there. There is no evidence that Trachuk intended to exclude workmen such as the four defendants or any other representatives of the petroleum companies involved in the surface lease, the well, or the easements, from entering upon the well site premises and from effecting any installations or changes there. The evidence is to the contrary. Olinek said that before arriving at the well site he had had no discussion whatsoever with Trachuk or Marathon about going to the well site, that he himself decided how and where to work on site, and that there had been no direction from Trachuk as to how Olinek was to do his work at the well site. The four defendants were on the well site premises with permission and with implied authority to excavate.

With respect to any contention that Trachuk had the right to possess the lands in question, the evidence is also to the contrary. First of all, one should consider the existence of the surface lease and the concept of possession inherent in a lease of land. In the text Williams & Rhodes, *Canadian Law of Landlord and Tenant*, 6th edition, Vol. I, 1988, on p. 1-1, the authors state as follows:

> 1:1 The Relation Defined
>
> At common law the relation of landlord and tenant is a contractual one, arising when one party, retaining in himself a reversion, permits another to have *exclusive possession* of a corporeal hereditament, for some definite period or for a period which can be made definite by either party. (Italics mine.)

[p. 1-4:]

> 1:1:3 Exclusive Possession
>
> To create the relation of landlord and tenant of real property it is essential that the tenant have the right to *exclusive possession* of the demised premises . . . in which it was held that exclusive possession may be found although the parties have agreed to certain reservations or restrictions of the purpose for which the possession may be used, such as the reservation to the lessor to recover merchantable timber or firewood. . . .

> One of the provisions of the surface lease requires the lessee thereunder to erect and maintain upon the boundaries of the surface lease a good and substantial fence if required by the lessor. There is no evidence of implementing any such requirement against the lessee. I do not accept the argument for Trachuk that the existence of that provision anticipates occupancy of the well site premises by a lawful user of the balance of the quarter section. Even though the surface lease anticipates the possibility of livestock being on the quarter section because of the provision for fencing and installation of gates, that does not thereby infer a grant of any rights of occupancy or possession of the surface lease premises to the person who runs the cattle on the quarter section.

One should consider the intended uses under the surface lease which were expressed as follows in it:

> For a well site and access roadway for the purpose of drilling a well for petroleum and/or natural gas and related hydrocarbons and the operation thereof and the taking of production therefrom with the right, liberty and privilege in, upon, under or across the demised premises to lay down, construct, maintain, inspect, remove, replace, reconstruct and repair pipes or pipelines and all structures and equipment necessary or incidental thereto for use in connection with all operations of the Lessee . . .

While the surface lease document is entitled "Surface Lease," it is clear that the lessee thereunder has subsurface rights in connection with well drilling, and development of pipelines and structures and equipment under the surface, without limitation as to depth. Amoco, holding the Lessee's interest under the surface lease, enjoyed the right of exclusive possession of the well site premises including the subsurface thereof . . .

When one considers the exclusionary clauses in the agricultural use leases (which probably applied during the oral arrangements for Trachuk's occupancy of the quarter section), the sale and purchase agreement between Marathon and Trachuk, the grant of exclusive possession under the provisions of the surface lease, and the grants of occupancy without interference under the easements, Trachuk is unable to show that he, at the time of finding of the money, had a scintilla of dominion to exercise over the portion of the lands where the money was uncovered. That applies *a fortiori* to the subsurface of that portion of the lands and to any chattels discovered under the surface of that portion of the lands.

Not only does it appear that Trachuk had no right to restrict the four defendants from entering upon the well site premises and excavating therein, but Trachuk could probably have been restrained by the lessee under the surface lease or the grantees under the easements from entering upon and excavating that portion of the quarter section.

Even if Marathon or its representative regarded Trachuk to be in continuous occupation of the entire quarter section, as counsel for Trachuk argued, that would be an error as it relates to the premises of the surface lease . . .

Trachuk had the onus to make out that he had possession of the premises in question with a manifest intention to exercise control of them and over things which may be in them: *Parker v. British Airways Board, supra*; *Armory v. Delamirie, supra*; *Grafstein v. Holme, supra.* Trachuk has not discharged that onus.

On the facts I find that the money was not in the possession of Trachuk when it was uncovered by the four defendants.

As between Trachuk, a party who was a non-occupier of the well site premises and having no right to occupation thereof, and the four defendants, who were lawfully on the well site premises, uncovered the hidden money thereunder, and having taken possession of the money, those defendants have rights to possessory title to the money (and any interest from investment thereof) superior to Trachuk.

Accordingly, I find in favour of the four defendants . . .

QUESTIONS AND COMMENTS

1. A finder of lost property acquires title good against the whole world except the true owner. True or false?

2. On what basis can we justify granting property rights to a finder? What would be the likely effect if the law refused to recognise that a finder acquires a property right in found objects?

3. In *Trachuk*, the Court concluded that where money is cached, not lost, the occupier of the land has a higher right than a finder? If so, why did the Court award the money to the four finders?

4. In *Clark v. Maloney* 3 Har. 68 (Del. S.C., 1840), A found 10 pine logs floating in Delaware Bay. Some time later they turned up in the possession of B, who alleged that the logs had been found "adrift and floating up the creek". Can A recover? Bayard C.J. charged the jury, in part, in these terms:

> [I]t is a well settled rule of law that the loss of a chattel does not change the right of property; and for the same reason that the original loss of these logs by the rightful owner, did not change his [sic] absolute property in them . . . so the subsequent loss did not divest the *special* property of the plaintiff [A]".

5. The leading English decision on finding is, arguably, *Parker v. British Airways Board* [1982] 1 Q.B. 1004 (C.A.). The case involved a gold bracelet that had been found by a passenger on the floor of an executive lounge at Heathrow Airport. Parker's rights as finder were found to be superior to those of the occupant of the premises, British Airway Board. In the course of delivering the principal judgment (Eveleigh L.J. and Sir David Cairns delivered concurring judgments), Donaldson L.J. (as he then was) set out some basic propositions of the law of finding (at 1017-8):

Rights and obligations of the finder

1. The finder of a chattel acquires no rights over it unless (a) it has been abandoned or lost and (b) he takes it into his care and control.

2. The finder of a chattel acquires very limited rights over it if he takes it into his care and control with dishonest intent or in the course of trespassing.

3. Subject to the foregoing and to point 4 below, a finder of a chattel, whilst not acquiring any absolute property or ownership in the chattel, acquires a right to keep it against all but the true owner or those in a position to claim through the true owner or one who can assert a prior right to keep the chattel which was subsisting at the time when the finder took the chattel into his care and control.

4. Unless otherwise agreed, any servant or agent who finds a chattel in the course of his employment or agency and not wholly incidentally or collaterally thereto and who takes it into his care and control does so on behalf of his employer or principal who acquires a finder's rights to the exclusion of those of the actual finder.

5. A person having a finder's rights has an obligation to take such measures as in all the circumstances are reasonable to acquaint the true owner of the finding and present whereabouts of the chattel and to care for it meanwhile.

Rights and liabilities of an occupier

1. An occupier of land has rights superior to those of a finder over chattels in or attached to that land and an occupier of a building has similar rights in respect of chattels attached to that building, whether in either case the occupier is aware of the presence of the chattel.

2. An occupier of a building has rights superior to those of a finder over chattels upon or in, but not attached to, that building if, but only if, before the chattel is found, he has manifested an intention to exercise control over the building and the things which may be upon it or in it.

3. An occupier who manifests an intention to exercise control over a building and the things which may be upon or in it so as to acquire rights superior to those of a finder is under an obligation to take such measures as in all the circumstances are reasonable to ensure that lost chattels are found and, upon their being found, whether by him or by a third party, to acquaint the true owner of the finding and to care for the chattels meanwhile. The manifestation of intention may be express or implied from the circumstances including, in particular, the circumstance that the occupier manifestly accepts or is obliged by law to accept liability for chattels lost upon his "premises", e.g., an innkeeper or carrier's liability.

4. An "occupier" of a chattel, e.g., a ship, motor car, caravan or aircraft, is to be treated as if he were the occupier of a building for the purposes of the foregoing rules.

In *Trachuk*, it was said that "[a]s a general principle, where a person has possession of a house or land, with a manifest intention to exercise control over it, then, if something is found on or under the land . . . the presumption is that the possession of that thing is in the owner of the location in question". Do you agree?

6. In *Bird v. Fort Frances* [1949] 2 D.L.R. 791, 1949 CarswellOnt 35 (H.C.), a 12-year-old boy found a stash of money on private property. He was trespassing at the time. The money was taken by the police, who in due course refused to return it to the boy. No claim was made for the money by the owner of the land on which the money was discovered, nor by any alleged true owner. It was held that the boy was entitled to the money. Compare *Baird v. British Columbia* 1992 CarswellBC 1113, 77 C.C.C. (3d) 365 (C.A.). Baird admitted having stolen a large sum of money, though he was never charged criminally. Nevertheless, his request that the money be returned to him was denied by the Crown, and that refusal was upheld on the grounds that a person should not be able to gain from one's own wrongdoing (*ex turpi causa non oritur actio*). But what about *Bird v. Fort Frances*? For the Court, Gibbs J.A. (at para. 21) reasoned that "*Bird* can be distinguished on the grounds that it was a kind of finders keepers case where there was not that degree of criminality or culpable immorality necessary to support an *ex turpi causa* plea". Is there a clear line between the two cases?

7. Assume that all of the parties referred to in *Trachuk* had decided to assert a claim to the money; even the four claimants are making separate claim to the entire amount of money found. Rank each claim. Identify the additional information that one might wish to know to gauge the strength of these claims.

8. In *Perry v. Gregory* 2003 CarswellPEI 97 (T.D.), the plaintiff and the defendant were scanning on a potato farm with metal detectors, with the permission of the landowners. Then,

> [n]ear the end of the day, the plaintiff received a signal from his machine but because it was a new machine he wanted to have verification. He asked the defendant to verify the reading. The plaintiff testified this had happened on at least two to four occasions in the past. He stated he had begun to dig the hole at the site and he thought he had it either two-thirds to three-quarters dug. He stated the defendant came over and, using his own metal detecting machine, he also received a positive reading. He said the defendant then started to dig without asking the plaintiff whether he should. Apparently this too had happened in the past. However, on those other occasions anything dug by the defendant in this way, in a hole that had been indicated by the plaintiff, was always given to the plaintiff.
>
> The plaintiff testified that in order to ensure his machine did not interfere with that of the defendant, he stepped back about 15 to 25 feet. He said he assumed the defendant was going to dig, so he simply allowed him to do so. He stated he continued to watch the defendant and when he saw the defendant take something out of the hole he went over to see what it was. The defendant held up a metal object which he told the plaintiff was a belt plate used by the PEI Regiment in the late 1700's. The plaintiff stated he reached for it and the defendant gave it to him, although he noted he did so somewhat reluctantly.

Ibid. at paras. 4-5 (*per* DesRoches C.J.T.D.).

In time, a dispute arose between the plaintiff and the defendant as to who was entitled to the find. Who should prevail?

10. In *Millas v. B.C. (A.G.)* (December 20, 1999) Doc. Vancouver 10324-I [1999] B.C.J. No. 3007 (Prov. Ct.), an off-duty police officer found $1 million in a trash can in a public park. A court later awarded the money to the officer. What should the officer do with the money? His lawyers said — to the press — that he should hold on to it for six years (or some appropriate period to be determined). Is this good advice?

Charrier v. Bell
496 So.2d 601 (La., 1986) [footnotes omitted]

Ponder J.:

Plaintiff appealed the trial court's judgment denying both his claim as owner of Indian artifacts and his request for compensation for his excavation work in uncovering those artifacts under the theory of unjust enrichment. We affirm.

Plaintiff . . . describes himself as an "amateur archeologist". After researching colonial maps, records and texts, he concluded that Trudeau Plantation, near Angola, was the possible site of an ancient village of the Tunica Indians. He alleges that in 1967 he obtained the permission of Mr. Frank Hoshman, Sr., who he believed was the owner of Trudeau Plantation, to survey the property with a metal detector for possible burial locations. After locating and excavating approximately 30 to 40 burial plots, lying in a circular pattern, plaintiff notified Mr. Hoshman that he had located the Tunica village. Although the evidence is contradictory, plaintiff contends that it was at that time that Mr. Hoshman first advised that he was the caretaker, not the owner, of the property.

Plaintiff continued to excavate the area for the next three years until he had located and excavated approximately 150 burial sites, containing beads, European ceramics, stoneware, glass bottles; iron kettles, vessels and skillets; knives, muskets, gunflints, balls and shots; crucifixes, rings and bracelets; and native pottery. The excavated artifacts are estimated to weigh two to two and one-half tons . . .

Confronted with the inability to sell the collection because he could not prove ownership, plaintiff filed suit against the six non-resident landowners of Trudeau Plantation, requesting declaratory relief confirming that he was the owner of the artifacts. Alternatively, plaintiff requested that he be awarded compensation under the theory of unjust enrichment for his time and expenses.

The State of Louisiana intervened in the proceeding on numerous grounds, including its duty to protect its citizens in the absence of the lawful heirs of the artifacts. In 1978, the State purchased Trudeau Plantation and the artifacts from the six landowners and agreed to defend, indemnify and hold the prior owners harmless from any and all actions.

In 1981 the Tunica and Biloxi Indians were recognized as an American Indian Tribe by the Bureau of Indian Affairs of the Department of the Interior. The Tunica-Biloxi Indians of Louisiana, Inc. intervened in the instant suit seeking title to the artifacts and the site of the burial ground . . . [T]he State subordinated its claim of title or trust status over the artifacts in favor of the Tunicas.

. . .

The issues before this court are the adequacy of proof that the Tunica-Biloxi Indians are descendants of the inhabitants of Trudeau, the ownership of the artifacts, and the applicability of the theory of unjust enrichment.

Plaintiff first argues that the evidence that the members of the Tunica-Biloxi Indians of Louisiana, Inc., are legal descendants of the inhabitants of Trudeau Plantation was insufficient to entitle them to the artifacts. He asserts that federal recognition of the tribe "merely proves that the Tribe is the best representative of the Tunica Indians for purposes of receiving federal benefits," and points to evidence of intermixing by the Tunica tribe with other tribes.

The fact that members of other tribes are intermixed with the Tunicas does not negate or diminish the Tunicas' relationship to the historical tribe. Despite the fact that the Tunicas have not produced a perfect "chain of title" back to those buried at Trudeau Plantation, the tribe is an accumulation of the descendants of former Tunica Indians and has adequately satisfied the proof of descent. This is evident from the "Final Determination for Federal Acknowledgment of the Tunica-Biloxi Indian Tribe of Louisiana", Fed.Reg. Vol. 46, No. 143, p. 38411 (July 27, 1981), which specifically found that the "contemporary Tunica-Biloxi Indian Tribe is the successor of the historical Tunica, Ofa and Avoyel tribes, and part of the Biloxi tribe". The evidence supports the finding that at least some portion of the Tunica tribe resided at Trudeau Plantation from 1731-1764. No contrary evidence, other than that suggesting intermixing, was presented at the trial of this case. Plaintiff's argument is without merit . . .

Plaintiff contends that the artifacts were abandoned by the Tunicas and that by finding them he became the owner.

Both sides presented extensive expert testimony on the history of the Tunica Indians, the French, English and Spanish occupation of the surrounding territory and the presence or absence of duress causing the Tunicas to abandon the Trudeau site.

However, the fact that the descendants or fellow tribesmen of the deceased Tunica Indians resolved, for some customary, religious or spiritual belief, to bury certain items along with the bodies of the deceased, does not result in a conclusion that the goods were abandoned. While the relinquishment of immediate possession may have been proved, an objective viewing of the circumstances and intent of the relinquishment does not result in a finding of abandonment. Objects may be buried with a decedent for any number of reasons. The relinquishment of possession normally serves some spiritual, moral, or religious purpose of the descendant/owner, but is not intended as a means of relinquishing ownership to a stranger. Plaintiff's argument carried to its logical conclusion would render a grave subject to despoliation either immediately after interment or definitely after removal of the descendants of the deceased from the neighborhood of the cemetery . . .

The term *res derelictae* refers to "things voluntarily abandoned by their owner with the intention to have them go to the first person taking possession." P. Esmein, *Aubry & Rau Droit Civil Francais*, Vol. II, §168, p. 46 (7th Ed. 1966). Some examples of *res derelictae* given by *Aubry and Rau* include things left on public ways, in the cities or to be removed by garbage collectors.

The artifacts fall into the category of *res derelictae*, if subject to abandonment. The intent to abandon *res derelictae* must include the intent to let the first person who comes along acquire them. Obviously, such is not the case with burial goods.

French sources have generally held that human remains and burial goods located in cemeteries or burial grounds are not "treasure" under article 716 of the French Civil Code and thereby not subject to occupancy upon discovery . . . The reasoning has been that any contrary decision would lead to and promote commercial speculation and despoilment of burial grounds . . .

The same reasoning that the French have used to treat burial goods applies in determining if such items can be abandoned. The intent in interring objects with the deceased is that they will remain there perpetually, and not that they are available for someone to recover and possess as owner.

For these reasons, we do not uphold the transfer of ownership to some unrelated third party who uncovers burial goods. The trial court concluded that La.C.C. art. 3421, as it read prior to passage of Act No. 187 of 1982, was not intended to require that objects buried with the dead were abandoned or that objects could be acquired by obtaining possession over the objections of the descendants. We agree with this conclusion.

The cases cited by plaintiff are distinguishable.

In *Touro Synagogue v. Goodwill Industries of New Orleans Area, Inc.*, 233 La. 26, 96 So.2d 29 (1957), the court found that a cemetery had been abandoned for burial purposes and the owner had the right to sell the property; however, the court conditioned the sale on the disinterment and reinterment (in another cemetery) of the remains of the deceased.

In *Ternant v. Boudreau*, 6 Rob. 488 (1844), jewelry interred with the decedent was stolen and recovered. The plaintiff claimed the ownership of all such goods on the basis that he purchased the decedent's succession from defendant who was the heir. The court found that the plaintiff was the lawful owner of the jewelry since there had been a valid sale from the descendant. The sale evidenced an express intent by the descendant not to retain ownership of the burial goods . . .

Plaintiff strongly argues that a finding that Indians did not abandon the artifacts will necessarily require the federal court to conclude that the Tunicas did not abandon the real property at Trudeau Plantation and could work havoc with the stability of Louisiana land titles. However, the question of the abandonment of the real property was excluded from the case. This opinion should not be interpreted as making any expression thereon . . .

[The Court then addressed and ultimately rejected the plaintiff's claim for compensation for his services and expenses in recovering the artifacts.]

QUESTIONS AND COMMENTS

1. In various jurisdictions in Canada, special rules apply to the finding of certain historical resources. For example, under the *Ontario Heritage Act*, R.S.O. 1990, c. O.18, the appropriate minister may direct that any artifact taken under the authority of a licence or a permit be deposited in a designated public institution and is regarded as being held in trust for the people of Ontario: s. 66(1). An artifact that is taken in violation of the Act may be seized by and dealt with in the same way: s. 66(2). Are these appropriate measures?

2. The decision in *Charrier v. Bell* turns in part on the issue of whether an abandonment had occurred. As a general matter, when is property abandoned? In *Stewart v. Gustafson* 1998 CarswellSask 581, [1999] 4 W.W.R. 695 (Q.B.) at paras. 11-7, Klebuc J. outlined the basic principles:

> The principle of abandonment has been reviewed in a few scholarly works. Lee Aitken, in "The Abandonment and Recaption of Chattels" (1994), 68 A.L.J. 263 states the principle at p. 272 as follows:
>
>> Precisely how "abandonment" works juristically is interesting and important. The cases make it clear, in Australia at least, that *an express intention to abandon coupled with an occupation by a newcomer is required before abandonment is complete.* Proof of this intention will be difficult: . . . There is sound moral sense in *not* depriving the possessor of his or her interest in a chattel until it is positively acquired by someone else. The act of abandonment, in Pollock's terms, confers a revocable licence which is only terminated when a subsequent possessor manifests dominion over the chattel with the intention of possessing it to the exclusion of others, including the former possessor. (Emphasis added)
>
> The different view of the principle was taken by A.H. Hudson in his article, "Is Divesting Abandonment Possible at Common Law?" (1984), 100 L.Q.R. 110. Therein he opined that an owner or possessor of a chattel can divest herself or himself of ownership by abandoning the chattel with the intention of surrendering ownership thereof. Such action, referred to as "divesting abandonment", in his view only requires the requisite intention and conduct by the owner manifesting the requisite intent.
>
> The question of whether either of the aforesaid approaches is applicable in this jurisdiction has not been judicially considered to date and need not be in the instant case in order to dispose of the issues before the Court. However, the divesting abandonment approach

was applied by the British Columbia Supreme Court in *Canada (Attorney General) v. Brock* (1991), 59 B.C.L.R. (2d) 261 (B.C. S.C.). There the Court relied on American jurisprudence which provides that upon an owner relinquishing title to a chattel it ceases to be owned by anyone until it is appropriated by someone with the intent of acquiring ownership thereof.

What constitutes the act of abandonment?

R.A. Brown in *The Law of Personal Property*, 2nd ed. (Chicago: Callaghan, 1955) defined "abandonment" as follows:

> Abandonment occurs when there is "a giving up, a total desertion, and absolute relinquishment" of private goods by the former owner. It may arise when the owner with the specific intent of desertion and relinquishment casts away or leaves behind his property . . .

The act of abandonment is essentially a question of fact to be proven by the party relying on the principle of abandonment: *Simpson v. Gowers* (1981), 121 D.L.R. (3d) 709 (Ont. C.A.) . . . The burden of proof is an onerous one where the owner's actions do not clearly manifest an intention to surrender ownership of the chattel in issue. In the result, intention often must be inferred by using the approach commonly employed in criminal law where intention is of paramount importance.

The authorities reviewed suggest that the following factors in the appropriate factual context support an inference of intention to abandon : (1) passage of time; (2) nature of the transaction; and (3) the owner's conduct. I am of the view the nature and value of the property also may be an indicator of intent. . . .

3. In 1996, $24,000 was found in the battery case of a Volkswagen Jetta. After an investigation, the money was seized on the grounds that it constituted the proceeds of crime. The vehicle was also seized because it had been used to transport drug money. The car was later sold by an agent of the United States government at an auction. Shortly afterwards, a mechanic who had been hired by the new owner to undertake repairs on the car found $84,000 in the gas tank. Who is entitled to that money? See *Chappell v. United States* 119 F.Supp.2d 1013 (U.S. Dist. Ct., W.D. Missouri, 2000).

5. TRANSFER OF TITLE THROUGH DELIVERY: GIFTS

J.B. Baron, "Gifts, Bargains, and Form" 64 Ind.L.J. 155 (1989) at 155-7, 198-201 [footnotes omitted]

It is a truism of Anglo-American law that there is a difference between gifts and bargains, between donative transfers and contractual exchanges. The two types of transactions are commonly presumed to accomplish divergent purposes in distinct settings. Donative transfers carry out benevolent urges in the context, usually, of the family, whereas contractual exchanges carry out self-interested aims in the context, usually, of the market. In addition, gifts and bargains are subject to divergent legal requirements, taught and learned in separate law school courses. Gifts require formalities such as delivery, signature, or attestation, whereas contracts require offer, acceptance and consideration.

The divergence between the requirements is, under accepted principles, not arbitrary; rather, it is thought to be a rational response to the respective goals and settings of the two different fields of law. Thus, with respect to gifts, where the primary legal goal is to effectuate donative intent, formalities are said to be required to put that intent beyond question. In contrast, with regard to contracts, where the primary legal goal is protection of expectations and security of transactions, consideration is said to be required to mark off those promises customarily understood, in a market economy, to be binding.

The divergent doctrinal treatment of gifts and bargains is thought to be appropriate not only in light of the different purposes of the two transactions, but also in light of their relative importance. Traditional discussions of gifts and contracts posit a world in which legal resources are scarce and costly; legal intervention must, in consequence, be rationed. In these discussions, gifts are treated as one-sided transfers which merely redistribute existing wealth, and they thus are not thought to warrant legal enforcement unless their formality renders administration of them simple. Bargains, on the other hand, are considered two-sided exchanges which create wealth, and due to their substantive importance they are thought to warrant enforcement without formality.

The divergence between the doctrinal requirements for gifts and bargains, and the particular requirements applicable to each, are thus alike considered appropriate responses to the true nature of each distinct kind of transfer. The notion that there is a "fit" between the nature of a given transaction and the legal rules applicable to it is comforting. It suggests the law is rational, responsive to reality.

There are, however, reasons to question this notion of "fit." First, it rests on assumptions about human behaviour in giving and bargaining which are at odds with conventional views of the contexts in which such transfers are ordinarily said to arise. Despite the benevolent motives and family settings usually associated with gifts, the accepted justification of donative formality assumes that, in giving, people are fundamentally unreliable and deceitful. Despite the self-interested aims and arm's length relationships usually associated with bargains, the accepted justification of the consideration doctrine assumes that, in business, people are trusting and trustworthy. These justifications turn the world topsy-turvy. We are to be suspected when we give, relied on when we trade.

Second, the notion of "fit" — the entire structure of rule and justification in the field of gifts — requires that gifts and bargains be truly different transactions. Only if gifts are not exchanges can they be characterized as so unimportant that they warrant enforcement on the basis of form alone. The now-accepted legal definition of a gift as a transfer without consideration is designed to assure that any particular transaction can be placed on one and only one side of the gift/bargain line. Yet there is nothing inevitable about this definition, which developed late in the life of the common law and which has never been used in the civil law. Indeed, the definition contrasts sharply with non-lawyers' understandings of gifts. Anthropological, sociological and psychological studies of gifts all suggest that gifts and bargains are alike exchanges, differing only in that bargains involve the exchange of commodities, while gifts may involve the exchange of noncommodities such as status, obligation, "psychic reward" or the like. The "purely" one-sided donative transfer is not part of the "reality" non-legal social scientists have studied.

In the light of this historical, comparative and social scientific evidence, the presumed dichotomy between gifts and bargains is difficult to sustain . . .

If gifts are exchanges rather than one-sided transfers, should the law treat them differently than it currently does? This question can be approached in two ways. First, we might ask whether, if this alternative view of giving is accepted, formalities and the functional explanation which has been offered for them would seem as necessary as they now do. Second, we might ask whether, if gifts are exchanges, there is any persuasive reason to treat gifts differently than we do conventional economic bargains.

Assuming gift-exchange merely replicates in social or affective terms the self-interested struggle of the commodities markets, the need for formalities becomes questionable. If the donor, like the contract promisor, acts out of self-interest and in expectation of future gain, his or her gift is a calculated act; if a gift is by hypothesis the product of deliberation, the donor needs a separate ritual to underscore the significance of his or her act no more than a market participant does. Nor is evidentiary reliability necessarily of greater concern in gift-exchange than in market-exchange. The selfish urge toward perjury is prevalent in respect to contracts as well as gifts, yet the Statute of Frauds provisions applicable to the former impose requirements considerably less onerous than those applicable to the latter. If a simple signed writing meets the problem in the one case, why is more needed in the other?

As we have seen, not everyone shares the view that gift-exchange is truly analogous to market exchange. Yet even for those who view gift-exchange as a process by which egoistical, self-interested motivations are channelled in ways that ultimately connect individuals more closely to one another, the utility of formalities is questionable. To the extent that formalities foster deliberation, calculation, precision and quantification, they are at odds with the spirit of giving. Gifts are socially important precisely because they are spontaneous, approximate and unspecifiable. Why should the law impose requirements which are inconsistent with these attributes and which seek to make gifts like bargains?

The question whether the law ought to retain the formalities currently applicable to gifts is related to another, more important question: Is there a reason to treat conventional market bargains as more worthy of legal intervention than gifts? In the consideration context, as we have seen, the affirmative justification for enforcing bargains is to protect the social interest in securing the commonly-held expectations customarily engendered by business promises. If, as social scientists claim, there are not equally strong and established expectations with respect to giving, it is not immediately obvious why these expectations should not be protected as well.

One answer, of course, is that the economic expectations produced by market bargains are easily distinguishable from the imprecise, non-quantifiable expectations involved in gift-exchange. Yet it is not entirely clear why the expectations of gift-exchange should be any less important for being non-economic. Wealth consists of more than commodities. Objects can be valuable not just as means of producing additional material rewards but because "they are part of the way we constitute ourselves as continuing personal entities in the world." The giving of objects can be part of this process of self-definition. Are these social and personal attributes of gift-exchange necessarily of less dignity than the economic attributes of market bargains? Only if wealth is defined solely in terms of commodities is it fair to characterize a gift as a "sterile transmission."

Yet even conceding the importance of the non-economic values of gift-exchange, there might nonetheless be reasons for the law to minimize its involvement in donative transfers. If in fact the obligations of gift-exchange are satisfied through the non-legal pressures exerted by trust, gratitude and the like, legal intervention may be both unnecessary and inappropriate. In any event, the law may be unsuited to engaging in the complicated emotional and social calculus of the gift-exchange process.

None of these arguments seems compelling. The business-related, non-legal pressures that cause most market participants to fulfill their bargains voluntarily are not thought to eliminate the need for judicial involvement in contracts; why should the social or psychological pressures that underlie gift-exchange require a different approach for donative transfers? Moreover, the notion that the law should avoid entanglement with gifts because its enforcement mechanisms — awards of damages and the like — are ill-suited to the connected, socially cohesive qualities of gifts suggests that the law should not involve itself with gifts at all; that suggestion conflicts with our legal system's ostensible commitment to lend its power to private decisions in the field of donative transfers. Finally, our legal system is not always adverse to tackling questions of enormous social and emotional complexity. In areas such as family law and reproductive rights it takes on such questions routinely.

In the end, the persistence of formal requirements for donative transfers and the reluctance to enforce such transfers except on purely formal grounds carries a message. Gifts are uncommon, untrustworthy, and unimportant. The formalities and the differential treatment of gifts and bargains have been justified as responses to "real" phenomena: the "needs" of individuals, of the economy, and of the judicial system. There is, however, reason to question whether these needs "really" exist or, if they do, whether they exist — at least in part — because of the system of legal rules that has been adopted. The legal rules now in effect treat "gifts" as distinct from "bargains". The qualities shared by these two "kinds" of transactions — including the possibility that they both involve exchange — are submerged, hidden in the very structure of distinction. We are thereby encouraged to think of donative and commercial transfers as being "truly" distinct, and to act accordingly. It is possible to ask whether the divergent mores and norms we bring to gifts and to bargains are not in some degree a product of that consciousness.

Nolan v. Nolan & Anor
[2003] V.S.C. 121 [footnotes omitted]

[This case concerns the ownership of three paintings: "Hare in Trap" (1946), "Royal Hotel" (1948), and "Italian Crucifix" (1955) by the well-known Australian artist Sidney Nolan (1917-92). The plaintiff, Jinx Nolan, was Sidney Nolan's daughter by adoption. She claimed that Sidney Nolan had made a gift of the paintings to her mother, Cynthia Nolan, sometime before Cynthia's death in 1976. Jinx was a major beneficiary of her mother's estate. That estate included various other Nolan originals, however, the paintings in dispute were not included in the estate inventories. Following Cynthia's death, the three paintings essentially remained in Sidney Nolan's possession until his death. The plaintiff alleged that proof of the claim that a gift had been made to her mother (largely based on documents from exhibitions) had only recently come to light.]

Dodds-Streeton J.: . . .

Gifts of Chattels

There are three recognised methods for making a valid gift of a chose in possession, such as a painting, *inter vivos*.

They are: (a) deed (b) declaration of trust (c) delivery.

In the present case, the plaintiff does not assert that a gift was effected by deed or declaration of trust. No deed has been identified or pleaded. Although various constructive trusts are pleaded, they are relevant only in reply to defences of limitations legislation and delay. They depend, for their effect, on the prior establishment of a valid gift to Cynthia by Sidney Nolan.

In establishing a valid gift of a chose in possession *inter vivos*, which is fundamental to her claim in this proceeding, the plaintiff encounters several significant hurdles represented by well-recognised principles and maxims applicable in this context.

First, it is well established that equity will not assist a volunteer. From that flows the equally venerable principle that equity will not complete an imperfect gift.

Secondly, possession is prima facie evidence of property. As Isaacs and Rich JJ. observed in *Russell v. Wilson* —

> Possession in the relevant sense, is not merely evidence of absolute title; it confers a title of its own, which is sometimes called a "possessory title". This possessory title is as

good as the absolute title as against, it is usually said, every person except the absolute owner.

Limitations of action legislation reflects the policy that lengthy possession must ultimately operate to preclude a remedy in relation to a title, "however clear and indisputable", when a title holder comes "too late". The legislation recognises the public's interest in having "a certain fixed period, after which the possessor may know that the title and right cannot be called in question" in order to avoid an opening to "interminable litigation, exposing parties to be harassed by stale demands, after the witnesses of the facts are dead, and the evidence of the title lost".

In the present case, Sir Sidney Nolan and the first defendant, Lady Nolan, as his beneficiary, have successively been in continuous peaceable possession of the disputed paintings for an unbroken period of approximately 27 years. The "witnesses of the facts" of the alleged gift transactions are dead.

Thirdly, the plaintiff bears the onus of establishing the necessary elements of a gift of chattels effected by delivery . . .

The plaintiff also contended that the fact that Sidney Nolan made many undisputed gifts of his paintings to Cynthia demonstrated a propensity on his part to make such gifts, which should assist the plaintiff in the present case. In my opinion, the fact that Sidney Nolan made many gifts to Cynthia which he did not dispute during her life or after her death, is more consistent with the conclusion that he did not make gifts to his wife of those paintings he retained after her death. There is evidence that Sidney Nolan was upset by the terms of his wife's wills, under which he took no benefit. Nevertheless, he made no attempt to challenge Cynthia's estates' entitlement to a considerable number of paintings. Such conduct suggests that Sidney Nolan "honoured" gifts and recognised them as binding.

The essential elements of a valid gift of a chattel inter vivos, in the absence of a deed of gift or a declaration of trust, are

(a) an intention to make a gift, usually expressed by words of present gift;

(b) intention on the part of the donee to accept the gift; and

(c) delivery.

Intention to Make a Gift

Donative intention is characteristically accompanied by words of gift which evince the intention and delineate the object and extent of the intended benefaction.

The plaintiff in the present case, although reliant on a valid gift, is unable to produce any witnesses to the alleged gift transactions. Instead, reliance is placed on documents, the admissibility of which is largely disputed. Those documents, to the extent to which they contain admissible statements, must be approached not only with the degree of caution generally applicable to claims against a deceased estate, but with added caution based on circumstances peculiar to the present case, discussed in detail below.

Are Words of Gift Essential?

The documents on which the plaintiff relies contain statements which, even if admissible, do not amount to words of present gift by Sidney Nolan.

Many of the decided cases have involved undisputed "words of present gift". It was submitted by the plaintiff that words of gift are not required provided that donative intention is established. The issue has not received detailed consideration in any of the authorities of which I am aware.

This method of effecting a gift of chattels is commonly characterised as "delivery".

In many of the cases, however, reference is made to a "parol gift" or a "gift by word of mouth". The question arises whether words of gift are an essential constituent of this method. It is clearly established that donative intention and delivery are required. In most decided cases, words of gift have been undisputed or appear to have been assumed. Argument has centred on whether the requirement of delivery was satisfied. *In re Cole, (a bankrupt) Ex parte The Trustees v. Cole* the Court of Appeal appeared to assume that "words of gift" must be spoken. Words of gift had indisputably been spoken in that case, so the effect of the absence of words of gift was not addressed. Recently, in *Horsley v. Phillips Fine Art Auctioneers Pty Ltd.*, Santow J. expressly stated that oral words of gift with delivery were required. The plaintiff's submission, however, draws support from the observation of Mason C.J. and McHugh J. in their joint judgment in *Corin v. Patton* that "Just as a manifestation of intention plus sufficient acts of delivery are enough to complete a gift of chattels at common law, so should the doing of all necessary acts by the donor be sufficient to complete a gift in equity". *Corin v. Patton* did not concern a gift of chattels, but a voluntary transfer of an interest in Torrens land. The observation is therefore *obiter*.

If donative intention and delivery only are essential for a valid gift of chattels, that intention must nevertheless be made manifest and expressed with certainty. Words of present gift show "an intention to give over property to another, and not to retain it in the donor's hands for any purpose, fiduciary or otherwise". Words of gift are usually necessary to achieve that certainty in relation to matters such as defining the extent of the benefit the donor intends to confer.

Nevertheless, in my opinion, the better view, as expressed in the *dictum* in *Corin v. Patton*, is that donative intention need not be manifested by words of gift. Although donative intention would normally be manifested, and its extent defined, by words, unusual circumstances may be imagined where other means fulfil those functions.

If a valid gift may be effected without words of gift in unusual cases, the putative donee who seeks to rely on alternative means of establishing donative intention, would bear the onus of proving the existence of a present, unequivocal donative intention, attended by the requisite certainty as to object, extent, and whether the gift would take immediate effect.

The question is relevant to the present case, because, in contrast to most decided cases, the plaintiff adduces no evidence of words of present gift. Rather, statements in the documents on which the plaintiff relies constitute, at their highest, *ex post facto* admissions or acknowledgments by Sidney Nolan, the alleged donor, that a particular painting belongs to Cynthia, is "Cynthia's" or is part of "Cynthia's collection".

In my opinion, evidence that Sidney Nolan believed that he had made a gift to Cynthia of an absolute interest, which had already taken effect and which he did not desire to retract, would be capable of manifesting donative intention. A comparable case is that of *Re Ridgeway*, in which the alleged donor apparently believed that he had made a gift of port to his children and thereafter acknowledged the port's reputation as "Tom's port" or "Alice's port". It was apparently accepted in *Re Ridgeway* that the putative donor intended to make a gift and believed that he had done so. That belief was found to be mistaken as a matter of law, because the essential requirement of delivery was not fulfilled. The port remained within the father's possession in the cellar. The gift, although intended, was held to be incomplete and equity will not perfect an imperfect gift.

Further, although a putative donor's acquiescence in an ascription of ownership to the donee may, in my opinion, constitute evidence that donative intention existed at a particular time, it may be more equivocal than words of present gift. Where the donor or donee is available to give direct evidence of the matter, any ambiguity or doubt may be resolved. That is not possible in the present case.

A further problem which arises in the present case in relation to the plaintiff's reliance on the alleged donor's apparent acknowledgment of the alleged donee's ownership is that, although delivery can precede, accompany or follow the gift, delivery must occur while the donative intention subsists. At any stage until delivery occurs, the donor can validly retract the gift.

The authorities establish that a promise to make a gift, or an expression of gift by words of future intention, however clear and unqualified, is not sufficient to establish a perfect gift. It follows that the donor's expression of belief or conclusion that he or she has made a gift which has taken effect, so that property has passed to the intended donee, is equally insufficient. At best, it satisfies only the first requirement of a valid gift of chattels. It manifests donative intention. The second necessary element of delivery must also be satisfied in order to give complete effect to the donative intention. That is a question of law which the putative donor rarely addresses and would usually be unqualified to determine, when expressing a conclusion that property in the chattel had passed to the donee . . .

In the present case, both the alleged donor and the alleged donee are dead, the donee for nearly 30 years. In seeking to discharge the onus of establishing the necessary elements of a perfect gift, the plaintiff must rely on documents, rather than on oral testimony which may be tested by cross-examination. Where the alleged donor is dead, the authorities require the claimant donee's account of events to be approached with caution. Where both the alleged donor and donee are dead, and reliance is placed on documents, caution is particularly necessary.

In *Re Garnett, Gandy v. McCauly* Brett M.R. observed:

> The law is that when an attempt is made to charge a dead person in a matter, in which if he was alive he might have answered the charge, the evidence ought to be looked at with great care; the evidence ought to be thoroughly sifted and the mind of any judge who hears it ought to be, first of all, in a state of suspicion.

He nevertheless noted that:

> . . . if, in the end the truthfulness of the witnesses is made perfectly clear and apparent, initial suspicion would yield to belief.

In *Thomas v. The Times Book Co.*, Plowman J. applied the approach of Brett M.R. in a case where the poet, Dylan Thomas, had died shortly after allegedly making a gift of the manuscript of his poem "Under Milk Wood" to a BBC executive. Plowman J stated:

> . . . [N]ot only in this case is the onus of proof on the defendants, but I am enjoined by authority to approach their story with suspicion, having regard to the fact that the other actor in this story, the late Dylan Thomas, is dead and cannot therefore give his own version of what took place . . .

Recent decisions of this Court have reiterated the need for caution, if not suspicion, in determining claims made against the estate of a deceased person . . .

[The Court then undertook an extensive review of the documentary evidence and the rules of evidence pertaining to their admissibility. It was then concluded that donative intent had not been proven.]

Delivery

As I have found that the plaintiff has not established words of gift or the requisite donative intention in relation to any of the three paintings, it is unnecessary to consider the further requirement of delivery. However, for the sake of completeness I do so.

Delivery in the present context does not function merely as evidence of donative intention. It is the legal act essential to complete the gift. It transfers both possession and (by perfecting the gift) ownership of the chattel to the donee. Accordingly, a valid delivery marks the termination of the donor's dominion. A continuation of control or power in the donor is inconsistent with a valid delivery and hence inconsistent with a perfect gift.

This was well-expressed in *Young v. Cockman* a decision of the Maryland Court of Appeals, in which Delaplaine J., delivering the judgment of the court, observed:

> To make an effectual delivery the donor must not only part with possession of the property, but must relinquish all present and future dominion and control over it beyond any power on his part to reclaim it. It is obvious that a transfer is not a transfer of possession unless the transferor intends that it shall take effect immediately. If he retains the same control over the property that he had before the transfer was made, there remains a *locus poenitentiae*, in which he may revoke what he has done, and consequently there is no delivery.

It is well-established that delivery may be actual (by way of manual or physical transfer of the goods), or constructive. Constructive delivery may take various forms. Where the nature or bulk of the goods renders manual delivery impossible or impractical, acts falling short of manual delivery have been held sufficient to signal a change in possession.

A further form of constructive delivery occurs when the donee is already in possession or, according to some authorities, when the donee already has custody, of the chattels. Delivery can also occur after the manifestation of intention, or (in the usual case) contemporaneously with it.

As the gift can be retracted at any time prior to delivery, where delivery takes place subsequently, it would be necessary to establish that the previously expressed donative intention was still on foot when delivery occurred.

Alternatively, it would be necessary to establish that the chattels were already in the possession (or at least the custody — see discussion below) of the purported donee at the time when the words of gift were expressed or donative intention was otherwise made manifest.

Where possession of the chattels by the intended donee precedes the words of gift, the gift may be perfected without the necessity for the donor to retake possession of the chattels in question in order to effect a valid delivery. In *Re Stoneham; Stoneham v. Stoneham*, the chattels in question were already situated in a house occupied by the donee when the donor spoke the words of gift. Laurence J., having reviewed *Cochrane v. Moore*, held that where the chattel the subject matter of a parol gift is already in the possession of the donee at the time when the gift is made, a further delivery or a change of possession is unnecessary. Rather, "in order to constitute a perfect gift by word of mouth of chattels capable of delivery the donee must have had the chattels delivered into his possession by the donor or by someone on his behalf. In principle, I can see no distinction between a delivery antecedent to the gift and a delivery concurrent with or subsequent to the gift. Nor can I see any reason in principle why the rule should not apply to a case where chattels have been delivered to the donee before the gift as bailee or in any other capacity, so long as they are actually in his possession at the time of the gift to the knowledge of the donor" . . .

Delivery in Common Establishments

The question of how delivery of household goods or chattels is to be validly effected between spouses or other cohabitants in a common establishment poses special difficulties. The determination of whether an establishment is "common" is a question of fact. There is no reason why the concept should be restricted to particular categories of social or familial relationships.

The National Trustees Executors and Agency Company Limited v. O'Hea is an early Victorian decision dealing with a purported gift from employer to employee within a shared establishment. The deceased, when close to death, stated clear words of gift of his coach and horses to his servant, the coachman. There was no doubt that the deceased intended to make a gift. However, no change in possession occurred. The coach and horses continued to be maintained at the deceased's premises.

A'Beckett J. found that the requirement of delivery was not satisfied. Although delivery could be antecedent, in the present case, although the servant had actual possession, it was not possession as a bailee, but legally, was the possession of the donor, his master. Further, nothing was done which would indicate a change in possession. "It could not be said that the [donor] had at any time made delivery to his coachman of any of the chattels which were in his custody at the time when they were given to him, or that the custody differed from the ordinary custody by a servant of his master's goods. When things are in such custody I hold that there can be no effectual gift of them by the master merely telling the servant that he may keep them as his own."

In requiring delivery, A'Beckett stated, "It would be dangerous to relax a rule which requires some visible act as an essential, when the only other essential is that certain words should be spoken."

The question of delivery between spouses in a common establishment was considered in *Re Cole, (a Bankrupt) Ex p. The Trustees v. Cole.* In that case, a husband purchased a house as a family home, equipped it with valuable furniture and introduced his wife to the house, escorting her through the house indicating items and stating, "Look, it's all yours". The spouses continued to reside together in the house.

On the husband's subsequent bankruptcy, the trustee in bankruptcy claimed entitlement to the house contents. The wife contested that claim, on the ground that she was the beneficiary of a valid gift.

Cross J., at first instance, held that there was a valid gift, observing, "I do not see what more Mr Cole could have done to put Mrs Cole into possession of the gift which he thought he was making".

On appeal, the Court of Appeal held that there was no valid gift. Harman L.J. observed:

> It is, I think, trite law that a gift of chattels is not complete unless accompanied by something which constitutes an act of delivery or a change of possession. The English law of the transfer of property, dominated as it always has been by the doctrine of consideration, has always been wary of the recognition of gifts . . . in the absence of consideration, delivery is still necessary, except in the cases of a gift by will or by deed, which latter itself imports both consideration and delivery. . . .

The peculiar problems posed by spouses or other cohabitants in a common establishment have received recent consideration in two Australian cases, which evince differing and perhaps irreconcilable approaches.

In *Horsley v. Phillips Fine Art Auctioneers Pty Ltd.*, Santow J. questioned the authority of *Re Cole.* His Honour held that where chattels are situated in a residence of which the intended donee is occupier or titleholder, and there is no shared control of the chattels, the chattels may be regarded as being in the pre-existing possession, or at least the custody, of the donee, and subsequent words of gift may suffice to perfect the gift, without any requirement for the donor first to retake possession or to execute a deed. His Honour's observations also evinced an expansive approach to delivery, suggesting that prior custody by a donee in a common establishment may suffice.

In *Horsley v. Phillips Fine Art Auctions Pty Ltd.* a credit corporation which seized certain valuable household chattels as assignee of a bill of sale resisted a cross-claim for conversion on the grounds that the cross-claimant had, *inter alia*, divested himself of that interest by joining with his brother in an effective gift of their half interests in the chattels to their mother, prior to the granting of the bill of sale from which the credit corporation purportedly derived title.

The brothers (who held joint title to the chattels in question) occupied a very large mansion property with their parents. The cross-claimant occupied a separate cottage and his brother, although residing within the main house with the parents, occupied a separate suite. Santow J. held that the arrangement did not constitute a "common establishment".

The relevant furniture was kept in those parts of the main house which were under the control of the parents, so that if the brothers used the rooms they did not do so "as co-possessors with their parents, but by leave of their parents; though no doubt their access was in practice untrammelled". Santow J. accepted the cross-claimant's evidence that the brothers "did unequivocally state to their mother that they were gifting the furniture to her and had the celebratory drink".

His Honour considered that the cross-claimant probably walked around the various items of furniture, but was unable to determine whether he was accompanied by his mother or brother, or, if his mother accompanied him, whether he placed his hand on the items, although he did not hand anything to his mother.

Santow J. concluded that a valid gift of the chattels had been effected. In that context, he relied upon the principle that further delivery is unnecessary if the intended donee "already had possession or at the least custody of the chattels at the time of the words of gift".

His Honour discussed the distinction between legal possession (*animus possidendi* and a degree of physical control sufficient to exclude strangers from interfering) and mere custody (*de facto* possession or mere physical control). He referred to *Flinn v. White* in which words of gift by a father to his daughter in relation to a piano, which remained throughout situated in the family home of which the father was occupier, were held to be ineffective, for want of pre-existing possession or custody in the donee, or a further act of delivery.

Santow J. questioned whether, although the daughter had "no more than a licence, revocable by the father at will" to use the piano, she did not in fact have custody. In his view, "status as a licensee, as such, need not be fatal; a licensee can have the degree of physical control required for custody". His Honour found, however, that the decision could, in any event, be justified by reference to onus. The daughter had not dispelled the implication of her having only limited access, a right to use the piano at the father's pleasure, which was shared with at least one other family member. More directly relevant were *Hislop v. Hislop* and *Re Cole* which involved a purported gift between husband and wife residing together in the matrimonial home. Santow J. considered the results in *Hislop v. Hislop* and *Re Cole* were explicable because joint *de facto* control of the furniture, (based on being permitted to use and enjoy it) did not suffice to establish pre-existing possession.

In *Horsley v. Phillips Fine Art Auctioneers Pty Ltd.*, Santow J. held that the intended donee, the mother, had (jointly with her husband) physical control and therefore custody of the chattels. On one view, she also had exclusive possession of the house and therefore of the rooms in which they were situated. The fact that the mother had such custody or possession jointly with her husband was, in his view, irrelevant.

On Santow J.'s findings, there was no joint custody or possession between the putative donors and donee. Although not deciding the question, Santow J. was inclined to think that shared control between a putative donor and donee should not be fatal. He observed —

> This is especially where there is no suggestion of shared control between putative donor and donee. I do not need to decide whether the feature, absent here, should be fatal to an effectual gift, though I am inclined to think it should not be fatal.

In *Horsley v. Phillips Fine Arts Auctioneers Pty Ltd.*, Santow J. questioned the authority of *Re Cole* and *Hislop v. Hislop* because the cases failed to deal with custody as a separate basis from possession. His Honour considered that, "They appear to have proceeded on an implicit, and I suggest, questionable assumption. That is, that where goods are in the shared use of the putative donor and donee, but where the putative donor has the superior right to those goods through ownership of the home in which kept [sic] that necessarily precludes a finding of custody on the part of the claimant donee".

Santow J.'s observation may suggest that the purported donors in *Re Cole* and *Hislop v. Hislop* had de facto mixed possession, but a superior right to the goods, not because they had legal ownership of the goods, but because they had legal title to the house in which they were situated. However, the reference to "possession following title" in those cases related to the title to the chattels, not title to the residence in which they were situated.

Horsley v. Phillips Fine Art Auctioneers Pty Ltd. did not concern a common establishment or a situation of shared control and Santow J.'s observations were therefore *obiter dicta*.

In *Tudberry v. Sutton*, a case decided after *Horsley v. Phillips Fine Art Auctioneers Pty Ltd.*, Judge McGill S.C. strongly reaffirmed the primacy of the requirement for an identifiable act of delivery. He considered that recognised exceptions based on prior possession or custody should not be extended. In *Tudberry v. Sutton*, the deceased's sister and her family resided in his house, visiting from interstate, while he was gravely ill in hospital. The sister gave evidence that her brother expressed an intention to make an immediate gift of a memento to her children (his niece and nephew). The sister selected and named two paintings in her brother's house, informed him, and he appeared to nod assent. The sister then removed the paintings from the brother's residence. The brother subsequently died.

Judge McGill S.C. held that there was no valid gift. He adverted to the necessity for the donor to give, rather than the donee to take, possession. He questioned the status of *Thomas v. Times Book Co Ltd*, which he identified as the only decision in which the taking of possession by the donee had been upheld. He considered that if it correctly decided that an effective delivery had occurred, such delivery was effective not because the donee took possession with consent, but because, on proper analysis, the custodian of the place where Thomas had mislaid the manuscript gave it to the donee in the capacity as the bailee of the donor. Nevertheless, Judge McGill S.C. concluded that, taken at face value, the decision in *Thomas v. Times Book Co Ltd* is "simply wrong and is an example of a hard case making bad law".

Judge McGill S.C. considered that Santow J.'s unqualified extension of prior possession to prior custody in any capacity at all in *Horsley v. Phillips Fine Art Auctioneers Pty Ltd.* failed to accord with the tenor of applicable authority and with the underlying governing principle that delivery is the formal step which effects the gift.

He considered that the only case where mere custody, as distinct from possession, is legitimately within the exception would be where the donee is in the degree of physical control that would otherwise require the donor first "to retake" the chattels. That would have been the case in both *Re Stoneham* and *Horsley v. Phillips Fine Art Auctioneers Pty Ltd.*, as the donees were in exclusive occupation of the residences in which the chattels were situated. It would not be the case where the donor and donee occupied a common establishment and where there was only "such custody as is afforded by actual use from time to time". In such cases, mere words of gift unaccompanied by any further act of delivery would not suffice. Some manual or constructive act of delivery would be necessary "unless the donee already has 'such a degree of possession that there would have to be re-delivery before there could be delivery'." On that basis, *Re Cole* was correctly decided.

In reiterating a preference for continued observance of the strict requirement of delivery, and confining the exception of pre-existing possession to strict limits, Judge McGill S.C. noted "I suspect that part of the reason for the survival of the rule in its strict form has been a desire to prevent a deathbed gift *inter vivos* or *donatio mortis causa* from evading statutes which require wills to be made in a particular form, coupled with a general suspicion as to the genuineness of claims of oral gifts from persons who were either unable to dispute them (because they were dead) or happy to connive at them (because they were bankrupt). There is, however, in my opinion, no justification for relaxing these rules.

Judge McGill S.C. held that the temporary residence of the deceased's sister as a guest in his house did not confer custody of the premises or the chattels therein, although the owner was temporarily absent. The exception did not apply, because re-delivery to the donor was not necessary in order to complete the gift.

In my opinion, there is force in Judge McGill S.C.'s insistence on maintaining delivery as a pre-eminent independent requirement. In the absence of an unambiguous act, the enforcement of voluntary transfers against donors and their successors in title could produce unjust outcomes. That approach does, on occasion, result in the failure of some purported gifts which were genuinely intended. However, greater harm may result from undue relaxation of the delivery requirement, particularly in the context of common establishments. A proliferation of claims between cohabitants, trustees in bankruptcy and executors, together with increased uncertainty in the determination of such claims, may result. In my opinion, the principles expressed in *The National Trustees Executors and Agency Company Limited* and *Re Cole* should be maintained.

In the present case if, contrary to my findings, the relevant documents expressed Sidney Nolan's clear donative intention or acknowledgment of Cynthia's ownership, the plaintiff must also establish a delivery of the paintings.

There is no direct evidence of any act of delivery, whether manual or constructive, by Sidney Nolan to Cynthia.

In the present case, it is undisputed that Sidney Nolan and Cynthia occupied a common matrimonial home during the course of their marriage.

The question arises whether there is any basis on which the plaintiff can discharge the onus of establishing delivery . . .

[T]here is no evidence that the paintings in dispute were situated in the Nolans' matrimonial home during the course of their marriage. Other than for the period from 1974 to mid 1976 (in relation to "Hare in Trap" 1946 and "Italian Crucifix" 1955) and the periods of the relevant exhibitions, there is no evidence as to where the paintings were situated.

Further, other than for the period from 1974 to mid-1976 there is no evidence of Cynthia's level of access to, or power, rights of user and control over, any of the paintings in dispute.

Given such *lacunae*, the liberal approach of Santow J. in *Horsley v. Phillips Fine Art Auctioneers Pty Ltd.* to pre-existing custody in a common establishment, even if extended, cannot assist the plaintiff to establish delivery in the present case.

There is no evidence that Cynthia was, at any stage, in possession of "Royal Hotel" 1948. There is evidence that Cynthia caused 26 paintings including "Hare in Trap" 1946 and "Italian Crucifix" 1955 to be despatched to Australia in 1974 and that she exercised control and dominion over "Hare in Trap" 1946 and (probably) "Italian Crucifix" 1955 until at least June 1976.

Cynthia at that time took possession of the paintings in question and assumed the rights of an owner in relation to them. There is no evidence that Sidney Nolan delivered possession to Cynthia. On the contrary, he did not know of, or consent to, her actions. If, contrary to the views expressed in *Tudberry v Sutton*, a valid delivery may be established by the donee's taking possession with the knowledge and consent of the donor, that did not occur in the present case. Unauthorised appropriation by the purported donee could not constitute a valid delivery on any view. In the circumstances, the plaintiff has failed to establish the essential element of delivery.

Conclusion

In this proceeding, the cases for the plaintiff and the defendants have been clearly presented and well-argued. For the reasons set out above, in my opinion, the plaintiff has failed to establish the requisite elements of donative intention and delivery in relation to the three paintings. I conclude that a valid gift of the paintings to Cynthia, on which the plaintiff's claim to relief in this proceeding depends, is not made out . . .

Re Bayoff Estate
[2000] 3 W.W.R. 455, 2000 CarswellSask 25 (Q.B.)

Krueger J.:

Antoinette Simard, the executrix of the estate of Peter Ivan Bayoff, deceased, applied with the consent of the residuary beneficiaries, for a ruling as to the validity of certain gifts made to her by Bayoff shortly before his death . . .

Agreed Facts and Documents

The agreed statement of facts reads as follows:

#1 The Deceased was a long time resident of the Town of Meadow Lake, Saskatchewan and had been a dentist for approximately fifty-five years.

#2 The Deceased moved and married in California and has one daughter, Marina Bayoff Morrissey. He was subsequently divorced in 1965 and returned to live in Meadow Lake.

#3 The facts concerning the matters in issue arose (in) or about September, 1997 when the deceased summoned solicitor, Daniel Lamontagne, to his bedside to prepare his Last Will and Testament.

#4 The Deceased was at that time aware he was afflicted (with) what he described as "terminal cancer" and had been aware of that diagnosis since February, 1997 at which time he began to liquidate the bulk of his investments including stocks and GICs for the purposes of preparing for the distribution of his estate.

#5 That on September 23, 1997 he provided verbal instructions to Daniel Lamontagne and a fellow solicitor, Mr. Arnold Goodman, for the preparation of his Last Will and Testament.

#6 That Will was prepared on those instructions and when presented for his signature on September 25, 1997 he requested that a number of changes be made with respect to the residual beneficiaries, deleting one Daisy Bayoff (his sister-in-law) and substituting his niece (Daisy's daughter).

#7 That it was after the execution of the Last Will and Testament that he proceeded to retrieve what he described as his safety deposit box key and in the presence of Goodman and Daniel Lamontagne gave the same to Antoinette Simard with the words "everything there is yours".

#8 That on the same occasion he also instructed Mrs. Antoinette Simard (who he had also just named as his Executrix in his Last Will and Testament) to go to the CIBC to clean out his safety deposit box and signed a paper authorizing her to access the box. This was not sufficient authorization for the CIBC as they required that such an authorization be filled out on their forms and when Mrs. Simard attended at the CIBC, she was denied access to the safety deposit box.

#9 That Dr. Bayoff passed away on October 1, 1997 without signing the necessary bank papers required to permit Mrs. Simard to access his safety deposit box.

#10 That on October 2, 1997 Mrs. Simard again attended at the CIBC and removed the following contents from the safety deposit box in the presence of Daniel Lamontagne and CIBC Bank Employee, Jackie Cheze.

#11 That the contents of the safety deposit box were removed and itemized. They consisted of the following:

13 silver dollars (Canadian)

3 Bahamas coins (in package)

Canada Savings Bond Registered in the Name of Peter Bayoff

Bond #RS42L0131248J in the amount of $10,000.00

Bond #RS47L0186299C in the amount of $10,000.00

Bond #RS47L0186298D in the amount of $10,000.00

Bond #RS47L0186297H in the amount of $10,000.00

Bond #RS42L0131249H in the amount of $10,000.00

Province of Saskatchewan Savings Bond #0319171 $20,000.00

Series III

DCT to Lot 7 Block 1 Plan BQ8006 Greig Lake, Saskatchewan

DCT to lot 8 Block 5 Plan AV3919 Meadow Lake, Saskatchewan

Combination to his safe

#12 The position of all parties is that the real property was disposed of by the Testator in his Last Will and Testament and these do not form part of any gift nor could they properly form part of any *donatio mortis causa*. . . .

The Last Will and Testament of Bayoff leaves specific bequests in varying small amounts to a number of named beneficiaries. It then provides that the residue of the estate is to be divided equally amongst the applicant, Antoinette Simard, a niece, Diana Bayoff, and a daughter, Marina Margaret Bayoff Morrissey. The estate has a value of $739,182.65 and Letters Probate issued to Simard on December 30, 1997.

Issue

The issue in this case is whether Bayoff made a valid gift *mortis causa* or *inter vivos* of $70,000.00 worth of Canada and Saskatchewan Bonds and sixteen coins which were then in his bank safety deposit box. I have concluded that he did make a valid gift *inter vivos* for the reasons that follow.

Analysis

A. *Donatio Mortis Causa*

A gift is a gratuitous transfer of the ownership of property. It is usually effected by a transfer during the lifetime of the donor or through the donor's Will. A gift that has the same characteristics as an *inter vivos* gift, but does not take effect until death is known as a *donatio mortis causa* (gift in contemplation of death). There are three essential elements that must be present for a transfer of property to be classified as a *donatio mortis causa*. Those elements were set out in *Rushka v. Tuba* (1986), 50 Sask. R. 152 (Sask. Q.B.) as:

1. impending death from an existing peril,

2. delivery of the subject matter; and

3. the gift is only to take effect upon death and will revert to the donor should he/she recover.

See also *Shawaga Estate, Re*, [1944] 2 W.W.R. 407 (Sask. Q.B.); *Brown, infra*; *Cain v. Moon,* [1896] 2 Q.B. 283 (Eng. Q.B.) at 286; *Wilkes v. Allington*, [1931] 2 Ch. 104 (Eng. Ch. Div.) at 109; *Delgoffe v. Fader*, [1939] Ch. 922 (Eng. Ch. Div.) at 97. Each of the elements of a *donatio mortis causa* is dealt with separately.

Impending Death From An Existing Peril

There is little doubt that this element has been satisfied. Bayoff was aware that he was terminally ill with cancer. That, by any standard, qualifies as impending death from an existing peril.

Delivery Of The Subject Matter

After signing his Will, Bayoff attempted to deliver the contents of the safety deposit box to Simard by giving her the key to the box and instructing his lawyer to complete the necessary paperwork which would permit access to the box for removal of its contents. Although he did not actually deliver the contents of the safety deposit box to Simard, his actions may have been enough to constitute a delivery for a *donatio mortis causa*: *Brown v. Rotenburg*, [1946] O.R. 363 (Ont. C.A.). Merely handing over the key to a trunk in which was located the key to a safety deposit box containing some jewellery the testator wished to give to a donee was enough to establish a *donatio mortis causa* in *Pembery v. Pembery,* [1952] 2 All E.R. 184 (Eng. Ch. Div.).

In *McDonald v. McDonald* (1903), 33 S.C.R. 145 (S.C.C.) the deceased, being ill and not expected to recover, stated that he wanted $6,000.00 to be divided equally between his wife, brother and a sister. The brother wrote out three cheques, one to each for $2,000.00, payable out of a receipt account. The wife of the deceased placed the cheque payable to her back in the trunk where the bank receipt book had been. Those actions were found to constitute a valid *donatio mortis causa*. The gift was complete when the cheques were written. The *McDonald* situation is analogous to the case before me. Delivery of the gift was, in my view, complete when Bayoff handed the safety deposit box key to Simard. Completing the paperwork to allow her to access the safety deposit box occurred after delivery had been completed and was incidental to the delivery.

In *Brown v. Rotenburg, supra*, the court held that delivery of the key for a safety deposit box was a valid and effectual delivery of the contents of the box. Here Bayoff gave up the only means he had of getting to the contents of the safety deposit box. Therefore, he parted with control over the contents. Had Simard not become the personal representative she would have been in a position to demand from Bayoff's executor the contents. I find that care and control over the contents of the safety deposit box had been transferred to Simard notwithstanding that the appropriate and necessary paperwork had not been completed prior to Bayoff's death. If delivery of the key to the safety deposit box did not constitute a transfer of control of the contents for the purposes of a *donatio mortis causa* in this case it is difficult to imagine a case where such a delivery would.

Gift To Take Effect Only Upon Death

The donor of a *donatio mortis causa* may revoke the gift at any time before death: Feeney, *The Canadian Law of Wills*, Vol. 2, 2nd ed. (Toronto: Butterworths, 1982) at 4. The gift is conditional until the donor dies.

The essence of a *donatio mortis causa* is that the property will revert to the donor if the imminent death does not occur. Two difficulties arise here. Bayoff was terminally ill when he made the gift; recovery was not a possibility. And by his words he indicated that he wished Simard to have immediate ownership of the contents of the safety deposit box. Bayoff did not, either by words or actions, suggest that the gift was to take effect only if he died. He had just finished signing a Will in contemplation of his death. It is likely that any gifts which he intended to take effect on death were included in his Will. The gift of the contents of the safety deposit box, in my opinion, was intended to be a gift *inter vivos*.

B. Inter Vivos Gifts

An *inter vivos* gift is one that is intended to take effect during the lifetime of the donor. Ziff, in *The Principles of Property Law*, 2nd ed. ([Toronto]: Carswell, 1996) sets out three elements of a perfectly constituted gift *inter vivos*:

1. an intention to donate;

2. acceptance of the gift; and

3. a sufficient act of delivery.

Of these three only delivery is in issue in this case. There was clearly an intent to donate and that intention was expressed in the presence of independent witnesses. Simard accepted the gift when she accepted the key and attended at the bank to remove the contents of the safety deposit box. I am satisfied that Bayoff had full intention of parting with ownership of the contents of the safety deposit box and that Simard, as donee, was not to return the property, but to treat it as her own.

What remains to be established is sufficient delivery of the *inter vivos* gift. The court will not complete an imperfect gift. See *Kooner v. Kooner* (1979), 100 D.L.R. (3d) 76 (B.C. S.C.).

Delivery of possession of an object by the donor to the donee, with intention to give, is a valid and irrevocable means of making a gift: Crossley Vaines, *Personal Property*, 5th ed. (London: Butterworths). In this case delivery was made of the key to the safety deposit box, but not the contents thereof. Once Simard had the key she had some control over the subject matter of the gift. That control was sufficient delivery to amount to a *donatio mortis causa*. But, was there a change of possession of the contents of the safety deposit box sufficient to amount to delivery of an *inter vivos* gift?

Where it is not possible to physically deliver a gift due to its size or bulk, symbolic delivery will suffice: *Lock v. Heath* (1892), 8 T.L.R. 295 (Eng. Div. Ct.). I doubt, however, that simple delivery of a key can or should be regarded as symbolic delivery of a gift contained in a safety deposit box. In *Watt v. Watt Estate* (1987), [1988] 1 W.W.R. 534 (Man. C.A.) delivery of a duplicate set of keys to a "thunder-bird" boat was found not to be sufficient delivery of a gift. In that case there was no relinquishment of control over the boat.

The donor must give up control of the gift and do everything possible to vest title in the donee. Bayoff did all that he thought he had to do. The court in *Kooner, supra* stated that:

> The methods of making a gift were authoritatively stated by Turner, L.J., in *Milroy v. Lord* (1862), 4 De G.F. & J. 264 at p. 274, 45 E.R. 1185:
>
> > I take the law of this Court to be well settled, that, in order to render a voluntary settlement valid and effectual, the settler must have done everything [page 80] which, according to the nature of the property comprised in the settlement, was necessary to be done in order to transfer the property and render the settlement binding upon him. He may of course do this by actually transferring the property to the persons for whom he intends to provide, and the provision will then be effectual . . .

In *Beavis v. Adams* (February 9, 1995), Doc. 41793/92 (Ont. Gen. Div.), the Ontario Court dealt with the gift of a GIC by a donor to her son. The mother physically delivered the certificate after completing the transfer form incorrectly. The mistake was not discovered until after her death. In that case the Ontario Court upheld the gift stating that simply completing the transfer in an uninformed manner would not defeat the gift. Here the paperwork allowing Simard to access the contents was also inadequate, but delivery had not yet been completed. Simard did not have access to the contents of the safety deposit box. The gift, in my opinion, was unfulfilled.

An unfulfilled gift will be treated as complete if the donee becomes an executor under the Will of the donor. See *Strong v. Bird* (1874), [1874-80] All E.R. Rep. 230 (Eng. Ch. Div.). So long as the intent to make the gift continues until death, by administering the estate, the donee receives control over the donor's property and can perfect the gift. That constitutes delivery of the gift. The Saskatchewan Court of Appeal affirmed this principle in *Rennick v. Rennick* (1962), 33 D.L.R. (2d) 649 (Sask. C.A.) when it stated at 652-53:

> The learned trial judge applied the principle of law which was laid down by Jessel, M.R., in *Strong v. Bird* (1874), L.R. 18 Eq. 315, 48 L.J. Ch. 814. That principle is [headnote, *Re Stewart*, (1908) 2 Ch. 251]:
>
> > that where a testator has expressed in his lifetime an intention to give personal estate belonging to him to one who becomes his executor, the intention to give continuing, the donee is entitled to hold the property for his own benefit.

A similar view had been expressed by Parker J. in *Innes, Re* (1909), [1910] 1 Ch. 188 (Eng. Ch. Div.) when, in referring to *Strong v. Bird, supra*, and *Stewart, Re*, [1908] 2 Ch. 251 (Eng. Ch. Div.), at pp. 193-4 he wrote:

> What is wanted in order to make that principle applicable is certain definite property which a donor has attempted to give to a donee, but has not succeeded. There must be in every case a present intention of giving, the gift being imperfect for some reason at law, and then a subsequent perfection of that gift by the appointment of the donee to be executor of the donor, so that he takes the legal estate by virtue of the executorship conferred upon him. It seems to me that it would be exceedingly dangerous to try to give effect by the appointment of an executor to what is at most an announcement of what a man intends to do in the future, and is not intended by him as a gift in the present which though failing on technical considerations may be subsequently perfected.

Based on the above cases I am satisfied that Bayoff intended to make an immediate gift to Simard, but failed to perfect the gift. His intention did not change before he died. The gift was perfected when Simard became the executrix of Bayoff's estate and was able to take delivery of the contents of the safety deposit box . . .

Conclusion

The Government of Canada and Saskatchewan Bonds and the coins contained in the safety deposit box of the deceased, Peter Ivan Bayoff, were gifted by him during his lifetime to Antoinette Simard. That *inter vivos* gift was perfected when she became his executrix and was able to take possession of the property.

QUESTIONS AND COMMENTS

1. What function does delivery perform in the law of gifts?

2. What alternatives to actual delivery are mentioned in *Nolan* and *Bayoff*?

3. The terms constructive and symbolic delivery are sometimes used in cases involving *inter vivos* gifts. Tim Youdan and Ben Hovius explain the accepted uses of those terms:

> The requirement that the subject-matter of a gift be transferred by the donor to the donee is subject to some qualifications of uncertain scope and effect. First, reference is sometimes made in the case law to "symbolic delivery". Occasionally, this term is used to describe what is here used to describe constructive delivery. Other times, "symbolic delivery" is used to describe cases "when instead of the thing itself, some other object is handed over in its name and stead". Although there is some slight authority in favour of symbolic delivery, the predominant view is that symbolic delivery will not be sufficient to make a gift.
>
> The term "constructive delivery" describes a fiction: something that is not a delivery is treated as if it were one. Although constructive delivery may be generalized as occurring where the donor gives up to the donee power and control over the subject-matter of the gift, there are two factually distinct situations in which it may occur. The first of these is where, although there is no direct handling over of the subject-matter of the gift, the means of getting at it and controlling it is conferred on the donee. The most obvious example of this would be the handing over of a key thereby giving access to the things contained in the place or receptacle whose lock the key will open. Although there is no decision in Anglo-Canadian law on the effect of such delivery with respect to an *inter vivos* gift, it is probable that such delivery would be held effective, subject to two likely qualifications. It is probably not sufficient to give access to the intended donee; the donee must be given power and control to the exclusion of others, including the donor. Also, this form of constructive delivery may, for pragmatic reasons, be restricted to cases where ordinary delivery is not reasonably possible. It may be that it would be restricted to one particular situation, where the subject-matter of the gift "comprises goods of a bulky, ponderous nature or the like". In principle, however, this sort of constructive delivery should apply generally when ordinary delivery is not practicable, whether because of the nature of the subject-matter or because of the "situation of the parties".
>
> The second type of constructive delivery occurs where there is no change [of] factual possession, but there is a change in the capacity in which that person has possession . . . [such as] where the donee is in possession of the subject-matter of the gift before the making of the gift . . .

B. Hovius & T. Youdan, *The Law of Family Property* (Toronto: Carswell, 1991) at 18-20.

4. In appropriate cases a gift may be perfected by deed, which is a document under seal. Actual delivery is not required: the deed becomes effective once the grantor has demonstrated an intention to be bound by it. See *Zwicker v. Zwicker* 1899 CarswellNS 58, 29 S.C.R. 527, applied in *Re Deeley Estate* 1995 CarswellOnt 1120, 10 E.T.R. (2d) 30 (Gen. Div.). Should the delivery of an ordinary piece of paper (i.e., not a deed) that clearly states that an immediate gift of defined property to a specified person suffice?

5. For an ordinary *inter vivos* gift of land, the counsel of perfection is to complete the transfer just as in the case of a sale. However, even in jurisdictions where legal title does not pass until registration, providing the donee with all of the documents necessary to obtain registration will satisfy the delivery requirement: see *Macleod v. Canada Trust Co.* 1979 CarswellAlta 269, [1980] 2 W.W.R. 303 (C.A.) at 311. See also *Hooper v. Hooper* [1953] O.R. 753, [1953] 4 D.L.R. 443, 1953 CarswellOnt

84 (C.A.). *Cf. Re Eisert-Graydon Estate* 2003 CarswellAlta 227, 49 E.T.R. (2d) 170 (Q.B.).

6. What purpose is served by recognising a *donatio mortis causa* (DMC)?

7. Delivery was not initially required to perfect a DMC. It remains the case that the delivery element is diluted where a DMC is concerned. A transfer of partial control, one that might be ineffective to perfect an incomplete gift, can be adequate for a DMC: see *Kooner v. Kooner* 100 D.L.R. (3d) 76, 1979 CarswellBC 786 (S.C.) at 80 (*per* Locke J.). Is that concession warranted?

8. Canadian and, until recently, English courts have refused to recognise the validity of a DMC of land: see, *e.g., Sorensen v. Sorensen* 1977 CarswellAlta 196, [1977] 2 W.W.R. 438 (C.A.). In England, such a gift is now possible: *Sen v. Headley* [1991] Ch. 425 (C.A.). And in *Cooper v. Severson* (1955) 1 D.L.R. (2d) 161 (B.C. S.C.), it was held that a DMC of land was tenable where properly executed documents of title were delivered to the donee.

9. Must the donor die of the contemplated peril? Must the contemplation of death be based on reasonable grounds? Must the donor be caught within imminent peril (*in extremis*) at the time of the gift? Should a DMC be permissible if death is certain to occur? The case law is not uniform in response to these questions. See further B. Ziff, *Principles of Property Law*, 3rd ed. (Toronto: Carswell, 2000) at 147-8.

REVIEW QUESTION

On August 21, 2003, Jim O'Connor died. In his will, he devised his home to his son, Adam.

Shortly after the funeral, Adam, Beth, and Carl, a good friend of the deceased, went to the property to help clean it out and prepare the property for Adam to move in. While working near the fence to the property, Carl found 17 old copper coins. Beth said at the time: "I think those are part of a collection that belonged to dad [Jim]. He made a gift of the collection to me before he died. He said I could have them and handed me the prize he had once won for them in a contest in Toledo."

Once the property transfer of Blackacre was registered in the Land Titles office, and just after Adam had moved in, it was discovered that the fence beside which the 17 copper coins were found had been wrongly placed by Jim's predecessor in title. The land on which the 17 copper coins were found is contained in the certificate of title of the adjoining property, Whiteacre. Adam, Carl, Beth, and David (the present owner of Whiteacre) all claim to be entitled to the 17 coins.

Of the four parties named above, rank their claims to the 17 coins. Identify uncertainty on the facts and in the law.

CHAPTER 5
THE DOCTRINE OF ESTATES

1. INTRODUCTION

This chapter is devoted to the doctrine of estates, a concept associated with ownership of land within the Anglo-Canadian system of property rights. Absolute ownership of land is, in theory, unavailable. In Chapter 2 it was seen that under the doctrine of tenures associated with feudal landholding one held property of a lord. What was held was an estate in land. Indeed, one's place within the feudal social network — one's *status* — was bound up with the idea of an *estate* in land.

Several different estates arose under law. At the upper echelons of the feudal structure, land was held under what are called freehold estates. It is also common to refer to an entitlement under a lease as a leasehold estate (to be studied in Chapter 8). A third form, copyhold, is now obsolete in England and was never part of the law of real property in Canada.

The common law recognizes three forms of freehold estate: the fee simple, which most closely approximates absolute ownership; the fee tail (an inheritable right of conceptually more limited duration), and the life estate. These three forms are canvassed in this chapter, as will be the relevance of the doctrine of estates to personalty.

This chapter also contains an introduction to Aboriginal land rights. It is now well understand that Aboriginal rights generally are unique (*sui generis*). Therefore it would be an error treat Aboriginal title as equivalent to fee simple ownership. However, Aboriginal land rights can be usefully compared to their mainstream counterparts.

2. THE ESTATE IN FEE SIMPLE

R.C. Ellickson, "Property in Land"
102 Yale L.J. 1315 (1993) at 1368–71 [footnotes omitted]

The Fee Simple: The Advantages of Perpetual Land Ownership . . .

Although economic historians have only recently begun to give the fee [simple] its due, Blackstone was able to articulate many of its benefits two centuries ago. Perpetual ownership rights greatly simplify land-security transactions. But the pre-eminent advantage of an infinite land interest is that it is a low transaction cost device for inducing a mortal landowner to conserve natural resources for future generations.

Although the assertion may seem counterintuitive, the key to land conservation is to bestow upon living persons property rights that extend perpetually into the future. The current market value of a fee in Blackacre is the discounted present value of the eternal stream of rights and duties that attach to Blackacre. A rational and self-interested fee owner therefore adopts a infinite planning horizon when considering how to use his parcel, and is spurred to install cost-justified permanent improvements and to avoid premature exploitation of resources. The fee simple in land cleverly harness human selfishness to the cause of altruism toward the unborn, a group not noted for its political clout or bargaining power.

An illustration may help convince the skeptical. Suppose that Mae, a selfish 80-year-old without a bequest motive, owns a house in the Hollywood Hills in fee simple. Mae is considering installing a screening room that would last, with luck, for centuries. In making her decision, would Mae consider the room's benefits that would accrue after her death? If private property rights are transferable — as . . . they usually are — Mae could sell her house at any time and use the proceeds during her dotage. Although she does not expect to live much longer, Mae has a fee simple and can convey perpetual rights. She might well be able to find a younger buyer, such as Rock, who could enjoy the screening room for several decades. When considering the purchase, Rock would recognize that this room would be a sales asset when it came time for *him* to unload the house, say to Demi (someone still younger). By installing the room, Mae would therefore elicit a higher bid from Rock not only because he could enjoy the facility himself, but also because it would add to the house's resale value. So far, the screening room's benefits to Mae, Rock, and Demi have been capitalized into the house's market value; it is easy to see that the same calculations continue in infinite regress, with Rock imagining Demi taking into account resale value to persons currently unborn, and on and on. In short, benefits and costs from here to eternity are capitalized into Rock's bid. If the screening room were to be cost-justified over the long haul, Mae would have an incentive to build it, because she could reap the capitalized value of its remaining net benefits when she sold the house.

Throughout history, many close-knit agricultural groups have recognized that perpetual private ownership makes for better land stewardship. As land in a preliterate society becomes scarcer and its economic development advances, it is increasingly likely to confer potentially infinite entitlements in croplands and homesites upon kinship lines. Especially until a group masters literacy, it may honor a variety of non-Blackstonian rules, such as that private parcels are descendible only to kin, inalienable to outsiders, and forfeitable for nonuse. But once it develops a written language, a group will almost invariably recognize unending private rights in some of its lands. For example, the ancients in Egypt and Greece, two cradles of Western civilization, conferred perpetual land entitles on private owners. In medieval England, farmers' copyholds were inheritable. And when private plots were parceled out at Jamestown and Plymouth, settlers received infinitely long interests. Perpetual private land rights are most emphatically not a uniquely Western institution, however. Land interests of potentially infinite duration evolved separately among the Japanese, the Ibo of Nigeria, and the Navajo of the American Southwest. In sum, the inherent efficiencies of perpetual private land rights have led to their spontaneous appearance on every continent.

Thomas v. Murphy
107 N.B.R. (2d) 165, 1990 CarswellNB 263 (Q.B.)

Creaghan J.: . . .

The plaintiffs retained the defendant to act on their behalf on the purchase of a property. By virtue of his retainer he undertook to report on title and must be seen to have given assurance to the plaintiffs that they had acquired marketable title.

The title acquired by the plaintiffs derived from a deed given by the residual beneficiaries under a will. . . .

The purpose of the conveyance and the intent of the grant is set out in the recitals to the deed as follows:

> Whereas the Grantors herein have executed this Indenture for the purpose of conveying all of their interest in the lands and premises hereinafter described to the Grantees as Executors and Trustees of the Estate of Reuben E. McLeod, in trust, so that they may give a good and sufficient deed thereof to any purchaser;

The terms under which the grantees were to hold the property are set out in the habendum to the deed as follows:

> To have and to hold tthe said lot, piece and parcel of land and premises hereby granted, bargained and sold, or meant, mentioned or intended so to be, and every part and parcel thereof with the appurtenances unto the said Grantees, in their capacity as Executors and Trustees under the Last Will and Testament of Reuben E. McLeod, deceased, late of St. Martins aforesaid, their successors and assigns to the only proper use, benefit and behoof of the said Grantees, their successors and assigns for the purpose of granting, bargaining, selling, alienating, releasing and conveying by Deed the lands and premises hereinabove described and retaining the proceeds therefrom in trust for the use of the Grantors herein in accordance with the provisions of the Last Will and Testament of the said Reuben E. McLeod dated July 11th 1955, a copy of which is filed in the Registry Office for the County of Saint John in Book 338, page 212 as No. 167441 on October 20th, 1956.

The grant of the property was to the grantees, their successors and assigns, in trust in their capacity as executors and trustees with specific power of sale for such price and pursuant to such terms as they may in their discretion determine.

The plaintiffs maintained that because the grantees in this deed did not receive a grant to themselves and their heirs, they could not dispose of a fee simple to the property and accordingly the title the plaintiffs subsequently received was defective and had to be repaired by further quit claim conveyances from the beneficiaries.

The plaintiffs claim costs associated with the repair of their title as damages against the defendant for negligence in reporting that they had obtained marketable title when they purchased the property.

The only issue here is whether the grantees in the trust deed received a fee simple interest in the property which they could convey.

There can be no question about the intention of the grantors. They held the property in fee simple pursuant to the grant under the will and they clearly indicated that the deed was executed for the purpose of conveying all of their interest in the property so that the grantees as trustees might give good and sufficient title to all their estate in the property to any purchaser.

There can be no question that the grantees as trustees had the power of sale for this power is specifically set out in the grant and the habendum.

The plaintiffs argue that because the property was conveyed to the trustees as grantees, their successors and assigns, rather than to the trustees as grantees, their heirs, successors and assigns, they therefore took and could only grant something less than a fee simple to the property and an interest remained vested in the beneficiaries as grantors.

I had hoped that the strict imperative of using magic words in the grant of an estate in real property had gone out of our law. I must say that the argument presented persuades me that that is not entirely the case.

Here the conveyance was to trustees as grantees, their successors and assigns, to hold and dispose of the property under terms of a specific trust. The defendant argues that there can be no limitation with respect to the heirs of the trustees, for the heirs of the trustees can take no interest in the property in any event.

The problem with this argument is that use of the word "heirs" in the grant is a matter of limitation of title not a question of succession to title, and absent the word "heirs" the fee simple is found at law not to have been granted.

The legislature has attempted to deal with this anarchism in the law by passage of section 12(3) of the *Property Act*, R.S.N.B. 1973, c. P-19:

> In a conveyance, it is not necessary in the limitation of an estate in fee simple to use the words "heirs", but it is sufficient if the words "in fee simple" are used.

The issue in this case would be much simpler if the *Property Act* of New Brunswick were to accept the principle set out in the much broader provisions contained in the Ontario *Conveyancing and Law of Property Act,* R.S.O. 1980, c. 90 which by s. 5 specifically provides that if no words of limitation are used, a deed can pass all the estate or interest held by the grantor, unless a contrary intention appears in the deed.

In this case the grantors in question held the property in fee simple. The recitals and the habendum contained in the deed to the trustees can leave no doubt of the intention of the conveyance to pass all the interest of the grantors to the grantees. I am satisfied that the conveyance taken as a whole clearly explains the intention of the parties to the conveyance and that the requirement of words of limitation in the grant should be seen to have been supplied by the clear intention in the deed to pass the fee simple interest of the grantors.

> It was stated in *Spencer v. Registrar of Titles* that "although the habendum cannot retract the gift in the premises, it may construe and explain the sense in which the words in the premises should be taken". Hence, in that case, where the grant was to a person in trust for another person, his heirs and assigns, and the habendum was to the grantee and his heirs, the lack of limitation of an estate in the operative words was supplied by the habendum so that the grantee took a fee simple in trust.
>
> Anger and Honsberger, *Real Property*, Vol. 1, (2nd Ed.), Canada Law Book (1985), at p. 105.

More importantly, as our Court of Appeal stated in *Wheeler v. Wheeler and Wheeler's Estate (No.2)* (1979), 25 N.B.R. (2d) 376 at p. 378:

> It is a fundamental principle of construction applicable to any written instrument that the instrument will be construed as a whole in order to ascertain the true meaning of its several clauses.

Accordingly, the appeal is allowed and the plaintiffs' action is dismissed.

QUESTIONS AND COMMENTS

1. The kernel of the problem that gave rise to this dispute in *Thomas v. Murphy* can be simply stated. At common law the words necessary to create an *inter vivos* grant in fee simple were "To A and her/his heirs." The phase "To A, her/his heirs, executors and assigns" would also suffice. This strict language requirement is a rule of law, meaning that even if it was apparent that a fee simple was intended, the absence of the appropriate language (as above) meant that A would receive a only a life estate. In the case of property devised by will, a more relaxed position developed: a fee simple would be found so long as the language was sufficiently clear to convey that meaning. A devise that simply read "To A" would not meet this requirement. Why might a different rule for wills have arisen?

The stock phrase "To A and her heirs" translates into the transfer of a fee simple in the following way. The words "To A" are *words of purchase*, describing the intended recipient of the property. The phrase "and her heirs" are *words of limitation*. They delineate the extent of the right conferred on A. The fee simple will endure so long as A has some designated heir: someone who, whether by sale, gift, will, or by operation of law, can take the property. Accordingly, a fee simple can last forever.

2. What rights do the heirs acquire? The case of *Thomas v. Murphy* hints at this answer: nothing of substance. The term heirs is purely descriptive of the rights given to A and confers on the heirs no enforceable claim to the land. It seems to have been so for centuries, as one can see from this ancient case reported in Bracton's Notebook:

> D'Arundel's Case, Brac. N.B. 1054 (1225)
>
> Radulf the son of Roger sought against William of Arundel five acres of land in Trelley, three acres in Treberned, two acres in Tredeiset and one acre in Hendrie and their appurtenances of which Roger his father was seized in law and in feudal services in the time of Lord Henry the King, and which descended from Roger by the law of the land to this same Radulf as his son and heir.
>
> And William came and defended his right, and said that the same Roger, the father, conveyed with quiet enjoyment all the land and its appurtenances to William, the father of William, in the King's Court all his right and inheritance therein; to William and his heirs solely and free from himself and his heirs forever, and offered a deed of Roger by which these things were attested.
>
> And Radulf came and admitted the deed of his father and covenant of quiet enjoyment, but asked judgment whether his father could convey all the land which he held by military tenure, retaining no service to himself and his heirs.
>
> And since Radulf admitted his father's deed and it was attested by the deed that his father Roger conveyed all his land and warranted quiet enjoyment from his heirs, it was adjudged that William should go in peace and Radulf be in mercy.

3. The traditional hyper-technical approach to drafting has been significantly altered by legislative reform. But, as can be seen from *Thomas v. Murphy*, the New Brunswick version introduces a quite limited change to the common law: the word "heirs" is no longer essential in the creation of a fee simple by deed; the use of the term "fee simple" will do. In *Thomas v. Murphy*, reference is made to the broader language of section 5 of the *Conveyancing and Law of Property Act*, R.S.O. 1990, c. C.34. That section reads:

> (1) In a conveyance, it is not necessary, in the limitation of an estate in fee simple, to use the word "heirs".
>
> (2) For the purpose of such limitation, it is sufficient in a conveyance to use the words "in fee simple" or any other words sufficiently indicating the limitation intended.
>
> (3) Where no words of limitation are used, the conveyance passes all the estate, right, title, interest, claim and demand that the conveying parties have in, to, or on the property conveyed, or expressed or intended so to be, or that they have power to convey in, to, or on the same.
>
> (4) Subsection (3) applies only if and as far as a contrary intention does not appear from the conveyance, and has effect subject to the terms of the conveyance and to the provisions therein contained.

(5) This section applies only to conveyances made after the 1st day of July, 1886.

Notice that the above provision applies only to *inter vivos* transfers (i.e., not to wills). However, a comparable principle applies to testamentary gifts:

> Except when a contrary intention appears by the will, where real property is devised to a person without words of limitation, the devise passes the fee simple or the whole of any other estate or interest that the testator had power to dispose of by will in the real property.

Succession Law Reform Act, R.S.O. 1990, c. S.26, s. 26.

One can see that these rules are more flexible than the common law. Under these provisions, one presumes a fee simple even absent words of limitation; but that presumption may be rebutted in appropriate cases. Any rule such as this — which establishes a provisional but not definitive meaning for language found in a dispositive document — is referred to as a *rule of construction.* What factors should influence the framing of a rule of construction?

4. Interpret the following devises of real property, using the Ontario provisions:

(a) " . . . to A and her heirs."

(b) " . . . to A."

(c) " . . . to A or her heirs."

(d) " . . . to A, her heirs, executors and administrators."

(e) " . . . I will, bequeath and devise the following tracts of real estate to ARTHUR L. GARBER, Route # 2, Washburn, Illinois, and his heirs, absolutely and in fee . . ." *Noll v. Garber*, 784 N.E.2d 388 at 389-390 (Ill.App. 3 Dist., 2003).

(f) " . . . to my granddaughter Sarah A. Whiton and her heirs on her father's side" *Johnson v. Whiton* 34 N.E. 542 (Mass. Sup. Ct., 1893).

5. Although a fee simple estate may last forever, it is equally true that it may not. What occurs when the current holder of a fee simple estate dies without heirs within the meaning of the rules for the succession to property?

Under the common law, the land escheats to the overlord as an incident of feudal tenure. In Canada that now means that the property ascends to the Crown. A number of jurisdictions regulate the escheat process by statute. For example, the *Escheats and Forfeitures Act*, S.N.B. 2002, c. E-10, provides in part as follows:

> 1. When any lands, tenements or hereditaments situate in this Province have become liable to be escheated to the Crown by reason of the person last seised thereof or entitled thereto having died intestate and without lawful heirs, or by reason of the same having

become forfeited for any cause, the Attorney General may cause possession of such lands, tenements or hereditaments to be taken in the name of the Crown, or in case possession is withheld he may cause an action to be brought for the recovery thereof, without any inquisition being first necessary. . . .

3. The Lieutenant-Governor in Council may make any grant of lands, tenements or hereditaments that have so escheated or become forfeited, or to which the Crown may hereafter become entitled by reason of any such escheat or forfeiture as herein mentioned, or of any portion thereof, or of any interest therein, to any person for the purpose of transferring or restoring the same to any person or persons having a moral claim to the property, or upon the person to whom the same had belonged, or of carrying into effect any disposition thereof that such person may have contemplated, or of rewarding any person making discovery of the escheat or forfeiture, as to the Lieutenant-Governor in Council seems meet.

4. Any such grant may be made without actual entry or inquisition being first necessary, and although the lands, tenements or hereditaments are not in the actual possession of the Crown, and notwithstanding that some person may claim title thereto adversely to the person whose estates the same had been; and if possession of the said lands, tenements and hereditaments is withheld, the person to whom such grant is made is thereupon entitled to institute proceedings for the recovery of said lands, tenements or hereditaments. . . .

3. THE FEE TAIL

J.V. Orth, "Does the Fee Tail Exist in North Carolina?" 23 Wake Forest L. Rev. 767 (1988) at 767, 773-8 [footnotes omitted]

The fee tail, one of the ancient freehold estates, was an interest in land impressed with a special rule of descent: it passed to the heirs of the body of the first taker until the particular line of descent became extinct. By contrast, the fee simple descended to the heirs of successive owners, whether or not those heirs were "of the body," that is, issue or offspring of the decedents. From the fact that decedents' collateral relatives were excluded the fee tail took its peculiar name from the French *tailler*, "to cut." Limiting the line of descent had a substantial practical consequence: if the line of descent of the estate in tail became extinct, the land reverted to the original grantor or his heirs. The fee simple did not, on the contrary, revert on the complete failure of heirs; it escheated.

The aim of those who first created the fee tail was to establish, in effect, a series of life estates in successive generations of the same family. Unlike the owner of a fee simple, who could convey the entire estate, the owner of an estate in tail could transfer only his present right to possess. At a time when land was the principal source of wealth and an indispensable element of social status, the fee tail represented an attempt to tie up real property in a family, secure from the risk that the family's representative in any one generation would dispose of the land or otherwise lose it. Although the fee tail long outlived the Middle Ages in which it had originated, the estate carried forward a distinctive outlook on property. Land was not the absolute possession of an individual to use or abuse as he saw fit; it was rather the asset of a family, literally its patrimony, designed to support its members from generation to generation. As such, the fee tail secured the economic basis — originally in a simple form, later, in a complex set of arrangements known as the strict settlement — of the English aristocracy and gentry. The fee tail was used to protect, to render permanent if possible, the wealth of the well-to-do. . . .

The freehold estate of fee tail is directly traceable to a statute adopted in 1285. As Sir Thomas Littleton quaintly put it two hundred years later: "tenant in fee taile is by force of the statute of Westminster the second." This statute was the result of dissatisfaction among the great landowners with some early judicial decisions. Grants had been made in the form "O to A and the heirs of his body" with the intention of endowing the grantee *and his descendants* with landed wealth. The judges, apparently hostile even at that early date to tying up land for too long, had construed such grants as empowering the grantee to convey the land in fee simple if he first began a living child (an "heir of his body"). In later years this estate was referred to as a fee simple conditional. To counter this judicial interpretation and give effect to the intentions of the grantor, King Edward I and his barons assembled at Westminster and enacted the statute *De donis conditionalibus*, "concerning conditional grants," which directed the judges to recognize the estate of fee tail. In a lively metaphor Dean Mordecai once described the result: "The conditional fee at common law was the tadpole state of estates tail; the metamorphosis being brought about by the statute *de donis conditionalibus*." This statute may also be viewed as the ancestor of a long line of statutes passed to alter the common law — and, ironically, as an early expression of the public policy in favor of respecting intention.

Over the next century various types of entailed estates emerged. The fee tail could be general or special: general, if all heirs of the body were qualified to succeed; special, if only heirs of the body begotten of a particular spouse were qualified. Furthermore, the heirs of the body could be limited by sex: if only male heirs of the body were qualified, the estate was in fee tail male; if only female heirs of the body were qualified, the estate was in fee tail female. Finally, the succession could be limited to heirs of the body of a certain sex begotten of a particular spouse: fee tail male special or fee tail female special.

For about two hundred years the fee tail continued in its original purity. Indeed, during the Wars of the Roses in the mid-fifteenth century, it demonstrated its usefulness to the warring barons. Not only did the fee tail secure dynastic property against spendthrift heirs who could affect the title only for their own lives, it also protected the landowner against the risk of loss due to political miscalculation or defeat. At that time traitors forfeited their estates. In the midst of the internecine Wars all the participants at one time or another ran the risk of being branded traitors. Whether the family estates were held in fee simple or in fee tail determined how much they stood to lose. At last, near the end of the military struggle, the judges renewed their legal attack on the fee tail. King Edward IV, praised for his efforts by Blackstone as "an active and politic prince," encouraged their offensive. By an elaborate fiction known as the common recovery, a tenant in tail in possession was permitted to convey a fee simple, thus defeating the expectations of the heirs of his body — barring or docking the entail, as it was called. . . .

The legal effect of the recognition of the common recovery was to empower tenants in tail in possession to bar the entail at any term of court. The common recovery defeated the intention of the grantor of the entailed estate; it defeated the expectations of the heirs of the body of the tenant in tail; and it destroyed the reversion in the grantor which would have become a possessory fee simple if the line of the first tenant in tail became extinct. The implementation of an individual's intention was not so predominant a factor in earlier land law as it has become in the modern law of property. Barring the entail by suffering a common recovery did not raise the problem of taking property without compensation that it would in a modern constitutional regime.

Over the next two hundred years, the fee tail (as qualified in practice by the possibility of suffering a common recovery) was utilized by conveyancers for wealthy families in developing the ingenious legal arrangement known as the strict settlement. The purpose of the strict settlement was to preserve land as a family asset, available to discharge the ramifying obligations to various family members, including widows, daughters, and younger sons, while providing enough flexibility to permit periodic adjustments in the interest of both present and future generations. The strict settlement was constructed out of recognized legal interests, specifically the life estate and the fee tail (usually the fee tail male), plus one novelty: a remainder to trustees to preserve contingent remainders. At common law contingent remainders, future interests to unborn persons or to living persons who had not yet satisfied some condition, were susceptible to destruction. The acceptance by the judges of the remainder to preserve contingent remainders ensured the success of the strict settlement as an arrangement to secure the economic basis of the aristocracy during its era of predominance after the Glorious Revolution of 1688 until the triumph of democracy in the nineteenth century.

In schematic form and stripped to its bare essentials, the strict settlement can be exemplified by the grant of an estate by a father (*O*) *to his son* (*A*) who is about to marry: "*O* to *A* for life, remainder to trustees for the life of *A* to preserve the contingent remainder, then to the first son of *A* and the heirs male of his body." Until a son is born to *A*, the remainder in tail is contingent; thus, there was need for the remainder to trustees to preserve the contingent remainder. At the birth of a son to *A*, designated *B*, the remainder in tail vests, thereby eliminating the need for trustees. For present purposes, it is important to note the role of the fee tail. The remainderman in tail (*B*), even after he comes of age, is incapable of suffering a common recovery and conveying a fee simple because he is *not in possession*. Only a tenant in tail in possession was empowered to use the device of the common recovery. Of course, as the conveyancers intended, the life tenant (*A*) and the remainderman in tail (*B*) could *together* do anything with the estate. If *A* surrendered his life estate to *B*, then *B* would be seized in tail and could suffer a common recovery to bar the entail. The land would not be lost to the family. The common recovery normally would be in favor of a "strawman," often the family solicitor, who would promptly convey it back to the family. Usually the strict settlement would merely advance one generation; that is, the conveyance back would be "to *A* for life, then to *B* for life, remainder to trustees for the lives of *A* and *B* to preserve the contingent remainder, then to the first son of *B* and the heirs of his body."

The strict settlement proved to be an admirable device. Land was treated as an asset to be conserved and managed: quick profits for any one generation were discouraged. Indeed, by consulting the interests of at least two generations before a re-settlement, the arrangement institutionalized a long-term perspective far more effectively than a regime favoring the fee simple absolute. The key to its effectiveness was the rule that estates in fee tail could not be converted into estates in fee simple until they became possessory. Yet the common recovery on which strict settlement depended was a cumbersome proceeding. Writing on the eve of American independence, Blackstone candidly assessed the situation.

> The design, for which these contrivances were set on foot, was certainly laudable; the unrivetting the fetters of estates-tail, which were attended with a legion of mischiefs to the commonwealth: but while we applaud the end, we cannot admire the means. [I]t hath often been wishes, that the process of this conveyance was shortened, and rendered less subject to niceties. . . .

Blackstone went on to catalog three possible reforms:

> [1] by either totally repealing the statue *de donis*, which perhaps, by reviving the old doctrine of conditional fees, might give birth to many litigations;
>
> [2] or by vesting in every tenant in tail of full age the same absolute fee-simple at once, which now he may obtain whenever he pleases, by the collusive fiction of a common recovery; though this might possibly bear hard upon those in remainder or reversion, by abridging the chances they would otherwise frequently have, as no recovery can be suffered in the intervals between term and term [of court], which sometimes continue for near five months together:
>
> [3] or, lastly, by empowering the tenant in tail to bar the estate-tail by a solemn deed, to be made in term time and enrolled in some court of record; which is liable to neither of the other objections, and is warranted not only by the usage of our American colonies . . . but also by the precedent of the statute 21 Jac. I. c.19 [1623-24] which, in case of a bankrupt tenant in tail, empowers his commissioners to sell the estate at any time, by deed indented and enrolled.

In fact, reform of the common recovery in England was long delayed. At last, in 1833 the *Fines and Recoveries Act* adopted Blackstone's third option: a tenant in tail in possession and of full age could bar the entail by deed. However, a remainder[er] in tail expectant on a life estate had to have the consent of the life tenant in possession.

QUESTIONS AND COMMENTS

1. Consider also this description of the family settlement in England, found in E. Spring, *Law, Land, & Family* (Chapel Hill: U.N.C. Pr., 1993) at 124-5 [footnotes omitted]:

> [T]hrough a system of making and remaking settlements each generation between father and son, a family estate might be made to descend generation after generation from one life tenant to another. . . .
>
> The scenario runs thus: The legal situation between father and son, as the son came to marry, was that under a settlement that had been made a generation earlier on the father's marriage, the father was possessed of an estate for life and the son was possessed of an estate tail, that is, an entail. Or in other words, the one was tenant for life and the other tenant in tail. If the son were to succeed to the inheritance still possessed of the entail, he would be able to make himself owner in fee simple, entails being barrable. Before he succeeded, however, father and son acting together was what made for settlement's aspect of entail. Were it not for this fact, every settlement must have shortly ended in an owner in fee, usually after one generation. The old settlement would be brought to an end, however, in circumstances that were likely to lead to a new one. The father, grown responsible with his years, would be anxious to ensure the inheritance for a further generation. The son would be in need of an income for himself and his wife during the years before he would succeed to the inheritance. Thus, in return for a present income, the son would agree to a new settlement in which his future interest would be cut down to a life tenancy after his father's and in which the inheritance would be entailed upon his as yet unborn son. The son would be expected someday to make a similar resettlement with his father. In this manner the estate would descend in the family generation after generation with an absolute owner in possession.

2. Incidentally, Professor Orth concluded that the fee tail does not exist in North Carolina as a present possessory estate, but that it can possibly exist as a future interest. In consequence, he cautioned (at 795) that "it is unwarranted to assert categorically that the fee tail does not exist in North Carolina."

3. For all intents and purposes the fee tail no longer exists in Canada. In Nova Scotia, for example, this kind of landholding was abolished prior to Confederation. Section 6 of the *Real Property Act*, R.S.N.S. 1989, c. 385 states:

> All estates tail are abolished and every estate, which before the second day of May, 1865, would have been adjudged a fee tail, shall on or after the second day of May, 1865, be adjudged a fee simple and may be conveyed and devised or descend as such.

4. At common law a gift that read "to A, but should A die without issue, then to B" gave a fee tail to A. The effect of a modern use of that language is contemplated in section 28 of the *Wills Act*, R.S.N.S. 1989, c. 505:

> In any devise or bequest of real or personal property, "die without issue", "die without leaving issue", "have no issue" or any other words which import either a want or failure of issue of any person in the persons lifetime or at the time of the person's death or an indefinite failure of the persons issue shall be construed to mean a want or failure of

issue in the lifetime or at the time of the death of such person and not an indefinite failure of the persons issue, unless a contrary intention appears by the will by reason of such person having a prior estate tail or of a preceding gift being, without any implication arising from such words, a limitation of an estate tail to such person or issue, or otherwise, but this Act does not extend to cases where such words so import if no issue described in a preceding gift are born or if there are no issue who live to attain the age or otherwise answer the description required for obtaining a vested estate by a preceding gift to such issue.

Given section 6 of the *Real Property Act*, why is this provision necessary?

5. Interpret the following clause, assuming that the above provisions are in effect:

(a) "To A, but if A or his heirs shall die without having issue, then to B"

(b) "To A, but if A shall die without issue, then immediately to B"

6. For six generations the McDonald family has farmed a hardscrabble patch of land in Cape Breton. Throughout these years it has passed down to successive members of the family. The current fee simple owner, Eleanor McDonald, attends at your office to prepare her will. She wants to make sure that the property remains within the McDonald family for all time. Her hope is that it will pass down to the eldest child of each owner for as long as possible. Thinking creatively, can you imagine ways in which this might be accomplished even absent the estate tail? (You might want to return to this question once you have completed Chapter 7, since it will then become apparent that there on some serious constraints on one's ability to craft an effective disposition that can accomplish this client's goal.)

4. THE LIFE ESTATE

(a) introduction

The duration of a life estate is determined by reference to continued existence of a life or lives. A gift of land "To A for life" confers on A what is termed an estate *pur sa vie*. It lasts so long as A is alive. Such an interest is fully transferable, though the initial designation of the measuring life (the *cestui que vie*) is fixed at the time that the interest is conferred. Therefore, where A owns a life interest, a transfer to B gives to the latter a life estate for the life of A; this is called an estate *pur autre vie* (for the life of another). Such an estate may even be initially granted in such terms (for example, a gift to A, B and C, for the life of A: see *Bank of Ireland v. Gaynor* [1999] I.E.H.C. 210. Where A holds a life estate for the life of B, and A predeceases B, there remains an unexpired portion of the life interest. At common law, rules of first occupancy governed ownership of this residual portion. Modern wills legislation now provides for the property to devolve along with the rest of A's estate: see, *e.g.*, *Wills Act, 1996*, S.S. 1996, c. W-14.1, s. 21. (As for the rules of occupancy, see A.W.B. Simpson, *A History of the Land Law*, 2nd ed. (Oxford: Clarendon Pr., 1986) at 92.)

(b) creation

Re Walker
(1924) 56 O.L.R. 517 (C.A.)

Middleton J.A.: . . .

John Walker died on the 27th March, 1903, and first made his will, bearing date the 17th November, 1902, which was in due course admitted to probate, his widow being his sole executrix. At the time of his death his estate amounted to approximately $16,000. By his will he provided as follows:

> I give and devise unto my said wife all my real and personal property saving and expecting thereout as follows namely my gold watch and chain I give to my nephew John Noble Walker son of my brother William Walker and all other jewelry I may have at the time of my decease I give to my nephews William Craig Walker and Percy Dugald Walker brothers of the said John Noble Walker share and share alike and also should any portion of my estate still remain in the hands of my said wife at the time of her decease undisposed of by her such remainder shall be divided as follows. . . .

The widow survived until 1922. Her will has been duly admitted to probate. Her estate, including all that remained of her husband's estate, was valued at $38,000.

Those claiming under the husband's will seek to have some portion of this estate earmarked as being an "undisposed of" portion of the husband's estate. Those claiming under the wife's will contend that under the provision of the husband's will the widow took absolutely. Mr. Justice Riddell decided in favour of those claiming under the husband's will. From this decision an appeal is now had.

From the earliest times the attempt has been made to accomplish the impossible, to give and yet to withhold, to confer an absolute estate upon the donee, and yet in certain events to resume ownership and to control the destiny of the thing given. By conveyance this is impossible. Where there is absolute ownership, that ownership confers upon the owner the rights of an owner and restrains an alienation; and similar attempts to mould and control the law are void: *In re Rosher* (1884), 26 Ch. D. 801.

As long ago as 1498 (13 Hen. VII. 22, 23, pl. 9), Bryan, C.J., interrupted counsel arguing before him that a condition on a fee simple not to alien was good, saying that the Court "would not hear him argue this conceit, because it is simply contrary to common learning and is now, so to speak, a principle . . . because in this way we should transpose all our old precedents. Therefore speak no more of this point." *Gray's Restraints on the Alienation of Property*, 2nd ed., pp. 9, 10.

By an executory devise testators succeed in many cases in attaining that which would have otherwise been impossible — creating a future right which would on the happening of certain events come into existence and terminate a pre-existing estate in fee simple, but limits have been placed upon this right constituting exceptions to the general rule that an estate given by will may be defeated on the happening of any event.

> One of these exceptions may, in my opinion, be expressed in this manner, that any executory devise, defeating or abridging an estate in fee by altering the course of its devolution, which is to take effect at the moment of devolution and at no other time, is bad. The reason alleged for that is the contradiction or contrariety between the principle of law which regulates the devolution of the estate and the executory devise which is to take effect only at the moment of devolution, and to alter its course. . . . Another exception to the general proposition which I have stated is this, that any executory devise which is to defeat an estate, and which is to take effect on the exercise of any of the rights incident to that estate, is void; and there again the alleged reason is the contrariety or contradiction existing between the nature of the estate given and the nature of the executory devise over. A very familiar illustration is this, that any executory devise to take effect on an alienation, or an attempt at alienation, is void, because the right of alienation is incident to every estate in fee simple as to every other estate. Another illustration of the same principle is that which arises where the exercise of the executory devise over is made to take effect upon not alienating, because the right to enjoy without alienation is incident to the estate given. . . .

> (*Show v. Ford* (1877), 7 Ch. D. 669, 673, 674) . . .

When a testator gives property to one, intending him to have all the rights incident to ownership, and adds to this a gift over of that which remains *in specie* at his death or at the death of that person, he is endeavouring to do that which is impossible. His intention is plain but it cannot be given effect to. The Court has then to endeavour to give such effect to the wishes of the testator as is legally possible, by ascertaining which part of the testamentary intention predominates and by giving effect to it, rejecting the subordinate intention as being repugnant to the dominant intention.

So the cases fall into two classes: the first, in which the gift to the person first named prevails and the gift over fails as repugnant; the second, in which the first named takes a life-estate only, and so the gift over prevails. Subject to an apparent exception to be mentioned, there is no middle course, and in each case the inquiry resolves itself into an endeavour to apply this rule to the words of the will in question. The sheep are separated from the goats; and, while in most instances there is not much doubt, in some instances the classification is by no means easy.

Speaking generally, no aid can be derived from reported decisions which do not establish a principle but simply seek to apply an established principle to a particular document. Nothing can well be added to the statements of Jessel, M.R., in *Aspden v. Seddon* (1874), L.R. 10 Ch. 397, note, and of Collins, M.R, in *Foulger v. Arding*, [1902] 1 K.B. 700. These being readily accessible, I refrain from quoting at length, only extracting a few words from the earlier decision (p.397):

> I think it is the duty of a Judge to ascertain the construction of the instrument before him, and not to refer to the construction put by another Judge upon an instrument, perhaps similar, but not the same. . . .

I have referred to an apparent exception to the rule which might be regarded as constituting a third class of cases into which some fall. These are cases in which all that is given to the first taker is a life — estate, but the life-tenant is given a power of sale which may be exercised at any time during the currency of his estate. There is no doubt that this may be validly done. It is not uncommon in cases where property is held in trust. In such cases power of sale is frequently vested in trustees who are empowered to sell and pay the purchase-money to the life-tenant for his maintenance. *Re Johnson* (1912), 27 O.L.R 472, is a good example. These cases constitute only an apparent exception to the rule because in them there is no conflict upon the face of the gift. Whether a case can be brought within this class is altogether a matter of construction, and the will here in hand plainly does not fall within it. . . .

Turning now to the will before the Court. I agree with the judgement in review that the words "undisposed of" do not refer to a testamentary disposition by the widow but refer to a disposal by her during her lifetime. I am, however, unable to agree with the construction placed upon the will otherwise. It appears to be plain that there is here an attempt to deal with that which remains undisposed of by the widow, in a manner repugnant to the gift to her. I think the gift to her must prevail and the attempted gift over must be declared to be repugnant and void.

I would therefore allow the appeal and declare the construction of the will accordingly. Costs may well come out of the wife's estate.

QUESTIONS

1. What possible constructions are available to a court when faced with the type of ambiguity that arose in *Re Walker*?

2. How did the Court in *Re Walker* determine the testator's dominant intention?

Re Taylor
12 E.T.R. 177, 1982 CarswellSask 196 (Surr. Ct.)

Scheibel J.:

This is an application by notice of motion on behalf of the executors of the estate of Kathleen Augusta Edith Taylor to determine the meaning, intent and effect of the following portion of the last will and testament of John Hillyard Taylor namely:

> I Give, Devise and Bequeath all my real and personal estate of which I may die possessed to my wife Kathleen Augusta Edith Taylor, to have and use during her lifetime.
>
> Any Estate, of which she may be possessed at the time of her death is to be divided equally between my daughters namely . . .

John Hillyard Taylor died on 26th February 1965 leaving his wife Kathleen Augusta Edith Taylor surviving. His will was probated on 13th April 1965. Mrs. Taylor used portions of his estate until her death.

The testatrix Kathleen Augusta Edith Taylor died on 27th December 1981. In her will there is a general direction to her executors to convert the assets comprised in her estate into money and to establish two equal funds, one of which is to go to charity with the remaining one half to go to five individuals.

Issue

The question raised in this case is whether the testatrix takes an absolute interest under the will of John Hillyard Taylor or only a life interest. If she takes an absolute interest, then any property which she acquired by devise or bequest under the will of John Hillyard Taylor forms part of her estate for distribution according to the terms of her will. If she takes only a life interest, then any part of the estate of John Hillyard Taylor remaining in her hands at her death passes to the daughters upon a gift over under the will of John Hillyard Taylor. The executors of the testatrix seek to have these questions determined as affecting the administration of her estate.

Decision

In my view, the meaning to be given to these clauses is clear. The language used evinces an intention on the part of the testator to give to his wife a life interest coupled with a power to encroach on capital for her own proper maintenance.

Counsel for the executors argues that this construction should be rejected. He states that on a true construction of these clauses the words operate as a devise of the whole estate of the testator to his wife absolutely. Any attempt to cut down this absolute gift fails *ex hypothesi* for repugnancy. Counsel argues that an absolute gift must be presumed or inferred from that clause in the will of the testator by which a power to encroach on capital is given to the wife.

It is argued that a right to encroach on capital which is not subject to any limitation and which may result in a depletion of the entire corpus of the estate amounts to an absolute interest. In such a case, the donee can by her own free act defeat the gift over so that the effect produced by the gift is the same as if it had been an absolute gift. In both cases the donee has the benefit of the entire estate. If the donee can have the whole estate, then the law presumes him to have what he can accomplish by his own free act. Several authorities are cited by counsel for the executors supporting this conclusion.

I have no hesitation in reaching the conclusion that the line of reasoning advanced by counsel for the executors should be rejected. The initial premise on which the argument rests cannot be supported. It assumes that because the same result can be achieved by a gift of an absolute interest and by a gift of a life interest with a power to encroach on capital, the two interests are identical.

The judgment of Thomson J. in *Re Rankin* (1951), 2 W.W.R. (N.S.) 562, affirmed 3 W.W.R. (N.S.) 433 (Sask. C.A.), is relied on as supporting this conclusion. In that case the testator gave the residue of his estate to his sister . . . "to be used by her and at her death if any of the money is left . . ." to X. Thomson J. held that the sister took an absolute interest. The words used by the testator were found to be inadequate to create a life interest. There was no sufficient reference to the life of the donee as being a limitation on the enjoyment of the estate by the donee. . . . In my view, this case is not authority for the proposition that a life interest becomes an absolute interest when it is accompanied by a power to encroach on capital which may result in the depletion of the entire corpus of the estate. No intention to create a life interest was found in the words used by the testator in the *Rankin* case. Once that construction was placed on the words used by the testator the only conclusion left was that he intended the donee to take an absolute interest.

No such difficulty arises here. The form of words used by the testator in this case evinces a clear intention to give to the donee a life interest. The words "during her lifetime" operate as words of limitation. They define the size of the estate which the donee is to take. In their grammatical sense, they qualify the words "to have and to use". It is difficult to see how more apt words could be used to create a life interest. . . .

The case of *Re Minchell's Will Trusts*, [1964] 2 All E.R. 47 is perhaps a stronger authority for the proposition advanced by counsel for the executors. In that case the testator gave all his property to his wife "for her lifetime" followed by a gift over "if anything should be left over" to X. Chancellor Salt held that the wife took an absolute interest. The words "for her lifetime" were found to be ineffectual to cut down the interest of the wife to a life interest. One reason given for this construction seems to be that the words "for her lifetime" are preceded by words which when taken alone would support an absolute gift. I find it difficult to see how the fact that words of gift necessarily precede words which in their grammatical sense are intended to qualify the gift, can have the effect of destroying the plain and ordinary meaning of the qualifying words.

If this method of construction were correct it would mean the grammatical sense of the words used in a will would have no significance at all. No combination in form of words would be adequate to express the intention of the testator because no reliance could be placed on the accepted meaning of the words in their ordinary grammatical sense.

I do not think that the learned chancellor intended to adopt such an approach. Some other factor must be found which would have the effect of destroying the plain meaning of the words used by the testator. There are statements by Salt, Chancellor which suggest that a right to encroach on capital had this effect. At p. 49 of his judgment he states:

> . . . by the words "for her lifetime" there arises the prima facie view that the widow's interest is cut down to a life interest in income. This might have been the true construction, if the will had stopped there. But it does not stop there. It proceeds on the assumption

> that thereafter all or nothing or some part of the capital and income may be "left over after her death" . . . (T)he words "after her death if anything should be left over" contemplate all or nothing or something being "left over" . . .

This case would seem, therefore, to be authority for the proposition that where a testator declares that the donee is to take a life interest, and in order to give effect to his intention of providing for the proper maintenance of the donee adds to this life interest a power to encroach on capital, the donee takes an absolute interest.

Some authority for this view may be found in *Williams on Wills* 5th ed., Vol. 1, at p. 630, where the authors cite this case as authority for the proposition that "A gift for life with a further disposition if anything left over is an absolute gift". If that is the effect of the decision in *Re Minchell's Will Trusts* , then, in my opinion, it is wrong and I should decline to follow it. However, if it stands for the proposition that where no intention to cut down the interest of the donee to a life interest appears in the words used by the testator, an unlimited right to encroach on capital may be taken as some evidence of an intention to give an absolute interest, then I would agree that the correct principle was applied, although I doubt that I would have come to the same conclusion with respect to the construction of the words used by the testator. On this latter interpretation of *Re Minchell's Will Trusts*, the case does not assist counsel for the executors.

In this case, the testator used clear words to indicate his intention to give the donee a life interest. Any significance a right to encroach on capital may have as evidencing an intention to give an absolute interest is displaced by the clear words of the testator. . . .

If I understand the argument of counsel for the executors, he is not suggesting that the words "to have and use during her lifetime" should be construed as a gift of an absolute interest, and that therefore, the gift over should be rejected as repugnant. He argues that a gift over of what remains in the hands of the donee at her death operates as a gift of an absolute interest to the first donee, and that this result is not affected by the use of clear words indicating an intention on the part of the testator that the donee is to have only a life interest.

On counsel's argument, the question of repugnancy arises not because the testator tried to accomplish two things which cannot logically stand one with the other; that is the true sense of the doctrine of repugnancy. Instead, on his argument the repugnancy arises because the law ascribes to a gift over of what remains at the death of the donee the effect of giving to the first donee an absolute interest. Because the testator is taken to have given the whole interest, the gift over is void *ab initio*. This is the crux of the argument of counsel for the executors.

Logically viewed, I cannot see why a gift over of what remains at the death of the donee should have the effect of giving an absolute interest to the donee. Where the testator uses clear words to indicate an intention to give only a life interest and then makes a gift over of what remains at the death of the donee, the gift over is no more than the logical result of an express intention to give a limited interest. . . .

An examination of basic principles shows at once that such an approach cannot be supported. The fundamental rule to be applied by a court in construing a will is that the intention of the testator is to be ascertained from a consideration of the will taken as a whole. Where that intention is plain, the court must give effect to it without being diverted by rules of construction which if applied, would produce a result which could not have been intended by the testator. . . .

On this ground alone, I would reject the proposition that a gift over of what remains at the death of the donee is to be construed as giving to the donee an absolute interest, notwithstanding that the testator uses clear words to indicate that the donee is to have only a life interest.

Any such rule would be opposed to fundamental principles which the courts have always regarded as governing the construction of wills. It is not a case where the testator has tried to accomplish something impossible on any logical ground, or where the testator has transgressed any rule of public policy limiting a testator's testamentary capacity and for which the law prescribes that the gift is void. These may be stated as qualifications to the principle that the intention of the testator is to be ascertained and given effect to. But they have no application here, where the rule relied on by counsel for the executors more closely resembles a rule of construction. There is no other possible characterization for the rule. The practical effect of its application is that the testator has produced a result which he did not intend and which follows as a result of a preconceived effect being given to the kind of disposition he makes without any logical ground for so doing.

Counsel for the executors also relies on the case of *Re Walker* [(1924), 56 O.L.R. 517 (C.A.)]. In that case the testator gave all his property to his wife excepting only certain items of personalty which were made the subject of specific bequests. This was followed [pp. 520-21] by a gift over "should any portion of my estate still remain in the hands of my said wife at the time of her decease undisposed of by her . . .". It was held that the wife took an absolute interest. Middleton J.A. took the view that the initial words of gift operated to pass the entire interest of the testator to his wife and that, therefore, the gift over should be rejected as repugnant. The testator was found to have had an intention to give an absolute interest and at the same time an intention to give a limited interest. This was said to give rise to a problem of repugnancy which could only be resolved by giving effect to what appeared to be the dominant intention of the testator.

No such difficulty arises here. There is no logical inconsistency requiring the court to choose between two alternative intentions which are opposed. The testator has used clear words to indicate an intention to give only a limited interest, and the gift over, far from being repugnant, completes the intention of the testator to dispose of all his property in the event that any should be left when the prior life interest comes to an end at the death of the donee.

Re Walker has no application to a case such as this. Support for this conclusion can be found in the case of *Re Scott*, 58 O.L.R. 138, [1926] 1 D.L.R. 151, a decision of the Ontario Court of Appeal rendered only a few months after *Re Walker* was decided. In *Re Scott* the testator gave all his property to his wife with directions to convert any real estate into money and to pay a small bequest to the wife's sister. This was followed by a gift over to the wife's sister of "whatever property remains in her [wife's] hands at the time of her death". It was held that the wife took an absolute interest and that the gift over was void for repugnancy. Middleton J.A. stated the rule to be applied as follows [pp. 140-41 O.L.R.]:

> [T]he cases in which a testator after apparently conferring a benefit purports to deal with the property upon the death of the person upon whom the first benefit is conferred fall into two classes: first, those in which the later provision shows that the first taker was not intended to take absolutely, but was intended to have a life-estate only; and the second in which it was clear that the first taker was intended to take absolutely, and, therefore, the attempted gift over of all that might remain on the death of the first taker was repugnant and void, and that in each case the problem was to determine within which of the classes the particular will under consideration fell . . . I can find nothing in the will to justify the view that all that was given to the widow was a life-estate, or a life-estate with power to encroach upon the *corpus* . . . It is plain to me that what the testator intended was to give absolutely to his wife and to control, upon her death, the destiny of that which he had already given, something . . . which cannot be done under the common law.

The effect of these two cases is to distinguish between those cases where the testator has so described the interest to be taken so as to leave the impression that the donee is to have an absolute interest but where at the same time the testator purports to engraft onto the prior absolute gift a gift over, with the result that the gift over cannot be given effect to; and those cases where the testator uses clear words to indicate an intention to give only a limited interest so that the gift over presents no problem of repugnancy. This instant case falls into the latter class of cases.

It was suggested in the foregoing that a gift of a life interest coupled with a power to encroach on capital does not change character because that power is expressed in terms which leaves open the possibility that the entire corpus of the estate may be depleted. One can see how, conceptually understood, the proposition that a life interest becomes enlarged to an absolute interest when it is coupled with a wide power to encroach on capital cannot rest on any logical ground.

Also we have seen how that proposition is opposed to fundamental principles of construction. It is not surprising, therefore, that there are numerous cases which have held that a gift of a life interest followed by a gift over of what remains in the hands of the donee operates as a gift of a life interest with a power to encroach on capital. The possibility that there may be nothing left on which the gift over can take effect does not enlarge the interest of the donee to an absolute interest. . . .

In *Townshend v. MacInnis* (1973), 4 Nfld. & P.E.I.R. 211, 35 D.L.R. (3d) 459 (P.E.I.C.A.), the testator gave all his property to his sister "to be used and disposed of as she wishes during her lifetime" followed by a gift over "any that is left at her death" to X. The Prince Edward Island Supreme Court on appeal held that the sister took an absolute interest.

The court took the view that the words "to be used and disposed of as she wishes during her lifetime" gave to the sister the whole estate so that nothing remained on which the gift over could take effect. Accordingly, the gift over was held to be repugnant. The decision in *Re Jones*, [1898] 1 Ch. 438, was relied on as supporting this conclusion. There is the suggestion in the judgment of Trainor C.J.P.E.I. that, where a life interest is coupled with a power of disposition inter vivos, the donee takes an absolute interest. At p. 216 of his judgment he said:

> [T]he words, "to be used and disposed of as she wishes during her lifetime" conferred upon the said Blanche C. MacDonald the full title in fee simple . . . and that the proposed gift over of any that is left is void as an attempt to cut down the interest of the said Blanche C. MacDonald to a life interest with a power to dispose in her lifetime.

In the present case there is no power of disposition inter vivos attached to the life interest of the donee. On that ground the decision of *Townshend* is distinguishable. The donee in this case has a power to encroach on capital for purposes of her own proper maintenance. She has no power to divest herself of corpus of the estate by transfer inter vivos. However, it might be argued that if the court can construct an absolute interest out of a life interest when coupled with a power of disposition, because the donee has it in her power to deplete the entire corpus of the estate by a transfer inter vivos, then the same result should follow where the corpus of the estate may be depleted by a power to encroach on capital.

In both cases the practical effect is the same. It is unnecessary to examine the correctness of this argument. If the rule laid down in *Townshend* is that a life interest coupled with a power of disposition operates as a gift of an absolute interest, then in my opinion it was wrongly decided . . . .

If a life interest coupled with a power of disposition does not change character even though the entire corpus of the estate may be depleted by the exercise of the power, I find it difficult to see how a life interest coupled with a power to encroach on capital becomes an absolute interest because it may have that result.

The case for such a change of character is much stronger where there is a power of disposition than in the case where the donee has only a power to encroach on capital for purposes of maintenance. In the latter case, the donee's enjoyment of the subject of the gift is limited to uses conforming with the requirement that the property is to be used for her own maintenance. She cannot give the property away because such a gift does not contribute to her maintenance, but instead diminishes the capacity of the estate to provide her with maintenance.

There is no such limitation where a general power of disposition *inter vivos* is given to the donee of a life interest. The interest more closely approximates an absolute interest because he may exercise for himself one of the incidents of ownership; namely, the right to freely alienate during his lifetime the subject matter of the gift. But we have seen that this feature does not have the effect of giving to the donee an absolute interest. *A fortiori*, such a conclusion cannot be supported in a case such as this, where the donee has only a power to encroach on capital for the purposes of maintenance.

Where the testator uses plain language to indicate an intention to give a life interest only, that interest is not enlarged to an absolute interest because the testator has declared that the donee is to have the right in her discretion to encroach on capital for her own proper maintenance. There is nothing in such a provision which can have the effect of displacing the clear intention of the testator.

. . .

Christensen v. Martini Estate
1999 CarswellAlta 289, [1999] 10 W.W.R. 417 (C.A.)

Hunt J.A.:

This case concerns the interpretation of a specific bequest in a will. The Appellant ("Martini") is the widow of the testator. She is shown in the will as "Sharie Raby." The sister Respondents Sandra Christensen and Sonya Nadon ("the Christensens") were longtime friends and neighbours of the testator, especially prior to his divorce from his first wife and his marriage to Martini.

The relevant facts may be stated briefly.

The testator and his first wife owned a duplex as tenants in common ("the property"). For many years the Christensens lived in a suite in the duplex with their parents, while the testator and his first wife lived in part of the duplex. It was during this time that the close relationship developed between the testator and the Christensens. Among other things, in 1988 the testator loaned a large sum of money to Sandra Christensen.

In 1990 the testator and his wife divorced. The testator married Martini the following year and they resided together in half the duplex, being the part that bore the street address of "2203." The testator commenced a matrimonial property action against his former wife on August 8, 1991 concerning, among other things, the property. A certificate of *lis pendens* was filed against the property by the testator a few days later.

On April 26, 1991, the testator had executed a will. . . .

This is the Last Will and Testament of me, Peter Anthony Martini of the city of Calgary, in the province of Alberta.

1. I hereby Revoke all former Wills and Testamentary dispositions heretofore made by me and Declare this to be and contain my Last Will and Testament. . . .

4. I give, Devise and Bequeath all of my estate, both real and personal, including any property over which I may have a general power of appointment to my Trustee, upon the following trusts, namely:

(a) I direct my Trustee to transfer my savings account in the Alberta Treasury Brach [sic] at 34th Ave. S.W. — 2140 34 Ave S.W. Calgary AB T2T 5P6 to Sandra Christensen of the city of Calgary.

(b) I forgive any money that Sandra Christensen owes me.

(c) I give to my wife Sharie Raby of Calgary 2203 31 Ave S.W. Calgary for her use. When she no longer needs 2203 31 Ave S.W. Calgary that she give said property to Sandra and Sonya Christensen of the city of Calgary.

(d) I direct my trustee to distribute the rest and residue of my estate equally amongst my wife Sharie Raby, Bruse Martini of 522 Walker Ave Winnipeg Manitoba, Valleyveiw [sic] Presbyterian Church in Calgary and the Children's Hospital Calgary. . . . (Emphasis added.)

Martini applied for and received probate of the will in late 1996. The Christensens thereafter applied for a declaration as to their interest, and that of Martini, in the property.

In a brief decision concerning the interpretation of clause 4(c) of the will, the learned chambers judge said that the testator's intent to confer a limited estate upon Martini had been "frustrated by virtue of the uncertainty of the nature and extent of such estate or interest. The gift over to Sandra and Sonya Christensen prevails and they are entitled to become the registered owners of the whole of the property immediately." . . .

In my view, the preferable interpretation of clause 4(c) is that the testator gave Martini a life estate without a power of encroachment in the undivided half-interest he owned at death. As for the matrimonial property settlement, in my opinion the undivided half-interest received by the estate thereunder must be distributed as on an intestacy, with the result that Martini receives title to it.

It follows that the appeal must be allowed.

1. What are the Interests in the Property of Martini and the Christensens?

It is trite law that, in interpreting provisions in a will, a court should endeavour to give effect to the testator's intentions as ascertained from the expressed language of the instrument and the surrounding circumstances.

Leading principle of construction. The only principle of construction which is applicable without qualification to all wills and overrides every other rule of construction is that the testator's intention is collected from a consideration of the whole will taken in connection with any evidence properly admissible, and the meaning of the will and of every part of it is determined according to that intention. (Emphasis added.)

Halsbury's Laws of England, vol. 50, 4th ed. reissue (London: Butterworths, 1998) at 332, para. 462.

Indeed, in approaching a problem of this kind it is important never to lose sight of the true principle of construction in such cases — that it is the duty of the Court to discover the meaning of the words used by the testator, and, from them and from such surrounding circumstances as it is permissible in the particular case to take into account to ascertain his intention. For this purpose, it is important to have regard not only to the whole of the clause which is in question, but to the will as a whole which forms the context to the clause.

Unless this is done, there is grave danger that the canons of construction will be applied without due regard to the testator's intention, tending thereby to ascertain his wishes by rules which, in the particular case, may produce consequences contrary to that intention. Per Lord Birkenhead, L.C., *Lucas-Tooth v. Lucas-Tooth*, [1921] A.C. 594 (U.K. H.L.) at 601. (Emphasis added.)

Courts will also endeavour to reconcile apparently conflicting provisions in a will, rather than ignore one of them or finding one of them void for uncertainty.

A Court will make every effort to reconcile two apparently conflicting provisions of a will, rather than absolutely ignore one or the other of them, or call either or both of them void for uncertainty.

T.G. Feeney, *The Canadian Law of Wills: Construction*, vol. 2 (Toronto: Butterworths, 1987) at 35.

Many arguments were made by both sides concerning how the bequest in clause 4(c) ought to be interpreted. The following possibilities have been mentioned:

1. An absolute gift to Martini, with words expressing the testator's hope (but not his direction) that she will give what remains of the property (if anything) to the Christensens, when she no longer needs it herself.

2. A determinable fee to Martini, with a gift over to the Christensens when Martini no longer needs the property.

3. A conditional fee to Martini with a gift over to the Christensens, the gift being conditional upon Martini's need for the property.

4. A life estate to Martini, with or without the power to encroach on the estate, with a gift over to the Christensens.

5. A licence of occupation to Martini, with a gift over to the Christensens.

It seems that the learned chambers judge interpreted the bequest as providing a determinable fee, which gift failed because the determining event was too uncertain. It appears that, in his view, the gift over had to take effect immediately due to this uncertainty.

Both sides cited many authorities to support the interpretations they put forward. Unfortunately, none of those authorities is particularly helpful. Each involved a will containing different language than that which must be interpreted in this case.

In my view, it is apparent that the testator intended to benefit both Martini and the Christensens. This interpretation is supported by the language of clause 4(c) itself, the entire will, and the surrounding circumstances. It seems to me that neither side seriously disputed this view during oral argument, although for various reasons each asserted that there were compelling legal reasons why effect could not be given to this intention. I do not, however, agree.

In my view, the most likely interpretation is that the testator intended Martini to have a life estate without a power of encroachment, with a gift over to the Christensens. It is apparent that he intended that the Christensens ultimately receive the property, because of his reference in clause 4(c) to the "said property." If the gift is interpreted as a life estate to Martini with a power of encroachment, "the said property" could be significantly diminished by the time it comes into the hands of the Christensens. That does not appear to be what the testator intended, given his choice of language.

In asserting that, at most, the testator intended Martini to have a licence of occupation, counsel for the Christensens pointed out that, had the testator intended to give Martini a life estate, he could have used words such as "during her lifetime." Counsel also suggested that the language used by the testator implied that the gift over to the Christensens had to occur while Martini was still alive ("that she give"). This, too, he argued, militates against interpreting the gift as a life estate.

I do not think the absence of the words such as "during her lifetime" necessarily means that the testator did not intend to grant his wife a life estate. The use of such words evidently would have rendered easier the task of interpreting the will. But the testator was a lay person who, it appears, drafted the will himself. Under such circumstances, I think it would be inappropriate to decide the case based upon a standard that would normally be applied to a will drafted by someone with legal training. Feeney, *supra*, at 17.

As for the argument that clause 4(c) seems to anticipate the property going to the Christensens during the lifetime of Martini, I agree that such an interpretation is possible. But it is equally plausible that the testator, a lay person, would assume that Martini would "no longer need" the gifted property upon her death. Additionally, there is no mechanism to force Martini to make an *inter vivos* transfer of the property to the Christensens. In other words, if it is up to her to decide when she "no longer needs" the property, it is extremely possible that she would not make that determination during her lifetime in any event.

The testator and Martini, as I have mentioned, lived together in part of the property following their marriage. This is another factor that makes it likely the testator intended that she have the right to continue to occupy the property after his death, for the duration of her life. . . .

Appeal allowed.

QUESTIONS

Interpret the following testamentary provisions:

(a) "I give to my Daughter Audrey Lillian Duncan, my half share in the Home 629 Government Ave Morse Place & all I die possessed of. [A]t Her Death all is to be sold and Equally [divided] between my Grandchildren, Albert Charles Duncan and Beverly Claire Duncan & William Alexander. Should either child die, His or Her share is to go to the surviving Children to be put in trust until they attain the age of Twenty one, 21 years, in the Event of Audrey & both children dying all belonging to me is to be divided between Mr. Walter Andrews & Mrs. Wm Seaman, on no account is anything to go to any Duncan other than those mentioned above." *Re Ingram Estate* 32 D.L.R. (2d) 152, 1961 CarswellMan 45 (Q.B.).

(b) "I GIVE, DEVISE AND BEQUEATH, to my wife, Katherine Mayhew and my son, Charles Mayhew all my real estate consisting of farms, stock, and all farm equipment, together with all cash, bonds, notes, mortgages, and all personal effects of every kind and nature which I may be possessed with at the time of my decease, share and share alike. *At the time of my wife's decease, her share to be the property of my son, Charles.*" *Re Mayhew Estate* 63 D.L.R. (4th) 198, 1989 CarswellPEI 40 (T.D.).

(c) "1. My Wife Denise gets all. 2. When we [the testator and his wife] both are gone everything to be split 3 ways or families Muriel Gourley Marjorie Stewart Dennis McEvoy. Also if I go first $5,000.00 each to Mr and Mrs Maloney. When both Denise and I die $5,000 each to Mark Shipclark & David Etheridge." *Re Armstrong Estate* (May 22, 1985), Doc. Ottawa 20589/84 [1985] O.J. No. 418 (H.C.).

(d) "I give, devise and bequeath and appoint all the rest, residue and remainder of my estate, both real and personal, of whatsoever kind and wheresoever situate, including any real or personal property to which I may be entitled at my death or over which I may have a general power of appointment, unto my trustees to hold upon the following trusts: (a) To pay and transfer the same to my wife Estella Maude Burke for her own use absolutely, if she is living at the time of my death. (b) If my said wife has predeceased me, and in any event upon her decease, in respect to any balance of my estate which may remain, I give the same as follows . . .". *Re Burke* [1960] O.R. 26, 1959 CarswellOnt 98 (C.A.).

(e) "I give, devise and bequeath all my real and personal estate of which I may die possessed in the following manner, that is to say: The SE 1/4 12-44-20 W. 3rd consisting of 160 acres more or less, including house, horse barns, implement sheds, workshop, four portable granaries, one tractor and threshing machine, and all other machinery and tools, horses, cattle and all livestock to my wife Ethel Blackstock and in the event of the death of my wife Ethel Blackstock this property to go to my son, Wesley Ivan Blackstock. The portion of the NW 1/4 12-44-20 W. 3rd consisting of 89 acres more or less, to my daughter Joyce Ina Blackstock on the advent of her twenty-first birthday, the fourteenth day of October, Nineteen hundred and thirty-nine. The NW 1/4 1-44-20 W3rd consisting of 160 acres more or less I leave to my son, Wesley Ivan Blackstock on his twenty-first birthday. All the residue of my estate not hereinbefore disposed of I give, devise and bequeath unto my wife Ethel Blackstock. And I nominate and appoint my wife Ethel Blackstock to be executrix of this my last Will and Testament." *Re Blackstock Estate* 1957 CarswellSask 13, 10 D.L.R. (2d) 192 (C.A.).

(f) "I APPOINT my daughter JOSEPHINE WALTON and my son MICHAEL EDWARD DUFFY (hereinafter called 'my Trustees') trustees and executors of this my will. . . . I GIVE DEVISE AND BEQUEATH to my grand-daughter Dallas Mary Duffy that pieceof land containing approximately one acre situate at Ransley's Road Glenlusk in Tasmania and bounded by the said Ransley's Road and other land now or formerly belonging to Mr Zeigler for her own use absolutely. . . . I GIVE DEVISE AND BEQUEATH the whole of the rest and residue of my property including my house and land situate at Berriedale in Tasmania to my Trustees upon trust for my son Michael Edward Duffy if he shall survive me by one calendar month PROVIDED HOWEVER that he shall have paid all rates and taxes and payments due on the present Mortgage on the said property from the date of this my will until my death then UPON TRUST for my daughters Dorothy Norah Dixon, Pauline Lillian Tutty, Josephene (sic) Elizabeth Walton, and Mary Winifred Geappen as tenants in common in equal shares." *Re Duffy* (February 27, 1997), Tasmania 10/1997 (S.C.).

(g) "I give, devise and bequeath all my realand personal estate of which I may die possessed in the manner following, that is to say: My house located at 20 Arrowsmith Aven., in Toronto, Ontario and all of its contents . . . unto my wife, ERMINIA MARCHETTI married FINUCCI, for her use absolutely . . .

All the rest and residue of my estate, whether it be real or personal and wheresoever situated, whether in possession or expectancy of which I am seized, possessed or entitled to, unto my wife ERMINIA MARCHETTI married FINUCCI for her use absolutely

In the event that my said wife ERMINIA MARCHETTI married FINUCCI should predecease me, or if we should die together, then my estate, both real and personal shall be equally divided amongst my brother MARIO SANTE FINUCCI'S three children: GIUSEPE FINUCCI, VERNA FINUCCI and MARIA LUISA FINUCCI. However, should my wife be my survivor, at the time of her death, my half of the estate shall go to my bother's children, as stated." *Finucci v. Finucci Estate* 2002 CarswellOnt 4184 (Div. Ct.).

(c) powers and obligations

Ontario Law Reform Commission, *Report on Basic Principles of Land Law* (Toronto: A.G. (Ont.), 1996) at 24-7 [footnotes omitted]

Waste

Where different persons are entitled to successive interests in property, a system of rules is required to balance the interests of those in present possession against the interests of those who will or may become entitled to possession in the future. Outside of the law of trusts, the main body of law designed to do this balancing is the law of waste.

Apart from laws — such as the law of nuisance, zoning by-laws or planning controls — created in the interests of neighbouring land-owners or the general public, the owner of an estate in fee simple is not generally subject to control in his or her possession of the land. This is not surprising in the case of an estate in fee simple absolute, since the owner of such an estate is in effect absolute owner: "The holder of [such an estate] has, as an incident of his estate, the right to exercise acts of ownership of all kinds, including the commission of waste, such as felling trees, mining and pulling down buildings." Even where the estate is qualified — where it is determinable or subject to a condition subsequent — it seems that the holder of the fee is generally not impeachable for waste. However, it has been said that the holder of an estate in fee simple subject to an executory gift over "is in the same position as a life tenant without impeachment for waste and may not commit equitable waste, that is, wanton or malicious acts, such as destruction of houses or felling of trees left for ornament or shelter." In addition, a will or settlement may expressly prohibit waste and such a provision can be enforced by injunction.

The law of waste has been developed mainly in the context of possession of land by tenants for life, although even in this context the relevant statutory provisions are based on early medieval English statutes and there has been little recent case-law.

The *Conveyancing and Law of Property Act* provides as follows:

> 29. A dowress, a tenant for life or for years, and the guardian of the estate of a minor; are impeachable for waste and liable in damages to the person injured.
>
> 30. An estate for life without impeachment of waste does not confer upon the tenant for life any legal right to commit waste of the description known as equitable waste, unless an intention to confer the right expressly appears by the instrument creating the estate.

31. Tenants in common and joint tenants are liable to their co-tenants for waste, or, in the event of a partition, the part wasted may be assigned to the tenant committing the waste at the value thereof to be estimated as if no waste had been committed.

32. Lessees making or suffering waste on the demised premises without license of the lessors are liable for the full damage so occasioned.

The essence of "waste" is that it is an act that causes injury, or does lasting damage, to the land. There are four types of waste: ameliorating, voluntary, permissive and equitable.

Ameliorating waste is defined as follows by *Anger and Honsberger's Law of Real Property*:

> Any act which changes the character of property is, technically, waste. Ameliorating waste is that which results in benefit and not in an injury, so that it in fact improves the inheritance. Examples of this kind are the turning of pasture land into arable land and vice versa and the conversion of rundown dwellings into modern, productive shops. Unless the character of the property is completely changed, it is unlikely that a court will award damages or grant an injunction for ameliorating waste as between a life tenant and remainderman.

Permissive waste connotes failure to act, for example, allowing buildings to become dilapidated by failing to repair. A tenant for life is, it seems, not impeachable for such waste, unless a duty to repair is provided by the instrument of grant.

Voluntary waste connotes the committing of a positive, wrongful action. It may be, for example, an act of voluntary waste to tear down and remove a building. Although there is little Canadian authority on this point, it seems that it is also voluntary waste for a life tenant to open and work a mine, but not to work an already open mine. It is also voluntary waste for a tenant to cut timber, and this is the aspect of waste that has provoked the most judicial discussion. It has been said that whether the cutting of any kind of tree is waste depends on whether the act is such as a prudent farmer would do upon his own land, having regard to the land as an inheritance, and whether there is, as a result, a diminution in the value of the land. The traditional approach has been to separate trees into timber and non-timber trees. Generally, it is an act of waste to cut down timber trees and whether trees are classified as timber trees depends on local custom and value in the area. Exceptionally, even timber trees may be cut without committing waste. For example, it has been held not to be waste to clear land by the removal of timber trees, for the purpose of bringing it into cultivation.

A tenant for life is liable for voluntary waste, although he or she may by the term of the grant be made unimpeachable for such waste.

Where a tenant for life is so exonerated for liability for waste, there was no liability for waste at common law. Nevertheless, where the waste amounts to acts of wanton destruction, the tenant for life could be restrained, in equity, by injunction. Activity of this character came to be called equitable waste. Section 30 of the

Conveyancing and Law of Property Act makes such sort of waste actionable at common law as well as in equity although it also expresses the principle that a tenant for life may be expressly permitted by the instrument of grant even to commit equitable waste.

The remedies available for waste are summarized as follows by *Anger and Honsberger's Law of Real Property*:

> If a life tenant commits waste he is liable in damages which generally amount to the decrease in the value of the reversion, less an allowance for immediate payment. In certain cases, exemplary damages may be awarded. Alternatively, or in addition, an injunction may be granted to prevent threatened or apprehended waste or the repetition of waste. However, as an injunction is discretionary, it may be refused where the waste is minor and not likely to be repeated. If the waste has resulted in a profit to the life tenant, for example, by the sale of minerals or timber, the money can be recovered by an accounting. Whether waste has been committed is a question of fact and the onus is on the plaintiff to prove the damage.

QUESTIONS

1. What is the function of the law of waste?

2. Can the life tenant and remainderperson(s) contract-out of the law of waste?

3. Should the law care about the commission of ameliorating waste?

4. The notion of waste applies to other property law relationships, most notably as between co-owners, mortgagor and mortgagee, and landlord and tenant. Some form of waste doctrine should also constrain the owner of a conditional or determinable fee simple. (These kinds of interests will be discussed in Chapter 7; for now it is important to appreciate only that the rights are not absolute, and there will exist an interest akin to a remainder after a life estate.)

Yet every human owner, even one holding fee simple absolute, will eventually die. Why then do we not apply the doctrine of waste to every owner, even one holding in fee simple absolute? See further E.J. McCaffery, "Must We Have the Right to Waste?" in S. Munzer, ed., *New Essays in the Legal and Political Theory of Property* (Cambridge: C.U.P., 2001) at 76.

Powers v. Powers Estate
182 Nfld. & P.E.I.R. 341, 1999 CarswellNfld 175 (T.D.)

Cameron J.A.:

This is an application . . . for a declaratory order respecting responsibility for certain expenses related to a property, in which the applicant has a life interest. . . .

For ease of reference, the operative part of the last will and testament of Gordon Eric Parsons is reproduced:

> All the rest and residue of my Estate of whatsoever kind and wheresoever situate I give, devise and bequeath unto my Executor, in particular my interest in the lands and premises located at Carpasian Road in the City of St. John's, in the Province of Newfoundland, to hold the same for the use and benefit of my mother, Susanna B. Powers during her natural lifetime, with power to draw on such of the income and capital of my Estate as my Executor in his absolute discretion deems advisable for the purposes of properly maintaining and supporting my mother and maintaining and paying for taxes, heat, electricity and other utilities in respect of any property in which my mother should reside. After the death of my said mother I direct that my executor shall hold the said property for the use and benefit of my brother Raymond Victor Powers during his natural lifetime and direct that my Executor shall have absolute discretion as to using such of my assets as he may deem necessary for the purposes of maintaining and providing heat and other services to any property in which he, the said Raymond V. Powers, might reside. On the death of my brother, Raymond Victor Powers, I give, devise and bequest all the rest and residue of my Estate unto my brother Ronald Warwick powers absolutely and forever.

. . . I held, in a decision of January 7, 1988 that by virtue of the last will and testament of Gordon Eric Powers, the applicant had received an equitable life interest and that the executor was given additional powers:

> at his discretion, to encroach upon the assets of the estate for the limited purpose of maintaining and providing services to the property in which the plaintiff [applicant] may reside. The word "assets" is broad enough in meaning to include all types of property. Encroachment upon the estate for the general purpose of maintaining the plaintiff is not permitted by the will.

I added:

> To what is the plaintiff, who holds an equitable life interest, entitled? In respect of the Carpasian Road property the parties do not seem to dispute that the plaintiff may occupy the property . . . the plaintiff may exercise the usual incidents of a life tenant. He may occupy [the Carpasian Road property] or he may lease it and collect the rents. . . . Of course, being the life tenant is not without responsibilities. For example, it is for the life tenant to pay annual taxes . . . and provide utilities to the property.
>
> The other major asset of the estate is savings held in a number of different accounts. The executor has an obligation to invest the savings, as permitted by law, and pay the interest to the plaintiff subject, of course, to those fees which may be payable out of income.

The cost of heating the premises in which the applicant lives

. . . [C]ounsel for the applicant concedes that on the application of the common law, normally the cost of heating a property would be borne by the life tenant. She submits, however, that in this case, the will requires the executor to pay this amount out of the capital of the estate. I am unable to accept that suggestion. Further, that matter was addressed in the last decision when I said:

> As to encroachment upon the estate the executor has the power to do so only for the limited purpose stated in the will, that is, for maintaining and providing services to the property in which the plaintiff may reside. The plaintiff has no right to require the encroachment.

The provisions of the will do not, in my view, alter the general law relating to the responsibilities to be born by the holder of a life estate. It permits the executor to encroach upon the capital in his "absolute discretion" and in the absence of evidence that these powers are being exercised unfairly, the court will not interfere (See: *Courage's Will, Re* (1975), 10 Nfld. & P.E.I.R. 511 . . . (Nfld. T.D.)) Had the testator wished to do what the applicant says he intended, it would have been very easy to state that the executor should pay out of the capital the costs of providing heat or other services to the premises occupied by the applicant. I understand that the applicant has no objection to the costs being paid by the executor out of the interest, as has been the case in the past, if I conclude, as I have, that there is no obligation on the executor to pay heating costs out of the capital of the estate. That is only an indirect method of the life tenant paying the heating costs. Over the course of the administration of the estate there has been sufficient income to meet the expenses which are, by law, to be paid out of income, pay the heating costs and a further sum to the applicant.

Repairs

. . . In *Dwyer, Re,* [1930] 2 D.L.R. 897 (N.S. S.C.) the court held that repairs necessary for the proper preservation of the building should be paid out of capital. Those of a recurrent or "periodical" nature were to be paid from income. In *Woods, Re* (1926), [1927] 1 D.L.R. 63 (Ont. Surr. Ct.) a similar division of costs was made. In *Woods* the restoration of the heating apparatus and painting, which was sworn to be a pressing need, was to be paid by the capital. These two cases are illustrative of the general principle. However, the principle is often difficult to apply, particularly for the trustee who has a duty to act impartially between beneficiaries.

While I am prepared to give general guidance to the parties, I am not in a position to answer definitively every situation which may arise in the future. Though para. 10(ii) of the Agreed Statement of Facts does not make it clear that this has been done, counsel for the executor states that the executor should and did pay the expense of replacement of the furnace and the re-shingling of the roof out of the capital of the estate. I agree that these expenses are directed to the preservation of the house and therefore should be paid out of capital.

As to lawn care, regular care of the lawn is for the life tenant. Unless one requires replacement of a retaining wall to protect the property or the felling of a tree that might endanger the property or replacement of trees or the lawn, it is difficult to imagine garden work which should be paid for by the capital. Replacement of a deck would fall within those items paid for by capital. Repair should be paid out of income. Interior painting, unless it can be shown to be necessary for the preservation of the property should be paid for by the life tenant. Replacement of a fence is to paid out of capital.

Insurance

. . . Counsel for the executor argues that the recurring nature of the expense suggests that insurance premiums should be paid by the life tenant. (See: *Caulfield, Re*, [1933] O.W.N. 233 (H.C.)) Further, he argues that the *Trustee Act* permits the executor to pay the cost of premiums from income. Counsel for the applicant argues that the primary beneficiary of the insurance is the remainderman and therefore the cost of premiums should be paid out of the capital of the estate. She also makes the point that since any payment out of the capital results in a reduction in interest and therefore the amount payable to the life tenant, the life tenant contributes in that way to the cost of insurance. The position taken by the applicant is supported by cases such as *Betty, Re . . .*, [1899] 1 Ch. 821 (Eng. Ch.) at p. 829. As to the *Trustee Act* she submits that it addresses only the immediate source of payment not whether ultimately the cost of premiums is to be paid out of capital or income.

Section 18(1) of the *Trustee Act*, R.S.N. 1990, c. T-10, permits a trustee (which by definition includes an executor or administrator) to insure against loss or damage by fire. It states:

> A trustee may insure against loss or damage by fire a building or other insurable property to an amount including the amount of an insurance already on foot not exceeding 75% of the full value of that building or property, and pay the premiums for that insurance out of the income of the building or property or out of the income of another property subject to the same trusts, without obtaining the consent of a person who may be entitled wholly or partly to that income.

The respondents argue that section 18 is determinative of the issue, not only as to the fire insurance but also as to furnace insurance. Counsel for the applicant agrees that the section is permissive. It permits, rather than directs, the executor to insure the Carpasian Road property for up to 75% of its value. However, she submits that the section is not so clear respecting how the premiums are to be paid. First, she argues that in Section 18(1), "property" must be construed to mean real property and since the income is not produced by real property there is not "income" from a source which may be used to pay the costs. I do not accept this restrictive interpretation. The word "property" is defined by the *Act*. The definition is a wide one not restricted to interests in land and nothing in section 18(1) suggests that the definition contained in the *Act* should not be applied or should be restricted when applying s. 18(1). Contrary to the submission of the applicant, the use of the word "includes" in the definition signals the intent of the legislature that the word "property" not have a restricted meaning.

In the alternative, Counsel for the applicant submits that in interpreting section 18 this Court should be guided by the reasoning of the Ontario Court of Appeal in *Rutherford, Re*, [1933] 4 D.L.R. 222. In *Rutherford* the equivalent section of the Ontario *Act* was interpreted as permitting the trustee to resort to income to get the funds to pay the premium in the first place. However, it was held not to determine which of income or capital should ultimately pay the costs. Middleton, J.A., discussing the Ontario section, said at p. 239:

> This, I think, gives to the trustee the right to resort to the income for the purpose of making the payment, and will be his protection in passing his accounts, but I do not think that it in any way interferes with the right of the life tenant to contend that the insurance or some portion thereof being for the benefit of the reversion, should, upon the accounting between the life tenant and the reversioner be dealt with in accordance with pre-existing law. . . .

As with the second question, one could find cases to support the positions taken by each of the parties. In my view, it is helpful to keep in mind the historical development of the law. The following points are generally accepted:

> 1. At common law there is generally no obligation on a life tenant to insure, although the life tenant must pay certain other recurring expenses such as the taxes imposed on the land. (See: *Kingham v. Kingham*, [1897] 1 I.R. 170.) However, if the life interest is in a leasehold estate, then the life tenant assumes the duty to pay the rent and the insurance if that is required by the lease.
>
> 2. The *Trustee Act* does not impose an obligation to insure on the life tenant. That is, the life tenant is not directed by the *Act* to obtain fire insurance nor to pay the premiums on fire insurance purchased by the trustee.
>
> 3. In England, at least historically, there was no obligation on the trustee to insure. However, if the executors were directed to insure the trust property against loss or damage by fire then the income payable to a party under the will would be net income after payment of certain expenses, including insurance.
>
> 4. The *Trustee Act* does not impose a duty on a trustee to insure. Rather, it grants the trustee the power to insure in the manner and to the extent specified in the *Act*.
>
> 5. However, in Canada, the failure of a trustee to insure for loss by fire would probably be seen as negligence in the performance of ones duties as a trustee. See *Gamble, Re* (1925), 57 O.L.R. 504 (H.C.) and *Jeffery Estate v. Rowe* (1989), 36 E.T.R. 217 (Ont. H.C.).

The question then becomes, if a trustee does the prudent thing and insures the property, does he or she look to the income or the capital of the estate to pay the premiums? As is self evident, if a trustee pays the premiums out of income, the beneficiary of the life interest has his or her income reduced by the equivalent amount. On the other hand, if the payments are made from capital, the estate is reduced by that amount and the income of the life tenant is reduced by the interest on that amount.

Leaving aside, for the moment, the effect of section 18 of the *Trustee Act*, the cases respecting whether the cost of insurance premiums should be paid by the income or capital are inconsistent. At least three different approaches emerge from the case law in Canada, England and the United States of America. The American view appears to be that insurance premiums are like repairs, taxes and mortgage interest, they should be borne by the life tenant. The prevalent approach is that, absent a clear directive in the trust instrument to do otherwise, the recurring expenses including insurance premiums are to be paid from income so that the capital is preserved. To those who argue that the premiums do not benefit the life tenant, the answer given is that neither do taxes or mortgage interest. (See: *Widdifield on Executors' Accounts* by Frederick D. Baker (5th ed) (1967) Carswell at p. 132.) There are Canadian cases which support this position, for example, *Caulfield, Re.* Garrow J., in *Caulfield*, cites *Halsbury's Laws of England* (1st ed), Vol 25, p. 615 in support of the general statement that recurring expenses are to be paid by the life tenant. However, the section from *Halsbury*'s quoted by Garrow J. does not deal specifically with insurance and that same edition of *Halsbury*'s, at p. 614, states that in the absence of a special contract or obligation, a tenant for life is not bound to insure the settled premises.

In Canada, at least two approaches can be identified in the cases. The first, and more frequently expressed view, consistent with the view expressed in the early English cases that there is no obligation on the life tenant to insure, is that premiums are a capital outlay. Others have expressed the view that premiums should be apportioned upon equitable principles as between the life tenant and the reversioner. (See: Middleton, J.A. in Rutherford.)

In *Widdifield on Executors' Accounts*, the author suggests at p. 134 that the dilemma be solved by requiring that insurance premiums on an income producing property be paid out of income while that on property not producing income be paid out of capital. The theory behind this proposal appears to be that in the case where the property is income producing, the insurance can also be said to be for the benefit of the life tenant. (See: *Woods* where the insurance was considered to be to the sole benefit of the life tenant as the existence of the buildings were absolutely necessary for the production of revenue. The life tenant received the whole of the income from the estate.) In *Law of Trusts in Canada* by D.W.M. Waters (2nd ed.) (1984) the author suggests at p. 860:

> It seems clear to the writer that trustees should always insure trust property, dissuade trust beneficiaries from taking out insurance of their own on any part of that property, and allocate appropriate responsibility to both the income and capital accounts for the premiums. In this way there can be no argument that all beneficial interests are insured, and also that even hand considerations have been met.

As to the impact of section 18 of the *Trustee Act*, there are surprisingly few cases on the subject. As already noted, in Ontario the equivalent section of the *Trustee Act* has been held to merely give the trustee who chooses to exercise the power to insure a ready source of revenue for the premium. It is not considered to answer where, as between the income and capital, the cost is ultimately charged. I have not been referred to cases in any other jurisdiction which have interpreted similar sections as being limited in such a manner. Rather, the commentary would indicate that the sections are intended to specify the source of funds for any premiums authorized to be paid by the sections. See for example: Pettit, *Equity and the Law of*

Trusts , 6th ed. (1989) and *Lewin on Trusts* by W. J. Mowbray 16th ed. (1964) at p. 224.

The *Trustee Act* grants permission to a trustee to insure. With respect to the view espoused by the Ontario courts, I am unable to adopt the position that as to the power to pay the premiums from income the legislature intended only to give the trustee access to immediate funds until capital could be accessed to pay the premium. I conclude that s. 18 provides the trustee with power to do what he or she would have done if directed by the testator to insure, that is, pay the premiums from income. Section 18 further clarifies that the trustee is not limited to income from the property being insured but may use income from other property subject to the same trust.

Since the enactment of the *Trustee Act*, the law, at least in Canada, has developed to require a trustee to insure against loss by fire. It seems to me that the approach to payment should be the same whether the trustee is directed to insure by the testator or does so as a prudent trustee in accordance with his duty imposed by law. The premiums should be paid from income. This is consistent with the directive of the legislature under s. 18 and, on the reasoning used in the American cases, is a modern day expense like taxes or interest on mortgage.

However this reasoning does not hold for all types of insurance. For example, furnace insurance would not necessarily be a required step to be taken by a trustee to protect and preserve the trust property. Further, s. 18 addresses only fire insurance. Assuming that the obtaining of furnace insurance is within the power of the trustee (no party argued otherwise) the purpose of the insurance becomes relevant to the determination of the issue. If the insurance is for replacement of the furnace in the event that the need arises, the insurance would seem to be primarily for the benefit of the remainderman and the cost of the premiums should be borne by capital. If, on the other hand, furnace insurance is for the regular maintenance and repair of the furnace it is directed to matters which are the responsibility of the life tenant. If the executor does not pay the premiums from interest, he may pay the maintenance costs from interest. The premiums for this type of insurance should be paid from income.

Costs

The costs of the parties shall be taxed on a solicitor and client basis and shall be paid out of the estate of Gordon Eric Parsons. I would add that were it not for the third question, about which there is genuine debate, I would not have awarded the applicant his costs in this matter, the first question having been answered in an earlier application and the principles applicable on the second question being relatively clear.

Application granted.

QUESTIONS

1. In general terms, how does the law characterize the rights of a life tenant as compared with those of a fee simple owner?

2. As between the life tenant and those entitled to the remainder, who is responsible for the payment of property taxes and to what extent? See *Mayo v. Leitovski* [1928] 1 W.W.R. 700, 1928 CarswellMan 21 (K.B.).

3. Assume that A, owner of Blackacre including mines and minerals, conveys the property "to B for life, remainder in fee simple to C." May B extract the minerals? See *Re Hall* [1916] 2 Ch. 448.

4. Is a life tenant (not holding under a trust) required to insure the premises? See *Re Darch* 16 D.L.R. 875, 1914 CarswellOnt 149 (H.C.).

5. As noted at the outset, a life estate is freely alienable. How might one calculate the value of that estate?

This issue arose in *Aho v. Kelly* 57 B.C.L.R. (3d) 369, 1998 CarswellBC 1285 (S.C.) where an order was granted for the sale of property subject to a life estate. The Court was then called upon to determine the portion of the proceeds of sale that should be allocated to the holder of the life estate. Bauman J. said this (at 375, 380-1):

> Clearly a common law life estate is a property interest having some "value". I use that word in the sense of an amount of money or goods for which a thing can be exchanged in the open market. At common law, a life estate is alienable. Upon a transfer it becomes an estate *pur autre vie*. . . .
>
> The petitioner, a life tenant, enjoys the right to rents from property during her lifetime. She as well has the right to sell her life interest. Without the respondents' co-operation, she could enjoy some financial return for her life interest. . . .
>
> As to the value of [the] life estate, the petitioner filed the Affidavit of Mark Zlotnik, a chartered accountant. Mr. Zlotnik notes that [the life tenants's] life expectancy is 18.7 years. He notes the present yield on Government of Canada bonds, for a duration in that range to be 5.75%. He concludes:
>
>> On the basis of a property with a value of $295,000.00 discounted at 5.75% over 18.7 years, the current value of a life interest of a 69 year old woman in the property is $191, 3000.00 and the value of the remainder is $103,7000.00.
>
> The resulting ratio is 76% to the petitioner [the life tenant], 24% to the respondents.

6. Compare the approach taken in *Child v. Child* 787 N.E.2d 1121 (Mass. App. Ct., 2003). That case concerned the division of marital assets on divorce. The wife held a life estate in a 14 room co-operative apartment in the posh Boston neighbourhood

of Beacon Hill, which she had received under her mother's will. The method of valuation of that interest was described by Gelinas J. (at 1123-5):

> In valuing the cooperative apartment, the judge essentially adopted the testimony of Edward Berger, the wife's expert. In arriving at his expert opinion of the value, Berger first accepted the estimate of the current fair market rental value of the parties' joint expert, Steven Elliot, who testified that the current rental value of the apartment was $7,500 per month. Berger then deducted the monthly charges of $3,403 that the wife was obligated to pay as a condition both of her retaining the life estate and the right to live in the apartment; the difference amounted to $4,097 per month. Berger then computed the present value of a single life annuity, paid to the wife for her lifetime, of $4,097 per month. The value of the wife's interest in the apartment thus achieved was $476,222. In his findings the judge accepted this method of valuation, but reduced the expenses, as he determined that the cost of heating the apartment had been double counted. The present value after this correction computed to $493,657.
>
> The husband claims that this method of valuing the apartment is speculative, as the net income that might hypothetically flow to the wife from the rental of 81 Beacon Street for the rest of her life is at best contingent and there could well be changes in the rental value and the costs during her lifetime; and, further, that the wife was prohibited under her mother's will from renting the apartment for more than a period of two years, and the opinion and facts relied upon by Berger were devoid of evidentiary support, as he had no information as to future fair market rental value and future expenses. We think that the judge was correct, and that the husband's arguments ignore the fact that the value of the wife's life estate must be taken at the time of divorce (or the time that consideration is given to the property division). . . . The trial judge has a certain flexibility in determining the exact date at which assets must be considered and valued. . . . To insist, as does the husband here, that the valuation must take into account potential future increases (or decreases) in the rental value and expenses, is to vitiate the partnership principle upon which property division is predicated. . . . Further, we find no merit in the husband's argument that the valuation was predicated on annuity tables established by the United States Treasury rather than on the table of values for life estates established in a similar Treasury regulation, as urged by the husband's expert. Here, there were substantial limitations on the wife's life estate. In order to avail herself of the life estate, and the concomitant right to live in the unit, the wife was required to pay all of the monthly expenses associated with the apartment. Her ability to rent the apartment was limited to a term of less than two years. Her mother's estate retained the right to sell the apartment, and in the case of a sale, the wife would lose the use of the apartment and would be entitled, under the mother's will, to receive only the income from one-half of the net sale proceeds. While styled a life estate, the wife's actual opportunity here was more in the nature of a limited tenancy at will, as distinguished from a traditional life estate, defined by the husband's expert as the "right to the use, possession, and income from a piece of property for the lifetime of an individual. . . ."

Which of these two approaches is best? Is it necessary to use a single method in all circumstances?

7. Although alienable in principle, it is obvious that the acquisition of a life estate is a risky undertaking. It might end tomorrow. Where the life tenant and all those entitled to the remainder can agree, the entire fee simple may be conveyed. Or, as

seen in cases such as *Re Taylor*, the generic life interest can be enhanced by appending rights that allow the life tenant to encroach on the remainder.

Still, the life estate can inhibit the transferability of the affected land. Indeed, the strict settlement was essentially deployed to impede transfer. The increasing regard to land as a market commodity in nineteenth century England led to reforms that were designed to augment the standards rights of life tenants. In England today, settled estates legislation confers rights of considerable breadth on a life tenant.

There is little comparable legislation in Canada. Under Ontario's *Settled Estates Act*, R.S.O. 1990, c. S.7, a court may authorize certain leases, sales and mortgages of settled land. A life tenant may grant a lease for up to 21 years, provided that the right to do so is not precluded by the original settlement. Such a lease will bind the remainder should the life tenant die before the lease expires.

See further O.L.R.C., *Report on Basic Principles of Land Law* (Toronto: A.G. (Ont.), 1996) at 30-60.

5. LIFE ESTATES ARISING BY OPERATION OF LAW

The life estates described above arise by virtue of a volitional disposition of property by a private land owner. At common law, two types of life interests in land could arise by operation of law, that is, irrespective of the intention of the landowner. Both arose in the context of marriage, and were of some considerable importance under the regime of inheritance known as primogeniture. Under that system, absent a valid testamentary gift, property devolved to the heirs of the landowners. Heirs were premised on consanguinity (blood) not affinity (marriage). As a result, widows and widowers fell outside of the primogeniture rules.

In response, a husband could, in defined circumstances, acquire a life estate in his deceased wife's landholding known as "curtesy". A widow's corresponding right was called "dower". In B. Murdoch, *Epitome of the Laws of Nova Scotia*, vol. 2 (Halifax: Joseph Howe, 1832) at 92-4, 97-100), these interests are described:

Tenancy by the curtesy of England

> According to the laws of England, where a man marries a woman seised of an estate of inheritance (whether fee simple or entail) and there arises issue from the marriage born alive, which issue is capable of inheriting the estate of the wife as her heir, the husband if he survive his wife is entitled to hold the property during the rest of his life to the exclusion of the children or other heirs of the woman, and this life estate in him is called tenancy by the curtesy of England, on the birth of the child who was to be heir, the interest of the husband is said to be initiate, because he then must be considered as having an interest in the land for his own life time, while before the birth his interest would entirely cease by the death of the wife. . . .

Tenancy in Dower

Where the husband is seized of any estate of inheritance at any time during the coverture, if the wife survive him, she is entitled by common law to the third part of the estate for the remainder of her life. The wife, to be entitled to dower, must be the actual wife of the deceased at the period of his death. For a total divorce, decreed before, destroys the right to dower, and so by the stat. West, 2. 13 E. 1 c. 34, does a voluntary elopement with an adulterer, unless the husband be reconciled to her voluntarily, but a divorce from bed and board under other circumstances does not affect her claim to dower. . . .

By the common law as it was understood by Littleton, and so stood in Lord Coke's time, a female could be endowed if she were above 9 years of age at the time of marriage, but younger if she was excluded from dower. Co. Lit. 33. We may conclude that in the present age the marriage of a person so young would be regarded as void, not having the essential requisites of a contract, and consequently neither giving room for the consequences in law that attend a regular marriage. A wife is by English law entitled to be endowed of all lands and tenements of which her husband was seized in fee simple or fee tail, at any time during the coverture, and of which any issue she might have had might by possibility have been heir. Therefore in an estate in special tail, where the wife is dead, who alone could be mother to the heir, the second wife of the donee cannot have dower of these lands.The wife may be endowed where the seisin of the husband was only a seisin in law, and not actual, for which Ld. Coke and the learned commentator give reason that it did not lie in her power to compel him to take actual seisin as he might take in her hands. 2 B.C. 131, Co. Lit. 31. To this principle which goes to distinguish the estates of dower and curtesy, C.J. Belcher affords us another, in his note on Co. Lit. 31, viz: "that the tenant in dower shall not be attendant to the Lord Paramount, but to the heir, therefore she shall be endowed as a seisin in law. 8 Co. 36 a. Paine's case." This estate of dower arises by operation of the law, and is therefore called dower at the common law. There were formerly other kinds of dower in use, arising by local customs or by verbal agreement before marriage, or at the time of its celebration. These are pointed out in the commentaries, 2nd vol., 122. 3, but as they are not in use among us in the colonies, and entirely inapplicable to our situation, there can be little use in dwelling on them here.

The seisin of the husband must be a *legal* seisin to entitle the wife to dower, therefore of an *equitable* estate a wife is not entitled to dower; for instance of a trust estate. 2 Atk 526. Ca. Temp, Talbot 139. Upon this principle if the estate be mortgaged in fee previous to the marriage and the legal estate vested in the mortgagee during the whole period of the coverture or marriage, the wife of the mortgagor has no right to dower because her husband was *not legally seized*, and by a singular construction, the wife of the mortgagee is equally excluded, because her husband held *legal* seisin *only*, and not the equitable title, the one losing her remedy in the courts of law, and the other being liable to the injunction of a court of equity if she were to seek it. . . .

We have seen that where the legal estate is out of the husband at the marriage, and during coverture, no dower can be derived. This gives rise to a variety of forms of marriage settlement usual in England, but very rare in the Colonies, and forming an intricate branch of English conveyancing, by which the legal estate is taken from the husband to deprive the wife of dower, and wherein her interests are generally provided for by some particular settlement.

Although dower and curtesy were once part of the law of property in common law Canada, they became increasingly irrelevant. As Murdoch suggests, in England dower could be avoided by manipulating the way in which property was transferred to a husband. And despite his comments about the state of affairs in Nova Scotia at the time of his writing, various avoidance techniques had already been adopted in Canada. For example, property held by a corporation was not subject to dower rights. Nor was property transferred to a husband under a document called a "deed to uses". This form of conveyancing was commonplace.

In addition, dower and curtesy came to be replaced by other measures designed to serve, roughly, the same purpose. These life estates arising by operation of law emerged within a legal context in which there were virtually no other death benefits for widows and widowers. Under modern intestate and family relief legislation that is no longer so. Moreover, family property legislation now provides for additional property rights for spouses (a term that itself has been expanding in scope). The advent of the mairtal property reforms in the late 1970s led to the phasing out of dower and curtesy in Atlantic Canada and Ontario.

In western Canada common law dower was abolished decades earlier, only to be reborn in the form of homestead legislation, an American innovation that was heavily dependent on the fundamentals of common law dower. In W. Renke, "Homestead Legislation in the Four Western Provinces," part of which is reproduced below, the demise and revival of dower rights in the west, and their current elements, are summarized.

W. Renke, "Homestead Legislation in the Four Western Provinces" in J.G. McLeod & M. Mamo, eds., *Matrimonial Property Law in Canada* (Toronto: Carswell, 1995) I-47*ff* [footnotes omitted]

(a) The English Dower Inheritance

The common-law dower rules have only historical significance. These rules predate the Norman Conquest. The common law recognized two relevant types of interests: (a) the "dower" interest of a surviving wife — a life interest in one-third of all lands owned at any time during the marriage by her husband; and (b) the "curtesy" of a surviving husband — a life interest in all lands owned by the wife during the marriage (both at law and in equity) that had not been disposed of *inter vivos* or by will, if there were children of the marriage. Land sold by a husband during his lifetime remained subject to his wife's dower interest, unless his wife "barred" her rights or, before marriage, the husband conveyed his lands to certain "uses to bar dower". The latter expedient gave the husband the incidents of ownership while avoiding the application of dower. The *Dower Act, 1833* abolished dower in land disposed of in the husband's lifetime or by his will and left dower effective only on certain intestacies.

The common law, as modified by the *Dower Act, 1833*, became the received law in British Columbia in 1867, and was later incorporated by statute. The English law as of July 15, 1870 was received in the Northwest Territories. The life of the English law of dower on Canadian soil was short.

In 1885, *The Real Property Act of 1885* eliminated common law dower and curtesy in Manitoba; in 1886, *The Territories Real Property Act* eliminated these rules in what is now Saskatchewan and Alberta; and in 1925 these rules were eliminated in British Columbia by the *Administration Act Amendment Act, 1925*. The western provinces now recognize "dower" interests only under statute.

(b) Effects of the Repeal of English Dower

The main reason for the elimination of the dower and curtesy rules in the western provinces was their inconsistency with the principles of the emerging land titles systems. Dower and curtesy impaired the freedom to transfer lands, and provided for interests which were not disclosed on certificates of title for lands. But while the elimination of these interests did facilitate commerce, a further practical effect was to imperil farm wives and farm families.

This effect arose at the conjuncture of two main streams of events. First, to promote the settlement of the West, Parliament had passed the *Dominion Lands Act*. This Act permitted settlers to purchase certain unappropriated Dominion lands for $1.00 per acre, and permitted settlers to take quarter sections of certain unappropriated lands free, if the settlers homesteaded the lands for three years. The lands were granted to the "head of the family" who was, in most cases, the husband. Husbands, therefore, usually became the sole registered owners of family lands.

Second, the prairies experienced a land boom in the early 20th century, leading a substantial number of land-owning husbands to sell or mortgage the family farm, without compensating their wives or sharing the proceeds. The frequent concomitant of speculation is ruin; lands not sold or foreclosed were seized from under families.

The economic tragedies that fell on farm women motivated some of the first feminist activism in Canada. Women demanded some legislative protection from the depredations of the marketplace and irresponsible husbands. To some extent, they succeeded. A mark of their success is the homestead legislation in the four western provinces. The homestead legislation provides a counterbalance (slight as it may be) to the free and efficient alienation of lands promoted by modern title systems; it promotes the security of the home.

(c) The Evolution of the Homestead Legislation

The models for Canadian homestead legislation were drawn not from the common law, but from American homestead legislation. American homestead legislation has three main features:

(i) it fetters the ability of an owner spouse to dispose of a homestead, without the consent of the non-owner spouse;

(ii) it provides the non-owner spouse with a life estate in the homestead upon the death of the owner spouse; and

(iii) it wholly or partially exempts the homestead from execution by unsecured creditors.

6. ABORIGINAL PROPERTY RIGHTS

(a) introduction

What was once a trickle of jurisprudence on the topic of Aboriginal land rights in Canada is now a steady stream with a strong current. Since the early 1970s, a broad array of issues have come before Canadian courts or have been a matter of public debate. These include (i) the interpretation and enforceability existing Aboriginal treaty rights and the negotiation of new ones; (ii) rights on federally created reserve lands; (iii) the misappropriation of Aboriginal cultural property, both tangible and intangible; (iv) the constitutional protection of Aboriginal rights; (v) Aboriginal self-governance; and (vi) land rights.

Some of these matters have already been touched on in earlier chapters: cultural appropriation (Chapter 1); Aboriginal conceptions of property (Chapter 2); the delimitation of reserve and treaty lands (Chapter 3); and entitlements to Aboriginal artifacts (Chapter 4). Moreover, various issues will be picked up later on: the role of equity in protecting Aboriginal intellectual property (Chapter 6); the rules governing the conditional surrender of reserve lands (briefly in Chapter 7); conceptions of communal property (Chapter 9); the recognition of Aboriginal hunting rights (briefly in Chapter 10), and the interplay between Aboriginal land rights and land registration (Chapter 12).

The focus is this chapter is Aboriginal land rights, especially the common law rules for the recognition of historic title. The law governing Aboriginal entitlements on federal reserve lands will also be considered. Within the vast corpus of case law on point, one can safely identify the decision of Chief Justice Antonio Lamer in *Delgamuukw v. British Columbia* (1997) as essential reading.

(b) Aboriginal title at common law

Delgamuukw v. British Columbia [1997] 3 S.C.R. 1010, 1997 CarswellBC 2358, 1997 CarswellBC 2359

Lamer C.J.C.:

I. Introduction

This appeal is the latest in a series of cases in which it has fallen to this Court to interpret and apply the guarantee of existing aboriginal rights found in s. 35(1) of the *Constitution Act, 1982.* Although that line of decisions, commencing with *R. v. Sparrow*, [1990] 1 S.C.R. 1075, proceeding through the *Van der Peet* trilogy (*R. v. Van der Peet*, [1996] 2 S.C.R. 507, *R. v. N.T.C. Smokehouse Ltd.*, [1996] 2 S.C.R. 672, and *R. v. Gladstone*, [1996] 2 S.C.R. 723), and ending in *R. v. Pamajewon*, [1996] 2 S.C.R. 821, *R. v. Adams*, [1996] 3 S.C.R. 101, and *R. v. Côté*, [1996] 3 S.C.R. 139, have laid down the jurisprudential framework for s. 35(1), this appeal raises a set of interrelated and novel questions which revolve around a single issue — the nature and scope of the constitutional protection afforded by s. 35(1) to common law aboriginal title.

In *Adams*, and in the companion decision in *Côté*, I considered and rejected the proposition that claims to aboriginal rights must also be grounded in an underlying claim to aboriginal title. But I held, nevertheless, that aboriginal title was a distinct species of aboriginal right that was recognized and affirmed by s. 35(1). Since aboriginal title was not being claimed in those earlier appeals, it was unnecessary to say more. This appeal demands, however, that the Court now explore and elucidate the implications of the constitutionalization of aboriginal title. The first is the specific content of aboriginal title, a question which this Court has not yet definitively addressed, either at common law or under s. 35(1). The second is the related question of the test for the proof of title, which, whatever its content, is a right in land, and its relationship to the definition of the aboriginal rights recognized and affirmed by s. 35(1) in *Van der Peet* in terms of activities. The third is whether aboriginal title, as a right in land, mandates a modified approach to the test of justification first laid down in *Sparrow* and elaborated upon in *Gladstone*.

In addition to the relationship between aboriginal title and s. 35(1), this appeal also raises an important practical problem relevant to the proof of aboriginal title which is endemic to aboriginal rights litigation generally — the treatment of the oral histories of Canada's aboriginal peoples by the courts. In *Van der Peet*, I held that the common law rules of evidence should be adapted to take into account the *sui generis* nature of aboriginal rights. In this appeal, the Court must address what specific form those modifications must take.

Finally, given the existence of aboriginal title in British Columbia, this Court must address, on cross-appeal, the question of whether the province of British Columbia, from the time it joined Confederation in 1871, until the entrenchment of

s. 35(1) in 1982, had jurisdiction to extinguish the rights of aboriginal peoples, including aboriginal title, in that province. Moreover, if the province was without this jurisdiction, a further question arises — whether provincial laws of general application that would otherwise be inapplicable to Indians and Indian lands could nevertheless extinguish aboriginal rights through the operation of s. 88 of the *Indian Act*, R.S.C. 1985, c. I-5. . . .

C. What is the content of aboriginal title, how is it protected by s. 35(1), and what is required for its proof?

(1) Introduction

The parties disagree over whether the appellants have established aboriginal title to the disputed area. However, since those factual issues require a new trial, we cannot resolve that dispute in this appeal. But factual issues aside, the parties also have a more fundamental disagreement over the content of aboriginal title itself, and its reception into the Constitution by s. 35(1). In order to give guidance to the judge at the new trial, it is to this issue that I will now turn.

I set out these opposing positions by way of illustration and introduction because I believe that all of the parties have characterized the content of aboriginal title incorrectly. The appellants argue that aboriginal title is tantamount to an inalienable fee simple, which confers on aboriginal peoples the rights to use those lands as they choose and which has been constitutionalized by s. 35(1). The respondents offer two alternative formulations: first, that aboriginal title is no more than a bundle of rights to engage in activities which are themselves aboriginal rights recognized and affirmed by s. 35(1), and that the *Constitution Act, 1982*, merely constitutionalizes those individual rights, not the bundle itself, because the latter has no independent content; and second, that aboriginal title, at most, encompasses the right to exclusive use and occupation of land in order to engage in those activities which are aboriginal rights themselves, and that s. 35(1) constitutionalizes this notion of exclusivity.

The content of aboriginal title, in fact, lies somewhere in between these positions. Aboriginal title is a right in land and, as such, is more than the right to engage in specific activities which may be themselves aboriginal rights. Rather, it confers the right to use land for a variety of activities, not all of which need be aspects of practices, customs and traditions which are integral to the distinctive cultures of aboriginal societies. Those activities do not constitute the right *per se*; rather, they are parasitic on the underlying title. However, that range of uses is subject to the limitation that they must not be irreconcilable with the nature of the attachment to the land which forms the basis of the particular group's aboriginal title. This inherent limit, to be explained more fully below, flows from the definition of aboriginal title as a *sui generis* interest in land, and is one way in which aboriginal title is distinct from a fee simple.

(2) Aboriginal title at common law

(a) General features

The starting point of the Canadian jurisprudence on aboriginal title is the Privy Council's decision in *St. Catharines Milling & Lumber Co. v. The Queen* (1888), 14 A.C. 46, which described aboriginal title as a "personal and usufructuary right" (at p.54). The subsequent jurisprudence has attempted to grapple with this definition, and has in the process demonstrated that the Privy Council's choice of terminology is not particularly helpful to explain the various dimensions of aboriginal title. What the Privy Council sought to capture is that aboriginal title is a *sui generis* interest in land. Aboriginal title has been described as *sui generis* in order to distinguish it from "normal" proprietary interests, such as fee simple. However, as I will now develop, it is also *sui generis* in the sense that its characteristics cannot be completely explained by reference either to the common law rules of real property or to the rules of property found in aboriginal legal systems. As with other aboriginal rights, it must be understood by reference to both common law and aboriginal perspectives.

The idea that aboriginal title is *sui generis* is the unifying principle underlying the various dimensions of that title. One dimension is its *inalienability*. Lands held pursuant to aboriginal title cannot be transferred, sold or surrendered to anyone other than the Crown and, as a result, is inalienable to third parties. This Court has taken pains to clarify that aboriginal title is only "personal" in this sense, and does not mean that aboriginal title is a non-proprietary interest which amounts to no more than a licence to use and occupy the land and cannot compete on an equal footing with other proprietary interests: see *Canadian Pacific Ltd. v. Paul*, [1988] 2 S.C.R. 654, at p. 677.

Another dimension of aboriginal title is its *source*. It had originally been thought that the source of aboriginal title in Canada was the *Royal Proclamation*, 1763: see *St. Catharines Milling*. However, it is now clear that although aboriginal title was recognized by the *Proclamation*, it arises from the prior occupation of Canada by aboriginal peoples. That prior occupation, however, is relevant in two different ways, both of which illustrate the *sui generis* nature of aboriginal title. The first is the physical fact of occupation, which derives from the common law principle that occupation is proof of possession in law: see Kent McNeil, *Common Law Aboriginal Title* (1989), at p. 7. Thus, in *Guerin* [*Guerin v. The Queen*, [1984] 2 S.C.R. 335], Dickson J. described aboriginal title, at p. 376, as a "legal right derived from the Indians' historic occupation and possession of their tribal lands". What makes aboriginal title *sui generis* is that it arises from possession *before* the assertion of British sovereignty, whereas normal estates, like fee simple, arise afterward: see Kent McNeil, "The Meaning of Aboriginal Title", in Michael Asch, ed., *Aboriginal and Treaty Rights in Canada* (1997), 135, at p. 144. This idea has been further developed in *Roberts v. Canada*, [1989] 1 S.C.R. 322 (S.C.C.), where this Court unanimously held at p.340 that "aboriginal title pre-dated colonization by the British and survived British claims to sovereignty" (also see *Guerin*, *supra*, at p.378). What this suggests is a second source for aboriginal title — the relationship between common law and pre-existing systems of aboriginal law.

A further dimension of aboriginal title is the fact that it is held *communally*. Aboriginal title cannot be held by individual aboriginal persons; it is a collective right to land held by all members of an aboriginal nation. Decisions with respect to that land are also made by that community. This is another feature of aboriginal title which is *sui generis* and distinguishes it from normal property interests.

(b) The content of aboriginal title

Although cases involving aboriginal title have come before this Court and Privy Council before, there has never been a definitive statement from either court on the content of aboriginal title. In *St. Catharines Milling*, the Privy Council, as I have mentioned, described the aboriginal title as a "personal and usufructuary interest", but declined to explain what that meant because it was not "necessary to express any opinion on the point" (at p.55). Similarly, in *Calder* [*Calder v. Attorney-General of British Columbia* [1973] S.C.R. 313], *Guerin*, and *Paul*, the issues were the extinguishment of, the fiduciary duty arising from the surrender of, and statutory easements over land held pursuant to, aboriginal title, respectively; the content of title was not at issue and was not directly addressed.

Although the courts have been less than forthcoming, I have arrived at the conclusion that the content of aboriginal title can be summarized by two propositions: first, that aboriginal title encompasses the right to exclusive use and occupation of the land held pursuant to that title for a variety of purposes, which need not be aspects of those aboriginal practices, customs and traditions which are integral to distinctive aboriginal cultures; and second, that those protected uses must not be irreconcilable with the nature of the group's attachment to that land. For the sake of clarity, I will discuss each of these propositions separately.

Aboriginal title encompasses the right to use the land held pursuant to that title for a variety of purposes, which need not be aspects of those aboriginal practices, cultures and traditions which are integral to distinctive aboriginal cultures

The respondents argue that aboriginal title merely encompasses the right to engage in activities which are aspects of aboriginal practices, customs and traditions which are integral to distinctive aboriginal cultures of the aboriginal group claiming the right and, at most, adds the notion of exclusivity; i.e., the exclusive right to use the land for those purposes. However, the uses to which lands held pursuant to aboriginal title can be put are not restricted in this way. This conclusion emerges from three sources: (i) the Canadian jurisprudence on aboriginal title, (ii) the relationship between reserve lands and lands held pursuant to aboriginal title, and (iii) the *Indian Oil and Gas Act*, R.S.C. 1985, c. I-7. As well, although this is not legally determinative, it is supported by the critical literature. In particular, I have profited greatly from Professor McNeil's article, "The Meaning of Aboriginal Title", *supra*.

[Lamer C.J. then reviewed these three sources and concluded (at 1087) that "the content of aboriginal title is not restricted to those uses which are elements of a practice, custom or tradition integral to the distinctive culture of the aboriginal group claiming the right. However, nor does aboriginal title amount to a form of inalienable fee simple . . ."]

> (c) Inherent Limit: Lands held pursuant to aboriginal title cannot be used in a manner that is irreconcilable with the nature of the attachment to the land which forms the basis of the group's claim to aboriginal title.

The content of aboriginal title contains an inherent limit that lands held pursuant to title cannot be used in a manner that is irreconcilable with the nature of the claimants' attachment to those lands. This limit on the content of aboriginal title is a manifestation of the principle that underlies the various dimensions of that special interest in land — it is a *sui generis* interest that is distinct from "normal" proprietary interests, most notably fee simple.

I arrive at this conclusion by reference to the other dimensions of aboriginal title which are *sui generis* as well. I first consider the source of aboriginal title. As I discussed earlier, aboriginal title arises from the prior occupation of Canada by aboriginal peoples. That prior occupation is relevant in two different ways: first, because of the physical fact of occupation, and second, because aboriginal title originates in part from pre-existing systems of aboriginal law. However, the law of aboriginal title does not only seek to determine the historic rights of aboriginal peoples to land; it also seeks to afford legal protection to prior occupation in the present-day. Implicit in the protection of historic patterns of occupation is a recognition of the importance of the continuity of the relationship of an aboriginal community to its land over time.

I develop this point below with respect to the test for aboriginal title. The relevance of the continuity of the relationship of an aboriginal community with its land here is that it applies not only to the past, but to the future as well. That relationship should not be prevented from continuing into the future. As a result, uses of the lands that would threaten that future relationship are, by their very nature, excluded from the content of aboriginal title.

Accordingly, in my view, lands subject to aboriginal title cannot be put to such uses as may be irreconcilable with the nature of the occupation of that land and the relationship that the particular group has had with the land which together have given rise to aboriginal title in the first place. As discussed below, one of the critical elements in the determination of whether a particular aboriginal group has aboriginal title to certain lands is the matter of the occupancy of those lands. Occupancy is determined by reference to the activities that have taken place on the land and the uses to which the land has been put by the particular group. If lands are so occupied, there will exist a special bond between the group and the land in question such that the land will be part of the definition of the group's distinctive culture. It seems to me that these elements of aboriginal title create an inherent limitation on the uses to which the land, over which such title exists, may be put. For example, if occupation is established with reference to the use of the land as a hunting ground, then the group that successfully claims aboriginal title to that land may not use it in such a fashion as to destroy its value for such a use (e.g., by strip mining it). Similarly, if a group claims a special bond with the land because of its ceremonial or cultural significance, it may not use the land in such a way as to destroy that relationship (e.g., by developing it in such a way that the bond is destroyed, perhaps by turning it into a parking lot).

It is for this reason also that lands held by virtue of aboriginal title may not be alienated. Alienation would bring to an end the entitlement of the aboriginal people to occupy the land and would terminate their relationship with it. I have suggested above that the inalienability of aboriginal lands is, at least in part, a function of the common law principle that settlers in colonies must derive their title from Crown grant and, therefore, cannot acquire title through purchase from aboriginal inhabitants. It is also, again only in part, a function of a general policy "to ensure that Indians are not dispossessed of their entitlements": see *Mitchell v. Peguis Indian Band*, [1990] 2 S.C.R. 85 (S.C.C.) at p. 133. What the inalienability of lands held pursuant to aboriginal title suggests is that those lands are more than just a fungible commodity. The relationship between an aboriginal community and the lands over which it has aboriginal title has an important non-economic component. The land has an inherent and unique value in itself, which is enjoyed by the community with aboriginal title to it. The community cannot put the land to uses which would destroy that value.

I am cognizant that the *sui generis* nature of aboriginal title precludes the application of "traditional real property rules" to elucidate the content of that title (*St. Mary's Indian Band v. Cranbrook (City)*, [1997] 2 S.C.R. 657, at para. 14). Nevertheless, a useful analogy can be drawn between the limit on aboriginal title and the concept of equitable waste at common law. Under that doctrine, persons who hold a life estate in real property cannot commit "wanton or extravagant acts of destruction" (E. H. Burn, *Cheshire and Burn's Modern Law of Real Property* (14th ed. 1988), at p. 264) or "ruin the property" (Robert E. Megarry and H. W. R. Wade, *The Law of Real Property* (4th ed. 1975), at p. 105). This description of the limits imposed by the doctrine of equitable waste capture the kind of limit I have in mind here.

Finally, what I have just said regarding the importance of the continuity of the relationship between an aboriginal community and its land, and the non-economic or inherent value of that land, should not be taken to detract from the possibility of surrender to the Crown in exchange for valuable consideration. On the contrary, the idea of surrender reinforces the conclusion that aboriginal title is limited in the way I have described. If aboriginal peoples wish to use their lands in a way that aboriginal title does not permit, then they must surrender those lands and convert them into non-title lands to do so.

The foregoing amounts to a general limitation on the use of lands held by virtue of aboriginal title. It arises from the particular physical and cultural relationship that a group may have with the land and is defined by the source of aboriginal title over it. This is not, I must emphasize, a limitation that restricts the use of the land to those activities that have traditionally been carried out on it. That would amount to a legal straitjacket on aboriginal peoples who have a legitimate legal claim to the land. The approach I have outlined above allows for a full range of uses of the land, subject only to an overarching limit, defined by the special nature of the aboriginal title in that land.

(d) Aboriginal title under s. 35(1) of the Constitution Act, 1982

Aboriginal title at common law is protected in its full form by s. 35(1). This conclusion flows from the express language of s. 35(1) itself, which states in full: "[t]he *existing* aboriginal and treaty rights of the aboriginal peoples of Canada are hereby recognized and affirmed" (emphasis added). On a plain reading of the provision, s. 35(1) did not create aboriginal rights; rather, it accorded constitutional status to those rights which were "existing" in 1982. The provision, at the very least, constitutionalized those rights which aboriginal peoples possessed at common law, since those rights existed at the time s. 35(1) came into force. Since aboriginal title was a common law right whose existence was recognized well before 1982 (e.g., *Calder, supra*), s. 35(1) has constitutionalized it in its full form.

I expressed this understanding of the relationship between common law aboriginal rights, including aboriginal title, and the aboriginal rights protected by s. 35(1) in *Van der Peet*. While explaining the purposes behind s. 35(1), I stated that "it must be remembered that s. 35(1) did not create the legal doctrine of aboriginal rights; aboriginal rights existed and were recognized under the common law" (at para. 28). Through the enactment of s. 35(1), "a pre-existing legal doctrine was elevated to constitutional status" (at para. 29), or in other words, s. 35(1) had achieved "the constitutionalization of those rights" (at para. 29).

Finally, this view of the effect of s. 35(1) on common law aboriginal title is supported by numerous commentators: Patrick Macklem, "First Nations Self-Government and the Borders of the Canadian Legal Imagination" (1991), 36 *McGill L.J.* 382, at pp. 447-48; Kent McNeil, "The Constitutional Rights of the Aboriginal Peoples of Canada" (1982), 4 *Sup. Ct. L. Rev.* 255, at pp. 256-57; James O'Reilly, "*La Loi constitutionnelle de 1982*, droit des autochtones" (1984) 25 *C. de D.* 125, at p.137; William Pentney, "The Rights of the Aboriginal Peoples of Canada in the *Constitution Act, 1982* Part II — Section 35: The Substantive Guarantee"[(1988) 22 U.B.C. L. Rev. 207] at pp. 220-21; Douglas Sanders, "The Rights of the Aboriginal Peoples of Canada" (1983), 61 *Can. Bar Rev.* 314, at p. 329; Douglas Sanders, "Pre-Existing Rights: The Aboriginal Peoples of Canada", in Gérald-A. Beaudoin & Ed Ratushny, eds., *The Canadian Charter of Rights and Freedoms* (2nd ed. 1989), 707 at pp. 731-32; Brian Slattery, "The Constitutional Guarantee of Aboriginal Treaty Rights"[(1982-83) 8 *Queen's L.J.* 232] at p. 254; Brian Slattery, *Ancestral Lands, Alien Laws: Judicial Perspectives on Aboriginal Title* [(Saskatoon: University of Saskatchewan Native Law Centre, 1983)] at p. 45.

I hasten to add that the constitutionalization of common law aboriginal rights by s. 35(1) does not mean that those rights exhaust the content of s. 35(1). As I said in *Côté, supra*, at para. 52:

> [s]ection 35(1) would fail to achieve its noble purpose of preserving the integral and defining features of distinctive aboriginal societies if it only protected those defining features which were fortunate enough to have received the legal recognition and approval of European colonizers.

I relied on this proposition in *Côté* to defeat the argument that the possible absence of aboriginal rights under French colonial law was a bar to the existence of aboriginal rights under s. 35(1) within the historic boundaries of New France. But it also follows that the existence of a particular aboriginal right at common law is not a *sine qua non* for the proof of an aboriginal right that is recognized and affirmed by s. 35(1). Indeed, none of the decisions of this Court handed down under s. 35(1) in which the existence of an aboriginal right has been demonstrated has relied on the existence of that right at common law. The existence of an aboriginal right at common law is therefore sufficient, but not necessary, for the recognition and affirmation of that right by s. 35(1).

The acknowledgement that s. 35(1) has accorded constitutional status to common law aboriginal title raises a further question — the relationship of aboriginal title to the "aboriginal rights" protected by s. 35(1). I addressed that question in *Adams, supra*, where the Court had been presented with two radically different conceptions of this relationship. The first conceived of aboriginal rights as being "inherently based in aboriginal title to the land" (at para. 25), or as fragments of a broader claim to aboriginal title. By implication, aboriginal rights must rest either in a claim to title or the unextinguished remnants of title. Taken to its logical extreme, this suggests that aboriginal title is merely the sum of a set of individual aboriginal rights, and that it therefore has no independent content. However, I rejected this position for another — that aboriginal title is "simply one manifestation of a broader-based conception of aboriginal rights" (at para. 25). Thus, although aboriginal title is a species of aboriginal right recognized and affirmed by s. 35(1), it is distinct from other aboriginal rights because it arises where the connection of a group with a piece of land "was of a central significance to their distinctive culture" (at para. 26).

The picture which emerges from *Adams* is that the aboriginal rights which are recognized and affirmed by s. 35(1) fall along a spectrum with respect to their degree of connection with the land. At the one end, there are those aboriginal rights which are practices, customs and traditions that are integral to the distinctive aboriginal culture of the group claiming the right. However, the "*occupation and use of the land*" where the activity is taking place is not "*sufficient to support a claim of title to the land*" (at para. 26). Nevertheless, those activities receive constitutional protection. In the middle, there are activities which, out of necessity, take place on land and indeed, might be intimately related to a particular piece of land. Although an aboriginal group may not be able to demonstrate title to the land, it may nevertheless have a site-specific right to engage in a particular activity. I put the point this way in *Adams*, at para. 30:

> Even where an aboriginal right exists on a tract of land to which the aboriginal people in question do not have title, that right may well be site specific, with the result that it can be exercised only upon that specific tract of land. For example, *if an aboriginal*

> *people demonstrates that hunting on a specific tract of land was an integral part of their distinctive culture then, even if the right exists apart from title to that tract of land, the aboriginal right to hunt is nonetheless defined as, and limited to, the right to hunt on the specific tract of land.* [Emphasis added.]

At the other end of the spectrum, there is aboriginal title itself. As *Adams* makes clear, aboriginal title confers more than the right to engage in site-specific activities which are aspects of the practices, customs and traditions of distinctive aboriginal cultures. Site-specific rights can be made out even if title cannot. What aboriginal title confers is the right to the land itself.

Because aboriginal rights can vary with respect to their degree of connection with the land, some aboriginal groups may be unable to make out a claim to title, but will nevertheless possess aboriginal rights that are recognized and affirmed by s. 35(1), including site-specific rights to engage in particular activities. As I explained in *Adams*, this may occur in the case of nomadic peoples who varied "the location of their settlements with the season and changing circumstances" (at para. 27). The fact that aboriginal peoples were non-sedentary, however (at para. 27):

> does not alter the fact that nomadic peoples survived through reliance on the land prior to contact with Europeans and, further, that many of the practices, customs and traditions of nomadic peoples that took place on the land were integral to their distinctive cultures.

(e) Proof of aboriginal title

(i) Introduction

In addition to differing in the degree of connection with the land, aboriginal title differs from other aboriginal rights in another way. To date, the Court has defined aboriginal rights in terms of *activities*. As I said in *Van der Peet* (at para. 46):

> [I]n order to be an aboriginal right an *activity* must be an element of a practice, custom or tradition integral to the distinctive culture of the aboriginal group claiming the right. [Emphasis added.]

Aboriginal title, however, is a *right to the land* itself. Subject to the limits I have laid down above, that land may be used for a variety of activities, none of which need be individually protected as aboriginal rights under s. 35(1). Those activities are parasitic on the underlying title.

This difference between aboriginal rights to engage in particular activities and aboriginal title requires that the test I laid down in *Van der Peet* be adapted accordingly. I anticipated this possibility in *Van der Peet* itself, where I stated that (at para. 74):

> *Aboriginal rights arise from the prior occupation of land, but they also arise from the prior social organization and distinctive cultures of aboriginal peoples on that land.* In considering whether a claim to an aboriginal right has been made out, courts must look

> at both the relationship of an aboriginal claimant to the land *and* [emphasis in original] at the practices, customs and traditions arising from the claimant's distinctive culture and society. Courts must not focus so entirely on the relationship of aboriginal peoples with the land that they lose sight of the other factors relevant to the identification and definition of aboriginal rights. [Emphasis added.]

Since the purpose of s. 35(1) is to reconcile the prior presence of aboriginal peoples in North America with the assertion of Crown sovereignty, it is clear from this statement that s. 35(1) must recognize and affirm both aspects of that prior presence — first, the occupation of land, and second, the prior social organization and distinctive cultures of aboriginal peoples on that land. To date the jurisprudence under s. 35(1) has given more emphasis to the second aspect. To a great extent, this has been a function of the types of cases which have come before this Court under s. 35(1) — prosecutions for regulatory offences that, by their very nature, proscribe discrete types of activity.

The adaptation of the test laid down in *Van der Peet* to suit claims to title must be understood as the recognition of the first aspect of that prior presence. However, as will now become apparent, the tests for the identification of aboriginal rights to engage in particular activities and for the identification of aboriginal title share broad similarities. The major distinctions are first, under the test for aboriginal title, the requirement that the land be integral to the distinctive culture of the claimants is subsumed by the requirement of occupancy, and second, whereas the time for the identification of aboriginal rights is the time of first contact, the time for the identification of aboriginal title is the time at which the Crown asserted sovereignty over the land.

(ii) The test for the proof of aboriginal title

In order to make out a claim for aboriginal title, the aboriginal group asserting title must satisfy the following criteria: (i) the land must have been occupied prior to sovereignty, (ii) if present occupation is relied on as proof of occupation pre-sovereignty, there must be a continuity between present and pre-sovereignty occupation, and (iii) at sovereignty, that occupation must have been exclusive.

The land must have been occupied prior to sovereignty

In order to establish a claim to aboriginal title, the aboriginal group asserting the claim must establish that it occupied the lands in question at the *time at which the Crown asserted sovereignty over the land subject to the title.* The relevant time period for the establishment of title is, therefore, different than for the establishment of aboriginal rights to engage in specific activities. In *Van der Peet,* I held, at para. 60 that "[t]he time period that a court should consider in identifying whether the right claimed meets the standard of being integral to the aboriginal community claiming the right is the period prior to contact. . . ." This arises from the fact that in defining the central and distinctive attributes of pre-existing aboriginal societies it is necessary to look to a time prior to the arrival of Europeans. Practices, customs or traditions that arose solely as a response to European influences do not meet the standard for recognition as aboriginal rights.

On the other hand, in the context of aboriginal title, sovereignty is the appropriate time period to consider for several reasons. First, from a theoretical standpoint, aboriginal title arises out of prior occupation of the land by aboriginal peoples and out of the relationship between the common law and pre-existing systems of aboriginal law. Aboriginal title is a burden on the Crown's underlying title. However, the Crown did not gain this title until it asserted sovereignty over the land in question. Because it does not make sense to speak of a burden on the underlying title before that title existed, aboriginal title crystallized at the time sovereignty was asserted. Second, aboriginal title does not raise the problem of distinguishing between distinctive, integral aboriginal practices, customs and traditions and those influenced or introduced by European contact. Under common law, the act of occupation or possession is sufficient to ground aboriginal title and it is not necessary to prove that the land was a distinctive or integral part of the aboriginal society before the arrival of Europeans. Finally, from a practical standpoint, it appears that the date of sovereignty is more certain than the date of first contact. It is often very difficult to determine the precise moment that each aboriginal group had first contact with European culture. I note that this is the approach has support in the academic literature: Brian Slattery, "Understanding Aboriginal Rights" [(1987), 66 *Can. Bar Rev.* 727] at p. 742; Kent McNeil, *Common Law Aboriginal Title, supra*, at p. 196. For these reasons, I conclude that aboriginals must establish occupation of the land from the date of the assertion of sovereignty in order to sustain a claim for aboriginal title. McEachern C.J. found, at pp. 233-34, and the parties did not dispute on appeal, that British sovereignty over British Columbia was conclusively established by the Oregon Boundary Treaty of 1846. This is not to say that circumstances subsequent to sovereignty may never be relevant to title or compensation; this might be the case, for example, where native bands have been dispossessed of traditional lands after sovereignty.

There was a consensus among the parties on appeal that proof of historic occupation was required to make out a claim to aboriginal title. However, the parties disagreed on how that occupancy could be proved. The respondents assert that in order to establish aboriginal title, the occupation must be the physical occupation of the land in question. The appellant Gitksan nation argue, by contrast, that aboriginal title may be established, at least in part, by reference to aboriginal law.

This debate over the proof of occupancy reflects two divergent views of the source of aboriginal title. The respondents argue, in essence, that aboriginal title arises from the physical reality at the time of sovereignty, whereas the Gitksan effectively take the position that aboriginal title arises from and should reflect the pattern of land holdings under aboriginal law. However, as I have explained above, the source of aboriginal title appears to be grounded both in the common law and in the aboriginal perspective on land; the latter includes, but is not limited to, their systems of law. It follows that both should be taken into account in establishing the proof of occupancy. Indeed, there is precedent for doing so. In *Baker Lake* [*Baker Lake v. Minister of Indian Affairs and Northern Development*, [1980] 1 F.C. 518],

Mahoney J. held that to prove aboriginal title, the claimants needed both to demonstrate their "physical presence on the land they occupied" (at p. 561) and the existence "among [that group of] . . . a recognition of the claimed rights . . . by the regime that prevailed before" (at p. 559).

This approach to the proof of occupancy at common law is also mandated in the context of s. 35(1) by *Van der Peet*. In that decision, as I stated above, I held at para. 50 that the reconciliation of the prior occupation of North America by aboriginal peoples with the assertion of Crown sovereignty required that account be taken of the "aboriginal perspective while at the same time taking into account the perspective of the common law" and that "[t]rue reconciliation will, equally, place weight on each". I also held that the aboriginal perspective on the occupation of their lands can be gleaned, in part, but not exclusively, from their traditional laws, because those laws were elements of the practices, customs and traditions of aboriginal peoples: at para. 41. As a result, if, at the time of sovereignty, an aboriginal society had laws in relation to land, those laws would be relevant to establishing the occupation of lands which are the subject of a claim for aboriginal title. Relevant laws might include, but are not limited to, a land tenure system or laws governing land use.

However, the aboriginal perspective must be taken into account alongside the perspective of the common law. Professor McNeil has convincingly argued that at common law, the fact of physical occupation is proof of possession at law, which in turn will ground title to the land: *Common Law Aboriginal Title, supra,* at p. 73; also see *Cheshire and Burn's, Modern Law of Real Property, supra*, at p. 28; and Megarry and Wade, *The Law of Real Property, supra*, at p. 1006. Physical occupation may be established in a variety of ways, ranging from the construction of dwellings through cultivation and enclosure of fields to regular use of definite tracts of land for hunting, fishing or otherwise exploiting its resources: see McNeil, *Common Law Aboriginal Title* at pp. 201-202. In considering whether occupation sufficient to ground title is established, "one must take into account the group's size, manner of life, material resources, and technological abilities, and the character of the lands claimed": Brian Slattery, "Understanding Aboriginal Rights", at pp. 758.

In *Van der Peet*, I drew a distinction between those practices, customs and traditions of aboriginal peoples which were "an aspect of, or took place in" the society of the aboriginal group asserting the claim and those which were "a central and significant part of the society's culture" (at para. 55). The latter stood apart because they "made the culture of that society distinctive . . . it was one of the things which truly *made the society what it was*" (at para. 55). The same requirement operates in the determination of the proof of aboriginal title. As I said in *Adams*, a claim to title is made out when a group can demonstrate "that their connection with the piece of land . . . was of central significance to their distinctive culture" (at para. 26).

Although this remains a crucial part of the test for aboriginal rights, given the occupancy requirement in the test for aboriginal title, I cannot imagine a situation where this requirement would actually serve to limit or preclude a title claim. The requirement exists for rights short of title because it is necessary to distinguish between those practices which were central to the culture of claimants and those which were more incidental. However, in the case of title, it would seem clear that any land that was occupied pre-sovereignty, and which the parties have maintained a substantial connection with since then, is sufficiently important to be of central significance to the culture of the claimants. As a result, I do not think it is necessary to include explicitly this element as part of the test for aboriginal title.

If present occupation is relied on as proof of occupation pre-sovereignty, there must be a continuity between present and pre-sovereignty occupation

In *Van der Peet*, I explained that it is the pre-contact practices, customs and traditions of aboriginal peoples which are recognized and affirmed as aboriginal rights by s. 35(1). But I also acknowledged it would be "next to impossible" (at para. 62) for an aboriginal group to provide conclusive evidence of its pre-contact practices, customs and traditions. What would suffice instead was evidence of post-contact practices, which was "directed at demonstrating which aspects of the aboriginal community and society have their origins pre-contact" (at para. 62). The same concern, and the same solution, arises with respect to the proof of occupation in claims for aboriginal title, although there is a difference in the time for determination of title. Conclusive evidence of pre-sovereignty occupation may be difficult to come by. Instead, an aboriginal community may provide evidence of present occupation as proof of pre-sovereignty occupation in support of a claim to aboriginal title. What is required, in addition, is a *continuity* between present and pre-sovereignty occupation, because the relevant time for the determination of aboriginal title is at the time before sovereignty.

Needless to say, there is no need to establish "an unbroken chain of continuity" (*Van der Peet,* at para. 65) between present and prior occupation. The occupation and use of lands may have been disrupted for a time, perhaps as a result of the unwillingness of European colonizers to *recognize* aboriginal title. To impose the requirement of continuity too strictly would risk "undermining the very purposes of s. 35(1) by perpetuating the historical injustice suffered by aboriginal peoples at the hands of colonizers who failed to respect" aboriginal rights to land (*Côté*, *supra* at para. 53). In *Mabo* [*Mabo v. Queensland* (1992), 107 A.L.R. 1 (H.C.)], the High Court of Australia set down the requirement that there must be "substantial maintenance of the connection" between the people and the land. In my view, this test should be equally applicable to proof of title in Canada.

I should also note that there is a strong possibility that the precise nature of occupation will have changed between the time of sovereignty and the present. I would like to make it clear that the fact that the nature of occupation has changed would not ordinarily preclude a claim for aboriginal title, as long as a substantial connection between the people and the land is maintained. The only limitation on this principle might be the internal limits on uses which land that is subject to aboriginal title may be put, i.e., uses which are inconsistent with continued use by future generations of aboriginals.

At sovereignty, occupation must have been exclusive

Finally, at sovereignty, occupation must have been exclusive. The requirement for exclusivity flows from the definition of aboriginal title itself, because I have defined aboriginal title in terms of the right to *exclusive* use and occupation of land. Exclusivity, as an aspect of aboriginal title, vests in the aboriginal community which holds the ability to exclude others from the lands held pursuant to that title. The proof of title must, in this respect, mirror the content of the right. Were it possible to prove title without demonstrating exclusive occupation, the result would be absurd, because it would be possible for more than one aboriginal nation to have aboriginal title over the same piece of land, and then for all of them to attempt to assert the right to exclusive use and occupation over it.

As with the proof of occupation, proof of exclusivity must rely on both the perspective of the common law and the aboriginal perspective, placing equal weight on each. At common law, a premium is placed on the factual reality of occupation, as encountered by the Europeans. However, as the common law concept of possession must be sensitive to the realities of aboriginal society, so must the concept of exclusivity. Exclusivity is a common law principle derived from the notion of fee simple ownership and should be imported into the concept of aboriginal title with caution. As such, the test required to establish exclusive occupation must take into account the context of the aboriginal society at the time of sovereignty. For example, it is important to note that exclusive occupation can be demonstrated even if other aboriginal groups were present, or frequented the claimed lands. Under those circumstances, exclusivity would be demonstrated by "the intention and capacity to retain exclusive control" (McNeil, *Common Law Aboriginal Title* , *supra*, at p. 204). Thus, an act of trespass, if isolated, would not undermine a general finding of exclusivity, if aboriginal groups intended to and attempted to enforce their exclusive occupation. Moreover, as Professor McNeil suggests, the presence of other aboriginal groups might actually reinforce a finding of exclusivity. For example, "[w]here others were allowed access upon request, the very fact that permission was asked for and given would be further evidence of the group's exclusive control" (at p. 204).

A consideration of the aboriginal perspective may also lead to the conclusion that trespass by other aboriginal groups does not undermine, and that presence of those groups by permission may reinforce, the exclusive occupation of the aboriginal group asserting title. For example, the aboriginal group asserting the claim to aboriginal title may have trespass laws which are proof of exclusive occupation, such that the presence of trespassers does not count as evidence against exclusivity. As well, aboriginal laws under which permission may be granted to other aboriginal groups to use or reside even temporarily on land would reinforce the finding of exclusive occupation. Indeed, if that permission were the subject of treaties between the aboriginal nations in question, those treaties would also form part of the aboriginal perspective.

In their submissions, the appellants pressed the point that requiring proof of exclusive occupation might preclude a finding of joint title, which is shared between two or more aboriginal nations. The possibility of joint title has been recognized by

American courts: *United States v. Santa Fe Pacific Railway Co.*, 314 U.S. 339 (1941). I would suggest that the requirement of exclusive occupancy and the possibility of joint title could be reconciled by recognizing that joint title could arise from shared exclusivity. The meaning of shared exclusivity is well-known to the common law. Exclusive possession is the right to exclude others. Shared exclusive possession is the right to exclude others except those with whom possession is shared. There clearly may be cases in which two aboriginal nations lived on a particular piece of land and recognized each other's entitlement to that land but nobody else's. However, since no claim to joint title has been asserted here, I leave it to another day to work out all the complexities and implications of joint title, as well as any limits that another band's title may have on the way in which one band uses its title lands.

I should also reiterate that if aboriginals can show that they occupied a particular piece of land, but did not do so exclusively, it will always be possible to establish aboriginal rights short of title. These rights will likely be intimately tied to the land and may permit a number of possible uses. However, unlike title, they are not a right to the land itself. Rather, as I have suggested, they are a right to do certain things in connection with that land. If, for example, it were established that the lands near those subject to a title claim were used for hunting by a number of bands, those shared lands would not be subject to a claim for aboriginal title, as they lack the crucial element of exclusivity. However, they may be subject to site-specific aboriginal rights by all of the bands who used it. This does not entitle anyone to the land itself, but it may entitle all of the bands who hunted on the land to hunting rights. Hence, in addition to shared title, it will be possible to have shared, non-exclusive, site-specific rights. In my opinion, this accords with the general principle that the common law should develop to recognize aboriginal rights (and title, when necessary) as they were recognized by either *de facto* practice or by the aboriginal system of governance. It also allows sufficient flexibility to deal with this highly complex and rapidly evolving area of the law.

(f) Infringements of aboriginal title: the test of justification

(i) Introduction

The aboriginal rights recognized and affirmed by s. 35(1), including aboriginal title, are not absolute. Those rights may be infringed, both by the federal (e.g., *Sparrow*) and provincial (e.g., *Côté*) governments. However, s. 35(1) requires that those infringements satisfy the test of justification. In this section, I will review the Court's nascent jurisprudence on justification and explain how that test will apply in the context of infringements of aboriginal title.

(ii) General Principles

The test of justification has two parts, which I shall consider in turn. First, the infringement of the aboriginal right must be in furtherance of a legislative objective that is compelling and substantial. I explained in *Gladstone* that compelling and substantial objectives were those which were directed at either one of the purposes underlying the recognition and affirmation of aboriginal rights by s. 35(1), which are (at para. 72):

> the recognition of the prior occupation of North America by aboriginal peoples or . . . the reconciliation of aboriginal prior occupation with the assertion of the sovereignty of the Crown.

I noted that the latter purpose will often "be most relevant" (at para. 72) at the stage of justification. I think it important to repeat why (at para. 73) that is so:

> Because . . . distinctive aboriginal societies exist within, and are part of, a broader social, political and economic community, over which the Crown is sovereign, there are circumstances in which, in order to pursue objectives of compelling and substantial importance to that community as a whole (taking into account the fact that aboriginal societies are part of that community), some limitation of those rights will be justifiable. *Aboriginal rights are a necessary part of the reconciliation of aboriginal societies with the broader political community of which they are part; limits placed on those rights are, where the objectives furthered by those limits are of sufficient importance to the broader community as a whole, equally a necessary part of that reconciliation.* [Emphasis added; "*equally*" emphasized in original.]

The conservation of fisheries, which was accepted as a compelling and substantial objective in *Sparrow*, furthers both of these purposes, because it simultaneously recognizes that fishing is integral to many aboriginal cultures, and also seeks to reconcile aboriginal societies with the broader community by ensuring that there are fish enough for all. But legitimate government objectives also include "the pursuit of economic and regional fairness" and "the recognition of the historical reliance upon, and participation in, the fishery by non-aboriginal groups" (para. 75). By contrast, measures enacted for relatively unimportant reasons, such as sports fishing without a significant economic component (*Adams, supra*) would fail this aspect of the test of justification.

The second part of the test of justification requires an assessment of whether the infringement is consistent with the special fiduciary relationship between the Crown and aboriginal peoples. What has become clear is that the requirements of the fiduciary duty are a function of the "legal and factual context" of each appeal (*Gladstone, supra*, at para. 56). *Sparrow* and *Gladstone*, for example, interpreted and applied the fiduciary duty in terms of the idea of *priority*. The theory underlying that principle is that the fiduciary relationship between the Crown and aboriginal peoples demands that aboriginal interests be placed first. However, the fiduciary duty does not demand that aboriginal rights always be given priority. As was said in *Sparrow*, *supra*, at pp. 1114-15:

> The nature of the constitutional protection afforded by s. 35(1) *in this context* demands that there be a link between the question of justification and the allocation of priorities in the fishery. [Emphasis added.]

Other contexts permit, and may even require, that the fiduciary duty be articulated in other ways (at p. 1119):

> Within the analysis of justification, there are further questions to be addressed, depending on the circumstances of the inquiry. These include the questions of whether there has been as little infringement as possible in order to effect the desired result; whether, in a situation of expropriation, fair compensation is available; and, whether the aboriginal group in question has been consulted with respect to the conservation measures being implemented.

Sparrow did not explain when the different articulations of the fiduciary duty should be used. Below, I suggest that the choice between them will in large part be a function of the nature of the aboriginal right at issue.

In addition to variation in the *form* which the fiduciary duty takes, there will also be variation in degree of scrutiny required by the fiduciary duty of the infringing measure or action. The degree of scrutiny is a function of the nature of the aboriginal right at issue. The distinction between *Sparrow* and *Gladstone*, for example, turned on whether the right amounted to the exclusive use of a resource, which in turn was a function of whether the right had an internal limit. In *Sparrow*, the right was internally limited, because it was a right to fish for food, ceremonial and social purposes, and as a result would only amount to an exclusive right to use the fishery in exceptional circumstances. Accordingly, the requirement of priority was applied strictly to mean that (at p. 1116) "any allocation of priorities after valid conservation measures have been implemented must give top priority to Indian food fishing".

In *Gladstone*, by contrast, the right to sell fish commercially was only limited by supply and demand. Had the test for justification been applied in a strict form in *Gladstone*, the aboriginal right would have amounted to an exclusive right exploit the fishery on a commercial basis. This was not the intention of *Sparrow*, and I accordingly modified the test for justification, by altering the idea of priority in the following way (at para. 62):

> . . . the doctrine of priority requires that the government demonstrate that, in allocating the resource, it has taken account of the existence of aboriginal rights and allocated the resource in a manner respectful of the fact that those rights have priority over the exploitation of the fishery by other users. This right is at once both procedural and substantive; at the stage of justification the government must demonstrate both that the process by which it allocated the resource and the actual allocation of the resource which results from that process reflect the prior interest of aboriginal rights holders in the fishery.

After *Gladstone*, in the context of commercial activity, the priority of aboriginal rights is constitutionally satisfied if the government had taken those rights into account and has allocated a resource "in a manner respectful" (at para. 62) of that priority. A court must be satisfied that "the government has taken into account the existence and importance of [aboriginal] rights" (at para. 63) which it determines by asking the following questions (at para. 64):

> Questions relevant to the determination of whether the government has granted priority to aboriginal rights holders are . . . questions such as whether the government has accommodated the exercise of the aboriginal right to participate in the fishery (through

reduced licence fees, for example), whether the government's objectives in enacting a particular regulatory scheme reflect the need to take into account the priority of aboriginal rights holders, the extent of the participation in the fishery of aboriginal rights holders relative to their percentage of the population, how the government has accommodated different aboriginal rights in a particular fishery (food *versus* commercial rights, for example), how important the fishery is to the economic and material well-being of the band in question, and the criteria taken into account by the government in, for example, allocating commercial licences amongst different users.

(iii) Justification and Aboriginal Title

The general principles governing justification laid down in *Sparrow*, and embellished by *Gladstone*, operate with respect to infringements of aboriginal title. In the wake of *Gladstone*, the range of legislative objectives that can justify the infringement of aboriginal title is fairly broad. Most of these objectives can be traced to the *reconciliation* of the prior occupation of North America by aboriginal peoples with the assertion of Crown sovereignty, which entails the recognition that "distinctive aboriginal societies exist within, and are a part of, a broader social, political and economic community" (at para. 73). In my opinion, the development of agriculture, forestry, mining, and hydroelectric power, the general economic development of the interior of British Columbia, protection of the environment or endangered species, the building of infrastructure and the settlement of foreign populations to support those aims, are the kinds of objectives that are consistent with this purpose and, in principle, can justify the infringement of aboriginal title. Whether a particular measure or government act can be explained by reference to one of those objectives, however, is ultimately a question of fact that will have to be examined on a case-by-case basis.

The manner in which the fiduciary duty operates with respect to the second stage of the justification test — both with respect to the standard of scrutiny and the particular form that the fiduciary duty will take — will be a function of the nature of aboriginal title. Three aspects of aboriginal title are relevant here. First, aboriginal title encompasses the right to *exclusive use* and occupation of land; second, aboriginal title encompasses *the right to choose* to what uses land can be put, subject to the ultimate limit that those uses cannot destroy the ability of the land to sustain future generations of aboriginal peoples; and third, that lands held pursuant to aboriginal title have an inescapable *economic component.*

The exclusive nature of aboriginal title is relevant to the degree of scrutiny of the infringing measure or action. For example, if the Crown's fiduciary duty requires that aboriginal title be given priority, then it is the altered approach to priority that I laid down in *Gladstone* which should apply. What is required is that the government demonstrate (at para. 62) "both that the process by which it allocated the resource and the actual allocation of the resource which results from that process reflect the prior interest" of the holders of aboriginal title in the land. By analogy with *Gladstone*, this might entail, for example, that governments accommodate the participation of aboriginal peoples in the development of the resources of British Columbia, that the conferral of fee simples for agriculture, and of leases and licences for forestry and mining reflect the prior occupation of aboriginal title lands, that economic barriers to aboriginal uses of their lands (e.g., licensing fees) be somewhat reduced. This list is illustrative and not exhaustive. This is an issue that may involve an assessment of the various interests at stake in the resources in question. No doubt, there will be difficulties in determining the precise value of the aboriginal interest in the land and any grants, leases or licences given for its exploitation. These difficult economic considerations obviously cannot be solved here.

Moreover, the other aspects of aboriginal title suggest that the fiduciary duty may be articulated in a manner different than the idea of priority. This point becomes clear from a comparison between aboriginal title and the aboriginal right to fish for food in *Sparrow*. First, aboriginal title encompasses within it a right to choose to what ends a piece of land can be put. The aboriginal right to fish for food, by contrast, does not contain within it the same discretionary component. This aspect of aboriginal title suggests that the fiduciary relationship between the Crown and aboriginal peoples may be satisfied by the involvement of aboriginal peoples in decisions taken with respect to their lands. There is always a duty of consultation. Whether the aboriginal group has been consulted is relevant to determining whether the infringement of aboriginal title is justified, in the same way that the Crown's failure to consult an aboriginal group with respect to the terms by which reserve land is leased may breach its fiduciary duty at common law: *Guerin*. The nature and scope of the duty of consultation will vary with the circumstances. In occasional cases, when the breach is less serious or relatively minor, it will be no more than a duty to discuss important decisions that will be taken with respect to lands held pursuant to aboriginal title. Of course, even in these rare cases when the minimum acceptable standard is consultation, this consultation must be in good faith, and with the intention of substantially addressing the concerns of the aboriginal peoples whose lands are at issue. In most cases, it will be significantly deeper than mere consultation. Some cases may even require the full consent of an aboriginal nation, particularly when provinces enact hunting and fishing regulations in relation to aboriginal lands.

Second, aboriginal title, unlike the aboriginal right to fish for food, has an inescapably economic aspect, particularly when one takes into account the modern uses to which lands held pursuant to aboriginal title can be put. The economic aspect of aboriginal title suggests that compensation is relevant to the question of justification as well, a possibility suggested in *Sparrow* and which I repeated in *Gladstone*. Indeed, compensation for breaches of fiduciary duty are a well-established part of the landscape of aboriginal rights: *Guerin*. In keeping with the duty of honour and good faith on the Crown, fair compensation will ordinarily be required when aboriginal title is infringed. The amount of compensation payable will vary with the nature of the particular aboriginal title affected and with the nature and severity of the infringement and the extent to which aboriginal interests were accommodated. Since the issue of damages was severed from the principal action, we received no submissions on the appropriate legal principles that would be relevant to determining the appropriate level of compensation of infringements of aboriginal title. In the circumstances, it is best that we leave those difficult questions to another day. . . .

E. Did the province have the power to extinguish aboriginal rights after 1871, either under its own jurisdiction or through the operation of s. 88 of the *Indian Act*? . . .

[By virtue of s. 91(24) of the *Constitution Act ,1867,* the power to legislate regarding "Indians and Lands Reserved for Indians" is given to the federal government. Lamer C.J. held that the Court found that this exclusive federal jurisdiction over Indians and Indian lands precluded the provinces from having power to extinguish Aboriginal title, and that any law of specific application that attempted to extinguish Aboriginal title, even (or especially) if it manifested a clear and plain intent to do so, would be *ultra vires* the province and therefore void. A law of general application could not extinguish Aboriginal title, as Aboriginal interests in land relate to the core of "Indianness" which is protected from provincial intrusion. It was reasoned (at 1118) that if the provinces had the power to extinguish native title "the government vested with primary constitutional responsibility for securing the welfare of Canada's aboriginal peoples would find itself unable to safeguard one of its most central of native interests—their interest in land".

British Columbia also argued that s. 88 of the *Indian Act*, which states that "all laws of general application from time to time in the province are applicable to and in respect of Indians of the province, except to the extent that those laws are inconsistent with this Act" gave the province power to extinguish native title through laws of general application. Again, the Supreme Court held that Aboriginal title was part of the protected core of "Indianness." A provincial law of general application thus could not function to extinguish Aboriginal title.]

VI. Conclusion and Disposition

For the reasons I have given above, I would allow the appeal in part, and dismiss the cross-appeal. Reluctantly, I would also order a new trial.

I conclude with two observations. The first is that many aboriginal nations with territorial claims that overlap with those of the appellants did not intervene in this appeal, and do not appear to have done so at trial. This is unfortunate, because determinations of aboriginal title for the Gitksan and Wet'suwet'en will undoubtedly affect their claims as well. This is particularly so because aboriginal title encompasses an *exclusive* right to the use and occupation of land, i.e., to the *exclusion* of both non-aboriginals and members of other aboriginal nations. It may, therefore, be advisable if those aboriginal nations intervened in any new litigation.

Finally, this litigation has been both long and expensive, not only in economic but in human terms as well. By ordering a new trial, I do not necessarily encourage the parties to proceed to litigation and to settle their dispute through the courts. As was said in *Sparrow*, at p. 1105, s. 35(1) "provides a solid constitutional base upon which subsequent negotiations can take place". Those negotiations should also include other aboriginal nations which have a stake in the territory claimed. Moreover, the Crown is under a moral, if not a legal, duty to enter into and conduct those negotiations in good faith. Ultimately, it is through negotiated settlements, with good faith and give and take on all sides, reinforced by the judgments of this Court, that we will achieve what I stated in *Van der Peet*, *supra*, at para. 31, to be a basic purpose of s. 35(1) — "the reconciliation of the pre-existence of aboriginal societies with the sovereignty of the Crown". Let us face it, we are all here to stay.

NOTE

Cory and Major JJ. concurred with Lamer C.J. The reasons of LaForest, L'Heureux-Dubé and McLachlin JJ. have been omitted. Sopinka J. took no part in the judgment.

QUESTIONS

1. In what way does the *sui generis* concept of Aboriginal title differ from the rights inherent in fee simple ownership?

2. Proof of occupation is central to a claim of common law aboriginal title. What does occupation mean in this context?

3. In Lamer C.J.'s judgment, an analogy was drawn between the limitations on use inherent in lands held under common law Aboriginal title, and the ancient doctrine of equitable waste (discussed earlier in this chapter). Is this analogy apt?

4. In *Delgamuukw* it was held that lands held under Aboriginal title must not be used in a way that is irreconcilable with the nature of the group's attachment to the land underlying the entitlement. What is the legal effect of an irreconcilable use?

5. Outline the test used in Canadian law for the recognition of Aboriginal rights other than rights to Aboriginal title. Does it make sense to have different criteria? Is a site-specific Aboriginal right a *sui generis* interest in land? Using the analysis of Russell Barsh introduced in Chapter 2, analyse Lamer C.J.'s spectrum of Aboriginal rights.

6. Based on the analysis in *Delgamuukw*, describe the nature of the Crown's fiduciary obligations to Canada's First Nations.

7. In *Delgamuukw*, a line seems to be drawn between state action that *infringes* an Aboriginal right and action that *extinguishes* such a right. For example, it was held the provinces lacked authority to extinguish Aboriginal title. However, it was also said (at para. 160) that "[t]he Aboriginal rights recognized and affirmed in s. 35(1), including Aboriginal title, are not absolute. Those rights may be *infringed*, both by the federal (*e.g., Sparrow*) and *provincial (e.g., Côté) governments*". In other words, even though provincial governments cannot extinguish Aboriginal title, they may validly infringe such rights. Again, at para. 165 it is said that "[t]he general principles governing justification laid down in *Sparrow*, and embellished by Gladstone, operate with respect to *infringements* of Aboriginal title." Likewise, in *R. v. Van der Peet*

[1996] 2 S.C.R. 507, 1996 CarswellBC 2309, 1996 CarswellBC 2310, reconsideration refused (January 16, 1997), Doc. 23803 (S.C.C.), Lamer C.J. stated (at para. 28) that "[s]ubsequent to s. 35(1) Aboriginal rights cannot be extinguished and can only be regulated or infringed consistent with the justificatory test laid out by this Court in *Sparrow*". [Emphasis added throughout.]

Does all of this mean that the federal government is no longer constitutionally competent to expropriate Aboriginal title lands? Is the distinction between infringement and extinguishment a stable one? What does the general law of takings suggest?

8. In 1839, the Chippewas of Southwestern Ontario purported to sell lands to C. The Crown had been advised of the negotiations for the sale, and the agreement for sale was approved by an order in council. Title to the lands did not pass until 1853, at which time letters patent for the lands were issued to C by the colonial governor. The sale was not a surrender properly so-called. However, the order in council was consistent with the idea that there would be a formal surrendering of the lands, and the letters patent were apparently issued under the mistaken belief that a valid surrender had occurred. About 150 year later, the Band disputed title to the patented lands. During the intervening period, the property had been sold and resold on numerous occasions by private owners who were unaware of the irregularities of the initial acquisition from the Chippewas. Applying the principles set out in *Delgamuukw*, can the Band succeed in reclaiming title? See *Chippewas of Sarnia Band v. Canada (A.G.)* 41 R.P.R. (3d) 1, 2000 CarswellOnt 4836 (C.A.), leave to appeal refused 2001 CarswellOnt 3952, 2001 CarswellOnt 3953 (S.C.C.), reconsideration refused 2002 CarswellOnt 1903, 2002 CarswellOnt 1904 (S.C.C.), to be studied in Chapter 12, and also K. McNeil, "Extinguishment of Aboriginal Title in Canada: Treaties, Legislation, and Judicial Discretion" (2001-2) 33 Ottawa L. Rev. 301.

T. Flanagan, *First Nations? Second Thoughts* (Montreal & Kingston: McGill-Queen's U.P., 2000) at 130-3 [footnotes omitted]

While it is beneficial to have the legal question of extinguishment in British Columbia settled [by *Delgamuukw*], in a practical sense it does not make much difference. This is because the provincial government had already admitted that modern treaties were necessary and had embarked in 1993 upon a course of tripartite negotiations with First Nations and the federal government. Debates over extinguishment may move now to Quebec and the Atlantic provinces, where the seventeenth- and eighteenth-century treaties of submission do not mention surrender of Indian title to the land. *Delgamuukw's* principle of federal extinguishment will not apply straightforwardly in eastern Canada, where the issue is complicated by the transition from French to British sovereignty. I would not presume to predict the outcome of the litigation that, I think, is certain to arise sooner or later.

Second, the Lamer doctrine makes an intellectual advance beyond the *St Catherine's Milling* case. As noted earlier, the JCPC recognized only the lowest common denominator of usufructuary rights. Lamer's spectrum of aboriginal rights, including site-specific usu-fructuary practices as well as the ownership right of aboriginal title, can recognize the variety of property rights that had emerged in different aboriginal cultures. In particular, it may offer a better fit than *St Catherine's Milling* ever could with the relatively sedentary culture of the West Coast Indians.

Unfortunately, however, the Lamer doctrine defines aboriginal title as collective without considering any argument to the contrary. There is in fact considerable historical evidence that aboriginal property rights were, if not individual in the modern sense, held by families rather than by the community at large. The anthropologist Adrian Tanner concludes that "the model of aboriginal title laid out in Delgamuukw . . . exclusively involving a collective right, one that can be sold, although only to the Crown, thus already represents a major transformation and simplification of not only prehistoric aboriginal practice, but also of some practices of aboriginal people that have continued to the present."

The Lamer doctrine, moreover, by typecasting aboriginal title as collective, makes its own application in a modern market economy difficult. Even if the courts in British Columbia were to award substantial tracts of land under the heading of aboriginal title, the owners would have to manage those lands through internal political processes. Communal ownership is an awkward instrument in a dynamic market economy. Profitable opportunities are likely to pass before all the meetings and votes necessary to make a decision can be held. Prospective business partners may not be absolutely deterred, but they will perceive higher risk and cost and will have to adjust their terms accordingly.

Similarly, the principle of inalienability except to the Crown limits the usefulness of aboriginal title. It will prohibit the owners not only from selling any of their lands but also from mortgaging them to raise investment capital. It raises all of the same problems that have plagued Canada's Indian reserves in the past, where the principle of inalienability has also applied. Similarly, Lamer's "inherent limit" on the use of land held under aboriginal title restricts its economic usefulness. Land is most valuable when it can be put to its most profitable use. Potential restrictions on use that in particular cases can be articulated only by the courts cannot help but detract from economic value by introducing uncertainty.

A market economy has to be undergirded by a set of rules about ownership that make efficient exchanges possible. It took centuries for English property law to progress from feudal notions of entailment to the modern conception of ownership in fee simple. Property law now unites the owner with the decision-maker and facilitates all sorts of transactions, including subdivision, sale, mortgage, and inheritance, thereby allowing land and natural resources to find their most efficient, highest-value usage. Collective, inalienable title, on the other hand, will tend to render land and resources legally immobile. Michael Warby's comments about Aboriginal property rights in Australia are equally applicable here: "It is not possible to achieve industrial-age life expectancies in an industrial-age society with hunter-gatherer notions of illness, causality and nutrition. Similarly, it is not possible to achieve industrial-age standards of living with hunter-gatherer notions of asset management or social organization. In particular, the choice of communal, inalienable title is the choice of poverty: as the experience of the command economies have shown very clearly."

In the Canadian context, Chief Justice Lamer's theory of infringement is the sword that cuts the Gordian knot of communal, inalienable, aboriginal title. Government can legally do the things that the aboriginal owners cannot, as long as it engages in appropriate consultation and pays appropriate compensation, both subject to judicial review. This notion of infringement may save the day in a practical sense, but as legal theorist Kent McNeil points out, its logical status is questionable. Aboriginal title, as part of aboriginal rights, is constitutionally protected under section 35(I) of the *Constitution Act, 1982*. In fact, aboriginal title is the only kind of property right to enjoy constitutional protection in Canada. "Since when," asks McNeil, "can constitutional rights be overridden for the economic benefit of other Canadians who do not have equivalent rights? Isn't this turning the Constitution on its head by allowing interests that are not constitutional to trump rights that are?" He has a point. The criticism is particularly relevant since Chief Justice Lamer relied on McNeil's publications at several key points in his opinion.

There are problems of economic efficiency as well as logic. Only government can infringe aboriginal title. That is, the blockages imposed by one collectivist institution — aboriginal title — can be overcome only by another collectivist institution — government. In this scenario, politics is likely to trump economic rationality as elected officials use the power of government to make allocative decisions that ought to emerge from market transactions.

These are all serious issues, but they may be dwarfed in significance by the legal uncertainty *Delgamuukw* has created. In spite of its attempt at conceptual sophistication, the Lamer doctrine leaves most of the pressing practical issues unsettled. As one critic has said, *Delgamuukw* "undermined everything but settled nothing." How much of British Columbia is subject to aboriginal title and site-specific aboriginal rights? How will aboriginal title and rights be proved? How much consultation and compensation will be required in cases of infringement? The only answer to these vital questions is that the courts will have to decide through further litigation. It is a lawyer's dream but an entrepreneur's nightmare.

Sadly, Canada's aboriginal people seem as far as ever from attaining a workable system of property rights. The treaties and the *Indian Act* have conspired to imprison them within a regime of collective rights that fit badly with the needs of a market economy. Now the Supreme Court of Canada, while asserting and redefining aboriginal property rights, has carved their collective and inalienable character in judicial stone. If there is anything for which Canadians should feel guilty, it is that our government, laws, and courts have kept Indians outside the world of individual property rather than encouraging them to step inside. . . .

(c) Aboriginal "estates" on reserves

The legislative regime governing Canada's reserve system is contained in the *Indian Act*, R.S.C. 1985, c. I-5 [as am.]. For land on reserves, as with Aboriginal title recognized by the common law, the rights are regarded as communal: *Joe v. Findlay Jr.* [1981] 3 W.W.R. 60, 1981 CarswellBC 35 (C.A.). Nevertheless, the Act contemplates that individual allotments may be made. Consider the effect of the following provisions, together with the case of *Okanagan Indian Band v. Bonneau*, which is reproduced below.

Indian Act
R.S.C. 1985, c. I-5 [as am.]

20. (1) No Indian is lawfully in possession of land in a reserve unless, with the approval of the Minister, possession of the land has been allotted to him by the council of the band.

(2) The Minister may issue to an Indian who is lawfully in possession of land in a reserve a certificate, to be called a Certificate of Possession, as evidence of his right to possession of the land described therein. . . .

(4) Where possession of land in a reserve has been allotted to an Indian by the council of the band, the Minister may, in his discretion, withhold his approval and may authorize the Indian to occupy the land temporarily and may prescribe the conditions as to use and settlement that are to be fulfilled by the Indian before the Minister approves of the allotment.

(5) Where the Minister withholds approval pursuant to subsection (4), he shall issue a Certificate of Occupation to the Indian, and the Certificate entitles the Indian, or those claiming possession by devise or descent, to occupy the land in respect of which it is issued for a period of two years from the date thereof.

(6) The Minister may extend the term of a Certificate of Occupation for a further period not exceeding two years, and may, at the expiration of any period during which a Certificate of Occupation is in force

> (*a*) approve the allotment by the council of the band and issue a Certificate of Possession if in his opinion the conditions as to use and settlement have been fulfilled; or
>
> (*b*) refuse approval of the allotment by the council of the band and declare the land in respect of which the Certificate of Occupation was issued to be available for re-allotment by the council of the band. . . .

24. An Indian who is lawfully in possession of lands in a reserve may transfer to the band or another member of the band the right to possession of the land, but no transfer or agreement for the transfer of the right to possession of lands in a reserve is effective until it is approved by the Minister.

25. (1) An Indian who ceases to be entitled to reside on a reserve may, within six months or such further period as the Minister may direct, transfer to the band or another member of the band the right to possession of any lands in the reserve of which he was lawfully in possession.

(2) Where an Indian does not dispose of his right of possession in accordance with subsection (1), the right to possession of the land reverts to the band, subject to the payment to the Indian who was lawfully in possession of the land, from the funds of the band, of such compensation for permanent improvements as the Minister may determine. . . .

28. (1) Subject to subsection (2), any deed, lease, contract, instrument, document or agreement of any kind, whether written or oral, by which a band or a member of a band purports to permit a person other than a member of that band to occupy or use a reserve or to reside or otherwise exercise any rights on a reserve is void.

(2) The Minister may by permit in writing authorize any person for a period not exceeding one year, or with the consent of the council of the band for any longer period, to occupy or use a reserve or to reside or otherwise exercise rights on a reserve. . . .

38. (1) A band may absolutely surrender to Her Majesty, conditionally or unconditionally, all of the rights and interests of the band and its members in all or part of a reserve. . . .

42. (1) Subject to this Act, all jurisdiction and authority in relation to matters and causes testamentary, with respect to deceased Indians, is vested exclusively in the Minister and shall be exercised subject to and in accordance with regulations of the Governor in Council. . . .

45. (1) Nothing in this Act shall be construed to prevent or prohibit an Indian from devising or bequeathing his property by will. . . .

(3) No will executed by an Indian is of any legal force or effect as a disposition of property until the Minister has approved the will or a court has granted probate thereof pursuant to this Act. . . .

48. (1) Where the net value of the estate of an intestate does not, in the opinion of the Minister, exceed seventy-five thousand dollars or such other amount as may be fixed by order of the Governor in Council, the estate shall go to the survivor.

(2) Where the net value of the estate of an intestate, in the opinion of the Minister, exceeds seventy-five thousand dollars, or such other amount as may be fixed by order of the Governor in Council, seventy-five thousand dollars, or such other amount as may be fixed by order of the Governor in Council, shall go to the survivor, and

(*a*) if the intestate left no issue, the remainder shall go to the survivor, (*b*) if the intestate left one child, one-half of the remainder shall go to the survivor, and

(*c*) if the intestate left more than one child, one-third of the remainder shall go to the survivor,

and where a child has died leaving issue and that issue is alive at the date of the intestate's death, the survivor shall take the same share of the estate as if the child had been living at that date.

(3) Notwithstanding subsections (1) and (2),

(*a*) where in any particular case the Minister is satisfied that any children of the deceased will not be adequately provided for, he may direct that all or any part of the estate that would otherwise go to the survivor shall go to the children; and

(*b*) the Minister may direct that the survivor shall have the right to occupy any lands in a reserve that were occupied by the deceased at the time of death.

(4) Where an intestate dies leaving issue, his estate shall be distributed, subject to the rights of the survivor, if any, per stirpes among such issue.

(5) Where an intestate dies leaving no survivor or issue, the estate shall go to the parents of the deceased in equal shares if both are living, but if either of them is dead the estate shall go to the surviving parent.

(6) Where an intestate dies leaving no survivor or issue or father or mother, his estate shall be distributed among his brothers and sisters in equal shares, and where any brother or sister is dead the children of the deceased brother or sister shall take the share their parent would have taken if living, but where the only persons entitled are children of deceased brothers and sisters, they shall take per capita.

(7) Where an intestate dies leaving no survivor, issue, father, mother, brother or sister, and no children of any deceased brother or sister, his estate shall go to his next-of-kin.

(8) Where an estate goes to the next-of-kin, it shall be distributed equally among the next-of-kin of equal degree of consanguinity to the intestate and those who legally represent them, but in no case shall representation be admitted after brothers' and sisters' children, and any interest in land in a reserve shall vest in Her Majesty for the benefit of the band if the nearest of kin of the intestate is more remote than a brother or sister.

(9) For the purposes of this section, degrees of kindred shall be computed by counting upward from the intestate to the nearest common ancestor and then downward to the relative, and the kindred of the half-blood shall inherit equally with those of the whole-blood in the same degree. . . .

50. (1) A person who is not entitled to reside on a reserve does not by devise or descent acquire a right to possession or occupation of land in that reserve.

(2) Where a right to possession or occupation of land in a reserve passes by devise or descent to a person who is not entitled to reside on a reserve, that right shall be offered for sale by the superintendent to the highest bidder among persons who are entitled to reside on the reserve and the proceeds of the sale shall be paid to the devisee or descendant, as the case may be.

(3) Where no tender is received within six months or such further period as the Minister may direct after the date when the right to possession or occupation of land is offered for sale under subsection (2), the right shall revert to the band free from any claim on the part of the devisee or descendant, subject to the payment, at the discretion of the Minister, to the devisee or descendant, from the funds of the band, of such compensation for permanent improvements as the Minister may determine.

Okanagan Indian Band v. Bonneau
2003 CarswellBC 1155 (C.A.)

The Court:

I. *Overview*

This appeal concerns the proper construction of the intestate succession provisions of the *Indian Act*, R.S.C. 1985, C. I-5 (the "*Indian Act*").

In the trial court, the parties sought determination of a question of law arising from the following agreed facts. The late Tommy Alexander was an Indian and a member of the Okanagan Indian Band. He died intestate on 7 April 1995. The Okanagan Indian Reserve No. 1 is a "reserve" as defined in the *Indian Act*. The Okanagan Indian Band's right to the use and benefit of Okanagan Indian Reserve No. 1 is subject to any lawful right of possession that an individual member of the Band may have in respect to any portion of it, pursuant to the *Indian Act*. Prior to his death, Tommy Alexander was in lawful possession, pursuant to the provisions of the *Indian Act*, of a parcel of land situated within the boundaries of Okanagan Indian Reserve No. 1. At the time of his death, Tommy Alexander's closest living relatives were his five nieces and nephews, none of whom were members of the Okanagan Indian Band.

The action was brought by the respondent, who is the elected Chief of the Okanagan Indian Band, and was prompted by the administratrix of Tommy Alexander's estate having purported to sell the deceased's right of possession in the parcel of land to the appellants, who are members of the Okanagan Indian Band. The Attorney General of Canada was joined as the representative of Her Majesty.

The question of law the parties sought to have determined was this:

When an Indian dies intestate, and his closest living relatives at the time of his death are nieces and nephews, does any right of possession to land in a reserve held by that Indian pursuant to the *Indian Act*, R.S.C. 1985, c. I-5 (the "*Indian Act*"):

(a) go to those nieces and nephews pursuant to s. 48(6) of the *Indian Act*; or

(b) does it vest in Her Majesty for the benefit of the band pursuant to s. 48(8) of the *Indian Act*?

In his judgment dated 6 August 2002, Mr. Justice Taylor held that the right of possession vests in Her Majesty for the benefit of the band. His decision is reported at (2002), 216 D.L.R. (4th) 210, 2002 BCSC 748 (B.C. S.C. [Chambers]).

In our opinion, the conclusion the learned chambers judge reached on the question of law he was asked to determine accords both with the legislative history and purpose of the intestate succession provisions found in s. 48 of the *Indian Act* and with the relevant principles of statutory construction. . . .

[The Court of Appeal then recited the appropriate statutory provisions, including section 48, which is recited above.]

The appellants argue that the phrase "next-of-kin" as it appears in the first clause of subsection (8) must obtain its meaning from and be interpreted in the same way as "next-of-kin" in subsection (7). Thus they argue that the opening phrase of subsection (8) must modify the whole of the section, including the final portion, so that the interest in favour of Her Majesty on behalf of the Band would arise only where an intestate's interest in land in a reserve devolves to his next-of-kin by reason of the operation of subsection (7), and subsection (7) applies only where the intestate dies leaving no spouse, issue, parent, sibling and "no children of any deceased brother or sister".

IV. *Discussion*

We cannot agree with the construction of s. 48 of the *Indian Act* urged by the appellants.

First, their submission misconceives the purpose and effect of ss. (8) of s. 48. The submission that "next-of-kin" in the first clause of ss. (8) must be interpreted in the same way as "next-of-kin" in ss. (7) cannot be supported. "Next-of-kin" means "blood relatives". Clearly, the reference to "next-of-kin" in ss. (7) is to blood relatives beyond the degree of consanguinity of nieces and nephews. That is the plain and ordinary meaning of the phrase in its immediate context. However, that cannot be its meaning in ss. (8). If it were, the subsection would read (substituting "blood relatives beyond nieces and nephews" for the phrase "next-of-kin" and "nieces and nephews" for "brothers' and sisters' children"):

(8) Where an estate goes to [blood relatives beyond nieces and nephews], it shall be distributed equally among the [blood relatives beyond nieces and nephews] of equal

> degree of consanguinity to the intestate and those who legally represent them, but in no case shall representation be admitted after [nieces and nephews]

Read in that way, the subsection is self-contradictory and makes no sense. Parliament could not have intended such a result.

The true meaning of "next-of-kin" as the phrase is used in ss. (8) becomes clear upon considering the phrase in the context of the whole of s. 48 and its legislative history. As already observed, s. 48 sets out a scheme for intestate succession in respect of Indians who reside on a reserve. Subsections (1) to (7) of s. 48 rank the beneficiaries of such intestate succession. The surviving spouse and close blood relatives (that is, father, mother, brothers, and sisters) are ranked expressly for purposes of devolution in s-ss. (1) to (6). Subsection (6) provides further for nieces and nephews to take *per stirpes* [that is, they take the share that their parent would have taken if he or she had survived] if one or more of the intestate's siblings survives and *per capita* [that is, they share equally] if none of the intestate's siblings survives. If there is no surviving spouse and none of the specified blood relatives is surviving, ss. (7) provides that the next closest surviving blood relatives take.

Subsection (9) sets out the manner of computing degrees of consanguinity of blood relatives, and resort must be had to this subsection when there is no surviving spouse and the next-of-kin other than those specified in s-ss. (2) to (6) are to be considered.

Subsection (8) must be viewed in this context. While s-ss. (1) to (7) provide a comprehensive list of all who may be entitled to share in the estate and ss. (9) provides a formula for ranking all who are not expressly mentioned, ss. (8) deals with other subjects, namely, representation and the devolution of interests in land. We will return to the second of these later in these reasons. The first part of ss. (8) summarizes s-ss. (2) to (7) in respect of representation and adds that representation is not permitted for beneficiaries other than those specified. Thus, "next-of-kin" in ss. (8) refers to blood relatives generally, including those blood relatives expressly mentioned in s-ss. (2) to (7). The phrase is not qualified in ss. (8), as it is in ss. (7).

Accordingly, it is not correct to say, as the appellants urge, that ss. 48(6) applies in the circumstances of this case and that ss. 48(8) does not apply because it serves to identify the beneficiaries of devolution in other circumstances. Rather, ss. (8) does not apply because no question of representation arises on the question posed in this case, since it is an assumed fact that Tommy Alexander has no surviving siblings. Therefore, his nieces and nephews take *per capita* as provided in s. 48(6). Thus, the appellants' submission is founded on a misapprehension of the purpose of ss. 48(8).

This analysis can be supported by reference to the *Report on Statutory Succession Rights* (Vancouver: Law Reform Commission of British Columbia, December 1983) to which the chambers judge referred. The Report contains (in chapter II) helpful references to the evolution of the law of intestate succession along with an analysis of the scheme of distribution in force in British Columbia. In the Report, the following appears under the heading "Next-of-kin":

At common law, rules were developed to determine who was entitled to succeed to the property of one who died intestate. Because various courts had jurisdiction to determine rights of succession the rules which were developed to determine successors varied depending on the nature of the property concerned. The descent of real property was determined, for example, by courts of common law. The distribution of personal property was within the jurisdiction of ecclesiastical courts, which developed rules modelled on the civil law.

The rules to determine next-of-kin for the purposes of distributing personal property were codified in the English Statute of Distribution, 1670. In Canada, all the common law provinces enacted legislation patterned after that Act. In 1919 the Commissioners on Uniformity of Legislation in Canada commenced a project on devolution of real estate and intestate succession. Two uniform Acts were adopted in 1925. These have been revised periodically. The last revision was made in 1963. Our present legislation, which defines the next-of-kin for the purposes of intestate succession and which makes real and personal property subject to the same rules, is based upon that uniform legislation. Intestate succession is currently being reconsidered by the Uniform Law Conference. A new Uniform *Intestate Succession Act* has recently been tentatively accepted in principle.

As the chambers judge observed [at paras. 52-53] by reference to the *House of Commons Debates* (20 April 1951), during a meeting of the Special Committee, Indian intestacy, which preceded the repeal and re-enactment of the *Indian Act* S.C. 1951, c. 29, section 48 of the re-enacted statute was based on the proposed uniform *Intestate Succession Act* that had been prepared by the Conference of Commissioners on Uniformity of Legislation in Canada in August 1925. Thus, the provisions in the two acts regarding intestate succession are similar. . . .

[Subsection] 48(8) is concerned, save for its last clause, with representation. It has no application to the question posed in this case because no question of representation arises. The conflict between the phrase "next-of-kin" as it is used in ss. (7) and ss. (8) is therefore illusory. There is no conflict. Subsection 48(6) applies and the first three clauses of ss. 48(8) are irrelevant in the circumstances of this case.

We come now to the arguments concerning the alleged conflict between ss. 48(6) and the last clause of ss. 48(8). Subsection 48(6) provides for distribution of the estate down as far as nephews and nieces but the last clause of ss. 48(8) appears to take away the right of nearest of kin more remote than brother or sister to receive an interest in reserve land.

After consideration of the intestate succession provisions in s. 48 in the context of other provisions of the *Indian Act*, the chambers judge concluded that the specific provision in ss. 48(8) governing the disposition of any on-reserve interest in land to kin more distant than brothers and sisters must prevail over the more general provisions of ss. 48(6) dealing with the intestate distribution of any realty or personalty where the intestate person is survived by brothers and sisters or their children, and that the right of possession in the reserve land would therefore vest in Her Majesty the Queen for the benefit of the Band.

The chambers judge's analysis was in accord with applicable principles of statutory construction . . . In our view, he correctly identified a fundamental purpose of the Indian Act as the preservation of the land base or ancestral territory for the benefit of the band and its individual members. . . . Accordingly, he properly applied the above principles in his analysis of the alleged conflict between subsections (6) and (8) of s. 48 of the *Indian Act* in reaching his conclusion that the specific provision must prevail over the general.

Although we do not disagree with the approach adopted by the trial judge, it is not necessary to rely on the rule of statutory construction that he invoked. A consideration of the historical evolution of both the general laws of intestacy and s. 48 of the *Indian Act* leads to the same conclusion.

It is useful to remember at the outset that, until relatively recently in the history of the common law, the intestate devolution of land and of personal property were governed by different rules. That they might be treated differently under s. 48 of the *Indian Act* should, therefore, come as no surprise.

There are many authoritative accounts of this history. Because of their accessibility, we have found S.F.C. Milsom, *Historical Foundations of the Common Law*, 2nd ed. (Butterworths: London, 1981), Part II, pp. 99-239 and Theodore F. T. Plucknett, *A Concise History of the Common Law*, 5th ed. (Little Brown and Company: Boston, 1956), Part 6, pp. 711-746 to be helpful references, and the following remarks are drawn from those works.

The law of real property has its roots in Anglo-Saxon customary law and, later, in the feudal system of tenures. Succession to land was, for centuries, based on the rules of inheritance. As Professor Plucknett observed (at p. 712):

> The sanctity of inheritance as the great safeguard of family security is a theme which runs continually through the history of property. It would be hard to find a more striking illustration than the charter of 1066: the Conqueror's message of reassurance to the nation was in terms which all could appreciate: "I will that every child be his father's heir."

Rules were developed in early times to identify the proper heir. They were based on the doctrine of primogeniture, whereby the decedent's land devolved directly to the eldest living male descendant to the exclusion of all others and without the intervention of a representative. If there were no lineal descendants, the law looked to the descendants of the decedent's father (the decedent's brothers, sisters, nephews, nieces, and their issue); if no heir could be found in the father's lineal descendants, resort was had to the descendants of the decedent's grandfather (his uncles, aunts, cousins, etc.), and so on, until an heir was found. Throughout, males excluded females of the same degree and, if an heir was found on the intestate's side, the intestate's widow and her side were excluded entirely. Disputes as to who was entitled to inherit were resolved summarily by the assize of *mort d'ancestor* or by writs of right in the royal courts.

The devolution of personal property, on the other hand, was within the purview of the Church and the ecclesiastical courts, since intestacy was considered to be a sin. The process on an intestate death involved the appointment by the local Bishop of a personal representative to collect and make inventory of the intestate's personal property, to pay his debts, and to divide the remainder into three shares, one for the widow, one for the children, and one (the "dead man's share") for worthy causes. Abuses arose out of jurisdictional conflicts between the ecclesiastical institutions and the royal courts and, as a consequence, the *Statute of Distributions*, 1670, 22 & 23 Charles II, c. 10, was enacted. This statute prescribed a new scheme of distribution of personal property: heirs at law were now entitled to share, a deceased child could now be represented by his or her descendants, and the personal estate was now to be divided one-third to the widow and two-thirds to the children. If there were no children, the widow took one-half and the other half went to next-of-kin; if there were no widow, the children took the whole estate; and if there were no widow or children, the estate went to the next-of-kin. As the Law Reform Commission Report, *supra*, points out, at p. 6, all of the common law provinces of Canada enacted legislation patterned on the 1670 statute as a result of the recommendations of the Conference of Commissioners on Uniformity of Legislation. Moreover, the uniform legislation brought real property under the same regime as personal property . . .

The first *Indian Act*, 31 Vict. c. 42, S.C. 1869, c. 6, reflected the pre-1925 state of the law of devolution in respect of land. . . . Thus, as with land in English law, the interest in land and the personalty of an intestate descended lineally to his children; if there were no children surviving, the benefit of the intestate's land and personal property was transferred to the band. However, the intestate's widow was recognized by imposing, in both cases, an obligation to support her from the estate.

In the *Indian Act, 1876*, S.C. 1876, c. 18 (39 Vict.), an amendment and consolidation of the earlier statute, we find, in s. 9, a different scheme for distribution upon intestacy:

> 9. Upon the death of any Indian holding under location or other duly recognized title any lot or parcel of land, the right and interest therein of such deceased Indian shall, together with his goods and chattels, devolve one-third upon his widow, and the remainder upon his children equally; and such children shall have a like estate in such land as their father; but should such Indian die without issue but leaving a widow, such lot or parcel of land and his goods and chattels shall be vested in her, and if he leaves no widow, then in the Indian nearest akin to the deceased, but if he have no heir nearer than a cousin, then the same shall be vested in the Crown for the benefit of the band: But whatever may be the final disposition of the land, the claimant or claimants shall not be held to be legally in possession until they obtain a location ticket from the Superintendent-General in the manner prescribed in the case of new locations.

Thus, we see the influence of the *Statute of Distributions, 1670* with the introduction of the widow of the intestate into the scheme of distribution. Now, the intestate's land and personal property could devolve to the children, to the widow, or to the next-of-kin as distant as cousins. However, in the absence of anyone in these classes, the benefit of the land and personal property reverted to the band. Moreover, to ensure that the land remained in the hands of band members, no one within the permitted classes of beneficiaries could take possession of the land without obtaining a location ticket. Thus, there was a limitation on the devolution of land that did not apply to the devolution of personal property.

This scheme was maintained in the 1880 consolidation (S.C. 1880, c. 28 (43 Vict.), s. 20), the 1884 amendment (S.C. 1884, c. 27 (47 Vict.), s. 20), and the 1886 revision (R.S.C. 1886, c. 43, s. 20). However, the scheme set out in s. 20 was amended significantly by S.C. 1894, c. 32, s. 1. Now, representation was permitted among all lineal descendants of the intestate by providing for devolution *per stirpes* to that line (ss. 20(2)). Again, land and personal property were treated differently within the scheme. By ss. 20(4), if the intestate left no issue or widow, "all his property of whatever kind" would devolve upon his "nearest of kin"; however, "any interest which he may have had in land in a reserve shall be vested in Her Majesty for the benefit of the band owning such reserve if his nearest of kin is more remote than a brother or sister." Thus, personal property could devolve to more remote kin than could real property. As before, the beneficiary could not take possession of the land without obtaining a location ticket.

The scheme for intestacy remained essentially in this state until 1951, when the *Indian Act* was repealed and re-enacted by S.C. 1951, c. 29, s. 123. It is in the 1951 statute that the definition of "estate" appears for the first time in this statute, in terms identical to those in the statute under consideration, i.e., by ss. 2(1)(f): "'estate' includes real and personal property and any interest in land."

The appellant's contend that, because s. 2 of the current *Indian Act* defines "estate" to include interests in land and personal property, and because ss. 48(7) provides for devolution of a decedent's "estate" to next-of-kin beyond "children of deceased brothers and sisters", the provision in ss. 48(8) that any interest in land shall revert to the band if the nearest of kin is more remote than a brother or sister creates a manifest inconsistency. How can the estate, which includes the interest in land, pass to next-of-kin more remote than nieces and nephews pursuant to ss. (7), they ask, if ss. (8) means that the land, which is part of the estate, cannot devolve upon anyone more remote than a brother or sister?

Since the alleged inconsistency that is said to create the ambiguity arises initially from the definition of "estate" in the 1951 statute, it is instructive to consider the state of the relevant provisions of the statute before their repeal and re-enactment, that is, the provisions of the *Indian Act*, R.S.C. 1927, c. 98 and amendments.

Section 26 of the 1927 statute provided that the intestate's "property of all kinds, real and personal, movable and immovable, including any recognized interest he may have in land in a reserve, shall descend as follows. . . ." The scheme was as already outlined.

Section 29 provided for the situation where there were no children entitled:

> 29. In case any Indian dies intestate without issue, leaving a widow, all his property of whatever kind shall devolve upon her, and if he leaves no widow the same shall devolve

> upon the nearest of kin to the deceased: *Provided that any interest which he may have had in land in a reserve shall be vested in His Majesty for the benefit of the band owning such reserve if his nearest of kin is more remote than a brother or sister.* [Emphasis added.]

As already noted, the 1927 Act was repealed and re-enacted in 1951. The relevant sections of the 1951 statute are, for all intents and purposes, identical to the provisions under consideration. On examining them, we see that s. 48 has replaced s. 26 and that there have been some changes. Now, by s-ss. 48(5) and (6), parents, brothers, sisters, nieces and nephews are expressly mentioned whereas, in the prior statute, they were referred to generally as "nearest of kin" under s. 29. More importantly, we see that the words "property of all kinds, real and personal, movable and immovable, including any recognized interest he may have in land in a reserve" in s. 26, and "all his property of whatever kind" in s. 29, have been replaced, in s. 48, by the word "estate", which, as already noted, is defined in s. 2 as "includes real and personal property and any interest in land". Further, the proviso in s. 29 that an interest in reserve land cannot pass to nearest of kin more remote than a brother or sister is now expressed as a sub-clause of ss. 48(8).

In our view, the changes in language enacted by S.C. 1951, c. 29 and carried through into the current statute do not effect substantive changes to the law as it existed before 1951. The definition of "estate" is merely a comprehensive and more convenient mode of describing the property of an intestate. The proviso in the pre-1951 legislation that an interest in reserve land could not devolve to next-of-kin beyond brothers and sisters clearly excepted such interests in land from the general rule for devolution and resulted in a different rule in those circumstances for land and for personalty. Consequently, the expression of that exception in ss. 48(8) of the *Indian Act* represents merely a formalistic change and was not intended by Parliament to effect a substantive change in the law.

In the result, by operation of ss. 48(8), in all circumstances where the estate devolves to next-of-kin, an interest in reserve land is excepted if the next-of-kin is more remote than a brother or sister of the intestate. In those cases, the interest in land reverts to the Crown for the benefit of the band. It follows, in our view, that the chambers judge answered the question correctly. . . .

As we have concluded that the chambers judge answered the question correctly, the appeal must be dismissed.

QUESTIONS

1. In what way are the entitlements set out in the *Indian Act* the same as, or different from: (a) the rights of a fee simple owner; (b) entitlements arising under common law Aboriginal title?

2. Did the British Columbia Court of Appeal in this case treat the rights conferred under the *Indian Act* as *sui generis*?

3. What conception of the family or family relations inform the scheme of inheritance rights contained in the *Indian Act*?

7. ESTATES IN PERSONALTY

N. Crago, "Bequests of Tangible Chattels in Succession" (1999) 28 U.W.A. L. Rev. 199, at 199, 201-4, 213 [footnotes omitted]

Many testators bequeath chattels by way of successive interests — usually, but not always, to members of their families. This will typically be for the purpose of passing on, and keeping within the family, heirlooms or especially valuable chattels such as antiques, works of art and jewellery, and collections of various kinds.

In many cases this is done by way of a simple trust. The chattel may be given by the will to the trustee of the estate upon trust, say, to permit the testator's eldest child to use and enjoy the chattel for life, and possibly, after that person's death, upon a similar trust for his or her eldest child for life and, in any event, upon trust for the testator' s eldest great-grandchild then living, absolutely. Many variants of this basic scheme of disposition are possible and come readily to mind. . . .

It is well settled that the fundamental doctrines of estates and tenures in real property have no application to chattels at common law. Life estates and remainders may, of course, exist with respect to chattels in equity as incidents of a trust; and it is the certainty and flexibility associated with these that make the use of an express trust attractive where successive interests in chattels (or other kinds of property) are given by will. But the common law had, and still generally has, no concept of the limited ownership of a chattel such as a life interest or a term of years. "A gift of a chattel for an hour", it has been said, "is a gift of it forever". Historically, the reasons for this were said to be threefold: first, the inherently perishable nature of chattels; secondly, the interests of trade and commerce in goods; and thirdly, against this background, the discouragement of litigation. As Blackstone put it:

> By the rules of the ancient common law, there could be no future property, to take place in expectancy, created in personal goods and chattels; because, being things transitory, and by many accidents subject to be lost, destroyed or otherwise impaired, and the exigencies of trade requiring also a frequent circulation thereof, it would occasion perpetual suits and quarrels, and put a stop to the freedom of commerce, if such limitations in remainder were generally tolerated and allowed.

At common law, the ownership of a chattel, as distinct from its possession, is absolute and indivisible. Ordinarily there can be no *legal* life estate or entailed estate, and no *legal* remainder, and hence no *inter vivos* settlements of chattels analogous to strict settlements of land. Equity, therefore, duly made good this deficiency in the common law, and came to recognise and protect its own limited interests in chattels arising by way of trust, broadly analogous to those existing in real property. Trusts of chattels, like trusts of other property, have long been recognised and enforced in equity; but they are not our present concern. . . .

Looking at the matter historically, there appear to be at least four possible modes by which this type of bequest may validly operate. Each of these modes has emerged from ancient case law and has been espoused by one or more fo the commentators referred to above. It also appears that there is no clear authority in favour of any one mode. The four modes are as follows:

First, it is possible that the entire ownership of the chattel is given immediately by the will to L, R having merely an executory interest, which is not itself a form of property but which is analogous to an executory interest in land. Secondly, it is possible that the entire ownership is given immediately to R, L having merely possession of the chattel, for the purpose of use and enjoyment for life. The technical term for L's interest in this case, derived from Roman law, is a "usufruct". Thirdly, it is possible that, even though L is, by definition, *not* made an express trustee by the will, nevertheless he or she might be regarded in equity as a trustee by operation of law for himself or herself for life and then for R. Fourthly, although there is again, by definition, no express trust, the testator's personal representative, whether executor or administrator, might be regarded as trustee by operation of law for L for life, and then for R. For purposes of discussion, these four possible modes of operation may be called, respectively, the executory bequest mode, the usufruct mode, the life tenant-trustee mode, and the executor-trustee mode. Each of these modes, as one would expect, carries its own particular incidents and effects; and these will be noticed below. . . .

Because the common law recognises no limited ownership interest in chattels it follows that a non-trust disposition by will of a chattel in successive interests can only create a regime which is sui generis. Historically, the English courts enforced such a disposition, independently of equity, either as an executory bequest, or as a usufructary interest (or, in equity, by imposing a constructive trust upon the life tenant or, possibly, upon the testator's personal representative).

It is suggested that to treat such a disposition as valid at law is, essentially, anomalous — it is to salvage it by recourse to the dubious application of principles derived, on the one hand, from the common law of real property or, on the other, from Roman law. In either case, the legal and practical difficulties inherent in such a salvage operation significantly exceed the benefits.

The case is one requiring legislative reform under which the life tenant for the time being would be fixed with duties of trusteeship of the chattel. Such a regime would create a framework of accountability in which the rights of life of life tenants and remainder[er], and also third parties, would be clearly determined under the supervision of the Supreme Court in accordance with established equitable principles.

Re Troup
[1945] 2 D.L.R. 450, 1944 CarswellMan 57 (K.B.)

Dysart J.:

This is an originating motion for the interpretation of the holograph will of the late Elizabelth E. Troup. It is a friendly application, in which, by the consent of all interested parties, Mr. Stubbs acted as sole counsel. In the discharge of his conflicting duties, Mr. Stubbs has acted with fairness to all concerned.

The specific language to be interpreted is as follows:

> I Elizabeth Ede Troup of the City of Winnipeg in the Province of Manitoba, Herewith bequeath all my worldly goods & Money to my husband Forbes Paterson Troup.
>
> And at his demise all goods property & Money shall be divided between our family.
>
> Winnifred to take half and Dorothy 1 quarter. And 1 quarter to our son Forbes Robinson

The testatrix made the will in 1937 and died in 1944, having been predeceased by her daughter Winnifred.

Two questions are raised for determination, the first of which is:

> 1. The meaning of the words, "all my worldly goods & Money" that is, does this bequest cover both personalty and realty;

In order to determine the meaning of any particular words in a will, all other qualifying words of the document must be scrutinized — the whole context must be studied. It is only thus that the intention of the testator, as expressed, can be discovered and given effect to: *Perrin v. Morgan,* [1943] A.C. 399 at p. 406; *Re Bampfield,* [1944] 4 D.L.R. 593 at p. 604.

Standing by themselves, the terms "goods" and "money" relate only to personalty. The epithet "worldly" adds nothing to them, because "goods" and "money" are necessarily "worldly" things. The verb "bequeath", as expressing a gift by will, generally refers to personalty as distinguished from realty But that meaning is not necessarily so limited.

In the sentence which follows the quoted bequest, the subject-matter of the gift is referred to as "all goods property & Money". The added term "property" indicates that something more than goods and money were being disposed of, because the term "property" includes realty as well as personally. In as much as the estate in fact includes realty, the words "all . . . property" suggest that the real property was intended to be included in the bequest; especially so because there is no other reference to real estate, and the whole will suggests that the whole estate was intended to be disposed of.

There is also the rule of construction, that where a will has been made there is a presumption of law against intestacy of any part of the estate: *Re Harrison, Turner v. Hellard* (1885), 30 Ch. D. 390 at. pp. 393 and 395; *Re Bampfield* at pp. 604-5.

This possible view is supported by Jarman on Wills, 7th ed., vol. 2, p. 978, where it is said: "The phrase 'worldly goods,' though properly applicable only to personal estate, will include the realty if aided by the context." In support of this proposition, *Wright v. Shelton* (1853), 18 Jur. 445, is cited.

The answer to the first question must therefore be that the bequest covers both personalty and realty.

The second question is:

2. What limitation is imposed upon the estate passing to the husband by the words, "*And at his demise all goods property & Money shall be divided between our family*".

Clearly the testatrix attempted to limit the estate which she bequeathed to her husband by cutting it down, from an estate absolutely or in fee, to an estate for life. Estates in real property may be so limited, but it is otherwise with personalty.

In Williams on Personal Property, 18 ed., p. 438, which deals with attempts to limit estates in personally, it is said: "Personal property . . . is essentially the subject of absolute ownership. At common law, therefore, the settlement of such property, by the creation of estates in it, cannot be accomplished; nor can such property, by the present law, be so settled in equity, except by means of an imperative trust for investment of the money constituting such property . . ."

And at p. 439: "As by the common law there can be no estate in personal property, it follows that there can be no such thing as an estate for life in such property in the strict meaning of the phrase. Thus, if any chattel, whether real or personal, be assigned to A for his life, A will at once become entitled at law to the whole. By the assignment the property in the chattel passes to him, and the common law knows no thing of a reversion in such chattel remaining in the assignor."

I hold that the personalty cannot be affected by the attempted limitation; that no limitation is imposed upon the personalty, which I therefore passes absolutely to the husband alone.

As to the realty, the considerations are different. Real property may be limited in its estate, and it is possible to confer upon one person an estate for life, with a remainder to others. But the actual words of the bequest in this case appear without any such limitation. They amount to a devise of the entire land estate absolutely in fee simple. Those operative words are then followed by words purporting to limit the estate to one for life. The two bequests are repugnant to each other and cannot be brought into harmony. They cannot both stand; one or the other must give way. Authorities agree that in such circumstances the chief words of a bequest must prevail over the subsidiary words; that the whole estate so conferred must pass without the limitation.

It would be different if the words of limitation could be construed as an alternative gift; but there is no room for any such alternative in the language of the present case.

In *Re Phillips* (1944), 52 Man. R. 331, I had to deal with a will which devised and bequeathed all the testator's property to several named persons "to be equally divided between them, their heirs and assigns absolutely and forever." I held that the words "heirs and assigns" did not add to, nor detract from, the absolute estate, and were futile.

The case of *Re Foss,* [1940] 4 D.L.R. 791, 3 W.W.R. 61 is in point.

There the will read:

> I give, devise and bequeath my property, both real and personal to my wife Anne Foss to have and to hold to her my said wife and to her heirs and assigns forever.
>
> After my wife's death, the property shall be divided equally between they [sic] heirs . . . (p. 792)

It was there held that the gift to the widow was absolute, and that the attempted gift over to the heirs was merely the expression of a wish. See also *Re Masterson; Trevanion v. Dumas,* [1901] W.N. 172; affirmed on appeal, [1902] W.N. 192.

I therefore answer the second question by declaring that no limitation is imposed upon either the personal estate or the real estate; and that all the property passed to the husband absolutely. The children take nothing.

Costs out of the estate.

QUESTION

An Editorial Note at [1945] 2 D.L.R. 450 contains this assessment of the above judgment: "A clearer case of frustrating the evident intention of the testator to create life interests and remainders would be difficult to find." What other analyses were open to the Court in *Re Troup*?

CHAPTER 6

THE ORIGINS AND NATURE OF EQUITABLE INTERESTS

1. INTRODUCTION

It is a remarkable feature of English, and later Canadian law, that two quite separate rule systems developed, virtually side-by-side. Common law courts, administering common law principles (as interstitially altered by statute) were complemented by courts whose province was to apply principles of equity. This chapter focuses on equity and its impact — which is considerable — on rights over property.

In the period following the Norman Conquest, as local customs were coalescing into the common law of England, a separate development was underway. A vague, flexible, and discretionary form of justice, later to be called equity, was emerging as a juridical cure for the perceived shortcomings of the law. The source of this new body of doctrine was, at base, the Crown, to which special petitions were presented in appropriate circumstances. The task of reviewing these supplications was delegated to the office of the Lord Chancellor, and in time to a Court of Chancery presided over by the Chancellor.

The modern trust, as Peter Butt's discussion below reveals, is a creation not of the common law, but of the Chancery in the exercise of its equitable jurisdiction. The rudiments of a trust and its development are outlined below. So, too, are some of the episodes in the development of property doctrine in which equity has played a vital role. In this chapter we consider how equity has affected the property rights of women, as well as the place of equity in the context of Aboriginal rights. Moreover, equitable principles will have a prominent place in the remaining chapters.

2. THE ORIGINS OF EQUITY

P. Butt, *Land Law*, 4th ed. (Sydney: Law Book Co., 2001) at 89-97 [footnotes omitted]

The doctrines of tenures and estates provided an adequate basis for the land law of the early Middle Ages. They were the legal interpretation of the existing facts of feudalism. But when the feudal organisation fo society began to disappear and the relationship of lord and vassal ceased to represent a fact of political and economic importance, the feudal-based land law began to lose contact with the requirements of everyday life. We have already observed how the incidents of feudal tenure degenerated into forms of financial extortion; and their existence, together with the common law's refusal to permit the disposal of land by will ("devise"), provided an ever-growing incentive to find means to escape the restrictions of the land law.

The means of escape were discovered outside the common law, not within it. By the end of the 13th century, the distinction between judicial and executive functions had become sufficiently well marked to deter the royal courts from broadening the common law on their own initiative. The common law had become rigid, bound by a formalism that insisted that a remedy could be obtained only through the medium of an existing form of writ; and in the case of land law, the number of writs was effectively closed.

Faced with the rigidity of the common law, the landowner turned to the "use". The basis of this institution was the transfer of property to a trusted friend, who was to hold it not for personal benefit but for the purpose of carrying out the transferor's instructors. Throughout the Middle Ages, indeed, even back beyond the Norman Conquest to Anglo-Saxon times, there can be traced a thin stream of these transactions, carried out for a multitude of purposes. For example, they were employed by knights who, going overseas on the Crusades, were anxious to leave their lands in safe hands; and by Franciscan friars, whose vows of poverty forbade ownership of land but not the enjoyment of land owned by others.

The person to whom the land was conveyed for this purpose was the "feoffee to uses". The person for whose benefit the land was conveyed — the beneficiary — was the "*cestui que use*" (in the plural, "*cestuis que usent*"), from the law French "*cestui a que use le feoffment fuit fait*".

For our purposes, conveying land to uses had three chief advantages. First, feudal burdens could be evaded. Land was conveyed to two or more joint feoffees ("joint tenants") in fee simple "to the use of" the grantor. The feoffees thus became the legal owners of the fee simple, and they alone were subject to the tenurial incidents. The most burdensome incidents took effect on inheritance of the land; but they did not apply on the death of one of a number of joint tenant(s) by right of survivorship and not by inheritance. And when the number of joint tenants dropped to one, the tenurial incidents on inheritance could be avoided by a conveyance from the surviving tenant to a new set of joint feoffees to uses. Though the feoffees were "seised", they allowed the beneficiary into possession. In this way the beneficiary enjoyed the advantages of ownership without suffering its burdens. And since the beneficiary had possession but not seisin, no feudal incidents arose on the beneficiary's death.

The second advantage was that uses could be disposed of by will. A landowner could convey land to feoffees to hold to the uses declared in the conveyor's will. This bypassed the common law prohibition against devises of land. The feoffees held the land to the conveyor's use until the conveyor died, and thereafter to the uses declared by the conveyor's will.

Thirdly, uses provided a means of overcoming many of the rigid rules of common law conveyancing. . . .

The Court of Chancery and the Use

The success of the use depended on the extent to which feoffees could be trusted or coerced. Until the 14th century, the frequency of uses had not been sufficient to provoke serious litigation; perhaps that was why they had not been incorporated into the common law. But their increasing popularity led to inevitable frauds by dishonest feoffees, and if the use was to survive some remedy had to be found. The common law refused to protect the cestui que use, for the accepted doctrines of the common law had no place for separate legal and beneficial ownership of land. The feoffees to uses had seisin; the *cestui que use* did not, and no forms of action were available to protect a beneficial interest divorced from seisin.

Thus it was that the Chancellor began to receive petitions to redress grievances arising out of the use. Precisely when the Chancellor first intervened in the interest of the *cestui que use* is not known; but certainly by the second half of the 15th century he was applying consistent principles to protect beneficial interests behind the use. The Chancellor based his intervention on the premise that consciences of the feoffees bound them to observe the terms of the use — that it was unconscionable, even though not strictly illegal, for feoffees to disregard the terms of the use. While the common law regarded the feoffees as the owners of the land, the Chancellor compelled them to exercise their legal rights consistently with the terms of the use.

The Chancellor enforced the beneficial interest not merely against the original feoffees, but against all who came to the land in such a way that in conscience they could not disregard the interest. So, for example, the use bound a person who received the land as a gift; this included heirs or devisees of a sole remaining feoffee. In conscience, a donee could not claim a greater interest than that of the donor. The use bound even a purchaser for value from the feoffee if, at the time of the purchase, the purchaser knew or ought to have known of the existence of the use, for to purchase with notice that the feoffee was selling in breach of the beneficiary's interest was to be a party to the breach. On the other hand, the conscience of a purchaser buying the legal interest from the feoffees was not bound if the purchaser acted honestly and without knowing of the beneficiary's interest; and so here the purchaser was allowed to disregard the beneficiary's claims. In this lay the origin of the modern doctrine of "notice". In its developed state, the doctrine of notice ensures that a beneficial interest affecting the legal ownership of land binds all who come to the land, except those who are *bona fide* purchasers for value of a legal interest in the land without notice of the beneficial interest.

Once the interest of the *cestui que use* came to be enforceable against third parties in this way, it had acquired the characteristics of a proprietary interest. Nevertheless, the juridical basis of the Chancellor's intervention remained unchanged: what was bound was the conscience of the person into whose hands the legal estate fell, not the land or the estate itself. Hence the maxim, "equity acts in personam".

We have seen the feoffee to uses was the legal owner of the estate, but that behind the legal ownership lay a beneficial ownership enjoyed by the *cestui que use*.

This division between legal ownership and equitable ownership proved pivotal in the history of land law.

In developing the concept of equitable ownership, successive Chancellors largely followed the common law by analogy. For example, they adopted the doctrine of estates: the *cestui que use* might have an equitable fee simple, and equitable fee tail, or an equitable life interest. But the Chancellors regarded themselves as free to depart from the rigid rules of the common law, enabling the creation in equity of interests that had no parallel in the courts of common law. As we will see, this freedom — perhaps an accidental by-product of the use — became the most important feature in the development of land law. It served to perpetuate the use long after the disappearance of the tenurial incidents which had been the first cause of its popularity.

The Statute of Uses

Purpose

During the 15th and 16th centuries, it became a common practice for large landowners in England to have the legal title held for their use. This considerably reduced their exposure to the burdensome feudal tenurial incidents. This in turn reduced the income for the royal coffers — for, as we have seen, the process of escheat and the abolition of subinfeudation had slowly but surely concentrated the financial benefits of tenurial incidents into the royal coffers. In order to avoid such losses in the future, in 1535 Henry VIII forced upon an unwilling Parliament the *Statute of Uses*.

The purpose of the statute was disarmingly simple: to divest the legal estate from the feoffee to uses and vest it in the *cestui que use*. The chief section, s. 1, provided essentially as follows:

> Where any person is seised of any lands to the use, confidence or trust of any other person or corporation, the latter person or corporation shall be deemed in lawful seisin, estate and possession of the lands for the same estate as he or it had in the use, confidence or trust.

The purpose was not to abolish uses, but to preclude their employment as a revenue-defeating device. By converting the *cestui que use*'s equitable interest into a legal interest, the feudal incidents would be revived. The statute applied not only to uses in existence when the Statute came into operation, but also to all future limitations.

Operation

The operation of the statute may be illustrated by the following example. Assume a conveyance of land to a feoffee to uses (F) to the use of a *cestui que use* (A). The conveyance would take the following form:

to F and his heirs to the use of A and his heirs.

(The words "and his heirs" — known technically as "words of limitation" — ensured that a fee simple interest was conferred, not a lesser interest such as a life estate or an estate tail. We discuss words of limitation in later chapters.) Before 1535, a conveyance in this form would have passed the legal fee simple to F and the equitable fee simple to A. After the *Statute of Uses*, however, the same conveyance would vest the legal fee simple in A. The statute "executed" the use, and F took nothing. Further, by the terms of the statute, A was deemed to be in possession of the land, even though A had never in fact entered it.

The *cestui que use* obtained by force of the statute a legal estate corresponding in quantum to the interest which, but for the statute, the *cestui que use* would have taken in equity. To illustrate, assume a grant

to F and his heirs to the use of A for life, with remainder to the use of B and her heirs.

Before the statute, this grant would have passed the legal fee simple to F, an equitable life estate to A, and an equitable remainder in fee simple to B. After 1535, F took nothing. A took a legal life estate, and B took a legal remainder in fee simple.

The *Statute of Uses* proved to be fundamentally important in the later development of land law, although in a manner unimagined in 1535. A number of chief aspects of the statute's operation may be noted:

Resulting uses

The statute executed resulting uses as well as uses expressly created (express uses). Consider a conveyance before 1535

to F and his heirs to the use of A for life.

The conveyor has conveyed the whole legal estate (to F) but only part of the equitable estate, namely, a life estate (to A). The remnant of the equitable estate — the reversion in fee simple — stays vested in the conveyor: there is a "resulting use" of this reversionary interest. The statute executed this resulting use. Accordingly, in the same conveyance after 1535, F took nothing. A took a legal life estate, and the conveyor took the legal fee simple in reversion.

Active uses

By contrast, the courts held that the statute did not execute active uses, that is, uses where the feoffee had active duties to perform. This conclusion appears to have been based on the premise that the statute effected a "Parliamentary conveyance" of the land from the feoffee to the *cestui que use* in the same way as the feoffee could lawfully have done before the statute — and a feoffee with active duties to perform could not lawfully have conveyed the legal estate to the *cestui que use*, for that would breach the terms by which the feoffee held the land. Thus, if the land were conveyed

> to F and his heirs to the use that F should collect the rents and profits and pay them to A and her heirs

the legal fee simple remained in the feoffee, A taking an equitable fee simple only (implied by the right to the rents and profits).

Feoffee must be seised

The statute applied only where the feoffee to uses was *seised.* And so it did not apply where the feoffee to uses held only a leasehold interest, for a leaseholder had no seisin. And so in a conveyance of a leasehold interest

> to F for 999 years to the use of A and his heirs

the statute did not execute the use. The conveyance took effect in equity as it had done before 1535. But as long as the feoffee was seised, the statute would apply even where the *cestui que use* was a leaseholder, as in a conveyance

> to F and his heirs to the use of A for 21 years.

Here F was seised, so the statute would vest the legal leasehold in A and the legal reversion in fee simple in the conveyor.

Not seised to own use

The statute did not apply where the feoffee was seised to his or her own use. It applied only where a person was seised to the use of another person. Thus, in a conveyance

> to F and his heirs to the use of F and his heirs

F held the legal fee simply by virtue of the common law, not be operation of the statute. The declaration of the use in F's favour simply showed that the use was also vested in F.

Use upon a use

Tyrrel's Case decided that the statute did not execute a use upon a use. To explain: it had been established before 1535 that in a conveyance

> to F and his heirs to the use of A and her heirs to the use of B and her heirs

F took the legal fee simple and A took the equitable fee simple, but B took nothing. The second use was "repugnant" to the first, and was invalid. By parity of reasoning, if there was no valid use in favour of B before 1535, then there was no use the statute could execute in B after that date. And so in the same conveyance after 1535 F took nothing. A took the legal fee simple, and B took nothing. . . . [H]owever, the Chancellor eventually changed his ruling on this. . . .

The Development of the Trust

Earlier we referred to *Tyrrel's Case* (1557), which held that a use upon a use was void. We saw that as a result of that decision, in a conveyance after 1535

to F and his heirs to the use of A and his heirs to the use of B and her heirs

A took the whole legal fee simple by the *Statute of Uses* and B took nothing. Doubtless the intention behind a conveyance in such terms would have been to separate the legal ownership from the equitable fee simple. But *Tyrrel's Case* rendered the attempt ineffectual. That remained the position for at least a century after the *Statute of Uses*. However, when in 1660 the *Tenures Abolition Act* abolished the burdensome feudal incidents, the Crown's financial interest in prohibiting equitable ownership ceased, and the Chancellors began to enforce the use upon a use. In the result, equitable interests in land could now be created as freely as before 1535.

To illustrate the change before 1535, in order to vest the legal fee simple in A for the benefit of B, the land would have been conveyed

to A and his heirs to the use of B and her heirs.

After the *Statute of Uses* and once the use came to be enforced, the same result could be achieved by conveying

to F and his heirs to the sue of A and his heirs to the use of B and her heirs.

The statue executed the use in A, giving A the legal fee simple (F taking nothing) and B the equitable fee simple. Of course, after 1535 a conveyance simply "to A and his heirs to the use of B and his heirs to the use of B and her heirs" would give B the *legal* fee simple, the statute executing the use in B's favour, A taking nothing.

The first instances of this development occurred before 1660. They appear to have been accompanied by some form of fraud, which on general equitable principles would be sufficient to take the case out of the statute. But after 1660 the existence of fraud ceased to be essential. Conveyancers began using the use upon a use for the avowed purpose of creating equitable ownership — not now to avoid feudal incidents or to acquire the power to devise, but to take advantage of the freedom the use allowed in manipulating beneficial interests.

A change in terminology also occurred. The new relationship became the 'trust", with the legal owner the "trustee". The old expressions "use", "feoffee to uses", and "*cestui que use*" were in practice reserved for those uses intended to be executed by the statute. The terminology in the form of grant also changed the phrase "in trust for" was employed to indicate the creation of an equitable interest, and the phrase "to the use of" was reserved for uses executed by the statute. The grant would now be expressed

to F and his heirs to the use of A and his heirs in trust for B and her heirs.

However, this change in terminology did not alter the reality that by an obvious ruse the statute had successfully been set aside and the Chancellor's jurisdiction over equitable ownership completely restored.

A further development was the increasing use of the formula "unto and to the use of". To illustrate, consider a conveyance

to A and his heirs to the use of A and his heirs in trust for B and her heirs.

Here A was seised to his own use, and so the statute did not operate. A took the legal fee simple by virtue of the common law. Nevertheless, the trust in favour of B was a use upon a use; it was not executed by the statute, but (by the time of which we are now speaking) it was enforced by the Chancellor. The formula "unto and to the use of A and his heirs" developed as a shorthand form of "to A and his heirs to the use of A and his heirs". In the result, trusts could now be created by the simple expedient of conveying land "unto and to the use of" the trustee "upon trust for" the beneficiary. Of course, if the drafter inadvertently drew the conveyance in the form "to" the trustee "upon trust for"the beneficiary, then (unless the trustee (feoffee) had active duties to perform) the *Statute of Uses* would execute the use, giving the intended equitable beneficiary the legal estate.

QUESTIONS AND COMMENTS

1. Analyse the following dispositions:

(a) Crown grant to John Snyder "in *trust* for his son Isaac Snyder, a lunatic, his heirs and assigns for ever, to have and to hold the same land to him the said John Snyder, his heirs and assigns for ever." *Doe d. Snyder v. Masters* (1852) 8 U.C.Q.B. 55.

(b) "To A in trust for B."

(c) "To A, to collect the rents and profits over Blackacre and to use these for the benefit of B for life; then in trust for C."

(d) To "Jane Long . . . To have and to hold to the said Jane Long, for the use and benefit of herself and children, Margaret, Robert, and Mary Long, their heirs and assigns for ever; and also to have and to hold the said parcel or tract of land hereby granted, conveyed, and assured unto the said Jane Long upon the conditions above stated, her heirs and assigns forever." *Long et al. v. Anderson* 1880 CarswellOnt 89, 30 U.C.C.P. 516.

(e) "to Annie Goldie, widow of the late Francis Goldie, deceased, formerly a sergeant in the 91st regiment of foot, her heirs and assigns, for ever, to have and to hold the said parcel or tract of land thereby given and granted to her the said Annie Goldie, in trust for herself and her children, Martha Goldie and Francis Goldie." *Goldie v. Taylor* 1856 CarswellOnt 373, 13 U.C.Q.B. 603.

2. As mentioned above, the principles of equity were administered through the Chancery and not by common law judges. By the latter half of the nineteenth century, this administrative structure became increasingly under attack. In consequence, reforms were introduced in England and elsewhere to combine the two court systems into one. The net effect of the fusion remains a matter of some debate. The better view, I believe, is that these measures created a procedural fusion but no more. In brief, superior courts were clothed with the capacity to apply both common law and equitable principles. Hence, for example, *The Court of Queen's Bench Act*, C.C.S.M. c. C280, s. 33(3) states: "The court shall administer concurrently all rules of equity and the common law." As this section implies, the principles of law and equity remain distinct. However, it is also true that the fusion has occasionally meant that equitable ideas have filtered into common law doctrine and *vice versa*: see generally *Canson Enterprises Ltd. v. Boughton & Co.* 1991 CarswellBC 269, [1991] 3 S.C.R. 534. *Cf. Chippewas of Sarnia Band v. Canada (Attorney General)* 2000 CarswellOnt 4836, 51 O.R. (3d) 641, 195 D.L.R. (4th) 135 (C.A.), leave to appeal refused 2001 CarswellOnt 3952, 2001 CarswellOnt 3953 (S.C.C.), reconsideration refused 2002 CarswellOnt 1903, 2002 CarswellOnt 1904 (S.C.C.), which is considered in Chapter 12.

3. As we have seen, the common law might regard one person as the holder of legal title, while equity will enforce a beneficial (equitable) entitlement held by someone else. Although it is conventional to say that equity does not contradict the law, but merely complements it, there is an inherent and obvious conflict when the two systems point to two different persons as *the* owner of a given property. When that does occur, the general rule is that the equitable right that will trump. That is a centuries-old proposition, one that is sometimes enshrined in legislation. For example, s. 33(4) of *The Court of Queen's Bench Act*, C.C.S.M., c. C280 provides that "Where a rule of equity conflicts with a rule of the common law, the rule of equity prevails."

This sweeping rule is qualified in various ways. For instance, equitable remedies have always been discretionary; in theory, one is never entitled to equitable relief, and a plaintiff may be disqualified from receiving redress by conduct. So, a party asserting an equitable right may be barred from enforcing it where there has been an unjustifiable delay in pursing that right; such a party is said to be precluded by the doctrine of laches from seeking the aid of equity. Second, in the context of property rights, equity may accord priority to a legal interest. As Professor Butt notes, equity will not impose an obligation on a person who is a *bona fide* purchaser for value of a legal interest when that person acquired the interest without notice of a prior equitable right. The rules governing priorities in equity will be reviewed in Chapter 12; for now, a simple example will help introduce the concept.

Assume that A holds title to Blackacre in fee simple. A then enters into a valid agreement to sell the land to B. We will see in more detail below that B is considered to hold an equitable interest in the property even before the formal conveyance of legal title. B's interest is equitable, provided always that equity would be willing to order specific performance of the contract for sale; let us assume so here.

Assume now that the real estate market is hot, and that A decides that a better price for the property might be obtained. In due course the land is sold again, this time to C. Legal title is conveyed to C, who all the time remains oblivious to the outstanding deal with B. We must also assume that even if C had made reasonable inquiries, the prior equitable interest held by B would not have been uncovered.

The situation now is this: B holds an equitable right, and C has subsequently obtained the legal title. On these facts, C is a *bona fide* purchaser of the legal title without notice (even constructive notice) of B's claim to the same land. Equity will prefer C in such a case, leaving B to sue A for damages arising from the blatant breaches of contract and trust.

In sum, an equitable right will trump a legal one, so long as equity considers that justice is served by doing so.

M. Conway, "Equity's Darling?" in S. Scott-Hunt & H. Lim, eds., *Feminist Perspectives on Equity and Trusts* (London: Cavendish, 2001) 27 [footnotes omitted]

INTRODUCTION

It is a truth universally acknowledged that equity has been the special friend of womankind, even that equity is a Sister. However, what is universally acknowledged is not necessarily true. While it is undeniably the case that equity has, from time to time, assumed the white knight role and ridden to the rescue of some damsel caught in the toils of the common law, it is much less certain that equity could ever rightfully claim to be a girl's best friend. . . .

Equity's credentials as the protector of women, historically, stem from the particular legal disabilities attaching to the married woman in English jurisprudence. Blackstone was able to put a positive "spin" on this. "Even the disabilities which the wife lies under, are for the most part intended for her protection and benefit. So great a favourite is the female sex of the laws of England." These disabilities are well known. During coverture, the woman's identity was merged with that of her husband — the fiction of marital unity. A married woman could not own property in her own right, she could neither sue nor be sued, had no rights over her own children, was not entitled to her own earnings, and did not even have to wait for her wedding day to find herself coming under the dominion of her husband-to-be, with the doctrine of restraint on anticipation. Single women were, of course, disenfranchised, but did have legal capacity, which their married sisters lacked. "It was not the fact of being female, but the status of wife that entailed severe legal disabilities." . . .

Christianity played a part in advocating the notion of the desirability of submissive and obedient wives, but was not the origin of the idea. "There is no doubt that Greeks and Romans, both men and women, had always accepted wifely subordination as an integral part of a well ordered family. The church fathers certainly thought that male domination was an important constituent of the Christian family. But, although they often cited the Bible for the submissive role of the wife, they never claimed that it would have been a particularly Christian idea. On the contrary, they believed that it was a commonly accepted part of the natural order." The idea of the "natural order" was also invoked to support the idea that men and women, or at least husbands and wives, occupied separate spheres, public and private respectively.

The disabilities within marriage were not addressed directly by equity; but women from wealthy families could have their property protected by trustees and specified to be for their sole and separate use, so that a husband would not have access to the property, nor be able to use it to settle his debts. When the marriage was in difficulty, and the parties had separated or divorced further problems arose. Not the least of these was the confusion of jurisdictions dealing with particular matters. No civil divorce was available before 1857, but in the preceding centuries, different procedures and arrangements were possible to enable the parties to live apart. "From the Middle Ages to 1857, there was no formal change at all in the official doctrine and practice of the canon law." The common law and equity had both complementary and conflicting roles in the process. The theoretical difficulties of the exact nature of marriage were not satisfactorily resolved — status or contract.

Marriage, at least amongst the landed classes, was often an exercise in dynastic engineering. The use of entails, settlements and the observance of primogeniture were inconsistent with the public policy of free alienability of land. However, the landed classes and the conveyancers combined were able to overcome these difficulties to their own satisfaction. The net effect of such practices was to limit severely the possibility of wives owning and dealing with property in their own right or daughters inheriting and thereby interfering with the male line of succession. Equity in these developments, as far as women were concerned, was by no means an invariably benign influence.

Throughout the 19th century, most of the legal disabilities for wives were eventually dealt with by legislation. The various *Married Women's Property Acts*, from the 1870s, enabled married women to own property and keep their own earnings. Civil divorce, in 1857, changed the marital landscape and the *Settled Land Act 1882*, by giving the powers of management to the tenant for life, took much of the sting out of the strict settlement. Such changes, of course, were not taking place in a political and social vacuum, but a lengthy consideration of the wider political, social, economic and religious forces, which wrought such changes in the 19th century, is beyond the scope of the present discussion.

Equity's traditional role of alleviating the harshness of the common law was perhaps more evident historically in protecting the rights of wives than of women generally. This practice continued into modern times: for example Lord Denning's famous campaign to create the "deserted wives' equity". It could be argued, however, that equity in some instances was used to defeat and destroy women's common law rights in order to protect succession in the male line.

. . . [F]ar from being the inevitable defender of women's rights, equity has occasionally provided the mechanism by which women's rights have been postponed or even eliminated. The common law, on the other hand, has not historically been the inevitable enemy of women. Nor should the role of legal practitioners, in and out of parliament, be ignored in this history.

IS THERE YET ANY PORTION OR INHERITANCE FOR US IN OUR FATHER'S HOUSE?

(Leah and Rachel, *Genesis*)

As Eileen Spring argues, the common law was not hostile to women in terms of inheritance. Where a daughter was the heiress at law, that is, a family with no sons but a daughter, she had a common law right to inherit. "The most important rules governing succession to lands were those of the common law. Of these the principal was primogeniture. Males excluded females of equal degree. Among males of equal degree only the eldest inherited, but females inherited together as co-heiresses." Operation of law, then, would transfer property to women, although only in default of a male heir. Where there was no power to alter the common law rule, daughters could inherit. It is the processes by which the common law rules were avoided that Eileen Spring investigates:

> From beginning to end, then, landowners' legal history is much to be seen as the effect to overcome the common law rights of daughters. It was heiresses whose rights threatened to divide estates. It was heiresses whose rights threatened to leave titles bare of land. It was heiresses who would alter the name tags associated with estates. . . . From the entail, to the use, to the strict settlement, what landowners were above all seeking was a means of dealing with the problem that female inheritance posed.

It is Equity's role in these processes which will be addressed. Eileen Spring identified the heiress at law as the target of these various devices — what she calls "ordinary daughters", that is, daughters who were not the heiress at law, ranked with younger sons in that the estate might have to provide for them, but who would inherit neither title nor land. Clearly, if landowners considered it necessary and desirable to maintain patrilineal succession, then it was incumbent upon them and their conveyancers to devise means of avoiding the common law rules. . . .

The strict settlement came to be the preferred method of arranging the transmission of property from one generation to the next. The modern form of settlement first emerged in the 17th century, as an elegant and typically English device to avoid the most stringent of the penalties for choosing the wrong side in the civil war. Land of traitors was forfeit, but if the traitor held only a life interest, then only the life interest could be forfeit. When land was settled, the form of the trust employed also operated very effectively to make inheritance in the female line a rare and precious thing. An example of equity not mitigating the harshness of the common law, but depriving women of their common law rights to inherit.

"In the simplest case, when it took place at the marriage of the eldest son, the settlement . . . limited the interest of the father to that of a life tenant, and made the eldest son a life tenant after the death of the father, the estate was to descend to his eldest son in tail." The purpose of this rather odd sounding arrangement was to keep the estate intact, by arranging for unitary, rather than partible inheritance, and to fragment the title, to reduce the possibility of any life tenant or tenant in tail endangering the estate by debt or sale. It was also, of course, an effective device to privilege sons over daughters.

Except for intestacy, primogeniture was not a legal requirement, and yet many landowners continued to observe the practice as though it were an obligation, not a choice. "It was natural for an established landowner to feel hat he was the temporary custodian of the family estate for his descendants." The settlement leaned in favour of primogeniture. . . .

Just as primogeniture was not obligatory, neither was the strict settlement ever given any official sanction. It was essentially a private matter between the landowner and his conveyancer. The landowner willed the end and the conveyancer provided the means. The third element required to make the settlements effective was that should they come to court, they would be enforced. . . . Once again, equity, by way of the trust, was used to defeat the common law rights of daughters to inherit. "The strict settlement was biased towards primogeniture; there was never any doubt that the elder son and his issue inherited before his younger brother, and that the sons took precedence over daughters." There was evidently a voluntary element to these arrangements. "The settlement of landed estates would not have lasted so long had it not commanded the acquiescence of the younger siblings . . ."

. . .

[T]he tide of law reform was gathering pace in the 19th century and, eventually, even the strict settlement had to yield. The *Settled Land Act 1882*, by giving powers of management to the tenant for life, effectively ended the power of the father to rule from beyond the grave. The entail, the compromise between the living and the dead, managed to hang on a bit longer, and was not finally ended until 1996. The same Act, although it preserved existing settlements, prevented the creation of new strict settlements. . . .

In terms of inheritance, then, it could be argued that the common law was a better friend to women than equity, and that equity by way of an alliance between dynastically minded landowners and artful conveyancers was deployed to deprive women of their rights which the common law would have provided. "It was on the large rights that the common law gave to females that landowners had their eyes fixed, and against which their conveyancing stratagems were fundamentally designed."

HIS DESIGNS WERE STRICTLY HONOURABLE, AS THE PHRASE IS: TO ROB A LADY OF HER FORTUNE BY WAY OF MARRIAGE

(Henry Fielding, *The History of Tom Jones*)

The legal disabilities of the married woman before 1882 have been well rehearsed, in particular, that the common law did not recognise the existence of the wife during the marriage. There can be no doubt that the circumstances surrounding marriage and the transmission of property in England, historically, were patriarchal.

> Patriarchy, I take it, is a form of social organisation in which fathers appear as political and legal actors, acting publicly for themselves and as representatives of the women and children subordinated to them and dependent on them in families. in the property regimes of patriarchy, descent and inheritance are reckoned in the male line; women function as procreators and as transmitters of inheritance from male to male.

"The provision of money and the getting of heirs was still the main function of women." Where the well endowed bride-to-be acquired her wealth is an interesting question, in the light of the foregoing discussion on inheritance. One route, of course, was the operation of law, whereby heiresses at law were allowed to inherit. Another is provision made in family settlements, where the land and title, if any, passed to the oldest son, and the estate provided portions for daughters and younger sons. "From the second half of the 17th century, the evolution of the strict settlement meant it had become customary to make provision for younger sons and daughters." Eileen Spring argues that writers of legal history have often represented portions for daughters as both generous and growing in size without taking into account the fact that portions were often paid to the heiress at law, who would, but for the machinations of landowners and their conveyancers, have inherited.

The main engines of perpetuating the system were the idea of primogeniture, entails and the strict settlement. "Within the family itself, the strict settlement also represented an important patriarchal weapon against any, other form of delinquency by heirs and heiresses." Within this very limited space, the common law made some provision for married women, and, more particularly, for widows. Common law dower provided that a widow should have one-third of the income of any real property of which her husband had been seised during his life. This provision had the potential to act as a fetter on the free alienability of land, and was eventually replaced by the jointure.

In those circumstances, it could be argued that equity assisted in the process of depriving widows of their dower. . . . Dower could not attach to property held in trust. . . .

The move from dower to jointure has been the subject of much academic debate. It clearly represents a move from status to contract, and it is equally clear that there was a trade off between portions and jointures. Not all commentators have interpreted the data as Spring has done, or accepted her argument that heiresses have been effectively cheated, and that equity has been instrumental in a kind of fraud. "The female disinheritance thesis is framed by the glow of common law rights. But no adequate theory or explanation for why the common law rules . . . took the form that they did is developed. It is as if it suffices that these rules were there. And that there was a later self-evident male conspiracy against dower."

What is less contentious is the contractual nature of the relationship between portion and jointure. "Women who contributed portions to their marriage expected in return to be maintained should they be widowed. By the 16th century fewer and fewer wives put their faith in the common law right of dower enshrined in *Magna Carta* . . .". The ratio was an indication of the relative bargaining powers of the families, and there is some evidence to support the view that the size of portions increased over time in relation to the value of the jointure which it could secure. "It has been pointed out that the average ratio of dowry (given by the father) to jointure (settled on the girl by the bridegroom's family) rose from four or three to one in the middle of the 16th century to between eight and 10 to one by the end of the 17th."

In marriages between equals in aristocratic circles, portions of £10,000 to £50,000 were perhaps normal, and the bride would expect a jointure of 10% at least on her fortune . . . In fact, the tariff laid down at the time of the marriage, both in respect of jointure and of portions for younger children whose numbers were unpredictable, was a minimum which was quite often augmented by will as circumstances and affection allowed. It was thus a complicated matter to arrive at the going rates of the marriage market and negotiations of some delicacy might be called for, with the family solicitor in reserve to say what was normal in any given case.

Paraphernalia, the personal clothing and ornaments which the bride brought to the marriage, was an exception to the general common law rule that all the wife's personal property at the time of the marriage belonged absolutely to the husband. Since the wife was the "shadow" of her husband, she had no capacity to contract on her own behalf, but was entitled to pledge her husband's credit for necessaries. This corresponded to the common law duty of the husband to maintain his wife. The law of agency was used to explain the wife's ability to pledge, and it is interesting to observe that this agency argument has, until relatively recently, still been employed in the husband-wife nexus. . . .

"Marriage is the only actual bondage known to our law. There remain no legal slaves, except the mistress of every house." Equity could offer some relief by safeguarding some property to the wife's sole use. However, even this required that the trustees, as the legal owners, had the control and management of the property, and not the wife. Nevertheless, this was of some benefit and, given the difficulty of obtaining a divorce, ecclesiastical or civil this could be of crucial importance.

Such settlements were not uncommon amongst the landed classes: all part of the extended and complex negotiations attendant upon a dynastic marriage. Pin money, income secured to the wife from her husband's estate during his lifetime, might also be agreed. The purpose of pin money is somewhat uncertain. It was clearly not intended to be used for the provision of necessaries, since the husband was under a common law obligation to provide those. Even this small measure of potential separate property for married women was of concern, and not permitted to flourish unchecked. . . . [T]he development of the legal doctrines concerning pin money between the Restoration and the early 19th century shows that the law having created a potentially threatening source of women's power in the married women's separate estate, soon appreciated that threat and responded by creating idiosyncratic rules for pin money and other forms of married women's separate property . . .

It was clear that, by the 19th century, calls for reform were growing, and not only amongst the married women themselves. "For law reformers in the 19th century the common law relating to a wife's property was the most basic disability suffered by married women . . ."

. . .

Property law was notoriously slow to change. "Between the Restoration and the *Reform Act of 1832* . . . the one notable change, the evolution of the strict settlement took place towards the middle of the 18th century." It would not have been possible to effect a system of separate property for wives without a comprehensive and radical overhaul of property law generally. That was not seriously contemplated until the 19th century was well advanced, and the role of the legal profession in stoutly resisting change has been well documented.

A WILD LATITUDINARIAN AND MISCHIEVOUS PRINCIPLE

(Sir Charles Wetherell AG on the *Divorce Bill*)

The most striking feature of married life in 18th century England was the theoretical, legal and practical subordination of wives to their husbands . . . even worse than the condition of the unhappily married, however, was the lot of those women who were separated or divorced. They automatically lost all contact whatsoever with their children, unless their husbands were willing to allow it, and they were also financially reduced to very small allowances, even if they were innocent parties.

Once married, though, it was no small matter to separate or divorce. During the interregnum, when the ecclesiastical courts were in abeyance, a practice of informal private separation agreements began to develop. The form of these agreements was essentially contractual in that, often, the husband would agree to pay an allowance and, in return, would be indemnified from responsibility for the wife's future debts. "There was great initial reluctance by common lawyers to accept such a transfer of financial freedom and responsibility to a wife, since it ran counter to the ancient legal concept that a married woman had no legal personality and lacked powers to borrow, sue, or transact any legal business." And, furthermore: "All these clauses made concessions to wives which were in partial or total contradiction with the common law, equity law in Chancery and canon law in the ecclesiastical courts."

The conflicting principles led to attempts by the common law courts to refuse to enforce the financial aspects of the agreements, on the basis that marriage was indissoluble, whereas equity would enforce the financial agreements but refused to enforce the separation. By the beginning of the 19th century, a *modus operandi* had emerged, whereby the separation agreements would be enforced provided they were made via trustees. "It therefore seems likely that an important cause of the spread of these agreements in the last half of the 18th century was the willingness of the court of Chancery to enforce the financial terms swiftly and cheaply, so long as trustees were involved."

Although still married, both parties derived some benefit from these arrangements. Wives received some financial control, while husbands were able to make an announcement that they were no longer liable for their wives' debts. The husband had the additional bonus that, should his wife enter into an adulterous relationship, he would be entitled to seek an ecclesiastical divorce and pay no alimony. Separated husbands, on the other hand, had more leeway. For a husband to be divorced in the ecclesiastical courts, there had to be both adultery on his part, and also cruelty. Given that, until the landmark case of *Jackson*, husbands had the common law right to chastise their wives, cruelty was notoriously difficult to establish.

[T]here comes a tide in the affairs of women, and finally, in 1857, civil divorce was introduced. Men and women did not have equal access to divorce until 1932, and women who did not divorce, but remained married, did not have full rights to separate property at common law until the *Married Women's Property Act 1882*. The *Married Women's Property Act 1870* permitted wives to keep their own earnings and property acquired after the marriage.

It could be argued that equity played at best a marginal role in these momentous developments for women. Some women; if they came from wealthy families, and if a settlement had been arranged for them whereby property was secured in trust for their sole use, might have some protection from the common law rules which applied to married women. Where parties had privately agreed to separate, equity would enforce the financial aspect of the agreement, where the common law would not recognise them. In terms of rights, the married woman in England suffered the most severe legal disabilities — she effectively ceased to exist as far as the common law was concerned, and equity availed her little. Such protection as equity did provide was not byway of a bonus, making women a "specially protected class", but, instead, the barest recognition that married women existed at all, if only through the medium of a trust.

CONCLUSION

A discussion of the historical legal aspects of marriage, widowhood, divorce and inheritance from a feminist perspective relies primarily on legal developments. However, it should always be borne in mind that "the law" is not an autonomous monolithic structure; it does not function in a hermetically sealed world, above and unaffected by social, political, economic, cultural and religious developments.

The strict settlement did not arise accidentally or inevitably. It was the result of landowners with dynastic ambitions, aided and abetted by the conveyancers' art, to design a vehicle which would safeguard inheritance in the male line, keep the estate intact for future generations and provide financial provision for other family members. The net result was to prefer males, even collateral males, to heiresses.

Equity's role in the development is complex. The strict settlement relied on the trust. It was also the method by which merger and unity of the title in the tenant in tail were avoided, by interposing contingent remainders held on trust, which both the common law and equity treated as vested interests. This was also the method by which the common law dower was rendered less effective, eventually being replaced by jointure provisions. In those circumstances, far from being woman's protector, equity appeared to be used to defeat existing common law rights.

"How can it be, then, that this court [equity], self-consciously protective of women and children, and apparently progressive in their interests, appears to strip widows of their dower?" Staves, who posed this question, answers it thus from a feminist viewpoint: ". . . basically nothing changed — not because English society as it changed continued to find appropriate forms of married women's property, but rather because the deeper structures of male domination and female subordination persisted from the Anglo Saxons right through to the *Family Provision Act* of 1975 and beyond."

At the same time, the move from status to contract was facilitated by the assistance equity afforded to the process of removing status-based rights and replacing them with rights of a contractual nature. Between 1500 and 1760 . . . communal protection by custom gave way to free competition in which women might need to go to law to enforce a contract. Marriage itself began to assume contractual status. Whether this development benefited women is doubtful, given the subordinate position women traditionally occupied in society, whether as women generally, or as wives in particular. The validity of contracts is predicated on the assumption that the contracting parties are bargaining on equal terms, and that the terms have been mutually agreed. The marriage contract does not fit that model and Carole Pateman argues that patriarchy was not defeated by the victory of contract over status, but merely consolidated in a modern form.

Stretton argues that the common law is frequently represented as antagonistic to women's rights. However, as he points out, when women were acting as ordinary litigants and not in some woman-specific role, the common law courts presented no extra obstacles. Equity, on the other hand, with its traditional approach of substance over form, was undoubtedly beneficial to women, as women, in that the procedures were more forgiving. Women, because of their exclusion from access to legal documents and proofs, would not readily be able to prosecute actions in common law courts, even where they had the capacity. The flexibility of equity was also evident in permitting widows to pursue actions which originated before or during coverture, often after many years. Widowhood was the first opportunity these women had to bring their cases, since they lacked legal personality during the marriage. The Masters in the Court of Requests would even permit women to sue their husbands in exceptional circumstances, but this anomaly served only to highlight the precarious position of the married woman in the eyes of the law, only slightly modified by equity.

Ultimately, the removal of the legal disabilities attaching to wives was brought about not by equity, but as part of the 19th century reform movements which saw the widening of the franchise, and other momentous social changes. Not that women were enfranchised at that time, but, nevertheless, change was afoot, and Parliament, in the end, recognised the separate existence of wives and granted them separate property rights. Wives had custody rights over their infant children, could keep their own wages and obtain civil divorces. Full legal equality with men in the eyes of the law was not to come until very much later, if it has come at all, but, again, without the agency of equity playing a particularly prominent role.

Equity, then, has been a friend to some women in some circumstances, particularly to married women before legislation made them discernible to the stern eye of the common law. In particular, women from wealthy families were able to avail themselves, through their fathers, their brothers, their husbands or their trustees, of equity's assistance. Single women and widows could, and did, use the common law courts freely and successfully for all kinds of legal matters. It was the married woman who truly needed a friend and it is arguable that offering some slight mitigation to a human being in a condition of theoretical, if by no means always actual, enslavement was a rather poor sort of friendship. . . .

3. RESULTING TRUSTS

The trusts described above are mainly express in nature: property was settled on trustees who were directed to hold the interest for the benefit of someone. (In appropriate case the object of the trust might not be person but some purpose.) However, trusts may arise in other ways, including by virtue of statute. One such means is through the principles governing resulting trusts.

A resulting trust will be recognised in two main circumstances. First, it can arise when a trust document has failed to dispose fully of all beneficial rights. Assume property is given "To Acme Trust in fee simple to hold in trust for B for life". Here, one would normally conclude that a resulting trust exists. There is no express mention as to the fate of the equitable title once the life estate ends. One might be tempted to conclude that once B dies no other interest encumbers the estate conferred on Acme Trust; hence it would hold the fee simple absolute. Yet it is unlikely that such a windfall to the trustee was intended. Instead it seems more sensible to regard the settlor as having retained that which was not expressly conferred. In other words, it is said that the undisposed of equitable interest results back to the settlor (or that person's estate).

Consider also a gift "to Acme Trust in trust for all of my grandchildren who reach 18 years of age". Assume that at this point no grandchildren qualify for the gift; indeed, it is possible that no one ever will. Given that there is no person to whom the gift can now be conferred, a resulting trust again arises. And should it come to pass that no one ever qualifies for the gift, the equitable title will remain where it has been reposed in the meantime: with the settlor.

The second principal situation in which a resulting trust may be found involves gratuitous transfers. Equity, it is commonly explained, prefers bargains not gifts. In consequence, when A purchases property and asks that title be placed in the name of B, it is presumed that A has chosen to retain the equitable interest. Legal title may be in B — equity does not ignore the law — but the beneficial interest is treated as resulting back to A, unless it can be shown that a gift was intended. The same result would obtain if A transfers a currently held interest to B. It might look like a gift to the outside world but equity starts with the view that a resulting trust was intended.

(A variant on this theme — called the common intention resulting trust — can arise when it is shown that the parties expressly or impliedly shared an intention that property held in the name of A was to be shared by A and B. Typically, these situations arise where a husband holds property, though the wife had made some indirect contribution.)

Some exceptions to the presumption of resulting trust have been recognised. If a father confers an interest on his child, or a child in which he stands in the place of the father (*in loco parentis*), a rebuttable presumption of advancement (or gift) arises. The same rule should apply to a gift by a mother. Many cases say so; some do not. See further *Cho Ki Yau Trust (Trustees of) v. Yau Estate* 1999 CarswellOnt 3232, 29 E.T.R. (2d) 204 (S.C.J.), where parental parity is adopted.

It was also once the case that a transfer from husband to wife was presumed to be an advancement (but not *vice versa*). In *Rathwell v. Rathwell* [1978] 2 S.C.R. 436, 83 D.L.R. (3d) 289, 1978 CarswellSask 36, 1978 CarswellSask 129, Dickson J. (as he then was) cast doubt on that presumption, saying that it was no longer a credible guide to intention. At this point, more than 25 years later, it can be ventured that the presumption of gift, at the very most hanging by a thread, is probably no longer operative as between spouses.

In many provinces the rules for interspousal transfers have been settled by statute. For example, the *Family Law Act*, R.S.O. 1990, F.3, s. 14, provides:

> The rule of law applying a presumption of a resulting trust shall be applied in questions of the ownership of property between husband and wife, as if they were not married, except that,

(a) the fact that property is held in the name of spouses as joint tenants is proof, in the absence of evidence to the contrary, that the spouses are intended to own the property as joint tenants; and

(b) money on deposit in the name of both spouses shall be deemed to be in the name of the spouses as joint tenants for the purposes of clause (a).

(Compare the *Matrimonial Property Act*, R.S.A. 2000, c. M-8, s. 36.)

QUESTION

Do you believe that the presumption of resulting trust — assuming it is applied in a gender-neutral fashion — actually reflects the probable intention in most gratuitous transfers between spouses?

Cooper v. Cooper Estate
1999 CarswellSask 327, [1999] 11 W.W.R. 592 (Q.B.)

Klebuc J.:

The plaintiff seeks a declaration under ss. 44(1) of *The Queen's Bench Act*, R.S.S. 1978, c. Q-1, that two guaranteed investment certificates registered in the joint names of the second defendant, Aurene Darlene Markwart, and Alfred Douglas Cooper , now deceased, are the property of the latter's estate. The principal issue is whether Aurene holds a legal and beneficial interest in such certificates as trustee for the estate of Alfred Douglas Cooper pursuant to a "presumed resulting trust" or whether both legal and beneficial ownership passed to her pursuant to the application agreement governing their purchase, and on application of the "presumption of advancement."

Facts

Alfred Douglas Cooper, age 85, died at Humboldt, Saskatchewan, on October 1, 1996, and was survived by three children, Aurene Markwart ("Aurene"), Edward Cooper ("Edward") and Lee Cooper ("Lee"). He left a last will and testament dated August 27, 1993, ("the Will") wherein he made the following bequests:

4. (a) TO DELIVER to my son, Edward Alfred Cooper . . .

(i) the portion of the NE 17-36-16 W2nd comprising of 120 acres more or less.

(ii) My John Deere 4640 tractor and all of my farm tools and equipment.

(b) TO DELIVER to my son Douglas Lee Cooper , the following property, namely:

(i) my house, lot and contents located on Lots 1 and 2, Block 22, Quill Lake, Saskatchewan. . . .

> (ii) any personal vehicle I may own at the time of my death.
>
> (c) TO DELIVER to my daughter, Arena (sic) Darlene Markwart the sum of fifty thousand ($50,000.00) dollars. . . .
>
> (e) TO DIVIDE all the rest and residue of my estate . . . into three equal shares and pay one such share to each of my children. . . .

At the time of his death the father owned the following property relevant to the issues before the Court: the NE 1/4 17-36-16 W2nd; two guaranteed investment certificates registered in the joint names of himself and his daughter for the principal sums of $30,000.00 and $10,000.00, respectively (the "certificates"); a John Deere 4640 tractor; a 1994 GMC half-ton truck; and miscellaneous undescribed farm tools and equipment.

To facilitate the purchase of the certificates solely with his own funds, the father executed and arranged for his daughter to execute an application form dated December 21, 1994. The form provides, *inter alia*:

> . . . We agree jointly and severally . . . with BMMC and with each other that: . . .
>
> b) BMMC may pay all principal and interest under the Certificate to any one of us. . . .
>
> d) in the event of the death of any one of us, BMMC may make payment under the Certificate to the surviving survivors of us, subject to the requirements of any succession duty or similar laws. . . .

The value of the certificates and the half-ton truck are not an issue, but the value of the NW 1/4 17, the tractor, the "other farm equipment" and the miscellaneous tools are. Aurene alleged that the farmland was worth in excess of $40,000.00 but provided no credible evidence to support her non-expert opinion. Edward placed in evidence an appraisal report which established the value thereof at $30,000.00 as of August 1, 1993, and $40,000.00 as of October 1, 1996. With respect to the tractor, two conflicting informal evaluations prepared by implement dealers were put before the Court. The one tendered by Edward estimated the value of the tractor to be approximately $25,000.00 whereby the one tendered by Aurene estimated its value at $32,000.00, subject to a number of repairs referred to therein. Other than for a fuel tank valued at $200.00 by the executors in their application for probate, no acceptable description or evaluation of the farm equipment or tools owned by the father was provided by the parties. The absence of a meaningful inventory by the executors and lack of any claim for capital cost allowance for tools or equipment in the father's 1996 income tax return suggests they were of nominal value.

Alfred Cooper's wife died on July 7, 1993, leaving a will naming her husband and son, Lee, as co-executors of her estate. Difficulties encountered in administering her estate annoyed the father. Lee deposed in his affidavit that subsequent to the father's execution of the Will on August 27, 1993, the father expressed his intention to execute another will after the administration of his wife's estate was completed.

Lee further deposed that he was aware of the father's intended purchase of the certificates and that at the time of their purchase the father advised him that his intention was to simplify the administration of his estate and to avoid the difficulties encountered with his wife's estate.

In August, 1995, the father transferred his home located in Quill Lake, Saskatchewan to Lee at a value of $45,000.00. The title issued in the name of Lee. No evidence was led as to who executed the affidavit of value comprising the transfer by the father. Aurene and her husband in their affidavits opined that the home was worth $75,000.00 and that its contents, including a lawn tractor, were worth in excess of $10,000.00. They based their evaluation of the home on an alleged statement by the father that the manager of the local Credit Union offered to purchase the home at a purchase price in the range of $74,000.00 to $76,000.00. . . .

In the circumstances, I am satisfied that the value attributed to the home in the father's transfer is the best evidence available of its fair market value at the time he transferred it. I am further satisfied that the father transferred title to the home in order to fulfil his testamentary intention and to pass on the cost of maintaining the home to his son immediately rather than at the time of his death. On the very limited description of the household goods gifted to Lee and the opinion of Aurene, I fix the value thereof at $10,000.00.

In January, 1996, the father gave Aurene $20,000.00.

The father retained legal title to the NE 1/4 17 and thereby preserved various tax benefits he would have forfeited upon conveying legal title thereto to Edward. More specifically, his arrangement with Edward whereby they shared the crop grown on the NE 1/4 17 — with the father paying property taxes, some input costs, and providing some assistance — enabled him to properly claim motor vehicle expenses, telephone expenses, and other expenses set out in his income tax return and to generate some income. Such arrangements are common in Saskatchewan.

Positions Taken by the Parties

Edward submitted that Aurene holds a legal and beneficial interest in the certificates as trustee for his father's estate pursuant to a resulting trust. He relies on the fact that the father at all times retained beneficial ownership and control of the certificates and had collected all interest accruing thereon. His position is that the father placed the funds jointly in his and Aurene's name for the purpose of reducing the cost of administering his estate and to ensure that his $50,000.00 bequest to her could be funded immediately. He further argued that if Aurene were entitled to the proceeds of the certificates and the sum of $50,000.00 under the terms of the Will, she would receive a disproportionate share of the father's estate in contravention of the father's intention.

Aurene in para. 4 of her statement of defence admitted the following:

> . . . the terms of the Last Will and Testament, wherein a bequest of Fifty Thousand ($50,000.00) Dollars is made to her, reflects the intention of the Testator to treat his three children with equality, and that it was the intention of the Testator that the Defendant, Aurene Darlene Markwart would receive Guaranteed Investment Certificates valued at Forty thousand ($40,000.00) Dollars by right of survivorship immediately upon his death.

In support of her position, she submitted the value of the father's bequest to Edward was approximately $103,000.00 and that Edward had received additional benefits by way of the father paying a disproportionate share of farm expenses and $3,000.00 to Edward's son for farm labour. She presented no specific evidence of the alleged "disproportionate share" of expenses or any evidence to indicate that Edward's son did work for his grandfather.

With respect to Lee, she submitted the *inter vivos* gifts he received from the father and the bequest of the truck under the Will had a total value of $110,000.00.

Lee took the position that the certificates form part of his father's estate and were not to pass to Aurene by way of right of survivorship.

The Law

The arguments advanced by Edward and Aurene rely heavily on the doctrine of presumed resulting trust and the doctrine of presumption of advancement. Both of these doctrines are fully discussed in Waters, *Law of Trusts in Canada*, 2d ed. (Toronto: Carswell, 1984) and therefore an in-depth analysis is not required herein.

A *presumption of resulting trust* arises when one person has gratuitously transferred his property into another party's name, that party, either because he is a fiduciary or gave no value for the property, is under an obligation to return the property to the transferor or the person who gave value for it: Waters, at p. 300. Underpinning the doctrine is the premise that equity does not assume a gift and hence the transferor of the property is presumed not to have given or advanced the property to another by way of gift: *Dyer v. Dyer* (1788), 30 E.R. 42 (Eng. Ch. Div.). Such presumption is an evidentiary one that may be rebutted by clear and convincing evidence . . .

The *presumption of advancement* essentially provides that where a transferor transfers his property to his wife or child, it is presumed that he intended to make a gift and therefore the presumption of a resulting trust does not arise. This presumption, like the presumption of a resulting trust, is an evidentiary one which the transferor may rebut . . .

In Saskatchewan, s. 5(1) of *The Matrimonial Property Act*, 1997, S.S. 1997 c. M-6.11 abolished the presumption of advancement as between spouses and declared that the presumption of resulting trust will apply between spouses as if they were not married to each other. While Waters acknowledges that the presumption of advancement as between husband and wife has lost its persuasiveness with the courts, the doctrine remains in effect with respect to children. At p. 315 he cites the following authorities: *B. v. B.* (1975), 65 D.L.R. (3d) 460 (B.C. S.C.); *O'Brien v. Bean* (1957), 7 D.L.R. (2d) 332 (B.C. S.C.); *Larondeau v. Laurendeau*, [1954] O.W.N. 722 (Ont. H.C.) at p. 724; [1954] 4 D.L.R. 293 (Ont. H.C.); *Young v. Young* (1958), 15 D.L.R. (2d) 138 (B.C. C.A.).

I have serious doubts as to whether presumption of advancement continues to apply with any degree of persuasiveness in Saskatchewan in circumstances where an older parent has transferred property to an independent adult child who is married and lives apart from his parent. However, because I am able to determine the issues before me without diminishing the nature and scope of the presumption of advancement, I will refrain from any further comments *in obiter*. Instead I will apply the doctrine of presumption of advancement in the manner outlined in the authorities applicable to the joint ownership of property between an older parent and an adult child.

The within action involves guaranteed investment certificates issued by a chartered bank , in the joint names of the father and Aurene, pursuant to the application form previously discussed. I am satisfied that the authorities governing the operational effect of joint bank account agreements executed among co-holders of a bank account and the bank, and the presumptions of result trust and advancement as applied thereto, apply equally to the joint certificates in the instant case. The Supreme Court of Canada definitively addressed their application to joint bank accounts in *Mailman, Re*, [1941] S.C.R. 368 (S.C.C.); *Niles v. Lake*, [1947] S.C.R. 291, [1947] 2 D.L.R. 248 (S.C.C.); and *Edwards v. Bradley*, [1957] S.C.R. 599, 9 D.L.R. (2d) 673 (S.C.C.).

In *Mailman, Re* the wife deposited her own money in the joint names of her husband and herself. Both of them signed an agreement with the bank which entitled either of them to draw cheques on the account and which gave the survivor the right to withdraw all funds in the account. The wife kept the bank book and was the only person to draw on the account during her lifetime. Shortly before her death, she handed her husband the bank book saying "This is yours." The majority held that the bank agreement only affects the relationship of the joint account holders with the bank and went on to hold that neither the bank agreement nor the evidence indicated any intention on the part of the wife to create a beneficial interest in the joint account in favour of her husband. In writing for the majority, Crocker J. stated the applicable law to be as follows at p. 374:

> That both law and equity interpose such a presumption against an intention to create a joint tenancy, except where a father makes an investment or bank deposit in the names of himself and a natural or adopted child or a husband does so in the names of himself and his wife, is now too firmly settled to admit of any controversy. This presumption, of course, is a rebuttable presumption, which may always be overborne by the owner's . . . real purpose in making the investment or opening the account in that form may reasonably be inferred to have been otherwise. In the absence, however, of any such evidence to the contrary the presumption of law must prevail. . . .

Any question as to the operational effect of a joint bank account agreement or the applicable presumptions was eliminated in *Niles*, where the Supreme Court of Canada definitively stated that a joint bank account agreement merely defines a relationship between the holders of the account and the bank and is not to be deemed decisive as to the relationship between the joint holders of the account. Neither *Mailman, Re* nor *Niles* is instructive on the legal effect of a joint account agreement where the facts indicate that the joint account holder who contributed all of the funds intended to make a gift to the volunteer joint account holder effective as of the former's death.

Waters, at pp. 335-336; advances three alternative arguments of which two are relevant to the issues before me. First, when A (the sole contributor) opened the joint bank account with B (the volunteer) as a co-holder and the joint bank account agreement was signed, B acquired a joint legal interest, including the legal interest in the right of survivorship. If the beneficial interest is also intended to pass to B at the same time, then an *inter vivos* gift of both the legal and equitable interest in the right of survivorship occurs. The second argument flows along the lines that the beneficial or equitable interest in the account is contingent on survivorship, hence the volunteer survivor acquires his or her interest only as of the moment of A's death. If A dies first, then A will have made a testamentary gift to B which must comply with the testamentary requirements of the jurisdiction in which the same was made. . . .

There are numerous decisions where *Mailman, Re* and *Niles* have been applied . . . In many of these cases, the volunteer joint holder or owner was the child of a father with respect to whom the courts required minimal evidence to rebut the presumption of advancement. In *Lavergne v. Lavergne* (1981), 131 D.L.R. (3d) 246 (Ont. H.C.) the daughter lived with and cared for the testatrix for a long period of time. As to the issue of whether the proceeds of a joint bank account created by the testatrix was the property of her estate or that of the daughter, Grange J. found that the evidence rebutted the presumption of resulting trust and that the doctrine of presumption of advancement did not apply between a mother and her child.

In order to adjudicate the instant case, I need not consider whether the presumption of advancement applies to both male and female parents, or, if only to male parents, whether the doctrine is contrary to the *Canadian Charter of Rights and Freedoms*, Part I of the *Constitution Act, 1982*, being Schedule B of the *Canada Act, 1982* (U.K.), 1982, c. 11. . . .

Analysis

All three children agree that their father's intention was to treat them equally. Aurene, in her evidence-in-chief and during her cross-examination, stated that such objective could only be achieved if she receives the proceeds of the certificates plus the bequest of $50,000.00 under the Will. The evidence in my view does not support her opinion that her brothers each obtained by way of gifts and bequests amounts approximating $110,000.00. To the contrary, the evidence confirms the total benefits bestowed on Lee had a value of approximately $69,000.00 while those bestowed on Edward were likely for a slightly smaller amount. Aurene had received an *inter vivos* gift of $20,000.00 plus $50,000.00 under the Will for a total of $70,000.00. In my view the distribution sought by Aurene is inconsistent with the father's intention to treat his children equally. . . .

The principal question is whether the father intended to vest Aurene with both the legal right and beneficial right of survivorship upon the certificates being purchased. In my opinion, the application agreement and the father's actions established a *prima facie* intention on his part to vest her with the legal right of survivorship as of the moment the certificates were purchased. Thus, in the absence of evidence to the contrary, the first element outlined in *Edwards v. Bradley* is proven. With respect to the question of whether beneficial right of survivorship vested in Aurene at the time the certificates were purchased, I am satisfied the presumption of advancement relied on by Aurene effectively overrides the presumption of resulting trust relied on by Edward. The burden thereby shifted to Edward to prove that the father did not intend to vest Aurene with the beneficial right of survivorship. I conclude that he has discharged that burden. The father retained the beneficial ownership of the certificates as evidenced by the fact that he kept control of the same and collected all interest accruing thereon. Such conduct, when coupled with his statement to Lee regarding the purpose of buying the certificates in the joint names of himself and Aurene, in my view effectively rebuts the presumption of advancement relied on by Aurene and establishes that the father intended the beneficial ownership thereof to pass to Aurene at the time of his death.

On the whole of the father's conduct, I am satisfied that he intended on his death that the proceeds of the certificates be used to fund the bequest of $50,000.00 to Aurene under his Will. . . . In the result his proposed distribution constituted a testamentary disposition which must comply with s. 7 of *The Wills Act*, 1996, S.S. 1996, c. W-14.1. It does not and therefore beneficial ownership of the certificates comprise part of the father's estate. . . .

Application allowed.

QUESTIONS AND COMMENTS

1. Should the presumption of advancement apply where an older parent has transferred property to an independent adult child?

2. It is not uncommon for property to be transferred into the name of another (often a family member) for, let us say, questionable purposes. Sometimes that purpose is to insulate the property from the transferor's creditors. (Some types of fraudulent conveyances can be attacked by legislation designed for that send: see, *e.g.*, *Fraudulent Conveyances Act*, R.S.O. 1990, c. F.29.) On occasion, the transferor seems to want to have it both ways, claiming as against creditors that no title is retained, but perhaps later saying to the transferee that in fact the beneficial interest had not

passed, but rather resulted back. As Lord Denning, in his inimitable style, said: "that simply will not do": *Tinker v. Tinker* (1969) [1970] P. 136 (C.A.) at 141.

In *Tribe v. Tribe* [1996] Ch. 107 (C.A.), Millett L.J. (with whom Otton L.J. agreed) set out what he regarded as the basic principles governing the effect of an illegal purpose on the operation of the presumptions of advancement and resulting trust (at 134-5):

> In my opinion the following propositions represent the present state of the law. (1) Title to property passes both at law and in equity even if the transfer is made for an illegal purpose. The fact that title has passed to the transferee does not preclude the transferor from bringing an action for restitution. (2) The transferor's action will fail if it would be illegal for him to retain any interest in the property. (3) Subject to (2) the transferor can recover the property if he can do so without relying on the illegal purpose. This will normally be the case where the property was transferred without consideration in circumstances where the transferor can rely on an express declaration of trust or a resulting trust in his favour. (4) It will almost invariably be so where the illegal purpose has not been carried out. It may be otherwise where the illegal purpose has been carried out and the transferee can rely on the transferor's conduct as inconsistent with his retention of a beneficial interest. (5) The transferor can lead evidence of the illegal purpose whenever it is necessary for him to do so provided that he has withdrawn from the transaction before the illegal purpose has been wholly or partly carried into effect. It will be necessary for him to do so (i) if he brings an action at law or (ii) if he brings proceedings in equity and needs to rebut the presumption of advancement. (6) The only way in which a man can protect his property from his creditors is by divesting himself of all beneficial interest in it. Evidence that he transferred the property in order to protect it from his creditors, therefore, does nothing by itself to rebut the presumption of advancement; it reinforces it. To rebut the presumption it is necessary to show that he intended to retain a beneficial interest and conceal it from his creditors. (7) The court should not conclude that this was his intention without compelling circumstantial evidence to this effect. The identity of the transferee and the circumstances in which the transfer was made would be highly relevant. It is unlikely that the court would reach such a conclusion where the transfer was made in the absence of an imminent and perceived threat from known creditors.

See also *Tinsley v. Milligan* (1993) [1994] 1 A.C. 340 (H.L.)

3. A conveys land to B for no consideration. Accordingly, a resulting trust is presumed in favour of A. B is now holding in trust for A. Is the *Statute of Uses* triggered? If so, would the legal estate return to A (who is already holding the equitable title, thus nullifying the entire transfer? Consider the analysis of Ritchie C.J. in *Wortman v. Ayles* 1867 CarswellNB 21, 12 N.B.R. 62 (C.A.), at para. 1:

> The question in this case is, whether any estate passed to the grantee under a registered deed in the following form:
>
> > Know all men by these presents, that Ralph Ayles, of Coverdale, in the County of Albert, and Province of New Brunswick, farmer, for and in consideration of the sum of—lawful money of said Province, to the said Ralph Ayles in hand, well and truly paid by Charles Ayles, of Coverdale aforesaid, the receipt whereof is hereby acknowledged, hath granted, bargained 'and sold, and by these presents, doth grant,

> bargain and sell, unto the said Charles Ayles, his heirs and assigns, a tract of land situate in Coverdale aforesaid, &c., (here follows the description), together with all the estate, right, title, interest, dower, right of dower, claim, or demand, of the said Ralph Ayles, of, in, or to the said described and bargained premises, with the appurtenances; to have and to hold the before described premises with all the improvements and privileges belonging to the same, unto the said Charles Ayles, his heirs and assigns, forever. And the said Ralph Ayles, for himself, his heirs, executors and administrators, doth hereby, covenant to, and with, the said Charles Ayles, his heirs, and assigns, that he is lawfully siesed of the before granted and bargained premises, and hath good right to bargain and sell the same in manner and form as before written, and that he will warrant and forever defend the same, unto the said Charles Ayles, his heirs and assigns, against the lawful claims or demands of all persons whomsoever. In witness whereof, etc.

It was contended that there must be either a valuable consideration or a declaration of the uses of the conveyance, otherwise there would be a resulting use back to the grantor, and that by the statute of uses (27 Hen. 8, c. 10), the legal estate was transferred to such resulting use.

The rule which requires a deed of bargain and sale to be founded on pecuniary consideration, is held to be matter of form only, and sufficiently complied with if the conveyance purport to be so founded; and for this purpose any trivial sum may be inserted. It is also immaterial whether the sum so inserted be actually paid or not. 1 Steph. Com. 495. In Cruise's Dig. Title 'Deed,' c. 9, §20, it is said, that if a person in consideration of "a certain sum of money" bargains and sells, this is a good consideration to raise a use without an averment of any sum in certain; for the quantity of the sum is not material, as any sum, however small, is a sufficient consideration. In the American cases cited from Washburn on Real Property, 613, the words "for value received," and "a certain sum in hand paid," were held to be sufficient.

The statement in the deed in this case, "lawful money of New Brunswick" shews us clearly that a pecuniary consideration was intended to be given for the land, as if the words had been "a certain sum of money." The amount not being material, all that is necessary to appear is that the consideration was 'money' or something valuable. We think, under these authorities, that this deed might operate either as a feoffment, or a bargain and sale. But admitting that it could not so operate, is it not good as a conveyance of land under the registry Act?

By the 1 Rev. Stat., c. 112, §10,—"Every conveyance duly acknowledged and registered, shall be effectual for transferring the lands therein described, and the possession thereof according to the intent of such conveyance, without livery of seisin, or any other Act."

The word "conveyance" is defined to mean any instrument by which any interest in real estate may be transferred or affected (1 Rev. St., 462). . . .

Can any one read this deed, and say that it was not the intention of the parties that the land should pass to the grantee? The deed contains all that is essential to make a valid deed at common law, even if it should be considered that a valuable consideration is not stated; for by the rules of the common law no consideration is necessary to the validity of a deed (2 Prest. Conv. 420). In this deed the names of the grantor and grantee, and the land professed to be conveyed, are sufficiently described. The grantor declares that by that deed he "doth grant, bargain and sell," the land to the grantee, and the habendum states that the grantee is "to have and to hold" the same to him and his heirs and assigns forever. To apply the strict and technical rules applicable to conveyances in England, and to hold that such a deed is not sufficient, under our Registry Act, to transfer the title and possession of the land to the grantee would, we think, be entirely to defeat, not only the intention of the parties to the deed, but the object which the Legislature had in view in passing the Act (26 Geo. 3, c. 3), from which the Revised Statute, c. 112, does not materially differ.

If, as the authorities show, the insertion of the most trivial sum in the deed, even one cent, without any proof of payment, will prevent the creation of a resulting trust in the grantor, it shows how entirely technical the rule is, which it is contended must be applied; on what a slight foundation the defendant's case rests; and what injustice would be done if we were bound to give effect to such objections. We think the Registry Act relieves us from applying the strict rules applicable to conveyances in England. The policy of the law of this Province, from its very foundation, has been to simplify and facilitate the transfer of real property, and to ignore, as unsuitable for this country, those considerations of every complex and subtle kind in the English jurisprudence, which Mr. Stephens (Vol. 1, p. 466) describes as having "been elaborated into a highly artificial system, known under the denomination of conveyancing; a system which maintains its own separate body of practitioners and professors, and constitutes a science of itself." . . .

4. CONSTRUCTIVE TRUSTS

Equity will impress a trust on property in appropriate circumstances. The interest so created is called a constructive trust. Two main kinds are found in Canadian law. The first is sometimes called an institutional constructive trust. This tag refers to the fact that such a trust can arise in discrete circumstances, such as where a person knowingly meddles with trust property (thereby becoming a trustee *de son tort*). The case of *Soulos*, reproduced below, explores the essence of this institutional form, in search of a thread that can unify all its established variants. From these specific instances, can an organizing principle be found?

The second type is the remedial constructive trust. It is remedial because it serves as one response to a finding of unjust enrichment. Here, then, the use of the remedial constructive trust is affected by an overarching concept (unjust enrichment), as applied to specific circumstances. The critical question is: under what circumstances is it appropriate to respond to an enrichment by awarding a proprietary interest through the imposition of a constructive trust?

Various institutional constructive trusts have been part of the law for centuries. By contrast, the modern Canadian doctrine of unjust enrichment is relatively new, having been developed mainly in the context of claims arising within family law cases over the last 30 years. Despite this chronology, the first case reproduced below, *Peter v. Beblow*, involves a remedial constructive trust. The emergence of a trust designed to respond to such a broad concept as unjust enrichment raises questions about whether the antecedent institutional constructive trust retains a useful role. That issue is explored in *Soulos v. Korkontzilas*, which follows *Peter v. Beblow*.

Peter v. Beblow
[1993] 1 S.C.R. 980, 1993 CarswellBC 44, 1993 CarswellBC 1258

[The following statement of facts is derived from the judgment of Cory J., which has otherwise been omitted.

In April 1973, the respondent asked the appellant to come and live with him. That same month, the appellant together with her four children moved into the respondent's home in Sicamous, B.C. At the time, two children of the respondent were living in the home. The parties continued to live together in a common law relationship for over 12 years, separating in June 1985. During this entire time the appellant acted as the wife of the respondent. She was a stepmother to his children until 1977 while they remained in the home. As well, she cared for her own children, the last one leaving in 1980.

During the 12 years, the appellant cooked, cleaned, washed clothes and looked after the garden. As well, she worked on the Sicamous property, undertaking such projects as painting the fence, planting a cedar hedge, buying flowers and shrubs for the property and building a rock garden. She built a pig pen. She kept chickens for a few years, butchering and cooking them for the family. During the winters, the appellant shovelled snow, chopped wood and made kindling. The respondent did not pay the appellant for any of her work. Both the appellant and the respondent contributed to the purchase of groceries and household supplies, although the respondent contributed a greater share.

In the first year of the relationship the appellant did not undertake outside work and spent eight hours a day doing housework and work on the Sicamous property. In subsequent years, she took part-time work as a cook from June to October. During these months she worked some six hours a day at a rate of $4.50 per hour. Except for one winter when she worked at a bakery, the appellant received unemployment insurance benefits in the winter months.

Throughout the relationship, the respondent worked on a more or less full-time basis as a grader operator. His work frequently took him out of town to various locations in British Columbia.

Before he met the appellant, the respondent had lived in a common law relationship with another woman for five years. When she left his home he hired housekeepers. The last housekeeper he had before the appellant came to his home was paid at a rate of $350 per month.

The trial judge accepted the appellant's testimony that the respondent had asked her to live with him because he needed someone to care for his two children. This need arose when the welfare authorities expressed some concern that the respondent left the children alone when he was working away from home.

When the parties met, the appellant had savings of $100. In 1976, she purchased a property in Saskatchewan for $2,500. She sold this property in 1980 for $8,000 and purchased a property at 100 Mile House for $6,500. She used the remainder of the sale proceeds for a trip to Reno. At the time of trial, the appellant still owned the 100 Mile House property.

The respondent had purchased the Sicamous property in 1971 for $8,500. Some $900 was paid in cash and the balance of $7,600 was secured by a mortgage. The respondent was able to pay off the mortgage in 1975. The estimated market value of the Sicamous property as of 1987 was $17,800. The property's assessed value in that year was $23,200. In that same year, the respondent rented the property. The tenants were given an option to purchase it for $28,000. The option was not exercised.

With the passage of time, the respondent began to drink heavily and became verbally and physically abusive to the appellant. As a result, the appellant moved out of the Sicamous home on June 7, 1985. At the time of the trial, she was on welfare and lived in a trailer court in Sicamous. The respondent by that time had retired and was living on a houseboat in Enderby, B.C. The Sicamous house and property were vacant.

The appellant brought an action claiming that the respondent had been unjustly enriched over the years of the relationship as a result of the work that she performed in his home without payment of any kind. She sought to have a constructive trust imposed on her behalf in respect of the Sicamous property or in the alternative, monetary damages as compensation for the labour and services she provided to the respondent.]

McLachlin J.: . . .

In recent decades, Canadian courts have adopted the equitable concept of unjust enrichment *inter alia* as the basis for remedying the injustice that occurs where one person makes a substantial contribution to the property of another person without compensation. The doctrine has been applied to a variety of situations, from claims for payments made under mistake to claims arising from conjugal relationships. While courts have not been adverse to applying the concept of unjust enrichment in new circumstances, they have insisted on adhering to the fundamental principles which have long underlain the equitable doctrine of unjust enrichment. . . .

The basic notions are simple enough. An action for unjust enrichment arises when three elements are satisfied: (1) an enrichment; (2) a corresponding deprivation; and (3) the absence of a juristic reason for the enrichment. These proven, the action is established and the right to claim relief made out. At this point, a second doctrinal concern arises: the nature of the remedy. "Unjust enrichment" in equity permitted a number of remedies, depending on the circumstances. One was a payment for services rendered on the basis of *quantum meruit* or *quantum valebat*. Another equitable remedy, available traditionally where one person was possessed of legal title to property in which another had an interest, was the constructive trust. While the first remedy to be considered was a monetary award, the Canadian jurisprudence recognized that in some cases it might be insufficient. This may occur, to quote Justice La Forest in *Lac Minerals Ltd. v. International Corona Resources Ltd.*, [1989]

2 S.C.R. 574, at p. 678, "if there is reason to grant to the plaintiff the additional rights that flow from recognition of a right of property." Or to quote Dickson J., as he then was, in *Pettkus v. Becker*, [1980] 2 S.C.R. 834, at p. 852, where there is a "contribution [to the property] sufficiently substantial and direct as to entitle [the plaintiff] to a portion of the profits realized upon sale of [the property]." In other words, the remedy of constructive trust arises, where monetary damages are inadequate and where there is a link between the contribution that founds the action and the property in which the constructive trust is claimed.

Notwithstanding these rather straightforward doctrinal underpinnings, their application has sometimes given rise to difficulty. There is a tendency on the part of some to view the action for unjust enrichment as a device for doing whatever may seem fair between the parties. In the rush to substantive justice, the principles are sometimes forgotten. Policy issues often assume a large role, infusing such straightforward discussions as whether there was a "benefit" to the defendant or a "detriment" to the plaintiff. On the remedies side, the requirements of the special proprietary remedy of constructive trust are sometimes minimized. . . . Occasionally the remedial notion of constructive trust is even conflated with unjust enrichment itself, as though where one is found the other must follow.

Such difficulties have to some degree complicated the case at bar. At the doctrinal level, the simple question of "benefit" and "detriment" became infused with moral and policy questions of when the provision of domestic services in a quasi-matrimonial situation can give rise to a legal obligation. At the stage of remedy, the trial judge proceeded as if he were making a monetary award, and then, without fully explaining how, awarded the appellant the entire interest in the matrimonial home on the basis of a constructive trust. It is only by a return to the fundamental principles laid out in cases like *Pettkus v. Becker* and *Lac Minerals*, that one can cut through the conflicting findings and submissions on these issues and evaluate whether in fact the appellant has made out a claim for unjust enrichment, and if so what her remedy should be.

1. Is the Appellant's Claim for Unjust Enrichment Made Out?

. . . The appellant's housekeeping and child-care services constituted a benefit to the respondent (1st element), in that he received household services without compensation, which in turn enhanced his ability to pay off his mortgage and other assets. These services also constituted a corresponding detriment to the appellant (2nd element), in that she provided services without compensation. Finally, since there was no obligation existing between the parties which would justify the unjust enrichment and no other arguments under this broad heading were met, there is no juristic reason for the enrichment (3rd element). Having met the three criteria, the plaintiff has established an unjust enrichment giving rise to restitution.

The main arguments on this appeal centred on whether the law should recognize the services which the appellant provided as being capable of founding an action for unjust enrichment. It was argued, for example, that the services cannot give rise to a remedy based on unjust enrichment because the appellant had voluntarily assumed the role of wife and stepmother. It was also said that the law of unjust enrichment should not recognize such services because they arise from natural love and affection. These arguments raise moral and policy questions and require the Court to make value judgments.

The first question is: where do these arguments belong? Are they part of the benefit — detriment analysis, or should they be considered under the third head — the absence of juristic reason for the unjust enrichment? The Court of Appeal, for example, held that there was no "detriment" on these grounds. I hold the view that these factors may most conveniently be considered under the third head of absence of juristic reason. This Court has consistently taken a straightforward economic approach to the first two elements of the test for unjust enrichment: *Pettkus v. Becker, supra*; *Sorochan v. Sorochan*, [1986] 2 S.C.R. 38 [[1986] 5 W.W.R. 289]; *Peel (Regional Municipality) v. Canada,* [1992] 3 S.C.R. 762 (hereinafter "*Peel*"). It is in connection with the third element — absence of juristic reason for the enrichment — that such considerations may more properly find their place. It is at this stage that the court must consider whether the enrichment and detriment, morally neutral in themselves, are "unjust".

What matters should be considered in determining whether there is an absence of juristic reason for the enrichment? The test is flexible, and the factors to be considered may vary with the situation before the court. For example, different factors may be more relevant in a case like *Peel*, *supra*, at p. 803, a claim for unjust enrichment between different levels of government, than in a family case.

In every case, the fundamental concern is the legitimate expectation of the parties: *Pettkus v. Becker, supra*. In family cases, this concern may raise the following subsidiary questions:

(i) Did the plaintiff confer the benefit as a valid gift or in pursuance of a valid common law, equitable or statutory obligation which he or she owed to the defendant?

(ii) Did the plaintiff submit to, or compromise, the defendant's honest claim?

(iii) Does public policy support the enrichment?

In the case at bar, the first and third of these factors were argued. It was argued first that the appellant's services were rendered pursuant to a common law or equitable obligation which she had assumed. Her services were part of the bargain she made when she came to live with the respondent, it was said. He would give her and her children a home and other husbandly services, and in turn she would look after the home and family.

This Court has held that a common law spouse generally owes no duty at common law, in equity or by statute to perform work or services for her partner. As Dickson C.J., speaking for the Court put it in *Sorochan v. Sorochan*, *supra*, at p. 46, the common law wife "was under no obligation, contractual or otherwise, to perform the work and services in the home or on the land." So there is no general duty presumed by the law on a common law spouse to perform work and services for her partner.

Nor, in the case at bar was there any obligation arising from the circumstances of the parties. The trial judge held that the appellant was "under no obligation to perform the work and assist in the home without some reasonable expectation of receiving something in return other than the drunken physical abuse which she received at the hands of the respondent." This puts an end to the argument that the services in question were performed pursuant to obligation. It also puts an end to the argument that the appellant's services to her partner were a "gift" from her to him. The central element of a gift at law — intentional giving to another without expectation of remuneration — is simply not present.

The third factor mentioned above raises directly the issue of public policy. While it may be stated in different ways, the argument at base is simply that some types of services in some types of relationships should not be recognized as supporting legal claims for policy reasons. More particularly, homemaking and childcare services should not, in a marital or quasi-marital relationship, be viewed as giving rise to equitable claims against the other spouse.

I concede at the outset that there is some judicial precedent for this argument. Professor Marcia Neave has observed generally that "analysis of the principles applied in English, Australian and Canadian courts sometimes fails to confront this question directly . . . Courts which deny or grant remedies usually conceal their value judgments within statements relating to doctrinal requirements." (Marcia Neave, "Three Approaches to Family Property Disputes — Intention/Belief, Unjust Enrichment and Unconscionability," in T.G. Youdan, ed., *Equity, Fiduciaries and Trusts*, at p. 251). More pointedly, Professor Farquhar has observed that many courts have strayed from the framework of *Sorochan* for public policy reasons: "the courts . . . have, after *Sorochan,* put up warning signs that there are aspects of relationships that are not to be analyzed in the light of unjust enrichment and constructive trust." (Keith B. Farquhar, "Causal Connection in Constructive Trust After *Sorochan v. Sorochan*" (1989), 7 Can. J. of Family Law 337, at p. 343). The public policy issue has been summed up as follows by Professor Neave at p. 251: "whether a remedy, either personal or proprietary, should be provided to a person who has made contributions to family resources." On the judicial side, the view of the respondent is pointedly stated in *Grant v. Edwards*, [1986] 2 All E.R. 426, at p. 439, per Browne-Wilkinson V.C.:

> Setting up house together, having a baby and making payments to general housekeeping expenses . . . may all be referable to the mutual love and affection of the parties and not specifically referable to the claimant's belief that she has an interest in the house.

Proponents of this view, Professor Neave, *supra*, at p. 253 argues, "regard it as distasteful to put a price upon services provided out of a sense of love and commitment to the relationship. They suggest it is unfair for a recipient of indirect or non-financial contributions to be forced to provide recompense for those contributions." To support this position, the respondent cites several cases. *Kshywieski v. Kunka Estate* (1986), 50 R.F.L. (2d) 421 [[1986] 3 W.W.R. 472] (Man. C.A.); *Houghen v. Monnington* (1991), 37 R.F.L. (3d) 279 (B.C.C.A.); *Prentice v. Lang* (1987), 10 R.F.L. (3d) 364 (B.C.S.C.); *Hyette v. Pfenniger*, B.C.S.C., Dec. 19, 1991 [now reported (1991), 39 R.F.L. (3d) 30, additional reasons at 39 R.F.L. (3d) at 44].

It is my view that this argument is no longer tenable in Canada, either from the point of view of logic or authority. From the point of view of logic, I share the view of Professors Hovius and Youdan in *The Law of Family Property* (1991), at p. 136, that "there is no logical reason to distinguish domestic services from other contributions." The notion that household and childcare services are not worthy of recognition by the court fails to recognize the fact that these services are of great value, not only to the family, but to the other spouse. As Lord Simon observed nearly thirty years ago: "The cock-bird can feather his nest precisely because he is not required to spend most of his time sitting on it" ("With All My Worldly Goods," *Holdsworth Lecture* (University of Birmingham, 20th March 1964), at p. 32). The notion, moreover, is a pernicious one that systematically devalues the contributions which women tend to make to the family economy. It has contributed to the phenomenon of the feminization of poverty which this Court identified in *Moge v. Moge*, [1992] 3 S.C.R. 813 [[1993] 1 W.W.R. 481], *per* L'Heureux-Dubé J., at pp. 853-54.

Moreover, the argument cannot stand with the jurisprudence which this and other courts have laid down. Today courts regularly recognize the value of domestic services. This became clear with the Court's holding in *Sorochan*, leading one author to comment that "the Canadian Supreme court has finally recognized that domestic contribution is of equal value as financial contribution in trusts of property in the familial context" (Mary Welstead, "Domestic Contribution and Constructive Trusts: The Canadian Perspective," [1987] *Denning L.J.* 151, at p. 161). If there could be any doubt about the need for the law to honestly recognize the value of domestic services, it must be considered to have been banished by *Moge v. Moge*, *supra*. While that case arose under the *Divorce Act*, R.S.C. 1985 c. 3 (2nd Supp.), the value of the services does not change with the legal remedy invoked.

I cannot give credence to the argument that legal recognition of the value of domestic services will do violence to the law and the social structure of our society. It has been recognized for some time that such services are entitled to recognition and compensation under the *Divorce Act* and the provincial Acts governing the distribution of matrimonial property. Yet society has not been visibly harmed. I do not think that similar recognition in the equitable doctrine of unjust enrichment will have any different effect.

Finally, I come to the argument that, because the legislature has chosen to exclude unmarried couples from the right to claim an interest in the matrimonial assets on the basis of contribution to the relationship, the court should not use the equitable doctrine of unjust enrichment to remedy the situation. Again, the argument seems flawed. It is precisely where an injustice arises without a legal remedy that equity finds a role. This case is much stronger than *Rawluk v. Rawluk*, [1990] 1

S.C.R. 70, where I dissented on the ground that the statute expressly pronounced on the very matter with respect to which equity was invoked.

. . . I conclude that the plaintiff was enriched, to the benefit of the defendant, and that no justification existed to *vitiate* the unjust enrichment claim. The claim for unjust enrichment is accordingly made out and it remains only to determine the appropriate remedy.

2. Remedy — Monetary Judgment or Constructive Trust?

The other difficult aspect of this case is the question of whether the remedy which the trial judge awarded — title to the matrimonial home — is justified on the principles governing the action for unjust enrichment. Two remedies are possible: an award of money on the basis of the value of the services rendered, i.e., *quantum meruit*; and the one the trial judge awarded, title to the house based on a constructive trust.

In Canada the concept of the constructive trust has been used as a vehicle for compensating for unjust enrichment in appropriate cases. The constructive trust, based on analogy to the formal trust of traditional equity, is a proprietary concept. The plaintiff is found to have an interest in the property. A finding that a plaintiff is entitled to a remedy for unjust enrichment does not imply that there is a constructive trust. As I wrote in *Rawluk*, *supra*, for a constructive trust to arise, the plaintiff must establish a direct link to the property which is the subject of the trust by reason of the plaintiff's contribution. This is the notion underlying the constructive trust in *Pettkus v. Becker*, *supra*, and *Sorochan v. Sorochan*, *supra*, as I understand those cases. It was also affirmed by La Forest J. in *Lac Minerals*, *supra*.

My colleague Cory J. suggests that, while a link between the contribution and the property is essential in commercial cases for a constructive trust to arise, it may not be required in family cases. He writes at p. 1022:

> . . . La Forest J. concluded [in *Lac Minerals*, *supra*] that the constructive trust should only be awarded when the personal monetary award is insufficient; that is, when there is reason to grant to the plaintiff the additional rights that flow from recognition of a right to property.
>
> I agree with my colleague that there is a need to limit the use of the constructive trust remedy in a commercial context. Yet I do not think the same proposition should be rigorously applied in a family relationship.

I doubt the wisdom of dividing unjust enrichment cases into two categories — commercial and family — for the purpose of determining whether a constructive trust lies. A special rule for family cases finds no support in the jurisprudence. Neither *Pettkus,* nor *Rathwell [Rathwell v. Rathwell,* [1978] 2 W.W.R. 101], nor *Sorochan* suggest such a departure. Moreover, the notion that one can dispense with a link between the services rendered and the property which is claimed to be subject to the trust is inconsistent with the proprietary nature of the notion of constructive trust. Finally, the creation of special rules for special situations might have an adverse effect on the development of this emerging area of equity. The same general principles should apply for all contexts, subject only the demonstrated need for alteration. Wilson J. in *Hunter Engineering Co. v. Syncrude Canada Ltd.*, [1989] 1 S.C.R. 426 [35 B.C.L.R. (2d) 145, [1989] 3 W.W.R. 385], at p. 519 (adopted by La Forest J. in *Lac Minerals*, *supra*, at p. 675), warns against confining constructive trust remedies to family law cases stating that: "to do so would be to impede the growth and impair the flexibility crucial to the development of equitable principles." The same result, I fear, may flow from developing special rules for finding constructive trusts in family cases. In short, the concern for clarity and doctrinal integrity with which this Court has long been preoccupied in this area mandates that the basic principles governing the rights and remedies for unjust enrichment remain the same for all cases.

Nor does the distinction between commercial cases and family cases on the remedy of constructive trust appear to be necessary. Where a monetary award is sufficient, there is no need for a constructive trust. Where a monetary award is insufficient in a family situation, this is usually related to the fact the claimant's efforts have given her a special link to the property, in which case a constructive trust arises.

For these reasons, I hold the view that in order for a constructive trust to be found, in a family case as in other cases, monetary compensation must be inadequate and there must be a link between the services rendered and the property in which the trust is claimed. Having said this, I echo the comments of Cory J. at p. 1023 that the courts should exercise flexibility and common sense when applying equitable principles to family law issues with due sensitivity to the special circumstances that can arise in such cases.

The next question is the extent of the contribution required to give rise to a constructive trust. A minor or indirect contribution is insufficient. The question, to quote Dickson C.J. in *Pettkus v. Becker*, *supra*, at p. 852, is whether "[the plaintiff's] contribution [was] sufficiently substantial and direct as to entitle her to a portion of the profits realized upon sale of the . . . property." Once this threshold is met, the amount of the contribution governs the extent of the constructive trust. As Dickson C.J. wrote in *Pettkus v. Becker*, *supra*, at pp. 852-53:

> Although equity is said to favour equality, as stated in *Rathwell*, it is not every contribution which will entitle a spouse to a one-half interest in the property. *The extent of the interest must be proportionate to the contribution, direct or indirect, of the claimant. Where the contributions are unequal, the shares will be unequal.* [Emphasis added.]

Cory J. advocates a flexible approach to determining whether a constructive trust is appropriate; an approach "based on common sense and a desire to achieve a fair result for both parties" (at p. 1023). While agreeing that courts should avoid becoming overly technical on matters which may not be susceptible of precise monetary valuation, the principle remains that the extent of the trust must reflect the extent of the contribution.

Before leaving the principles governing the remedy of constructive trust, I turn to the manner in which the extent of the trust is determined. The debate centres on whether it is sufficient to look at the value of the services which the claimant has rendered (the "value received" approach), or whether regard should be had to the amount by which the property has been improved (the "value survived" approach). Cory J. expresses a preference for a "value survived" approach. However, he also suggests, at p. 1025, that "there is no reason why *quantum meruit* or the value received approach could not be utilized to quantify the value of the constructive trust." With respect, I cannot agree. It seems to me that there are very good reasons, both doctrinal and practical, for referring to the "value survived" when assessing the value of a constructive trust.

From the point of view of doctrine, "the extent of the interest must be proportionate to the contribution" to the property: *Pettkus v. Becker*, *supra*, at p. 852. How is the contribution to the property to be determined? One starts, of necessity, by defining the property. One goes on to determine what portion of that property is attributable to the claimant's efforts. This is the "value survived" approach. For a monetary award, the "value received" approach is appropriate; the value conferred on the property is irrelevant. But where the claim is for an interest in the property one must of necessity, it seems to me, determine what portion of the value of the property claimed is attributable to the claimant's services.

I note, as does my colleague, that there may also be practical reasons for favouring a "value survived" approach. Cory J., alludes to the practical problems with balancing benefits and detriments as required by the "value received" approach, leading some to question whether it is the least attractive approach in most family property cases (see *Davidson v. Worthing* (1986), 6 R.F.L. (3d) 113 [9 B.C.L.R. (2d) 202] (S.C.), McEachern C.J.S.C.; Hovius and Youdan, *supra*, at pp. 136 *et seq.*). Moreover, a "value survived" approach arguably accords best with the expectations of most parties; it is more likely that a couple expects to share in the wealth generated from their partnership, rather than to receive compensation for the services performed during the relationship.

To summarize, it seems to me that the first step in determining the proper remedy for unjust enrichment is to determine whether a monetary award is insufficient and whether the nexus between the contribution and the property described in *Pettkus v. Becker* has been made out. If these questions are answered in the affirmative the plaintiff is entitled to the proprietary remedy of constructive trust. In looking at whether a monetary award is insufficient the court may take into account the probability of the award's being paid as well as the special interest in the property acquired by the contributions: *per* La Forest J. in *Lac Minerals*. The value of that trust is to be determined on the basis of the actual value of the matrimonial property — the "value survived" approach. It reflects the court's best estimate of what is fair having regard to the contribution which the claimant's services have made to the value surviving, bearing in mind the practical difficulty of calculating with mathematical precision the value of particular contributions to the family property.

I turn now to the application of these principles to the case at bar. The trial judge began by assessing the value received by the respondent (the *quantum meruit*). He went on to conclude that a monetary judgment would be inadequate. The respondent had few assets other than his houseboat and van, and no income save for a War Veteran's Allowance. The judge concluded, as I understand his reasons, that there was a sufficiently direct connection between the services rendered and the property to support a constructive trust, stating that "[the appellant] has shown that there was a positive proprietary benefit conferred by her upon the Sicamous property." Accordingly, he held that the remedy of constructive trust was made out. This approach accords with principles discussed above. In effect, the trial judge found the monetary award to be inadequate on the grounds that it would not be paid and on the ground of a special contribution to the property. These findings support the remedy of constructive trust in the property.

The remaining question is the quantification of the trust. The trial judge calculated the *quantum meruit* for her housekeeping for 12 years at $350 per month and reduced that figure by 50% "for the benefits she received." The final amount was $25,200. He then reasoned that, since the services rendered amounted to $25,200 after appropriate deductions, it follows that the appellant should receive title to the respondent's property, valued at $23,200. The missing step in this analysis is the failure to link the value received with the value surviving. As discussed above, a constructive trust cannot be quantified by simply adding up the services rendered; the court must determine the extent of the contribution which the services have made to the parties' property.

Notwithstanding the trial judge's failure to make this link, his conclusion that the appellant had established a constructive trust entitling her to title to the family home can be maintained if a trust of this magnitude is supported on the evidence. This brings me to a departure from the methods used below. The parties and the Court of Appeal appear to have treated the house as a single asset rather than as part of a family enterprise. This led to the argument that the appellant could not be entitled to full ownership in the house because the respondent had contributed to its value as well. The approach I would take — and the approach I believe the trial judge implicitly to have taken — is to consider the appellant's proper share of all the family assets. This joint family venture, in effect, was no different from the farm which was the subject of the trust in *Pettkus v. Becker*.

With this in mind, I turn to the evidence on the extent of the contribution. The appellant provided extensive household services, over a period of 12 years, including care for the children while they were living at the house and maintenance of the property. The testimony of the plaintiff's son provides a general idea of her contribution to the family enterprise:

Q. What sort of things did she do?

A. She did all the motherly duties for all of us . . .

A. When [the defendant's] two sons and my brother and I were there still, even when my sisters were there, that was quite a long time ago, I was quite young, so there was nothing really bad then, but after the sisters left, she took care of all the duties, cooking and stuff like that, cleaning, laundry. She had her ringer washer, she would do the laundry, she'd worked in the garden, things like that. She took care of all things around the house, when he was gone especially . . .

Q. Do you remember what work your mother did in the yard outside?

A. M'hm, they both got together doing the garden, he would do the roto-tilling, they would both take care of the planting and stuff; when he was gone, she would do all the weeding and keeping up. They would share the watering of the garden. She put together three or four flower gardens all herself, except for the hard heavy work, like lifting rocks, when she first started, that was shared by all of us, including the kids.

Of all the chores performed around the property, the son states that the various siblings had minor chores, such as chopping wood and making beds. "Everything else, the major stuff, she would take care of." Other evidence, including testimony from Catherine Peter and William Beblow, supports this picture of the appellant's contribution. The trial judge held that while the respondent worked in the construction business:

. . . he would be away from home during the week and would return on the weekend whenever possible. While he was absent, the plaintiff would care for the property in the home and care for the children while he was away . . .

In effect, the plaintiff by moving into the respondent's home became his housekeeper on a full-time basis without remuneration except for the food and shelter that she and the children received until the children left home.

The respondent also contributed to the value of the family enterprise surviving at the time of breakup; he generated most of the family income and helped with the maintenance of the property.

Clearly, the appellant's contribution — the "value received" by the respondent — was considerable. But what then of the "value surviving"? It seems clear that the maintenance of the family enterprise through work in cooking, cleaning, and landscaping helped preserve the property and saved the respondent large sums of money which he was able to use to pay off his mortgage and to purchase a houseboat and a van. The appellant, for her part, had purchased a lot with her outside earnings. All these assets may be viewed as assets of the family enterprise to which the appellant contributed substantially.

The question is whether, taking the parties' respective contributions to the family assets and the value of the assets into account, the trial judge erred in awarding the appellant a full interest in the house. In my view, the evidence is capable of supporting the conclusion that the house reflects a fair approximation of the value of the appellant's efforts as reflected in the family assets. Accordingly, I would not disturb the award.

I would allow the appeal with costs.

NOTE

La Forest, Sopinka and Iacobucci JJ. concurred with McLachlin J. (as she then was). L'Heureux-Dubé and Gonthier JJ. agreed with Cory J.

QUESTIONS

1. A drives back to Toronto after a trip to the Fort Erie Racetrack. While waiting at a traffic light, and before A can react, two young men begin to clean A's windshield. The windshield had been covered with dirt and dead sand flies, and it is patent that the cleaning has conferred a benefit on A. Is this a case of unjust enrichment?

2. A agrees to sell land to C, subject to a right of first refusal held by B. B, believing in error that he had acquired the land, begins clearing rock, spraying, fertilizing and seeding. Title is shortly afterwards validly acquired by C. Does B have a claim based on the work undertaken? See *Olchowy v. McKay* 1995 CarswellSask 283, [1996] 1 W.W.R. 36 (Q.B.).

Soulos v. Korkontzilas
[1997] 2 S.C.R. 217, 1997 CarswellOnt 1489, 1997 CarswellOnt 1490

McLachlin J.:

I

This appeal requires this Court to determine whether a real estate agent who buys for himself property for which he has been negotiating on behalf of a client, may be required to return the property to his client despite the fact that the client can show no loss. This raises the legal issue of whether a constructive trust over property may be imposed in the absence of enrichment of the defendant and corresponding deprivation of the plaintiff. In my view, this question should be answered in the affirmative.

II

The appellant Mr. Korkontzilas is a real estate broker. The respondent, Mr. Soulos, was his client. In 1984, Mr. Korkontzilas found a commercial building which he thought might interest Mr. Soulos. Mr. Soulos was interested in purchasing the building. Mr. Korkontzilas entered into negotiations on behalf of Mr. Soulos. He offered $250,000. The vendor, Dominion Life, rejected the offer and tendered a counter-offer of $275,000. Mr. Soulos rejected the counter-offer but "signed it back" at $260,000 or $265,000. Dominion Life advised Mr. Korkontzilas that it would accept $265,000. Instead of conveying this information to Mr. Soulos as he should have, Mr. Korkontzilas arranged for his wife, Panagiota Goutsoulas, to purchase the property using the name Panagiot Goutsoulas. Panagiot Goutsoulas then transferred the property to Panagiota and Fotios Korkontzilas as joint tenants. Mr. Soulos asked what had happened to the property. Mr. Korkontzilas told him to "forget about it"; the vendor no longer wanted to sell it and he would find him a better property. Mr. Soulos asked Mr. Korkontzilas whether he had had anything to do with the vendor's change of heart. Mr. Korkontzilas said he had not.

In 1987 Mr. Soulos learned that Mr. Korkontzilas had purchased the property for himself. He brought an action against Mr. Korkontzilas to have the property conveyed to him, alleging breach of fiduciary duty giving rise to a constructive trust. He asserted that the property held special value to him because its tenant was his banker, and being one's banker's landlord was a source of prestige in the Greek community of which he was a member. However, Mr. Soulos abandoned his claim for damages because the market value of the property had, in fact, decreased from the time of the Korkontzilas purchase. . . .

In my view, the doctrine of constructive trust applies and requires that Mr. Korkontzilas convey the property he wrongly acquired to Mr. Soulos.

III

The first question is what duties Mr. Korkontzilas owed to Mr. Soulos in relation to the property. . . . The trial judge rejected the submission of Mr. Soulos that an agreement existed requiring Mr. Korkontzilas to present all properties in the Danforth area to him exclusively before other purchasers. He found, however, that Mr. Korkontzilas became the agent for Mr. Soulos when he prepared the offer which Mr. Soulos signed with respect to the property at issue. He further found that this agency relationship extended to reporting the vendor's response to Mr. Soulos. This relationship of agency was not terminated when the vendor made its counter-offer. The trial judge therefore concluded that Mr. Korkontzilas was acting as Mr. Soulos' agent at all material times.

The trial judge went on to state that the relationship of agent and principal is fiduciary in nature. He concluded that as agent to Mr. Soulos, Mr. Korkontzilas owed Mr. Soulos a "duty of loyalty". He found that Mr. Korkontzilas breached this duty of loyalty when he failed to refer the vendor's counter-offer to Mr. Soulos.

The Court of Appeal did not take issue with these conclusions. The majority did, however, differ from the trial judge on what consequences flowed from Mr. Korkontzilas' breach of the duty of loyalty.

IV

This brings us to the main issue on this appeal: what remedy, if any, does the law afford Mr. Soulos for Mr. Korkontzilas' breach of the duty of loyalty in acquiring the property in question for himself rather than passing the vendor's statement of the price it would accept on to his principal, Mr. Soulos?

At trial Mr. Soulos' only claim was that the property be transferred to him for the price paid by Mr. Korkontzilas, subject to adjustments for changes in value and losses incurred on the property since purchase. He abandoned his claim for damages at an early stage of the proceedings. This is not surprising, since Mr. Korkontzilas had paid market value for the property and had, in fact, lost money on it during the period he had held it. Still, Mr. Soulos maintained his desire to own the property.

Mr. Soulos argued that the property should be returned to him under the equitable doctrine of constructive trust. The trial judge rejected this claim, on the ground that constructive trust arises only where the defendant has been unjustly enriched by his wrongful act. The fact that damages offered Mr. Soulos no compensation was of no moment: "It would be anomalous to declare a constructive trust, in effect, because a remedy in damages is unsatisfactory, the plaintiff having suffered none" (p. 69). Furthermore, "it seems simply disproportionate and inappropriate to utilize the drastic remedy of a constructive trust where the plaintiff has suffered no damage" (p. 69). The trial judge added that nominal damages were inappropriate, damages having been waived, and that Mr. Soulos had mitigated his loss by buying other properties. . . .

The trial judge took the view that in the absence of established loss, Mr. Soulos had no action. To grant the remedy of constructive trust in the absence of loss would be "simply disproportionate and inappropriate", in his view. The majority in the Court of Appeal, by contrast, took a broader view of when a constructive trust could apply. It held that a constructive trust requiring reconveyance of the property could arise in the absence of an established loss in order to condemn the agent's improper act and maintain the bond of trust underlying the real estate industry and hence the "integrity of the laws" which a court of equity supervises.

The appeal thus presents two different views of the function and ambit of the constructive trust. One view sees the constructive trust exclusively as a remedy for clearly established loss. On this view, a constructive trust can arise only where there has been "enrichment" of the defendant and corresponding "deprivation" of the plaintiff. The other view, while not denying that the constructive trust may appropriately apply to prevent unjust enrichment, does not confine it to that role. On this view, the constructive trust may apply absent an established loss to condemn a wrongful act and maintain the integrity of the relationships of trust which underlie many of our industries and institutions.

It is my view that the second, broader approach to constructive trust should prevail. This approach best accords with the history of the doctrine of constructive trust, the theory underlying the constructive trust, and the purposes which the constructive trust serves in our legal system.

V

The appellants argue that this Court has adopted a view of constructive trust based exclusively on unjust enrichment in cases such as *Becker v. Pettkus*, [1980] 2 S.C.R. 834 (S.C.C.). Therefore, they argue, a constructive trust cannot be imposed in cases like this where the plaintiff can demonstrate no deprivation and corresponding enrichment of the defendant.

The history of the law of constructive trust does not support this view. Rather, it suggests that the constructive trust is an ancient and eclectic institution imposed by law not only to remedy unjust enrichment, but to hold persons in different situations to high standards of trust and probity and prevent them from retaining property which in "good conscience" they should not be permitted to retain. This served the end, not only of doing justice in the case before the court, but of protecting relationships of trust and the institutions that depend on these relationships. These goals were accomplished by treating the person holding the property as a trustee of it for the wronged person's benefit, even though there was no true trust created by intention. In England, the trust thus created was thought of as a real or "institutional" trust. In the United States and recently in Canada, jurisprudence speaks of the availability of the constructive trust as a remedy; hence the remedial constructive trust.

While specific situations attracting a constructive trust have been identified, the older English jurisprudence offers no satisfactory limiting or unifying conceptual theory for the constructive trust. As D. W. M. Waters, *The Constructive Trust* (1964), at p. 39, puts it, the constructive trust "was never any more than a convenient and available language medium through which . . . the obligations of parties might be expressed or determined". The constructive trust was used in English law "to link together a number of disparate situations . . . on the basis that the obligations imposed by law in these situations might in some way be likened to the obligations which were imposed upon an express trustee": J. L. Dewar, "The Development of the Remedial Constructive Trust" (1981), 6 *Est. & Tr. Q.* 312, at p. 317, citing Waters, *supra*.

The situations in which a constructive trust was recognized in England include constructive trusts arising on breach of a fiduciary relationship, as well as trusts imposed to prevent the absence of writing from depriving a person of proprietary rights, to prevent a purchaser with notice from fraudulently retaining trust properties, and to enforce secret trusts and mutual wills. See Dewar, *supra*, at p. 334. The fiduciary relationship underlies much of the English law of constructive trust. As Waters, *supra*, at p. 33, writes: "the fiduciary relationship is clearly wed to the constructive trust over the whole, or little short of the whole, of the trust's operation". At the same time, not all breaches of fiduciary relationships give rise to a constructive trust. As L. S. Sealy, "Fiduciary Relationships", [1962] *Camb. L.J.* 69, at p. 73, states:

> The word "fiduciary," we find, is *not* definitive of a single class of relationships to which a fixed set of rules and principles apply. Each equitable remedy is available only in a limited number of fiduciary situations; and the mere statement that John is in a fiduciary relationship towards me means no more than that in some respects his position is trustee-like; it does not warrant the inference that any particular fiduciary principle or remedy can be applied. [Emphasis in original.]

Nor does the absence of a classic fiduciary relationship necessarily preclude a finding of a constructive trust; the wrongful nature of an act may be sufficient to constitute breach of a trust-like duty: see Dewar, *supra*, at pp. 322-23.

Canadian courts have never abandoned the principles of constructive trust developed in England. They have, however, modified them. Most notably, Canadian courts in recent decades have developed the constructive trust as a remedy for unjust enrichment. It is now established that a constructive trust may be imposed in the absence of wrongful conduct like breach of fiduciary duty, where three elements are present: (1) the enrichment of the defendant; (2) the corresponding deprivation of the plaintiff; and (3) the absence of a juristic reason for the enrichment: *Becker v. Pettkus, supra.*

This Court's assertion that a remedial constructive trust lies to prevent unjust enrichment in cases such as *Becker v. Pettkus* should not be taken as expunging from Canadian law the constructive trust in other circumstances where its availability has long been recognized. The language used makes no such claim. A. J. McClean, "Constructive and Resulting Trusts — Unjust Enrichment in a Common Law Relationship — *Pettkus v. Becker*" (1982), 16 *U.B.C.L. Rev.* 156 at p. 170, describes the ratio of *Becker v. Pettkus* as "a modest enough proposition". He goes on: "It would be wrong . . . to read it as one would read the language of a statute and limit further development of the law".

Other scholars agree that the constructive trust as a remedy for unjust enrichment does not negate a finding of a constructive trust in other situations. D. M. Paciocco, "The Remedial Constructive Trust: A Principled Basis for Priorities over Creditors, (1989), 68 *Can. Bar Rev.* 315, at p. 318, states: "the constructive trust that is used to remedy unjust enrichment must be distinguished from the other types of constructive trusts known to Canadian law prior to 1980". Paciocco asserts that unjust enrichment is not a necessary condition of a constructive trust (at p. 320):

> . . . in the largest traditional category, the fiduciary constructive trust, there need be no deprivation experienced by the particular plaintiff. The constructive trust is imposed to raise the morality of the marketplace generally, with the beneficiaries of some of these trusts receiving what can only be described as a windfall.

Dewar, *supra*, holds a similar view (at p. 332):

> While it is unlikely that Canadian courts will abandon the learning and the classifications which have grown up in connection with the English constructive trust, it is submitted that the adoption of the American style constructive trust by the Supreme Court of Canada in Pettkus v. Becker will profoundly influence the future development of Canadian trust law.

Dewar, *supra*, at pp. 332-33, goes on to state: "In English and Canadian law there is no general agreement as to precisely which situations give rise to a constructive trust, although there are certain general categories of cases in which it is agreed that a constructive trust does arise". One of these is to correct fraudulent or disloyal conduct.

M. M. Litman, "The Emergence of Unjust Enrichment as a Cause of Action and the Remedy of Constructive Trust", (1988), 26 *Alta. L. Rev.* 407, at p. 414, sees unjust enrichment as a useful tool in rationalizing the traditional categories of constructive trust. Nevertheless he opines that it would be a "significant error" to simply ignore the traditional principles of constructive trust. He cites a number of Canadian cases subsequent to *Becker v. Pettkus, supra*, which impose constructive trusts for wrongful acquisition of property, even in the absence of unjust enrichment and correlative deprivation, and concludes that the constructive trust "cannot always be explained by the unjust enrichment model of constructive trust" (p. 416). In sum, the old English law remains part of contemporary Canadian law and guides its development. As La Forest J.A. (as he then was) states in *White v. Central Trust Co.* (1984), 17 E.T.R. 78 (N.B. C.A.), at p. 90, cited by Litman, *supra*, the courts "will not venture far onto an uncharted sea when they can administer justice from a safe berth".

I conclude that the law of constructive trust in the common law provinces of Canada embraces the situations in which English courts of equity traditionally found a constructive trust as well as the situations of unjust enrichment recognized in recent Canadian jurisprudence.

VI

Various principles have been proposed to unify the situations in which the English law found constructive trust. R. Goff and G. Jones, *The Law of Restitution* (3rd ed. 1986), at p. 61, suggest that unjust enrichment is such a theme. However, unless "enrichment" is interpreted very broadly to extend beyond pecuniary claims, it does not explain all situations in which the constructive trust has been applied. As McClean, *supra*, at p. 168, states: "however satisfactory [the unjust enrichment theory] may be for other aspects of the law of restitution, it may not be wide enough to cover all types of constructive trust." McClean goes on to note the situation raised by this appeal: "In some cases, where such a trust is imposed the trustee may not have obtained any benefit at all; this could be the case, for example, when a person is held to be a trustee *de son tort*. A plaintiff may not always have suffered a loss." McClean concludes (at pp. 168-69): "Unjust enrichment may not, therefore, satisfactorily explain all types of restitutionary claims".

McClean, among others, regards the most satisfactory underpinning for unjust enrichment to be the concept of "good conscience" which lies at "the very foundation of equitable jurisdiction" (p. 169):

> "Safe conscience" and "natural justice and equity" were two of the criteria referred to by Lord Mansfield in *Moses v. MacFerlan* (1760), 2 Burr. 1005, 97 E.R. 676 (K.B.) in dealing with an action for money had and received, the prototype of a common law restitutionary claim. "Good conscience" has a sound basis in equity, some basis in common law, and is wide enough to encompass constructive trusts where the defendant has not obtained a benefit or where the plaintiff has not suffered a loss. It is, therefore, as good as, or perhaps a better, foundation for the law of restitution than is unjust enrichment.

Other scholars agree with McClean that good conscience may provide a useful way of unifying the different forms of constructive trust. Litman, *supra*, adverts to the "natural justice and equity" or "good conscience" trust "which operates as a remedy for wrongs which are broader in concept than unjust enrichment" and goes on to state that this may be viewed as the underpinning of the various institutional trusts as well as the unjust enrichment restitutionary constructive trust (at pp. 415-16). . . .

[McLachlin J. (as she then was), then reviewed American, English and New Zealand caselaw which, on the whole, embrace the idea of good conscience as underlying the recognition of the various institutional constructive trusts.]

Good conscience addresses not only fairness between the parties before the court, but the larger public concern of the courts to maintain the integrity of institutions like fiduciary relationships which the courts of equity supervised. As La Forest J. states in *Hodgkinson v. Simms*, [1994] 3 S.C.R. 377 (S.C.C.), at p. 453:

> The law of fiduciary duties has always contained within it an element of deterrence. This can be seen as early as *Keech* in the passage cited supra; see also *Canadian Aero, supra*, at pp. 607 and 610; *Canson, supra*, at p. 547, *per* McLachlin J. In this way the law is able to monitor a given relationship society views as socially useful while avoiding the necessity of formal regulation that may tend to hamper its social utility.

The constructive trust imposed for breach of fiduciary relationship thus serves not only to do the justice between the parties that good conscience requires, but to hold fiduciaries and people in positions of trust to the high standards of trust and probity that commercial and other social institutions require if they are to function effectively.

It thus emerges that a constructive trust may be imposed where good conscience so requires. The inquiry into good conscience is informed by the situations where constructive trusts have been recognized in the past. It is also informed by the dual reasons for which constructive trusts have traditionally been imposed: to do justice between the parties and to maintain the integrity of institutions dependent on trust-like relationships. Finally, it is informed by the absence of an indication that a constructive trust would have an unfair or unjust effect on the defendant or third parties, matters which equity has always taken into account. Equitable remedies are flexible; their award is based on what is just in all the circumstances of the case.

Good conscience as a common concept unifying the various instances in which a constructive trust may be found has the disadvantage of being very general. But any concept capable of embracing the diverse circumstances in which a constructive trust may be imposed must, of necessity, be general. Particularity is found in the situations in which judges in the past have found constructive trusts. A judge faced with a claim for a constructive trust will have regard not merely to what might seem "fair" in a general sense, but to other situations where courts have found a constructive trust. The goal is but a reasoned, incremental development of the law on a case-by-case basis.

The situations which the judge may consider in deciding whether good conscience requires imposition of a constructive trust may be seen as falling into two general categories. The first category concerns property obtained by a wrongful act of the defendant, notably breach of fiduciary obligation or breach of duty of loyalty. The traditional English institutional trusts largely fall under but may not exhaust (at least in Canada) this category. The second category concerns situations where the defendant has not acted wrongfully in obtaining the property, but where he would be unjustly enriched to the plaintiff's detriment by being permitted to keep the property for himself. The two categories are not mutually exclusive. Often wrongful acquisition of property will be associated with unjust enrichment, and vice versa. However, either situation alone may be sufficient to justify imposition of a constructive trust.

In England the law has yet to formally recognize the remedial constructive trust for unjust enrichment, although many of Lord Denning's pronouncements pointed in this direction. The courts do, however, find constructive trusts in circumstances similar to those at bar. Equity traditionally recognized the appropriateness of a constructive trust for breach of duty of loyalty simpliciter. . . .

Both categories of constructive trust are recognized in the United States; although unjust enrichment is sometimes cited as the rationale for the constructive trust in the U.S., in fact its courts recognize the availability of constructive trust to require the return of property acquired by wrongful act absent unjust enrichment of the defendant and reciprocal deprivation of the plaintiff. Thus the authors of *Scott on Trusts* (3rd ed. 1967), Vol. V, at p. 3410, state that the constructive trust "is available where property is obtained by mistake or by fraud or by other wrong".

Canadian courts also recognize the availability of constructive trusts for both wrongful acquisition of property and unjust enrichment. Applying the English law, they have long found constructive trusts as a consequence of wrongful acquisition of property, for example by fraud or breach of fiduciary duty. More recently, Canadian courts have recognized the availability of the American-style remedial constructive trust in cases of unjust enrichment: *Becker v. Pettkus, supra.* However, since *Becker v. Pettkus* Canadian courts have continued to find constructive trusts where property has been wrongfully acquired, even in the absence of unjust enrichment. While such cases appear infrequently since few choose to litigate absent pecuniary loss, they are not rare.

Litman, *supra*, at p. 416, notes that in "the post-*Pettkus v. Becker* era there are numerous cases where courts have used the institutional constructive trust without adverting to or relying on unjust enrichment". The imposition of a constructive trust in these cases is justified not on grounds of unjust enrichment, but on the ground that the defendant's wrongful act requires him to restore the property thus obtained to the plaintiff. . . .

I conclude that in Canada, under the broad umbrella of good conscience, constructive trusts are recognized both for wrongful acts like fraud and breach of duty of loyalty, as well as to remedy unjust enrichment and corresponding deprivation.

While cases often involve both a wrongful act and unjust enrichment, constructive trusts may be imposed on either ground: where there is a wrongful act but no unjust enrichment and corresponding deprivation; or where there is an unconscionable unjust enrichment in the absence of a wrongful act, as in *Becker v. Pettkus, supra*. Within these two broad categories, there is room for the law of constructive trust to develop and for greater precision to be attained, as time and experience may dictate.

The process suggested is aptly summarized by McClean, *supra*, at pp. 167-70:

> The law [of constructive trust] may now be at a stage where it can distill from the specific examples a few general principles, and then, by analogy to the specific examples and within the ambit of the general principle, create new heads of liability. That, it is suggested, is not asking the courts to embark on too dangerous a task, or indeed on a novel task. In large measure it is the way that the common law has always developed.

VII

In *Becker v. Pettkus, supra*, this Court explored the prerequisites for a constructive trust based on unjust enrichment. This case requires us to explore the prerequisites for a constructive trust based on wrongful conduct. Extrapolating from the cases where courts of equity have imposed constructive trusts for wrongful conduct, and from a discussion of the criteria considered in an essay by Roy Goode, "Property and Unjust Enrichment", in Andrew Burrows ed., *Essays on the Law of Restitution* (1991), I would identify four conditions which generally should be satisfied:

> (1) The defendant must have been under an equitable obligation, that is, an obligation of the type that courts of equity have enforced, in relation to the activities giving rise to the assets in his hands;
>
> (2) The assets in the hands of the defendant must be shown to have resulted from deemed or actual agency activities of the defendant in breach of his equitable obligation to the plaintiff;
>
> (3) The plaintiff must show a legitimate reason for seeking a proprietary remedy, either personal or related to the need to ensure that others like the defendant remain faithful to their duties and;
>
> (4) There must be no factors which would render imposition of a constructive trust unjust in all the circumstances of the case; e.g., the interests of intervening creditors must be protected.

VIII

Applying this test to the case before us, I conclude that Mr. Korkontzilas' breach of his duty of loyalty sufficed to engage the conscience of the court and support a finding of constructive trust for the following reasons.

First, Mr. Korkontzilas was under an equitable obligation in relation to the property at issue. His failure to pass on to his client the information he obtained on his client's behalf as to the price the vendor would accept on the property and his use of that information to purchase the property instead for himself constituted breach of his equitable duty of loyalty. He allowed his own interests to conflict with those of his client. He acquired the property wrongfully, in flagrant and inexcusable breach of his duty of loyalty to Mr. Soulos. This is the sort of situation which courts of equity, in Canada and elsewhere, have traditionally treated as involving an equitable duty, breach of which may give rise to a constructive trust, even in the absence of unjust enrichment.

Second, the assets in the hands of Mr. Korkontzilas resulted from his agency activities in breach of his equitable obligation to the plaintiff. His acquisition of the property was a direct result of his breach of his duty of loyalty to his client, Mr. Soulos.

Third, while Mr. Korkontzilas was not monetarily enriched by his wrongful acquisition of the property, ample reasons exist for equity to impose a constructive trust. Mr. Soulos argues that a constructive trust is required to remedy the deprivation he suffered because of his continuing desire, albeit for non-monetary reasons, to own the particular property in question. No less is required, he asserts, to return the parties to the position they would have been in had the breach not occurred. That alone, in my opinion, would be sufficient to persuade a court of equity that the proper remedy for Mr. Korkontzilas' wrongful acquisition of the property is an order that he is bound as a constructive trustee to convey the property to Mr. Soulos.

But there is more. I agree with the Court of Appeal that a constructive trust is required in cases such as this to ensure that agents and others in positions of trust remain faithful to their duty of loyalty: see *Hodgkinson v. Simms, supra, per* La Forest J. If real estate agents are permitted to retain properties which they acquire for themselves in breach of a duty of loyalty to their clients provided they pay market value, the trust and confidence which underpins the institution of real estate brokerage will be undermined. The message will be clear: real estate agents may breach their duties to their clients and the courts will do nothing about it, unless the client can show that the real estate agent made a profit. This will not do. Courts of equity have always been concerned to keep the person who acts on behalf of others to his ethical mark; this Court should continue in the same path.

I come finally to the question of whether there are factors which would make imposition of a constructive trust unjust in this case. In my view, there are none. No third parties would suffer from an order requiring Mr. Korkontzilas to convey the property to Mr. Soulos. Nor would Mr. Korkontzilas be treated unfairly. Mr. Soulos is content to make all necessary financial adjustments, including indemnification for the loss Mr. Korkontszilas has sustained during the years he has held the property.

I conclude that a constructive trust should be imposed. I would dismiss the appeal and confirm the order of the Court of Appeal that the appellants convey the property to the respondent, subject to appropriate adjustments. The respondent is entitled to costs throughout.

NOTE

La Forest, Gonthier, Cory and Major JJ. concurred with McLachlin J. (as she then was). The dissenting opinion of Sopinka J., with which Iacobucci J. concurred, has been omitted.

COMMENT

One of the established forms of institutional constructive trust arises on the sale of real estate. Land transactions typically occur in stages. In a garden-variety house sale, the property is listed with an agent. A prospective buyer is found and, after an anxiety-raising spate of offers and counter-offers, an agreement is reached, the details of which are scribbled on a standard-form agreement. Among the small print one will invariably find a date at which the transaction is to "close". It is on the closing date that the land is transferred to the purchaser and the money fully paid to the vendor. Until then, legal title does not pass. In the interim period between the contract and the closing the necessary searches, inquiries and other preparations are carried out, as need be.

During that interim period, what interest, if any, does the purchaser acquire in the property? In Canada, the conventional response is that the land is held upon a constructive trust, so long as a court of equity would be prepared to grant the remedy of specific performance of the contract. Technically speaking, specific performance is available only once the time for performance arrives (i.e., at the closing date). However, courts in Canada, normally without addressing the issue, consider that if specific performance is available, the trust relates back to the point in time at which the contract was made. See further *Martin Commercial Fueling, Inc. v. Virtanen* 144 D.L.R. (4th) 290, 1997 CarswellBC 600 (C.A.).

As just mentioned, this brand of constructive trust is premised on the availability of specific performance, and in the past a purchaser could generally count on a court of equity to conclude that the uniqueness of a parcel of land would point to specific performance as the appropriate remedy. Damages were routinely treated as an inadequate response to a breach. Land is special; they've stopped making it. However, in *Semelhago v. Paramadevan* [1996] 2 S.C.R. 415, 1996 CarswellOnt 2737, 1996 CarswellOnt 2738, Sopinka J. cast doubt on that point of view. There, in *obiter*, he suggested (at 428-9) that:.

> It is no longer appropriate . . . to maintain a distinction in the approach to specific performance as between realty and personalty. It cannot be assumed that damages for breach of contract for the purchase and sale of real estate will be an inadequate remedy in all cases. . . .
>
> Specific performance should, therefore, not be granted as a matter of course absent evidence that the property is unique to the extent that its substitute would not be readily available.

These words have been influential, as is evident from the review of the authorities in *Cross Creek Timber Traders Inc. v. St. John Terminals Ltd.* 49 R.P.R. (3d) 35, 2002 CarswellNB 80 (Q.B.), below.

Cross Creek Timber Traders Inc. v. St. John Terminals Ltd. 49 R.P.R. (3d) 35, 2002 CarswellNB 80 (Q.B.)

[Cross Creek Timber Traders agreed to purchase lands from St. John's Terminals. A cheque for $30,000 was given as a deposit to the real estate agent who was acting for both parties. Mistakenly believing that the deposit cheque had not been paid on time, the vendor withdrew from the agreement. The trial judge found that the vendor had in fact been searching for a reason to back out of the deal, and that its conduct constituted an anticipatory breach of contract. In this action, the purchasers sought the equitable remedy of specific performance of the agreement for sale.]

Glennie J.: . . .

Remedy

Cross Creek seeks specific performance. Specific performance of a contract for the sale of reality is the appropriate remedy where the land has a special or unique value such that damages may not provide an adequate remedy.

> Specific performance should, therefore, not be granted as a matter of course absent evidence that the property is unique to the extent that its substitute would not be readily available. (*Semelhago v. Paramadevan* (1996), 136 D.L.R. (4th) 1 (S.C.C.), at 11) . . .

In his text, *Injunctions and Specific Performance*, Canada Law Book Inc., Justice Robert J. Sharpe writes:

> 8.10 The remedy of specific performance has, until recently, almost invariably been granted when sought to enforce contracts for the purchase and sale of land. However, in light of a recent decision of the Supreme Court of Canada (*Semelhago*), this appears to no longer be the case, and it will now be necessary to consider the extent to which the property in question may be said to be unique. Discussion of the issues arising here will be facilitated by dealing in turn with the purchaser's and vendor's rights to specific performance. . . .
>
> Specific performance should, therefore, not be granted as a matter of course absent evidence that the property is unique to the extent that its substitute would not be readily available.

Justice Sharpe writes at p. 8-4, *Injunctions and Specific Performance*:

> Since *Semelhago*, lower courts have frequently found that from the purchaser's perspective, properties are unique: see e.g. *Morsky v. Harris*, [1997] 6 W.W.R. 557, 155 Sask.R. 193, 10 R.P.R. (3d) 133 (Q.B.) revd on other grounds [1998] 8 W.W.R. 340, 168 Sask.

> R. 27, 173 W.A.C. 27 (C.A.) (homestead unique as land fertile and rarely available on the open market); *Tropiano v. Stonevalley Estates Inc.* (1997), 36 O.R. (3d) 92 (Gen. Div.) (subdivision lot unique due to border with ravine); 11 *Suntract Holdings Ltd. v. Chassis Service & Hydraulics Ltd.* (1997), 36 O.R. (3d) 328, 15 R.P.R. (3d) 201 (Gen. Div.), supp. reasons 15 R.P.R. (3d) 234 (Gen. Div.) (industrial property unique as crucial component of larger development plan); *Mc-Carthy v. Amiss* (1997), 14 R.P.R. (3d) 27 (B.C.S.C.) (specific performance ordered without any discussion of uniqueness requirement); 11 *Suntract Holdings Ltd. v. Chassis Service & Hydraulics Ltd.* (1997), 36 O.R. (3d) 328, 15 R.P.R. (3d) 201, supp. reasons 15 R.P.R. (3d) 234 (Ont. Ct. (Gen. Div.)); *1252668 Ontario Inc. v. Wyndham Street Investments Inc.* (1999), 27 R.P.R. (3d) 58 (Ont. S.C.J.), supplementary reasons 91 A.C.W.S. (3d) 303, leave to appeal to C.A. granted 92 A.C.W.S. (3d) 302; at p. 64, per Lamek J.: *I do not consider that the plaintiff has to demonstrate that the premises are unique in a strict dictionary sense that they are entirely different from any other piece of property. It is enough . . . for the plaintiff to demonstrate that the premises have a quality that makes them especially suitable for the proposed use and that they cannot be reasonably duplicated elsewhere.* [My emphasis.]

In a case comment entitled "The Supreme Court of Canada's Lost Opportunity: *Semelhago v. Paramadevan*" the author, Orlando Da Silva (1998), 23 Queens L.J. 475, comments on the *Semelhago* decision as follows:

> Unfortunately, although the court replaced centuries old presumptions about the value of land with a "uniqueness analysis," it did so without guiding lower courts and practitioners on how to conduct such an analysis (i.e., whether it should be objectively or subjectively based). The court merely identified the starting point of the analysis as being a review of the "uniqueness" of the land. Uniqueness apparently means, according to the court, that there are no "readily available substitutes." Apart from using the word "readily," the Supreme Court of Canada merely held that the land is unique when it is unique. There ends the analysis - and with it three centuries of legal jurisprudence. . . .

It is relevant to note that in *Semelhago v. Paramadevan*, Justice Sopinka writes at Para 20:

> While at one time the common law regarded every piece of real estate to be unique, with the progress of modern real estate development this is no longer the case. *Both residential, business and industrial properties are mass produced much in the same way as other consumer products.* If a deal falls through for one property, another is frequently, though not always, readily available.
>
> It is no longer appropriate, therefore, to maintain a distinction in the approach to specific performance as between realty and personalty. It cannot be assumed that damages for breach of contract for the purchase and sale of real estate will be an inadequate remedy in all cases. [My emphasis.]

It would appear that Justice Sopinka was referring to the mass production of residential, business and industrial properties in the sense of development which would include the subdivision and servicing of land and the construction of buildings thereon. In the case at bar, we are not dealing with a mass produced or cookie cutter property. We are dealing with 800 acres of unharvested, undeveloped, unsubdivided heavily wooded timberland in Southern New Brunswick which is especially suitable for Cross Creek's proposed use.

I am satisfied on the evidence that the Lake Retreat property is unique. It has a particular mixture of wood product including cedar, hardwood, high quality spruce and low quality pulpwood that makes it especially suitable for Cross Creek's proposed use. There is no evidence that 800 acres of heavily wooded timberland can be reasonably duplicated elsewhere. A related company owns an adjacent parcel of land. The Lake Retreat property has a quality that makes it especially suitable for Cross Creek's proposed use. I conclude on the evidence that a substitute property was not readily available. Mr. Hargrove was asked if there have been any other 800 acre parcels of land with the kind of growth that's on the Lake Retreat property available to buy since Terminals failed to complete the transaction, and he responded in the negative. When asked if there have been other pieces of land this size with that kind of a stand of wood that he has been able to buy, Mr. Hargrove responded in the negative. He says he has not been able to buy any. Mr. Hargrove used forest inventory maps to determine the age, class and distribution of the trees and the species on the Lake Retreat property. It must be remembered that this is a heavily wooded property. I am satisfied on the evidence that its duplicate is not readily available. Terminals offered no evidence from a forester, real estate agent or assessor to counter Mr. Hargrove's testimony. I have no hesitation in accepting Mr. Hargrove's testimony in this regard. There is no evidence that the features of the Lake Retreat property can be reasonably duplicated elsewhere. I have also taken into consideration the size of the property. It is not, for example, a building lot in a subdivision or in the nature of "mass produced" property referred to by Justice Sopinka in *Semelhago*. I have also taken into consideration that because of its equitable nature, specific performance is a discretionary remedy, not available as of right as are common law damages. Cross Creek chose to keep the contract in this case alive. It did nothing to allow a conclusion to be drawn from July 20, 2000, forward that it was not ready, willing and able to complete the Agreement of Purchase and Sale it had entered into with Terminals. It acted in good faith at all times.

In an article on *Semelhago,* written by Professor Donald H. Clark entitled "Will That Be Performance . . . Or Cash?: *Semelhago v. Paramadevan* and the Notion of Equivalence" (1999) 37 A.L.T.A. L.rev (no. 3) 589-619, the author writes at Para. 6:

> There is a neatness about assimilating real estate transactions of all kinds with personalty in this context. However, symmetry has to be weighed against the considerable downside for both litigants and their legal advisers: inevitable uncertainty as to what characteristics or combination of characteristics will qualify as "unique" (for example, size, shape, view, proximity to shops/parks/schools/relatives/friends, "character"), with the resultant dilemma of how much evidence to call and of what kind; the equally inevitable inconsistency of decisions on something so intangible as the attraction of a particular property. The critical determination, unless a finding of the plaintiff's sincerity were itself to be sufficient to discharge the onus, will have to be an objective judgment-call by the court.
> . . .

It would be an entirely different situation if Terminals had subdivided the 800 acre Lake Retreat property into 800 one acre serviced building lots and Cross Creek had offered to purchase one of those building lots. . . .

Conclusion and Disposition

Accordingly, there shall be judgment in favour of Cross Creek for specific performance of the Agreement of Purchase and Sale relating to the Lake Retreat property. Cross Creek is also entitled to damages, if any, caused by Terminals failure to close at the specified time.

Action allowed.

QUESTIONS AND COMMENTS

1. Consider also Spiegel J.'s assessment of the post-*Semelhago* caselaw in *Neighbourhoods of Cornell Inc. v. 14401066 Ontario Inc.* 2003 CarswellOnt 2757 (S.C.J.) at paras. 109-111:

> When one looks at the rationale behind the equitable remedy of specific performance, uniqueness is just one of several factors to consider. The essential question is whether damages are not sufficient to do justice and there is "some fair, real and substantial justification for the claim." Uniqueness, in the sense that there is no replacement property available, is one indicator that damages might not be adequate compensation for the loss of the land. However, if the purchaser's intention was not to use the land but to resell it, then the land's uniqueness becomes less important in determining if specific performance is necessary to do justice.
>
> The purchase of land as an investment is different than the purchase of land in order to run a business on it (as was the case in *John E. Dodge* [2003 CarswellOnt 342 (C.A.)]) or the purchase of land as one's home (as in *Semelhago*). In *Semelhago*, at least part of the motivation was the personal enjoyment of the unique aspects of the land — a non-monetary benefit. In *John E. Dodge*, the benefit, while not purely non-monetary, was derived from the continued use of the land such as the ability to attract business at that particular location. When the purchaser gets a non-monetary benefit from the uniqueness of the land, damages cannot adequately compensate this loss; therefore, specific performance is an appropriate remedy.
>
> With an investment, the goal is to sell the land either before or after development for profit; the only benefit for the purchaser from the special qualities of the land is monetary. The loss of these benefits can usually be adequately assessed and compensated for in the award of damages. It does not matter that the land is unique if the only benefit to be derived from its uniqueness is monetary. Even if it is a uniquely good investment, damages are adequate compensation for a monetary loss. To borrow the words of Weatherston J. in *Heron Bay Investments*, [2 C.P.C. 338 (Ont. H.C.)] at 339, "True, it may be a uniquely good investment, but it was not being purchased by the plaintiffs for their own use but only to develop and resell at a profit. Obviously, any loss of profits can be compensated for in damages."

2. Under what circumstances would it be appropriate to deny specific performance for an agreement concerning residential property? Consider *De Sena v. Allure Homes Ltd.* 2002 CarswellAlta 763 (Master), and also *Kelly v. Dosch* 2003 CarswellOnt 330, 8 R.P.R. (4th) 306 (S.C.J.).

3. *Semelhago* has been treated as an innovation, whether for better or worse. Is it really new?

Bulun Bulun v. R. & T. Textiles Pty. Ltd. (1998) 157 A.L.R. 193 (Fed. Ct.)

von Doussa J.:

These proceedings arise out of the importation and sale in Australia of printed clothing fabric which infringed the copyright of the first applicant Mr Bulun Bulun, in the artistic work known as "Magpie Geese and Water Lilies at the Waterhole" ("the artistic work").

The proceedings were commenced on 27 February 1996 by Mr Bulun Bulun and the second applicant, Mr George Milpurrurru. Both applicants are leading Aboriginal artists. The respondents were at that time, R & T Textiles Pty Ltd ("the respondent") and its three directors. Mr Bulun Bulun sued as the legal owner of the copyright pursuant to the *Copyright Act* 1968 (Cth) for remedies for the infringement, for contraventions of sections of Pt. V of the *Trade Practices Act* 1974 (Cth) dealing with misleading or deceptive conduct, and for nuisance. Mr Milpurrurru brought the proceedings in his own right and as a representative of the traditional Aboriginal owners of Ganalbingu country which is situated in Arnhem Land, in the Northern Territory of Australia. He claims that the traditional Aboriginal owners of Ganalbingu country are the equitable owners of the copyright subsisting in the artistic work.

These proceedings represent another step by Aboriginal people to have communal title in their traditional ritual knowledge, and in particular in their artwork, recognised and protected by the Australian legal system. The inadequacies of statutory remedies under the *Copyright Act* 1976 as a means of protecting communal ownership have been noted in earlier decisions of this Court: see *Yumbulul v. Reserve Bank of Australia* (1991) 21 IPR 481 at 490 and *Milpurrurru v. Indofurn Pty Ltd* (1994) 54 FCR 240 at 247. . . .

> While joint authorship of a work by two or more authors is recognised by the *Copyright Act*, collective ownership by reference to any other criterion, for example, membership of the author of a community whose customary laws invest the community with ownership of any creation of its members is not recognised.
>
> [Ellison, "Stopping the Rip-Offs: Intellectual Property Protection for Aboriginal and Torres Strait Islander Peoples" (1994) National Capital Printing at 6].

Mr Bulun Bulun's claim

As soon as the proceedings were served the respondent admitted infringement of Mr Bulun Bulun's copyright in the artistic work, and pleaded that the infringement had occurred in ignorance of the copyright. The respondent immediately withdrew the offending fabric from sale. At that time approximately 7600 metres of the fabric had been imported and approximately 4231 metres sold in Australia. . . .

Counsel for the applicants informed the Court that the artistic work incorporates within its subject matter much that is sacred and important to the Ganalbingu people about their heritage. Counsel emphasised that copyright infringements of artworks such as the artistic work affect interests beyond those of the copyright owner, and that the Ganalbingu people considered it to be of great importance that the Court recognise the rights of the Ganalbingu people and the injury caused to them by the respondent's infringement. Counsel said that Mr Milpurrurru therefore proposed to continue with his claim notwithstanding the consent orders in favour of Mr Bulun Bulun. . . .

Evidence in Mr Milpurrurru's claim . . .

Much of the evidence in these proceedings relates to customary rights and obligations recognised and observed by the individual members of the Ganalbingu people and the group as a whole. For a discussion of the reception of customary law into evidence see *Delgamuukw v. British Columbia* (1997) 153 DLR (4th) 193 at para. 81-87 [3(1) AILR 35], per Lamer C.J. Counsel for the Minister submitted that customary rights and interests are not enforceable in Australian courts. As Lamer C.J. in the Supreme Court of Canada observed in *Delgamuukw v. British Colombia*, customary rights and obligations are not easily explicable and definable in terms of ordinary western jurisprudential analysis or common law concepts. The High Court's decision in *Mabo v. Queensland (No. 2)* (1992) 175 CLR 1 [66 ALJR 408]; 107 ALR 1 shows that customary indigenous law has a role to play within the Australian legal system. Indeed the conclusion that native title survived the Crown's acquisition of sovereignty was dependent upon the Court's acceptance of antecedent traditional laws and customs acknowledged and observed by the indigenous inhabitants of the land claimed. Whilst Mason C.J. observed in *Walker v. New South Wales* (1994) 182 CLR 45 at 49-59; [2(1) AILR 35; 71 ALJR 173;] 126 ALR 321 that it is not possible to use evidence about indigenous customs and traditions to operate as "customary law" in opposition to or alongside Australian law (see also *Coe v. Commonwealth* (1993) 118 ALR 193 at 200, and *Wik Peoples v. Queensland* (1996) 187 CLR 1 at 214 . . . per Kirby J.), Australian courts cannot treat as irrelevant the rights, interests and obligations of Aboriginal people embodied within customary law. Evidence of customary law may be used as a basis for the foundation of rights recognised within the Australian legal system. Native title is a clear example. In *Milpurrurru v. Indofurn* the Court took into account the effect of the unauthorised reproduction of artistic works under customary Aboriginal laws in quantifying the damage suffered. In my opinion the evidence about Ganalbingu law and customs is admissible.

The amended application in this case alleges that the Ganalbingu people are the traditional Aboriginal owners of Ganalbingu country who have the right to permit and control the production and reproduction of the artistic work under the law and custom of the Ganalbingu people. . . .

The amended statement of claim pleads that the Ganalbingu people are the traditional Aboriginal owners of the corpus of ritual knowledge from which the artistic work is derived, including the subject matter of the artistic work and the artistic work itself.

Mr Milpurrurru is the most senior person of all the Ganalbingu people. The Ganalbingu people are divided into "top" and "bottom" people as is the Ganalbingu country. Mr Milpurrurru is a "top" Ganalbingu. Mr Bulun Bulun is the most senior person of the "bottom" Ganalbingu and is second in line to Mr Milpurrurru of the Ganalbingu people generally. . . .

The artistic work was painted by Mr Bulun Bulun in 1978 with permission of senior members of the Ganalbingu people. He sold it to the Maningrida Arts and Crafts Centre. At that time Mr Peter Cooke was the arts adviser at the Centre. Mr Cooke then arranged the sale of the artistic work to the Northern Territory Museum of Arts and Sciences. It was reproduced with Mr Bulun Bulun's consent in the book *Arts of the Dreaming — Australia's Living Heritage* by Jennifer Isaacs at p. 198. The artwork was copied without the consent of Mr Bulun Bulun by a Queensland T-shirt manufacturer in 1988, which led to proceedings being taken by Mr Bulun Bulun in the Federal Court of Australia in 1989. These proceedings received wide publicity. They were settled prior to a hearing. In the present case, the artistic work has not been exactly reproduced on the infringing fabric, but the design of the fabric obviously reproduces substantial aspects of the artwork, and constitutes a substantial reproduction of it. So much was acknowledged by the respondent as soon as the copyright was brought to its attention. . . .

Why the claim is confined to one for recognition of an equitable interest

The submissions of counsel for the applicants reflected a wide ranging search for a way in which the communal interests of the traditional Aboriginal owners in cultural artworks might be recognised under Australian law. This exercise was painstakingly pursued by counsel for the applicants (and later by counsel for the Minister). That the claim was ultimately confined to one for recognition of an equitable interest in the legal copyright of Mr Bulun Bulun is an acknowledgment that no other possible avenue had emerged from the researches of counsel.

Whilst it is superficially attractive to postulate that the common law should recognise communal title, it would be contrary to established legal principle for the common law to do so. There seems no reason to doubt that customary Aboriginal laws relating to the ownership of artistic works survived the introduction of the common law of England in 1788. The Aboriginal peoples did not cease to observe their *sui generis* system of rights and obligations upon the acquisition of sovereignty of Australia by the Crown. The question however is whether those Aboriginal laws can create binding obligations on persons outside the relevant Aboriginal community, either through recognition of those laws by the common law, or by their capacity to found equitable rights *in rem*.

In *Mabo (No. 2)* Deane and Gaudron JJ., after analysing the effects of the introduction of the common law of England into Australia in 1788 said, (at CLR 79):

> The common law so introduced was adjusted in accordance with the principle that, in settled colonies, only so much of it was introduced as was 'reasonably applicable to the circumstances of the colony'. This left room for the continued operation of some local laws or customs among the native people and even the incorporation of some of those laws and customs as part of the common law [some footnotes omitted].

In 1788 there may have been scope for the continued operation of a system of indigenous collective ownership in artistic works. At that time the common law of England gave the author of an artistic work property in unpublished compositions which lasted in perpetuity: *Mansell v. Valley Printing Company* [1908] 1 Ch 567 and Laddie, Prescott and Vitoria, *The Modern Law of Copyright* 1980, para 4.64. That property was lost upon publication of the artistic work. Exhibition for sale or sale constituted publication: *Britain v. Hanks Bros and Co.* (1902) 86 LT 765. This property interest was separate from the right recognised in equity to restrain a breach of confidence, a right which continues and was invoked in *Foster v. Mountford and Rigby Ltd.* (1976) 14 ALR 71. The common law of England did not protect an author of an artistic work after publication. If the common law had not been amended in the meantime by statute, an interesting question would arise as to whether Aboriginal laws and customs could be incorporated into the common law. However, the common law has since been subsumed by statute. The common law right until first publication was abolished when the law of copyright was codified by the *Copyright Act* of 1911 in the United Kingdom. That Act, subject to some modifications, became the law in Australia by s. 8 of the *Copyright Act 1912* (Cth). Copyright is now entirely a creature of statute: McKeough and Stewart, *Intellectual Property in Australia* (1991) at para. 504; *Copinger and Skone James on Copyright* (13th ed.), para. 1-43. The exclusive domain of the *Copyright Act 1968* in Australia is expressed in s. 8 (subject only to the qualification in s. 8A) namely, that "copyright does not subsist otherwise than by virtue of this Act".

Section 35(2) of the *Copyright Act 1968* provides that the author of an artistic work is the owner of the copyright which subsists by virtue of the Act. That provision effectively precludes any notion of group ownership in an artistic work, unless the artistic work is a "work of joint ownership" within the meaning of s. 10(1) of the Act. A "work of joint authorship" means a work that has been produced by the collaboration of two or more authors and in which the contribution of each author is not separate from the contribution of the other author or the contributions of the other authors. In this case no evidence was led to suggest that anyone other than Mr Bulun Bulun was the creative author of the artistic work. A person who supplies an artistic idea to an artist who then executes the work is not, on that ground alone, a joint author with the artist: *Kenrick & Co v. Lawrence & Co.* (1890) 25 QBD 99. Joint authorship envisages the contribution of skill and labour to the production of the work itself: *Fylde Microsystems Ltd v. Kay Radio Systems Ltd.* (1998) 39 IPR 481 at 486.

In *Coe v. Commonwealth* (1993) 118 ALR 193 at 200 Mason C.J. rejected the proposition that Aboriginal people are entitled to rights and interests other than those created or recognised by the laws of the Commonwealth, its states and the common law. See also *Walker v. New South Wales* (at 45-50) and Kirby J. in *Wik Peoples v. Queensland* (at CLR 214). To conclude that the Ganalbingu people were communal owners of the copyright in the existing work would ignore the provisions of s. 8 of the *Copyright Act*, and involve the creation of rights in indigenous peoples which are not otherwise recognised by the legal system of Australia.

Do the circumstances in which the artistic work was created give rise to equitable interests in the Ganalbingu People?

The statement of claim alleges "on the reduction to material form of a part of the ritual knowledge of the Ganalbingu people associated with Djulibinyamurr by the creation of the artistic work, the first applicant held the copyright subsisting in the artistic work as a fiduciary and/or alternatively on trust, for the second applicant and the people he represents". The foundation for this contention is expanded in written submissions made on Mr Milpurrurru's behalf. It is contended that these rights arise because Mr Milpurrurru and those he represents have the power under customary law to regulate and control the production and reproduction of the corpus of ritual knowledge. It is contended that the customs and traditions regulating this use of the corpus of ritual knowledge places Mr Bulun Bulun as the author of the artistic work in the position of a fiduciary, and, moreover, make Mr Bulun Bulun a trustee for the artwork, either pursuant to some form of express trust, or pursuant to a constructive trust in favour of the Ganalbingu people. The right to control the production and reproduction of the corpus of ritual knowledge relating to Djulibinyamurr is said to arise by virtue of the strong ties which continue to exist between the Ganalbingu people and their land.

Was there an express trust?

The possibility that an express trust was created in respect of the artistic work or the copyright subsisting in it was not at the forefront of the applicants' submissions. In my opinion that possibility can be dismissed on the evidence in this case. The existence of an express trust depends on the intention of the creator. No formal or technical words constituting an expression of intention are necessary to create an express trust. Any apt expression of intention will suffice: *Registrar, Accident Compensation Tribunal v. FCT* (1993) 178 CLR 145 at 166; 117 ALR 27. What is important is that intention to create a trust be manifest in some form or another. There must be an intention on the part of the putative creator to divest himself or herself the beneficial interest, and to become a trustee of the property for another party: *Garrett v. L'Estrange* (1911) 13 CLR 430. An intention to create a trust may be inferred even where the creator has not in words expressed such an intention: see *Jacobs' Law of Trusts* (6th ed), para. 309. The intention to create a trust may be inferred from conduct: *Gissing v. Gissing* [1971] AC 886 at 900, 906, and *A-One Accessory Imports Pty Ltd. v. Off Road Imports Pty Ltd.* (1996) 143 ALR 543 at 557. A trust created in such circumstances remains an express trust based on the actual intention of the creator as inferred from his or her conduct: *Bahr v. Nicolay (No. 2)* (1988) 164 CLR 604 at 618-19; 78 ALR 1.

In the present case it is suggested that it should be inferred that by creating the artistic work with the permission of those of the Ganalbingu people who had the right to control the corpus of ritual knowledge associated with Djulibinyamurr Mr Bulun Bulun intended to hold the copyright subsisting in the artistic work for the benefit of the Ganalbingu people.

The artwork, when completed, was sold by Mr Bulun Bulun to the Maningrida Arts and Crafts Centre. It is not suggested that he did not receive and retain the sale price for his own use. Moreover, the evidence indicates that on many occasions paintings which incorporate to a greater or lesser degree parts of the ritual knowledge of the Ganalbingu people are produced by Ganalbingu artists for commercial sale for the benefit of the artist concerned.

On the evidence there is no suggestion that ownership and use of the artistic work itself should be treated separately from ownership in the copyright to the artistic work. The evidence was directed to uses made of the artwork itself that were permissible or impermissible under Ganalbingu law and customs. Notions of copyright ownership have not developed under Ganalbingu law. If it were possible to infer an express trust, on the evidence the subject matter of the trust would be the artistic work itself and all the rights that attach to its creation under the Australian legal system.

There is no usual or customary practice whereby artworks are held in trust for the Ganalbingu people. In the present case neither Mr Bulun Bulun's djungaye or Mr Milpurrurru suggest that the commercial sale of the artwork by Mr Bulun Bulun was contrary to customary law, or to the terms of the permission which was given to him to produce the artwork. In these circumstances, the fact of the sale and the retention of the proceeds for his own use is inconsistent with there being an intention on the part of Mr Bulun Bulun to create an express trust. Further, the fact that the artwork was sold commercially, and has been the subject of reproduction, with the apparent permission of those who control its reproduction, in *Arts of the Dreaming — Australian Living Heritage*, forecloses any possibility of arguing that the imagery in the artwork is of such a secret or sacred nature that it could be inferred that the artist must have had the intention in accordance with customary law to hold the artwork for the benefit of the Ganalbingu people.

If the evidence were consistent with there being an intention by Mr Bulun Bulun to hold the artwork and the copyright on an express trust, a further question would arise whether the express trust was for a charitable purpose. If not, the trust might fail for want of certainty as to the identity of the objects of the trust. This would be so if the intention were to create a trust in favour of both present and future members of the Ganalbingu people. Whilst it could be argued that the requisite certainty existed because the trust should be construed as being for the immediate beneficial enjoyment of present members of the clan (*Leahy v. Attorney-General (NSW)* [1959] AC 475 at 478-9), the nature of Aboriginal communal ownership, insofar as it is described in the evidence, suggests that the beneficiaries of such a trust would be regarded as being all present and future members of the clan as a whole and not for the immediate enjoyment of present members. These questions are not addressed either by the evidence or by the applicants' submissions.

Did Mr Bulun Bulun hold the copyright as a fiduciary?

In *Breen v. Williams* (1996) 186 CLR 71 at 82; 138 ALR 259, Brennan C.J. identified two sources of fiduciary duties, the first being the circumstances in which a relationship of agency can be said to exist, and the other is founded in a relationship of ascendancy or influence by one party over another, or dependence or trust on the part of that other. The applicants' counsel did not seek to characterise the fiduciary relationship for which he contends as derived from either source in particular. The existence of a fiduciary relationship is said to arise out of the nature of ownership of artistic works amongst the Ganalbingu people. . . .

The factors and relationships giving rise to a fiduciary duty are nowhere exhaustively defined: *Mabo (No. 2)* (at CLR 200) per Toohey J.; *Hospital Products v. United States Surgical Corp* (1984) 156 CLR 41 at 68, 96-97; 55 ALR 417; P.D. Finn, *Fiduciary Obligations* (1977), p. 1, and *News Ltd. v. Australian Rugby Football League Ltd.* (at IPR 564). It has been said that the term "fiduciary relationship", defies definition: *Breen v. Williams* (at CLR 106) per Gaudron and McHugh JJ., see also Gibbs C.J. in *Hospital Products v. United States Surgical Corp* (at CLR 69). For this reason the fiduciary concept has developed incrementally throughout the case law which itself provides guidance as to the traditional parameters of the concept. The essential characteristics of fiduciary relationships were referred to by Mason J. in *Hospital Products* (at CLR 96-7; ALR 454):

> The critical feature of [fiduciary] relationships is that the fiduciary undertakes or agrees to act for or on behalf of or in the interests of another person in the exercise of a power or discretion which will affect the interests of that other person in a legal or practical sense. The relationship between the parties is therefore one which gives the fiduciary a special opportunity to exercise the power or discretion to the detriment of that other person who is accordingly vulnerable to abuse by the fiduciary of his position . . . It is partly because the fiduciary's exercise of the power or discretion can adversely affect the interests of the person to whom the duty is owed and because the latter is at the mercy of the former that the fiduciary comes under a duty to exercise his power or discretion in the interests of the person to whom it is owed.

In *Mabo,* Toohey J. said (at CLR 200; ALR 156):

> Underlying such relationships is the scope for one party to exercise a discretion which is capable of affecting the legal position of the other. One party has a special opportunity to abuse the interests of the other. The discretion will be an incident of the first party's office or position.

In *Wik Peoples v. Queensland* (1996) 187 CLR 1 at 95; 141 ALR 129 at 160 Brennan C.J. said with respect to the asserted existence of a fiduciary duty owed by the Crown to the indigenous inhabitants of the leased areas under consideration:

> It is necessary to identify some action or function the doing or performance of which attracts the supposed fiduciary duty to be observed: *Breen v. Williams* (1996) 186 CLR 71 at 82; 138 ALR 259. The doing of the action or the performance of the function must be capable of affecting the interests of the beneficiary and the fiduciary must have so acted that it is reasonable for the beneficiary to believe and expect that the fiduciary will act in the interests of the beneficiary (or, in the case of a partnership or joint venture, in the common interest of the beneficiary and fiduciary) to the exclusion of the interest of any other person or the separate interest of the beneficiary. [Some footnotes omitted].

See also the discussion of fiduciary relationships in *News Ltd v. Australian Rugby Football League Ltd* (at IPR 563-7), and Weinrib, "The Fiduciary Obligation" (1975) 25 *University of Toronto Law Journal* 1 at 4-8.

In *Hodgkinson v. Simms* (1994) 117 DLR (4th) 161, La Forest J. expressed the question whether a fiduciary relationship existed as being "whether, given all the surrounding circumstances, one party could reasonably have expected that the other party would act in the former's best interests with respect to the subject-matter at issue" (see also *LAC Minerals Ltd. v. International Corona Resources Ltd.* (1989) 61 DLR (4th) 14 at 40. As the statement of Brennan C.J. in *Wik* at 95 (above) reflects, the law of fiduciary relations in this country has followed that of Canada in recognising the protection of reasonable expectations as a fundamental purpose of the fiduciary concept: see also *The Principles of Equity* (Parkinson (Ed.)) (1996), P.D. Finn, "The Fiduciary Principle" in T.G. Youdan (Ed.), *Equity, Fiduciaries and Trusts* (1989), p. 46 and *Commonwealth Bank of Australia v. Smith* (1991) 102 ALR 453 at 476.

The Court was not referred to any authority in support of the imposition of equitable principles to govern relations amongst members of a tribal group. However, the application of the principles of equity in this situation is not unknown to the common law as it has been applied outside of this country. Amongst tribal communities of African countries tribal property is regarded as being held on "trust" by the customary head of a tribal group: see S. K. B. Asante "Fiduciary Principles in Anglo-American Law and The Customary Law of Ghana" (1965) 14 *International & Comparative Law Quarterly* 1144 at 1145. This principle received judicial recognition in *Kwan v. Nyieni* (1959) 1 GLR 67 at 72-3 where the Court of Appeal of Ghana held that members of the tribal group were entitled to initiate proceedings for the purpose of preserving family property in the event of the failure of the head of the tribal group to do so. The head of the tribal group is regarded as a fiduciary: S. K. B. Asante, at 1149.

The relationship between Mr Bulun Bulun as the author and legal title holder of the artistic work and the Ganalbingu People is unique. The "transaction" between them out of which fiduciary relationship is said to arise is the use with permission by Mr Bulun Bulun of ritual knowledge of the Ganalbingu People, and the embodiment of that knowledge within the artistic work. That use has been permitted in accordance with the law and customs of the Ganalbingu People.

The grant of permission by the djungayi and other appropriate representatives of the Ganalbingu People for the creation of the artistic work is predicated on the trust and confidence which those granting permission have in the artist. The evidence indicates that if those who must give permission do not have trust and confidence in someone seeking permission, permission will not be granted.

The law and customs of the Ganalbingu People require that the use of the ritual knowledge and the artistic work be in accordance with the requirements of law and custom, and that the author of the artistic work do whatever is necessary to prevent any misuse. The artist is required to act in relation to the artwork in the interests of the Ganalbingu People to preserve the integrity of their culture, and ritual knowledge.

This is not to say that the artist must act entirely in the interests of the Ganalbingu People. The evidence shows that an artist is entitled to consider and pursue his own interests, for example by selling the artwork, but the artist is not permitted to shed the overriding obligation to act to preserve the integrity of the Ganalbingu culture where action for that purpose is required.

In my opinion, the nature of the relationship between Mr Bulun Bulun and the Ganalbingu People was a fiduciary one which gives rise to fiduciary obligations owed by Mr Bulun Bulun.

The conclusion that in all the circumstances Mr Bulun Bulun owes fiduciary obligations to the Ganalbingu People does not treat the law and custom of the Ganalbingu People as part of the Australian legal system. Rather, it treats the law and custom of the Ganalbingu People as part of the factual matrix which characterises the relationship as one of mutual trust and confidence. It is that relationship which the Australian legal system recognises as giving rise to the fiduciary relationship, and to the obligations which arise out of it. . . .

[Justice von Dousa then considered and dismissed the suggestion that there was a contract between Bulun Bulun and the Ganalbingu people to create the artwork.]

The fiduciary obligation

Central to the fiduciary concept is the protection of interests that can be regarded as worthy of judicial protection: Glover, *Commercial Equity — Fiduciary Relationships* (1995), para. 3.4. The evidence is all one way. The ritual knowledge relating to Djulibinyamurr embodied within the artistic work is of great importance to members of the Ganalbingu People. I have no hesitation in holding that the interest of Ganalbingu People in the protection of that ritual knowledge from exploitation which is contrary to their law and custom is deserving of the protection of the Australian legal system.

Under the *Copyright Act*, the owner of the copyright has the exclusive right to reproduce the work in a material form, and to publish the work. The copyright owner is entitled to enforce copyright against the world at large. In the event of infringement, the copyright owner is entitled to sue and to obtain remedies of the kind actually obtained by Mr Bulun Bulun in this case.

Having regard to the evidence of the law and customs of the Ganalbingu People under which Mr Bulun Bulun was permitted to create the artistic work, I consider that equity imposes on him obligations as a fiduciary not to exploit the artistic work in a way that is contrary to the laws and custom of the Ganalbingu People, and, in the event of infringement by a third party, to take reasonable and appropriate action to restrain and remedy infringement of the copyright in the artistic work.

While the nature of the relationship between Mr Bulun Bulun and the Ganalbingu People is such that Mr Bulun Bulun falls under fiduciary obligations to protect the ritual knowledge which he has been permitted to use, the existence of those obligations does not, without more, vest an equitable interest in the ownership of the copyright in the Ganalbingu People. Their primary right, in the event of a breach of obligation by the fiduciary is a right in personam to bring action against the fiduciary to enforce the obligation.

In the present case Mr Bulun Bulun has successfully taken action against the respondent to obtain remedies in respect of the infringement. There is no suggestion by Mr Milpurrurru and those whom he seeks to represent that Mr Bulun Bulun should have done anything more. In these circumstances there is no occasion for the intervention of equity to provide any additional remedy to the beneficiaries of the fiduciary relationship.

However, had the position been otherwise equitable remedies could have been available. The extent of those remedies would depend on all the circumstances, and in an extreme case could involve the intervention of equity to impose a constructive trust on the legal owner of the copyright in the artistic work in favour of the beneficiaries. Equity will not automatically impose a constructive trust merely upon the identification of a fiduciary obligation. Equity will impose a constructive trust on property held by a fiduciary where it is necessary to do so to achieve a just remedy and to prevent the fiduciary from retaining an unconscionable benefit: *Muschinski v. Dodds* (1985) 160 CLR 583 at 619-20; 62 ALR 429 and *Baumgartner v. Baumgartner* (1987) 164 CLR 137 at 148; 76 ALR 75. By way of example, had Mr Bulun Bulun merely failed to take action to enforce his copyright, an adequate remedy might be extended in equity to the beneficiaries by allowing them to bring action in their own names against the infringer and the copyright owner, claiming against the former, in the first instance, interlocutory relief to restrain the infringement, and against the latter orders necessary to ensure that the copyright owner enforces the copyright. Probably there would be no occasion for equity in these circumstances to impose a constructive trust.

On the other hand, were Mr Bulun Bulun to deny the existence of fiduciary obligations and the interests of the parties asserting them, and refuse to protect the copyright from infringement, then the occasion might exist for equity to impose a remedial constructive trust upon the copyright owner to strengthen the standing of the beneficiaries to bring proceedings to enforce the copyright. This may be necessary if the copyright owner cannot be identified or found and the beneficiaries are unable to join the legal owner of the copyright: see *Performing Right Society Ltd v. London Theatre of Varieties* [1924] AC 1 at 18.

It is well recognised that interlocutory injunctive relief can be claimed by a party having an equitable interest in copyright . . .

I do not consider Mr Milpurrurru and those he seeks to represent have established an equitable interest in the copyright in the artistic work. In my opinion they have established that fiduciary obligations are owed to them by Mr Bulun Bulun, but as Mr Bulun Bulun has taken appropriate action to enforce the copyright, he has fulfilled those obligations and there is no occasion to grant any additional remedy in favour of the Ganalbingu People. However, in other circumstances if the copyright owner of an artistic work which embodies ritual knowledge of an Aboriginal clan is being used inappropriately, and the copyright owner fails or refuses to take appropriate action to enforce the copyright, the Australian legal system will permit remedial action through the courts by the clan.

For these reasons, the proceedings by Mr Milpurrurru must be dismissed. . . .

QUESTIONS

1. In what way, if at all, does the ruling in *Bulun Bulun* create a form of property right, cognizable in a domestic court, in favour of the Ganalbingu people?

2. By what means might Canadian law recognize a property right of the kind asserted in *Bulun Bulun*?

CHAPTER 7

CONDITIONAL GIFTS AND FUTURE INTERESTS

1. INTRODUCTION

Colonel Reuben Wells Leonard placed his signature on the third and final version of the Leonard Foundation Trust deed in late December, 1923. He had, with this act, donated over $500,000 to create a fund for scholarships tenable across Canada. It was at the time the largest gift of its kind in Canada and, along with a myriad of other benefactions, had served to earn for Leonard a reputation as one of the country's most generous philanthropists.

The deed contains a lengthy preamble that was designed to explain the underlying principles of the trust. It begins with a statement of Leonard's belief that "the White Race is, as a whole, best qualified by nature to be entrusted with the development of civilization and the general progress of the world along the best lines." The document also recites that the progress of the world depends in the future, as it has in the past, on the maintenance of the Christian religion, and that the advancement of civilization throughout the world rests upon the independence, stability and prosperity of the British Empire. The Empire, the deed asserts, must remain under the control of British nationals who are not beholden to foreign powers, whether temporal or spiritual. Based on these premises, the student awards created under the trust were available only to white Protestants of British nationality or parentage. Both males and females were eligible, although no more than one-quarter of the funds awarded annually could be given to female recipients.

Odd-sounding, even disturbing, as this language may now appear, the Leonard Foundation operated under these terms for over sixty years. Throughout this period, hundreds of scholarships were awarded, the recipients selected by a board of governance that included at various times university presidents, high-placed Anglican clerics, a justice of the Supreme Court of Canada and a Member of Parliament.

B. Ziff, *Unforeseen Legacies: Reuben Wells Leonard and the Leonard Foundation Trust* (Toronto: Osgoode Society & U.T.P., 2000) at 3-4.

Is such a trust valid?

A testator provides that money shall be paid to a legatee so long as she resides in Canada? What could that mean? What type of sojourn might result in the termination or forfeiture of this entitlement?

Sylvia Usniak enters your office seeking assistance in the preparation of her last will and testament. Her house is located on an acreage that her great-grandparents homesteaded in the 1880s. It has been in the family ever since, and she wants that to remain so. Her instructions are that the property is never to be transferred to anyone outside of her immediate family; never, from generation to generation. Is it possible to create that type of restriction? Should it be permissible?

A philanthropist wishes to reward the first person to find a cure for AIDS with a large bequest, and so a term of his/her will provides that a large fund of money shall be set aside to be awarded to the person who finds a cure. Can the money be held for an indefinite period?

These questions concern the limits to proprietary freedom — both of current owners as well as future ones. That is the main focus of this chapter.

2. BASIC CONCEPTS

Stuartburn (Municipality) v. Kiansky
2001 CarswellMan 155, [2001] 8 W.W.R. 145 (Q.B.)

[An application was brought to determine whether David Kiansky, the Reeve of Stuartburn, was entitled to hold that office. Under Manitoba election law, in order to hold elected office, a person must, among other requirements, be an owner of land which is assessed in the latest revised realty assessment roll, or else a tenant or occupier of land whose name is entered on the latest roll as the owner of a right, interest or estate in the land: section 5 of the *Local Authorities Election Act*, R.S.M. 1987, c. L180 ("the *LAE Act*"). At the time of the court application, Reeve Kiansky had sold his home and moved from the relevant district. But he continued to hold an interest in other Stuartburn real estate. His entitlement to that other land was subject to a prior life estate in favour of his grandmother, Mary Kiansky. Did this satisfy the ownership requirements of the election laws?]

Wright J.: . . .

Kiansky does not deny that he sold his home and related land and moved out of the Municipality as the Municipality says, but he contests the claim he was then disqualified from being an elector. He relies on the fact that when he moved from the Municipality he was the holder of a remainder interest in other real property in the Municipality expectant on the death of his grandmother, Mary Kiansky, who held the life interest. . . .

The subject land is a quarter section of real property in the Municipality. At all material times Kiansky was recorded in the land titles office in relation to this land as "registered owner of an estate in remainder expectant upon the decease of Mary Kiansky of Vita, Manitoba . . .". Mary Kiansky herself was recorded as "registered owner of a life estate during the term of her natural life . . .".

The land is and was assessed in the latest revised realty assessment roll.

The first issue then on the application is whether Kiansky's remainderman interest is sufficient to classify him as "an owner of land" despite the sale of his residence property and move from the Municipality. The exact phraseology in s. 5(1) is "is, in his own right . . . an owner of land . . .". These words have to be considered in the context of the meaning of "owner" and the nature of the remainder interest. . . .

I take this definition, in the context of the wording of s. 5(1), to mean the person must be the *present* owner of a freehold estate in land. The ownership must be of a currently existing freehold estate. In the case of Kiansky this means that his remainder interest must be capable of identification as a freehold estate owned by him at the same time as his grandmother was exercising her rights in respect of the life estate.

What then is a freehold estate?

Freehold is a measure of the nature and degree of a person's interest in land. It includes a life interest and a fee simple. Both are for an indeterminate period. The life interest will expire on the death of the owner (or tenant as it is often termed). The fee simple may be inherited.

At common law, both the life interest and the fee simple could be alienated but any disposition was subject to the limitations of the freehold. The fee simple interest is the broadest freehold.

The word "estate", when used in conjunction with "freehold" can be thought of as synonymous with the words "right", "title" and "interest" [*Black's Law Dictionary* (6th ed.) at 547]. Thus, freehold estate can be interpreted to mean a freehold right, title, or interest in land.

The nature of Kiansky's remainder interest is of a right to a freehold interest in fee simple. This can also be described as a right to a freehold *estate* in fee simple.

Most importantly, the remainder interest is a *present* right. It co-exists with the life estate even though enjoyment and possession of the real property is postponed until termination of the life interest. This arises from the common law requirement that there could be no abeyance of seisin; that is, that there could be no abeyance of the ownership or transfer of the ownership of the freehold interest if the transfer was to be effective. Therefore, an instant vesting took place. Thus, as in the present circumstances, a grant of a life estate to one person with the remainder in fee simple to another, was and remains a grant to each effective as of the time of the grant. Seisin did not require *actual* possession, although it did require possession in the sense of title or ownership.

Support for these legal interpretations can be found in *Anger and Honsberger Real Property*, Vol. 1 (2nd ed., 1985), and in particular from the following passages from that text:

The doctrine of estates is one of the most remarkable and enduring in the history of English land law. The term "estate" is probably derived from status, for in a landholding society the relationship one had to one's land no doubt defined one's standing in the community. Later, however, the term "estate" described the quantity of a person's interest in land. The concept of the estate is unique to English law. It is an abstraction, interposed between the tenant and the land so that a person does not own the land itself absolutely or allodially as in the civil law. Indeed, he cannot own the land for the Crown owns it. Instead, he owns an estate or interest in the land. Furthermore, it is the concept of seisin which links the abstract concept of the estate with the physical thing, the land. The person who has the seisin, or who is entitled to it in the future, has an estate in the land. Moreover, the idea of estates, as distinct from ownership of land, makes possible the fragmentation of ownership among different persons in succession. Thus, for example, land may be granted "to A for life, then to B in tail, remainder to C in fee simple". In this example all three persons have estates in the land and they exist in the present, that is, they are capable of present ownership. The latter is a precondition of an estate. Even though the seisin rests in A only for the time being, the ownership of B and C also exists in the present. [at 26-27]

. . . An estate is an abstract concept distinct from the land itself. In essence, the word describes the rights a person may have in land for a period of time. The *quantum* of the estate thus varies with time. The largest estate possible is the *fee simple*. In theory it may last forever, being passed on by transfer or succession. It ends only when the owner of it dies intestate without an heir. In that event it passes to the Crown. It may be carved up into lesser estates, namely, the *fee tail*, which lasts only so long as the direct descendants of the original tenant in tail survive, and the life estate which lasts for the duration of the life specified. These three estates are known as estate of *freehold* and they are thus distinguishable from *leaseholds*. . . . [at 11]

These several estates may exist in *possession*, in *remainder*, or in *reversion*. The first of these terms is self-explanatory. When X is entitled to an immediate life estate he is entitled to enjoy it in possession. An estate in remainder is created when a person is given an estate but he is not entitled to possession until the expiration of a prior estate created by the same instrument. An estate in reversion is the estate retained by the grantor when he conveys away a lesser estate. Thus, in a conveyance by G to "A for life and then to B in fee tail", A has a life estate in possession, B has an estate in fee tail in remainder and G retains an estate in fee simple in reversion. Moreover, these estates are said to be *vested* in that they are presently existing, even though the owners are not all immediately entitled to possession. Vested thus normally means "vested in interest" and not "vested in possession". . . . [at 11-12]

In other words, a remainder limited to take effect automatically upon the expiration of the prior particular estate is a vested remainder because a present estate is conferred although it is not to be enjoyed until that future time. . . . [at 395]

A future interest is an interest in property in which the right to possession or enjoyment of the property is postponed to a future time. Nevertheless, it is a presently existing interest in the property and it is thus part of the total ownership of the property. . . . [at 335]

. . . at common law, livery of seisin was necessary to grant any freehold estate and the freehold could never be in abeyance, for there had to be someone at all times to perform the feudal services and against whom actions could be brought. . . . [at 392] . . .

For all the reasons above expressed, the conclusion I have reached, therefore, is that Kiansky's remainder interest allows him to be classified as a present owner of a freehold estate in the Municipality. This meets the requirement of s. 5(1) of the *LAE Act*.

However, this does not end the matter. The Municipality also supports its application on the ground the early English common law has been altered by legislation in Manitoba that includes *The Perpetuities and Accumulations Act*, R.S.M. 1987, c. P33 ("the *Perpetuities Act*"), *The Trustee Act*, R.S.M. 1987, c. T160, *The Law of Property Act*, R.S.M. 1987, c. L90, and *The Real Property Act*, R.S.M. 1988, c. R30. The submission on behalf of the Municipality is that the legislation has removed any common law right of ownership of successive legal estates because any such rights are now subject to a statutory trust.

I do not disagree that the effect of this legislation, and in particular the *Perpetuities Act*, is to create a trust relationship involving the life tenant and the holder of the remainder interest. The *Perpetuities Act* provides that their successive legal interests take effect in equity behind a trust. The *Perpetuities Act* makes the beneficiaries of those legal interests the trustees [s. 4(2)]. It also provides that the trust property vests in the trustees [s. 4(3)]. However, I do not believe the creation of this kind of trust, which admittedly removes the legal ownership of the freehold estates (or interests) from the life estate holder and the remainderperson, has caused those persons to lose the kind of ownership required to meet the terms of the *LAE Act*. On the contrary, they still remain the owners of freehold estates. Because of the trust created by statute, they have become *beneficial* owners but that makes them, no less, owners. The trust creates a new relationship which affects the way in which the freehold estates may be handled but it does not annul the vested ownership rights in those estates simply because the rights have become beneficial rather than legal. . . .

Application dismissed.

COMMENTS

1. The settlement in this case resembles those studied in Chapter 5: Mary Kiansky holds a life estate in Blackacre; B holds the *remainder* in fee simple. Consider now a transfer of realty that reads simply: "To A for life". The full fee simple not having been given away, this creates a *reversion* in favour of the grantor. This same idea was studied in Chapter 6 in relation to equitable interests: if S creates a trust in favour of A for life, with no allocation of the remainder of the beneficial interest, it was seen that the settlor holds the rest of the equitable entitlement as a *resulting trust.*

2. The passages from the Anger and Honsberger treatise on real property quoted in *Kiansky* refer to the terms "vested in possession" and "vested in interest". Mary Kiansky's life estate is vested in possession: she is presently entitled to enjoyment of her freehold life estate. David's remainder is vested in interest; it is a present right (as the Court held) to future enjoyment. Once Mary dies, David will then be vested

in possession of the fee simple. Should he predecease Mary, this right would pass to whomever was entitled to this part of his estate.

3. Not all future interests are vested in interest. Imagine a gift "to A for life, remainder to B when and not before B turns 25 years of age". Here the grantor has added a stipulation that before B is vested — even in interest — the prescribed age must first be attained. Such an interest is said to be *contingent* on B meeting that requirement. A contingent interest can also be described as one subject to a *condition precedent*. Put another way, it is the existence of a condition precedent that makes the interest contingent. Note, however, that the natural ending of the prior estate does not make the subsequent one contingent. The condition must relate to some other event, one which is not inevitable.

4. A stipulation may be framed as a condition subsequent. If so this means that the property is first given — the recipient is vested — though the entitlement may later be taken away should the identified event occur. A gift "To A, but should the land ever be used as a hospital, this interest shall revert" would appear to give A vested interest. However, should — subsequently — the stipulated event occur, the entitlement may be brought to an end. When property is held subject to a condition subsequent, it is sometimes said that the interest is vested subject to being divested. (As we will soon see, there are other constructs that might be created; these are, in effect, variations on this theme.)

5. In sum, interests in property are either: vested in possession, vested in interest or contingent. In the above examples, the classifications are relatively simple to make. That is not always so: the decisions in *McKeen Estate*, *Kotsar v. Shattock* and *Village of Caroline v. Roper*, below, illustrate the interpretive difficulties that occasionally emerge.

6. Coincidentally, a problem somewhat similar to that in *Stuartburn (Municipality) v. Kiansky* occurred in 1990 at the federal level. That was the year that Prime Minister Mulroney appointed eight additional Senators so as to ensure the safe passage of the G.S.T. legislation through the Senate.

To qualify for the red chamber a person must, according to the *Constitution Act, 1867*, be seised of lands worth at least $4,000. One appointee, Michael Forrestall, held only a remainder interest; as with Kiansky, he would be entitled to possession only once an existing life estate ended. On these facts was Forrestall seised of land? The answer depends on the meaning of the word seisin. This Senate speech suggests, correctly, that the answer is no:

> Section 23(3) states that he must be seised for ". . . his own use and benefit . . ." Clearly, at the present time, he may neither use it nor benefit from it. The authorities suggest, anyway, that seisin must always be full and cannot be divided.
>
> By way of a buttress for these conclusions I refer to authorities, first *Black's Law Dictionary* at pages 1218-1219, says:

> Seisin means possession and the right to immediate possession.

The authorities cited are mostly United States authorities.

The next authority is *Canadian Law of Real Property* by Anger and Honsberger, at page 553, which states:

> Seisin is synonymous with possession.

The third authority is *Property Law, Cases, Texts and Materials* by Mendes Da Costa and Balfour, a 1982 publication, and a leading Canadian authority.

The research notes that I have state:

> At page 739 they describe a fact situation which corresponds to the one Senator Forrestall is in. The person who holds the life estate and has possession of the property is clearly the one who holds seisin.

Remember that "seisin" is the word used in the Constitution.

Continuing:

> The vested remainder interest does not entitle the remaindermen to seisin since he is not entitled to possession.
>
> At pages 745-746 the concept is further illustrated with a diagram. Those with life interests have seisin. In *The Law of Real Property*, by Megarry and Wade, leading United Kingdom authorities, from which we derive a good deal of our property law, as I am sure many honourable senators know, it is at pages 48-49 that the requirements for seisin are listed, and they include possession.

In *Cheshire's Modern Law of Real Property*, another United Kingdom authority, states:

> At page 296, it states seisin means possession and it must always be full (i.e. it is not possible to have partial seisin).

The notes further state:

> Apparently Senator Forrestall has stated that he made sure his interest satisfies the property requirement.

I believe him. I also believe that the Clerk acted properly when he accepted Senator Forrestall's sincere belief that his interest satisfied the property requirement of the Constitution. But belief is not the test so these authorities raise serious questions about it. In fact, I am prepared to say that they negate that assertion.

I am told the Atlantic Television System obtained a legal opinion that concluded Mr. Forrestall did not meet the minimum requirement, and I agree with it.

For all of the above material on seisin I am indebted to Senator Stanbury, and also his research assistan[t], Mr. Andrew Kavchak, who did the research on that subject.

Senate Debates, 2nd Sess., 34th Parl. vol. 133, at 3265-6, October 26, 1990 (Royce Firth).

The importance of seisin in the law of future interests will be addressed in Part 4 of this chapter.

McKeen Estate v. McKeen Estate 1993 CarswellNB 35 (Q.B)

[The testator died in 1981. His will directed that his entire estate be held in trust for his wife for life, and on her death, the trustees were directed, after payment of several pecuniary legacies and the devise of his house,

> To divide the residue of my estate equally between my sisters [AM] and [BM] if they are both alive at the time of the death of the survivor of me and my third wife. If only one of my said sisters is alive at the time of the death of the survivor of me and my said wife, I direct my Trustees to deliver the residue of my estate to the surviving sister, the same to be hers absolutely.

The two sisters died in 1989; the testator's wife died in 1992. In other words, neither sister survived the testator and his wife. As a question of construction, did the requirement of survival make the gifts to AM and BM contingent? If so, they did not — and now of course could not — satisfy that condition. If that were the case, the fate of the property could not be governed by the quoted clause. In fact, it would fall into intestacy, and devolve to the testator's next of kin in accordance with New Brunswick's statutory intestacy rules. If however, the gifts to AM and BM could be considered as vested, the property would then pass to their estates.]

Landry J.: . . .

1. The testator's intention

There is no doubt that of paramount importance is the determination of the actual and subjective intention of the testator. . . .

In the Supreme Court of Canada case *Merchants Bank of Canada v. Keefer* (1885), 13 S.C.R. 515, Henry J., said at page 539:

> A construction which gives a vested interest is, no doubt, favored by the courts where there is ambiguity or doubt, but where the intention to create a contingent estate or interest is reasonably evident or clear that intention must be respected and carried out.

2. *The presumption against intestacy*

There is a presumption against intestacy. Halsbury, 3d ed., vol. 39, states at page 996:

> A testator may well intend to die partially intestate; when he makes a will, he is testate only so far as he has expressed himself in his will. Accordingly, there is no reason for the court in all cases to lean too heavily against a construction which involves a partial intestacy. Where, however, the construction of the will is doubtful, the court acts on the presumption that the testator did not intend to die either wholly or even partially intestate, provided that on a fair and reasonable construction there is no ground for a contrary conclusion. In cases where the will shows an intention of the testator to dispose of the whole of his property, but, as regards the interests created, two constructions are possible, according to one of which the will effects a complete disposition of the whole, but according to the other the will leaves a gap, the court inclines to the former construction.

3. *Construction in favour of vesting*

Feeney, in *The Canadian Law of Wills* (*supra*), said at page 225:

> Where the condition must happen for the gift to take effect in the first place, the gift is said to be subject to a condition precedent. On the other hand, where the language shows that the gift is to take effect but terminate on the happening of the condition, it is said to be subject to a condition subsequent. It is not always easy to tell whether a condition attached to a gift creates an interest subject to a condition precedent, in which case the gift is said to be contingent, or whether it creates a vested interest which is subject to divestment. The whole matter of whether a gift is vested or contingent is reserved for the next chapter. The crucial distinction is whether the happening of the condition (or the cessation of a certain state of affairs) is an event that causes the gift to spring into being (causes a contingent gift to become vested) or whether the happening signifies that an existing (vested) interest has come to an end.

and at page 257:

> When an interest is vested but the enjoyment of it is postponed, it is presently owned; it has come into being. A vested interest, the enjoyment of which is postponed, may be one that is not subject to a condition, in which case it is bound to be enjoyed at some future date. Often, however, such a vested interest is subject to a condition that may totally divest it. When this is so, the interest, like a contingent interest, may never be enjoyed, but until the happening of the divesting event (an event which may never happen) it is vested.

and at pages 259 and 260:

> A contingent interest is one that is subject to the prior happening of an event which may never happen, for example, the birth of a child, the attainment of a certain age, or marriage. For instance, it may be subject to the condition precedent that the donee become a citizen. Sometimes, the condition is the satisfaction of some requirement not personal to the donee, for example, a condition that some other person do something or that another donee survive or not survive an event. Usually where the gift is contingent the words of

futurity are introduced by the conjunction "if", but *prima facie* the construction will be the same and the legacy will be treated as contingent, in the first instance at least, when the reference to the future event is introduced by the word "when". Similarly, the cases hold that in a bequest to A, words such as "at" a given age, or "upon" attaining a given age, or "as" he shall attain, or "from and after" his attaining a given age, *prima facie* introduced a contingent gift.

Yet, as will be shown, some words are more contingent than others. When the words are not clearly contingent, and when various other circumstances to be considered in determining the question are favourable to a vested construction, the courts are inclined to call a gift that is *prima facie* contingent, "vested". . . .

Whether or not it can be said that in every case there is a presumption in favour of vesting, *the courts are inclined to hold a gift vested rather than contingent wherever the words used and the will as a whole admit of a construction that will result, as is said, in "early vesting"*. That inclination has always been said to be particularly strong where the property is land. It would seem proper to refer to the tendency of courts to call devises "vested" as a presumption to that effect, so it can be said that devises, if not legacies, are to be held to be vested unless there is a clear condition precedent. Accordingly, a gift, whether a devise or a legacy, that makes no reference to the time of vesting should always be held to take effect at the testator's death, unless that date of vesting would disturb provisions already made in the will, or unless the will as a whole evinces a clear intention that the gift operate contingently and at a later date. (The emphasis is mine.)

4. *The rule in* Browne v. Moody

The leading case *Browne v. Moody*, [1936] O.R. 422 (P.C.) establishes the proposition that a gift is *prima facie* vested if the postponement is to allow for a prior life estate. In that case the testatrix provided that a large sum be invested during her son's lifetime and that the income be paid to him provided that " 'on the death of my said son . . . I direct that the said fund . . . is to be divided as follows: one half . . . to my granddaughter . . . and the remainder . . . to be divided equally between my daughters Florence . . . Constance . . . and Helen . . . share and share alike' " [p. 423]. In another clause the testatrix directed that should any of the women predecease the son "leaving issue", then the issue were to take their mother's share.

The Privy Council held that the vesting of the gifts to the women in remainder was not postponed until the death of the life tenant but took place immediately on the death of the testator. Lord Macmillan said at pages 426 and 427:

Their Lordships observe in the first place that the date of division of the capital of the fund is a *dies certus*, the death of the son of the testatrix, which in the course of nature must occur sooner or later. In the next place, the direction to divide the capital among the named beneficiaries on the arrival of that *dies certus* is not accompanied by any condition personal to the beneficiaries, such as their attainment of majority or the like. The object of the postponement of the division is obviously only in order that the son may during his lifetime enjoy the income. The mere postponement of distribution to enable an interposed life-rent to be enjoyed has never by itself been held to exclude vesting of the capital. . . .

> But where there is a direction to pay the income of a fund to one person during his lifetime and to divide the capital among certain other named and ascertained persons on his death, even although there are no direct words of gift either of the life interest or of the capital, the rule is that vesting of the capital takes place *a morte testatoris* in the remaindermen. . . .

5. *The rule in* Re Francis

In *Re Francis*, [1903] 2 Ch. 295, the testator devised two houses to his niece "when she shall attain the age of twenty-five years". The court held that the devise was contingent and the attainment of twenty-five years of age was a condition precedent to the estate vesting in the niece.

Feeney in *The Canadian Law of Wills* (*supra*) said at pages 263 and 264:

> Where, however, the reason for the postponement of the gift is one personal to the donee, *prima facie* the gift is contingent. This may be shown by words descriptive of the donee or by words that state some qualification or other that the testator requires of the donee if he is to become the object of the testator's bounty. The testator may show that he wishes the donee to become a lawyer, or to marry, or, in the case of a class gift, that the members attain a specified age. The testator may show this so clearly, for example, by a devise or bequest to "the first son of A to become a lawyer", "the first daughter of A to marry", or "only such children as shall attain the age of 25", that there can be no question but that the gift is contingent. On the other hand, it may not be so very clear that the gift is subject to a condition precedent, but in such a case the court, seeing that the reason for the postponement is one personal to the donee, will regard the gift as contingent, at least in the first instance.

Having considered the authorities which I believe are applicable to the within fact situation, I will now deal with the clause of the will to be interpreted, which Sub-Paragraph *XII* of the Paragraph 3(e) provides:

> To divide the residue of my estate equally between my sisters, Alice McKeen and Beatrice McKeen if they are both alive at the time of the death of the survivor of me and my said wife. If only one of my said sisters is alive at the time of the death of the survivor of me and my said wife, I direct my Trustees to deliver the residue of my estate to the surviving sister, the same to be hers absolutely. . . .

Dr. McKeen's will reflects the precision to which a surgeon is accustomed in the specific bequests directed to selected relatives. Dr. McKeen wanted mainly to provide for his wife during her life and also ultimately to deliver the bulk of his estate to benefit his sisters Alice and Beatrice McKeen or the survivor of them. Dr. McKeen did not intend a partial intestacy.

On reading the will as a whole, one finds that it is the act of a well-informed and careful testator. He, for example, recognizes the frailty of his wife by providing for a substitute executor, and within four months of his death, his wife is replaced by Alice McKeen.

The residue of the testator's estate was dedicated to his two sisters Alice and Beatrice McKeen as mentioned above.

The clause in question . . . cannot be split and must be read as a whole, with the result that the actual and subjective intention of the testator is as follows: "I want the residue of my estate divided between my sisters, Alice and Beatrice, or the survivor of them".

Applying the authorities which I have reviewed and in particular the Rule in *Browne v. Moody*, I find that the residue of the estate of Harry L. McKeen vested in Alice McKeen and Beatrice McKeen equally at the date of death of Harry L. McKeen, subject to the possibility of divesting of the interest of the deceased sister if only one sister survived the life tenant.

In this case, the reason for the postponement of the distribution is simply that a life interest was previously given to the widow, so that the residue could not be paid until her death and is not a reason personal to the legatees. I disagree with the solicitors for the Respondents, Harry Cody and Gladys Flowers, that the gift was accompanied by a condition personal to both sisters, that is that they had to be alive.

A construction which gives a vested interest is favoured by the courts where there is ambiguity or doubt. There most certainly is a good amount of ambiguity or doubt in this case, a case which is not at all an easy one to rule upon.

I'm of the opinion that the testator did not contemplate an intestacy. I also find that the interpretation which I am giving to the clause in question more closely reflects the intention of the testator as gathered by the reading of the will as a whole.

In *Re Stillman* (1965), 52 D.L.R. (2d) 601, the Ontario High Court followed the rule in *Browne v. Moody*. That case which I have found most helpful in arriving at my decision (as it closely resembles the case at hand) was commented upon as follows at pages 268 and 269 of Feeney's *The Canadian Law of Wills* (*supra*):

> The rule that the "survivors" referred to in a will are to be ascertained as of the date of distribution applies equally to a simple gift to the survivors of several named persons as well as to class gifts. Thus in a 1966 Ontario case, *Re Stillman*, this rule was applied where the testator, after making provision for his widow, disposed of the capital of the residue of his estate among three named cousins "or the survivors or survivor of them". The three named cousins all survived the testator but predeceased his widow, the life tenant. The question was whether the residue vested in the three cousins on the testator's death by virtue of their having survived him. The court answered the question in the affirmative, holding that the words of survivorship in the clause leaving the residue to the three cousins was referable to the date of payment or distribution and not the date of vesting. Each cousin had acquired a vested interest upon the death of the testator, and as none of the three cousins survived the date of payment or distribution (they predeceased the life tenant, the widow), these interests had never been divested. Accordingly, the judge held that the estates of the three cousins took equal shares. Thus, it was the gift over to the survivor or survivors of the three, not the gift to the three cousins, that was contingent on surviving the widow; the gift to the three cousins was vested subject to being divested in favour of one or two of the cousins who satisfied the description

"survivor or survivors" of the three; and since the latter event could never happen (as all three predeceased the widow) their estates were unconditionally entitled to the residue. . . .

Order accordingly.

Kotsar v. Shattock
[1981] V.R. 13 (S.C. Full Ct.)

Crockett J.:

The relevant provisions in the will of the testatrix giving rise to the construction question out of which this appeal arises are as follows:

> 6. My Trustees shall hold the net proceeds of such sale calling in and conversion together with any ready moneys upon the following trusts: . . .
>
> (d) Upon the death of my said husband to pay his daughter Elva Blackmore of 5 Williams Road, Ringwood a legacy of a sum equal to ten per centum of the net value of my residuary estate.
>
> (e) To pay and transfer the remainder of my residuary estate to Oilme Kotsar of Venevere Side Jaoskond, Poltsamaa Rajoon Estonia N.S.V. if and when she shall attain the age of twenty-one years provided that upon the attainment of such age she shall then be resident in one of the countries of the British Commonwealth of Nations.
>
> (f) In the event of the failure of either of the above trusts in favour of the said Elva Blackmore or the said Oilme Kotsar to pay and transfer the part of my residuary estate affected by such failure to such charitable institutions as my Trustees shall think fit but it is my wish that the greater part thereof shall be paid and transferred to institutions whose object is the relief of hardship among elderly people.

By a codicil the testatrix subsequently revoked the gift to Elva Blackmore and declared that the bequest fall into and form part of the residue. The testatrix died on 12 March 1971. The residuary beneficiary attained the age of 21 years on 13 November 1975. On that date she lived in Estonia which at all material times has been one of the Soviet Socialist Republics. In these events the originating summons asked the question whether, on the proper construction of the will, Oilme Kotsar is entitled to the residue of the estate of the testatrix.

The learned Judge to whom the question fell for decision held that she was not. He reached this conclusion by construing the provision in cl. 6(e) as a condition precedent. Whilst recognizing that the law favours early vesting and that, in cases of doubt, a condition should therefore be treated as subsequent, he held that because "the words in the *proviso* are expressly in the language of a condition precedent" a contrary intention was to be found in the will. In the result no interest vested in the residuary beneficiary unless and until the conditions imposed by the *proviso* were fulfilled. Furthermore, when treated as a condition precedent the terms of the *proviso* were not so uncertain — either as to the expression "resident" or the expression "the British Commonwealth of Nations" — as to render it void. Being certain and not having been complied with the gift to the residuary legatee failed. . . .

In my view, properly interpreted, the *proviso* operates so as to create a condition subsequent. Moreover, despite the frequent readiness of the law not so to find in such circumstances, I consider the terms of the *proviso* to be expressed with sufficient certainty.

I should state briefly why I differ from the learned Judge on each of these questions.

In my view the rule in *Phipps v. Ackers* (1842), 9 C. & Fin. 583 governs the question of the correct classification of the contingencies. The "rule" in that case (as later extended to property other than realty) provides that, when a gift to a devisee is made subject to compliance with a condition, with a gift over in the event the condition be not fulfilled, the condition is held to be a condition subsequent. Being a rule of construction it gives way to a direction as to vesting. However, the direction must be express or explicit. In the present case there is no such direction. The words which the Judge found amounted to an expression of a contrary intention were no more than words of contingency *Ex hypothesi* they must always be present before the question of characterization of the condition can arise.

This is explained by Ungoed-Thomas J. in *In re Penton's Settlements*, [1968] 1 W.L.R. 248, at p. 256; [1968] 1 All E.R. 36, where, having pointed out that the principle of law on which the rule in *Phipps v. Ackers* was founded was based on intention ascertained as a matter of construction, his Lordship went on to say: "Further — and this is crucial — an examination of the cases clearly reveals that the intention is ascertained, not by reference to the non-disposal of income which would arise before the contingency occurred if the gift were treated as contingent, but by reference to the gift over being dependent upon that contingency not occurring. The contingency applicable to the prior gift and the gift over, are the counterparts of each other, hinging on the same event. When read together, as they should be, as a matter of construction, they thus indicate an intention that the prior donee should take, subject only to the subsequent contingency of the gift over being satisfied."

. . .

Nor, it may be added, does the rule have any less application should there be more than one condition: *Public Trustee v. Gower*, [1924] N.Z.L.R. 1233; and *Re Leury*, [1975] V.R. 601.

Consequently, upon the reason for the rule's existence and the circumstances of its application being understood, it becomes plain that words constituting a more explicit direction than are to be found in clause 6(e) of the will must be present before the operation of the rule will be displaced. . . . Accordingly, the gift to the primary beneficiary is to be construed as operating to vest the interest in that gift in that beneficiary subject to divestment in favour of those taking under the gift over in the event that the conditions imposed for retention of the interest should not be met . . .

NOTES

1. Southwell J. concurred with Crockett J. Starke J. wrote a separate concurring judgment.

2. A portion of this case is reproduced below in Part 3 of this chapter.

QUESTIONS AND COMMENTS

1. What is the rule in *Phipps v. Ackers*? Is it a rule of law or construction? What policy does it advance?

2. Clause (f) of the will at issue in *Kotsar v. Shattock* provides:

> In the event of the failure of either of the above trusts in favour of the said Elva Blackmore or the said Oilme Kotsar to pay and transfer the part of my residuary estate affected by such failure to such charitable institutions as my Trustees shall think fit but it is my wish that the greater part thereof shall be paid and transferred to institutions whose object is the relief of hardships among elderly people.

Some ostensible conditions in will are treated as precatory, meaning that they create no enforceable rights. However, such stipulations are to be distinguished from so-called "precatory trusts", which, while employing polite and gentle language, are nonetheless to be regarded as obligatory. In your view, to what extent, if at all, are the trustees duty-bound to comply with the terms of clause (f)?

3. In addition, apparent conditions in wills may be treated as *in terrorem*; the law regards them as empty threats. Accordingly, it has been held that provisions calling for the loss of an interest should the donee marry or contest a term of the will have been treated as *in terrorem* when the will provides for no gift over in the event of a breach.

In *Bellinger v. Nuytten Estate* 2003 CarswellBC 845 (S.C.) the will read:

> 7. IT IS MY FURTHER DESIRE, because of an expressed intention of one of the legatees to contest the terms of this my Will, that should any person do so then he or she shall forfeit any legacy he or she may be otherwise entitled to.

It was held by Hood J. (at paras. 6–9) that the clause was *in terrorem*:

> Mr. Hamilton drew my attention to the ancient English Law on the subject of conditions not to dispute a Will annexed to gifts in the Will and the doctrine of *in terrorem*; referring to Volume 1 of *Williams on Wills*, 7th ed. (London: Butterworths, 1995) at p. 366; *Cooke*

v. Turner (1846), 153 E.R. 1044 (Eng. Exch.) and *Evanturel v. Evanturel* (1874), L.R. 6 P.C. 1 (England P.C.), for the proposition:

> . . . that a Testamentary gift given on the condition that the Recipient not dispute the Will is not void for uncertainty, nor as being contrary to good morals or public policy, nor prohibited by any positive law, . . .

A perusal of these and other authorities makes it clear to me that there should be no dispute as to the law in the area applicable to the case at bar. While it is as stated in the above passage, the passage does not go far enough for present purposes. The gift must be accompanied by an effective gift over which vests in the recipient on the condition being breached. If there is no gift over, then the condition will be treated as merely *in terrorem*, that is a mere threat, and will be found to be void. And nothing short of a positive direction of a gift over, of vesting in another, even in the case where the forfeited legacy falls in the Residue, will suffice. There must be an express disposition made of what is to be forfeited. . . . Thus the application of the general rule that a failed gift falls into Residue is insufficient for the purpose of the rule.

Compare *Kent v. McKay* 1982 CarswellBC 187, [1982] 6 W.W.R. 165 (S.C.) which the Court in *Bellinger v. Nuytten Estate* treated as binding authority. There, the will read:

> [I]f any person who may be entitled to any benefit under this my Will shall institute or cause to be commenced any litigation in connection to any of the provisions of this my Will other than for any necessary judicial interpretation thereof or for the direction of the Court in the course of administration all benefits to which such person would have been entitled shall thereupon cease . . . [the] said benefits so revoked shall fall into and form part of the residue of my Estate to be distributed as directed in this my Will . . .

It was held in *Kent* that this clause was not *in terrorem*. However, it was also held that it could not prevent a beneficiary from attacking the will under the *Variation of Wills Act*. That Act permits a challenge on the grounds that the will does not contain adequate provision for a dependant of the decedent.

Caroline (Village) v. Roper
1987 CarswellAlta 363, 37 D.L.R. (4th) 761 (Q.B.)

[This case concerns the construction of a deed executed in 1949. At issue was the applicability of the common law rule against perpetuities, to be studied in the last part of this chapter. In short, in the event that the document created a fee simple subject to a condition subsequent, the rule against perpetuities would render that fee simple absolute; i.e., the condition would be removed. However, if the interest was a determinable fee simple, no perpetuities problem would exist. Which was it?]

Cavanagh J.:

In 1925, Thomas Roper allowed a community group to build a community hall on an acre of his land. This was on the strict understanding that it would be used for community purposes only. He retained title to the land. He died in 1946. His widow, Rosina, inherited the land and title was transferred into her name.

In 1949, representatives of the Community Association told Mrs. Roper that they wanted to install a basement under the community hall and that it would assist them to do so if the title was transferred into their names.

She and her son, the Respondent, said Thomas Sr. had only agreed to the use of the land as long as it was being used for a community centre. The representatives said that that condition would be preserved by a document they would prepare. Acting upon that assurance, she signed a transfer of title to Mr. Dix and Mr. Forsyth, trustees for the Caroline Community Hall on March 5, 1949 and was given a document dated the same day which reads as follows:

> Hamlet of Caroline
>
> March 5, 1949
>
> In regard to Mrs. Rosina Rennie Roper:
>
> This acre (SE corner of the NE quarter of 14-36-6-W5th) Transferred to the Caroline Community Hall, this day, Shall revert back to the Late Thomas Roper Estate if used for other than a community centre. . . .

Since then, there have been other transfers and now the title is in the name of the Village of Caroline, the within Applicant. This Applicant and intervening title holders were aware of the document recited above, although it was not registered in the Land Titles Office.

In 1961, Rosina Roper died and her son, the Respondent, succeeded to her Estate.

In 1982, the Community Hall burned down. It has not been rebuilt and the Village has no intention of using the land for a Community Centre any longer. In fact, the Village wants to sell the land to be used for a commercial purpose.

The Applicant now brings an application for a declaration that the trust contained in the above document is void and unenforceable. The basis on which the Village relies is that the document, if it is a trust, is one which by its wording offends against the rule against perpetuities and is, therefore, unenforceable.

In support of its position, the Applicant relies on a number of Ontario cases, being *Re Tilbury West Public School Board and Hastie* (1966) 55 D.L.R. (2d) 407; *Re North Gower Township Public School Board and Todd* (1967) 65 D.L.R. (2d) 421; *Re McKellar* (1972) 27 D.L.R. (3d) 289; *Re Essex Country Roman Catholic Separate School Board and Antaya* (1977) 80 D.L.R. (3d) 405 and *Missionary Church, Canada East v. Township of Nottawasage et al* (1980) 120 D.L.R. (3d) 489.

The leading case in this series is the first one, *Re Tilbury*, in which Grant J. made a comprehensive study of the problem. At p. 410 he said:

> It must be determined first if the grant in question was a determinable fee simple subject to a right of reverter or a fee simple subject to a condition subsequent . . . The essential distinction appears to be that the determining event in a determinable fee itself sets the limit for the estate first granted. A condition subsequent, on the other hand, is an independent clause added to a complete fee simple absolute which operates so as to defeat it: Megarry and Wade, p. 76. At p. 77 it is stated:
>
>> Words such as "while", "during", "as long as", "until" and so on are apt for the creation of a determinable fee, whereas words which form a separate clause of defeasance, such as "provided that", "on condition that", "but if", or "if it happens that", operate as a condition subsequent.
>
> In Cheshire at p. 280, the words "until", "so long as", and "whilst", are stated to be expressions creating determinable interests while phrases such as "on condition", "provided that", "if", "but if it happens", raise interests subject to condition subsequent.
>
> Cheshire at p. 281, points out the difference in the following words
>
>> In short, if the terminating event is an integral and necessary part of the formula from which the size of the interest is to be ascertained, the result is the creation of a determinable interest; but if the terminating event is external to the limitation, if it is a divided clause from the grant, the interest granted is an interest upon condition.

Then on p. 411 he said:

> Thus a devise to a school in fee simple "until it ceases to publish its accounts" creates a determinable fee, whereas a devise to the school in fee simple "on condition that the accounts are published annually" creates a fee simple defeasible by condition subsequent: *Re Da Costa*; *Clarke v. Church of England Collegiate School of St. Peter*, [1912] 1 Ch. 337.
>
> *Goodeve and Potter's Modern Law of Real Property* (1929) states at p. 124:
>
>> With a fee simple determinable the estate determines *ipso facto* by the happening of the event but where there is a condition, external to the limitation, the estate is not determined until entry by the person entitled to take advantage of the condition.
>
> It is my view that the deed in question created a fee simple determinable with a right of reverter. I am influenced to such a conclusion by reason that the words "so long as it shall be used and needed for school purposes and no longer" are used in the granting clause and they are words denoting a determinable fee.

The key words in the document given Mrs. Roper are "This acre . . . shall revert . . . if used for other than a community centre". Those words use the future tense and the future action depends on something occurring which may not occur or may occur in the indefinite future, thus offending against the rule against perpetuities. The words seem to make the fee simple that was given that day defeasible if a future event occurs. They do not put a condition on the fee simple that it is good only so long as a certain use is made of it. For these reasons, I would hold that the document in its present form is void and unenforceable. . . .

QUESTIONS AND COMMENTS

1. The fee simple subject to a condition subsequent was alluded to in the earlier analysis. Such an interest is regarded as being vested (in this case in the municipality) subject to being divested. The interest that is retained is called a right of re-entry. It is contingent: do you see why? The answer: before this right of re-entry can be exercised, an event (i.e., a condition precedent) must occur — the land must no longer be needed as a community centre.

The decision also addresses whether the interest granted was a determinable fee simple. That interest is vested, though it might come to an end the happening of the designated event. If that is the correct interpretation, the grantor retains a possibility of reverter. Is that interest vested or contingent?

The tempting response is to say that the interest is contingent, just as is its first cousin, the right of re-entry. That position prevailed in one English case: *Hooper v. Liverpool Corp.* (1944) 88 So.J. 213. The common law in Canada is thought to be different. In *Re Tilbury West Public School Board and Hastie* (1966) 55 D.L.R. (2d) 407, 1966 CarswellOnt 76 (H.C.) it was held, after an extensive review of the authorities, that the possibility of reverter is to be treated as vested. Hence, when a determinable interest is created, a fiction is adopted: the stipulated event giving rise to the possibility of reverter is seen as marking the full duration of the state, and is not a supervening event that cuts short the interest granted. (As we will see in the discussion of perpetuities, this reading has been altered, for perpetuity purposes only, in some jurisdictions.)

2. Interpret the following clauses:

(a) "[To] [t]he Temiskaming and Northern Ontario Railway Commission for the purposes of a right of way for a Wye at the Town of Timmins. . . .

In the event of the whole or any portion of the land hereby transferred not being required for the purposes of the railway Commission as hereinbefore set forth, the said Railway Commission agrees to re-convey and transfer the said lands or the portion thereof not so required for the purposes of a railway to the Timmins Townsite Company Limited." *Ontario Northland Transportation Commission v. Timmins (City)* 1991 CarswellOnt 1956 (Gen. Div.).

(b) "[To the City of Moncton] on the condition that this property is to be held and used for all time for civic purposes in perpetuity". *Moncton (City) v. Canada (Minister of National Defence)* 1987 CarswellNB 71 (Q.B.).

(c) To A, "to be used for the purpose of constructing a flood control facility on Bear Creek and thereafter to be used solely for flood control purposes" and "for so long as the Property is used for the purpose of constructing a flood control facility or used for flood control purposes. . . . If and when the Property is ever used for the purposes other than flood control or is abandoned by Grantee, his successors and assigns, this conveyance shall be null and void, and title to the Property shall absolutely revert to Grantor, his successors and assigns without the necessity of re-entry or suit; and no act or omission on the part of any beneficiary of this clause shall be a waiver of the operation and enforcement of such condition." *Cypress-Fairbanks Independent School Dist. v. Glenn W. Loggins, Inc.* 2003 WL 21502414 (Tex.App. San Antonio).

(d) "[My daughter Verna Powell] . . . shall have the right to the occupation, possession and use of my house . . . for as long as she remains in possession of the said premises . . . and that in the event my said daughter ceases to remain in possession of the said premises or married [sic] or upon her death . . . the said premises . . . shall be held . . . in trust for my four (4) children, Marie Mitchell, William Albert Powell, Verna Powell and James Andrew Powell." *Powell v. Powell* 1988 CarswellAlta 193 (Q.B.).

(e) "the . . . [grantor] doth grant unto the . . . [Railway Company] its successors and assigns for ever. . . . [B]ut upon the express condition and understanding that so soon as the said Railway Company shall cease to occupy and use the lands first hereinbefore recited for the purposes set out in said by-law, and the same thereby revert to the said Corporation then the fee simple in the last described lands shall revert to the party of the first part and he shall thereupon become entitled to enter thereon and possess the same as heretofore.

TO HAVE AND TO HOLD unto the said party of the second part its successors and assigns to and for its and their sole and only use forever subject nevertheless to the reservations, limitations, *provisos* and conditions expressed in the original Grant thereof from the Crown, and subject to the above mentioned condition and understanding" *Re McKellar* [1972] 3 O.R. 16, 1972 CarswellOnt 350 (H.C.), affirmed 1972 CarswellOnt 449 (C.A.).

(f)(i) "To have and to hold the said lands unto the said Corporation, its successors and assigns forever upon and subject to the following trusts and uses that is to say that the said lands are to be used by the said Corporation its successors and assigns as a site upon which to erect a Hospital and for purposes in connection with such Hospital and for no other purpose or purposes whatsoever; And it is hereby declared to be an express condition of the Grant hereby made that if the said lands or any part thereof shall at any time hereafter be used for any purpose or purposes other than those hereinbefore set forth then these Presents and everything therein contained shall become and be null and void, and it shall be lawful for Us, Our successors or Assigns thereupon or at any time thereafter into and upon the said lands or any part thereof in the name of the whole to reenter and the same to have again re-possess and enjoy as of Our and their former estate therein anything herein contained to the contrary notwithstanding."

(f)(ii) "To have and to hold the same unto the said Corporation its successors and assigns, so long as the same are or is as the case may be, and upon the trust and subject to the condition that the same shall be used for hospital purposes and for no other purpose or purposes whatsoever."

(f)(iii) "To have and to hold the same unto the said Corporation its successors and assigns so long as the same are, and upon the trust and subject to the condition that the same shall be used for Hospital purposes and for no other purpose or purposes whatsoever . . . Provided always and these presents are issued upon and subject to the following condition namely: that if the Corporation, its successors or assigns shall at anytime hereafter fail or neglect to use the said lands for the purposes aforesaid or if the Corporation, its successors or assigns shall use the said lands for any other purpose, then and in any of the said cases it shall be lawful for Our Minister of the Interior of Canada by writing under his hand to cancel these presents and upon such cancellation these presents and the grant thereby made shall become and be null and void and the said that lands shall thereupon become and be vested in Us as of Our former estate and interest therein." *Friends of the Calgary General Hospital Society v. Canada* 2000 CarswellAlta 66 (Q.B. [Chambers]), affirmed 2001 CarswellAlta 825 (C.A.), leave to appeal refused: 2002 CarswellAlta 184, 2002 CarswellAlta 185 (S.C.C.).

(g)(i) "I Give and Devise to the Women's Christian Association of the City of London, lots number thirty-eight (38) and thirty-nine (39) on the east side of Richmond Street in the said City of London, together with the large brick building erected thereon by me and known as the T. McCormick Home for Aged People to have and to hold the same for the purposes of such home as long as the Association shall maintain the same, but if at any time the said Association ceases to maintain and support the said Home, then the said property is to revert to my general estate, and form a part thereof. . . .

Now this Indenture Witnesseth that (in pursuance of the powers vested in them) the said Grantors as personal representatives of the said Thomas McCormick deceased, in consideration of the sum of five of lawful money of Canada, to them in hand paid by the said Grantees the receipt whereof is hereby acknowledged, Do Grant and Convey unto the said Grantees, their Successors, and assigns FOREVER: All and Singular those certain parcels of land and premises situate in the City of London in the County of Middlesex and being composed of lots numbers thirty-eight and thirty-nine on the east side of Richmond Street."

(g)(ii) Habendum: "To have and to hold the same unto the said Grantees, their successors, and assigns FOREVER: Subject to the restrictions and reservations contained in the said last will and testament of Thomas McCormick." *Women's Christian Assn. of London v. McCormick* 1989 CarswellOnt 533 (H.C.).

(h) To the School Board in fee simple. "It is further covenanted that the above described property is to be used for school purposes only and the said grantor reserves to himself and his heirs the preference to buy the said property at the current price should the same ceased [sic] to be used for the purposes intended." *Re Essex County Roman Catholic Separate School Bd.* 1977 CarswellOnt 429, 80 D.L.R. (3d) 405 (H.C.).

3. *St. Mary's Indian Band v. Cranbrook (City)* [1997] 2 S.C.R. 657, 1997 CarswellBC 1259, 1997 CarswellBC 1258 concerns Aboriginal reserve land in British Columbia. In 1966, the appellants surrendered approximately 600 acres of their reserve to the Federal government for use as a municipal airport. It was agreed "that should at any time the said lands cease to be used for public purposes they will revert to the St. Mary's Indian Band free of charge". A question arose as to the effect of this latter stipulation. Drawing on the *sui generis* nature of Aboriginal rights, Lamer C.J. (at 668) rejected the idea that the interpretive devices used to distinguish between a condition subsequent and a determinable fee should be invoked:

> [W]e do not focus on the minutiae of the language employed in the surrender documents and should not rely upon traditional distinctions between determinable limitations and conditions subsequent in order to adjudicate a case such as this. Instead, the Court must "go beyond the usual restrictions" of the common law and look more closely at the respective intentions of the St. Mary's Indian Band and the Crown at the time of the surrender of the airport lands.
>
> The reason the Court has said that common law real property concepts do not apply to native lands is to prevent native intentions from being frustrated by an application of formalistic and arguably alien common law rules. Even in a case such as this where the Indian band received full legal representation prior to the surrender transaction, we must ensure that form not trump substance. It would be fundamentally unjust to impose inflexible and technical land transfer requirements upon these "autonomous actors" and conclude that the "cease[d] to be used for public purposes" stipulation was a condition subsequent solely because the band made the mistake of using the word "should" instead of the word "until".

It was concluded, *inter alia*, that in looking at the document as a whole the surrender was intended to be absolute.

3. STATE LIMITATIONS ON PRIVATE POWER

(a) introduction

Proprietary freedom is extensive in Canadian law, but it is not absolute. Not all conditional dispositions will be enforced. To take a clear example, no court would give effect to a transfer conditioned on the donee committing a criminal act before being entitled to receive property. In this part, some critical limits on proprietary freedom are considered. What forces drive the imposed limitations? To what extent are these limits informed by the property-based values (such as efficiency), or factors external to property law (such as respect for human dignity and equality under law)?

Assuming that a gift contains an invalid element, what then happens to the property? The effect of invalidity depends on the form that the gift takes. For example, it is accepted that when a condition subsequent is invalid, it is removed (and with it the right of re-entry), thereby rendering the gift absolute. An invalid determinable limitation results in the entire gift failing: here both the determinable interest and the related possibility of reverter are destroyed. Likewise, an invalid condition precedent of land will be removed, and this destroys the gift. The rule concerning conditions precedent of personalty may well follow that established for land. However, as will be seen in *Unger v. Gossen*, below, a different approach seems to be adopted.

Unger v. Gossen
1996 CarswellBC 1248 (S.C.)

Stromberg-Stein J.:

This Petition is brought by Abraham Philip Unger, the Executor of the estate of Malvina Henry Toews for an order pursuant to Rule 10 of the *Supreme Court Rules* for construction of paragraph 6(e) of the Will.

All the potential beneficiaries, except the Eastern European Mission, are in agreement that the estate should be divided into three equal portions and immediately distributed to the three nephews of Malvina Toews — Ernst, Heinrich and Erich Gossen (also known as Ernest, Henry, and Erich Goossen). The children of Ernst and Erich have signed a Waiver and Renunciation of any interest in the estate on the condition that the estate is so distributed. Heinrich Gossen does not have children.

The Eastern European Mission no longer exists under that name and is no longer registered as a charity in California. It has not been served with this Petition.

At issue is whether the Court can or should direct a distribution of the estate as desired by all the potential beneficiaries. This involves consideration of the effect of a residency condition in paragraph 6(e) in the Will. It is necessary to consider the intent of the Testator in drafting the condition and the fact that it is impossible to fulfil the condition at this time.

Malvina Toews died on May 8, 1994. She left a Will dated December 15, 1980. Her estate consists of approximately $150,000.00 held by her Executor in term deposits. Letters Probate were granted to her Executor on July 15, 1994.

The Will provides that the entire estate should be held by the Executor and Trustee in trust and the income paid annually to the Testator's sister, Anna Toews, during her lifetime. Anna Toews died on February 3, 1994. On her death the entire estate was to be divided among the three nephews, Ernst, Heinrich and Erich Gossen provided that, severally, they qualified by becoming residents in Canada within fifteen years of the date of the death of Malvina Toews.

At the time the Will was drawn, Ernst, Heinrich and Erich Gossen were citizens of the Soviet Union.

The Will provides that if any of the nephews should die before qualifying, or fail to qualify within the fifteen year period, the share that would have gone to that nephew would be paid to his children then living in equal shares provided that each child eligible for such payment qualifies by becoming resident in Canada within sixteen years of the date of the death of Malvina Toews.

The Will provides that in the event that one or more persons qualifies by becoming a resident of Canada within the specified time, they would receive interest only on their nominal share for the first five years of their residency. Upon the expiration of the five years, they would receive their nominal share of the capital. The nominal share would be calculated as if all beneficiaries of the same class qualify at the same time.

Any one-third interest not qualified for by a nephew or his children within sixteen years of the date of death is to be distributed equally among the beneficiaries who have qualified. The payment of each portion in that event is to be paid upon completion of the five year residency requirement.

In the event that no nephew or any child of any nephew qualifies, then the whole of the residue of the estate is to be paid to the Eastern European Mission of Pasadena, California. In the event that the Eastern European Mission would otherwise be entitled but had ceased to exist, then the residue of the estate is to be given to its successor and if no successor existed, the Executor and Trustee is to use his discretion and give the entire residue to a Church Mission doing missionary work in Eastern Europe and the U.S.S.R.

Anna Gossen, the daughter of Erich Gossen has "qualified" by becoming a resident of Canada so the Eastern European Mission, even if it did exist, has no interest in the estate.

It is clear from the evidence that the overriding concern of Malvina Toews at the time her Will was drafted was that she did not want any of her funds to go to any beneficiary residing in a communist state, particularly the U.S.S.R. She believed that the state would confiscate all or most of the funds designated for any relatives living there. This was the reason her Will contained the residency requirement.

The evidence reveals that beginning in 1989, Malvina Toews suffered from dementia and lost her capacity to make or alter her Will. When Soviet communism collapsed and her three nephews were able to emigrate from the former Soviet Union to Germany, she was not able to alter her Will to reflect the changed circumstances.

All three of Malvina Toews' nephews are still alive and they reside in Germany.

Heinrich Gossen is 71 years old. He has the equivalent of a grade seven education and is a retired truck driver. He speaks no English and has no funds to invest in Canada for the purpose of qualifying as an investor immigrant. He has no children.

Erich Gossen is 70 years old. He speaks no English. He has the equivalent of a grade five education and is a retired farm machinery mechanic. He has no funds to invest in Canada for the purpose of qualifying as an investor immigrant. He has six children: Jacob Gossen, Agnes Gossen-Gisbrecht, Olga Gossen-Tshugunova, Elisabeth Gossen-Brozio, Anna Gossen and Helena Gossen. All live in Germany or the U.S.S.R. except for Anna who lives in Canada.

Ernst Gossen is 65 years old. He has the equivalent of a grade four education and is currently working as a driving instructor and auto mechanic. He has no funds to invest in Canada for the purpose of qualifying as an investor immigrant. Ernst Gossen has two children, Andreaas Gossen and Rudolf Gossen, both of whom reside in Germany.

None of the children are under the age of nineteen. Other than Anna Gossen who is already in Canada, none of the children of Ernst and Erich Gossen wish to reside in Canada.

An opinion has been obtained from a Canadian lawyer with ten years' experience and with a legal practice restricted to immigration law. He has deposed that, in his opinion, none of the three nephews would be eligible to immigrate to Canada under the selection criteria set out in the *Immigration Act Regulations*.

Of all the potential beneficiaries in the estate, only Anna Gossen, the daughter of Erich, has apparently "qualified" by becoming a resident of Canada. Her share in the estate would, pursuant to the terms of the Will, be postponed until it was determined if her father or either of his brothers qualified by becoming a resident in Canada before May 8, 2009, which would be the fifteenth anniversary of the Testator's death.

Although the Testator does not appear to have considered this possibility, it seems from the wording of the Will that any other qualifying beneficiary would lose their entitlement to their share in the capital of the estate if, having become a resident in Canada, they ceased to be a resident before the expiration of five years from the date of residency. . . .

[T]he condition has become impossible to fulfil due to the operation of Canadian law. The relevant law consists of the regulations passed pursuant to the *Immigration Act* which make it impossible for the nephews to immigrate to Canada. This impossibility was not known to the Testator as it arose after the making of the Will.

Counsel submits that the law regarding impossible condition precedents is somewhat obscure. In Feeney, *The Canadian Law of Wills*, 3rd ed. (Toronto: Butterworths, 1987) at 246 the author states:

> Thus, with regard to legacies of personal property, the Canadian law can be stated as follows: Conditions precedent impossible of performance (so known to the testator) are to be disregarded and the gift upheld. Also, where the condition is made impossible by the act or default of the testator the condition is void but the legacy is good. Moreover, regardless of the testator's knowledge, where the condition cannot be performed because it is contrary to law, then, too, the bequest is absolute. It must be shown, however, that the performance of the condition was not the sole motive for the bequest. Also, if the impossibility was unknown to the testator, or if the condition when created was possible but has since become impossible by an act of God, or a law making it illegal, or some act not attributable to the testator, then both the legacy and the condition are void.

This passage seems to suggest the impossibility of the condition by reason of law had to exist at the outset in order for the condition to be ignored leaving the gift intact.

I have not been referred to any authorities dealing directly with the situation where a condition has become impossible by operation of law after the making of the Will and the reason for the condition no longer exists. . . .

In *Re MacDonald* (1971), 18 D.L.R. (3d) 521 (Ont. H.C.), a gift was made to the Windsor Library Board to be used in collecting historical objects for showing and presentation in a certain house on the condition that the City of Windsor give the necessary assurances that the house, itself of some historical significance, would never be moved. The City was not the owner of the house and could give no such assurances. The Court found that this gift was subject to a condition which was, at the time of its creation and to the knowledge of the Testator, impossible.

The Court in *Re MacDonald* reasoned that where a Testator grants a bequest, subject to a condition which is impossible, the dominant intent must be the gift, because to intentionally draft into a will a void condition is an absurdity. Unless it could be shown that the principal concern of the Testator was the condition, and not the gift, the condition alone must fail. . . .

In the present case there is clear evidence that the dominant consideration of the Testator was to make the gift to her nephews. The purpose of the condition was to ensure the gift did not fall into the hands of the government of the U.S.S.R.

I conclude on the evidence before me that the condition of residency is a condition precedent. However the gift, not the condition, was the Testator's motivation and the performance of the condition was not the very reason for the gift.

The condition that her nephews come to Canada is impossible to fulfil by operation of law. In this case the question whether the Testator knew of the impossibility of the performance of the condition when she drafted the condition is not determinative. Clearly her intent was to benefit her nephews. The condition was drafted to ensure that the nephews were the beneficiaries and not the Soviet government. She was incapacitated and unable to change her Will when her nephews' circumstances changed and there was no longer any reason for concern on her part. Her nephews cannot immigrate to Canada due to present immigration policies.

All potential beneficiaries agree that the estate should be distributed in accordance with the wishes of Testator. I agree with counsel that having regard to the Testator's wishes, and because the condition in the Will is impossible to fulfil by operation of law, the condition fails and the estate should be distributed at this time in accordance with the terms of the Will and the wishes of all potential beneficiaries.

There will be an order for costs to all parties payable from the estate.

Application allowed.

(b) uncertainty

Kotsar v. Shattock
[1981] V.R. 13 (S.C., Full Ct.)

[Note: a portion of this case was reproduced above in the discussion of basic concepts. The following clause of the will is relevant to the issue of uncertainty:

> (e) To pay and transfer the remainder of my residuary estate to Oilme Kotsar of Venevere Side Jaoskond, Poltsamaa Rajoon Estonia N.S.V. if and when she shall attain the age of twenty-one years provided that upon the attainment of such age she shall then be resident in one of the countries of the British Commonwealth of Nations.]

Crockett J.:

The remaining question is — are those conditions void for uncertainty? A condition that is void will not, of course, act in bar of the beneficiary's taking absolutely. The necessity for attainment of a specified age (which in fact has occurred) affords no difficulty. However, it is said by counsel for the primary residuary beneficiary that the requirement that, upon the attainment of such age, she shall then be resident in one of the countries of the British Commonwealth of Nations is so uncertain as to be void. The contention was that either one or both expressions "resident" and "British Commonwealth of Nations" were too uncertain to be enforceable.

With regard to the requirement of "residency" reliance was placed upon the Privy Council decision in *Sifton v. Sifton*, [1938] A.C. 656; [1939] 1 All E.R. 109. In that case the critical clause provided that: "The payments to my said daughter shall be made only so long as she shall continue to reside in Canada." That clause was held void for uncertainty on the ground that there was insufficient definition as to how much absence from Canada was permissible and for what purposes and occasions. But, as Dixon C.J. pointed out in *Perpetual Trustees Executors and Agency Co. of Tasmania Ltd. v. Walker* (1953), 90 C.L.R. 270, at p. 283, when discussing *Sifton's Case*, "not a little turned on the word 'continue' ". And, as Lord Romer, in the judgment of the Privy Council delivered by him, observed at ([1938] A.C.) pp. 675-6, the meaning of the words "reside" and "residence" depends on the context in which the words are used, his Lordship giving as an example that would present no difficulty, the words "reside in the house for at least six weeks in a year".

Now, in the present case, whilst the requirement is residence in a country, it is residence in that country on one particular day only, namely the day upon which the beneficiary attains the age of 21 years. The lack of certainty and precision associated with the requirement of continuity of residence in a country can have no application to such a provision. What may be needed to comply with such a requirement can be determined in advance. If the expressions "reside" or "be resident" are themselves inherently understandable then their employment in the testamentary instrument will not *ipso facto* operate as a ground for a forfeiture unless the context of their use compels that result. The expression "be resident in a country" is an expression of ordinary speech and I should think plainly means that the person at the material time has his ordinary dwelling in which he lives in that country. As the learned Chief Justice said in the course of that part of his judgment in *Walker's Case*, *supra*, at p. 279, with which all other members of the Court agreed: "The amount of absence from a man's dwelling which is necessary to rob it of that character and make it no longer his residence may be a matter of degree. But everyone understands that if it is the place to which he returns from temporary absences, from journeys abroad and from peregrinations upon pleasure or business, where he maintains an establishment, and keeps his more permanent personal belongings and household furniture, it is his home and he resides there."

It follows, in my opinion, that the country in which that home is, is the country in which he is resident.

The lack of certainty ascribed by the Privy Council in *Sifton v. Sifton*, *supra*, to the requirement of residency in a country arose from the provision that the residency was to continue. But, limited to a particular and definable day, a requirement that extends to residence in a particular country can be no less certain than was the condition in *Walker's Case*. Lord Cranworth in *Clavering v. Ellison* (1859), 7 H.L.C. 707, at p. 725, expressed the rule to govern the question in these words: "Where a vested estate is to be defeated by a condition on a contingency that is to happen afterwards, that condition must be such that the court can see from the beginning precisely and distinctly upon the happening of what event it was that the preceding vested estate was to determine."

In my view in this case that event can be seen. Authorities which suggest the contrary in relation to conditions as to "residency" in, or "occupancy" of, a house (a number of which are to be found discussed in the judgment of Dixon C.J. in *Walker's Case*, *supra*) should not be treated as having application to the present case. *Sifton v. Sifton*, in my view, is clearly distinguishable.

Is then the expression "British Commonwealth of Nations" so uncertain as to render invalid the condition in which it is incorporated? I think not. The Court was given instances by counsel of supposed difficulties in interpretation of the expression as demonstration of the allegation of obscurity of the relevant words. But in regard to such an approach the cautionary words of Lord Simonds in *Bromley v. Tryon*, [1952] A.C. 265, at pp. 275-6; [1951] 2 All E.R. 1058 should be borne in mind. The Lord Chancellor observed that: "It does not follow because the words of a defeasance clause are sufficiently clear to give the clause validity, that there may not be cases in which its application is difficult, and I apprehend that, if there is a real doubt, the court will show the same favour to a vested estate in applying the clause as it does in construing it."

It was submitted (the submission being reinforced by reference to passages in texts dealing with the structure of the British Commonwealth) that, as a matter of international law, it is not possible, or at least was not at the relevant time, (and assuming that there is no significance in the tendency in recent years to omit the adjective "British" from the expression) to determine whether membership of the Commonwealth was limited to independent nations in voluntary association or also included those states that were, in turn, under the sovereignty in some degree of an independent member nation. The existence of this uncertainty was (so it was said) itself fatal to the validity of the defeasance clause. Then, it was further contended that, should the correct definition be the latter of the two alternatives, as it was notorious that the precise political status of states commonly described as, for example, Crown colonies, dependencies, mandated territories or protectorates was often a matter of dispute, it could not be said with certainty whether such a state was within the Commonwealth at the relevant time.

I am disposed to think that the correct definition of the expression — at least as it is used in the will — is the first of the two postulated alternatives which may be described as the preliminary sense in which the term is used. Compare *Halsbury* 4th ed., vol. 6, para. 801. However, should this view be incorrect, the short answer to the appellant's contention is that the term must be amenable to curial definition with all the certainty that such a definition implies. It must be so amenable because it is to be found employed statutorily. See, for example, the *Matrimonial Causes Act* (Commonwealth) 1959–1966, s. 101(2) and the *Foreign Judgments Act* (Victoria) 1962, s. 3(1). The extension of the meaning of the Commonwealth of Nations by specific statutory definition in the Victorian Act leaves unaffected the requirement in the administration of the relevant aspects of that Act to ascribe an unequivocal meaning to the expression "British Commonwealth of Nations". Doubtless the term may also be found in other enactments.

In discussing the question whether the word "residence" was too uncertain to be made the ground of a forfeiture, Dixon C.J., in *Walker's Case*, *supra*, at p. 279, said: "The legislature has had no hesitation in making 'residence' in a given place the criterion of liability to taxation, of rateability and of the right to vote. Indeed the jurisdiction of this court may depend upon the residence of a litigant in a State. It seems strange that a testator should be denied the power of prescribing residence in a given dwelling place as a qualification for his bounty."

By analogy those observations have no less force in relation to the selection by the testatrix of a country in the British Commonwealth of Nations in which residence must occur if the appellant's entitlement to the gift of residue is to be satisfied.

As the condition as to residency has not been fulfilled the appellant is not entitled to the residue of the estate of the deceased. The answer is given by the learned Judge to the question in the summons is, therefore, correct, although, as I would hold, for reasons different from those upon which the Judge relied. The appeal should be dismissed. . . .

Appeal dismissed.

QUESTIONS AND COMMENTS

1. Southwell J. concurred with Crockett J. Starke J. wrote a separate concurring judgment. At 16, he discussed the distinction between issues of uncertainty as they affect conditions subsequent and precedent:

> I turn then to the question of certainty or uncertainty of the condition as to residence. It is I think well established that the tests relating to conditions subsequent differ from those relating to conditions precedent.
>
> In *Re Allen deceased*, [1953] Ch. 810; [1953] 1 All E.R. 308, Evershed, M.R. said at ([1953] Ch.) p. 816: "It has long been established that the courts (which are inclined against the divesting of gifts or estates already vested) will hold a condition subsequent void if its terms are such that (apart from mere difficulties of construction of the language or of the ascertainment of the facts) it cannot be clearly known in advance or from the beginning what are the circumstances the happening of which will cause the divesting or determination of the gift or estate."
>
> At ([1953] Ch.) p. 817 he said: "In any case and whether the formula be a condition precedent or qualification it seems to me no such general or academic test is called for as a condition subsequent requires. All that the claiming devisee has to do is at the relevant date to establish if he can that he satisfies the condition or qualification whatever be the appropriate test. If the formula is such as to involve questions of degree (as *prima facie* is implicit in any requirement of adherence or attachment to a particular faith or creed), the uncertainty of the test contemplated well may invalidate the formula as a condition subsequent but will not, in my judgment, necessarily do so in the case of a condition precedent; for if the claimant be able to satisfy any, or at least any reasonable test, is he to be disentitled to the benefit of the gift?"

2. Do you think that the majority in *Shattock* successfully distinguished the *Sifton* decision?

3. Assume that you are retained to draft a clause designed to pursue the same objectives as those in *Sifton*. How would you try to do so without running afoul of the rules relating to uncertainty? Assume also that in the event that the clause is found to be uncertain, your client would not want the donee to have the gift at all. Instead, she prefers that the money be given to charity. What legal construct would you use to achieve that result?

4. In 1996 the Ontario Law Reform Commission recommended:

> that the continuing distinctions between a determinable interest and an interest subject to a condition subsequent should be abrogated. This abrogation should apply to interests held under trusts, as well as common law interests, and should extend to interests in personal as well as real property. It should be achieved, we recommend, by providing that language that at common law would create a determinable interest will instead create an interest subject to a condition subsequent (O.L.R.C., *Report on Basic Principles of Land Law* (Toronto: A.G.(Ont.), 1996) at 158).

What implications flow from this proposal?

5. Comment on the meaning and validity of the following clauses:

(a) ". . . to my son STEWART BERNARD all my estate, real and personal, of whatsoever nature and kind and wheresoever situate to be his absolutely subject only that should my son FLOYD BERNARD decide to return to live here, that a lot of land of three acres along highway No. 2 be transferred to him." *Bernard Estate v. Bernard* 1986 CarswellNB 47 (Q.B.).

(b) "I give and bequeath to my son James . . . [Blackacre] . . . on the following conditions: that my son James reside on said land and cultivate the same; should my said son James desire not to reside on said property or cultivate same then that portion hereby bequeath to be the property of my son Harold he paying to my said son James the sum of one thousand dollars." *H.J. Hayes Co. v. Meade* 1987 CarswellNB 66 (Q.B.).

(c) ". . . As regards the remaining one-half of the residue, I direct my Trustee to use the fund until the same is fully exhausted to purchase parcels of food stuffs and other necessities of life and to send such parcels to certain members of my family now living in the Ukraine. I shall furnish my Trustee with the names and addresses of all of my relatives and I give my Trustee absolute discretion in regards to purchasing the parcels, and the frequency of such purchase and the number of parcels that he shall send to each member of my family. If my Trustee is of the opinion that my family is not benefiting from receiving such parcels, and if there is evidence to show that the members of my family are not receiving these parcels, then I authorize my Trustee in his absolute and uncontrolled discretion to discontinue sending parcels to members of my family, and in the event that this event take place I Give, Devise and Bequeath the residue of my funds to my Trustee, and the said Walter Dubrowskij for his own use absolutely." *Re Czykalenko* (1983) 42 O.R. (2d) 631 (H.C.).

(d) "All my property of whatsoever kind and wheresoever situate I leave to my wife, Veronica, for her use during her lifetime, and upon her death, to my youngest son, Robert, to be his absolutely subject, however, to the *proviso* that should any of my children require a building lot out of my land, the same shall be made available to them either by my wife during her lifetime, or by my son, Robert, upon the death of my wife, provided however, that should any of my children require a building lot out of my land, they shall request it from Robert within five years of the death of my wife, at the end of which time all the rest and residue of my estate shall become the property of my son, Robert, to be his absolutely." *Fitzgerald v. Fitzgerald Estate* 1993 CarswellNfld 265 (C.A.).

(e) "I give and bequeath to my grandson Bruce Greening my dwelling house and all its contents as well as all my part of the land situated at Jamestown. . . . It is to be clearly understood that the said Bruce Greening is to take care of his grandfather, the aforesaid Gilbert Philpott and to see that in the event of death to be decently and properly interred in a properly constituted cemetery." *Philpott v. Philpott Estate* 1989 CarswellNfld 117 (T.D.).

(f) "I leave my house and land and all buildings on this land to my son Henry George Fry of Summerville. The boat & motor and shed and fishing gear will go to my son Henry George Fry. My wishes are that all of my daughters and my son William James Fry will be allowed and welcome to stay at our house when they come home for a holiday. All of my dishes and household things will be divided equally between my five daughters and two sons. Any monies left when funeral expenses are paid will be divided equally between my seven children." *Re Fry Estate* 2001 CarswellNfld 281 (T.D.).

(g) "[To my trustees] . . . To permit my friends LARRY PAIKE and CONNIE SMITH, or either of them to have the personal USE, occupation and enjoyment thereof as a place of RESIDENCE for a trial period of three years upon their or his or her undertaking to preserve the Admirals Road House in its current state and condition and on the condition that given such undertaking then during this period . . . Upon expiration of the trial period of three years, then upon his or her undertaking to continue to preserve the Admirals Road House in its current state and condition then to my friends, LARRY PAIKE and CONNIE SMITH, or either of them, absolutely." *Small v. Cotton* 1982 CarswellBC 612 (S.C.).

(h) "This house at 792 Mapleton Place, Victoria, B.C. V8Z 6W2 — to Gerald F. Thomas — my husband's 2nd cousin of 1832 West Burnside Rd., Victoria, B.C. V8X 3X3. *if* he wishes to live in it. If he doesn't wish to live here — then it shall be sold and *half* the money shall go to him. One quarter to go to my cousin Mrs. Joan Richardson of 7 Castle Court, Castle Lane, Hadleigh, Benfleet, Essex, England. One quarter to the Fairbank Calligraphy Society." *Davis Estate v. Thomas* 1990 CarswellBC 559 (C.A.).

(c) public policy

Re Leonard Foundation Trust
1990 CarswellOnt 486 (C.A.)

Robins J.A.:

The principal question in this appeal is whether the terms of a scholarship trust established in 1923 by the late Reuben Wells Leonard are now contrary to public policy. If they are, the question then is whether the *cy-près* doctrine can be applied to preserve the trust.

The appeal is from the order of McKeown J. [reported (1987), 27 E.T.R. 193 (H.C.)] on an application under s. 60 of the *Trustee Act*, R.S.O. 1980, c. 512 and rr. 14.05(2) and (3) of the *Rules of Civil Procedure*, by the Canada Trust Company, as the successor trustee of a scholarship trust known as "The Leonard Foundation", for the advice, opinion and direction of the Court upon certain questions arising in the administration of the trust. The questions put before the Court are as follows:

> 1. Are any of the provisions of, or the policy established under the Indenture made the 28th day of December, 1923 between Reuben Wells Leonard, Settlor of the First Part, and The Toronto General Trusts Corporation, Trustee of the Second Part (the "Indenture") set out in Schedule A hereunder void or illegal or not capable of being lawfully administered by the applicant The Canada Trust Company, successor trustee thereunder, and/or the General Committee and other committees referred to in the Indenture, by reason of
>
> (i) public policy as declared in the *Human Rights Code*, 1981 (the "*Code*");
>
> (ii) other public policy, if any;
>
> (iii) discrimination because of race, creed, citizenship, ancestry, place of origin, colour, ethnic origin, sex, handicap of otherwise; or
>
> (iv) uncertainty?
>
> 2. If the answer to any of the questions propounded above is in the affirmative with respect to any of the said clauses or policy, does the trust created by the Indenture fail in whole or in part and if so, who is entitled to the trust fund under the Indenture?
>
> 3. If the answer to any of the questions propounded in paragraph 1 above is in the affirmative with respect to any of the said clauses or policy, but the answer to question

2 is in the negative, is there a general charitable intention expressed in and by the Indenture such that the Court in the exercise of its inherent jurisdictions in matters of charitable trusts will direct that the trust be administered *cy-près*?

4. If the answer to any of the questions propounded in paragraph 1 above is in the affirmative with respect to any of the said clauses or policy, but the answer to question 3 above is also in the affirmative, how should the Trustee and/or the General Committee and other committees referred to in the Indenture administer the trust?

5. Does the application form as employed in the administration of the trust constitute a publication, display or other similar representation that indicates the intention of the Trustee or of the General Committee or other committees administering the trust to infringe or to incite the infringement of rights under Part 1 of the *Code*?

6. If the answer to question 5 is in the affirmative, how should the Committee on Scholarships of The Leonard Foundation and its Honorary Secretary carry out the provisions of the Indenture which require an official application form to be submitted to the Honourary Secretary by a member of the General Committee on behalf of an applicant for a Leonard Scholarship?

McKeown J. found that the trust provisions were not invalid for any of the reasons set out in Question 1, which made it unnecessary for him to answer Questions 2, 3 and 4. He answered Question 5 in the negative, which made it unnecessary to answer Question 6.

The order has been appealed by two of the parties to the proceedings. The first appellant, the Ontario Human Rights Commission, takes the position that the learned Weekly Court Judge should have declined to answer Questions 1(i), 1(iii) and 5 on the ground that these questions concern the applicability of the *Human Rights Code, 1981*, S.O. 1981, c. 53, and relate to matters within the exclusive primary jurisdiction of the Commission and, therefore, are not properly before the Court.

The appellant, the Royal Ontario Museum (the "ROM"), has status in these proceedings as one of the charitable institutions named in the last will of Reuben Wells Leonard. Under this will, any amount that falls to be administered in the residuary estate is to be divided among certain individuals and charitable institutions as set out by the testator. The ROM's position on this appeal is that the scholarship trust violates public policy and fails completely. In its submission, the Judge erred in not holding that the trust fund falls into the Leonard estate and must be distributed to the residual beneficiaries, including the ROM, in accordance with the provisions of the will.

The Public Trustee and the Class of Persons Eligible to Receive Scholarships from the Leonard Foundation are intervenors in the case. They both support the judgment below and ask that the appeal be dismissed. However, should the Court find that the terms of the scholarship trust violate public policy, the Public Trustee submits that the trust nonetheless has a valid charitable purpose and should not fail but should be applied *cy-près*, without the offending conditions. On the other hand, counsel for the Class of Persons Eligible to Receive Scholarships takes the position that if the trust violates public policy, it fails completely and is incapable of being applied *cy-près*.

The respondent, Canada Trust Company (the "trustee"), takes no position other than to suggest that: (1) the Court below had jurisdiction to hear the application and (2) the Indenture in 1923 created a valid charitable trust, and should this Court determine by reason of the *Human Rights Code, 1981*, or other grounds of public policy that the conditions are now void then either (a) such conditions are merely *malum prohibitum* and the Court should strike them out and leave the charitable trust to operate freed therefrom or (b) a reference should be directed to apply the fund *cy-près*.

The Issues

The preliminary issue as to jurisdiction, raised by the Ontario Human Rights Commission, can be disposed of very briefly. In my opinion, this application is properly before the Court. I agree with McKeown J. and Tarnopolsky J.A. in this regard and have nothing to add to their reasons. On the remaining issues, while I agree with Tarnopolsky J.A. that the appeal must be allowed, my reasons for reaching that conclusion differ from those of my learned colleague.

The remaining issues, in my view, reduce themselves to these questions:

1. Do the provisions of the trust contravene public policy or are they void for uncertainty?

2. If the answer to that question is in the affirmative, can the doctrine of *cy-près* be applied to save the trust?

Before considering these issues, I think it important to examine the trust and review the circumstances that compelled the trustee to launch this application for advice and direction.

The Facts

A. The Trust Document

By Indenture dated December 28, 1923, (the "Indenture" or "trust document") Reuben Wells Leonard (the "settlor") created a trust to be known as "The Leonard Foundation" (the "trust" or the "scholarship trust" or the "Foundation"). He directed that the income from the property transferred and assigned by him to the trust (the "trust property" or "trust fund") be used for the purpose of educational scholarships, to be called "The Leonard Scholarships". The Canada Trust Company has been appointed successor trustee of the Foundation.

The Indenture opens with four recitals which relate to the race, religion, citizenship, ancestry, ethnic origin and colour of the class of persons eligible to receive scholarships. These recitals read as follows:

> WHEREAS the Settlor believes that the White Race is, as a whole, best qualified by nature to be entrusted with the development of civilization and the general progress of the World along the best lines:
>
> AND WHEREAS the Settlor believes that the progress of the World depends in the future, as in the past, on the maintenance of the Christian religion:
>
> AND WHEREAS the Settlor believes that the peace of the World and the advancement of civilization depends very greatly upon the independence, the stability and the prosperity of the British Empire as a whole, and that this independence, stability and prosperity can be best attained and assured by the education in patriotic Institutions of selected children, whose birth and training are such as to warrant a reasonable expectation of their developing into leading citizens of the Empire:
>
> AND WHEREAS the Settlor believes that, so far as possible, the conduct of the affairs of the British Empire should be in the guidance of christian [sic] persons of British Nationality who are not hampered or controlled by an allegiance or pledge of obedience to any government, power or authority, temporal or spiritual, the seat of which government, power or authority is outside the British Empire. For the above reason the Settlor excludes from the management of, or benefits in the Foundation intended to be created by this Indenture, all who are not Christians of the White Race, all who are not of British Nationality or of British Parentage, and all who owe allegiance to any Foreign Government, Prince, Pope, or Potentate, or who recognize any such authority, temporal or spiritual.

The schools, colleges and universities in which the scholarships may be granted are described in the body of the Indenture in these terms:

> 2. The Schools, Colleges and Universities in which such Scholarships may be granted and enjoyed, are such one or more of Schools and Colleges in Canada and such one or more of Universities in Canada and Great Britain as the General Committee hereinafter described may from time to time in its absolute discretion select, *but subject always to the requirements, terms and conditions concerning same as hereinbefore and hereinafter referred to and set out*, and to the further conditions that any School, College or University so selected *shall be free from the domination or control of adherents of the class or classes of persons hereinbefore referred to*, whom the settlor intends shall be excluded from the management of or benefits in the said Foundation: . . .
>
> PROVIDED further and as an addition to the class or type of schools above designated or in the Schedule "A" hereto attached, the term "School" may for the purposes of Scholarships hereunder, include Public Schools and Public Collegiate Institutes and High Schools in Canada of the class or type commonly known as such in the Province of Ontario as distinguished from Public Schools and Collegiate Institutes and High Schools (if any) *under the control and domination of the class or classes of persons hereinbefore referred to as intended to be excluded from the management of or benefits in said Foundation*, and shall also include a Protestant Separate School, Protestant Collegiate Institute or Protestant High School in the Province of Quebec.
>
> PROVIDED further that in the selection of Schools, Colleges and Universities, as herein mentioned, preference must always be given by the Committee to the School, College or University, which, being otherwise in the opinion of the Committee eligible, prescribes

physical training for female students and physical and military or naval training for male students. [Emphasis added.]

The management and administration of the Foundation is vested in a permanent committee known as the General Committee. The Committee consists of 25 members, all of whom must be possessed of the qualifications set out in the Indenture's recitals:

The administration and management of the said Foundation is hereby vested in a permanent Committee to be known as the General Committee, consisting of twenty-five members, men and women *possessed of the qualifications hereinbefore in recital set out*. [Emphasis added.]

The General Committee is given, *inter alia*, the following power:

(c) *Power* to select students or pupils *of the classes or types hereinbefore and hereinafter described* as recipients of the said Scholarship or for the enjoyment of same, as the Committee in its discretion may decide. [Emphasis added.]

The class of students eligible to receive scholarships is described as follows:

SUBJECT to the provisions and qualifications hereinbefore and hereinafter contained, a student or pupil to be eligible for a Scholarship shall be a British Subject of the White Race and of the Christian Religion in its Protestant form, as hereinbefore in recital more particularly defined, who, without financial assistance, would be unable to pursue a course of study in any of the Schools, Colleges or Universities hereinbefore mentioned. Preference in the selection of students or pupils for Scholarships shall be given to the sons and daughters respectively of the *following classes or descriptions of persons who are not of the classes or types of persons whom the Settlor intends to exclude from the management or benefit of the said Foundation as in the preamble or recital more particularly referred to*, but regardless of the order of priority in which they are designated herein, namely:

(a) Clergymen,

(b) School Teachers,

(c) Officers, non-commissioned Officers and Men, whether active or retired, who have served in His Majesty's Military, Air or Naval Forces,

(d) Graduates of the Royal Military College of Canada,

(e) Members of the Engineering Institute of Canada,

(f) Members of the Mining & Metalurgical [sic] Institute of Canada.

PROVIDED further that in the selection, if any, of female students or pupils in any year under the provisions of this Indenture, the amount of income to be expended on such female students or pupils from and out of the moneys available for Scholarships under

> the terms hereof, shall not exceed one-fourth of the total moneys available for Scholarships for male and female students and pupils for such year. [Emphasis added.]

The settlor expressed the wish that:

> [T]he students or pupils who have enjoyed the benefits of a scholarship . . . will form a Club or association for the purpose of . . .
>
> (b) Encouraging each other when the occasion arises and circumstances will permit, to personally afford financial assistance to pupils and students of *similar classes as in recital hereinbefore described* to obtain the blessings and benefits of education. [Emphasis added.]

The trustee is empowered at the expense of the trust to apply to a Judge of the Supreme Court of Ontario, possessing the qualifications set out in the recitals, for the opinion, advice and direction of the Court:

> 9. The Trustee is hereby empowered at the expense of the trust estate to apply to a Judge of the Supreme Court of Ontario *possessing the qualifications required of a member of the General Committee as hereinbefore in recital set out*, for the opinion, advice and direction of the Court in connection with the construction of this trust deed and in connection with all questions arising in the administration of the trusts herein declared. [Emphasis added.]

I should perhaps note that no challenge was put forth on this basis in either this Court or the Court below.

The Leonard Scholarships have been available for more than 65 years to eligible students across Canada and elsewhere, and are tenable at eligible schools, colleges and universities in Canada and Great Britain. Application forms are available upon request from members of the General Committee. An applicant submits the application through a member of the General Committee, who conducts a personal interview of the applicant, completes the nomination and recommendation and forwards the application to the General Committee.

The Committee on Scholarships meets in April or May of each year to consider all of the applications and to make recommendations to the General Committee. Finally, the General Committee meets and, after consideration of the recommendations of the Committee on Scholarships, approves the awards for the following academic year.

B. The Circumstances Leading Up to the Application

The circumstances leading up to this application are described in the affidavit of Jack Cummings McLeod, a trust officer with Canada Trust Company who has been the secretary of the General Committee since 1975. In light of the public policy aspects of the application, the circumstances described by Mr. McLeod become significant.

Mr. McLeod deposes that, since 1975, he, as secretary, and various members of the General Committee have received correspondence from students, parents and academics expressing concerns and complaints with regard to the terms of eligibility for scholarships under the trust. Since 1956, numerous press articles, news reports and letters to the editor have appeared in the daily and university press of Canada commenting on or reporting on comments about the eligibility conditions. Mr. McLeod is aware of approximately 30 such articles, all generally critical of the eligibility requirements. The tenor of these articles is evident from their headings, which include "A Sorry Anachronism", "Act Now on Racist Funding" and "Whites Only Scholarship is Labelled 'Repugnant'."

Since 1971, the Human Rights Commissions of Alberta and Ontario and the Human Rights Branch of the Department of Labour of British Columbia have complained to the trustee and officials of the General Committee about the conditions of eligibility. Other bodies, such as the Saskatoon Legal Assistance Clinic and units of the Anglican Church of Canada, have made similar complaints.

Over the years 1975 to 1982, various schools and universities, including the University of Toronto, the University of Western Ontario and the University of British Columbia, have also complained, without success, to the Foundation about the eligibility requirements. In 1982, the University of Toronto discontinued publication of the Leonard Scholarships and refused to continue processing award payments because of the University's policy with respect to awards containing discriminatory or irrelevant criteria. The University of Alberta has taken similar action.

In January, 1986, the chairman of the Ontario Human Rights Commission advised the Foundation that the terms of the scholarships appear to "run contrary to the public policy of the Province of Ontario" and requested "appropriate action to have the terms of the trust changed." In response, the Foundation took the position that it was administering a private trust whose provisions did not offend the *Human Rights Code, 1981*.

At various times over the past 25 years, members of the General Committee and officials of the trustee have themselves expressed concern about the eligibility criteria. The matter has been considered internally and, it appears, has been the subject of "divisive" debate at meetings of the General Committee.

In April, 1986, the Most Reverend Edward W. Scott, then Primate of the Anglican Church of Canada, the church of which the late Colonel Leonard was a prominent member, wrote to the Foundation expressing his "deep concerns" about the trust. He recorded, in strong terms, his view that the eligibility criteria are discriminatory and against public policy and not "in keeping with the spirit and intent of the Canadian Charter of Rights." He urged the Committee to apply to the courts to have the offensive terms "read out of the trust deed . . . with the ultimate result that effect will continue to be given to the trust deed and gift as a whole." He concluded his letter stating:

I have every confidence that if the kind benefactor of this Trust were living in 1986, rather than those many years ago, there would be agreement that the scope of possible recipients be widened bringing the document in line with standards of public acceptance of today. There is every reason why the good works of the generous benefactor of the Foundation should live on in perpetuity but, in my view, they must be in keeping with the society of today just as what was written those many years ago was, no doubt, although regretfully, in keeping with the society of that day.

In August, 1986, the Ontario Human Rights Commission, not satisfied with the response to its earlier letter, filed a formal complaint against the Leonard Foundation, alleging that the trust contravened the *Human Rights Code, 1981*. This prompted the trustee to seek the advice and direction of the Court. In his affidavit, Mr. McLeod explains the Trustee's position in bringing the application as follows:

21. . . . the Trustee has been advised that it is, and has hitherto seen it to be its duty to support, maintain and administer the trusts which were accepted by the original Trustee until such time as a Court of competent jurisdiction determines that the trust is illegal or void. This the Trustee and its predecessor corporations have done for upwards of 63 years since the inception of the trust, without serious difficulty or opposition until the more recent of the events described in paragraphs 14 to 20 hereof.

22. The inquiries from the press, complaints of universities, schools, Human Rights Commissions and similar agencies, academics, members of the public and certain members of the General Committee, as well as the Complaint referred to in paragraph 17 hereof, the press articles and reports referred to in paragraphs 14 and 18 hereof, the divisive effect of the motion and vote referred to in paragraph 20 hereof, and other similar recent events have, in my view, had an unsettling effect and have interfered with the due administration of the trusts declared by the Indenture and the ability of the Trustee to carry on such administration effectively. They have also impacted and can be expected to continue to impact unfavourably on the efficient administration of the scholarship programme by the General Committee, its Committee on Scholarships and its officials.

23. Although there has not to date been any serious difficulty experienced by the General Committee in identifying and making awards to students who fulfil the eligibility requirements of the Indenture, there have obviously been great changes in Canadian society and in the British Empire that have occurred in the 63 years since the inception of the Foundation. It may become more difficult than in the past to interpret and apply such eligibility terms as "British Nationality", "British Parentage", "allegiance to any Foreign Government, Prince, Pope or Potentate", "Christians of the White Race", "British Subject" and "of the Christian Religion in its Protestant Form". The Trustee has received an opinion of its counsel that a charitable trust is exempt from the requirement of certainty of objects and cannot fail for uncertainty so long as there are some eligible persons who are with certainty within the ambit of the qualifications. Nevertheless, in the context of modern Canadian life and society, the increasingly multi-cultural makeup of Canada and the attention which has now been focused on the eligibility requirements of the Indenture, these difficulties may be expected to increase.

24. The Trustee accordingly believes that it requires the opinion, advice and direction of this Honourable Court as to the essential validity of the Indenture under which it

operates, pursuant to the provisions of section 60 of the *Trustee Act* and the Court's inherent jurisdiction to supervise charitable trusts.

The Public Policy Issue

A. Can the Recitals Be Considered in Deciding this Issue?

In holding that the provisions of the trust did not violate either the *Human Rights Code, 1981* or public policy, McKeown J. took into account only the operative clauses of the trust document and the second sentence of the fourth recital. In his view, the balance of the recitals were merely expressions of the settlor's motive and, hence, irrelevant to a determination of the issues before him. While he found the motives offensive to today's general community, he concluded that these recitals could play no part in interpreting the trust document or in resolving the question of whether the trust contravened public policy.

In my opinion, the recitals cannot be isolated from the balance of the trust document and disregarded by the Court in giving the advice and direction sought by the trustee in this case. The document must be read as a whole. While the operative provisions of an instrument of this nature will ordinarily prevail over its recitals, where the recitals are not clearly severable from the rest of the instrument and themselves contain operative words or words intended to give meaning and definition to the operative provisions, the instrument should be viewed in its entirety. That, in my opinion, is the situation in the case of this trust document.

The recitals here in no way contradict or conflict with the operative provisions. The settlor made constant reference to them throughout the operative part of the document. He restricted the class of persons entitled to the benefits of the trust by reference to the recitals, he set the qualification for those who might administer the trust and give judicial advice thereon by reference to the recitals and he stipulated the universities and colleges which might be attended by scholarship winners by reference to the recitals.

Moreover, the recitals were intended to give guidance and direction to the General Committee in awarding scholarships. They go beyond the restriction in the second sentence of the fourth recital excluding "all who are not Christians of the White Race, all who are not of British Nationality or of British Parentage, and all who owe allegiance to any Foreign Government, Prince, Pope or Potentate, or who recognize any such authority, temporal or spiritual" from benefits in the Foundation. They indicate that not all white Protestants of British parentage should be eligible for the benefits of the trust but, rather, only those "whose birth and training are such as to warrant a reasonable expectation of their developing into leading citizens of the Empire" and "who are not hampered or controlled by an allegiance or pledge of obedience to any government, power or authority, temporal or spiritual, the seat of which government, power or authority is outside the British Empire." Those statements were intended as standards which, if not binding, were meant to be taken into account in the making of awards. I would not regard them as irrelevant. Nor would

I regard any other of the recitals as irrelevant. The operative provisions were intended to be administered in accordance with the concepts articulated in the recitals. As this document is framed, its two parts are so linked as to be inextricably interwoven. In my opinion, one part cannot be divorced from the other.

Furthermore and perhaps more fundamentally, even if the recitals are properly treated as going only to the matter of motive, I would not think they can be ignored on an application of this nature in which a trustee seeks advice with respect to public-policy issues. While the Foundation may have been privately created, there is a clear public aspect to its purpose and administration. In awarding scholarships to study at publicly supported educational institutions to students whose application is solicited from a broad segment of the public, the Foundation is effectively acting in the public sphere. Operating in perpetuity as a charitable trust for educational purposes, as it has now for over half a century since the settlor's death, the Foundation has, in realistic terms, acquired a public or, at the least, a quasi-public character. When challenged on public-policy grounds, the reasons, explicitly stated, which motivated the Foundation's establishment and give meaning to its restrictive criteria are highly germane. To consider public-policy issues of the kind in question by sterilizing the document and treating the recitals as though they did not exist is to proceed on an artificial basis. In my opinion, the Court cannot close its eyes to any of this trust document's provisions.

B. Does the Trust Violate Public Policy?

Viewing this trust document as a whole, does it violate public policy? In answering that question, I am not unmindful of the adage that "public policy is an unruly horse" or of the admonition that public policy " 'should be invoked only in clear cases, in which harm to the public is substantially incontestable, and does not depend on the idiosyncratic inferences of a few judicial minds' ": *Re Millar*, [1938] S.C.R. 1, [1938] 1 D.L.R. 65, at 7 [S.C.R.]. I have regard also to the observation of Professor Waters in his text on the *Law of Trusts in Canada*, 2d ed. (Toronto: Carswell, 1984), at 240 to the effect that:

> The courts have always recognized that to declare a disposition of property void on the ground that the object is intended to contravene, or has the effect of contravening public policy, is to take a serious step. There is the danger that the judge will tend to impose his own values rather than those values which are commonly agreed upon in society and, while the evolution of the common law is bound to reflect contemporary ideas on the interests of society, the courts also feel that it is largely the duty of the legislative body to enact law in such matters, proceeding as such a body does by the process of debate and vote.

Nonetheless, there are cases where the interests of society require the court's intervention on the grounds of public policy. This, in my opinion, is manifestly such a case.

The freedom of an owner of property to dispose of his or her property as he or she chooses is an important social interest that has long been recognized in our society and is firmly rooted in our law: *Blathwayt v. Lord Cawley*, [1976] A.C. 397, [1975] 3 All E.R. 625 (H.L.). That interest must, however, be limited in the case of this trust by public-policy considerations. In my opinion, the trust is couched in terms so at odds with today's social values as to make its continued operation in its present form inimical to the public interest.

According to the document establishing the Leonard Foundation, the Foundation must be taken to stand for two propositions: first, that the white race is best qualified by nature to be entrusted with the preservation, development and progress of civilization along the best lines, and second, that the attainment of the peace of the world and the advancement of civilization are best promoted by the education of students of the white race, of British nationality and of the Christian religion in its Protestant form.

To say that a trust premised on these notions of racism and religious superiority contravenes contemporary public policy is to expatiate the obvious. The concept that any one race or any one religion is intrinsically better than any other is patently at variance with the democratic principles governing our pluralistic society, in which equality rights are constitutionally guaranteed and in which the multicultural heritage of Canadians is to be preserved and enhanced. The widespread criticism of the Foundation by human rights bodies, the press, the clergy, the university community and the general community serves to demonstrate how far out of keeping the trust now is with prevailing ideas and standards of racial and religious tolerance and equality and, indeed, how offensive its terms are to fair-minded citizens.

To perpetuate a trust that imposes restrictive criteria on the basis of the discriminatory notions espoused in these recitals according to the terms specified by the settlor would not, in my opinion, be conducive to the public interest. The settlor's freedom to dispose of his property through the creation of a charitable trust fashioned along these lines must give way to current principles of public policy under which all races and religions are to be treated on a footing of equality and accorded equal regard and equal respect.

Given this conclusion, it becomes unnecessary to decide whether the trust is invalid by reason of uncertainty or to consider the questions raised in this regard in para. 23 of Mr. McLeod's affidavit, which I reproduced earlier. Nor is it necessary to make any determination as to whether other educational scholarships may contravene public policy.

On the material before the Court, it appears that many scholarships are currently available to students at colleges and universities in Ontario and elsewhere in Canada which restrict eligibility or grant preference on the basis of such factors as an applicant's religion, ethnic origin, sex, or language. None, however, so far as the material reveals, is rooted in concepts in any way akin to those articulated here which proclaim, in effect, some students, because of their colour or their religion, less worthy of education or less qualified for leadership than others. I think it inappropriate and indeed unwise to decide in the context of the present case and in the absence of any proper factual basis whether these other scholarships are contrary to public policy or what approach is to be adopted in determining their validity should the issue arise. The Court's intervention on public-policy grounds in this case is mandated by the, hopefully, unique provisions in the trust document establishing the Leonard Foundation.

The Cy-Près *Issue*

On this issue, I agree with the learned Weekly Court Judge that the trust established by the Indenture is a charitable trust. I am persuaded that the settlor intended the trust property to be wholly devoted to the furtherance of a charitable object whose general purpose is the advancement of education or the advancement of leadership through education.

It must not be forgotten that when the trust property initially vested in 1923 the terms of the Indenture would have been held to be certain, valid and not contrary to any public policy which rendered the trust void or illegal or which detracted from the settlor's general intention to devote the property to charitable purposes. However, with changing social attitudes, public policy has changed. The public policy of the 1920s is not the public policy of the 1990s. As a result, it is no longer in the interest of the community to continue the trust on the basis predicated by the settlor. Put another way, while the trust was practicable when it was created, changing times have rendered the ideas promoted by it contrary to public policy, and hence it has become impracticable to carry it on in the manner originally planned by the settlor.

In these circumstances, the trust should not fail. It is appropriate and only reasonable that the Court apply the *cy-près* doctrine and invoke its inherent jurisdiction to propound a scheme that will bring the trust into accord with public policy and permit the general charitable intent to advance education or leadership through education to be implemented by those charged with the trust's administration. . . .

Disposition

To give effect to these reasons, I would strike out the recitals and remove all restrictions with respect to race, colour, creed or religion, ethnic origin and sex as they relate to those entitled to the benefits of the trust and as they relate to the qualifications of those who may be members of the General Committee or give judicial advice and, as well, as they relate to the schools, universities or colleges in which scholarships may be enjoyed. (The provision according preferences to sons and daughters of members of the classes of persons specified in the trust document remains unaffected by this decision.) . . .

Tarnopolsky J.A.: . . .

Is the Trust Void in Whole or in Part Either for Uncertainty or Because it Violates Public Policy?

We are concerned here with a charitable trust. In order to be considered charitable, a trust must have been established for one of the following four purposes: relief of poverty, advancement of education, advancement of religion or other purposes beneficial to the community as a whole as enunciated by the courts. . . .

The general rule is that in order to achieve charitable status, a trust must satisfy three conditions. It must have as its object one of the four purposes stated above, its purpose must be wholly and exclusively charitable and it must promote a public benefit . . . To satisfy the public benefit requirement, the trust must be beneficial and not harmful to the public, and its benefits must be available to a sufficient cross-section of the public . . .

In the case at Bar, all of these tests are met. The trust is dedicated to the advancement of education and it is wholly charitable. Education is clearly a benefit to the public. Because the class was not ascertainable by the settlor, there was no personal nexus between him and the beneficiaries. The benefit, although not available to everyone, is available to a sufficiently wide cross-section of the public.

Next, it is necessary to consider whether the trust could be invalid because of uncertainty. It is important to note that in analyzing the validity of the trust on this basis, the Court may refer only to the operative words, unless they are ambiguous, in which case it can refer to the recitals. Regular rules of statutory construction apply (*Re Moon; Ex parte Dawes* (1886), 17 Q.B.D. 275, 34 W.R. 753 (C.A.)). Since recitals are descriptions of motive and are normally irrelevant to determining validity, McKeown J. held that they were irrelevant and inoperative. However, it could be argued that many sections of the Indenture refer to the recitals and thereby incorporate them. In fact, McKeown J. noted eight references, after the recitals, to the definition of the class of beneficiaries but then went on to state [at 214-215]:

> At no time throughout the operative clauses does Colonel Leonard refer back to the three opening recitals; thus his beliefs as stated therein are not incorporated into the operative words and play no part in the interpretation of this instrument.

Without deciding whether the recitals are incorporated in the trust instrument by subsequent references to them, I would agree that Colonel Leonard's beliefs as stated in the opening recitals are evidence of motive and are irrelevant. However, that part of the trust instrument which matters for the purpose of assessing certainty is the second sentence in the first full paragraph on p. 2 of the instrument, which reads as follows:

> For the above reason the Settlor excludes from the management of, or benefits in the Foundation intended to be created by this Indenture, all who are not Christians of the White Race, all who are not of British Parentage, and all who owe allegiance to any

> Foreign Government, Prince, Pope or Potentate, or who recognize any such authority, temporal or spiritual.

This definition of the class of beneficiaries is a condition precedent. A condition precedent is one in which no gift is intended until the condition is fulfilled. A condition subsequent differs in that non-compliance with the condition will put an end to an already existing gift. A condition precedent will not be void for uncertainty if it is possible to say with certainty that any proposed beneficiary is or is not a member of the class . . . The condition will not fail for uncertainty unless it is clearly impossible for anyone to qualify . . . It is well established that a charitable trust should not fail for uncertainty (see *Re Gott*, [1944] Ch. 193, [1944] 1 All E.R. 293). Historically, courts have been reluctant to strike down such gifts if it can be avoided. If a condition is uncertain, the court can consider it inoperative, but rarely will a trust fail because of uncertainty if the condition is a condition precedent.

In this case, there has been no difficulty over some 6 decades in ascertaining whether students qualify. The clause referred to above is sufficiently certain, except possibly for the "allegiance" exclusion. In my view, however, the clause as a whole meets the requirements established for a condition precedent, and the provisions containing the conditions are sufficiently certain. If I am wrong, however, I would find only the clause referring to "allegiance" to be uncertain and I would hold that it is severable from the other restrictions as to class.

Turning now to the public-policy issue, it must first be acknowledged that there has been no finding by a Canadian or a British court that at common law a charitable trust established to offer scholarships or other benefits to a restricted class is void as against public policy because it is discriminatory. In some cases, British courts have chosen to delete offensive clauses as "uncertain", as in *Re Lysaght; Hill v. Royal College of Surgeons of England*, [1966] Ch. 191, [1965] 2 All E.R. 888 . . . or "impracticable" as in *Re Dominion Students' Hall Trust*, [1947] Ch. 183. In the latter case, the Court found a general charitable intention and then applied the trust property *cy-près*. The attitude of British courts, however, is probably best summed up in the words of Buckley L.J. in *Re Lysaght*, *supra*, at 206, quoted by McKeown J. at 220:

> I accept that racial and religious discrimination is nowadays widely regarded as deplorable in many respects and I am aware that there is a Bill dealing with racial relations at present under consideration by Parliament, but I think that it is going much too far to say that the endowment of a charity, the beneficiaries of which are to be drawn from a particular faith or are to exclude adherents to a particular faith, is contrary to public policy. The testatrix's desire to exclude persons of the Jewish faith or of the Roman Catholic faith from those eligible for the studentship in the present case appears to me to be unamiable, and I would accept Mr. Clauson's suggestion that it is undesirable, but it is not, I think, contrary to public policy.

However, in considering these observations of Buckley L.J., it is necessary to keep in mind two points. First, the observations themselves indicate that they were made *before* the enactment of the first comprehensive statute in the United Kingdom to prohibit discrimination on racial grounds — the *Race Relations Act*, (U.K.), 1968, c. 71. Second, religion, as a prohibited ground of discrimination, is conspicuously left out of the anti-discrimination laws of the United Kingdom. I do not, therefore, find the English cases on point to be of any help or guidance.

In Canada, the leading case on public policy and discrimination at the commencement of World War II was *Christie v. York Corp.*, [1940] S.C.R. 139, [1940] 1 D.L.R. 81, wherein the majority of the Supreme Court of Canada found that denial of service on grounds of race and colour was *not* contrary to good morals or public order.

After the war, this Court, in *Noble and Wolf v. Alley*, [1949] O.R. 503, [1949] 4 D.L.R. 375, rev'd [1951] S.C.R. 64, [1951] 1 D.L.R. 321, upheld a racially restrictive covenant in the course of deciding that there was insufficient evidence to conclude that racial discrimination was contrary to public policy in Ontario. In this, the Court specifically overruled Mackay J., in *Re Drummond-Wren*, [1945] O.R. 778 (H.C.), who had found such covenants void as against public policy. The Supreme Court of Canada struck down the covenant in *Noble and Wolf*, *supra*, on technical grounds but did not refer to the public-policy argument.

Subsequently, in *Bhadauria*, [*Seneca College of Applied Arts & Technology (Board of Governors) v. Bhadauria* (1979), 105 D.L.R. (3d) 707 (C.A.)] at 715 , in concluding that the common law had evolved to the point of recognizing a new tort of discrimination, Wilson J.A. referred to the preamble to the *Ontario Human Rights Code*, R.S.O. 1970, c. 318, the first two paragraphs of which then provided:

> WHEREAS recognition of the inherent dignity and the equal and inalienable rights of all members of the human family is the foundation of freedom, justice and peace in the world and is in accord with the Universal Declaration of Human Rights as proclaimed by the United Nations;
>
> AND WHEREAS it is public policy in Ontario that every person is free and equal in dignity and rights without regard to race, creed, colour, sex, marital status, nationality, ancestry or place of origin.

She then observed: "I regard the preamble to the Code as evidencing what is now, and probably has been for some considerable time, the public policy of this Province respecting fundamental human rights." That the *Human Rights Code* recognizes public policy in Ontario was acknowledged a few years later by the Supreme Court of Canada in *Ontario Human Rights Commission v. Borough of Etobicoke* (1982), 3 C.H.R.R. D/781, 82 C.L.L.C. 17,005, 132 D.L.R. (3d) 14, 40 N.R. 159, at 23-24 [D.L.R.].

Therefore, even though McKeown J. referred to the caution of Duff C.J.C. in *Re Millar*, [1938] S.C.R. 1, [1938] 1 D.L.R. 65, at 7-8 [S.C.R.], to the effect that public policy is a doctrine to be invoked only in clear cases where the harm to the public is substantially incontestable and does not depend upon the "idiosyncratic inferences of a few judicial minds," the promotion of racial harmony, tolerance and equality is clearly and unquestionably part of the public policy of modern day Ontario. I can think of no better way to respond to the caution of Duff C.J.C. than to quote the assertion of Mackay J. of nearly 45 years ago in *Re Drummond-Wren*, *supra*, at 783:

> Ontario and Canada too, may well be termed a province, and a country, of minorities in regard to the religious and ethnic groups which live therein. It appears to me to be a moral duty, at least, to lend aid to all forces of cohesion, and similarly to repel all fissiparous tendencies which would imperil national unity. The common law courts have, by their actions over the years, obviated the need for rigid constitutional guarantees in our policy by their wise use of the doctrine of public policy as an active agent in the promotion of the public weal. While courts and eminent judges have, in view of the powers of our legislatures, warned against inventing new heads of public policy, I do not conceive that I would be breaking new ground were I to hold the restrictive covenant impugned in this proceeding to be void as against public policy. Rather would I be applying well-recognized principles of public policy to a set of facts requiring their invocation in the interest of the public good.

Further evidence of the public policy against discrimination can be found in several statutes in addition to the preamble and content of the *Human Rights Code, 1981*: s. 13 of the *Conveyancing and Law of Property Act*, R.S.O. 1980, c. 90; s. 4 of the *Ministry of Citizenship and Culture Act, 1982*, S.O. 1982, c. 6; s. 117 of the *Insurance Act*, R.S.O. 1980, c. 218; and s. 13 of the *Labour Relations Act*, R.S.O. 1980, c. 228. All of these indicate that this particular public policy is not circumscribed by the exact words of the *Human Rights Code, 1981*, alone. Such a circumscription would make it necessary to alter what the courts would regard as public policy every time an amendment were made to the *Human Rights Code*. This can be seen just by comparing the wording of the second paragraph of today's preamble with that considered by Wilson J.A. in 1979 and quoted above. Currently this paragraph reads:

> AND WHEREAS it is public policy in Ontario to recognize the dignity and worth of every person and to provide for equal rights and opportunities without discrimination that is contrary to law, and having as its aim the creation of a climate of understanding and mutual respect for the dignity and worth of each person so that each person feels a part of the community and able to contribute fully to the development and well-being of the community and the Province.

It is relevant in this case to refer as well to the "Ontario Policy on Race Relations" (Race Relations Directorate, Ministry of Citizenship) as well as the Premier's statement in the Legislature concerning the policy (*Hansard Official Report of Debates of Legislative Assembly of Ontario*, 2nd Session, 33rd Parliament, Wednesday, May 28, 1986, at 937–941). The Policy on Race Relations states:

> The government is committed to equality of treatment and opportunity for all Ontario residents and recognizes that a harmonious racial climate is essential to the future prosperity and social well-being of this province . . . The government will take an active role in the elimination of all racial discrimination, including those policies and practices which, while not intentionally discriminatory, have a discriminatory effect . . . The government will also continue to attack the overt manifestations of racism and to this end declares that: (a) Racism in any form is not tolerated in Ontario.

In introducing it in the Legislature, Premier David Peterson said (*Hansard* at 937):

> This policy recognizes that Ontario's commitment to equality has grown from benign approval to active support. It leaves no doubt that the path we will follow to full racial harmony and equal opportunity is paved, not just with good wishes and best intentions but with concrete plans and active measures.

Public policy is not determined by reference to only one statute or even one province, but is gleaned from a variety of sources, including provincial and federal statutes, official declarations of government policy and the Constitution. The public policy against discrimination is reflected in the anti-discrimination laws of every jurisdiction in Canada. These have been given a special status by the Supreme Court of Canada in *Ontario Human Rights Commission v. Simpsons-Sears Ltd.*, [1985] 2 S.C.R. 536, 52 O.R. (2d) 799 (headnote only), 17 Admin. L.R. 89, 9 C.C.E.L. 185, 7 C.H.R.R. D/3102, 86 C.L.L.C. 17,002, 23 D.L.R. (4th) 321, [1986] D.L.Q. 89 (headnote only), 64 N.R. 161, 12 O.A.C. 241, at 329 [D.L.R.]:

> The accepted rules of construction are flexible enough to enable the court to recognize in the construction of a human rights code the special nature and purpose of the enactment (see Lamer J. in *Insurance Corp. of B.C. v. Heerspink et al.* . . . [1982] 2 S.C.R. 145 at pp. 157-158 . . .), and give to it an interpretation which will advance its broad purposes. Legislation of this type is of a special nature, not quite constitutional, but certainly more than ordinary — and it is for the courts to seek out its purpose and give it effect.

In addition, equality rights "without discrimination" are now enshrined in the *Constitution Act, 1982* [*Canadian Charter of Rights and Freedoms*] in s. 15; the equal rights of men and women are reinforced in s. 28, and the protection and enhancement of our multicultural heritage is provided for in s. 27.

Finally, the world community has made anti-discrimination a matter of public policy in specific conventions like the *International Convention on the Elimination of All Forms of Racial Discrimination*, 1965, and the *Convention on the Elimination of All Forms of Discrimination Against Women*, 1979, as well as arts. 2, 3, 25 and 26 of the *International Covenant on Civil and Political Rights*, all three of which international instruments have been ratified by Canada with the unanimous consent of all the provinces. It would be nonsensical to pursue every one of these domestic and international instruments to see whether the public-policy invalidity is restricted to any particular activity or service or facility.

Clearly this is a charitable trust which is void on the ground of public policy to the extent that it discriminates on grounds of race (colour, nationality, ethnic origin), religion and sex.

Some concern was expressed to us that a finding of invalidity in this case would mean that any charitable trust which restricts the class of beneficiaries would also be void as against public policy. The respondents argued that this would have adverse effects on many educational scholarships currently available in Ontario and other parts of Canada. Many of these provide support for qualified students who could not attend university without financial assistance. Some are restricted to visible minorities, women or other disadvantaged groups. In my view, these trusts will have to be evaluated on a case by case basis, should their validity be challenged. This case should not be taken as authority for the proposition that all restrictions amount to discrimination and are therefore contrary to public policy.

It will be necessary in each case to undertake an equality analysis like that adopted by the Human Rights Commission when approaching ss. 1 and 13 of the *Human Rights Code, 1981*, and that adopted by the courts when approaching s. 15(2) of the *Charter*. Those charitable trusts aimed at the amelioration of inequality and whose restrictions can be justified on that basis under s. 13 of the *Human Rights Code* or s. 15(2) of the *Charter* would not likely be found void because they promote rather than impede the public policy of equality. In such an analysis, attention will have to be paid to the social and historical context of the group concerned (see *Andrews v. Law Society of British Columbia*, [1989] 1 S.C.R. 143, 34 B.C.L.R. (2d) 273, 25 C.C.E.L. 255, [1989] 2 W.W.R. 289, 10 C.H.R.R. D/5719, 36 C.R.R. 193, 56 D.L.R. (4th) 1, 91 N.R. 255, at 152-153 [S.C.R.] per Wilson J. and 175 per McIntyre J.) as well as the effect of the restrictions on racial, religious or gender equality, to name but a few examples.

Not all restrictions will violate public policy, just as not all legislative distinctions constitute discrimination contrary to s. 15 of the *Charter* (*Andrews*, *supra*, at 168-169 per McIntyre J.). In the Indenture in this case, for example, there is nothing contrary to public policy as expressed in the preferences for children of "clergymen", "school teachers", etc. It would be hard to imagine in the foreseeable future that a charitable trust established to promote the education of women, aboriginal peoples, the physically or mentally handicapped, or other historically disadvantaged groups would be void as against public policy. Clearly, public trusts restricted to those in financial need would be permissible. Given the history and importance of bilingualism and multiculturalism in this country, restrictions on the basis of language would probably not be void as against public policy, subject, of course, to an analysis of the context, purpose and effect of the restriction.

In this case, the Court must, as it does in so many areas of law, engage in a balancing process. Important as it is to permit individuals to dispose of their property as they see fit, it cannot be an absolute right. The law imposes restrictions on freedom of both contract and testamentary disposition. Under the *Conveyancing and Law of Property Act*, s. 22, for instance, covenants that purport to restrict sale, ownership, occupation or use of land because of, *inter alia*, race, creed or colour are void. Under the *Human Rights Code*, discriminatory contracts relating to leasing of accommodation are prohibited. With respect to testamentary dispositions, as mentioned earlier, one cannot establish a charitable trust unless it is for an exclusively charitable purpose (see Waters, *supra*, at 601–603 and 626; and *Ministry of Health v. Simpson*, *supra*). Similarly, public trusts which discriminate on the basis of distinctions that are contrary to public policy must now be void.

A finding that a charitable trust is void as against public policy would not have the far-reaching effects on testamentary freedom which some have anticipated. This decision does not affect private, family trusts. By that I mean that it does not affect testamentary dispositions or outright gifts that are not also charitable trusts. Historically, charitable trusts have received special protection: (1) they are treated favourably by taxation statutes; (2) they enjoy an extensive exemption from the rule against perpetuities; (3) they do not fail for lack of certainty of objects; (4) if the settlor does not set out sufficient directions, the court will supply them by designing a scheme; (5) courts may apply trust property *cy-près*, providing they can discern a general charitable intention. This preferential treatment is justified on the ground that charitable trusts are dedicated to the benefit of the community (Waters, *supra*, 502). It is this public nature of charitable trusts which attracts the requirement that they conform to the public policy against discrimination. Only where the trust is a public one devoted to charity will restrictions that are contrary to the public policy of equality render it void. . . .

Appeal allowed.

QUESTIONS AND COMMENTS

1. What is the *ratio decidendi* of the *Leonard Foundation Trust* case?

2. How do the majority and minority judgments differ?

3. How did Robins and Tarnoplosky JJ.A. ascertain public policy? What role if any did the *Canadian Charter of Rights and Freedoms* play in that determination?

4. In *Re Ramsden Estate* 1996 CarswellPEI 98 (T.D. [Chambers]), a bequest was left to the University of Prince Edward Island. A scholarship was to be established under the following terms:

> (f) To pay to the Board of Governors of the University of Prince Edward Island one-half of the rest and residue of my general estate for the purpose of founding in the said University as a memorial to both my late husband and myself, one or more University scholarships, or bursaries, to be known as "A.G. and Eliza Jane Ramsden" Scholarship or Bursary, as the case may be, the net annual income from this fund to be awarded to protestant students annually, the amounts, conditions, and recipient of such Scholarships or Bursaries to be determined from time to time and in such manner as the Board may direct. Notwithstanding the foregoing, it is my express wish and desire that the University shall, in making such awards, take into consideration the financial needs and requirements of students and also those students who are most deserving but not necessarily in accordance with academic merit. I further wish the University to give preference, if possible, to students intending to enter the field of ministry. . . .

It was held that, owing to the terms of the *University of Prince Edward Island Act*, the University could not serve as a trustee of this gift. Therefore, the Court ordered that another trustee be appointed. However, this did not dispose of the question of whether the bequest contravened the doctrine of public policy. Did *Leonard* govern? MacDonald C.J.T.D. (at para. 13) said no:

> In *Re: Leonard Foundation Trust* . . . a general educational trust with discriminatory conditions attached was held to fail on a ground of public policy. In my view, that case is distinguishable from the present one, in that the trust in that case was based on blatant religious supremacy and racism. There is no such basis for the trust in this case. Therefore, I can see no ground of public policy which would serve as an impediment to the trust proceeding, if it were administered by a body other than the University itself.

(See also *University of Victoria v. British Columbia* 2000 CarswellBC 529 (S.C. [Chambers]).) Is the *Ramsden* holding consonant with the *Leonard* case?

5. Both judgments in the *Leonard* case draw a distinction between "public" and "private." How does one describe the dividing line between these domains? In what way might the Leonard Foundation trust be characterized as private? In what way might a family trust (a term used by Tarnopolsky J.A.) be regarded as public?

6. In *Fox v. Fox Estate* 1996 CarswellOnt 317 (C.A.), leave to appeal refused: (1996) 207 N.R. 80 (note) (S.C.C.), A, the widow of the decedent, was also named as the executor of his will. In that capacity, she was accorded broad discretionary powers to allocate property under the will. Her son, B, was given the residue of the capital in the event that he survived his mother. A exercised her powers in such a way as to exhaust the residue. Her motivation for doing so was (at least in part) to deprive her son of any benefit of the estate because he had entered into a relationship with a woman of a different religious faith. The question before the court was whether the mother had improperly exercised her power. The Ontario Court of Appeal held that she had. In the course of so holding, one member of the Court of Appeal, Galligan J.A., suggested (at paras. 16–20) as follows:

> There is another reason why the discretion which Miriam exercised in this case was improper and must be set aside. It is abhorrent to contemporary community standards that disapproval of a marriage outside of one's religious faith could justify the exercise of a trustee's discretion. It is now settled that it is against public policy to discriminate on grounds of race or religion. This is made clear in the reasons delivered by Robins J.A. in *Canada Trust Co. v. Ontario Human Rights Commission* . . .
>
> In that case, Robins J.A. was discussing the restraint which public policy puts upon the freedom of the settlor to dispose of his property as he saw fit. If a settlor cannot dispose of property in a fashion which discriminates upon racial or religious grounds, it seems to me to follow that public policy also prohibits a trustee from exercising her discretion for racial or religious reasons.
>
> I am of the view that in this case it would be contrary to public policy to permit a trustee effectively to disinherit the residual beneficiary because he dared to marry outside the religious faith of his mother. While there were decisions in the past which have upheld discriminatory conditions in wills, in response to a query from the bench, counsel in this case were not prepared to argue that any court would today uphold a condition in a will which provides that a beneficiary is to be disinherited if he or she marries outside of a particular religious faith. I find compelling Mr. Eastman's argument that if a testator could not do so then his trustee could not do it for him.

Counsel for the grandchildren argued that if Ralph were still alive there would have been nothing to prevent him from revoking his will and making a new one in which he left nothing to Walter. She argued therefore, that in the exercise of her absolute power to encroach Miriam should be able to do that for him. Even if it were accepted that Ralph, if alive, would have disinherited Walter because of his intention to marry out of Ralph's religious faith, that argument cannot succeed.

It is of course a given, assuming testamentary capacity, that a person is entitled to dispose of property by will in any fashion that he or she may wish. The exercise of a testator's right of disposition is not subject to supervision by the court. But a trustee's exercise of discretion is subject to curial control. Admittedly, because he would not be subject to judicial supervision, Ralph, if alive, could have disinherited Walter for reasons which would have contravened public policy. However, Ralph is not alive and is not preparing a new will. Miriam, while acting as a trustee, on the other hand is subject to judicial control and that control can and must prevent her from exercising her discretion in a fashion which offends public policy.

Would the approach suggested by Galligan J.A. in *Fox* constitute a welcome extension of the reasoning in the *Leonard* case? Compare *Shapira v. Union Nat. Bank* 315 N.E.2d 825 (Ohio Com.Pl., 1974), and *Blathwayt v. Lord Cawley* (1975) [1976] A.C. 397 (H.L.).

B. Ziff, *Unforeseen Legacies: Reuben Wells Leonard and the Leonard Foundation Trust* (Toronto: Osgoode Society & UTP, 2000) at 146-58 [footnotes omitted]

Exploring The Deeper Problems . . .

Putting aside the intricacies of Ontario statute law, and the identification of the precise ruling in the Ontario Court of Appeal judgments, it is possible to understand the *Leonard* case as exposing some important features of the legal treatment of equality in Canada.

There are several reasons why discriminatory conduct is difficult to regulate. One concerns a problem of efficacy — there are limits on the law's capacity to alter beliefs and prejudices in a meaningful way. It is unrealistic to suppose that even stringently enforced equality principles can eradicate deep-seated racial hatred. Another difficulty involves the limits of the forensic process. Proving racial prejudice that runs contrary to provincial human rights protections is often a difficult task. The presence of such a code can itself induce guarded, nuanced conduct, driving discriminatory conduct underground.

Two other problems concerning equality under law are especially evident in the Leonard Foundation dispute. One concerns the way in which we measure the importance of equality against other social values. There are occasions in which the law fails to respond to acts of discrimination on the ground that the public policy costs are too high. The law provides no remedy because the losses are seen as outweighing the gains of a legal response when measured in normative or utilitarian terms. Accordingly, even in cases where it is accepted that it is possible to affect conduct through law (that is, there is no problem of efficacy), and where we know that discrimination has occurred (so that there is also no problem of proof), there are times when no action will be taken because, on balance, it is seen as counter-productive. We may, for example, allow certain forms of racist speech in the name of protecting freedom of expression.

Second, the idea of equality is itself a contested matter, so that just what we are trying to achieve when we use that term to define a social good is sometimes unclear. Principles of equal treatment under law stress the essence of human nature and the need to acknowledge the moral worth of all people. These measures also recognize that discrimination is degrading and disabling. However, this begs questions about the form of equality that societies should strive to achieve. Is the aim equality of opportunity or equality of condition? To what extent can equality be achieved by the unequal treatment of individuals and groups? What is the proper place of affirmative action in Canadian law? To what extent should the law promote, protect or encourage difference as a value? Or, more generally, in what ways can we distinguish between pernicious and justifiable discriminatory action?

The *Leonard* case touches on these issues: the balancing of equality and other rights, and the contested meanings of equality. These are considered in turn.

Equality v. Other Liberal Values

The International Convention on the Elimination of All Forms of Racial Discrimination (1965) declares that all parties to the convention "condemn racial discrimination and undertake to pursue by all appropriate means and without delay a policy of eliminating racial discrimination in all its forms." The convention provides also that all parties undertake "not to sponsor, defend or support racial discrimination by any persons or organizations." Although Canada is a signatory to this instrument, there remain instances in which Canadian law chooses to resist responding to prejudicial conduct for the sake of advancing or protecting other accepted values. In the context of the *Leonard Foundation* case, or more generally, in the realm of what one might call "documentary discrimination", the countervailing values include freedom of religion and expression and the rights inherent in the concept of private ownership. None of these rights exists in pure-form under Canadian law. There is inevitably a balancing or accommodation of conflicting interests, and a favouring of some of these over others.

Consider the ways in which one might exercise racial or religious preferences. At one extreme one can envision acts that are openly antagonistic to members of racial or religious groups. It is likely that most Canadians deplore the activities of organizations such as the Aryan Nations and would dread being the target of its vitriol of bigotry. For this reason, it is a crime in Canada to promote racial hatred. In addition, human rights statutes prohibit the publication of materials promoting discrimination. Here, equality values have prevailed over claims to free speech.

However, at the other end of a continuum of discrimination, one finds the exercise of preferences that are not only permitted but protected; not just tolerated, but facilitated. The constitutional right to freedom of religion is designed toward that end. At a pivotal point in the Court of Appeal ruling in *Leonard*, Mr Justice Robins stated that the trust contravened public policy because it was predicated on notions of racism and religious superiority. To claim that one race or religion is intrinsically superior was said to be offensive to the values of a pluralistic, democratic society. However, in relation to religious belief, this statement may be misleading or wrong. A modern-day R.W. Leonard may prefer low church Anglicanism over any other type of religion. He may feel that its doctrine expresses the true word of God. Moreover, nothing will prevent him from donating money to that cause, even though this means that all other religions on earth will receive nothing from him. Even if he wished to donate to each and every religion known to him, except one, this would be permitted. Likewise, he might wish to endow an educational institution that taught the scripture based solely on specific theological principles. All of this would be sanctioned, protected, and encouraged; his donations would be tax deductible. In these instances, religious freedom would easily prevail over equality under law.

Instead of focusing on freedom of religion or speech as the countervailing values, one can understand the problem as pitting the protection of private property against the promotion of equality. This is the essence of the Leonard Foundation controversy, in which concerns over discrimination were set against the rights of private property. The support for Leonard that appeared in the press was founded on an appeal to property rights as an important liberal value. This was a dominant theme within the public debate over the Leonard Foundation Trust: almost every public defence of the Leonard Foundation contains an argument along these lines. It was said that Reuben Leonard's rights, even more than fifty years after his death, should be respected. Part of the rationale was that to do otherwise would have a chilling effect on philanthropic practice. What the discourse does not reveal is just how complex these concepts can be. The rights of property owners are limited. Both the judge at first instance and the Court of Appeal in the *Leonard* case saw the problem in those terms, that is, as a response, for instance, to equality concerns, the composition on the bundle of rights that constitute property ownership can be altered so as to limit rights of transfer. Where the judgments at the two levels differ is, primarily, as to how these rights should be ordered.

This dilemma can be illustrated by reference to another continuum. At one end can be placed the well-accepted limits on property entitlements. For example, the ownership of contraband may be prohibited altogether; the possession of certain inherently dangerous objects is also heavily regulated. Some transfers are prohibited (the sale of cigarettes to children) or regulated (the sale of prescription drugs) in the public interest. However, in general, property rights are extensive: by and large owners are entitled to do whatever they wish with their belongings, even to the extent of destroying their property. Assume, for example, that Reuben Leonard bestowed a gift on some perfect stranger. When asked about this bewildering action, Leonard replied as follows: "I selected him because he is white, and because I believe that he is a Protestant and of British parentage." Even after the *Leonard* case there is no basis in law for treating this (outright) gift as invalid. Nor would it be unlawful to confer a gift on the Aryan Nations. What is more, there is a large ambit of offensive discriminatory conduct that is not contrary to human rights protections. People are entitled to decide that whites only may enter their home. In that domain, rights of ownership continue to prevail over the values inherent in equal treatment.

A host of reasons have been advanced to explain why the law confers broad powers and privileges as part of the ownership bundle. Some of the rationales for property are consequentalist. Hence it is sometimes asserted that private property rights allow for economic efficiency and therefore produce material well-being. Property allows for freedom, and it promotes privacy and full human development. Property rights are also sometimes justified as apt rewards for labour and productivity. Although all of these assertions are contentious, they nonetheless serve to fuel the powerful ideological engine of property rights in Canadian law and society. As a result, when other values come into conflict with those underscoring rights of ownership, a strong case for curtailing property entitlements is often demanded.

Bearing this reasoning in mind, one can imagine a modern-day Reuben Leonard marshalling a defence along the following lines: I may express my view on racial or national preferences provided that I do not promote racial hatred or otherwise violate various statutory prohibitions. I may demonstrate my devotion to one religion by a direct donation, though by doing so I effectively discriminate against all other religions. I may destroy all of my savings or indulge in frivolous gifts as much as I wish, though no public good otherwise results. I may choose who may walk on my lawn, and in doing so I may happen to exercise preferences that my neighbours see as racist and therefore inexcusably objectionable. That being so, why is it that the law does not allow me to exercise *the very same preferences* through the instrumentality of the Leonard Foundation?

The answers given in the Court of Appeal rely upon the "public" dimension of his so-called "private" foundation. Mr Justice Robins emphasized what he termed the quasi-public nature of the Foundation, a status that arose from the fact that it was a charitable trust, designed (therefore) to benefit the public. Moreover, the awards were tenable at publicly funded educational institutions. Similarly, Tarnopolsky J.A. was careful to distinguish between charitable trusts, such as the one in issue, and family trusts. The rationale for the distinction under each approach is clear: public action is to be assessed in law by reference to a different (that is, more rigorous) standard than that applied to private dealings. In a sense, even Reuben Leonard understood this way of thinking. He regarded his fortune as being held as a "public trust." He accepted, therefore, that a sense of public duty attended his actions. Indeed, it is ironic that this very characterization was so instrumental in defeating his 1923 scheme.

The public/private dichotomy is often invoked in legal analysis, especially in relation to human rights issues, but the dividing line between the two is not always clear. This is because the dichotomy is actually deployed in two different ways, producing not two but three categories of conduct. The public/private divide is sometimes used to separate state from non-state action. It is this use that explains why the Canadian Charter of Rights and Freedoms is not directly applicable to the Leonard Foundation Trust. [T]he Charter applies to state (public) conduct. The Foundation is treated as private for the purposes of Charter analysis. The category of private conduct is further bifurcated. One speaks of acts done in the public arena and those done in private. For instance, it is understood that in a market economy resources are primarily allocated by private transactions, not by public authority. However, private enterprise in the marketplace is construed as public when compared to the private domain of the home. The three categories that emerge therefore are as follows: (1) state action; (2) private conduct in the public domain (such as the conduct of private enterprise); (3) private conduct treated as being outside of the public arena (such as family life).

The effect of defining three forms of action is seen in the rules for scrutinizing conduct. With regard to equality concerns, the state is subject to the highest level of scrutiny because it is duty-bound to treat each citizen with an even hand. In contrast, citizens are permitted, indeed invited, to pursue self-interest and to exercise their personal preferences in a host of ways. Between these two realms lies conduct that partakes of both private and public elements, and it is in this region that the debate over the Leonard Foundation occurred. The initial inquiries made by the Ontario Human Rights Commission to the Leonard trustees were met with the response that the Foundation was a private trust. This, of course, is no answer to the commission's jurisdiction to investigate, since its province is the regulation of private discriminatory conduct. In this context, the term "public" refers to actions ordinarily occurring in a public forum. This is category (2) conduct.

Even if we accept this three-part description, the dividing lines remain imprecise. This is because the private and the public are not really as separate as this above analysis suggests. Rather, they overlap. All discriminatory action regarding private property can be seen, at bottom, as state action. It is sometimes said that property is understood in the law as a set of rights created under law, and that, therefore, absent state sanction and enforcement, property rights vanish. As a result, in allowing property to be used in a discriminatory way, the state is therefore acting complicitously. On occasion this complicity is apparent: consider again the cases of *Franklin v. Evans* (1924) and *Christie v. York* (1939), which were discussed in Chapter 3. Both disputes involved the refusal of services to black patrons. In both, under the law as it then stood, the legal attack on the discriminatory conduct failed. In short, any legitimate private discriminatory conduct will, by definition, receive the backing of the state. In this sense, then, all *private* property dealings have a *public* dimension. Property rights can be seen as a state delegation of the decision-making power (about property) into private hands.

This line of reasoning applies not just to the category (2) type of conduct but to category (3) as well, that is, to private action occurring in a non-public setting. Consider another situation discussed in Chapter 3: a testamentary gift conditioned on the recipient adhering to a particular religious faith. We saw in that chapter that these gifts have generally been treated as valid. It was here that Tarnopolsky J.A. felt his reasoning should stop. Family trusts, as he called them, would not be subject to the rigorous rules he proposed for discriminatory scholarships. Similarly, category (3) conduct is generally thought to be outside the reach of human rights instruments.

I am not sure that these limitations make sense. First, a gift subject to a stipulation concerning religious adherence (as in the above example) is subject to legal enforcement. It is therefore public in the sense that the courts will enforce all valid testamentary gifts. And it is only private (in the category (3) sense) if we assume that the recipients of such gifts are denied the status of being members of the public at large. To put it another way, it is not clear that we should tolerate discriminatory action that affects family members to any greater extent than that tolerated in the community at large.

One answer to this issue is sometimes suggested. If a gift is given, say, from father to son, on the *proviso* that the son does not marry outside the Jewish religion, it is always open to the son simply to disclaim the gift. He need not sacrifice his moral beliefs concerning religious adherence because he can walk away from the "offer" contained in the bequest. Therefore, no harm is done by allowing such a gift to stand.

My reply to this reasoning is based on an apparent extrapolation of the *Leonard* case. We know that Colonel Leonard could have chosen to destroy his fortune in a bonfire or to make an absolute gift to some person he thought to be a worthy recipient. However, having chosen to endow a scholarship, the law now demands that he adhere to a certain level of fairness. Likewise, where a testator decides to confer a conditional gift on a small set of the outside world (that is, family members), one could argue that he or she is equally bound to comply with an appropriate public-policy standard. This closeness of these two situations would, perhaps, be more apparent if another example is given. Imagine a testamentary gift under which a college fund is promised "to all the members of my family who are white, British subjects and adherents to the Christian religion in its Protestant form. It is provided also that no more than one quarter of the monies set aside shall be allocated to female relatives." In assessing the "publicness" of such a gift, the difference is purely one of degree. It is not clear to me that, if the Leonard Foundation trust of 1923 is unacceptable, such a family gift should pass muster. . . .

Let me summarize this last point. In the *Leonard Foundation Trust* case we see the law resolving a competition between conflicting values. In *Leonard*, a distinction was drawn between public and private action, and this dichotomy was instrumental in the reasoning in both appellate judgments. However, I find the attempt to explain the line between permissible and impermissible discrimination by relying on a distinction between private and public conduct to be unhelpful. What results from such an approach is not a bright line at all but three overlapping categories that obscure rather than clarify what the law should be.

Contested Meanings of Equality

The problem in the law governing equality discussed above pertains to the balancing of conflicting rights. The issue addressed in this section involves competing conceptions of equality. Unlike the contest between equality on the one hand and values external to it (such as property rights) on the other, the dilemma here involves a conflict contained *inside* the concept of equality itself. That problem can be described in this way: Although we live in a world in which no two individuals are or can be equal in every conceivable biological, legal or other way, the pursuit of equality has nevertheless become an important goal. At the same time, in a multicultural society that aspires to respect and value difference, it is obvious that equality (defined as sameness) may not be a desirable end.

The tension between competing notions of equality can be found in human rights legislation. Anti-discrimination codes tend to stress the common elements of the human condition. As a result, Ontario's law mandates that in the provision of goods and services we must not take account of certain differences. We all need decent accommodation, whatever the colour of our skin or our religious beliefs. In relation to these needs, we are all to be treated as equals. Put another way, what is required by such a law is neutrality. We are being asked to ignore some considerations in the way that we treat people. That demand might encompass intentional acts that demonstrate differential treatment, as well as systemic factors that wind up producing the same result. In both situations, all that such equality rules require is that there be no correlation between our conduct and a prohibited ground of discrimination.

However, neutrality is only one way of conceiving of the idea of equality. If, by contrast, it is considered important that each member of society enjoy certain material conditions in life, neutrality normally will not suffice. An unrestrained egalitarian might argue, for instance, that the law should ensure that each and every one of us can enjoy an equal measure of property or prosperity. A more tempered approach might suggest that the demands of substantive equality are met when, say, everyone is accorded some minimal standard of living. Rather than ignoring differences (that is, acting neutrally), people would have to be treated differently, that is, their present position would have to be assessed and reassessed until the goal of material equality (whatever the specific target may be) is achieved.

It is in relation to the pursuit of this type of equality goal that the idea of affirmative action emerges. Affirmative action occurs when some positive steps are taken in a differential way to achieve some form of equal standing. Often at work here is the appreciation that past acts of discrimination (in effect, prior breaches of the idea of neutrality) can have lasting and harmful effects. Therefore, affirmative action has been used to improve the lot of historically marginalized and disadvantaged groups. To place matters within the context of the present study, it may be observed that both Reuben Wells Leonard and advocates of affirmative action accept the privileged status of the white Anglo-Saxon males. For Leonard, it was both natural and beneficial. Affirmative action is predicated on the view that that privileged position is historically contingent and deeply damaging.

Equality, then, is multidimensional. Even so, it remains an important liberal precept, and in many ways Canadian law is committed to achieving some version (or other) of this ideal. Because equality (choose your meaning) is treated by most people as virtuous, it carries rhetorical weight: It is nowadays hard to be against equality, even though there may be vehement disagreement as to what that term should mean. Given its protean character and its popular appeal, it is understandable that equality-based arguments could be found on both sides of the Leonard Foundation controversy. Both groups felt it useful to resort to equality claims to bolster their respective positions. So the Human Rights Commission alleged that the Foundation was in violation of the equal rights protections found in the Ontario Human Rights Code. Those writing in support of the Leonard Foundation argued that the scholarships should be governed by the same rules that apply to other discriminatory scholarships, such as those open only to South African blacks, Jews, persons of Greek descent, and so on. McKeown J.'s reasons for judgment comport with this point of view. The Leonard Foundation Trust was like other scholarships that discriminated on the basis of race or nationality. The implication to be drawn from his reasons for judgment was that to strike down the Leonard Trust would be to imperil a host of other ostensibly worthy scholarships and bursaries. Again, such is the rhetorical force of the word "equality" that both camps sought to enlist its support.

However, the reasons of McKeown J., like all of the pro-Leonard arguments that appeared in the press, adopt a "neutrality" definition of equality. What is called for is the application of a type of "moral algebra," one that mandates that dominant and marginalized groups be treated equally. We have just seen that this is only one meaning that can be given to the term. The pursuit of substantive equality through affirmative action was almost totally ignored in the public discourse about the Leonard Foundation. This is surprising since the concept of affirmative action has a firm footing under current Canadian law. With regard to governmental action, the Canadian Charter of Rights and Freedoms contains a basic guarantee of equality before the law. However, this is qualified by an exemption in favour of governmental action directed at the amelioration of conditions of disadvantaged individuals or groups. In addition, generally speaking, provincial human rights codes, such as Ontario's, exempt certain forms of reverse discrimination.

In Canada, as elsewhere, the adoption of affirmative action programs, in employment, education and so forth, has been controversial. At the heart of the critiques is the complaint that affirmative action is, by definition, discriminatory and therefore wrong. The argument is based on the view that the legal conception of equality should be confined to the idea of neutrality; the law should take no notice of differences (such as race or religion). Moreover, it is said that the application of affirmative action can produce harmful and unfair results. In seeking to respond to existing patterns of discrimination, it can serve to confer a benefit on those who have not in fact suffered injustice while at the same time imposing burdens on those who were not responsible for past wrongs. For instance, when an affirmative action policy is applied, the most competent members of a benefitted group will receive an advantage at the expense of the most competent members of the non-benefitted group. In addition, whether affirmative action is effective in pursuing equality goals is an open question; some complain that it cannot begin to address the entrenched problems of social inequality. Where it is effective, the intended beneficiaries may in time enjoy an undue advantage. As well, affirmative action can be difficult to apply, that is, it is not always easy to identify or prove the specific area of disadvantage and to construct a remedy that responds to that concern, no more and no less. Another claim is that affirmative action can be counter-productive, breeding resentment and hostility against the groups to be benefitted and devaluing the accomplishments of those who have received assistance under an affirmative action program. And it is argued that affirmative action leads to mediocrity because merit factors are given subordinate importance.

I believe that it is important to employ devices like affirmative action, though it is, one must concede, a blunt instrument. Problems of application, some of which are described in the preceding paragraph, surface when endeavouring to assess the validity of discriminatory scholarships. What precisely are we seeking to ameliorate? Is it necessary to demonstrate material disadvantage in Canadian society at large? Or in the institution at which the award is tenable? Or in the program of study? In some fields, such as nursing, women have been historically over-represented. Would affirmative action be justified here? Conversely, might this be a case in which scholarships to induce men to enter nursing might be acceptable as a form of affirmative action? Just how Canadian courts will treat these issues as they relate to affirmative action scholarships and bursaries is not yet known.

Is there an element of affirmative action to be found within the 1923 Leonard Trust? It was, in essence, a bursary, financial need being an absolute prerequisite. In the selection of recipients, the General Committee has always treated this consideration as central. That remains true. Hence, an argument can be made that the scholarship can be said to have a valid purpose even having regard to contemporary public policy dictates. Put another way, the trust identifies a marginalized segment of the population, namely *poor*, white, Protestant, British subjects. Viewed in this way (and absent reference to the recitals), the trust is designed to help not a dominant elite but an underclass.

Attractive at first glance, this argument must ultimately fail. The requirement of financial stringency was never challenged in the litigation and remains part of the trust. It was unassailable. That being so, the question that emerges is whether there are grounds for favouring poor white students over poor black ones, poor Protestants over poor Catholics, Muslims or Jews, and so on. Also, one would want to know why more help should be afforded to needy men than women. It is entirely appropriate to set aside the invidious distinctions while preserving the valid one (poverty). So, if we control for poverty, no justification exists in this instance for favouring Leonard's selected group of poor over the others. Under the scholarship program as reshaped by the court order, white, Protestant, British subjects may still apply for a Leonard award. That aspect of the original design is unaltered, and therefore that segment of Canada's underclass is still aided. What has changed is that they must now compete with a broader range of similarly situated candidates. To put it still another way, one good apple does not save the whole barrel. If it were not so, one virtuous act of charity could work to insulate other elements that are deplorable.

(d) restraints on alienation

Trinity College School v. Lyons
1995 CarswellOnt 403 (Gen. Div.)

Sheard J.:

This application is brought to enforce an option to purchase lands adjacent to the applicant's lands, pursuant to an agreement made in 1965 between the applicant and the parents of the respondents.

The respondents have brought a cross-application, which includes a number of issues that would require a trial to determine disputed allegations of fact. It was agreed by counsel and me that I would reserve judgment to consider, first, the issues as to which there was no disagreement on the facts, and state my decision on those issues, before addressing the request by the respondents for a trial of issues involving disputed allegations of fact.

What follows are my reasons for judgment on the first issues, prefaced by an outline of the undisputed facts.

The applicant is a residential school in Port Hope, where it began more than a century ago. I will refer to it as TCS, by which initials it is usually known.

Adjacent to the TCS lands is what was once a small farm owned and operated by successive generations of the Bennett family since 1891, when it was purchased by the grandparents of the respondents. Thomas Bennett, their father, was born there in 1898. He and his brother Frank, as had their father, provided TCS with milk for many years. Thomas also worked as a maintenance man for the school, and did gardening, snow ploughing and odd jobs, as well as running his farm.

In 1963, when he reached the age of 65, he decided to retire. He had a partial disability pension for lameness, for which he had been discharged from the army in the First World War. He and Mildred, his wife, who was two years older, were entitled to the Old Age Security pension. Since they were giving up working the farm, they decided to sell off portions of the land to TCS.

As a result, there were two agreements between TCS and Thomas and Mildred Bennett, one in 1963 and another in 1965, the latter agreement giving rise to this application.

By the 1963 agreement, the Bennetts (described therein as the "optionors") sold to TCS (the "optionee") a parcel of their farm referred to as the "north vacant lands," for $3,500. With respect to the balance of the property, they agreed not to sell to any purchaser other than TCS, unless it had been previously offered for sale to TCS at the fixed purchase price of $12,000.

A related term was that the Bennetts could offer a piece of the remaining land (the "south vacant lands") for the price of $1,500, and that, if TCS accepted that offer, the previously mentioned option price of $12,000 would be reduced by $1,500 to $10,500. (This parcel was purchased by TCS as part of the 1965 agreement.)

The 1963 agreement also included that TCS would pay the taxes on the lands retained by the optionors, the Bennetts. If they sold to TCS according to the agreement, no "adjustment" was required to be made for the taxes. If, however, the Bennetts sold to a third party, in consequence of TCS not exercising its option, TCS was entitled to a rebate of the taxes it had paid. Finally, if TCS did purchase, it would be entitled to a credit on the purchase price for any taxes paid beyond 10 years, that is, taxes paid after July 15, 1973.

In 1965, negotiations between TCS and the Bennetts began anew, and the agreement dated February 4, 1965, resulted. By this agreement, TCS purchased, for $2,625, the parcel known as the south vacant lands, plus a parcel that adjoined it, called the "additional lands."

What was left was the Option Lands — a piece with 150 feet frontage on Ward Street by a depth of 200 feet, on which stood the Bennett house — a two-storey frame dwelling. Here, Thomas and Mildred Bennett continued to reside, but in the 1965 agreement they gave TCS a right of first refusal — as they had in the 1963 agreement, plus — and this was new — an option to purchase on the death of the survivor of them. A significant feature of the right of first refusal was that the TCS purchase price, in the event the Bennetts received an offer from any other purchaser that they were willing to accept, would be the lower of that offered price or the sum of $9,375. By the same token, what might be called the post mortem option was for the same price: $9,375.

As it turned out, Thomas Bennett died in 1978, and Mildred Bennett lived on to December 1991, having survived the option agreement by almost 27 years. In the month following her death, TCS served notice to exercise its option. The relief requested in this application is an order for specific performance of the option, directing the respondents to convey the option lands to the applicant for the option price of $9,375, or, "in the alternative damages in the amount of $135,000, being the current fair market value of the option lands."

According to an appraisal obtained by the respondents, $135,000 was the market value of the property as of March 30, 1992. Counsel for the applicant said that her client would accept that figure for the purpose of calculating damages, less, of course, the amount of the option price.

The 1965 agreement, like the 1963 agreement, included that TCS would pay the taxes on the Option Lands, with different terms as to rebate of these payments. These were:

> (1) if the optionors sell to the optionee at any time prior to July 15, 1973, no rebate required;

(2) if the sale of the optionee occurs after July 15, 1973, all taxes paid by the optionee after that date shall be rebated to it up to the date of closing, without interest;

(3) if the optionee does not purchase the option lands it shall be entitled to a rebate of all taxes paid by it since July 15, 1963, without interest, out of the proceeds of the sale to another purchaser or one year after the death of the survivor of the two optionors.

Under the terms of the agreement, the option did not arise unless the optionors, or either of them, had beneficial ownership at the death of the survivor:

4. In the event that the Optionors or either of them have beneficial ownership of the lands and premises described in Schedule "B" hereto at the date of death of the survivor of them, the Optionee shall have the option, irrevocable from the date of death of the survivor of the Optionors until one month after receiving written notice of the death of such survivor, to purchase the said lands and premises. If the Optionee exercises such option the resultant purchase shall be for the price or sum of NINE THOUSAND, THREE HUNDRED AND SEVENTY-FIVE ($9,375.00) DOLLARS . . .

In March 1976, the Bennetts advised TCS that they intended to pay the property taxes themselves. TCS said it had no objection to that, and did not pay the 1976 taxes, or thereafter.

By a deed given in September 1978 and registered in October, Thomas and Mildred Bennett conveyed the Option Lands to their three daughters, now the respondents, as a gift to them. The Bennetts did not inform TCS of this at the time; it learned of this conveyance after Mildred Bennett's death.

Thomas Bennett died shortly after the conveyance to the daughters.

Much of the argument in the application was directed to the question of whether TCS was entitled to assert an option at all, since at the date of the death of Mildred Bennett, the surviving optionor, and indeed for some 13 years prior to that, she had ceased to be an owner.

What had occurred — the conveyance of the Option Lands by gift — was not contemplated in the language of the agreement conferring the option. For the right of option to survive, it thus became necessary for the optionee to request the Court to imply a term in the agreement that the optionors would not convey the Option Lands without first offering them to the optionee. . . .

Mr Zucker referred in his submissions to the carefully reasoned and instructive judgment of Lane J. in *Law-Woman Management Corp. v. Peel (Regional Municipality)* (1991), 2 O.R. (3d) 567. At page 586, Lane J. says: "To imply a term into an agreement is not to be done lightly nor merely because it represents a sensible agreement which the parties might well have made. There must be an evidentiary foundation for finding that the implied term is one which the parties would both have agreed to, or if they had thought of the point (as, for example, a trade custom); *or is one that is necessary for the business efficacy of the transaction and is in accord with the parties' intentions.*" (Emphasis added.)

It is argued that the evidentiary foundation is lacking to support the conclusion that the Bennetts would have agreed to a clause forbidding them from giving away the Option Lands to their daughters. In my opinion, the evidentiary analysis need not be pursued if, as here, there is compelling reason to imply the missing term to maintain the business efficacy of the transaction in accord with the apparent intention of the parties.

I agree that the Bennetts should not be able to defeat the right of first refusal by giving the property away to their daughters.

However, a fundamental question underlies the whole arrangement embodied in the 1965 agreement. That is, whether the option, for a fixed price, was unenforceable or void as an improper restraint on alienation of an estate in fee simple.

As is pointed out in A.H. Oosterhoff and W.B. Rayner, *Anger and Honsberger: Law of Real Property*, 2d ed. (Aurora, Ont.: Canada Law Book), Vol. 1, section 503.1, page 114, since the *Statute of Quia Emptores* in 1290 [(U.K.), 18 Edw. 1, St. 1], the right of alienation has been an inseparable incident of an estate in fee simple. "As a result, the courts have viewed with disfavour any restraints on alienation. . . . A condition that would take away the necessary incidents of the estate, such as that the holder shall not take the profits, or shall not have the power to alienate, either generally or for a limited time, is void as being repugnant to the estate created. The reason such restraints are void is because they keep property out of commerce and tend to result in a concentration of wealth."

That last statement is taken from the judgment of Howland J.A. (as he then was) in *Stephens v. Gulf Oil Canada Ltd.* (1975), 65 D.L.R. (3d) 193, at page 220:

> The objections in principle to restraints on alienation are twofold. They keep property out of commerce and have a tendency to result in concentration of wealth. They also tend to prevent improvement of property, since a landowner will be reluctant to make improvements when he cannot sell the property.
>
> The case of *Re Rosher* (1884), 26 Ch. D. 801, is of particular importance as it dealt with a right of pre-emption which was considered to be an absolute restraint. In that case the testator devised certain property to his son, but provided that if his son desired to sell it during the lifetime of the testator's wife, then she should have the option to purchase it at a price of £3,000 for the whole, and at a proportionate price for any part or parts, and it should be first offered to her at such price or proportionate price. The value of the property at the testator's death was £15,000. Pearson J., considered that to require the son, if he desired to sell, to do so at one-fifth of its value, was equivalent to an absolute restraint against sale during the life of the widow. He also concluded that a condition imposing a restraint on alienation during a particular time, here the lifetime of the widow, was void in law as being repugnant to the estate in fee.
>
> *Re Rosher* was applied in *Re Cockerill*, [1929] 2 Ch. 131. In that case the testator devised certain land to the devisee on condition that if he or his personal representatives desired to sell the lands within 20 years from the testator's death, then the governors of the Northampton Old Grammar School Foundation should be given the option to purchase

it at £300 per acre, subject to payment of certain annuities and roadmaking charges. At the testator's death the land was in fact worth £670 an acre. Eve J., considered that the condition requiring the land to be offered to the governors was void as a restraint on alienation.

In *Stephens v. Gulf Oil*, Howland J.A. reviews at length the development of the law forbidding restraint on alienation, starting with the foundation principle that "[a] power of alienation is an inseparable incident of an estate in fee simple. Consequently, where there is a condition annexed to a grant or devise of land in fee simple, which is an absolute restraint on alienation, it will be void as being repugnant to that estate." (At page 219.)

At page 224, Howland J.A. compares an option to purchase to a right of pre-emption:

> An option to purchase is more objectionable as a restraint on alienation, than a right of pre-emption. Giving Palen a right of pre-emption is very different from requiring that the property be sold to Palen, or prohibiting its sale without Palen's consent. There would also seem to be a distinction between a pre-emptive right to meet any offer which is received, and a pre-emptive right exercisable at a fixed price which makes no provision for an increase in the value of the property. The latter provision may involve a very substantial sacrifice by the person who granted it.
>
> Fratcher in his text on *Perpetuities and Other Restraints* (1954), states at p. 87:
>
> > *The Restatement of Property* takes the position that a pre-emptive provision is a restraint on alienation. It asserts, nevertheless, that such a provision is valid if the optionee is required to meet any offer received by the optionor as a condition of exercising his option. *If, however, the optionee need pay only a fixed price or a percentage of any offered price, the Restatement treats the provision as one governed by the general rules as to restraints on alienation of estates in fee simple.*
>
> A similar distinction was drawn by Merrill I. Schnebly in three learned articles on "Restraints Upon the Alienation of Legal Interests", 44 Yale L.J. 961, 1186, and 1380 (1935), at p. 1391, where he stated:
>
> > Any preemption exercisable at a fixed price is likely to involve sacrifice to the person bound to offer, since a fixed price is usually based upon the value of the land when the preemptive provision is executed. *It might be held, therefore, that any preemptive provision fixing a price without reference to future increase in value is void as a restraint upon alienation in substance.* If the preemptioner must pay the offeror's price, however, there is no material impediment to alienation. A preemptive provision of this type might be enforced in so far as the rule against restraints upon alienation is concerned. *In my view, if the right of pre-emption at a fixed price substantially deprives the person who granted it of his right of alienation, then it will not be valid.* [Emphasis mine.]

In *Stephens v. Gulf Oil*, Stephens wanted to purchase part of Palen's land, for the price of $37,207, which was acceptable to Palen, but it was necessary to obtain the concurrence of Gulf, to whom Palen had given a right of first refusal. The purchase by Stephens was, in fact, approved by Gulf, but on terms that included a right of first refusal from Stephens to Palen at the fixed price of $37,207, Stephens's purchase price. These arrangements (the "Three Party Agreement") also included that Palen gave Stephens a right of first refusal of Palen's remaining land, at the price of $64,174.

Howland J.A. distinguished between the right of first refusal that had been imposed on Stephens as a term of the sale to him, holding that it was void as a restraint on alienation, and the pre-emptive right given by Palen to Stephens. The latter right was held not to be void. "That right of pre-emption was in no sense a condition imposed on Palen's property which might be void as a restraint on alienation. Palen was not acquiring title at the time of the Three Party Agreement, but was simply granting a right of pre-emption in respect of land which he already owned."

On that reasoning, it could be said that the right of first refusal given by Thomas and Mildred Bennett was not void as a restraint on alienation, notwithstanding that it specified a fixed price of no more than $9,375.

In my opinion, however, the right of option triggered by the death of the survivor of the Bennetts was of an essentially different nature, and is void as an unlawful restraint on alienation.

That conclusion is compatible with the views expressed by Howland J.A. in the passages in *Stephens*, aforementioned.

In particular, there is an obvious analogy between the post mortem option in the 1965 agreement and the testamentary pre-emptive provisions in *Re Rosher; Rosher v. Rosher* [(1884), 26 Ch. D. 801, 32 W.R. 821] and *Re Cockerill; Mackaness v. Percival* [[1929] 2 Ch. 131] ruled in each of those cases to have been void.

All the more so should the post mortem option in the 1965 agreement be declared void, since it was an even greater restraint on alienation, because it was exercisable at the choice of TCS, whether or not the executrix of the will of Mildred Bennett wished to sell.

The acquisition of the land by the executrix on the death of Mrs. Bennett is comparable to the conveyance to Stephens. He got less than a title in fee simple because the conveyance to him was saddled with a right of first refusal, at a fixed price, in favour of Palen. Howland J.A. found that to be a void condition.

If the post mortem option were valid, the executrix of Mildred Bennett would get even less, and not by her decision or agreement. The words of Mills J. in *Blackburn v. McCallum* (1903), 33 S.C.R. 65, quoted by Howland J.A., are appropriate:

> It is reasonable to say that where an estate is bestowed, of which the power of alienation is an incident, that one conveying such an estate to another shall not have the power to

> alter its character, and to make it something wholly different from what it has been made by the law. To do so is to assume the power to make an estate unknown to the law. It is an attempt not simply to convey away an estate, but to exercise a legislative power, and to create a new form of property in land. . . .

The application on the agreed facts argued before me must be dismissed.

QUESTIONS AND COMMENTS

1. What policies underlie the law governing restraints on alienation? Suppose the law did not invalidate such restraints. Is it certain that the policies giving rise to the existing law would, in fact, be offended?

2. The English case of *In re Macleay* (1875) L.R. 20 Eq. 186, dealt with a devise that read: "I give unto my dear brother *John* the whole of the property given to me by my late dear aunt *Clara Perkins*, consisting of the manor of *Bletchingly*, in the county of *Surrey* and the *Pendell Court Mansion*, with the land belonging to it, on the condition that he never sells it out of the family." In course of the judgment, Jessel M.R. observed (at 189):

> Now, you may restrict alienation in many ways. You may restrict alienation by prohibiting a particular class of alienation, or you may restrict alienation by prohibiting it to a particular class of individuals, or you may restrict alienation by restricting it to a particular time.

In *Trinity College School v. Lyons* there were no express prohibitions. The owners were free to sell the property, albeit on certain terms. Why then was the law of restraints on alienation in issue?

3. What would have occurred if the restraint in *Macleay* (see note 2) had been violated by the donee? In some instances the language of the gift makes it clear that the entitlement will be forfeited completely, as would be the result for any breached condition subsequent. Alternatively, it might be the case that the purported violation is treated a void. This type of restraint disables the holder from exercising a normal power of disposition. So, in *Blackburn v. McCallum* (1903) 33 S.C.R. 65, 1903 CarswellOnt 804, at 74, Tachereau C.J. described the effect of an attempt to breach a prohibition on the transferring or encumbering of a devised parcel of land:

> A void act cannot operate a forfeiture. *Quod nullum est nullum producit effectum*. The testator willed this land with prohibition to the devisee to alienate or incumber it. But what is the consequence if he attempts to alienate or incumber? Nothing else but the complete nullity of any act done in contravention of the prohibition, but not forfeiture or nullity of the devise.

4. Under Canadian law, it is not clear whether a purely contractual (or "promissory") restraint is subject to these rules. Should it be?

5. To what extent should a grantor's reasons for the imposed restraint affect the outcome of the case?

6. Comment on the meaning and validity of the following dispositions:

(a) "I BEQUEATH the property being 1075 Crawford to my sons, namely; MARVIN KATZMAN and NELSON KATZMAN, with the bequest to MARVIN KATZMAN being conditional upon NELSON KATZMAN being able to purchase MARVIN KATZMAN'S interest at a purchase price of $75,000.00 to be repaid in monthly payments of $310.00 a month, without interest, until paid in full." *Re Katzman Estate* 1983 CarswellOnt 622 (H.C.).

(b) "[To my trustees] TO TRANSFER AND DELIVER my home situate at 413-4th Street, New Westminster, British Columbia to my nephew DONALD BEADLE for his own use absolutely, PROVIDED AND ONLY IN THE EVENT that he shall use it as his home by residing in it for a continuous period of ten (10) years, AND PROVIDED FURTHER that he shall not during said period of ten (10) years mortgage, pledge, encumber in any manner, or use said home as collateral security for any loan; IN THE EVENT that my said nephew Donald Beadle shall not continuously use said home as his residence for the continuous period of ten (10) years as aforesaid, I DIRECT that my said home shall be sold by my Trustees and that the proceeds from the sale thereof be paid and distributed to and among my nephews and nieces who shall survive me in equal shares." *Beadle v. Gaudette* 1985 CarswellBC 619 (S.C.).

(c) "*I further direct* that after the death of my said wife that the Northwest quarter of Section two (2), and the Southwest quarter of Section eleven (11), all in Township thirty-six (36) in Range three (3) West of the third meridian in the Province of Saskatchewan, *to be divided in equal shares* among my three (3) daughters, Alice S. Allen, Grace Elizabeth Allen and Lorraine Willis Allen. . . .

I further direct that my executors hereinafter named give my son, George Rae Allen, *the first opportunity of purchasing* the said Northwest quarter of section two (2), and the Southwest quarter of Section eleven (11), all in township thirty-six (36) in Range three (3) West of the third meridian in the Province of Saskatchewan *at its then market price at the date of my death*, and on terms to be agreed on among my said children, beneficiaries of the said property." *Allen v. Allen* 1994 CarswellSask 199 (Q.B.).

(d) "I will that the aforesaid parcels of land shall not be at their disposal at any time until the end of twenty-five years from the date of my decease, and farther, I will that the said parcels of land shall remain free from all incumbrance, and that no debts contracted by my sons, William Chisholm and Hugh Chisholm, shall by any means incumber the same during twenty-five years from the date of my decease." *Blackburn v. McCallum* 1903 CarswellOnt 804, 33 S.C.R. 65.

(e) To H and W for life. "Upon the Death of the Survivor, we will, devise and bequesth to our son, SONNY DYER, our farm and homeplace. However, it is our express desire that this farm and homeplace not be sold, but is to stay in the Worth Dyer family. In the event he should at any time desire to sell his property, he is to sell it to one of my male heirs at the amount for which property is selling for at that time." *Dyer v. Dyer* 2002 WL 1517662 (Geo. S.C.).

REVIEW PROBLEM

Comment on the meaning and validity of the following clauses:

"I appoint Stephen Kay . . . to be Executor and Trustee of this my Will. & I expect him to carry out my orders without any changes and no one can contest it.

I give Royal North Shore Hospital $10,000 for the Liver Department . . . I give The Children's Hospital at Randwick $10,000 for treatment of White [and white is underlined twice] babies. I give the Blind Dogs $10,000 for dog pets for the elderly.

I give the Pink Ladies at Ryde Hospital $5000 & my finished craft to sell in their shop . . . My brother, his wife or any of their descendants are not [not is underlined twice] to get anything out of the house or 1 cent of any money. If Stephen Kay wants to sell the house he must sell it to a young White [white is underlined twice] Australian Couple for a reasonable price & not sell at auction or to a developer.

If Stephen Kay does not want to handle this he can pay someone else to do so but not his solicitor as I don't like him. Stephen Kay is to get house contents & any money left after expenses have been paid. The money is in St Georges Bank & investments with Esanda Finance.

Nothing in the house is to be sold. It is to be given to anyone who needs it or to charity, even Rotary for their garage sale but not the Smith Family or St Vincent de Paul. What no one wants is to go to the tip. So goodbye to anyone who is interested."

Kay v. South Eastern Sydney Area Health Service [2003] N.S.W.S.C. 292.

4. THE LEGAL REMAINDER RULES

Ontario Law Reform Commission, *Report on Basic Principles of Land Law* (Toronto: A.G. (Ont., 1996)) at 14-7 [footnotes omitted]

The Legal Remainder Rules

The validity of contingent remainders in the early common law is obscure. However, in time their creation was allowed at common law but subject to certain restrictive rules. These rules are described here as the legal remainder rules.

An argument can be made that these rules were not, and should not have been, received into Ontario as part of the general adoption of English law since their rationales were obviously irrelevant to circumstances in Upper Canada at the end of the eighteenth century. However, in a few cases these rules have been applied in Ontario, including a case decided in 1984; it has never been held or stated judicially that they are inapplicable; and it is generally assumed that they are applicable.

The first rule is that there can be no remainder after a grant in fee simple. This rule appears reasonable even to the modern mind where the first grant is an estate in fee simple absolute. For example, if A purported to grant an estate in fee simple to B with remainder to C in fee simple the remainder to C would be void. The rationale appears to be that the grant to B exhausts A's interest in the property so that there is nothing left to give to C after B's interest. However, the rule was applied even where the grant to B was a qualified fee simple. Although A can grant a determinable fee simple and retain an interest known as a possibility of reverter or can grant a conditional fee simple and retain an interest known as a right of re-entry, A cannot at common law limit a remainder in favour of C to take effect on the termination of B's interest.

The second rule is that a

> remainder must be supported by a prior particular state of freehold created by the same instrument. It cannot be allowed to spring up in the future after a hiatus . . .

For example, if A purports to convey an interest to B (who at the time is aged 19) and if when B attains 21, the conveyance will be void at common law and B will obtain no interest. On the other hand, an interest could have been validly created if, for example, A had conveyed to X for life, remainder to B in fee simple if and when B attains 21. As long as B attains 21 during the lifetime of X the contingent remainder would vest in interest at that time and would vest in possession on the death of A. In this example, the remainder is supported by a prior particular estate of freehold: X's life interest.

The basic idea behind this rule was that there must, at the time of grant, be an immediate passage of seisin. This, in turn, was required since the method of conveying a freehold estate in land was originally feoffment with livery of seisin. A feoffment required the transferor at the moment of feoffment to make a symbolic delivery of seisin to the transferee. This could only be achieved if there existed at that time a grantee capable of receiving seisin. In addition, this rule may be explained by the closely-related reason that the importance of seisin within the feudal system required that there always be someone with seisin since the person seised of land was the person subject to feudal obligations and the only person against whom certain actions relating to land could be brought. It was, therefore, a maxim of the common law that seisin must not be in abeyance.

The third rule is that a remainder must await the regular ending of the prior particular estate. We have already mentioned that an interest may be made subject to a condition subsequent along with the retention by the grantor of a right of re-entry — a right to terminate the estate if the condition is broken. For example, A can convey land to B for life provided that B does not marry C. However, pursuant to the common law rule under consideration here, A cannot give a third party an interest that takes effect on the termination of a prior estate by reason of the operation of a condition subsequent. Assume, for example, that A conveys land to B for life on condition that B does not marry C and if B does marry C his life estate to terminate and an estate in fee simple in favour of D to take effect. The provision in favour of D would be void.

The rule is based on the common law principle that only the party from whom a condition moves — the grantor or his heirs — can take advantage of a condition broken. This principle was itself related to the common law attitude towards the passage of seisin. An estate in remainder was regarded by the common law as an estate that was created by and that commences upon the original livery of seisin. A grantor, by the act of re-entry, would re-acquire that seisin which had passed from him by the original feoffment. But, according to the common law, it was not otherwise possible validly to interrupt the passage of seisin set in motion by the initial act of livery of seisin.

Even at common law this rule could easily be circumvented by appropriate drafting. For example, if A conveyed land to B for life or until B should marry C, remainder to D in fee simple, the remainder to D would be valid. B would take a determinable life estate; that is, B's interest may continue for his life or may determine sooner on the occasion of B's marriage to C. The limitation in favour of D would constitute a valid limitation by way of remainder since the event of B's marriage to C would not operate to determine B's life estate prematurely. It would merely mark the duration of B's estate so that, on the marriage, B's life estate would end regularly.

As stated in *Anger and Honsberger's Law of Real Property*,

> [the] fourth common law remainder rule requires that a remainder vest during the continuance of the prior particular estate or at the moment that it determines.

The operation of the rule is explained as follows:

> The limitation may be so worded as to stipulate for a gap, in which case it is void, as in a grant "to A for life, remainder to B when he reaches age 21 after A's death." On the other hand, if the gap may or may not occur at the time of the determination of the prior estate, the law permits the remainderman to wait and see until that time. If the remainder is then vested, it is allowed to take effect; if it is not, it is void. Hence, a grant to "A for life, remainder to B when he marries" (B being a bachelor), B's remainder will be valid if he has married when A dies; if he has not, it will fail.

Where a remainder is initially valid under this rule but will be invalidated if it does not turn out to vest during or at the moment of determination of the prior estate, the validity of the remainder will depend on the date of termination of the prior estate. This may terminate naturally, for example, by the death of a prior life tenant, or it may occur artificially. For example, the prior estate could be destroyed by forfeiture, surrender, merger or disclaimer. Section 35 of the *Conveyancing and Law of Property Act* has partially abolished artificial destruction of contingent remainders:

> 35. Every contingent remainder is capable of taking effect notwithstanding the determination by forfeiture, surrender or merger of any preceding estate of freehold.

The abolition is only partial since destruction of a prior estate may occur in other ways, notably disclaimer which is not mentioned in section 35. In addition, section 35 does not apply to the natural determination of a prior estate.

This rule, which is closely related to the second legal remainder rules, rests, like the second rule, on the importance attached by the common law to seisin and thus to the idea that there must always be someone with seisin. The second and fourth legal remainder rules also carried out a policy of preventing the creation of interests operating too far into the future. However, because of the development of uses and the impact of the *Statute of Uses*, they were not an effective way of controlling perpetuities. This policy was more effectively carried out by the modern rule against perpetuities, the main principles of which were developed in the last quarter of the seventeenth century.

QUESTIONS AND COMMENTS

1. Apply the legal remainder rules to the following *inter vivos* dispositions:

(a) Under a deed dated November 2003: "to my son on his next birthday [August 15th]."

(b) "To A for life, remainder to his widow, should A marry and leave a widow."

(c) "To A for life, to his eldest son, provided that he attends his father's funeral."

(d) "To A for life, remainder to B if and only if B attends university."

(e) "To A for life, but should B attend university then immediately to B."

(f) "To A for life or until then to B attends university, and then immediately to B."

(g) "To A in fee simple, but should B marry, then to B in fee simple."

2. Re-examine the transfer in *Caroline (Village) v. Roper* 1987 CarswellAlta 363, 37 D.L.R. (4th) 761 (Q.B.), discussed above in Part 2. Does that transfer comply with the legal remainder rules?

3. I suspect that very few would challenge the conclusion that the legal remainder rules have ceased to have contemporary significance; hence the Ontario Law Reform Commission proposed that they be abolished. In theory, absent statutory alteration, they can apply to simple *inter vivos* transfers. They do not apply to interests that are purely equitable; these rules, after all, are only concerned with legal remainders. The rules no longer apply in Manitoba. There, *The Perpetuities and Accumulations Act*, C.C.S.M., c. P33, sub. 4(1) provides:

> Successive legal interests, whether valid or invalid at common law or as executory interests, take effect in equity behind a trust, except that any successive legal interest which would not be valid as an equitable interest behind a trust is invalid for all purposes.

It is also well-established that the legal remainder rules do not apply to most interests that are affected by the operation of the *Statutes of Uses*. The Statute, it will be recalled, operates in the following manner: Where A is seised to the use of B, the Statute would operate so as to remove the legal estate from A and place it in B. The resulting entitlement in B is referred to as a legal executory interest; it is legal by virtue of the operation of the Statute.

It is likewise part of the established doctrine that gifts of legal interests in wills are treated in the same way as these executory interests (and in wills are commonly referred to as executory devises), even if the language of uses is not employed in the will. Therefore a devise of the legal estate "To A, but should A re-marry then to B" is valid even though it creates a fee after a fee. The interest of B is called a shifting executory interest. And a devise of legal title in a will "to A upon A graduating from University" is valid even though it is a gift *in futuro*. This is a springing executory devise.

However, there is an exception to the general rule that legal executory interests are not subject to the legal remainder rules. The exception is embodied in the rule in *Purefoy v. Rogers*, the applicability of which was at issue in *Re Crow*, below. Moreover, as it will also be seen in the commentary following *Re Crow*, another school of thought maintains that the legal remainder rules *never* apply in wills.

Re Crow
1984 CarswellOnt 556 (H.C.)

[In 1926, the testator passed away. His will provided in part that certain real property should be devised "to my grandsons Robert and William the sons of my son Orville for and during the term of their natural lives and upon their death to their children." The will further provided that should William and Robert die without having children, the remainder should go to their nieces or nephews.

William Crow died in 1944 having no children; and at that time there were also no nieces and nephews then alive who could inherit the remainder. Robert died in 1983. He had no children, but there were nieces and nephews alive at the time of his death. The question then arose as to the fate of the remainder of the interest once held by William Crow. In particular, was it subject to the rule of timely vesting described above?]

Krever J.: . . .

In the absence of any contrary intention to be discerned from a reading of the codicil, the period of distribution with relation to the class gift over after the life estate of the undivided one-half interest of William must, in my opinion, be the termination of William's life estate and not the testator's death. The critical date, in other words, was December 12, 1944, at which date no children of Joseph, Charles or Robert, that is, children "of my grandchildren mentioned in paragraphs 5, 6 and 7", had been born. That brings me to what has been called the fourth rule of the rules governing legal remainders. That rule and its explanation, as stated in Megarry's *Manual of the Law of Real Property* (4th ed., 1969), at pp. 92-93, though put in the past tense because of subsequent statutory changes in the land of its origin, are as follows:

> A remainder was void —
>
> (i) unless it was so limited that it could take effect during the continuance of the particular estate or at the moment of its determination; and
>
> (ii) unless it did in fact take effect in this way.
>
> Each branch of this rule was founded on the common law abhorrence for an abeyance of seisin; when the particular estate determined, it must be possible for the seisin to pass forthwith to the next remainderman . . . .
>
> The second branch of the rule meant that even if the remainder complied with the first part of the rule and so escaped being void *ab initio*, it nevertheless failed unless it in fact vested during the continuance of the particular estate or at the moment it determined.

The second branch of the rule became known as a "wait and see" rule. If at the date the will took effect, that is, at the date of the testator's death, the remainder could take effect during the life estate because, to apply the rule to the facts of the instant case, the grandchildren mentioned in paragraphs 5, 6 and 7, that is, Joseph, Charles or Robert, might have children during the life estate of William the remainder was not void simply because at the testator's death they did not, in fact, have children. Rather, according to the second branch of the rule, one would wait and see whether at the date of William's death, there were, in fact, children of Joseph and Charles and Robert. As I have pointed out more than once, however, though Joseph and Charles, the grandchildren mentioned in paras. 5 and 6 of the codicil did eventually have children, no such children had been born at the date of the termination of William's life estate. In the absence of any statutory provision abrogating the common law rule and unless the gift over is not a legal remainder but is an executory devise, the gift over must fail. I have not been referred to nor have I myself found a statutory abrogation of the rule. With respect to the characterization of the gift over as an executory devise, however, the result would not differ from that which results from treating the gift over as a legal remainder. The reason for that is that it is the second branch of the fourth rule that is offended, that is to say, the "wait and see" rule. It could not be said that at the time of its creation the gift over might not take effect at the end of William's prior life estate. According to the rule in *Purefoy v. Rogers* (1671), 2 Wms. Saund. 380, 85 E.R. 1181, the devise must be treated as a remainder and not as an executory devise.

The following concise and clear explanation of the rule, described in the paragraph preceding the explanation as the "notorious" rule in *Purefoy v. Rogers*, is taken from Megarry and Wade, *The Law of Real Property*, at pp. 192-93:

> This rule probably originated as a rule of construction, but it became a sanctified dogma of the law, to be applied without exception and without regard to the grantor's intentions. "Now, if there be one rule of law more sacred than another, it is this, that no limitation shall be construed to be an executory or shifting use, which can by possibility take effect by way of remainder." This meant that if any limitation, even though contained in a grant to uses or a will, was on any assumption *capable* of complying with the legal remainder rules, it was to be treated as a legal contingent remainder and not as an executory interest. Clearly this would not endanger limitations which were bound to comply with the rules when so treated. But equally clearly it endangered those limitations whose validity, when treated as contingent remainders, was placed in suspense by rule 4. If in the event such a limitation did not vest in time, it failed, because although it might have complied with the legal remainder rules it had not in fact done so. There were accordingly three possibilities. A contingent interest in a grant to uses or a will, when scrutinised as at the moment of its creation, might either
>
> (i) defy the legal rules from the outset, and be certain to infringe them if it took effect at all, as did springing and shifting interests; or
>
> (ii) comply with them from the outset, and be certain to vest within the limits and in the way required at common law; or
>
> (iii) be capable of complying with them, but not certain to do so unless events turned out favourably.
>
> Interests in class (i) were unaffected by the rule in *Purefoy v. Rogers*; they remained legal executory interests, and were free from the legal rules.
>
> Interests in classes (ii) and (iii) were required to conform to the legal rules and became legal contingent remainders. This could in no way injure class (ii). But class (iii) was exposed to the danger that if events turned out adversely the interest would be invalidated under the "wait and see" rule at some time in the future.

In this case events have turned out adversely to the interest because at the time of William's death none of Joseph, Charles or Robert had had any children and, therefore, in my opinion, the gift over to them . . . was invalidated.

Order accordingly.

QUESTIONS AND COMMENTS

1. Was Krever J. bound by the rule in *Purefoy v. Rogers*? Should he have applied it?

2. The following Editorial Note accompanies *Re Crow* in the Dominion Law Reports (1984) 12 D.L.R. (4th) 415 (H.C.) at 416:

> We understand that *Re Robson*, [1916] 1 Ch. 116, was not cited to the court. That case reached the opposite conclusion on the application of the rule in *Purefoy v. Rogers et al.* (1671), 2 Wms. Saund. 380, 85 E.R. 1181, in circumstances in which the statutory trust created by the English equivalent of s. 2 of the *Estates Administration Act*, R.S.O. 1980, c. 143, applied, and further held that an interest which was equitable by reason of the statutory trust did not become destructible merely because administration of the estate had been completed.

The case of *Re Robson* concerned a devise of property to A for life, remainder to such of A's children as attain the age of 21. At the time of A's death, some of A's children had reached 21 years of age; others had not. The issue was whether those children who were under 21 were unable to take an interest once they turned 21, because of the same rule that was invoked in *Re Crow* (the timely vesting rule). It was held that those younger children were not foreclosed.

The reasoning adopted in *Robson* was that under the *Land Transfer Act, 1897*, the legal estate conferred under the will is first reposed in the personal representative(s) of the decedent. Therefore, during this transitional phase in the administration of the estate, the beneficiaries hold only equitable entitlements. Moreover, even when the property is ultimately dispersed in accordance with the terms of the will, the legal entitlements (somehow) retain the initial immunity from the legal remainder rules that existed when those interests were deemed by the Act to be equitable. If this reasoning is sound, the result is that the legal remainder rules do not apply in wills.

3. As the editorial recognizes, the applicability of the reasoning in *Re Robson* presupposes a statutory provision equivalent to that found in the *Land Transfer Act, 1897*. The relevant part of that Act reads:

> 1(1) Where real estate is vested in any person . . . it shall, on his death, notwithstanding any testamentary disposition, devolve to and become vested in his personal representatives or representative from time to time as if it were a chattel real vesting in them or him.

Is there a provision in your home jurisdiction that serves as the functional equivalent of this subsection?

4. What is the effect of section 13 of the *Real Property Act*, R.S.P.E.I. 1974, c. R-4, on the operation of the legal remainder rules:

> Every contingent remainder . . . which would have been valid as a springing or shifting use or executory devise or other limitation had it not had a sufficient estate to support it as a contingent remainder, in the event of the particular estate determining before the contingent remainder vests, shall be . . . capable of taking effect in all respects as if the contingent remainder had originally been executed as a springing or shifting use or executory devise or other executory limitation.

5. THE RULE AGAINST PERPETUITIES

L.A. McCrimmon, "Understanding the Rule Against Perpetuities: Adopting a Five-Step Approach to a Perpetuities Problem" (1997) 5 Aust. Prop. L.J. 130 [footnotes omitted]

Introduction

"The Rule Against Perpetuities". For most of us these words evoke an image of tortuous hours spent in Real Property lectures while a well-intentioned, but in our minds sadistic, lecturer attempted to explain the intricacies of the Rule. Mention the Rule to a colleague today and you'll likely receive the response, "Never did understand it". Those of us who profess a fondness for the Rule must endure looks usually reserved for the bankrupt and destitute.

While strong arguments can be made for the abolition of the Rule, the fact remains that it is part of our law and legal practitioners and law students should have an understanding of its application. The observations of the late Professor Barton Leach, contained in an article written over 40 years ago, apply with equal force today.

> Our students, entering a great profession which carries increasingly important burdens, should spend their time upon more constructive studies. Yet, at the deadly peril of their client's welfare and of their own reputations, they cannot neglect the Rule as it now stands.

The discussion which follows is not intended to be an exhaustive review of the law relating to perpetuities. Rather, the article focuses on a *schema* which can be used to tackle a perpetuities problem. The article revisits briefly the origins and policy of the modern Rule Against Perpetuities. It is then suggested that a perpetuities problem can be "solved" by adopting a five-step approach. This approach conveys the "inner consistency", which enables the Rule to be applied, "with remorseless logic and predictable outcome".

The origins and policy of the rules against perpetuities

In feudal England, control of land equalled wealth, power and social prestige. A prerequisite to maintaining one's position in society was the ability to maintain control over the family landholdings. For reasons of public policy, the common law courts took the position that land must remain freely alienable. Hence, from an early date the courts were involved in a battle to restrict the ability of a landholder to exercise, from the grave, control over real property. During the course of this battle the courts formulated rules to invalidate interests which vested at too remote a time in the future. These rules became known as the rules against perpetuities.

The word "perpetuity" literally means, "the state or quality of being perpetual". In other words, "lasting or enduring forever or for an indefinitely long time". It has been noted that:

> [t]he word perpetuity was probably first used in the English courts about the end of the sixteenth century. It has since been used in at least three different senses, namely (1) a limitation in the nature of an unbarrable entail, or (2) an inalienable interest, or (3) an interest which vests in interest at too remote a time in the future.

It is the third meaning of the word, namely an interest which vests at too remote a time in the future, which is the subject matter of the rules against perpetuities.

Historically two rules to restrict the power of a landholder to control the future ownership and enjoyment of land have been developed by the courts. These are sometimes referred to as the "old rule against perpetuities", or the *Whitby v. Mitchell*, and the "modern rule against perpetuities". While the ultimate object of both rules is the same, namely to invalidate interests which may vest in interest at too remote a time in the future, the two rules are separate and distinct.

The rule in *Whitby v. Mitchell* originated in the latter part of the sixteenth century; however, it has become known as the rule in *Whitby v. Mitchell* after the seventeenth century English Court of Appeal case which fully discussed the issue. The rule voids any interest given to the issue of an unborn person, together with any subsequent limitations. It applies to both legal and equitable contingent remainders in real property, but it does not apply to personal property. The rule has been abolished by statute in New South Wales, Victoria, Queensland, Western Australia and Tasmania. It is for this reason that the primary focus today, and hence the focus of this article, is on the "modern Rule Against Perpetuities".

The Modern Rule Against Perpetuities

With the rise of the executory interest following the passage of the Statute of Uses 1535, the courts began to uphold the validity of executory devises of potentially long duration. By the latter part of the seventeenth century it became clear that the use of the executory devise could defeat the policy of the courts to restrict the power of landholders to control, from the grave, the use and enjoyment of land; a fact which disturbed members of both the bench and the bar. In the *Duke of Norfolk's Case*, a decision which has been described as "one of the classics of English legal literature and a landmark in the field of equity jurisdiction", Lord Nottingham L.C. laid the foundation of the "modern Rule Against Perpetuities".

Lord Nottingham held that the validity of a future interest is governed by the time within which the interest is to vest. If that time is too remote, the future interest is invalid. In determining whether the time is too remote, consideration was to be given to possible, rather than actual, events. On the facts of the case Lord Nottingham held that a future interest which had to vest, if it vested at all, no later than the expiration of a life in being when the interest was created, was a valid interest.

During the ensuing 200 years, the period of time within which the future interest must vest, if it vests at all, was gradually extended; first to include any actual period of gestation plus a gross period of 21 years after some life in being. By 1833 the courts had sculptured the modern Rule Against Perpetuities, which may be stated as follows:

> An interest is only good if it must vest, if it vests at all, not later than 21 years after the death of some life in being who was alive or *en ventre sa mere* at the creation of the interest. If no such life in being was in existence at the creation of the interest, then the term of 21 years only is allowed.

Elements of the Rule — the general law

The Rule Against Perpetuities can be dissected into a number of elements. When followed sequentially, these elements evolve into a five step process of analyzing a perpetuities problem. These elements will be considered in turn.

ELEMENT: The Rule Against Perpetuities applies to contingent remainders and executory interests, not to vested interests.

The Rule Against Perpetuities invalidates attempts to create interests which will *vest* at too remote a time in the future. Hence, if an interest is vested as at the date of the creation of the interest, the Rule will not apply.

Example 1

Testator (T) devises Blackacre to A for life, then to B for life, then to C for life, then to D in fee simple. (At T's death, A is three years old, B is two years old, C is one year old and D is 10 years old.)

The fact that a substantial period of time may elapse before B, C or D's interest vests in possession is irrelevant, because at the date of the creation of the interest, the life estates in remainder to B and C, and the fee simple remainder to D, are vested in interest. The focus of the Rule is on the nature of the interest created, not on the person to whom the interest is conveyed. If a contingent remainder or an executory interest is created by the instrument, the Rule may apply. If the interest is vested as at the date of the creation of the interest, the Rule will not apply.

ELEMENT: The date of the creation of the interest is dependent upon the nature of the instrument containing the gift.

If the interest is one to which the Rule Against Perpetuities may apply, it is necessary to determine when the perpetuity period begins to run. Under the general law, the perpetuity period begins to run as at "the creation of the interest". The date of creation of the interest will depend on the nature of the instrument containing the gift. If the gift is contained in a will, the perpetuity period will begin to run from the date of the death of the testator. If the gift is contained in an instrument *inter vivos*, the perpetuity period will begin to run from the date the instrument takes effect. For example, if the gift is contained in a deed, the perpetuity period will take effect from the date of execution and delivery of the deed. If the gift is revocable, the perpetuity period runs from the date the settlor releases the power of revocation (if the power of revocation is not revoked, the power will terminate on the settlor's death).

ELEMENT: To constitute a life or lives in being, four conditions must be satisfied: the measuring life or lives must be human; such person or persons must be living at the date of the creation of the interest; if a group of persons is used as the measuring lives, that group cannot be capable of increasing in number after the date of the creation of the interest; and if a group of persons is used as the measuring lives, that group must be ascertainable. In other words, it must be possible to determine what members of the group were alive at the date of the creation of the interest so that it can be determined when the last survivor of that group dies.

Ascertaining the life in being (or "lives in being" in that more than one measuring life can be designated either expressly or by implication) is the major stumbling block in the application of the Rule Against Perpetuities. When determining whether a person or group of persons can constitute a life or lives in being, such a person or group must be viewed as a yardstick against which the validity of the gift can be measured. For the reasons discussed below, the focus should not be on physical capabilities of such person or persons.

When determining whether a person, or group of persons, can constitute a life or lives in being within the meaning of the Rule Against Perpetuities, *all* of the conditions noted above must be satisfied. Each of the four conditions is discussed below.

Condition 1 — measuring lives must be human

This prerequisite is self-explanatory. To quote Meredith J. in *Re Kelly, Clary v. Dillon*:

> If the lives of the dogs or other animals could be taken into account in reckoning the maximum period of "lives in being and 21 years afterwards" any contingent or executory interest might be properly limited, so as only to vest within the lives of specified carp, or tortoises, or other animals that might live for over a hundred years, and for 21 years afterwards, which, of course, is absurd. "Lives" means human lives.

Condition 2 — person(s) must be living at the date of creation of the interest

Condition 3 — group of persons, if used, must not be capable of increasing in number

When analyzing a limitation to determine whether it offends the Rule Against Perpetuities, these conditions, although separate and distinct, are often considered together. To satisfy these conditions it is essential first to determine the date of the creation of the interest. For example, a limitation contained in a will may be valid, whereas the same limitation, if contained in a deed *inter vivos*, may offend the Rule.

Example 2

Testator (T) devises Blackacre to all of my grandchildren in fee simple.

(At T's death, T had two children, X and Y.)

This gift is contained in a will, therefore, the date of creation of the contingent fee simple remainder to T's grandchildren is the date of the death of T. The measuring lives for the purpose of the Rule may be expressly or impliedly designated in the instrument containing the gift. No express designation is contained in this example; however, X and Y are impliedly designated. Obviously, the grandchildren of T must be the issue of the children of T, namely X and Y, therefore X and Y are lives which are necessarily involved in the limitation and which satisfy all of the criteria necessary to constitute lives in being. They are human, they are live at the date of creation of the interest, their number, given the death of T, is not capable of increasing and their number is ascertainable. T's grandchildren cannot be lives in being because subsequent to the date of creation, namely the date of the death of T, X and Y may have more children, therefore conditions 2 and 3 above are not satisfied.

The contingent fee simple remainder to T's grandchildren does not offend the Rule against Perpetuities because the gift to the grandchildren must vest, if it vests at all, within death of the survivor of X and Y plus 21 years. In fact, in this example all of the grandchildren of T will be ascertained as at the death of the survivor of X and Y (neither X nor Y can have any more children — i.e., grandchildren of T — after their death), therefore the fee simple interest will vest in the grandchildren of T immediately upon the death of such survivor. There is no need to employ the 21 years. . . .

If this same gift were contained in a deed *inter vivos*, it would offend the Rule Against Perpetuities and would be invalid under the general law.

Example 3

Grantor (G) gives Blackacre to trustees upon trust for all of G's grandchildren.

(At the date of the deed establishing the trust, G has two children, X and Y, who are both alive).

This gift is contained in a deed *inter vivos*, therefore the date of creation is the date of the execution and delivery of the deed. No express designation of a life in being is contained in the deed. G's children are impliedly designated for the reasons noted in example 2; however, they cannot constitute lives in being. Subsequent to the date of creation, namely the date of the execution and delivery of the deed, G, who is still alive, may have more children and therefore condition 3 necessary to constitute G's children as lives in being, namely that they belong to a class that is not capable of increasing in number, is not satisfied. The only other person impliedly designated in the deed is G and therefore G will be the life in being.

The gift to the grandchildren will be invalid as infringing the Rule Against Perpetuities. It is possible that when G dies, any children alive at her death may have children more than 21 years after G's death. Hence, there is a possibility that the contingent fee simple interest in the grandchildren may vest, if it vests at all, more than 21 years after the death of the life in being at the creation of the interest, namely G. Hence, the gift to the grandchildren will infringe the Rule Against Perpetuities and will be invalid.

Taking this analysis one step further, it was noted above that the measuring lives can be implied in the instrument, as in the above examples, or the measuring lives can be designated expressly. The person or persons designated expressly as a life or lives in being can be selected at random and there is no requirement that they have any connection with the settlor or with the beneficiaries of the gift.

Example 4

Grantor (G) grants Blackacre to trustees on trust for such of my lineal issue who shall be living at the expiration of 20 years from the day of the death of the last survivor of all of the lineal descendants of the late Sir Owen Dixon who shall be living at the date of the execution and delivery of this deed.

The lineal descendants of the late Sir Owen Dixon alive at the date of creation can (admittedly with difficulty and expense) be ascertained, and, given the wording of the grant, that group is not capable of increasing in number subsequent to the date of the creation of the interest. Therefore, such a group constitutes expressly designated measuring lives.

To maximize the perpetuity period, it became a common practice in England, and to a lesser extent in Australia, to include a "royal lives clause" in the instrument. Through the use of the "royal lives clause", vesting of some interests are postponed until 21 years after the death of the last lineal descendant of a named sovereign living at the date of the creation of the interest.

Example 5

Testatrix (T) devises Blackacre to trustees on trust for such of my lineal issue living at the expiration of 20 years from the day of the death of the last survivor of all of the lineal descendants of His late Majesty King George VI who shall be living at the time of my death.

The lineal descendants living at the date of the creation of the interest, namely at the death of T, can be ascertained, are not capable of increasing in number given the *proviso* in the devise that such descendants must be living at T's death, and therefore such an express designation of measuring lives results in a gift which does not offend the Rule Against Perpetuities.

Condition 4 — group of persons, if used, must be ascertainable at the date of creation of the interest.

The group designated, either expressly or impliedly, as the lives in being cannot be so numerous as to be unascertainable.

Example 6

Testator (T) devises Blackacre to trustees to be held for A for life, then for B for life, then for all of my lineal descendants living at the time of the last survivor of all persons who shall be living at the time of my death.

The gift of a life estate in possession to A, and a life estate in remainder to B, are vested interests which fall outside the purview of the Rule Against Perpetuities and are therefore valid. The contingent fee simple remainder to the lineal descendants of T does not escape the Rule. The gift cannot vest until such time as the last measuring life, namely the last survivor of all persons alive at T's death, dies. It would be impossible to determine what members of this group were alive at the date of the creation of the interest, therefore the gift would be void for uncertainty.

Ascertaining who, or what group, constitutes a life or lives in being is a two-step process. First, all of the conditions necessary to constitute a life or lives in being noted above must be satisfied. Secondly, it must be kept firmly in mind that lives in being are used as a yardstick to measure the validity of a limitation contained in an instrument. They are part of the perpetuity formula and therefore the focus should not be on the actual physical attributes of such measuring lives. In other words, when applying the perpetuity formula, the focus is on theoretical possibilities, not on actual events or probabilities. This concept is fundamental to an understanding of the next element of the Rule.

ELEMENT: If, at the commencement of the perpetuity period, it is theoretically possible to construct circumstances in which vesting would occur outside of the period, then the Rule Against Perpetuities is infringed.

Ford and Lee note that the facts existing at the commencement of the perpetuity period, namely the date of the creation of the interest, must be examined to determine whether it is possible for vesting to occur outside the perpetuity period.

If it is logically possible to construct circumstances in which vesting would occur outside the period, then the rule is infringed. This is so even if the postulated circumstances are highly improbable and even if later events make them impossible. In other words, the rule is concerned only with logical possibilities open at the commencement of the period; it is not concerned with practical probabilities, or with actual later events.

The determination of whether there is a theoretical possibility that the interest will not vest within the perpetuity period must be made at the commencement of that period, namely at the date of the creation of the interest. This is sometimes referred to as the "initial certainty rule". To illustrate this point reference often is made to extreme examples of its application, two of which have been metaphorically referred to as the "fertile octogenarian", and the "precocious toddler".

The fertile octogenarian and *the precocious toddler*

Under the general law there is a conclusive presumption of fertility. Males are deemed to be capable of begetting children, and females are deemed to be capable of giving birth to children, regardless of age or physiological facts.

Example 7

The fertile octogenarian

Testator (T) devises Blackacre to trustees on trust for his wife, A, for life, then for A's children for their lives, then for such of A's grandchildren who attain the age of 21 years.

(At the date of creation of the interest, namely the death of T, A is 80 years old and has two children, X and Y, aged 60 and 55 years respectively. A also has three grandchildren, the eldest of which is 18 years).

The gift to A's grandchildren infringes the Rule Against Perpetuities and is invalid. The Rule is concerned with theoretical possibilities, not probabilities, therefore A, notwithstanding her age, is presumed to be capable of having more children subsequent to the death of T. A's children belong to a group which is capable of increasing in number; therefore A's children cannot be lives in being for the purposes of the Rule. A is the only person impliedly designated in the instrument who satisfies all of the conditions necessary to constitute a life in being; therefore, for the contingent fee simple interest to the grandchildren to be valid, it must vest, if it vests at all, within 21 years from the death of A. There is a theoretical possibility that A may have a child, Z, and then die. Z may then have a child who will not have attained the age of 21 years within 21 years after A's death. Hence, under the general law the gift to the grandchildren of A is void as infringing the Rule Against Perpetuities.

Example 8

The precocious toddler

Testator (T) devises Blackacre to A for life, then for such of A's grandchildren living at T's death or born within five years thereafter who shall attain the age of 21 years.

(At the date of the creation of the interest, namely the death of T, A is a widow aged 65. She has two children, and one grandchild aged eight years.)

The gift to A's grandchildren infringes the Rule Against Perpetuities and is invalid. Pursuant to the presumption of fertility, A, as in Example 7, is presumed to be capable of having more children subsequent to the death of T. A's children, therefore, belong to a group which is capable of increasing in number and cannot be lives in being for the purposes of the Rule. Given the wording of the limitation, A's grandchildren cannot be lives in being for the same reason. How is this possible? Theoretically, A could have a child after T's death, and that child could, in turn, have a child within five years of T's death. Admittedly A's child would have to become a parent when aged less than five years; a "precocious toddler".

Examples 7 and 8 illustrate clearly that the focus for the purposes of the Rule is on theoretical, not physiological, possibilities.

Tackling a perpetuities problem

Having outlined and discussed the essential elements of the Rule Against Perpetuities, a four-step approach to solving a perpetuities problem under the general law can be distilled.

Step 1: is the limitation contained in the instrument one to which the Rule Against Perpetuities may apply?

Applicable element: *The Rule Against Perpetuities applies to contingent remainders and executory interests, not to vested interests.*

Step 2: What is the date of creation of the interest?

Applicable element: *The date of the creation of the interest is dependent upon the nature of the instrument containing the gift.*

• will: date of death of testator

• instrument *inter vivos*: date the instrument takes effect

Step 3: Who is/are the life/lives in being?

Applicable element: *To constitute a life or lives in being, four conditions must be satisfied*:

• *condition 1*: measuring life/lives must be human

• *condition 2*: measuring life/lives must be living at the date of the creation of the interest

• *condition 3*: if a group of persons is used as the measuring lives, that group cannot be capable of increasing in number after the date of the creation of the interest

• *condition 4*: if a group of persons is used as the measuring lives, that group must be ascertainable.

Step 4: Is it theoretically possible to construct circumstances in which vesting would occur outside of the perpetuity period?

Applicable element: *If, at the commencement of the perpetuity period, it is theoretically possible to construct circumstances in which vesting would occur outside of the period, then the Rule Against Perpetuities is infringed.*

• The rule is only concerned with theoretical possibilities open at the commencement of the perpetuity period; it is not concerned with practical probabilities, or with actual events occurring after the date of creation of the interest.

The application of this four step process is illustrated in the following example:

Example 9

By settlement inter vivos *settlor (S) conveys Blackacre to trustees upon trust for such of my grandchildren as shall attain the age of 21 years.*

(Settlor, at the date of settlement, has two children, B aged three years and C aged one year.)

Step 1: Given that the beneficiaries are not yet ascertained, the limitation is a contingent remainder to which the Rule Against Perpetuities applies.

Step 2: The date of creation of an instrument *inter vivos* is the date the instrument takes effect, in this case the date of settlement.

Step 3: The only person who satisfies all four conditions to constitute a life in being is S. Her children cannot be lives in being because, subsequent to the date of creation, namely the date of settlement, S could have more children; therefore, conditions 3 and 4 are not satisfied. At the date of creation S has no grandchildren; therefore, pursuant to condition 2, her grandchildren cannot be lives in being. Hence, the maximum perpetuity period is S's lifetime plus 21 years.

Step 4: It is theoretically possible to construct circumstances in which vesting would occur outside of the perpetuity period. S's children could have children who are born after the death of S and therefore will not reach the age of 21 years within the perpetuity period. The limitation offends the Rule Against Perpetuities and is invalid under the general law. . . .

Statutory Modification of the Rule Against Perpetuities — the final step

In an attempt to remove some of the problems associated with the general law application of the Rule Against Perpetuities, a number of Australian jurisdictions have introduced legislation which modifies the Rule.

The fifth step can be expressed as follows:

Step 5: Can the limitation which is invalid under the general law be saved through an application of the statutory modifications to the Rule?

One thing must be kept in mind; in most cases the legislation modifies, but does not abrogate, the Rule. The applicable statute may save the interest once it is clear that the Rule has been infringed, but generally reference to the statute only follows a determination of the validity of the limitation under the general law. . . .

Conclusion

If understood and applied methodically, the five-step approach to a perpetuities problem outlined in this article may dispel the aura of confusion which surrounds the Rule Against Perpetuities. The focus has been on the general law application of the Rule, as it is this aspect of the law which causes the most difficulty. If the *schema* proposed is followed, a once painful experience may be transformed into a pleasurable pursuit. At the very least, those tackling a perpetuities problem will survive the encounter with their reputations intact.

QUESTIONS

1. *Hees v. Higgins* 1983 CarswellBC 459 (C.A.) involved a 10-year lease with a right to renew for a further 10-year term. The lease also contained the following clause which created an option to purchase the leased property:

> Whether or not this Lease or any renewal hereof shall have meanwhile expired from effluxion of time, and subject to the Lessor's rights under Sub-paragraph (1) and Sub-paragraph (2) above, the Lessees shall on the death of the survivor of the Lessor and his wife Florence Louise McMeeken, have an option to purchase the lands herein for the aforesaid price of $12,000.00 cash within one (1) year of the death of the survivor of the Lessor and his said wife (provided that the time shall run from the time the Lessees receive notice of the death of such survivor) . . .

Does this clause contravene the rule against perpetuities?

2. In *Elward Estate v. McBay* 1996 CarswellOnt 3556 (Gen. Div.), a will provided that the testator's widow was to receive income from the estate for her life, plus the right to occupy the farm during her lifetime. The will further provided as follows:

> 5. It is my intention to provide a fund for the education and training of my grandchildren and great grandchildren or other deserving children chosen by my executors, and for that purpose I authorize my executors, during the lifetime of my said wife, to expend any amount up to but not exceeding one-fifth of the capital of my estate as it exists after

the payment of any succession duties, the costs of probating my estate and payment of my debts for the following purposes, namely;

6. To apply such portions of the said fund as my executors shall think fair and reasonable towards the higher education or training of any or all of my grandchildren or great-grandchildren or other child or children chosen by my executors to benefit by this fund. To avoid any ambiguity I hereby state that higher education or training shall mean a course or term in a college or university or such other course or training as my executors may decide for any person benefitting from this fund.

7. Upon the decease of my said wife I direct that the residue of my estate remaining undisposed of at that time shall be apportioned in five shares. Two shares thereof shall be paid or transferred to my son Franklin Elward and two shares to my son Edwin Elward and the remaining one share shall remain in my estate as the fund to be used for education and training as provided in paragraph five hereof.

8. I FURTHER DIRECT that when the youngest child of any of my said grandchildren, which grandchild is living at the time of my decease, attains the age of 21 years, then the balance remaining in the said fund shall be divided in equal shares among all my grandchildren and great grandchildren living at the time of such distribution.

Is there a perpetuity problem? Here is what was said by Sheard J. at para. 37:

Mr. Cullity's submission is that "the Residue Trust was intended to continue unless and until the youngest great-grandchild of the deceased attained the age of 21 years. As, at the death of the deceased, there was no certainty that the event would ever occur, it was possible — and it remains possible — that the Residue Trust might continue indefinitely. In consequence, beneficial interests under the Residue Trust might vest outside the perpetuity period. . . ." I agree.

Do you agree?

3. Comment on the meaning and validity of the following clauses. Assume that the common law rule against perpetuities applies.

(a) "[To the trustees of the New Mills Presbyterian Church . . . in trust for the] *continuing Presbyterian Congregation of New Mills. . . .* Provided that said Congregation should at any time unite with any other denomination then said property to revert to the original owner, his heirs and assigns." *McNair v. Creighton* 1999 CarswellNB 87 (Q.B.).

(b) "[To my executor upon the following trusts, namely:] to transfer the residue of my estate to the Communist Party of Canada and in the event my property cannot legally be transferred to the Communist Party of Canada, to be delivered to my nephew, MICHEL LEPAGE, son of JEAN-GUY LEPAGE, during his lifetime and at his death, to be transferred to his son, JOSEPH ERIC YAN LEPAGE." *Lepage v. Communist Party of Canada* 1999 CarswellNB 37 (Q.B.).

(c) "This transaction of purchase and sale is to be closed on or before the 1st day of August, A.D., 1985, or whenever water and sewerage installation has been completed along the aforesaid described lot." *Bérubé v. Babin* 1993 CarswellNB 361 (C.A.).

(d) "I hereby give, devise, and bequeath all the rest, residue, and remainder of my estate, both real and personal, of every nature, and wherever situate to my grandchildren, to be held in trust by my son, Thomas H. Lantz, and my daughter-in-law, Becky Lantz, and used for the educational benefit of all of my grandchildren." *Richards v. Maiden* 34 Va.Cir. 494 (2000).

(e) "I . . . give to my son Albert VanNess Ransom the use of one half of the remainder of my land joining my home farm on the North and running North to the Town of Hubbardton . . . I give to said Albert that part of the same lying North of such line. I give the same to the said Albert during his natural life and after his decease should children survive him I give the use of said land to them during their natural lives and to the survivor of them, and at the decease of the survivor of such children I direct that said land be divided among their children equally share and share alike." *Ransom v. Bebernitz* 782 A.2d 1155 (Ver. S.C., 2001).

(f) To A in fee simple, "SUBJECT TO AND RESERVING UNTO THE VENDOR or his estate, the right to repurchase and receive for the sum of One Dollar Canadian Funds, ($1.00) a re-conveyance thereof, free from mortgages, charges or other encumbrances, of ALL THAT piece or parcel of land herein more particularly described as parcel "C" annexed hereto, upon the provision and availability by appropriate municipal and/or governmental authorities of water and sewage facilities to the property boundaries hereinbefore more particularly described AND the Purchasers, their heirs, executors, administrators, successors and assigns hereby covenant and agree, jointly and severally, that they will immediately undertake, at their cost, to hook up and install the water and sewage facilities in Parcel "B" when they become available and to concurrently reconvey and reassign ALL THOSE lands and premises hereinbefore more particularly described." *Brennan v. Stokes* 2002 CarswellNfld 280, 5 R.P.R. (4th) 266 (T.D.).

4. As Les McCrimmon notes, a child *en ventre sa mere* is treated as a life in being under the common law rule. In recent years questions have emerged about the effect of the new reproductive technologies on the operation of the rule against perpetuities. For instance, should frozen embryos be regarded as lives in being? If they are, what problems arise? What if they are not? See further S. Hoffman & A.P. Morriss, "Birth After Death: Perpetuities and the New Reproductive Technologies" (Ga. L. Rev. forthcoming, 2004).

Scurry Rainbow v. Taylor
2001 CarswellSask 539 (C.A.)

Tallis J.A.:

The principal question on this appeal is whether the appellants' oil and gas "top lease" with the late Harry Herbert Taylor should be rendered void by the rule against perpetuities. In reasons now reported [(1998), 170 Sask. R. 222 (Sask. Q.B.)], the learned trial judge held that the lease was void because it breached that rule and allowed the respondents' action for a declaration to that effect.

I

The background and essential facts with respect to this controversy are not in dispute.

On April 26, 1949, the late Harry Herbert Taylor (father of the respondent Harry Ernest Taylor) granted a ten-year primary term lease to Imperial Oil Ltd. of "all the petroleum and natural gas and related hydrocarbons, except coal and valuable stone, within, upon or under" the land described as The East Half of Section Fifteen (15), in Township Four (4), Range Thirty-two (32), West of the Principal Meridian in the Province of Saskatchewan, in the Dominion of Canada, containing One Hundred and Sixty (160) acres, more or less, according to Dominion Government Survey thereof. Minerals Included. Under the *habendum* clause in this lease, the primary term was for ten years from April 26, 1949, and "for so long thereafter as leased substances were produced from the lands". There was no production and the lease expired at the end of the primary term — April 25, 1959.

On August 7, 1950, Harry Herbert Taylor signed an agreement entitled "Assignment and Conveyance of Petroleum and Natural Gas Royalty and Lease of Minerals" in which he was the grantor and Freeholders Oil Company Limited was the grantee. Under the terms of this "top lease" Mr Taylor granted petroleum rights in the same half section to Freeholders upon expiration of the Imperial Oil lease dated April 26, 1949. (A "top lease" is one which takes effect upon the termination of a prior existing lease: *Meyers v. Freeholders Oil Co. Ltd.*, [1960] S.C.R. 761 (S.C.C.), at 766 *per* Martland J.).

Since the threshold issue at trial was whether this agreement of August 7, 1950 was void by reason of the common law rule against perpetuities, we find it convenient to reproduce the relevant parts of it: . . .

> AND WHEREAS by Petroleum and Natural Gas Lease dated the "26th" day of "April", A.D. "1949", (hereinafter referred to as "the drilling lease"), made between the GRANTOR as lessor and "Imperial Oil Limited" (hereinafter called "the lessee"), the GRANTOR has demised and leased to the LESSEE the petroleum, natural gas and related hydro-carbons within, upon or under the above described land subject to the payment to the GRANTOR of a gross royalty of twelve and one-half per cent. (12 1/2%) of all of the production of the said petroleum, natural gas and related hydro-carbons or any of

them, produced, saved and marketed from the said lands during the currency of the said drilling lease; . . .

AND WHEREAS it has been further agreed by and between the parties hereto that should the said drilling lease between the GRANTOR and the LESSEE terminate from whatsoever cause, or be avoided, or become null and void, or become unenforceable by the LESSEE at any time within a period of forty-two (42) years from the day of the date hereof, then and in that event, all the mines, minerals and mineral rights within, upon or under the above described land shall be subject to the terms of the lease as hereinafter provided, and the GRANTEE will allot and issue to the GRANTOR additional fully paid-up shares in the capital stock of the GRANTEE in such amount as shall increase the number of shares allotted and issued to the GRANTOR to one share for every acre of the above described land, which shares shall be allotted and issued to the GRANTOR upon receipt of actual notice from the GRANTOR that the said drilling lease has been terminated, cancelled, avoided, or has expired;

NOW THEREFORE THIS INDENTURE WITNESSETH and it is agreed by and between the parties hereto as follows:

2. Lease to Grantee —

UPON AND IN THE EVENT OF the termination, cancellation, avoidance or expiration of the said drilling lease between the GRANTOR and the LESSEE, and in consideration of the covenants of the GRANTEE herein contained, the GRANTOR DOTH HEREBY GRANT AND LEASE UNTO THE GRANTEE all the mines, minerals and mineral rights, including the petroleum, natural gas and all related hydro-carbons (hereinafter referred to as "the minerals") within, upon or under the above described lands and all the right, title, estate and interest of the GRANTOR in and to the minerals or any of them within, upon or under any lands excepted from, or roadways, lanes, or rights-of-way adjoining the lands aforesaid together with the exclusive right and privilege to explore, drill for, win, take, remove, store and dispose of, the minerals, and insofar as the GRANTOR has the right so to grant, and for the said purposes, the right of entering upon, using and occupying the said lands or so much thereof and to such extent as may be necessary or convenient, TO HAVE AND TO ENJOY the same for a term of ninety-nine (99) years from the date hereof, renewable at the option of the GRANTEE, and so long thereafter as the minerals or any of them are produced from the said lands. . . .

II

The concept of "top leases" is not unique or unusual in the Saskatchewan oil and gas industry. The evidence adduced at trial established that there are hundreds of such leases in this Province. Tarragon holds approximately 180 leases in the same form as the lease in question. . . .

In some jurisdictions "top leases" are considered accepted business practice in the oil and gas industry: See for example Roach: *The Rule Against Perpetuities — The Validity of the Oil and Gas Top Deed in Texas After Peveto Starkey* (1983) 35 *Baylor Law Review* 399 particularly at 409.

Although these "top leases" have been attacked on other grounds, this is the first case before the Saskatchewan Courts in which the rule against perpetuities has been advanced to void such a lease. . . .

III

The Rule Against Perpetuities

The learned trial judge adopted the classic statement of the modern rule as stated by Professor J.C. Gray (see 170 Sask. R. 231, para. 21.):

> . . . No interest is good unless it must vest, if at all, not later than twenty-one years after some life in being at the creation of the interest.

The learned author of *Halsbury's Laws of England*, (4th ed.), Volume 35, summarizes the rule in the following passage at p. 615:

> 1008. . . . An executory devise or other future limitation to be valid must vest, if at all, within a life or lives in being and 21 years and a possible period for gestation after; it is not sufficient that it may vest within that period. It must be good in its creation, and, unless it is created in such terms that it cannot vest after the expiration of a life or lives in being and 21 years and the period allowed for gestation, it is not valid, and subsequent events cannot make it valid. [Footnotes omitted.]

The exact period of 21 years is the full extent of the perpetuity period in all cases where no life is indicated for the purpose, or where every life indicated has predeceased the testator (*Halsbury's Laws of England*, (4th ed.), Vol. 35, p. 624, para. 1016).

The term "perpetuity" literally means something that lasts forever, but as used in this context it is generally used to refer to limitations of contingent future interests which may or will not vest beyond the period prescribed by the rule. In this context a perpetuity is a limitation upon the common law right of every person to dispose of his land to any other person at his or her discretion. This has led some writers to suggest that the rule against perpetuities is really a rule against remoteness of vesting rather than a rule against perpetuities. (See for example *Appeal of Mifflin* (1888), 121 Pa. 205, 15 A. 525 (U.S. Penn. S.C.) at 526 with particular reference to Gray: *Rule Against Perpetuities*.)

Before the enactment of the *Statute of Wills*, 32 Hen. VIII and the *Statute of Uses*, 27 Hen. VIII, c. 10 (1535) in England, it appears that no question of remoteness in the creation of estates and interests had come before the English Courts.

Executory limitations, like other classes of future interest, were ordinarily created and were a common testamentary method of providing for the future disposition of a testator's property. Such executory limitations created by will were, as to real property, called executory devises and were employed in creating future interests which the strict common law rules of conveyancing did not countenance. The common law did not allow a remainder or other legal estate to be limited after a fee. But under the *Statute of Uses*, and even before they were legalized by that statute, a species of limitations known as "shifting or springing uses" was recognized, which permitted ulterior estates to be created to arise on the defeasance of prior estates in the same property, contrary to the strict rules of the common law.

The *Statute of Uses* provided that the legal title should follow the beneficial interest and vest in the *cestuis que use* "after such quality, manner, form and condition as they had before in or to the use confidence or trust that was in them". Prior to the statute, deeds of bargain and sale and of covenant to stand seised did not operate to convey the title, but only the right to beneficial use. As affecting the land itself, they were regarded as executory contracts. At law they were of no force as conveyances. In equity they were enforced by requiring the person in whom was the legal title to hold that title for the benefit of the person to whom the right of use had been transferred. The result of the *Statute of Uses* was the coming into use of several new modes of conveying legal estates that were wholly unknown to the common law.

After the passage of the *Statute of Wills* and following the analogies furnished by conveyances to uses and in support of the intention of the testator, Courts gradually came to recognize the validity of limitations not permitted in conveyances under the common law.

Executory devises came into use after the *Statute of Wills* and were allowed out of indulgence to testators, that they might, without the intervention of trustees to preserve remainders, establish future interests in strict settlement beyond the reach of those who had the prior estates. The original purpose of such devises was to carry into effect the will of the testator and give effect to limitations over which could not operate as contingent remainders by common law rules. Such stringent rules were derived from a principle of English feudal law that an estate of freehold must be created to commence immediately. . . .

In the period after passing of the *Statute of Uses* and *Statute of Wills*, the transfer of estates to take effect in the future began to encounter restrictions in various ways. Express covenants against alienation were introduced but English Courts of the day thwarted this means of preserving family estates by refusing, on grounds of public policy, to enforce such covenants.

Executory limitations were another method adopted to further the objects of the landowning class. Under the early law and the *Statute of Uses* these limitations were created by deed as springing and shifting uses which had various aspects of perpetuity.

A means of limiting their scope was found in the "rule against perpetuities" so that a shifting or springing use, to be valid, must not by possibility be so limited that it will not take effect within the time allowed by this rule.

As matters developed, the rule's usual application and effect was to prohibit or invalidate attempts to create by limitation, whether executory or by way of remainder, future interests or estates, the vesting of which is postponed beyond the prescribed period.

We do not find it necessary to trace the historical development of this rule against perpetuities in connection with executory limitations, but it is important to observe that the rule had its origin in reference to executory devises of chattels real, and may be traced to early English decisions that certain testamentary decisions were void as against public policy because the estates devised were inalienable or indestructible. The objection of remoteness was not at first suggested but over time it became the doctrine now embodied in the rule.

The origins of the rule must be passed upon and considered in light of the economic, social and political forces at work in seventeenth century England. (For an interesting analysis of the political and legal historical background to this rule See: Haskins: *Extending the Grasp of the Dead Hand: Reflections on the Origins of the Rule Against Perpetuities*, 126 U. of Pa. L. Review 19 (November 1977)).

The genesis of the rule that became known as the rule against perpetuities is the *Duke of Norfolk's Case* (1682), 22 E.R. 931, 3 Chan. Cas. 1 (Eng. Ch.) (1681–1698). In this case Lord Nottingham held that the validity or invalidity of a future interest depended on its remoteness, and not on the nature of the contingency, and that the contingency was required to occur within a life or lives in being. . . .

In *Canadian Long Island Petroleums Ltd. v. Irving Wire Products* (1974), [1975] 2 S.C.R. 715 (S.C.C.), the Court held that a clause in an agreement between joint owners governing operation and development of certain oil properties did not engage the operation of the rule. Under this clause in the agreement each party was given the right of first refusal to acquire the other party's participating interest. Since each party argued that upon the occurrence of a certain event, which was within its own control, the other party would have a first right of purchase for a 30 day period. Given the language of the governing clause, the Court held that the agreement was personal and did not create an interest in land to which the rule could be applicable.

In the course of his reasons, Martland J., speaking for the Court, distilled the history of the rule in the following passages at pp. 726-27:

> In considering the application of the rule against perpetuities in the circumstances of the present case it is useful to consider its background. The history of the rule is outlined in Cheshire's *Modern Real Property*, 10th ed., at pp. 234 and 235, as follows:
>
>> The history of the rules whereby settlors have been prevented from limiting remote interests, is the history of a conflict between two antagonistic ideas. On the one hand there is the desire of the man of means to regulate the future enjoyment of his property for as long a period as possible. The right of making a settlement or a will is a potent weapon in the hands of a declining man, and unless human nature is transformed, the opportunity it offers of fixing the pecuniary destinies of the coming

> generations will not be neglected. A landowner, unless he gives thought to the fiscal consequences, is not always content to leave a large estate at the free disposal of a son. Old age especially, satisfied with its own achievements and often irritated by the apparent follies of a degenerate time, is inclined to restrain each generation of beneficiaries within close limits, and to provide for a series of limited interest. A landowner views the free power of alienation with complacency when it resides in his own hand, but he does not feel the same equanimity with regard to its transfer to others.
>
> But the freedom of alienation and devise was not congenial to the spirit in which great landowners viewed their land. To preserve their family name and position, "to keep the land in the family," seemed to them a desirable and even laudable object, to restrain any individual holder of the land from dealing with it so as to interfere with the interest of subsequent generations of the family in the family land was a necessary means to this end. To contrive restraints on alienation and succession which the law would enforce, to ascertain the furthest limits up to which the law would allow the grasp of the dead hand to be kept on the hand of the living, was the task set by the great landowners before their legal advisers. (Scrutton, *Land in Fetters*, p. 108.)

This aspiration, however, soon aroused the antagonism of the courts. The law is moved, and from the earliest times always has been moved, by a deep-seated antipathy to this human love of power. It is one thing to permit the free power of alienation, another to allow it to be exercised to its own destruction. The view of the law is that no disposition should be allowed which tends to withdraw land from commerce, and in pursuance of this policy two rules have emerged which have successfully prevented the particular evil of "perpetuities," though they are essentially different from each other in nature. The first, directed against inalienable interests and often called the *old rule against perpetuities*, forbids the creation of any form of unbarrable entail; the second, the *modern rule against perpetuities*, invalidates an interest that may vest at too remote a date in the future.

In *Scurry-Rainbow Oil Ltd. v. Galloway Estate*, [1993] 4 W.W.R. 454 (Alta. Q.B.), Hunt J. (now J.A.) addressed the question whether certain gross royalty trust agreements were void under the rule against perpetuities. In the course of her reasons she referred to the policy behind the rule in the following passages at pp. 509-10:

169 It is also worth considering the purpose behind the Rule and its relationship to decisions as to when the Rule has been offended. Morris and Leach, *The Rule Against Perpetuities*, 2nd ed. (London: Stevens & Sons, 1962), have observed at p. 26:

> The Rule against Perpetuities is one of those precepts of judge-made law which, in the interest of producing a workable and satisfactory law fashioned in the public interest, declares that certain intentions of a settlor or testator may not be carried out. *In any system of private property a prohibitory rule is not lightly to be invoked. The prohibition should be imposed only upon interests the creation of which would offer a real threat to the public interest.* The method by which or the words in which a person seeks to create a particular series of interests should be immaterial; if the series of interests ties up the property for too long, the offending interests should be held void, *but if the series of interests is found not to violate sound policy, they should be held valid.* There is no justification for declaring that a given series of

> interests can be created by one method or one formula of language and not by others; the policies underlying the Rule against Perpetuities have no relation to types of instruments or forms of expression. [Emphasis added.]

171 There is nothing in the nature of these royalty arrangements that in any way prevents the development and utilization of the lands. Therefore, the policy behind the Rule is not offended.

IV

Object and Purpose of the Rule

Given the historical background of the rule and in light of the social, economic and political times in which it was formulated, the object and purpose of the rule is obvious. However, we find it convenient to restate the basis for the rule.

The underlying and fundamental purpose of the rule is founded in the public policy of preventing the fettering of the marketability of property over long periods of time by indirect restraints upon its alienation. The general purpose of the rule is to prevent the tying up of property to the detriment of society in general.

The exclusion of property from the stream of commercial development for extended periods of time was perceived by the law as a public evil. Since alienability is the object, the destruction of future interests is the means employed to obtain this object. The rule against perpetuities was developed as a device to cut out the limitations which, if they were allowed to take effect, would produce the consequences which were sought to be avoided. Since this approach was adopted particularly in relation to devolution of estates, the judge-made rule limited the extent to which the "dead hand" could control contingent devolution.

The basis for the rule is succinctly summed up in *Halsbury's Laws of England*, *supra*, in this way at p. 605 at para. 1001:

> *1001. Basis of the rules affecting perpetuities.* The rules of law affecting perpetuities are based upon considerations of public policy. Although the principle of private ownership requires that an owner of property is to have power to dispose as he thinks fit, either during life or on death, of his whole interest in the property he owns, public policy requires that the power should not be abused. Accordingly, from early times, the law has discouraged dispositions of property which either impose restrictions on future alienations of that property, or fetter to an unreasonable extent its future devolution or enjoyment. [Footnote omitted.]

In [*Halisbury's*], the learned author refers to these considerations of public policy articulated in early decisions:

> 1 These considerations were stated in *Stanley v Leigh* (1732) 2 P Wms 686 at 688 per Jekyll M.R., to be "the mischief that would arise to the public from estates remaining for ever or for a long time inalienable or untransferable from one hand to another, being

a damp to industry and prejudice to trade, to which may be added the inconvenience and distress that would be brought on families whose estates are so fettered". . . .

V

Rule Prevailing Over Intention

The common law rule against perpetuities prevails over intention because it is not a rule of construction, but a rule of property. Given the nature of the rule, and under a strict mechanistic application of the rule, it is to be applied irrespective of the question of intention. This means that in the field of administration of estates, the intent of the testator, if it runs counter to the rule, is defeated. In some instances the *cy pres* doctrine had been invoked to ameliorate the harshness of the rule against perpetuities.

Accordingly, the orthodox rule against perpetuities is not to be tested by actualities, but by possibilities. Vesting within the period must be evident at that time without regard to subsequent events. One of the essential elements of the orthodox rule is that at the time the future interest is created, it must appear that the condition precedent to vesting must necessarily happen, if it happens at all, within the prescribed period. A mere possibility, or even a probability, that the estate or interest may vest within the time is not enough.

VI

Given the historical object and purpose of this judge-made rule against perpetuities, the appellants argue that the principal justification for application of the rule does not exist in this case and accordingly the rule should not be applied to the "top lease" in question.

Although a number of other grounds of appeal were raised and fully argued, this threshold issue proceeds on the assumption that a rigid and mechanistic application of the rule would render the top lease void. Having raised this threshold issue in this way, the appellants stress the trial judge's finding that the policy behind the rule was not offended by this top lease. . . .

The respondents contend that this judge-made rule is of such extensive application and so firmly imbedded in our system of jurisprudence as not to be disturbed except by statute.

We now turn to a consideration of this threshold issue. As earlier noted in our consideration of the object and purpose of this rule, it was designed to further alienability and to prevent the tying up of property within the family line for generation on generation. The exclusion of property from the channels of commercial development for extended periods of time was considered to be a public evil.

Since the judge's finding that the policy behind the rule is not offended by the "top lease" in this case, we only need to refer to its commercial background in brief terms. In *Meyers v. Freeholders Oil Ltd., supra*, the Supreme Court of Canada outlined the nature of the Freeholders "top leasing" programme that dates back to the 1950s. As earlier noted, the evidence at trial indicated that there are hundreds of such leases in existence in Saskatchewan — leases that might run afoul of the orthodox rule notwithstanding the fact that parties and their successors relied upon them for fifty years.

"Top leases" are an accepted business practice in the oil and gas industry. They increase actual drilling and competitiveness because oil companies whose leases have been "topped" have a greater incentive to drill on leased lands. If they do not, they stand to lose the lease and make way for someone else to drill.

This top leasing programme is not limited to Saskatchewan. Such leases are considered accepted business practice in other jurisdictions and one can trace their origin to the American oil and gas industry which pre-dates the development of the industry in Western Canada. In *Nantt v. Puckett Energy Co.* (1986), 382 N.W.2d 655 (U.S. N.D.), the North Dakota Supreme Court described top leasing as a "useful and widespread business practice in the oil and gas industry in North Dakota, as well as other regions".

In the case before this Court, the Freeholders "top lease" does not offend the policy behind the rule against perpetuities. The provisions in this "top lease" encourage commercial development and drilling activity on the land. In a commercial sense, the provisions do not clog alienation.

Given the development of top leasing as a useful and desirable type of transaction in the oil and gas industry, the application of the orthodox rule against perpetuities does not reflect modern realities. When the rule was formulated by judges in earlier times, top leases in the oil and gas industry were not contemplated.

It could not have been intended to apply to such transactions and no worthwhile social or economic purpose is served by applying it to this type of transaction in the oil and gas industry. When the rule is transposed from its original setting and is placed among interests unknown at the time, the appellants contend that it must be justified by new conditions before being permitted to strike down considered transactions of this nature.

The appellants argue that these factors militate against a rigid mechanistic operation and application of the rule in the present case. Since the "top lease" encourages commercial development in the industry rather than offending the object and purpose of the rule, they argue that its application cannot be justified. In this case the "lease", which has existed since 1950, was entered into in good faith and acted upon by all the parties involved for many decades.

In many instances exceptions have been created to this rule. Speaking generally, some of these exceptions might well have the effect of allowing an interest to remain uncertain beyond the rule period. Nevertheless, several exceptions of this type are well established, such as gifts to charities, rights of entry, possibilities of reverter, resulting trusts, and covenants running with the land: Also see *Halsbury's Laws of England, supra*, p. 612, para. 1006, *Unobjectionable perpetual interests*.

Furthermore, application of the "wait and see" doctrine would validate the impugned top lease in this case because the interest actually vested within the perpetuity period. Dissatisfaction with the harshness of the "certainty of vesting" requirement under the orthodox rule of perpetuities spawned what has become known as the "wait and see" doctrine. In some jurisdictions this doctrine has been adopted by statute. . . . In other jurisdictions the dissatisfaction with the harshness of the "certainty of vesting" requirement led some courts, even in the absence of a statute modifying the rule, to relieve against such severity by substituting for the "certainty of vesting" requirement, a rule permitting consideration of events occurring after inception of the instrument which are relevant to the vesting of a future instrument, so that if the contingency upon which the interest is limited actually occurs within the period of the rule, the interest is valid.

VIII

The respondents vigorously argue that this judge-made rule against perpetuities is of such extensive application and so firmly imbedded in our legal system that it should not be modified or disturbed except by statute. They submit that it is the exclusive province of the legislature to abolish or limit the application of the rule.

The respondents further point to the fact that Bill No. 42 — *An Act to abolish the Rules Against Perpetuities and The Accumulation Act and to enact Consequential Amendments* — was introduced in 1995. When presented for second reading, the debate was adjourned on April 25, 1995 and apparently the matter died on the Order paper. The tone of the short debate indicated some concern with the complete abolition of the rules as recommended by the Law Reform Commission. There was also an expressed appreciation of the need to improve competitiveness in the oil and gas industry. . . .

Given the trial judge's conclusion and our concurring view that the object and purpose of the rule against perpetuities is not offended by the top lease in question, we are persuaded that this is an appropriate case for this Court to intervene and determine that the top lease in question is not rendered void. In arriving at this conclusion, we find the reasoning and approach of the Supreme Court of Canada in cases such as *Salituro*, *Tolofson* and *Morguard Investments Ltd.* to be persuasive. As well, the decision of the House of Lords in *Arthur J S Hall & Co.* demonstrates the need to reexamine archaic rules of common law which cannot be justified in modern society.

The genius of the common law lies in its adaptiveness to changing times. Its basic principles were not meant to become rigid formulae, inflexible and resistant to new developments or changing concepts in the commercial world. Since common law rules are judge-made rules, the Court can make exceptions to such rules when changing conditions so mandate. Common law rules may be tweaked to do justice between the parties when a rigid and mechanistic application of a rule would run counter to the object and purpose of the rule. . . .

Appeal allowed.

NOTE

The dissenting opinion of Jackson J.A. has been omitted.

QUESTIONS AND COMMENTS

1. Why was the top lease contingent?

2. What policies support this ruling?

3. The case of *PanCanadian Petroleum Ltd. v. Husky Oil Operations Ltd.* 1994 CarswellAlta 293 (Q.B.) involved rights to extract petroleum (classified as *profits à prendre*, to be discussed in Chapter 10). Two separate agreements were entered into, both of which contained the following clause:

> TO HAVE AND ENJOY the same for the primary term of twenty-five (25) years from the date hereof and so long thereafter as the leased substances, or any of them, are produced from the said lands or the pooled lands, subject to the sooner termination of the said term, and subject also to the renewal of the said term, all as hereinafter set forth.

A clause gave the grantee the option to a "renewal lease of the leased substances in the said lands for a further primary term of twenty-five (25) years . . ."

What would be the rights of the parties in the event that production was ongoing at the end of the first 25 year period? What if it was not?

4. In *PanCanadian* it was held that the option to renew was void as contrary to the rule against perpetuities. Can that case be distinguished from *Scurry Rainbow*?

5. *Scurry Rainbow* represents a rare attempt at judicial reform of the common law rule against perpetuities. A number of reform initiatives have been undertaken over the last 40 years or so. Generally speaking, these statutes soften the application of the rule. Indeed, in Manitoba, the rule has been abolished altogether: *The Perpetuities and Accumulations Act*, C.C.S.M., c. P33.

6. The approach followed in the Northwest Territories (and Nunavut) reflects a common strategy found among the Canadian reforms. Set out below are provisions

drawn from the *Perpetuties Act*, R.S.N.W.T. 1988, c. P-3. As a general rule, the Act applies to dispositions taking effect after July 8, 1968. Identify the changes to the common law rule introduced by these sections. In what way, if at all, do the reforms curtail or expand the ambit of the rule against perpetuities?

Perpetuities Act
R.S.N.W.T. 1988, c. P-3

1. In this Act,

"in being" means living or *en ventre sa mere*;

"limitation" includes any provision by which property or any interest in property is disposed of, created or conferred. . . .

3. The rule of law known as the rule against perpetuities continues to have full effect except as provided in this Act.

4. No limitation creating a contingent interest in real or personal property shall be treated as or declared to be invalid as violating the rule against perpetuities by reason only of the fact that there is a possibility of that interest vesting beyond the perpetuity period.

5.(1) Every contingent interest in real or personal property that is capable of vesting within or beyond the perpetuity period is presumptively valid until actual events establish

(a) that the interest is incapable of vesting within the perpetuity period, in which case the interest, unless validated by the application of s. 9 or 10, shall be treated as void or declared to be void; or

(b) that the interest is incapable of vesting beyond the perpetuity period, in which case the interest shall be treated as valid or declared to be valid. . . .

7.(1) Except as provided in s. 10 and ss. 14(3), 16(2) and (3), the perpetuity period shall be measured in the same way as if this Act has not been passed, but, in measuring that period by including a life in being when the interest was created, no life shall be included other than that of any person whose life, at the time the interest was created, limits or is a relevant factor that limits in some way the period within which the conditions for vesting of the interest may occur.

(2) A life that is a relevant factor in limiting the time for vesting of any part of a gift to a class shall be a relevant life in relation to the entire class.

(3) Where there is no life satisfying the conditions of subsection (1), the perpetuity period is 21 years.

8.(1) Where, in any proceeding respecting the rule against perpetuities, a question arises that turns on the ability of a person to have a child at some future time, it shall be presumed

(a) that a male is able to have a child at the age of 14 years or over, but not under that age, and

(b) that a female is able to have a child at the age of 12 years or over, but not under that age or over the age of 55 years,

but, in the case of a living person, evidence may be given to show that he or she will or will not be able to have a child at the time in question. . . .

9.(1) For the purpose of this section, a person shall be treated

(a) as a member of a class if in his or her case all conditions identifying a member of a class are satisfied; and

(b) as a potential member of a class if in his or her case some only of those conditions are satisfied but there is a possibility that the remainder will in time be satisfied.

(2) Where

(a) a limitation creates an interest in real or personal property by reference to the attainment by any person or persons of a specified age exceeding 21 years, and

(b) actual events existing at the time the interest was created or at any subsequent time establish that the interest would, but for this section, be void as incapable of vesting within the perpetuity period, but that it would not be void if the specified age had been 21 years,

the limitation shall be read as if, instead of referring to the age specified, it had referred to the age nearest the age specified that would, if specified instead, have prevented the interest from being so void.

(3) Where the inclusion of any persons, being potential members of a class or unborn persons who at birth would become members or potential members of the class, prevents s. (2) from operating to save a limitation creating an interest in favour of a class of person from being void for remoteness, such persons shall be excluded from the class for all purposes of the limitation, and the limitation takes effect accordingly.

(4) Where

(a) a limitation creates an interest in favour of a class to which subsection (3) does not apply, and

(b) actual events at the time of the creation of the interest or at any subsequent time establish that, but for this subsection, the inclusion of any persons, being potential members of a class or unborn persons who at birth would become members or potential members of the class, would cause the limitation to the class to be void for remoteness,

such persons shall be excluded from the class for all purposes of the limitation, and the limitation takes effect accordingly.

10. Where

(a) any disposition is made in favour of any spouse of a person in being at the commencement of the perpetuity period, or

(b) a limitation creates an interest in real or personal property by reference to the time of the death of the survivor of a person in being at the commencement of the perpetuity period and any spouse of that person,

for the purpose of validating any such disposition or limitation that but for this section would be void as offending the rule against perpetuities as modi fied by this Act, the spouse of such person shall be deemed to be a life in being at the commencement of the perpetuity period even though the spouse was not born until after that time. . . .

14.(1) The rule against perpetuities does not apply to an option to acquire for valuable consideration an interest reversionary on the term of a lease

(a) if the option is exercisable only by the lessee or his or her successors in title; and

(b) if the option ceases to be exercisable at or before the expiration of one year following the determination of the lease.

(2) Subsection (1) applies to an agreement for a lease as it applies to a lease, and "lessee" shall be construed accordingly.

(3) In the case of all other options to acquire for valuable consideration any interest in land, the perpetuity period under the rule against perpetuities is 21 years, and any such option that according to its terms is exercisable at a date more than 21 years from the date of its creation is void on the expiration of 21 years from the date of its creation as between the person by whom it was made and the person to whom or in whose favour it was made and all persons claiming through either or both of them, and no remedy lies for giving effect to it or making restitution for its lack of effect.

(4) The rule against perpetuities does not apply, nor does s. (3) apply, to options to renew a lease.

15. In the case of an easement, *profit a prendre* or other similar interest to which the rule against perpetuities may be applicable,

(a) the perpetuity period is 40 years from the time of the creation of the easement, *profit a prendre* or other similar interest;

(b) the validity or invalidity of the easement, *profit a prendre* or other similar interest, so far as remoteness is concerned, shall be determined by actual events within the 40-year period; and

(c) the easement, *profit a prendre* or other similar interest is void only for remoteness if, and to the extent that, it fails to acquire the characteristics of a present exercisable right in the servient land within the 40-year period.

16.(1) In the case of

(a) a possibility of reverter on the determination of a determinable fee simple, or

(b) a possibility of a resulting trust on the determination of any determinable interest in any real or personal property,

the rule against perpetuities as modified by this Act applies in relation to the provision causing the interest to be determinable as it would apply if that provision were expressed in the form of a condition subsequent giving rise on its breach to right of re-entry or an equivalent right in the case of personal property and, where the event that determines the determinable interest does not occur within the perpetuity period, the provision shall be treated as void for remoteness and the determinable interest becomes an absolute interest.

(2) In the case of

(a) a possibility of reverter on the determination of a determinable fee simple,

(b) a possibility of a resulting trust on the determination of any determinable interest in any real or personal property,

(c) a right of re-entry following on a condition subsequent, or

(d) an equivalent right in personal property,

the perpetuity period shall be measured as if the event determining the prior interest were a condition to the vesting of the subsequent interest, and failing any life in being at the time the interests were created that limits or is a relevant factor that limits in some way the period within which that event may take place, the perpetuity period is 21 years from the time when the interests were created.

(3) Even though some life or lives in being may be relevant in determining the perpetuity period under s. (2), the perpetuity period for the purposes of this section shall not exceed a period of 40 years from the time when the interests were created and shall be the lesser of a period of 40 years and a period composed of the relevant life or lives in being and 21 years. . . .

QUESTIONS

1. The use of a "wait and see" test is common among the patchwork reforms of the rule against perpetuities found in Canada and elsewhere. What drawbacks are associated with such an approach?

2. Using both the common law rule against perpetuities and the provisions of the Northwest Territories statute, analyze the following dispositions. Assume that all of the property interests mentioned below are equitable and, unless otherwise stated, are contained in a will.

(a) "To my widow for life. On her death, to such of my grandchildren as reach 30 years of age."

(b) "To my son [a bachelor] for life. Thereafter to his widow for her life. The property shall then pass to their oldest surviving child."

(c) "To the Y.M.C.A. for so long as the land is used for recreational purposes."

(d) "To my daughter Kate Rowlands, provided that should she cease to be a Canadian citizen, the land shall revert to my estate."

(e) "To such of my children as shall attain the age of 25 and marry." Assume that at the time of her decease, the testator had two children, aged 6 and 9.

(f) *Inter vivos* transfer: "To such of my grandchildren as attain 18 years of age." Assume that at the time of the grant the testator has 3 children, aged 8, 12 and 16, but no grandchildren.

(g) "I give Whiteacre unto and to the use of my executors to hold in trust for whichever of my granddaughters is the first to turn 21 and marry. If none do, then a gift over in trust for my son, Phipson Ackers."

3. What are the drafting lessons that emerge from the materials covered in this chapter?

CHAPTER 8

LEASES, LICENCES AND BAILMENTS

1. INTRODUCTION

Many of the topics covered in this Casebook may seem removed from the life experiences of law students. However, it is probably the case that most Canadians are tenants at one point or another in their life. In that role it is hard not to have a sense of powerlessness; it is hard not to regard one as perilously living under a roof owned by someone else. The ostensible jumble of rules that govern that kind of property relationship has a deeply embedded legal structure. These foundational elements will be considered in this chapter.

Leases, as we saw in Chapter 2, are described as "chattels real". This curious designation owes its origins to the writ system developed in the common law, and denotes that while a lease was initially regarded as personalty (a chattel), it obviously resembles other land (or real) rights. The lease did not initially hold a place within the feudal scheme of estates. In other words, it did not run with the land, and so could not bind new owners of the freehold. And the real actions were not available to the tenant.

In time, the law's treatment of the leased changed, largely as a means to bolster the otherwise precarious position of tenant farmers. A tenant wrongly ousted could seek an order of ejectment, a remedy that also serves as a convenient and effective means of redress for freeholders.

The law of landlord and tenant continues to change, and indeed its contractual facets are again prominent, especially in the shaping of remedies. Moreover, the law has become bifurcated. Common law doctrine, with some modifications, lies at the core of the law of commercial leases. Residential tenancies have undergone a far greater degree of statutory reconfiguration, largely in response to the power relationship typically found between landlords and tenants.

This chapter also addresses two related concepts: licences and bailments. The former occupies the space once occupied by the lease itself, for a licence *simpliciter* is an *in personam* right even though it may relate to a given parcel of land. A bailment is a lease-like right to chattels.

2. THE NATURE OF A LEASE

There are four kinds of leases recognised by the common law: a fixed term lease (*e.g.*, for ten years), a period lease (such as from month-to-month), a tenancy at will (which may be terminated at any time by either the landlord and tenant), and a tenancy at sufferance (which arises when a tenant overholds after the expiration of a term. It is acknowledged that the treatment of this situation as a true tenancy is somewhat fictional). A perpetual lease, being by definition without a certain term, can be created by statute; it is a creature unknown to the common law.

A lease must relate to a given property between ascertained persons (landlord(s) and tenant(s)). When the tenancy is for a fixed term, its starting date must be ascertainable, and its maximum duration must be certain or ascertainable at the commencement of the term: see *Black v. Blair Athol Farms Ltd.* 1996 CarswellMan 123, [1996] 5 W.W.R. 516 (C.A.) where the leading authorities are cited. The payment of a rent is not an essential ingredient: a leasehold right may be given as a gift. A lease must also contain a grant of the leasehold interest; a "demise" as it is called.

But what rights of ownership — dominion and control — are conferred by the granting of a tenancy? That question is occasionally posed this way: is the right conferred a leasehold properly so-called, or is it a mere licence — a permission to do that which otherwise would amount to a trespass? The lease-licence distinction was at the centre of the dispute in the recent New Zealand case of *Fatac Ltd. (in liquidation) v. Commissioner of Inland Revenue*, below.

Fatac Ltd. (in liquidation) v. Commissioner of Inland Revenue [2002] NZCA 269

[Puhinui was the owner of a 9.9021 ha property in South Auckland. Part of the land was a quarry. In 1991 Puhinui granted Atlas the right to operate the quarry for a period of twelve years, renewable for a further three years. In 1996 Puhinui agreed to sell the entire property to Mt Wellington. This case involved a determination of which of the parties to the sale agreement was liable for the payment of GST. This in turn depended on whether the lands were "tenanted property" as described in the sale document.]

Fisher J.:

Introduction

This case is mainly about the distinction between tenancies and licences. The distinguishing feature of a tenancy always used to be the right to exclusive possession. A broader approach held sway for 30 years of the mid-twentieth century, largely at the instigation of Lord Denning. England returned to orthodoxy in 1985 but in the meantime New Zealand had followed the broader path. It has prevailed in this country ever since. There is an irony in New Zealand's continuing legacy of an English adventure since abandoned by the English. We do not think that the broader approach stands close scrutiny in logic or principle. The conclusion reached in this judgment is that it is time to return to exclusive possession as the fundamental test. . . .

Distinction between tenancy and licence

In its conventional sense a tenancy is an interest in land conferring the right to possess it for a limited period. A licence is a mere permission to be on the land, with or without additional permission to perform specified acts there. The former creates an estate in the land; the latter does not.

The distinction has usually assumed significance for occupiers who would enjoy statutory protection against eviction only if they were tenants rather than licencees. It has also affected the availability of relief against forfeiture, the right to distrain for unpaid rent, proprietary interests as against third parties, assignability and liability to pay local body rates. Unsurprisingly, policy considerations and implied legislative intentions have sometimes influenced the outcome in those contexts. Authorities are to be read with that caution in mind. . . .

In the present case the object is purely to ascertain the intention of the parties when they used the expression "tenanted" for the purpose of allocating GST obligations between themselves. Nevertheless it seems reasonable to infer that, in the absence of any express indications to the contrary, when they used that expression the parties contemplated "tenancy" in the sense usually understood by lawyers. . . .

Developments in the tenancy/licence distinction in England

Over the past hundred years the English approach to the tenancy/licence distinction has effectively described a circle: Cheshire & Burn's *Modern Law of Real Property* (15th ed., Butterworths, 1994) p. 362 and see further *Street v. Mountford* [1985] A.C. 809 (H.L.). Traditionally, the crucial question was whether the occupier had the right to exclusive possession. Typical was *Glenwood Lumber Co. Ltd v. Phillips* [1904] A.C. 405 where the grant of a right to hold an area of land for the cutting and removal of timber was held to constitute a tenancy. Delivering the advice of the Privy Council, Lord Davey said this (409):

> In the so-called licence itself it is called indifferently a licence and a demise but in the Act it is spoken of as a lease, and the holder of it is described as the lessee. It is not, however, a question of words but of substance. *If the effect of the instrument is to give the holder an exclusive right of occupation* of the land, though subject to certain reservations or to a restriction of the purposes for which it may be used, it is in law a demise of the land itself. [Emphasis added.]

Chiefly under the influence of Lord Denning, the mid-twentieth century saw a temporary English departure from that approach — see, for example, *Errington v. Errington* [1952] 1 K.B. 290 at 298; *Cobb v. Lane* [1952] 2 All E.R. 1119 at 1120–2; *Isaac v. Hotel de Paris Limited* [1960] 1 W.L.R. 239 at 245; *Shell-Mex & BP Limited v. Manchester Garages Limited* [1971] 1 W.L.R. 612 at 615; and *Marchant v. Charters* [1977] 3 All E.R. 318 (C.A.). Speaking for the Privy Council in *Isaac v. Hotel de Paris, supra*, at 245 Lord Denning said:

> The intention of the parties is the paramount consideration and while the fact of exclusive possession together with the payment of rent is of first importance, the circumstances in which exclusive possession has been given and the character in which money paid as rent has been received are also matters to be considered.

In *Shell-Mex*, *supra*, at 615 he went further, stating:

> Broadly speaking, we have to see whether it is a personal privilege given to a person (in which case it is a licence) or whether it grants an interest in land (in which case it is a tenancy). At one time it used to be thought that exclusive possession was a decisive factor. But that is not so. It depends on broader considerations altogether. Primarily on whether it is personal in its nature or not.

The English Courts returned to orthodoxy in 1985. Delivering the unanimous judgment of the House of Lords in *Street v. Mountford*, *supra*, Lord Templeman rejected the passage just quoted from Lord Denning's judgment, pointing out that (824E):

> In my opinion the agreement was only "personal in its nature" and created "a personal privilege" if the agreement did not confer the right to exclusive possession of the filling station. No other test for distinguishing between a contractual tenancy and a contractual licence appears to be understandable or workable.

The right to exclusive possession has remained the core test in England ever since — see, for example, *AG Securities v. Vaughan* [1990] 1 A.C. 417 (H.L.).

For their part, the Australian Courts never departed from the traditional reliance on the right to exclusive possession. Declining to follow the temporary English foray into other approaches, the High Court of Australia reasserted the exclusive possession test in *Radaich v. Smith* (1959) 101 C.L.R. 209 (H.C. of A.) and in subsequent decisions such as *Goldsworthy Mining Limited v. Federal Commissioner of Taxation* (1972) 128 C.L.R. 199, 212 (H.C. of A.).

Rationale for the exclusive possession test

In our view first principles support the right to exclusive possession as the litmus for tenancies. Exclusive possession allows the occupier to use and enjoy the property to the exclusion of strangers. Even the reversioner is excluded except to the extent that a right of inspection and/or repair is expressly reserved by contract or statute. A tenant enjoys those fundamental, if temporary, rights of ownership that stem from exclusive possession for a defined period. Stipulated reservations stem from that premise. The reverse is true for a licensee. Lacking the right to exclusive possession, a licensee can merely enter upon and use the land to the extent that permission has been given. It is this reversal of starting point that provides the rationale for recognising an estate in the land, in the one case, and a mere personal right or permission to enter upon it, in the other: see further *Street v. Mountford*, *supra*, at 816B–D.

Because the tenancy/licence distinction turns on those substantive rights granted to the occupier, it remains unaffected by the label which the parties choose to place upon their transaction. It has sometimes been said that the distinction between tenancies and licences turns on the intention of the parties. This can be misleading unless it is appreciated that the only intention that matters is intention as to substantive rights, not intention as to legal classification. As Lord Templeman put it in *Street v. Mountford, supra*, at 819:

> . . . The consequences in law of the agreement, once concluded, can only be determined by consideration of the effect of the agreement. If the agreement satisfied all the requirements of a tenancy, then the agreement produced a tenancy and the parties cannot alter the effect of the agreement by insisting that they are only creating a licence. The manufacture of a five-pronged implement for manual digging results in a fork even if the manufacturer, unfamiliar with the English language, insists that he intended to make and has made a spade. . . .

Refinements to the exclusive possession test

Analysis of the case law reveals a series of ancillary principles for the purpose of distinguishing tenancies from licences. None of these, however, undermines exclusive possession as the fundamental test. Exclusive possession terminable by the owner at will would, at least as against the owner, be possession in name only. Accordingly a necessary incident of a meaningful right to exclusive possession is a defined term, whether fixed or periodic (see further *Street v. Mountford, supra*, at 816G). The same is true of an intention to be legally bound (*ibid.*, at 819–822).

Rent would seem relevant to the presence or absence of an intention to be legally bound but not a precondition for a tenancy *per se*. In *Street v. Mountford, supra*, at 816G Lord Templeman spoke of rent as one of the central features of a tenancy but provided no rationale for elevating it to a critical requirement. In *Ashburn Anstalt v. Arnold* [1988] 2 All E.R. 147 at 154 (C.A.) Fox L.J. observed that "we are unable to read Lord Templeman's speech in *Street v. Mountford* as laying down a principle of 'no rent, no lease' ". . . .

Limitations upon the purposes to which the occupier can put the land do not negate a tenancy: *Glenwood Lumber Co Ltd v. Phillips, supra*, at 408-409 (P.C.). Exclusive possession is not synonymous with an unqualified range of permitted uses. Equally consistent with the critical role of exclusive possession is the refusal to recognise a tenancy where the owner is prevented by statute from granting a tenancy (*Street v. Mountford* at 821), where the landlord's right of entry to provide services is inconsistent with exclusive possession (*ibid.*, at 818, 824-825), or where the right to exclusive possession can be terminated pursuant to some legal relationship extraneous to that of landlord and tenant.

We would see the last point as the rationale for withholding recognition as a tenancy where an employee occupies an employer's premises in order to perform the employee's duties (*Street v. Mountford* at 818), where there is a purchaser in occupation pursuant to an agreement for sale and purchase (*ibid.*, at 826-827), where occupation is incidental to the holding of an office, and where there is a mortgagee in possession (*ibid.*, at 818). In all of these cases the owner has the legal right to terminate occupation for reasons extraneous to any conventional relationship as landlord and tenant. Tenancies can be prematurely terminated for non-payment of rent or breach of a covenant relating to use of the land. Employee-occupiers can be required to vacate when they are dismissed for redundancy. In the latter case the trigger for the eviction arises independently of the owner-occupier relationship. Consequently there is no tenancy.

A refinement of the last point occurs where the occupier enjoys exclusive possession of only a small proportion of the total area of land that is the subject of the overall contract (see *Waimiha Sawmilling Co Ltd (in liquidation) v. Howe* [1920] N.Z.L.R. 681 (S.C. and C.A.) and *John Fuller and Sons Limited v. Brooks* [1950] N.Z.L.R. 94 (S.C. and C.A.) discussed *infra*). If the contract is primarily concerned with the use of the land as a whole, and occupation of the exclusively possessed portion can be terminated for reasons extraneous to its use and payment, there is no tenancy. All of these matters can be traced back to the indefeasibility of the occupier's possession.

Equally consistent with the exclusive possession test are the many decisions concerned with interpretation of the contract or grant conferring the right to occupation. The fundamental question here is whether the parties intended that the occupier would have the right to exclusive possession. On that subject *de facto* exclusive possession can be an important guide to contractual intentions. That would seem the best explanation for the significance often attached to possession in fact — see, for example, *Isaac v. Hotel de Paris Limited, supra*, at 245; *Street v. Mountford, supra*, at 823 and *Daalman v. Oosterdijk* [1973] 1 N.Z.L.R. 717.

Terminology traditionally used to describe a tenant's right of occupation (e.g. the right "to enter upon, use and enjoy" the land) is significant only if and to the extent that it indicates an intention that the occupier enjoy exclusive possession (*Addiscombe Garden Estates Ltd & Anor v. Crabbe & Ors* [1957] 3 All E.R. 563 (C.A.) at 567). An express right to enter and inspect can imply a general foundation of exclusive possession to which exceptions must be expressly stated (*ibid.*, at 568). Conversely, a requirement that the occupier not impede the owner's "right of possession and control" (*Shell-Mex & BP Limited v. Manchester Garages Limited, supra*, at 616), or that the occupier move from one part of the premises to another at the owner's direction (*Dresden Estates Limited v. Collinson* [1987] 1 E.G.L.R. 45 (C.A.) at 47), tends to negate exclusive possession. All such refinements remain consistent with the right to exclusive possession as the fundamental test.

Recent approaches to the tenancy/licence distinction in New Zealand

Until the mid-20th century New Zealand decisions reflected orthodox reliance upon exclusive possession. . . .

[The Court of Appeal then reviewed the New Zealand caselaw that had adopted the intention approach, including *John Fuller and Sons Limited v. Brooks* [1950]

N.Z.L.R. 94 (S.C. and C.A.) and *Baikie v. Fullerton-Smith & Another* [1961] N.Z.L.R. 901 (C.A.).]

Should New Zealand return to exclusive possession?

Current understanding in this country is reflected in Hinde McMorland & Sim, *Butterworths Land Law in New Zealand* at para 5.008 where the learned authors say:

> In distinguishing between a lease and a licence two factors need to be considered: first, whether a legal right of exclusive possession has been given; and secondly, the intention of the parties to be inferred from the circumstances and from their conduct.

What this passage has in common with *John Fuller, Baikie v. Fullerton-Smith*, and the English counterparts of their day, is the assumption that the right to exclusive possession and the intention of the parties are discrete topics. In our view this is misconceived. Whether the occupier has the right to exclusive possession turns on the effect of the contract or grant. The effect of the contract or grant is a matter of interpretation. Interpretation is the search for the intention of the parties. The quarry is intention as to exclusive possession.

It adds nothing to the exclusive possession test to say that the Court must search for the intention of the parties on that subject. In this context their intention on any other subject is irrelevant. In particular it is for the Court alone to determine the legal classification of the transaction. To the extent that *John Fuller* and *Baikie v. Fullerton-Smith* suggest otherwise, we would no longer follow them. They can not be supported in principle and are no longer supported by overseas authority. . . .

A more principled basis may be discerned for some of the refinements to the exclusive-possession test discussed earlier. Occupation pursuant to an employment relationship, a purchaser in occupation, a mortgagee in possession, occupation pursuant to the holding of an office and exclusive occupation of an area that is small in proportion to the total area affected by the agreement, were examples. Difficult questions of degree will be unavoidable in some of these cases. At times the connection with exclusive possession may seem tenuous. But the sounder analysis would seem to be that in all cases of that type where the occupier is found to have a mere licence, it will be because the initial appearance of a right to exclusive possession is found to be critically undermined by the potential for termination for reasons extraneous to the occupation of the exclusively occupied area. A tenant is safe if he pays the rent and other specified outgoings and observes all covenants relating to use of the property. Not so an employee, purchaser, mortgagee, office holder or business partner. In the latter cases possession is defeasible for reasons unconnected with tenancies.

Conclusions as to the tenancy/licence distinction in New Zealand

Our conclusion is that in this country, as elsewhere, the fundamental distinction between a tenant and a licensee is that the former alone has the right to exclusive possession. For exclusive possession to be meaningful there must be a minimum finite term, whether fixed or periodic. Rent is an important indicator of an intention to be legally bound but its absence does not *per se* negate a tenancy.

The terminology employed by the parties in describing their relationship will be immaterial unless it helps in deciding whether there is a right to exclusive possession. Restrictions upon the use to which the occupier may put the land are not inconsistent with exclusive possession. On the other hand there will be no tenancy where there is no intention to enter into a legally binding relationship or where a tenancy is precluded by statute.

There will similarly be no tenancy where the occupier's right to possession may be terminated for reasons extraneous to the occupation of the land. Examples are occupation pursuant to an employment relationship, a purchaser in occupation, a mortgagee in possession, occupation pursuant to the holding of an office and exclusive occupation of an area that is small in proportion to the total area affected by the agreement. In cases of this kind questions of degree will be unavoidable but the answer is not to be found in the perceived intention of the parties as to the legal classification or dominant purpose of their transaction.

Was the arrangement in this case a tenancy or a licence?

In the present case the relevant transaction is recorded in Mt Wellington's letter of 13 September 1996 read together with the Licence Agreement of 30 April 1991. The lack of provision for rent does not preclude a tenancy. The parties clearly intended to be legally bound. The use of the word "licence" in both documents is irrelevant, as is the purported "right of re-entry" (1991 agreement cls. 11.1 and 11.2) and the right to "distrain for royalty" (cl. 11.3). The focus is not the terminology of the parties but the exclusivity of Atlas's right of occupation.

Even under the 1991 agreement Puhinui and its associated companies had a general right of access to the land so long as they did not obstruct the permitted activities of Atlas (cl. 9.2). The 1996 letter took this further, reserving to Mt Wellington the right to all quarried materials other than basalt. In association with its own right to quarry those materials, Mt Wellington enjoyed the right to set up a screening plant in the quarrying area, and to stockpile and remove all material other than basalt, so long as this did not impede Atlas's quarrying operations. Atlas's right of occupation was far from exclusive.

The point is reinforced by the dwindling area still yielding basalt rock. Atlas's quarrying rights were limited to the residue. As para. 15 of the 1996 letter records, by 1996 a substantial proportion of the original area had already been quarried. The stockpiling referred to in para. 6 of the letter, and the related purposes provision in cl. 6.1 of the original licence, implied continued use of other areas by Atlas but the location and duration of these was not fixed. Coupled with the uses reserved for Mt Wellington, it could not be said that there was any clearly defined area of which Atlas would have the exclusive use, let alone an area that was substantial in relation to the licensed area as a whole. We conclude that the arrangement with Atlas was a licence in the strict sense. It was not a tenancy. . . .

QUESTIONS

1. The following terms are drawn from *Metro-Matic Services Ltd. v. Hulmann* 1973 CarswellOnt 916, 4 O.R. (2d) 462 (C.A.) where, as in *Fatac*, the test of exclusive possession was applied. Based on these terms, has a lease or licence been created?

> Lease Agreement
>
> THIS INDENTURE OF LEASE made the *twentieth* day of November, 1963, BETWEEN: *130 Jameson Apartments* hereinafter called "the Landlord" — and — METRO-MATIC SERVICES LIMITED, hereinafter called "the Tenant"
>
> WHEREAS the Landlord is the owner of certain lands and apartment building(s), known as *130 Jameson Apartments* located at *130 Jameson Avenue*, in the *City* of *Toronto*, hereinafter called the "Landlord's premises".
>
> NOW THIS INDENTURE WITNESSETH:
>
> 1. In consideration of the rents, covenants and agreements hereinafter reserved and contained on the part of the Tenant, the Landlord does demise and lease unto the Tenant the laundry room or rooms located on the *ground* floor(s) of the Landlord's premises.
>
> 2. To have and to hold the demised premises for and during the term of five (5) years to be computed from the *20* day of *November, 1963*; provided that this lease shall automatically renew itself for a further term of Five (5) years, unless either party, at least three months prior to the end of the term hereby granted or any renewal thereof, gives notice in writing to the other party of its intention to terminate this Lease.
>
> 3. Yielding and paying therefor during the term hereby granted and any renewal thereof, unto the Landlord the sum of: *ONE DOLLAR AND TWENTY-FIVE CENTS ($1.25) per suite per month* payable quarterly, the first of such payments to become due and payable on the *31st* day of *December 1963.*
>
> 4. The Tenant covenants and agrees that the demised premises shall be used only for the purpose of carrying on the business of an automatic laundry.
>
> 5. The Landlord covenants with the Tenant for quiet enjoyment.
>
> 6. The Landlord further covenants and agrees as follows:
>
> > (a) the Tenant shall have the sole and exclusive right to install and maintain as many automatic washing machines and dryers, coin changers and soap machines as the

Tenant in its absolute discretion shall deem necessary to properly serve the tenants of the Landlord's premises, as well as installing from time to time such other machines and equipment as the Tenant shall deem necessary.

(b) the authorized employees and agents of the Tenant shall have free access to the demised premises at all reasonable times to install, inspect, service, repair or remove the said machines and equipment and to collect the monies deposited therein;

(c) notwithstanding anything contained in the Landlord and Tenant Act, Revised Statutes of Ontario, 1960, Chapter 206, and amendments thereto (the benefit of which the Landlord hereby irrevocably waives) or any other Act of the Province of Ontario both present and future, the said machines and equipment referred to herein shall not be subject to distress or seizure by the Landlord or its agents by reason of any default whatever by the Tenant, its employees and agents; and the said machines and equipment shall not become fixtures of the Landlord, but shall remain the personal property of the Tenant;

(d) to pay all charges for water and electricity incurred as a result of the use of the said machines and equipment;

(e) to permit the tenants of the Landlord's premises to have free access to the demised premises and to have the use of the machines and equipment at all reasonable times;

(f) in the event the Landlord's premises shall be sold during the term hereby granted or any renewal thereof, then the Landlord shall, prior to the closing of any such purchase and sale, obtain from the purchaser and remit to the Tenant a written acknowledgment by the purchaser that he agrees to be bound by the terms, covenants and conditions set forth herein;

(g) the Landlord will pay all taxes, duties and assessments whatsoever whether municipal, parliamentary or otherwise which during the said term may be charged upon the demised premises or upon the Landlord or Tenant in respect hereof;

(h) no part of the Landlord's premises shall during the term hereby granted or any renewal thereof, be leased, licensed or in any other way granted to any other person or corporation other than the Tenant for any of the aforementioned purposes.

7. Provided that the Tenant may remove the said machines and equipment.

8. Provided that in the event the demised premises are damaged by reason of fire, lightning, tempest or any of the other elements, then rent shall cease until the demised premises are rebuilt.

9. Provided that in the event the Landlord's premises other than the demised premises are rendered wholly unfit for occupancy by the tenants thereof, by reason of fire, lightning, tempest or for any other reason whatever, then the rent provided for herein shall cease until such time as the Landlord's premises are restored to the condition they were in prior to being rendered unfit for occupancy and the said Landlord's premises are again reoccupied to the extent of the occupancy prior to such damage; provided further that in the event only part of the Landlord's premises normally occupied by

tenants are rendered unfit for occupancy, then the rent provided for herein shall abate in the proportion that the part of the Landlord's premises occupied by tenants after such damage bears to that part of the Landlord's premises ordinarily occupied by tenants.

10. Provided that if in the opinion of the Tenant, the Landlord has been in breach of any of the terms, covenants and agreements contained herein, the Tenant may terminate this Lease upon seven (7) days' written notice to the Landlord.

11. Any notice required or contemplated by any of the provisions of this Lease or which the Landlord or Tenant may desire to give to the other shall be sufficiently given to the Tenant by personal delivery or by registered letter, postage prepaid addressed to the Tenant at 153 Viewmount Avenue, Toronto 19, Ontario, and to the Landlord by registered mail postage prepaid and addressed to the said Landlord at *130 Jameson Avenue, Toronto, Ontario*.

12. This Lease shall enure to the benefit of and be binding upon the parties hereto, their heirs, executors, administrators, successors and assigns respectively.

2. In most jurisdictions, formal requirements are mandated for leases of three-years' duration or longer. The origins of these formal requirements can be found in the *Statute of Frauds, 1677*. In *Rogers v. National Drug and Chemical Company* (1911) 24 O.L.R. 486 (C.A.) at 488, Garrow J.A. succinctly described the course of the law on this point:

> Prior to the Statute of Frauds, a demise for a term of years by parol was perfectly lawful. That statute made a writing necessary. And a subsequent statute . . . required the writing to be under seal. If, however, at law, possession had been taken under the parol demise, and rent paid, the tenant was regarded as a tenant, not at will merely, as described in the Statute of Frauds, but as a tenant from year to year, upon the terms contained in the writing, so far as appropriate to such a tenancy; while in equity his rights were much larger, for there the Courts would in a proper case decree specific performance, treating the parol demise, if otherwise sufficient, as an agreement for a lease, with the result that the parties were regarded in equity as landlord and tenant from the time possession was taken.

Notice that according to this statement, the law presumes one type of lease, while at the same time equity may regard it as another. Based on the general principles discussed in Chapter 6, which is it? See *South Shore Venture Capital Ltd. v. Haas* 1994 CarswellNS 161, 371 A.P.R. 9 (S.C.), describing and applying the rule in *Walsh v. Lonsdale* (1882) 21 Ch. D. 9 (C.A.), which provides that an agreement for a lease is as good as a lease.

3. THE NATURE OF THE LANDLORD'S AND TENANT'S INTERESTS

Under a tenancy, the lessee obtains a leasehold interest in the land. As we saw in the *Fatac* case, this confers upon the lessee a right of exclusive possession, a right that is good against even the lessor. At common law, a right of the lessor to enter the premises (say, to inspect the state of repair) must be negotiated with the lessee.

The interest in the property held by lessor under a lease is referred to as a reversion, and both that right and the leasehold interest may be transferred. A transfer of the leasehold can occur in two distinct ways: the tenant may transfer the remainder of the term (called an assignment), or some smaller portion (a sub-lease).When an assignment is made, the assignee will be placed in a direct tenurial relationship with the original landlord. There is no privity of contract between these two people as there was with the original parties, but there is what is called "privity of estate". In the case of a sub-lease, the original tenant retains an interest in the lease. That tenant now wears two hats: as tenant under the original (or head) lease, and as sub-landlord to the sub-tenant. There is neither privity of contract nor estate between the landlord under the initial lease and the sub-tenant.

The distinction between these two situations can be significant. All else being equal, an assignee's liability as against the landlord is controlled by the privity of estate that exists between them. The common law rule, established in *Spencer's* case (1583) 5 Co.Rep.16, 77 E.R. 72, is that all of the "real covenants" in the lease run with an assignment. A comparable principle applies to assignees of the landlord (by virtue of the *Grantees of Reversions Act, 1540*, 32 Hen. 8, c. 34 and its modern counterparts). A real covenant is one that is said to touch and concern the leased property. In other words, it is one that affects the landlord *qua* landlord and the tenant *qua* tenant. This rather vague definition is described further in the case of *Merger Restaurants v. D.M.E. Foods Ltd.*, below.

The rule in *Spencer's Case* concerns the automatic running of benefits and burdens. It presupposes that the parties can be taken to have intended — expressly or impliedly — that these obligations should run. Moreover, the benefits (though not the burdens of a contract) may be assigned under the general law of contract. A contractual assignment obviates the need to rely on *Spencer's* case or the *Grantees of Reversions Act*.

As noted, there is no privity of contract or estate between the landlord and a sub-tenant. Therefore, a default by a sub-tenant gives the landlord no direct recourse against that person. That may not always matter in practice. Consider a situation where L leases Blackacre to T for a term of five years, charging a rent of $1,000 per month. One year later, T validly sub-lets the premises to ST for one year. A sub-tenancy has been created, with T retaining the right to possession once the one-year lease ends. As part of the sub-tenancy, ST agrees to pay rent of $1,000, and out of convenience, it is agreed that the rent will be paid directly to L.

Assume now that ST defaults on the rent payment. L has no direct recourse against ST. But the failure to pay rent under the head lease would (in a conventionally drafted lease) give L the right to re-enter and terminate the head lease. If that were to occur, the sub-lease — which has been carved out of the head lease — would also crumble. The head tenant may wish to stave off that outcome, by paying the landlord, and that tenant could then seek to recover from the sub-tenant. In sum, when a breach of the sub-lease leads to a breach of the head lease, the landlord can pursue a remedy against the head tenant that can redound to the detriment of the sub-tenant.

Merger Restaurants v. D.M.E. Foods Ltd. 1990 CarswellMan 212, 71 D.L.R. (4th) 356 (C.A.)

Philp J.A.:

At issue in this action [appeal from 65 D.L.R. (4th) 142, 63 Man. R. (2d) 183] is the plaintiff's (Merger) parking entitlement under the terms of its lease. It seeks declaratory and injunctive relief.

Merger operates a restaurant, now called Merk's Family Dining, on Pembina Highway in south Winnipeg. The defendant D.M.E. Foods Ltd. (Bonanza Restaurant) operates a restaurant on a neighbouring property. The properties, almost contiguous, are owned by the common landlord, the defendant Lakeview.

Merger's restaurant occupies leased premises in an open mall shopping plaza fronting on the west side of Pembina Highway. The property is designated as lot 2 in a plan of subdivision and its civic address is 1855 Pembina Highway. Bonanza Restaurant occupies a building previously free-standing, located on property designated as lot 5 and known as 1863 Pembina Highway. Lot 2 and lot 5 are separated by a strip of land approximately 50 feet in width owned by the city of Winnipeg and designated as a drainage right-of-way. By agreement with the city, the drainage right-of-way provides motor vehicle access from Pembina Highway to and from lots 2 and 5, and areas lying to the west of lots 2 and 5, and parking for those properties.

Merger has operated a restaurant in the leased premises in the shopping plaza since 1982. It is the assignee of a lease made with the then-owner of the property, Brousseau Bros. Ltd., on 10th June 1980. Bonanza Restaurant has been operated on lot 5 under several ownerships since 1973. Brousseau Bros. Ltd., at the time the owner of lot 2 (more accurately, but of no significance in this action, then the owner of lot 6 which was later subdivided into lots 1 and 2), purchased lot 5 on 18th June 1980. Lakeview purchased lots 2 and 5 from Brousseau Bros. Ltd. in August 1986.

The dispute that forms the background of this action has its origin in construction that took place on lot 5 in the summer and fall of 1987. At that time Lakeview constructed an addition to the Bonanza Restaurant premises and, as well, constructed a multi-tenant commercial addition to the Bonanza Restaurant building. In the result there was a sizeable reduction in the parking stalls available on lot 5 for Bonanza Restaurant and its customers. Prior to the construction there were 74 parking stalls on lot 5 adjacent to the Bonanza Restaurant building.

By an amending agreement dated 6th August 1987, Lakeview agreed with Bonanza Restaurant that its patrons are entitled to park at certain designated stalls and at any available non-designated stalls in parking areas located on lot 5, on lot 2 and on the drainage right-of-way.

Lakeview asserts the right to permit Bonanza Restaurant and its patrons to use the parking lot on lot 2 in common with others, and to designate parking stalls on lot 2 for the exclusive use of Bonanza Restaurant and its patrons. Merger, on the other hand, claims that under its lease it was granted the right to exclusive parking, along with the other tenants of lot 2, their employees and invitees, on the lot 2 parking area that was contemplated at the time its lease was entered into.

The trial before Jewers J. proceeded on the basis of an agreed statement of facts, the relevant leases and agreements, and read-ins from the examinations of the parties on discovery. The trial judge concluded that the parking areas on lot 2 are restricted to the use of Merger and other tenants of lot 2, and their employees and invitees; and that Lakeview is not entitled to designate parking stalls in the parking areas on lot 2 for the exclusive use of Bonanza Restaurant and its patrons. . . .

Although expressed in different ways by the parties, the issues that arise on the appeal may be stated:

1. Do the provisions in Merger's lease restrict the use of the parking areas in lot 2 to Merger and other tenants of lot 2, and their employees and invitees?

2. Is Lakeview entitled, from time to time, to alter the common areas, including parking spaces, on lot 2, and to designate parking spaces on lot 2 for the exclusive use of Bonanza Restaurant and its patrons?

A third issue, not raised in the notice of appeal or in the *factums* of Lakeview and Bonanza Restaurant, but considered by the trial judge and argued on appeal, is the question as to whether the provision in the Merger lease granting common area rights to Merger is a covenant running with the land, and consequently binding upon Lakeview as the successor in title to the lessor, Brousseau Bros. Ltd. . . .

[The Court of Appeal then concluded *inter alia* that the lease under which Merger claimed could not be construed so as to allow Lakeview to permit Bonanza to use parking on Lot 2.]

I turn to the question as to whether the provision in the Merger lease granting common area rights is a covenant running with the land, and consequently binding upon Lakeview as the successor in title to the original lessor, Brousseau Bros. Ltd. Counsel cited, but the trial judge declined to follow, *Kontogonis Hldg. Ltd. v. North West Trust Co.*, 38 A.C.W.S. (2d) 273, B.C.S.C., 29th May 1986 (unreported). In that case, the plaintiff operated a restaurant on the ground floor of a two-storey building. Its landlord was obligated under the lease to "provide . . . an area . . . suitable for and in sufficient size and reasonable proximity to the premises to permit parking during business hours of the lessee for all customers of the restaurant . . ." The defendant sought a declaration that the parking provision did not bind it as the successor in title to the landlord.

The trial judge, Lander J., stated that:

> One could not seriously argue that the parking provision is not beneficial to the plaintiff's operation as a restaurant because common sense dictates that if there is parking in close proximity, particularly in that cold climate, this is a benefit to the business.

Nevertheless, he concluded that the parking provision was not a covenant that ran with the land. He said:

> I find that the parking clause is one which accrues to the tenant or business rather than the demised premises itself. Further, I find that this particular clause is a separate contract which may exist regardless of the landlord/tenant relationship. I find therefore that the successor in title to the lessor is not bound by this covenant.

Although similar in some respects to the case on appeal, *Kontogonis* can be distinguished. Firstly, it would appear that the restaurant in *Kontogonis* occupied premises in a commercial building, not in a shopping plaza. Secondly, the lease in *Kontogonis* obligated the landlord to provide a suitable area for parking; it did not grant common area rights to the restaurant. In any event, I have some difficulty with the finding in *Kontogonis* "that this particular clause is a separate contract which may exist regardless of the landlord/tenant relationship"; and, like Jewers J., I decline to make a similar finding in this case.

The traditional test for a covenant to run with the land is that it must "touch or concern" the subject matter of the lease: *Spencer's Case* (1583), 5 Co. Rep. 16a, 77 E.R. 72. His Honour Judge Forbes, in The General Law of Landlord and Tenant, 7th ed. (1947 Hamish Hamilton Law Books), notes that to run with the land, covenants must either affect the land itself, that is, the "nature, quality or value" of the thing demised (see *Dyson v. Forster*, [1909] A.C. 98 (H.L.)); or the value of the land at the end of the term (see *Congleton Corp. v. Pattison* (1808), 10 East 130, 103 E.R. 725).

There can be no doubt that the extent and availability of parking spaces in a shopping plaza will directly affect the nature and value of the land. The importance of parking facilities to a shopping centre was recognized in a paper ["Parking Provisions"] by Lawrence M. Keay in Shopping Centre Leases (Canada Law Book, 1976), vol. 1, at p. 533:

> The parking facilities included in a shopping centre are an essential element both of the basic concept of a shopping centre and of the economic well-being of the tenant and the landlord.

Jewers J. made the express finding, quoted above, that "parking is essential for the viability" of Merger's restaurant.

The passage of time has not affected the rule of law laid down in *Spencer's Case*, that covenants which touch or concern the land run with the land and are binding upon successors in title. Applying that centuries-old rule to the circumstances of this appeal, I conclude that Merger's common area rights touch or concern the demised premises. Parking facilities are so essential to the operation of Merger's restaurant, and to the well-being of both Merger and Lakeview, that such rights cannot be considered as merely collateral to the demise. It is more than speculation to say that the common area rights immediately affect the nature, quality and value of the demised premises; and that without parking facilities Merger's restaurant and Lakeview's shopping plaza on lot 2 would be doomed to failure. . . .

Appeal dismissed.

NOTE

Leave to appeal to the Supreme Court of Canada was refused: [1991] 3 W.W.R. xxii (S.C.C.).

QUESTIONS AND COMMENTS

1. Consider also this definition of the touch and concern requirement:

> Formulations of definitive tests are always dangerous, but it seems to me that, without claiming to expound an exhaustive guide, the following provides a satisfactory working test for whether, in any given case, a covenant touches and concerns the land: (1) the covenant benefits only the reversioner for time being, and if separated from the reversion ceases to be of benefit to the covenantee; (2) the covenant affects the nature, quality, mode of user or value of the land of the reversioner; (3) the covenant is not expressed to be personal (that is to say neither being given only to a specific reversioner nor in respect of the obligations only of a specific tenant); (4) the fact that a covenant is to pay a sum of money will not prevent it from touching and concerning the land so long as the three foregoing conditions are satisfied and the covenant is connected with something to be done on to or in relation to the land.

P. & A. Swift Investments (A Firm) Respondent v. Combined English Stores Group Plc. [1989] A.C. 632 (H.L.) at 642 (*per* Lord Oliver of Aylmerton).

2. Which of the following promises touch and concern demised land?

(a) the payment of rent: *Parker v. Webb* (1703) 3 Salk. 5, 91 E.R. 656.

(b) a covenant to repair: *Perry v. Bank of Upper Canada* (1866) 16 U.C.C.P. 404, 1865 CarswellOnt 274.

(c) a guarantee by a third party to pay the rent owed by the tenant under the lease: *Lee v. Simmons* [1998] Q.C.A. 1.

(d) a covenant by the landlord to provide housekeeping services for offices: *Barnes v. City of London Real Property Co.* [1918] 2 Ch. 18.

(e) a covenant to pay taxes owing on the land: *Mackinnon v. Crafts, Lee & Gallinger* (1917) 33 D.L.R. 684, 1917 CarswellAlta 15 (C.A.); *Cf. McDuff v. McDougall* (1889) 21 N.S.R. 250, 1889 CarswellNS 2 (C.A.).

(f) an option to purchase the reversion at the end of the lease: *Woodfall v. Clifton* [1905] 2 Ch. 257, affirmed [1905] 2 Ch. 266 (C.A.).

(g) a covenant by the tenant to redecorate the premises at the end of the leasehold: *Boyer v. Warbey* [1953] 1 Q.B. 234 (C.A.).

3. At common law, the lessee has a plenary right to alienate the remainder of the lease. However, a given lease might limit, even eliminate, the lessee's rights of transfer. The lease may provide, for example, that the term may not be transferred at all, or only on the consent of the lessor. It is quite common for the right to transfer to be conditioned on the consent of the landlord with the *proviso* that the landlord's consent cannot be unreasonably withheld. What counts as a valid reason for withholding consent? That is a multi-faceted question. The case of *Sundance Investment Corp. v. Richfield Properties Ltd.*, below, and the notes that follow it, discuss some of the key considerations.

Sundance Investment Corp. v. Richfield Properties Ltd. 1983 CarswellAlta 4, [1983] 2 W.W.R. 493 (C.A.)

Belzil J.A.:

The issue in this appeal is whether the respondent Richfield Properties Limited has unreasonably withheld its consent to a proposed sublease by its lessee, the appellant Sundance Investment Corporation Ltd. The appellant lessee had sought a declaration that it was relieved from obtaining the consent of the respondent lessor to the proposed sublease on the ground that consent was unreasonably withheld.

The respondent Richfield owns the Heritage Hill Plaza, a relatively small neighbourhood shopping centre located on the north-east corner of Heritage Hill Drive and Macleod Trail South in the city of Calgary. There are two major tenants of the shopping centre who between them lease almost the entire shopping centre. The appellant holds a lease of over 60,000 square feet for a 25-year term from 1st February 1973 to 31st January 1998. The second respondent, Beaver Lumber Limited, is the other major tenant, leasing approximately 40 per cent of the available space, where it operates the retail business of a home improvement centre.

Under the terms of the head lease between Richfield and Sundance, Sundance may not assign or sublease any of the lease premises without the prior written consent of the lessor. This consent is not to be "arbitrarily or unreasonably withheld" with the further qualification that a withholding of consent is deemed not to be unreasonable if the other major tenant objects to the "*nature of the business*" to be carried on by the proposed subtenant. The assignment clause in the lease reads as follows:

> The Lessee shall not be entitled to assign this lease or sublet any portion of the demised premises without the prior written consent of the Lessor which consent shall not be arbitrarily or unreasonably withheld, *however it is understood and agreed that the withholding of consent by the Lessor shall not be construed or pleaded as being unrea-*

sonable if the other major tenant occupying the building objects to the nature of the business to be conducted by any sub-tenant or assignee, provided however that the Lessor shall not object to any subletting in respect of a use which would fall within the normal business of a drug store, variety store or junior department store, including food and refreshment services of a kind appropriate thereto. (The italics are Belzil J.A.'s.)

It is common ground that "the other major tenant" referred to in this clause is Beaver.

The appellant is successor to Super S Drugs Ltd. From or about 1st February 1973, to or about 6th September 1978, the appellant carried on business within the leased premises under the name "Super S Drugs". The business was that of a drug store, variety store and junior department store. On or about 6th September 1978, the appellant sold that business to White Cross Pharmacy (1965) Ltd. and approximately half the space leased by the appellant was sublet to White Cross, which has continued to carry on business under the name of "Super S Drugs".

For a period of something in excess of five years, the appellant sublet a portion (3,266 square feet) of its leased space to Town 'N Country Restaurant Ltd. ("Town 'N Country"). The sublease was consented to by Richfield. The space formerly occupied by the restaurant has been vacant since September 1978.

The appellant now proposes to sublet approximately 9,600 square feet of the leased premises, including the space formerly occupied by Town 'N Country, to Foodcorp Western Limited for the operation of a Swiss Chalet Restaurant. It is to this proposed sublease that Richfield refuses to give its consent.

Beaver advised Richfield of its absolute objection to the proposed restaurant and Richfield in turn refused its consent on the basis of Beaver's objection.

The appellant's primary submission is that the learned chambers judge erred in holding that Richfield was entitled to rely on Beaver's objection in withholding consent because Beaver's objection did not relate to the nature of proposed use of the premises but rather to a normal incident of any use of the premises being the need for parking. In the alternative, the appellant submits that the learned chambers judge erred in failing to find that the objection was unreasonable as being based upon a matter extraneous to the landlord-and-tenant relationship.

In response to the appellant, the respondent Richfield advances, first of all, that it was entitled to rely on Beaver's objection and, secondly, that apart from Beaver's objection its refusal to consent to the sublease was reasonable in the circumstances because the operation of the proposed sublessee would seriously jeopardize the business of its other major tenant, Beaver, with serious financial repercussions not only upon Beaver, but upon Richfield itself because Richfield collects rent from Beaver calculated on a percentage of Beaver's sales. . . .

The layout of the parking lot is of special significance in this case. Leaving aside the parking stalls at the north end of the site, which are on a separate level and are intended to service a separate medical centre and office building which is not connected with the shopping centre, the remaining portion of the parking lot designed to service the shopping centre comprises approximately 400 stalls laid out in rows of from 15 to 20 stalls in front of and at right angles to the left wing of the building, with more stalls to the north beyond it. Beaver's main entrance is at the south end of this elongated parking lot.

It is common ground that customers of shopping centres tend to park as close as possible to the entrance to the place where they are going to shop. That has been particularly true in the case of Beaver because heavy and bulky merchandise such as plywood sheets represents 60 per cent of its sales. According to Beaver, its customers have tended to use the southerly 70 stalls closest to its entrance out of the 400 stalls designed to service the shopping centre. Beaver alleges that its customers will simply take their business elsewhere if they are required to park much further.

Swiss Chalet requires as a condition of acceptance of the sublease that the main entrance to its proposed premises be located at the south end of the appellant's lease premises closest to Beaver's entrance at the south end of the parking lot so that the parking stalls closest to Swiss Chalet's entrance would be those very stalls which are closest to Beaver's entrance and which Beaver's customers have tended to use in the past. Beaver would have no objection if the entrance to the proposed restaurant were moved to the other end of the sublease premises.

If the sublease is approved with the entrance where proposed, congestion at the south end of the parking lot is inevitable. Not even the appellant disputes that. The proposed Swiss Chalet Restaurant would seat 335 customers at one time. Both it and Beaver have the same peak hours of business, that is to say after 4:30 p.m. Beaver's objection is not only to the overall increased demand for parking as a result of this large proposed restaurant, but also to the particular "static" type of parking which the restaurant will attract.

In its letter of 29th September 1981 to the respondent landlord, Beaver outlined its objections as follows:

> Further to your letters of September 15th and 24th, Beaver Lumber Company Limited clearly and absolutely objects to a *restaurant as described by you* in the Heritage Hill Complex. There are a number of places in our lease where we have this right to object. There is one clause which specifically deals with changes, additions, design, etc. of the complex. There is the standard quiet enjoyment clause and there is the various use clause outlining the nature of the project and others.
>
> When this project was conceived it was to be a complex containing a hard goods store, Beaver; a drug based store, Super S; a few miscellaneous convenience type operations as part of Super S, a medical centre and an office tower. A *substantial sit-down family restaurant was never contemplated or planned for in this centre*. Surely you, as the landlord, and the other tenants of this shopping centre must recognize the existing parking problem and can imagine *the problem that will result from a restaurant as described*. Myself and my family have eaten many times at Swiss Chalet Restaurants — they *are extremely popular and generate a lot of traffic. Their evening activity is in direct conflict*

> *with the evening activity at our store*. We object to this proposal and intend to take whatever action we can to protect our rights in the event you approve of this activity. [The italics are Belzil J.A.'s.] . . .

Clearly the objection to a substantial sit-down family restaurant generating a lot of "static" parking is an objection to the nature of the business to be conducted by the proposed sublessee within the meaning of cl. 7 of the lease. If the clause had been intended to mean "use" instead of "nature", it would have said so, as it does in the last *proviso* of the clause. It is the particular characteristic of the proposed restaurant which is objected to. The Town 'N Country restaurant, which had formerly occupied a third of the premises, had not been objectionable to Beaver because it was a small 80-seat restaurant with access through the appellant's business premises only and catering primarily to staff and customers of the shopping centre. It did not have the same characteristic and popular attraction as the proposed Swiss Chalet with its 335 seats.

The parties have themselves agreed that the withholding of consent by the lessor in these circumstances shall not be construed as unreasonable. The learned chambers judge was accordingly right to dismiss the appellant's application.

I am also satisfied that even if the special feature in cl. 7 recognizing the other major tenant's right to object were not considered, the appellant would still fail to show that the lessor's withholding of consent was unreasonable. In my view, the present case is governed by *Coopers & Lybrand Ltd. v. William Schwartz Const. Co. Ltd.* (1980), 36 C.B.R. (N.S.) 265, 116 D.L.R. (3d) 450, a decision of the Court of Queen's Bench affirmed by this court in an unreported decision of 5th February 1981. The principles of law on the issue of unreasonable withholding of consent to a sublease are adequately reviewed by Egbert J. in his reported reasons.

The first principle stated by Egbert J. and applicable here is taken from Halsbury's Laws of England:

> (b) In Halsbury's Laws of England, Vol. 27 "Landlord and Tenant" (4th ed) [p. 289] it is said at paragraph 371:
>
> The landlord is not bound to give any reason for refusing his consent to an assignment: *the burden of proof is on the tenant to show that the landlord has unreasonably withheld his consent, and is not on the landlord to prove that he was justified in withholding it.* (The italics are Belzil J.A.'s.)

The second applicable principle is stated by Kerans J.A. in the unreported decision affirming *Coopers & Lybrand*:

> In our view, the landlord may rely on any reason, if genuine, for refusal, whether or not earlier told to the tenant.

So while Richfield based its first letter of refusal on Beaver's objection, the affidavit filed on its behalf before the learned chambers judge also raised the adverse impact of parking congestion at Beaver's entrance on Beaver's sales, and hence on its own percentage rental receipts. This ground is accordingly properly to be considered in this appeal.

In *Coopers & Lybrand* it was held not unreasonable to withhold consent on the grounds that the competition from the proposed subtenant could adversely affect other tenants of the shopping centre and thereby adversely affect the landlord's own interest in the entire mall. The underlying principle here is that consent is not unreasonably withheld if the landlord's own financial interest will be adversely affected. It is immaterial whether this adverse effect results from competition in sales or from other causes such as congested parking. Parking is not an extraneous matter. It is an integral part if not the very *raison d'etre* of shopping centres such as the one in this case.

We are advised that the percentage rents which Richfield receives from Beaver have increased from $3,000 in 1978 to a figure in excess of $80,000 in 1981. Both Beaver and Richfield believe that the congestion resulting from the proposed Swiss Chalet would seriously and adversely affect Beaver's sales and the rents payable by it to Richfield. The concern is a valid one and it is not challenged by the appellant. It was for the appellant to show that the apprehensions of the respondents were so unfounded as to be unreasonable. It has not attempted to do so.

If the test of reasonableness is what a reasonable landlord would do in the circumstances, would a reasonable landlord be expected to consent to an assignment of lease which might result in his direct loss of $80,000 annual rental income? Surely not! . . .

Harradence J.A. (dissenting): . . .

The first point to be considered is this: whether the objection of Beaver goes to "the nature of the business" within the meaning of the contract provision quoted above.

The point is one of construction, and therefore, the authorities brought to the attention of the court are of somewhat restricted usefulness. They can give the court guidance as to general principle, but cannot decisively define what is meant in the particular contract which the court is considering. The court must inquire whether the matters enumerated by the learned chambers judge are matters going to "the nature of the business" within the meaning of this lease. It was submitted for the landlord, Richfield, that "the nature of the business" does not simply mean "kind or species" but includes those features of a business that are integral to the conduct of it. For the tenant, Sundance, it was submitted that "nature", at bottom, means "kind", that parking and volume of customers, in any case, do not go to "the nature of the business" but are quantitative matters and matters which should be covered by some arrangement other than the provisions for sublease. Finally, it is said that matters like customer volume and the need for parking are part of the nature of every business, and that the construction contended for by the landlord would allow Beaver to exercise an arbitrary power which the lease specifically denies to the landlord.

It is undoubted that availability of parking is of the greatest importance to any business, particularly a retail business in a shopping centre. Again, there is considerable substance in the contention that the behaviour of the clientele of a business may be part of the nature of the business. A useful example of this might occur in the case of a salon selling *haute couture*, the proprietor of which objects to having a penny arcade next door. The penny arcade would attact an adolescent clientele whose comportment would be objectionable to the patrons of the salon. An objection of that kind would be one going to the nature of the business.

However, the term "nature of the business" cannot be extended so far as to include something inherent in every business. Every business must have customers, who need a place to park. The more successful the business is, the more space its customers occupy. Granted that the customers of a family style restaurant will park for longer than the customers of other businesses, the question whether this goes to "the nature of the business" can be tested by the following example. One business may have a small number of customers parking for, say, one hour at a time. Another business may have twice as many customers, who park for half as long. A customer coming into the parking lot may be able to slip his car into a parking space more readily in the latter case, but the difference is very slight. The same use is being made of the space. An objection to the amount of parking space occupied by the customers of a business is, as this example shows, not an objection to the nature of the business, but to its success. Beaver could readily accommodate itself to an unsuccessful neighbour, whether a restaurant, a bowling alley, or a saddlery, but not to a successful neighbour, no matter what kind of business was conducted.

Moreover, when the provision in question is examined, the manner in which it has been drawn bears a strong implication that the essential element in it is prevention of destructive competition. If Sundance proposed to sublet to someone who carried on a form of endeavour in direct competition with Beaver, an objection by Beaver would undoubtedly be to the nature of the business; the matter of parking is not clearly within the meaning of the phrase, and there are compelling reasons for restricting the phrase to a narrow compass. In the first place, it is to be observed that in the arrangements among the parties to this case no tenant had any exclusive sovereignty over any particular area of the parking lot. Though the lease provides for the manner in which parking regulations may be made, the parties have chosen not to do so prior to this date. Consequently, it should not be open to Richfield to use the subletting and assignment clause to accomplish that end.

Secondly, it is of the greatest importance that a provision restricting subletting is a restraint on alienation. A preferable construction is one which imposes fewer restraints rather than more. As it was put by Joyce J. in *Grove v. Portal*, [1902] 1 Ch. 727 at 731:

> . . . these covenants have always been construed with the utmost jealousy to prevent the restraint from going beyond the express stipulation.

It would, in my view, be contrary to the principle expressed by Joyce J. to allow Richfield and Beaver to found an objection on parking problems with the result that all of the space held by Sundance would be sterilized.

The extent to which Beaver's objection, though it is said to be to the nature of the business, really rests on smaller matters for which other remedies are provided in the lease is illustrated by Beaver's concern with the location of the doors to the restaurant. That concern emerges from cross-examination on the affidavit of Mr. Aries, division manager of Beaver Lumber Co. Ltd., in the following way (Appeal Book, p. 288):

> Q. Okay. And I gather that the conversation which you had with Mr. Reynolds related to the possibility of being an alternative entrance to the restaurant on the west side?
>
> (Note: The west side of the building is the opposite side from the parking lot.)
>
> A. That is correct.
>
> Q. And could that make a difference to Beaver?
>
> A. I think yes.

The second point to be considered is this. Under its arrangements with Beaver, Richfield takes a share of Beaver's revenue. If Beaver's business is interfered with, Richfield will suffer a loss of rental revenue. It is said for Richfield that this gives Richfield, in addition to the right to object on the basis of harm to Beaver, the right to object in order to protect its own position. A similar point was considered in *Can. Safeway Ltd. v. Triangle Accept. Ltd.*, [1980] 3 W.W.R. 352, 11 R.P.R. 279, 5 Man. R. (2d) 22 (Co. Ct.), an appeal from which was dismissed at [1980] 5 W.W.R. 259, 14 R.P.R. 90 (Man. C.A.). That case was in some respects the converse of this one: the consent of the landlord was withheld mainly because the proposed subtenant would not attract a sufficient volume of shoppers. It was decided that the reduced volume of shoppers could not found the landlord's objection to subletting.

At pp. 358-59 Philp Co. Ct. J. said:

> I also consider that to give effect to the ground upon which Triangle bases its objection amounts to re-writing the assignment and subletting covenant *ex post facto* to include a very substantial condition. To include in the covenant the condition that a proposed assignee or subtenant must generate the same or a greater volume of shoppers may, in a practical sense, render the assignment or subletting of the lease impossible.

That reasoning is respectfully adopted as applicable to this case, though it is not applicable to all cases, particularly where the loss of volume of business is large. It is applicable to this case because if the landlord were allowed to withhold consent to subletting on the basis of a change in volume of business, that would amount to re-writing the lease so as to give a minimum revenue to the landlord. The landlord has freely entered into an arrangement by which it takes a share of revenue. If volume is increased, the landlord prospers. If volume is decreased, the landlord should not in this case be allowed to decide that it no longer cares to bear any of that risk.

A similar conclusion was reached by the English Court of Appeal in *Bromley Park Garden Estates v. Moss*, [1982] 1 W.L.R. 1019, though in a slightly different factual context. There a landlord refused consent to assignment of a lease of an apartment. It was not in the interest of the landlord to permit assignment. The court made it clear that only in rare cases will it be held to be reasonable to withhold consent where the landlord is seeking in effect to modify the agreement.

Referring to earlier authorities, Dunn L.J. said at pp. 1032-33:

> It is true that in deciding the question of unreasonableness the courts did not confine themselves to narrow considerations as to the personality of the proposed assignee or the subject matter of the lease, as had been done in some of the older cases — and it may be that the passage in *Woodfall* [Woodfall, Landlord and Tenant, 28th ed. (1978), p. 485, para. 1181] was intended to draw attention to that — but there is nothing in the cases to indicate that the landlord was entitled to refuse his consent in order to acquire a commercial benefit for himself by putting into effect proposals outside the contemplation of the lease under consideration, and to replace the contractual relations created by the lease by some alternative arrangements more advantageous to the landlord, even though this would have been in accordance with good estate management.

In the view which I take of this case, the landlord was, at the time the lease was executed, prepared to assume the risk of expansion of Sundance's business and was bound by that assumption of risk. Had the parking difficulties emerged as a result of the expansion of the business of Sundance the landlord would be unable to interfere. The situation now is in principle no different from the situation which would have been present had the parking problems arisen in the absence of subletting. The fact of subletting does not alter the contemplation of the parties at the time when the lease was made and, in my view, it was not within the contemplation of the parties to the lease that the landlord would be able to prevent Sundance from making use of its space in what is essentially a commercially acceptable manner. If the submissions of Richfield were given effect Sundance would be restricted to subletting to unsuccessful, even insolvent, subtenants for fear that a successful one would present a risk of congestion of the parking facilities associated with the premises. The adequacy of those parking facilities is not a matter with which the tenant could deal. In consequence I am of the view that their inadequacy is a burden which must be shouldered by the landlord. The indirect impact of the inadequacy of the parking facilities on the revenue of the landlord cannot bring about the consequence that the landlord could keep the space originally let to Sundance empty in order to protect the revenue of Beaver.

An unreported decision of this court, *Coopers & Lybrand Ltd. v. William Schwartz Const. Co. Ltd.*, affirmed the decision of Egbert J., which is reported at (1980), 36 C.B.R. (N.S.) 265, 116 D.L.R. (3d) 450. There, the landlord withheld consent to subletting and was held to be doing so reasonably. That case, however, was different from this one in important aspects. There, the proposed subtenant proposed to sell goods in competition with the other tenants; the proposed subtenant would also have sold live pets, which emitted an unpleasant odour; the subtenant had other stores whose goods were displayed in disarray. The proposed sublease arguably permitted uses different from those permitted by the head lease, and the result which could be anticipated was that the subtenant could with impunity carry on business in a manner forbidden to the tenant under the head lease. It was argued in that case that the landlord's real objection to subletting was that the proposed subtenant would not have a sufficient volume of business and thus the landlord would derive less money; but Egbert J. made no finding on the point. The tenant also argued in that case that the landlord should not be able to rely in litigation on objections which were not raised before consent was refused. It was decided that the landlord's objection was to the use of the premises; that that objection had been made known to the tenant before consent was withheld; and that the landlord could justify the refusal on the basis of matters which had not originally been stated to the tenant. Further, in the decision of this court, the *Can. Safeway* decision was distinguished expressly on the basis that in the *Coopers & Lybrand* case the head lease expressly provided for the matters on which the landlord's objection was founded.

For those reasons the decision in the *Coopers & Lybrand* case does not govern this one. Indeed, it has often been observed that cases of this kind vary so much that there will rarely be a case in which precedent precisely determines the outcome. The authorities are of value mainly in indicating a general approach.

In my view the landlord's consent has been unreasonably withheld. Where consent is unreasonably withheld, the tenant is released from the obligation to obtain it: Williams, *The Canadian Law of Landlord and Tenant*, 4th ed. (1973), p. 719.

Accordingly, I would allow the appeal, answer both questions in the originating notice in the affirmative, and declare the rights of the parties as above stated.

Appeal dismissed.

QUESTIONS AND COMMENTS

1. Which opinion do you find most convincing?

2. In *International Drilling Fluids Ltd. v. Louisville* [1986] Ch. 513 (C.A.), Balcombe L.J. (at 519–21) set out this summary of the law governing assignments and subletting:

> (1) The purpose of a covenant against assignment without the consent of the landlord, such consent not to be unreasonably withheld, is to protect the lessor from having his premises used or occupied in an undesirable way, or by an undesirable tenant or assignee: *per* A. L. Smith L.J. in *Bates v. Donaldson* [1896] 2 Q.B. 241, 247, approved by all the members of the Court of Appeal in *Houlder Brothers & Co. Ltd. v. Gibbs* [1925] Ch. 575.
>
> (2) As a corollary to the first proposition, a landlord is not entitled to refuse his consent to an assignment on grounds which have nothing whatever to do with the relationship

of landlord and tenant in regard to the subject matter of the lease: see *Houlder Brothers & Co. Ltd. v. Gibbs*, a decision which (despite some criticism) is binding on this court: *Bickel v. Duke of Westminster* [1977] Q.B. 517. A recent example of a case where the landlord's consent was unreasonably withheld because the refusal was designed to achieve a collateral purpose unconnected with the terms of the lease is *Bromley Park Garden Estates Ltd. v. Moss* [1982] 1 W.L.R. 1019.

(3) The onus of proving that consent has been unreasonably withheld is on the tenant: see *Shanly v. Ward* (1913) 29 T.L.R. 714 and *Pimms Ltd. v. Tallow Chandlers Company* [1964] 2 Q.B. 547, 564.

(4) It is not necessary for the landlord to prove that the conclusions which led him to refuse consent were justified, if they were conclusions which might be reached by a reasonable man in the circumstances: *Pimms Ltd. v. Tallow Chandlers Company* [1964] 2 Q.B. 547, 564.

(5) It may be reasonable for the landlord to refuse his consent to an assignment on the ground of the purpose for which the proposed assignee intends to use the premises, even though that purpose is not forbidden by the lease: see *Bates v. Donaldson* [1896] 2 Q.B. 241, 244.

(6) There is a divergence of authority on the question, in considering whether the landlord's refusal of consent is reasonable, whether it is permissible to have regard to the consequences to the tenant if consent to the proposed assignment is withheld. In an early case at first instance *Sheppard v. Hongkong and Shanghae Banking Corporation* (1872) 20 W.R. 459, 460, Malins V.C. said that by withholding their consent the lessors threw a very heavy burden on the lessees and they therefore ought to show good grounds for refusing it. In *Houlder Brothers & Co. Ltd. v. Gibbs* [1925] Ch. 575, 584, Warrington L.J. said:

> An act must be regarded as reasonable or unreasonable in reference to the circumstances under which it is committed, and when the question arises on the construction of a contract the outstanding circumstances to be considered are the nature of the contract to be construed, and the relations between the parties resulting from it.

In a recent decision of this court, *Leeward Securities Ltd. v. Lilyheath Properties Ltd.* (1983) 271 E.G. 279 concerning a sub-letting which would attract the protection of the Rent Act, both Oliver L.J. and O'Connor L.J. made it clear in their judgments that they could envisage circumstances in which it might be unreasonable to refuse consent to an underletting, if the result would be that there was no way in which the tenant (the sub-landlord) could reasonably exploit the premises except by creating a tenancy to which the Rent Act protection would apply, and which inevitably would affect the value of the landlord's reversion. O'Connor L.J. said, at p. 283:

> It must not be thought that, because the introduction of a Rent Act tenant inevitably has an adverse effect upon the value of the reversion, that that is a sufficient ground for the landlords to say that they can withhold consent and that the court will hold that that is reasonable.

To the opposite effect are the *dicta, obiter* but nevertheless weighty, of Viscount Dunedin and Lord Phillimore in *Viscount Tredegar v. Harwood* [1929] A.C. 72, 78, 82. There are numerous other *dicta* to the effect that a landlord need consider only his own interests: see, e.g., *West Layton Ltd. v. Ford* [1979] Q.B. 593, 605, and *Bromley Park Garden Estates Ltd. v. Moss* [1982] 1 W.L.R. 1019, 1027. Those *dicta* must be qualified, since a landlord's interests, collateral to the purposes of the lease, are in any event ineligible for consideration: see proposition (2) above. But in my judgment a proper reconciliation of those two streams of authority can be achieved by saying that while a landlord need usually only consider his own relevant interests, there may be cases where there is such a disproportion between the benefit to the landlord and the detriment to the tenant if the landlord withholds his consent to an assignment that it is unreasonable for the landlord to refuse consent.

(7) Subject to the propositions set out above, it is in each case a question of fact, depending upon all the circumstances, whether the landlord's consent to an assignment is being unreasonably withheld: see *Bickel v. Duke of Westminster* [1977] Q.B. 517, 524, and West Layton Ltd. v. Ford [1979] Q.B. 593, 604, 606-607.

See further *Ashworth Frazer Ltd v. Gloucester City Council* [2001] 1 W.L.R. 2180 (H.L.)

3. See also Cullity J.'s summary in *1455202 Ontario Inc. v. Welbow Holdings Ltd.* 2003 CarswellOnt 1761 (S.C.J.) at para. 9:

In determining whether the Landlord has unreasonably withheld consent, I believe the following propositions are supported by the authorities cited by counsel and are of assistance:

1. The burden is on the Tenant to satisfy the court that the refusal to consent was unreasonable: *Shields v. Dickler*, [1948] O.W.N. 145 (Ont. C.A.), at pages 149-50; *Sundance Investment Corp. v. Richfield Properties Ltd.*, [1983] 2 W.W.R. 493 (Alta. C.A.), at page 500; cf. *Welch Foods Inc. v. Cadbury Beverages Canada Inc.* (2001), 140 O.A.C. 320 (Ont. C.A.)., at page 331. In deciding whether the burden has been discharged, the question is not whether the court would have reached the same conclusion as the Landlord or even whether a reasonable person might have given consent; it is whether a reasonable person could have withheld consent: *Whiteminster Estates v. Hodges Menswear* (1974), 232 E.G. 715, at pages 715-6; *Zellers Inc. v. Brad-Jay Investments Ltd.*, [2002] O.J. No. 4100 (Ont. S.C.J.), at para 35.

2. In determining the reasonableness of a refusal to consent, it is the information available to — and the reasons given by — the Landlord at the time of the refusal — and not any additional, or different, facts or reasons provided subsequently to the court — that is material: *Bromley Park Garden Estates v. Moss*, [1982] 2 All E.R. 890 (Eng. C.A.), at page 901-2 per Slade L.J. Further, it is not necessary for the Landlord to prove that the conclusions which led it to refuse consent were justified, if they were conclusions that might have been reached by a reasonable person in the circumstances: *Pimms Ltd. v. Tallow Chandlers in London (City)*, [1964] 2 All E.R. 145 (Eng. C.A.), at page 151.

3. The question must be considered in the light of the existing provisions of the lease that define and delimit the subject matter of the assignment as well as the right of the Tenant to assign and that of the Landlord to withhold consent. The Landlord is not entitled to require amendments to the terms of lease that will provide it with more advantageous terms: *Jo-Emma Restaurants Ltd. v. A. Merkur & Sons Ltd.* (1989), 7

R.P.R. (2d) 298 (Ont. Dist. Ct.); *Town Investments Underlease, Re*, [1954] Ch. 301 (Eng. Ch. Div.) — but, as a general rule, it may reasonably withhold consent if the assignment will diminish the value of its rights under it, or of its reversion: *Federal Business Development Bank v. Starr* (1986), 55 O.R. (2d) 65 (Ont. H.C.), at page 72. A refusal will, however, be unreasonable if it was designed to achieve a collateral purpose, or benefit to the Landlord, that was wholly unconnected with the bargain between the Landlord and the Tenant reflected in the terms of the lease: *Bromley Park Garden Estates v. Moss*, above, at page 901 per Dunn L.J.)

4. A probability that the proposed assignee will default in its obligations under the lease may, depending upon the circumstances, be a reasonable ground for withholding consent. A refusal to consent will not necessarily be unreasonable simply because the Landlord will have the same legal rights in the event of default by the assignee as it has against the assignor: *Ashworth Frazer Ltd. v. Gloucester City Council*, [2001] H.L.J. No. 57 (U.K. H.L.).

5. The financial position of the assignee may be a relevant consideration. This was encompassed by the references to the "personality" of an assignee in the older cases see, for example, *Slanly v. Ward* (1913), 29 T.L.R. 714 (Eng. C.A.); *Dominion Stores Ltd. v. Bramalea Ltd.*, [1985] O.J. No. 1874 (Ont. Dist. Ct.).

6. The question of reasonableness is essentially one of fact that must be determined on the circumstances of the particular case, including the commercial realities of the market place and the economic impact of an assignment on the Landlord. Decisions in other cases that consent was reasonably, or unreasonably, withheld are not precedents that will dictate the result in the case before the court: *Bickel v. Duke of Westminster*, [1976] 3 All E.R. 801 (Eng. C.A.), at pages 804-5; *Ashworth Frazer Ltd. v. Gloucester City Council*, above, at para 67; *Dominion Stores Ltd. v. Bramalea Ltd.*, above, at para 25.

4. Should a landlord be allowed to raise objections which have come to mind after the refusal to allow the assignment or sub-letting? Compare *Sundance Investment Corp. v. Richfield Properties Ltd.* with *1455202 Ontario Inc. v. Welbow Holdings Ltd.* on this point.

5. The tables were turned in *First Capital (Northgate) Corp. v. 137th C.T. Grill Inc.* 2003 CarswellAlta 1440 (C.A.). There, the tenant had a right of veto under the lease, should the landlord wish to construct additional units on designated zones within a shopping-centre complex. The tenant's consent could not be unreasonably withheld.

The landlord wanted to use part of the existing parking lot (a no-build zone) for a restaurant. The tenant, also in the restaurant business, refused to consent because it was concerned that the new operation would have a "negative impact on the business of the tenant". The landlord argued that the tenant's refusal could only be maintained if the objection related to the potential loss of parking space for its customers. How would you resolve the dispute?

4. OBLIGATIONS OF LANDLORDS AND TENANTS

Under the common law, the terms of a lease are a matter of contractual intention, and freedom of contract is the guiding precept. Some terms are implied under law, very few in fact, and even these can be negated by the parties; such terms are, therefore, merely rules of construction.

One term is central to the tenant's rights under a lease: the right to quiet enjoyment. It may be that this right is not essential to a lease, not inherent in the very idea of exclusive possession, though it is hard to imagine how the latter can have real meaning without the former. To say that one has a right to exclusive possession but that the landlord is liable for disruptions that make the right unusable, seems wrong. In any event, one is hard-pressed to find case law under which absolutely no right to quiet enjoyment has been found. Issues do arise as to the extent of the right and whether a breach has occurred on the facts.

Southwark LBC v. Mills
[2001] 1 A.C. 1 (H.L.)

Lord Hoffmann:

My Lords, the appellants in these two appeals, Mrs Tracey Tanner and Ms Yvonne Baxter, are respectively tenants of the London Boroughs of Southwark and Camden. Mrs Tanner lives in a block of flats on Herne Hill. Ms Baxter occupies the first floor flat in a converted Victorian house in Kentish Town. They both complain of being able to hear all the sounds made by their neighbours. It is not that the neighbours are unreasonably noisy. For the most part, they are behaving quite normally. But the flats have no sound insulation. The tenants can hear not only the neighbours' televisions and their babies crying but their coming and going, their cooking and cleaning, their quarrels and their love-making. The lack of privacy causes tension and distress. . . .

Neither tenancy agreement contains any warranty on the part of the landlord that the flat has sound insulation or is in any other way fit to live in. Nor does the law imply any such warranty. This is a fundamental principle of the English law of landlord and tenant. In *Hart v. Windsor* (1843) 12 M & W 68, 87-88 Parke B. said: "There is no contract, still less a condition, implied by law on the demise of real property only, that it is fit for the purpose for which it is let." And in *Edler v. Auerbach* [1950] 1 K.B. 359, 374 Devlin J. said:

> It is the business of the tenant, if he does not protect himself by an express warranty, to satisfy himself that the premises are fit for the purpose for which he wants to use them, whether that fitness depends upon the state of their structure, the state of the law, or any other relevant circumstances.

It is true that in each tenancy agreement the council agreed to keep the structure in *repair*. Such an obligation would in any case be implied by s. 11 of the *Landlord and Tenant Act, 1985*. But the appellants do not rely upon this covenant and cannot do so. Keeping in repair means remedying disrepair. The landlord is obliged only to restore the house to its previous good condition. He does not have to make it a better house than it originally was: see *Quick v. Taff Ely Borough Council* [1986] Q.B. 809.

In many cases, of course, the tenant does not have the bargaining power to exact an express warranty as to the condition of the premises or the freedom of choice to reject property which may not meet his needs. This is often the case with local authority housing. For this reason, Parliament has in various ways intervened to protect certain tenants from the bleak *laissez-faire* of the common law. . . .

In the absence of any modern statutory remedy which covers their complaint, the appellants have attempted to fill the gap by pressing into service two ancient common law actions. They are the action on the covenant for quiet enjoyment and the action of nuisance. My Lords, I naturally accept that if the present case falls squarely within the scope of either of these actions, the appellants must succeed. But if the question is whether the common law should be developed or extended to cover them, your Lordships must in my opinion have regard to the fact that Parliament has dealt extensively with the problem of substandard housing over many years but so far declined to impose an obligation to install soundproofing in existing dwellings. No doubt Parliament had regard to the financial burden which this would impose upon local authority and private landlords. Like the Court of Appeal in *McNerny v. Lambeth London Borough Council* 21 H.L.R. 188, 194, I think that in a field such as housing law, which is very much a matter for the allocation of resources in accordance with democratically determined priorities, the development of the common law should not get out of step with legislative policy.

I shall consider first the covenant for quiet enjoyment. This is contained in cl. 1 of Mrs Tanner's tenancy agreement. It says: "The tenant's right to remain in and to enjoy the quiet occupation of the dwelling house shall not be interfered with by the council . . ." Clause B4 of Ms Baxter's agreement says: "The council shall not interfere with the tenants' rights to quiet enjoyment of the premises during the continuance of the tenancy." Read literally, these words would seem very apt. The flat is not quiet and the tenant is not enjoying it. But the words cannot be read literally. The covenant has a very long history. It has been expressed or implied in conveyances and leases of English land for centuries. It comes from a time when, in a conveyancing context, the words "quiet enjoyment" had a technical meaning different from what they would today signify to a non-lawyer who was unacquainted with their history. So in *Jenkins v. Jackson* (1888) 40 Ch. D. 71, 74 Kekewich J. felt obliged to point out that the word "quietly" in the covenant:

> does not mean undisturbed by noise. When a man is quietly in possession it has nothing whatever to do with noise . . . "Peaceably and quietly" means without interference — without interruption of the possession.

Likewise in *Kenny v. Preen* [1963] 1 Q.B. 499, 511 Pearson L.J. explained that:

> the word "enjoy" used in this connection is a translation of the Latin word "*fruor*" and refers to the exercise and use of the right and having the full benefit of it, rather than to deriving pleasure from it.

The covenant for quiet enjoyment is therefore a covenant that the tenant's lawful possession of the land will not be substantially interfered with by the acts of the lessor or those lawfully claiming under him. For present purposes, two points about the covenant should be noticed. First, there must be a substantial interference with the tenant's possession. This means his ability to use it in an ordinary lawful way. The covenant cannot be elevated into a warranty that the land is fit to be used for some special purpose: see *Dennett v. Atherton* (1872) L.R. 7 Q.B. 316. On the other hand, it is a question of fact and degree whether the tenant's ordinary use of the premises has been substantially interfered with. In *Sanderson v. Berwick-upon-Tweed Corpn* (1884) 13 Q.B.D. 547 the flooding of a substantial area of agricultural land by water discharged from neighbouring land occupied by another tenant of the same landlord was held to be a breach of the covenant. In *Kenny v. Preen* [1963] 1 Q.B. 499 a landlord's threats to evict the tenant, accompanied by repeated shouting and knocking on her door, was held to be a breach. It is true that in *Browne v. Flower* [1911] 1 Ch. 219, 228 Parker J. said that:

> to constitute a breach of such a covenant there must be some physical interference with the enjoyment of the demised premises, and that a mere interference with the comfort of persons using the demised premises by the creation of a personal annoyance such as might arise from noise, invasion of privacy, or otherwise is not enough.

And in *Phelps v. City of London Corpn* [1916] 2 Ch. 255, 267 Peterson J. said it was "at least doubtful" whether a nuisance by noise was a breach of the covenant. For my part, however, I do not see why, in principle, regular excessive noise cannot constitute a substantial interference with the ordinary enjoyment of the premises. . . .

There is however another feature of the covenant which presents the appellants with a much greater difficulty. It is prospective in its nature: see *Norton on Deeds*, 2nd ed (1928), pp. 612-613. It is a covenant that the tenant's lawful possession *will* not be interfered with by the landlord or anyone claiming under him. . . .

If one stands back from the technicalities of the law of landlord and tenant and construes the tenancy agreement in accordance with ordinary contractual principles, I think that one reaches the same conclusion. In the grant of a tenancy it is fundamental to the common understanding of the parties, objectively determined, that the landlord gives no implied warranty as to the condition or fitness of the premises. *Caveat* lessee. It would be entirely inconsistent with this common understanding if the covenant for quiet enjoyment were interpreted to create liability for disturbance or inconvenience or any other damage attributable to the condition of the premises. Secondly, the lease must be construed against the background facts which would reasonably have been known to the parties at the time it was granted. . . .

In the present case, there was no evidence about what the tenants had known about the lack of soundproofing before they took their tenancies. But in my opinion a requirement of consent to the noise goes too far. It is sufficient that the tenants must reasonably have contemplated that there would be other tenants in neighbouring flats. If they cannot complain of the presence of other tenants as such, then their complaint is solely as to the lack of soundproofing. And that is an inherent structural defect for which the landlord assumed no responsibility. The council granted and the tenant took a tenancy of that flat. She cannot by virtue of the terms of that tenancy require the council to give her a different flat.

It remains only, on this part of the case, for me to comment on two authorities upon which the appellants strongly relied. The first is *Sanderson v. Berwick-upon-Tweed Corpn* 13 QBD 547, to which I have already referred in another context. The corporation let a farm to Sanderson. It reserved in favour of Cairns, another tenant farmer, the rights to use a drain across one of Sanderson's fields and to enter and repair it. Water discharged by Cairns leaked through the drain and flooded Sanderson's land. He sued the landlord on the covenant for quiet enjoyment. Fry L.J., giving the judgment of the Court of Appeal, said, at p. 551:

> the damage here has resulted to the plaintiff from the proper user by Cairns of the drains passing through the plaintiff's land which were improperly constructed. In respect of this proper use Cairns appears to us to claim lawfully under the defendants by virtue of his lease, and to have acted under the authority conferred on him by the defendants. The injury caused to the field appears to us to have been, within the meaning of the covenant in that behalf contained in the lease to the plaintiff, a substantial interruption by Cairns, who is a person lawfully claiming through the defendants, of the plaintiff's enjoyment of the land, and so to constitute a breach of the covenant for quiet enjoyment for which the defendants are liable in damages.

The appellants argue that their neighbouring tenants are likewise making "proper use" of their flats but the improper construction of the building, like the improper construction of the drain, results in an interference with the appellants' lawful use and possession of their own premises. In my opinion, however, these parallels are misleading. Fry L.J., in the passage which I have cited, is not saying that Cairns, in flooding the plaintiff's land, was making a "proper use" of the drain as against the plaintiff. He makes it quite clear that it was not. The reference to "proper use" is for the purpose of deciding whether the landlord is liable for what Cairns had done. This depended upon whether Cairns was "lawfully claiming under" the landlord and that in turn depended upon whether he was using the drains in a manner authorised by his lease. It is in this sense that he describes his use of the drains as "proper".

The present case is not concerned with whether the neighbouring tenants, in using their flats in the ordinary way, are lawfully claiming under the landlord. They obviously are. The question is rather whether their conduct amounts to a breach of the covenant for quiet enjoyment at all. In *Sanderson's* case the flooding of the land by Cairns was improper and a breach because he had a very limited right to discharge water onto the plaintiff's land. He could do so only through the drains. If the drains were badly made so that they would not hold the water, it was his or his landlord's responsibility to ensure that they did. A right to entry had been reserved to enable him to do so. But in the present cases, the rights of the tenants of neighbouring flats to use them in a normal way are not qualified in any way. As against the appellants, there is nothing improper about their neighbours' use of their flats.

In the Court of Appeal in Mrs Tanner's case Mantell L.J. [2001] Ch. 1, 17b-c, said that he regarded *Sanderson v. Berwick-upon-Tweed Corpn* 13 Q.B.D. 547 as indistinguishable from the case before him. But he said that it was in conflict with the decision of the Court of Appeal in *Duke of Westminster v. Guild* [1985] Q.B. 688. In that case, the question was whether a landlord was obliged to repair a drain serving the demised premises which passed under the landlord's retained land. The Court of Appeal held that no such obligation could be implied and that it did not fall within the scope of the covenant for quiet enjoyment. Slade L.J. said, at p. 703:

> The express covenant for quiet enjoyment and implied covenant against derogation from grant cannot in our opinion be invoked so as to impose on [the plaintiffs'] positive obligations to perform acts of repair which they would not otherwise be under any obligation to perform.

Mantell L.J. said that he preferred the latter case and applied the principle stated by Slade L.J. But I do not regard the two cases as being in conflict. The landlord in *Sanderson* was obliged to repair the drain on Sanderson's land only if he or his other tenant wanted to use it. Otherwise they ran the risk of exceeding their right to discharge water onto the tenant's land. But the drain in *Duke of Westminster v. Guild* [1985] QB 688 was on the landlord's land and he was not using it. Nor was anyone claiming under him. The tenant wanted it repaired for his own benefit. This the landlord was not obliged to do. It is a general principle that the grantor of an easement of way or drainage is not obliged to keep the way or drain in repair. In my opinion, therefore, Mantell L.J. was quite right to apply the principle stated by Slade L.J. in *Duke of Westminster v. Guild* and need not have been troubled by *Sanderson*. That principle seems to me to apply *a fortiori* to the present appeals. The appellants are attempting to use the covenant for quiet enjoyment to create not an obligation to repair but a more onerous obligation to improve the demised premises.

The second authority relied upon by the appellants is *Sampson v. Hodson-Pressinger* [1981] 3 All E.R. 710. The plaintiff was statutory tenant of a flat (flat 6) in a converted house in Belgravia. On 31 March, 1978, the landlord granted him a lease for 99 years with the usual covenant for quiet enjoyment. The landlord made alterations to the flat above (flat 7) which included the construction of a tiled terrace on the roof over the plaintiff's living room. On a date which does not appear in the report, the landlord granted a 99-year lease of the upper flat to a tenant who took possession on 11 August, 1978. The tiles had not been properly laid and as a result the plaintiff was seriously disturbed in his living room by the impact noise of people walking about on the terrace. The Court of Appeal held that the landlord was liable in nuisance. It does not appear that the pleadings placed reliance on the covenant for quiet enjoyment, but Eveleigh L.J. mentioned it in passing, at p. 714:

> The contemplated use for which the original landlord let flat 7 to the first defendant was one which interfered with the reasonable enjoyment of the plaintiff's flat. Consequently that landlord was, in my opinion, in breach of the covenant for quiet enjoyment.

I think with respect that this reasoning, while possibly correct on the facts, omits some essential steps. At the time when the plaintiff was granted his lease, it must have been contemplated by the parties that the flat upstairs would be used for ordinary residential occupation in accordance with the way it was constructed. It could not therefore have been intended that such use would be a breach of the covenant for quiet enjoyment. It could have amounted to a breach only if the cause of the noise was some act of the landlord or the tenant of flat 7 claiming under him which could not fairly have been within the contemplation of the parties when the plaintiff took his lease. If the terrace had not then been in existence, I can see the argument for saying that the parties could not have contemplated that the plaintiff would have people walking about on his roof. As the building then stood, that may have been an unreasonable use to make of the roof. If people did so regularly, with the authority of the landlord, in such a way as to cause substantial interference with his enjoyment of the premises, it could have been a breach of the covenant for quiet enjoyment. And if the landlord adapted the roof to enable his tenant and her guests to walk upon it, he would be obliged to do so in a way which protected the tenant beneath from unreasonable noise. But this argument depends entirely upon the adaptation of the terrace taking place after the grant of the plaintiff's lease. It has no application to the present case in which the premises were in their present condition when the appellants took their tenancies. . . .

[Lord Hoffman then discussed and dismissed the claim in private nuisance.]

Lord Millett:

My Lords, most people in England today live in cities. Many of them live cheek by jowl with their neighbours. They live in terraced houses, purpose-built blocks of flats, or flatlets created by the conversion of houses into separate residential units. Modern building regulations require proper sound insulation to be installed, but this is often lacking in older buildings or conversions. In its absence each occupier is likely from time to time to be disturbed in the enjoyment of his property by noise caused by the activities of his neighbours, as they are by his. Where the disturbance is intermittent and relatively slight the parties usually accept the need to put up with the annoyance they cause each other. But what if it is continuous and intolerable?

Where the offending noise is occasioned by the ordinary use of residential premises, so that it cannot be brought to an end except by leaving them vacant, the only practical solution is to install proper sound insulation; but that is expensive. Where the sufferer is an owner-occupier, he must either bear the cost himself or persuade his neighbour, who is likely to be suffering similar disturbance by noise emanating from his premises, to share the cost with him. Where the sufferer is a tenant, he would obviously like his landlord to carry out the work, but there is normally no legal obligation on him to do so. The law has long been settled that there is no implied covenant on the part of the landlord of a dwelling house that the premises are fit for human habitation, let alone that they are soundproof. Parliament has intervened in the case of furnished tenancies and tenancies at a low rent, but subsequent inflation has deprived the legislation of any practical application to unfurnished tenancies. In its report, Landlord and Tenant: Responsibility for State and Condition of Property (1996) (Law Com. No. 238) the Law Commission recommended that a covenant that the premises are fit for human habitation should be implied in leases of dwelling houses of less than seven years, but rejected a proposal that this should cover sound insulation.

The question in these appeals is whether the position is different where the tenant and his neighbour share a common landlord. Can the tenant, who cannot sue his landlord because his own property admits noise, have an action against him because his neighbour's emits it? Can the tenant, who cannot compel his landlord to install sound insulation in his own property, oblige him to install it in his neighbour's? And since each tenant is both the victim of the disturbance caused by his neighbour and the cause of similar disturbance to his neighbour, can they join forces to compel their common landlord to install sound insulation to make both their properties soundproof?

The answer is to be found in the words of Martin B in *Carstairs v. Taylor* (1871) L.R. 6 Ex. 217, 222: "Now, I think that one who takes a floor in a house must be held to take the premises as they are, and cannot complain that the house was not constructed differently." Goddard L.J. spoke to the same effect in *Kiddle v. City Business Properties Ltd* [1942] 1 K.B. 269, 274-275:

> [The plaintiff] takes the property as he finds it and must put up with the consequences. It is not to be supposed that the landlord is going to alter the construction, unless he consents to do so. He would say to his intending tenant: "You must take it as it is or not at all."

The doctrine does not depend on fictions, such as the ability of the tenant to inspect the property before taking the lease. It is simply a consequence of the general rule of English law which accords autonomy to contracting parties. In the absence of statutory intervention, the parties are free to let and take a lease of poorly constructed premises and to allocate the cost of putting them in order between themselves as they see fit. The principle applies whether the complaint relates to the state and condition of the demised premises themselves or, as in the cases cited, of other parts of the building in which the demised premises are located. Of course, the tenants of local authority housing do not negotiate the terms of their tenancy agreements. They take what they are offered on terms set by the local authority. But the meaning and effect of contractual arrangements cannot be made to depend on the parties' relative bargaining power. If it is thought right to redress any imbalance by importing terms in favour of the weaker party, this is a matter for Parliament.

The tenants accordingly accept that, in the absence of a statutory or contractual obligation to such effect, they cannot compel their landlords to install sound insulation. They invoke the tort of nuisance and the covenant for quiet enjoyment to obtain indirectly that which they cannot obtain directly. They complain of the sound emanating from the adjoining property, allege that it constitutes a legal wrong for which the landlord is responsible, and seek orders to restrain its continuance. In theory the landlord could avoid the cost of installing sound insulation by obtaining possession of the flat where the sound originates and leaving it vacant; though he might equally well choose to obtain possession of the flat belonging to the complainant. This solution is not, however, available in practice, since all the flats are subject to secure tenancies. . . .

Breach of the covenant for quiet enjoyment

The covenant for quiet enjoyment is one of the covenants of title formerly found in a conveyance of land, and the only such covenant found in a lease of land. It has long been understood that the word "quiet" in such a covenant does not refer to the absence of noise. It means without interference. The covenant for quiet enjoyment was originally regarded as a covenant to secure title or possession. It warranted freedom from disturbance by adverse claimants to the property: see *Dennett v. Atherton* L.R. 7 Q.B. 316; *Jenkins v. Jackson* 40 Ch. D. 71; *Hudson v. Cripps* [1896] 1 Ch. 265. But its scope was extended to cover any substantial interference with the ordinary and lawful enjoyment of the land, although neither the title to the land nor possession of the land was affected: *Sanderson v. Berwick-upon-Tweed Corpn* (1884) 13 Q.B.D. 547, 551.

Despite this there has lingered a belief that, although there need not be physical irruption into or upon the demised premises, there must be "a direct and physical" interference with the tenant's use and enjoyment of the land. On this ground the courts have dismissed complaints of the making of noise or the emanation of fumes, of interference with privacy or amenity, and other complaints of a kind commonly forming the subject matter of actions for nuisance. Little harm seems to have been done, since in cases where a remedy was appropriate the tenant has been able to have recourse to the landlord's implied obligation not to derogate from his grant. But the existence of the limitation has been questioned: (see *Kenny v. Preen* [1963] 1 Q.B. 499) or circumvented by the round assertion that it is satisfied in what might be thought somewhat doubtful circumstances: (see *Owen v. Gadd* [1956] 2 Q.B. 99), and I think that we should consider whether it is a proper one.

There is nothing in the wording of the conventional covenant that would justify the limitation. I do not know whether it owes its existence to a desire to maintain some connection with the original scope of the covenant as a covenant securing title or possession, or to the mistaken notion that actions for nuisance "productive of sensible personal discomfort" were actions for causing discomfort to the person rather than for causing injury to the land: see *Hunter v. Canary Wharf Ltd* [1997] A.C. 655, 706. Now that this fallacy has been exposed, however, I can see no sound reason for confining the covenant for quiet enjoyment to cases of direct and physical injury to land.

Accordingly, I agree with the tenants that the covenant for quiet enjoyment is broken if the landlord or someone claiming under him does anything that substantially interferes with the tenant's title to or possession of the demised premises or with his ordinary and lawful enjoyment of the demised premises. The interference need not be direct or physical. Nor, in my opinion, is it a necessary precondition of liability on the covenant that the acts alleged to constitute the breach would support an action in nuisance. I do not doubt that this will usually be a sufficient condition of liability, but there is nothing in the language of the conventional form of the covenant that would justify holding it to be a necessary one.

Once these artificial restrictions on the operation of the covenant for quiet enjoyment are removed, there seems to be little if any difference between the scope of the covenant and that of the obligation which lies upon any grantor not to derogate from his grant. The principle is the same in each case: a man may not give with one hand and take away with the other. Whether a particular matter falls within the scope of the covenant for quiet enjoyment depends upon the proper construction of the covenant. As ordinarily drafted, however, the covenant shares two critical features in common with the implied obligation. The first is that they are both prospective in their operation. The obligation undertaken by the grantor and covenantor alike is not to do anything after the date of the grant which will derogate from the grant or substantially interfere with the grantee's enjoyment of the subject matter of the grant: see *Anderson v. Oppenheimer* 5 Q.B.D. 602. In the present case the tenancy agreement contained a covenant on the part of the council that "the tenant's right . . . *shall* not be interfered with . . ." (emphasis added). That form of words clearly looks to the future.

The second feature that the implied obligation and the covenant for quiet enjoyment have in common is that the grantor's obligations are confined to the subject matter of the grant. Where the covenant is contained in a lease, its subject matter is usually expressed to be the demised premises. In an oft quoted passage in *Leech v. Schweder* (1874) L.R. 9 Ch. App. 463, 474 Mellish L.J. said:

> It is perfectly true that the lessee is "to hold and enjoy without any suit, let, or hindrance". But what is he to hold and enjoy? "The premises." What are the premises? The things previously demised and granted. The covenant does not enlarge what is previously granted, but an additional remedy is given, namely, an action for damages if the lessee cannot get, or is deprived of that which has been previously professed to be granted. Nothing, I apprehend, can be plainer than that at law it would not, in the least degree, enlarge what was granted.

In *Spoor v. Green* L.R. 9 Ex. 99 buildings collapsed because of subsidence caused by mining operations which had taken place before the lease. There was held to be no breach of the covenant for quiet enjoyment. The subject matter of the lease, and therefore of the covenant was land already liable to subsidence in consequence of the prior removal of the coal.

In the present cases the covenants guaranteed "the tenant's right to remain in and to enjoy the quiet occupation of *the dwelling house*" (emphasis added), that is to say the dwelling house comprised in the tenancy. This must be identified at the date when the tenancy was granted. In each case it consisted of a flat in a building constructed or adapted for multiple residential occupation and having inadequate sound insulation. An undesirable feature of the flat was its propensity to admit the sounds of the everyday activities of the occupants of adjoining flats. The landlord covenanted not to interfere with the tenant's use and enjoyment of a flat having that feature. It has not done so. It has not derogated from its grant, nor has it interfered with any right of the tenant to make such use and enjoyment of the premises comprised in the tenancy as those premises are capable of providing. To import into the covenant an obligation on the part of the landlord to obtain possession of the adjoining premises and not relet them, or to install sound insulation, would extend the operation of the grant.

The subject matter of the grant extends, of course, not only to the demised premises but to everything that is appurtenant or incident to the grant to which it relates. If the demised premises enjoy a right to ancient lights over adjoining property, the landlord must not interfere with the tenant's enjoyment of the right. This would be a nuisance at common law, but it would also be a breach of the covenant for quiet enjoyment. If, however, the demised premises enjoy no such right over adjoining land, the landlord is free to build upon it without thereby committing an actionable nuisance or breach of the covenant: *Leech v. Schweder* L.R. 9 Ch. App. 463. This may have given rise to the notion that it is a necessary condition of liability on the covenant that the acts complained of would constitute an actionable nuisance. But this is not the reason for the distinction. The true reason is that the covenant must be construed by reference to its subject matter, and what amounts to an interference with land which enjoys an easement over adjoining property may not amount to an interference with the enjoyment of land which does not. Thus in *Davis v. Town Properties Investment Corpn Ltd* [1903] 1 Ch. 797 the scope of the covenant was limited by the fact that the owner of land adjoining the demised premises (which did not belong to the lessor at the date of the lease) might build on it at any time so as to interfere with the draught from the lessee's chimneys.

In construing the covenant, therefore, the location of the demised premises and the use to which adjoining premises are put at the date of the tenancy agreement, or the use to which they may then reasonably be expected to be put in future, must always be a material consideration. In *Lyttleton Times Co Ltd v. Warners Ltd* [1907] A.C. 476, the parties agreed that the appellants' printing house should be rebuilt, that the respondents should take a lease of the upper floors as additional bedrooms for their hotel, and that the appellants should use the ground floor for an engine house and printing machinery. Both parties believed that the noise and vibration caused by the operation of the machinery would be so slight that it might be disregarded. The Privy Council held that the respondents had no cause of action. In giving the opinion of the Board, Lord Loreburn L.C. said, at p. 481:

> In this case their Lordships think that both parties agreed upon a building scheme with the intention that the building should be used for bedrooms and also for a printing house according to a design agreed upon. Both parties believed these two uses could co-exist without clashing, and that was why both of them accepted the scheme. Neither would have embarked upon it if he had not thought his intended enjoyment of the building would be permitted, and both intended that the other should enjoy the building in the

way contemplated. They were mistaken in their anticipation. But if it be true that neither has done or asks to do anything which was not contemplated by both, neither can have any right against the other.

The case was argued in nuisance and the implied obligation not to derogate from the grant, but the reasoning is equally applicable to the covenant for quiet enjoyment. This is why it is important to bear in mind that the subject matter of each of the tenancies in the present case was not merely a residential flat, but a flat in a building constructed or adapted for multiple occupation. The adjoining flats appear to have been already let at the date of each of the tenancy agreements in question; but it would make no difference if they were not. It must have been within the contemplation of the prospective tenants that the adjoining flats would be let to residential tenants, and that the occupiers would live normally in them. Neither landlord, and none of occupiers of adjoining properties, has done or asks to do anything since the tenancy agreements were entered into which was not contemplated by everyone concerned. . . .

Any tenant who complains of the state and condition of his property is right to consider whether the tenancy agreement, possibly modified by statute, provides him with a remedy. Where the complaint cannot be remedied without expensive improvements to the premises, this will require a clear contractual obligation to be expressed in the agreement. The covenant for quiet enjoyment is an unsuitable vehicle for such an obligation.

Conclusion

My Lords, these appeals illuminate a problem of considerable social importance. No one, least of all the two councils concerned, would wish anyone to live in the conditions to which the tenants in these appeals are exposed. For the future, building regulations will ensure that new constructions and conversions have adequate sound insulation. But the huge stock of pre-war residential properties presents an intractable problem. Local authorities have limited resources, and have to decide on their priorities. Many of their older properties admit damp and are barely fit for human habitation. Southwark London Borough Council has estimated that it would cost £1.271 billion to bring its existing housing stock up to acceptable modern standards. Its budget for 1998-1999 for major housing schemes was under £55m. The average cost of installing sound installation in the flats in Casino Avenue is £8,000 per flat. There are 34 similar flats in the estate, so that the total cost would be about £272,000. The borough-wide cost could be of the order of £37m. The relevant local residents' association has considered that the installation of sound insulation is not a priority need.

These cases raise issues of priority in the allocation of resources. Such issues must be resolved by the democratic process, national and local. The judges are not equipped to resolve them. All that we can do is to say that there is nothing in the relevant tenancy agreements or current legislation, or in the common law, which would enable the tenants to obtain redress through the courts.

I would dismiss both appeals.

COMMENTS

1. Canadian courts have adopted the broadly based meaning of quiet enjoyment found in the modern English cases. A leading example is *Pellatt v. Monarch Investments Ltd.* (1981) 23 R.P.R. 8, 1981 CarswellOnt 557 (Co. Ct.). While completing her Bar Admission program in Toronto, Anna lived in a small apartment. During the course of her tenancy extensive renovations to the property were undertaken by the landlord. The tenants were invited to terminate their leases, but Anna chose to stay. The disruptions caused by the renovations having made her living conditions intolerable, she commenced an action claiming a breach of the covenant of quiet enjoyment. In holding in her favour, Borins Co. Ct. J. (as he then was) drew upon the existing English case law (at 13–16):

> In my view, the landlord has, despite the result of renovations to 117 Old Forest Hill Road, acted reasonably in the circumstances. They made efforts to apprise the tenants as early as January of this year of their intention. As well, they tried to keep the tenants up to date by way of a newsletter on October 16 informing them of what work was intended to be carried out in the apartment building over the succeeding period of time. I indicated earlier they did offer Miss Pellatt alternative accommodation for study purposes and had she continued as a tenant I assume that the landlord would have, as they intended to do with other tenants, offered her free accommodation in an empty suite in the building while the new kitchen was installed in her premises. In other words, there is an intention of the landlord with respect to each unit in the building to remove the tenants at the landlord's expense for that period of time which will be required to install the new kitchen. Even though the landlord has acted reasonably throughout, the question still remains as to whether or not the renovations and consequent inconvenience to the tenant is sufficient in law to entitle the tenant to the relief sought. . . .
>
> Was the landlord in breach of its covenant for quiet enjoyment? From the earliest days, the covenant for quiet enjoyment protected against the interference with the tenant's title or possession: *Morgan v. Hunt* (1860), 2 Vent. 213, 86 E.R. 400. In more recent times the Courts have tended to a wider interpretation of covenant. In *Browne v. Flower*, [1911] 1 Ch. 219 at 228, Parker J. said:
>
>> It appears to me that to constitute a breach of such covenant there must be some physical interference with the enjoyment of the demised premises, and that a mere interference with the comfort of persons using the demised premises by the creation of a personal annoyance such as might arise from noise, invasion of privacy or otherwise is not enough.
>
> In *Owen v. Gadd*, [1956] 2 Q.B. 99 at 107-108, [1956] 2 All E.R. 28 (C.A.), Lord Evershed Master of the Rolls, took this sentence as being correct, and Romer L.J. said:

> It has become quite well established by the authorities that no act of a lessor will constitute an actionable breach of a covenant for quiet enjoyment unless it involves some physical or direct interference with the enjoyment of the demised premises.

So too Buckley J. in *Jaeger v. Mansions ConsoL Ltd.* (1902), 87 L.T. 690 at 692, affirmed (1903), 87 L.T. 694 (C.A.): "The disturbance must be of a physical and not a metaphysical nature." In *Phelps v. London*, [1916] 2 Ch. 255, temporary inconvenience due to noise from alterations to the passageway under offices was held insufficient to constitute a breach of the covenant. Finally, in *McCall v. Abelesz*, [1976] Q.B. 585 at 594, [1976] 1 All E.R. 727 (C.A.), Lord Denning M.R. said:

> This covenant is not confined to direct physical interference by the landlord. It extends to any conduct of the landlord or his agents which interferes with the tenant's freedom of action in exercising his rights as a tenant . . . It covers, therefore, any acts calculated to interfere with the place or comfort of the tenant, or his family.

In this case I am satisfied that the construction with respect to the tenant's apartment itself and in a larger sense to the apartment building in which she lived, as a result of the noise, the odours and the mess, constituted an invasion of the tenant's right to the "peace and comfort", to use the words of Lord Denning, of her apartment. In this sense I am satisfied that there was a breach of the covenant for quiet enjoyment . . .

2. A common form of the covenant for quiet enjoyment applies to the landlord and those holding under the landlord. So worded, the covenant does not protect against a claim by someone asserting a better right to the property than the landlord (a person claiming title paramount). Such a person is not claiming *under* the landlord.

Other tenants, however, do claim under the landlord. Their leaseholds are derived from the landlord. In *Mills* it was argued that the noise emanating from other flats counted as a contravention of the covenant. Does this mean that, putting aside the peculiar problem of soundproofing that was so central in *Mills*, persistently noisy tenants can be relied upon as constituting a breach of the covenant of quiet enjoyment? Some Canadian courts seem to think so, when another tenant causes a disturbance under circumstances in which the landlord was in a position to take action but stood idly by: see, *e.g.*, the authorities cited in *Albamor Construction & Engineering Inc. v. Simone* 1995 CarswellOnt 2664 (Gen. Div.).

3. However, consider *Curtis Investments Ltd. v. Anderson* 1981 CarswellMan 332, 24 Man. R. (2d) 220 (Co. Ct.), where the breach of the covenant of quiet enjoyment was founded on the intolerable noise from an upstairs apartment which had not been remedied by the landlord. Jewers Co. Ct. J. (at paras. 10–16) found that no breach had occurred:

> In my view, though, there was here no breach of the covenant of quiet enjoyment. The plaintiff, itself, was not causing, or responsible for causing the noise and disturbance emanating from the apartment upstairs.
>
> In *Woodfall's Landlord and Tenant* (27th Ed.) vol. 1, p. 570, Article 1322, it is stated that, unless the lessor has let adjacent premises for a purpose which must necessarily involve a nuisance amounting to an interruption or disturbance of the enjoyment of

demised premises, he is not liable merely because he knows the other lessee is causing a nuisance and takes no steps to prevent it: there must be consent or active participation on the lessor's part to make him liable for breach of covenant in such a case.

The case of *Malzy v. Eichholz*, [1916] 2 K.B. 308 (C.A.), is in point. There, a common landlord let adjacent premises to two tenants. One tenant operated a restaurant business in his premises, and the other permitted an auction business to be carried on in his premises. The auction business was carried on in such a way as to cause great disturbance and noise which interfered with the restaurant business. The lessee operating the latter business brought action against the landlord alleging breach of the covenant for quiet enjoyment in his lease. The court of Appeal dismissed the action, and the headnote of the case is as follows:

> A lessor is not liable in damages to his lessee under a covenant for quiet enjoyment for a nuisance caused by another of his lessees because he knows that the latter is causing the nuisance and does not himself take any steps to prevent what is being done. There must be active participation on his part to make him responsible for the nuisance. A common lessor cannot be called upon by one of his tenants to use for the benefit of that tenant all the powers he may have under agreements with other persons.

To the same effect, see the cases referred to in Williams' *Canadian Law of Landlord and Tenant* (4th Ed.), pp. 354 and 355.

This view of the law appears to have been accepted by the Ontario Law Reform Commission in their *Report On Landlord and Tenant Law*, p. 92, where it is stated:

> With respect to acts committed by tenants of adjacent premises, there would appear to have to be some consent or active participation by the common landlord in the act of the adjoining tenant in order to render that landlord liable for the breach of the covenant for quiet enjoyment, and this would appear to extend also to acts of nuisance committed by the adjacent tenant. A distinction is drawn between acts authorized or assented to by the landlord on the one hand, and unauthorized acts by persons admitted onto adjoining lands with his authority or assent on the other.

The Ontario Law Reform Commission recommended a change in the law to broaden the landlord's liability for breach of the covenant to cover acts done by his adjacent tenants, irrespective of his active participation in, or consent to, the acts. However, that would appear not to be the present law which, of course, I am bound to apply and follow.

In the instant case, there was no active participation or consent on the part of the landlord; quite the contrary. The plaintiff was concerned about the noise and did investigate it. There was no evidence of complaints from other tenants, and the plaintiff had to rely entirely upon the word of the defendant. As I have mentioned, the information which the plaintiff received from its investigation was that apparently the upstairs tenant was not home at the time of the noises complained of, and the plaintiff was not able to establish the truth of the matter. I accept that, if the plaintiff's representatives had been genuinely convinced that the noises existed, they would have taken steps to eliminate the problem. . . .

4. Allied to the covenant for quiet enjoyment is the implied obligation of a landlord not to derogate from the grant. The meaning of that concept in the context of leasehold premises is explored in the following case.

Petra Investments Ltd v. Jeffrey Rogers plc [2000] L. & T.R. 451 (Ch. D.)

[L owned a small shopping centre in London. The units were rented to firms marketing mainly women's clothing. T entered into a 25-year lease in 1988. The centre was not a financial success, and in 1996, L converted a central atrium into commercial space which was then leased to Virgin as a music "megastore" in the hope of increasing business. During the period of construction, T's business suffered. In response, L offered to provide what was termed a "service charge holiday" until the work was completed. The *quid pro quo* was that T would not bring legal action in relation to the disturbances caused by the work undertaken to build the new unit, or in relation to the creation of the unit.

After the Virgin megastore opened, T's trade did not improve, which T attributed to the new store. T ceased trading on February 15, 1999. L sued for unpaid rent; T claimed, *inter alia*, that the landlord was liable for derogation of grant.]

Hart J.: . . .

As Nicholls L.J. pointed out in *Johnson & Sons Ltd v. Holland* [1988] 1 E.G.L.R. 264 at 267, "the expression 'derogation from grant' conjures up images of parchment and sealing wax, of copperplate handwriting and fusty title deeds", but, as he went on to demonstrate, the principle is not based on some quaint technicality of real property. It is a principle "which merely embodies in a legal maxim a rule of common honesty" (see per Younger L.J. in *Harmar v. Jumbil (Nigeria) Tin Arms Ltd* [1921] 1 Ch. 200 at 225). After citing the classic statements of the doctrine (in particular Lord Loreburn's formulation in *Lyttleton Times Co. v. Warners* [1907] A.C. 476 at 481 and Lord Denning M.R.'s in *Molton Builders Ltd. v. City of* (1975) 30 P. & C.R. 182 at 186, Nicholls L.J. stated the problem thus (*ibid.*, at 268):

> . . . the exercise involves identifying what obligations, if any, on the part of the operator can fairly be regarded as necessarily implicit, having regard to the particular purpose of the transaction when considered at the time the transaction was entered into.

In carrying out this exercise, which in the usual case will involve questions of fact and degree, the starting point is to examine the circumstances subsisting at the time of the original transaction, which circumstances include, but are not limited to, the obligations expressly undertaken by the parties. In the present case neither the Agreement for Lease (into which the defendant entered on September 14, 1988) nor the lease granted in due course pursuant thereto, offers much clue as to the "particular purpose of the transaction" beyond the fact that the defendant was taking a lease of a unit in a building which was to be used "as a retail shopping centre" (recital 2 of the Agreement for Lease) and was to be restricted in its use of the unit to "the sale of ladies wear and associated accessories"; that permitted use could be changed to any other retail use with the consent of the landlord, such consent not to be unreasonably withheld: see Schedule 1, Part 5, and Schedule 2, paragraph 4.2.1 to the lease. The expression "the Shopping Centre" was defined as meaning "the Shopping Centre comprising the Building", the latter expression being defined by reference to plans showing the centre in the form which it took at the date of the lease.

Paragraph 6 of the Second Schedule, Part 2, of the lease reserved to the landlord the following:

> The right at any time during the Term and for any purposes to execute works and erections upon or build or rebuild or alter the remainder of the buildings and any other premises now or during the Specified Period belonging to the Landlord in any manner whatsoever and to use or let the same for any purpose or otherwise dealt herewith notwithstanding that the access of light or air to the Premises may be obstructed diminished or interfered with or that any other liberty privilege easement quasi-easement right benefit or advantage now or from time to time appertaining to or reputed to appertain to or enjoyed or intended to be enjoyed by the Premises or by the Tenant is thereby diminished or prejudicially affected and notwithstanding that the carrying out of such works or such use letting or dealing as aforesaid may temporarily cause obstruction disturbance annoyance or inconvenience to the Tenant in the Tenant's occupation or use of the Premises on the condition that any damage or disturbance covered to the Premises in the exercise of such right is minimised and any such obstruction disturbance annoyance or inconvenience is minimised.

Mr Gaunt Q.C. on behalf of the claimant did not seek to argue that the effect of this reservation was to oust entirely the doctrine of non-derogation from grant. He submitted, however, that the paragraph could be relied upon as indicating various types of activity by the landlord (namely alteration of the Building, the letting of any part of the Centre for any purpose or "otherwise dealing therewith") which were plainly contemplated as not necessarily being inconsistent with the irreducible minimum implicit in the grant itself. In broad terms I accept that submission, but I do not find it helpful in identifying what that irreducible minimum was, or what obligations (either positive or negative) are thereby owed by the landlord. If the paragraph is construed as ousting the doctrine in its entirety it is repugnant to the lease and should itself be rejected in its entirety. If it does not, it has itself to be read subject to a saving of the irreducible minimum. The most that the clause shows is that not every alteration to the centre, either physical or in terms of its use, was contemplated as being incompatible with the rights expected to be enjoyed by the defendant. That does not, however, take one very far.

One thing clearly demonstrated by the evidence was that the original conception of a sophisticated cosmopolitan department store was never anything more than a unrealised aspiration. Short of that ideal what the defendant had hoped for was to be one of a number of ladies' fashion retailers on the ground floor broadly competing for, and thus, as a "clustering", attracting the same customer profile. That also seems to have been the landlord's aim in its initial letting policy, and that aim appears to have been realised by the initial lettings on the ground floor, unstable as they were in the event to prove.

The extent to which these shared expectations of landlord and tenant as to tenant-mix can be translated into an enduring obligation on the landlord to maintain that, or some similar, tenant-mix throughout the vicissitudes to be expected during the initial 25 years of the centre's life might be a matter of some difficulty were it squarely before me. As my summary of the history has shown, there were several significant lease determinations in the early years, as well as the radical transformation of the centre's original philosophy represented by the introduction of The GAP. As an abstract matter, one can see that it can, on the one hand, be argued that lessees such as the defendant took the risk that commercial pressures might lead the landlords, by degrees or otherwise, to depart from their original philosophy, and, on the other hand, that there was a reasonable expectation that the landlords would take positive steps to maintain the tenant-mix. As to the latter argument, I am far from persuaded that the existence of a "reasonable expectation" leads to the conclusion that the landlord was under a "necessarily implicit" obligation to satisfy the expectation. The reasonable expectation may be founded on no more than a belief that market forces would themselves lead the landlords to pursue policies which conduced to the benefit of its original tenants. The question is not, however, squarely before me since it is no part of the defendant's pleaded case that either the claimant or its predecessor was at fault in allowing the situation to develop to the point which it had reached by the end of 1996.

The point is, however, still relevant in the sense that, on the authorities, the relevant comparison is not between the purpose for which the property was fit at the date immediately preceding the action complained of and its state as a result of this action. The test is whether the action complained of rendered the premises "unfit or materially less fit to be used for the particular purpose for which the demise was made": see per Parker J. in *Browne v. Flower* [1911] 1 Ch. 219 at 226. The camel with the broken back is entitled to complain about the last straw.

In considering whether the introduction of the Virgin Megastore rendered the defendant's unit materially less fit for the purpose for which it was let, it was submitted on behalf of the claimant that the mere fact that changes in the centre had rendered the defendant's business less profitable could not, as a matter of law, amount in itself to a derogation. Reliance was, for this purpose, placed on the decision in *Port v. Griffith* [1938] 1 All E.R. 295 as authority for the proposition that the doctrine of derogation does not extend to an act, such as letting adjoining premises to a competitor, which merely decreases the profitability of trading. The correctness of the decision in *Port v. Griffith* has been the subject of recent judicial consideration and decision that the principle which it illustrates is still good law: see *Romulus Trading Co. Ltd v. Comet Properties Ltd* [1996] 2 E.G.L.R. 70. The narrow point decided in *Port v. Griffith* was that, if premises are let for a particular trade, there is nothing to prevent the lessor from letting adjoining premises for the same purpose. The reasoning which led to that conclusion was essentially based on the unreasonableness of attributing to the parties a common intention that the landlord should have been under any such restrictive obligation. Such an obligation must be bargained for if it is to be imposed.

In my judgment the approach taken in *Port v. Griffith* and *Romulus Trading Co. Ltd v. Comet Properties Ltd* requires some qualification in a case involving a letting in a purpose-built centre such as the present. In such a case it is not so obviously unreasonable to suppose that the parties contemplated that the landlords were to be subject to obligations which had not been expressly bargained for but which were implicit in the use for which the landlord had designed the centre and for which the defendant had taken the lease of its unit. A recent decision of the Court of Appeal illustrates the potential significance of this having been a letting in a shopping centre. *Chartered Trust v. Davies* [1997] 2 E.G.L.R. 83 concerned the lease of one unit out of five in a small mall which had been developed by the original landlord on Bognor Regis High Street. The claimant's business was the sale of puzzles and executive toys. The initial lettings were not all in accordance with the landlord's originally stated aim of attracting "high class retail outlets", and, of those that were, two failed within the first year or two of trading and the units concerned remained empty for over a year. This in itself had a depressing effect on the claimant's ability to trade. The landlord then let one of the empty units to a pawnbroking business. This business attracted hosts of scruffy clients whose presence in the mall, while queuing for service, had a deterrent effect on what might otherwise have been the claimant's passing trade. The trial judge found that the letting to the pawnbroker had created a nuisance, and was in derogation from grant.

The Court of Appeal rejected the submission that the doctrine of derogation from grant was limited to situations where the landlords were responsible for some act which made it either physically or legally less fit for the purpose for which it had been let. Henry L.J. said:

> The central point to be got from the circumstances surrounding the lease at the time Mr Davies took it was that what the landlords were marketing was not just a separate and independent retail unit, but such a shop in its place in a shopping arcade or (in the modern usage) mall. That was the "particular purpose for which the land was hired". The lease makes that clear.

He then listed various provisions in the lease which made that observation good, for each of which there is a counterpart in the lease provisions in the present case. He went on, however, to accept the landlord's submission that the judge had been wrong to find that the mere fact of letting to a pawnbroker had been a derogation from grant: while pawnbroking was not a retail use, there was no evidence that pawnbrokers "were necessarily such unsuitable neighbours that the fact of letting was such a substantial interference with Miss Davis' business to be a derogation" (see 86C). He was inclined also to accept the submission that the actual manner of conduct of the pawnbroking business had not on the evidence before the trial judge, been foreseeable.

Despite accepting these submissions, the Court of Appeal nevertheless rejected the landlord's appeal. It did so on the basis that the actual conduct of the pawnbroking business amounted to a legal nuisance, that the landlord had power, either by enforcing the pawnbroker's covenants or by making new rules for the conduct of its business, to control that nuisance, and that the landlord had been in breach of duty owed to the claimant is not exercising that power. Although it is not entirely clear whether the source of that duty was located in the covenant for quiet enjoyment or the duty not to derogate, the reference in a passage at 88 B-C to what is required by "the principle of fair dealing" supports the view that it was the latter duty which was principally involved. The Court of Appeal distinguished its own earlier decision in *Malzy v. Eichholz* [1916] 2 K.B. 308, where a landlord had been held not liable for failing to abate a nuisance created by one of his tenants and complained of by another, on the ground partly of subsequent developments in the law but essentially on the ground that:

> the critical factual distinction between Malzy and the present case is that here the nature of the grant to a large measure depended upon the proper management of the shopping mall, and the common parts thereof. This development was marketed as a shopping mall, was legally set up in a way which gave the landlord rule-making powers in relation to the development, and the tenants were charged a service charge to finance the necessary management. Proper management might, in appropriate cases, require the provision of security, whether men or cameras, to police the mall. Here it may be that determined use of the rule-making powers to preserve the shared rights of way over the common parts would have sufficed. Instead the landlords did nothing.

While the case illustrates that the context of duty not to derogate may be affected by the fact that the letting is of a unit within a centrally managed mall, its limitations need to be recognised. It was concerned with the landlord's duty to control the nuisance which the conduct of the pawnbroking business caused in the common parts. The thesis that the mere letting of the unit on a non-retail use involved a derogation was rejected. I do not overlook that one of the tenant's complaints related to the dominating pawnbroker's signage permitted at the entrance to the arcade (making it look as though it was Pawnbroker's Arcade) but the Court of Appeal plainly did not regard that as central to its decision.

In the present case the "particular purpose for which the land was hired" was certainly as a retail unit within a centrally managed centre. One cannot, however, proceed directly from that proposition to the proposition that the landlord had assumed a general responsibility not to do anything in the exercise of its reserved powers which might cause damage to the businesses of its tenants. To do so would not be to show a proper respect for the complete absence of any such obligation in the express provisions of a lease entered into between parties of equal bargaining power. I am inclined, however, to think that the circumstances of the grant in this case did impose an obligation on the landlord not so to alter or use the common parts of the centre in such a manner as to cause it to lose its character as a retail shopping mall. The extent to which the landlord was also under an obligation to maintain the initial "clustering" of ladies' fashion retail at ground floor level is much more doubtful. The original leases envisaged that there might be circumstances in which the landlords would, indeed might be compelled to, consent to a change of use. One cannot therefore say that it was implicit in the defendant's lease that the landlord would, throughout its 25-year term, exercise its rights over unlet parts or its powers under other leases so as to maintain the original mix of user. I doubt if one can go further than to say that the landlord was under a duty when exercising those rights and powers to take account of the expectations of its existing lessees. Taking proper account of such expectations might entail not doing or permitting something which, at the time it was contemplated, was reasonably foreseeable as rendering a particular lease materially less fit for the commercial purpose for which it had been granted. I do not, however, think that the duty could ever be so strict as to entail a liability on the landlord for every adverse effect on that commercial purpose, whether foreseeable or not. To be imposed, such a wide-reaching obligation should, in my judgment, be expressly bargained for.

If I am right, then the claimant's proposal to create a new unit encompassing a large proportion of the total square footage of retail selling space in the mall, and to let it to a non-fashion retailer, risked being in breach of at least the first of those obligations. The difficulty for the defendant, however, is that, with full knowledge of the proposal, it agreed to accept a reduction in service charges in full and final settlement of any claim which it had or might seek to make "in respect of the carrying out of the works to create the Virgin unit or in *respect of the creation of the unit*" (italics supplied). In my judgment the italicised words encompass not only the effect of the creation of the new trading unit but also the effect of letting it to Virgin, a non-fashion retailer. All that is left untouched by the phrase, is the effect of the subsequent conduct by Virgin of its business, including in particular the signage subsequently permitted to Virgin by the claimant.

The defendants sought to escape from this conclusion in two ways. First, it was submitted that the word "creation" referred to the process of creation, rather than the state of having been created. That construction, however, renders otiose the words "the works to create the Virgin unit". Secondly, it was submitted that the formula did not catch what had in fact been effected by the construction of the new unit coupled with the letting to Virgin, namely what Mr Berry Q.C. described as the transformation of what had once been a retailing shopping centre with a ground floor orientation towards female fashion into what was now in essence a Virgin Megastore with a few separate retail outlets leading off it at ground floor level. I am not satisfied that, even if this were an accurate description of what has taken place, it would not have been caught by the wording of the compromise agreement. The location and dimensions of the new unit were such that, by whomsoever it was to be occupied, it would to a great extent dominate the character of the centre in a way which it had not previously been dominated. Knowing that it was to be occupied by Virgin, the defendant contracted to make no claim thereafter in respect of its creation. In any event, on the facts this is not, in my judgment, an accurate description of what has taken place. At least once inside the mall it is clear that what remains at ground floor level is a shopping centre, albeit a small one. The fact that the non-Virgin units now have no particular focus has not been shown to be a by-product of the pleaded breach by the claimant in permitting Virgin to trade in the manner in which it does from the new unit. It is conceded that the introduction of Virgin did not displace any existing tenant whose business was of assistance to the defendants and that it did not reduce the number of units on the ground floor.

On those findings the only complaint which the defendant can have is as to the manner in which the claimant has permitted Virgin to trade, in particular in the aggressive exterior signage which it enjoys and the extent to which the whole of the ramped entrance has been allowed to be incorporated, both visually and to some extent functionally, into the Megastore. As to this I have found that these features may well have made some contribution to the unexpectedly adverse effect of the whole on the defendant's trading. In permitting it, however, the claimant was simply pursuing the logic of introducing the Virgin Megastore as an anchor or "magnet" tenant. The fact that the magnet has not only not exerted the attractive force which was expected by both parties but appears to have had an opposite effect in relation to the defendant's business does not entail that the claimant is legally responsible for the consequences. All that it demonstrates is that commercial judgments made from time to time may turn out to be wrong. The lease into which the defendant entered left the landlords free to make such commercial judgments. Moreover, the claimant has not in my judgment been shown to have stood in the way of any constructive proposal by the defendant to counter-balance the allegedly offending Virgin signage with additional advertising of its own.

Accordingly I am unable to conclude that any of the alleged breaches by the claimant of its duty not to derogate can be relied on by the defendant.

Judgment for the landlord.

COMMENT

In *Clark's-Gamble of Can. Ltd. v. Grant Park Plaza Ltd.* [1967] S.C.R. 614, 1967 CarswellMan 48, space in a shopping centre had been leased to T for use as a discount department store. Some time later, L expanded the centre, and agreed to rent one of the new units to F.W. Woolworth's for use as a Woolco store. T argued, among other things, that this amounted to a derogation of grant by L. For the Court, Spence J. rejected that argument (at 625-6):

> In the present case, the landlord, whether it be considered to be Grant Park Plaza Ltd. or either of its subsidiary companies, does not propose to utilize any part of the balance of its land in a fashion which would result in any part of the lands leased to the appellant being rendered unfit for doing business. It proposes to erect a building more than twice the size of that leased to the appellant and lease the said building to the F.W. Woolworth Company for the carrying on of a Woolco store. It is true that one could only expect the operation of the Woolco Store to be stern competition for the appellant. But this is far from conduct which would render the premises leased to the appellant unfit for it to carry on its business. To adopt the words from *Browne v. Flower*, [[1911] 1 Ch. 219, at 227], "after all, a purchaser can always bargain for those rights which he deems indispensable to his comfort". Certainly the responsible officers of the appellant were well aware of the rights and interests of their employer. They had had long experience in both merchandising and leasing and would have found it a matter of no particular complication whatsoever to have drafted and insisted on a clear and exact covenant against leasing to a competing enterprise . . . .

5. TERMINATION AND REMEDIES

Tenancies may terminate in a number of ways. A lease for a set term will expire once the terminating date has been reached. Periodic leases can be ended by either party giving the appropriate notice. At common law, this meant notice equivalent to the period of the lease (a monthly lease requires a month's notice), except for a yearly lease for which only six-months notice is required. A tenancy at will can be brought to an end by either party serving notice to that effect.

When events trigger the doctrine of frustration the lease is treated as having ended (see especially *National Carriers Ltd. v. Panalpina (Northern) Ltd.* (1980) [1981] A.C. 675 (H.L.). See also *Carnell v. Carson* (1818) 1 Nfld. L.R. 131 (S.C.)). A lease will also end when the tenant buys the freehold, or a third party acquires the leasehold and freehold entitlements; in either case these separate estates merge into one.

The landlord may also reacquire the property where the tenant surrenders the lease, if the surrender is accepted by the landlord. Surrender may arise under an express agreement, or impliedly. When, for example, the tenant abandons the premises, and the landlord decides to retake possession (a question of facts which can sometimes be contentious), this may give rise to a finding that a surrender has occurred.

A breach can lead to an action for damages, or an action in debt to collect unpaid rent (if such is the case). Likewise, when the tenant fails to pay the rent, a landlord may levy distress. That is, goods of the tenant on the premises may be seized — held hostage — until the rent is duly paid. Legislation now regulates the distraint process, and typically allows distrained goods to be sold to make good any shortfall in rent. It is an extraordinary power: most creditors cannot simply seize other property of the debtor to make good some debt obligation; instead, the creditor must obtain a judgment before invoking this type of creditor's remedy.

A breach can also, in appropriate circumstances, lead to a termination of a tenancy. Until recently, it was generally understood that when a breach of a lease occurs the lessor's ability to terminate depends on how the obligation was created under the lease. Where a term is couched as a condition, the lessor retains a right of re-entry for breach. This construct is no more than a leasehold version of the fee simple subject to a condition subsequent, coupled with a right of re-entry for condition broken, studied in Chapter 7. (Is there a potential perpetuities problem here? See R. Megarry and W. Wade, *The Law of Real Property*, 6th ed. (London: Sweet & Maxwell, 2000, Charles Harpum) at 355.)

Terms might be explicitly stated to be conditions. Or, as is commonly the case, the document might list a string of tenant obligations and thereafter recite that a breach of any covenant gives rise to a right of re-entry. Under either style of drafting, the landlord may re-enter. However, until re-entry has occurred, the lease continues in effect. Moreover, if there is a failure to follow the appropriate steps for the recovery of possession, or the actions of the lessor suggest that the right of forfeiture is not being exercised (waiver), this may preclude the landlord from terminating. In addition, the tenant may be in a position to set matters right and seek equitable relief from forfeiture by court order.

The case of *Highway Property v. Kelly, Douglas* reformed the law of landlord remedies, and, as will be seen, the case holds implications for the covenant/condition dichotomy.

Highway Properties v. Kelly, Douglas & Co. 1971 CarswellBC 239, [1971] S.C.R. 562

Laskin J.:

The issue in this appeal arises out of the repudiation of an unexpired lease by the major tenant in a shopping centre and the resumption of possession by the landlord, with notice to the defaulting tenant that it would be held liable for damages suffered by the landlord as a result of the admittedly wrongful repudiation. This issue raises squarely the correctness of the decision of the Ontario Court of Appeal in *Goldhar v. Universal Sections & Mouldings Ltd.*, [1963] 1 O.R. 189, 36 D.L.R. (2d) 450, which was followed by the majority of the British Columbia Court of Appeal in the present case.

The substantial question emerging from the facts is the measure and range of damages which the landlord, the appellant before this Court, may claim by reason of the repudiation by the tenant, the respondent herein, of its lease of certain premises, and its consequent abandonment of those premises, where the landlord took possession with a contemporaneous assertion of its right to full damages according to the loss calculable over the unexpired term of the lease. It will be necessary, in dealing with this question, to consider the situations where, upon the tenant's repudiation and abandonment, the landlord does not resume possession but insists on enforcing the lease, or takes possession on his own or on the tenant's account. A common characterization of the problem in this appeal is whether it is to be resolved according to the law of property or according to the law of contract; but, in my opinion, this is an over-simplification.

The dispute between the parties stems from a lease of 19th August 1960 under which the landlord demised certain premises in its shopping centre to the tenant "to be used for grocery store and super market". A term of 15 years from 1st October 1960 was specified at a prescribed annual rent, payable monthly in advance, plus an additional rent based on a certain formula which need not be reproduced here. The tenant covenanted, *inter alia*, to pay rent, certain taxes and maintenance costs; not to do or suffer anything to be done on the demised premises without the landlord's consent whereby insurance policies thereon might become void or voidable or the premiums increased; and to pay into a promotion fund to be used for the benefit of the shopping centre. There were covenants for repair and provisions for renewal but their terms are not germane to the disposition of this appeal. There was also a covenant by the landlord for quiet enjoyment. Clause 5(a), so far as relevant here, provided that if the rent or any part thereof be in arrears for 15 days or if any covenant by the tenant should be unfulfilled, and the failure to pay rent or fulfill the covenant should continue 15 days after notice thereof to the tenant, then the current month's rent and three months' additional rent should immediately become due and the landlord might forthwith re-enter, and thereupon the demise should absolutely determine, but without prejudice to any right of action in respect of any antecedent breach of the tenant's covenants.

Clause 9, which was central to the landlord's claim for damages, was as follows:

> The tenant further covenants and agrees that it will commence to carry on its business within thirty (30) days from the completion of the demised premises and will carry on its business on the said premises continuously. The demised premises shall not be used for any other purpose than as to conduct the Tenant's business in the said premises during such hours as the Landlord may from time to time require on all business days during the term hereby created and in such manner that the Landlord may at all times receive the maximum amount of income from the operation of such business in and upon the demised premises. The Tenant shall install and maintain at all times in the demised premises first class trade fixtures and furniture adequate and appropriate for the business of the Tenant thereon. The Tenant further agrees to conduct its business as aforesaid in the said premises during such evenings and for such hours thereof during the term hereby created as permitted by the By-laws of the Corporation of the District of North Vancouver, B.C. and consistent with the practices generally acceptable by retail outlets in the area.

The shopping centre built by the appellant consisted of 11 stores, including the supermarket premises let to the respondent. Before buying the land on which the shopping centre was later built, the appellant obtained the commitment of the respondent to lease space therein for a food supermarket to be constructed according to its specifications. This commitment was evidenced by a lease dated blank day of May 1960, whose terms were carried into the document of 19th August 1960. The respondent went into possession through a subtenant (with the appellant's consent) on or about 20th October 1960. By February 1961 only five other stores in the shopping centre had been let, and the venture did not prosper. The supermarket subtenant indicated its intention to close the business down on 24th March 1962, and did so. The appellant drew the respondent's attention to cl. 9 of the lease and received an assurance in a letter from the respondent of 26th March 1962 that it was standing by the lease and was endeavouring to sublet its leasehold. Nothing came of its endeavours.

The closing down of the supermarket adversely affected the other tenants in the shopping centre, and by 22nd November 1963 (a date whose relevance will appear later) three of those tenants had moved out. The shopping centre began to take on a "ghost-town" appearance and suffered from petty vandalism. On 13th April 1962, following the closing down of the supermarket, the appellant's solicitors wrote to the respondent, again drawing attention to cl. 9 of the lease, complaining that the appellant was suffering damage and advising that they would seek compliance to have the business reopened or would claim damages. The appellant learned in July

1962 that the respondent was removing fixtures, and its solicitors wrote in objection on 11th July 1962, relying on cl. 9 and on the covenant in cl. 10(a) permitting removal if the tenant is not in default. The letter threatened resort to an injunction unless the removal was halted.

The action, out of which this appeal arises, was commenced on 16th July 1962, and an interlocutory injunction was sought but refused. Rent was paid by the respondent to June 1963. The statement of claim, which was delivered on 31st May 1963, asked for a declaration that the lease was binding upon the respondent, asked for a decree of specific performance and for a mandatory order and an injunction, and also sought damages. The respondent delivered a defence and counter-claim on 12th September 1963. Paragraph 8 of the counter-claim said flatly: "The Defendant hereby repudiates the said agreement dated August 19, 1960". As a result of this repudiation, the appellant's solicitors wrote to the respondent's solicitors on 22nd November 1963 (a date mentioned earlier in these reasons) in these terms:

> Dear Sirs:
>
> *Re: Highway Properties Limited and Kelly Douglas & Co. Ltd.*
>
> This is to advise you that in view of your pleadings, our client takes the position that your client has repudiated the lease in question.
>
> Our client, therefore, intends to take possession of the premises and will attempt to lease these upon the same terms and conditions as set out in the lease of the 19th of August, 1960.
>
> We would further advise you that our client intends to hold your client responsible for any damages suffered by them as a result of your client's breach and wrongful repudiation of the said lease.

Following this letter the appellant took possession of the supermarket premises and attempted, without success, to relet them for the unexpired term of the lease of the respondent. Subsequently, the appellant subdivided the premises into three stores which were eventually rented, two under a lease of 1st March 1965, and the third under a lease of 1st November 1965. At the opening of trial on 29th November 1966 the appellant obtained leave to amend its statement of claim. The amendment referred to the respondent's rescission of the agreement thereunder in accordance with the letter of 22nd November 1963 and claimed damages not only for loss suffered to the date of the so-called rescission but also, and mainly, for prospective loss resulting from the respondent's failure to carry on a supermarket business in the shopping centre for the full term of the lease. . . .

I approach the legal issue involved in this appeal by acknowledging the continuity of common-law principle that a lease of land for a term of years under which possession is taken creates an estate in the land, and also the relation of landlord and tenant, to which the common law attaches various incidents despite the silence of the document thereon. For the purposes of the present case, no distinction need be drawn between a written lease and a written agreement for a lease. Although by covenants or by contractual terms, the parties may add to, or modify, or subtract from the common-law incidents, and, indeed, may overwhelm them as well as the leasehold estate by commercial or business considerations which represent the dominant features of the transaction, the "estate" element has resisted displacement as the pivotal factor under the common law, at least as understood and administered in this country.

There has, however, been some questioning of this persistent ascendancy of a concept that antedated the development of the law of contracts in English law and has been transformed in its social and economic aspects by urban living conditions and by commercial practice. The judgments in the House of Lords in *Cricklewood Property & Investment Trust Ltd. v. Leighton's Investment Trust Ltd.*, [1945] A.C. 221, [1945] 1 All E.R. 252, are illustrative. . . .

In the various common-law provinces, standard contractual terms (reflected, for example, in Short Forms of Leases Acts) and, to a degree, legislation, have superseded the common law of landlord and tenant; for example, in prescribing for payment of rent in advance; in providing for re-entry for non-payment of rent or breaches of other covenants exacted from the tenant; in modifying the absoluteness of covenants not to assign or sublet without leave; and in blunting peremptory rights of termination or forfeiture. The contractual emphasis, even when reinforced by commercial clauses testifying to the paramount business considerations in a lease of land, has hitherto stopped short of full recognition of its remedial concomitants, as, for example, the principle of anticipatory breach and the principle governing relief upon repudiation. I note that this Court had no hesitation in applying the doctrine of anticipatory breach to a contract for the sale of land, even to the point of allowing an immediate suit for specific performance (but, of course, at the time fixed for completion): see *Kloepfer Wholesale Hardware & Automotive Co. v. Roy*, [1952] 2 S.C.R. 465, [1952] 3 D.L.R. 705. I think it is equally open to consider its application to a contractual lease, although the lease is partly executed. Its anticipatory feature lies, of course, in the fact that instalments of rent are payable for future periods, and repudiation of the lease raises the question whether an immediate remedy covering the loss of such rent and of other advantages extending over the unexpired term of the lease may be pursued notwithstanding that the estate in the land may have been terminated.

The developed case law has recognized three mutually exclusive courses that a landlord may take where a tenant is in fundamental breach of the lease or has repudiated it entirely, as was the case here. He may do nothing to alter the relationship of landlord and tenant, but simply insist on performance of the terms and sue for rent or damages on the footing that the lease remains in force. Second, he may elect to terminate the lease, retaining of course the right to sue for rent accrued due, or for damages to the date of termination for previous breaches of covenant. Third, he may advise the tenant that he proposes to re-let the property on the tenant's account and enter into possession on that basis. Counsel for the appellant, in effect, suggests a fourth alternative, namely, that the landlord may elect to terminate the lease but with notice to the defaulting tenant that damages will be claimed on the footing of a present recovery of damages for losing the benefit of the lease over its unexpired term. One element of such damages would be, of course, the present value of the unpaid future rent for the unexpired period of the lease less the actual rental value of the premises for that period. Another element would be the loss, so far as provable, resulting from the repudiation of cl. 9. I say no more about the elements of damages here in view of what has been agreed to in that connection by the parties.

There is no need to discuss either the first or second of the alternatives mentioned above other than to say, in respect of the second, that it assumes a situation where no prospective damages could be proved to warrant any claim for them, or even to warrant taking the third alternative. I wish, however, to examine the underpinnings and implications of the third course because they have a decided bearing on whether the additional step proposed by counsel for the appellant should be taken in this case.

Where repudiation occurs in respect of a business contract (not involving any estate in land), the innocent party has an election to terminate the contract which, if exercised, results in its discharge *pro tanto* when the election is made and communicated to the wrongdoer. . . . Termination in such circumstances does not preclude a right to damages for prospective loss as well as for accrued loss.

A parallel situation of repudiation in the case of a lease has generally been considered in the language of and under the principles of surrender, specifically of surrender by operation of law or implied surrender. It is said to result when, upon the material breach or repudiation of a lease, the innocent party does an act inconsistent with the continued existence of that lease. The *Goldhar* case applied the doctrine where, upon a tenant's repudiation of a lease, the landlord re-let the premises. The further consequence of this was said to be not only the termination of the estate in the land but also the obliteration of all the terms in the document of lease, at least so far as it was sought to support a claim thereon for prospective loss.

The rule of surrender by operation of law, and the consequences of the rule for a claim of prospective loss, are said to rise above any intention of the party whose act results in the surrender, so long as the act unequivocally makes it inconsistent for the lease to survive. Even if this be a correct statement of the law, I do not think it would apply to a case where both parties evidenced their intention in the lease itself to recognize a right of action for prospective loss upon a repudiation of the lease, although it be followed by termination of the estate. There are cases in other jurisdictions which have recognized the validity of covenants to this effect: see 11 Williston on Contracts (Jaeger) 3rd ed., 1968, para. 1403. . . .

English and Canadian case law has given standing to a limitation on the operation of surrender, although there is repudiation and repossession, if the landlord, before repossessing, notifies the defaulting tenant that he is doing so with a view to re-letting on the tenant's account. No such notice was given in the *Goldhar* case; and although it was argued in the present case that the letter of 22nd November 1963 asserted that position, neither the trial Judge nor the Court of Appeal accepted the argument. I agree that the letter is not sufficiently explicit to that end, but I would think that the recognition of such a modifying principle would suggest a readiness to imply that a re-letting was on the repudiating tenant's behalf, thus protecting the landlord's rights under the lease and at the same time mitigating the liability for unpaid rent. . . . I know that under the present case law the landlord is not under a duty of mitigation, but mitigation is in fact involved where there is a re-letting on the tenant's account.

Since the limiting principle under discussion is based on a unilateral assertion of unauthorized agency, I find it difficult to reconcile with the dogmatic application of surrender irrespective of intention. One of the earliest of the cases in England which gave expression to this limiting principle was *Walls v. Atcheson* (1826), 3 Bing. 462, 130 E.R. 591. I read it as indicating that a landlord upon an abandonment or repudiation of a lease by his tenant may qualify his re-entry to make it clear that he is not foregoing his right to insist on continuation of the tenant's obligation to pay rent. Since rent was regarded, at common law, as issuing out of the land, it would be logical to conclude that it ceased if the estate in the land ceased. But I do not think that it must follow that an election to terminate the estate as a result of the repudiation of a lease should inevitably mean an end to all covenants therein to the point of denying prospective remedial relief in damages.

I appreciate, however, that this principle of denial has been carried into modern doctrine from the older cases that were founded on the relation of surrender to a continuing claim for rent. *Woodfall on Landlord and Tenant*, 1968, vol. 1, 27th ed., p. 869 cites only the *Goldhar* case for the proposition, but it is evident from other English cases such as *Richmond v. Savill*, [1926] 2 K.B. 530, that the English law is to the same effect. I have the impression from a reading of the cases that the glide into this principle was assisted by translating repudiation or abandonment into an "offer" of surrender and by compounding this legal solecism by a further lapse into the language of rescission. . . .

As long ago as 1906, the High Court of Australia in *Buchanan v. Byrnes* (1906), 3 C.L.R. 704, held that upon an abandonment by a tenant, in breach of covenant, of the hotel property which he had leased, the landlord was entitled to claim damages over the unexpired term of the lease notwithstanding a surrender. It is coincidence that the lease in that case was for 15 years and that it also included a covenant by the tenant, similar to the covenant here, to carry on the business for which the lease was given, for the full term of the tenancy. . . .

The approach of the High Court of Australia commends itself to me, cutting through, as it does, artificial barriers to relief that have resulted from overextension of the doctrine of surrender in its relation to rent. Although it is correct to say that repudiation by the tenant gives the landlord at that time a choice between holding the tenant to the lease or terminating it, yet at the same time a right of action for damages then arises; and the election to insist on the lease or to refuse further performance (and thus bring it to an end) goes simply to the measure and range of damages. I see no logic in a conclusion that, by electing to terminate, the landlord has limited the damages that he may then claim to the same scale that would result if he had elected to keep the lease alive.

What is apparently the majority American view is to the same effect as the view taken in Australia and that I would take: see 4 *Corbin on Contracts*, 1951, para. 986, p. 955. *The American Law of Property*, 1952, vol. 1, pp. 203-4, states that "If the lessee abandons the premises and refuses to pay rent, the cases quite generally hold, in accordance with the doctrine of anticipatory breach, that the lessor may sue for complete damages without waiting until the end of the term"; and I may add that, under the case law, this is so at least where the suit is for damages and not for rent as such.

There are some general considerations that support the view that I would take. It is no longer sensible to pretend that a commercial lease, such as the one before this Court, is simply a conveyance and not also a contract. It is equally untenable to persist in denying resort to the full armoury of remedies ordinarily available to redress repudiation of covenants, merely because the covenants may be associated with an estate in land. Finally, there is merit here as in other situations in avoiding multiplicity of actions that may otherwise be a concomitant of insistence that a landlord engage in instalment litigation against a repudiating tenant.

Lest there be any doubt on the point, cl. 5(a) of the lease (previously referred to in these reasons) does not preclude the claim made herein for prospective damages. The landlord did not invoke the clause, and hence no question arises of an irrevocable election to rely on it.

I would, accordingly, allow his appeal, with costs to the appellant throughout, and remit the case to the trial Judge for assessment of damages. It follows that I would overrule the *Goldhar* case.

J.W. Lem, "Annotation: *Unisys Canada Inc. v. York Three Associates Inc.*" (2002) 44 R.P.R. (3d) 140

Many Canadian legal academics and leasing practitioners alike have advocated the demise of Laskin's "first remedy" from *Highway Properties Ltd. v. Kelly, Douglas & Co.*, [1971] S.C.R. 562, 1971 CarswellBC 239, 1971 CarswellBC 274 (S.C.C.). That is, they have argued that, as a matter of policy, a landlord under a commercial lease really ought not have a right, in the face of a tenant repudiation, to ". . . do nothing to alter the relationship of landlord and tenant, but simply insist on performance . . .". In other words, those who rail against the "first remedy" argue that a commercial lease, like any other contract, cries out for an obligation on the part of the landlord to mitigate in circumstances where the tenant has purported to repudiate its lease (for a truly persuasive piece, see A. Sternberg, "The Commercial Landlord's Duty to Mitigate Upon a Tenant's Abandonment of the Premises" (1984-85) 5 Adv.Q.385). Notwithstanding such learned protestations, however, the commercial landlord's exemption from the duty to mitigate has remained a central tenet of the Canadian law of landlord and tenant, and was re-affirmed, at least in Ontario, as recently as 1992 in *607190 Ontario Inc. v. First Consolidated Holdings Corp.*, 26 R.P.R. (2d) 298, 1992 CarswellOnt 609 (Div. Ct.).

The now seemingly long-standing *status quo* on the landlord mitigation issue established in *Highway Properties* was almost upset, however, by the recent trial decision in *Unisys Canada Inc. v. York Three Associates Inc.*, 1999 CarswellOnt 4100, 39 R.P.R. (3d) 220 (S.C.J.). At trial in *Unisys*, it was held that a landlord had a duty to mitigate its damages, not only by terminating and seeking a replacement tenant, but by actually renegotiating with the repudiating tenant itself! Although the trial court did not exactly compel the landlord to mitigate, it did deny the landlord recovery for prospective damages as a result of its failure to enter into a compromise with the defaulting tenant. This startling *ratio* did seem, however, somewhat susceptible to scrutiny (see *e.g.* this annotator's comments on the trial decision at 39 R.P.R. (3d) 221).

The Ontario Court of Appeal drilled the coffin shut on the trial court's reasoning by concluding, somewhat unceremoniously, as follows:

> Unisys [*i.e.* the Landlord] takes the position that it had a valid sublease with York Three and that it was under no obligation to renegotiate with it in order to mitigate its damages in the event that York Three should default. It is correct in this. The trial judge should not have penalized Unisys for its failure to mitigate.

What many may have thought was the best hope in decades at a serious run at the Landlord's duty to mitigate has fizzled-out on appeal. Practitioners, at least in Ontario, should simply "get over it" and continue practising knowing that Laskin's "first remedy" lives on, and that commercial landlords, at least in Ontario, still do not have a duty to mitigate.

QUESTIONS AND COMMENTS

1. Does the reasoning in *Highway Properties* mean that the distinction between covenants and conditions is now irrelevant?

2. In leases the landlord's obligations are typically stated as covenants. And the covenants of a landlord are independent of those of the tenant. As a result, the tenant's only recourse for breach was an action for damages. Unless evicted, actually or constructively, the tenant was required to continue to pay rent even in the face of a landlord's other (even egregious) breaches. Does *Highway Properties* change that?

Since that decision, it has been held that a fundamental breach of a lease by a landlord triggers a right of termination on the part of the tenant. See, *e.g.*, *Shun Cheong Holdings B.C. Ltd. v. Gold Ocean City Supermarket Ltd.* 2002 CarswellBC 1892, 2 R.P.R. (4th) 198 (C.A.).

3. What would be the effect of a term stating "the tenant may not terminate the lease by reason of a fundamental or material breach by the landlord"?

4. Could the landlord have received the same compensation by using the third remedy? If so, why is it necessary to add a fourth?

5. In quantifying the measure of damages in a case such as *Highway Properties*, Laskin J. stated (at para. 14) that: "[o]ne element of such damages would be, of course, the present value of the unpaid future rent for the unexpired period of the lease less the actual rental value of the premises for that period". Is that the right method of computation?

6. In *Foresight Projects Ltd. v. Tyee Plaza Development Inc.* 2003 CarswellBC 770 (C.A.), T entered into a lease which provided that it would "use the Premises for the purpose of a WORKWEAR WORLD STORE and for no other purpose without the written consent of the Lessor": cl. 9. T also covenanted that:

> 17.1. The Lessee covenants with the Lessor, and it is a condition of this Lease that:
>
> (d) if the Premises at any time during the lease term become vacant in consequence of their abandonment by the Lessee, or the removal of the lessee by legal process for non-payment of rent, breach of covenant or any other cause;
>
> (h) in case the Premises are used by any other person or for any other purpose than as herein provided without the written consent of the Lessor,
>
> then and in any such case the Lessor in addition to any other remedy now or hereafter provided by law may at its option cancel this Lease forthwith and upon such cancellation the term hereof and any right of renewal herein will be determined and forfeited and the then current month's Basic Rent and Additional Rent and a further three month's Basic Rent and Additional Rent will thereupon immediately become due and payable and the Lessor may re-enter and take possession immediately ... and such cancellation and re-entry will not operate as a waiver or satisfaction in whole or in part of any right, claim or demand of the Lessor arising out of or connected with any breach or violation by the Lessee of covenants or agreement on his part to be performed.

T closed its Workwear World store in July 1999, and it moved into a different shopping centre. At that time the lease still had 24 months to run. In October 1999, L served T with a notice of termination based on breaches of cls. 9 and 17(1)d, and reserved the right to recover "all outstanding amounts." L later sued, claiming *inter alia* for prospective losses under *Highway Properties*. Was that case applicable to these circumstances?

Here is what the British Columbia Court of Appeal said (*per* Mackenzie J.A. (orally) at paras. 17-18):

> [L] relied upon *Highway Properties Ltd. v. Kelly, Douglas & Co.*, [1971] S.C.R. 562 (S.C.C.) for the proposition that when a landlord terminates a lease because of repudiation or a fundamental breach, damages are not limited to those that have accrued to the date of termination.
>
> However, in *Highway Properties* the lease contained a continuous use covenant. The shopping centre there was not a success and the tenant, faced with declining business, closed its supermarket and repudiated the lease. This case differs from *Highway Properties* in that the trial judge here held that the intention of s. 9 was only to limit the tenant's use of the premises to operating a store. In my view, clause 9 is, by its terms,

> essentially a negative covenant limiting the lessee's use of the premises to a Workwear World store and prohibiting any other use without the lessor's consent. I agree with the trial judge's finding that there was no contractual obligation to continue to operate a business. In that regard I am of the opinion that clause 9 does not go that far . . .

7. The letter of November 22nd played an important part in *Highway Properties*: it gave the tenant notice that the landlord treated the tenancy as over, but was reserving the right to sue for prospective loss. Courts continue to require such notice. In *Langley Crossing Shopping Centre Inc. v. North-West Produce Ltd.* 2000 CarswellBC 261, [2000] 4 W.W.R. 560 (C.A.), L had leased commercial property to T for a five-year term. The lease was assigned three times — all with the consent of L. All of the assignors agreed to remain obligated to indemnify the landlord for the tenant's obligations.

The third assignee, MDJ, defaulted on the rent payments, and on November 16th, 1995, MDJ was asked to leave the premises, which it did. An action was brought against the original tenant and all three assignees. In January 1997, the property was re-let at a substantially lower rent. In the course of the litigation, questions arose as to whether a sufficient and timely notice was required under *Highway Properties*, and if so, whether such notice was given here. The landlord relied on two letters. One was sent on October 30, 1995, before the lease was terminated. It read:

> Further to our letter of October 06, 1995 (copy enclosed) please be advised that the current tenant has paid $4,000.00 towards this account since our letter.
>
> As the November 1995 rent payment is due on Wednesday of this week, we hereby demand that the current amount outstanding in the amount of $23,135.80 be paid in full on or before close of business of October 31, 1995. *Failing such, we will be enforcing our rights under our lease and indemnity agreements.*

A second letter was sent on December 21:

> We wrote to you on October 30, 1995 indicating that we would be enforcing our rights under the lease with your client. . . .
>
> *As you are aware, your clients are under an obligation to continue to pay all rent as per the terms of the lease as well as the arrears outstanding currently in the amount of $41,228.44.*
>
> We have not heard from you since our October 30, 1995 letter and as such hereby demand payment for arrears on or before December 29, 1995. Failing such, we shall have no alternative but to turn this matter over to our solicitor for collection pursuant to the terms and conditions of the lease. [Emphasis as in trial reasons.]

The British Columbia Court of Appeal found that these missives failed to meet the notice requirement: they were vague as to what rights were to be pursued. But is notice required at all?

For the Court, Esson J.A. wrote (at para. 13):

> Before us, there was discussion of the question whether there could be any utility in the landlord being required to give express notice in a timely way of its election to seek prospective damages. There is sound reason for requiring the landlord to make clear which of the four mutually exclusive courses it proposes to follow. If it intends to follow the first course of doing nothing other than insisting on performance of the terms, or if it intends to follow the fourth course of terminating and suing for prospective damages, it behooves those liable on the lease to take steps to rectify the situation, perhaps by securing a new tenant or applying for relief against forfeiture. The second and third courses do not create the same threat to a solvent tenant or indemnitor. For the very reason that the landlord's remedies are mutually exclusive, it is not sufficient to simply give notice of its intention to exercise its "rights" under the lease. The need for timely notice is most obvious in relation to persons who, like these appellants, played no part in the default but remained liable for the consequences of it.

8. Can a claim for prospective loss contained in a statement of claim constitute a sufficient notice? See *North Bay T.V. & Audio Ltd. v. Nova Electronics Ltd.* 1984 CarswellOnt 1202 (C.A.).

9. As we have seen, the landlord and an assignee stand in privity of estate with each other; there is no privity of contract between them. Absent an express agreement to the contrary (which appears to have been the case in *Langley Crossing*), would an assignee be subject to the contractual approach adopted in *Highway Properties*?

6. THE PROPRIETARY STATUS OF LICENCES

At the beginning of this chapter the distinction between a lease and a licence was discussed. It was seen that, as a general matter, a licence is not regarded as an interest in land. At root, a licence is no more than a permission to do that which would otherwise amount to a trespass. So, when a customer enters a retail store, the store owner (or occupier) is taken to have impliedly authorized the entry. At the same time, that owner may, without ado, ask any patron to leave so long as the reason for doing so does not contravene human rights legislation or any other protective measures under law. The licence is a bare one, subject to revocation at any time.

At one time, the common law regarded even a contractual licence as inherently revocable; a revocation in breach of the agreed terms gave rise only to a right of damages in favour of the licensee. That has now changed: a licence may be made irrevocable, or revocable only on terms. The case of *Davidson v. Toronto Blue Jays Baseball Ltd.* 1999 CarswellOnt 626, 170 D.L.R. (4th) 559 (Gen. Div.) concerned a fan who refused to show his ticket when requested to do so by staff at the Skydome in Toronto during a baseball game. Following this refusal, Davidson was escorted by the police from the stadium. In an action by Davidson for false arrest, a question arose as to whether the Blue Jays management was able to revoke the patron's licence to attend the game. It was held by Wilson J. (at paras. 11–19) that no such right existed on the facts as alleged:

I turn to consider first the fine print of the contractual provisions on the reverse of the Blue Jays ticket. It provides:

> Notice and Agreement — This ticket is a personal, revocable licence, which cannot be replaced if destroyed, lost or stolen, and the holder agrees that the management may refuse admission or remove from the premises any person who has obtained admission by this ticket by refunding purchase price. Holder further agrees to observe all municipal, provincial and federal regulations and by-laws, and may be refused admission, or may be removed from the premises for failure to do so without compensation.

It is not disputed that the plaintiff was never offered, nor did he receive, a refund for the purchase price of his tickets. Further it is agreed that the plaintiff was not in breach of any municipal, provincial or federal regulation or by-law prior to his arrest. By the terms of the ticket itself, the plaintiff was at the baseball game with a personal, revocable licence to be present. In accordance with the contractual terms of the ticket there were no grounds to validly revoke the plaintiff's licence to attend the baseball game to its conclusion. It is the plaintiff's position that the contractual terms should be strictly construed against the Blue Jays whose counsel drafted the terms of the ticket.

The decision of *Hurst v. Picture Theatres Ltd.*, [1915] 1 K.B. 1 (Eng. C.A.) confirms that the purchaser of a ticket for a seat at the theatre has the right to remain and attend the entire performance. The licence granted by the ticket includes a contract not to arbitrarily revoke the licence during a performance. The right to remain is subject to the implied contractual condition that the patron behaves properly, and complies with the rules of management. It appears clear that a ticket holder for a performance is "acting under a right or authority conferred by law", and therefore *prima facia* [*sic*] the trespass provisions of the Act do not apply. . . .

Hurst was considered and adopted in *Winter Garden Theatre (London) Ltd. v. Millenium Productions Ltd.* (1947), [1948] A.C. 173 (U.K. H.L.). The licence for value granted by a ticket for a performance is specifically discussed in *Wintergarden*:

> There is yet a third variant of a licence for value which constantly occurs, as in the sale of a ticket to enter premises and witness a particular event, such as a ticket for a seat at a particular performance at a theatre or for entering private ground to witness a day's sport. In this last class of case, the implication of the arrangement, however it may be classified in law, plainly is that the ticket entitles the purchaser to enter and, if he behaves himself, to remain on the premises until the end of the event which he has paid his money to witness. Such, for example, was the situation which gave rise to the decision of the Court of Appeal in *Hurst v. Picture Theatres, Ld. (2)*. I regard this case as rightly decided, and repudiate the view that a licensor who is paid for granting his licensee to enter premises in order to view a particular event, can nevertheless, although the licensee is behaving properly, terminate the license before the event is over, turn the licensee out, and leave him to an action for the return of the price of his ticket. The licence in such a case is granted under contractual conditions, one of which is that a well-behaved licensee shall not be treated as a trespasser until the event which he has paid to see is over, and until he has reasonable time thereafter to depart, and in *Hurst v. Picture Theatres, Ld. (2)*, where these rights were disregarded and the plaintiff was forced to leave prematurely substantial damages for assault and false imprisonment rightly resulted.

> The Ontario Court of Appeal in *Heller v. Niagara Racing Assn.* (1924), [1925] D.L.R. 286 (Ont. C.A.) considered and adopted *Hurst.* A ticket is a licence for value and is an enforceable right to attend the event in question until its conclusion, provided the ticket holder complies with the implied contractual condition that he or she behaves properly in accordance with the rules of management. *Hurst* and *Heller* were recently adopted by Ground J. in *Livent Inc., Re* (December 17, 1998), Doc. 98-CL-3162 (Ont. Gen. Div. [Commercial List]) at para. 10:
>
>> In *Heller v. Niagara Racing Association* (1924), 56 O.L.R. 355, dealing with the right of a ticket holder to enter a race track and witness the race, Hodgins J.A. stated at p. 361:
>>
>>> It appears to be settled law in England that a license granted by the sale of a ticket includes a contract not to revoke the license arbitrarily, which contract entitles the purchaser to stay and witness the whole performance, provided he behaves properly and complies with the rules of the management, and that this license and agreement, if given for value is an enforceable right: *Hurst v. Picture Theatres Ltd.*, [1915] 1 K.B. at p. 10. There is no reason why this Court should not adopt what seems to be a most reasonable view, having regard to modern conditions.
>
> In the case at bar, there were no posted rules by the SkyDome or by the Blue Jays management. The programme, which may be purchased by those attending each game, contains the rules of fan conduct. The rules of fan conduct are common sense courtesies to ensure the safety of the players and the fans alike. If these rules are intended to be enforceable with respect to all ticket holders, it would be appropriate to bring them to the attention of all the fans by making them clearly visible to all. In any event, there is nothing in the rules of fan conduct stipulating that fans must present their tickets upon demand once on the premises.
>
> Prior to this incident there is no allegation that the plaintiff was misbehaving or not in compliance with the rules of management. He was simply enjoying the ball game with his friend. It is clear that the plaintiff was vocal and rude when he was requested to accompany the Blue Jays personnel and the police to discuss this incident. The plaintiff refused to leave his seat. The issue is who was responsible for escalating the situation — the plaintiff or the Blue Jays' personnel. I concur with the findings of the jury that it was unfortunate that the Blue Jays personnel escalated the situation to the point of unnecessary conflict culminating in the plaintiff's arrest.
>
> I conclude after review of the terms of the ticket, and the relevant case law that the defendants are not entitled to revoke at will the licence granted to the plaintiff, and to treat the plaintiff as a trespasser after he refused to voluntarily leave the SkyDome.

A licence might well be thought of as proprietary, at least to the extent that it is a kind of *personal* property. Depending on the terms of the licence, the benefit may be capable of assignment: see further *Dorling v. Honnor Marine Ltd.* [1965] Ch. 1 (C.A.). A long-standing debate concerns the circumstances under which a licence can be regarded as an interest in *land.* Sometimes it is said that a licence coupled with a recognised interest in land (such as a *profit à prendre* (see Chapter 10)) represents an example of a licence that can run with land. However, such a licence merely piggybacks on an otherwise valid real property right, and so adds little to the analysis of the property nexus of licences.

English law once flirted with the broad proposition that a licence can be considered as an equitable interest in land, where the parties so intend. That radical idea — floated by Lord Denning in *Errington v. Errington* (1951) [1952] 1 K.B. 290 (C.A.) — has been rejected in the most recent case law on point (see, *e.g.*, the *dictum* in *Ashburn Anstalt v. Arnold* [1989] Ch. 1 (C.A.)). However, this is not to say that there are no circumstances under which a licence can give rise to an entitlement that runs with the land, as will be seen below.

Toronto (City) v. Jarvis
1895 CarswellOnt 24, 25 S.C.R. 237

Strong C.J.:

In 1877 John Severn was seized in fee of the *locus in quo* and in that year gave permission to the corporation of Yorkville, now represented by the appellant, to construct a drain through the land in question for the purpose of carrying off surface and other water. The municipality made the drain accordingly.

In 1879 John Severn sold the land to his son George Severn. John Severn died in February, 1880. The sale to George Severn was completed before the death of John Severn. . . . It does not appear to have been disputed that this conveyance was registered; the title is spoken of in the judgment of the Court of Appeal as a registered title, and the only question as regards the registry laws seems to have been whether the interest of the municipality was an interest to which the registry laws applied, and I find it nowhere suggested that if it was there had not been such registration of the deeds as to bring the case within the operation of those laws.

George Severn, having acquired title as before mentioned, made certain mortgages. Under a power of sale contained in some of these mortgages the late Sheriff Jarvis, the father of the respondent, became a purchaser of the property for valuable consideration. Subsequently the land became vested in the respondent under a conveyance from the trustees of his father's will. These mortgages and the deed to the respondent were all duly registered.

The city authorities having entered and performed certain works in connection with the drain the respondent brought the present action to recover damages for trespasses committed in so entering; also damages for maintaining the drain.

The appellant pleaded the agreement with John Severn. The respondent replied that he and those under whom he claimed were purchasers for value and set up the registry laws.

The agreement by John Severn with the municipality of Yorkville, under which the drain was constructed, was proved beyond doubt. It was, however, also established that there was no by-law of the Yorkville council authorising the taking of the land for the drain. Further, it was established by the evidence of George Severn himself, that he had direct notice of the agreement between his father and the municipality before he purchased.

Upon this state of facts Chief Justice Armour and the Court of Appeal have successively held that the respondent is entitled to recover. Their judgments both proceed upon the ground that the respondent is entitled to the benefit of the registry laws.

It is not necessary that we should define with exactitude the nature of the interest in the land taken by the municipality under the agreement with John Severn. Whether that agreement is to be taken as conferring the property in the land required and taken for the purposes of the drain, or whether it is to be considered as conferring a *quasi easement* for that purpose, or was a mere license, can make no difference. In either case it was an interest in land to which the registry laws apply.

If it was the intention to give a title to the property in the land or an easement, it matters not which, then the agreement must be deemed to have been a contract for an interest in land partly performed, one which, being for the valuable consideration involved in the expenditure on the drain, a court of equity would have decreed specific performance of. If it was a mere license it would have been revocable at first, but if not countermanded before money had been expended in the execution of the purpose for which it was conferred it would have by that expenditure become irrevocable, and therefore an interest in land. *Plimmer v. Mayor of Wellington* [(1884) 9 App. Cas. 699.] . . . .

[The Chief Justice then held that the respondent did not have adequate notice of the appellant's interest, and so was not bound by it. As a result, the appeal was dismissed.]

QUESTIONS AND COMMENTS

1. *Toronto v. Jarvis* concerns the equitable doctrine of proprietary estoppel, the application of which is not confined to licences: see generally E. Cooke, *The Modern Law of Estoppel* (Oxford: O.U.P., 2000) at 42*ff.* The estoppel underscores the conclusion that an irrevocable licence arose. However, does it necessarily follow that an irrevocable licence is an interest in land?

2. A cluster of cases have found that a constructive trust will be imposed in defined circumstances against an new owner of land affected by an existing licence. *Toronto v. Jarvis* might well be understood as such a case, though the imposition of the constructive trust was resisted because the putative trustee took the land without adequate notice of the licence. In *Lloyd v. Dugdale* 2001 WL 1476179 (C.A.), Sir Christopher Slade described the guiding principles (at para. 52):

> (1) Even in a case where, on a sale of land, the vendor has stipulated that the sale shall be subject to stated possible incumbrances or prior interests, there is no general rule that

the court will impose a constructive trust on the purchaser to give effect to them. In *Ashburn and Anstalt v. Arnold* [[1989] Ch. 1 (C.A.)] at p. 25E, Fox L.J., delivering the judgment of the court, expressed agreement with the following observations of Dillon J. in *Lyus v. Prowsa Development Ltd.* [[1989] Ch. 1] at p. 1051: "By contrast, there are many cases in which land is expressly conveyed subject to possible incumbrances when there is no thought at all of conferring any fresh rights on third parties who may be entitled to the benefit of the incumbrances. The land is expressed to be sold subject to incumbrances to satisfy the vendor's duty to disclose all possible incumbrances known to him, and to protect the vendor against any possible claim by the purchaser . . . So, for instance, land may be contracted to be sold and may be expressed to be conveyed subject to the restrictive covenants contained in a conveyance some 60 or 90 years old. No one would suggest that by accepting such a form of contract or conveyance a purchaser is assuming a new liability in favour of third parties to observe the covenants if there was for any reason before the contract or conveyance no one who could make out a title as against the purchaser to the benefit of the covenants."

(2) The court will not impose a constructive trust in such circumstances unless it is satisfied that the conscience of the estate owner is affected so that it would be inequitable to allow him to deny the claimant an interest in the property: (see *Ashburn Anstalt v. Arnold* at pp. 22E-F and 25H).

(3) In deciding whether or not the conscience of the new estate owner is affected in such circumstances, the crucially important question is whether he has undertaken a new obligation, not otherwise existing, to give effect to the relevant incumbrance or prior interest. If, but only if, he has undertaken such a new obligation will a constructive trust be imposed. The importance of this point was repeatedly stressed in *Ashburn Anstalt v. Arnold* (*supra*): see for example at pp. 23G, 25A–26A, and 27B. See also *Lyus v. Prowsa Development Ltd.* (*supra*) at p. 1051; *IDC Group Ltd v. Clark* (1992) 1 E.G.L.R. at p. 190B-C; *Melbury Road Properties 1995 Ltd. v. Kreidi* [(1993) 3 E.G.L.R. 10] at p. 110G.

(4) Notwithstanding some previous authority suggesting the contrary, a contractual licence is not to be treated as creating a proprietary interest in land so as to bind third parties who acquire the land with notice of it, on this account alone: see *Ashburn Anstalt v. Arnold* (*supra*) at pp. 15H and 24D.

(5) Proof that the purchase price by a transferee has been reduced upon the footing that he would give effect to the relevant incumbrance or prior interest may provide some indication that the transferee has undertaken a new obligation to give effect to it: see *Ashburn Anstalt v. Arnold* (*supra*) at p. 23F-G. However, since in matters relating to the title to land certainty is of prime importance, it is not desirable that constructive trusts of land should be imposed in reliance on inferences from "slender materials"; *ibid.*, at p. 26E.

7. RESIDENTIAL TENANCY REFORM

Over the last forty years, the basic law of landlord and tenant has been reformed in relation to residential tenancies. The impetus was a felt need to strengthen the rights of tenants by providing, among other things, greater security of tenure.

The reforms follow common themes. In *Principles of Property Law*, 3rd ed. (Toronto: Carswell, 2000) at 277, I describe the main types:

1. greater security of tenure for tenants and lodgers;

2. increased termination notice periods;

3. the fixing of standard obligations of both landlords and tenants in a way that endeavours to allocate responsibilities and rights in a rational and fair manner;

4. an increase in tenants' remedies;

5. the curtailment of landlords' self-help remedies;

6. the establishment of dispute resolution procedures that are designed to be informal, effective, expeditious and inexpensive;

7. the establishment of prohibitions on the bargaining away of statutory rights;

8. the elimination of various anachronisms affecting the general law of landlord and tenant;

9. the creation of landlord and tenant advisory boards; and

10. rent control mechanisms.

The operational details of these elements vary across the country. To what extent are they present in the residential tenancies legislation found in your home jurisdiction?

Rent control regulation is not common in Canada, and it has proven to be controversial wherever it has been tried. It is easy to understand why. In the absence of rent controls, the market governs. If one removes the marketplace, how are rents to be set? A scheme that allows for a fixed annual increase is possible, but will not be fair to all concerned. Some rents may have been historically low; landlords may have introduced upgrades and feel entitled to increased rental income. Hence, an administrative mechanism must be established to deal with unconventional circumstances.

There are other problems that must be addressed for a system of rent control to be effective. For example, a landlord faced with a cap on income may choose to reduce maintenance of the premises as a way to increase the profit margin. If the value of the property as a rental unit drops too low, it might induce the landlord to change uses: creating a condominium or transforming the premises to commercial purposes are common options. Some means of responding to these options is required or else the quality and quantity of rental accommodations will likely diminish. And, of course, the presence of rent controls can inhibit the dedication of new developments for rental purposes. Controls are useful for those presently in rental accommodations, but a low rent creates incentives for tenants to stay put, leaving the next generation of renters with fewer options. A black market in controlled premises, in which tenants exact "key money" to assign a tenancy, can also emerge.

More important is a matter of principle. In some real estate markets the cost of freehold housing has gone through the roof. Should landlords as a class of entrepreneurs/citizens be called upon to shoulder the problem of a lack of affordable housing? Is that not a form of taking?

At the same time, consider a residential tenancy regime that confers security of tenure on tenants in good standing. In Nova Scotia, a tenant under a periodic tenancy who has been in the premises for five years cannot be asked to vacate (absent breach) unless specified grounds exist. Assume that a landlord lacks such grounds, but nevertheless wishes to recover possession of the premises, say because of a dislike of the tenants. What is to prevent such a person from duly issuing a notice of rent increase, raising the rent to $1 million per month. A general rent control system no longer operates in that province, though only one increase in rent can be introduced in a given year. If that type of increase is not precluded, security of tenure is a sham.

Landlords may wish not to evict, but only to gouge. A significant rent increase may induce a tenant to look elsewhere; assuming that there is ample choice in the marketplace. Even where there is, not every rental increase, even if it places the cost above market value, will prompt the tenant to leave. There is a certain inertia that builds up; the place might otherwise be fine; the kids might like the neighbourhood school; and moving is a hassle. Hence, a properly calibrated increase can yield a high return for the landlord.

In Nova Scotia, it was reasoned that this type of hold-up problem strikes the mobile-home market the hardest. Commonly, a mobile home site is rented while the home is owned by the occupant. Picking up stakes is expensive, so a landlord can increase the rent for the pad quite substantially before the tenant reaches the breaking point. As a result, rent controls for mobile homes — but only for mobile homes — have been reinstated in Nova Scotia.

QUESTIONS

1. Many of the logistical problems associated with rent control (such as neglect and conversion to other uses) can be dealt with in some manner. But how can one respond to the question of principle, namely, that landlords are being called upon to suffer a financial loss owing to the fact that inexpensive housing happens to be in scarce supply? (Of some relevance to this question is *Highmark Residences Inc. v. Ontario* 1997 CarswellOnt 5236, 152 D.L.R. (4th) 692 (C.A.), leave to appeal refused: (1998) 50 C.R.R. (2d) 376 (note) (S.C.C.).)

2. Sections 6 and 17 of *The Residential Tenancy Act*, R.S.S. 1978, c. R-22 provide:

> 6.(1) For the purposes of this Act, the relationship of landlord and tenant whether created under a lease or under a tenancy agreement entered into under this Act is one of contract only and does not create any interest in land in favour of the tenant.

(2) A lease or tenancy agreement to which this Act applies shall be deemed not to be a lease within the meaning of *The Land Titles Act* or *The Landlord and Tenant Act*.

17. Covenants in a tenancy agreement concerning things related to the residential premises run with the land whether or not the things are in existence at the date the tenancy agreement is entered into.

What is the combined effect of these two provisions? In what way, if at all, does section 6 alter the rule in *Spencer's* case?

C.R. Vernon, "Life Lease Housing: An Ownership Alternative for Ontario Seniors" (2001) 37 R.P.R. (3d) 40, at 40–4, 65–9 [footnotes omitted]

Introduction

The life lease housing concept has primarily been marketed to senior citizens, although it is not necessarily limited to that group. This paper will provide an overview of the background and development of life lease housing in Ontario and will address current legal concerns relating to it. Life lease housing in this province is essentially unregulated. Condominium ownership is governed by the *Condominium Act* and all rental residential accommodation is subject to the provisions of the *Tenant Protection Act*. Accordingly, there will be a survey of the existing legislative and regulatory framework within which the life lease concept has developed and grown in Ontario. Since the focus of this paper is the purchaser/user, special attention will be paid to the consumer protection issues that arise in the context of life lease housing.

Basic Framework of the Life Lease Concept . . .

[T]he life lease concept, in Ontario at least, is a hybrid beast that is undefined by statute, but governed and circumscribed in its creation and operation by numerous statutes of general application, both federal and provincial.

There is a wide range of tenure/ownership models for seniors' retirement housing available to potential providers and users. It extends from the traditional landlord/tenant relationship of a relatively short-term tenancy, with or without a lease, to freehold ownership of an individual condominium unit, most often a single-storey, apartment-type unit. In between these extremes fall life tenancies, life leases and shared equity arrangements. These various alternatives, rather than being separate and distinct, really form a continuum of housing possibilities for seniors and, in fact, their characteristics often blend together and overlap.

A research paper prepared for CMHC in 1991 contains a useful general definition of the term "life lease":

A life lease is a rental agreement which entitles seniors the right to occupy a unit for the rest of their lives in exchange for the payment of a lump sum. Life leases are usually terminated by the death of the tenant (or in the case of a couple by the death of the last surviving spouse) or at the option of the tenant, upon giving a specific amount of notice.

At termination an amount is usually reimbursed. This amount is determined by a method included in the lease documentation. The nature of redemption formulas is what distinguishes life-lease agreements . . .

In addition to the initial lump sum payment, the residents are also responsible for monthly payments, similar to condominium fees, which pass on the sponsors operating costs, usually including property taxes, utilities, maintenance, and replacement reserves.

In Canada, the history of life lease projects is quite limited and confined to Ontario and the Western provinces. While a few such projects were created as early as 1975, the great majority find their origin in the last 10 to 12 years.

Essentially, the term "life lease" has become a buzz-word for a category of proprietary interests in real estate which are also variously described by their promoters as "life occupancy estate" and "right to occupy". Regardless of how it is described, the two essential ingredients of life lease are:

(i) a sole and exclusive right to both occupy a designated apartment or townhouse unit, fee simple title to which is owned by a third party, and enjoy shared use of the common areas appurtenant to it, and

(ii) an entitlement to realize, in whole or in part, the equity in the unit at such time as the period of occupancy comes to an end.

The first distinguishes the life lease concept from owner-occupancy of freehold or condominium dwelling units. The second distinguishes it from the freehold interest known by the common law as a life estate.

Life lease documentation varies greatly from project to project, and generalizations and assumptions about the subject can be very dangerous. In fact, a 1993 CMHC research project reported that its survey found "many differences among life lease projects across the country — in fact there are more differences than similarities." . . .

The Misnomer of "Life Lease"

Although the term "life lease" is commonly used throughout Ontario and the four western provinces, it is useful, at the outset of any discussion about this concept, to recognize what a disservice the term does to its understanding. Unlike a month to month tenancy or a lease for a fixed period of time, both of which define or determine the term of the lease, a life lease is usually not in fact a lease for the life of the purchaser. Likewise, it is not usually a life estate — a freehold interest terminated automatically by the death of the current owner (life tenant), after which the remainderman automatically becomes the owner. Rather, it is an interest in property that cannot extend beyond the life of its owner, and possibly a brief period thereafter.

The confusion regarding the meaning of the term is often exacerbated by statements in marketing literature, such as the following:

> Life lease residents are not tenants. Conversely, life lease residents are not owners. Life lease residents own a leasehold interest in the development through a contract with the sponsoring organization of the development.

However, upon its expiry, whether by virtue of the owner's death, inability to continue to live independently or conscious decision to move from the unit, the life lease interest usually continues to have an equity value to its owner. This value is typically realized by open market resale of the unit to a qualified or approved new purchaser, or by repurchase by the sponsor based on a price formula and subsequent resale, in both cases followed by the issuance of a new life lease to the new purchaser.

The major distinguishing feature between a leasehold estate and a freehold estate is that of certainty of duration. An interest that has a fixed term, or a term that is capable of being rendered certain, is a leasehold interest. An interest that has an uncertain duration is a freehold interest.

Whether the purchaser's interest is a life estate, the product of a landlord and tenant relationship, or simply a revocable licence to occupy the unit will depend on the terms of the occupancy agreement. Some such agreements limit the term to less than 50 years, thereby creating, at most, a leasehold interest. Others expressly state that they do not create any interest in land. . . .

Tenant Protection Act

The *Tenant Protection Act, 1997*, may have an enormous impact on life lease housing, if the relationship between sponsor and owner is determined to be a landlord-tenant relationship. On the other hand, it may well fall within other established categories of relationship between landowner and user/beneficiary of land, such as trust, security interest or licence. Alternatively, it may simply be a life estate — a type of freehold interest.

An interesting case, although not raised in the context of life lease housing, is the decision of Blair J. in *Charboneau v. Peterson*. This involved the sale of a three unit apartment building, subject to the reservation by the vendor, Mrs. Charboneau, of a "lifetime interest" in a particular unit. She had agreed to pay a nominal monthly rent of $200.00 and was responsible for her own hydro electric charges and one third of any realty tax increases after the fifth year of the arrangement. An issue arose after Mrs. Charboneau moved out and rented her unit to Peterson for $950.00 per month. Several years later, Peterson claimed that, under the then-applicable rent control legislation, he was entitled to the benefit of Mrs. Charboneau's $200.00 rent as the "first rent" charged for the unit and accordingly entitled to a refund of approximately $80,000.00 of the rent that he had paid over a six-year period. The Rent Officer under the *Rent Control Act* held that the relationship between Mrs. Charboneau and the building owner was that of life tenant and remainderman, rather than that of landlord and tenant. The result was that the amount paid by her was not subject to the rent control legislation and the "first rent" charged was the amount that Peterson had agreed to pay when he rented the unit from her. An appeal by Peterson from the Rent Officer's decision was dismissed by the Divisional Court, which stated:

> The Rent Officer was therefore correct in finding that the first landlord and tenant relationship which existed for Unit No. 1 was between Mrs. Charboneau and Mr. Peterson in 1986, and that the first rent that was subject to the rent control legislation was the rent charged in accordance with the Charboneau/Peterson lease.
>
> While parties used a standard residential lease form in drawing up the terms of the interest which Mrs. Charboneau reserved to herself at the time of the sale, she did not in our view become a "tenant" of the Purchaser, that is to say, a landlord and tenant relationship was not created. Rather, so far as Unit 1 was concerned, Mrs. Charboneau retained a life estate, and the Purchaser held the remainder of the fee. In common parlance, it may be thought that a "lease for life" is a leasehold interest in land. However, at law that is not the case . . . an estate for life is a freehold interest in land.

The result of the Charboneau decision, if followed, is that a "life lease" expressly stated to be for the life of the purchaser would create a life estate, rather than a leasehold interest, and accordingly not be subject to the provisions of the *TPA*. However, most life lease agreements are, in substance, leases or licences that on their face appear to fall within the ambit of the *TPA*. Rarely does the agreement specifically define its "term". . . .

Assuming that a life lease arrangement does in fact create a lease, does or should the *TPA* apply? In reviewing the provisions of the *TPA*, it is clear that life lease housing was not contemplated or taken into account. Many of its provisions are contrary to the basic concept of life lease housing and are undesirable to both the sponsor and the resident. The definition of "rent", previously quoted, is clearly broad enough to encompass the purchase price paid by the purchaser upon and in consequence of entering into the life lease agreement. It is certainly a payment given for the right to occupy a unit but, since it is not a recurring payment, what is its nature in the scheme of the *TPA*? Likewise, monthly occupancy charges fit within the definition of rent, but since the components thereof are all directly related to the expenses of operating the project, how can rent control guideline limits be applied without jeopardizing the viability of the project? . . .

There do not appear to have been any successful legal challenges to life lease projects, and their structure and operation, under the *TPA* or its predecessors or, for that matter, under any other relevant legislation. Ronald A. Crane attributes this as follows:

> What has kept challenges and confrontation to a minimum is the nature of a life lease community, There is a shared vision, a collective desire to protect the lifestyle and the

> protective and focused will of the sponsor group to make it work. Such a setting tends to treat people with equity and fairness and most people respond to that treatment by respecting the rules. The other fact that mitigated against challenges is the market. Life Leases have been around long enough that there is empirical evidence that, despite the fear that they don't work, they are resold to a growing market for prices which are competitive to more traditional forms of housing.

Nevertheless, the uncertainty that arises by virtue of the apparent inconsistencies between the *TPA* and the provisions of a typical life lease agreement cry out for legislative intervention. . . .

QUESTIONS

1. As Robert Vernon notes (at 44): "[w]hether the purchaser's interest is a life estate, the product of a landlord and tenant relationship, or simply a revocable licence to occupy the unit will depend on the terms of the occupancy agreement". Draft three separate clauses, each of which creates "a life lease" with the basic attributes described by Vernon. The first should do so by creating a freehold; the second a lease; and the third a licence.

2. Manitoba has legislation governing life leases: *The Life Leases Act*, C.C.S.M., c. L130. Under subsection 1(1), a life lease is defined, in part, as "a written tenancy agreement under or in respect of which . . . the person first entitled to occupy the rental unit under the agreement is granted a right of occupancy for life or for a fixed term of not less than 50 years." Taking that definition as standing alone, what type of proprietary interest does it contemplate?

8. BAILMENT

A bailment can likened to a "lease" of a chattel, for it involves at its core a transfer of possession of goods from a bailor to a bailee. It was shown earlier in this chapter that the line between a lease of land and a licence is drawn by reference to whether or not there has been a grant of exclusive possession. Likewise it may be necessary — for reasons that will soon be apparent — to distinguish a bailment from a licence. Again, that questions turns on whether possession has been transferred — in this setting from the bailor to the bailee. If, for instance, I park my car in a commercial lot, I may be regarded as having bailed it to those controlling the lot. That conclusion is likely (but not a lock) if I hand over the car keys. If I retain control over the car, a licence has been granted. Notice that the land/chattel analogy is slightly askew in this example. In the land context, one is either a tenant or a licensee. However, in the case of a deposited chattel, one becomes either the bailee or the licens*or*. Do you see why?

It will also be recalled that there is no direct juridical nexus between a head landlord and a sub-tenant. One cannot sue or be sued by the other. That is not true under the law of bailment, as will be seen in the case of *Punch v. Savoy*, below.

With land, not every transfer of possession occurs under the terms of a lease: a sale also involves a transfer of possession. Here again a comparable issue occurs in the context of bailment. Imagine a case where A's grain is stored in B's silo. When the period of storage has ended, A is given back an allotment of grain, but there is no certainty that the very same items have been returned; indeed there is no expectation that the same grains will be returned. Is this a bailment, or something else, such as trade or barter? The analysis of bailment begins with that issue.

Mercer v. Craven Grain Storage Ltd. [1993] E.W.J. No. 736 (C.A.)

Simon Brown and Russell L.JJ.: . . .

The plaintiffs are three farmers working in partnership. During the 1980s they became members of a Farmers Co-operative Grain Marketing Scheme whereby, through a company called Craven Grain Limited, they disposed of their grain. There were over one hundred farmers who took part in the scheme. . . .

The defendants, Craven Grain Storage Limited, a separate legal entity from Craven Grain Limited, was likewise incorporated at the same time as Craven Grain Limited. Its primary function was to provide storage and drying facilities for the grain deposited with the company by members of the scheme, and then to release grain to Craven Grain Limited for sale by the latter company.

Between the 3rd August and the 4th September 1990 the plaintiffs deposited with the defendants over 2,200 tonnes of milling wheat. Immediately upon deposit it was mixed with grain already in the possession of the defendants from other farmers. Accordingly it could never thereafter be identified as a separate parcel.

Grain deposited with the defendants was withdrawn from them on the instructions of Craven Grain Limited. The general manager of both companies was a Mr. Muxlow. He was told by the plaintiffs that they were not prepared to sell their wheat through Craven Grain Limited unless and until a minimum price of £160 per tonne was achieved.

Contrary to those instructions all but a very small quantity of grain stored at the defendants' premises was removed from store upon the instructions of Craven Grain Limited. The price of £160 per tonne was never achieved. The plaintiffs were never paid, and by July 1991 Craven Grain Limited was hopelessly insolvent.

The plaintiffs instituted proceedings by a writ and statement of claim dated the 5th November 1991. Paragraph 6 of the statement of claim alleges ". . . the defendant has failed and refuses to re-deliver to the plaintiffs any of the balance of their grain whereby the plaintiffs have suffered loss and damage". The amount claimed was just over £300,000 said to represent the value of the grain lost.

Paragraph 7 of the statement of claim reads "Further or in the alternative the defendant has delivered the plaintiffs' grain to third parties on the instructions of the servant or agent of the defendant or Craven Grain Limited, which instructions were without the actual authority of the plaintiffs whose grain has been lost and the defendant is liable therefore pursuant to the said express term." The express term there referred to is clause 8 of the storage agreement to which we shall shortly return.

It would be convenient now to look briefly at the two contracts which the plaintiffs entered into pursuant to the scheme, one with the defendants and the other with Craven Grain Limited, the marketing company. The storage agreement with the defendants provided for the plaintiffs storing with the defendants not less than a minimum quantity of their grain each year. The defendants were entitled to handling charges. Clause 8 of the storage agreement provides:

(a) Whilst in the possession of the Society the grain shall remain the property of the Grower, but subject to paragraph (b) the risk or (sic) loss of or damage to the grain shall be on the Society.

(b) Any liability of the Society arising under this Clause shall not exceed the amount recoverable by the Society under its insurance policy details of which shall be made available to the Grower on request.

The contract with the marketing company, Craven Grain Limited, provided by clause 2:

(a) In each year in which this Contract is in operation the Grower shall sell through the agency of the Society, which shall sell on behalf of and as agent for the Grower not less than the required proportion of the tonnage of grain produced by the grower that year.

Clause 6(a) provides

Before the first day of June in every year the Society should give the Grower written notification of the categories of grain to be harvested by members that year in respect of which the Society will operate price pools.

We were told that in practice grain was disposed of by the marketing company either pursuant to such price pools or as spot sales dependent upon instructions from the growers. The documentation in this case supported the plaintiffs' assertion that they directed spot sales of their grain.

Paragraph 7 of the Schedule to the Agreement so far as material provides:

(a) Before the first day of July in each year the Directors shall estimate the amounts of the charges either as a percentage of sale prices or as a fixed sum per tonne of grain sold, whichever they think fit.

(b) On a sale of grain not included in any price pool on behalf of a member the Society shall pay to that member within 28 days after receipt of the purchase price from the buyer a sum equivalent to that price after deduction of the appropriate charge as estimated under paragraph (a) of this Regulation.

So much for the material facts and the contractual terms relevant to this appeal.

Mr. Edward Bannister Q.C. for the appellants, developed a number of submissions, but central to them all was the contention that whilst the plaintiffs doubtless had a valid claim against the marketing company for an account, no parallel or other claim existed against the defendants. As to paragraph 6 of the statement of claim he submitted that the defendants were never bailees of the plaintiffs' grain, that once the grain became intermixed with other grain the plaintiffs' property in the grain was eliminated and the defendants ceased to have any obligation to return the plaintiffs' grain to them, nor could the plaintiffs call for the return of their grain. In these circumstances a claim pleaded as it was in conversion could not be sustained in law. Mr. Bannister reminded us that in practice the defendants' store of grain was constantly fluctuating in terms of both quality and quantity, and that the plaintiffs' grain was mixed with other grain not only upon storage with the defendants but upon sale when grain stored at entirely different premises might be drawn down by the marketing company to supplement grain held by the storage company. The defendants, submitted Mr. Bannister, had done no more than release, according to the instructions they had received from the marketing company, grain in bulk for disposal by the marketing company. They had not received instructions directed to the plaintiffs' grain exclusively, for there was no specific parcel identifiable at the defendants' premises. The alternative claim, pleaded under paragraph 7 of the statement of claim, was therefore likewise unsustainable.

Mr. Bannister relied heavily upon a passage to be found at page 97 of *Palmer on Bailment* (2nd Edition):

1. The Wheat Cases:

The essence of bailment is that the bailed property should be returned to the bailor or applied in accordance with his instructions when the bailment terminates. The goods need not be in their precise original form when this event occurs in order for the transaction to qualify as a bailment; if this rule were imposed, it would remove main bailments (such as those for repair or alteration) from the sphere of that relation altogether. What is necessary is that the goods themselves, whether in altered or original form, should be returnable and not merely some other goods of equivalent character or value. There must be a clear physical heredity between what has been delivered to the bailee and what must be returned.

This rule has given rise to difficulty in the area of milling or storage contracts where consumable goods are delivered by their owners for a process of treatment which necessarily involves the intermingling of those goods with similar merchandise belonging to other parties. The facts of *South Australian Insurance Company Limited v. Randell* [1869] LR 3 PC 101 epitomize the problem. A firm of millers were attempting to enforce a claim against their insurers in respect of a quantity of wheat and flour which had been destroyed by fire on their premises. The insurer's defence was that the millers held the wheat as mere bailees for the farmers who delivered it to them to be ground, and that the terms of the relevant policy did not cover goods that were subject to a bailment because the millers had not insured them specifically as "goods held in trust or on commission". The millers denied that they were bailees. They showed that their established trade practice, known to all farmers with whom they dealt, was to intermingle individual deliveries of wheat within a central pool and to use this pool as their current stock. The intermixture took place immediately upon receipt of the wheat and in the presence of the farmer who delivered it. Once it had occurred, the millers might sell any part of the wheat, or grind any part into flour at their sole discretion; the farmer's part of the bargain was that he could at any time demand payment for an equal quantity of wheat to that originally delivered at the price which was current at the time of demand. Sometimes the millers made advances to farmers upon individual deliveries. It was not directly shown that any farmer could demand an equal quantity of wheat.

The Privy Council held that the above course of dealing clearly failed to create a bailment of each consignment of wheat, and gave rise instead to a sale of such consignments, subject (if one took the construction most favourable to the insurers) to the seller's right to re-purchase an equivalent quantity at a future time. Even if individual farmers could, under the terms of trade, demand the return of an equivalent quantity of wheat, they could not demand the identical consignment and thus had not cast the millers in the position of bailees. The case was no different from the deposit of money with a banker, and the fact that the millers made a small charge "for storage" did not affect the complexion of the agreement.

As to the part played by Mr. Muxlow, Mr. Bannister contended that what he had done was in his capacity as manager of the marketing company; it was contrary to his contract of employment with the marketing company and was possibly fraudulent *viz-a-viz* his employers. It could not involve the defendants in any breach of their contract with the plaintiffs or in any breach of any duty owed by the defendants to the plaintiffs. . . .

For the plaintiffs Mr. R. King of counsel submitted that the facts which were common ground between the parties coupled with the contractual documents made it plain that upon liability there was no defence to the plaintiffs' claim and that the judge was right to enter judgment.

He dealt first with the appellants' submissions based upon the passage in Palmer to which we have referred and the supporting authority. Mr. King pointed out that in Randell's case the millers retained a discretion as to how they were to deal with the wheat deposited with them. No such discretion existed in the instant case. Nor was there in Randell any contractual provision retaining property in the depositor remotely akin to clause 8 of the storage agreement here. Upon a proper analysis, submitted Mr. King, the bulk held by the defendants after intermixture was the common property of all growers who had contributed to the bulk, and their interest was an aliquot share of the bulk in the proportions of the individual contributions to the bulk. For this proposition he referred us to and relied upon "The Law of Restitution" by Lord Goff of Chieveley and Jones, 3rd edition, at p. 65. The aliquot share of the bulk would go up or down dependent upon the addition to or depletions from the bulk, but property in common with others was a continuing feature so long as the whole or any part of the individual contributions formed a part of the bulk. This analysis was the only one which could give any effect to cl. 8 in the storage agreement which in terms retained the property in the wheat in the individual growers. The appellants' analysis ignored the existence of cl. 8 or deprived it of any meaning. Likewise in the marketing agreement cl. 2 meant what it said. The marketing company did not sell its own wheat; it sold wheat on behalf of the grower and as agent for the grower; that could not happen, submitted Mr. King, if the growers retained no property in the bulk. The appellants' analysis flew in the face of the plain meaning of cl. 2.

The contract between the plaintiffs and the defendants was in the nature of a bailment submitted Mr. King. Whilst the plaintiffs could not demand a return of their individual grain, once there had been an intermixing, to give effect to the contractual terms, it was necessary to conclude that the plaintiffs retained property in the bulk in common with the other depositors. That afforded them rights against the defendants and created obligations which were owed by the defendants to the plaintiffs.

Mr. King concluded his submissions by advancing the following propositions:

1. The storage agreement should be given effect according to its plain intention. The agreement was for storage screening and drying. It provided for nothing more and was intended by the parties to be separate from the marketing agreement.

2. As such it was implicit in the storage agreement that the defendants would store grain to the amount deposited by the plaintiffs until they ordered its release either to themselves or to the marketing company properly authorised to dispose of the wheat.

3. The plaintiffs never ordered release of any grain until they demanded delivery to themselves in August 1991, and neither did they authorise the marketing company to order the release of grain from the storage company.

4. The defendants were precluded from submitting that the plaintiffs ordered or consented to any delivery of grain because:

(a) the plaintiffs told Mr. Muxlow that grain was to be sold on spot sales at £160 per tonne. This was plainly evidenced by the documents already disclosed and amongst the bundles before the court.

(b) the price of £160 was never achieved.

(c) the marketing company did not have any authority to dispose or order movement of grain which was referable to the plaintiffs, save pursuant to the terms of the spot sales.

(d) the defendant company knew of the lack of authority in the marketing company through the knowledge of their own manager Mr. Muxlow.

5. The plaintiffs were the owners in common of the whole grain in storage to the proportion of grain deposited by them. This proportion varied dependent upon the extent

of the bulk. This last proposition is the only way to give effect to the storage and marketing agreements without doing violence to the terms of both agreements.

6. In August 1991 the plaintiffs were entitled to delivery of their share of the grain and because the defendants were unable to deliver they are liable in conversion in disposing of the plaintiffs' share of the mass, in breach of contract in the nature of a bailment, under an implied term that the grain would be delivered to the plaintiffs or their order, and pursuant to Clause 8 because the defendants had lost the plaintiffs' share of grain.

For all these reasons, submitted Mr. King, the defendants had failed to show any arguable defence and the judge was right to make the order that he did.

We are satisfied that the propositions advanced by Mr. King are valid, that his analysis of the legal relations between the plaintiffs and the defendants is an accurate and realistic one, that any other analysis does violence to the language used in the written contracts, and that consequently the learned judge was right to make the order that he did for the reasons that he identified.

This appeal will be dismissed.

NOTE

The decision of the Court of Appeal was reversed on other grounds: *Mercer v. Craven Grain Storage Ltd.*, Unreported, March 17, 1994. The House of Lords affirmed the Court of Appeal's conclusion that title to the grains remained in the growers even after the mixing.

L.D. Smith, "Bailment With Authority to Mix and Substitute" (1995) 111 LQ.R. 10, at 12-5

The decision [in *Mercer v. Craven*] is (with respect) clearly correct. It is well established that there mere fact of a mixture does not destroy proprietary rights (*Spence v. Union Marine Insurance Co.* (1868) L.R. 3 C.P. 427; *Nelson v. Brown* 53 Iowa 555; 5 N.W. 719 (1880); *Coleman v. Harvey* [1989] 1 N.Z.L.R. 723, C.A.). Absent an agreement, the effect of the mixture is debatable. Some cases suggest that contributors become tenants in common of hte mixture (*Buckley v. Gross* (1863) 3 B. & S. 566; *Moore v. Erie Ry Co.* 7 Lansing 39 (N.Y.S.C., 1872); *Indian Oil Corpn v. Greenstone Shipping S.A.* [1988] Q.B. 345; others are consistent with the idea that original proprietary rights are retained, and artificial rules are available to identify each contributor's contribution (. . . *McDonald v. Lane* (1882) 7 S.C.R. 462). Either way, there is no difficulty with the retention of proprietary rights so long as the quantity in the mixture does not fall below the total of all contributions, as that total varies from time to time. If proprietary rights are retained in an inadvertent mixture, then *a fortiori* they are retained when there is a contractual provision to that effect, express or implied (*Re Stapylton Fletcher*, [1994] 1 W.L.R. 118. A storage arrangement is most likely to be seen as a bailment where the depositor pays storage charges (*Barnes v. McCrae* 75 Iowa 267; 39 N.W. 392; 9 A.m. St. Rep. 473 (1888)); where the grain is stored at his risk (*Moffatt v. Grand Trunk Ry Co.* (1865) 15 U.C.C.P. 392; *Clark v. McClellan* (1893) 23 O.R. 465); where he is required to pay for the insurance (*Busse v. Edmonton Grain & Hay Co.* [1932] 1 D.L.R. 744); and where the warehouse is obliged to keep enough grain to answer to all receipts that are out (*Ledyard v. Hibbard* 48 Mich. 421; 42 Am. Dec. 474 (1882); *Rice v. Nixon* 97 Ind. 97; 49 Am. Rep. 430 (1884)). Of course, there is nothing in these principles which confines them to grain. In *Liggett v. Kensington*, [*sub nom. Re Goldcorp Exchange Ltd.*], Thorp J. at first instance applied them to mixtures of gold bullion, in relation to bullion depositors and to the Walker & Hall claimants (see (1993) 110 L.Q.R. 509); and the decision on the Walker & Hall claimants was affirmed in this respect by the Privy Council. The effect is that there can be a bailment even though it is known from the start that the bailor will not recover possession of the very goods bailed.

Slightly more difficult is the case in which the quality in the mixture does fall below the total of all contributions. It might be that at some point the grain warehouse stands empty. If there is a bailment which only allows mixing, then this is obviously a breach of its terms. Equally obviously, the bailors lose their proprietary rights; they can establish no proprietary rights in grain added subsequently, unless there was an intention to make good the breach (*Clark v. Western Assurance Co.* (1866) 25 U.C.Q.B. 209; *Liggett v. Kensington*, *supra*, depositors and Walker & Hall claimants). That is the lowest intermediate balance rule. But in a grain storage situation, the storer might have the authority to make sales from the mixture even though he did not contribute to it. On the other hand, the depositors might be able to demand a like quantity and quality of grain to their deposit, even though there is an intervening balance lower than the total of all contributions. If depositors are to have proprietary in this situation, a more sophisticated explanation is required. It was provided many years ago by Oliver Wendell Holmes ("Grain Elevators" (1872) 6 American L.R. 450; this article is unsigned, but is attributed to Holmes in Williston, *Sales* (rev. ed., 1948), at p. 412, n. 16). It rests on the idea that the bailee is authorised to substitute other goods for those deposited. The effect of the substitution is that the subject-matter of the bailment changes, with the consent of both the bailor and the bailee. This arrangement is analytically distinct from the idea of mixture; it could apply to a bailment of a single book, which the bailee is authorised to replace with another copy. As before, it is easier for courts to recognise this type of arrangement when it is express, but it can also be implied. If the parties intended that the depositor should have proprietary rights, then that intention will be effective.

If the bailee is allowed to make sales out of the bailed goods, then upon such a sale, the erstwhile bailor has only a personal right (to the price, or to a like quantity of grain) against the erstwhile bailee. Roman law admitted the possibility of such an arrangement (Buckland, *Textbook of Roman Law* (3rd ed. by Stein, 1963) pp. 469-470; D.12.1.9.9). The bailee therefore has the power to turn the bailment into a sale or loan. If, in addition, the bailee has the authority to substitute other goods, then he has the power to turn the loan back into a bailment. When the bailee alienates the bailed goods, he becomes a borrower from the erstwhile bailor, who is deprived of his proprietary rights and so converted into a lender. During this period, there is no priority in the event of the insolvency of the bailee/borrower; conversely, the bailor/

lender bears no risk for the destruction of any goods (*Nelson v. Brown* 53 Iowa 555; 5 N.W. 719 (1888); *Sering v. Shafroth* 137 Ill. 393; 27 N.E. 702 (1891)). When the borrower replaces the goods, he transfers proprietary rights back to the lender; he repays the loan and converts the relationship back into a bailment. Such an authority to substitute appears to be inconsistent with an obligation to keep enough goods to answer all claims; unless the mixture contains the bailee's own goods (in which case no authority to substitute would be required), it is impossible to use the authority to substitute without breaching the obligation to keep enough goods. If there is an obligation to keep enough goods to answer all claims, as where the receipts are sought to be made negotiable securities backed by proprietary rights (*Bucher v. Commonwealth* 103 Penn. 528 (1883)), there can be no authority to sell or to substitute. Even here, though, it might be found (albeit at the expense of general creditors) that grain wrongfully taken could be effectively replaced with other grain appropriated to bailors. . . .

QUESTIONS AND COMMENTS

1. Compare *Lawlor v. Nicol* (1898) 12 Man. R. 224 (C.A.) at 230 (*per* Killam J.): "Whether the party supplying the grain is receive a price in money or an equivalent quantity of grain, or has the option to do either, it is really a sale. The property passes to the warehouseman and he is to pay in grain or money," following *South Australian Insurance Co. v. Randell* (1869) L.R. 3 P.C. 101.

2. In *Crawford v. Kingston* [1952] 4 D.L.R. 37 (Ont. C.A.), Crawford entered into a verbal agreement with Murray, under which Murray was to keep and care for two of Crawfords's cows. Murray was to raise two heifers and at the end of three years, the four cows were to be returned to Crawford. Murray was entitled to retain any income derived from the cattle during this period. Similar arrangements were made between the parties over the next few years. Importantly, they also agreed that Murray could sell and replace any of the cows so long as the same number of cattle were returned to Crawford.

Before this arrangement had come to an end, creditors of Murray seized and sold the cattle. That action was lawful provided that the cattle belonged to him. Was the arrangement regarding the cattle a sale (in which case the seizure was unobjectionable), or was it a bailment, so that title to the cattle remained in Crawford (and therefore not liable to seizure on the basis of the debt owed by Murray)?

The Ontario Court of Appeal (*per* Mackay J.A. at 39), held that the transaction was a sale:

> When the original chattel delivered is to be returned in the same or an altered form the title does not pass but the transaction constitutes a bailment with the title in the bailor, but if the transaction as made by the contract between the parties does not require the party receiving the chattel to return it in its original or an altered form but permits the possessor to return another chattel of equal value or to pay the money value thereof, the relation of vendor and purchaser is created and the title to the property passes to him and is in him.

> The essential difference between bailment and sale is the *locus* of the title. In the instant case Murray, under the contract, was required to return a certain number of cattle to the plaintiff. From 1944 Murray was at liberty to sell or dispose of any or all of the stock and to make a profit by means of increase in the stock or otherwise. If the animals were destroyed by fire or killed by lightning, would it be any answer for Murray to say to the plaintiff [Crawford] when, under the terms of the contract, demand was made for the return of the required number of cattle, "They were all destroyed by fire or killed by lightning"? The plaintiff would in all probability reply: "The stock was delivered to you to be used as you saw fit for your own use and benefit. You acquired absolute and complete dominion over them and you must therefore bear the loss."
>
> We are respectfully of opinion that even if there should be one or more of the original cattle in the herd of Murray (which was not established at trial) there would be no substantial, if any, difference in law. It is not upon the exercise of dominion, not subject to control, but upon the fact of having such dominion in the property of other cattle, was not bound to exercise it in any particular way or at any particular time, but his having had such power to use the stock as his own with the notion of holding such stock as bailee rather than that of beneficial ownership.

Can *Mercer* be distinguished?

Letourneau v. Otto Mobiles Edmonton (1984) Ltd. 2002 CarswellAlta 1431, [2003] 3 W.W.R. 389 (Q.B.)

Johnstone J.:

INTRODUCTION

A trailer owned by Ray and Karen Letourneau (the "Plaintiffs") was stolen in July of 1999. The Plaintiffs had delivered the trailer to a parking lot located adjacent to the business premises of Otto Mobiles Edmonton (1984) Ltd. (the "Defendant") in order for the Defendant to repair the trailer the following day. The Plaintiffs claim damages from the Defendant for the loss of their trailer.

ISSUES

The parties agree that the damages amount to $27,500.00. This trial is concerned with liability only. The following issues arise:

1. Did the relationship of bailor-bailee exist between the Plaintiffs and Defendant?

2. If so, did the Defendant fail to meet the standard of care owed to the Plaintiffs?

3. If so, was the Plaintiffs' loss caused by the Defendant's failure to meet this standard of care?

4. Did the Plaintiffs' negligence contribute to their own loss?

5. Did the Defendant breach its contractual obligation to the Plaintiffs?

BACKGROUND FACTS

The Plaintiffs were the owners of a 1998 Triple E Topaz trailer (the "Trailer").

In June of 1999 they retained the Defendant to perform certain repairs on the Trailer. The Defendant was the only approved dealer in Edmonton that serviced Topaz trailers. The work order, executed by Mr. Letourneau and dated June 19, 1999, contained a waiver of liability clause which provided as follows:

> I hereby authorize the repair work hereinafter set forth to be done along with the necessary material and agree that to the extent permitted by law, you are not responsible for loss or damage to the vehicle or articles left in [sic] vehicle in case of fire, theft or any other cause beyond your control . . .

The Letourneaus were invoiced and paid $631.82 for the repairs. However, further work was required on the Trailer as these repairs were unsatisfactory. Mr. Letourneau testified that he visited the Defendant's repair facility on July 5 or 6, 1999 and spoke with the Defendant's Service Manager, Darrell Faryna. As a result of extensive work commitments Mr. Letourneau was unable to drop the Trailer off during the Defendant's normal weekday working hours, or on Saturday.

I accept Mr. Letourneau's evidence that when he visited the repair facility, he and Mr. Faryna exited the building to have a cigarette. Mr. Faryna then took the opportunity to show Mr. Letourneau where to park after hours, namely the Intuit lot adjacent to the repair facility. Mr. Faryna indicated that the Trailer would be picked up the following morning in accordance with the customary practice of the Defendant.

It is notable that Mr. Faryna is no longer in the employ of the Defendant and could not be located by his former employer to testify. As a result, the evidence of the Plaintiffs, both of whom did testify, is uncontradicted relative to their contact with Mr. Faryna.

Following Mr. Faryna's directions, on the evening of July 6, 1999 between approximately 6:45 p.m. and 7:00 p.m. the Plaintiffs attended at the Intuit lot and endeavoured to park their Trailer. However, another couple, Phyllis and Re'al Provencher had already taken their appointed spot.

Phyllis Provencher testified at trial. I found her to be a very credible and reliable witness. Her evidence was that she received the same direction from the Defendant's service department as did the Plaintiffs regarding an after hour drop-off. Although she felt a little apprehensive about leaving her trailer in the adjacent Intuit lot, when she questioned the representative of the Defendant, he assured her that it was fine to leave her vehicle at that location.

She further confirmed that the Plaintiffs did arrive at the same time to drop-off their Trailer and insisted that Mr. Provencher move his trailer because it was smaller and could be more easily accommodated elsewhere on the Inuit lot. Mr. Provencher obliged.

When Mr. and Mrs. Provencher were trying to find an alternative place to leave their trailer, a woman came out of the Intuit building and told them they could not leave their trailer on the lot because it would be towed away. They reluctantly left their trailer on the street adjacent to the Defendant's repair facility.

Mr. Letourneau testified that he was in a hurry on the evening of July 6, 1999 as he had a ball game to attend at 7:30 p.m. He stabilized the Trailer with blocks as he normally would and padlocked the hitch. As suggested by Darrell Faryna, he secreted the key to the padlock in the water compartment of the Trailer and then locked the compartment.

The next day, July 7, 1999, he called Mr. Faryna and asked him to look at an additional problem he was encountering with the Trailer. Mr. Faryna indicated he would do so. There was no mention made of any work having been started on the Trailer nor did Mr. Letourneau confirm that he had dropped the Trailer off the night before. The Defendant has no work order for the requested service on the Trailer.

At approximately 8:55 a.m. the following day Mr. Faryna contacted Mr. Letourneau advising that the Trailer could not be located. It was then concluded that the Trailer had been stolen. The Plaintiffs reported the theft to the police at approximately 2:55 p.m. that day. The Trailer was never recovered.

The Defendant called two witnesses at trial, one of whom, Terrence Hobbs, held the position of Assistant General Manager at the time of the loss. Mr. Hobbs' testimony clearly revealed that he had no personal knowledge of the discussion between employees of the Defendant's service department and either Mr. Letourneau or Mrs. Provencher. He confirmed that the Defendant has not been able to locate a work order nor any paper work relative to the July 6th drop-off of the Trailer.

The other witness was Elizabeth Buysen who was employed with Intuit Canada at the lot adjacent to the Defendant's repair facility in July of 1999. She indicated that on the night of July 6th she encountered a couple who were endeavouring to park their trailer in the Intuit lot. She specifically recalled that when she left work that night a trailer had been parked in the Intuit lot but was not there the next morning when she returned to work.

ARGUMENTS OF THE PARTIES

The Plaintiffs' Position

The Plaintiffs argue that their evidence, which is uncontradicted and was corroborated by the testimony of Mrs. Provencher, clearly establishes a bailment of the Trailer.

As with the Plaintiffs, the Provenchers dropped off their trailer after receiving instructions from the Defendant's service department. The Defendant's Service Manager agreed that certain repairs would be affected and that was the reason the Plaintiffs left the Trailer as directed by Mr. Faryna. According to the Plaintiffs, this was a case of bailment for reward given that possession, custody and control of the Trailer passed to the Defendant based upon the clear intention of the parties. The onus now reverts to the Defendant and the evidence is overwhelming that the Defendant did not take reasonable care to ensure the safekeeping of the Trailer during the period of bailment.

The Plaintiffs contend there is no contributory negligence on their part as they strictly complied with the instructions of the Defendant, parking in the designated area and secreting the key in the manner directed.

In addition, they maintain the waiver of liability clause appearing in the work order of June 19 did not apply to the work instructed on either July 5 or July 6, 1999.

The Defendant's Position

At trial, the Defendant acknowledged it is vicariously liable for the actions of its employee, Mr. Faryna. However, the Defendant maintains that nothing turns on that admission given that bailment has not been established. In order to establish bailment, constructive or actual possession must be transferred from the bailor to the bailee with the latter undertaking control of the chattel. There must be an expectation by the bailor that the bailee take possession and control. The Plaintiffs never gave up exclusive possession and control of the Trailer but rather retained a key and could have accessed the Trailer at any time after it was dropped off. Furthermore, there is no evidence that the Defendant knew when the Trailer would be left. When Mr. Letourneau contacted Mr. Faryna on July 7th, he did not confirm that the Trailer had been dropped off.

The Defendant suggests the Letourneaus left the Trailer at their own risk and did not take any security precautions prior to doing so. A bailor cannot thrust bailment on the bailee. The Defendant argues there was uncertainty in its undertaking. Further, the bailment was not to commence until it took actual possession of the Trailer to effect the repairs. The Defendant makes a similar argument in denying negligence on its part or a breach of its contractual obligations. As the agreement to repair did not commence until the morning of July 7th, 1999, the contract was frustrated by the theft of the Trailer.

DETERMINATION

Definition of Bailment

Mr. Justice Cory in *Punch v. Savoy's Jewellers Ltd. et al.* (1986), 26 D.L.R. (4th) 546 at 551 (Ont. C.A.) defined bailment as:

> . . . the delivery of personal chattels on trust, usually on contract, express or implied, that the trust shall be executed and the chattels be delivered in either their original or an altered form as soon as a time for which they were bailed has elapsed. It is to be noted that the legal relationship of bailor and bailee can exist independently of a contract. It is created by the voluntary taking into custody of goods which are the property of another.

The Existence of a Bailment

The first issue that requires my determination is whether a bailment relationship has been established. A bailment in these circumstances would be one of location *operis faciendi*, defined by *Palmer on Bailment*, 2nd ed. (Agincourt: Carswell, 1991) at p. 881 as a bailment which contains two elements: "a contract for services, coupled with a bailment of the article upon which those services are to be performed" (*Coggs v. Bernard* (1703), 92 E.R. 107 at p. 109). The workman performing the services is considered a "bailee for reward" for as long as the chattel upon which the work is done is in the workman's possession: Palmer at p. 893.

One of the essential elements of the bailor-bailee relationship is possession of the chattel by the bailee. In this case, the Plaintiffs claim the Defendant was in possession of their vehicle from the point in time when they left the Trailer in the Intuit lot, in accordance with the instructions of the Defendant's Service Manager. The Defendant claims that it never took possession of the Trailer.

Most cases of bailment are fact-based and this case is no exception. Nevertheless, some of the case law in the area is instructive. In *Hefferman v. Elizabeth Irving Service Center et al.* (1980), 29 Nfld. & P.E.I.R. 470 (Nfld. S.C. (T.D.)), the plaintiff parked his truck at the side of the defendant's service station. The truck subsequently was demolished when it was taken from that location without the plaintiff's consent. Mahoney J. found it was "only too evident" that a bailor-bailee relationship existed. He noted that the plaintiff would only leave the truck whenever repairs were necessary. It was typical practice for the plaintiff to leave the truck, turn the keys over to an employee, and telephone the service station a day or so later and indicate what repairs were required.

The case of *Appleton et al v. Ritchie Taxi et al.*, [1942] O.R. 446 (C.A.) involved a parking lot where customers would pay for parking and then leave their vehicles and keys with an attendant at the front gate. The attendant would move each vehicle to a final destination in the lot. The plaintiff left his vehicle and keys with an attendant but the vehicle was stolen from the lot. The trial judge held that no bailment existed; the relationship was one of licensor-licensee. On appeal, Gillanders, J.A. held that the defendants became bailees when the attendant, as agent of the defendants, took charge of the car at the front gate, since possession of the car was delivered to the defendants for safe custody.

The defendant in *St-Isidore Asphalte Ltee v. Luminex Signs Ltd.* (1996), 176 N.B.R. (2d) 135 (Q.B.), aff'd [1997] A.N.B. no. 72 (C.A.) was a sign manufacturer that performed lettering work on the plaintiff's truck. Upon completion of the work, the defendant notified the plaintiff that his truck was ready for pick-up. Under the impression that the plaintiff or its agent would be picking up the truck, the defendant closed its shop and left the plaintiff's vehicle in the shop parking lot, unlocked with the keys inside. McIntyre J. held at para. 6 that the defendant's duties as bailee did not terminate upon completion of the contracted work but continued until the truck was picked up or the plaintiff clearly relieved the defendant of its contractual obligation.

In the case at bar, the Plaintiffs never physically delivered possession of the Trailer by direct delivery of the keys to the Defendant. However, they did comply precisely with the instructions of the Service Manager regarding drop-off of the Trailer.

Much the same as the plaintiff's drop-off practice in *Hefferman*, I find that this method of after-hours delivery was a common practice at the Defendant's repair facility, as corroborated by the evidence of Mrs. Provencher who testified that she and her husband had dropped their trailer off under the same arrangement and at the same time as the Plaintiffs.

Palmer indicates that possession can be inferred when it is a necessary incident of some other function. *Appleton* supports this principle. In *Appleton*, although the plaintiff's contract with the defendants was merely for parking on the defendants' lot, the manner in which the parking was executed, namely using an attendant, made possession a necessary incident to the parking.

In the present case, the Plaintiffs had a service contract with the Defendant. Possession by the Defendant was necessarily incidental to the service contract, since the Defendant had to assume control of the Trailer in order to perform the required repairs.

The Defendant makes much of the fact that the Trailer was not left on its property. Case law establishes that this is not a bar to creating the relationship of bailor-bailee. For example, in *Edelson v. Musty's Service Station and Garage*, [1956] O.W.N. 848 (C.A.), an employee of the defendant service station parked the plaintiff's vehicle on a nearby public street, since there was a lack of space on the service station premises. The trial judge held the defendant was a bailee and responsible for the car, notwithstanding that it was parked on a public street. Possession was not at issue in that case, however, as the plaintiff had clearly delivered the car for servicing. The trial decision was upheld on appeal, although the appeal was based on other grounds.

In *Costello Equipment Co. v. Shaw GMC Trucks Ltd.*, [1975] A.J. No. 85 (S.C.(T.D.)), the plaintiff left his truck "in some mysterious fashion" at the defendant service station and indicated to an employee at the station that he had done so. Overnight, the truck rolled down an incline and was damaged in a collision. Dechene J. held that a bailment existed.

The more recent case of *Luider v. Nguyen*, [1994] A.J. No. 494 (Prov. Ct. (Civ. Div.)) places import on knowledge of the defendant in determining whether the defendant is a bailee. The plaintiff in that case delivered a heifer to the defendant's premises for later pick-up by a third party. Neither the plaintiff nor the third party contacted the defendant with respect to this arrangement. The trial judge held the defendant did not have the requisite "possession, custody and control" to be a bailee. He also noted it was not a custom of the trade to deliver animals under such an arrangement.

In the present case, the Defendant had the requisite knowledge as its employee specifically instructed the Plaintiffs to leave their Trailer in the manner in which they did; a practice which I find to have been customary.

Further, the Defendant argued vigorously that there was no change in possession, a factor which would be fatal to establishing the relationship of bailment. A holistic approach to the change of possession was advocated in *Maritime Coastal Containers Ltd. v. Shelburne Marine Ltd.* (1982), 52 N.S.R. (2d) 51 (NSSC (T.D.)). The defendant shipyard in that case was contracted to unload steel from the plaintiff's ship onto an adjacent lot. The steel sat ignored for over three years until the plaintiff discovered it was missing. At p. 63, Hallett J. discussed the difficulty in determining a change of possession, citing the following passage from *Palmer* at p. 196:

> Identifying this change of possession has, however, caused considerable difficulty, for although the parties' intention should always be a material element, this will rarely be decisive and the courts have had to fall back on the physical facts and circumstances of each individual case.

Hallett J. concluded it was a question of fact, after considering all relevant circumstances, whether the defendant was a bailee. There had been no instructions flowing between the plaintiff and the defendant in respect of the steel and the defendant had discharged all of its obligations under the contract. Further, there was no ancillary function to be performed by the defendant on the steel. Hallett J. held that the relationship of bailment had not been established.

In the present case, there were explicit instructions given by the Defendant's Service Manager to the Plaintiffs which resulted in the Plaintiffs dropping off their Trailer for the specific purpose of having it repaired.

The decision of *Munroe v. Belinsky* (1995), 103 Man.R. (2d) 12 (Q.B.) is also instructive. In that case, the defendant agreed to make arrangements to have the plaintiff's truck transported by semi-trailer truck to another city for repair by the truck dealer. The defendant told the plaintiff where to leave the truck for loading and said the keys should be left in the ignition. The driver of the transport vehicle left the plaintiff's truck at a scrap yard on learning from the dealer that no arrangements had been made with respect to the truck. The truck subsequently went missing. Beard J. held at p. 16 that under the circumstances the defendant was a bailee and had taken possession of the truck.

Given that the Defendant's Service Manager in the present case specifically directed the Plaintiffs to leave their Trailer in a certain spot and designated the manner in which the keys were to be hidden, I find that temporary possession of the Trailer passed to the Defendant. This occurred when the Plaintiffs left the Trailer and not, as argued by the Defendant, when the Defendant's employee should have picked up the Trailer the following morning.

Duty and Standard of Care

As bailment has been established, the burden shifts to the Defendant to prove on a balance of probabilities that it met the standard of care required of it:

> The bailee for reward must exercise due care for the safety of the article entrusted to him by taking such care of the goods as would a prudent man of his own possessions. Significantly, the bailee is liable for the loss of goods arising out of his servant's theft on the grounds that he is responsible for the manner in which the servant carries out his duty. In the result, it matters not whether the servant is careless, whether the goods are stolen by a stranger, or if the servant himself steals them: *Punch* at p. 552 and see *Longley v. Mitchell Fur Co. Ltd.* (1983), 45 N.B.R. (2d) 78 (C.A.) at p. 80

Baillee For Reward vs. Gratuitous Bailee

Historically, it was held that a higher standard of care was placed on a bailee for reward than on a gratuitous bailee, since in the latter case the bailment was only for the benefit of the bailor. The distinction, however, has blurred with the passage of time.

For purposes of assessing the appropriate standard of care I find it unnecessary to ascertain whether this was a gratuitous bailment or bailment for reward. Rather than deal with this distinction, I prefer to adopt the principle enunciated by my colleague Purvis J. in *Carpenter v. Gargil Grain Co.*, [1982] 4 W.W.R. 292 (Alta. Q.B.) citing with approval *Palmer on Bailment* (1979) at p. 275:

> This principle, in fact, entitled him [the bailee] to avoid liability by two distinct avenues: either he may show that he had taken reasonable care of the goods, or he may show that his acknowledged or established failure to take reasonable care did not contribute to the loss. In either event the burden of proof rests on him [the bailee].

The significance of bailment for reward has declined considerably in recent years as recognized by Binder J. in *Dorico Investments Ltd. v. Weyhaeuser Canada Ltd. / Weyerhaeuser Canada Ltée* (1999), 249 A.R. 53 (Q.B.) and by my colleague

Acton J. in *Gaudreau v. Belter* (2001), 290 A.R. 377 (Q.B.). In the latter case, after noting that Canadian cases were in conflict on this issue, Acton J. concluded at para. 9 that it was "not helpful to try to create watertight compartments of types of bailment." At para. 10 she attempted to provide some certainty in the law of bailment in Alberta, stating:

> A test that focuses on what is reasonable in the circumstance is more flexible and more appropriate than trying to force facts into pigeon hole classifications . . . . The relevant circumstances will include whether the bailment was gratuitous or for reward, but will also include circumstances such as how the bailment came about, the relationship between the bailee and the bailor, the value and nature of the bailed item, and the cause of the damage or loss.

I agree that it makes little difference today whether bailment is gratuitous or for reward. The obligation of a bailee in either case is to take the same care of the goods received as a prudent owner, acting reasonably, might be expected to take of his or her own chattels.

Waiver of Liability Clause

Should an action of bailment be looked upon as a cause of action in contract or in tort, or do unique obligations and duties arise in bailment? It may be said that bailment is, in essence, a consensual matter whereby the bailee consents to receive goods for a specific purpose. If it is consensual, any limitation of liability for the loss of goods is a fundamental aspect of that consent as the arrangement is basically contractual. Therefore, the Defendant should be entitled to rely on any limitation clause available to it.

The Defendant directs me to the waiver of liability clause appearing in the June 19th work order.

A waiver of liability clause must be strictly construed: *Murray v. Bitango* (1996), 184 A.R. 68 (C.A.), following *Canada Steamship Lines Ltd. v. The King*, [1952] 2 D.L.R. 786 (P.C.).

In *Brown v. Toronto Auto Parks Ltd.*, [1955] 2 D.L.R. 525 at 527 (Ont. C.A.), Laidlaw J.A. discussed the duty of a bailee of reward and how contractual limitations of liability factor into the bailor-bailee relationship:

> A custodian for reward may limit or relieve himself of his common law liability by special provisions and special conditions in the contract made by him. In such cases it has been held that such provisions and such conditions will be strictly construed and will be held not to exempt the bailee from responsibility for losses due to his negligence unless the words used are clear and adequate for the purpose or there is no other liability to which they can apply.

In the case at bar there was no written contract and no work order but rather a verbal agreement whereby the Defendant through its Service Manager agreed to repair the Trailer. The waiver of liability clause appearing in the previous work order must be strictly construed and confined only to that work and not to the July 5th or July 6th and July 7th oral agreements.

Was the Loss Caused by the Defendant's Failure to Meet the Duty of Care?

It is apparent from the case of *Calgary Transport Services Limited v. Pyramid Management Ltd.*, [1976] 6 W.W.R. 631 (Alta. S.C. (A.D.)) that a plaintiff must establish that loss or damage to the bailed goods occurred while the goods were in the possession of the bailee. Only then does the onus of proof shift to the bailee to negative negligence.

The bailee's burden of proof was summarized well by Cory J.A., as he then was, in the more recent case of *Punch* at p. 552:

> . . . when goods are damaged or lost while in the possession of a bailee, the bailee must prove either that he took appropriate care of them or that his failure to do so did not contribute to the loss. If the goods are lost or damaged while they are in possession of the bailee, the burden is on the bailee to show that the damages occurred without any neglect, default or misconduct on the part of himself or any of his servants to whom he delegated a duty. To escape liability, he must demonstrate that the loss was without any fault on his part or the part of his servants. Only if he satisfies the owner that he took due care to employ trustworthy servants and that he and his servants exercised all diligence will he be excused from liability.

In *Gray v. Canwest Parking Limited* (1965), 52 W.W.R. 56 (B.C. Co. Ct.), the defendant parking lot was held to have taken possession of the plaintiff's car when the parking attendant, as the defendant's servant, requested that the plaintiff leave his keys in the car after parking it. The defendant was held negligent when the car was stolen, largely due to the fact the car was left unlocked with the keys in plain sight.

The defendant parking lot in *Appleton* left the plaintiff's car unlocked but secreted the keys away from view. The Court held the lot was negligent even though it took steps to hide the keys, since an unknown third party evidently found them and used them to steal the plaintiff's vehicle.

The defendant bailee in *Sabean v. Moran* (1991), 117 N.B.R. (2d) 329 (Q.B.) was successful in demonstrating care and diligence. The defendant operated a repair shop that performed work on the plaintiff's vehicle. Upon completion of the work, the defendant parked the vehicle in an adjacent lot to await pick-up by the plaintiff. The vehicle was locked. While in the lot, the vehicle was vandalized. Jones J. held the defendant was not negligent in his care of the plaintiff's vehicle, since the parking lot was well lit by street lights, the defendant regularly parked his own vehicle in the same lot, and there had been no previous instances of vandalism in the lot.

Once the Defendant in the present case accepted the possession, care and control of the Trailer for the purpose of doing the requisite repairs, it became a bailee and assumed responsibility for safe keeping of the Trailer.

The Defendant has failed to establish that the conduct of employees was consistent with the standard of care that a prudent owner, acting reasonably, might be expected to take of his or her own chattels. The Trailer was left on the Intuit property not only with the consent and agreement of the Defendant's Service Manager but at his direction. In my view, the Defendant is responsible for not providing a safe location for storage of the Trailer given that it invited the Plaintiffs to deliver possession of the Trailer to it during off-business hours.

Further, looking at the bailment action as tortious in nature, I reach the same conclusion. The Defendant under the circumstances breached its duty of care to properly secure the vehicle. Its failure to take reasonable steps to do so resulted in the loss. Simply put, if a bailment action is tortious in nature so that a claim can be based on negligence alone, the Defendant would be liable to the Plaintiffs for its negligence in the unexplained loss of the trailer.

Contributory Negligence

Contributory negligence reflects the failure of a plaintiff to take reasonable care with the result that the plaintiff contributes to his or her own loss. For contributory negligence to succeed as a defence, the defendant must prove that the plaintiff was negligent and that the plaintiff's negligence was a cause of his or her loss. The test is reasonable foreseeability of probable or possible risks: *Heller v. Martens*, [2002] A.J. No. 638, 2002 ABCA 122 (Alta. C.A.).

Contributory negligence on the part of a bailor is rarely found in bailment cases. However, the case of *Edelson* is of assistance. When the defendant parked the plaintiff's car on the nearby public street, the defendant left the car unlocked but took care to remove the keys and bring them inside the service station. Unbeknownst to the defendant, however, the plaintiff had placed a second set of keys in the locked glove compartment of the car. It was argued by the defendant that the plaintiff had been contributorily negligent in doing so, since the car had been stolen with the use of the second set of keys. The trial judge held the plaintiff was not contributorily negligent. This ruling was upheld on appeal, the Court concluding that the plaintiff was entitled to expect the car would be locked if it was to be left on a public street all day. The Court did note, however, that the plaintiff had *locked* the keys away in the glove compartment.

In the present case, the Plaintiffs pad-locked the hitch of the Trailer and secreted the key in a locked compartment at the request of the Defendant. In his Examination for Discovery, Mr. Letourneau indicated the Trailer was dropped off while it was still daylight. Consequently, he did not notice whether there was sufficient lighting in the area. Mrs. Letourneau indicated that she neither noticed nor discussed with her husband the presence of any security measures, devices or cameras.

The Plaintiffs were comfortable in leaving the Trailer at the Intuit lot based in large part on the representations and instructions given by the Defendant's Service

Manager and no doubt confirmed when they encountered the Provenchers dropping off their trailer at the same location.

The Defendant argues that the Plaintiffs never asked Mr. Faryna about security measures extant for the Intuit lot and should have taken reasonable steps to secure the Trailer. I find that Mr. Faryna at no time indicated to the Plaintiffs that they were parking in the Intuit lot at their own risk. To the contrary, I accept the evidence of the Plaintiffs that the direction by the Service Manager to park in the designated spot assured them that the Trailer could be left safely in that location. This factor is corroborated by the testimony of Mrs. Provencher. For these reasons, I find no contributory negligence on the part of the Plaintiffs.

Given my earlier findings I need not deal with the issue of contractual breach.

CONCLUSION

A bailment relationship existed. The Defendant has not discharged the burden of proving that it satisfied the duty and standard of care required. I find there was no contributory negligence on the part of the Plaintiffs. In the result, the Defendant is liable for the Plaintiffs' loss, quantified at $27,500.00. . . .

QUESTIONS AND COMMENTS

1. Is the existence of a contract essential in order to give rise to a bailment?

2. Why does it matter whether or not a licence or a bailment has been created?

3. Could it be said that possession had not been transferred to the defendant in this case since the plaintiffs had a spare key for the trailer?

4. For several centuries, the law has categorized bailments by reference to whom they benefited: either the bailor (as where goods are stored as a favour), or the bailee (as where A borrows B's property casebook to prepare for class), or for mutual benefit (as where goods are stored or borrowed for a fee). This approach resulted from a distillation of the categorization of bailments laid down in the pivotal case of *Coggs v. Bernard* (1703) 2 Ld. Raym. 909, 92 E.R. 107. In brief, where the bailment is found to be for the sole benefit of the bailee, a higher duty of care is expected: even slight negligence is actionable; where the bailment is for the benefit of the bailor, liability attaches if gross negligence has occurred. For bailments of mutual benefit, ordinary negligence is the standard of care required of the bailee.

The proper characterization of a bailment under this taxonomy is not always easy. Consider this situation: A car is stolen from a restaurant parking lot for which valet parking is provided. The car owner sues the restaurant alleging breach of bailment. There is no direct charge for parking cars in the lot. Assuming that a bailment has occurred (and not a licence), is it gratuitous bailment for the benefit of the bailor, or one for mutual benefit? In *Martin v. Town N' Country Delicatessen*

Ltd. 1963 CarswellMan 77, 42 D.L.R. (2d) 449 (C.A.) a majority of the Manitoba Court of Appeal (*per* Miller C.J.M. at para. 13) said that such a bailment was gratuitous:

> The facilities of the parking lot were made available gratuitously for the convenience of plaintiff and others desirous of using the restaurant and arriving by car. The supply of a parking lot for the convenience of patrons was not a service covered by a consideration paid by patrons of the restaurant. Presumably the same prices would be charged people who walked to the restaurant, or who came by bus or taxicab, without any consideration for the furnishing of a parking lot for motorists. It would surely not be a bailment for reward.

In dissent, Schultz J.A. opined (at paras. 51-52) that:

> The bailment was one of mutual benefit. To constitute such a bailment it is not necessary that the bailee receive compensation in cash. If the bailee derives a benefit to himself by taking possession of the bailor's property, that in itself is a sufficient consideration. Nor is the court primarily concerned with the sufficiency or non-sufficiency of such consideration and generally will not inquire into the nature, or amount, or sufficiency of consideration or to its certainty of being realized. It will only determine whether there was a consideration
>
> In regard to the question of sufficiency of consideration, I have already referred to one minor advantage accruing to defendant by taking possession of plaintiff's car and keys — that of increasing the efficiency of its parking lot. But there is a more important advantage conceded by defendant, namely, its admission that it operated its parking lots for the convenience and accommodation of patrons of its restaurant — an operation that obviously was incidental to and important for its business. While the defendant made no direct charge for the parking-lot accommodation it provided for its customers, it is reasonable to infer that an indirect consideration accrued to it and constituted a benefit. That benefit was the profit which defendant might reasonably anticipate would result by way of increased patronage. There are many cases which indicate that courts infer a consideration although there was no direct payment.

This dissenting view accords with the holding in *Murphy v. Hart* 1919 CarswellNS 13, 46 D.L.R. 36 (C.A.), where a restaurant offered a "free" coat check. For the Court, Harris C.J. (at para. 5) wrote:

> The depositing of the overcoat in the place provided by the defendant for that purpose was for the benefit of both parties, and, while no price was paid directly or specifically to the defendant for the care of the plaintiff's overcoat, it was part of the accommodation for which the defendant received his recompense from his customers. It is obvious that the defendant derived some advantage in the way of increased trade by making his premises attractive, and the providing of a place in which customers could leave their coats and hats while eating was a necessary incident to the business just as it is the case of a barber shop, or a bathing house.

Which view do you prefer?

5. Some courts have moved away from the rigid formula based on the taxonomy of bailments; *Letourneau* provides an illustration. What test of liability did the trial judge use? Does that approach mark a change for the better?

6. It can be seen from this case that there is a shift in the normal burden of proof in bailment cases. In civil actions, a plaintiff is required to prove alleged and relevant facts on the balance of probabilities. By contrast, in actions against a bailee, if it can be shown that the goods have been damaged or lost (as the case may be) during the course of the bailment, the onus shifts to the bailee to disprove negligence.

The reversal of the onus of proof was not applied, however, in the case of *National Trust Co. v. Wong Aviation Ltd.* [1969] S.C.R. 481, 1969 CarswellOnt 125. There, a plane crash led to the death of the bailee. In an action brought to recover damages for the loss of the plane, the Supreme Court of Canada held that the presumption of negligence could not be triggered. Why not?

7. A bailee's liability is not restricted to negligent acts or omissions. Bailed goods cannot be dealt with in a manner that falls outside of the terms, express or implied, of the bailment. If items are stored in a manner that falls outside of the arrangement, liability is strict if a loss occurs as a result. Likewise, if goods are misdelivered, the bailee will be liable even if care was shown. And, of course, the bailee cannot deliberately misappropriate the items.

8. The applicability of the defence of contributory negligence in a bailment context is unresolved. In N.E. Palmer, *Bailment*, 2nd ed. (Sydney: Law Book Co., 1991) at 69–71, the author inclines toward the view that the defence is available for both contractual and non-contractual bailments provided that the wrong complained of is actionable in tort, that is, independently of the contract itself. However, when the breach relates to an obligation for which liability is strict, Palmer suggests that the defence may not be available.

The defence of contributory negligence was introduced by statute, and so whether or this partial defence is applicable in a bailment action is, in truth, a matter of statutory interpretation. Palmer's analysis must be understood in that light. In your view, to what extent would the defence be tenable in a bailment action, given s. 3 of Ontario's *Negligence Act*, R.S.O. 1990, c. N.1:

> In any action for damages that is founded upon the fault or negligence of the defendant if fault or negligence is found on the part of the plaintiff that contributed to the damages, the court shall apportion the damages in proportion to the degree of fault or negligence found against the parties respectively.

Compare the language of s. 1 of the *Negligence Act*, R.S.B.C. 1996, c. 333:

> If by the fault of 2 or more persons damage or loss is caused to one or more of them, the liability to make good the damage or loss is in proportion to the degree to which each person was at fault.

9. In *Minichiello v. Devonshire Hotel (1967) Ltd.* 1978 CarswellBC 441, 87 D.L.R. (3d) 439 (C.A.), the plaintiff parked his car in a lot owned by the defendant. Those using the lot were instructed to leave their keys in the ignition so that the cars could be moved when necessary by the attendant. The plaintiff testified that he had an attaché case full of jewellery from his store, and that as he left the lot he notified the attendant that there were valuables in the trunk. The car was stolen.

There was little doubt that the car had been bailed; but what of the jewellery? The British Columbia Court of Appeal held that the defendant/bailee was liable for that loss. Craig J.A., for the Court, stated (at para. 10):

> The evidence reasonably supports the finding that the appellant was bailee for reward with respect to the automobile. The bailment would cover the contents of the automobile which one would reasonably expect to be in the car and contents which one might not reasonably expect to be in the car but of which the bailee has knowledge. Counsel for the appellant submits that the appellant could be responsible for the contents of the attaché case only if the respondent told the attendant that there were valuable diamonds and rings in the car . . . I think that the statement that there were "valuables" in the car was sufficient to constitute the appellant a bailee for reward of the contents of the attaché case.

10. It is a well-established doctrine of bailment that a bailee is estopped from denying the title of the bailor unless and until a person with a better right to the bailed goods (a title paramount) intervenes: *Biddle v. Bond* (1865) 6 B. & S. 225, 122 E.R. 1179. How, if at all, does this idea fit with basic principles governing possession and the relative nature of title?

11. At common law, special rules apply to innkeepers. These doctrines were explained by Gorham Co. Ct. J., in *Fraser v. McGibbon* 1907 CarswellOnt 25, 10 O.W.R. 54 (Co. Ct.) at paras. 2–4, 7, 12:

> Th[e] law and custom of England — the common law — originally imposed upon an innkeeper certain liabilities to prevent him from acting in collusion with the bad characters who in old times infested the roads, and to protect wayfarers and travellers who on their journeys brought goods into the inn. The wayfaring guest had no means of knowing the neighbourhood or the character of those whom he met at the inn. It was therefore thought right to cast the duty of protecting the guests upon the host. Knowing that this is one of his duties, one of the liabilities he incurs, the innkeeper can make such charge for the entertainment of his guest as will compensate him for the risk. It may be observed that, unless the law cast upon him this burden, a dishonest innkeeper might be tempted to take advantage of a wealthy traveller. With that view the innkeeper was placed in the position of an insurer of the goods of his guest, and correlative to his liability is his right of lien upon the goods which the guest brings with him into the inn.
>
> The innkeeper must be the keeper of a common inn, that is, one who makes it his business to entertain wayfarers, travellers, and passengers, and provide lodgings and necessaries for them, their horses and attendants, and receive compensation therefor. He must admit and entertain to the extent of his accommodation all persons of the class for whose entertainment he holds out his house and against whom no reasonable objection can be shewn. He may exclude such as are not sober, orderly, able to pay his reasonable charges,

or such as ply his guests with solicitations for patronage in their business, or whose filthy condition would annoy other guests. It appears that he may limit his accommodation and entertainment to a certain class. . . . An innkeeper by opening his house — his inn — offers it to the use of the public as such, and thereupon the common law imposes on him certain duties and gives him certain rights. Those duties and rights, as well as the attendant liabilities, have been changed, in some respects made heavier and in some respects made lighter, by statute. . . .

It is important to ascertain when the relation of innkeeper and guest commences, in cases involving liability for the loss of or injury to the guest's effects. This is a question of fact, the solution of which generally depends on the facts of each case. It is obvious that when a person goes to an inn as a traveller or wayfarer, and the innkeeper receives him as such, the relation of landlord and guest attaches at once. The intention to avail himself of the entertainment, that is, to obtain refreshment, or lodging, or both, is material, and if the party should engage and pay for a room merely to secure a safe place for the deposit of his valuables, or without any intention of occupying it, he would not be a guest. Under some circumstances too, the relation may commence before the party actually reaches the inn [Am. & Eng. Encyc. Of Law, vol. 16, p. 520] . . .

The relation of innkeeper and guest having been established, it becomes the duty of the innkeeper to keep such goods as the guest brings with him into the inn safely night and day. And this although the guest does not deliver his goods to the innkeeper or his servant, nor acquaint him with them: *Calye's Case*, 8 Coke 32, 1 Sm. L. C., 10th ed., p. 115. This, it has been said, is necessary for the protection of those resorting to the inn, from the negligence and dishonest practices of innkeepers and their servants: *Holder v. Solby*, 8 C. B. N. S. 254. As will appear hereafter, it is not necessary at common law that the guest's goods should be in the special keeping of the innkeeper, it is generally sufficient that they are within the inn under his implied care, and as soon as the goods are brought into the inn, though there is no actual delivery of the goods, nor any notice of them given to the innkeeper, this custody begins. If he desires to avoid liability for their loss or injury he must give the guest direct notice. Hanging up a coat in the place allotted for that purpose is placing it infra hospitium, that is, in charge of the innkeeper and under the protection of the inn, though it is done in the absence of the landlord and his servant . . .

An innkeeper cannot discharge himself of the duty imposed upon him by the common law by a general notice. If he desires to limit his liability in any way he must give the guest express notice, that is, the notice must be brought home to the guest. The posting up of, or the putting upon the hotel register book, a notice, is not sufficient unless it can be shewn that the guest saw it and read it: *Richmond v. Smith*, 8 B. & C. 9; *Packard v. Northcraft*, 2 Met. (Ky.) 442. In *Bernstein v. Sweeny*, 33 N. Y. Super. Ct. 271, it was decided that the signing of a register under a printed heading containing an agreement that the innkeeper shall not be responsible for the loss of valuables unless deposited in the safe, is not the contract of the guest, in the absence of any proof that it was seen or assented to by him.

12. Consider the statutory modification of these duties contained in the *Hotel Keepers Act*, R.S.B.C. 1996, c. 206:

3 (1) No innkeeper is liable to make good to a guest loss of or injury to goods or property brought to the inn, except if the goods or property have been

(a) stolen, lost or injured through the wilful act, default or neglect of the innkeeper or the innkeeper's servant, or

(b) deposited expressly for safe custody with the innkeeper, except that in case of the deposit the innkeeper may require as a condition of liability that the goods or property be deposited in a box or other receptacle, fastened and sealed by the person depositing the goods or property.

(2) If the vehicle of a guest has been delivered to the custody of the innkeeper or the innkeeper's servant expressly for storage or parking in a place specifically reserved and designated by the innkeeper for the storing or parking of vehicles, the liability of the innkeeper is that of a bailee for reward. . . .

(4) If an innkeeper refuses to receive for safe custody, as mentioned, goods or property of a guest, or if a guest, through a default of the innkeeper, is unable to deposit the goods or property, the innkeeper is not entitled to the benefit of this Act for the loss of or injury to the goods or property unless the innkeeper proves that the inn was not equipped with a proper safe or vault or did not have a place for the storing or parking of vehicles and that the innkeeper informed the guest at the time of refusing or failing to receive the goods or property.

An innkeeper who fails to satisfy the provisions of s. 4 "is not entitled to the benefit of" the Act. What is the significance of such a consequence?

13. A hotel guest hands a package to a hotel clerk for storage in the safe. The package disappears. Unknown to the clerk it contained valuable jewellery. Is the hotel liable for the loss, and if so to what extent? See *Bendera v. C.E. & V. Holdings* 1983 CarswellBC 28, 43 B.C.L.R. 96 (C.A.).

14. A bailor assumes responsibility for the state of the goods bailed. What is the standard to which the bailor will be held? See *M. et al. v. Sinclair c.o.b. Sinclair's Riding Stables* (1980) 15 C.C.L.T. 57, 1980 CarswellOnt 621 (H.C.), reproduced below.

M. et al. v. Sinclair c.o.b. Sinclair's Riding Stables (1980) 15 C.C.L.T. 57, 1980 CarswellOnt 621 (H.C.)

[The Millers rented horses from Sinclair Riding Stables. George Miller Sr. requested slow horses for himself and his daughter, but rented a more spirited horse for Michael Miller, his son. During the group ride, Michael fell from his horse injuring his left hip. The trial judge accepted the evidence of Michael that the stirrup had fallen off while he had been riding and this had caused the fall. Was the bailor liable?]

Lerner J.:

This case was founded in bailment for reward that carried an implied warranty of fitness and also in negligence.

Hyman v. Nye (1881), 6 Q.B.D. 685 appears to form the basis for the law in Ontario on the applicable standard of care. The plaintiff was injured when a horse-drawn carriage which he rented fell apart. Although the action was based in negligence, the Court held that the plaintiff could possibly recover on a breach of warranty. Lindley, J. stated at page 689:

> It was objected on the part of the defendant that the plaintiff had in his statement of claim based his case on negligence on the part of the defendant, and not on any breach of warranty express or implied, and consequently that the plaintiff could not recover in this action, at least, without amending. But the absence of such care as a person is by law bound to take is negligence; and whether the plaintiff sues the defendant in tort for negligence in not having supplied such a fit and proper carriage as he ought to have supplied, or whether the plaintiff sues him in contract for the breach of an implied warranty that the carriage was as fit and proper as it ought to have been, appears to me wholly immaterial. Upon this point I adopt the opinion of Baron Martin in *Francis v. Cockrell* [Law Rep. 5 Q.B. 509], which is based upon and warranted by *Brown v. Boorman* [11 Cl. & Fin.1.].

The duty placed upon the lender of carriages was set out at pages 687-88:

> . . . A person who lets out carriages is not, in my opinion, responsible for all defects discoverable or not; he is not an insurer against all defects; nor is he bound to take more care than coach proprietors or railway companies who provide carriages for the public to travel in; but in my opinion, he is bound to take as much care as they; and although not an insurer against all defects, he is an insurer against all defects which care and skill can guard against. His duty appears to me to be to supply a carriage as fit for the purpose for which it is hired as care and skill can render it; and if whilst the carriage is being properly used for such purpose it breaks down, it becomes incumbent on the person who has let it out to shew that the break down was in the proper sense of the word an accident not preventible by any care or skill.

In other words, a person who lets out carriages for hire is not responsible for all defects. Rather, he is responsible for all defects which care and skill could guard against.

The expression "reasonably fit and proper" was further defined in *Hyman* at page 688:

> In many of the cases bearing on this subject, the expression "reasonably fit and proper" is used. This is a little ambiguous, and requires explanation. In a case like the present, a carriage to be reasonably fit and proper must be as fit and proper as care and skill can make it for use in a reasonable and proper manner, *i.e.*, as fit and proper as care and skill can make it to carry a reasonable number of people, conducting themselves in a reasonable manner, and going at a reasonable pace on the journey for which the carriage was hired; or (if no journey was specified) along roads, or over ground reasonably fit for carriages. A carriage not fit and proper in this sense would not be reasonably fit and proper, and vice versa. . . .

Factually, I find that the infant plaintiff, Michael Miller, fell from the horse and was injured because the strap holding the stirrup to the saddle was either defective or improperly secured. There was a breach of implied warranty against a defect which care and skill could have avoided, and also negligence in not ensuring that such care and skill was used in securing the strap or observing that it was defective. The fact that on her own evidence MacFarlane testified that she adjusted the stirrup straps for Michael after he was in the saddle, makes the principles stated *supra* eminently applicable in this case.

In addition to denying breach of warranty and negligence, the defendant also denied liability on the further grounds that (1) as a condition of the bailment, the plaintiffs executed a waiver of liability for bodily injury or property damage; (2) that the maxim *volenti non fit injuria* applied to the facts thus absolving the defendant.

Waiver

The defendant displayed signs on his premises to the effect that riders rented horses at their own risk, allegedly absolving him from liability for personal injuries and property damage. Each rider was required to sign a register upon which there appeared, at the top of each page, the words:

PLEASE READ CAREFULLY

NO LIABILITY - AGAINST SINCLAIR STABLE

- FOR INJURY - TO BODY DAMAGE

- CLOTHING OR GLASSES

Mr. Miller, his ten-year-old son Michael and eight-year-old daughter were each required to sign the register before being assigned a riding horse. It is hardly necessary to state that the infant plaintiff Michael Miller and his sister were clearly not bound by their undertakings to waive any rights to claim because they were under the age of accountability. But, apart from that disability and assuming that Mr. Miller, on his own behalf, could waive any right to claim and if the tenuous agreement was successfully made that he could bind his children, the waiver would still fall on other grounds.

Without discussing the other defects in the notice of alleged exemption from liability, it must be remembered that on the principle of *contra proferentem* the notice, if inadequate, ambiguous or restrictive, must be interpreted against the author thereof for whose benefit it was intended. The notice merely purported to exempt Sinclair from bodily injury or property damage (whatever that was supposed to mean) but did not specifically exempt Sinclair from his negligence or that of his employees. To be effective, injury or damage as a result of negligence would have to be excluded in clear terms. Respectfully, I adopt the reasoning of Verchere, J. in *Collins v. Richmond Rodeo Riding Ltd. et al* (1966), 55 W.W.R. 289, 56 D.L.R. (2d) 428 (B.C.) wherein the learned judge dealt exhaustively with many authorities pertinent to exemptions clauses.

Volenti Non Fit Injuria

On the facts of this accident as found, it cannot be said that Mr. Miller or his son Michael freely and voluntarily, with full knowledge of the nature and extent of the risks that they accepted, impliedly agreed to accept them. The risk here turned out to be that Michael thus knowingly agreed or undertook to ride a horse with an improperly secured stirrup on the saddle. Nothing more need be said of that defence. . . .

QUESTION

Compare this analysis of the bailor's duty, drawn from *Cottee v. Franklins Serve-Service Pty. Ltd.* [1997] 1 Q.R. 469 (C.A.) at 477-8 (*per* Macrosan C.J.):

> In *Derbyshire Building Co. Pty Ltd. v. Becker* (1962) 107 C.L.R. 633 which was a case where damages were claimed for personal injuries, McTiernan J. at 645 accepted as a correct statement of the law the proposition of Jordan C.J. in *Gemmell Power Farming Co. Ltd. v. Nies* (1935) 35 S.R. (N.S.W.) 469 as follows:
>
> > When one person, for value, supplies a chattel to another to be used for an agreed or stated purpose, or for a purpose indicated by the nature of the chattel, he impliedly promises, in the absence of some provision to the contrary, that it is reasonably fit for such use.
>
> In *Derbyshire* at 649 Kitto J. accepted that the weight of judicial opinion was "in favour of applying to all contracts for the supply of chattels, including contracts of bailment, the principles laid down with respect to sales" in the *Sale of Goods Act* and in particular where an implication as to the fitness of a chattel arose under a contract it was not limited to fitness extending only so far as the supplier knew or ought to have known. Taylor J. at 656-657 accepted that the same rule of implication concerning the reasonable fitness of a chattel for a specified purpose applied in the case of sale, hire purchase and hire, and Windeyer J. at 659 accepted that the same rule applied for sale as for hire and the ordinary implication was that chattel should be reasonably fit for its contemplated use.

Punch v. Savoy's Jewellers Ltd.
(1986) 54 O.R. (2d) 383, 1986 CarswellOnt 154 (C.A.)

Cory J.A.:

A number of issues are raised on this appeal. They pertain to the duty of care owed by bailees and sub-bailees to the bailor; the interpretation of a clause limiting the liability of a sub-bailee carrier; and whether there has been a fundamental breach of the contract of carriage by that carrier.

Factual Background

Lenore Punch received from her aunt a very attractive antique ring. It was of considerable value and had been appraised by Savoy's Jewellers Ltd. (Savoy), a local jeweller in Sault Ste. Marie, at $11,000. The ring was in the nature of a family heirloom and the understanding was that eventually it would be passed on to a daughter of Lenore Punch.

The ring was in need of repair. Lenore Punch, who lived in Sault Ste Marie, took it to Savoy. Savoy was unable to carry out the repairs on its premises so it sent the ring to Harry Walker Jewellery Manufacturers Co. Limited (Walker) in Toronto. The ring was transmitted by registered mail with a value of $100 shown for insurance purposes. This seems to have been the practice in the jewellery trade. Certainly Savoy had used this method of transmitting jewellery for repair for over 25 years without experiencing any loss.

Walker duly carried out the repairs on the ring and was ready to send it back to Sault Ste. Marie. Unfortunately a postal strike had intervened. An employee of Walker had heard that Rapidex, a branch of Canadian National Railway (C.N.), was being used to transport jewellery. The use of C.N. as a carrier was discussed by employees of Walker and Savoy. The Savoy employee agreed tht the ring might be sent back by means of the C.N. carrier. However, there was no discussion of the terms or details of the carriage. At the trial, Mr. Antoine, the principal officer of Savoy, agreed that he probably would have "gone along" with C.N. if Walker had spoken directly to him. He said that he had found the mail reliable in the past and would have used C.N. if he was satisfied its system was good.

The Walker employee then called C.N. Rapidex and a driver of that company attended at the Walker premises. He appeared to be in a hurry. The Walker employee explained that she had no experience with the C.N. bill of lading form and did not know how to complete it. The driver then filled in the form including the value of the five items that were included in the package. When it came to filling in the valuation of the articles, the Walker employee mentioned that when transmitting by mail the value was usually shown at $100. The driver suggested that the same amount should be used in the C.N. form. This was done for the items other than those which belonged to Walker. In the case of the two Walker items, the values were shown at $300 and $700. When the form was completed, the driver for C.N. signed it, left a copy with Walker and departed.

It was conceded by the only C.N. employee who testified that a number of errors had been made by the driver who attended at Walker's. It was the policy of Rapidex and indeed it was set out in their brochures that customers were not to use Rapidex for jewellery worth more than $300. It was admitted that in light of the valuations shown for these five articles they should not have been accepted. C.N. does not instruct its drivers to advise customers of the conditions in the contract of carriage. In the usual course, it is C.N. sales personnel who explain such conditions when they are soliciting customers and obtaining orders. C.N. agreed that it was very important to advise customers to set a proper valuation on their goods to be shipped, as C.N. employs a higher standard of care in the handling of valuable goods. In any event, the driver ought to have telephoned the C.N. office staff to obtain permission to carry such valuable items. He failed to take this step. Further, the driver ought not to have signed the shipping invoice.

The ring was never delivered by C.N. to Savoy. In fact, there is no record of the ring ever being in C.N.'s possession other than the shipping invoice. When it came to the attention of Walker and Savoy that the ring had not been delivered, Walker telephoned C.N. and was told to instruct Savoy to call C.N. Mr. Antoine of Savoy called a C.N. employee who told him in no uncertain terms that he should "forget it" for he had only a $50 coverage. In light of that advice, Savoy did not put in a written claim.

At trial, C.N. gave no explanation for the loss of the ring. Indeed, it went further and admitted that the loss could have been due to the theft of the ring by its driver. C.N. conceded that it was aware of the driver's address but it did not see fit to call him. C.N. did not know if the driver had been questioned although this would have been a standard investigative procedure that could easily have been verified.

With regard to the notice of the claim, C.N. stated that it had received oral notice of the claim well within the twelve-month limitation period set out in the shipping invoice which was the contract of carriage. It conceded that it would not have taken any further steps to investigate the matter had it received a written claim.

Although Lenore Punch was not aware that her ring would be sent out of Sault Ste. Marie for repairs, she testified that if such a step was necessary she would have expected the ring to have been shipped to Toronto for those repairs. At one point she called at Savoy to pick up her ring and was told it had been sent to Toronto for repairs. She did not express any objection to this.

The Rapidex form that the Walker employee signed contained the following warnings immediately below the space left for the shipper's signature:

> Subject to terms and conditions approved by General Order T-43, referred to on reverse side hereof.
>
> Liability limited to $50.00 per shipment.
>
> Increased liability may be purchased in accordance with existing tariffs.

Continuing on the reverse side in small print the following conditions are set out:

> 1.(a) In this contract "Carrier" means the Carrier issuing this shipping document . . .
>
> 1.(b) This contract shall inure to the benefit of and be binding upon the shipper and consignee and all persons claiming or asserting any right to the ownership or possession of the shipment, and shall inure to the benefit of and be binding upon any Carrier to whom the shipment may be delivered for furtherance to destination, and shall apply to any reconsignment or return of the shipment.
>
> 2.(a) When in accordance with the terms of this contract the Carrier is liable for any damage (which damage shall mean herein any complete or partial loss, or destruction, injury or delay) with respect to any shipment, whether such damage arises through

negligence or otherwise, the amount for which the Carrier shall be liable in accordance with clauses 2(b), 2(c), 2(d) hereof, shall not exceed, in any event, the actual value of the shipment.

2.(b) The maximum liability of the Carrier with respect to the shipment shall be limited for any shipment of one hundred pounds or less to Fifty Dollars ($50.00 and for any shipment in excess of one hundred pounds to any amount not exceeding fifty cents (50 cents) per pound (actual weight) unless the shipper indicates in the shipping contract his intention to take advantage of the provisions of sub-clauses (c) or (d) hereof.

2.(c) The maximum liability of the Carrier shall be the amount of the value declared by the shipper and embodied in the shipping contract and provided that valuation charges are assessed in accordance with the applicable tariffs. . . .

3.(b) The liability of the Carrier for a shipment of . . . jewelry . . . will not be for a greater sum than that stated in the shipping contract, or for more than the actual value of the shipment at the time and place of receipt thereof by the Carrier, whichever may be the lesser amount . . .

6.(b) The Carrier shall not be liable: . . .

(VIII) For non-delivery or complete loss or destruction of the shipment in Canada, unless a claim is filed at any office of the Carrier within twelve (12) months from the date the shipment was delivered by the shipper to the Carrier. . . .

12. Any alteration, addition or erasure in the shipping contract shall be signed or initialled by an agent of the Carrier issuing the same and the shipper and, if not so signed or initialled, shall be without effect, and the shipping contract shall be enforceable according to its original tenor.

Decision at Trial

The trial Judge found that Savoy was a bailee and Walker and C.N. were sub-bailees of the ring. He determined that Walker and C.N. were in breach of the duty they owed to Lenore Punch but that Savoy was not.

Walker, he observed, had failed to discuss the terms and conditions of the shipment with Savoy. Further, the trial Judge found that it failed to take proper care of the ring by not insuring it against loss for its true value and by setting a grossly inadequate valuation of the ring on the bill of lading.

The trial Judge found C.N. responsible for failing to deliver the ring without advancing any explanation for its loss. He was of the view that C.N. could not rely upon the condition that a written claim be filed within a year. He concluded that C.N. was "estopped" from complaining of the absence of a written claim within the specified time as Savoy had been told to "forget it" and that, in any event, C.N. was fully aware of the claim shortly after the ring was lost. He found the reference on the face of the bill of lading that there were conditions on the reverse side and the stipulation limiting liability to $50 unless otherwise specified to be inconspicuous.

He held that, in those circumstances, the conditions did not bind Walker as C.N. had not taken reasonable measures to draw the conditions to Walker's attention.

In the result, Walker and C.N. were found liable to the plaintiff but her claim against Savoy was dismissed. However, she was permitted to recover the costs payable to Savoy resulting from her action against it being dismissed from C.N. Walker was to be indemnified by C.N. for Walker's liability to the plaintiff.

Duty of Bailees

It may be helpful to first consider the nature of bailment and the duty of bailees. Bailment has been defined as the delivery of personal chattels on trust, usually on a contract, express or implied, that the trust shall be executed and the chattels be delivered in either their original or an altered form as soon as the time for which they were bailed has elapsed. It is to be noted that the legal relationship of bailor and bailee can exist independently of a contract. It is created by the voluntary taking into custody of goods which are the property of another. Such is the situation in cases of sub-bailment. See *Halsbury's*, 4th ed., Vol. 2, p. 689, para. 1501. The facts of this case demonstrate that Savoy was a bailee for reward and that Walker and C.N. were sub-bailees for reward. The transfer of the ring to each of these entities fell within the definition of "bailment".

The bailee for reward must exercise due care for the safety of the article entrusted to him by taking such care of the goods as would a prudent man of his own possessions. Significantly, a bailee is liable for the loss of goods arising out of his servant's theft on the grounds that he is responsible for the manner in which his servant carries out his duty. In the result, it matters not whether the servant is careless, whether the goods are stolen by a stranger, or if the servant himself steals them.

In *Morris v. C.W. Martin & Sons Ltd.*, [1965] 2 All E.R. 725, Lord Denning M.R. confirmed that when goods are damaged or lost while in the possession of a bailee, the bailee must prove either that he took appropriate care of them or that his failure to do so did not contribute to the loss. If the goods are lost or damaged while they are in possession of the bailee, the burden is on the bailee to show that the damage occurred without any neglect, default or misconduct on the part of himself or any of his servants to whom he delegated a duty. The escape liability, he must demonstrate that the loss was without any fault on his part or the part of his servants. Only if he satisfies the owner that he took due care to employ trustworthy servants and that he and his servants exercised all diligence will he be excused from liability.

How should bailment principles be applied to the facts of this case?

(a) Duty owed by Walker to the owner of the ring

A prudent owner would wish to make certain that this valuable antique ring was transported and carried in the safest possible manner. It may be that the past history of jewellers sending articles by registered post for over 25 years without a loss was sufficient to establish that this was a safe method of carriage. In any event, in this case, the matter went further. When the mail strike intervened, Walker and Savoy agreed that the ring would be returned through C.N. Walker was clearly remiss in not discussing the manner of carriage and the possibility of obtaining insurance with Savoy.

This family heirloom deserved to be carried with all due care and caution. A prudent owner, when asked whether he would wish to insure a ring valued at $11,000 during transportation, would answer in the affirmative. If the owner was concerned about the safety of the unproven transportation by C.N., he would undoubtedly say, "Insure it for its full value to make certain it is carried safely". Alternatively, the owner might say, "Wait and, if you vouch for it, send the ring in the usual way that has proved safe for the last 25 to 30 years." Mrs. Punch was never given the opportunity to consider the alternatives. Rather, Walker negligently and falsely fixed the value of the ring at only $100 when it arranged for its shipment.

In those circumstances, I cannot see how it could be said that Walker took such care of a valuable ring as would a reasonable and prudent owner. Walker was in breach of the duty owed to Lenore Punch and is liable to her for the damages flowing from the loss of her ring.

(b) Duty owed by Savoy

Savoy, without consulting the owner, accepted a new method of carriage without inquiring as to the feasibility and cost of obtaining insurance coverage on the goods during their transportation.

It is said that there is no duty on a bailee to insure goods. That principle may be true in the case of goods stored, for example, in a warehouse: see *Mason v. Morrow's Moving & Storage Ltd.* (1978), 87 D.L.R. (3d) 234, [1978] 4 W.W.R. 534, 5 C.C.L.T. 59 (B.C. C.A.). In the case at bar, insurance for the value of the goods was, in essence, a term and condition of their transportation. Any prudent owner of a ring such as this would make certain that insurance coverage was available for its true value. This step would be taken not only to provide insurance *qua* insurance but primarily to ensure that adequate and proper care was taken in the transportation of a valuable belonging. This would be a particularly important factor when employing an untried carrier. I would characterize the provision of insurance as an essential term of this contract of carriage. It is a minimal step that a prudent owner would take for goods of this type. Savoy was, on the facts of this case, in breach of its duty to the owner of the ring.

(c) Duty owed by C.N.

What then is the position of C.N.? It has lost the goods. No attempt has been made to explain their disappearance. The admitted possibility of theft by the driver looms large in light of C.N.'s failure to call him, although aware of his place of residence. C.N. relies entirely upon the term set out in the bill of lading that its liability for non-delivery is limited to $50 or, at most, $100, the amount claimed by the shipper.

The determination of C.N.'s obligations will depend in part upon what duties and obligations, if any, are found to be owed by C.N. to each of Walker, Savoy and Lenore Punch and in part upon the nature of the action that arises from the bailment of articles.

Should an action in bailment be looked upon as a cause of action in contract or in tort, or do unique obligations and duties arise in bailment? While it is true in modern times that liability in tort and contract have overlapped to an ever greater extent, some distinctions remain, and this may be particularly true of an agreement for bailment. It may be said that bailment is, in essence, a consensual matter whereby the bailee consents to receive goods for a specific purpose. If it is consensual, limitation of liability for the loss of the goods is a fundamental aspect of that consent and the arrangement is basically contractual. On this view, C.N. should be entitled to rely on the limitation clause.

If a bailment action is tortious in nature so that a claim can be based on negligence alone, then C.N. would be liable to Savoy and to Lenore Punch for its negligence in the unexplained failure to deliver the ring. One can be sympathetic to this position as well, where neither the owner Punch nor the original bailee Savoy consented to the terms of the sub-bailment to C.N., particularly the clause limiting liability.

The relationship of bailment combines elements of both contract and tort. For example, if a sub-bailee carrier is aware when it enters into a contract of the existence of an owner who is not a party to the contract, it would owe a duty of care to such an owner. If that owner did not give express or implied consent to the terms of carriage, then the owner might not be bound by any terms exempting or limiting liability.

Since Walker advised Savoy of its intention to use C.N. as the shipper and Savoy agreed to that method of carriage, this was a duly authorized sub-bailment of the ring to C.N. From that it would follow that C.N. would owe the same duty and enjoy the same limitations of liability with regard to Savoy as it did with regard to Walker. Support for this proposition is to be found in the reasons of Lord Denning M.R. in the *Morris* case, *supra*, at p. 733:

> Can the defendants [sub-bailees] rely, as against the plaintiff, on the exempting conditions although there was no contract directly between them and her? There is much to be said on each side. On the one hand, it is hard on the plaintiff if her just claim is defeated by exempting conditions of which she knew nothing and to which she was not a party. On the other hand, it is hard on the defendants if they are held liable to a greater responsibility than they agreed to undertake . . . The answer to the problem lies, I think, in this: the owner is bound by the conditions if he expressly or impliedly consented to the bailee making a sub-bailment containing those conditions, but not otherwise.

However, the reasons specify that a sub-bailee is able to rely on the exempting clause as against the owner only if the owner expressly or impliedly consented to the bailee making a sub-bailment "*containing those conditions, but not otherwise*". In the case at bar, Savoy and Walker never discussed the terms of carriage, including the aspect of insurance. In those circumstances, Savoy did not consent expressly or impliedly to the sub-bailment on the terms agreed to by Walker. Thus Savoy was not bound by the limitation of liability clause.

What is the relationship between the owner of the ring, Lenore Punch, and C.N.? What duty, if any, did C.N. owe to the owner in the circumstances of this case? Clearly there was no contractual relationship between them. It is unlikely that Mrs. Punch was aware of the existence of Rapidex and still less likely that C.N. knew of Lenore Punch. However, the possibility of someone claiming through Savoy is clearly contemplated in cl. 1(b) of the contract of carriage which states that the provisions pertaining to the limitation of liability are to be binding upon *all* persons claiming any right to the ownership or possession of the shipment. In light of this clause, it can be said that the carrier contemplated the loss or damage which the ultimate owner would suffer as a result of the disappearance of the ring. Thus, such a loss could not be considered too remote a risk to form the basis of a claim in negligence.

Can such a concept apply to bailment? At least one author, Palmer on *Bailment* (1979), at p. 801, considers that the reasons in the *Morris* case widened the scope of liability of sub-bailees to include someone in the position of Lenore Punch. There, the learned author states:

> The decision . . . marks the final stage in the emancipation of bailment from contract, for it enables the former relation to arise not only without consideration but without communication or agreement of any kind.

It has been seen that Savoy cannot be bound by a limitation of liability clause to which it did not consent. Obviously Lenore Punch, who knew nothing of the clause, the contract of carriage or the carrier, cannot be bound by it. C.N. is liable to her for the full value of the ring since its contract of carriage specifically contemplates the existence of an owner to whom a duty of care is owed.

(d) The Effect of the Limitation of Liability Clause in Determining the Claim of Walker for Indemnity from C.N.

Clauses which exempt or limit the liability of a contracting party in situations where there is a failure to carry out the contractual obligations have long troubled the Courts. Often these clauses are included in a standard form of contract where the contracting parties are of very unequal status. They are frequently difficult to find in the contract and even more difficult to understand. It appears frustrating that a contracting party should undertake to do something and then specify that it will not be liable if it fails to fulfill its undertaking. On the face of it, there is something very unfair about this sort of clause, yet it may be the only economical basis upon which the contract can be undertaken. . . .

In *Beaufort Realties (1964) Ltd. v. Chomedey Aluminum Co. Ld.*, [1980] 2 S.C.R. 718, 116 D.L.R. (3d) 193, 13 B.L.R. 119, Ritchie J., speaking for the Court, stated that the question of whether an exclusionary clause applied when there had been a fundamental breach of the contract was to be determined according to the true construction of that contract.

In this case, the validity of the limitation clause must be determined on the basis of the construction of the contract between Walker and C.N. By cl. 2(a) the carrier is liable for damage which is defined to mean any complete or partial loss, destruction, injury or delay with respect to any shipment, whether such damage arises through negligence or otherwise. The damages for such loss are to be limited to $50 or the value stipulated; here, to $100. It would seem C.N. was primarily interested in excluding liability for damages flowing from negligence. Nowhere in the contract is reference made to loss occasioned by theft by an employee. It is true that the term "or otherwise" is an apparently broad one. Nonetheless, I cannot see it as encompassing theft by an employee. If an employer wishes to exclude any responsibility for loss arising from theft by his own employees then good conscience requires that such an exclusion be spelt out with clarity and precision. It is the employer who hires and has some basis for knowing his employees. His customers (including bailors) cannot be expected to know anything about those employees. If the responsibility for their theft is sought to be avoided then the bailor customer should be aware of it in order that he can make an informed decision as to whether to deal with a bailee on those terms.

Can it be said that the terms of the contract limited liability to $50 or $100 in the case of an unexplained loss that might well have been occasioned by theft of an employee? I think not. In this case, all trace of the ring was lost from the moment C.N. picked it up from Walker. It has been held that a bailee is liable if goods bailed to him are lost as a result of theft by his employees. . . . It follows that unless a clause excluding or limiting liability exempts a bailee from liability for loss resulting from theft by employees the bailee remains liable for such loss. That principle should be extended to the factual situation present in this case. Where there is an unexplained loss of goods which may have been occasioned by theft by an employee, the bailee should be liable for that loss unless the contract of bailment contained a clause clearly exempting the bailee from loss occasioned by the theft of an employee. My construction of this contract leads me to the conclusion that the disappearance of the ring without any explanation in circumstances where the possibility of theft existed amounted to a fundamental breach of the contract.

This finding does not make the position of the bailee an impossible one. For example, in this case, if C.N. had given evidence as to the care it had exercised in the selection and hiring of its drivers, and if the driver had explained what care he and other employees took of the ring when it was in their possession, then if it transpired that the article had nevertheless been stolen, C.N. would have incurred no liability.

Further, I agree with the finding of the trial Judge that C.N. cannot rely upon the contractual requirement that a written notice of the claim be given within 12 months of the loss. The C.N. employee's advice to the claimant that he should forget the claim is sufficient to dispose of this argument of the railway. Further, it is conceded that there was prompt oral notice given of the claim and no prejudice was occasioned by the failure to give written notice.

Summary and Conclusion

The following then is the result. Both Savoy and Walker are liable to Lenore Punch for breach of their duty as bailees. They breached this duty by failing to obtain instructions from the owner as to the means of carriage in light of the postal strike; by failure to give a proper evaluation of the ring to the carrier; and by failure to stipulate as a term of the carriage insurance coverage for the true value of the ring itself. C.N. also is liable to the owner for the unexplained loss of the ring. Savoy and Walker are to be indemnified by C.N. for any loss which they must make good to the owner.

Walker, however, should not be entitled to recover any costs against C.N. It was Walker which fixed the value of the article to be shipped at $100 and it must accept some responsibility for that action.

The judgment at trial will be varied. The plaintiff will have judgment in the amount of $11,000 and costs against all three defendants. The plaintiff will have prejudgment interest from January 31, 1980 at the rate of interest prescribed by s. 36(3) of the *Judicature Act*, R.S.O. 1980, c. 223, to the date of the judgment. There was no objection taken to the plaintiff's cross-appeal on this issue. Savoy and Walker are to be indemnified by C.N. for any amount of the claim and costs they may have to pay to the plaintiff. Savoy will have its costs of defending the action against C.N. Walker will not recover any costs against C.N. apart from those costs of the plaintiff which it may be required to pay.

The appeal of C.N. will be dismissed with costs payable to the plaintiff. The appeal of Walker will be dismissed with costs to the plaintiff. The cross-appeal of the plaintiff against Savoy will be allowed with costs payable by Savoy. . . .

QUESTIONS

1. In this case it was noted that Lenore Punch was unaware that her jewellery had been sent to Toronto. Was that action by Savoy not itself a breach of the bailment?

2. A bails goods to B, who in turn sub-bails to C. C sub-sub-bails to D. (B, C and D are all express delivery businesses.) In due course, B seeks a return of the goods from D, which refuses to comply. B brings an action (in detinue) against D, seeking an order for the return of the goods. Should it succeed? See *Followmont Transport P/L v. Premier Group P/L* [1999] Q.C.A. 232.

3. It is open to the parties to alter the normal rules governing obligations of care. Indeed, in the last three cases reproduced above, a purported waiver of liability was

involved. Notice, however, that in none of these cases was the limiting clause actually effective. Review these judgments, and outline the ways in which the clauses were circumvented. Can you think of other grounds for circumventing an exculpatory clause?

4. It is possible to contract out of liability for even for a fundamental breach of contract provided that one does so with sufficient clarity: see *Syncrude Canada Ltd. v. Hunter Engineering* [1989] 1 S.C.R. 426, 1989 CarswellBC 37, 1989 CarswellBC 703. However, it was also recognized in *Syncrude* that circumstances may arise that would render it unconscionable to enforce an exculpatory clause.

The case of *Solway v. Davis Moving & Storage Inc.* 2002 CarswellOnt 4257, 62 O.R. (3d) 522 (C.A.), leave to appeal refused: 2003 CarswellOnt 2018, 2003 CarswellOnt 2019 (S.C.C.) was just such a case. There, goods moved and stored by a moving company had been stolen during the course of the bailment. There seemed to be little question that the bailee was negligent. However, a term of the contract limited the defendant's liability to a monetary amount far below the value of the stolen items. For a majority of the Ontario Court of Appeal, Labrosse J.A. considered (at paras. 13–20) the effect of *Syncrude* on the instant case:

> In *Fraser Jewellers (1982) Ltd. v. Dominion Electric Protection Co.* (1997), 34 O.R. (3d) 1 (Ont. C.A.), at 8, this court reviewed the decision in *Hunter Engineering* and noted that, in that case, the Supreme Court of Canada was unanimous in holding that, while limitation of liability provisions, *prima facie*, were enforceable according to their true meaning, a court was empowered in limited circumstances to grant relief against provisions of this nature. The Supreme Court of Canada, however, was evenly divided on the question of the test to be used to determine when or in what circumstances the power to grant relief should be exercised.
>
> In *Hunter Engineering*, Chief Justice Dickson, writing for himself and La Forest J., rejected the doctrine of fundamental breach and the uncertainty that was related thereto. As an alternative, he adopted a more direct approach to dealing with potentially unfair contracts. He stated, at p. 342:
>
>> Only where the contract is unconscionable, *as might arise* from situations of unequal bargaining power between the parties, should the courts interfere with agreements the parties have freely concluded. The courts do not blindly enforce harsh or unconscionable bargains . . . Explicitly addressing concerns of unconscionability *and* inequality of bargaining power allow the courts to focus expressly on the real grounds for refusing to give force to a contractual term said to have been agreed to by the parties. [Emphasis added].
>
> By way of contrast, Wilson J., writing for herself and L'Heureux-Dubé J., adopted an approach first accepted by the Ontario Court of Appeal and then by the Supreme Court of Canada in *Chomedy Aluminium Co. v. Belcourt Construction (Ottawa) Ltd.* (1980), 116 D.L.R. (3d) 193 (S.C.C.). In explaining this approach at p. 376, Madam Justice Wilson was of the view that courts need "to determine whether *in the context of the particular breach which had occurred* it was fair and reasonable to enforce the clause in favour of the party who had committed the breach." [Emphasis in original].

> McIntyre J., the other member of the court, did not address this issue.

Robins J.A., speaking for this court, reconciled these two approaches in *Fraser Jewellers*, at p. 10, as follows:

> [W]hether the breach is fundamental or not, an exclusionary clause of this kind, in my opinion, should, *prima facie*, be enforced according to its true meaning. Relief should be granted only if the clause, seen in the light of the agreement, can be said, on Dickson C.J.C.'s test, to be "unconscionable" or, on Wilson J.'s test, to be "unfair or unreasonable". The difference in practice between these alternatives, as Professor Waddams has observed, "is unlikely to be large": Waddams, *The Law of Contract*, 3rd ed. (1993), at p. 323. . . .

In this case, the plaintiffs' goods were highly valuable, both in monetary and sentimental terms. As such, they took special care to choose a moving company that would provide the security they felt was essential. Based on their past experience with Kennedy Moving, its apparent professionalism, and its affiliation with Atlas Van Lines, the plaintiffs made what they thought was an informed decision to opt for Kennedy Moving.

Despite Kennedy Moving's assurances to the contrary, the plaintiffs' goods were not, however, kept in secure conditions. The trailer containing their goods was left overnight on the street with no surveillance. As the trial judge noted, Kennedy Moving should have anticipated that a theft might occur if the trailer was left unattended overnight on a public street. The plaintiffs were never advised that their goods would be stored in these conditions, and they certainly never agreed to such an arrangement.

In deciding not to enforce the limitation clause, the trial judge appears to have equated the words, "unconscionable" and "unreasonable" as these terms were discussed in *Hunter Engineering*. In our view, on the facts as found by the trial judge, to limit the loss of the plaintiffs to $7,089.60 would, in the words of Dickson C.J.C. be "unconscionable", or in the words of Wilson J. be "unfair or unreasonable". This is one of those cases where relief should be granted.

5. In *The Pioneer Container* [1994] 2 A.C. 324 (Hong Kong P.C.) at 341-2, Lord Goff of Chieveley wrote:

> [Is] it a prerequisite of a bailment that the bailor should have consented to the bailee' s possession of the goods? An affirmative answer to this question (which is the answer given by Mr. Bell in his *Modern Law of Personal Property in England and Ireland* at pages 88-89) leads to the conclusion that, if the owner seeks to hold a sub-bailee responsible to him as bailee, he has to accept all the terms of the sub-bailment, warts and all; for either he will have consented to the sub-bailment on those terms or, if not, he will (by holding the sub-bailee liable to him as bailee) be held to have ratified all the terms of the sub-bailment. A negative answer to the question is however supported by other writers, notably by Professor Palmer in his book on *Bailment* at pages 31 *et seq.*, where he cites a number of examples of bailment without the consent of the owner, and by Professor Tay in her Article on The Essence of Bailment in (1966) 5 Sydney Law Review 239. On this approach, a person who voluntarily takes another person's goods into his custody holds them as bailee of that person (the owner); and he [*sic*] can only invoke, for example, terms of a sub-bailment under which he received the goods from

an intermediate bailee as qualifying or otherwise affecting his responsibility to the owner if the owner consented to them.

Which approach to the characterization of a bailment is implicitly adopted in *Punch v. Savoy Jewellers*?

6. Given the Ontario Court of Appeal's ruling on the applicability of the exculpatory clause against Lenore Punch, how, if at all, can a sub-bailee in the position of CN insulate itself from liability at the suit of the head bailor?

In answering this question, consider the holding in *Marcq v. Christie Man & Woods Ltd. (trading as Christie's)* [2002] 4 All E.R. 1005 (Q.B.). There, a painting was consigned by S to Christie's for sale at auction. The reserve bid not having been achieved at the auction, the painting was returned to S, who subsequently sold it privately. M then came forward alleging that the painting had been stolen from him several years earlier. In the aftermath, an action was brought against Christie's, alleging *inter alia* that they were sub-bailees of the painting as against M, the true owner. Acting for the plaintiff was Professor Norman Palmer, author of the leading treatise on bailment law (N.E. Palmer, *Bailment*, 2nd ed. (Sydney: Law Book Co., 1991). In preliminary proceedings, Jack J. dealt (at 1026-7) with the bailment claim:

> Professor Palmer submitted that Christie's were to be treated as the bailees of Mr. Marcq and so were under the duties of a bailee. He said that they were in the position of a finder or an unconscious bailee. Mr. McCaughran's answer was that as Christie's had no knowledge of the existence of Mr. Marcq, they were not his bailees and owed no duty to him. He submitted that Christie's were the bailees of Mr. Schunemann only. He said that this was not to be treated as equivalent to the position where there is a bailment and sub-bailment, where the sub-bailee is found to owe duties to the bailor, for, he said, it is essential to the existence of such duties that the sub-bailee has some knowledge of the existence of the bailor, even if he does not know his identity.
>
> Judge Hallgarten dealt with these submissions quite shortly, rejecting those made on behalf of Mr. Marcq. I think that he was right. For otherwise, as Mr. McCaughran submitted, the law of bailment and conversion would be quite different. Sufficient authority can be found in the judgment of the Privy Council given by Lord Goff of Chieveley in *The Pioneer Container, KH Enterprise (cargo owners) v. Pioneer Container (owners)* [1994] 2 All ER 250 at 262, [1994] 2 AC 324 at 342:
>
>> Their Lordships wish to add that this conclusion, which flows from the decision in [*Morris v. C W Martin & Sons Ltd.* [1965] 2 All ER 725, [1966] 1 QB 716] and [*Gilchrist Watt & Sanderson Pty Ltd. v. York Products Pty Ltd.* [1970] 3 All ER 825, [1970] 1 WLR 1262], produces a result which in their opinion is both principled and just. They incline to the opinion that a sub-bailee can only be said for these purposes to have voluntarily taken into his possession the goods of another if he has sufficient notice that a person other than the bailee is interested in the goods so that it can properly be said that (in addition to his duties to the bailee) he has, by taking the goods into his custody, assumed towards that other person the responsibility for the goods which is characteristic of a bailee. This they believe to be the underlying principle. Moreover, their Lordships do not consider this principle to impose obligations on the sub-bailee which are onerous or unfair, once it is recog-

nised that he can invoke against the owner terms of the sub-bailment which the owner has actually (expressly or impliedly) or even ostensibly authorised. In the last resort the sub-bailee may, if necessary and appropriate, be able to invoke against the bailee the principle of warranty of authority.

7. Assume that, contrary to the holding of Cory J.A., the law provided that in order for Lenore Punch to sue CN, she was required to either accept the terms of the sub-bailment — warts and all — or not at all. See, *e.g.*, *Johnson Matthey v. Constantine Terminals* [1976] 2 Lloyd's Rep. 215 (Q.B.). Could Punch still obtain some form of legal remedy against CN?

8. Some academic legal writers subscribe to the view that the concept of bailment contributes to the intelligibility or rationality of English personal property law. Bailment is said to straddle the domains of obligations and property. The purpose of this paper is to enquire whether English law does in fact benefit from having and over-arching concept of bailment as a tool for regulating diverse fact situations occupying a broad spectrum, embracing from one extreme the honest finder of goods to multi-million pound aircraft finance leases. The argument is that the alleged concept of bailment does more harm than good, stultifying the development of a rational law of personal property. The supposed concept of bailment is too elusive or too over-inclusive in its scope to be of any normative significance. Indeed, where legal conclusions have been derived from the deployment of the concept, they usually turn out to be unsound. Furthermore, sometimes the label of bailment acts as an unnecessary straitjacket, confining principles of potentially broad application to the particular context of chattels. Another insidious tendency of the current attachment to bailment reasoning is to downplay the deliberate contractual structuring of relationships between commercial parties. Overall it will be argued that the category of bailment has no autonomous legal content which cannot be better attributed to concepts of consent, wrongdoing, unjust enrichment or property.

G. McMeel, "The Redundancy of Bailment" [2003] L.M.C.L.Q. 169.

Do you agree? Comment.

CHAPTER 9
SHARED OWNERSHIP

1. INTRODUCTION

To equate private property with individual ownership would be a miscue. Private ownership rights are shareable and infinitely divisible. Indeed, the modern corporation is a form of common enterprise in which participants hold a portion of the venture, their respective entitlements being aptly called *shares*.

In this chapter the various forms of private co-ownership will be outlined, with special reference being given to two types of common holdings — the tenancy in common and the joint tenancy.

Beyond these two basic forms lie other kinds of shared property rights. Some apply in the context of marital property; others concern condominiums and co-operative housing. We have also seen that Aboriginal title is communal. In the last part of the chapter, we return to these forms of collective rights, as well as others.

2. BASIC CONCEPTS

Ontario Law Reform Commission, *Report on Basic Principles of Land Law* (Toronto: A.G. (Ont.), 1996) at 73–7 [footnotes omitted]

The two main types of co-ownership are joint tenancy and tenancy in common. The fundamental concept behind joint tenancy is that two or more people together own the same interest. This was traditionally expressed by saying joint tenants were seised "*per mie et per tout*", meaning that "each joint tenant holds the whole and holds nothing, that is, he holds the whole jointly and nothing separately". This fundamental concept gives rise to two main features: the four unities and the right of survivorship.

The four unities that must be present for the creation and continuation of a joint tenancy are the unities of possession, interest, title and time. The unity of possession "refers to the fact that each joint tenant is entitled, concurrently with the other joint tenants, to possession of the whole of the land that is the subject of the joint tenancy". The unity of interest requires that the interest of each joint tenant be "the same in extent, nature and duration". For example, there can be no joint tenancy if one person's interest is indefeasibly vested and another's is subject to a condition subsequent.

The unity of title means that each joint tenant's title must be derived from the same document or occurrence. The unity of time means that each joint tenant's title must vest at the same time. However, unity of time is not required for a joint tenancy created by will or by a conveyance employing a use. For example, a joint tenancy may be created by a gift by will of land to the children born to A, even though the children's interests will each vest at the time of their respective births.

The right of survivorship (or *jus accrescendi* as it is often called) is the right of the surviving joint tenants to take the interest of a pre-deceasing joint tenant. However, in theory this is a misleading way of expressing the right: the death of one joint tenant does not cause an interest to pass to, or be taken by, the survivors; they are left as before but simply share their ownership with one less person. . . .

As we shall discuss below, a joint tenancy may be converted into a tenancy in common (which carries no right of survivorship) by a process known as severance. However, severance may not be effected by will, so that if a joint tenant purports to devise his or her interest in the property by will, the surviving joint tenants will benefit from the right of survivorship and the devisee will take nothing.

A tenancy in common differs from a joint tenancy in two main ways. First, the only unity that is required is unity of possession. Unlike joint tenants, tenants in common have distinct, separate interests so that there is no reason why they should have unity of interest, title or time. Tenancy in common does require unity of possession. Tenants in common have equal rights of possession over the whole of the land. Otherwise, they would not be co-owners at all.

Secondly, tenants in common do not have a right of survivorship. When one tenant in common dies, his or her interest in the land does not pass to the surviving tenants in common but forms part of the deceased's estate and passes in accordance with the will or intestacy rules.

Two other forms of co-ownership are no longer important and, indeed, probably no longer exist in Ontario. Tenancy by the entireties was an arrangement that at one time applied to married persons.

> At common law, when property was conveyed to a husband and wife in any estate in such a way that had they been strangers they would have taken as joint tenants, they took rather as tenants by the entireties. This was so because of the doctrine of unity of legal personality, according to which husband and wife were considered in law as one: to the four unities of time, title, interest and possession was added a fifth unity, unity of the person. The unity was so complete that neither spouse was regarded as having even a potential share in the property, both were seised together as one individual of the whole, that is, of the entirety. They were, in other words, together tenants of the entirety. From this flows one of the most important features of a tenancy by the entireties: its unseverability. And it follows from this unseverability that the right of survivorship is indestructible.

In some provinces tenancies by the entireties have been explicitly abolished. In England and Australia, the married women's property legislation, which substantially diminished the concept of unity of husband and wife, has been treated as removing the basis of tenancy by the entireties and consequently of impliedly abolishing that form of co-ownership. The same position was taken in Ontario until the decision in *Campbell v. Sovereign Securities & Holdings Co.*, when the Court of Appeal approved the view that tenancy by the entireties could still be created in Ontario. Since the decision in that case the *Family Law Reform Act* and more recently the *Family Law Act* have replaced the *Married Women's Property Act* and have restated the abrogation of the concept of unity of husband and wife. . . .

One commentator has argued that the predecessor to this provision — s. 1 of the *Family Law Reform Act* — did not necessarily abrogate tenancy by the entireties. The argument goes as follows. The provision clearly removes a husband's marital rights over his wife's property so that, among other things, the provision abrogates his common law right during the parties' joint life times to the control and enjoyment over property held as tenants by the entireties. However, that leaves the husband and wife on an equal footing so that, in accordance with section 64(3) of the *Family Law Act*, section 64(1) has no application to a tenancy by the entireties.

Against this, it can be strongly argued that the unity of husband and wife was the basis of tenancy by the entireties and that the basis has been clearly removed. In addition, survival of tenancy by the entireties is inconsistent with the very widely shared assumption that husbands and wives can hold land as joint tenants and that they can sever their joint tenancies and convert them into tenancies in common. . . .

The fourth kind of co-ownership that at one time could exist was coparcenary. This occurred where at common law or by custom land descended on intestacy not, as usually was the case, to a single heir but to two or more persons. For example, if a person died intestate survived only by two daughters, the daughters took as coparceners. In Ontario, coparcenary on intestacy is expressly abrogated by section 14 of the *Estates Administration Act* which has the effect that if real property becomes vested in two or more persons on intestacy, they take as tenants in common.

QUESTION

Why might one choose to create a joint tenancy or a tenancy in common with other co-owners?

3. METHODS OF CREATION

Ontario Law Reform Commission, *Report on Basic Principles of Land Law* (Toronto: A.G. (Ont.), 1996) at 77–80 [footnotes omitted]

At common law there was a presumption of joint tenancy (rather than tenancy in common) so that a transfer of title to co-owners produced a joint tenancy if the four unities were satisfied and an intention to create a tenancy in common was not established. However, in at least three sets of circumstances equity took a different view and presumed a tenancy in common rather than a joint tenancy, and to some extent this equitable position remains relevant today. First, where two or more persons advance money on mortgage, it is presumed in equity that their title as mortgagees is held as tenants in common. Second, it is the orthodox view that partnership property is presumed in equity to be held by partners as tenants in common. A different position might appear to have been taken by Middleton J. in the briefly reported case of *Harris v. Wood* where he stated as follows:

> Partners carry on business jointly, and upon the death of one partner the whole partnership estate vests in the survivor. The surviving partner then asserts in his own name the rights of the firm. It, therefore, follows that the style of cause should be amended . . . The more material question is as to the ability of the surviving partner to give a good title if the defendant is entitled to a reconveyance. It is admitted that the transaction was a partnership transaction, and it follows . . . that the whole property, upon the dissolution of the partnership, became vested in the surviving partner . . .
>
> I had some doubt whether [section 13] of the *Conveyancing and Law of Property Act* affects the matter in hand. On consideration, I do not think it does. The fact that the transaction is a partnership transaction, and that the property was conveyed to the partners, as partners, sufficiently demonstrates that the holding is as joint tenants and not as tenants in common.

Although the reasoning in *Harris v. Wood* is somewhat confusing, it seems that it is not in fact inconsistent with the traditional view that partners are presumed in equity to take partnership property as tenants in common. The findings in *Harris v. Wood* that in litigation involving the partnership the surviving partner represents the firm and that the surviving partner is able to convey title to partnership property involve only the view that the partners were joint tenants at common law and that the surviving partner became at common law the sole owner by survivorship. This does not imply that the survivor did not hold the property on trust from himself and the state of the deceased partner as tenants in common in equity.

The third situation where equity presumes a tenancy in common is where the purchase price for the property is provided unequally. For example, assume that A and B purchase property, A paying seventy-five percent and B twenty-five percent, and title is put in the name of B alone. Subject to proof of a contrary intention, B would hold the property on a resulting trust for A and B as tenants in common with A having a seventy-five percent share and B a twenty-five percent share. A similar result would follow if title had been put in the names of A and B. Subject to the effect of s. 13 of the *Conveyancing and Law of Property Act*, A and B would be joint tenants at common law but they would hold title on trust for themselves as tenants in common in the proportions described above. It is not clear what the position is if title is put in the name of A alone but A and B contributed equally to the purchase price. It is clear that A would, in the absence of proof of a contrary intention, hold title on a resulting trust for A and B. What is not clear is whether in equity A and B are joint tenants or tenants in common with equal shares. In *Delehunt v. Carmody* the High Court of Australia, relying on the indirect effect of a provision equivalent to s. 13 of the *Conveyancing and Law of Property Act*, held that A and B were equitable tenants in common with equal shares. In fact, it is strongly arguable that, even apart from the indirect effect of s. 13, a beneficial tenancy in common is presumed to be created when interests are created under a resulting trust, whether those interests are unequal or equal.

We have made several references to s. 13 of the *Conveyancing and Law of Property Act*. In circumstances in which it applies this provision reverses the common law presumption and creates a presumption in favour of tenancy in common. It provides as follows:

> 13.(1) Where by any letters patent, assurance or will, made and executed after the 1st day of July, 1834, land has been or is granted, conveyed or devised to two or more persons, other than executors or trustees, in fee simple or for any less estate, it shall be considered that such persons took or take as tenants in common and not as joint tenants, unless an intention sufficiently appears on the face of the letters patent, assurance or will, that they are to take as joint tenants.
>
> (2) This section applies notwithstanding that one of such persons is the spouse of another of them.

In addition, s. 14 of the *Estates Administration Act*, which has been mentioned above in the context of the abolition of coparcenary, provides:

> 14. Where real property becomes vested under this Act in two or more persons beneficially entitled under this Act, they take as tenants in common in proportion to their respective rights, unless in the case of a devise they take otherwise under the will of the deceased.

In addition, s. 14 of the *Conveyancing and Law of Property Act* provides:

> 14. Where two or more persons acquire land by length of possession, they shall be considered to hold as tenants in common and not as joint tenants.

Section 13 of the *Conveyancing and Law of Property Act* applies only to "land". The common law presumption in favour of joint tenancy has therefore not been altered with respect to pure personalty. Consequently, where there is a composite gift to two or more persons consisting of both land and pure personalty there will be a presumption of joint tenancy with respect to the personalty and a presumption of tenancy in common with respect to the land.

It appears that s. 13 does not apply to a partnership property. Section 23 of the *Partnership Acts* provides as follows:

> 23. Where land or any heritable interest therein becomes partnership property, unless the contrary intention appears, it is to be treated as between the partners, including the representatives of a deceased partner, and also as between the heirs of a deceased partner and his or her executors or administrators as personal or movable and not real or heritable estate.

Since land which is partnership property is treated as between the partners as if it is personal property, s. 13 does not apply and as far as common law title is concerned the common law presumption in favour of joint tenancy continues. This, it must be emphasized, does not affect the equitable presumption in favour of tenancy in common, affecting the equitable interests of the parties. Even with respect to land, s. 13 of the *Conveyancing and Law of Property Act* does not apply in all circumstances in which persons become co-owners since it only applies where land is "granted, conveyed or devised" by "any letters patent, assurance or will". There are two main situations outside the scope of this provision. First, it was held in *Campbell v. Sovereign Securities & Holding Co.* that a written contract for the purchase of land is not an "assurance" within the section and that therefore the section does not apply in the determination of the effect of such a contract. Second, co-ownership may arise because of such doctrines or remedies as proprietary estoppel, constructive trust or resulting trust, in circumstances where the co-ownership is not derived from any instrument at all.

Re Bancroft, Eastern Trust Co. v. Calder [1936] 4 D.L.R. 571 (N.S. S.C.)

Ross J.:

The late Samuel E. Bancroft died on December 24, 1971. His will is dated October 24, 1913, and a codicil is dated the ____ day of October, 1917. He left surviving him, his widow Clara E. Bancroft, two sons Percy and Aubrey and a daughter Florence. The widow is still living. A daughter Minnie B. Calder predeceased the testator, leaving two children Paul B. Calder and Jean W. Cooke. Paul died on or about January 31, 1933. Surviving him are four children all living, namely John Mills, Hugh MacKeen, Edward Cullen and Paul Alexander. Jean W. Cooke is still living. Helena Valetta Calder, one of the defendants, is the sole executor of the last will and testament of Paul B. Calder deceased. The Eastern Trust Co., the plaintiff, is the sole trustee under the testator's will.

Under the will the widow is bequeathed the fuel, house-keeping provisions, and other consumable stores in the dwelling-house and furniture during her lifetime and after her lifetime and after her death they fall into and form part of the residuary estate. The rest and residue of the estate goes to the trustee upon certain trusts. Briefly, the trustee is to convert the residue into money and dispose of it as follows:

> (a) To divide the same into two equal shares and invest one of the said shares in any investment for the time being authorized by law for the investment of trust moneys and pay the income thereof unto my said wife Clara E. Bancroft during her lifetime.
>
> (b) To invest the other of the said shares in any investment for the time being authorized by law for the investment of trust moneys and divide the income thereof annually during the term of the life of my said wife Clara E. Bancroft into four equal shares and pay one of the shares to my son Percy, one of the said shares to my sin Aubrey, one of the said shares to my daughter Florence and the other of the said shares to the children of my deceased daughter Minnie B. Calder.

Up to the death of Paul B. Calder, the trustee paid one fourth of the income arising from the fund set up under para. 6(b) to Jean W. Cooke and the said Paul B. Calder in equal shares. Since the death of the latter, the question has arisen whether the share heretofore paid to him should go to Jean W. Cooke or to the estate or to the children of Paul B. Calder. An originating summons was accordingly taken out by a trustee for the determination of the following question:

> Whether the share heretofore paid by virtue of para 6(b) of the said will dated October 25, 1913, to Paul B. Calder, deceased, one of the children of the testator's deceased daughter Minnie B. Calder, is payable after January 31, 1933, being the date of the death of said Paul B. Calder to: (a) The estate of the said Paul B. Calder; or (b) The children of the said Paul B. Calder; or, (c) The surviving sister of the said Paul B. Calder.

The important question to be determined is whether the children of Minnie B. Calder took as joint tenants or tenants in common.

Now, there is not much dispute about the law to be applied. It seems clear, under the authorities that a bequest to a number of persons without ant accompanying explanatory words creates a joint tenancy. The law is laid down in *Jarman on Wills*, 7th ed., vol. 3, p. 1764:

> A bequest of chattels real or personal, unaccompanied by any explanatory words, confers a joint, not a several interest, and that whether the gift be by way of trust or not and notwithstanding the disposition of courts of late years to favour tenancies in common, the same rule is now established as to money legacies and residuary bequests. . . .

On the other hand, the Courts have leaned strongly against joint tenancies and Jarman in the same volume at p. 1769, says:

> Anything which in the slightest degree indicates an intention to divide property must be held to abrogate the idea of a joint tenancy and to create a tenancy in common.

He then goes on to state that such words as "equally amongst them" or "equally to them" or "equally" or "in equal moieties" etc., have been held to make the objects tenants in common.

It is true that under the paragraph of the will now being considered the word equal is used in the same sense that the income from one share of the residue of the estate is to be divided into four equal shares, one share to go to Percy, one to Aubrey, one to Florence and the remaining share to "the children of my deceased daughter Minnie B. Calder," but there are no such words as are set out in Jarman qualifying the bequest to the children of minnie B. Calder, such words, for instance, as "equally" or "share and share alike" or "respecting" *etc.* It seems to me to be a plain case of a bequest to a plurality of persons unaccompanied by any explanatory words.

It is strongly urged by counsel representing respectively the estate and the children of Paul B. Calder that a tenancy in common was intended by the testator because under para. 6(c) the testator showed a clear intention of benefiting the children of Paul B. Calder and Jean W. Cooke. That clause of the will is as follows:

> (c) Upon the death of my said wife Clara E. Bancroft, if either of my children shall then be living, then in the case, during the lives of such of them as may be living and during the life of the survivor of them, my said trustee shall pay the whole of the income arising from the whole of my estate to my sons Percy and Aubrey and to my daughter Florence and to the children of my deceased daughter Minnie B. Calder, or to the issue of either of them that shall be dead laving issue then livng, in equal shares *per stirpes*.

To say that he intended to benefit those children under that paragraph is only to state the obvious. Under cl. (b) he provides for the disposition of the income during the lifetime of he wife and under cl. (c) for its disposition after her death. I cannot adopt the reasoning that because the testator showed clearly that he intended benefiting the grandchildren of Minnie B. Calder under (c), that is, after the death of his wife, that you can therefore read into cl. (b) an intention to benefit them under that clause as well, and thus make a tenancy in common where otherwise, on the face of the will, there would be a joint tenancy. The testator was dealing with the apportionment of the income at two entirely different periods — one before and the other after his wife's death.

Although it may be true that not one in a hundred testators appreciate the distinction between a joint tenancy and a tenancy in common, yet to me, it is not inconceivable, that the testator might well have intended that the income during his wife's lifetime should go to the children of Minnie B. Calder of the survivor of them, while making an entirely different disposition after her death. That is exactly what he did. To decide otherwise would in my opinion be making a will and not interpreting it.

It was argued by counsel upholding the theory of joint tenancy that if cl. (c) showed an intention to benefit the grandchildren of Minnie B. Calder the cl. (h) of the will showed a contrary intention. That clause is as follows:

> (h) Any of my said trustees shall pay the remaining such equal shares to the issue, if any, of my deceased daughter Minnie, then living, and if there shall be no issue of my deceased daughter Minnie, then living, my dais trustees shall pay one half of such shares to the United Baptist Convention of the Maritime Provinces to be used by them as they shall think best, and the other half thereof shall be divided equally among my issue, then living, *per stirpes*.

It is quite unnecessary for me to decide whether the word "issue" in this clause is restricted to the children of Minnie B. Calder or whether it means her lineal descendants. If the former it gives some support to the argument in favour of a joint tenancy. If the latter then I could only repeat what I have said in regard to the provision made for the grandchildren of Minnie B. under (c).

I have only to add that in my opinion the conclusion to which I have come seems to me at least to be in harmony with the whole letter of the will, and I find nothing in the will which in the slightest degree indicates an intention to divide the income between the children of Minnie B. and which can be held to abrogate the idea of a joint tenancy and to create a tenancy in common.

Accordingly the answer to the question submitted will be that the share heretofore paid to Paul B. Calder by virtue of para. 6(b) of the will is payable after January 31, 1933, to the surviving sister Jean W. Cooke. . . .

QUESTIONS

1. Interpret the following clauses:

(a) "The rest and residue of my Estate, both real and personal, of whatsoever nature or wheresoever situate [shall go] to my son Charles Merrill Woodley and my two daughters, Hazel Woodbury and Dorothy McCullough, to be theirs jointly in equal shares.

In the event that one or more of the above named beneficiaries should predecease me the residue [is] to become the property of the successor or successors of them." *Winchester v. McCullough* (2000) 31 E.T.R. (2d) 321, 2000 CarswellNB 33 (Q.B.).

(b) "[I devise] Unto my nephew, Walter Sellon, and my niece, Dolena Huston, jointly, my real estate situated at Englishtown, Nova Scotia." *Sellon v. Huston Estate* (1991) 107 N.S.R. (2d) 6, 1991 CarswellNS 188 (T.D.).

(c) "[I direct my executors] to convey the larger of the two cottages and the land on which it is situated and being part of my summer property to my two daughters Shirley Joyce Williston and Wilma Jean Meyers to their joint and absolute use and to convey the smaller of the two cottages and the land on which it is situated and being part of my summer property to my two sons Robert Melbourne MacGregor and Gordon Ross MacGregor to their joint and absolute use, and that if either one of the two cottages on my summer property should be destroyed or otherwise cease to exist at any time following my death and before the death of my wife, the party to which the cottage was to be conveyed shall be paid the insurance on the full value of the cottage, and that the remaining portion of my summer property shall be conveyed in equal shares between the two aforementioned parties so that each of the two parties can have full utilization of their cottage and a good and sufficient access to the shore of East Bay." *Re MacGregor* 2001 CarswellNS 30 (S.C.).

(d) "To my Common Law wife Ellen Power and to Elizabeth Power daughter of my Common Law wife I leave my Land and House at Ferndale Jersey Side with all the Contents of said Land and House share and share alike. All and Personal I GIVE, DEVISE AND BEQUEATH unto Ellen Power my Common Law wife of Ferndale Jersey Side absolutely." *McCarthy v. Pittman* 1991 CarswellNfld 177 (T.D.).

2. A devised Blackacre "to B and C as joint tenants, but should B become a lawyer, then B's interest shall pass to D". B died before becoming a lawyer. Describe the state of title.

3. Section 11 of the *Property Law Act*, R.S.B.C. 1996, c. 377, provides as follows:

11. (1) In this section, "transferred" includes a vesting by declaration of trust or order of court.

(2) If, by an instrument executed after April 20, 1891, land is transferred or devised in fee simple, charged, or contracted to be sold by a valid agreement for sale in which the vendor agrees to transfer the land to 2 or more persons, other than personal representatives or trustees, they are tenants in common unless a contrary intention appears in the instrument.

(3) If the interests of the tenants in common are not stated in the instrument, they are presumed to be equal.

Does this provision apply to an assignment of a lease? See *Robb v. Robb* 1993 CarswellBC 110 (S.C.). Would the Ontario provision apply to that assignment?

4. It is possible for parties to hold property as joint tenants in law but as tenants in common in equity. (Some of the these circumstances are referred to by the Ontario Law Reform Commission, above.) For example, consider a situation where A and B of Vancouver purchase a car in unequal shares, with title in the name of A and B. In British Columbia, the presumption in favour of a joint tenancy continues to apply to personal property. However, the purchase having been made in unequal shares, equity presumes a tenancy in common. This is one of the classic situations in which equity does not follow the law. Assume that A dies. Describe the state of title.

4. SEVERANCE OF JOINT TENANCIES

In the context of co-ownership, the word "severance" is used in two different ways. In the determination of whether a joint tenancy or a tenancy in common has been initially created, the use of appropriate words of severance (such as "share and share alike") are taken to denote a tenancy in common. The word severance is also used to refer to the transformation of an existing joint tenancy into a tenancy in common. The following two cases concern severance of that type.

Re Sorensen & Sorensen
1977 CarswellAlta 196, [1977] 2 W.W.R. 438 (C.A.)

McDermid J.A.:

This appeal is concerned with whether there has been severance of the joint tenancy titles of three lots in the city of Calgary, which are registered in the name of Marrian Alwilda Sorensen (hereinafter referred to as "the wife") and Marshall Kitchener Sorensen (hereinafter referred to as "the husband") as joint tenants. All of the parties joined in an application by notice of motion to the court to decide their rights upon an agreed statement of facts.

I shall summarize the facts as so agreed upon. The husband and wife were married in 1940 and had three children, one son and two daughters. The oldest, the son, is mentally retarded and was a dependant in the care of the wife up until the time of her death. The husband and wife were divorced, the decree absolute being granted on 19th September 1969. After the divorce the parties entered into minutes of settlement.

There were three separate titles for the lots in question. The title to the land on which the matrimonial home was situated at one time contained an additional lot, but the husband and wife in the said settlement agreed that the title to these lots on which the matrimonial home was situated should be divided and the vacant lot sold, and that the wife should receive the proceeds, which she should spend upon the matrimonial home. The parties further agreed that the lot on which the matrimonial home was situated was to be leased to the wife for her lifetime at a rental of $1 a year. It was further agreed that "Whereas the said infant son . . . is by reason of disability unable to withdraw himself from the charge of his mother and to provide himself the necessities of life by reason of mental retardation" the husband was to pay to the wife as maintenance for the son the monthly sum of $100, and that such amount was to be charged by way of security against the interest of the husband in the matrimonial home. In the month of September 1974 the wife was given a tentative medical diagnosis of malignancy and as a result she decided she wished to partition the lots in question so as to provide an estate for her son. The son, although mentally retarded, does have a normal life expectancy, and is capable of simple work. He is presently living in a government of Alberta provincial home, and his basic needs are provided by the government of Alberta. The wife executed the following trust deed on 6th September 1974:

> THIS TRUST DEED made this 16 day of September, A.D. 1974.
>
> I, MARRIAN ALWILDA SORENSEN of the City of Calgary in the Province of Alberta, being the registered owner of an undivided one-half interest as joint tenant subject however to such encumbrances, liens and interests as are notified by Memorandum underwritten in all those certain tracts of land situate in the Province of Alberta being composed of:
>
> > [three properties are then described]
>
> do hereby declare that I hold said lands upon trust for my son ARTHUR FREDERICK SORENSEN of the City of Calgary in the Province of Alberta, his heirs and assigns forever.
>
> I DECLARE that I have executed a Transfer of Land, said Transfer of Land being pursuant to the Land Titles Act, Chapter 170 R.S.A. 1955 with respect to each of the above mentioned lands.
>
> I FURTHER DECLARE that my son ARTHUR FREDERICK SORENSEN is the named Transferee in the said Transfers and I have delivered the said Transfer documents to my solicitor, said delivery shall be deemed to be an effective delivery to be held by him until my passing whereupon said Transfers shall be immediately registered at the Land Titles Office in the City of Calgary in the Province of Alberta.

> I ALSO DECLARE that I have executed said Transfers and this Trust Deed to sever the aforementioned joint tenancy and that said execution shall be deemed to be an effective severance.
>
> DATED at the City of Calgary in the Province of Alberta this 16 day of September A.D. 1974.
>
> "Marrian Alwilda Sorensen" (seal)
>
> In the presence of: (Signature illegible)

On the same date she executed her last will and testament, in which she appointed her two daughters to be the executrixes and trustees of her will. The statement of facts set out that the only significant assets of the wife were the lots in question. The wife gave all of her property to the daughters upon the trusts that after paying her debts to hold the property:

> (c) If my son ARTHUR FREDERICK SORENSEN who is physically and mentally incapable of conducting his own affairs survives me for a period of thirty (30) days after my decease, to set aside as a fund the residue of my estate and to pay the net annual income therefrom solely to or for my son during his life time in approximately equal monthly installments with power and authority to my Trustees to pay to or use for the benefit of my son, such part or parts of the whole of the capital of this fund as in their absolute discretion that my Trustees consider advisable to the intent and purpose that my son shall continue to enjoy the standard of living to which he has become accustom during my life time and to receive every care, attention and advantage requisite to his health and happiness.
>
> (d) Upon the death of my son, if he survives me for a period of thirty (30) days, any balance then remaining in his fund is to be distributed as follows:
>
> 1. To divide and distribute the residue of my estate then remaining among my daughters alive at the death of my son in equal shares provided that if any daughter of mine shall then be dead leaving any children then alive, such children shall take in equal shares the share of which such deceased daughter would have taken if living.

On 26th November 1974 an originating notice of motion was issued on the wife's behalf, asking for partition of the said lots. On the day that the motion came on for a hearing the wife died early in the morning and, as a result, the motion was not heard. Immediately upon the death of the wife the husband filed caveats against the said lands claiming that he was the person solely entitled to the lots, as the surviving tenant. . . .

I shall deal with the actions which it was submitted severed the joint tenancy in the chronological order in which they took place. They are:

> the execution of the Settlement Agreement dated September 27th, 1971 which agreed to the division of the title to the matrimonial home into two titles, provided for a lease of the Husband's interest in the lot on which the matrimonial home was situated and a charge on the Husband's interest in the said lot to the Wife for her life;

> the Trust Deed (set out *supra*) dated September 16th, 1974 which declared the Wife was holding the lots in question in trust for her son and declared she had executed transfers of the lots to her son which were not to be registered until her death;
>
> the execution of her Will dated September 16th, 1974; and
>
> the commencement of the action for partition of the lands. . . .

As was said by Lord Denning in *Burgess v. Rawnsley*, [1975] Ch. 429 at 438-39, [1975] 3 All E.R. 142, in referring to the manners in which a joint tenancy may be severed,

> Nowdays everyone starts with the judgment of Sir William Page Wood V.C. in *Williams v. Hensman* (1861), 1 John & H. 546, 70 E.R. 862 at 867, where he said:
>
> A joint-tenancy may be severed in three ways: in the first place, an act of any one of the persons interested operating upon his own share may create a severance as to that share. The right of each joint-tenant is a right by survivorship only in the event of no severance having taken place of the share which is claimed under the *jus accrescendi*. Each one is at liberty to dispose of his own interest in such manner as to sever it from the joint fund—losing, of course, at the same time, his own right of survivorship. Secondly, a joint tenancy may be severed by mutual agreement. And, in the third place, there may be a severance by any course of dealing sufficient to intimate that the interests of all were mutually treated as constituting a tenancy in common. When the severance depends on an inference of this kind without any express act of severance, it will not suffice to rely on an intention, with respect to the particular share, declared only behind the backs of the other persons interested. You must find in this class of cases a course of dealing by which the shares of all the parties to the contest have been effected, as happened in the cases of *Wilson v. Bell* (1843), 5 Ir. Eq. R. 501, and *Jackson v. Jackson* (1804), 9 Ves. 591, 32 E.R. 732.

The onus to demonstrate that there has been a severance lies on those who so contend: *Re Denny; Stokes v. Denny*, [1947] L.J.R. 1029 at 1032, and *Flynn v. Flynn*, [1930] I.R. 337 at 343.

I am of the opinion that the execution of the settlement agreement on 27th September 1971 and the actions therein provided for did not constitute a severance of the titles to the lots.

It was argued that, from the fact that the husband and wife agreed in the settlement agreement to the sale of the vacant lot next to the lot on which the matrimonial home was situated, it can be inferred they intended that the joint tenancy in respect to the matrimonial lot be severed. As stated in *Re Denny* at p. 1033:

> . . . distribution in severalty of portions of the fund or estate may well be evidence of an intention to sever as to the whole, it is not every distribution, no matter how small and unimportant, that will support such an inference.

The subsequent conduct of the wife is against drawing any such inference, for she clearly thought she had to do something further to sever the title as is shown by her conduct in executing the trust deed and commencing an action for partition. There is no evidence that the husband at any time considered that the joint tenancy of the properties had been severed.

I am, therefore, of the opinion that the conduct of the parties in this respect was not intended by them to sever the title as to the lot on which the matrimonial home was situated and it was not severed.

The settlement agreement further provided that the lot on which the matrimonial home was situated was to be leased to the wife. Clause 6 of the said agreement provided:

> 6. The parties finally agree hereto that they as joint tenants shall lease the aforesaid matrimonial home located at 1316 - 17th "A" Street North West, to Mrs. Sorensen, the said lease to be a lease for the life of Mrs. Sorensen and further, that the parties hereto enter into a lease agreement to be annexed hereto and marked as Schedule "A" to this agreement, the said lease agreement to provide that the rental for the said property shall be at the rate of ONE DOLLAR ($1.00) a year and further that all repairs and upkeep on the said property is to be paid for by Mrs. Sorensen.

Pursuant to this clause a lease was made between the parties for the term of the wife's life.

It was argued that by this clause and the lease the unity of possession—one of the four unities—was destroyed and therefore a severance was effected. In Megarry and Wade, *The Law of Real Property*, 4th ed. (1975), p. 404, it is stated:

> Severance was effected by destroying one of the unities. Unity of time could not be severed, and severance of the unity of possession meant partition, but severance of the unity either of title or of interest converted a joint tenancy into a tenancy in common.

The question becomes, Does the granting of a lease by one joint tenant to the other work a severance of the tenancy? In 24 Hals. (1st), 205, para. 389, it is stated:

> A lease for years by one of two joint tenants in fee of his share does not, it seems, sever the joint tenancy, and it is binding on the other joint tenant after the death of the lessor, whether the lessee enters during the life of the lessor or not.

I have referred to the first edition of Halsbury as the law in England has been substantially changed by statute since then. It should be noted that the lease referred to was for a term of years. The question of whether a lease for a term of years effects a severance is discussed in Megarry and Wade at p. 405 and the authors are of the opinion the matter is not free from doubt.

In an article in January (1944), Australian L.J., vol. 17, p. 292, the author, after stating that Lord Blackburn in *Cowper v. Fletcher* (1865), 6 B. & S. 464, 122 E.R. 1270, expressed the opinion that a lease for a term of years by one joint tenant severs the tenancy and at p. 293 goes on to say:

> No reasons are given by Lord Blackburn for this conclusion, but his opinion appears to have been adopted in subsequent judgments. The writer has been able to find only one attempt to explain the proposition and that appears in an Irish case, *Re Armstrong*, [1920] 1 L.R. 239, where in the course of his judgment, Ross, J., stated: "In the case of a term of years held in joint tenancy a lease by one joint tenant for a term less than the residue does sever the joint tenancy. So it has been laid down in Co. Lit. (ss. 289, 319), but why this should be so is far from clear. It would seem reasonable when an act is done by either joint tenant inconsistent with the chief characteristic of a joint tenancy, namely, survivorship, that such an act should effect a severance. Now a lease must effect the survivorship to some extent, because it is binding after the death of the lessor. We are not, however, left to depend on the ancient authorities, because the matter was considered by Lord Blackburn in the case of *Cowper v. Fletcher* and he expressed the opinion that the effect of making a separate demise does sever a joint tenancy."
>
> Even this explanation does not seem very satisfactory and convincing but by reason of weight of authority the proposition that such a lease severs the joint tenancy must be accepted.
>
> One would have thought, however, that a lease from A. and B. (joint tenants) of the whole of the land to A. would be an effective method of leasing without severance of the joint tenancy resulting, but the difficulties become more complex when this type of lease is examined in the light of the authorities. . . .

However, in all of the cases cited the lease was for a term of years. Here the lease was only for the lifetime of the tenant, the wife. Upon the death of the wife the lease would terminate and upon the death of the husband, if the wife was still living, she would succeed to the whole of the tenancy and, as a result, the lease would merge in the fee. Therefore the lease did not interfere with the chief characteristic of a joint tenancy, viz., survivorship. The fact that the tenancy was only for the lifetime of one of the joint tenants might well be evidence that the intention was not to sever. . . .

I have therefore come to the conclusion that the lease by the husband to wife, being only for the lifetime of the wife, did not sever the tenancy.

In the minutes of settlement it was also provided that the monthly sum of $100 maintenance for the son to be paid by the husband to the wife was to be "charged by way of security against the interest of the Husband in the matrimonial home."

The question of whether a mortgage by one joint tenant works a severance is dealt with in articles in 15th January (1936), Australian L.J., vol. 9, 322, and 15th April (1936), 431. The author explains the meaning of "*per mie et per tout*" which is so often used in referring to the seisin of joint tenants. He says:

> Let us first examine the peculiar standing at law of a joint-tenant. In foot-notes to *Daniel v. Camplin* (1845), 7 M. & G. 172 , and to *Murray v. Hall* (1849), 7 C.B. 441, 137 E.R. 175, it is shewn that when joint tenants are said in the law French (Old Norman) to be seised per my et per tout the word "my" is equivalent in modern French to "mie" which means "a half". Hence the statement of the law by Bracton in Latin, "*Quilibet totum tenet et nihil tenet; scilicet, totum in communi, et nihil separatim per se*". So Blackstone (2 Bl. Com. 182) attempts to explain the position in the words. "They have not, one of

> them a seisin of one half or moiety, and the other of the other moiety; . . . but each has an undivided moiety of the whole, and not the whole of an undivided moiety."

In my opinion the same reasoning would apply here as I applied in deciding the lease for life did not work a severance. The charge did not affect the chief characteristic of a joint tenancy, viz., survivorship, for upon the death of either the husband or wife the security would not continue as a charge on the property. This is assuming there were no arrears. If there were arrears by the husband the husband's estate would still be liable but as for the security the wife would have succeeded to the husband's interest instead of having only a charge on it. So, therefore, as there has been no interference with the *jus accrescendi*, the charge by the husband did not work a severance.

I turn now to the question of whether the execution of the trust deed and the execution of the transfers effected a severance.

In the case at bar the wife declared in the trust deed that she was severing the joint tenancy, but there is no evidence that this trust deed ever came to the attention of the husband. I think it clear, as stated by Sir John Pennycuick in *Burgess v. Rawnsley*, *supra*, at p. 154, a declaration by one party uncommunicated to the other cannot operate as a severance.

It is difficult to reconcile all of the actions of the wife in her attempts to sever the properties and make a gift to her son.

There are four ways a gift can be made:

1. by transfer, conveyance or delivery (whichever mode is appropriate) of the property to the donee;

2. by transferring, conveying or delivering the property to a third party, trustee for the donee;

3. by the donor declaring himself a trustee of the property for the donee; and

4. by will.

The wife attempted to give the property to her son by all of these ways except by giving the properties to a third party as trustee.

The learned trial judge said [at p. 145]:

> In my view the wife's actions in 1974 do not amount to a severance. The documents and transfers executed by the wife do not convey an immediate interest, but merely defer the transfer of any interest until her death. She retained control of her interest in the property. If Arthur (the son) had predeceased her would she have thought that the interest in the properties belong to his estate? Surely not! Clearly she only intended to deliver documents to her solicitor to be held in trust for her. The solicitor is trustee for her alone

> under the trust document. If any further proof is required one must only look at the affidavit supporting the application for partition and sale signed by the wife a few days before her death.

He then goes on to point out that in the wife's affidavit taken in connection with her application to the court to partition the properties she does not mention that she has given the properties to her son, but in fact says she is the owner. I think, however, when she says she was the owner she meant she was the legal owner, and that she was.

I would agree with the learned trial judge that there was no severance except for the declaration of trust for the son. The wife declared in the trust deed, "I . . . do hereby declare that I hold the said lands upon trust for my son ARTHUR FREDERICK SORENSEN of the City of Calgary in the Province of Alberta, his heirs and assigns forever." The presumption of advancement applied and the result was that there was a valid gift of the beneficial interest in the properties to the son. This gift, although only of the equitable title, severs the joint tenancy: *Stonehouse v. A.G. B.C.*, 37 W.W.R. 62, [1962] S.C.R. 103, 31 D.L.R. (2d) 118; *Public Trustee v. Mee*, [1972] 2 W.W.R. 424, 23 D.L.R. (3d) 491 (B.C. C.A.). . . .

Turning now to the execution of the transfers and the instructions in the trust deed that the wife's solicitor was to hold them until her passing and then immediately to register them—there are several reasons why this alone would not work a severance. The solicitor was the wife's solicitor and not the son's so, there being no effective delivery of the transfers, the gift would be incomplete and not effective: *Walker v. Foster* (1900), 30 S.C.R. 299; *Macedo v. Stroud*, [1922] 2 A.C. 330.

Secondly, if the intention of the wife was to make a gift *mortis causa* in this manner it would also be ineffective, for real property cannot be the subject of a *donatio mortis causa*. That it cannot appears to be a historical anomaly, and it has been questioned why it cannot, but I have found no case in Canada or England where it has been held that land could be given *mortis causa*. . . .

As I have stated, an explanation for the execution and delivery of the transfers is that the wife was not intending to make a gift *mortis causa* but was only intending to expedite the conveyancing of her estate.

Although counsel for the wife in his *factum* contended that the execution by the wife of her will severed the properties, no authority was quoted to us which would justify such a statement.

The execution of a will cannot sever a joint tenancy: 37 Hals. (3d) 337; Megarry and Wade, *The Law of Real Property*, 1st ed. (1957), p. 403. This statement refers to the execution of a will by one joint tenant only, for in *Szabo v. Boros* (1967), 60 W.W.R. 754, 64 D.L.R. (2d) 48, it was held by the British Columbia Court of Appeal that, where both joint tenants executed wills leaving the property in question to the other, this evidenced a common intention to treat the property as severed and fell within the third category of ways that a joint tenancy might be severed, as enunciated in *Williams v. Hensman*, *supra*, viz., a course of dealing showing that the tenants intended their interests to be treated as tenants in common and not joint tenants.

If the titles were not severed the will was ineffective to give the wife's interest in the properties to the son. As stated in *Wharton's Law Lexicon*, 11th ed., "*Jus accrescendi praefertur ultimae voluntati*. Co. Litt. 185b. — the right of survivorship is preferred to the last will."

Coming to the action for partition which it was contended severed the titles, in *Munroe v. Carlson*, [1976] 1 W.W.R. 248, 21 R.F.L. 301, 59 D.L.R. (3d) 763 (B.C.), Macdonald J. decided that the bringing of an action alone for partition where the action is subsequently discontinued is not sufficient to constitute a severance. He founded his view on *Re Wilks; Child v. Bulmer*, [1891] 3 Ch. 59, and stated it was followed in *Grant v. Grant*, [1952] O.W.N. 641, and *Nielsen-Jones v. Fedden*, [1975] Ch. 222, [1974] 3 All E.R. 38. He refused to follow *Hawkesley v. May*, [1956] 1 Q.B. 304, [1955] 3 All E.R. 353, and *Re Draper's Conveyance; Nihan v. Porter*, [1969] 1 Ch. 486, [1967] 3 All E.R. 853. The English cases are discussed in *Burgess v. Rawnsley*, *supra*, and there is a difference of opinion in the English courts as to whether under the common law before the English *Law of Property Act*, 1925, c. 5, notice by one joint tenant to another was sufficient to sever the joint tenancy. . . .

I am of the view that the weight of authority is that the declaration by one party of an intention to sever alone without any other act and without acceptance by the other joint tenants does not sever the tenancy.

Under the present English law it would seem the joint tenancy in equity can now be severed by notice by one joint tenant to the other; 32 Hals. (3d), 337. This would appear to be a sensible provision, but I do not think such an amendment of the common law can be made by judicial decision of this court.

In my opinion the only act that severed the titles was the gift to the son by declaration of trust of the wife of the beneficial interest in the titles. . . .

NOTE

Leave to appeal to Supreme Court of Canada was granted: (1977) 6 A.R. 540 (S.C.C.); but the action was discontinued: [1979] 1 S.C.R. xiii.

QUESTIONS

1. What policies should inform the rules governing severance?

2. What potential acts of severance are discussed in this case? How were they assessed by the Court of Appeal? In view of the Court's holding, describe the state of title.

3. Was the interest granted to the wife a leasehold? Does the characterization of that right affect the determination as to whether a severance had occurred?

4. Under California law, a lease by a joint tenant expires on the death of that tenant, and does not produce a severance: see, *e.g.*, *Lindseth v. Huffman* 2002 WL 1380344 (Cal.App. 4 Dist.). Is that an appropriate approach?

5. A, B and C hold title as joint tenants. A sells her interest to D. What is the state of title? Assume instead that A sells her interest to B.

6. At common law, a legal mortgage is perfected by the borrower conveying the legal title (under a deed of mortgage) to the lender. The borrower then retains an equitable interest (today known as the equity of redemption). Does a mortgage by one joint tenant sever the joint tenancy?

7. In some jurisdictions, the legal characterization of mortgage has been altered. For example, Ontario law now provides that "A charge does not operate as a transfer of the legal estate in the land to the chargee": *Land Registration Reform Act*, R.S.O. 1990, c. L.4, s. 6. Under that Act, a charge "means a charge on land given for the purpose of securing the payment of a debt or the performance of an obligation, and includes a charge under the *Land Titles Act* and a mortgage": s. 1. Should a charge by one joint tenant result in severance?

8. A and B hold as joint tenants. A enters into an agreement to sell his interest to C. Before the sale closes and the transfer is perfected, A drops dead. Who is entitled to A's interest?

9. What effect do the following provisions have on the ability of a joint tenant to sever by unilateral action?

Land Titles Act, S.S. 2000, c. L-5.1, s. 156:

No title or interest held in joint tenancy may be alienated by an instrument purporting to grant the title or interest unless the alienation is authorized:

(a) by all the joint tenants, in writing; or

(b) by court order, on the application of one of the joint tenants.

Land Titles Act, R.S.A. 2000, c. L-4, s. 65:

65. The Registrar shall not register a transfer that has the effect of severing a joint tenancy unless

(a) the transfer is executed by all the joint tenants,

(b) all the joint tenants, other than those executing the transfer, give their written consent to the transfer, or

(c) the Registrar is provided with evidence satisfactory to the Registrar that all the joint tenants who have not executed the transfer or given their written consent to the transfer have by

(i) personal service, or

(ii) substitutional service pursuant to a court order,

been given written notice of the intention to register the transfer.

Havlik v. Whitehouse
2000 CarswellAlta 355, 34 R.P.R. (3d) 128 (Q.B.)

[This dispute involved a cottage property jointly held by a woman and her uncle. When the uncle died, his widow claimed that the joint tenancy had been severed. It was argued that all three of the forms of severance set out in *Williams v. Hensman* had occurred. The claim based on unilateral action was premised on (a) an expressed intention by the deceased to sever (which is ineffective under current Canadian law) and (b) action taken by the deceased to complete a transfer of the property to himself. Under Alberta law, a transfer by a joint tenant to that same person as a tenant in common can produce a severance, provided the transfer is registered. In this case, no registration occurred. Both arguments based on unilateral action therefore failed. The court then considered whether severance under the second and third heads in *Williams v. Hensman* had occurred.]

Johnstone J.: . . .

Mutual agreement between the owners to sever the joint tenancy

The Applicant in fact addresses both the second and third methods of severance under this heading, *i.e.* mutual agreement, and a course of dealing sufficient to intimate that the interests of all were mutually treated as constituting a tenancy in common. I will deal with each of these methods separately.

The relevant facts are:

* The Deceased executed a will in February of 1999, which contemplated the possibility that there would be no severance prior to his death.

* On March 3, 1999, the Deceased communicated through his counsel that he wished to sever the joint tenancy and to leave his one-half interest to the Applicant. The Respondent was given a deadline to respond. The Deceased's solicitor also demanded payment for taxes for 1997 and 1998 on or before March 17, 1999.

* The Respondent's solicitor forwarded a "without prejudice" letter dated March 25, 1999 and apparently received March 30, 1999, stating that the Respondent was agreeable to severing the joint tenancy, but indicating that the Defendant in the past

had refused any contribution from the Respondent for the taxes, and therefore she would be willing to contribute only from 1999 onwards.

* The Deceased's solicitor wrote on May 5, 1999, enclosing a transfer executed by the Deceased. The Deceased agreed the Respondent would not have to pay taxes for 1997 and 1998 and was "considering his position with respect to future taxes".

* A further letter dated June 9, 1999 was sent by the Deceased's solicitor, asking whether the Respondent would execute the Transfer, and stating that if there was no response by June 14, 1999, there would be an application to the Courts to sever.

* The Respondent's solicitor forwarded a letter dated July 9, 1999, apparently received July 12, 1999 asking whether the Deceased would be interested in selling his interest.

* The Respondent deposes she advised her counsel she did not wish to sever the joint tenancy and was surprised to receive a copy of his letter of March 25, 1999.

* There is no evidence that the Deceased ever took the steps available to him to unilaterally sever the joint tenancy.

Mutual Agreement

The Respondent submits, as a preliminary issue, that the "without prejudice" communication of March 25, 1999 is privileged.

In J. Sopinka, *et al*, *The Law of Evidence in Canada*, 2d ed. (Butterworths: Toronto, 1998) at 810, the authors set out the conditions to establish privilege for communications in furtherance of settlement:

— a litigious dispute must be in existence or within contemplation;

— the communication must be made with the express or implied intention that it would not be disclosed to the court in the event negotiations failed; and

— the purpose of the communication must be to attempt to effect a settlement.

In the present case, a litigious dispute was within contemplation. The letter of March 3, 1999 demanded severance and payment of $2,000 for taxes, failing which an application for an Order severing and legal action for the taxes would be commenced. Clearly, litigation was contemplated by the Deceased's solicitor, and that prospect was communicated to the Respondent.

The letter from the Respondent's counsel dated March 25, 1999 was marked "without prejudice". The intention of non-disclosure may be implied from the use of that phrase, thereby constituting *prima facie* evidence of intention (Sopinka, *supra*, at 810, 811). . . .

In the present case, the issue of severance and that of liability for taxes went hand-in-hand. From the correspondence of May 5, 1999, it can be concluded that the Respondent was "left hanging" with respect to the Deceased's position on future taxes. It is not clear what it is he was considering, as the Respondent had already agreed to contribute front 1999 onwards. Did the Deceased envisage a greater future contribution on the part of the Respondent to make up for past years, or was he considering whether to pay all taxes in the future, as he had in 1997 and 1998 (which would not be particularly consistent with ownership as tenants in common)? The tax issue was never resolved.

The parties themselves were obviously of the view that the matter was not finalized. As was the case in *Sorensen* [*Sorensen v. Sorensen*, 1977 CarswellAlta 196 (C.A.)], the Deceased thought he had to do something further to sever the title, and although the Respondent canvassed the possibility of purchasing the Deceased's share, there is no evidence that she at any time considered that the joint tenancy of the property had in fact been severed. The Respondent's letter of July 9, 1999 is internally inconsistent, as it purports to suggest an alternative to severance — a buy-out — which implies a severance. However, the Respondent's suggestion of a buy-out was likely not based on the niceties of the law of severance, but rather on her desire to end up with the entire property one way or another.

Also noteworthy is the fact that in the June 9, 1999 letter, the Deceased's solicitor simply asked for advice as to whether the Respondent would sign the transfer, again failing which an application to sever would be initiated. There is nothing in that correspondence which would indicate that the Deceased's solicitor was of the view that the "without prejudice" communication had resulted in a final agreement.

I am of the view that the issue was never resolved so that it could be said that the negotiations were successful, and therefore the "without prejudice" letter of March 25, 1999 is privileged. Even were I to find otherwise, however, I am disturbed by the conflict between the Respondent's affidavit evidence to the effect that she had not instructed her solicitor to agree to sever, and the contents of the "without prejudice" letter. If nothing else, the "without prejudice" notation on that letter (whether effective to result in privilege or not), indicates that the Respondent's solicitor viewed it as part of ongoing negotiations, and not as a conclusion thereof. The evidence simply does not persuade me on a balance of probabilities that a mutual agreement was reached.

Course of Dealing

Prior to embarking on an analysis of the "course of dealing" in this case, I wish to make two observations. The first is that much of the case law on severance involves joint tenancies between husband and wife. McClean ["Severance of Joint Tenancies" (1979) 57 Can. Bar Rev. 1] at 25 states:

> It is no doubt significant if the co-owners are husband and wife who are negotiating . . . a property settlement on Separation or divorce; and that may explain some of the cases . . .

Veit J. in *McNaughton* [1999 CarswellAlta 519 (Q.B.)] went so far as to ponder at para. 19:

> It may well be that in every case where one spouse owning real property jointly with the other spouse issues a statement of claim claiming an interest in the real property as matrimonial property, that is a sufficient indication of an intention to no longer wish to be bound by the attributes of joint tenancy to sever that tenancy. . . .

In most cases of marital break-up (particularly those before the courts), it is reasonable to infer that the couple intends at some point to sever their joint tenancies. There are typical inferences in such cases which do not necessarily follow where the joint tenancy is held by non-spouses, even where the facts are similar.

The second observation is that some commentators have expressed the opinion that in those jurisdictions where there is no longer a presumption in favour of joint tenancy, but rather where the creation of a joint tenancy requires cognizant and deliberate action, the use of severance as a way to avoid the dramatic results of survivorship may be excessive or unfair. . . . In Alberta, individuals must purposefully set out to establish a joint tenancy, and therefore a right of survivorship. That intention forms part of the relevant background within which the course of dealings must be viewed.

The case law on common law severance is replete with analyses of the "course of dealing" method of severance. In some cases, the courts have been prepared to draw an inference as to severance from negotiations which do not lead to a final agreement. However, each case must be decided on its own facts, and as indicated above the onus is on the party alleging severance to prove it.

I find the course of dealing of the parties in this case to be ambivalent. There is evidence that each contemplated severance at a certain point in time, however, I do not find that the entire course of dealing was the equivalent of "mutually treating all interests as constituting a tenancy in common". The Deceased's actions can be seen as indicating an intention to sever even in the absence of the consent of the Respondent. However, the s. 68.1 mechanism was open to him at all times, and although he was represented by counsel in the matter, he failed to avail himself of the same. For some reason, the Deceased remained of the view that an application for severance was necessary.

The circumstances in this case are unlike those in matrimonial property proceedings, where it would be difficult to conceive of the possibility that the parties who have experienced animosity and separation would wish to maintain for the other the right of survivorship. Here the Deceased clearly contemplated the possibility of a continuation of the Respondent's right of survivorship in his Will within months of his death.

I find the Deceased's actions difficult to understand. Perhaps the Deceased simply did not intend to force the matter against the wishes of the Respondent. After reviewing the evidence of the entire course of dealing, I simply am not persuaded on the evidence that common law severance in fact occurred. . . .

Application dismissed.

NOTE

In a brief judgment, the Alberta Court of Appeal stated that "we are not persuaded that the chamber judge reached any erroneous, let alone reversible, conclusion": *Havlik v. Whitehouse* 2001 CarswellAlta 1408, [2002] 1 W.W.R. 270 (C.A.) at para. 4 (*per* McClung J.A.).

QUESTIONS AND COMMENTS

1. Some Canadian courts have held that even where negotiations between joint tenants do not lead to a binding contract concerning their property holdings, the process of negotiation can count as a course of dealing sufficient to intimate that they regard their interests as no longer being held under a joint tenancy: see, *e.g.*, *Re Walters* 1977 CarswellOnt 404, 79 D.L.R. (3d) 122 (H.C.), affirmed (1978) 17 O.R. (2d) 592 (note) (C.A.). *Cf. Gore and Snell v. Carpenter* (1990) 60 P. & C.R. 456 (Ch.). Is severance based on inconclusive negotiations consistent with the ruling in *Havlik*?

2. Severance can arise by operation of law. For example, bankruptcy gives rise to a severance of all of the jointly held property of the bankrupt: see, *e.g.*, *Kansra (Trustee of) v. Kansra* 2003 CarswellOnt 1994 (S.C.J.).

3. The murder of one joint by the other produces what amounts, functionally, to a severance in equity. The victim's share is held on a constructive trust by the perpetrator for the benefit of the victim's heirs: *Schobelt v. Barber* (1966) [1967] 1 O.R. 349, 1966 CarswellOnt 179 (H.C.).

4. A, B and C hold as joint tenants. A murders B. What is the state of title? See the solution offered in *Rasmanis v. Jurewitsch* (1970) 70 S.R. (N.S.W.) 407 (C.A.).

5. Is it possible to create an unseverable joint tenancy? Drawing on the concepts studied in Chapter 7, can you create a set of entitlements that produce, functionally, a right of survivorship that cannot be destroyed by unilateral action?

5. RESOLVING CONCURRENT OWNERSHIP DISPUTES

T.J. Micelli & F. Sirmans, "Partition of Real Estate; Or, Breaking Up is (Not) Hard to Do" 29 J. Legal Stud.783 (2000) at 783-4 [footnotes omitted]

Common ownership can promote efficient use of land (or any asset) if the bargaining costs among the co-owners are lower than the cost of arm's-length transactions between them. . . . Circumstances can change, however, and what was once a productive union may become an inharmonious association, thus creating a threat of inefficient land use due to the "anticommons" problem. In this case, the law offers each owner an escape route in the form of the right to partition. Under the common law, partition involved a physical division of the land (partition in kind) into separate, individually owned parcels. While this remedy overcomes the high transaction costs among the co-owners, the problem is that it may cause an excessive fragmentation of the land with a resulting reduction in its value. And while reassembly is possible, this would require additional transactions that at some point may prove too costly.

In response to this problem, state partition statutes provide for a second remedy — namely, sale of the undivided parcel with division of the proceeds in proportion to each owner's share. This remedy preserves the scale of the parcel without the need for reassembly, but it too has a drawback. In particular, it subjects nonconsenting owners to a forced sale, thereby depriving them of any value that they attach to the land in excess of its market value. In effect, each owner's share is protected by a liability rule rather than a property rule *vis-à-vis* the other owners. In recognition of this problem, courts and legislatures have traditionally urged that forced sales be used only in exceptional circumstances. Actual practice, however, seems to be the reverse — forced sale is the norm and partition the exception.

Greenbanktree Power Corp. v. Coinamatic Canada Inc. 2002 CarswellOnt 1486, 5 R.P.R. (4th) 1 (S.C.J.)

[In this case, the applicant company, Greenbanktree, held small percentage interests (ranging from about to 5.5 % to 8.3%) in five properties. In 1998, the applicant registered a notice on the titles to two of these properties stating that: there was no co-tenancy agreement pertaining to the property; unanimity among the co-owners was required to effect a sale; and that Greenbanktree must consent to any change in management of the property.

In 1999, the respondent entered into an agreement to acquire the properties, and was successful in reaching a deal to buy all but the Greenbaktree interests. In 2001, two days before the closing of the sale of the other interests to the respondent, the notices were taken off the titles by Greenbanktree. It then brought an application for the sale of the properties under the *Partition Act*. Such a sale, the Court was advised, could result in the imposition of a penalty of about $2 million under the respondent's mortgage, and tax consequences also ranging in the millions. Moreover, the cost of the 2001 closing was in the range of $1 million.]

Pitt J.:

This case raises the following issues:

1. When should a Court deny a tenant-in-common its *prima facie* right under the *Partition Act* to compel the sale of commercial property owned jointly with an unwilling co-tenant?

(a) How much significance, if any, should be given to the difference in size of the respective interests, especially where the applicant's interest is significantly smaller?

(b) What constitutes bad faith (maliciousness, oppressiveness or vexatiousness) on the part of an applicant?

(c) In the context of the need for fairness, what weight should a Court give to the large costs that would be incurred in the premature discharge of a mortgage, and the large costs already incurred in the very recent acquisition and mortgaging, and real possibility or indeed probability that the respondent will be required to pay land transfer tax to reacquire the property — which it had only recently purchased?

2. Can the applicant, in such an application, be required by the Court to sell only its own interest? . . .

Discussion of the Law

Sections 2 and 3(1) of the *Partition Act* R.S.O. 1990, c. P.3 read as follows:

> 2. *All* joint tenants, tenants in common and coparceners, all doweresses, and parties entitled to dower, tenants by the curtesy, mortgagees or other creditors having liens on, and all parties interested in, to or out of, any land in Ontario, may be compelled to make or suffer partition or sale of the land, or any part thereof, whether the estate is legal and equitable or equitable only. R.S.O. 1980, c. 369, s.2. [My emphasis.]
>
> 3.(1) Any person interested in land in Ontario, or the guardian of a minor entitled to the immediate possession of an estate therein, may bring an action or make an application for the partition of such land or for the sale thereof under the directions of the court if such sale is considered by the court to be more advantageous to the parties interested. R.S.O. 1980, c. 369, s. 3(1); 1984, c. 11, s. 200(1).

The most recent decision in Ontario brought to the Court's attention was that of Nordheimer J. in *Gartree Investments Ltd. v. Cartree Enterprises Ltd.*, [2000] O.J. No. 2078, 33 R.P.R. (3d) 85 (Ont. S.C.J.); upheld by the Divisional Court (Gravely, Taliano, Epstein JJ.); [2001] O.J. No. 1184, 39 R.P.R. (3d) 138 (Ont. Div. Ct.) leave to appeal to OCA dismissed.

In that case the Court reviewed the key authorities and re-emphasized the view that cases after *Davis v. Davis* (1953), [1954] O.R. 23 (Ont. C.A.) have narrowly defined the basis for any finding of a sufficient reason to deny an application. In *Gartree Investments Ltd.*, the issue was whether the applicant's request for sale could be described as malicious, vexatious or oppressive because of "(a) tax liability that will be visited on all of the parties if the sale takes place and (b) the refusal of the applicant to accept the respondent's offer to buy her (the applicant's) interest in the properties at more than the market value" (at page 87). *Gartree Investments Ltd.*, like this case, involved commercial property, although the parties were sisters.

Understandably, most of the cases under the *Partition Act* involve spouses and more often than not matrimonial property. It was such a case, *Davis v. Davis*, *supra*, that initially established the approach to the construction of the Act following the legislature importing the Court's discretionary jurisdiction in the statute in 1913. Laidlaw J.A. speaking for the Court said at page 29 (*Davis*, *supra*):

> In my opinion the change made in the legislation in 1913, whereby the Court obtained discretionary power to allow or refuse an application for partition or sale of lands, did not alter the policy of law theretofore existing or the fundamental considerations which ought to prevail in reaching a decision in the matter. There continues to be a *prima facie* right of a joint tenant to partition or sale of lands. There is a corresponding obligation on a joint tenant to permit partition or sale, and finally the Court should compel such partition or sale if no sufficient reason appears why such an order should not be made. I do not attempt to enumerate or describe what reasons would be sufficient to justify refusal of an order for partition or sale. I am content to say that each case must be considered in the light of the particular facts and circumstances and the Court must then exercise the discretion vested in it in a judicial manner having due regard to those particular facts and circumstances as well as to the matters which I have said are, in my opinion, fundamental.

Nordheimer J. referred in *Gartree Investments Ltd.*, *supra*, (at page 87) to the following passage, in *Silva v. Silva* (1990), 1 O.R. (3d) 436 (Ont. C.A.), where Finlayson J.A. speaking for the Court said at page 441:

> Cases subsequent to *Hutcheson* [[1950] O.R. 265, 2 D.L.R. 751 (C.A.)] agreed that the courts had discretion to refuse to grant an order for partition and sale, but limited that discretion to cases where the applicant had behaved maliciously, oppressively or with a vexatious intent toward the respondent.

While marriage or common-law breakdowns tend to generate the kind of emotion that may tend to engender conduct of a malicious, vexatious or oppressive character, business relationships generally do not tend to engender such conduct. What tends to emerge more often than not from the break up of business relationships are approaches or decisions designed to secure the best financial interest of one or both of the parties. It is, therefore not surprising that not many cases can be found where co-tenants, not related to each other by marriage, are found to have acted maliciously, vexatiously or oppressively in seeking relief under the *Partition Act*.

In *Yale v. MacMaster* (1974), 3 O.R. (2d) 547 (Ont. H.C.), Mr Justice Galligan said unambiguously that the court may take the relative hardship of the respective parties into account on an application under the *Partition Act* involving parties other than spouses. It is to be noted, however, that the parties before the Court in that case were former spouses.

The respondent cited *Jabs Construction Ltd. v. Callahan* (1991), 61 B.C.L.R. (2d) 383 (B.C. S.C.) for the proposition that "the Court's primary goal in crafting a process of sale must be fairness to both parties." It is notable that in that British Columbia case, the parties had agreed the property should be sold pursuant to the British Columbia *Partition Act* and Rule 43, and the issue was the nature of the process to be used in effecting the sale. In addition, the British Columbia statute and rules are not identical to those of Ontario. However, Madam Justice Huddart, in her analysis, referred to *Dibattista v. Menecola* (1990), 75 O.R. (2d) 443 (Ont. C.A.), also cited by the respondents, where our Court of Appeal at page 449 [O.R.] said:

> In the contest between interests motivated solely by profit potential, the risks that the parties have assumed are customarily left to be resolved by the forces of the market place. We should remember these sections were not concerned with encouraging or favouring development. They do not favour one interest over the other but provide for sale only when it is "more advantageous to the parties interested." The sections are therefore not intended to be a means by which one tenant in common can acquire the interests of the other . . .

It is clear, however, that the issue in *Dibattista v. Menecola*, *supra*, was whether a sale or partition was the appropriate relief, not whether one joint owner's *prima facie* right to sell or partition should be thwarted or vindicated.

Issues

Size of respective interests. . . .

Logic and common sense would suggest that the difference in size of the respective interests is a factor that should be recognized. No case law, however, has indicated whether or not it should be a significant factor; perhaps for the reasons that no such cases have been reported or perhaps, interests tend, more often than not, to be equal. However, I cannot on principle find this to be a significant factor, especially as s. 2 of the statute imposes the obligation to suffer partition on all joint owners.

What constitutes bad faith?

The respondent has made much of the registered notices referred to earlier, both on the grounds that their contents were false and also the lateness of the timing of their discharges, two days before closing, suggesting that they were used as leverage in bargaining for a higher price.

The first ground runs against the obvious obstacle that when the notices were registered the respondent was not, as it were, "in the picture", at all. As to the lateness of their withdrawal, it was for the vendors, i.e. the parties who were selling their interests to the respondent in the fall of 2001, to clear the title if they thought it was necessary to preserve the sale transaction, which it probably was not. In any event, the filing of those notices is evidence that there was a need for caution by anyone considering the purchase of those properties without the concurrence of all the owners.

In my view, that whole "issue" cannot be considered bad faith on the question of the applicant's motive or objective in seeking the Court's intervention.

Although there was no agreement between the parties requiring the applicant not to exercise its *prima facie* right to partition in the short run, the respondent asserts that the applicant represented to the respondent that it had such an intention.

The basis for this assertion is a letter written by the applicant during negotiations for an exchange of properties between the parties. In the letter dated October 28, 2001, a response to a proposal dated October 22, 2001, the applicant said,

> We are not a seller or a mortgagor of properties, so "maximizing the value of these properties" means something completely different to us than it means to you. We have owned the properties for 45 years and hope to own them for another 45 years.

That, frankly, is no more than another illustration of the different approaches of the parties, which partly account for the impasse in the management dispute that appears to be the genesis of this proceeding.

The respondent also asserts that the timing of the application is evidence of its malicious, vexatious or oppressive nature. The argument is that the applicant should have brought the application prior to the purchase by the respondent, presumably since the applicant ought to have known that it could not work cordially with the respondent.

The short answer to that proposition is that there is no evidence of a desire on the part of the applicant to have ended the relationship with its former co-owners.

Hardship — Costs

It seems to me that the issue of costs is one that ought to be given careful consideration by a Court which is required by authority, and statute, to balance the interests of the parties.

The Divisional Court considered the issue of hardship in *MacDonald v. MacDonald* (1976), 14 O.R. (2d) 249 (Ont. Div. Ct.). The Court made it clear that there is always a *prima facie* right to partition or sale under the Act. However, the Court recognized that it must determine whether substantial hardship would result to the respondent in the event the order was granted. Although the Court did not enunciate the factors to be weighed in such a test, it rejected the notion that the test is on a mere balance of probabilities of hardship to the respective parties.

In *Re Yale v. MacMaster, supra*, Galligan J. said at page 562:

> Having come to the conclusion that a consideration of relative hardship is a relevant consideration in determining how a Court ought to exercise the discretion conferred upon it by the *Partition Act*, I feel obliged to consider it in this case. It goes without saying that in some cases the Court may be very hesitant to give great weight to that factor, while in other cases it may have very considerable importance. I think the weight that such a factor may have in each case will depend upon the *circumstances of how, when and why the property was purchased, the relationship of the parties or their predecessors in title at the time the property was purchased and the circumstances which have resulted directly from the relationship of the parties which existed at the time*. [My emphasis.]

In denying the application, the Court found that the situation of the respondent wife would have been disastrous if she were forced to sell.

It is well to remember, firstly, that the respondent knew, or ought to have known, from the communications between the parties, that it was entering into a relationship with a joint owner who appeared to be uncompromising. The applicant was the classic "holdout" encountered in land assemblies. The applicant also made it clear prior to the respondent's purchase that it did not relish the prospective association with the respondent.

Can the applicant be required to sell its own interest? I would think that either the applicant has a right to a sale or it does not. It does not need an order of the Court to sell its own interest. The co-tenants, who sold to the respondent, did not need the intervention of the Court. In addition to which, a sale of such a minority interest may well have to be done at a discount.

With due respect, this argument is a rather creative attempt to resolve a difficult problem, but I do not believe there is any support for it either in the authorities or in logic.

Summary

The only rational basis for denying the application would be the costs to the Respondent. If that were a proper basis for refusing the application, the applicant's *prima facie* right would not be exercisable until such time as the mortgage matures, which will not be for five years, and/or when the respondent has received a Promise of Waiver of Land Transfer Tax from the Minister of Finance, and/or when it has earned enough profit to absorb comfortably the legal costs incurred on the purchase and mortgage. That is a very difficult position to defend.

The parties cannot agree on the appropriate management of the properties. This seems to be precisely the kind of problem the *Partition Act*, s. 3(1) is designed to remedy. As was said in *Fellows v. Lunkenheimer*, [1998] O.J. No. 4923 (Ont. Gen. Div.) at p. 33:

> Partition or sale was the law's answer when joint owners can no longer get along.

As I said earlier, the applicant did not consider the 2001 offer to purchase the entire interest, made by the respondent, acceptable. Here, there is no evidence of a generous offer as was found by Cameron J. in another incarnation of *Gartree Investments Ltd.*, [2002] O.J. No. 753 (Ont. S.C.J.) [5 R.P.R. (4th) 13], where the only issue was whether the applicant could force a sale on the open market or accept a generous offer by the respondent.

Disposition

For the reasons set out above, the applicant shall have a judgment . . . for the sale of the lands. . . .

NOTE

In a short judgment, the decision of Pitt J. was affirmed by the Divisional Court: 2003 CarswellOnt 3775 (Div. Ct.).

J.W. Lem & B.G. Clark, "Annotation" (2002) 5 R.P.R. (4th) 2

Greenbanktree is but one of a flurry of recent cases dealing with the application of the *Partition Act*, R.S.O. 1990, Chapter P.4, with the "Gartree-Cartree" litigation (*Gartree Investments Ltd. v. Cartree Enterprises Ltd.* (2000), 33 R.P.R. (3d) 85 (Ont. S.C.), affirmed (2001), 39 R.P.R. (3d) 138 (Ont. Div. Ct.), (hereinafter, "*Gartree (No. 1)*") and *Gartree Investments Ltd. v. Cartree Enterprises Ltd.* (2002), 5 R.P.R. (4th) 17 (Ont. S.C.), (hereinafter, "*Gartree (No. 2)*"). . . .

The *Partition Act* governs co-ownership arrangements where there are no formal contractual agreements between co-owners of real property. Greatly paraphrased, the *Partition Act* provides that, where co-owners of real estate cannot agree on how to govern the real estate, then, at the demand of any one or more co-owners, the co-ownership relationship will be ended by court order and the co-owned property will be "partitioned" (divided up, with discrete portions of the fee granted exclusively to each co-owner by the court in accordance with the co-owners' proper co-ownership interests therein). Where the property does not lend itself to partitioning (as is frequently the case in single buildings), the court can, instead, order the co-owned property to be sold, with the net proceeds from the sale distributed amongst the co-owners in their proper proportions. This partition and sale can be compelled upon any co-owner and any mortgagee with an interest in the co-owned land, regardless of the comparative size of the co-owner or mortgagee suffering the sale. Conversely, a partition and sale can be initiated by any aggrieved co-owner or mortgagee with an interest in the co-owned land, regardless of the comparative size of the interest of the aggrieved co-owner calling for the sale.

While this sounds intuitively fair, the consequences of a forced sale are not always entirely equitable. Aside from the shared loss arising from the natural price discounting inherent in any distressed sale, a court-ordered sale under the *Partition Act* triggers a host of additional costs that speak directly to realizable value. In *Greenbanktree*, for instance, a forced sale by the minority co-owner would have resulted in not only immediate capital gains taxes and other closing costs, but more significantly, a sizeable yield maintenance penalty payable to the fixed-term mortgagee. The question before the court in *Greenbanktree* was whether a very small minority co-owner could, using the *Partition Act*, compel the sale of the co-owned party against the wishes and with ultimate prejudice to the majority co-owner.

In concluding in the affirmative, the Ontario Superior Court made some interesting observations about the nature of the partition and sale remedy under the *Partition Act*. First of all, the court found that it was not relevant that the majority co-owner held a much larger percentage than the minority co-owner (although it varied across the portfolio, the minority co-owner in *Greenbanktree* generally held less than a 10% undivided interest in any one of the portfolio properties). Secondly, while the forced sale caused additional costs to both of the co-owners, including the large yield maintenance penalty, such additional costs were not, in and of themselves, a reason to take away the minority co-owner's *prima facie* right to force a sale. In order for a co-owner to jeopardize this *prima facie* right to partition and sale, the moving co-owner's conduct had to amount to behaviour in bad faith to the extent of being "malicious, oppressive or vexatious".

While it initially seems quite fair to protect minority co-owners from oppressive conduct by majority co-owners, the relatively high bar to remedial disqualification gives minority co-owners unanticipated negotiating leverage. Without a statutory regime for less than unanimous co-owner decision-making, or an effective judicial will to police the abuse of a unanimity-only based co-ownership rule, it is possible that the partition and sale remedy will become a weapon in the arsenal of an aggressor, rather than its original intended use as a shield in the hands of the oppressed. In fact, as recent case law might suggest, there is a real risk that the partition and sale remedy could be used offensively by a clever co-owner to extract a "last man standing" premium (whether from a prospective purchaser or from the other co-owners anxious for a sale) simply for being the last (or amongst the last) to sell.

The case law running up to *Greenbanktree* is somewhat mixed but is, for the most part, consistent with *Greenbanktree*. In *Gartree (No. 1)*, the judge did not feel that, just because the majority co-owners would collectively suffer large capital gains on the premature sale of the jointly held property (as would the minority co-owner instigating the sale), the adverse tax consequences of the premature sale entitled the court to refuse the minority co-owner's *prima facie* right to a sale of the co-owned property under the *Partition Act*. As stated in *Greenbanktree*, especially in non-matrimonial circumstances, the finding of the requisite "malicious, oppressive or vexatious" conduct would be rare and *Gartree (No. 1)* and the other cases seem to support this contention, for the most part.

That being said, it is not impossible to find the requisite "malicious, oppressive or vexatious" conduct, even in a commercial context. So, for example, in *Gartree (No. 2)*, on facts only slightly different than those in *Gartree (No. 1)*, the minority co-owner's application for partition and sale was actually denied as being, *inter alia*, "malicious, oppressive or vexatious" (in fairness to the assertion, it is not entirely correct to suggest that the *Gartree* litigation was purely commercial since the litigious co-owners were in fact sisters, although the co-owned portfolios at stake were all quite commercial in nature and not at all the typical co-owned property involved in most family disputes). In *Gartree (No. 2)*, the majority co-owners had offered to buy out the minority co-owner at 110% of the fair market value of her minority interest (based on independent appraisals and assessed without the usual minority discount). The minority co-owner refused the other co-owners' buyout offer but then sought a forced sale of the entire co-owned portfolio under the *Partition Act*, arguing that she should not be forced into recognizing capital gains when the other co-owners would not have to. Of course, the irony was that, had the co-owned properties been sold in the open market under the *Partition Act*, as demanded by the minority co-owner, that minority co-owner would also have had to endure the exact same capital gains tax of which she had originally complained. Of course, the obvious difference was that, in a third party sale of the whole portfolio, the minority co-owner would be comforted in knowing that her income tax problems would also be visited on the other co-owners. The judge in *Gartree (No. 2)* was obviously discomforted by the patent "scorched earth" philosophy behind the minority co-owner's application for partition and sale under the *Partition Act*, and the court ultimately refused the minority co-owner's request.

Gartree (No. 2) goes somewhat further than has generally been the case in *Partition Act* jurisprudence to date. In addition to simply denying the minority co-owner's application for a forced sale of the whole co-owned portfolio, the judge actually compelled the dissenting co-owner to sell out her minority share of the jointly held portfolio to the majority co-owners at 110% of fair market value. The reasoning is somewhat sophisticated, but with compliments to the ingenuity of winning counsel, the court in *Gartree (No. 2)* was persuaded that the undocumented co-ownership relationship in *Gartree (No. 2)* was more akin to a partnership than a simple co-ownership. This finding was critical so that the court could avail itself of the additional remedy of compelling the minority partners to sell out to the majority partners, following the law as set out in *80 Wellesley St. East Ltd. v. Fundy Bay Builders Ltd.*, [1972] 2 O.R. 280 (Ont. C.A.).

Although there is no doubt that *Gartree (No. 2)* was correctly decided on its facts, readers are however cautioned not to interpret *Gartree (No. 2)* as necessarily being an authority for the proposition that "all real estate co-ownerships are *de facto* partnerships". Such a conclusion might be too aggressive given the actual wording in *Gartree (No. 2)*, and it is probably more appropriate to conclude that the partnership finding by the court in *Gartree (No. 2)* is limited to the case's unique facts (for an excellent recent commentary on the fact-specific nature of partnerships, see the comments of Lord Nicholls of Birkenhead in the House of Lords' comments on the issue in *Dubai Aluminium Company Limited v. Salaam*, [2002] UKHL 48). Furthermore, it should be noted that a finding of partnership in the context of partition and sale need not necessarily be a finding of partnership for all purposes. That is, there is nothing in *Gartree (No. 2)* that would suggest that a finding of partnership for partition and sale purposes would translate into a finding of partnership for the purposes of civil liability or taxation. For those interested in the co-ownership versus partnership debate, one can find a great deal of interesting commentary in the U.S. jurisprudence and academic literature surrounding "§1031 Exchanges", the tax-free exchanges of real property permitted under 26 USC §1031. Curiously, there seems to be a well-developed secondary market in the United States for the brokering of such land barters and the exchanges apparently occur fairly frequently. The issue in §1031 Exchanges is whether or not a given co-ownership arrangement is a true undivided tenant-in-common ownership in real property (which would then be eligible for §1031 Exchange treatment) or merely an interest in a business entity such as a partnership (in which case the interest would not be eligible for §1031 Exchange treatment). The debate engendered by §1031 Exchanges seems to have gained a revivalist following in the United States with the repeal of Revenue Procedure 2000-46 and the replacement thereof with Revenue Procedure 2002-22, which sets out a fairly detailed code as to what the IRS believes would distinguish the two concepts for the purposes of any "advance rulings" requested of the IRS on the matter. While Revenue Procedure 2002-22 is a great read and of considerable academic interest, it has, of course, very little authority in Canada (or for that matter, for civil issues in the United States). Typical of taxing statutes, Revenue Procedure 2002-22, by its own opening words, declares its federal jurisdiction and limits its own application to tax matters, deliberately staying outside the jurisdiction of the state laws that would otherwise govern the relationship for other purposes.

Readers interested in the issues raised in *Partition Act* litigation are encouraged to consider the excellent short article on the subject by Craig R. Carter in "The Partition Act", *The Six-Minute Real Estate Lawyer*, 2002, The Law Society of Upper Canada, November 27, 2002. The article provides a great summary of the leading cases preceding *Greenbanktree* and offers some fascinating insights on the normative role of the *Partition Act* in modern real property law. In his article, Carter indicates that there are over 800 searchable Canadian cases dealing with partition and sale and that the vast majority of these cases arise in the context of family members or spouses who together co-own real estate. From that observation (which was largely echoed by Mr. Justice Pitt in *Greenbanktree)*, Carter postulates that the *Partition Act* was originally enacted largely as an adjunct to family law and that it is this original family law function which gives rise to the unusually high "malicious, oppressive or vexatious" standard for disqualifying partition and sale as of right (*i.e.* since familial disputes were inherently "messy" at the best of times, the courts wanted a truly high bar to disqualification so that they would not have to regularly consider and arbitrate petty inequities). Carter also laments the lack of remedies available under the *Partition Act*, arguing that, while a simple "yeah" or "nay" on a partition and sale application might have been sufficient for the resolution of most family real estate disputes, there is a need for a broader range of remedies to effectively police commercial co-ownership disputes (although not specifically referred to by Carter, he contemplates, as and by way of example, the very call right ultimately awarded to the majority co-owners in *Gartree (No. 2)*, but "shotgun" options, rights of first refusal and other like rights might also be useful). Carter unequivocally concludes that ". . . [t]here is a case to be made that the *Partition Act* should never be employed in commercial disputes . . . "and suggests that, by allowing the minority co-owner in *Greenbanktree* to succeed in a statutory sale of the whole co-owned portfolio, the court sanctioned ". . . using the [p]artition process to extract a premium on [the minority co-owner's] interest in circumstances where it wanted to sell its minority interest", a result that the *Partition Act* was clearly never intended to have.

However, therein perhaps lies the lesson solicitors should be drawing from these *Partition Act* cases. As Carter himself concludes (begrudgingly it would seem), the overall pattern of these *Partition Act* cases is "entrenched", with *Gartree (No. 1)* and *Greenbanktree* reflecting the judicial attitude of the overwhelming majority of the cases and *Gartree (No. 2)* perhaps representing the "flyers". Notwithstanding the success of the barristers in *Gartree (No. 2)*, given the relative longevity of the *Partition Act* (the operative provisions have remained largely intact for over 150 years) and no realistic grounds for optimism in increased judicial activism in real property matters generally . . . it is unlikely that there will be much movement in the law of partition and sale in the near future. Since the law countenances contracting-out of partition and sale (see, *e.g.*, *Sylvester v. Feldman* (2001), 39 R.P.R. (3d) 25), it behoves business persons choosing to own real property in co-ownership to contractually exclude statutory partition and sale remedies *ab initio*, and settle, instead, upon dissolution and dispute resolution procedures well in advance of a dispute (and for such purpose, even a rudimentary co-ownership agreement would probably prove more equitable than unbridled partition and sale under the *Partition Act*).

QUESTION

Compare the holding in *Greenbanktree* with section 15 of the *Law of Property Act*, R.S.A. 2000, c. L-7.

> 15.(1) A co-owner may apply to the Court by originating notice for an order terminating the co-ownership of the interest in land in which the co-owner is a co-owner.
>
> (2) On hearing an application under subsection (1), the Court shall make an order directing
>
> > (a) a physical division of all or part of the land between the co-owners,
> >
> > (b) the sale of all or part of the interest of land and the distribution of the proceeds of the sale between the co-owners, or
> >
> > (c) the sale of all or part of the interest of one or more of the co-owners' interests in land to one or more of the other co-owners who are willing to purchase the interest.

(3) A sale under subsection (2)(b) or (c) and the distribution of the proceeds of the sale shall be under the direction of the Court.

(4) In making an order under subsection (2)(c), the Court shall fix the value of the land sold and the terms of the sale.

Ontario Law Reform Commission, *Report on Basic Principles of Land Law* (Toronto: A.G. (Ont.), 1996) at 80–7 [footnotes omitted]

(i) Accounting for Benefits of Occupation

The unity of possession is an essential characteristic of both joint tenancy and tenancy in common: each co-owner has the same right to possession of the whole of the property. It is therefore a general rule that a co-owner does not have an obligation to account to other co-owners for the benefits derived from possession.

> Mere occupation by a co-owner will not impose a liability to account even if the occupation is sole or one co-owners has made more by his or her occupation. This is so because the non-occupying co-owner cannot, by failing to exercise his or her right to occupation, establish a claim for compensation against another co-owner who is lawfully exercising his or her own rights.

There are exceptional situations in which one co-owner may be required to account to other co-owners for the benefits of occupation — for what is often referred to as "occupation rent".

a. Ouster

Liability to pay an occupation rent occurs when one co-owner has unlawfully "ousted" another. Clearly, ouster includes actual expulsion. It probably also includes violent or threatening conduct on the part of one that makes it intolerable for the other to remain. It may extend further to cases where one party's conduct (whether or not violent) "made conditions intolerable" for the other or even to cases where the circumstances (whether or not fault is attributed to either party) makes it intolerable to unreasonable for the parties jointly to possess the property.

b. Agreement

An agreement between co-owners may make one liable to account. There are two main types of such agreement. First, the co-owners may have agreed to one having sole possession on the terms of making rental or other payments. Second, one co-owner may have agreed to act as agent or, as it is often put in archaic language in this context, as bailiff of the other co-owner with responsibility to account to the latter for her or his shares of the profits of the land.

c. The "Statute of Anne"

Statute provides for an accounting in certain circumstances. The relevant provision, which was first passed in England in 1704 and is often referred to as the "*Statute of Anne*", has been re-enacted in Ontario as section 122(2) of the *Courts of Justice Act*, which provides:

> 122.(2) An action for an accounting may be brought by a joint tenant or tenant in common, or his or her personal representative, against a co-tenant for receiving more than the co-tenant's just share.

It is well established that under this provision,

> a co-owner must account to his fellows for benefits which he *receives*, as co-owner, from third parties, but not for benefits which he *takes* from the soil as a result of his own exertions.

For example, in *Henderson v. Eason* one co-owner who was in sole occupation and farmed the property, was not liable to account for the profits obtained. In *Osachuk v. Osachuk* husband and wife were co-owners of a house divided into two apartments. On their separation the husband remained in sole occupation of one apartment and the other apartment subsequently became vacant. It was held that the husband wasn't liable to account for the benefit of his sole occupation or for the rents that might have been obtained from the vacant apartment.

d. Waste

The law of waste applies to co-owners, s. 31 of the *Conveyancing and Law of Property Act* providing:

> 31. Tenants in common and joint tenants are liable to their co-tenants for waste, or, in the event of a partition, the part wasted may be assigned to the tenant committing the waste at the value thereof to be estimated as if no waste had been committed.

However, the law of waste curtails the enjoyment of land by a co-owner less stringently than it does that of a tenant for life.

> Unlike a life tenant or a lessee, a co-tenant in fee simple may use the property in the same manner as would an owner who did not share title with co-owners, subject only to a duty to act reasonably. A co-owner can cut mature timber which is not of special value as ornamental timber. . . Similarly, a co-tenant can develop and operate mines. Therefore, if these acts are not waste, what acts would constitute waste as between co-tenants? The answer is, any conduct, which would unreasonably diminish the value of the property. Malicious conduct would be included.

Ontario authority, it may be added, places emphasis on whether the act of the co-owner amounts to *destruction* of the property. Spragge V.C. stated in *Dougall v. Foster*.

> It is clear that a tenant in common has not an *unlimited* power to do as he will with the estate, for though the court is slow to interfere between tenants in common, yet where one commits any act amounting to *destruction*, he will be restrained . . .

And in that case the digging of clay for making bricks was restrained.

e. equitable accounting

It is sometimes argued that there is a general equitable jurisdiction to make allowances between co-owners. It appears, however, that this jurisdiction only applies in partition and sale or analogous proceedings and even in such proceedings the court's power to order payment of occupation rent may be limited to the situation where the party to be charged claims an allowance in respect of outgoings related to the property. Moreover, it seems that a claim for contribution in respect of certain outgoings will not open the claimant up to being charged with occupation rent. In *Mastron v. Cotton* it was held that a joint tenant was entitled to credit for making mortgage payments and paying taxes, and for repairs if she submitted to an allowance for use and occupation. Claiming an allowance for payment of mortgage principal did not similarly render her liable to occupation rent.

The rationale that has been suggested for this special treatment of payments of mortgage principal is that they increase the capital value of the co-owners's equity in the property. However, this rationalization is unconvincing since a claim for the cost of improvements which have increased the capital value of the property does give rise to liability for occupation rent. In Australian cases co-owners have been entitled to obtain reimbursement, without becoming liable for occupation rent, for "rates and roadmaking charges" and mortgage payments, rates and taxes, and fire insurance premiums. The rationale in these cases was that the payments were in respect of joint liabilities of the co-owners. In some Canadian cases co-owners have been held entitled to credit for various payments without the court adverting to liability of occupation rent. The best view may be that the court has flexibility in determining whether allowance of credit for payments by a co-owner should open that co-owner up to liability for occupation rent. In the leading Ontario case of *Mastron v. Cotton*, Ferguson J.A. expressed the relevant principle as giving the court such flexibility:

> While the general rule is that one joint tenant, unless ousted by his co-tenant, may not sue another for use and occupation, it seems clear that when the joint tenancy is terminated by a Court order may in such proceedings make all just allowances and should give such directions as will do complete equity between the parties . . .
>
> What is just and equitable depends on the circumstances of each case. For instance if the tenant in occupation claims for upkeep and repairs, the Court, as a term of such allowance, usually requires that the claimant shall submit to an allowance for use and occupation . . . Again, if one tenant has made improvements which have increased the selling value of the property, the other tenant cannot take the advantage of increased price without submitting to an allowance for the improvements . . . And, once again, when, as here, one tenant has paid more than his share of encumbrances, he is entitled to an allowance for such surplus.

> These allowances being made as equitable allowances, there may as matter of course be circumstances under which they should not be made. For instance, the circumstances may indicate that the improvements were made or the surplus payments were made or intended to be made as gifts by one tenant to the other . . .

In cases where a co-owner is required to pay occupation rent, no clear principle has emerged for measuring the occupation rent payable. In *Irrsack v. Irrsack* the amount ordered was one-half of the rent "that these premises would attract". In *Dennis v. McDonald*, in the context of a jurisdiction with a rent control system providing for rent of some properties at a "fair rent" without account being taken of scarcity, it was held that a co-tenant in possession should pay compensation by reference not to a market rent but "a fair rent . . . eliminating the scarcity element". In *Leake v. Bruzzi*, the court in effect treated the occupation rent as equivalent to the interest element of the mortgage payments made by the co-tenant in possession. In *Baker v. Baker*, Craig J. said that "occupation rent is not necessarily measured by either the rental value of the property or the rent which an ousted owner may have to pay for accommodation elsewhere" and decided that "[h]aving regard to all the circumstances" it was "just to fix the occupation rent in this case at $125 a month, that is, the same amount as the mortgage payments [made by the co-tenant in possession]". . . .

(ii) Claiming for Expenditures Related to Property

In certain circumstances one co-owner can obtain reimbursement from other co-owners with respect to expenditures relating to the property. In numerous cases reimbursement has been obtained for mortgage payments, improvements, taxes, fire insurance premiums, upkeep and repairs and expenses from litigation with a third party.

Where the expense relates to a joint obligation of the parties, it appears that the claim for reimbursement may be made at any time since the right of reimbursement is a right of contribution analogous to that between co-sureties and co-insurers.

Although it has been suggested that there is a general equitable jurisdiction to account as between co-owners, it appears that outside of the right of contribution mentioned above, the right of reimbursement may be claimed only in proceedings for partition and sale or analogous proceedings. A rationale for denying relief while co-ownership lasts was given by Brett M.R. in *Leigh v. Dickeson:*

> The cost of repairs to the house was a voluntary payment by the defendant partly for the benefit of himself and partly for the benefit of his co-owner; but the co-owner cannot reject the benefit of the repairs, and if she is held to be liable for a proportionate share of the cost, the defendant will get the advantage of the repairs without allowing his co-owner any liberty to decide whether she will refuse or adopt them.

Maddaugh and McCamus comment as follows on this rationale:

The analysis offered by Brett M.R. would account for the denial of relief where the repairs or improvements are unnecessary or of no use to this inactive co-tenant. But where, for instance, the repairs in question may be viewed as an unavoidable burden of ownership, on what policy basis should recovery be denied? A more comprehensive explanation for the "no liability" rule would be that the relationship of co-owners generates a number of complex cost allocation problems which ought, for reasons of convenience, to be resolved on the basis of mutual agreement. Where the co-tenants cannot agree on such fundamental question, partition is an appropriate and available solution to their problems. At that point, an accounting will be taken in order to prevent the unjust enrichment of one co-tenant at the expense of the other.

Accounting at the time of partition or sale is justified on the basis that,

. . . the benefit conferred is now, in effect, a liquid asset in the hands of the co-tenant. This being so, the benefited co-tenant will not be unfairly prejudiced by the imposition of liability and, accordingly, a restitutionary liability to account arises.

Two comments should be made on reimbursement for improvements. First, it is established in Australia that a co-owners's claim for an allowance arising from improvements creates a proprietary interest, in the nature of an "equity", but this view has not been accepted in Canada. Secondly, the measure of compensation with respect to improvements is the amount of the outlay to the extent that the value of the property has been improved. . . .

QUESTIONS

1. "[T]he traditional principles relating to accounting between co-owners may properly be treated as based on the principle of unjust enrichment (although they were developed before the articulation of unjust enrichment as part of Canadian law) and their development is capable of being guided by reference to that principle": Ontario Law Reform Commission, *Report on Basic Principles of Land Law* (Toronto: A.G. Ont., 1996) at 89. Do you agree?

2. The following provision governs accounting on partition and sale in Alberta. To what extent does this subsection codify the common law rules discussed above?

17.(2) In determining if an accounting, contribution or adjustment should take place or compensation be paid for an unequal division of the land, the Court shall, without limiting itself from considering any matter it considers relevant in making its determination, consider whether

(a) one co-owner has excluded another co-owner from the land;

(b) an occupying co-owner was tenant, bailiff or agent of another co-owner;

(c) a co-owner has received from third parties more than the co-owner's just share of the rents from the land or profits from the reasonable removal of its natural resources;

(d) a co-owner has committed waste by an unreasonable use of the land;

(e) a co-owner has made improvements or capital payments that have increased the realizable value of the land;

(f) a co-owner should be compensated for non-capital expenses in respect of the land;

(g) an occupying co-owner claiming non-capital expenses in respect of the land should be required to pay a fair occupation rent; . . .

Law of Property Act, R.S.A. 2000, c. L-7, sub. 17(2).

6. SHARED OWNERSHIP OF PERSONALTY

Personal property, as with realty, may be co-owned either under a joint tenancy or tenancy in common. However, typically the statutes that reverse the presumption in favour of a joint tenancy do not extend to personal property. Hence, the old learning concerning words of severance applies. Likewise, the right to partition and sale is unavailable for chattels.

A problem of especial importance in the co-ownership of personalty, which has no direct counterpart in connection with land, concerns rights held under joint bank accounts. We have already seen that in the establishment of a joint account questions can arise as to whether or not the beneficial title to the money sitting on deposit is shared: see, for example, *Cooper v. Cooper Estate* 1999 CarswellSask 327, [1999] 11 W.W.R. 592 (Q.B.), which is reproduced in Chapter 6. Assuming that beneficial title is co-owned, do the account holders take as tenants in common or as joint tenants? See *Frosch v. Dadd*, immediately below.

Frosch v. Dadd
[1960] O.R. 435, 1960 CarswellOnt 114 (C.A.)

Schroeder J.A.:

This is an appeal from a judgment of Aylen J., pronounced on March 17, 1960, following the trial of the action without a jury at Hamilton, whereby it was adjudged that the plaintiff, as administratrix, do recover from the defendant the sum of $14,199.84, being one-half of the credit balance in joint savings account No. 3683 in the Bank of Montreal, Hamilton Branch, Main and James Sts., standing in the names of the deceased and the defendant.

The plaintiff administratrix and the defendant are brother and sister and the deceased, Henry Edward Dadd, was their brother. The defendant and the deceased were bachelors and they, the plaintiff and her husband, and another sister, Violet, lived together in a house owned by the deceased and the defendants as tenants in common. The plaintiff, and her husband, paid a nominal sum of $20 per month for board and lodging and the sister Violet paid $6 per week. The plaintiff was the housekeeper and her services were evidently taken into account by the brothers when they fixed the charge at such a moderate rate.

The defendant was a coat trimmer by trade and the deceased was a printer. They would appear to have lived very frugally and to have invested their money carefully. Their first real estate venture was made in 1921 when they purchased the house in which they were living at the time of Henry's death. In 1929, they purchased, as tenants in common, a property known as the Arva Apartments in Hamilton, each brother contributing one-half of the purchase-money. The rents of this property were collected by the deceased and deposited by him in an account which originally stood in his own name but which, in 1933, was converted into a joint account in the names of the two brothers. All necessary expenditures in connection with the operation of the apartment building were paid out of this account. In 1946, the Arva Apartments were sold; the proceeds of the sale were deposited in the joint account referred to and divided in equal shares between the brothers.

In 1942 the deceased brother and the defendant bought a property known as the Canterbury Apartments in Hamilton, taking title in their names as tenants in common. Later, in 1951, they purchased a property known as the Stanley Apartments, the title being taken in their names as tenants in common. They were so owned at the time of Henry Dadd's death.

Prior to their acquisition of the Canterbury Apartments, that property was managed by the real estate firm of Lounsbury & Lounsbury in Hamilton and this arrangement was continued by them. That firm collected the rents and made disbursements necessitated by the operation of the building up to an amount of $100 without authorization, but was required to obtain the defendant's approval before paying out any greater sum. They remitted a monthly cheque to the defendant covering the net rentals derived from the Canterbury Apartments, and the same course was pursued with respect to the Stanley Apartments after the latter property was acquired.

On receipt of the monthly cheques from the real estate agents, the defendant deposited them in an account in the Bank of Montreal which was then in his own name. It is not suggested that the deceased was not entitled to a one-half share of the moneys standing to the credit of that account and in fact the Stanley Apartments were purchased with the moneys then on deposit therein. That account remained in the name of the defendant until February 15, 1955, on which date it was closed and the money re-deposited to the credit of the joint account in question.

It was claimed by the defendant that before the said joint account was opened a discussion had occurred between the deceased and himself which resulted in an agreement between them that the survivor of them should be entitled to the money on deposit in the account at the time of the other's death. Responding to a question put by the trial Judge, the defendant stated that although the title to the real estate was in the name of the deceased and himself as tenants in common, a different arrangement was made with respect to the joint bank account to ensure that the surviving brother would have "something to carry on with". Later in cross-examination he added that the arrangement was made to enable the survivor to continue to meet expenses for taxes etc. out of this account. On March 6, 1957, the deceased, Henry Edward Dadd, suffered a heart attack and was removed to the hospital where he died on March 19, 1957. Two days prior to his death he made a short and informally worded will, which reads as follows: "I want the ranch to go to Vera and Clark Frisk and $1,000.00 to Zion Tabernacle and the residue to be divided between Violet and Vera." The "ranch" was a vacant lot which had been jocularly referred to by the members of the family in that way. The defendant was not present when the will was executed, although he had been sent for and had arrived a short time afterwards. When informed of its contents he made no comment except to observe that some provision should have been made for his nephew, the plaintiff's son.

On Monday March 18, 1957, the day before his brother's death, the defendant withdrew the entire balance standing to the credit of the joint account, namely $28,399.68 and at once deposited it in an account standing in his own name at the same branch of the Bank of Montreal.

Approximately 10 days after the death of Henry Edward Dadd, all the members of the family attended at the office of the late Mr. Kerr, the family solicitor. The plaintiff testified that the defendant on that occasion delivered the bank book relating to the joint account to the solicitor and informed him that one-half of the money on deposit belonged to the deceased. This was denied by the defendant but he admitted having stated that there was a joint account and that he then furnished particulars thereof. He does not deny that on this occasion he did not assert a claim to the whole of the moneys by right of survivorship. He evidently was displeased with the testamentary disposition of his brother's property and at that time requested his sisters to share the residue of the estate equally with him. This they declined to do. Cross-examination elicited from him the admission that if his sister had acceded to his request he would nevertheless have asserted his claim to the entire balance of the joint account. The learned trial Judge did not accept the defendant's evidence given in support of his claim and expressed the opinion that the claim which he now asserts was an afterthought which did not arise in his mind until his sisters declined to divide the residue with him.

It is beyond controversy that when the joint account was opened one-half of the money transferred to it belonged to the deceased, and that he and the defendant made equal contributions to the account thereafter to the date of Henry Dadd's death. The defendant attempted to establish by his own evidence an oral agreement whereby he was to receive all the moneys on deposit in the joint account if he should survive his brother. Such a claim advanced against the estate of a deceased person must be authenticated by the most convincing and unimpeachable testimony. This was pointed out by Aylesworth J.A. in *Lahay v. Brown*, 8 D.L.R. (2d) 728 at p. 735, [1957] O.W.N. 210 at p. 214 [affd 12 D.L.R. (2d) 785, [1958] S.C.R. 240] where he quoted from the judgment of Middleton J.A. in *Bayley v. Trusts & Guarantee Co.*, [1931] 1 D.L.R. 500 at p. 505, 66 O.L.R. 254 at p. 258 as follows:

> The proper judicial attitude at the first place towards the evidence of the living claimant ought to be one of suspicion, even when that evidence is corroborated within the meaning

> of the statute, and effect ought not to be given to it unless the effect of the entire evidence, including that which is relied upon as corroboration, is to remove all reasonable doubt from the judicial mind.

The learned trial judge not only held that the defendant's evidence upon this point was uncorroborated, but he disbelieved it.

While he acknowledged that the defendant's own evidence would not be sufficient to support his claim unless it was corroborated by some other material evidence, it was contended by his counsel that corroboration is to be found, first, in the formal deposit agreement signed by the parties, and secondly, that the failure of the deceased to mention the defendant in his will must be imputed to his recognition of the fact that the defendant was entitled on survivorship to all the moneys on deposit in the joint account. This fact, he maintained, constituted further corroboration. In my respectful opinion such a negative fact can be corroborative of nothing. The form of agreement signed by the parties on opening the joint bank account is substantially similar to the form of agreement which was involved in *Re Mailman*, [1941], 3 D.L.R. 449, S.C.R. 368, there Crocket J. stated at pp. 456-7 D.L.R., pp. 377-8 S.C.R.:

> Looking at the whole agreement form, as signed by Mrs. Mailman and her husband, I cannot see how it can well be regarded as other than a mere compliance with the usual requirements of the bank for the opening of any joint deposit account. Even if one were disposed to regard it as an agreement between the parties themselves as to their respective rights concerning the deposit fund, those rights, as already appears, are definitely restricted to the authority of each to withdraw money from the account in the manner stated in the first paragraph. This does not itself necessarily imply the right of the appellant to take the money as his own. Otherwise there could be no joint bank account, to which any presumption of law could apply one way or the other, in view of the fact that such authority to withdraw is a necessary incident of the establishment of every joint bank account.

In *Niles v. Lake*, [1947], 2 D.L.R. 248, S.C.R. 291, the form of joint deposit agreement was much more favourable to the claim of the defendant in that case. Using the bank's standard form of agreement in that case the parties "for valuable consideration (receipt whereof is hereby acknowledged)" mutually agreed "jointly and each with the other or others of us" and also with the bank "that all moneys now or which may be hereafter deposited to the credit of the said account, and all interest thereon, shall be and continue the joint property of the undersigned with right of survivorship" and each of them "in order effectually to constitute the said joint deposit account hereby assigns and transfers to all of the undersigned jointly and to the survivor or survivors" of them any and all moneys theretofore, then or thereafter deposited to the credit of the account together with all interest "to be the joint property of the undersigned and the property of the survivor or survivors of them" and each irrevocably authorized the bank to accept from time to time as a sufficient discharge for any sum or sums withdrawn any receipt, cheque etc. "signed by any one or more of the undersigned without any further signature or consent of the other or others of the undersigned thereto"; they agreed "with each other and with the said Bank that the death of one or more of the undersigned shall not affect the right of the survivors or any one of them or of the sole survivor to withdraw all of the said moneys and interest" from the bank and to give a valid and effectual discharge or receipt therefor. It was held, reversing the judgment of the Court of Appeal for Ontario, [1946], 2 D.L.R. 177, O.R. 102, and restoring the judgment of Greens J. at trial, [1945], 4 D.L.R. 795, O.R. 652, that the document in question should, under the circumstances and in its language, be construed as being for the protection of the bank and to facilitate its dealing with the account; further that neither the terms of the document nor other circumstances in evidence served to rebut the presumption of a resulting trust in favour of the deceased depositor or to cut down the beneficial interest of the deceased raised in equity under the agreement. I would refer also to the judgment of the Supreme Court in *Edwards v. Bradley*, 9 D.L.R. (2d) 673, [1957] S.C.R. 599.

The standard form of agreement signed with the bank in the present case is not unequivocal in its terms but is as consistent with the non-existence as with the existence of any prior or contemporaneous oral agreement between the depositors. It follows that it does not afford any corroboration of the alleged oral agreement upon which the defendant relies.

For the appellant it is argued that such cases as *Re Mailman*, *supra*, *Niles v. Lake*, *supra*, . . . are distinguishable from and have no application to the case at bar on the ground that in those cases all the money deposited to the credit of the joint account was the sole property of the deceased whereas here the funds deposited were the mutual funds of the deceased and the defendant, and it was clearly intended that the joint account would at all times consist of mutual funds. He maintains that there was a genuine joint fund created and that the mutuality of its creation excludes the primary presumption of a resulting trust in favour of the deceased; that the underlying principle of the creation of a resulting trust by operation of law is founded on the beneficial ownership being in one person and the legal ownership in another having no beneficial interest when that legal ownership is created by the act of the beneficial owners. No authority was cited for that proposition. Reference was made, however, to *Williams on Personal Property*, 18th ed., p. 518 where the following proposition is stated:

> If personal property, whether in possession or in action, be given to A. and B. simply, they will be joint owners, having equal rights, as between themselves, during the joint ownership, and being, with respect to all other persons than themselves, in the position of one single owner . . . As a further consequence of the unity of joint ownership, the important right of survivorship, which distinguishes a joint tenancy of real estate, belongs also to a joint ownership of personal property.

It is contended that since the brothers were the joint owners of the moneys in the joint bank account, "the law would be sufficient of itself to carry the property to the survivor". The fallacy of this argument lies in the fact that there is no acceptable evidence to substantiate the defendant's claim that the money deposited in the joint bank account was a *gift* to the two of them, and to give effect to this contention would be to hold that a joint tenancy could be created by inadvertence, a proposition which I find wholly untenable. No doubt when the joint bank account was opened, half the monies deposited therein belonged to the deceased and it is indisputable that one-half of all further money deposited was money belonging to the deceased. The fact that only a portion of the moneys placed in the joint account belonged to him does not in any way alter or modify the operation of the well settled principle, and it follows that the deposit of the deceased brother's share in the joint account raised the presumption of a resulting trust in his favour as to that portion which the defendant was unable to rebut.

The history of the dealings between the brothers makes abundantly plain the purpose for which the joint account was opened. They had carried on this enterprise in combination for a period of approximately 25 years. Appellant's counsel contests the claim that a partnership existed between the brothers, but there can be no doubt that in the carrying out of the undertaking in which they were mutually interested the relationship of principal and agent was created between them within the test laid down in *Cox v. Hickman* (1860), 8 H.L.C. 268 at p. 306, 11 E.R. 431, applied and followed by the Judicial Committee of the Privy Council in *Ross v. Can. Bank of Commerce, Ross v. Northern Canada Supply Co., Ross v. Taylor Hardware Co.*, [1923] 3 D.L.R. 339, 54 O.L.R. 59. The [O.R.] headnote of that case, which accurately summarizes the judgment, is as follows:

> It was immaterial whether the combination was called a partnership or a joint adventure — probably it was a partnership — but in any case it was a combination, and it was part of the terms upon which the combination was made that a business should be carried on and liabilities should be incurred; and liabilities incurred by the combination or by a member on its behalf, within the limit of the adventure, bound both members, and not only the one by whom the liability was actually incurred.

Even on the assumption that the defendant and the deceased became joint owners of a chose in action, the fact that they were partners or stood in a like relationship to each other, had the effect in equity that the share of the deceased partner in the chose in action belonging to the partnership devolved on his legal personal representatives. The equitable maxim "equality is equity" is demonstrated in those cases where equity leans in favour of a tenancy in common and will, in many cases, treat persons who are joint tenants at law as tenants in common of the beneficial interest, so that although at law the survivor is entitled to the whole estate he will hold in part as trustee for the representatives of the deceased: *Snell's Principles of Equity*, 23rd ed., p. 19, where the author states:

> For instance, if A and B purchase property with purchase-money provided in *unequal* shares, and take the conveyance to themselves jointly, on A's death B becomes entitled to the whole of the property at law, but in equity he is treated as a trustee for A's representatives to the extent of the share of the purchase-money advanced by A.

The author points out at p. 20: "In the case of a mortgage made to A and B jointly, it is immaterial whether the money is advanced equally or unequally; the mere circumstance of the transaction being a loan is sufficient to repel the presumption of an intention to hold the mortgage on a joint tenancy, and the survivor is therefore a trustee for the representatives of the deceased mortgagee to the extent of his proportion of the loan." Citing *Morley v. Bird* (1798), 3 Ves. 628 at p. 631, 30 E.R. 1192.

The court will not treat the mortgage as joint in equity merely because it contains a clause to the effect that the money belongs to the lenders on a joint account. It was pointed out in Snell that before the *Conveyancing Act, 1981*, such a clause was usually inserted in a mortgage made to two mortgagees in order to enable the surviving mortgagee to give a receipt to the mortgagee for the whole of the mortgage money; it was simply conveyancing machinery and did not conclude the question whether the survivor was entitled beneficially to the whole of the money or must hold part as trustee for the representatives of the deceased mortgagee. Citing *Brown v. Raindle* (1796), 3 Ves. 256, 30 E.R. 998; *Burnaby v. Equitable Reversionary Interest Society* (1885), 28 Ch. D. 416; *Re Hewett, Hewett v. Hallett*, [1894] 1 Ch. 362. In *Re Sutcliffe & Sons Ltd., Ex p. Royal Bank* [1933], 1 D.L.R. 562 at p. 565, OR 120 at p. 125, Middleton J.A. clearly described the relationship between a banker and his customers as that of a debtor and creditor, the banker being liable to an action at law for money had and received by him to the use of the customer. He points out that money paid into a bank ceases altogether to be the money of the principal but becomes the money of the banker who is bound to return an equivalent by paying a similar sum to that deposited with him when he is asked for it. The deposit of these moneys to the credit of the joint account in question was in effect a loan made to the bank. In that respect the transaction bears some analogy to the loan of money upon a mortgage. If the analogy holds good, then the defendant having failed to prove that he was beneficially entitled to the whole of the money in the account must be taken to hold it as the one-half portion of the deceased brother for the latter's legal personal representatives. This line of reasoning raises a very interesting point, but I do not rest my judgment upon it. I mention the point only out of deference to the argument presented to us.

Counsel for the respondent urged that since it is necessary, if a joint tenancy with the right to survivorship is to exist in either real of personal property, the four unities of possession, interest, title and time must exist and continue to exist until the date of death of one of the joint tenants, otherwise there can be no right of survivorship; that the destruction of any of the four unities will terminate the tenancy and therewith the right of survivorship as discussed by Grant J.A. in *Power v. Grace*, [1932], 2 D.L.R. 793 at pp.795-6, O.R. 357 at p. 360. Hence it is argued, the defendant by withdrawing the money, and placing it in his own personal account on the day before the date of his brother's death, destroyed the unities and lost whatever right of survivorship he might have had. In view of the decision to which I have come, however, upon the other grounds, it is unnecessary to explore further the very interesting point thus raised.

The judgment of the learned trial Judge was right and the appeal should be dismissed with costs.

Appeal dismissed.

QUESTION AND COMMENT

Even assuming shared beneficial entitlements to the money while in the account (either under a joint tenancy or a tenancy in common), who owns items purchased from that account? In *Rathwell v. Rathwell* [1978] 2 S.C.R. 436, 1978 CarswellSask 36, 1978 CarswellSask 129, Dickson J. (as he then was) advanced this position (at 459):

> Where a husband and wife have a joint bank account, the beneficial ownership of money in it and of assets acquired from it, will depend upon the intention of the parties. *Jones v. Maynard*, [[1951] Ch. 572, [1951] 1 All E.R. 802] is authority for the proposition that when the intention is that the account is to be a pool of their resources, or in the words of the trial judge in the present proceedings, "a common purse", the money in it will be treated as belonging to them jointly and if investments are purchased out of the account in the name of the husband, he holds a one-half interest in them as trustee for the wife. It is true that in *Re Bishop, National Provincial Bank Ltd. v. Bishop* [[1965] Ch. 450, [1965] 1 All E.R. 241] Stamp J. said that so far as the decision in *Jones v. Maynard* related to investments, it was based on its own particular facts and, in general, where spouses open a joint account on terms that cheques may be drawn by either, then (unless the account is kept for some specific or limited purpose) each spouse can draw on it for his or her own benefit, and any investment purchased out of the account belongs to the spouse in whose name the purchase was made. I have difficulty in understanding the basis upon which it can be said that the joint owner who reaches the bank first can divert jointly-owned funds to the purchase of investments upon which the other joint owner will have no claim. In a decision of this Court, *Re Daly*; *Daly v. Brown* [(1907), 39 S.C.R. 122] at p. 148, a joint bank account case, MacLellan J. said: "In a case of joint tenancy neither party is exclusive owner of the whole. Neither can appropriate the whole to himself."

7. CO-OWNERSHIP THROUGH MARITAL PROPERTY LAW

Co-ownership is common among spouses, and much of the case law concerning accounting and termination has arisen in the context of marriage breakdown. Today these disputes often fall to be considered under matrimonial property legislation.

Issues involving marital property law have already been touched on in this casebook. It will be recalled for example that in Maggie Conway's discussion of equity and women in Chapter 6 ("Equity's Darling?") it was observed that equity has played a role, albeit imperfectly, in preserving property rights for married women prior to the introduction of married women's property legislation. The use of the remedial constructive trust marked an effort by equity to provide proprietary recourse for married women and unmarried cohabitees who had contributed — usually by dint of hard work — to property owned by their familial partners.

The martial property regimes introduced in the 1970s provide a more convenient mechanism for dividing marital contributions. In the common law provinces and territories of Canada rules of deferred equal sharing have dominated. These systems are described as "deferred" because until a designated event transpires — such as marital breakdown or in some provinces the death of a spouse — the generic rules of property apply, more or less. Once a triggering event occurs, a right to seek a division of assets arises.

Two basic approaches emerged to identify those property interests that gave rise to a presumptive right of equal sharing. One focuses on the nature of the property. Hence, under Ontario's first-generation statute, the *Family Law Reform Act, 1978*, items used by the family ("family assets"), whensoever acquired, were subject to the presumption of equal sharing. Another approach, now far more common, is to treat most assets accumulated during marriage as being subject to a presumption of equality. The Ontario *Family Law Act*, R.S.O. 1990, c. F.3 adopts that style, and will be used below to work through the crucial issues.

Part 1 of the Act deals with the division of property. In s. 4 the term "property" is defined to mean:

> . . . any interest, present or future, vested or contingent, in real or personal property and includes,
>
> (a) property over which a spouse has, alone or in conjunction with another person, a power of appointment exercisable in favour of himself or herself,
>
> (b) property disposed of by a spouse but over which the spouse has, alone or in conjunction with another person, a power to revoke the disposition or a power to consume or dispose of the property, and
>
> (c) in the case of a spouse's rights under a pension plan that have vested, the spouse's interest in the plan including contributions made by other persons.

In general, the Act treats property acquired by the parties during marriage as subject to division unless it was received by gift (as long as it is not a gift of the matrimonial home), as damages for personal injury, or under a life insurance policy. The exemption attaching to these properties can be traced into later-acquired property (except the home). This means that the new property retains the initial exemption from sharing. (See Part 5 of Chapter 3, where this tracing rule was mentioned in the discussion of intermixture.) By means of a domestic contract the parties may also exclude or include shareable property.

In essence, the parties are entitled to walk away from the marriage with an equal share of the accumulated property unless it can be shown that it would be unconscionable to demand equality. This is a strong presumption: notionally, unconscionability is a more demanding hurdle than simple "unfairness". Put in other words, a court might well conclude that an equal division is unfair, but would nevertheless be duty-bound to divide the property in half. What is the policy justification for overlooking "mere" unfairness?

In giving effect to an award for the division of assets a court has several options. It may order an equalization payment: here the spouse with more net property makes a payment to the other. A court can also order that the property be charged or transferred. The Act also allows for partition and sale. In addition, under Part 2 both spouses have a right to possession of the matrimonial home. In Ontario, this is an immediate not a deferred entitlement. To preserve this occupancy right, the Act imposes restraints on alienation by the owning spouse. These rules, which generally speaking give the non-owning spouse a veto on dispositions, are derived from the Western Canadian homestead protections discussed in Chapter 5.

As the Ontario Law Reform Commission remarked, there has been little attention paid to the interplay between these matrimonial property systems and the conventional law of co-ownership: O.L.R.C., *Report on Basic Principles of Land Law* (Toronto: A.G. (Ont.), 1996) at 88. Here several observations can be made.

First, given that separate property rights are preserved during marriage breakdown, the general law of property must be invoked to determine who owns what. Then and only then can an order for reallocation be made.

Second, minor alterations to the general law have been introduced under marital property legislation. As seen in Chapter 6, the law governing the presumption of advancement has been reformed. In Ontario, s. 14 of the *Family Law Act* provides that:

> The rule of law applying a presumption of a resulting trust shall be applied in questions of the ownership of property between husband and wife, as if they were not married, except that,
>
> (a) the fact that property is held in the name of spouses as joint tenants is proof, in the absence of evidence to the contrary, that the spouses are intended to own the property as joint tenants; and
>
> (b) money on deposit in the name of both spouses shall be deemed to be in the name of the spouses as joint tenants for the purposes of clause (a).

Third, it has been established that the law governing unjust enrichment, largely made redundant in this context by the legislative sharing regime, is nevertheless not altogether ousted. Often it will not matter whether a spouse receives an award based on unjust enrichment or under the *Family Law Act*. Still, in select cases it may be pertinent to determine whether the principles of unjust enrichment should be invoked: see *Rawluk v. Rawluk* [1990] 1 S.C.R. 70, 1990 CarswellOnt 217, 1990 CarswellOnt 987.

Fourth, the Ontario Act contemplates the possibility that the decedent spouse may have held property under a joint tenancy with someone else. The right to share in that property on death would of course be lost to the surviving spouse because the "other" joint tenant would instead take by survivorship. To avoid that outcome, the Act provides for a deemed severance just before the spouse/joint tenant's death.

Fifth, when the parties are co-owners under the general law, certain financial readjustments are undertaken when partition and sale is sought. There is no reason why such adjustments should not also be carried out when a share of marital property is being awarded. With regard to accounting, it has been seen that under partition and sale legislation a claim for occupation rent may be tenable against a co-owner in possession. Such a claim can be made when one co-owner has been ousted by the other. The idea of ouster includes the straightforward case in which one owner prevents the other from entering the premises. In addition, it can encompass situations in which the conduct of the remaining party is so egregious that the other owner has felt compelled to leave; this is known as constructive ouster: see, *e.g.*, *Baker v. Baker* 1976 CarswellBC 153, [1976] 3 W.W.R. 492 (S.C.). Occupation rent can also be charged when the remaining spouse makes a claim for current expenses or, in some jurisdictions, for improvements to the property.

In recent years, the courts have shown a greater flexibility when entertaining claims for occupation rent in a family law setting. In *Braglin v. Braglin*, below, the nature of occupation in the context of a division under marital property law was considered.

Braglin v. Braglin
2002 CarswellAlta 1143 (Q.B.)

Veit J.:

Summary

Ms. Braglin asks the court to order her husband to pay her occupation rent. He has occupied the matrimonial home since she left the home with the children of the marriage in October 2001.

The application is denied.

Awarding occupation rent in a domestic dispute is a discretionary remedy which depends on all of the circumstances of the case. Just because one joint tenant left the property voluntarily rather than by "ouster" does not deprive the departing owner from a claim for occupation rent. In a family law situation, a departing joint tenant who has not been asked to contribute to the payments associated with the property and who does not in fact contribute to the financial support of the property is not, for those reasons, prevented from bringing a claim for occupation rent.

Here, Ms. Braglin was not ousted from the matrimonial home and she does not contribute to the expenses connected with maintaining the matrimonial home. Her claim for occupation rent is a claim for matrimonial property. Her claim is premature: all of the issues relating to matrimonial property are not yet before the court. . . .

1. Background

In October 2001, Ms. Braglin, and the two children of the marriage, moved out of the matrimonial home. In March 2001, Ms. Braglin commenced proceedings asking for a divorce judgment and for an "equitable division" of the matrimonial property. Between her departure from the matrimonial residence and March 2001, Mr. Braglin paid $400 per month, and subsequently $600 per month for support. After Ms. Braglin initiated divorce proceedings, Mr. Braglin retained a lawyer. In April, 2002, Mr. Braglin commenced to pay child support pursuant to the Federal Child Support Guidelines; since that time, he has been paying $1,000 per month, based on his gross salary of approximately $80,000.

In May 2002, Ms. Braglin brought an application for various types of relief, including spousal support. That application has been adjourned *sine die*.

In June 2002, Ms. Braglin borrowed $25,000 from her parents and purchased a home in Calgary. She has moved into this home with the children and a partner.

In this application, Ms. Braglin asks for an order for the sale of the matrimonial home; that order was granted. The house will be sold and the proceeds placed in trust.

As another aspect of this application, Ms. Braglin asks for $300 per month in occupation rent. Ms. Braglin has never been asked to contribute to the mortgage and maintenance payments for the home; she has not been asked to contribute to the renovation loan repayment. Ms. Braglin has provided no evidence of the rental value of the matrimonial home.

2. Should Ms. Braglin be awarded occupation rent on an interlocutory application?

While the court has the jurisdiction to award occupation rent, even on an interlocutory application, it would not be appropriate to do so in this case. . . .

The most recent decision dealing with occupation rent of which I am aware is *Kazmierczak* [*Kazmierczak v. Kazmierczak*, 2001CarswellAlta 943 (Q.B.)], Slatter J.; in it, there is a careful outline of the evolution of the treatment of occupation rent in the domestic context. A few extracts from his decision are useful. . . .

> [para90] In my view, care must be taken in carrying forward the common-law concept of occupation rent into the family law context. Non-family joint tenants generally do not have mutual obligations of support for each other, and for children. In the family law context, such mutual obligations of support are generally present, and would usually dominate and outweigh the common-law property rights associated with joint tenancy. Occupation rent should only be awarded in the family law context with great caution.
>
> . . .
>
> [para92] In *Grinde v. Grinde* (1977), 5 A.R. 561 (decided before the Matrimonial Property Act was in force) the Court reviewed the common law relating to jointly-owned property. In Grinde a wife's claim for occupation rent from her husband on the partition of their jointly owned farmland was dismissed on the grounds that the husband had not elected to ask the wife for contribution towards his expenses as occupier of the premises. This election was held to vest in the co-owner in possession, and to be exercisable at

trial. Grinde was acknowledged as "good law" in *Aleksiuk v. Aleksiuk* (1991), 112 A.R. 298, but the Court added at p. 307 that "in view of the concept of the Matrimonial Property Act, and in particular the wording of s. 8(c), I do not think that the principles enunciated in *Grinde v. Grinde* would strictly apply to a matrimonial property division . . .". In Aleksiuk the Court held that ". . .in considering occupation rent one would have to take into account the fact that the parties' children resided in the property so that an adjustment would have to be made, the defendant being equally responsible for their maintenance". Aleksiuk therefore recognized the link between a claim for occupation rent, and the responsibilities of each party to support the children, and to potentially support each other. To the same effect is the *Balzar* case [*Balzar v. Balzar* (1990), 67 Man. R. (2d) 196 (Q.B.) at para. 57] where the husband and wife cohabited for 14 years and separated for 16 years. During the lengthy separation, the husband lived in the matrimonial home with the child of the marriage, supported the child, made all mortgage payments, and paid for the taxes, insurance and repairs. No occupation rent was allowed while the child was a child of the marriage.

[para93] In *Hantel v. Hilscher* (2000), 255 A.R. 187 (C.A.) the Court of Appeal held at para. 26 that:

> Occupation rent is a discretionary remedy. It depends largely on the circumstances of the case. Hantel and the two children had been residing in the home since the separation. The trial judge granted Hilscher occupation rent and left the value of the rent to be determined by the parties, taking into account the fact that Hilscher had a responsibility to maintain his two children who were in the home. The trial judge made no error in principle in exercising his discretion to award occupation rent on the evidence before him.

By describing occupation rent as a "discretionary remedy", the Court of Appeal moved away from the traditional analysis of occupation rent as a property right arising between co-tenants. This approach had previously been outlined in *Timms v. Timms* (1997), 203 A.R. 81, 51 Alta. L.R. (3d) 99, 29 R.F.L. (4th) 392, [1997] 7 W.W.R. 392 where a husband's claim for occupation rent for the time the wife resided in the matrimonial home with the child of the marriage was dismissed, as there was no evidence before the Court of the impact it would have on the maintenance order. Johnstone J. referred to the decisions of *Scott v. Scott* (1996), 183 A.R. 103 and *Crane v. Crane* (1997), 189 A.R. 81 and noted at paras. 56-57:

> . . . Neither of these decisions are of assistance to me given that in Scott, *supra*, Justice Gallant held that the exclusive possession of the wife of the matrimonial home was extravagant; and the wife and children did not require as much space and the parties could not afford the very high cost of servicing the mortgage, the realty taxes, insurance "and otherwise". Similarly in *Crane v. Crane*, *supra*, although Justice Veit indicates at page 86 as follows: "In a marriage, once there is a definitive separation that results in the exclusive occupation of the matrimonial home by one of the spouses, the occupying spouse has deemed notice that the excluded spouse has a notional claim for occupation rent", she dealt with the issue of pre-judgment interest. I do agree with her, however, that the occupying spouse has deemed notice that the non-occupying spouse has a notional claim. However, the operative word is "notional". The awarding of occupation rent is discretionary and is linked inextricably to the award of child and spousal maintenance. (Emphasis added.)

In *Lauderdale*, LoVecchio J. cited the following comment with approval:

> In assessing occupation rent, the court must exercise a certain amount of discretion in balancing the relevant factors in order to determine whether occupation rent is sensible in the totality of the circumstances of the case.

After reviewing the materials presented, I have concluded that a court can award occupation rent in a domestic dispute, see s. 9 of the *Matrimonial Property Act*, but that such an award is a discretionary remedy which depends on all of the circumstances of the case. Just because one joint tenant left the property voluntarily rather than by "ouster" does not deprive the departing owner from a claim for occupation rent. In a family law situation, a departing joint tenant who has not been asked to contribute to the payments associated with the property and who does not in fact contribute to the financial support of the property is not, for those reasons, prevented from bringing a claim for occupation rent.

In this case, Ms. Braglin did not make a claim for occupation rent when she issued divorce proceedings. Ms. Braglin does not contribute to the mortgage payments on the home or to the repayment of the home renovation loan. Mr. Braglin is paying child support under the Guidelines. Although there is no evidence of it on this application, it seems likely that Mr. Braglin has, at least on an interim basis, assumed responsibility for all of the matrimonial debts. Ms. Braglin's claim for spousal support has been adjourned *sine die*. The matrimonial home will be sold immediately, and the proceeds will presumably be available relatively quickly for distribution to the parties as a part of the matrimonial property claim.

3. Should Ms. Braglin be awarded occupation rent when she voluntarily left the matrimonial home?

As indicated above, my understanding of the law is that Ms. Braglin is not deprived of her right to ask for occupation rent merely because she left the matrimonial home voluntarily.

4. Is Ms. Braglin hampered in her request because she has not specifically asked for occupation rent in her Statement of Claim?

Ms. Braglin ought to have made a claim for occupational rent in order to become entitled to such relief. . . .

Ms. Braglin did not ask for occupation rent in her pleadings. . . . It is good pleading practice to let the party opposite know what your claim is.

Application granted in part

QUESTIONS

1. What is the rationale for a different approach to occupation rent in matrimonial cases?

2. In what way, if at all, does the following provision found in the *Family Law Act*, R.S.N.L. 1990, c. F-2, differ from the approach to marital property adopted under Ontario law?

> 8.(1) Notwithstanding the manner in which the matrimonial home is held by either or both of the spouses, each spouse has a 1/2 interest in the matrimonial home owned by either or both spouses, and has the same right of use, possession and management of the matrimonial home as the other spouse has.
>
> (2) Subsection (1) creates a joint tenancy with respect to the matrimonial home.
>
> (3) Notwithstanding subsection (2), where spouses hold a matrimonial home as tenants in common, either before or after July 1, 1980, that tenancy continues.
>
> (4) Where title to the matrimonial home is held by 1 spouse by virtue of adverse possession or a licence or easement relates to the use and enjoyment of the matrimonial home, the period of adverse possession, licence or easement that has accrued prior to the time the home becomes a matrimonial home accrues to the spouse who acquires an interest in the matrimonial home under this Act and the period of adverse possession, licence or easement continues to run notwithstanding the effect of Parts I and II upon the title to the home.
>
> (5) Notwithstanding anything contained in this Part and Part II, the joint tenancy created with respect to the matrimonial home by this section
>
> > (a) creates a right of survivorship in a surviving spouse; and
> >
> > (b) operates to vest beneficial ownership in the matrimonial home in the surviving spouse without the need for the probate or the administration of an estate of the deceased spouse.
>
> (6) Where the right of survivorship referred to in subsection (5) operates, the matrimonial home shall not be subject to division as a matrimonial asset under Part II.

8. THE NATURE OF CONDOMINIUMS AND CO-OPERATIVES

The condominium complex, now ubiquitous in Canadian urban centres, is a relatively recent innovation. The first of the modern statutes regulating condos began to emerge in Canada in the 1960s. The condominiums created under statute tend to be crafted from a mix of basic extant legal tools. So, for example, the owners hold a fee simple entitlement (a flying fee). The common areas are typically held by all owners as tenants in common. A corporate model is used to deal with the management of the entire entity, with the unit-owners also holding shares and voting rights in the corporation.

As in all collective endeavours, conflict is inevitable. What values influence the manner in which disputes are resolved? That issue was at the forefront in *2475813 Nova Scotia Ltd. v. Ali*, below.

2475813 Nova Scotia Ltd. v. Ali
2001 CarswellNS 18, 41 R.P.R. (3d) 129 (C.A.)

[This case concerned the proposed sale of a condominium. Eighty per cent of all of the units in the condo were held by a Mr. Bruce Brett. He had developed the project and served as a director of the condominium corporation. The proposed sale was to be to Brett's company, and he controlled enough votes of the condominium unit holders to secure approval of the sale. However, a minority of unit holders objected to the proposal. In the litigation that ensued, a motions judge held that s. 40 of the *Condominium Act*, R.S.N.S. 1989, c. 85 authorized the sale.

Section 40 provides as follows:

40.(1) Sale of the property or any part of the common elements may be authorized by

(a) a vote of owners who own eighty per cent of the common elements; and

(b) the consent of the persons having registered claims against the property or the part of the common elements, as the case may be, created after the acceptance for registration of the declaration and description.

(2) A conveyance shall be executed by all the owners and a release or discharge shall be given by all the persons having registered claims against the property or the part of the common elements, as the case may be, created after the acceptance for registration of the declaration and description, and shall be submitted for registration together with a supplementary report on title in prescribed form showing the persons signing the same to be all the owners and persons having registered claims and the Registrar shall accept the deed or transfer so submitted for registration.

(3) Upon the acceptance for registration of the instruments mentioned in subsection (2),

(a) the government of the property or of the part of the common elements by this Act is terminated;

(b) claims against the land and interests appurtenant to the land created before the acceptance for registration of the declaration and description are as effective as if the declaration and description had not been accepted for registration; and

(c) claims against the property or the part of the common elements created after the acceptance for registration of the declaration and description are extinguished.

(4) Subject to subsection (5), the owners share the proceeds of the sale in the same proportions as their common interests.

(5) Where a sale is made pursuant to this Section, any owner who dissented may elect to have the fair market value of the property at the time of the sale determined by arbitration under the Arbitration Act by serving notice to that effect on the corporation within ten days after the vote, and the owner who served the notice is entitled to receive from the proceeds of the sale the amount the owner would have received if the sale price had been the fair market value as determined by the arbitration.

(6) Where the proceeds of the sale are inadequate to pay the amount determined pursuant to subsection (5), each of the owners who voted for the sale is liable for a portion of the deficiency determined by the proportions of their common interests.

It was also held at first instance that the directors were not in a conflict of interest. Moreover, under the Act encumbrancers are given a veto over sales. It was held that they were under no obligation to exercise this right in a self-interested manner; they were not subject to a reasonableness standard.

The Nova Scotia Court of Appeal upheld all of these rulings. However, there remained two related issues: was Brett a fiduciary, and if so, what duties would thereby be imposed upon him?]

Cromwell J.A.:

Introduction:

This case concerns a proposed sale of a condominium development. One person, Mr. Brett, effectively controls 80% of the votes of all unit owners. He was also the controlling mind of the developer and a director of the condominium corporation. By exercising his 80% voting control, Mr. Brett has obtained the authorization necessary to require the sale of the condominium to a company under his control at a price of his choosing. There is a group of dissenting unit owners who, if the transaction proceeds, will be required to sell their units against their will. Their position is that the proposed transaction has not been properly authorized. While the appeal raises several interpretative and procedural issues under the *Condominium Act*, the fundamental question is this. Does the *Act* permit a person controlling 80% of the votes to purchase the condominium property, dispossess all of the unit holders and dictate the terms of the sale over the dissent of the remaining unit holders?

Before turning to the facts and issues, it will be helpful to set out an overview of the legal framework for the condominium out of which the specific questions to be answered on this appeal arise.

The term "condominium" refers to a system of ownership and administration of property with three main features. A portion of the property is divided into individually owned units, the balance of the property is owned in common by all the individual owners and a vehicle for managing the property, known as the condominium corporation, is established: see A.H. Oosterhoff and W.B. Rayner, *Anger and Honsberger Law of Real Property* (1985), Vol. II, s. 3801 and Alvin B. Rosenberg, *Condominium in Canada* (1969). The condominium may be seen, therefore, as a vehicle for holding land which combines the advantages of individual ownership with those of multi-unit development: Oosterhoff and Rayner at s. 3802. In a sense, the unit owners make up a democratic society in which each has many of the rights associated with sole ownership of real property, but in which, having regard to their co-ownership with the others, some of those rights are subordinated to the will of the majority: see Robert J. Owens *et al.* (eds), *Corpus Juris Secundum* (1996), *Estates* § 195, Vol. 31, p. 260.

As Oosterhoff and Rayner wisely observed, the success of a condominium depends in large measure on an equitable balance being struck between the independence of the individual owners and the interdependence of them all in a co-operative community. It follows, they note, that common features of all condominiums are the need for balance and the possibility of tension between individual and collective interests: at s. 3802.

From a more purely legal perspective, a modern condominium is created pursuant to detailed legislative provisions such as, in Nova Scotia, the *Condominium Act*, R.S.N.S. 1989, c. 85 (the "*Act*"). The condominium is, therefore, a creature of statute. But condominium legislation reflects the combination of several legal concepts and relies on, and to a degree incorporates by reference, principles drawn from several different areas of law. The law relating to individual ownership of real property is, of course, central because the owners of the individual units are, subject to certain limits, entitled to exclusive ownership and use of their units: see s. 27(2) of the *Act*. The law relating to joint ownership is significant because the owners are tenants in common with respect to the common elements: see s. 28(1). The law relating to easements and covenants is relevant because the unit owners have rights to compliance by the others with the provisions governing the condominium and certain easements are, by statute, appurtenant to each unit: see s. 30(2) and 29. The law relating to corporations is also of importance because the condominium is administered by the condominium corporation in which the unit holders are in a position analogous to shareholders: see, *e.g.*, ss. 13 and ff and s. 25. While the *Condominium Act* enables and, to a degree, regulates the legal aspects of condominium ownership, it does so against a vast background of general legal principles which will frequently be relevant to the interpretation and application of the *Act*. As has been said, "[i]n its legal structure, the condominium first combines elements of several concepts . . . and then seeks to delineate separate privileges and responsibilities on the one hand from common privileges and responsibilities on the other." *Corpus Juris Secundum*, *supra*, at p. 260.

Not all condominium developments succeed or last indefinitely. The *Act* provides for termination and sale.

Under s. 41, the owners may decide that the property will no longer be a condominium. To use the language of the statute, the government of the property by the *Act*, may be terminated. The effect of taking this step is that the property ceases to be a condominium, the unit owners become tenants in common and the condominium corporation is deemed to have been wound up: see ss. 42(a) and (b) and s. 22. This step may only be taken if approved by all unit owners and registered encumbrancers or by court order: ss. 41(1) and 43.

Under s. 40 of the *Act*, the property, that is, all units and common elements, may be sold. When this step is taken, the government of the property is terminated and the owners share the proceeds of sale in the same proportions as their common interests: ss. 40(3)(a) and 40(4). The practical effect is that individual owners are forced to sell their units. This step may be taken only with the approval of 80% of the unit owners and all registered encumbrancers: s. 40(1). Dissenting unit owners are afforded a measure of protection. They are given the right to have the fair market value of the property determined and, if this is greater than the sale price, all unit owners voting for the sale are liable for the deficiency: ss. 40(5) and 40(6).

Termination or sale of the condominium are fundamental steps which, when contemplated or pursued, are likely to escalate the inherent tension between individual and collective interests. And so it is in this case.

Overview of the Facts:

Halifax Condominium Corporation No. 151 was registered on March 29, 1988. It is a 200 unit residential building known as Granbury Place. Brett Pontiac Buick GMC Limited, a company controlled by Bruce Brett, was the declarant-owner of the property. The project was developed and marketed through Granbury Developments Limited, another Brett company.

Some initial sales of the units were made, but about 80 of the 200 units remained unsold and were acquired by another Brett company, 2475813 Nova Scotia Limited. It acquired additional units with the result that, as of January 12, 2000, that company owned or, together with Mr. Brett, controlled, in excess of 80% of the units and common elements. Most of these units were rented. The appellants, who in the main occupy their units, owned roughly 14%.

Since at least 1997, there have been disputes between the Brett interests and the appellants about the governance and future direction of the condominium. The Board of Directors of the condominium corporation made offers (the first being made in May of 1997) to acquire all the units owned by the Brett interests, but no agreement was reached. From roughly June of 1998, Mr. Brett undertook what he referred to as ". . . an extensive process of repurchasing units through 2475813 Nova Scotia Limited." The result of this process was that, according to Mr. Brett's disclosure statement in December, 1999, 2475813 Nova Scotia Limited owned 150 units and other persons related to Mr. Brett owned 13. He thus had effective control of just over 80% of the units.

In December of 1998, Mr. Brett wrote to unit owners that "[i]rritations left in the body of unit owners which remain in the Corporation are of such a significance and to such an extent that I now conclude that the sole appropriate resolution of this matter is to move to a termination of the governance of the Corporation under the *Condominium Act*." This is a reference to the procedure contemplated by s. 41 of the *Condominium Act*. To simplify, when this procedure is properly invoked, the *Act* ceases to apply to the property and the owners become tenants in common in the same proportions as their common interests.

Although a resolution to terminate was passed by votes representing over 80% of the units at a general meeting of owners in December of 1998, the termination did not become effective as the required documents were not accepted for registration by the Registrar of Condominiums.

In late December of 1999, 2475813 Nova Scotia Limited, acting through its President, Mr. Brett, petitioned the Board of Directors to call a meeting of owners for the purpose of considering resolutions (referred to as a Resolutions A and B) authorizing the sale of the property to 2475813 Nova Scotia Limited, for $13,200,000 and the construction of an addition to the property. The Board convened the requested meeting on January 12, 2000 and the resolutions were declared passed on the affirmative vote of the units owned or controlled by the Brett interests. However, for reasons that will become apparent, no agreement of purchase and sale has been entered into in furtherance of these resolutions.

For ease of reference, I will often refer to the various corporations owned or controlled by Mr. Brett as well as the units effectively under his control as the Brett interests and the appellants collectively as the individual unit holders. . . .

[Cromwell J.A. then reviewed the history of the litigation to date, and then dealt at length with the holdings of the chamber judge, and the issues on appeal as outlined above.]

Fiduciary Duty:

The appellants sought a declaration that:

> Section 40 of the Condominium Act does not apply to authorize or permit a non-arms' length acquisition of the condominium property, including the units, by a unit owner owning a majority of interest in the common elements and particularly by a unit owner who is deemed to be the declarant legally or beneficially owning an interest [of] 80% or more of the common elements.

In support of this position, they allege that the power conferred upon the Brett interests as holder of 80% control is subject to fiduciary duties owed to all the unit holders. The chambers judge held that there was nothing in the *Act*, the Declaration or the circumstances which prohibit any person from owning more than one unit or exercising the voting rights attached to the ownership of more than one unit.

As I have said, I agree with the judge's interpretation of the statute and the Declaration and with her rejection of the appellants' arguments based on statutory interpretation. However, to my mind, that is not the end of the matter. It does not follow automatically, in my view, that this transaction is one that may be authorized under s. 40 if there is some legal constraint on the exercise by the majority interest of its authority to approve the transaction. The key question is whether, in the circumstances of this case, the majority power may lawfully be used to approve this transaction.

For reasons which I develop, I have concluded that Mr. Brett owes fiduciary duties to act in the interests of the unit owners and the corporation. These duties arise from the particular circumstances and relationships present in this case in light of the power conferred by s. 40 of the *Act*. The fundamental duty of a fiduciary is loyalty to those to whom the duty is owed. It follows that Mr. Brett, having regard to his fiduciary position, cannot exercise his voting control in a situation such as this where his interest and duty conflict and where he stands to benefit personally from the exercise of the authority. However, a transaction which would otherwise be contrary to the fiduciary's duty may be undertaken if all unit holders give their informed consent or if the transaction receives court approval.

I will now set out in detail my reasons for this conclusion.

(a) Overview of Fiduciary Principles:

The parties have been helpful in referring us to some of the authorities, both in Canada and the United States, which deal with particular fiduciary duties that may arise in relation to condominiums. I have found it helpful, however, to place these authorities in the context of the general development of fiduciary principles.

Fiduciary principles have roots in equity extending to the early eighteenth century: see, for example, *Hodgkinson v. Simms*, [1994] 3 S.C.R. 377 at 407. As LaForest J. put it in *Hodgkinson*, the fiduciary duty is one of a ". . . species of a more generalized duty by which the law seeks to protect vulnerable people in transactions with others.": at 405. While many judicial decisions, including a series of cases in the Supreme Court of Canada, have given the law of fiduciary duties a well-defined analytical structure, one of their key elements is flexibility. Consistent with their equitable origins, fiduciary principles may be moulded to meet the needs of justice in a wide variety of circumstances. As LaForest J. said in *Canson Enterprises Ltd. v. Boughton & Co.*, [1991] 3 S.C.R. 534 (S.C.C.) at 585–6, ". . . the maxims of equity can be flexibly adapted to serve the ends of justice as perceived in our days. They are not rules that must be rigorously applied but malleable principles intended to serve the ends of fairness and justice." Or, as Laskin J. said in *Canadian Aero Services Ltd. v. O'Malley*, [1974] S.C.R. 592 (S.C.C.) at 609 ". . . new fact situations may require a reformulation of existing principle to maintain its vigour in the new setting."

In keeping with this thinking, the Supreme Court of Canada has emphasized that the categories of fiduciary should not be considered closed: see *Guerin v. R.*, [1984] 3 S.C.R. 335 (S.C.C.) at 384 and *Hodgkinson*, *supra*, at 408. Fiduciary obligations do not only arise in certain categories of relationships, such as principal and agent. A fiduciary duty may arise from the nature of a relationship in specific circumstances even though, in general, a fiduciary duty would not otherwise exist. The question in such cases is whether fiduciary obligations ". . . arise as a matter of fact out of the specific circumstances of that particular relationship.": *Hodgkinson*, at 408.

In considering whether a fiduciary relationship exists, the fundamental purposes of this equitable concept must be kept in mind. These purposes, which have been expressed in both scholarly and judicial writing, are to protect and foster the integrity of important social relationships and institutions where one party is given power to affect the important interests of another. The fiduciary principle helps to prevent, and may provide redress for abuse of such power, thereby ensuring that interdependence does not lead to subjugation. This point was made by Leonard I. Rotman, "*Fiduciary Obligations*", in Mark Gillen and Faye Woodman (eds), *The Law of Trusts A Contextual Approach* (2000), 739–806 at 742:

> Fiduciary law has its origins not only in equity but also in public policy. *The creation of fiduciary doctrine may be traced to the need to protect the continued existence of certain types of relationships within a given society. . . .*
>
> *Fiduciary law exists to preserve the integrity of socially valuable or necessary relationships that arise as a result of human interdependency.* Maintaining the viability of an interdependent society requires that interdependency be closely monitored to avoid the potential for abuse existing within such relations.
>
> *Protecting the integrity of socially valuable relationships requires that those who possess the ability to affect others' interests be prevented from abusing their powers for personal gain. . . .* (Emphasis added.)

To similar effect, LaForest J. said in *Hodgkinson, supra*, at 422:

> The desire to protect and reinforce the integrity of social institutions and enterprises is prevalent throughout fiduciary law. *The reason for this desire is that the law has recognized the importance of instilling in our social institutions and enterprises some recognition that not all relationships are characterized by a dynamic of mutual autonomy, and that the marketplace cannot always set the rules. . . .* (Emphasis added.)

An analytical framework for determining whether a fiduciary relationship exists was set out in the dissenting judgment of Wilson J. in *Frame v. Smith*, [1987] 2 S.C.R. 99 (S.C.C.) and subsequent cases have recognized it as helpful in identifying new categories of fiduciary relationships: see *Hodgkinson* at 408. Factors such as a person's scope for the exercise of some discretion or power, the right to exercise that power unilaterally to affect another's legal or practical interests and peculiar vulnerability to the exercise of that discretion are *indicia* of a fiduciary relationship: see *Hodgkinson* at 408. For present purposes, I find particularly helpful the statement of the characteristics of a fiduciary relationship as set out by McLachlin J. (as she then was), in her reasons in *Canson* at 544, where, citing Cooter and Freedman, "The Fiduciary Relationship: Its Economic Character and Legal Consequence" (1991), 66 N.Y.U.L. Rev. 1045 she identified three characteristics, each of which is potentially relevant here. First, fiduciary relationships are often characterized by a separation between ownership and control. Here, the individual unit holders own their units, but in relation to a sale of the condominium development, control is conferred by the *Act* on those with 80 per cent of the votes. Second, fiduciary relationships are often characterized by the fiduciary having open-ended obligations in that specific conduct and definite results are not stipulated. Here, the authority granted by the *Act* to those controlling 80 per cent of the votes is conferred in broad terms with no direction or guidance concerning the purposes of or the circumstances justifying its use. Third, a fiduciary relationship is often characterized by what Cooter refers to as "asymmetry of information concerning acts and results". By this I take it he means that the fiduciary is better informed than those to whom the duty is owed about the actions to be taken and their results. On the facts of this case, the chambers judge found that the directors failed to provide adequate information concerning the proposed transaction to the unit holders at large and there can be no doubt that Mr. Brett was in a much better position to evaluate the proposed sale than the individual unit holders.

Where, as here, it is alleged that the fiduciary obligation arises out of the specific circumstances of a particular relationship, the key consideration is whether, in all of the circumstances, one party could reasonably have expected that the other would act in the former's best interest with respect to the subject matter at issue: *Hodgkinson* at 409. This does not preclude the fiduciary from acting in the joint interests of him or herself and those to whom the duty is owed. LaForest J in *Hodgkinson* at 407 specifically approved the statement of Professor P. D. Finn in "Contract and the Fiduciary Principle" (1989), 12 U.N.S.W.L.J. 76 at 88 that the key consideration is whether ". . . the one has the right to expect that the other will act in the former's interests (*or, in some instances, in their joint interest*) to the exclusion of his own several interests." (Emphasis added.)

I emphasize that, in this case, the alleged fiduciary duty is one that arises, if at all, from the *specific* circumstances of a particular relationship. We are not here concerned with an attempt to establish a new category of fiduciary relationships or even to establish some generalized fiduciary duty in relation to the exercise of the power conferred by s. 40 of the *Act* to authorize sales of the property. The analysis here concerns the specific circumstances and relationships in this particular transaction and nothing more.

(b) Fiduciary Duties and the Condominium

I noted earlier that the fundamental purpose of the law relating to fiduciaries is to reinforce the integrity of social institutions and enterprises. It follows from this that fiduciary principles must be applied in the context of condominium law in a manner which will further strengthen the integrity of the socially valuable relationships upon which the condominium is based. In doing so, there are two potentially conflicting considerations. The first is that condominiums under the *Act* are created by a reasonably comprehensive statutory code and the courts should, therefore, be cautious about imposing rights and duties which are not expressly included: see, for example, *Eberts v. Carleton Condominium Corp. No. 396*, [2000] O.J. No. 3773 (Ont. C.A.); *National Trust Co. v. Grey Condominium Corp. No. 36*, [1995] O.J. No. 2079 (Ont. Gen. Div.); *Ceolaro v. York Humber Ltd.* (1994), 37 R.P.R. (2d) 1 (Ont. Gen. Div.). The other is that a residential condominium will often be the owner's home. Decisions of the corporation intimately affect their everyday lives as well as their financial security: see *Carleton Condominium Corp. No. 347 v. Trendsetter Developments Ltd.* (1992), 94 D.L.R. (4th) 577 (Ont. C.A.) at 586.

The stated legislative purpose of the *Act* reflects the need "to facilitate the division of land into parts that are to be owned individually, and parts that are to be owned in common", "to provide for the use and management of such properties" as well the need "to expedite the dealings therewith." see s. 2. It is, therefore, important in determining whether fiduciary obligations arise in particular circumstances to reflect the necessary balance between business efficacy required for effective management of the collective interests and security of individual ownership. It also must be remembered that, while condominium ownership has many of the attributes of individual ownership of real property, it is not identical with it. The joint ownership of common areas and the joint management of the property, which are central features of the condominium, necessarily limit or modify rights normally associated with the ownership of real property: see Oosterhoff and Rayner, *Anger and Honsberger Law of Real Property* (1985), vol. II, at s. 3902.

Effective joint ownership and management require that differences of opinion about what is in the best interests of the condominium be resolved and decisions taken in a timely fashion. The sale provisions in the *Act* and the provisions for termination of the government of the property in s. 41 are parts of the statutory scheme which reflect this requirement. They establish mechanisms for taking actions which fundamentally alter the condominium relationship. The ownership interests of unit holders are provided with considerable protection while recognizing that such extreme measures as a sale or termination of the condominium are, in fact, appropriate and necessary in some circumstances.

With respect to a sale of the property, the legislation requires a strong majority of unit holders (i.e., 80%) to approve, which, in most circumstances, will reflect a widely held view among the unit holders that the proposed sale is in their interest and the interest of the corporation. Aside from assuring that proper information is presented to them, as the chambers judge required in this case, there is no need, in most cases, for any other protection for unit owners. Their own, well-informed decision, by a strong majority, to authorize the sale vouches for the fact that it is in their interest and in the interest of the corporation. The fact that unanimity is not required guards against unreasonable obstruction and promotes business efficacy that might be thwarted by a requirement for unanimity, but the requirement for 80% approval vouches for the fact that the transaction is, reasonably viewed, in the unit holders' collective interest.

What, if any, aspects of the specific circumstances and relationship here would suggest that (to paraphrase LaForest J. in *Hodgkinson* at 409) Mr. Brett would reasonably be expected by all unit holders to act in their collective best interests?

First, I think it is relevant that Mr. Brett is not just a person who owns or controls the votes of 80% of the units. There is no dispute that Mr. Brett owned and controlled Brett Pontiac Buick GMC Limited. It was the declarant-owner of the property which became the condominium. There is also no dispute that he is the sole shareholder and an officer and director of the numbered company. At the relevant time, it owned 150 units and persons related to Mr. Brett owned 13 units. The numbered company was also the intended purchaser of the property.

The respondents have not submitted that it is necessary for the purposes of this aspect of the case to pay attention to the various separate corporate entities. It is apparently acknowledged that Mr. Brett is the directing mind of all of them. This is clear as regards the numbered company from his letter to the unit owners dated

December 3, 1998 in which Mr. Brett refers to "... the interests which [he] owned or controlled" and to the fact that he "... commenced an extensive process of repurchasing units through 2475813 Nova Scotia Limited."

Mr. Brett was also a director of the condominium corporation. While corporate law principles cannot simply be imported into condominium law without careful analysis, I note the strong line of authority that directors of corporations, including the directors of condominium corporations, owe fiduciary duties to the corporation to act in its best interests. As the Court put it in *Trendsetter, supra*, at p. 590, directors "... owe a fiduciary duty to the corporation and not to any other individual or organization. If they fail in the exercise of that duty, they are subject to the full force of the law." To the same effect, in the context of business corporations, Laskin J. said in relation to the fiduciary duties of directors in *O'Malley* at p. 610:

> *What these decisions indicate is an updating of the equitable principle whose roots lie in the general standards that I have already mentioned, namely, loyalty, good faith and avoidance of a conflict of duty and self-interest.* Strict application against directors and senior management officials is simply recognition of the degree of control which their positions give them in corporate operations, a control which rises above day-to-day accountability to owning shareholders ... *It is a necessary supplement, in the public interest, of statutory regulation and accountability which themselves are, at one and the same time, an acknowledgement of the importance of the corporation in the life of the community and of the need to compel obedience by it and by is promoters, directors and managers to norms of exemplary behaviour.* (Emphasis added.)

There is considerable authority for the view that the developer of a condominium owes certain fiduciary duties to those who purchase units in the property. While the existence and extent of these duties will depend on several considerations including the relevant legislation and the terms of the declaration and by-laws of the condominium, it has been widely accepted that the developer has certain fiduciary obligations to protect the interests of all unit owners, present and prospective, as well as the interests of the condominium corporation: see for example A. H. Oosterhoff and W.B. Rayner, *Anger and Honsberger Law of Real Property* (1985) vol II, s. 4008.1; *Condominium Plan No. 86-S-36901 v. Remai Construction (1981) Inc.* (1991), 84 D.L.R. (4th) 6 (Sask C.A.) at 14–19 and 22; *York Condominium Corp. No. 167 v. Newrey Holdings Ltd.* (1981), 32 O.R. (2d) 458; 122 D.L.R. (3d) 280 (Ont. C.A.). It bears noting, however, that this duty does not require the fiduciary to act in the interests of a few dissident unit holders but in the interests of all of the unit holders: see *e.g. Carleton Condominium Corp. No 347 v. Trendsetter Developments Ltd., supra*, at 585–6.

In summary, Mr. Brett's involvement in the development and marketing of the condominium and his position as one of the directors of the condominium corporation tend, in my view, to support a reasonable expectation on the part of the corporation and all the unit holders that he would act in their collective best interest.

The controlling position of the Brett interests is a highly relevant consideration: see *Trendsetter* at p. 586. Section 40 of the *Act* provides that, subject to the approval of the encumbrancers, votes representing 80% of the units may authorize a sale of the property. This power, conferred by the statute, places other unit owners in a position of special vulnerability as the facts of this case amply demonstrate. The Brett interests have the power under the *Act* to dispossess dissenting unit holders by forcing them to sell their homes. In my view, unit holders would reasonably expect that this power would not be exercised by a director of the condominium corporation or the controlling mind of the developer other than in their collective best interest.

Brooke J.A., in *Frontenac Condominium Corp. No.1 v. Joe Macciocchi & Sons Ltd.* (1975), 67 D.L.R. (3d) 199 (Ont.C.A.) spoke of what the "average person" understands about condominiums. I think his words are helpful on the issue of the reasonable expectations of unit holders in these circumstances. He said (at p. 202) that the average person would understand that ". . . no one, including the developer, would be in a position to put his economic interests against the interest of the group so far as joint ownership, management or enjoyment of the property was concerned, save through a mortgage or similar interest."

Section 40 of the *Condominium Act* gives a broad authority to 80% of the unit holders to approve a sale of the property. The existence of such a power granted by statute does not in any way preclude the existence of a fiduciary duty on the part of one individual exercising it. It may, in fact, be a key consideration in finding that such a duty exists. This is well illustrated by *Guerin, supra*, where the Supreme Court of Canada found that the Crown had fiduciary duties to Indians in its exercise of certain powers under the *Indian Act*. In rejecting the Crown's argument that the express statutory conferral on the Crown of a broad, discretionary power ousted the jurisdiction of the courts to intervene, Dickson J., for the majority, said at 384:

> *This discretion on the part of the Crown, far from ousting, as the Crown contends, the jurisdiction of the courts to regulate the relationship between the Crown and the Indians, has the effect of transforming the Crown's obligation into a fiduciary one.* Professor Ernest Weinrib maintains in his article *The Fiduciary Obligation* (1975), 25 U.T.L.J. 1, at p. 7, that "the hallmark of a fiduciary relation is that the relative legal positions are such that one party is at the mercy of the other's discretion." Earlier, at p. 4, he puts the point in the following way:
>
> > [W]here there is a fiduciary obligation] there is a relation in which the principal's interests can be affected by, and are therefore dependent on, the manner in which the fiduciary uses the discretion which has been delegated to him. The fiduciary obligation is the law's blunt tool for the control of this discretion.
>
> I make no comment upon whether this description is broad enough to embrace all fiduciary obligations. *I do agree, however, that where by statute, agreement, or perhaps by unilateral undertaking, one party has an obligation to act for the benefit of another, and that obligation carries with it a discretionary power, the party thus empowered becomes a fiduciary. Equity will then supervise the relationship by holding him to the fiduciary's strict standard of conduct.* (Emphasis added.)

As noted, the *Act's* requirement that a sale be authorized by 80% of the unit owners will, in most circumstances, provide adequate assurance that the sale is in the collective best interests of the unit owners and the condominium corporation.

The situation is completely different in the circumstances of this case, however. Where, as here, Mr. Brett controls 80% of the votes and the sale is to himself, it is apparent that the authorization of the sale by that majority does not carry with it any assurance that the sale is in the best interests of the unit holders or of the corporation. If unconstrained by equitable principle, the sale provisions in the Act would permit the unit owner with the controlling interest to impose a sale in his or her own interest and dispossess the others. Expressed in the language of fiduciary obligations, the controlling unit holder, in effect, is (i) approving a sale to himself; (ii) has control over the property interests of others which is conferred by the *Act* in open-ended terms; and (iii) is much better informed than the individual unit holders about the wisdom and benefits of the proposed sale.

In my view, there are several strong indicators of a fiduciary obligation on the part of Mr. Brett in the particular circumstances and relationships present in this case. Would the existence of such an obligation serve to enhance the integrity of the condominium and further the purposes of the *Condominium Act*?

The *Act*, it is true, provides a measure of protection to the dissenting unit holders by providing, in ss. 40(5) and 40(6) that they may have the market value of the property determined by arbitration and recover any deficiency from the owners who voted for the sale. I do not think, however, that these statutory provisions oust all other protections for unit holders that arise from general legal principles. I agree with the chambers judge that such would be ". . . an extreme view." Moreover, these rights are premised on the assumption that the sale was indeed in the best interests of the unit holders as a group as assured by at least 80% approval of it. They do not provide an answer to the problem that, where a controlling owner is selling to himself, there is no such assurance.

In my view, the imposition of a fiduciary relationship in these circumstances will further, rather than hinder, the implementation of the purposes of the *Act* to the extent that the existence of this duty requires some further assurance beyond the 80% approval that the proposed sale is, in fact, in the best interests of both the unit holders and the corporation.

I return to what was identified by LaForest J. in *Hodgkinson* as the key question. In all the surrounding circumstances, would the unit owners reasonably have expected that Mr. Brett would exercise his voting control with respect to a sale of the property in the best interests of all unit owners? In my view they would. Mr. Brett was the controlling mind of the developer who sold units in this condominium. He was a director of the condominium corporation. His voting control gave him a broad, discretionary power to affect not just the property rights of the other owners, but to dispossess them of their homes. That power made the other unit holders vulnerable to its exercise in matters affecting their vital interests. He was the directing mind and owner of the purchaser in the transaction for which his voting control assured approval. In these circumstances, justice and the proper administration of a condominium require that Mr. Brett be subject to a fiduciary obligation which disentitles him from authorizing this sale without other objective assurances that it is in the best interests of the corporation and the unit holders as a whole.

I conclude, therefore, that Mr. Brett was subject to two fiduciary duties. First, by virtue of being the owner and controlling mind of the developer and having effective voting control of the corporation, he owed a fiduciary duty to all of the unit holders not to use that voting control to authorize a sale of the property where, as here, their interests and his could conflict. Second, by virtue of Mr. Brett's position as a director of the corporation, he owed a fiduciary duty to the corporation of a similar character.

Having identified a fiduciary relationship, it is necessary to be specific about its nature and extent and its implications for a vote of unit owners authorizing a sale of the property pursuant to s. 40 of the *Act*. The term fiduciary refers to many different types of relationships and may give rise to a range of different duties. As was pointed out by Fletcher-Moulton L.J. in *Coomber, Re*, [1911] 1 Ch. 723 (Eng. C.A.) at 728–29:

> . . . *Fiduciary relations are of many different types*; they extend from the relation of myself to an errand boy who is bound to bring me back my change up to the most intimate and confidential relations which can possibly exist between one party and another . . . All these are cases of fiduciary relations, and the Courts have again and again, in cases where there has been a fiduciary relation, interfered and set aside acts which, between persons in a wholly independent position, would have been perfectly valid. . . . *[I]n some minds there arises the idea that if there is any fiduciary relation whatever any of these types of interference is warranted . . . Of course that is absurd. The nature of the fiduciary relationship must be such that it justifies the interference.* (Emphasis added.)

It is, therefore, necessary to define with precision the nature and extent of the duties attached to the particular fiduciary relationship. In this case, the only issue is whether the fiduciary relationship gave rise to any restriction on the right of Mr. Brett to proceed with the sale to himself which was authorized by voting his 80% interest as a unit holder.

I mention this to emphasize that, in this case, it is not necessary to determine the precise extent of the fiduciary duties, if any, that may arise in relation to other aspects of the condominium corporation's decision-making. We are dealing here only with the question of a resolution to sell the property in a situation in which the intended purchaser also has sufficient voting control to achieve the required authorization under the *Act* and where the person effectively exercising voting control is also the controlling mind of the developer and a director of the condominium corporation.

We are not here concerned with an alleged breach of the duty to act in the best interests of the corporation or the unit holders. The fact that such a duty exists does not lead to the conclusion that the proposed transaction is not in the best interests of all of the unit holders or of the corporation itself. That issue is not before the Court in these proceedings. The duty to act in the best interests of the unit holders does not mean that only actions to which they all assent may be considered in their best interests. The duty to act in the best interests of the corporation does not mean that only actions to which all unit holders agree may be taken. Moreover, there is nothing before the Court which would justify a conclusion that the proposed transaction is or is not in the best interests of the unit holders collectively or of the corporation.

The existence of the fiduciary duties does, however, limit the ability of the fiduciary to impose the sale on dissenting unit holders where the transaction is such that the fiduciary's duty and interest conflict and where the fiduciary stands to benefit from the transaction. This conflict and potential for personal gain on the part of Mr. Brett coupled with his voting control take away the assurance normally provided by the favourable vote of a strong majority that the decision is, in fact, in the best interests of the unit holders and of the corporation.

The fiduciary, in these circumstances, does not stand in the same position as a true trustee. The obligation is not to act selflessly, but to act in the best interests of all the unit holders and of the corporation. The duty does not preclude personal profit from the decision, but rather it precludes profit at the expense of others. Mr. Brett, through his company, has a large investment in the condominium. His right to act as he sees fit to protect that investment must not be unduly restricted. He must not be disenfranchised and the condominium corporation must not be left in an irreconcilable deadlock. What the fiduciary principle requires in the context of s. 40 of the *Act* and the circumstances of this case is some substitute mechanism for assuring that the proposed sale is in the interests of the unit holders and the corporation, an assurance normally provided by the vote of a strong majority of the unit holders.

In my view, that assurance may be provided here in each of two ways. First, the informed consent of all of the unit owners other than the Brett interests, in addition to the support of the Brett interests, would provide the assurance sought by the statute that the transaction is in the best interests of the unit holders as a group. Failing that, such assurance could be provided by approval of the transaction by an application to the Supreme Court of Nova Scotia on notice to all unit holders, the corporation and registered encumbrancers. The role of the Court on such an application would be to determine whether the proponents of the transaction have shown that, having regard to the circumstances of, and future prospects for, the condominium, there are sound reasons supporting the view that the proposed transaction is in the interests of unit holders and the corporation collectively. Having regard to the fact that the sale will result in the termination of government of the property (s. 40(3)), a Court hearing such an application for approval may find it helpful to consider some or all of the matters relevant to Court ordered termination as set out in the authorities and s. 43(2) of the *Act*.

For the reasons I have given, I would set aside paragraph 1 of the declaration made by the Chambers judge in file S.H. No. 162065 and in its place make the following declaration:

> 1. That, in the circumstances of the fiduciary duties owed by Mr. Brett to the unit holders and the to the corporation, a sale of the property of Halifax County Condominium Corporation No. 151 to a corporation under his control may be authorized pursuant to section 40 of the Condominium Act by unanimous approval of the other unit holders or by order of the Supreme Court of Nova Scotia.

The order in S.H. No. 162174 should be amended accordingly. To that extent, I would allow the appeals. As noted earlier, I would dismiss the cross-appeals. . . .

QUESTIONS AND COMMENTS

1. Theodore Rotenberg, in a scathing critique of the Court of Appeal decision, notes that directors of a condominium corporation, as with any other company, have fiduciary duties toward the corporation. That is trite law. Moreover, wrongful conduct by majority shareholders that prejudices a minority can be remedied by what is referred to as a derivative action. In addition:

> While Cromwell J.A. recognizes . . . that Brett in his capacity as a director of the condominium owes a legal duty, he does not follow through on this analysis and hold all the directors to their statutory duty to the corporation. The reasons why Cromwell J.A. does not pursue this point, it is respectfully argued, are legally questionable. At the end of the day Brett controls more than 80 per cent of the units, and he alone can decide whether the condominium can be sold either to his company at a higher price, or to a third party. Because Brett can in theory "dispossess" of the other owners through a sale, Cromwell J.A. therefore perceived a unique need to impose on that person a duty that deprived him of his statutory right to have the vote determined according to the Act. But the Act allows 80 per cent of the unit owners to do precisely this very thing. Nothing conceptually changes because one entity owns 80 per cent. The 80 per cent majority may by law always "dispossess" the minority; what the Act says is that this majority may not "dispossess" the minority by accepting an unfair price, a question that can be answered if the Board is required to obtain more information. . . .
>
> Only in the rarest of cases, and then only on unique and fact-specific events, will a director or officer owe a legal duty to shareholders. Moreover, while corporate law has always protected against the abuse of non-arm's length transactions by majority shareholders, it historically did so within the doctrine of a breach by the directors or officers of their fiduciary duties to the corporation, not by imposing a fiduciary duty on the majority shareholder. Shareholders wearing their ownership hats have historically owed no general duty to each other; otherwise, they would have chosen to be partners. The corporate structure is designed to separate out duties from ownership, so that there is no need for one owner to owe a legal duty to another owner or for a director or officer to owe a duty to anyone but the corporation.
>
> The author respectfully suggests that this corporate distinction works equally well in the condominium setting. Suppose, for example, that the offer had been from an arm's length third party and the directors had obtained evidence that this offer was at the best possible price and terms. Suppose further that only Brett wished to sell to recover his financial investment while every other unit owner was a resident who opposed a sale because they did not want to become tenants of a new owner or be forced to move. In this situation, it is respectfully suggested, the court would see the conflict as that of two competing self-interests, and leave the statutory scheme undisturbed. Thus, if Brett controlled 80 per cent of the units, the sale would be approved by the owners and could not be successfully challenged in court. The only reason that the court neutralizes Brett 's voting rights (requiring either the informed consent of all other owners or a court motion) is because Brett is both buyer and seller. This by itself is not a reason to impose a fiduciary duty on him when a proper legal duty to remedy the mischief already exists. Even a

Brett-controlled board can be required to perform due diligence. In a worst case scenario, the court could appoint a monitor (at the corporation's cost) to review the Board's due diligence. Imposing a fiduciary duty on one owner was unnecessary in this case.

T. Rotenberg, "The False Fiduciary" (2001) 41 R.P.R. (3d) 130, at 133-4.

2. Was justice done in this case? Why were the protections in s. 40 thought to be inadequate?

3. Analyse what might transpire in next phase in this controversy from a Coasean perspective.

4. Co-operatives are an additional form of concurrent ownership. In essence, the co-operative structure is used to provide members with a shared right of use and governance over the subject-matter of the association. In the context of housing, two main forms exist. Under one, so-called equity co-ops, members contribute financially to the enterprise in order (i) to defray costs associated with the premises (repairs, mortgage payments and so forth) and (usually) (ii) to augment the value of their investment. Commonly, though not universally, the property is owned by the corporation and the members hold shares in that entity. The right to live in a specific unit is contained in an occupancy agreement.

Additionally, co-op housing has developed on a non-profit basis as a means of providing low-cost accommodation coupled with the ability to participate in the governance of the community. The nature of non-profit co-operative housing in Ontario was described by the Divisional Court in *David B. Archer Co-operative Inc. v. D'Oliveira* 2003 CarswellOnt 1434 (Div. Ct.) at para. 5:

> [N]on-profit housing co-operatives . . . are democratic organizations governed by the *CCA* and the by-laws adopted by its Board of Directors and confirmed at general meetings of the membership. . . . Co-operatives operate on the principle of "one member, one vote". Boards of Directors are elected by and from among the members of the Co-operative. The members can requisition general meetings of members and also meetings of the Board of Directors. The members can remove all or some of the Board of Directors, and replace them. The relationship between the members and the Co-operative is based on a concept of collective ownership. Members have a right to participate fully in the collective operation and management of the Co-operative. Indeed, they are expected to. Members individually have a right of occupancy and security of tenure, *provided* they comply with the by-laws.

In Ontario, the residents in a non-profit co-operative are not governed by the *Tenant Protection Act*, or the *Commercial Tenancies Act: Co-Operative Corporations Act*, R.S.O. 1990, c. C.35, s. 171.7. The internal rules of the corporation provide the main source of rights and duties. Moreover, the return on investment is designed to be minimal. Under s. 171.2(1), "[a] non-profit housing co-operative shall not distribute or pay any of its property to its members during its existence or on its dissolution" except for "(a) amounts owed to the member including patronage returns and interest on a member loan or any other loan from the member at a rate not exceeding the prescribed maximum annual percentage; or (b) reasonable amounts for goods or services provided by the member": s. 171.2. On the bright side, the co-op is the landlord!

9. ALTERNATIVE CONCEPTIONS OF SHARED OWNERSHIP

In this part I present three forms of shared ownership. The first relates to communal property held by religious groups. There have been, and still are, many forms of such holdings in Canada. The communal ownership regime adopted among Hutterite colonies is used to illustrate the idea.

Second, Aboriginal conceptions of sharing are considered. It will be remembered that in *Delgamuukw v. British Columbia* [1997] 3 S.C.R. 1010, 1997 CarswellBC 2358, 1997 CarswellBC 2359, the Supreme Court of Canada endorsed the conventional view that Aboriginal title was communal. Yet, the judgments do not develop the meaning of that idea. Moreover, that characterization pertains only to the common law right itself. It says nothing about the rules/entitlements/duties and so forth that apply on Aboriginal lands among members of the Aboriginal collective *inter se.* James sakej Henderson's description of the approach to land among the Mikmaw of Canada's east coast invites some dramatic contrasts with the rules studied in this book and the premises of property law found in Chapter 1.

A final example concerns ownership of computer software, where the issues of common and private property have emerged anew.

Hofer v. Hofer
[1970] S.C.R. 958, 1970 CarswellMan 51, 1970 CarswellMan 80

Ritchie J.:

This is an appeal from a unanimous judgment of the Court of Appeal of Manitoba [(1967), 65 D.L.R. (2d) 607] affirming a judgment rendered by Dickson J. dismissing the appellants' action whereby they had sought a declaration that they were still members of the Interlake Colony of Hutterian Brethren (hereinafter referred to as the "Interlake Colony") together with an order for the winding-up of the affairs of that Colony, the appointment of a receiver to gather in its assets, an accounting of all assets and liabilities of the Colony, and a direction that its assets should be distributed equally among each of the appellants and the respondents.

The judgment of the Court of Appeal also affirmed the order and declaration made by Dickson J. allowing the respondents' counterclaim and declaring that the appellants were no longer members of the said Interlake Colony and were not entitled to any portion of the real and personal property of that Colony, and directing them to vacate permanently the real property owned by the Colony and deliver up possession of all personal property owned by it which may have come into their possession.

The appellants' main contention is that the provisions of the Articles of Association governing the conduct of the Interlake Colony to which all parties had agreed, in so far as they relate to the holding of meetings and the expulsion of members, were not complied with when the appellants were allegedly expelled from the Colony and that as a result of that unauthorized expulsion they and their families have been made to suffer abuses and indignities inconsistent with the concept of harmonious living as a Colony so that it is no longer possible for the Colony to continue and that a receiver should be appointed to wind up its affairs. In the alternative, the plaintiffs say that the Articles of Association purport to give ministers of the Church who are not parties thereto unlimited power and control over the life and property of the plaintiffs and that the agreement is therefore contrary to public policy and should be declared null and void.

In the further alternative the plaintiffs say that the Articles of Association create a form or partnership and that the provisions thereof whereby the plaintiffs purport to have been deprived of their property rights amount to a penalty or forfeiture against which a court of equity ought to grant relief by way of dissolution of the association. . . .

The origins of the dispute between the appellants and the respondents are rooted in religious controversy and in the differences of opinion existing between the respective parties as to the true nature of the religious way of life to which they had all subscribed. The history of the Hutterian Brethren has been analyzed in the Courts below, but it appears to me to be necessary for the purpose of these reasons to outline briefly those features of the Hutterian way of life which have a direct bearing on the matters here in issue.

The history of the Hutterian Brethren goes back to the 15th century when they adopted their own form of medieval monasticism as a result of which they were persecuted in Europe and after migrating from one country to another on that continent for nearly three centuries, a small group came to the United States. Today there are 15,000 Hutterites in North America living in colonies or communities of Brethren each of which is usually limited to about 100 people and in all of which the members devote themselves to a communal form of life in which private ownership is not recognized and all real and personal property is held for the purposes of the colony and for the benefit of each and all members thereof. Membership of the Hutterian Brethren Church is a prerequisite to membership in all such colonies and the daily tasks of the members are related to and an expression of their religious beliefs.

When it is decided that a Hutterian Colony is getting to be too large, the practice is for that colony to form a "daughter" colony and it is thus that the Interlake Colony was formed by the Rock Lake Colony of Hutterian Brethren. When the decision was made to create this new Colony, and after approval had ben obtained from all other colonies, it was agreed among the members of the Rock Lake Colony that they should divide into two groups, neither of which could decide whether it wished to go to the new Colony or not. This was finally decided by lot and the assets of Rock Lake were divided roughly in proportion to membership. 2,080 acres of land were then purchased for the new Colony at Interlake at $76 an acre and although these lands are referred to in the Articles of Association, which were later signed by all members of the Interlake Colony, as being held in the names of the defendants Zachariah Hofer, Jacob Hofer and Jacob S. Hofer as joint tenants and not as tenants in common as trustees for the new Colony, this is nevertheless not in accord with the certificate of title of the Interlake Colony's lands which shows them to be registered in the names of three members of the Rock Lake Colony who later, in July 1966, executed a document declaring that they had no right to tile or interest in the lands in question for their own use and benefit, but only upon trust to hold the same for the benefit of Zachariah, Jacob and Jacob S. Hofer.

It appears to me to be clear from the above that the lands in question are not held in trust for the individual members of the Interlake Colony but for the Colony as a whole and that the individual members have no beneficial interest whatever in the land upon which their Colony is situated. This is true of all colonies of Hutterian Brethren and it is in conformity with the acceptance of the principle of community of property which is fundamental to the Hutterite religion. The acceptance of this principle by all the parties to this action is made manifest by the provisions of paras. 30, 31 and 32 of the Articles of Association of the Interlake Colony to which all parties subscribed. These paragraphs read as follows:

> 30. All the property, real and personal, of said Colony from whomsoever, whensoever and howsoever it may have been obtained, shall forever be owned, used, occupied, controlled and possessed by the said Colony for the common use, interest and benefit of each and all members thereof, for the purposes of said Colony.
>
> 31. All the property both real and personal, that each and every member of the said Colony has or may have, own, possess or may be entitled to at the time that he or she joins such Colony, or becomes a member thereof, and all the property both real and personal, that each and every member of the said Colony may have, obtain, inherit, possess or be entitled to, after he or she becomes a member of the said Colony, shall be and become the property of the said Colony for the common use, interest and benefit of each and all of the members thereof as aforementioned.
>
> 32. None of the property, either real or personal, of the said Colony shall ever be taken, held, owned, removed or withdrawn from the said Colony, or be granted, sold, transferred or conveyed otherwise than by the Board of Directors, and if any member of the said Colony shall be expelled there from, or cease to be a member thereof, he or she shall not cease to be a member thereof, he or she shall not have, take, withdraw, grant, sell, transfer or convey, or be entitled to any of the property of the said Colony, or any interest therein; and if any member of the said Colony shall die, be expelled therefrom or cease to be a member thereof, he or she, or his or her representatives, heir-at-law, legatees or devisees or creditors or any other person shall not be entitled to, or have any of the property of the said Colony, or interest therein, whether or not he or she owned, possessed or had any interest in or to any of the property of the said Colony at the time he or she became member thereof, or at any time thereafter, or had given, granted, conveyed or transferred any property or property interest to the said Colony at any time.

I am satisfied after having read a great deal of the material submitted by both sides in this case and after having considered the analysis thereof as contained in the judgments of the learned trial judge and the Court of Appeal, that the Hutterite religious faith and doctrine permeates the whole existence of the members of any Hutterite Colony and in this regard I adopt the language which the learned trial judge employed in the course of his reasons for judgment where he said:

> To a Hutterian the whole life is the Church. The colony is a congregation of people in spiritual brotherhood. The tangible evidence of this spiritual community is the secondary or material community around them. They are not farming just to be farming — it is the type of livelihood that allows the greatest assurance of independence from the surrounding world. The minister is the spiritual and temporal head of the community.

It follows in my view that, notwithstanding the fact that the Interlake Colony was a prosperous farming community, it cannot be said to have been a commercial enterprise in the sense that any of its members was entitled to participate in its profits. The Colony was merely an arm of the church and the overriding consideration governing the rights of all the Brethren was the fulfilment of their concept of Christianity. To the Hutterian Brethren the activities of the community were evidence of the living church. In this context I find it impossible to view the Interlake Colony as any form of partnership known to the law.

In the case of *Barickman Hutterian Mutual Corpn. v. Nault et al.* [[1939] S.C.R. 223], this Court decided that the appellant corporation was a "farmer" within the meaning of *The Farmers' Creditors Arrangement Act, 1934*, and in the course of his reasons for judgment, Sir Lyman Duff had occasion to comment on the Hutterite way of life, saying, at p. 227:

> . . . as a religious community they aim at pursuing a way of life broadly conforming, as they conceive, economically as well as spiritually, to the "Christian principles described in the New Testament." Their tenets and their practice include ownership of all things in common, the administration of their goods and their worldly affairs generally by person nominated by themselves for that purpose. It is freely admitted, and it may be assumed, that the arrangements for the administration of their temporal affairs are only a means to enable them to govern their lives by what they believe to be the primitive Christian plan.

The plan to form the Interlake Colony had been conceived some time in 1960 and the seven members of the Hofer family who are now parties to this action all signed the Articles of Association in May of 1961.

There is no allegation anywhere in the pleadings that the Articles of Association were signed otherwise than as the free act and deed of the appellants. Although I conclude that the parties signed the Articles because they were Hutterian Brethren, I cannot find any submission made on behalf of the appellants to the effect that they were signed under any kind of duress. In this regard Mr. Justice Freedman in the course of his reasons for judgment in the Court of Appeal observed:

> Another characteristic of Hutterianism — one that is of special significance in the context of the present controversy — is that all members renounce in favour of the Colony any right to private property. They acknowledge that all property of the Colony and of its

members is forever to be owned and controlled by the Colony for the common use, interest and benefit of the members thereof. It is pertinent to note that an express affirmation of the renunciation of private property is part of the adult baptismal service and also of the marriage service. The plaintiffs, all of them baptized as adults, and all of them married have thus twice acknowledged this basic feature of Hutterian life and their obligation to abide by it. In addition, as is indicated below, the Articles of Association signed by them expressly recorded and declared their acceptance of this same principle, rule, and obligation. . . .

. . . [I]n my view adherence to the Hutterite faith was a prerequisite to membership in the Colony which by its very nature was required to be composed exclusively of Hutterian Brethren and their families. I am also of opinion that the decision as to whether or not any individual was a Hutterian Brethren so as to be entitled to continue as a member of the community was a decision which could only be made by the Hutterite Church. In the present case, as I have indicated, the decision to expel the appellants from the Colony was made by the Church, but it had the effect of making the appellants ineligible for continued membership in the Colony. It follows from this that the appellants' contention to the effect that the Articles of Association were not properly complied with in regard to expulsion is without merit, and in my view the alternative plea with respect to the unlimited power and control of the ministers of the Church over the personal life and property being contrary to public policy, is equally invalid. . . .

There is no doubt that the Hutterian way of life is not that of the vast majority of Canadians, but it makes manifest a form of religious philosophy to which any Canadian can subscribe and it appears to me that if any individual either through birth within the community or by choice wishes to subscribe to such a rigid form of life and to subject himself to the harsh disciplines of the Hutterian Church, he is free to do so. I can see nothing contrary to public policy in the continued existence of these communities living as they do in accordance with their own rules and beliefs, and as I have indicated, I think it is for the Church to determine who is an who is not an acceptable member of any of its communities.

For all these reasons, as well as for those so fully expressed by the learned trial judge and the Court of Appeal, I would dismiss this appeal with costs.

Hall J.:

I agree with my brother Ritchie that this appeal must be dismissed for the reasons given by him but with this reservation that in certain circumstances involving minors or others under disability as well as those who have not subscribed to the Articles of Association, the unlimited power and control of the ministers of the limited power and control of the ministers of the Church under the Articles of Association might be void as being contrary to public policy. The question to this extent should be left open at this time. The appellants here were adults and as my brother Ritchie points out they all signed the Articles of Association of their own free will.

While agreeing that this appeal fails, I must, however, express my abhorrence at the treatment accorded the appellants by their erstwhile co-religionists. The insults and gross indignities inflicted on these men and their families as disclosed in the evidence is foreign to the whole concept of life in Canada, whether lived in community or not. The rigidity of the law as declared in *Free Church of Scotland (General Assembly) v. Overtoun (Lord); Macalister v. Young* [[1904] A.C. 515.], which deprives a dissident group, whether small or large, of all rights in the property and the assets of a religious community should, I think, be softened by appropriate legislation under which a formula might be devised so as to permit a dissenter and his family to leave a community such as this one in dignity and with a severance adjustment corresponding in some degree to the contribution made by the dissident member in his years of service to the community. As it is, the dissenter, as my brother Pigeon points out, cannot even claim ownership to the clothes he is wearing as he departs. . . .

NOTE

Martland and Judson JJ. concurred. The concurring judgment of Cartwright C.J., Spence J. concurring, has been omitted, as has Pigeon J.'s dissenting opinion.

A.J. Esau, "The Judicial Resolution of Church Property Disputes: Canadian and American Models" (2003) 40 Alta.L.Rev. 767, at 768–70 [footnotes omitted]

I have been engaged for some time in an examination of the litigation of membership and property disputes at Hutterite colonies, particularly in Manitoba. Property entitlements are often linked to membership issues because the property of religious associations is usually held in trust for the beneficial use of members of the particular association. Thus in *Hofer v. Hofer*, the Supreme Court of Canada upheld the excommunication of a number of Hutterites at a Manitoba colony who had switched their religious faith from the Hutterite Church to the Radio Church of God. Once their expulsion from membership was affirmed, the court upheld the basic principle that the former members had no property claim to a *pro rata* share of the colony assets. More recently, the Supreme Court judicially reviewed the expulsion of a number of Hutterites on the ground of insubordination at another Manitoba colony [the *Lakeside* case]. The court asserted that when voluntary associations expel members, the court may judicially review the process to ensure that the association has first followed its own internal rules, whether customary or written, and then secondly that the process complies with the basic principles of natural justice in terms of notice and fair opportunity to be heard by an unbiased tribunal. The court voided the expulsion of the Hutterites because they allegedly had not been given adequate notice that their expulsions would be considered at a meeting of members. Following this decision, the colony in question simply returned to the drawing board, gave proper notice, and then proceeded to expel the members again. A Manitoba court upheld these expulsions and applied the basic principle that, so long as the expulsions were valid, the ex-members had no claim to any *pro rata* share of the assets of the colony, even though they had lived their whole lives on the colony.

However, the second round of the *Lakeside* case also dealt with the authority of the majority to expel the minority and was related to a considerable amount of additional Hutterite litigation that arose as a result of a schism in the Schmiedeleut branch of the Hutterite Church, which occurred after the Supreme Court decision. The immediate schism related to a basic disagreement as to whether the Senior Elder of the tribe had been voted out of office. Under that dispute lay a host of controversies related to the Schmiedeleut affiliation with the Bruderhof, a small group of Christian communalists centred in the Eastern United States with arguably more liberal cultural norms, and yet more authoritarian leadership styles as compared to the traditional Hutterites. There was also a host of allegations relating to various financial transactions involving the Senior Elder and other Hutterite managers and the alleged violations of the traditional anti-litigation norm of Hutterites. Today, there are about one hundred Hutterite colonies in Manitoba, which before the schism would have been associated as one branch of the wider Hutterian Brethren Church, but are now almost evenly divided into two separate groups, which I call Group One (those that supported the Senior Elder) and Group Two (those who claimed the Elder had lost a vote of confidence at a meeting of the wider Schmiedeleut Conference). During the course of the schism, various colonies were sometimes internally divided, with two opposing groups attempting to gain or retain control of the colony assets. Ultimately, the courts in Manitoba were engaged with disputes at the following colonies: Oak Bluff, Rock Lake, Huron, Cypress and Sprucewood.

When a few members of a religious group allegedly switch religions or are deemed by some hierarchy or by some majority vote of a congregation to have violated some norm of the group, it may not seem all that controversial to suggest that a court may enforce the expulsion of the ex-members from the use of the group's community property. Similarly, when the courts award all the property to a small minority on the ground that the larger majority has breached the affiliation or doctrinal trust on which the property must be held, the adequacy of the law may again come into question. In the wake of the schism in the Schmiedeleut, the highest level of the Hutterite Brethren Church, composed of all three tribes, passed a new Constitution and recognized Group Two as the true representatives of the Schmiedeleut. Group One, on the other hand, argued that the passing of the new Constitution was irregular and that they were the true Schmiedeleut. Most of the litigation took place at Group Two colonies where a minority of Group One loyalists attempted to seize or control assets under the theory that they were the true beneficiaries of the common property of the colony.

The courts in Manitoba came perilously close to having to adjudicate the competing property entitlements of the two groups. Would it be all-or-nothing, where one group of Hutterites would in effect be entitled to the property of every colony, because every colony was deemed to be entrusted to those properly affiliated with the higher Hutterite Brethren Church? And which group would that be? Would it be all-or-nothing, but only as determined by a majority vote at each individual colony as to whether the colony would affiliate with either Group One or Group Two? Or, could it be that a court would recognize *both* groups as within the Hutterite umbrella, properly so-called, and actually divide property on a *pro rata* basis between the two groups instead of using the all-or-nothing approach? If the court did that, would it be violating the internal norms of the Hutterian community that departing or excommunicated members are not entitled to a share? In part, this article examines the jurisprudence on church property entitlements in Canada to test whether there is any support for a division of assets, rather than an all-or-nothing approach.

The reason that the Manitoba courts were spared, at least for now, from allocating or dividing Hutterite property in the context of a schism, was that the defendants in the *Lakeside* case, who later were accepted into Group Two, were in the end unwilling to counterclaim for the assets because this would violate their religious convictions against bringing lawsuits. The leaders of Group One and Group Two came to an agreement several years later: in order to stop all the litigation at other colonies, assets would be divided at these colonies on a *pro rata* basis. While litigation arose about the meaning and application of that agreement, the voluntary agreement to divide assets ended the main litigation surrounding the schism. However, the issue of how courts deal with church property in the wake of a schism is hardly an answered question, even in the Hutterite context.

J.s. Youngblood Henderson, "Mikmaw Tenure in Atlantic Canada" (1995) 18 Dal. L.J. 196, at 232–5 [footnotes omitted]

The relationship between the Míkmaq and the land embodies the essence of [an] intimate sacred order. As humans, they have and retain an obligation to protect the order and a right to share its uses, but only the future unborn children in the invisible sacred realm of the next seven generations had any ultimate ownership of the land. In the custom of the Míkmaq, the Santé Mawíomi was and is the trustee of the sacred order and territory for the future generations. Part of its duty is to regulate the natural resources of Míkmáki among the allied people and through the Nikmanen trading customs increase the bio-diversity. This is more of a management right to ensure discipline in consumption of the resources, rather than the concept of ownership.

Inherent in this sacred order is the conviction that the resources had to be renewed as well as shared. Rather than managed, which implied human domination, the Míkmaq developed rituals for sharing or harmonizing the human and spiritual realms. These renewal rituals and ceremonies brought the people and the land into balance thereby achieving basic subsistence and material well-being. These rituals and ceremonies created a harmony which emphasized stability and the minimization of risk for the harvesting of the resources rather than growth and the accumulation of wealth. The quest for harmony also created the need for diversification by trade and modification of habitats thereby developing surplus capacities and sharing.

Sharing of resources is the equivalent of consensus in creating governing structures. Just as the managers of shared resources sustain them, the leaders of communities, districts, and nations are managers of shared authority and spaces. Sharing of the harvest is neither random nor universal, but based on patterns, kinship and correspondence. It is an honour, a duty and a privilege; those who have a little more to share may gain prestige, influence and dignity.

Managing a space and sharing is viewed as an integral part of the ethical development of a Míkmaq. It is important for the development of family, friendship and self. Míkmaq see no distinction between collective or individual interests. The goal of creating a sustaining space and a sharing and caring community in which everyone can participate and belong is the ultimate interest. Everyone must come to this realization; they must come to understand the beauty and dignity of maintaining, protecting, and renewing their family space and traditions. Through this developmental process, Míkmaq establish a clear understanding of oneself as a human and in relation to the environment. Through this process, Míkmaq understand the needs of the biological realms and the ethical significance of their desires, freedoms and responsibilities.

In Míkmaq language, "*netukulimk*" refers to the responsibility of a Míkmaq user to be mindful that the Life Givers and the keepers have consented to the conditional use of the resources being managed. The prime condition was sharing of the harvest among the communities of the place. Feasts were an integral part of the sharing of the resources. Míkmaw could rarely understand the possessive nature of the Europeans. Moreover, sharing manages demand, and serves to mitigate many of the incentives to consume a resource.

These sentiments of sharing are generated by the Míkmaw concept of space. Space is described as spirals of a relative network of family sites and paths among resources. Within the Míkmaq words for particular locations are encoded not only the use of the land but also its special significance for families. Certain families or peoples had "rights" to use certain animals, plants, materials and access sites (hunting and fish traps) because of their particular relationship. Their indigenous narratives, comprised in songs and stories, and the ceremonies associated with each space, link the present and the past.

Conceptually, these differences reflect the difference between the Míkmaw worldview and the European worldview. In the Euro-British world, sharing has traditionally been seen as a threat to the personal autonomy or choice, thus a threat to legal rights and responsibilities. Altruism, a European morality of sharing and sacrifice within a particular relationship, is usually seen as inconsistent with the modern theory of individualism.

The Míkmaw view provides an alternative vision of a proper social order. The indigenous nations were generous, sharing whatever they possessed with an open handedness that amazed the immigrants. Greed was always considered a wrong, while private management of the resource, along with a bundle of rights and duties, was the legal norm.

Míkmaw "property rights" were usually obtained through kinship rather than use or purchase. They were endowments or legacies. Everyone has relative claims, through birth and marriage, to the use of a great variety of sites and resources, which can also be claimed by others on the same ground. Often the word for kinship and ownership are the same. It is inconceivable in a Míkmaq worldview, however, that an individual could claim an exclusive use or entitlement to a particular site or that any family could lose their relationship to a site. This concept applied both to men and women.

Renewal ceremonies also emphasize the relationship between space and claims in the indigenous Míkmaw worldview. The places of certain ceremonies are bounded to a specific location and can be transported. They symbolically reiterated and renewed the ancient relationships between a particular family and people and a particular ecosystem. The grounding in a particular ecosystem has been categorized as "geopiety".

In the renewal ceremonies, various family claims are continually being asserted and adjusted. While each renegotiation affects family allegiance and identity, this is seen as relatively unimportant; the crucial factor is the periodic equalization of shared rights among the collective families.

This process of resource adjustment created considerable self-serving confusion among the Europeans. They deduced that the indigenous Míkmaw tenure systems were essentially collective or communal and that no individual owned the land. Indeed that is the case, but what created the perplexity was that those resources were a private family entitlement. The confusion is unraveled when one understands that in an indigenous tenure the role of the family or individual is more managerial rather than proprietary.

What is not understood by outsiders was that each family or personal claim to a resource or space is based on permissions by local, regional or national consensus. While these boundaries may be imprecise or shifting to an outsider, they are part of a complex tenure based on sharing rather than exclusive use. Very few distinctions exist between personal and real property. If these distinctions exist it is to give dignity and honour to the Míkmaw or family by sharing them, *e.g.*, to exhibit their generosity to others.

The sacred order itself is never individualized. The tenure is held for future generations. A family or an "individual" might enjoy wide administrative authority over a resource or space (a *legacy*) but they have no right to withhold the use of the resources or the products of their use to another insider. The system of kinship relations unites everyone in a web of complementary rights and responsibilities. Each person is simultaneously a parent, child, uncle, aunt or cousin to others. This implicit order is non-hierarchical and reproduces itself without the need to accumulate more people, land, or goods. The continued strength of any claim in the indigenous tenure is a function of sound management and generosity. These legacies are "strong" enough to create incentives to conserve, but "weak" enough to create incentives to share.

The Míkmaq legacy became vested in a family or person after seven generations of sound management and generosity. A right of succession or inheritance is based on actual services to the elderly managers as well as management of the resource, rather than kinship. . . .

QUESTIONS

1. Compare the concepts described by Professor Henderson with the fundamental precepts of Canadian property law.

2. Do the concepts described above comport with the law governing Aboriginal rights set out in *Delgamuukw*? See further K. McNeil, "Extinguishment of Aboriginal Title in Canada: Treaties, Legislation, and Judicial Discretion" (2001-2) 33 Ottawa L.Rev. 301, at Part II, *passim*.

P. J. Weiser, "The Internet, Innovation and Intellectual Property" 103 Colum. L. Rev. 534 (2003) at 534, 568–83 [footnotes omitted]

The Internet continues to transform the information industries and challenge intellectual property law to develop a competition policy strategy to regulate networked products. In particular, inventors of "information platforms" that support the viewing of content — be they instant messaging systems, media players, or Web browsers — face a muddled set of legal doctrines that govern the scope of available intellectual property protection. This uncertainty reflects a fundamental debate about what conditions will best facilitate innovation in the information industries — a debate most often played out at the conceptual extremes between the "commons" and "proprietary control" approaches to the Internet and intellectual property policy. . . .

The Current Battle in Intellectual Property Theory: The Commons Model Versus Proprietary Control

Intellectual property protection constitutes a first line of competition policy that provides open access to information platforms. By making access more difficult, intellectual property law can, like antitrust, discourage cooperation where competition would lead to more innovation and consumer choice. Alternatively, by allowing access . . . intellectual property law affords companies a self-help remedy that facilitates open access without the regulatory intervention characterized by antitrust or telecommunications regulation. How intellectual property law should function in this regard continues to spark heated debates between advocates of the commons and proprietary control models, each of which pushes for very different approaches. In particular, commons advocates point to the spectacular growth of the Internet based on open source technologies, claiming that this growth could never have occurred against a backdrop of proprietary standards. By contrast, the proprietary control model underscores that a dominant firm may be able to develop a uniform and continually evolving platform standard that can push the industry forward. . . .

The Commons Model. — In the current struggle over how the Internet will develop, the commons camp is often associated with the "cyber hacker rallying cry" that "information wants to be free." In the Internet world, the information infrastructure has been mostly free, as many of the main software programs that support Internet content are nonproprietary and distributed on an open source basis.

Under the open source model, no individual firm benefits directly from the creation of the product, as all open source licenses allow for free access to the source code for the software program. This model harkens back to the early era of software development, where developers viewed software not as a commercial product but as one that should be shared with society. Under this model, the sharing and cloning of software — like the free reuse of academic ideas — are viewed as natural and healthy. Most famously, the GNU-Linux operating system (which uses the GPL license developed by Richard Stallman) has capitalized on the popularity of open source development among independent programmers and continues to grow in popularity for use on Internet servers. Under open source development, programmers collaborate on the creation of software programs and allow all users free access to the programs' source codes. Within the realm of open source development, the GPL license reflects a particular vision of "free software," as it insists not only on openness, but prevents developers from using free software in conjunction with proprietary products. By contrast, software merely placed in the public domain enables any firm to repackage it — even with modest improvements — and sell it as proprietary software.

The commons model's fervent commitment to openness reflects the perspective that, at least in the information industries, proprietary control is not necessary or desirable to encourage innovation. This perspective finds support in a substantial body of literature that makes clear that a large number of all innovations would take place in the absence of any intellectual property protection. Indeed, then-Professor Breyer highlighted this point over thirty years ago, well before the wave of added intellectual property protection in recent legislation and judicial decisions. For advocates of the commons model, the legacy of the Internet's development provides even further reason for questioning the centrality of broad intellectual property protection as a means of spurring valuable innovation. In fact, this history underscores that intellectual property protection raises the costs of invention to would-be innovators.

In the Internet world, the commons model looks to the increasing use of open source licenses as well as standard-setting committees to regulate the development of new technologies. In particular, some argue that these institutions allow for a "bottom-up" system of norms and traditions that should replace current legal tools, such as intellectual property laws. Just recently, the World Wide Web Consortium (W3C), a group that endorses standards for the Web, took a commons model approach, concluding that patented technologies would not be permitted in that group's official standards. To the extent that the W3C is able to develop new standards without recognizing proprietary ownership — and licensing fees — for Internet technologies, it will offer a model of how the commons approach can govern an Internet where proprietary ownership is neither necessary nor desirable.

The commons model rests in part on the "path dependence" theory that network markets will almost invariably rely on a single standard. On this view, an information technology standard may become dominant not because of its relative merits and greater degree of technological sophistication, but because it came first. Among economists, there is an ongoing debate over which (if any) markets reflect this phenomenon, with the case study of the standard for keyboards — the choice of the "QWERTY" over the "Dvorak" model — being a topic of notable disagreement. Those invoking this example to demonstrate the path dependence phenomenon suggest that the Dvorak standard provided users with the ability to type more quickly, but lost out to the established QWERTY standard because QWERTY came first. On this view, QWERTY, which initially served the purpose of slowing down typists so that they would not jam the keys, benefited greatly from the fact that users continued to be locked into an inferior standard. Following the logic of this argument, path dependence theory claims that markets characterized by strong "network effects" — that is, where "the utility a user derives from consumption of the good increases with the number of other agents consuming the good" — are also ones where one standard or product will achieve dominance because its established value network will, once dominant, never be replaced.

In network markets where a single standard emerges as dominant, economists suggest that the market has "tipped" to a particular product. This tipping phenomenon does not suggest that the product is inherently superior, but merely that a sufficient mass of users have adopted it and are locked into it because the switching costs of moving to an incompatible product are sufficiently great to deter a move. In particular, where a company can build a proprietary value network and prevent others from gaining the critical mass to provide an alternative product — say, by refusing to make its dominant product compatible with rivals — it can establish a durable monopoly.

For intellectual property policy, the commons model suggests that the Internet and information industries function best when they are open and not susceptible to control by a proprietary firm. As commons model advocates explain it, the Internet's openness enables firms to introduce innovations without worrying about gaining access to the basic platform. Consequently, this model envisions that, by introducing proprietary standards to the Internet and allowing firms to exercise control over its development, the Internet will not only fail to realize its potential, but may fail as an emerging communications medium. On this view, reverse engineering should always be allowed. . . .

The Failings of the Commons Theory. — As an initial matter, it is important to understand that the commons conception of the Internet rests in large part on a community that can enforce norms committed to open architecture and nonproprietary development. In today's Internet, however, the conditions that once nurtured that environment — considerable government support, a small community of stakeholders, and the absence of proprietary development — are increasingly no longer in place. Thus, to the extent that the development of information platforms reflects the lessons of managing other common resources, the increasing number of interested parties and diversity of interests suggests that solutions like open source development and the creation of common, nonproprietary standards will become the exception, not the norm.

Second, in terms of standard-setting committees, there are good reasons to believe that the stance taken by the W3C in rejecting the use of patented technologies may be the exception in the Internet's future development. Most other standard-setting bodies . . . have tolerated patented technologies, provided that they are licensed at reasonable and nondiscriminatory terms. This acceptance reflects the fact that stakeholders in the Internet's development and participants in standard-setting bodies have become more diverse and focused on profits. Nonetheless, standard-setting committees like . . . the W3C still can provide a forum for negotiating between different proprietary interests and developing common standards that will benefit the entire community, but this role differs from a communal commitment to certain values. Finally, even to the extent that groups like the W3C reject the use of patents in their endorsed standards, it remains to be seen when and how this will be enforced.

Third, the claim that network markets will invariably tip to a single standard and thus platform standards should not be protected under intellectual property law overlooks important reasons why network competition can occur. Significantly, the tipping prediction does not take account of the likely scenario where a network effect (the value of additional customers) declines at some point in time because the network size has reached critical mass or where a rival network is able to overcome the first mover's initial advantage. In markets where the critical mass is small enough to accommodate multiple providers of a particular product or service, multiple firms will compete at the platform level, as they currently do in the market for video game consoles and cell phones. Moreover, it is quite clear that consumers' demand for variety can compensate for a lack of a strong network effect.

Finally, it merits noting that some advocates of a commons model, like Professor Lessig, view open source not as an optimal goal for economic regulation, but as a means of protecting broader public values. This endorsement is consistent with a recognition that experiences like the fragmentation of the Unix operating system suggest that strong government support may be necessary to support research and development of open and common standards. This response, after all, is the typical one for a public goods problem and was the posture that the U.S. government took during the earlier years of the Internet's development. Professor Lessig's writings, however, acknowledge that such levels of government support are unlikely, leading him to concede the likelihood that the Internet will increasingly be subject to the control of proprietary firms.

The Proprietary Control Model and the Schumpeterian Justification

The success of the Internet and open source development represents a fundamental challenge to the traditional model of proprietary software development, which still remains dominant and is exemplified (for good and bad) most clearly by Microsoft. Microsoft and other proprietary software vendors, unlike open source developers, do not rely on a dispersed community of developers contributing to a common project, but rather on a team of developers centralized at corporate headquarters. As such, proprietary firms expect to recoup substantial returns from their work and do not release the source code of their products for free (or at all, in most cases). Not surprisingly, such firms challenge the open source movement as foolhardy and counterproductive.

The Proprietary Control Model. — Believers in the proprietary control model view the challenges for supremacy among firms as part of an ongoing battle that the late economist Joseph Schumpeter called "creative destruction." On this view, any market power will be temporary, as a new technology will ultimately knock off every incumbent. As two commentators recently put it, Schumpeter's hypothesis is that "firms compete through innovation for temporary market dominance, from which they may be displaced by the next wave of product advancements." Although this position rests on three analytically distinct propositions, the strong version of the Schumpeterian contention is that monopolies are both acceptable and necessary to facilitate technological innovation. . . .

The proprietary control model embraces a rich tradition in intellectual property theory that without an appropriate incentive, inventors will not create new innovations. In the Internet context, both the Clinton Administration's embrace of strong intellectual property protection in the e-commerce area and the endorsement of the so-called "business method patents" reflect this perspective. In particular, this vision places a premium on ensuring that firms reap proprietary rewards for innovating in the Internet environment. On this view, proprietary control of intellectual property does not simply provide the important incentive to invent new technologies, but also ensures that such technologies are maintained carefully and put to their best use.

Relying on proprietary development provides a clear answer to a potential weakness of the open source model: It boasts a clear ability to develop and deploy talented leadership and coordination to ensure that a standard does not fragment within a wide user base. . . . Second, a real weakness of open source projects is that they do not generate any direct financial benefits for their inventors, so they can fall prey to the public goods problem of being subject to underinvestment. Sun's experience with its open Java standard (which relies on a "community source license" that is somewhat similar to the open source model) is telling on this score: "For all its hype and popularity, Java has made more money in direct software sales for competitors than for the company that invented it." To be sure, the invention of Java did bring considerable recognition and indirect benefits to Sun, but it is far from clear that Sun has appropriated enough benefits from Java to justify its investment in the technology.

In the computer world, the proprietary model relies on the ability of software firms to maintain close control over the application programming interfaces (APIs) for the programs they develop. These interfaces can be analogized to the "gear teeth, levers, pulleys, and belts that physical machines use to interoperate." In the context of proprietary software, control over these interfaces enables the platform owner to maintain control over its platform both defensively — to prevent rivals from cloning its products — as well as offensively — to prevent competitors from creating compatible products. In the government's antitrust case against Microsoft, for example, the government submitted evidence of a manager's statement that "'to control the APIs is to control the industry'" and established that Microsoft's monopoly rested, in part, on its firm control of its APIs.

The Failings of the Proprietary Control Theory. — Even though there are important reasons to allow for the development of proprietary technologies as a means of facilitating new innovations, there also are reasons to doubt Schumpeter's claim that complete control over an industry's standards by large firms like Microsoft will be good for consumers and will be checked by future innovation. As an initial matter, current economic thinking suggests that while larger firms may enjoy some advantages in fostering innovation, the Schumpeterian hypothesis is not supported by the evidence, in part because smaller firms tend to be more efficient, productive, and aggressive about pursuing innovation. Accordingly, Scherer and Ross conclude that "[t]echnological progress thrives best in an environment that nurtures a diversity of sizes and, perhaps, especially, that keeps barriers to entry by technologically innovative newcomers low."

Second, to the extent that some size may be helpful in more established industries, there is reason to think that this is less true for the information industries where there is a greater need for intellectual capital than physical capital, and the fixed costs necessary for research and development are considerably less. Cisco, for example, despite its overwhelming size, relies on outsourcing for much of its research and development through purchasing start-up companies. Similarly, start-up companies financed by venture capitalists have undertaken risky research and development efforts that have produced a significant number of patents.

Finally, two critical concerns underscore why pure Schumpeterian thinking should not drive intellectual property policy. First, although monopolies such as IBM and Microsoft may be dethroned at some point, the exercise of monopoly power in the meantime — which may well be several decades — still can injure consumers. In the case of Microsoft, its ability to maintain and control closed, *de facto* industry standards — as opposed to open, *de jure* ones endorsed by standard-setting committees — has enabled it to exercise great influence over other companies. In particular, Microsoft has used this control to undermine support for Sun Microsystems's open Java standard.

A second, and more fundamental, criticism of the proprietary control model is that numerous studies have shown that incumbent monopolies will often fail to develop and deploy radically new technologies, sometimes even using their current monopolies to distort and thwart the process of competing to introduce more innovative products. Indeed, this very concern motivated AT&T's decision not to embrace the Internet at its creation as well as to slow roll the deployment of wireless telephone service. Thus, an important role for regulation is to "keep entry open so that challengers with new ideas can force the pace of innovation."

In short, the commons model's basic insight — that the Internet provided an avenue for entry because of its open and common platform — can still guide the

Internet's future even with an allowance for the development of proprietary standards. By contrast, an acceptance of dominant platform standards may create more value for the individual companies, but can leave the Internet community itself worse off, where would-be improvers lack access to the particular proprietary platform (or only gain access under onerous terms). To solve this problem and to facilitate continued innovation in the Internet environment will require a combination of private and public responses: the leadership of standard-setting committees, enlightened self interest on behalf of companies in the marketplace, some well-targeted government subsidies for basic research, and appropriate antitrust and telecommunications regulation, as well as . . . a well-formulated and coherent intellectual property policy.

The GNU General Public License (GPL)
Version 2, June 1991
Copyright 1989, 1991 Free Software Foundation, Inc.
59 Temple Place, Suite 330, Boston, MA 02111-1307 USA

Everyone is permitted to copy and distribute verbatim copies of this license document, but changing it is not allowed.

Preamble

The licenses for most software are designed to take away your freedom to share and change it. By contrast, the GNU General Public License is intended to guarantee your freedom to share and change free software — to make sure the software is free for all its users. This General Public License applies to most of the Free Software Foundation's software and to any other program whose authors commit to using it. (Some other Free Software Foundation software is covered by the GNU Library General Public License instead.) You can apply it to your programs, too.

When we speak of free software, we are referring to freedom, not price. Our General Public Licenses are designed to make sure that you have the freedom to distribute copies of free software (and charge for this service if you wish), that you receive source code or can get it if you want it, that you can change the software or use pieces of it in new free programs; and that you know you can do these things.

To protect your rights, we need to make restrictions that forbid anyone to deny you these rights or to ask you to surrender the rights. These restrictions translate to certain responsibilities for you if you distribute copies of the software, or if you modify it.

For example, if you distribute copies of such a program, whether *gratis* or for a fee, you must give the recipients all the rights that you have. You must make sure that they, too, receive or can get the source code. And you must show them these terms so they know their rights.

We protect your rights with two steps: (1) copyright the software, and (2) offer you this license which gives you legal permission to copy, distribute and/or modify the software.

Also, for each author's protection and ours, we want to make certain that everyone understands that there is no warranty for this free software. If the software is modified by someone else and passed on, we want its recipients to know that what they have is not the original, so that any problems introduced by others will not reflect on the original authors' reputations.

Finally, any free program is threatened constantly by software patents. We wish to avoid the danger that redistributors of a free program will individually obtain patent licenses, in effect making the program proprietary. To prevent this, we have made it clear that any patent must be licensed for everyone's free use or not licensed at all.

The precise terms and conditions for copying, distribution and modification follow.

TERMS AND CONDITIONS FOR COPYING, DISTRIBUTION AND MODIFICATION

0. This License applies to any program or other work which contains a notice placed by the copyright holder saying it may be distributed under the terms of this General Public License. The "Program", below, refers to any such program or work, and a "work based on the Program" means either the Program or any derivative work under copyright law: that is to say, a work containing the Program or a portion of it, either verbatim or with modifications and/or translated into another language. (Hereinafter, translation is included without limitation in the term "modification".) Each licensee is addressed as "you".

Activities other than copying, distribution and modification are not covered by this License; they are outside its scope. The act of running the Program is not restricted, and the output from the Program is covered only if its contents constitute a work based on the Program (independent of having been made by running the Program). Whether that is true depends on what the Program does.

1. You may copy and distribute verbatim copies of the Program's source code as you receive it, in any medium, provided that you conspicuously and appropriately publish on each copy an appropriate copyright notice and disclaimer of warranty; keep intact all the notices that refer to this License and to the absence of any warranty; and give any other recipients of the Program a copy of this License along with the Program.

You may charge a fee for the physical act of transferring a copy, and you may at your option offer warranty protection in exchange for a fee.

2. You may modify your copy or copies of the Program or any portion of it, thus forming a work based on the Program, and copy and distribute such modifications or work under the terms of Section 1 above, provided that you also meet all of these conditions:

a) You must cause the modified files to carry prominent notices stating that you changed the files and the date of any change.

b) You must cause any work that you distribute or publish, that in whole or in part contains or is derived from the Program or any part thereof, to be licensed as a whole at no charge to all third parties under the terms of this License.

c) If the modified program normally reads commands interactively when run, you must cause it, when started running for such interactive use in the most ordinary way, to print or display an announcement including an appropriate copyright notice and a notice that there is no warranty (or else, saying that you provide a warranty) and that users may redistribute the program under these conditions, and telling the user how to view a copy of this License. (Exception: if the Program itself is interactive but does not normally print such an announcement, your work based on the Program is not required to print an announcement.)

These requirements apply to the modified work as a whole. If identifiable sections of that work are not derived from the Program, and can be reasonably considered independent and separate works in themselves, then this License, and its terms, do not apply to those sections when you distribute them as separate works. But when you distribute the same sections as part of a whole which is a work based on the Program, the distribution of the whole must be on the terms of this License, whose permissions for other licensees extend to the entire whole, and thus to each and every part regardless of who wrote it.

Thus, it is not the intent of this section to claim rights or contest your rights to work written entirely by you; rather, the intent is to exercise the right to control the distribution of derivative or collective works based on the Program.

In addition, mere aggregation of another work not based on the Program with the Program (or with a work based on the Program) on a volume of a storage or distribution medium does not bring the other work under the scope of this License.

3. You may copy and distribute the Program (or a work based on it, under Section 2) in object code or executable form under the terms of Sections 1 and 2 above provided that you also do one of the following:

a) Accompany it with the complete corresponding machine-readable source code, which must be distributed under the terms of Sections 1 and 2 above on a medium customarily used for software interchange; or,

b) Accompany it with a written offer, valid for at least three years, to give any third party, for a charge no more than your cost of physically performing source distribution, a complete machine-readable copy of the corresponding source code, to be distributed under the terms of Sections 1 and 2 above on a medium customarily used for software interchange; or,

c) Accompany it with the information you received as to the offer to distribute corresponding source code. (This alternative is allowed only for noncommercial distribution and only if you received the program in object code or executable form with such an offer, in accord with Subsection b above.)

The source code for a work means the preferred form of the work for making modifications to it. For an executable work, complete source code means all the source code for all modules it contains, plus any associated interface definition files, plus the scripts used to control compilation and installation of the executable. However, as a special exception, the source code distributed need not include anything that is normally distributed (in either source or binary form) with the major components (compiler, kernel and so on) of the operating system on which the executable runs, unless that component itself accompanies the executable.

If distribution of executable or object code is made by offering access to copy from a designated place, then offering equivalent access to copy the source code from the same place counts as distribution of the source code, even though third parties are not compelled to copy the source along with the object code.

4. You may not copy, modify, sublicense, or distribute the Program except as expressly provided under this License. Any attempt otherwise to copy, modify, sublicense or distribute the Program is void, and will automatically terminate your rights under this License. However, parties who have received copies, or rights, from you under this License will not have their licenses terminated so long as such parties remain in full compliance.

5. You are not required to accept this License, since you have not signed it. However, nothing else grants you permission to modify or distribute the Program or its derivative works. These actions are prohibited by law if you do not accept this License. Therefore, by modifying or distributing the Program (or any work based on the Program), you indicate your acceptance of this License to do so, and all its terms and conditions for copying, distributing or modifying the Program or works based on it.

6. Each time you redistribute the Program (or any work based on the Program), the recipient automatically receives a license from the original licensor to copy, distribute or modify the Program subject to these terms and conditions. You may not impose any further restrictions on the recipients' exercise of the rights granted herein. You are not responsible for enforcing compliance by third parties to this License.

7. If, as a consequence of a court judgment or allegation of patent infringement or for any other reason (not limited to patent issues), conditions are imposed on you (whether by court order, agreement or otherwise) that contradict the conditions of

this License, they do not excuse you from the conditions of this License. If you cannot distribute so as to satisfy simultaneously your obligations under this License and any other pertinent obligations, then as a consequence you may not distribute the Program at all. For example, if a patent license would not permit royalty-free redistribution of the Program by all those who receive copies directly or indirectly through you, then the only way you could satisfy both it and this License would be to refrain entirely from distribution of the Program.

If any portion of this section is held invalid or unenforceable under any particular circumstance, the balance of the section is intended to apply and the section as a whole is intended to apply in other circumstances.

It is not the purpose of this section to induce you to infringe any patents or other property right claims or to contest validity of any such claims; this section has the sole purpose of protecting the integrity of the free software distribution system, which is implemented by public license practices. Many people have made generous contributions to the wide range of software distributed through that system in reliance on consistent application of that system; it is up to the author/donor to decide if he or she is willing to distribute software through any other system and a licensee cannot impose that choice.

This section is intended to make thoroughly clear what is believed to be a consequence of the rest of this License.

8. If the distribution and/or use of the Program is restricted in certain countries either by patents or by copyrighted interfaces, the original copyright holder who places the Program under this License may add an explicit geographical distribution limitation excluding those countries, so that distribution is permitted only in or among countries not thus excluded. In such case, this License incorporates the limitation as if written in the body of this License.

9. The Free Software Foundation may publish revised and/or new versions of the General Public License from time to time. Such new versions will be similar in spirit to the present version, but may differ in detail to address new problems or concerns.

Each version is given a distinguishing version number. If the Program specifies a version number of this License which applies to it and "any later version", you have the option of following the terms and conditions either of that version or of any later version published by the Free Software Foundation. If the Program does not specify a version number of this License, you may choose any version ever published by the Free Software Foundation.

10. If you wish to incorporate parts of the Program into other free programs whose distribution conditions are different, write to the author to ask for permission. For software which is copyrighted by the Free Software Foundation, write to the Free Software Foundation; we sometimes make exceptions for this. Our decision

will be guided by the two goals of preserving the free status of all derivatives of our free software and of promoting the sharing and reuse of software generally.

NO WARRANTY

11. BECAUSE THE PROGRAM IS LICENSED FREE OF CHARGE, THERE IS NO WARRANTY FOR THE PROGRAM, TO THE EXTENT PERMITTED BY APPLICABLE LAW. EXCEPT WHEN OTHERWISE STATED IN WRITING THE COPYRIGHT HOLDERS AND/OR OTHER PARTIES PROVIDE THE PROGRAM "AS IS" WITHOUT WARRANTY OF ANY KIND, EITHER EXPRESSED OR IMPLIED, INCLUDING, BUT NOT LIMITED TO, THE IMPLIED WARRANTIES OF MERCHANTABILITY AND FITNESS FOR A PARTICULAR PURPOSE. THE ENTIRE RISK AS TO THE QUALITY AND PERFORMANCE OF THE PROGRAM IS WITH YOU. SHOULD THE PROGRAM PROVE DEFECTIVE, YOU ASSUME THE COST OF ALL NECESSARY SERVICING, REPAIR OR CORRECTION.

12. IN NO EVENT UNLESS REQUIRED BY APPLICABLE LAW OR AGREED TO IN WRITING WILL ANY COPYRIGHT HOLDER, OR ANY OTHER PARTY WHO MAY MODIFY AND/OR REDISTRIBUTE THE PROGRAM AS PERMITTED ABOVE, BE LIABLE TO YOU FOR DAMAGES, INCLUDING ANY GENERAL, SPECIAL, INCIDENTAL OR CONSEQUENTIAL DAMAGES ARISING OUT OF THE USE OR INABILITY TO USE THE PROGRAM (INCLUDING BUT NOT LIMITED TO LOSS OF DATA OR DATA BEING RENDERED INACCURATE OR LOSSES SUSTAINED BY YOU OR THIRD PARTIES OR A FAILURE OF THE PROGRAM TO OPERATE WITH ANY OTHER PROGRAMS), EVEN IF SUCH HOLDER OR OTHER PARTY HAS BEEN ADVISED OF THE POSSIBILITY OF SUCH DAMAGES.

END OF TERMS AND CONDITIONS . . .

QUESTIONS

1. How, if at all, does the GPL create a commons (let us call it a cyber-commons)?

2. Do you predict that there will be a tragedy of the cyber-commons?

3. Or, could the privatization of cyberspace produce the converse, namely, a tragedy of the anticommons? Consider this dire prediction:

> In 1992, the Internet opened to commercial exploitation. Relying on the public character of the Internet, and the vast public commons that was created before they ever arrived, commercial operators have grown exceedingly fat. They now have successfully exploited the cyberspace as place metaphor, convincing judges to carve out remarkable new property rights online. By tiny, almost imperceptible steps, commercial operators are enclosing cyberspace. They have mounted a campaign that has eroded cyberspace's public commons, and they threaten to create a genuine digital anticommons.

> We have been lucky. We have witnessed an unprecedented decade of innovation on the Internet. This innovation has flourished in part because of the dot-com bubble, but more importantly because of the commons that cyberspace has provided, and the opportunity that this presents. The cyberspace enclosure movement, dependent on the cyberspace as place metaphor, has not yet closed this off completely. However, if the current approach is not challenged, then little stands between us and an intractable digital anticommons — where low value uses beat out high value ones. It will be almost impossible to change this state. We will not be able to rebundle the various commons interests that we once shared. The opportunity will be lost forever.
>
> We may already be past the point where we can do anything about this. I hope it is still a little way off. But unless we do something, as we all stake out our little private claim in cyberspace, the commons that is cyberspace will be destroyed.
>
> And this would be the real tragedy.

D. Hunter, "Cyberspace as Place and the Tragedy of the Anticommons" 91 Calif. L.Rev. 439 (2003) at 518-9. See also J. Boyle, "The Second Enclosure Movement and the Construction of the Public Domain," 66-SPG Law & Contemp. Probs. 33 (2003).

CHAPTER 10
SERVITUDES OVER PROPERTY

1. INTRODUCTION

We saw in Chapter 1 that rights of ownership are divisible. That theme has recurred in the discussion of the spatial dimensions of property (where surface and subsurface ownership can be in different hands), estates and future interests (where sharing can be sequential), equity (where legal and equitable title may be split) as well as in relation to shared ownership *per se*, and the law of landlord and tenant. It will appear again in connection with the law of mortgages.

This chapter, too, involves a form of divided rights. In this instance, the possessory entitlements of an owner of a freehold or leasehold estate can be burdened with non-possessory rights. I adopt the Roman law term "servitudes" to describe such interests. In English and Canadian law, the term "incorporeal hereditaments" is used to describe most of the property interests discussed in this chapter.

The easement exemplifies this kind of holding. The right of the owner of Blackacre to use a path across Whiteacre is a simple example of an entitlement that can take the form of an easement. As will be seen, many other kinds of easements are recognised.

Other servitudes are considered below. The right to extract minerals or other natural products may be granted as a *profit à prendre*; this is a commonly used device in the oil and gas industry. Restrictive covenants are employed as private planning devices in both commercial and residential development contexts. A rentcharge, a right to exact a periodic payment against a freeholder, hitherto a rather neglected form of incorporeal hereditament in Canada, may also be of use in the context of complex real estate developments.

Some rights possess certain servitude-like features. If I wish to exercise my *Charter* rights of free expression or assembly on public land, can the government prevent this? The answer is no, unless of course that the means chosen by the state to interfere with these guarantees are demonstrably justified. Hence, the *Charter* can be seen as creating rights of access on public property. Might it even be the case (as it is in some American states) that certain rights of access can be exercised on venues such as privately owned (yet functionally *quasi*-public) shopping centres?

2. THE NATURE OF EASEMENTS

Ontario Law Reform Commission, *Report on Basic Principles of Land Law* (Toronto: A.G. (Ont.), 1996) at 126–9 [footnotes omitted]

Anger and Honsberger define an easement as follows:

> An easement is a privilege without profit annexed to land to utilize the land of a different owner (which does not involve the removal of any part of the soil or the natural produce of the land) or to prevent the other owner from utilizing his land in a particular manner for the advantage of the dominant owner.

Following the judgment of the English Court of Appeal in *Re Ellenborough Park* it is conventional to describe easements as comprising four characteristics:

> (1) there must be a dominant and a servient tenement;
>
> (2) an easement must "accommodate" the dominant tenement;
>
> (3) the dominant and servient tenements must "not be both owned and occupied by the same person";
>
> (4) a right over land cannot amount to an easement unless it is capable of forming the subject matter of a grant.

The first two requirements, as well as the definition of easements by Anger and Honsberger quoted above, emphasize that in Anglo-Canadian law an easement cannot exist independently of a benefitted piece of land; it cannot exist in gross. This is unlike . . . the law in the United States where the common law was developed to permit easements in gross. In addition, other jurisdictions, including New Zealand, have provided by statute for easements in gross.

The requirement that an easement must "accommodate" the dominant tenement is very similar, if not functionally the same, as the requirement in the law of covenants that a covenant "touch and concern" the land. In *Re Ellenborough Park* the English Court of Appeal approved Cheshire's statement that:

> one of the fundamental principles concerning easements is that they must be not only appurtenant to a dominant tenement, but also connected with the normal enjoyment of the dominant tenant . . . [W]e may expand the statement of the principle thus; a right enjoyed by one over the land of another does not possess the status of an easement unless it accommodates and serves the dominant tenement, and is reasonably necessary for the better enjoyment of that tenement. . . .

Emphasis on the "normal" enjoyment of the dominant tenement is, however, open to criticism and it may be that the principle should be more broadly stated so that "the test is whether the right makes the dominant tenement a better and more convenient property".

Three issues were considered in *Re Ellenborough Park* in relation to the fourth characteristic of an easement:

> Whether the rights purported to be given are expressed in terms of too wide and vague a character; whether, if and so far as effective, such rights could amount to rights of joint occupation or would substantially deprive the park owners of proprietorship or legal possession; whether, if and so far as effective, such rights constitute mere rights of recreation, possessing no quality of unity or benefit; and on such ground cannot qualify as easements.

The first of these issues does not distinguish an easement from other rights in property but it simply emphasizes that it must be sufficiently certain to be recognized as a property right. The second issue does identify an important characteristic of an easement: that it confers an entitlement falling short of possession. The third issue, which is framed in light of the facts in *Re Ellenborough Park*, does not relate to any general principle. However, it indicates, as also more generally do the other issues, that the courts maintain control over the rights which will be allowed recognition as easements. The list of easements may not be closed, but the courts control entry to the list.

There are two main categories of easements that have received recognition. "Positive" easements give "the owner of land a right himself to do something on or to his neighbour's land". Rights of way, right to take water, and right to have drainage pipes and sewers under land provide examples. "Negative" easements give the owner of land "a right to stop his neighbour doing something on his [the neighbour's] own land". A right to light or a right to create what would otherwise be a nuisance "by the discharge of gases, fluids, or smoke" provide examples.

There are in fact very few negative easements. . . .

QUESTIONS AND COMMENTS

1. Identify whether the following recognised easements are negative or positive:

(a) a right of way over nearby land: *Laurie v. Winch* [1953] 1 S.C.R. 49, 1952 CarswellOnt 118.

(b) use of a washroom: *Miller v. Emcer Products Ltd.* [1956] Ch. 304 (C.A.).

(c) receipt of light through a specific window: *Colls v. Home & Colonial Stores Ltd.* [1904] A.C. 179 (H.L.).

(d) the right to commit a nuisance: *B.C. Forest Products Ltd. v. Nordal* (1954) 11 W.W.R. (N.S.) 403, 1954 CarswellBC 20 (S.C.).

(e) use of a drainage pipe: *Israel v. Leith* (1890) 20 O.R. 361 (Q.B.).

(f) access to a water well: *Cross v. Malekow* 1996 CarswellBC 1158 (S.C. [Chambers]).

(g) overhead power lines: *Hillside Farms Ltd. v. B.C. Hydro & Power Authority* [1977] 3 W.W.R. 749, 1977 CarswellBC 355 (C.A.).

(h) support of buildings on the dominant tenement: *Wilton v. Hansen* 1968 CarswellMan 28, 65 W.W.R. 23 (Q.B.), affirmed 1969 CarswellMan 28 (C.A.).

(i) a sign placed on nearby property: *Moody v. Steggles* (1878) 12 Ch. D. 261.

(j) the right to wander along a beach: *Dukart v. District of Surrey* [1978] 2 S.C.R. 1039, 1978 CarswellBC 422, 1978 CarswellBC 557.

(k) use of a park as a garden: *Re Ellenborough Park* (1955) [1956] Ch. 131, affirmed (1955) [1956] Ch. 153 (C.A.).

(l) the right to use land for recreational purposes and to leave boats on a lake: *City Developments Ltd. v. Registrar General of the Northern Territory* [2000] N.T.S.C. 761.

(m) use of a stairway: *Fu v. Khan* 2001 CarswellOnt 4362 (S.C.J.).

See also R. Megarry & W. Wade, *The Law of Real Property*, 6th ed. (London: Sweet & Maxwell, 2000, C. Harpum) at 1151*ff.*

2. What is the rationale of the rule that an easement cannot exist in gross? What type of interest, if any, is created if there is no dominant tenement?

3. How can one distinguish between a licence and an easement? See *Imperial Oil Ltd. v. Young* 1998 CarswellNfld 224, 21 R.P.R. (3d) 65 (C.A.).

4. The requirement that an easement cannot include rights of joint occupation that substantially deprive the servient owner of proprietorship or legal possession has raised questions about the juridical status of pipeline easements. After all, the pipeline has a physical presence on the servient lands. In *Shelf Holdings Ltd. v. Husky Oil Operations Ltd.* 1989 CarswellAlta 34, 56 D.L.R. (4th) 193 (C.A.) that issue was confronted. At trial, it was held that a pipeline right-of-way owned by Husky Oil could not count as an easement because it amounted to a grant of a possessory interest. That decision was reversed on appeal. Haddad J.A. (at paras. 36–46) concluded that a flexible standard was required:

> By the very nature of an easement it is inevitable that some measure of occupation by the easement taker is present in all cases — and that the dominant tenement will to some extent, at least, interfere with the servient tenement. Moreover, because of the rights it carries, an easement, for its limited purpose, is an interest in land. . . .

Examination of the grant in this case discloses, in my view, that the privileges granted to Husky do not detract from the servient owner's rights of ownership.

The tenor of the grant is such that it reflects the intention of the parties that the grantee Husky acquire a benefit subject to its compliance with certain terms and conditions. The right of Shelf as the servient owner to use the land free from interference has been curtailed to the extent only of prohibiting it from interfering with the subsoil or to erect works on the strip comprising the right of way, "but otherwise the Grantor shall have the right fully to use and enjoy the said right-of-way except as the same may be necessary for the purposes herein granted to the Grantee".

I infer from the material filed and the comments of counsel that the lands are farm lands. It is apparent from the literal construction of the second term that curtailment of the appellant's use of its land does not deprive it completely of use of the surface of the right of way. All conventional rights of way will, to some degree, impair the use of the land.

The fourth term requires Husky to compensate the grantor (Shelf) for damages to crops, pasture, fences and livestock occasioned by the exercise of its rights and prohibits Husky from fencing the right of way thereby leaving Shelf free to cultivate and run cattle over the surface. This in effect allows Shelf full use of the entire parcel subject only to those limitations prescribed in the second term. Moreover, Husky in burying and maintaining its pipeline is prohibited from interfering with the drainage or ordinary cultivation of the lands.

The seventh term obliges Husky upon abandonment of the right of way to restore the lands to the same condition as they were prior to its use and entry thereon. This contemplates that the right of way will revert to Shelf after it has served Husky's purposes. I read this as confirmation that the parties intended the grant to create nothing more than an easement.

The ninth term is not consistent with the conveyance of an interest in land to Husky. It recognizes the mutual undertakings of the parties and it is explicit in providing that Husky is entitled to enjoy the rights it received under the grant subject to its "performing and observing the terms and conditions on its part to be performed and observed". I construe this paragraph to say that the rights conferred on Husky under the grant will be subject to termination in the event of its failure to perform and observe.

Husky acquired from Peregrym the privilege of using a corridor across a parcel consisting of 150 acres, and nothing more. The document reserves to the servient tenement a high degree of possession and control with only a low level of interference from the dominant tenement. The rights granted to Husky do not detract from the rights of the servient owner with the force required to raise the grant above the status of an easement. The grant is free of the words "appropriate" and "exclusive use" or words of that connotation. I view the document as having been devised to ensure that the servient owner's proprietary rights in the corridor are preserved.

It is common knowledge that grants of easements for pipelines have been widely used in the development of the petroleum industry and accepted and operate as easements.

Accordingly, in my judgment the grant to Husky is an easement valid and enforceable . . .

Does this holding mean that pipelines are invariably acceptable forms of easement?

5. Can the owner of a right-of-way easement repair the road on the servient lands? See *Cronkhite v. Miller* (1901) 2 N.B. Eq. 203 (S.C.).

3. CREATION OF EASEMENTS

Ontario Law Reform Commission, *Report on Basic Principles of Land Law* (Toronto: A.G. (Ont.), 1996)) at 129–37 [footnotes omitted]

(i) Introduction

There is a variety of methods by which easements may be created. All are to a greater or lesser extent related to the idea of acquisition by grant. The methods of acquisition may be classified into three groups. Acquisition may be by *express grant or reservation*, by *implied grant* or *reservation*, or by *prescription*. In this last case, the grant is presumed by law and is a fiction.

A deed is required for an express grant to be effective at common law but an equitable easement may be created where the parties enter into a specifically enforceable contract to grant an easement. At common law there was a technical difficulty in the making of a reservation of an easement in favour of land retained by a grantor. However, where the conveyance was executed by the grantee it was treated as making a re-grant of any easement expressed in favour of the grantor's retained land. Even in the absence of such execution by the grantee, "in equity the grantee would not be permitted to prevent the easement from being enjoyed by his grantor or those claiming under him". Statute has removed these technical difficulties, section 44 of the [Ontario] *Conveyancing and Law of Property Act* providing as follows:

> 44. Where by the terms of a conveyance of a land a right of way or easement is reserved or excepted from the land thereby transferred or charged, such reservation or exception is effectual and shall be deemed always to have been effectual to vest the right of way or easement in the transferor or chargor of the land notwithstanding that the transferee or chargee does not execute the instrument.

(ii) Easements Arising by Implication

Various doctrines provide the basis for the implication of an easement where one is not expressly created. Although these doctrines are all concerned with the circumstances in which the grant or reservation of an easement may be properly be inferred, they overlap considerably and the effect of their interrelationship is not always clear.

a. The Rule in Wheeldon v. Burrows

The Rule in *Wheeldon v. Burrows* is concerned with the "translation into easements" of rights over a grantor's retained land. As Megarry and Wade explain:

> It is natural for this purpose to look at the grantor's previous use of the land, and to allow the grantee to take easements corresponding to the facilities which the grantor himself found necessary. Before the grant they cannot have been easements because of the common ownership. They are therefore called "quasi-easements", *i.e.* rights which are potential easements in case of a division of the land.

The Rule provides that on the grant by the owner of a piece of land of part of that land there will pass to the grantee all those quasi-easements which, first, were "continuous and apparent" and, second, which are necessary to the reasonable enjoyment of the property granted, and which have been and are at the time of the grant used by the owners of the entirety for the benefit of the part granted. This rule operates only to create easements in favour of a grantee; it does not create any easement in favour of the grantor with respect to retained land.

b. The "General Words" Statutory Provision

Section 15(1) of the [Ontario] *Conveyancing and Law of Property Act* provides:

> 15.(1) Every conveyance of land, unless an exception is specifically made therein, includes all . . . ways, waters, watercourses, lights, liberties, privileges, easements, profits . . . hereditaments and appurtenances whatsoever to such land belonging or in anywise appertaining, or with such land demised, held, used, occupied and enjoyed or taken or known as part or parcel thereof . . .

The main purpose of the provision was to shorten conveyances by implying the verbiage that had previously had typically set out expressly in conveyances. For the most part the extraordinarily detailed list of items is unexceptional and is irrelevant to the creation of easements. Even the explicit references to easements or profits appurtenant to the land conveyed, which automatically pass with it, save that it precludes any argument that they were not intended to pass. However, the provision does have the important effect, unless there is provision to the contrary, of creating an easement . . . out of previously enjoyed ways, liberties, and privileges and so on. For example, in *International Tea Stores Co. v. Hobbs* a landlord has permitted his tenant to use a way across property that remained in the occupation of the landlord. Subsequently, the landlord sold the reversion to the previously leased property to the tenant. It was held that the tenant, by force of English legislation equivalent to s. 15, acquired an easement of way. What had previously been a way enjoyed by permission was converted into an easement of way.

Section 15 overlaps the Rule in *Wheeldon v. Burrows*. However, in important respects it has a considerably wider ambit. There is no requirement that the quasi-easement be "continuous" or "apparent" or that it be reasonably necessary to the enjoyment of the property conveyed. On the other hand, the House of Lords held in

Sovmots Investments Ltd. v. Secretary of State for the Environment that the equivalent of English provision only applies where there had been some diversity of ownership or occupation of the quasi-dominant and quasi-servient tenements prior to the conveyance.

c. "Intended" Easements

Even in circumstances outside those attracting the Rule in *Wheeldon v. Burrows* an easement, often referred to as an "intended" easement, may be implied on the basis that it is "necessary to give effect to the common intention of the parties". Although it is more difficult for a grantor than a grantee to establish an easement on this basis, an "intended" easement may be implied in favour of a grantor as well as a grantee.

d. Easements of Necessity

These easements are closely related to "intended easements" and may in fact merely be illustrations of them. The classic example of an easement of necessity occurs where there is a grant of land, resulting in the land granted or retained by the grantor having no means of access unless an easement is implied providing such access. As suggested by this example, an easement of necessity may be implied in favour of a grantor as well as a grantee.

The necessity requirement is more stringent in easements of necessity than in the Rule in *Wheeldon v. Burrows*. For example, a convenient second method of access may be acquired as an easement under the Rule in *Wheeldon v. Burrows*. On the other hand,

> [i]f some other way exists, no way of necessity will be implied unless that other way is merely precarious and not as of right, or unless, perhaps, it would be a breach of the law to use that other way for the purpose in question. Nor will there be a way of necessity if the other way is merely inconvenient, as where the land abuts on a highway in a cutting twenty feet below; for the principle is that an easement of necessity is one "without which the property retained cannot be used at all, and not one merely necessary at the reasonable enjoyment of that property".

(iii) Prescriptive Easements

The law of prescriptive easements was summarized in the Commission's *Report on Limitations of Actions* and it will be convenient to set out that summary here.

(b) Prescriptive Easements

For a prescriptive easement to arise, the claimant must show user "as of right". This means that he has enjoyed the easement as if he were entitled to it. The enjoyment must have been without force, without secrecy, and without permission. (*Nec vi, nec clam, nec precario* are the expressions used in legal terminology). A claimant to a right of way will not succeed if he had to break open a locked gate to achieve his use or where the adverse use has been continually contentious. Nor will he be successful if the adverse use is secret, although active concealment is not an essential ingredient of secrecy for this purpose. This may be illustrated by the underground discharge of waste from one property into another. Finally, if permission has been given by the owner of the land, a prescriptive easement cannot arise. It matters not how long ago that permission was given, or whether it was written or oral. Obviously, if an owner of land gives permission (i.e., a licence) to another to cross his land, the owner should not be subjected to a claim for an easement merely because the person to whom he has given permission has taken advantage of that permission for a considerable length of time.

The person claiming the easement must show that the owner of the land has acquiesced in his enjoyment. The latter must have acquiesced, yet not given permission. It is not always easy to tell whether or not there was, in fact, acquiescence or permission in a particular case.

Under English law, prescriptive easement can arise in three ways:

(i) at common law;

(ii) under the doctrine of the lost modern grant;

(iii) under the *Prescription Act*, 1832.

In Ontario, prescriptive easements can only be created by the second and third methods. The English statute was adopted for Upper Canada in 1847 and most of its provisions are now to be found in *The Limitations Act*.

The Limitations Act expressly excludes the operation of prescription in certain situations. It has not been possible to acquire a prescriptive easement with respect to light in Ontario since 1880. (See s. 33.) However, prescriptive easements of light which were acquired prior to 1880 are still valid today. Wires or cables on another's property cannot give rise to a prescriptive easement. (See s. 35) Nor can prescription under *The Limitations Act* work against unsurveyed Crown lands. (See s. 41) It does, however, apply to surveyed Crown lands. (See ss. 30 and 31.)

(i) At Common Law

At common law, a grant of an easement would be presumed if the enjoyment of the claimed right could be shown to have continued from time immemorial. Under the common law in England, this meant back to 1189, the first year of the reign of Richard I. Since it would be virtually impossible to show continuous enjoyment since 1189, the courts would presume that such long-term enjoyment existed if twenty years of user could be proved. However, the presumption could be rebutted by showing that at some time since 1189 the adverse use did not exist.

(ii) The Lost Modern Grant

To overcome the obvious difficulties in establishing a prescriptive easement at common law so that legal support could be given to long established enjoyment, the English courts developed what Cheshire had described as "the very questionable theory" of the lost modern grant. This judge-made rule was based on the court's presuming that, if actual enjoyment had been shown for a reasonable length of time, an actual grant had been made when the enjoyment began, but that the deed granting that easement had been subsequently lost. The speciousness of the fiction of the "lost" grant is demonstrated by the refusal of the courts (although there is some law to the contrary) to allow the presumption to be rebutted by evidence that no such grant was in fact made.

The doctrine of the lost modern grant is part of the common law as it exists in Ontario.

(iii) The Prescription Act of 1832

The relevant provisions of this statute were made applicable to Upper Canada in 1847 and are now contained in sections 30 to 32, 34, 39 and 40 of *The Limitations Act*.

The purpose of the 1832 statute was to reduce the uncertainties of establishing prescriptive easements at common law or under the lost modern grant doctrine, and avoid the problem of persuading juries to find that grants had been made and lost when it was obvious that this was not the case.

The statute did not replace the common law and lost modern grant methods of acquiring prescriptive rights. It merely supplied a new and supposedly simpler method. Thus, in England, a prescriptive easement can still be claimed in three different ways and, in Ontario, in two. Because of the requirements of the provisions of the statute, there are occasions when a prescriptive easement cannot be successfully claimed under it but, nevertheless, can be either at common law or under the doctrine of the lost modern grant in England and under the latter in Ontario.

The Act of 1832 is described by Megarry and Wade in their text on real property law as "ill-drafted" and Gale, the author of leading treatise on easements, wrote "it certainly is to be lamented that its provisions were not more carefully framed". These comments apply to the provisions as they have been carried forward into the present Ontario limitations statute. The prescription provisions of that enactment remain a mystery to many a practicing lawyer.

Under the provisions, the following are the points of significance:

1. Section 31 establishes two different periods for the creation of prescriptive easements. These periods are twenty and forty years.

The 20 year period

After twenty years of adverse use, an easement cannot be defeated by showing that user began after 1189. This merely facilities the operation of prescription at common law by eliminating one kind of defence. Thus, while an easement by prescription at common law could not be created in Ontario apart from this provision, section 31 makes 'time immemorial' irrelevant and enables a prescriptive easement to be created at common law in this province. Apart from showing user began after 1189, a claim for a prescriptive easement after twenty years' adverse use may still be defeated by any other defence that was available at common law.

The 40 year period

After forty years of adverse use, the easement becomes "absolute and indefeasible". This is not as definite as it appears. The basic rule that prescription must operate for and against a fee simple estate still applies. Thus, a tenant cannot prescribe against his landlord and it is doubtful if a corporation can be prescribed against if it does not have the power to grant an easement. Also a claim based on forty years' adverse use may be defeated, as could a twenty year claim, by showing that the user was forcible or secret, or enjoyed by written permission. On the other hand, a forty year claim cannot be defeated, as a twenty year claim can, by proving it was enjoyed by oral permission. Furthermore, the disabilities that have to be taken into account in the running of the twenty year period under section 39 do not apply to the running of the forty year period. (Note, however, section 40).

Thus, section 31 may be said to operate both negatively and positively. It facilitates the creation of common law prescription by the elimination of a defence, on the one hand, and establishes a right, on the other.

2. Section 31 only comes into play when there is litigation and the relevant period of user must immediately precede the bringing of the action. Thus, forty years of adverse use does not of itself create an "absolute" prescriptive easement. An action must be brought and the necessary period of employment must be immediately prior to the commencement of that action.

3. The period must be "without interruption". This does not mean mere non-user by the person claiming the easement. It means that the claimant has not been obstructed from enjoying the use.

4. No act is deemed to be an interruption for the purpose of section 31 unless the person claiming the easement has submitted to interruption for one year.

Example of the operation of sections 31 and 32

X has been crossing Y's property as if he had an easement for 19 years and one day. The next day Y prevents X from crossing by placing an obstruction in the way of passage. At this time, X has no right to cross as he cannot show twenty years of enjoyment.

However, if X sues for a prescriptive easement one year from the day after he had enjoyed the use for nineteen years, he will succeed. X will now be able to show after twenty years of enjoyment prior to bringing the action. The interruption will not count as it was for one year less a day. X could not have brought his action sooner as he would have been short of the twenty year period required.

An action brought by X on the following day will be too late as the interruption will now have lasted a year and section 31 can no longer apply.

The acquisition of an easement by adverse use or enjoyment is, of course, to be distinguished from the acquisition of title by adverse possession under sections 4 and 15 of *The Limitations Act*. Ten years of adverse possession gives rise to a possessory or "squatter's" title, which is good against the world. The adverse use required for an easement does not amount to a dispossession and, of course, must be for te benefit of adjacent land. Adverse possession entails dispossession and does not depend for its existence on other land which will benefit.

Furthermore, the adverse enjoyment which gives rise to prescriptive easement is based on a presumed grant. It is presumed that the claimant has been granted the right to use the lands in the first place. Adverse possession raises no such presumption but, once it has lasted ten years, results in:

(a) the dispossessed person being barred from suing for the recovery of the land; and

(b) the dispossessed person's title to the land being extinguished.

QUESTIONS AND COMMENTS

1. The ability to acquire prescriptive easements has been abolished in many places in Canada, either (i) completely, (ii) for lands under the land titles registration system (see Chapter 12), or (iii) in relation to particular easements. Here are illustrations of each kind of reform:

In Alberta, the acquisition of rights through prescription has been completely abolished:

> No right to the access and use of light or any other easement, right in gross or profit a prendre shall be acquired by a person by prescription, and no such right is deemed to have ever been so acquired.

Law of Property Act, R.S.A. 2000, c. L-7, sub. 69(3).

In Ontario, prescriptive rights (as well as rights via adverse possession) cannot be acquired for land covered by the *Land Titles Act*:

> Despite any provision of this Act, the *Real Property Limitations Act* or any other Act, no title to and no right or interest in land registered under this Act that is adverse to or in derogation of the title of the registered owner shall be acquired hereafter or be deemed to have been acquired heretofore by any length of possession or by prescription.

Land Titles Act, R.S.O. 1990, c. L.5, sub. 51(1).

For other lands, prescription has been abolished for particular easements:

> No person shall acquire a right by prescription to the access and use of light or to the access and use of air to or for any dwelling-house, work-shop or other building, but this

section does not apply to any such right acquired by twenty years use before the 5th day of March, 1880.

No easement in respect of wires or cables attached to property or buildings or passing through or carried over such property or buildings shall be deemed to have been acquired or shall hereafter be acquired by prescription or otherwise than by grant from the owner of the property or buildings.

Real Property Limitations Act, R.S.O. 1990, c. L.15, ss. 33, 35.

Why abolish some rights acquired through prescription but not others?

2. What are the features that distinguish prescription from adverse possession?

3. In addition to the modes of creation outlined by the Ontario Law Reform Commission, above, it is also possible for easements to arise by statute, or as a result of the application of the doctrine of proprietary estoppel. The case of *Depew v. Wilkes*, below, discusses easements created through estoppel. As to easements created by statute, see for example *The Condominium Act*, C.C.S.M., c. C170, which creates easements for the benefit of individual units and the common property within condominium complexes:

9.(1) The following easements are created and are appurtenant to each unit: . . .

(b) An easement for the provision of any service through any installation in the common elements or any other unit.

(c) An easement for support and shelter by the common elements and any other unit capable of providing support or shelter.

9.(2) The following easements are created and are appurtenant to the common elements:

(a) An easement for the provision of any service through any installation in any unit.

(b) An easement for support and shelter by any unit capable of providing support and shelter.

9.(3) All ancillary rights and obligations reasonably necessary to make easements effective apply in respect of easements implied or created by this Act.

Depew v. Wilkes
2002 CarswellOnt 2516, 60 O.R. (3d) 499 (C.A.)

Rosenberg J.A.:

This appeal and cross-appeal raise issues concerning prescriptive and equitable easements. The appellants own cottages on Lake Erie. The respondents own a cottage on Lake Erie and, more importantly, a strip of land the appellants have used for parking and other purposes for many years. The appellants submit that having found prescriptive easements for certain uses such as the parking, Marshall J. erred in dealing with those rights under the rubric of equitable proprietary estoppel. I agree with that submission and would allow the appeal.

The respondents by their cross-appeal submit that the trial judge erred in finding prescriptive and equitable easements. I do not agree with that submission and I would dismiss the cross-appeal.

The appellants also appeal from the costs order at trial. The trial judge found that success was divided and made no order for costs. Particularly in light of the disposition of the appeal, I would allow the appeal from the costs award. The appellants are also entitled to their costs of the appeal and the cross-appeal on a partial indemnity basis.

THE FACTS

The appellants and the respondents own cottages in Port Ryerse. To get to those cottages, one drives to the end of Commercial Road. The respondents' cottage abuts Commercial Road. The appellants' cottages are to the west of the respondents' cottage. To get to their cottages, the appellants turn west on to Willow Beach Lane, which runs between the cottages to the north and the beach to the south. Both Willow Beach Lane and the beach in front of the cottages lie on Lot 13. The respondents own Lot 13. The dispute in this case concerns the appellants' use of Lot 13. Lot 13 is subject to two express rights-of-way: access by the appellants' vehicles (ingress and egress) and access in common with the public to Lake Erie. Except for the appellant Wise, the appellants have rights of ingress and egress expressly stipulated in their deeds. The respondents concede that Wise has the same access rights as do the other appellants.

Over the years, the appellants have erected a number of structures on Lot 13 and have parked their cars on Lot 13 in front of their respective cottages. For reasons that are not now material, the respondents recently began to dispute these uses. At trial, the appellants claimed that they had acquired possessory title to parts of Lot 13 by way of adverse possession. Alternatively, they claimed prescriptive easements or easements by reason of equitable proprietary estoppel. The trial judge found against the appellants on adverse possession and that is no longer a part of the case. There is also no longer any dispute about some of the specific rights claimed by the appellants. I will summarize the facts in relation to the issues that are still outstanding.

Parking

It would seem that parking is the most contentious issue between the parties. For more than 20 years, the appellants have parked their vehicles in front of their cottages. Public parking is available on Commercial Road but the appellants much prefer to park at the side of Willow Beach Lane on Lot 13 in front of their cottages.

The respondents acknowledge that the appellants have many reasons for parking on Lot 13, including the following:

* Safety: If the appellants had to walk the 150 to 250 feet from Commercial Road at night, they would risk injury because of the potholes.

* Health: The appellants Crawford and Wise claim that they cannot walk from Commercial Road because of age or medical condition. The respondents dispute this claim with respect to Crawford.

* Vandalism: There is an increased risk of vandalism associated with parking on Commercial Road.

* Finding parking spots: At certain times of the year it is difficult to find parking spots on Commercial Road because the appellants have to compete with fishermen and day users of the beach.

* Emergencies: Occasional family emergencies make it more desirable to park vehicles immediately in front of the cottages.

* Inconvenience: Parking on Commercial Road results in some inconvenience when the appellants have to ferry children around.

The trial judge found that the appellants had made out a prescriptive easement to park on Lot 13 in front of their cottages. He also found that the appellants had established their alternative claim for proprietary estoppel. In the result, he ruled that the appellants were entitled to park in front of their cottages but required them to pay an annual "licence fee" of $250 per cottage.

The pier

In the 1950's, the predecessor in title to the appellant Wilkes built a large pier on Lot 13. The trial judge found that Wilkes had a prescriptive easement for the pier as well as an easement by proprietary estoppel. As with the parking, the trial judge granted an equitable remedy and required Wilkes to pay an annual $100 licence fee for the pier.

The well

Wilkes' predecessor in title installed a well on Lot 13 over 70 years ago, with the permission of the respondents' predecessor in title. For most of that time, the well covering has been plainly visible. In 1985, Wilkes abandoned that well and installed a "sand point" to obtain water for his cottage and the Wise cottage. The sand point is beneath the surface and is not visible. The respondents claim that they were not aware of the sand point until the litigation began. The trial judge found that, in view of its very recent installation, Wilkes had not acquired a prescriptive easement over the well. He found, however, that users of the well had acquired an easement by reason of equitable proprietary estoppel and assessed a $100 per year licence fee.

The concrete blocks

In the 1970's, the appellants erected cement pads south of Willow Beach Lane on Lot 13 to protect their cottages and Willow Beach Lane from high water. In 1986, the appellants Crawford and Wise placed one-ton concrete blocks on top of the cement pads to provide further protection from high water. These blocks are moveable and in fact have been moved by storms. The trial judge found that, because of their relatively recent placement, there was no prescriptive easement with respect to the blocks. However, he found that the appellants had established their claim for proprietary estoppel in respect of the blocks. The trial judge did not impose any licence fee because the blocks benefited the whole beach, including the respondents' property.

The other improvements

Over the years, the appellants made other improvements to Lot 13. The cement pads are an example. It is unnecessary to deal with those other improvements since neither side now complains about the trial judge's disposition.

ANALYSIS

The main appeal

The main appeal raises a single narrow issue. Having found that the appellants had made out a prescriptive easement with respect to the parking and the pier on Lot 13, did the trial judge err in considering the equitable claim? The trial judge gave these reasons for proceeding in that manner:

> In the end then, although I have found that some of the improvements the defendants have made qualify as easements under the *Limitations Act*, I would deal with them first under the rubric of equitable proprietary estoppel. I do that because of the necessity of answering equity or fairness in the result. . . .
>
> Here, for all these reasons, I have chosen the "path" of equitable proprietary estoppel giving rise to an equitable easement coupled to a rent or annual licence fee. In this way, in these instances, equity can best be done.
>
> Here the Depew family own and, presumably, have paid taxes on Lot 13. Though equity will assist the cottagers in establishing the easement by estoppel, equity to the titleholder of the land requires that a reasonable annual fee be paid to the titleholder for the use of the land.

In my view, the trial judge misdirected himself on the application of the equitable doctrine. The doctrine is described by the authors of *Megarry & Wade, The Law of Real Property*, 6th ed. (2000) at p. 727:

> Proprietary estoppel, which is also sometimes referred to as "estoppel by acquiescence" or "estoppel by encouragement", is a means by which property rights may be affected or created. The term describes the equitable jurisdiction by which a court may interfere *in cases where the assertion of strict legal rights is found to be unconscionable.* [Footnotes omitted; emphasis added.]

The trial judge found that, because of the expiration of the 20 year limitation period provided for in ss. 31 and 32 of the *Limitations Act*, R.S.O. 1990, c. L.15, the appellants had acquired prescriptive easements to park their cars in front of their cottages on Lot 13 and that Wilkes had established a prescriptive easement with respect to the pier. These were legal rights. It was nevertheless open to the trial judge to grant the respondents an equitable remedy, provided he found assertion of these strict legal rights unconscionable.

The trial judge made no such finding and it is difficult to see any basis for doing so. The appellants and their predecessors in title had been parking on Lot 13 for many decades without charge and with the acquiescence of the respondents and their predecessors in title. The Wilkes pier was erected in the 1950's and, as the trial judge said, it benefited all the cottagers, including the respondents, by protecting the beach, Willow Beach Lane and the cottages. The only reasons given by the trial judge for imposing the licence fees were that the respondents presumably were paying taxes on Lot 13 and that "equity to the titleholder of the land requires that a reasonable annual fee be paid to the titleholder for the use of the land." There was no evidence of how much, if anything, the respondents were paying in taxes.

While I appreciate that the trial judge turned to equity in order to effect what he thought was a fair result, I have concluded that he erred in doing so. His approach is based on nothing more than his sense of justice or fairness and could be applied in virtually every case where a prescriptive easement is made out. Adopting this approach would make the law of easements unpredictable. As Cory J.A. said in *Henderson v. Volk* (1982), 35 O.R. (2d) 379 (C.A.), at 384, the courts ought to proceed with caution before finding title by prescription because "[i]t tends to subject a property owner to a burden without compensation." However, notwithstanding that result, absent a finding of unconscionability there is no basis for proceeding to consider some further equitable remedy where a prescriptive easement has been found to exist. In the result, I would set aside the licence fees for parking and the pier.

This is sufficient to dispose of the main appeal, provided that the trial judge's finding of a prescriptive easement for parking can be sustained. That is one of the issues raised on the cross-appeal. The respondents had cross-appealed the trial judge's finding of an easement with respect to the pier, but they have abandoned that part of their cross-appeal. I will now turn to the cross-appeal.

The cross-appeal

Parking

The authors of *Anger and Honsberger: Law of Real Property*, 2nd ed. (1985) at p. 925 describe an easement as a "right annexed to land which permits the owner of the dominant tenement to require the owner of the servient tenement 'to suffer or not to do' something on such land". They describe the four essential qualities of an easement in these terms:

(i) there must be a dominant and a servient tenement;

(ii) an easement must accommodate the dominant tenement;

(iii) dominant and servient owners must be different persons; and

(iv) a right over land cannot amount to an easement unless it is capable of forming the subject-matter of a grant.

In this case, the servient tenement is Lot 13. The dominant tenements are the appellants' lots. On this part of the appeal, dealing with parking, the issue is condition two: the easement must accommodate the dominant tenement. The respondents submit that, while the appellants may find it convenient to park on Lot 13 in front of their cottages, this is not sufficient and they must show that the easement is "reasonably necessary for the better enjoyment" of the dominant tenements. The reasonable necessity elaboration of the accommodation requirement seems to have originated in a passage from *Cheshire's Modern Real Property* that was approved by the English Court of Appeal in *In re Davies Ellenborough Park* (1955), [1956] 1 Ch. 131 (Eng. C.A.). Evershed M.R. stated, at p. 170,

> We think it unnecessary to review the authorities in which the principle has been applied; for the effect of the decisions is stated with accuracy in Dr. Cheshire's Modern Real Property, 7th ed., at p. 457. After pointing out that "one of the fundamental principles concerning easements is that they must be not only appurtenant to a dominant tenement, but also connected with the normal enjoyment of the dominant tenement" and referring to certain citations in support of that proposition the author proceeded: "We may expand the statement of the principle thus: a right enjoyed by one over the land of another does not possess the status of an easement unless it accommodates and serves the dominant tenement, and is *reasonably necessary for the better enjoyment of that tenement*, for if it has no necessary connexion therewith, although it confers an advantage upon the owner and renders his ownership of the land more valuable, it is not an easement at all, but a mere contractual right personal to and only enforceable between the two contracting parties . . . [Emphasis added.]

The reasonable necessity requirement serves to emphasize that there must be a connection between the easement and the dominant tenement, as opposed to a personal right. In *MacKenzie v. Matthews* (1999), 46 O.R. (3d) 21 (C.A.) at para. 8, Sharpe J.A., speaking for the court, held that the grant of an express easement includes a grant of ancillary rights "which are reasonably necessary to the use and enjoyment of the easement which was contemplated by the grantor". In that case, the owners of two islands had been granted a 20-foot right-of-way over the appellants' property. The evident purpose of the right-of-way was for the owners of the island to gain access to their islands. The court found that the parking of vehicles while the users of the right-of-way enjoyed access to the islands was an ancillary right reasonably necessary to the use and enjoyment of the easement.

In *Caldwell v. Elia* (2000), 129 O.A.C. 379 (C.A.), this court considered the conditions for easements acquired by prescription and easements of necessity. The latter is described in *Gale on Easements*, 16th ed. (1997) at p. 148:

> A way of necessity, strictly so called, arises where, on a disposition by a common owner of part of his land, either the part disposed of or the part retained is left without any legally enforceable means of access. In such a case the part so left inaccessible is entitled, as of necessity, to a way over the other part.

In *Caldwell*, the original owner had created by deed a right-of-way over one lot to provide access to a land-locked lot. However, the owners had never used that right-of-way. Instead, for many years they had used a gravel road to get access to and from the properties. At some point, the respondents sought to block the gravel road. The trial judge held that the gravel road did not accommodate the appellant's property because it was not reasonably necessary; the appellant could simply use the right-of-way. This court allowed the appeal and held that the gravel road did accommodate the appellant's property and that the appellant had acquired an easement by prescription. Austin J.A., speaking for the court at para. 14, distinguished between an easement acquired by prescription and easements of necessity:

> What [the appellant] claims is *not* a way of necessity, but rather a prescriptive right accruing by virtue of use over a period of at least twenty years. *A prescriptive claim need have no element of "necessity"*. Accordingly, the existence of the 15' right-of-way created expressly by deed is irrelevant to [the appellant's] prescriptive claim. [Emphasis on "not" in original; other emphasis added.]

I do not understand the court in *Caldwell* to have held that reasonable necessity as understood in *Ellenborough Park* is not a requirement for a prescriptive easement. To the contrary, both before and after the passage quoted above, the court accepted the *Ellenborough Park* test.

In the present case, I agree with the respondents that the appellants had to establish that parking was, in the words of *Ellenborough Park*, "reasonably necessary for the better enjoyment" of the dominant tenements. The reasonable necessity requirement is fact specific and must be applied in a flexible manner. As was said in *Anger and Honsberger*, *supra*, at p. 927:

> What is reasonably necessary must be a flexible criterion and have reference to current social conditions and the prevailing patterns and trends of conduct. What today might not be regarded to be a reasonable amenity for the better enjoyment of a property might be regarded as a reasonable amenity tomorrow.

The trial judge found that parking on Lot 13 does accommodate the dominant tenements:

> Considering all of the evidence on the size of the lots and the availability of public parking, I would conclude that parking is reasonably necessary in this case. The lots are, for the most part, built in and only 50' by 60' in total. The public parking available is on Commercial Road and, in the Court's view, a less than satisfactory alternative. I would conclude that parking is reasonably necessary. . . .
>
> I am satisfied that the prescribed 20 years has long passed in regard to parking. I am satisfied there was acquiescence, that the parking was open and notorious and uninterrupted and, as I have said, reasonably necessary. In the result, then, I would grant an easement in regard to parking.

I agree with that conclusion. The parking is connected with the normal enjoyment of the property. As the *Caldwell* case demonstrates, the fact that an alternative exists does not preclude a finding that the easement is reasonably necessary for the better enjoyment of that tenement. Taken together, the appellants' reasons for parking on Lot 13 listed above demonstrate that there was an adequate basis for the trial judge's finding of reasonable necessity.

The well

The sand point well presents a different problem. The trial judge held that the appellants had not made out an easement by prescription because the sand point well was only recently installed and was not open or notorious. He went on to hold, however, that the appellants had acquired an equitable easement by virtue of equitable proprietary estoppel. The respondents challenge that holding in their cross-appeal. Of the conditions required to make out proprietary estoppel, the only one in issue in this part of the appeal is that of "encouragement", which is summarized as follows in *Snell's Equity*, 30th ed. (2000) at para. 39–16:

> A's belief must have been encouraged by O or his agent or predecessor in title. This may be done actively, as where a father persuades his son to build a bungalow on the father's land, or a mother assures her daughter that she will have the family home for her life, or a man assures his former mistress that the house in which they lived together is hers. *The equity will also arise where O merely encourages A's belief passively, as where a mortgagee stood silently by while a purchaser in ignorance of the mortgage built on the land. "The circumstance of looking on is in many cases as strong as using terms of encouragement." Before the equity can arise in such circumstances, O must have known of A's expenditure.* Further, normally he must also have known that the property was his, or that his property was being improved, or that he was entitled to interfere, for such knowledge makes it dishonest for him to remain wilfully passive and thereby afterwards profit by a mistake which he might have prevented. But this knowledge is not essential, for even without it, O's encouraging conduct considered in conjunction with A's actions and belief, may be such that it would be dishonest and unconscionable for O to seek to stand on his legal rights. Once it is shown that O gave assurances or other encouragement to A, and A suffers detriment, it will readily be inferred that the detriment was suffered as a result of the encouragement: the burden of proof is on O to show that A's conduct was not induced by the assurances. [Footnotes omitted; emphasis added.]

The respondents submit that the encouragement requirement was not made out because they were unaware of the sand point's existence until the litigation began. They, therefore, could not be said to have encouraged the appellants.

There has been a well on Lot 13 to serve the Wilkes and Wise cottages for over 70 years. That well was installed with the agreement of the respondents' predecessors in title. Originally, the well had a concrete cover. Around 1962, because of problems with the concrete cover being knocked off by storms, Mr. Wilkes replaced it with a stainless steel one. The cover, whether concrete or stainless steel, was virtually always visible; occasionally it would be covered by sand. In 1985, because of high water and because they were getting some taste from seaweed, Mr. Wilkes tried to drill a well on his own property. After spending $3,000, he had to give up because the water was contaminated by sulphur. Mr. Wilkes then decided to install the sand point. The sand point is not visible because it does not require rings. Mr. Wilkes testified that, "I had no idea I was going to have a problem with wells on the beach. I thought it was a right I had bought and acquired. It was always there".

The trial judge dealt with the well as follows:

> I am satisfied, on the evidence, that [the respondents] were aware of water wells being placed on the beach from time to time.
>
> The Wilkes ' well used by Lot 7 (Wise) and Lot 8 (Wilkes) for many, many years had a stainless steel cover that was, except in high water, clearly visible to all. These improvements were all made with the knowledge and acquiescence of the Depew family.

I agree with the trial judge's conclusion on this aspect of the cross-appeal. The evidence establishes that the wells were placed on Lot 13 first with the active encouragement of the respondents' predecessors in title and thereafter, at least with the respondents' acquiescence. In light of the appellants Wilkes and Wise's long-standing use of a well on Lot 13, I think it would be wrong to focus only on whether the respondents knew the location of the particular well in use at the time of trial. In fact, Mr. Depew testified that he did not object to the use of Lot 13 for a well to service the Wilkes and Wise properties. He testified that, "If permission is asked we normally grant it. We like to know what's on the property." The respondents' course of conduct and that of their predecessors in title encouraged the Wilkes and Wise families to install a well on Lot 13. It is regrettable that the parties could not reach their own arrangement over the well. However, the trial judge's solution of a $100 annual fee is a fair one.

The concrete blocks

The concrete blocks were recently installed and therefore the appellants did not make out a claim for a prescriptive easement. The trial judge held that the appellants were entitled to an equitable easement with respect to the concrete blocks. He did not impose a licence fee because the blocks benefit all of the owners, including the respondents.

On their cross-appeal, the respondents submit that the trial judge erred in finding that the appellants' claim for proprietary estoppel was made out. The principal submission is that the element of detriment was not made out. For proprietary estoppel to be made out, there must be detriment. The person making the claim "must have incurred expenditure or otherwise have prejudiced himself or acted to his detriment": *Snell's Equity, supra*, at para. 39–14.

The respondents submit that it is open to the appellants to move the blocks to their own property without any loss on their investment. Therefore, there is no detriment. The trial judge did not expressly deal with the issue of detriment as it relates to the concrete blocks. However, I am satisfied that there is an evidentiary basis for finding that the appellants had proved detriment. The blocks have been placed on the south side of Willow Beach Lane, on Lot 13, to protect the lane as well as the cottages. The lane is required so that the owners can access their cottages. The appellants have spent money to acquire and place the blocks in that location. . . .

DISPOSITION

Accordingly, the appeal is allowed and the Judgment varied as follows. With respect to parking, paragraph 4 of the Judgment is varied to remove reference to equitable easements by estoppel and paragraph 5 of the Judgment is struck out. With respect to the pier, paragraph 10 of the Judgment is varied to remove reference to an equitable easement by estoppel and paragraph 11 is struck out. I would allow the appeal with respect to costs and award the appellants their costs of the trial on a partial indemnity basis to be assessed.

The appellants are entitled to their costs of the appeal and the cross-appeal on a partial indemnity basis. At the hearing of the appeal, Ms. Bachmann provided the court with a draft bill of costs. I have reviewed the bill of costs in light of the issues raised on the appeal. I would fix the costs of the appeal at $16,000 inclusive of disbursements and GST.

Appeal allowed in part; cross-appeal dismissed.

QUESTION

What is the foundation for the existence of easements of necessity: is it a matter of public policy alone, or a question of imputed or implied intention? Under English law, an easement of necessity is said to arise from intention. Hence in *Nickerson v. Barraclough* [1981] Ch. 426 (C.A.), Brightman L.J. held (at 440-1):

> . . . [T]he doctrine of way of necessity is not founded on public policy at all but on an implication from the circumstances. I accept that there are reported cases, and textbooks, in which public policy is suggested as a possible foundation of the doctrine, but such a suggestion is not, in my opinion, correct. . . . [T]here would seem to be no particular reason to father the doctrine of way of necessity on public policy when implication is such an obvious and convenient candidate for paternity. . . . Furthermore, I cannot accept

> that public policy can play any part at all in the construction of an instrument; in construing a document the court is endeavouring to ascertain the expressed intention of the parties. Public policy may require the court to frustrate that intention where the contract is against public policy, but in my view public policy cannot help the court to ascertain what that intention was. . . .

Compare this view, drawn from the American case of *Frederick v. Consolidated Waste Services, Inc.* 573 A.2d 387 (Me., 1990) at 389 (*per* Clifford J.):

> [A]n easement created by strict necessity [arises] when a grantor conveys a lot of land from a larger parcel, and that conveyed lot is "landlocked" by the grantor's surrounding land and cannot be accessed by a road or highway. Because of the strict necessity of having access to the landlocked parcel, an easement over the grantor's remaining land benefiting the landlocked lot is implied as a matter of law irrespective of the true intent of the common grantor.

Likewise, see *Hirtle v. Ernst* (1991) 21 R.P.R. (2d) 95, 1991 CarswellNS 101 (T.D.) at 105 (R.P.R.).

Does the characterization matter?

4. SCOPE, LOCATION AND TERMINATION

Laurie v. Winch
[1953] 1 S.C.R. 49, 1952 CarswellOnt 118

Kellock J.:

The appellant is the owner of lots 18, 19 and 33 on registered plan 103 which fronts on the easterly side of a road known as the Lake Shore Road skirting the easterly shore of Lake Simcoe in the Province of Ontario. The respondent is the owner of lots on plan 320 which adjoins plan 103 to the east. Plan 103 consists of thirty-two lots, numbering from south to north, fronting on the east side of the Lake Shore Road, and also a long narrow lot, number 33, which adjoins the easterly limits of the other lots and fronts on the north limit of a road called the Mahoney Side Road which, in turn, runs east and west to the Lake Shore Road along the southerly limits of the two plans. Lots 1 to 32 are fifty feet in width, while lot 33 is thirty feet. The attached sketch sufficiently indicates the situation.

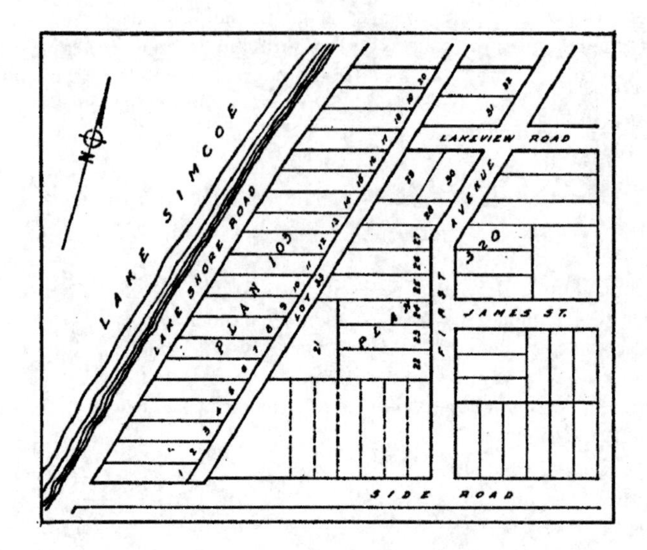

When plan 103 was registered in or about the year 1910, the lands covered by both plans, as well as other land to the east, were owned by one O.B. Sheppard, the lands now covered by plan 320 and the land to the east being in the occupation of a tenant, John T. Smith, who was engaged in farming operations thereon. Subsequently, Sheppard conveyed the farm to Smith and his wife as joint tenants.

The farm fronted on the north side of the Mahoney Side Road, but there had been in use for some time prior to the conveyance to the Smiths a farm lane running in an easterly and westerly direction from the farm buildings located some distance north of the side road, across the farm, over lot 33 to lot 17, plan 103, and thence to the Lake Shore Road. This lane was used as a means of access to and from the farm buildings.

The farm was fenced off from plan 103 by a wire fence running along the easterly boundary of lot 33, the only opening in it being a gate opposite lot 17 where the farm lane met the east limit of lot 33. There was also a gate opposite in the east limit of lot 17, while there was another gate in the west limit of lot 17 where the lane entered Lake Shore Road.

Lots on plan 103 were from time to time disposed of by Sheppard, usually together with a right-of-way over lot 33. Sheppard conveyed lot 17 on September 9, 1924, to one Lascelles, reserving to himself a right-of-way over the entire lot "for all purposes and at all times." At this time Sheppard remained the owner of lot 18 immediately to the south, as well as lot 33. On November 29, 1924, Lascelles conveyed lot 17 to the Smiths, subject to the above mentioned right-of-way. Subsequently, on September 21, 1925, Sheppard executed the following deed:

> In consideration of the sum of one dollar the receipt of which is herby acknowledged I hereby give to John Smith of the Township of North Gwillimbury in the County of York and Province of Ontario his heirs executors and assigns a perpetual right of way over

> Lot thirty-three (33) Plan one hundred and three (103) registered said Lot & Plan being in the Township of North Gwillimbury in the County of York and Province of Ontario. This is to be binding on my heirs executors or assigns.

In 1941 the Smith farm, as well as lot 17, plan 103, was conveyed (the latter subject to the right-of-way already mentioned) to the predecessor in title of the respondent, together with "a perpetual right-of-way over lot No. 33 according to plan No. 103". The registration of plan 320 followed on March 30, 1946. This plan shows a street known as Lakeview Road overlying the site of the westerly portion of the old farm lane, but this street is sixty-six feet in width, whereas that of the lane was about fifty feet between its fences.

This action was commenced by the appellant to restrain the respondent and certain other owners of lots on plan 320 from entering upon lot 33, and in the alternative, from using lot 33 to any greater extent than the same was actually used prior to the year 1945. . . .

The appellant [maintains] that the conveyance of 1925 was a personal license only. In the alternative, the appellant seeks a declaration that (1) the right-of-way granted to Smith was limited to the purposes for which the lane was at that time used, and (2) that by reason of the filing of plan 320 and the sale of lots according thereto, there was such a change in the circumstances as amounted to an extinguishment of that easement.

The basis upon which counsel founds his argument that the conveyance of 1925 amounted to nothing more than a personal license, is that there is no dominant tenement named in the conveyance. It is therefore said that the conveyance amounts to a grant of an easement in gross, something unknown to the law, with the consequence that the grant is to be construed as a personal license only.

It is to be observed that in the case at bar, there is in the deed of 1925 not only no mention of a dominant tenement but, apart from the words "over lot thirty-three," there is no indication as to the termini of the "right-of-way" granted by the instrument. The grantee of the right, John Smith, together with his wife, were owners as joint tenants, both of lot 17, plan 103, and of the farm lands to the east. To my mind, in addition to the silence of the instrument of 1925 with respect to any dominant tenement, there is also, when the terms of the grant are applied to the existing circumstances, ambiguity as to whether *the* right-of-way was intended to be granted over the entire length and breadth of lot 33 or over some lesser part of it only. It is to be noted that the lot extended some 700 feet north of the northerly limit of the farm lane and ended in a cul-de-sac.

As stated by Lord Chelmsford in *Waterpark v. Fennell* [(1859) 7 H.L.C. 650 at 678, 683]:

> Parol evidence is generally admissible to apply the words used in a deed, and to identify the property comprised within it. You cannot, indeed, show that the words were *intended* to include a particular piece of land, but you may prove facts from which you may collect

> the meaning of the words used, so as to include or exclude land, where the words are capable of either construction. . . .

In *Cannon v. Villars* [(1878) 8 Ch. D. 415], Sir George Jessel M.R. said at p. 419:

> In construing all instruments, you must know what the facts were when the agreement was entered into. . . .

In *Pettey v. Parsons* [[1914] 2 Ch. 653], Swinfen Eady L.J. at p. 667 said:

> It is a question of construction in a deed granting a right of way whether the way that is granted is a way so that the grantee may open gates, or means of access to the way, at any point of his frontage, or whether it is merely a way between two points, a right to pass over the road, and is limited to the modes of access to the road existing at the date of the grant. In each case it is a question of construction. . . .

I think, in the first place, that the dominant tenement intended by the parties to the deed of 1925 was the farm and not lot 17. The fact that that lot, although also owned by the Smiths, was subject to a right-of-way appurtenant to lot 33 indicates, I think, that it could not have been intended that the easement created by the instrument of 1925 was intended to be appurtenant to a lot which was, at that time at least, sterile so far as building upon it was concerned.

In the second place, as pointed out by the learned Chief Justice for Ontario, the right-of-way granted was "a" right-of-way, and the situation existing at the time, namely, the existence of the farm lane over that part of lot 33 between the gates and the non-user in connection with the farm of any other part of lot 33 indicates, in my opinion, that the way granted was over the site of the existing farm lane. I think this conclusion is very strongly reinforced by the existence of the fence along the entire easterly limit of lot 33, which indicates clearly that the only place of entry upon lot 33 from the farm which the grantee was intended to have was at the gate in the easterly boundary of the lot. It follows that the width of the way was limited to the width of such gate. In admitting that he had no other point of access to lot 33 from plan 320, I think the respondent was well advised.

The words "over lot thirty-three" are just as capable of referring to that part of the lot north of the old lane as to that part of the lot to the south. It is not suggested that Smiths had ever made use of the northerly part of the lot or that its use could have been of benefit to the farm. Similarly, with respect to any user by the Smiths of the southerly part of the lot, I think, with the learned Chief Justice of Ontario, there is no evidence of such user. . . .

The farm fronted on the side road and thus communicated with it directly. The lane was a means of communication between the farm buildings and the Lake Shore Road. There was little or no utility so far as the farm was concerned, in going to or from the farm buildings to the side road by means of lot 33.

With respect to the nature and extent of the easement granted, it is to be observed that the grant is one of a right-of-way *simpliciter* with no express restriction as to use. Just as the circumstances existing at the time of the grant may be looked at for the purpose of ascertaining the intention of the parties as to the dominant tenement and as to the location and termini of the way, the circumstances may also be looked at for the purpose of construing the conveyance as to the nature and extent of the rights conveyed.

In *White v. Grand Hotel* [[1913] 1 Ch. 118; 110 L.T. 209.], while the easement there in question was the subject of an express grant, there was no documentary evidence of its exact terms. The action was by the owner of the servient tenement to limit the user of the way, the dominant tenement having been changed from a private residence, at the time of the grant, to a hotel. It was held, that there being no limitation to be found in the grant in the nature of the width of the right-of-way or anything of that kind, full effect must be given to the grant and the way could not be restricted to such use as existed at the time of its execution. Hamilton L.J., as he then was, pointed out that the dominant tenement, although used as a private dwelling house at the time of the grant, might be, with the consent of a third person, as in fact it had been turned into a house which could be used for the purpose of trade. The decision on this point was upheld by the House of Lords.

In *South Eastern Railway Co. v. Cooper* [[1924] 1 Ch. 211], Warrington L.J. used the following language at p. 226:

> There is no question that if this were a grant of a way from one person to another, the grantee would be entitled to use it for any purpose without reference to the purpose for which the dominant tenement was used at the date of the grant, and notwithstanding that the burden on the servient tenement was thereby increased.

In *Todrick v. Western National Omnibus Co.* [[1934] 1 Ch. 190], Farwell L.J. at the trial said, at p. 206:

> In considering whether a particular use of a right of this kind is a proper use or not, I am entitled to take into consideration the circumstances of the case, the situation of the parties and the situation of the land at the time when the grant was made: see *United Land Co. v. Great Eastern Ry. Co.* [L.R. 10 Ch. 586 at 590], and in my judgment a grant for all purposes means for all purposes having regard to the considerations which I have already mentioned.

It was held by the Court of Appeal in *Todrick's* case [[1934] 1 Ch. 561] that having regard to the width of the land over which the right-of-way there in question was granted, it was not within the intention of the parties to the grant that it should be used for heavy omnibus traffic.

In *Robinson v. Bailey* [[1948] 2 All E.R. 791], Lord Green M.R. referred to the language of Farwell L.J. in *Todrick's* case, *supra*, and said at p. 795:

> While not in any way dissenting from that statement as a general proposition, I would like to give this word of caution, that it is a principle which must not be allowed to carry

> the court blindly. Obviously the question of the scope of the right of way expressed in a grant or reservation is *prima facie* a question of construction of the words used. If those words are susceptible of being cut down by some implication from surrounding circumstances, it being, to construe them properly, necessary to look at the surrounding circumstances, of course they would be cut down. *Todrick's* case is a very good example of the sort of application of the rule which Farwell J. was enunciating.

In *Robinson's* case the court found that there was no limitation upon the language of the grant to be implied from the nature of the land over which the right was granted, but rather the contrary, and although the dominant tenement in question in that case was at the date of the grant subject to restrictions, those restrictions, like the situation in *White's case* [[1913] 1 Ch. 118; 110 L.T. 209], could have been gotten rid of by the consent of a third party.

In the case at bar, while the Smith lands were, at the date of the grant, being used for agricultural purposes, there was no reason why they might not subsequently be subdivided into building lots as had been the case with the original part of the farm with respect to which plan 103 had been registered, and I cannot think that it is to be said that it was within the contemplation of the parties to the conveyance of 1925 that the farm would always remain a farm. I think, therefore there is nothing in the circumstances to restrict the plain words of the grant to the use being made of the farm lane at that time. Further, upon the severance of the dominant tenement into several parts the easement attached to those parts; *Codling v. Johnson* [(1829) 9 B. & C. 933], *Newcomen v. Coulson* [(1877) 5 Ch. D. 133].

I would therefore allow the appeal to the extent indicated. The farm lane having been obliterated and the gates having disappeared, I would, if the parties cannot agree, direct a reference to define the location of the right-of-way. . . .

Appeal allowed in part.

Malden Farms Ltd. v. Nicholson
[1956] O.R. 415, 1956 CarswellOnt 107 (C.A.)

Aylesworth J.A.:

Defendant appeals from the judgment of Spence J. dated 20th August 1954, granting respondent an injunction "that the Defendant, his servants and agents, be and they hereby are restrained from inviting and receiving the general public in such numbers that the use by the Plaintiff as a way of the lands described in Schedule A hereto will be substantially interfered with" and damages in the sum of $50 for the wrongful removal on two different occasions by appellant of respondent's gate. The right of respondent to maintain the gate in question cannot be seriously contested. . . .

The lands in question lie along the edge of Lake Erie south of provincial highway no. 18, also known as the Lake Shore Road, in the township of Malden in the county of Essex, and are a part of lot 56 in the 5th concession and lot 57 in the 6th concession and of a tract of land known as the Caldwell Grant.

In 1916 one Barron owned the easterly portion of these lands extending westerly from the lands of Lake Erie Country Club and the Lake Shore Road. The westerly portion of the lands in question was owned by Ledyard and Bulkley (respondent's predecessors in title) and was chiefly marsh lands, used and of much value for duck-hunting. The marsh cut across Barron's lands also, which to the north thereof were farm lands and which to the south thereof were in a state of nature with a wide sand beach extending to the lake. By conveyance dated 26th January 1916, and duly registered, Barron granted to Ledyard *et al.* "their heirs and assigns and their agents, servants and workmen, a free uninterrupted right of way ingress and egress for persons, animals and vehicles through along and over" a 20-foot strip of land on the easterly boundary of his lands from the Lake Shore Road towards the lake and then across the southern portion of his lands to the boundary of the grantees' lands. The grantor, for himself, his heirs and assigns, covenanted with the grantees, their heirs and assigns, to keep the way in proper repair and condition and to maintain fences on both sides of the way at his own expense and it was further agreed that the grantees "shall have the right to maintain a gate at each end of the said way with the privilege of having the said gates opened or locked, whichever they desire".

By conveyance dated 10th March 1917, and duly registered, Barron conveyed to Wallace and Marentette (appellant's predecessors in title) two parcels of land at the southerly portion thereof and abutting on either side the east-west portion of the right of way previously granted to Ledyard *et al.*, "together with a right of way for the Grantees their heirs and assigns over and upon the lands shown on each of the plans hereto attached marked Ledyard, Bulkley and Chappus right of way". Forming part of this conveyance is a plan attached thereto which sets out the right of way granted to Ledyard *et al.* and the lands being conveyed to Wallace and Marentette; in the conveyance itself, each of the two parcels conveyed is described by metes and bounds commencing at points in the Ledyard *et al.* right of way limits and the prior grant of that right of way is referred to by the registered instrument number.

By later conveyances the remaining lands of Barron, including the fee in his lands made subject to the rights of way mentioned, and the Ledyard and Bulkley lands, became vested in respondent and the Wallace and Marentette lands similarly became vested in appellant and his father as joint tenants. In July 1953 the father conveyed his interest to appellant. The predecessor in title to appellant and his father, one Frank Dayus, had acquired Wallace and Marentette's lands in 1941, and shortly thereafter, by agreement with respondent, the east-west portion of the right-of-way was shifted northward approximately 300 feet, respondent, however, never relinquishing the fee in any portion of the way as originally delimited. On 16th July 1952, Dayus threw open his premises as a beach-resort and, by extensive advertising, attracted large numbers of patrons who flocked to the premises by automobile over the right of way. In that year the travelled portion of the right of way was widened to 18 feet, gravelled, calcimined and rolled to a full two-car width. Appellant and his father in their turn, and later appellant, continued to advertise the premises as "Holiday Beach" and, in addition, held them out as a trailer-park and camp-site. It is unnecessary to detail the extent of the user of the right of way resulting from the establishment and maintenance of "Holiday Beach". Suffice it to say that, in the picnic and camping season each year, cars and patrons by the hundreds travelled up and down the way, cars were parked on appellant's lands, and the picnickers and campers spread out not only over those lands, but over the respondent's lands comprising the original east-west portion of the way. In other words, the burden of the easement has been markedly increased.

The fee in the way is now burdened, not with a private right of way in favour of appellant, his heirs and assigns, as originally contemplated, but with a use of the way for appellant's commercial purposes by great numbers of the public who travel over respondent's lands much as though the same constituted a public highway or a busy toll-road. At the time appellant's easement was created it was subject to the prior "free uninterrupted right-of-way" in respondent's predecessors in title. The chronology and contrasting language of the two grants, together with the surrounding circumstances as referred to by the learned trial judge, establish very clearly, in my opinion, that appellant's present user is much beyond the extent of his legal right and ought to be restrained. Appellant's use of the way constitutes as unauthorized enlargement and alteration in the character, nature and extent of the easement.

In ascertaining the rights of the parties I have applied the principles enunciated in *Gale on Easements*, 12th ed. 1950, p. 324, and in the judgment pronounced by the Supreme Court of Canada in *Laurie v. Winch*, [1953] 1 S.C.R. 49, [1952] 4 D.L.R. 449. I quote from Gale at pp. 324-5:

> According to the present state of the authorities, it appears that the grantee of a right of way is not entitled to increase the legitimate burden. But, on the other hand, the legal extent of his right may entitle him to increase the amount of inconveniences imposed upon the servient tenement — *e.g.*, by placing on the dominant tenement new buildings or increasing the size of old buildings. And the legal extent of the right (in other words, the mode as distinct from the extent of user) must, it seems, be ascertained from the intention of the parties at the time when the right was created.

It is useful, also, to quote two passages from *Laurie v. Winch*, *supra*. At p. 56 Kellock J., delivering the judgment of the Court, said:

> With respect to the nature and extent of the easement granted, it is to be observed that the grant is one of a right-of-way *simpliciter* with no express restriction as to use. Just as the circumstances existing at the time of the grant may be looked at for the purpose of ascertaining the intention of the parties as to the dominant tenement and as to the location and termini of the way, the circumstances may also be looked at for the purpose of construing the conveyances as to the nature and extent of the rights conveyed.

[Aylesworth J.A. then quoted from the references to *Todrick v. Western National Omnibus Co.*, [1943] Ch. 190, and *Robinson v. Bailey*, [1948] 2 All E.R. 791, found in the judgment of Kellock J. in *Laurie v. Winch*, above.] . . .

[T]he appellant ought to be restrained from continuing to use the right of way as he has been using it. I think, however, that respondent is entitled to its injunction in somewhat broader terms than those contained in para. 2 of the judgment. In the first place, since the original east-west portion of the way is no longer used as such, the parties by consent having substituted therefor a way of equal width lying to the north thereof, respondent is entitled to an order restraining appellant from any use of the lands comprising that original east-west portion. Then as to the whole of the way as presently constituted, appellant, his servants and agents, ought to be restrained from using it as a means for members of the public to have access to or egress from appellant's lands while used as a public commercial bathing-beach, public picnic-ground or trailer-camp, and from inviting members of the public so to use the way or any part thereof, and from otherwise using the way so as substantially to interfere with respondent's user thereof: see *Taff Vale Railway Company v. Gordon Canning*, [1909] 2 Ch. 48 at 58. If any difficulty arises as to the precise language of the injunction the parties may speak to a member of the Court.

In the result, the motion to vary the judgment will be allowed without costs and as to para. 2 thereof to the extent indicated and the appeal will be dismissed with costs.

Appeal dismissed with costs; motion to vary allowed in part without costs.

QUESTIONS

1. How does one determine the proper scope of an easement?

2. Is *Malden Farms* consistent with *Laurie v. Winch*?

Das v. Linden Mews Ltd.
[2002] 2 E.G.L.R. 76 (C.A.)

Buxton L.J.:

Introduction

Linden Mews is a small mews, containing only seven properties, in West London. At the further end of the mews, facing each other over what I will call the carriageway, are nos. 4 and 5. At the end of the mews, at right-angles to the carriageway and abutting on to nos. 4 and 5, is a substantial wall. Behind that wall is an area of garden ground. That ground has been used for the parking of cars since about 1988, at which time the whole of it was owned by the owner of no. 4, though held as a separate tenement from no. 4 itself. In 1998 the garden ground was divided between the owners of nos. 4 and 5, both of whom use it for the parking of cars. To facilitate access for vehicles, substantial gates have been opened in the wall by the owners of nos. 4 and 5.

For a long period the residents in the mews were uncertain as to who owned the carriageway. However, two of them succeeded in tracking down the owner, and formed the defendant company (LM Ltd) to purchase and hold the freehold of the carriageway. LM Ltd then required the payment by the various owners of substantial sums in order to park on the carriageway. The owners resisted those claims, claiming easements of way along the mews and easements to park their vehicles immediately adjacent to their respective properties. When that claim came on for trial at the Central London County Court all the frontagers apart from the owner of no. 1 agreed, on the first day of the trial, to enter into lease agreements for spaces in front of their houses. The only contest was on the part of the owner of no. 1, whom the judge held to have established a prescriptive right to park by his property, though with it left unresolved at that stage over what exact area of the carriageway that right extended.

However, LM Ltd additionally counterclaimed against the owners of nos. 4 and 5, claiming declarations that the owners of numbers 4 and 5 did not have a right to pass over the carriageway by foot or with vehicles for the purpose of gaining access to the garden ground, and injunctions to prevent their doing so.

The judge held that the owners of nos. 4 and 5 had no such right, and granted the injunctions sought. The owners appeal against that finding; and contend that in any event the judge should not have granted injunctions, but only have made an award of damages under Lord Cairns' Act. There are no significant differences between the case of no. 4 and the case of no. 5, and I shall deal only with no. 4, using the latter expression to refer to the premises of no. 4, excluding the garden ground; and referring to the owner of no. 4 for the time being as "the owner".

The easement and its extent

It is agreed that the owner has an easement of way over the carriageway, indeed in the terms asserted by LM Ltd in paragraph 1 of the relief sought by its counterclaim:

> a right to pass and repass over the [carriageway] to and from the highway to their respective properties by foot and with vehicles and a right to halt a single vehicle immediately adjacent to their respective properties for the purposes of loading and unloading the said vehicles

It was further agreed or assumed without challenge that the right would extend to driving a car into a garage contained within number 4, were such to exist.

LM Ltd, however argued, and the judge accepted, that any extension or use of that right of way to secure access to the garden ground, and to park a car there, fell foul of what is known as the rule in *Harris v. Flower* (1904) 74 L.J. Ch. 127. Because of the important role that that rule, and that case, played in the present appeal, it is necessary to make some general observations about it.

Rule in Harris

In *Harris*, the defendant owned land (the white land) immediately adjacent to the dominant tenement (the pink land) served by the way. He erected a single building, partly on the white land and partly on the pink land. The court had to decide whether use of the way to access the building as a whole by passing through the pink land would be for the purpose of obtaining access to the white land; and held that that was the case. It had to determine that question because of the rule as formulated by Romer L.J., in *Harris* at p. 132:

> If a right of way be granted for the enjoyment of Close A, the grantee, because he owns or acquires Close B, cannot use the way in substance for passing over Close A to Close B

However, that rule was only a particular application of the more general principle that the dominant owner can only use the way for the purposes of the dominant tenement, and not for other land. . . .

That more general proposition was recently set out by the House of Lords in *Alvis v. Harrison* (1991) 62 P. & C.R. 10 at pp. 15-16 (a Scottish appeal, which was however stated by the House equally to apply English law):

> A servitude right of access enures to the benefit of the dominant tenement and no other. Thus it cannot be communicated for the benefit of other tenements contiguous thereto . . . What they may not do . . . is to use the way, or permit its use by others, to obtain access to subjects other than the dominant tenement, whether or not they happen to be heritable proprietors of those other subjects.

It should also be noted at this stage that it is the general principle as stated in *Alvis*, rather than the factually constrained version of it stated in *Harris*, that arises on the facts of the present case. The owner does not assert a right to pass through no. 4 to the garden ground, or, at least, that is not his principal interest, since he seeks to access the garden ground not merely on foot but, principally, by vehicle. He does that, not by passing through no. 4, but by driving past no. 4 and into a different tenement.

The owner's case: "ancillary" use

In powerful submissions before this court Mr Lewison QC did not challenge the general correctness of either the rule in *Harris* or the more general statement of principle to be found in *Alvis* . He said, however, that they were subject to a gloss or qualification, on which the owner could rely. That qualification was that, because the agreed easement was to accommodate the use of no. 4 as the dominant tenement, the lawful exercise of that easement extended to accommodating any use that was ancillary to use of the dominant tenement. Access to the garden ground for the owner was clearly for the benefit of no. 4, and, thus, was a use ancillary to the agreed core of the right under the easement.

The books do not appear to adopt any principle at the level of generality contended for by Mr Lewison, but he contended that such could be drawn from, principally, three authorities, two of them in this court. However, before turning to those authorities it is necessary to look more closely at the formulation of the principle that they are said to establish. Mr Lewison was clear that the ancillary "use" that he asserted was a use ancillary to the beneficial use of no. 4: that is, that parking upon the garden ground by the owner was ancillary to his enjoyment of no. 4 as a dwelling-house. Thus, to drive up the carriageway to the garden ground was not to do something ancillary to the *easement*, rather, it was to use the easement for the very purpose for which the servient owner must be taken to have granted it, that of accommodating the dominant tenement. . . .

[The Court then addressed the first two authorities relied on by counsel: *Harris v. Flower* itself and *Peacock v. Custins* [2001] 1 EGLR 87. Both were found to be of little assistance in advancing the owner's position on ancillary use.] . . .

The case put before us that was nearest to the facts of this appeal was *National Trust for Places of Historic Interest or Natural Beauty v. White* [1987] 1 WLR 907. The Trust owned Figsbury Ring, a popular attraction, and had the benefit of an easement over a track leading to it. A car park was constructed at the side of the track, for visitors to leave their cars in order to proceed on foot to the Ring. Objection having been taken to that use, the Trust sought a declaration that it and persons authorised by it were entitled to use the track in conjunction with the car park for the purpose of visiting the Ring. Warner J. granted the declaration, saying, at p.p 912G–913D:

> [In *Harris v. Flower* the dominant owner] proposed to use the right of way for access to the factory as a whole. The Court of Appeal held that he was not entitled to do that because it would amount to increasing the size of the dominant tenement and thereby increasing the burden on the servient tenement. The Court of Appeal, however, recognised that it would have been otherwise if user of the right of way for access to the white land had been merely "subsidiary" and the "principal user" had been for access to the pink land . . .
>
> So applying in this case the distinction drawn by the Court of Appeal in *Harris v. Flower* . . . since the right claimed by the National Trust is no more than a right to authorise people to use the track for access to the car park for the purpose of visiting Figsbury Ring, it is properly to be regarded as ancillary to the enjoyment of Figsbury Ring. It is not as if the National Trust claimed a right to authorise people to use the track for access to the car park for the purpose of enjoying the car park itself, *e.g.* by picnicking there. Indeed, one way of describing the right claimed by the National Trust is as a right to authorise people to use the track to get to Figsbury Ring, in their vehicles as far as the car park and on their feet from there on.

Mr Lewison relied strongly not only on the result in that case, but also on the observations of Warner J. as to the use of the car park being "ancillary" to the enjoyment of Figsbury Ring. In our case, he said, parking on the garden ground was ancillary to the enjoyment of no. 4; and it could not make any difference in principle that the parking was at the end of the way rather than, as in *White*, half way up it. The inclusion of uses ancillary to the enjoyment of the dominant tenement was thus founded on the distinction drawn in *Harris*, which Warner J. had seen himself as applying.

There are two reasons why I cannot agree with that contention. First, although I accept that Warner J. did speak of use of the car park as ancillary to the "enjoyment of Figsbury Ring", the general structure of his judgment, and not least his references to the analysis of this court in *Harris*, makes it plain that what he had in mind was use of the car park as ancillary to, or in Mr Denehan's phrase part and parcel of, the use of the way for the purpose of the original grant, of getting to and from the Ring. That that is so is strongly supported by Warner J.'s statement of the practical effect of the provision of the car park that is to be found in the last sentence of the passage cited in [s.] 18 above. Second, although I agree that the mere fact of the location of the parking area cannot be decisive, it is of importance in the present case. Because the car park abutted on to the way, and was used for access to the way rather than separately for access to the Ring, it was possible for Warner J. to analyse the mechanics of its use as he did; and not possible for it to be said, as it can be said in the present case, that the principal or real use of the way that is asserted is a right to use the way to access land that is not part of the dominant tenement.

The distance between the decision in *White* and any principle that easements can be extended to access to any activity that can be said to ancillary to the beneficial use of the dominant tenement can be illustrated in a further way. Warner J. excluded any use of the way for the purpose of separate activities within the car-park, for instance picnicking. He undoubtedly so held because use of the way to accommodate a separate activity on the car-park would have extended the dominant tenement, contrary to the principle that Warner J. drew from *Harris* in the passage quoted in [s.] 18 above. But it might well occur to the trust, in line with similar arrangements at other beauty spots, that it would be agreeable for their visitors, and convenient for the trust in terms of protecting the Ring while pleasing the customers, to provide a picnic area in the car park. Provision and use of the picnic area would undoubtedly be ancillary to the enjoyment or beneficial use of the Ring. Warner J.'s judgment is, however, clear that the way could not be used to access the picnic area.

I therefore consider that *White* gives no support to a rule or principle that would justify the use of the way sought to be made in the present case. That conclusion is strongly reinforced by consideration of the actual facts of the present case, and of the implications within them of the principle that is sought to be established.

The facts of the present case

What the owner wishes to do is to drive a car up the carriageway, past no. 4, on to the garden ground, and then leave the car parked there while he enters no. 4: either by going through the garden ground or through the front door that abuts on to the carriageway. All that is said to accommodate the dominant tenement, in that it is an adjunct to, ancillary to, the owner's enjoyment of life in no. 4. But even if the latter were, in law, an available analysis in general terms, on the facts of this case it presents an insuperable problem. Mr Lewison pointed out that, unless the owner creates a garage within the building of no. 4, the admitted easement, as set out in [s.] 5 above, is of only limited use to him; because if the owner or his guests arrive by car at the front of no. 4, they have to put the passengers down while the driver takes the car off to park somewhere else, there being no easement of parking in front of no. 4. Quite so. The great benefit of access to the garden ground is not simply to be able to access no. 4, because that can already be done by using the easement according to the grant. What the garden ground adds is somewhere where the car can be left: a parking space.

I have no doubt that, for the practical reasons already given, that is a separate use from mere access. It is a use that takes place other than on the dominant tenement, and by using the carriageway to access that parking space the owner extends the dominant tenement. . . .

Conclusion as to the asserted use of the easement

I would uphold the judge's judgment, and declare that the appellants do not have a right to pass and repass over the carriageway either by foot or with vehicles for the purposes of gaining access to the garden ground. . . .

NOTE

Moses J. concurred. Thorpe L.J. wrote a separate concurring judgment.

Costa v. Janikas
2001 CarswellOnt 1691 (S.C.J.)

Brennan J.:

This case concerns part of a *mutual driveway* between *453 and 455 Mortimer Avenue in East York. The most southerly 16 feet*, more or less, has not been used as a mutual driveway, at least since 1937, and indeed, perhaps, before that. Mrs. McLaughlin gave evidence of the joy with which her sister, Anne Hayes, and her husband, took possession of the house at Number 433 in 1937. Then, or soon after, a fence was built dividing the most southerly 16 feet of the mutual driveway in half along its length.

Thereafter, the occupants of 453 and 455 have exercised exclusive possession of the area three and a half feet approximately, by 16 feet approximately, on their respective sides of the fence.

The Hayes family rented 453 until 1942 and then purchased it. They raised nine children there.

The yard, including the fenced-in part of the mutual driveway, was the playground for their children. That portion of the yard which (on the strength of photographic evidence and the recollections of the witnesses) I find included part of the mutual driveway,

> If the owner of the dominant tenement should make sufficiently substantial alterations to the dominant tenement so as to make the enjoyment of the easement impossible or unnecessary, or which would substantially increase the burden of an easement, it is evidence of an intention to abandon an easement.

I quote from the factum which was originally prepared by Mr. Tzekas, just at paragraph 24:

> In this particular case, that is the case before me, there is no suggestion that the right-of-way, south of the houses has ever been used to facilitate vehicular access, or parking. Both parties and their predecessors took active steps to physically obliterate the right-of-way and render such use impossible. Both parties and their predecessors took active steps to incorporate this portion of the registered right-of-way into their respective backyards, and the non-user has extended for a period of more than fifty years.

I quote again from the factum, paragraph Number 11, an express grant of a right-of-way can only be lost by express release, by merger, or by abandonment. The onus of proving the abandonment rests upon the respondents, in this case, the defendants.

And paragraph Number 12: "The inclusion of the right-of-way in a registered conveyance has been found to be of clear intention not to release the right-of-way."

In *Liscombe v. Maughan* [(1927), [1928] 3 D.L.R. 397 (Ont. C.A.)] is the authority cited for that proposition and for Paragraph 11. I accept that proposition but the fact is that there has been no registered conveyance until the conveyance to the present plaintiffs. It is the case of the defendants, I find, that the right-of-way had been extinguished by abandonment before that transaction.

Paragraphs 13 and 14, I accept as well, but distinguish the propositions that are made there. The prevention of use of the right-of-way for ten years or more is not by itself determinative of the issue. Something more than that is required, but I find that something more than that is in fact established in the case before me.

I hold that the expressly granted easement or mutual driveway, has been extinguished by its release by each owner by abandonment, and that that took place *prior to the transfer to the plaintiffs*. The application is therefore dismissed. Judgment will be for the defendants.

QUESTIONS AND COMMENTS

1. An easement may be released by express agreement between the holders of the dominant and servient tenements, or, as can be seen from *Costa v. Janikas*, by implied release (abandonment). What other events might give rise to the termination of an easement? Hint: consider the rules governing the four required elements of an easement, the analysis of abandonment found in *Costa*, the rule in *Harris v. Flower*, the doctrine of proprietary estoppel and adverse possession.

2. Does an easement of necessity come to an end when the necessity itself ceases, such as where another means of access is subsequently acquired?

See *B.O.J. Properties Ltd. v. Allen's Mobile Home Park Ltd.* 1979 CarswellNS 82, 108 D.L.R. (3d) 305 (C.A.) at paras. 50-3, 60-5 (*per* Coffin J.A.):

> ... In *Holmes v. Goring* (1824), 2 Bing, 76 at 84, 130 E.R. 233. Lord Best said at p. 237:
>
> > A grant, therefore, arising out of the implication of necessity, cannot be carried farther than the necessity of the case requires, and this principle consists with all the cases which have been decided.
>
> In *Barkshire v. Grubb* (1881), 18 Ch. D. 616, Fry J. remarked at p. 620:
>
> > I thought that the necessity must be judged of at the date of the conveyance. But the proposition laid down in *Holmes v. Goring* seems to have been only a dictum, for there appears to have been no necessity at the date of the grant.
>
> In *Proctor v. Hodgson* (1855), 10 Ex. 824 at 828; 156 E.R. 674, Park B. said at p. 675:
>
> > The extent of the authority of *Holmes v. Goring* is, that, admitting a grant in general terms, it may be construed to be a grant of a right of way as from time to time may be necessary. I should have thought it meant as much a grant for ever as if expressly inserted in a deed, and it struck me at that time that the Court was wrong: but that is not the question now.
>
> In *Gardner v. Horne* [(1848, 3 N.S.R. 278], the conclusion is indicated in the headnote:
>
> > A way of necessity is not superseded by the subsequent construction of a public road, to which the person claiming such right can have access through his own lands by a less convenient way.
>
> Bliss J. at p. 279 referred to *Holmes v. Goring's* reservation but remarked:
>
> > But still some regard must, I think, be had to convenience — for inconvenience, pushed to an extreme, amounts to a necessity. In all such cases, the question, I take it, will be, whether, fairly and reasonably considered with reference to the situation of the land and the circumstances of the case, the necessity which created the way has been removed or not by that which is alleged to have put an end to it. . . .
>
> Gale, *The Law of Easements* (14th ed.), pp. 120 to 121 citing *Barkshire v. Grubb, supra*, at p. 620 and *Proctor v. Hodgson, supra*, at p. 828 said:
>
> > In *Holmes v. Goring* the Court of Common Pleas considered that a way of necessity does not survive the necessity under which it arose, and that, if the person entitled to it acquires adjoining land which gives access to the dominant tenement, the right will cease. The case is not clear, however, and it may be that, at the time of the grant of the allegedly servient tenement, the necessity for a way over it had already ceased.

In the footnote it is stated that the facts in *Holmes v. Goring* were "unusual and complicated, and the leading judgment is difficult to analyse".

I notice, however, that at p. 309 the text again quotes *Holmes v. Goring* as authority for the view that,

> . . . a way of necessity is limited by the necessity which created it, and when such necessity ceases the right of way is extinguished.

Even if one accepts the authority of *Holmes v. Goring* or the position urged by the appellant, there still remains the question of the revival of the easement on the severance of the two properties (Gale (14th ed.), p. 311). The difficulty is that the older cases make a distinction between a type of apparent and continuous easement, such as ". . . a customary right in the city of London to have a gutter running in another man's land . . ." and something which is non-continuous.

The problem was discussed in Anger and Honsberger, *Canadian Law of Real Property* (1959), at p. 990:

> During unity of ownership no way or easement can exist in the land (*Morris v. Edgington*, (1810) 3 Taunt. 24, 128 E.R. 10). All easements, whether of convenience or necessity are extinguished by unity; but upon any subsequent severance, easements which, previous to such unity, were easements of necessity, are impliedly granted anew in the same manner as any other easement which would be held by law to pass as incident to the grant (Gale on Easements, 12th ed., 1950, p. 166).

The tone is somewhat modified on p. 988, where the author points out that a continuous and apparent easement such as an eave or downspout will pass on the severance by implication of law. Then he goes on to say:

> An easement which is in its nature not continuous and apparent such as an ordinary right of way will not pass on the severance of a tenement unless the grantor by appropriate language shows an intention that it should pass . . .

But see *McCulloch v. McCulloch* 1910 CarswellOnt 565, 2 O.W.N. 331 (H.C.).

3. In British Columbia, the rules governing the discharge of easements have been supplemented by statute: see *Property Law Act*, R.S.B.C. 1996, c. 377, s. 35:

> (1) A person interested in land may apply to the Supreme Court for an order to modify or cancel any of the following charges or interests against the land, whether registered before or after this section comes into force:
>
> (a) an easement;
>
> (b) a land use contract;
>
> (c) a statutory right of way;
>
> (d) a statutory building or statutory letting scheme;

(e) a restrictive or other covenant burdening the land or the owner;

(f) a right to take the produce of or part of the soil;

(g) an instrument by which minerals or timber or minerals and timber, being part of the land, are granted, transferred, reserved or excepted.

(2) The court may make an order under subsection (1) on being satisfied that the application is not premature in the circumstances, and that

(a) because of changes in the character of the land, the neighbourhood or other circumstances the court considers material, the registered charge or interest is obsolete,

(b) the reasonable use of the land will be impeded, without practical benefit to others, if the registered charge or interest is not modified or cancelled,

(c) the persons who are or have been entitled to the benefit of the registered charge or interest have expressly or impliedly agreed to it being modified or cancelled,

(d) modification or cancellation will not injure the person entitled to the benefit of the registered charge or interest, or

(e) the registered instrument is invalid, unenforceable or has expired, and its registration should be cancelled.

(3) The court may make the order subject to payment by the applicant of compensation to a person suffering damage in consequence of it but compensation is not payable solely for an advantage accruing by the order to the owner of the land burdened by the registered instrument.

(4) The court must, as it believes advisable and before making an order under subsection (2), direct

(a) inquiries to a municipality or other public authority, and

(b) notices, by way of advertisement or otherwise, to the persons who appear entitled to the benefit of the charge or interest to be modified or cancelled.

(5) An order binds all persons, whether or not parties to the proceedings or served with notice.

(6) The registrar, on application and the production of an order made or a certified copy of it must amend the registrar's records accordingly.

REVIEW QUESTION

Paul Durack owned both Lot 1 and Lot 2. He would frequently cross both lots over a path that connected the two properties. He would pick apples annually on Lot 2, and he also ran a clothesline from the back door of Lot 1 into the backyard of Lot

2. In 1999, he sold Lot 2 to Jason Armao. He also purported to grant Armao a "lease" (as they called it) which gave "the exclusive possession and use of any half of the double garage and driveway on Lot 1 that Armao or his assigns should require while Armao, or his assigns, are using the property as a residence." The transfer deed also contained the following term:

> It is hereby agreed and declared between the vendor and the purchaser that all easements and quasi-easements as are now existing between Lots 1 and 2 shall continue for the benefit of the respective properties.

A dispute has now arisen over the nature of the rights of each of the parties, especially as to which rights would continue in the event that either or both of the properties are later sold. Advise the parties of their rights. Identify uncertainty on the facts and in the law.

5. OTHER SERVITUDES AND SERVITUDE-TYPE RIGHTS

British Columbia v. Tener
[1985] 1 S.C.R. 533, 1985 CarswellBC 7

Wilson J.: . . .

A *profit à prendre* is defined in *Stroud's Judicial Dictionary* (4th ed.), vol. 4, at p. 2141 as "a right vested in one man [sic] of entering upon the land [page 541] of another and taking therefrom a profit of the soil". In *Black's Law Dictionary* (5th ed.), it is defined as "a right to make some use of the soil of another, such as a right to mine metals, and it carries with it the right of entry and the right to remove and take from the land the designated products or profit and also includes the right to use such of the surface as is necessary and convenient for exercise of the profit". Wells J. elaborated on the nature of a *profit à prendre* in *Cherry v. Petch*, [1948] O.W.N. 378 where he said, at p. 380:

> It has been said that a *profit à prendre* is a right to take something off the land of another person. It may be more fully defined as a right to enter on the land of another person and take some profit of the soil such as minerals, oil, stones, trees, turf, fish or game, for the use of the owner of the right. It is an incorporeal hereditament, and unlike an easement it is not necessarily appurtenant to a dominant tenement but may be held as a right in gross, and as such may be assigned and dealt with as a valuable interest according to the ordinary rules of property.

It is important to note that it is the right of severance which results in the holder of the *profit à prendre* acquiring title to the thing severed. The holder of the profit does not own the minerals *in situ*. They form part of the fee. What he owns are mineral *claims* and the right to exploit them through the process of severance. . . .

Profits à prendre may be held independently of the ownership of any land, i.e., they may be held *in gross*. In this they differ from easements. Alternatively, they may be *appurtenant* to land as easements are, i.e., they may be a privilege which is attached to the ownership of land and increases its beneficial enjoyment. . . .

Profits à prendre in gross are extinguished by unity of seisin, i.e., if the holder of the profit either:

(a) releases it in favour of the owner of the land in which the profit subsists; or

(b) becomes the owner of the land in which the profit subsists.

The extinguishment arises from the fact that if the ownership of the profit and the ownership of the land in which the profit subsists devolve on the same person, the profit can no longer exist as a separate interest in the land. The profit merges in the fee and is extinguished.

Bank of Montreal v. Dynex Petroleum Ltd. **[2002] 1 S.C.R. 146, 2002 CarswellAlta 54, 2002 CarswellAlta 55**

Major J.:

I. Introduction

This appeal arises from an application made by the appellant Bank of Montreal before the chambers judge in the Alberta Court of Queen's Bench for a determination that, as a matter of law, an overriding royalty is incapable of being an interest in land. . . .

II. Facts

The material filed and submissions of counsel indicated that royalty arrangements are common forms of arranging exploration and production in the oil and gas industry in Alberta. Typically, the owner of minerals *in situ* will lease to a potential producer the right to extract such minerals. This right is known as a working interest. A royalty is an unencumbered share or fractional interest in the gross production of such working interest. A lessor's royalty is a royalty granted to (or reserved by) the initial lessor. An overriding royalty or a gross overriding royalty is a royalty granted normally by the owner of a working interest to a third party in exchange for consideration which could include, but is not limited to, money or services (e.g., drilling or geological surveying). G. J. Davies, "The Legal Characterization of Overriding Royalty Interests in Oil and Gas" (1972), 10 Alta. L. Rev. 232, at p. 233. The rights and obligations of the two types of royalties are identical. The only difference is to whom the royalty was initially granted.

The appellant Bank of Montreal was a secured creditor of Dynex Petroleum Ltd. ("Dynex"), a corporation in liquidation. The trustee in bankruptcy wanted to sell all the oil and gas properties of Dynex. One issue was whether any such sale would be subject to overriding royalties arising out of the working interest held by Dynex. Also, there were several competing claims against the appellant, which by the time of this appeal had narrowed to the overriding royalties of the respondents Enchant and Willness, who claimed a preference by way of a caveat filed in the South Alberta Land Registration District, claiming an interest in Dynex's working interest as a result of services performed for Dynex and/or its predecessors. The respondents claimed their royalty rights comprised interests in land and claimed priority over the appellant because their interests, as protected by caveats, preceded the appellant's loans to Dynex and its predecessors. The appellant submitted that at common law an interest in land could not arise from an incorporeal hereditament and therefore the respondents' overriding royalties (which arose from a working interest, an incorporeal hereditament) did not rank higher in priority than the appellant's security interest.

This case pits this ancient common law rule against a common practice in the oil and gas industry. The Court is asked to resolve the apparent conflict. . . .

V. Analysis

At common law, an interest in land could issue from a corporeal hereditament but not from an incorporeal hereditament. "Corporeal hereditament" is defined by *The Dictionary of Canadian Law* (2nd ed., 1995) as:

> 1. A material object in contrast to a right. It may include land, buildings, minerals, trees or fixtures. . . .
>
> 2. Land.

"Incorporeal hereditament" is defined as:

> 1. [A right] . . . in land, which [includes] such things as rent charges, annuities, easements, *profits à prendre* and so on. . . .
>
> 2. Property which is not tangible but can be inherited.

In *Berkheiser v. Berkheiser*, [1957] S.C.R. 387 (S.C.C.), at p. 392, Rand J. held that an oil and gas lease, the interest from which an overriding royalty is created, can be a *profit à prendre*, an interest in land. A *profit à prendre* is an incorporeal hereditament. The appellant has submitted that at common law, an interest in land could not issue from an incorporeal hereditament and therefore overriding royalties cannot be interests in land.

Canadian case law suggests otherwise. In *Saskatchewan Minerals v. Keyes* (1971), [1972] S.C.R. 703 (S.C.C.), the majority declined to decide whether an overriding royalty could be an interest in land. However, Laskin J. in dissent specifically addressed that issue. He did not find the distinction between corporeal and incorporeal hereditaments to be useful in this context and discussed the difficulty of conforming new commercial concepts to anachronistic categories at p. 722:

> The language of "corporeal" and "incorporeal" does not point up the distinction between the legal interest and its subject-matter. On this distinction, all legal interests are "incorporeal", and it is only the unconfronted force of a long history that makes it necessary in this case to examine certain institutions of property in the common law provinces through an antiquated system of classification and an antiquated terminology. The association of rents and royalties has run through the cases (as in *Re Dawson and Bell, supra,* the *Berkheiser* case, *supra,* and cf. *Attorney-General of Ontario v. Mercer,* at p.777) but without the necessity hitherto in this Court to test them against the common law classifications of interests in land or to determine whether those classifications are broad enough to embrace a royalty in gross.

Laskin J. referred to *Berkheiser, supra,* where Rand J. held that a royalty was analogous to rent. While that case involved a lessor's royalty, Laskin J. found that although theoretically the holder of a lessor's royalty holds an interest in reversion, whereas the holder of an overriding royalty does not, since in essence the two interests are identical, there should be no distinction between the two royalty interests in their treatment as interests in land. The effect of Laskin J.'s reasons was to render inapplicable, at least insofar as overriding royalties, the common law rule against creating interests in land out of incorporeal interests.

Laskin J. concluded that the overriding royalty was an interest in land, analogous to a rent-charge. It is significant that he did not find all overriding royalty interests to be interests in land. He held that the intentions of the parties judged by the language creating the royalty would determine whether the parties intended to create an interest in land or to create contractual rights only. . . .

The appellant referred to cases that held royalty interests not to be interests in land. (See *St. Lawrence Petroleum v. Bailey Selburn Oil & Gas Ltd.*, [1963] S.C.R. 482 (S.C.C.) . . . *Vandergrift v. Coseka Resources Ltd.* (1989), 67 Alta. L.R. (2d) 17 (Q.B.); *Nova Scotia Business Capital Corp. v. Coxheath Gold Holdings Ltd.* (1993), 128 N.S.R. (2d) 118 (S.C.).) Although each of these cases held that the royalty therein is not an interest in land, they do not support the proposition that a royalty cannot be an interest in land. In each case the court found that the language used by the parties in creating the interest did not evidence the intention to create an interest in land.

That royalties can be interests in land finds support in W. H. Ellis' "Property Status of Royalties in Canadian Oil and Gas Law" (1984), 22 Alta. L. Rev. 1 at p. 10:

> Royalties, as used in the oil and gas industry, make sense only if they are property interests in unproduced minerals. Owners of mineral rights should be able to create them as such if they make clear their intent to do so. . . .

The oil and gas industry, which developed largely in the second half of the 20th century and continues to evolve, is governed by a combination of statute and common law. The application of common law concepts to a new or developing industry is useful as it provides the participants in the industry and the courts some framework for the legal structure of the industry. It should come as no surprise that some common law concepts, developed in different social, industrial and legal contexts, are inapplicable in the unique context of the industry and its practices.

The appellant could not offer any convincing policy reasons for maintaining the common law prohibition on the creation of an interest in land from an incorporeal hereditament other than fidelity to common law principles. Given the custom in the oil and gas industry and the support found in case law, it is proper and reasonable that the law should acknowledge that an overriding royalty interest can, subject to the intention of the parties, be an interest in land.

The Alberta Court of Appeal [1999 CarswellAlta 1271] offered compelling insight into the evolution of the law at para. 52:

> The principles inherent in the above argument need not be applied to prevent an overriding royalty from being an interest in land for a number of reasons. First, royalties and ORRs need not be classified into a traditional common law property category unsuited to the realities of the oil and gas industry and need not be subject to the arcane strictures of traditional categories. Second, some authorities suggest it is possible to have an incorporeal interest (an overriding royalty) created from an incorporeal interest. Third, even if it is not possible, the rule need not be blindly adhered to because, as stated by Mr. Justice Holmes in "The Path of the Law" (1897) 10 Harv. L. Rev. 457 at p. 469, it is "revolting to have no better reason for a rule of law than that so it was laid down in the time of Henry IV," and, "still more revolting if the grounds upon which it was laid down have vanished long since, and the rule persists from blind imitation of the past."

In *Friedmann Equity Developments Inc. v. Final Note Ltd.*, [2000] 1 S.C.R. 842, 2000 SCC 34 (S.C.C.), at para. 42, Bastarache J. outlined when changes to the rules of common law are necessary:

(1) to keep the common law in step with the evolution of society,

(2) to clarify a legal principle, or

(3) to resolve an inconsistency.

In addition, the change should be incremental, and its consequences must be capable of assessment.

In this appeal, to clarify the status of overriding royalties, the prohibition of the creation of an interest in land from an incorporeal hereditament is inapplicable. A royalty which is an interest in land may be created from an incorporeal hereditament such as a working interest or a *profit à prendre*, if that is the intention of the parties.

Virtue J. in *Vandergrift, supra*, at p. 26 succinctly stated:

> . . . it appears reasonably clear that under Canadian law a "royalty interest" or an "overriding royalty interest" can be an interest in land if:
>
> 1) anguage used in describing the interest is sufficiently precise to show that the parties intended the royalty to be a grant of an interest in land, rather than a contractual right to a portion of the oil and gas substances recovered from the land; and
>
> 2) the interest, out of which the royalty is carved, is itself an interest in land.

VI. Conclusion

The appeal is dismissed with costs to the respondents.

QUESTIONS

1. What is a "working interest"?

2. Why was it important to the litigants for the Supreme Court to determine whether or an overriding royalty was an interest in land?

3. What is the ancient rule that is rejected by the Supreme Court of Canada? What policy might be said to explain that rule?

4. What is accomplished by creating the "overriding royalty" arrangement used by the parties here? (Hint as to part of the answer: Before large deposits of oil were discovered in Alberta in the 1940s, dozens of dry holes were drilled. Even today, mineral sensing is not an exact science.) What other land law interests might also be employed in place of the overriding royalty?

5. Can the parties of an agreement declare an interest to be one of real property by simply stating that they intend it to be so? Is Major J. right in treating the question as one of intention?

Fredericton (City) v. Danielski
2003 CarswellNB 149 (Q.B.)

Garnett J. (Orally):

The City of Fredericton asks the Court for the following relief:

1. A declaration that White Court is a street in the City of Fredericton and a public thoroughfare;

2. An order that the Respondent, Betty Rose Danielski, or any person acting on her behalf, or any successor in title, be prohibited from interfering with the public's use and enjoyment of White Court as a public thoroughfare;

3. An order that the City of Fredericton immediately resume the administration, care and maintenance of White Court.

The Respondent, Betty Rose Danielski, says that the land, which the City asserts is a street, belongs to her and neither the City nor the public have a right to treat it as a public thoroughfare.

The Facts

White Court is an irregularly U-shaped, paved roadway which joins Duke Street at both ends.

Mrs. Danielski owns a property known as 29 Marshall Street which extends across the paved road to land in the center of the "U". She says that that portion of White Court (on the west and north side of the "U"), which she owns, is not a public street. . . .

The City admits that there is no known deed or other instrument establishing that the City has title to the land upon which the road is located.

Mrs. Danielski does have a deed (Danielski Affidavit, September 3, 2002).

The predecessors in title to Mrs. Danielski, James E. Lewis and Olga M. Brown, wrote to the City on October 3, 1983 and stated that they owned the portion of White Court now in dispute but would permit the City to use it (Record, Yerxa Affidavit, page 18).

On January 12, 1984, the City replied to their letter stating, among other things, that the road had been used by the public and maintained by the Town of Marysville and/or the City of Fredericton since at least 1959. Based on these facts, the City asserted that the court had been dedicated as a public street (Record, Yerxa Affidavit, page 20).

Notwithstanding this assertion by the City, Lewis and Brown continued to write letters to the City granting permission "to continue to use . . . our property" (Record, Yerxa Affidavit, pages 21–30 and 32–34). This continued on a yearly basis until 1999.

Mrs. Danielski purchased the property and when the City proposed to curb White Court in 2001 she would not permit the curbing of "my property" (Record, pages 36–38).

The City restated its position that the roadway was "dedicated" (Record, pages 40 & 41).

Correspondence continued and in June of 2002 Mrs. Danielski and/or her agents caused a portion of the roadway to be barricaded thereby inhibiting public use.

On September 4, 2002, Mrs. Danielski and/or her agents were enjoined and restrained from blocking the roadway and from asserting to the public that any portion of White Court was not a public street.

The Issue

The issue is whether the City has acquired the right to use the land in question for a public thoroughfare.

In Rogers, *The Law of Canadian Municipal Corporations* (2nd Edition), the author states that a municipality may acquire the right to use land as a street in four circumstances:

1. Dedication by the Crown;

2. Dedication by private individuals;

3. By statute;

4. By usurption and long enjoyment.

In this case the City relies on:

1. dedication by private individuals;

2. by usurption and long enjoyment.

1. Dedication by private individuals.

The City admits that there is no evidence of dedication by express act but says that it may be inferred by usage or other acts that the owner intended to dedicate the soil for a public road. The City relies on the following principles and authorities:

> The intention of the owner can be inferred from an owner's acquiescence in allowing public access and from the expenditure of public funds on the road over the years. *Delta (Municipality) v. Trim* (1982), 20 M.P.L.R. 208, 41 B.C.L.R. 58 (B.C. S.C.); *Cook's Road Maintenance Assn. v. Crowhill Estates*, [2001] O.J. No. 360 (Ont. C.A.) para 22-29.
>
> The use of a road by the public may be used as a presumption that the road was dedicated. *R. v. Moss* (1896), 26 S.C.R. 322 (S.C.C.).
>
> No formal acceptance of a dedication by a local authority is necessary in order to render it effective since the dedication is to the public and not to the corporation. *Rhodes v. Perusse* (1908), 41 S.C.R. 264 (S.C.C.).

> Once the street is accepted as a public road it maintains that character regardless of the subsequent circumstances. In effect, "Once a highway always a highway". *Stager v. Muskoka Lakes (Township)* (1989), 71 O.R. (2d) 126 (Ont. Div. Ct.).
>
> In addition to the use of the public, however, evidence of the expenditure of public money, the construction of pavements and the installation of mains have been considered as acceptance by the municipality by the public. The work or expenditure must be clear and unequivocal so as to indicate the intention of the municipality to assume the road. Rogers, Op Cit s. 227.24 at p. 1174; *Rorabeck v. Sidney (Township)* (1977), 16 O.R. (2d) 296 (Ont. H.C.). . . .

2. *By usurpation and long enjoyment.*

In *Lafferty v. Colborne (Township)* (1999), 45 O.R. (3d) 614 (Ont. S.C.J.), Justice Heeny of the Ontario Superior Court of Justice said at paragraph 11 and 12:

> The fourth option is usurpation and long enjoyment. Here it is argued that the owner of the road, the defendant Brindley, permitted the general public to use the road for the purpose of accessing his flea market and other purposes, and therefore an implied intention to dedicate the road can be inferred. It seems to me that the degree to which Brindley permitted the general public to use the road is a genuine question of fact. Thus, a triable issue does arise as to whether the road has been impliedly dedicated through Brindley's conduct and Mr. Smith conceded this point in argument.
>
> However, this does not determine the motion. Even assuming that the plaintiffs are able to prove dedication, they still must prove assumption by the municipality in order to succeed. It is only if the plaintiffs can demonstrate that evidence exists that could support a positive finding on both issues that a trial will be necessary.

I accept that these cases accurately state the law with respect to the issues before the Court.

The Evidence

The City submitted ten affidavits in support of its position. Walter Brown, who was born in 1940 and lived his entire life in the relevant area, is a City Councillor for the City of Fredericton. Prior to the amalgamation of the Town of Marysville with Fredericton in 1973, he was a Town Councillor for the Town of Marysville from 1970–1973. He says "as far back into my childhood as I can remember White Court was used as a public thoroughfare." He says, also, that the Town maintained White Court while he was a councillor.

Peter Grasman, who has been employed by the City since 1980, says the City has "maintained, plowed and administered" White Court during all of his employment. He says, also, that there are water pipes, storm sewers and sanitary sewer pipes in the ground below White Court which have been there since at least 1973.

George Saunders, who is 65, has lived in the relevant area his entire life. He was a Town Councillor for the Town of Marysville from 1960–1970 and was the Chairman of Public Works. He says that during that time the Town exercised administrative control over White Court by "paving and plowing, setting speed limits and generally maintaining it." In 1967–68 the Town installed new asphalt curbing and paving on the entire surface of White Court. He says, also, that as far back as he can remember White Court was used as a public thoroughfare.

Brian Parker, who has lived at the entrance to White Court for fourteen years, says the public has used it during all of that period.

Mrs. Danielski has submitted three affidavits all sworn by her. The only relevant information contained in these is that her predecessors in title disputed the City's assertion that White Court was a public street beginning in 1983.

Disposition

Since there was an objection to the City's assertion that White Court was a public street in 1983, I have examined the evidence from before that date to ascertain whether there is sufficient evidence to infer that the owners before that time intended to dedicate the soil for a public road and whether there is evidence that the municipality assumed responsibility for it on behalf of the public.

On the basis of the evidence of Walter Brown and George Saunders, I find White Court has been used by the public as a thoroughfare from at least the late 1940s. I find, also, on the basis of their evidence that the Town of Marysville assumed responsibility for its maintenance since at least 1960.

I therefore find that White Court is a public street. . . .

Order

I declare that White Court is a public street in the City of Fredericton and a public thoroughfare.

Mrs. Danielski does not have a right to interfere with the public's use of the street and is prohibited from doing so. . . .

Application granted.

QUESTIONS AND COMMENTS

1. What policy considerations should govern the determination of whether or not an intention to dedicate exists?

2. Under English common law, servitude-like rights can arise from customary usage. For example, in *Hall v. Nottingham* (1875) 33 L.T.R. 697 (Ex. D.), a right to dance around a maypole on private lands was protected on this basis. In *Adair v. National*

Trust [1998] N.I. 33 (Ch. D.), a customary right was asserted to dig for an unlimited quantity of lugworms on the foreshore of a lough in a locale in County Down. The elements needed to support a customary claim, and its application to the instant facts were dealt with by Girvan J. (at 44-5):

> A custom is a particular rule which has existed either actually or presumably from time immemorial and has obtained the force of law in a particular locality although contrary to or not consistent with the general law of the realm (see *Lockwood v. Wood* (1844) 6 QB 50 at 64 per Tindal C.J.). A custom is in the nature of a local common law within the particular locality.
>
> In relation to the plaintiff's claim to be entitled to take lugworms from the foreshore without limitation and for general commercial purposes it has been demonstrated that no such unlimited right exists at common law. If the plaintiff has such a right it must be on the basis of a customary right. To be valid a custom must have four essentials: (1) it must be immemorial; (2) it must be reasonable; (3) it must be certain in respect of its nature and in respect of the locality; (4) it must have continued without interruption.
>
> It has been held that an alleged custom is unreasonable on the grounds that it would destroy the subject matter of the right and for this reason a *profit à prendre* cannot ordinarily be acquired by custom (see *Tilbury v. Silva* (1889) 45 Ch. D. 98 at 107, *Lord Fitzharding v. Purcell* [1908] 2 Ch. 139 and *Payne v. Ecclesiastical Comrs* (1913) 30 T.L.R. 167). Furthermore the customary right must be limited to particular classes of persons or sections of the public and the category of persons so defined must be free from vagueness and uncertainty. The plaintiff alleged that members of the "fishing community of County Down" were entitled to assert the customary right. This class is vague and uncertain. Thus, for example, it is not clear whether it was being claimed that retired or unemployed fishermen or persons who in the past had some connection with the fishing industry or members of a family of such persons were within or without the custom. In any event the evidence does not satisfy the court that it has been established that there was in fact a widespread enjoyment of an alleged right to take lugworms for general commercial purposes from the Lough.
>
> The plaintiff's asserted claim to a customary right to take unrestricted supplies of lugworm for all purposes, accordingly, must fail.

(Time immemorial was established by statute to mean 1189, the year of the ascension to the throne of Richard I: *Statute of Westminster I*, 1275, c. 39.)

3. Assume that a similar right was alleged by an Aboriginal band in Canada. What criteria govern the recognition of such a right?

6. ACCESS TO PUBLIC AND PRIVATE PROPERTY

In recent years, courts in Canada and elsewhere have dealt with the rights of individuals to use both public and private property as venues for public assembly or the exercise of free speech. One can treat such entitlements as a form of servitude (using that term loosely).

Crown land is impressed with constraints on use that do not affect private owners. In *Director of Public Prosecutions v. Jones (Margaret)* [1999] 2 A.C. 240 (H.L.), the Law Lords were called upon to determine whether the use of a highway as a site of protest was permissible under the common law. In that case, several individuals had been convicted at trial of "trespassory assembly" contrary to the *Public Order Act, 1986.* They had participated in a protest to "free Stonehenge" from the fence that had been erected to protect the ancient monument from vandalism. By a 3:2 majority the convictions were set aside. Lord Irvine Lairg L.C. said that a highway is a public place which the public may enjoy for any reasonable purpose — such as peaceful assembly — provided that activity does not unreasonably impede traffic or otherwise constitute a nuisance. These were questions of fact, to be determined on a case-by-case basis. Lord Hutton added (at 288):

> If, as in my opinion it does, the common law recognises the right of public assembly, I consider that the common law should also recognise that in some circumstances this right can be exercised on the highway, provided that it does not obstruct the passage of other citizens, because otherwise the value of the right is greatly diminished. The principles of law in Canada governing the right of public assembly are different to those in England, in part because the *Canadian Charter of Rights and Freedoms* gives an express right of freedom of expression, but I consider that the reasoning in the following passage in the judgment of Lamer C.J.C. in the Supreme Court of Canada in *Committee for the Commonwealth of Canada v. Canada* (1991) 77 D.L.R. (4th) 385, 394 should also apply to the common law right of public assembly:
>
>> the freedom of expression cannot be exercised in a vacuum . . . it necessarily implies the use of physical space in order to meet its underlying objectives. No one could agree that the exercise of the freedom of expression can be limited solely to places owned by the person wishing to communicate: such an approach would certainly deny the very foundation of the freedom of expression.

The reference to the Canadian case of *Committee for the Commonwealth of Canada v. Canada* (1991) 77 D.L.R. (4th) 385, 1991 CarswellNat 827, 1991 CarswellNat 1094 (S.C.C.) is instructive. The most significant constraints in Canada on the right of exclusion and control of public property are the limitations that arise out of the *Canadian Charter of Rights and Freedoms*. The *Charter* applies to state action and can affect, *inter alia*, the state's power of exclusion over its property (i.e., public property). So, for example, in the *Commonwealth* case it was decided that the use of an airport as a site for distributing political pamphlets is constitutionally protected. The reasons for judgment in the *Commonwealth* case are extensively reviewed in *Cie generale des Establissements Michelin — Michelin & CIE v. C.A.W. — Canada* [1997] 2 F.C. 306, 1996 CarswellNat 2297, 1996 CarswellNat 2711 (T.D.), below.

An enforceable right of access to *private* property is a more controversial notion. A private owner's power to exclude is not inherently fettered by the *Charter*. At the same time, it has long been acknowledged that that power is not absolute. For example, human rights legislation prohibits private discriminatory conduct in relation to the provision of goods, services and rental accommodations. And under the common law, innkeepers and common carriers are obliged to accept all patrons unless there exist reasonable grounds to refuse service.

In the pre-*Charter* case of *Harrison v. Carswell* [1976] 2 S.C.R. 200, 1975 CarswellMan 58, 1975 CarswellMan 84, it was held that a mall owner was entitled to exclude a picketer from the premises. A conviction against Sophie Carswell under Manitoba's *Petty Trespass Act* for refusing a request to leave the shopping centre was therefore upheld. For the majority, Dickson J. (as he then was) wrote (at 219):

> Anglo-Canadian jurisprudence has traditionally recognized, as a fundamental freedom, the right of the individual to the enjoyment of property and the right not to be deprived thereof, or any interest therein, save by due process of law. The Legislature of Manitoba has declared in the *Petty Trespasses Act* that any person who trespasses upon land, the property of another, upon or through which he has been requested by the owner not to enter, is guilty of an offence. If there is to be any change in this statute law, if A is to be given the right to enter and remain on the land of B against the will of B, it would seem to me that such a change must be made by the enacting institution, the Legislature, which is representative of the people and designed to manifest the political will, and not the Court.

Shortly after the Supreme Court of Canada decision in *Harrison v. Carswell*, the Province of Manitoba amended *The Petty Trespass Act*, C.C.S.M. P50. Section 4 now reads:

> Any person who, on any walk, driveway, roadway, square or parking area provided outdoors at the site of or in conjunction with the premises in which any business or undertaking is operated and to which the public is normally admitted without fee or charge, communicates true statements, either orally or through printed material or through any other means, is not guilty of an offence under this Act whether the walk, driveway, roadway, square or parking area is owned by the operator of that business or undertaking or by any other person or is publically owned, but nothing in this section relieves the person from liability for damages he causes to the owner or occupier of the property.

In addition, section 57 of *The Court of Queen's Bench Act*, C.C.S.M. C280 states:

> (1) Subject to subsection (3), the court shall not grant an injunction that restrains a person from exercising the right to freedom of speech.
>
> (2) For the purposes of this section, the communication by a person on a public thoroughfare of information by true statements, either orally or through printed material or through any other means, is an exercise of the right to freedom of speech.
>
> (3) Nothing in this section affects
>
> > (a) enforcement by criminal or quasi criminal proceedings of an Act of Parliament or of the Legislature or of a by-law of a municipality respecting
> >
> > > (i) the use of public thoroughfares,

(ii) the protection of public property,

(iii) the general conduct of persons in public places, or

(iv) restrictions on or prohibitions against the making of certain statements or statements of certain types; or

(b) enforcement by a civil proceeding

(i) of an Act of Parliament or of the Legislature respecting restrictions on or prohibitions against certain statements or statements of certain types, or

(ii) of the law respecting defamation.

(4) In this section, "public thoroughfare" includes a walk, driveway, roadway, square and parking area provided outdoors at the site of and in conjunction with a business or undertaking and to which the public is usually admitted without fee or charge and whether or not the walk, driveway, roadway, square or parking area is owned by the person carrying on the business or undertaking or is publicly owned.

To what extent do these provisions alter the law as set out in *Harrison v. Carswell* in Manitoba?

In *Gameday Publication(s) Ltd. v. Keystone Agriculture & Recreation Centre Inc.* (1999) 170 D.L.R. (4th) 617, 1999 CarswellMan 69 (C.A.) a narrow reading was given to both provisions. Gameday distributed a magazine pertaining to the Brandon Wheat Kings hockey team and the Western Hockey League on the Keystone premises, the arena used by the Wheat Kings for home games. The magazine was supported by advertizing revenue and was distributed free of charge. It was, in effect, in direct competition with the Wheat Kings program that was sold at the arena. When the Gamesday agents attended at the arena in October 1997, they were asked to leave the premises and were peacefully evicted from the property by the security personnel. Gameday then sought an injunction that would allow them to enter the premises.

At first instance, the injunction was granted. That decision was reversed on appeal. The Manitoba Court of Appeal held that section 4 of the *PTA* merely provides a defence to a charge under that Act, and so was not engaged in the case. Section 57 of *The Queen's Bench Act* had the limited effect of removing the remedy of injunction but did not prevent a landowner from peaceably evicting a trespasser, as occurred in the case. Moreover, it was concluded that the actions here, which were purely commercial, were not protected speech with the meaning of section 57 of the *Court of Queen's Bench Act*. Still, it was offered that some commercial activity might fall with that provision. For the Court, Helper J.A. wrote (at para. 27):

> I am not prepared to attempt to enumerate all of the circumstances and actions that the Legislature contemplated would come within the provisions of s. 57. However, I agree with counsel . . . that arguably the legislative intent was not confined to the protection of those involved in peaceful picketing. Persons who are communicating information with a commercial component may well be protected by the legislation. Each situation

must be analyzed on its own facts by examining the manner of the distribution, the nature of the information being communicated, and the objective of the persons communicating to determine whether the actions taken constitute the exercising of a right to freedom of speech as envisioned by the statute.

In the end, it was Keystone that was granted the injunction. Do you agree with the conclusions of the Manitoba Court of Appeal?

Harrison v. Carswell remains the starting point in an analysis of the relevant law in Canada (even if it has not always been followed: see, *e.g.*, *R. v. Layton* (1986) 38 C.C.C. (3d) 550, 1986 CarswellOnt 792 (Prov. Ct.)). But is it still good law?

Cie generale des Establissements Michelin — Michelin & CIE v. C.A.W.-Canada [1997] 2 F.C. 306, 1996 CarswellNat 2297, 1996 CarswellNat 2711 (T.D.)

[In the course of an attempt by the Canadian Auto Workers to unionize labour at three Michelin tire plants, leaflets and posters were distributed containing the word "Michelin", as well as the corporate logo, the Michelin Man (Bibendum), both uses being without permission from the company. The company sued based on breach of trademark and copyright. The union responded that the right to freedom of expression protected their actions.

It was held that there was a copyright (but not a trademark) infringement. A substantial part of the copyrighted material (the Bibendum) had been reproduced, and the use by the C.A.W. could not be characterized as "fair dealing", an exception to liability under the *Copyright Act*. At the same time, it was decided that the reproduction of Bibendum constituted "expression" within the meaning of section 2(b) of the *Canadian Charter of Rights and Freedoms*, under which "Everyone has the . . . fundamental freedoms [of] freedom of thought, belief, opinion and expression. . . ." But was it *protected* expression under section 2(b)?]

Teitelbaum J.: . . .

Parody as an exception

As I have ruled that the Defendants have reproduced a substantial part of the Plaintiff's work and thus infringed the copyright, the burden now shifts to the Defendants to prove that they fall under an exception to copyright infringement. Like the Plaintiff in regards to the *Trade-marks Act*, the Defendants have offered a novel argument and radical interpretation of the law. In this case, the Defendants argue that parody is a form of "criticism" under Section 27(2)(a.1). . . .

Parody is not explicitly discussed in the *Copyright Act*. . . .

. . . Under the *Copyright Act*, "criticism" is not synonymous with parody. Criticism requires analysis and judgment of a work that sheds light on the original. Parody is defined in the *Collins* dictionary (Second Edition) as "a musical, literary or other composition that mimics the style of another composer, author, etc. in a humorous or satirical way". In *Zamacoïs v. Douville and Marchand*, [1943] 3 Fox Pat. C. 44 Justice Angers at page 71 held that the Court will consider the wider context, both the quantity and quality of quotations from the original, in its evaluation of a work as "criticism": "The right of literary criticism includes the right of citation of passages from the work criticized and the number or the importance of the citations does not modify the character of the publication if they serve only to contribute to the demonstration of the criticism undertaken". In the Canadian and Commonwealth courts, parody has never been held to figure as criticism although the term criticism is not confined to "literary criticism".

The Defendants have added a twist to this usual reasoning by urging the Court to consider, in line with the recent decision of the American Supreme Court in *Luther R. Campbell a.k.a Luke Skywalker v. Acuff-Rose Music, Inc.*, 114 S.Ct. 1164 (1994) [hereinafter "*Acuff-Rose*"] that parody is a form of "criticism" under Section 27(2)(a.1). The Defendants submitted that even though their "Bibendum" constituted a reproduction of a substantial part of the Plaintiff's copyright, this was a type of parody that by the very definition of the term parody required substantial reproduction of the original to make its point. The addition of the men under "Bibendum's" upraised leg, the dialogue and the alteration in "Bibendum's" expression created a new, integrated "Bibendum" design that was meant to ridicule and mock "Bibendum's" usual corporate image as a benign, smiling and safe father figure. The Defendants further argued that they had no need to cite the source, a requirement under Section 27(2)(a.1) since in a parody, the source is implicitly known to the onlooker.

As with the Plaintiff's creative and novel interpretations of the *Trade-marks Act*, I have rejected the Defendants' submissions. The Defendants fall short because American case law permitting parody as criticism under the American doctrine of "fair use" is not applicable nor terribly persuasive in the Canadian context of a different legal regime and a longstanding trend to deny parody as an exception. As well, exceptions to copyright infringement should be strictly interpreted. I am not prepared to read in parody as a form of criticism and thus create a new exception under Section 27(2)(a.1).

American Case Law and Strict Interpretation

The Defendants pointed to the recent unanimous decision of the American Supreme Court in *Acuff-Rose*, *supra*, as sole authority for reading in parody as a component of criticism or the exception to infringement. In effect, the Defendants are admitting, "Yes, we did infringe the Plaintiff's copyright by copying a substantial part of the original but as a defence, we can plead that we were parodying the original, a form of fair dealing for the purpose of criticism under Section 27(2)(a.1)". The Defendants admitted that they were urging the Court to accept a new interpretation of Section 27(2)(a.1) in the light of the American decision. In *Acuff-Rose*, the defendant had used the characteristic bass riff and opening line from Roy Orbison's classic rock song, "Pretty Woman" in its own rap song with new lewd and crude lyrics and distinctive rap background motifs. Justice Souter writing for the Court held at page 1173 that the Court of Appeals had erred in overstating the parodist's commercial motive to deny the fairness of the use: "In giving virtually dispositive weight to the commercial nature of the parody, the Court of Appeals erred. "The rap version of "Pretty Woman" could still qualify as a parody or critique of the romantic fantasy embodied in the original song and could be considered an exception to copyright infringement as fair use for the purpose of criticism under Section 107 of the American Statute. The United States Supreme Court remanded the case to the trial level to reconsider the rap version of "Pretty Woman" against all of the factors for "fair use" in Section 107.

While the American case is most fascinating from both a cultural and legal perspective, I have not found it to be persuasive authority in the context of Canada's particular copyright regime. Chief Justice Laskin in *Morgentaler v. The Queen*, [1976] 1 S.C.R. 616 held at page 629 that a Court should be prudent in applying American precedents to the Canadian context and should take into consideration the particular rules of each system of law: ". . . they do not carry any authority beyond persuasiveness according to their relevance in the light of context, with due regard to the obvious differences that exist . . . ". American decisions are only persuasive to the extent that the laws in both jurisdictions are similar: (see *Compo Co. Ltd. v. Blue Crest Music*, [1980] 1 S.C.R. 357 at page 367 [hereinafter "*Compo*"]). The Plaintiff rightly pointed out many distinctions between Section 107 of the American *Copyright Act* and our own system. Contrary to the opinion of James Zegers, author of an article entitled, "Parody and Fair Use in Canada after *Campbell v. Acuff-Rose*" in (1994) 11 C.I.P.R. 205, I hold that these distinctions are crucial. First, the American system is open-ended when it comes to exceptions. In other words, the list of exceptions is not exhaustive but should be on a case-by-case basis since Section 107 reads, "for purposes *such as criticism, comment* . . ." (emphasis added). As well, the four factors in Section 107 for determining whether use is fair are equally not exhaustive since they are prefaced by the phrase, "*shall include*". This is the not the case in Canada. The exceptions to acts of copyright infringement are exhaustively listed as a closed set in subsections 27(2)(a) to 27(2)(m) and 27(3) of the *Copyright Act*. They should be restrictively interpreted as exceptions. Justice McLachlin in *Bishop v. Stevens*, [1990] 2 S.C.R. 467 at pages 480–481 [hereinafter "*Bishop*"] cautioned the Court against reading in exceptions to copyright infringement given the detailed and explicit exemptions: "Furthermore, an implied exception to the literal meaning of s. 3(1)(d) is all the more unlikely, in my opinion, in light of the detailed and explicit exceptions in s. 17(2) (now s. 27(2)) of the Act, providing for matters as diverse as private study, research or critical review . . . ". I cannot accept that I should give the word "criticism" such a large meaning that it includes parody. In doing so, I would be creating a new exception to the copyright infringement, a step that only Parliament would have the jurisdiction to do.

Second, "fair use" in the American system is not equivalent to "fair dealing" in Canada. Unlike the explicit requirement in Section 27(2)(a.1), the American system does not require that the critic give the source and author of the copyright if this information is provided in the original. In sum, parody does not exist as a facet of "criticism", an exception to infringement in Canadian copyright law. I do accept that parody in a generic sense can be a form of criticism; however, it is not "criticism" for the purposes of the *Copyright Act* as an exception under the fair dealing heading. . . .

Conclusions on Copyright

I am not prepared to take the two leaps of faith urged by the Defendants. The first is that parody is synonymous with criticism. The second is that the Defendants can dispense with the need to mention the source and fair treatment because of the peculiar nature of parody with its implicit acknowledgment of the source. My role is not to create legislation but to apply the existing rules crafted by Parliament. If Parliament had wanted to exempt parody as a new exception under the fair dealing provision, it would have done so: (see *Bishop, supra*, at pages 483–484). Since the Defendants have shown little creativity in depicting the "Bibendum", I do not accept the Defendants' contention that their creativity is being fatally stifled by a repressive copyright regime. I am also not convinced by the Defendants' invocation of public policy. They raised the spectre of editorial cartoonists being barred from using the "Bibendum" in a parodic way. If the Plaintiff were to be thin-skinned enough to attack all unflattering depictions of the "Bibendum", I would suggest that such cartoons could be protected as sufficiently new works under Section 3(1) if they do not reproduce a substantial part of the original and display a modicum of thought such as to produce a new result. They would therefore not be considered acts of infringement. Parody would be protected against charges of infringement by its dissimilarity to the original work as long as it did not produce a substantial portion of the original. As Zegers, *supra*, noted at page 208 of his article on the *Acuff-Rose* decision in the Canadian context, written parodies would be protected because they could not hone so closely to the original as in a song parody. As well, creative works depicting some critical variation of the "Bibendum" could be protected under the umbrella of "criticism" within the context of a newspaper or journal article describing CGEM Michelin and its subsidiary Michelin Canada. . . .

The Use of Private Property and Freedom of Expression

I am not aware of any decisions from the Supreme Court of Canada providing direct guidance on how a Court should evaluate the use of a copyright in determining the scope of protection under Section 2(b) of the *Charter*. However, I take support for my position that the use of private property is a prohibited form of expression from the decision of the Supreme Court of Canada in *Committee for the Commonwealth of Canada v. Canada* (1991), 77 D.L.R. (4th) 385 (S.C.C.) [hereinafter "*Commonwealth*"]. In *Commonwealth, supra*, the Supreme Court suggested that choosing a *public* forum of expression can possibly limit the scope of protection under Section 2(b). By analogy, I reason that use of *private* property to convey expression can also warrant removing the expression from the protection of Section 2(b). . . .

In fact, the Defendants do not assert a right to hand out anti-Michelin leaflets inside the factory gates. That would constitute a trespass, a clearly illegal or prohibited form of expression. However, the Defendants do argue that their freedom of expression includes the right to use the Plaintiff's property to convey meaning. . . .

[I]n *Commonwealth* . . . the Court continued to recognize that private property is not available as a forum for free expression. Justice McLachlin at page 448 was the most unequivocal:

> It has not historically conferred a right to use another's private property as a forum for expression. A proprietor has had the right to determine who uses his or her property and for what purpose. Moreover, the *Charter* does not extend to private actions. It is therefore clear that s. 2(b) confers no right to use private property as a forum for expression. . . .

Chief Justice Lamer in *Commonwealth* did not expressly address the issue of the use of private property but he did draw a distinction at page 393 of his decision between the "quasi-fiduciary nature" of the government's right of ownership and the exclusive rights of the private owner who "benefits personally from the places he owns". Chief Justice Lamer went on to rule that the Court, in determining the scope of the individual's right to free expression on government property under Section 2(b), should first balance the government's interest in public property with the individual's right to free expression on that property. Only if the expression is compatible with the primary function of the property is the expression within the protected sphere of Section 2(b).

Justice L'Heureux-Dubé in *Commonwealth* gave the most expansive rights of access to public property and held that any restriction on the time, manner and use of public property had to be justified under Section 1. However, even she recognizes at page 422 in *Commonwealth* the different and distinct status of private property:

> If the government had complete discretion *to treat its property as would a private citizen, it could differentiate on the basis of content, or choose between particular viewpoints and grant access to* sidewalks, streets, parks, the courthouse lawn, and even to Parliament Hill *only to those whose message accorded with the government's preferences.* (My emphasis.)

For two reasons, *Commonwealth* does not bear directly on the particular facts of this case — the issue of the use of copyright as private property and freedom of expression. However, the *Commonwealth* decision still contains relevant principles of law on the status of private property and the balancing of the parties' interests under Section 2(b). In *Commonwealth*, the Supreme Court, in various ways, elaborated what Justice McLachlin at page 451 called "a threshold test . . . to screen out cases clearly falling outside the free speech guarantee before reaching the s. 1 analysis." What then are the differences between the facts in *Commonwealth* and the case at bar? The first difference is that the property in the *Commonwealth* case was used as a *location* or forum for the distribution of leaflets and other types of protected expression. The property was being "used" but only as a backdrop for expression and not to convey meaning. Unlike the case at bar, the property was not the vehicle for the Defendants' message. I do agree with Justice Thurlow in *New Brunswick* [*New Brunswick Broadcasting Co. Ltd. v. CRTC*, [1984] 2 F.C. 410 [hereinafter "*New Brunswick*"]], that the Court should reject as out of hand anyone who argues that Section 2(b) gives him or her the right to use without permission the printing press of another — more likely a computer in this day and age — merely because it is used to create leaflets that are legitimately protected as expression. It remains a more open question, however, whether parodic use of a copyright, the copyright itself already imbued with meaning, should be analogous to use of a printing press. The "Bibendum" is not property like a printing press that is devoid of meaning. A printing press is truly only a vehicle for conveying meaning.

Second, the property in *Commonwealth* was an airport or piece of *public* property. The Plaintiff's copyright is *private property*. The Defendants fought against the usual characterization of copyright as private property and urged the Court to consider the Plaintiff's copyright as a type of state sanctioned private property. The Defendants sought to diminish the "private" nature of the Plaintiff's property rights for a particular reason. They wanted the Court to apply Justice L'Heureux-Dubé's framework in *Commonwealth*, *supra*, at pages 429-430 for balancing public property rights and free expression under Section 1 of the *Charter* to the current case. I have no hesitation in stating that I can find no merit in the Defendants' characterization of the Plaintiff's copyright as a piece of quasi-public property. The fact that the Plaintiff's copyright is registered by a state-formulated system under the aegis of the *Copyright Act* in no way diminishes the private nature of the right. If one were to extend the Defendants' test of "state sanctioned private property" to its logical extreme, no one in Canada could properly say that his or her house was "private property" since houses are also registered under various province designed systems of land title! I therefore hold that Justice L'Heureux-Dubé's analysis of the balance of public property and free expression under Section 1 is not applicable to the case at bar.

A further wrinkle in extrapolating from the *Commonwealth* case is that the entire Supreme Court agreed on the outcome, but Justices McLachlin, L'Heureux-Dubé and Chief Justice Lamer issued three distinct approaches on the subject of public property and the scope of free expression. As Justice Linden stated at page 86 of *Weisfeld*, *supra*, "both Chief Justice Lamer and Madame Justice McLachlin, in their separate reasons, suggested that the scope of expression protected under paragraph 2(b) of the *Charter* may be somewhat different when the expression takes place on government-owned property than in other situations". It is difficult to discern the majority opinion on the methodology for determining the scope of protected expression in the use of public property by a individual asserting a right to free expression. One must carefully read the concurring opinions. Justice Sopinka concurred with the reasons of Chief Justice Lamer in their entirety while Justice Cory at page 446-447 concurred with the same reasons specifically on Chief Justice Lamer's balancing technique under Section 2(b) between the individual's interest in expression and the primary function of the government property. Justices Gonthier and La Forest agreed with several elements of both the reasons of the Chief Justice and Justices L'Heureux-Dubé and McLachlin but they ultimately decided that in future cases, they would adopt the approach of Justice McLachlin. Thus, neither the decision of Chief Justice Lamer nor Justice McLachlin has the numerical edge. Subsequent cases like *Peterborough (City) v. Ramsden* (1993), 106 D.L.R. (4th) 233 [hereinafter "*Peterborough*"] and *Weisfeld* [*Weisfeld v. Canada*, [1995] 1 F.C. 68 (C.A.) [hereinafter "*Weisfeld*"]] have considered all three approaches in reviewing the scope of protection for free expression on public property. Finally in *Toronto(City) v. Quickfall* (1994), 111 D.L.R. (4th) 687 (O.C.A), Justice Abella at page 690 held that Justice Iacobucci in *Peterborough, supra*, had in fact applied the approach of Chief Justice Lamer in balancing the interests of property owners with the freedom of expression guarantee: "Without disavowing the other two tests proposed respectively by L'Heureux-Dubé and McLachlin JJ., both of whose approaches he reiterated, Iacobucci J. utilized the approach of Chief Justice Lamer." I therefore have adopted by analogy the approach of Chief Justice Lamer in considering the interests of the individual asserting a right of free expression and the use of *private* property.

Although I have analyzed in some detail below the facts of this case under Chief Justice Lamer's balancing principle in *Commonwealth*, I also hold that the Defendants would have failed to prove that their expression was a protected form of expression even under the approach elaborated by Justice McLachlin in *Commonwealth*. Justice McLachlin acknowledged at page 449 of *Commonwealth* that "the protection conferred by a right, even *prima facie*, should not go beyond what can be justified, having regard to the history of the right and the purpose which it serves". Justice McLachlin established a test for when the scope of free expression is to be restricted under the Section 2(b) analysis. She stated at pages 455-456 of *Commonwealth, supra*, that the individual asserting a right to free expression on public property had to establish a link between the use of the public property and one of the purposes — truth, social participation and diversity of ideas — informing the protection of expression. Once again, this test from *Commonwealth* is not directly applicable to the case at bar since it concerns the use of *public* property as a *forum* for expression but it elaborates a helpful principle for distinguishing the nature of the parties' interests in this case. I agree with the Plaintiff's argument that use of its private property, the "Bibendum" copyright, was hardly consistent with all of the purposes informing free expression. Of course, there was certainly a link between the Defendants' leaflets and brochures that did not depict the "Bibendum" and the value of expression enhancing participation in social and political decision-making. However, one should not confuse the entirely socially acceptable and legitimate overarching goal of the Defendants' unionization activity with their inappropriate and unprotected means of expression under Section 2(b). The Defendants had no need to adopt a form of expression, the use of copyrighted material, that deprived the Plaintiff of its property and actually subverted the third value of promoting the diversity of ideas. In other words, if copyright is not respected and protected, the creative energies of authors and artists in furthering the diversity of ideas will not be adequately compensated or recognized.

(iv) Balancing Required at the Section 2(b) Stage:

The Defendants did not lightly dismiss the fact that they have used the Plaintiff's copyright. However, they urged the Court to consider this use as one element in the

Section 1 analysis in which the Court has to balance the nature of the parties' interests and rights. The Plaintiff also offered as evidence of the fact that the Defendants' freedom of expression was not restricted the multitude of anti-Michelin leaflets and brochures circulated by the Defendants that did not use the "Bibendum" copyright. The Plaintiff argued that freedom of expression is not impaired if the Defendants can say whatever they like against Michelin (aside from defamatory statements) as long as they do not use CGEM Michelin's property. Once again, the Defendants argued that the possibility of alternate forms of expression only becomes relevant at the Section 1 analysis under the question of whether the *Copyright Act* is a minimal impairment of the Defendants' right of free expression. The Defendants argued that it is premature under the Section 2(b) part of the Court's *Charter* analysis to consider the fact that the Defendants can so freely criticize Michelin's corporate policies and make their point without recourse to the Plaintiff's property.

I disagree with the Defendants' submission that the balancing of the parties' interests is only properly performed in the context of Section 1 of the *Charter*. Although the Defendants are correct in stating that the balancing of the parties' interests and rights most often occurs in the Section 1 analysis, some balancing, particular when it comes to the use of property, whether public or private, must take place even before the Court undertakes an inquiry under Section 1 to determine if the form of expression is prohibited. Chief Justice Lamer at page 392 in *Commonwealth*, *supra*, states:

> when a person claims that his freedom of expression was infringed while he was trying to express himself in a place owned by the government, the legal analysis must involve examining the interests at issue.

I acknowledge that this balancing principle from *Commonwealth* is not directly applicable to the case at bar since *Commonwealth* concerned use by a person of public property as a forum for expression. The Defendants have used private property not as a forum but as a means of conveying a message. However, despite these differences, I reason by analogy to *Commonwealth* that I am permitted to consider the parties' interests even before the Section 1 stage of the analysis in order to examine the scope of the Defendants' freedom of expression under Section 2(b) and determine if the expression is in a prohibited form. I hold that it is reasonable to equate doing something on private property as a forum for expression with using the property — the copyright — to convey expression.

(v) Interests of the Defendants and the Plaintiff

I recognize as Chief Justice Dickson stated at page 968 of *Irwin Toy* [*Irwin Toy Ltd. v. Quebec (A.G.)*, [1989] 1 S.C.R. 927 (S.C.C.) [hereinafter "*Irwin Toy*"]] how free expression is "fundamental because in a free, pluralistic and democratic society we prize a diversity of ideas and opinions for their inherent value both to the community and the individual". The Defendants were anxious to counter the Court's qualms that it would have to make a radical finding that all unauthorized uses of copyrighted material are protected forms of expression. The Defendants urged the

Court to consider the particular facts of this case in its consideration of the effects of the *Copyright Act* on the Defendants' freedom of expression. The Defendants argued that the Court could narrow the ambit of protected expression in its analysis of the effect of the *Copyright Act.* According to the Defendants, a Court might state that freedom of expression is only restricted when use of the copyright is for non-commercial purposes such as parody of a company symbol by a union during an organization campaign. I agree that the Defendants are distinct in that their expression is for a non-commercial purpose tied to such other fundamental *Charter* values as freedom of association: (see *Professional Institute of the Public Service of Canada v. Northwest Territories (Commissioner)* (1990), 72 D.L.R. (4th) 1 (S.C.C)). This is not to say, however, that the union is necessarily a non-commercial body. One cannot give free rein to unions to use the property of another merely because they are in the midst of an organizing campaign. Freedom of expression is not an absolute value: (see *Hill v. Church of Scientology of Toronto*, [1995] 2 S.C.R. 1130 at page 1173).

What then is the nature of copyright as private property? Copyright is an intangible property right. The owner therefore has a more challenging task in asserting his or her control over the use of the property. Launching an action for infringement under the aegis of the *Copyright Act* is the owner's prime tool for asserting his or her rights. But just because the right is intangible, it should not be any less worthy of protection as a full property right: (see *Ladbroke (Football) Ltd. v. William Hill (Football) Ltd.*, [1964] 1 W.L.R. 273 (H.L.) at 291). It may be easier to focus on the nature of the Plaintiff's property right in the copyright if we imagine the case of an infringer dealing with a painting, a piece of tangible private property that like the copyright is already imbued with meaning. No infringer could credibly allege that freedom of expression gives him or her the right to subvert the content or message of the painting by physically drawing a moustache on the painting. However, what if the infringer asserted the right to copy or substantially reproduce the painting with a moustache? Our instincts might not be so certain about the scope of the infringer's freedom of expression because our perceptions are coloured by the intangible nature of the copyholder's right. We should guard against our instincts in this instance since they might lead us to undervalue the nature of the Plaintiff's copyright and overestimate the breadth of the Defendants' freedom of expression. As Chief Justice Lamer stated at page 395 in *Commonwealth, supra,* "the fact that one's freedom of expression is intrinsically limited by the function of a public place is an application of the general rule that one's rights are always circumscribed by the rights of others". Rights also bring with them duties. The Defendants cannot logically assert a *right* to use the Plaintiff's private property within the scope of their freedom of expression, because then the Plaintiff would have a reciprocal *duty* to give the Defendants access to this property.

The Plaintiff argues that the Defendants' use of its property in fact subverts the third value — the diversity of ideas by enhancing self-fulfilment — of expression. Copyright promotes the third value by protecting and providing an incentive for authors to create works of expression because their works will be protected under the aegis of the *Copyright Act* from unauthorized reproduction. I have no reason to doubt that the Plaintiff is intent on protecting its interest in its copyright against all unauthorized users. The Defendants argue that the "Bibendum" is freely used by both pro- and anti-union forces without the permission of the owner by either side in the unionization campaign. However, the Plaintiff submitted evidence that it pursues any party, pro- or anti-union, who uses its intellectual property without permission. The Plaintiff offered as evidence on this point memos written by Mr. George Sutherland, in-house counsel for Michelin Canada. Mr. Sutherland had written to plant managers during an earlier unionization campaign in 1986. In these memos, Mr. Sutherland asked the managers to locate who had authored *anti-union* leaflets depicting the Bibendum. The managers were unable to locate the authors but the Plaintiff' intent on protecting its interests and private property against all comers is apparent.

It is now important to consider whether the Defendants' use of the Plaintiff's property is a prohibited form of expression. In *Commonwealth* at page 396, Chief Justice Lamer held that in instances of use of public property, expression is protected only if it is compatible with the primary function of the property. Thus, no one has a right to set up a peace camp in the middle of a public library because such obstreperous demonstrations would be incompatible with silent study, the prime function of the library. However, a peace camp on the lawn of Parliament Hill would be compatible with the function of Parliament Hill as an arena for public discourse and debate: (see *Weisfeld*, *supra.*) If freedom of expression in a public forum is limited by such factors as the function of the place, the conditions and restrictions for using private property should be even stronger. By analogy to Chief Justice Lamer's reasoning on the use of *public* property, I hold that a person using the *private* property of another like a copyright, must demonstrate that his or her use of the property is compatible with the function of the property before the Court can deem the use a protected form of expression under the *Charter*. In the present case, subjecting the Plaintiff's "Bibendum" to ridicule as the object of parody is *not* compatible with the function of the copyright. A "Bibendum" about to stomp hapless workers into submission does not present the original author's intent of a favourable corporate image or provide an incentive for compensating artists for the integrity of their vision.

(vi) Summary on the Scope of Protection Under Section 2(b)

I agree with the Defendants that the threshold for prohibiting forms of expression is high. Violent forms are certainly at the extreme end but a form need not be violent in order to be prohibited. In *Irwin Toy* at page 970, Chief Justice Dickson did not "delineate precisely when and on what basis a form of expression chosen to convey a meaning falls outside the sphere of the guarantee." The threshold for prohibiting forms of expression is not so high that use of another's private property is a permissible form of expression. Chief Justice Lamer in *Commonwealth*, *supra*, stated that the necessary balancing of the parties' interests in cases of a party asserting the right to use *public* property occurs before the Section 1 analysis. I have expanded this principle to conclude that a similar but stricter balancing of interests is to occur if the party, like the Defendants in the case at bar, asserts the right to use *private* property. In the balance of interests and rights, if the Defendants have no right to use the Plaintiff's "Bibendum", they have a multitude of other means for expressing their views. However, if the Plaintiff loses its right to control the use of its copyright, there is little left to the Plaintiff's right of private property. The Defendants seek to extend the scope of their right of free expression to include the use of another's property. . . .

[The Court held further that even if a violation of section 2(b) had been made out, the provisions of the *Copyright Act* would have been saved under section 1 of the *Charter* as a reasonable limitation on the rights contained in section 2(b).]

Sky City Auckland Ltd. v. Wu
[2002] 3 N.Z.L.R. 621 (C.A.)

Blanchard and Anderson JJ.:

This is an appeal from a judgment of Chambers J. [in the High Court at Auckland on 13 February 2002] granting the respondent, Mr Wu, an interlocutory injunction restraining the appellant operators of the Sky City Casino (Sky City)from preventing him under a banning notice dated 18 February 2001 for a period of two years from entering the casino or using its facilities. The appeal concerns the interpretation of s. 67 of the *Casino Control Act 1990* (the Act) against the background of the common law which underlies that section. The section reads:

67. Entry to and exclusion of entry from casino

(1) The fact that a casino is licensed under this Act shall not entitle any person to enter or to remain on the casino premises as against the holder of the casino premises licence or the casino operator's licence; and, subject to any right conferred by or under any other Act, every person shall leave the casino premises when required to do so by or on behalf of the holder of the licence.

(2) The provisions of subsection (1) of this section are in addition to, and not in derogation from, the Trespass Act 1982.

The notice given Mr Wu was in the following form:

SKYCITY Trespass Notice

To: Mr Zhangping Wu

17 Albert Street, 11th Floor, Auckland City

PURSUANT to section 67 of the Casino Control Act 1990 and under the general law, any person must leave SKY CITY AUCKLAND LIMITED when requested to do so.

TAKE NOTICE THAT YOU ARE FORBIDDEN FROM ENTERING SKY CITY LTD PREMISES WHICH INCLUDES ALL GAMING AREAS, SKY TOWER, SKY THEATRE, SKY CITY HOTEL, CARPARKS AND RESTAURANTS FOR A PERIOD OF TWO YEARS FROM THE DATE OF THIS NOTICE.

> If you re-enter Sky City Auckland Limited within two years from the date of this notice you will commit an offence under the Trespass Act 1980 and civil wrong of trespass. . . .

The issue is whether there is any obligation on Sky City to show that it acted reasonably in banning Mr Wu for the period which it has stipulated. Mr Wu contends that Sky City has banned him merely because he is a successful gambler and had raised with it an issue about discrepancies in pay-outs from slot machines in the casino. Sky City, while denying that this was the reason and saying that Mr Wu was ejected after threatening one of its staff members, says that under the general law, as confirmed by s. 67, it is entitled, as a landowner, to exclude people from its property, the casino, without giving any reason. We should interpolate at this early stage that no argument is made on Mr Wu's behalf that Sky City has acted towards him in breach of any of the anti-discrimination provisions of the *Human Rights Act* 1993. He does not say, for example, that he has been banned because he is Chinese. The parties are in agreement that the Casino Control Act must be read subject to those provisions. . . .

The Judge made his decision on the basis of a cause of action based in private law. The argument was made that Sky City owes casino patrons "a legal duty to serve and treat members of the public equally, without discrimination and in a fair and reasonable manner". So, it was said, the casino may not ban members of the general public without good cause. That alleged duty was pleaded as arising from:

> [a] The establishment and regulation of the casino industry in New Zealand by statute in the public interest;
>
> [b] The rights and privileges conferred on Sky City by virtue of its being the holder of a casino premises licence under s. 31 of the Act;
>
> [c] The rights and privileges conferred on Sky City by virtue of its being the holder of a casino operator's licence under s. 37 of the Act;
>
> [d] The status of the casino as a lucrative State-licensed monopoly affected with a public interest;
>
> [e] Sky City holding itself out to the public as being willing to serve all, thereby creating an expectation that access/entry will not be denied without warning, proper grounds and procedural fairness; and
>
> [f] The status of casinos as a common calling in New Zealand in 2001.

Chambers J. concluded that Sky City did owe a "special duty to the public" as alleged. He said that when property owners open their premises to the general public in the pursuit of their own property interests, they must not exclude people unreasonably. They have a duty not to act in an arbitrary or discriminatory manner towards people who come on to their premises. Probably, the Judge said, this is but a development of the old law of common callings. The general proposition of law was subject to a qualification contained in s. 67(1).That subsection empowered the casino premises licence holder and the casino operator's licence holder to require people to leave the casino premises and everyone must comply with such a request unless he or she can point to a statutory right to remain, which Mr Wu could not do. That did not mean, however, the Judge said, that licence holders could capriciously request people to leave. In exercising the s. 67 powers, licence holders were subject to public law constraints, which might also affect private law obligations and rights. That was not a matter which the Judge said he needed to decide, as Mr Wu's application for an interlocutory injunction was based not on Sky City's removal of him but rather on the purported ban against re-entry. Section 67(1) did not affect Sky City's powers to ban, which stemmed from its rights as occupier of the premises. But those rights were not absolute. They were subject to the restriction to which he had referred.

The Judge found that Sky City was under a duty not to ban members of the public without good cause. That duty arose from its holding itself out to the public as being willing to serve all. The duty did not arise by virtue of any licence under the Act or from the status of the casino as a state-licensed monopoly. It was not relevant that Sky City happened to be the only casino in Auckland." There cannot be one rule for Sky City because it is the sole casino in its city and another rule for towns like Queenstown where there is more than one casino". It was the fifth matter pleaded (see para . . . (e) above) which was the true basis of the duty, although the Judge was not necessarily to be taken as subscribing to the pleaded "expectation". The duty was not to exclude people unreasonably.

Chambers J. thought there was no need to determine whether casinos are a common calling in New Zealand in 2001 because the law of common callings has, at least in this respect, now been subsumed within a wider proposition. The Judge concluded . . . :

> Any land occupier under the general law can give notice to others requiring them to stay off his or her land. Those who defy such notices commit the tort of trespass. That power to exclude is subject to qualification, however, in the case of property owners who open their premises to the general public in pursuit of their own property interests. Such property owners cannot exclude or ban people unreasonably. . . .

On this appeal both sides agree that we should merely determine whether Sky City was under a duty to act reasonably in banning Mr Wu from the casino. If it was, as Chambers J. held, the appellants accept that there is a serious question to be tried and that, for the reasons given by him, the interlocutory injunction restraining them from enforcing the ban should remain in place pending trial. However, if there is no such obligation to act reasonably, Mr Wu's cause of action must fail and the interlocutory injunction against Sky City should be discharged.

Submissions for appellants

Mr Davison Q.C. took as a starting point the unfettered right of an owner or occupier of land to exclude others without giving justification or reasons. The right arises as an incident of property ownership or possession and is enforceable by means of the tort of trespass to property. It was submitted that Chambers J. had undertaken an inappropriate reformulation of this fundamental right. As expressed, it would embrace all kinds of private property, for example, a corner dairy, retail premises, sporting venues and restaurants. All would have to substantiate any exclusion of a member of the public with well-founded reasons. Any such reformulation, it was submitted, should and could occur only through legislation. It was wrongly undertaken by the Judge also because Parliament has already entered the field by placing some restrictions upon the conduct of occupiers by means of the Human Rights Act. In any event, s. 67(1) precluded application of any reformulated general rule to licensed casinos.

Counsel referred to the difficulties created by departing from the brightline rule that reasons were not required by the landowner, and to the danger that some people would be sure to litigate their exclusion and breaches of the peace might occur when disputes arose over the propriety of an owner's conduct. There would be uncertainty also over procedural obligations accompanying any exercise of a qualified right.

Questions of the reasonableness or fairness of an owner's actions towards persons on his or her property were said to be foreign to private law and, it was submitted, should not be imported from public law. Subject to an absence of any discrimination in breach of the Human Rights Act, the casino licence holder, as a property owner or occupier, must have the right to exclude someone without having to give any reason or justifying their action. They are entitled to exclude someone, for example, because they may be considered to be winning too much. . . .

Submissions for respondent

Mr Taggart submitted that at common law the right of a property owner or occupier to require persons to leave the property or to refuse them entry has been qualified where the owner or occupier is using the property to conduct a business affected by the public interest. A casino operator, by virtue of a licence from the State, is in the position of having a "virtual monopoly" (also put as a "relative monopoly") and therefore has such a business. Because of the status of the business the casino operator cannot exclude a member of the public from access to it without good reason. Section 67, it was submitted, merely confirms this position, but it does require the patron to leave first and argue afterwards about the reasonableness of the casino operator's requirement.

Counsel said that this Court in [*Vector Ltd. v. Transpower N.Z. Ltd.* [1999] 3 N.Z.L.R. 646 (C.A.)] had traced the common law doctrine of prime necessity back to passages in Sir Matthew Hale's *Treatise De Portibus Maris*, written about 1670 but published in 1787 (1 Harg L Tr 78) and had accepted that, where a relevant monopoly exists, property becomes affected with a public interest and subjected to the asserted common law obligations. The Court had recognised that the principle owed something to the rule that those who exercised a common calling had a duty to serve all and at a reasonable price. The modern form of the doctrine has developed by analogy and resembles the American law of public utilities. The concern is with the abuse of monopoly power. It was submitted that the point has been reached in New Zealand where the various doctrines have merged into one which has several aspects: businesses affected with a public interest are bound to supply goods and services to the public equally, without discrimination and unreasonable exclusion, and at a reasonable price. There are several factors which, it was submitted, either singly or in combination, trigger these obligations and temper the existence of property rights. They include the presence of monopoly or near monopoly, the source of the authorisation, presence of State licensing, the nature of the service and the importance of the service to the individual and/or the community, the holding out to the public and the furnishing of that service to a large number of people.

Mr Taggart argued that there is an analogy between the present case and *Allnutt v. Inglis* (1810) 12 East 527, where the proprietor of a bonded warehouse (in which imported goods could be deposited without payment of customs duty until their release from the warehouse) was held to be under a common law duty, derived from Hale's statement of principle, to make its facilities available to the plaintiff upon tender of reasonable compensation. (Because of s. 64 of the Act, under which casino operators may not charge for the "right of entry", no question of reasonableness of charges arises in the present case.) The remedy where goods were excluded without good reason or the price was too high was an action in tort (action on the case). (For a modern example of a tort action for exclusion involving racial discrimination by an innkeeper, Mr Taggart referred to *Constantine v. Imperial London Hotels Ltd* [1944] KB 693.) . . .

Discussion

The idea that a business invested with "the monopoly of a public privilege" must, in the absence of good reason in a particular case or situation, such as a lack of capacity to provide goods or services, make its facilities available to all, and at a reasonable price, is soundly based both in New Zealand law and in economic good sense. The phrase "affected with the publick interest" comes from Hale himself, as this Court noted in *Vector Ltd v. Transpower New Zealand Ltd*, at para [41]. We referred to the judgment of Lord Ellenborough C.J. in *Allnutt v. Inglis*. In that case the London Dock Company had been certificated under an Act of Parliament whereby it had become lawful for wine importers to store their wines in the company's warehouses and defer paying duties on them until the wines were taken out of store. The plaintiffs had been refused the use of this bond-store facility because they would not agree to pay the company's notified charges. There was no other place in the Port of London where such a facility was available, although the Court commented that if the exclusive privilege had been extended to a few others it would not appear to have varied the case. It was held that there was such a monopoly and public interest attaching to the company's property that it was bound by law to receive the goods into its warehouses for a reasonable hire and reward. Lord Ellenborough, in the leading judgment, recognised a general principle "that every man may fix what price he pleases upon his own property or the use of it". But "if, for a particular purpose, the public have a right to resort to his premises and make use of them, and he have a monopoly in them for that purpose, if he will take the benefit of that monopoly, he must as an equivalent perform the duty attached to it on reasonable terms". The Chief Justice said that the legislation enabling the deposit of the wines without payment of duties in the first instance had been passed "not merely for the benefit of the company but for the good of trade". The company's warehouses had been "invested with the monopoly of a public privilege, and therefore they must by law confine themselves to take reasonable rates for the use of them for that purpose". At p. 540 there is the following passage:

> If the Crown should hereafter think it advisable to extend the privilege more generally to other persons and places, so far as that the public will not be restrained from exercising a choice of warehouses for the purpose, the company may be enfranchised from the restriction which attaches upon a monopoly: but at present while the public are so restricted to warehouse their goods with them for the purpose of bonding, they must submit to that restriction: and it is enough that there exists in the place and for the commodity in question a virtual monopoly of the warehousing for this purpose, on which the principle of law attaches, as laid down by Lord Hale in the passage referred to, which includes the good sense as well as the law of the subject. . . .

The same principle, deriving from Hale, was accepted by the Supreme Court of the United States to be part of the common law in that country in *Munn v. Illinois* 94 US 1977 (1876). Waite C.J., delivering the opinion of the Court, said at p. 126:

> Property does become clothed with a public interest when used in a manner to make it of public consequence, and affect the community at large. When, therefore, one devotes his property to a use in which the public has an interest, he, in effect, grants to the public an interest in that use, and must submit to be controlled by the public for the common good, to the extent of the interest he has thus created. He may withdraw his grant by discontinuing the use; but, so long as he maintains the use he must submit to the control.

A subsequent reference to Hale makes it clear that the Court was contemplating a situation in which the person concerned had an effective monopoly.

Vector confirms the reception of the principle into New Zealand law and refers to a considerable body of authority in this country. The label given to it in that case — the doctrine of prime necessity — is a term appropriate to cases which concern the supply of electricity or water by a utility company but we think that Mr Taggart is correct in his submission that that doctrine is a strand of the broader principle which, as *Vector* recognised, is adaptable to meet new legal and social situations.

This Court viewed the doctrine of prime necessity as a "backstop common law remedy", to be applied in the absence of other remedies and where there are no statutory contra-indications to its use, such as were found in that case in the *Commerce Act*, reinforced by the *State Owned Enterprises Act*. As Thomas J. said in his concurring judgment in *Vector* at para [77], without such a remedy the law would be deficient. Thomas J. spoke of the law's objective of curbing the exploitation of monopoly power in the supply of essential services (para [80]).

In the United States it is not yet settled whether, and to what extent, licensed gambling facilities are properly to be regarded as businesses affected by the public interest. The Supreme Court of New Jersey has favoured the view that they are. In *Uston v. Resorts International Hotel Inc* [445 A 2d 370 (1982)] the appellant had excluded Mr Uston from blackjack tables in its casino because he was a practitioner of a complex strategy for playing blackjack known as card counting, which increased his chances of winning money. The Court held that New Jersey's Casino Control Act gave its Casino Control Commission exclusive authority to set the rules of licensed casino games, which included methods of playing those games. The Court held that the Act therefore precluded the appellant casino from excluding Mr Uston for card counting. Any common law right the casino may have had to exclude him for this reason was abrogated by the Act. But, in an obiter portion of its judgment, the Court made some observations about the position, as it saw it, at common law. It recognised that the majority American rule had for many years disregarded the right of reasonable access and had allowed proprietors of amusement places an absolute right arbitrarily to eject or exclude any person consistently with State and Federal civil rights laws. The New Jersey Court took a different view. It said that property owners have no legitimate interest in unreasonably excluding particular members of the public when they open their premises for public use. Whether a decision to exclude was reasonable must be determined from the facts of each case.

Uston can be contrasted with the decision of the United States Court of Appeals for the Seventh Circuit in *Brooks v. Chicago Downs Association Inc* 791 F.2d 512 (1986), which concerned whether the operator of a horse racetrack had the absolute right to exclude a patron from the track premises for any reason, or no reason, except race, colour, creed, national origin or sex. The Court allowed the exclusion. The argument for the racetrack owner had been that because it was a privately owned place of amusement it could exclude someone "simply for wearing a green hat or a paisley tie"; that it need give no reason for excluding the patron "because it is not a State-granted monopoly, but a State-regulated licensee operating on private property". The Seventh Circuit followed the decision of the New York Court of Appeals in *Madden v. Queens County Jockey Club* 72 N.E. 2d 697 (1947) in which the plaintiff had been barred from the Aqueduct Race Track by the club under the mistaken belief that he was a bookmaker with the same surname operating for a well-known mobster. The New York Court had concluded that the club had the power to admit as spectators only those whom it might select and could exclude others as long as the exclusion was not founded on race, creed, colour or national origin. The Court had rejected Mr Madden's argument that a licence to conduct horse racing was equivalent to a franchise or a monopoly to perform a public service.

The Seventh Circuit found that the defendant in the case before it, the racetrack owner, did not enjoy a State granted franchise or monopoly. It had "only a licence for 75 days of racing in any one year. "That licence had been imposed only to regulate and raise revenue, "as opposed to a franchise which grants a special privilege that does not belong to an individual as a matter of common right". The Court added at p. 516:

> Any one racetrack may or may not have a "quasi-monopoly" (a term that is subject to many interpretations) over opportunities available to jockeys, owners, or drivers, but they do not have a true monopoly over opportunities for the plaintiffs to bet on horses.

Accordingly, the Seventh Circuit found at p. 517, the proprietor of the racetrack did not have to prove or explain that the reason for exclusion was a just reason:

> He doesn't want to be liable to Coley Madden solely because he mistakenly believed he was a mobster. The proprietor wants to be able to keep someone off his private property even if they only *look like* a mobster. As long as the proprietor is not excluding the mobster look-a-like because of his national origin (or because of race, color, creed or sex), then the common law, and the law of Illinois, allows him to do just that.

The Seventh Circuit chose not to follow what it called the arguable — but not clear — abandonment of the common law rule in New Jersey in *Uston.* It said that it was clear that New Jersey had not *per se* abandoned the common law rule "but has adapted it, in a limited fashion, to the particular needs of its casino industry. The Seventh Circuit seems to have been considerably influenced by the fact that in the situation before it there was no monopoly. . . .

Counsel for the appellants placed reliance on the decision of the English Court of Appeal in *CIN Properties Ltd v. Rawlins* [1995] 2 EGLR 130, an extempore judgment which briefly referred to *Uston* and regarded it as based upon a previous decision of the Supreme Court of New Jersey in *State of New Jersey v. Schmid* 423 A 2d 615 (1980), which the English Court believed to have turned upon the constitutional freedoms of the First Amendment. Therefore, the general proposition in *Uston* was considered to have no application in English law. With respect, we regard this as an inaccurate reading of what the New Jersey Supreme Court was saying when it referred to *Schmid.* That case certainly had constitutional overtones but the New Jersey Court saw the decision in *Schmid* as being analogous to the position at common law. It is to be noted that, more recently, *dicta* from a differently constituted English Court of Appeal in *Porter v. Commissioner of Police of the Metropolis* (Court of Appeal, England, 1675 of 1999, 20 October 1999) has acknowledged the possibility of further incremental development of the common law.

Although we do not find it necessary to express a concluded view, we have found persuasive Mr Taggart's argument, based in part on the foregoing authorities, that the common law of New Zealand will now recognise a casino or other licensed gambling facility as a business affected by the public interest in circumstances where the operator enjoys a monopoly; and that in such a case, subject to any statutory provision to the contrary, the operator's right to exclude members of the public may be qualified by an obligation to do so only for an articulated good reason.

We do not, however, express a firm conclusion on this point because, even if that is assumed to be the law and the Sky City Casino is further assumed to be operating in monopoly conditions, in our view s. 67 expresses a legislative contra-indication, namely that the fact that the casino is licensed does *not* make it necessary for the licence holder to have a good reason for excluding someone from the premises. . . .

It can be seen that [s. 67] is directed to the effect of the licensing of the casino under the Act. That fact is not to entitle any person to enter or remain on the premises and, subject to any right conferred by or under any other Act — such as the *Human Rights Act* — every person is to leave the casino premises when required to do so by or on behalf of a holder of the licence. In addition, the *Trespass Act 1982* can be invoked. It seems to us that the very purpose of the section is to negate the doctrine upon which the respondent is relying — to negate any suggestion that because the casino is licensed, and in its particular situation therefore may operate as a monopoly created by the licence, patrons must not be excluded without good reason. The argument for the respondent is that the section merely states the position at common law modified to require an excluded patron to leave first and argue afterwards, but surely, if that had been intended, it would have been very directly stated that persons must not be excluded without good reason although they must leave if asked to do so and contest the validity of their exclusion thereafter. It is, we think, of significance, as the appellants submitted, that the word "reasonably" does not appear in the section. . . .

We have therefore concluded that the purpose of s. 67 is to make it clear that the holders of licences pertaining to casinos under the Act are entitled to exclude members of the public without assigning a reason so long as they do not commit any breach of the *Human Rights Act* or other relevant legislation, and that accordingly Mr Wu's cause of action must fail and the interlocutory injunction must be discharged.

Result

The appeal is allowed and the injunction granted by the High Court is discharged. . . .

McGrath J.:

I agree with the majority judgment that s. 67 of the *Casino Control Act 1990* (the Act) excludes any common law principle which otherwise might require the appellants to have good reason before refusing Mr Wu entry to their licensed casino . . .

As the Court is unanimous that, on its true construction, the application of s. 67 determines the appeal in the appellants' favour, it is not strictly necessary for me to discuss the scope of the underlying common law principle of prime necessity which was central to the respondent's argument. . . . Like the majority I do not wish to express a concluded view on the question but, in view of what they say, I wish to express my tentative views on the scope of prime necessity in New Zealand. . . .

In New Zealand, prior to 1918, attempts by litigants to avail themselves of the principle by reference to the early 19th century English cases were largely inconclusive in indicating whether it applied in New Zealand and if so in what forms. It was the Privy Council decision in 1918 in *Minister of Justice for the Dominion of Canada v. City of Lévis* [1919] A.C. 505 which was pivotal in recognition by the New

Zealand Courts of the common law principle of prime necessity. The *Vector Ltd* decision confirmed that recognition.

In *City of Lévis* Lord Parmoor, who delivered the judgment of the Privy Council, coined the term "prime necessity" in relation to supply of water for domestic and sanitary purposes (p. 513). It was on the premise that water is a matter of prime necessity that he applied, without acknowledgement of the earlier English authority, a principle akin to but, narrower than that stated in *Allnutt v. Inglis*. Thereafter in New Zealand the element of a necessary service or commodity appears constant in the cases which followed *City of Lévis* up to and including *Vector Ltd*. . . .

There is no common pattern of recognition in the common law countries of this aspect of the writings of Hale as expressed in *Allnutt v. Inglis*. The High Court of Australia, has rejected the argument that there is a principle of law that when a utility or other body exercised an exclusive franchise, it is under a duty to provide the service: *Bennett and Fisher Ltd v. Electricity Trust (SA)* (1962) 106 C.L.R. 492 per Dixon C.J. at pp. 500–501. . . . Nor has it been applied in modern times in England (see Constitutions, Property and Regulations, P.P. Craig, [1991] Public Law 538.On the other hand in the United States the relative popularity of Hale and *Allnutt v. Inglis* appears, at least in part, as a means of bypassing constitutional restraints on legislative price regulation . . . It was probably for this reason that in *Vector Ltd* this Court observed that United States cases "must be located in their own constitutional setting" (para. [42]). . . .

The effect of the submission to which the majority is attracted, would be to remove from the principle the requirement of the element of "public necessity". Only by doing that will there be a basis for applying it to restrain the operators of casinos, or other licensed gambling facilities, from excluding people from their premises without giving good reason. Given the rather anachronistic nature of the doctrine and its limited relevance in the modern political economy as *Vector Ltd* demonstrates, it would be strange for the Courts to attempt to broaden the scope of its traditional application in New Zealand. And, given the modern legislative practice of addressing situations possibly covered by it directly, it may well be no occasion arises in which it ever becomes necessary for this Court to decide the modern scope of the common law doctrine. . . .

QUESTIONS AND COMMENTS

1. The majority of the New Zealand Court of Appeal declined to make a final determination as to whether a casino was a business affected by the public interest given that the business enjoys a monopoly. Would you be prepared to go that far?

2. As McGrath J. noted, the catalyst for the development of this branch of the law is a Canadian case — *Minister of Justice (Canada) v. City of Lévis* (1918) [1919] A.C. 505 (Quebec P.C.) — where Lord Parmoor first used the term "prime necessity". There, it was held the City of Lévis had a duty to supply water at a fair and reasonable

rate to land owned by the federal Crown, even though the land was exempt from municipal property taxes.

However, the *City of Lévis* case been given a very narrow reading in Canada, its application being confined to the obligation governmental authorities to provide water and similar services at reasonable rates: see, *e.g.*, *500 Holding Ltd. v. Nanaimo (City)* (1995) 12 B.C.L.R. (3d) 181, 1995 CarswellBC 570 (S.C. [Chambers]); *Duquet v. Ste-Agatha-des Monts (Town)* (1976) [1977] 2 S.C.R. 1132, 1976 CarswellQue 57, 1976 CarswellQue 57F; *Chastain v. B.C. Hydro & Power Authority* (1972) [1973] 2 W.W.R. 481, 1972 CarswellBC 287 (S.C.); and *R. v. Three Rivers (City)* (1921) 21 Ex. C.R. 188, 1921 CarswellNat 31 (Ex. Ct.). See also *Burns Lake Indian Band v. Burns Lake (Village)* (2000) 13 M.P.L.R. (3d) 63, 2000 CarswellBC 1419 (S.C.); *Tsawwassen Indian Band v. Delta (City)* [1997] 9 W.W.R. 626, 1997 CarswellBC 1558 (C.A.), leave to appeal refused (1998) 227 N.R. 195 (note) (S.C.C.).

To what kinds of services in Canada could the more vigorous concept of prime necessity apply? What would be the implications of such applications?

Albertson's Inc. v. Young
131 Cal. Rptr. 2d 721 (App., 2003)

Scotland P.J.:

Over two decades ago, our state Supreme Court concluded that a privately owned shopping center that attracts large numbers of people to congregate in order to shop and take advantage of other amenities offered by the shopping center is the functional equivalent of the traditional town center, which historically is a public forum where persons can exercise the right to free speech. (*Robins v. Pruneyard Shopping Center* (1979) 23 Cal.3d 899, 910-911 & fn. 5, 153 Cal. Rptr. 854, 592 P.2d 341 (hereafter *Pruneyard*).) Therefore, the Supreme Court held that the free speech clause of California's Constitution precluded the Pruneyard Shopping Center from preventing a small group of individuals from setting up a table within the center to peacefully distribute handbills and solicit signatures on petitions. (*Ibid.*, at pp. 910-911, 153 Cal. Rptr. 854, 592 P.2d 341.)

James Young, Eloise Voneckert, John Slevin, Charles Noble, Christopher Noble, and Edward Noonan (defendants) are individuals who solicit and gather signatures on initiative petitions to place measures on election ballots. Armed with initiative petitions and the holding in *Pruneyard*, defendants attempted to solicit the signatures of shoppers by stationing themselves on the walkway immediately outside of the entrances to a grocery store owned and operated by Albertson's, Inc., in Nevada County.

Albertson's forbade them from doing so, took steps to stop their activity, and then commenced this action for injunctive and declaratory relief. Defendants cross-complained, alleging that Albertson's violated their constitutional rights to free speech and caused them harm.

The trial court ruled that the Albertson's store is not the functional equivalent of a traditional public forum and, therefore, defendants do not have a constitutional right to use it to solicit signatures on initiative petitions. Accordingly, the court entered judgment in favor of Albertson's, permanently enjoining defendants from coming onto the premise of the store for voter registration activity or to solicit and gather signatures on petitions to governmental or political bodies.

On appeal, defendants contend the court failed to consider that Albertson's permitted other noncommercial expressive activity at the store, and erred in viewing it as a stand-alone store rather than as part of the shopping center in which it is located. And, they argue, even if Albertson's store is considered a stand-alone business, the plurality, concurring and dissenting opinions of the California Supreme Court in (2001) 26 Cal.4th 1013, 111 Cal. Rptr.2d 336, 29 P.3d 797 (hereafter *Golden Gateway)* have, in the words of defendants' counsel, "delineated the reach of California's constitutional free speech provision in a manner which appears to extend the constitutional rights to stand-alone grocery stores."

We disagree with each of these contentions and shall affirm the judgment. As we will explain, *Golden Gateway* does not support defendants' position. The test that courts must apply is whether, considering the nature and circumstances of the private property, it has become the functional equivalent of a traditional public forum. Here, the nature and circumstances of the Albertson's store do not impress it with the character of a traditional public forum, nor do the setting and circumstances of the shopping center where it is located. And the fact that Albertson's has established content-neutral and nondiscriminatory rules and procedures by which expressive activity may be permitted on the store's premises does not impress it with the character of a traditional public forum. . . .

DISCUSSION

I

Defendants contend that, in accordance with the reasoning of *Pruneyard, supra*, 23 Cal.3d 899, 153 Cal. Rptr. 854, 592 P.2d 341, the privately owned walkway in front of Albertson's grocery store is a public forum for defendants' signature-gathering activity because the store is part of a large shopping center.

In the alternative, defendants argue that, even if Albertson's store is viewed as a stand-alone business, the Supreme Court's relatively recent decision in *Golden Gateway, supra*, 26 Cal.4th 1013, 111 Cal. Rptr. 2d 336, 29 P.3d 797 "indicates that stand-alone retail stores which are not modest retail establishments are constitutionally-protected forums for the exercise of non-commercial expressive activities in California."

For reasons that follow, we are not persuaded by either of these contentions.

A. Pruneyard

The privately owned shopping center in *Pruneyard* was located on approximately 21 acres, 5 acres of which were devoted to parking. (23 Cal.3d at p. 902, 153 Cal. Rptr. 854, 592 P.2d 341.) The other 16 acres of the center contained walkways, plazas, a central courtyard and various businesses, including 65 retail shops, 10 restaurants and a cinema. (*Ibid.*) The plaintiffs were high school students who were opposed to a United Nations resolution and who set up a table in a corner of the central courtyard of the shopping center and sought to discuss their concerns with shoppers and solicit signatures for a petition to be sent to the White House. (*Ibid.*) When the students were excluded from the shopping center, they brought an action to enjoin the owners of the center from denying them access to circulate their petition. (*Ibid.*, at p. 903, 153 Cal. Rptr. 854, 592 P.2d 341.)

Pruneyard recognized that the federal Constitution does not give individuals a general right of access to private property for free speech purposes. (. . . *Lloyd Corp. v. Tanner* (1972) 407 U.S. 551, 567–570, 92 S.Ct. 2219, 2228–2229, 33 L.Ed.2d 131, 141–143.) Nevertheless, *Pruneyard* concluded that federally protected property rights would "not preclude law-making in California which requires that shopping center owners permit expressive activity on their property." . . .

Pruneyard then turned to the question of whether California's Constitution creates broader speech rights with respect to private property than does the federal Constitution. . . . [T]he court held that "sections 2 and 3 of article I of the California Constitution protect speech and petitioning, reasonably exercised, in shopping centers even when the centers are privately owned." . . .

Pruneyard was affirmed by the United States Supreme Court in *Pruneyard Shopping Center v. Robins* (1980) 447 U.S. 74, 100 S.Ct. 2035, 64 L.Ed.2d 741, which rejected the contention that it impermissibly infringed upon the property owner's federally protected property rights or his own First Amendment rights. (*Ibid.*, at pp. 82–88, 100 S.Ct. at 2041–2044, 64 L.Ed.2d at pp. 752–756.) In holding that a shopping center may be required by the state to allow individuals to use the property for free expression and petition, the majority noted that nothing suggested "this sort of activity will unreasonably impair the value or use of [the] property as a shopping center." (*Ibid.*, at p. 83, 100 S.Ct. at 2042, 64 L.Ed.2d at p. 753.) In this regard, the majority emphasized that the shopping center "is a large commercial complex that covers several city blocks, contains numerous separate business establishments and is open to the public at large," that the California Supreme Court's ruling allows the shopping center to "restrict expressive activity by adopting time, place and manner regulations that will minimize any interference with its commercial functions," and that the students "were orderly, and they limited their activity to the common areas of the shopping center." (*Ibid.*, at pp. 83–84, 100 S.Ct. at 2042, 64 L.Ed.2d at p. 753.)

Justice Marshall concurred, stating that while there remains a federal constitutional barrier to the abrogation of common law property rights, this barrier is not "approached" by a decision "limited to shopping centers, which are already open to the general public." (447 U.S. at pp. 94–95, 100 S.Ct. at pp. 2047–2048, 64 L.Ed.2d at p. 760 (conc. opn. of Marshall J.).)

Justice Powell, joined by Justice White, also concurred because the decision "is limited to the type of shopping center involved in this case." (447 U.S. at p. 96, 100 S.Ct. at 2048, 64 L.Ed.2d at p. 761 (conc. opn. of Powell J.).) However, he warned: "Significantly different questions would be presented if a State authorized strangers to picket or distribute leaflets in privately owned, freestanding stores and commercial premises. Nor does our decision today apply to all 'shopping centers.' This generic term may include retail establishments that vary widely in size, location, and other relevant characteristics. Even large establishments may be able to show that the number or type of persons wishing to speak on their premises would create a substantial annoyance to customers that could be eliminated only by elaborate, expensive, and possibly unenforceable time, place, and manner restrictions." (*Ibid.*, at p. 96, 100 S.Ct. at 2048, 64 L.Ed.2d pp. 761–762.)

And Justice White wrote separately to emphasize that the California Supreme Court's decision dealt only with "the public or common areas in a large shopping center and not with an individual retail establishment within or without the shopping center. . . ." (447 U.S. at p. 95, 100 S.Ct. at 2048, 64 L.Ed.2d at p. 761 (conc. opn. of White J.).)

B. Golden Gateway

Over 20 years after its *Pruneyard* decision, the California Supreme Court acknowledged that the decision has been difficult to construe and apply. (*Golden Gateway, supra*, 26 Cal.4th at p. 1016, 111 Cal. Rptr.2d 336, 29 P.3d 797.) Therefore, the court sought to "clarify" the holding. (*Ibid.*)

At issue in *Golden Gateway* was whether the owner of a large, privately owned residential apartment complex could prohibit a tenants association from distributing newsletters by leaving them on or under apartment doors. (26 Cal.4th at pp. 1016, 1017–1018, 111 Cal. Rptr.2d 336, 29 P.3d 797.) The lead opinion, endorsed by three justices, concluded that California's constitutional free speech provision includes a "state action" requirement, *i.e.*, it guards against infringement on speech by the government, but not by private parties. (*Ibid.*, at pp. 1023, 1025, 1031, 111 Cal. Rptr.2d 336, 29 P.3d 797 (lead opn. of Brown J.).)

According to the lead opinion, the actions of the Pruneyard Shopping Center to exclude expressive activity could be considered "state action" for the purposes of California's free speech clause because of "the public character of the property." (26 Cal.4th at pp. 1032, 1033, 111 Cal. Rptr.2d 336, 29 P.3d 797.) Due to its "open and unrestricted invitation to the public to congregate freely" within the property, the shopping center had become "the functional equivalence of . . . a traditional public forum — the 'downtown [ ]' or 'central business district[ ].'" (*Ibid.*, at p. 1032, 111 Cal. Rptr.2d 336, 29 P.3d 797.) This impressed the shopping center with a "public . . . character" that warranted "treat[ing it] as publicly owned property for

First Amendment purposes. . . ." (*Ibid.*, at p. 1033, 111 Cal. Rptr.2d 336, 29 P.3d 797.)

The lead opinion went on to express a "threshold requirement for establishing state action," i.e., "the actions of a private property owner constitute state action for purposes of California's free speech clause only if the property is freely and openly accessible to the public." (26 Cal.4th at p. 1033, 111 Cal. Rptr.2d 336, 29 P.3d 797.)

Noting that access to the privately owned Golden Gateway apartment complex was limited to the tenants and their invitees, the lead opinion found that, unlike the Pruneyard Shopping Center, the apartment complex was "not the functional equivalent of a traditional public forum. Accordingly, Golden Gateway's actions [to preclude distribution of a tenant association newsletter] do not constitute state action . . ., and the Tenants Association has no right to distribute its newsletter [on the property]." (26 Cal.4th at pp. 1033–1034, 111 Cal. Rptr.2d 336, 29 P.3d 797.) . . .

From the opinions in *Golden Gateway*, defendants glean that the "decisive" criterion for determining whether private property constitutes a public forum for the purpose of expressive activity is whether "the property is freely and openly accessible to the public." Because Albertson's grocery store "is open to the public," defendants claim the plurality and concurring opinions "indicate [ ] that it is a site where members of the general public can exercise their constitutional non-commercial expressive activity rights."

This is merely wishful thinking. Nothing in *Golden Gateway* can be interpreted to support the conclusion that any large business establishment is a public forum for expressive activity simply because it is "freely and openly accessible to the public." The quoted language simply is the test set forth by three members of the Supreme Court as a "threshold requirement" for establishing that actions of a private property owner constitute state action for purposes of California's free speech clause. (26 Cal.4th at p. 1033, 111 Cal. Rptr.2d 336, 29 P.3d 797.)

Rather, the test appears to remain whether, considering the nature and circumstances of the private property, it has become the "functional equivalent of a traditional public forum." (26 Cal.4th at p. 1033, 111 Cal. Rptr.2d 336, 29 P.3d 797 (lead opn. of Brown J.); see *ibid.* at p. 1039, 111 Cal. Rptr.2d 336, 29 P.3d 797 (conc. opn. of George C.J.).)

Golden Gateway provides no help in resolving the dispute before us because (1) the Supreme Court was unable to reach a majority opinion in that case, (2) whether there is a state action requirement was not raised here and (3) the facts in *Golden Gateway* are not comparable to those regarding Albertson's store — among other things, *Golden Gateway* involved communication directly related to the use of the apartment complex, whereas the communication here was noncommercial activity unrelated to Albertson's business enterprise; and unlike the broader access to the Albertson's store, access to the apartment complex was limited to the tenants and their invitees. . . .

C. Pruneyard progeny

Appellate decisions applying *Pruneyard* focus on whether the property owner has so opened up his or her property for public use as to make it the functional equivalent of a traditional public forum. (*E.g., Trader Joe's Co. v. Progressive Campaigns, Inc.* (1999) 73 Cal. App.4th 425, 433–434, 86 Cal. Rptr.2d 442 (hereafter *Trader Joe's*) . . ..) The less that an owner has opened up the property for use by the general public, the less that the owner's rights are circumscribed by the statutory and constitutional rights of those who use it. . . .

Whether private property is to be considered quasi-public property subject to the exercise of constitutional rights of free speech and assembly depends in part on the nature, purpose and primary use of the property; the extent and nature of the public invitation to use the property; and the relationship between the ideas sought to be presented and the purpose of the property's occupants. . . .

As pointed out in *Trader Joe's, supra*, 73 Cal. App.4th 425, 86 Cal. Rptr.2d 442, "*Pruneyard* instructs us to balance the competing interests of the property owner and of the society with respect to the particular property or type of property at issue to determine whether there is a state constitutional right to engage in the challenged activity." (*Trader Joe's, supra*, at p. 433, 86 Cal. Rptr.2d 442.) *Pruneyard* did not hold that free speech and petitioning activity can be exercised only at large shopping centers or that such activities can be exercised on any property except for individual residences and modest retail establishments. (*Ibid.*) The size of the business is simply a factor to be weighed in balancing the competing interest of the owner and society — "[t]he smaller the business, the more weight the owners' rights will have." (*Allred v. Shawley* [232 Cal. App.3d 1489 (1991)] at p. 1496, 284 Cal. Rptr. 140.) . . .

D. Albertson's grocery store

Decisional authorities indicate that, in considering whether a particular business or business area is impressed with a public character for purposes of expressive activity, no single factor is determinative. When we consider Albertson's store in light of all the surrounding circumstances, we are satisfied the trial court correctly concluded that it is not the functional equivalent of a traditional public forum.

First, we consider the nature of the Albertson's store, which is a single structure, single-use grocery store, that contains no plazas, walkways, or courtyards for patrons to congregate and spend time together. It sells food but has no restaurant or any place for patrons to sit and eat, other than a courtesy bench for such things as waiting for a taxi. It does not have a theater or any other form of entertainment. Although the store attracts a large number of customers, they come for a single purpose, to buy goods. The store does not invite the public to meet friends, to eat, to rest, to congregate or to be entertained at its premises.

For their part, defendants demonstrated that they would like to set up at the entrance to the Albertson's store because of the many shoppers there. However, to establish a quasi-public forum at a particular store, it is not enough that a large number of people visit the store. A location will be considered a quasi-public forum only when it is the functional equivalent of a traditional public forum as a place where people choose to come and meet and talk and spend time. (*Pruneyard, supra,* 23 Cal.3d at pp. 907, 910, fn. 5, 153 Cal. Rptr. 854, 592 P.2d 341; *Trader Joe's, supra,* 73 Cal.App.4th at p. 434, 86 Cal. Rptr.2d 442.) The evidence does not establish that the Albertson's store is such a place.

Next, we consider whether its location in Fowler Center impresses the Albertson's grocery store with the character of a public forum. Among other things, we consider the physical layout of the center, which includes seven separate buildings situated around the perimeter of a central parking lot.

Albertson's store and the B & C True Value Hardware store are fairly large retail establishments housed in their own separate buildings. The other buildings, and the businesses they house, are relatively small and consist of ten retail stores, five restaurants or food retailers and five service businesses (including a travel agency, photo store, video library and mail box rental).

Albertson's store, in building 2, is located on the north side of the parking lot. The much smaller building 1 is located to the east of Albertson's, and the much smaller building 3 is located to the west of Albertson's. To the west of building 3 is the hardware store's large outside storage area, which is not a common area. The hardware store, in building 4, is to the southwest and across the parking lot from Albertson's. Buildings 5, 6 and 7, are south and across the parking lot from Albertson's.

Each of the buildings in Fowler Center, and each of the businesses they house, are supplied with sufficient, immediately contiguous parking spaces so that anyone wishing to patronize a particular business would generally have no need, and no occasion, to walk past any other business.

There are no enclosed walkways, plazas, courtyards, picnic areas, gardens or other areas that might invite the public to congregate at Fowler Center. And the center is not under unified ownership; it consists of seven parcels of land, with two parcels owned and occupied by Albertson's and the remaining parcels owned by members of the Fowler family. The property owners have entered into restrictive covenants to preclude the establishment of certain kinds of businesses, such as a bar, entertainment or recreational facility, training center, or educational facility and the like. A representative of Albertson's explained that Albertson's endeavors to do business as a convenience store and that its premises are designed to get customers in and out very quickly. Any type of business that would encourage members of the public to congregate or to remain on the premises for longer periods would be incompatible with Albertson's marketing plan.

In view of the physical layout of Fowler Center, the restrictions on the types of businesses that may open in the center, and the absence of any common areas that would invite the public to meet, congregate, or engage in other activities typical of a public forum, we conclude that Albertson's location in Fowler Center does not impress the walkways of Albertson's store with the character of a traditional public forum. It is obvious that, by setting up at the entrances to the grocery store, defendants target Albertson's customers rather than the patrons of Fowler Center in general. In fact, as the trial court noted, defendants' evidence focused on Albertson's, and they did not present evidence with respect to the number of persons who visit Fowler Center itself or with respect to the number of persons who might visit more than one retail establishment in the course of a shopping trip.

Under the circumstances presented here, we are satisfied that its location in Fowler Center does little, if anything, to distinguish the Albertson's store from an ordinary stand-alone grocery store.

Defendants disagree, claiming the reasoning of *Pruneyard* demonstrates that Fowler Center is a public forum and that, because of Albertson's location in the center, the grocery store must be considered a public forum as well. The argument is a leap in logic from the *Pruneyard* decision.

Pruneyard involved an effort to solicit initiative signatures in the central courtyard of a large shopping center. Similarly, *Savage v. Trammell Crow Co.* (1990) 223 Cal.App.3d 1562, 273 Cal. Rptr. 302, the other decision on which defendants place substantial reliance, involved an attempt to engage in expressive activity in the common parking lot of a large shopping center. (*Ibid.*, at p. 1581, fn. 7, 273 Cal. Rptr. 302.) Neither case involved the claim of a right to set up and solicit signatures at the entrance to a particular, individual business.

To establish a right to solicit signatures at the entrance to a specific store, it must be shown that the particular location is impressed with the character of a traditional public forum for purposes of free speech. For reasons stated above, the walkway at the entrance to Albertson's grocery store in Fowler Center is not such a public forum. . . .

V

Noting Albertson's does permit some noncommercial expressive activity to occur on the premises of its grocery store, defendants assert that this precludes Albertson's from excluding defendants.

The record shows Albertson's has a corporate policy that endeavors to accommodate persons or groups who wish to engage in petitioning and leafleting activity to the extent consistent with the primary commercial purposes of the supermarket. To that end, Albertson's has created written rules to govern the use of its property and the behavior of those who wish to engage in expressive activity. Among other things, the rules require an application for permission be submitted to the store director at least three days, but not more than twenty days, before the desired date of activity. And the rules provide that, in assigning the areas and times for political petitioning, the store director may not consider the content of the speech to be exercised.

Defendants argue that, because Albertson's will tolerate expressive behavior under some circumstances, its property thereby becomes a public forum from which it cannot exclude any expressive behavior. This is not the rule. (*Perry Ed. Assn. v. Perry Local Ed. Assn.* (1983) 460 U.S. 37, 46, 103 S.Ct. 948, 955, 74 L.Ed.2d 794, 805; *Leeb v. DeLong* (1988) 198 Cal. App.3d 47, 56, 243 Cal. Rptr. 494; *Gebert v. Patterson* (1986) 186 Cal. App.3d 868, 874, 231 Cal. Rptr. 150.)

Were defendants' argument to prevail, newspaper publishers would be required to print anything any member of the public desired to publish, and homeowners who post political signs in their yards would be required to allow anyone who desired to post additional signs to do so.

And the establishment of the rule urged by defendants would likely prove to be more detrimental to, than promotive of, speech and petitioning activity. Under defendants' standard, the owner of private property that is not otherwise a quasi-public forum, and who wished to retain primary control over the property, would have no choice but to prohibit all expressive activity on the property. Where, as here, a property owner endeavors to be a "good citizen" by agreeing to permit, on a content-neutral and nondiscriminatory basis, expressive activity to the extent consistent with the primary commercial use of the property, we should not lightly conclude that the owner thereby gives up the right to insist upon compliance with its rules.

The extent to which private property is actually used for expressive purposes by members of the public is relevant, together with all of the surrounding circumstances, in determining whether the property has taken on the characteristics of a traditional public forum. But defendants did not establish that the premises of Albertson's store are actually used for expressive purposes to such an extent that they must be considered such a public forum. . . .

In sum, the mere fact that Albertson's has established reasonable time, place and manner rules for use of its property for expressive activity does not give defendants a constitutional right to use its property in disregard of those very rules.

SUMMARY

For all the reasons stated above, we conclude the nature and circumstances of Albertson's grocery store do not impress it with the character of a traditional public forum for purposes of free expression. And, in light of the setting and circumstances of Fowler Center, Albertson's presence there does not impress its store with the character of such a public forum. We also conclude the fact that Albertson's has content-neutral and nondiscriminatory rules and procedures by which expressive activity may be permitted on the premises of its store does not in itself impress the store with the character of a traditional public forum.

Accordingly, defendants have no right to use the privately owned premises of the Albertson's store to solicit and gather signatures for initiative petitions or for other such expressive activity.

Our colleague [Sims J.] agrees the judgment must be affirmed, albeit "on a narrow ground: the appellants failed to prove that *this* Albertson's store had replaced the public downtowns of Nevada City and Grass Valley as a public forum."

Lamenting that "government at all levels in California has increasingly become subject to the domination and control of monied special interests, leaving the average citizen without an effective voice in government," he suggests that our legal conclusion will inflict a mortal blow to the "need to preserve the initiative process," which he perceives to be "the last avenue by which ordinary citizens can effect political change." However, even though stores in a shopping area like Fowler Center may not be compelled to allow signature gathering on their property, common sense suggests that, as a matter of goodwill, some will do so voluntarily. And it is an overstatement to suggest that there are no other areas in which signature-gatherers can be successful. So our conclusion does not mean that the sky is falling on the initiative process.

Nevertheless, our colleague feels that courts "should be adopting rules of law that encourage rather than discourage the initiative process." In this regard, he believes "a supermarket's interest in totally excluding speech from its vicinity is not strong." Thus, "[w]ith the allowance of reasonable time, place and manner restrictions," he does "not see how there is a burden on a supermarket that outweighs the strong public interest in allowing free speech in the vicinity of its store." We assume that, in referring to "speech in the vicinity of [the] store," he means expressive activity on the private property of the store — indeed, next to the entrance to the store as happened in this case.

In assessing the burden on a store like Albertson's, and the effectiveness of time, place and manner restrictions, courts must keep in mind the significant implications of concluding private property has become the functional equivalent of a traditional town center. This determination affects not only signature-gathering for initiative petitions, but other forms of expressive activity. Such private property could be used by individuals or groups to set up tables or carry signs voicing their views on a variety of matters on which persons strongly disagree, like advocates for or against a war in Iraq, for or against abortion, for or against restrictions on the ownership of firearms, *etcetera*.

Subject only to time, place and manner restrictions, the owners of such private property may be compelled to associate with, and to assist, those who are disseminating ideas with which the property owners vehemently disagree.

And a finding that private property has become the functional equivalent of a traditional town center inevitably will impose on its owner the financial and emotional costs of defending against a lawsuit whenever the owner resorts to time, place and manner restrictions to preclude its use for expressive activity. It takes little imagination to recognize that those precluded from using the property to advance their views will accuse the property owner of impermissibly prohibiting the expressive activity based on the content of the message.

Therefore, courts must be very careful before proclaiming private property to be a place for expressive activity.

NOTE

Morrison J. concurred with Scotland P.J. The concurring opinion of Sims J., referred to in the summary of the lead opinion, has been omitted.

QUESTIONS AND COMMENTS

1. Can a corporate e-mail system, such as that operated by the multi-national corporation Intel, count as a *Pruneyard* forum? If you believe, given the *Albertson's* case, that the answer is obviously no, then you are correct:

> Although Intel is a large company, it is not like a Pruneyard Shopping Center, in that it is not a place where the public gathers to engage in expressive activity such as gathering signatures to petition the government, nor is its e-mail system so used. The Intel e-mail system is private property used for business purposes. Intel's system is not transformed into a public forum merely because it permits some personal use by employees.

Intel Corp. v. Hamidi 114 Cal. Rptr. 2d 244 (App., 2001) at 257 (*per* Morrison J.).

2. There is another line of American authorities concerning access to private property. In the important case of *State v. Shack* 277 A.2d 369 (N.J. Sup. Ct., 1971), a lawyer and a field worker were charged with trespass. They had visited a farm with a view to meeting with migrant farm workers who lived and worked there. The defendants insisted on meeting with the workers in the privacy of their living quarters. The farm-owner refused that request. Following these discussions, a state trooper was called and a formal complaint alleging trespass was laid. At trial the defendants were convicted.

The New Jersey Supreme Court quashed the convictions. The judgment of Wientraub C.J. for the Court (at 372, 374), demonstrates an attempt to strike a balance between proprietary rights and other values:

> Property rights serve human values. They are recognized to that end, and are limited by it. Title to real property cannot include dominion over the destiny of persons the owner permits to come upon the premises. Their well-being must remain the paramount concern

of a system of law. Indeed their needs may be so imperative and their strength so weak, that the law will deny the occupants the power to contract away what is deemed essential to their health, welfare or dignity.

Here we are concerned with a highly disadvantaged segment of our society. We are told that every year farm workers and their families numbering more than one million leave their home areas to fill the seasonal demand for farm labor in the United States . . .

[W]e find it unthinkable that the farmer-employer can assert a right to isolate the migrant worker in any respect significant for the worker's well-being. The farmer, of course, is entitled to pursue his farming activities without interference, and this defendants readily concede. But we see no legitimate need for a right in the farmer to deny the worker the opportunity for aid available from federal, State, or local services or from recognized charitable groups seeking to assist him. Hence representatives of these agencies and organizations may enter upon the premises to seek out the worker at his living quarters. So, too, the migrant worker must be allowed to receive visitors there of his own choice, so long as there is no behavior hurtful to others, and members of the press may not be denied reasonable access to workers who do not object to seeing them.

It is not our purpose to open the employer's premises to the general public if in fact the employer himself has not done so. We do not say, for example, that solicitors or peddlers of all kinds may enter on their own; we may assume or the present that the employer may regulate their entry or bar them, at least if the employer's purpose is not to gain a commercial advantage for himself or if the regulation does not deprive the migrant worker of practical access to things he needs.

And we are mindful of the employer's interest in his own and in his employees' security. Hence he may reasonably require a visitor to identify himself, and also to state his general purpose if the migrant worker has not already informed him that the visitor is expected. But the employer may not deny the worker his privacy or interfere with his opportunity to live with dignity and to enjoy associations customary among our citizens. These rights are too fundamental to be denied on the basis of an interest in real property and too fragile to be left to the unequal bargaining strength of the parties.

3. What should the Canadian law be? Would it be necessary to invoke the *Charter* to produce a result similar to that found in the *Pruneyard* and *Shack* lines of authority?

7. COVENANTS RUNNING WITH PROPERTY

Tulk v. Moxhay
(1848) 2 Ph. 774, 41 E.R. 1143 (Ch.)

A covenant between vendor and purchaser, on the sale of land, that the purchaser and his assigns shall use or abstain from using the land in a particular way, will be enforced in equity against all subsequent purchasers with notice, independently of the question whether it be one which runs with the land so as to be binding upon subsequent purchaser at law.

In the year 1808 the Plaintiff, being then the owner in fee of the vacant piece of ground in Leicester Square, as well as of several of the houses forming the Square, sold the piece of ground by the description of "Leicester Square garden or pleasure ground, with the equestrian statue then standing in the centre thereof, and the iron railing and stone work round the same," to one Elms in fee: and the deed of conveyance contained a covenant by Elms, for himself, his heirs, and assigns, with the Plaintiff, his heirs, executors, and administrators, "that Elms, his heirs, and assigns should, and would from time to time, and at all times thereafter at his own costs and charges, keep and maintain the said piece of ground and square garden, and the iron railing round the same in its then form, and in sufficient and proper repair as a square garden and pleasure-ground, in an open state, uncovered with any buildings, in neat and ornamental order; and that it should be lawful for the inhabitants of Leicester Square, tenants of the Plaintiff, on payment of a reasonable rent for the same, to have keys at their own expense and the privilege of admission therewith at any time or times into the said square garden and pleasure ground."

The piece of land so conveyed passed by divers mesne conveyances into the hands of the Defendant, whose purchase deed contained no similar covenant with his vendor: but he admitted that he had purchased with notice of the covenant in the deed of 1808.

The Defendant having manifested an intention to alter the character of the square garden, and asserted a right, if he thought fit, to build upon it, the Plaintiff, who still remained owner of several houses in the square, filed this bill for an injunction and an injunction was granted by the Master of the Rolls to restrain the Defendant from converting or using the piece of ground and square garden, and the iron railing round the same, to or for any other purpose than as a square garden and Pleasure ground in an open state, and uncovered with buildings. . . .

Cottenham L.C.:

That this Court has jurisdiction to enforce a contract between the owner of the land and big neighbour purchasing a part of it, that the latter shall either use or abstain from using the land purchased in a particular way, is, what I never knew disputed. Here there is no question about the contract: the owner of certain houses in the square sells the land adjoining, with a covenant from the purchaser not to use it for any other purpose than as a square garden. And it is now contended, not that the vendee could violate that contract, but that he might sell the piece of land, and that the purchaser from him may violate it without this Court having any power to interfere. If that were so, it would be impossible for an owner of land to sell part of it without incurring the risk of rendering what he retains worthless. It is said that, the covenant being one which does not run with the land, this court cannot enforce it; but the question is, not whether the covenant runs with the land, but whether a party shall be permitted to use the land in a manner inconsistent with the contract entered into by his vendor, and with notice of which he purchased. Of course, the price would be affected by the covenant, and nothing could be more inequitable than the original purchaser should be able to sell the property the next day for a great price, in consideration of the assignee being allowed to escape from the liability which he had himself undertaken.

That the question does not depend upon whether the covenant runs with the land is evident from this, that if there was a mere agreement and no covenant, this Court would enforce it against a party purchasing with notice of it; for if an equity is attached to the property by the owner, no one purchasing with notice of that equity can stand in different situation from the party from whom he purchased. There are not only cases before the Vice-Chancellor of England, in which he considered that doctrine as not in dispute; but looking at the ground on which Lord Eldon disposed of the case of *The Duke of Bedford v. The Trustees of the British Museum*, (2 My. & K. 552), it is impossible to suppose that be entertained any doubt of it. In the case of *Mann v. Stephens* before me I never intended to make the injunction depend upon the result of the action: nor does the order imply it. The motion was, to discharge an order for the commitment of the Defendant for an alleged breach of the injunction, and also to dissolve the injunction. I upheld the injunction, but discharge the order of commitment, on the ground that it was not clearly proved that any breach had been committed; but their being any doubt whether part of the premises on which the Defendant was proceeding to build was locally situated, within what was called the Dell, on which alone he had under the covenant a right to build at all, and the Plaintiff insisting that it was not, I thought the pendency of the suit ought not to prejudice the Plaintiff in his right to bring an action if he thought he had such thought, and therefore, I give him liberty to do so.

With respect to the observations of Lord Brougham in *Keppell v. Bailey*, he never could have meant to lay down that this Court would enforce an equity attached to land by the owner, unless such circumstances as would maintain an action at law. If that be the result of his observations, I can only say that I cannot coincide with it.

I think the cases cited before the Vice-Chancellor and this decision of the Master of the Rolls perfectly right, therefore that this motion must be refused with costs.

B. Ziff, "Restrictive Covenants: The Basic Ingredients" in *Special Lectures of the Law Society of Upper Canada 2002, Real Property Law: Conquering the Complexities* (Toronto: Irwin Law, 2003) 293, at 293–309 [revised; footnotes omitted]

Introduction

Broad descriptions of the law of covenants running with land are never flattering. Almost a century ago it was observed that "[t]here is no branch of law so technical as that relating to covenants running with the land". Its doctrines have been decried as "arbitrary and . . . for the most part quite illogical". Regrettably, those sentiments still seem apt, perhaps even more so in Canada than England, where flexibility has occasionally prevailed over rigid adherence to technical doctrine.

Detailed and irrational though it may be, the law governing covenants is not uninteresting. In 1945, it was decided in the celebrated case of *Re Drummond Wren* that a covenant that prohibited the sale of land "to Jews, or to persons of objectionable nationality" was, among other things, void because it was contrary to public policy. The *Globe and Mail* applauded the decision, and the *Toronto Star* reported that properties valued at about $1 million in Hamilton could be affected by that ruling. A few years later the Ontario Court of Appeal upheld a covenant prohibiting, among other things, transfers of property in a cottage community to Jews, blacks or persons of "coloured race or blood". Curiously, the *Globe and Mail* also endorsed the Court of Appeal ruling, though that holding was ultimately reversed by the Supreme Court of Canada. These issues have receded into history, but the current law still involves important social questions. For example, the law of covenants allows private land rights to supplement (but not contravene) public planning instruments. In this way, there can be a collision of private and public interests concerning the ways our cities should develop, or about the complexion of the neighbourhoods in which we might choose to live.

Nor is the law, with all its imperfections, unimportant in practice. Covenants running with freehold land have both residential and commercial uses. In a residential setting they are used to create planned communities. Put less politely, they can work to create economic ghettos. Covenants may be used to control the types of homes that are built or to preserve the area as purely residential (even where zoning allows for mixed uses). One common commercial use concerns the regulation of business competition within a development (such as a shopping centre). A sale (or lease) to X Co. might be accompanied by a covenant given by the grantor that the remaining lands will not be leased or sold for certain specified competing purposes.

In this section the basic principles and policies governing covenants running with land will be the focus. This is a concept that arises out of, but is separate from, the idea of privity of contract. When an agreement concerning land use is struck, and the original parties to the covenant remain on title, the law of contract governs and no special real property rules are engaged. Likewise, where a landlord and tenant relationship exists, there is privity of estate between the parties. Different rules apply to the transmission of rights and obligations in that context. The rules considered here are applicable even when no privity of contract or estate is present. In this setting, contractual promises can be attached to the land and run with that land into the hands of new owners. This is true of both the benefit of a promise and its corresponding burden.

The general policies that inform the law in this area are straightforward enough. Property law as a whole is supposed to promote economic efficiency and this is accomplished in part by permitting and facilitating the transfer of entitlements into the hands of those who value them most (value being equated with willingness to pay). But property law tries to do more than that. It seeks to promote freedom, and to facilitate personal development. And as cases such as *Re Drummond Wren* illustrate, the law of covenants engages other social values (such as respect for human dignity and equality) which are relevant in a range of domains including property dealings.

At the level at which the rules considered below operate it is sometimes difficult to discern just how these ends are being served. A covenant under which a restriction is agreed to can increase the value of the benefited land. Yet the restriction can diminish the market value of the burdened property because the uses to which that land can be put are, by definition, limited. Likewise, covenants affect proprietary freedoms and personhood interests in different ways. The creation of a restrictive building scheme is a manifestation of the proprietary freedom of the original owners. Yet everyone who chooses to purchase lands within the scheme is agreeing to surrender some control over their property, often for an indefinite time span. Whether this trade-off results in a net gain or loss of freedom is debatable.

Most of this jurisprudence in this realm concerns equitable principles. This is so for two reasons. First, the circumstances under which the burden of a covenant will run with land so as to bind subsequent owners is of critical importance. Under law, the burden of a covenant will not run with the land; in equity it can. Second, it is often the case that the remedy sought for a breach of a covenant is an injunction; an equitable remedy. Damages will often simply not suffice, though even when monetary compensation is sought, equitable damages may be available. The principles of equity being dominant, these will first be outlined.

Burdens in Equity

It is trite law that the burdens of a simple contract are not assignable (though benefits may be). At least since the mid-nineteenth century landmark case of *Tulk v. Moxhay* it has been accepted that the burden of a covenant may run with the land in equity. That case concerned Leicester Square Garden in the centre of London. The covenant at issue was designed to ensure that the property would be maintained forever as a park. In other words, in the midst of Industrial Revolution, and as many ancient rules that hampered alienation were being chiselled away by reforms, a new land law interest — one which made private conservation possible — was born. Whether owing to the covenant or not, a small oasis of green space in Leicester Square has been preserved.

The ruling in *Tulk*, though it marked a breakthrough, did not say much. It seemed based chiefly on the idea that a purchaser with notice of a covenant should in conscience be bound by it. Notice of the enduring obligation was central. More is now demanded. Putting statutory exceptions to one side, there are four principal requirements.

First, the covenant must be negative in substance; only *restrictive* covenants will be enforced. Quite simply, a covenant is considered negative when compliance is possible by the obliged party doing absolutely nothing. For instance, a covenant on undeveloped land that provides that the land shall not be used for commercial purposes is negative. So, it has been held, is a promise that no construction may occur unless plans are first submitted for approval. Given that, a promise, say, that any dwelling built on the land shall have an area of at least 2,000 square feet would also appear to satisfy this requirement. Such a term does not mandate that the property be developed at all, so that compliance is possible through inaction, even though any development that does occur must be undertaken in a prescribed way. However, the question, it must be stressed, is a matter of substance not form. If the only use to which the land can realistically be put involves building on it, it is at least arguable that a promise to build in a certain manner is positive in substance.

The precise reasons for the negativity element have been much debated, though it has been faithfully applied in Canadian law over the years. In 1994 the House of Lords confirmed that this requirement remains a basic tenet of English law, and the Ontario Court of Appeal followed suit in March, 2002. The cogency of this limitation, and the meaning and scope of the various exceptions to it are discussed later on in this chapter.

Second, it must have been intended that the burden was to run with the servient land, and that land must be sufficiently described in the covenant. Put another way, the promise given must be one that was not intended to be applicable only to the covenantor. It is not ordained that a promise given by a landowner will run, and in fact it has been suggested that "there is a presumption against finding that a restrictive covenant runs with the land." Equity will not impose an obligation on a new owner if the original parties had no desire to do so.

Third, the covenant must be taken for the benefit of dominant lands, and those lands must also be sufficiently identified in the document. That proposition also relates to the idea that the covenant must not have been intended as personal. But there is more here than just that. This requirement, taken with the preceding one, means that two properties must be involved. Borrowing from the language of the law of easements, there must be a dominant tenement (the property to be benefited) and a servient tenement (the burdened property). As in the law of easements, apart from statute there cannot be a restrictive covenant in gross. It is not essential that the two properties be contiguous, though proximity is required. Nor it is necessary that the dominant tenement be a freehold estate. For instance, a lease can support a restrictive covenant, as can the interest of a mortgagee.

In the case of *Galbraith v. Madawaska Club Ltd.*, the Supreme Court of Canada confirmed that the dominant lands must be "easily ascertainable from the deed containing the covenant"; extrinsic evidence alone will not suffice as a means of locating the property to be benefited. The *Galbraith* ruling has been applied by a number of courts over the past 40 years. Arguably English law is different. There, the better view is that the property may be ascertainable even when it is not described in the initial covenant. Under either approach, if the requirement of ascertainability is not met, a party acquiring the servient lands is not bound by the covenant. The rationale is that such a person is entitled to know who may enforce the covenant; that is, the servient owner should be able to ascertain who holds the dominant lands.

Under the third requirement it is not enough that the covenant was intended to benefit some other (sufficiently identified) parcel. The promise must actually be capable of benefiting the dominant lands. Canadian courts have said that the covenant must "touch and concern" those lands. The phrase is derived the learning under the

Rule in *Spencer's* case, which concerns the transmission of covenants when privity of estate exists. In the context of covenants running in the absence of privity, it is sometimes recited that a covenant touches and concerns the dominant lands when it affects the mode of occupation of the land, or directly, and not merely from collateral circumstances, affects the value of the land. This is not a particularly helpful general statement. Examining the Canadian authorities allows one to understand the parameters of this requirement.

Restricting the property to residential uses is a common — and all else being equal an acceptable — covenant. However, terms that seek to regulate or restrict the class of acceptable purchasers have been held not to meet the touch and concern requirement under Canadian law. As a result, a covenant that attempts to prohibit alienation to members of a particular race or religion does not touch and concern the land (not to mention that it would otherwise almost certainly violate public policy). The same result occurs when the restriction is based on occupation and not purchase. Covenants that endeavour to preserve land for the use of amenities (such as parking) can run. Importantly, so can covenants aimed at restricting competitive business activities.

As with the negativity element, the requirement that there be a benefited property was not apparently critical in *Tulk* itself, though it was observed in that case that a covenantee's nearby land might suffer if burdens were not observed. Still, one wonders why a dominant tenement should be essential. The answer must have something to do with the balancing of respective proprietary freedoms. Should an owner who has otherwise completely parted with land nevertheless be able to control its use into the indefinite future? The touch and concern requirement demands there be a good reason to enforce a burden once the original covenantee has parted with the property. The requirement of a dominant land demands that this reason amount to a direct and palpable benefit that is enjoyed by the owner of some other land. At the same time, sufficiently "good reasons" can exist even absent a dominant tenement. For example, one might be interested in preserving the lands sold as an act of conservation. Naturally this is going to affect the amount the property can fetch in the real estate market, so it is not something one would decide to do lightly. However, because it is nevertheless rational to wish to impose such a term, Ontario law now permits conservation and heritage covenants to exist in gross. Furthermore, it might be sensible to allow homeowners' associations to enforce covenants designed for the community as a whole, even if the association has no land of its own. Even more boldly, it has been proposed that covenants be allowed to exist in gross, so long as this is coupled with a judicial power to remove covenants that are pointless.

Fourth, equity must otherwise be prepared to enforce the covenant. The starting point in equity, as reflected in *Tulk v. Moxhay*, was the importance of notice in binding a purchaser. This requirement is an application of equity's general rules concerning priorities. So, for example, in a contest between a prior equitable interest (such as the benefit of a restrictive covenant) and a subsequent legal interest (such as through a transfer of the burdened land), the covenant is not enforceable against a *bona fide* purchaser of the legal estate who had no notice of the prior equitable right.

Questions of notice are now affected by statute. For example, for land under the Ontario *Registry Act*, general principles governing priorities established under that Act apply. Specific registration requirements for restrictive covenants are set out in Ontario's *Land Titles Act* for parcels under that Act.

Notice is one aspect affecting the application of equitable remedies. As will be seen in the discussion of termination, other general equitable principles may stand in the way of the enforcement of a covenant.

Benefits in Equity

There are three means by which a benefit can be transmitted: by annexation; through contractual assignment; or via a building scheme. These three methods are outlined in turn.

(i) annexation

Equity also recognizes that the benefit of a covenant can be annexed so as to run automatically with the benefited land. In order to run, the benefit must touch and concern that land and it must be shown that the benefit was annexed so as to run with the land. Appropriate phrasing might include the term "annexation" (though there is no magic in that word) and would indicate that the benefit was to pass to all successors in title. Under the *Conveyancing and Law of Property Act* (Ontario) a covenant relating to land will be deemed to be made with the covenantee's heirs and assigns as if they had been expressly named. In England, a *somewhat* comparable provision has been held presume the annexation of the benefit, but it is unclear whether the language of the Ontario statute produces the same result. At common law it is not necessary that the transferee of the *benefited* lands have notice of the benefit to obtain it through annexation. It can be, as one court has said, "a hidden treasure which may be discovered in the hour of need." This remains true in Ontario, for even under the special and detailed registration rules set out in the *Land Titles Act*, there is no requirement that a covenant be registered on the title to the dominant lands.

English law contemplates the idea of implied annexation. Such an implication might be required when, for example, the initial document does not expressly provide that the benefit is to run with specified lands. By contrast, it has been said that Canadian law does not allow for the possibility of implied annexation. The explanation for that position relates to the Galbraith ruling discussed earlier. There it was held that the burden of a covenant does not run with the burdened land unless the land to be benefited is sufficiently identified in the document. By extension, it is said that if the land is not identified, then even express (let alone implied) annexation is impossible. In brief, Canadian law stresses the need for the holder of the burden (even the original covenantor) to know who it is that might seek to enforce the promise. If the land is mentioned but it is not explicitly set out that burden is to run with it — which is probably a rare situation — there might be room for implied annexation. That remains an open question.

(ii) assignment

The benefit of a restrictive covenant can be expressly assigned. This is a matter of contract law and is subject to the principles governing assignments of choses in action. Such an assignment will be effective against the original covenantor. In theory, it can also be effective against a subsequent purchaser who takes the assigned benefit when the land is bought, provided of course that the burden of the covenant has run. This is a major *proviso.* An express assignment is only required when annexation has not occurred. However, the very factors that prevent the benefit from running (such as the absence of an adequate reference to the dominant lands) will also mean that the burden has not run.

(iii) building schemes

It is common for restrictive covenants to be created *en masse* within the context of either a commercial complex or a residential development. One can understand such an arrangement as involving merely a cluster of similar, even identical, restrictive covenants. The rules discussed above would then apply individually to each and every one of these covenants. However, it is also possible that the widespread imposition of covenants can be accomplished more conveniently through the creation of a "building scheme". This is the term most commonly referred to in Canadian law, though it is variously called a common plan (that is the generic term), or scheme of development (or a development scheme), or, in the context of leasehold covenants, a rental scheme.

The function of a building scheme is to provide a reciprocal set of rights and obligations. It creates, in effect, a "local law" under which each property owner is subject to the burdens and is entitled to the benefits of the relevant covenants. Such a community of interest can be created using the tools described above, though the process required to do so is cumbersome. It is easy enough to extract the same burden from each purchaser on the sale the lots. However, the benefit of the covenants would, absent careful drafting, only attach to whatever lots the vendor then retained. The rules governing building schemes allow a more streamlined approach to be taken, and where a building scheme has been perfected, the result is that each lot owner may enforce the covenants no matter when the individual lots were acquired. In other words, the benefit of a covenant under a building scheme can be acquired by early purchasers even as against later ones.

The orthodox view is that, assuming the relevant covenants touch and concern the land, four additional prerequisites are needed to establish a building scheme. First, it must be shown that the titles to the properties in issue are derived from a common vendor. Second, that vendor must have laid out the relevant parcels subject to restrictions that could only be consistent with a general scheme of development. (Some minor variations for particular lots are nevertheless possible.) Third, the restrictions must be intended to be for the benefit of all the parcels within the scheme: there must be an element of mutuality. Fourth, the affected parcels must have been purchased on the understanding that the restrictions would enure to the benefit of all of the other parcels. Moreover, the area of the scheme must be properly defined.

Under modern English law, the need to satisfy these requirements has been relaxed, especially as regards the first two elements. What is now sought is proof that there is an identifiable scheme involving mutually enforceable obligations. In Ontario, however, the orthodox view has so far prevailed, so that if the conditions set out above are not met, a building scheme will not be established. However, all is not lost: The failure of a scheme does not necessarily mean that the covenants are not enforceable. They may be, if the burdens and benefits have been properly affixed in accordance with the rules discussed above.

There is some uncertainty in the Canadian jurisprudence surrounding the full impact of establishing a building scheme. One result is patent: under the scheme, every lot that is bound by the burdens also carries with it the reciprocal benefits. In short, the main advantage of a building scheme is that it provides a simple way to ensure that both the benefits and burdens attach more or less equally to all parcels within the designated area. Furthermore, it is obvious that in finding a scheme a court is prepared to draw inferences from the surrounding circumstances. Is there more than that? It is said that building schemes arise out of "[a]n independent equity," and that they are "quite immune from many of the normal rules governing the enforceability of restrictive covenants". But does this mean that through the use of a building scheme the rules governing burdens in equity can be outflanked?

At least one of the rules governing burdens is affected. It will be recalled that the burden must be made for the benefit of land retained by the covenantee. This is not strictly required under a building scheme. Instead, on the sale of the last lot, the covenantee retains no land within the scheme, yet that last promise is enforceable by all of the prior purchasers. More generally, the benefit can attach to lots already sold off.

By the same token, it is equally clear that some of the requirements for the passing of the burden are *not* affected by the existence of a building scheme. Positive covenants are not enforceable under a building scheme even if the four prerequisites under the orthodox position are in place. Likewise, the equitable rules governing notice (and so forth) remain relevant. In addition, the requirement that the dominant lands be properly described in the document for the burden to run remains applicable.

One might be tempted to think that in this instance extrinsic evidence could suffice to demonstrate the territorial ambit of the scheme of development. This is because anyone seeking to enforce a covenant under a scheme will be able to show that their own land is subject to the same restriction. That serves as the badge to prove that the benefit attaches to the party seeking enforcement. Some courts seem to favour that view. For instance, in *Concerned Citizens of Westwood Subdivision v. McCutcheon* an application was brought to enforce a restrictive covenant that prohibited, among other things, the placing of mobile homes on lots in a residential development. No dominant lands were identified in the governing documents. After a thorough review of the Canadian authorities on ascertainability it was held that the burden of the covenant could not run under *Tulk*. Yet the covenant was enforced nonetheless because it was found to be part of a building scheme. It was said that "when a restrictive covenant does not identify the lands to be benefited by it, then the applicants will only be able to enforce the restrictive covenant[] if it is found that there was a building scheme in existence covering the lands . . .".

I believe that this is incorrect. It may well be possible to determine if a given plaintiff has standing to sue. However, without a detailed search of title it will not be easy to determine all of the properties to which the benefit attaches. That would be essential information should an attempt be made to remove the covenant by agreement or court order. There must be a sufficient delineation of the land covered by the building scheme (even under the more flexible English approach). That being so, there seems no reason to depart from the standard required for basic restrictive covenants in Canada when a building scheme has been created.

The Running of Benefits and Burdens at Law

As mentioned above, the principles of equity dominate this field. One reason relates to the availability of the equitable remedy of injunction. A second concerns the law's refusal to enforce a burden against subsequent landowners. That remains the case, even when a negative covenant is involved. As in the law of contracts generally, a burden is incapable of assignment.

However, it is possible for the benefit of covenant to transferred at law, and such a transmission will allow the new holder of the benefit to enforce the covenant against the original covenantor. One simple method of accomplishing this end is through a contractual assignment. Although even the benefit of a contractual promise could not be directly assigned under the common law, this is now permitted under statute.

Even absent an express contractual assignment, the benefit may run at law if it has been annexed to the land so as to run with it. To perfect an annexation at common law three requirements must be satisfied: First, the covenant must touch and concern the dominant lands. Second, it must be shown that it was intended that the benefit should run. Third, at common law the transferee must acquire the entire interest of the original holder of the benefit. If these elements are present, the benefit of a covenant will automatically pass on the transfer of the dominant lands. And the benefits conferred in this way may be enforced even in relation to a positive covenant, given that the only person susceptible to an action at law is the original covenantor.
. . .

Berry v. Indian Park Assn.
1999 CarswellOnt 1248, 174 D.L.R. (4th) 511 (C.A.)
[footnotes omitted]

Laskin J.A.:

Sugarbush is a rural community near the Horseshoe Valley Ski Resort. It was developed in three phases. The homes in Phases I and II form a recreational cottage community. The homes in Phase III, which were built much later, form a modern residential subdivision. The appellant Indian Park Association maintains a recreation centre and other common areas in the community for the benefit of all the residents. The Association's by-laws require every resident of Sugarbush to be a member of the Association. The by-laws also contain a number of restrictive covenants, restricting how owners can use their land. The Association claims that these land use restrictions are enforceable because they are part of a valid building scheme covering all the lots in Sugarbush.

The respondents are a group of aggrieved neighbours who live in homes in Phase III of the Sugarbush community. They object to being required to join the Association and to being required to comply with the land use restrictions in the Association's by-laws. These owners applied to court to be relieved of their obligations under the by-laws. In a judgment dated November 19, 1997, Eberhard J. declared that the challenged by-laws of the Association were not enforceable against the lots in Phase III. She held that there was no valid building scheme over Phase III and that the challenged by-laws exceeded the powers of the Association in its letters patent and in the *Corporations Act*.

The Association appeals and submits that Eberhard J. erred both in failing to find a valid building scheme and in holding that the Association exceeded its powers in passing the by-laws in question.

The Facts

The homes in Phases I and II of the Sugarbush community were built in 1974 and 1975 by two developers, Kitwee Developments Incorporated and Modco Investments Ltd. Phase I consists of 94 lots, Phase II of 63 lots. Kitwee and Modco built small, rustic, wooden, chalets on these lots. These chalets were built for seasonal use by those who skied at Horseshoe Valley. They had few amenities and were located in quiet, wooded and somewhat isolated surroundings.

Under a development agreement with the local municipality, Kitwee and Modco provided the part-time residents of Sugarbush with a number of services that the municipality was unable or willing to provide, including snow and garbage removal and the supply of clean water. To maintain these services and to allocate their costs to the residents, Kitwee and Modco applied to turn Phases I and II into a condominium. However, their application was rejected. Kitwee then created a "mock" condominium scheme by incorporating the Association as a non-share capital corporation.

On August 30, 1974, Kitwee, Modco and the Association signed an agreement (the Kitwee agreement) which expressly established a building scheme governing the management of the land in Phases I and II. Under the Kitwee agreement, the Association undertook to manage and maintain for the residents the water supply and distribution system and the sewage disposal system. Kitwee also transferred some land in Sugarbush to the Association to be used for a common parking lot and a recreational centre. In addition, Kitwee and Modco agreed with the Association that when they sold lots in Phases I and II they would impose on the purchasers a number of restrictive covenants affecting how lot owners could use and enjoy their land. These land (or lot) use restrictions were contained in the Association's by-laws and were registered against title to each lot in Phases I and II. They provided:

> Provisions Respecting the Lots: The use of the Lots shall be in accordance with the following restrictions for the enhancement in value of all of the Lots and Land and the better enjoyment thereof by the members:
>
> > (i) No garage or fence shall be constructed or erected on any Lot save and except each lot owner may construct and install a pool which can be fenced in accordance with the by-laws and zoning restrictions of the Township of Oro.
> >
> > (ii) . . . no improvements, alterations or additions to any Lot or to the exterior of any premises thereon shall be made, performed or constructed without the prior written approval of the board, which approval shall not be unreasonably withheld.
> >
> > (iii) No trees shall be cut down other than those which are dead or diseased. . . .
> >
> > (iv) No motor vehicles of any kind other than snowmobiles or motorcycles shall be parked on any Lot, . . . only snowmobiles may be driven on or over the lands owned by the Corporation or parked on such lands.
> >
> > (v) There shall be no littering on any Lot. . . .
> >
> > (vi) No animal shall be kept or brought on any Lot other than domestic animals normally regarded as pets.
> >
> > (vii) No signs advertising any Lot for sale or rent shall be placed thereon without the prior written approval of the board which approval shall not be unreasonably withheld.
> >
> > (viii) The beneficial ownership in and to any Lot shall not be transferred by sale, gift, bequest or otherwise, other than to a person who shall acknowledge, in writing, to the Corporation his membership therein and accordingly his obligations to observe this and any other By-laws of the Corporation.

When Phases I and II were built in 1974 and 1975 no further development within the Sugarbush community was contemplated. However, in 1988 the directors of the

Association negotiated with Monica Interior Designs Ltd., the owner of the adjoining land, to amalgamate its land with the original Sugarbush community. Instead, however, of adding to the existing seasonal cottage community, Monica developed its land into a modern residential subdivision, consisting of year round homes with amenities including private driveways, garages, lawns and basements. Monica's development became Phase III of the Sugarbush community. Phase III consists of 178 lots on which Monica has built 82 permanent homes.

In November 1988 before any Phase III lots had been sold, the Association passed new by-laws, containing even more onerous restrictions on the use of lots in Sugarbush. These new restrictions included:

> 1. Board approval must be obtained for the construction or installation of any structure of all new dwellings prior to receiving a building permit, excepting those homes built by the developer.
>
> . . .
>
> 6. No pool or fence shall be constructed or erected on any Lot.
>
> 7. Except in authorized garages, Lots may not be used to store the following: unlicensed vehicles, boats, trailers, mobile vans, non-permanent structures not approved by the Board, heavy equipment, machinery, garbage and debris. These items will be removed at the Owner's expense.
>
> . . .
>
> 10. Only vehicles used for normal passenger transportation should be parked on the lots. Commercial trucks and other commercial vehicles may not be parked within Sugarbush.
>
> . . .
>
> 14. Lots cannot be used for commercial ventures. Home occupations are permitted as long as lots are not advertised for commercial use.
>
> . . .
>
> 17. Lots shall be used for single family use only. For the purpose of this By-law "family" means one human being or two or more human beings related by blood, marriage or legal adoption or a group of not more than three human beings who need not be related by blood or marriage living together as a single housekeeping unit . . .

In August 1991 Monica and the Association signed an agreement ("the Monica agreement") by which the Phase III lands were brought under the umbrella of the Association's management of Sugarbush. Monica agreed "on behalf of itself, its successors and assigns" to abide by the Association's by-laws, rules and regulations. In turn, the purchasers of lots in Phase III became members of the Association and also undertook in their agreements of purchase and sale to comply with the Association's by-laws, rules and regulations.

Although the Phase III development has commonly being considered part of the Sugarbush community, it differs in significant ways from the development in Phases

I and II. Phase III was built years later and by a different developer than Phases I and II. The Phase III land was developed as a modern permanent residential subdivision. The developer, Monica, built large, brick homes with basements and private driveways. The homeowners use municipal garbage collection. The land in Phases I and II was developed as a seasonal, recreational cottage community. The developers, Kitwee and Modco, built small, wooden cottages without basements or private driveways. The cottagers use common parking lots and garbage dumpsters. The Monica agreement covering Phase III does not refer to the establishment of a building scheme. The Kitwee agreement, covering Phases I and II, does refer to the establishment of a building scheme. Finally, the Association's restrictive covenants are not registered on title to the land in Phase III, but are registered on title to the land in Phases I and II.

These differences led to disputes between Phase III residents and the Association, which was controlled by the residents in Phases I and II. The Phase III residents complained that many of the services provided by the Association and for which they paid yearly maintenance fees, were irrelevant to them. For example, the Association provides garbage collection, sewage disposal, water supply and distribution, and snow removal from garbage dumpsters and common parking lots. The Phase III residents contributed to the costs of these services which they did not need and which benefited only the residents in Phases I and II. Eventually, many of the Phase III residents stopped paying their maintenance fees and these court proceedings were launched.

First Issue: Are the Phase III Lands Part of a Valid Building Scheme?

The Association seeks to enforce its by-laws, including those containing land use restrictions, against the owners of land in Phase III. These by-laws amount to restrictive covenants, restricting the way in which the owners may use their property. Because no privity of contract exists between the Association and the Phase III owners, the Association cannot enforce its by-laws under contract law.

But restrictive covenants relating to land are also governed by property law. In some circumstances, property law principles permit restrictive covenants relating to land to be enforced despite the lack of privity of contract. For example, one exception, in equity, provides that if certain conditions are met, both the burden and the benefit of a restrictive covenant may be annexed to the land and so "run with the land". This exception, which originates in the case of *Tulk v. Moxhay*, does not apply here. The Association concedes that the restrictive covenants in its by-laws do not run with the Phase III lands under the principles in *Tulk v. Moxhay*.

The Association relies on another equitable exception by which restrictive covenants relating to land may be enforced. This exception concerns building schemes. A restrictive covenant imposed for the purpose of land development may be enforceable despite the lack of privity of contract, if the land is included within a building scheme. A building scheme may exist when restrictive covenants are imposed during the course of development with the intent that once the scheme has crystallized on the sale of the first lot, the vendor will be bound by the scheme and the restrictions will be mutually enforceable by the purchasers of the various lots. The rationale for building schemes rests on the notion that because the restrictions are imposed for the general benefit of the development, all owners have a common interest in their enforcement. This underlying notion of community of interest imports reciprocity of obligation. Thus, under a valid building scheme, restrictive covenants are enforceable by and against the original purchasers and their assignees.

The Association submits that the Phase III land is included within a valid building scheme and thus it may enforce the land use restrictions in its by-laws against homeowners in Phase III. The Association frames this submission on two different footings — either the Phase III development became part of the pre-existing Phase I and II building scheme or an entirely separate building scheme exists for Phase III. The latter footing has no merit whatsoever. The Association has sought to enforce the same set of restrictions against Phases I, II and III; it has never treated the Phase III land as a separate scheme. The Association always considered that only one building scheme existed, which comprised Phases I, II and III of the Sugarbush community. Thus I focus on whether the Phase III development, when built in 1988, became part of an existing building scheme. As did the trial judge, I assume without deciding, that a valid building scheme exists for Phases I and II.

Elliston v. Reacher is still the leading case on the requirements of a building scheme. In that case Parker J. set out four requirements that must be met to enforce restrictive covenants as part of a valid scheme.

> . . . it must be proved
>
> (1) that both the plaintiffs and the defendants derive title under a common vendor;
>
> (2) that previously to selling the lands to which the plaintiffs and defendants are respectively entitled, the vendor laid out his estate, or a defined portion thereof (including the lands purchased by the plaintiffs and the defendants respectively), for sale in the lots subject to restrictions intended to be imposed on all the lots, and which, though varying in details as to particular lots, are consistent and consistent only with some general scheme of development;
>
> (3) that these restrictions were intended by the common vendor to be and were for the benefit of all the lots intended to be sold, whether or not they were also intended to be and were for the benefit of other land retained by the vendor; and
>
> (4) that both the plaintiffs and the defendants, or their predecessors in title, purchased their lots from the common vendor upon the footing that the restrictions subject to which the purchasers were made were to enure for the benefit of the other lots included in the general scheme whether or not they were also to enure for the benefit of other lands retained by the vendors.

Although its strict requirements have been relaxed in some jurisdictions, *Elliston v. Reacher* has been consistently applied by courts in Ontario including this court. However, the requirements of *Elliston v. Reacher* co-exist with the provisions of the

Land Titles Act, which permit restrictive covenants to be registered and thus annexed to land. Subsections 118(1), (3) and (5), the provisions of the *Act* in force when this case arose, prescribed the procedure and requirements for registration:

> 118.(1) Upon the application of the owner of land that is being registered or of the registered owner of land, the land registrar may register as annexed to the land a condition or restriction that the land or a specified part thereof is not to be built upon, or is to be or is not to be used in a particular manner, or any other condition or restriction running with or capable or being legally annexed to land. . . .
>
> (3) Upon the application of the owner of land that is being registered or of the registered owner of land, the land registrar may register as annexed to the land a covenant that the land or a specified part thereof is not to be built upon, or is to be or is not to be used in a particular manner, or any other covenant running with or capable of being legally annexed to land. . . .
>
> (5) The first owner and every transferee, and every other person deriving title from him, shall be deemed to be affected with notice of such condition or covenant, but any such condition or covenant may be modified or discharged by order of the court on proof to the satisfaction of the court that the modification will be beneficial to the persons principally interested in the enforcement of the condition or covenant.

The trial judge considered *Elliston v. Reacher* and s. 118 of the *Land Titles Act* and found that Monica did not establish a building scheme over the Phase III land. I think that for two main reasons the trial judge was correct in her finding. First, Monica did not apply to register the land use restrictions now sought to be enforced as restrictive covenants under s. 118 of the *Land Titles Act*. Instead, it simply registered notice of the Monica agreement (which included the Association's letters patent and by-laws as schedules) under s. 74 of the *Land Titles Act*. The trial judge held, and I agree with her, that registration of notice of the agreement did not have the effect of annexing the land use restrictions in the Association's by-laws to the Phase III lots. Monica's failure to register the restrictions on land use as restrictive covenants under s. 118 of the *Land Titles Act* stands in sharp contrast to the action taken by Kitwee concerning the land in Phases I and II. In 1974 Kitwee applied to the land registrar under s. 118 of the *Act* to annex to the Phase I and II lands the restrictive covenants underpinning the building scheme. The land registrar exercised his discretion by registering these restrictive covenants. I think that there is much to be said for the recommendation of the 1989 *Ontario Law Reform Commission Report on Covenants Affecting Freehold Land*:

> In the event that the formal requirements [of registration of a building scheme] are not satisfied, the instrument should be deemed conclusively not to create a land obligation or a development scheme (although, in such a case, the instrument might create a personal covenant or other obligation).

At least Monica's failure to register the land use restrictions as restrictive covenants affords strong evidence against the establishment of the building scheme over Phase III.

Second, apart from s. 118 of the *Land Titles Act*, the requirements of *Elliston v. Reacher* have not been met. The first requirement is a common vendor. There is no common vendor. The Association and the owners of Sugarbush received title to their lands from three vendors, Kitwee, Modco and Monica. Some courts, however, have relaxed the requirement of common vendor and instead focussed on the other requirements of *Elliston v. Reacher*.

Even if I were to ignore the common vendor requirement, the second requirement in *Elliston v. Reacher* has not been satisfied. Under the second requirement, before selling any land, the vendor must have laid out its property for sale in lots subject to restrictions intended to be imposed on all the lots and consistent with a general scheme of development. In 1974 and 1975 when Sugarbush was conceived and developed by Kitwee and Modco, Phase III was not laid out or defined as part of the Sugarbush community. Indeed, Phase III was not even contemplated at the time.

Moreover, I cannot find in the record any evidence that Monica intended to establish a valid building scheme and to impose the Association's by-laws on all Phase III lot owners. Again the contrast between what Kitwee did in 1974/75 and what Monica did in 1988 is instructive: in 1974 and 1975 Kitwee registered on title to the Phases I and II lands an agreement between it, Modco and the Association, which expressly recited that "the parties hereto have agreed to the establishment of a building scheme for the better enjoyment of and the enhancement of the value of the said lands." The Monica agreement contains no express intention to establish a building scheme. Although such an intention might be inferred in an appropriate case, all that the Monica agreement recited was that Monica "wished" all Phase III lot owners to become members of the Association. This wish falls short of intending to impose the Association's by-laws on each owner.

Also, the Phase III development is not consistent with the scheme of development established in Phases I and II. The scheme developed in Phases I and II preserves Sugarbush as a recreational cottage community; Phase III is a modern residential subdivision. Counsel for the respondent owners accurately described Sugarbush as an "incongruous marriage" between Phases I and II on the one hand, and Phase III on the other. The benefits of the building scheme are not shared by the Phase III residents.

In summary, the restrictive covenants were not registered under the *Land Titles Act*, and the Association has not met the *Elliston v. Reacher* requirements for establishing the existence of a building scheme. Accordingly, the Association must fail on this first issue.

Second Issue: Are the Association's By-laws Restricting Land Use and Requiring Mandatory Membership Enforceable?

In every agreement of purchase and sale between Monica and a purchaser of a lot or home in Phase III, the purchaser agreed to abide by the rules of the Association. The Association therefore submits that its by-laws are binding on Phase III owners.

The trial judge rejected this submission. She held that the Association exceeded its powers in passing by-laws that restricted the use to which Phase III owners could put their property and that required all owners to become members of the Association. She therefore concluded that the Association could not enforce its by-laws restricting land use and that the Phase III owners had the right to terminate their membership in the Association. I agree with her conclusion.

In addition to imposing a mandatory membership scheme the Association's by-laws, in effect, restricted members from:

* installing a swing set on their land without the approval of the Association's directors

* placing a dog house on their land without the approval of the Association's directors

* building a patio on their land without the approval of the Association's directors

* building a deck on their land without the approval of the Association's directors

* installing a shed on their land without the approval of the Association's directors

* building a garage on their land without the approval of the Association's directors

* planting trees on their land without the approval of the Association's directors

* painting their house without the approval of the Association's directors

* renting space in their home to a temporary lodger without the approval of the Association's directors

* altering, improving or adding to their property without the approval of the Association's directors

* installing a pool on their land

* paving their driveway

* building fences

* parking boats, trailers, mobile vans or other recreational vehicles on their land

* resigning from the Association

* transferring their membership in the Association unless they transfer ownership of their homes . . .

[Laskin J.A. concluded that the by-laws were beyond the powers of the association and were therefore unenforceable.]

Even if the Association had the power to pass these by-laws, I doubt that it could enforce them against Phase III owners. No privity of contract exists between the Association and these owners and, absent a valid building scheme covering Phase III, the Association does not have standing to enforce its by-laws.

Appeal dismissed.

QUESTIONS

1. Why should it be necessary for there to be a common vendor for a building scheme to exist?

2. In addition to restrictive covenants, what other means of controlling land-use are available? What are the advantages and drawbacks of these alternative methods?

3. In the *Indian Park* case, Laskin J.A. wrote (at para. 18): "[t]he trial judge held, and I agree with her, that registration of notice of the agreement did not have the effect of annexing the land use restrictions in the Association's by-laws to the Phase III lots." If covenants are stated to be annexed to the relevant lands, and a notice is duly recorded under s. 74 of the *Land Titles Act*, as occurred here, why should it be necessary to register the covenant under s. 118 of the *L.T.A*?

4. As mentioned above, the case of *Galbraith v. Madawaska Club Ltd.* [1961] S.C.R. 639, 1961 CarswellOnt 72, confirmed that in Canada in order for the burden of the covenant to run the benefited (or dominant) lands must be ascertainable from the covenant. It will be recalled that in *Laurie v. Winch* [1953] 1 S.C.R. 49, 1952 CarswellOnt 118, included in the section of the chapter on easements, the dominant tenement which was to enjoy the benefit of the right of way easement was not referred to in the granting document. Yet, that did not affect the outcome; instead the Supreme Court of Canada used extrinsic evidence to determine the property intended to enjoy the easement. Is this consistent with the later ruling in *Galbraith*? Does it make sense to differentiate between these two kinds of servitudes?

5. Does a covenant not to sever (subdivide) the burdened lands touch and concern the lands of the covenantee? See *Piazza v. Hopley* 2001 CarswellOnt 4313, 46 R.P.R. (3d) 133 (S.C.J.).

P. Filion, *The Impact of Restrictive Covenants on Affordable Housing and Non-Single Family Use of Homes: A Waterloo Region Case Study* (1993) [endnotes omitted]

[T]wo groups of writers . . . advocate an expansion in the role of restrictive covenants as instruments of land use control. The more moderate stand calls for an updating of the legislation pertaining to restrictive covenants in order to enhance their effectiveness and facilitate their use. Other proponents adopt a more radical stand: they see restrictive covenants as a potential free-market alternative to public sector regulations, in particular to zoning by-laws. . . .

For partisans of the more moderate position that is favourable to restrictive covenants, this form of private obligation can work to the advantage of property owners by complementing zoning by-laws. Their argument is that planning law is suitable to the setting of broad development standards, while restrictive covenants can narrow these standards by focussing on detailed obligations which are beyond the purview of zoning by-laws. Covenants are thus perceived as effective instruments to protect and enhance neighbourhood amenities. This perspective is shared, for example, by the Law Commission of England (1984, pp. 5-6), OLRC (1989, p. 99) and Preston and Newson (1976).

The OLRC goes beyond a mere justification of restrictive covenants by calling for legislative changes that would broaden their scope of application and ease their adoption and enforcement. Its recommendations to that effect include the running of both positive and negative covenants with the property and the entitlement of hired managers or homeowners' associations to enforce restrictive covenants for the benefit of all property owners in a building scheme. . . .

In essence, this first position recommends both a widening of restrictive covenants' scope of application and the preservation of the public sector regulatory system.

The second, more radical, position that is favourable to restrictive covenants, adopts a free-market stand to launch an all-out attack on zoning which is perceived as an ill-guided form of government intervention into property rights. It proposes restrictive covenants as one alternative to zoning. This position was developed in the United States in the 1970s by Ellickson (1973) and Siegan (1970; 1972; 1975), and achieved political prominence in the 1980s when the President's Commission on Housing (1982) portrayed zoning as a foremost cause of high housing costs (see also Dowall [1984] and Garrett [1987, pp. 66-77]). In Canada these views were espoused by Goldberg and Horwood (1980).

A major complaint levelled at the zoning process concerns its political nature and susceptibility to be seized by self-serving interests. According to this position's exponents, these interests would manipulate the zoning process to secure the social status of their residential areas and protect or improve their locality's fiscal balance. In these circumstances, zoning regulations would skew the free-market process against cheaper forms of housing and thus be detrimental to social groups with little influence on the zoning decision-making process (Goldberg and Horwood, 1980, pp. 26-9; Siegan, 1975, pp. 385-93). In this perspective, planners are another group that is advantaged by zoning: they derive power from administering the process (Siegan, 1975, p. 458). Those who adhere to this anti-zoning view maintain that zoning's political nature, which generally causes it to take the form of a compromise, is responsible for its inaptitude to offer the best planning solution to a neighbourhood.

Another major complaint aimed at zoning concerns its inability to provide a reliable protection of property values over the long term. This situation results from municipal governments' control over the zoning process and its sensitivity to political pressures. Local governments can grant variances which may be at odds with the character of a neighbourhood or the original intent of a zoning by-law (Ellickson, 1973, p. 694). Ironically some zoning opponents also criticize both zoning's rigidity, which causes it to perpetuate *status quo*, and its frequent lack of adaptation to future conditions because of the inaccuracy of the projections on which zoning by-laws are based (Goldberg and Horwood, 1980, pp. 26–9).

Costs associated with the planning process are another grievance. Whereas public sector costs, which result from the need for a municipal bureaucracy to prepare and enforce zoning by-laws are perceived as relatively modest, private sector expenses are deemed to be far more important. These expenses include the cost of conforming to, and challenging, zoning by-laws. Finally, the argument is made that since zoning serves the purpose of protecting private property rights, it should logically be privatised (Tarlock, 1972).

For adherents to this approach the fundamental problem with zoning is that it represents an excessive public sector involvement in the land development process (Siegan, 1975, pp. 456-7). It follows that their proposed solution does not involve a reform of zoning, but rather its abolition (Siegan, 1972, p. 247; Wolf, 1989, pp. 267-8). Ellickson proposes a return to nuisance laws which hark back to the pre-zoning era. Such laws would result in corrective actions when interferences arise, and would thus represent a more targeted instrument than zoning by-laws to deal with negative externalities.

Siegan, on the other hand, turns to Houston, which is the only large United States city without zoning legislation, as a model. On the basis of the Houston experience, he observes that land use specialization takes place as efficiently whether zoning regulations are in place or not, which prompts him to conclude that such a purpose cannot justify the existence of zoning (Siegan, 1972). He also attributes Houston's plentiful supply of affordable apartments to the absence of zoning, and uses this observation to highlight the inequitable nature of zoning in cities where it severely confines the areas where multi-unit buildings can be erected (Siegan, 1970, p. 128; see also Jones, 1980). Siegan contends that the broad land use control measures adopted by the city of Houston, which consist of sub-division controls and a building code, are sufficient; for him more encumbering public sector instruments such as zoning are both unnecessary and harmful.

Both Ellickson and Siegan perceive restrictive covenants as the foremost alternative to zoning. For example, Siegan describes the extensive role of restrictive covenants in protecting Houston's residential neighbourhoods and argues that they are mere effective than zoning in achieving this end (Siegan, 1970, pp. 72–82). For these authors, restrictive covenants are more closely tailored to the interests of the residents of a sub-division than zoning by-laws, since developers use covenants exclusively to enhance their profits. Accordingly, when formulating restrictive covenants developers would anticipate preferences of targeted home buyers (Ellickson, 1973, p. 713; Korngold, 1984). Anti-zoning exponents further argue that since restrictive covenants are employed for economic rather than political reasons, they are more efficient than zoning in protecting land values. In their perspective, restrictive covenants are less malleable than zoning because they remain unaffected by the political system, and thus provide a more reliable protection to homeowners.

And finally, according to these authors, social equity problems emanating from the use of restrictive covenants are infrequent despite their efficiency in excluding uses that can adversely affect property values. They ascribe this situation to the small proportion of a city's territory that is tied up by restrictive covenants at any given time (by contrast to zoning that affects all parcels of land). Indeed not all development plans are brought under covenants and, in any event, these obligations cease to be operative after their expiry date. It would follow that even if repelled by restrictive covenants, lower cost forms of housing can find plentiful alternative locations.

Some of the arguments raised by anti-zoning advocates do raise serious shortcomings with current planning practice, which are acknowledged by a wide variety of observers. For example, no one can repudiate the existence of social segregation caused by zoning by-laws, and the impediment they represent for the development of affordable forms of housing in certain jurisdictions. A closer attention to some of restrictive covenants' characteristics, however, raises grave questions about the appropriateness of covenants as a replacement for zoning regulations, and highlights the advantage of zoning over some aspects of private land use controls.

A major shortcoming of restrictive covenants — although hailed as an advantage by anti-zoning proponents — is their lack of flexibility. It is extremely difficult to alter or delete restrictive covenants once they are in place since such transformations must rely on the courts and may be subjected to unanimity rule (Korngold, 1989, pp. 963–5; Urban, 1974). This rigidity may frustrate the expression of value changes. One thinks here of covenants that ban clothes lines and compost bins, restrictions that are clearly out of tune with the present concern for the environment and energy conservation. Planning legislation, on the other hand, allows for variances and updating. Moreover, participatory planning instills a measure of neighbourhood democracy within the zoning process by enabling residents to influence the formulation of zoning by-laws.

Another deficiency of restrictive covenants pertains to enforceability difficulties. Enforcement requires legal action by the owner of the dominant land, or any property owner within a development scheme. In these circumstances, one can surmise that many breaches go unchallenged because of the deterring effect legal costs have on individuals responsible for the enforcement of covenants. Also the freeloading potential dissuades individuals within building schemes from incurring legal costs on their own for the benefit of the entire scheme (Ellickson, 1973, p. 717; Shelton *et al.*, 1989, p. 58).

Perhaps the major problem associated with restrictive covenants is that they treat sectors they affect as if they were cut off from the remainder of the city or even from society; those who adopt restrictive covenants are exclusively concerned with the territory they embrace and fail to heed broader city- and society-wide needs and objectives. Restrictive covenants' purpose is to protect a sector's property values irrespective of infrastructures and services required as a result of society's equity values and for the operation of an urban region as a whole. They thus result in the exclusion from the sectors they cover of land use types that are important to the operation of the city and of society, but may be damaging to property values within a given sector. It follows that in circumstances where a significant proportion of a city's territory is under restrictive covenants, the potential exists for the creation of "ghettoes" where these types of land use would be concentrated. Typically such ghettoes would accommodate low-income residential areas and land uses that are major sources of negative spillovers (such as urban expressways and incinerators).

On the other hand, zoning by-laws have to conform to official plans, the role of which is to address current and future needs of a city. These by-laws must also reflect provincial social objectives. At least in theory, therefore, the zoning of a specific area should accord with planning guidelines that consider the requirements of a city as a whole and provincial social policies (Griswold, 1984, pp. 190–1). . . .

In the current legal context, however, restrictive covenants have the capacity to frustrate these new planning objectives by isolating entire subdivisions from a requirement to support their fair share of affordable housing and other social facilities. This can be achieved through restrictions that stipulate a single-family use of homes and set building standards that *de facto* rule out the construction of affordable housing. A further problem may result from the aggregate effect of an ever greater number of development plans burdened by restrictive covenants, which would be employed precisely to resist the intent of planning objectives that promote affordable housing and inclusionary zoning. In these circumstances, a planning system that increasingly encourages affordable housing and inclusionary zoning would be set on a collision course with a growing reliance on restrictive covenants whose purpose is to shelter areas from the effects of this new planning approach. And the more extensive is the use of restrictive covenants, the harder it becomes to meet the objective of dispersing affordable housing and group homes (Guernsey, 1984, p. 456). . . .

The combined effect of an increased use of restrictive covenants, the large areas they burden, and the adoption of provincial and municipal planning objectives that promote affordable housing and inclusionary zoning, supported the expectation of clashes between these policy objectives and restrictive covenants. These clashes would have taken the form of an obstruction to planning objectives and could have led to repeated legal attempts to challenge restrictive covenants. . . . [H]owever, interviews with planners, officials and affordable housing advocates indicate otherwise.

It emerges from these observations that in Waterloo Region restrictive covenants do not necessarily threaten the meeting of city-wide affordable housing and non-single-family use objectives because of a plentiful availability of non-burdened sites. It is apparent, however, that covenants can produce major equity problems because of the uneven distribution of such land uses they cause. In their current utilization, restrictive covenants permit the sheltering of residential sectors from land use policy objectives purporting to assure a sharing of affordable housing and non-single-family uses by different residential areas.

Serious clashes between planning policy objectives and restrictive covenants seem inevitable in the future if current trends persist. On the one hand, the provincial commitment to affordable housing and inclusionary planning is about to be intensified by the policy to authorize an apartment in a house located in all residential zoning categories. Moreover current circumstances suggest that municipalities will adapt their zoning to provincial policy requirements and maintain their own inclusionary zoning objectives. On the other hand, we have witnessed a sharp increase in the reliance on restrictive covenants and can therefore expect that they will burden a very high proportion of newly developed residential areas in the future. Also, if current Waterloo Region trends hold, it is to be expected that restrictive covenants will cover the residential sectors of a wide range of income groups, possibly most single-family housing developments. The only sectors that would be left unburdened would be multi-unit housing sectors, which are often low-income residential areas. In fact, efforts to protect neighbourhoods from the impact of policies promoting affordable housing and inclusionary zoning may well lead to an even higher reliance on restrictive covenants.

Restrictive covenants' capacity to subvert this type of planning policies would be further enhanced were the Ontario Law [Reform] Commission recommendations adopted. As seen, such recommendations would ease the enforcement of covenants and allow the creation of building schemes in built up areas. Residents of such areas could then sue restrictive covenants as a device to deflect affordable housing and non-single-family use of homes (OLRC, 1989). . . .

8. COVENANTS AND CONSERVATION

B. Ziff, "Restrictive Covenants: The Basic Ingredients" in *Special Lectures of the Law Society of Upper Canada 2002, Real Property Law: Conquering the Complexities* (Toronto: Irwin Law, 2003) 293, at 309-10 [revised; footnotes omitted]

Currently, covenants are typically designed to produce controlled commercial and residential *development*. However, the origins of the law of covenants affecting freehold land lie in environmental *conservation*: remember that *Tulk v. Moxhay* involved a covenant designed to preserve a small patch of green space in the centre of London. Today, environmental control is largely accomplished through public law, though in recent years the idea that private covenants may have a useful part to play has re-surfaced. Owing to some of the limitations imposed under the general law (such as the rule concerning positive covenants), statutory schemes providing for purpose-built "conservation covenants" (sometimes called "conservation easements") have been enacted in a host of jurisdictions. See further J.D. Mahoney, "Perpetual Restrictions on Land and the Problem of the Future", 88 Va. L. Rev 739 (2002).

Consider, for example Ontario's *Conservation Land Act*, R.S.O. 1990, c. C.28, which provides, in part, as follows:

3.(1) In this section,

"conservation body" means, (a) the Crown in right of Canada or in right of Ontario, (b) an agency, board or commission of the Crown in right of Canada or in right of Ontario that has the power to hold an interest in land, (c) a band as defined in the *Indian Act* (Canada), (d) the council of a municipality, (e) a conservation authority, (f) a corporation incorporated under Part III of the *Corporations Act* or Part II of the *Canada Corporations Act* that is a charity registered under the *Income Tax Act* (Canada), (g) a trustee of a charitable foundation that is a charity registered under the *Income Tax Act* (Canada) or (h) any person or body prescribed by the regulations;

"owner" means the person registered on title in the proper land registry office as the owner of land.

(2) An owner of land may grant an easement to or enter into a covenant with a conservation body, (a) for the conservation, maintenance, restoration or enhancement of all or a portion of the land or the wildlife on the land; or (b) for access to the land for these purposes.

(3) The easement or covenant may be assigned by a conservation body to another conservation body.

(4) The easement or covenant is valid whether or not the conservation body or assignee owns appurtenant land or land capable of being accommodated or benefited by the easement or covenant and regardless of whether the easement or covenant is positive or negative in nature.

(5) The easement or covenant may be registered against the land affected in the proper land registry office and, once registered, it runs with the land against which it is registered.

(6) The conservation body or assignee may enforce the easement or covenant against the owner of the land and, if it is registered, against any subsequent owner of the land against which it is registered.

(7) If a conservation body ceases to be a conservation body, it shall be deemed to have assigned every easement and covenant to which it is a party to the Minister.

(8) The Minister may register notice of the deemed assignment against the land affected in the proper land registry office and may assign the easements and covenants, or any of them, or hold them as if he or she were a conservation body.

(9) Nothing in this section limits a right or remedy that a person may have under any other Act, at common law or in equity in respect of an easement or covenant, if the right or remedy is not inconsistent with this section.

(10) A covenant under this section, whether positive or negative in nature, shall be deemed to be a restrictive covenant.

(11) The Minister may make regulations, (a) prescribing persons or bodies for the purpose of clause (h) of the definition of "conservation body" in subsection (1); (b) respecting those records, information, reports and returns with respect to easements and covenants that a conservation body holds under this section that the conservation body must keep, must open for inspection or must submit to the Minister or other person designated in the regulations.

The *Ontario Heritage Act*, R.S.O. 1990. c. O.18, confers rights that are in some ways more expansive. The Act allows the Ontario Heritage Foundation to enter into agreements, covenants, and easements with owners of interests in land for the conservation, protection, and preservation of the heritage of Ontario. Likewise, a municipality may be empowered to enter into an easement or covenant with property owners for the conservation of buildings of historic or architectural value or interest. The covenants may be positive or negative, and may exist without a dominant tenement. Moreover, the class of potential assignees of the benefit is unlimited: the benefit may be transferred to anyone. (See further B.L. Wilkinson, "An Overview of the Law in Respect of the Conservation of Built Heritage in Ontario" (2003) 6 R.P.R. (4th) 175.)

QUESTION

In what way, if any, does the *Conservation Land Act* alter the general law of easements and covenants?

9. POSITIVE COVENANTS

Amberwood Investments Ltd. v. Durham Condominium Corp. No. 123 (2002) 211 D.L.R. (4th) 1, 2002 CarswellOnt 850 (C.A.)

Charron J.A.:

The sole issue on this appeal is whether a covenant to pay certain interim expenses contained in a reciprocal easement and cost sharing agreement (the "Reciprocal Agreement") between owners of adjoining parcels of land is enforceable against the successor in title to the covenantor. Stinson J. ruled that the covenant, being a positive covenant, does not run with the land and that, consequently, it was not enforceable against the respondents, Amberwood Investments Limited and 1018898 Ontario Inc. ("Amberwood"), as successors in title to the original covenantor. The appellant, Durham Condominium Corporation No. 123 ("DCC 123"), who is the original covenantee under the Reciprocal Agreement, appeals from this decision.

A. The Facts

Amberwood and DCC 123 are the registered owners of adjoining parcels of land in Whitby, Ontario. Originally, these two parcels were one, owned by a developer called WHDC Harbour Development Corporation ("WHDC").

WHDC intended to build two condominium high-rise residential buildings on the land, in two phases. The first phase, Phase 1, was completed and as a result, DCC 123 was registered on March 20, 1992. This registration divided the land into two parcels. WHDC started to build the Phase 2 condominium but, after putting in its foundation, ran into financial difficulties.

It was WHDC's intention that the two-phased project would share certain facilities and expenses, and that each Phase would have easements over the land of the other for the purposes of support and access. Particulars of these various rights and obligations were set out in the Reciprocal Agreement between WHDC and DCC 123, dated March 20, 1992, which applied to and was registered on the title of both parcels.

The original lender for the project was the Royal Bank of Canada ("RBC"). It advanced $50,000,000 in debenture financing to WHDC in May 1990, secured by a mortgage over both parcels of land. After DCC 123 was registered in 1992, RBC's mortgage on DCC 123's parcel was discharged. RBC retained the mortgage on the adjoining parcel. In 1995, RBC assigned this mortgage to Paarl Construction Inc. ("Paarl"), which later sold the second parcel under power of sale to The Shores of Whitby Land Corporation. This purchase was financed by Amberwood and secured by a first mortgage.

In October 1998, The Shores of Whitby Land Corporation defaulted under the mortgage held by Amberwood and, in consequence, quitclaimed its interest in the second parcel to Amberwood. DCC 123 was informed of this transfer the following month. As of the date of this application, no building had been constructed on the Phase 2 lands.

The developer's plan was for both condominiums to share a recreational facility. That facility has been constructed and is located within DCC 123, and is owned by DCC 123 and Amberwood.

The Reciprocal Agreement provides, amongst other things, for the sharing of the cost of maintaining certain shared services and facilities, including the recreational facility. It required WHDC to pay certain interim expenses until the second condominium was built and registered. These interim expenses are the subject-matter of this application. They are outlined in section 2.9:

> *Section 2.9 — Interim Costs*
>
> The parties agree that until completion of the building comprising Condominium 2, Phase I Condominium Corporation's [DCC 123's] share of certain operating expenses contained in its budget will be greater than they will be after completion of the building comprising Condominium 2. Accordingly, the owner [WHDC] agrees until the date of registration of Condominium 2, to pay the Proportionate Share of the Phase II Condominium Corporation for the following items listed in the budget of the Phase I Condominium Corporation:
>
> (a) Water Treatment; and
>
> (b) Air Conditioner Maintenance.
>
> The Owner further agrees, until the Transfer Date, to pay 35.417% of the costs of maintaining one full time security guard on the site.

The Reciprocal Agreement further contains general provisions that include the following:

> *Section 13.1 — Provisions Run with the Land*
>
> . . .
>
> (b) The parties hereto hereby acknowledge and agree that the Easements, rights and provisions as set forth in this Agreement establish a basis for mutual and reciprocal use and enjoyment of such Easements, rights and provisions and as an integral and material consideration for the continuing right to such use and enjoyment each party hereto does hereby accept, agree to assume the burden of, and to be bound by each and every of the covenants entered into by them in this Agreement.
>
> (c) The provisions of this Agreement are intended to run with the real property benefitted and burdened thereby, specifically, the Phase 1 Lands, the Phase 2 Lands and the Common Units and except as may otherwise be specifically provided shall bind and enure to the benefit of the respective successors in title thereof.

After WHDC ran into financial difficulty, it stopped paying its proportionate share of the interim expenses. Arrears accumulated. Paarl, as assignee of the RBC mortgage, refused to make the payments and DCC 123 registered a lien against the Phase 2 lands. When The Shores of Whitby Land Corporation purchased the lands, the arrears were paid. However, when Amberwood assumed ownership of the lands through the quitclaim deed, it paid the interim expenses for a few months and then refused to continue the payments. Amberwood's share of the expenses is estimated at $4,225 a month, or $50,700 a year. When the expenses remained unpaid by October 1999, DCC 123 registered a caution and issued notice of sale proceedings in accordance with the Reciprocal Agreement. . . .

(1) Analysis in a nutshell

The rule that positive covenants do not run with the land has been a settled principle of the English common law for well over a century and it is undisputed that it has clearly been adopted in Canada: *Parkinson v. Reid*, [1966] S.C.R. 162 (S.C.C.). It appears to be equally undisputed that the rule at times causes inconvenience, that its application in some cases may even result in unfairness, and that the present state of the law should be modified to meet the needs of modern conveyancing. However, it is my view that the call for reform is not one for the courts to answer but for the Legislature. Any change in the law in this area could have complex and far-reaching effects that cannot be accurately assessed on a case by case basis. The need to preserve certainty in commercial and property transactions requires that any meaningful reform be achieved by legislation that can be drafted with careful regard to the consequences.

Therefore, since positive covenants do not run with the land, Amberwood is not bound by the positive covenant to pay the interim expenses under the Reciprocal Agreement solely by virtue of having acquired the Phase 2 lands with notice of its terms. The question remains whether Amberwood is liable to pay the expenses under some other recognized legal principle.

First, DCC 123 places reliance on the doctrine of benefit and burden in *Halsall v. Brizell* [[1957] 1 All E.R. 371] as a method of avoiding the application of the rule. The nature and scope of this doctrine will be discussed more fully later in these reasons. Suffice it to say for the purpose of this overview that, in my view, the benefit and burden doctrine is not as wide or as settled in English law as contended by DCC 123. Furthermore, the adoption of this doctrine as a recognized exception to the rule in the common law of this province, in much the same way as the abolition of the rule itself, would have complex, far-reaching and uncertain ramifications that cannot be adequately addressed on a case by case basis.

The second method relied upon by DCC 123 is the conditional grant of easement. The question whether or not a provision in a conveyance is a conditional grant essentially turns on the construction of the relevant instrument, in this case the Reciprocal Agreement. In my view, there is no link between the easements conferred under the Reciprocal Agreement and the positive covenant to pay interim expenses so as to create a conditional grant within the meaning of this principle. The general clause of mutuality and reciprocity of easements, rights and provisions contained in the Reciprocal Agreement cannot be relied upon by DCC 123 to convert all positive obligations into conditional grants of easement so as to defeat the rule. As stated earlier, the rule that positive covenants do not run with the land applies despite the parties' express intention to the contrary. Hence, the applications judge erred in finding that, by virtue of section 13.1(b) of the Reciprocal Agreement, the grant of easements and benefits under section 2.3 and Article 3 was conditional upon payment of the interim expenses set out under section 2.9.

In the result, for different reasons than those of the applications judge, I am of the view that he was nonetheless correct in granting Amberwood's application, and I would dismiss the appeal.

(2) Introduction

In a relatively recent decision, *Rhone v. Stephens*, [1994] 2 All E.R. 65 ... (H.L.(E)), the House of Lords considered the question of the enforceability of positive covenants between owners of freehold estates including, in particular, the rule that positive covenants do not run with the land. The rule is commonly referred to as the rule in *Austerberry v. Oldham Corp.* (1885), 29 Ch. D. 750 (C.A.). It is unfortunate that this case was not brought to the attention of the applications judge because the judgment in *Rhone v. Stephens* provides a convenient framework for discussion of the issues raised in this case. Lord Templeman, in his reasons delivered on behalf of the court, set out a useful and succinct review of the law related to covenants, including the different rules governing restrictive and positive covenants, its historical development, and its underlying rationale. Lord Templeman also acknowledged the severe criticism of the present state of the law on positive covenants and the call for legislative reform made by the Law Commission in England. He also considered, and declined, the invitation to abolish the rule in *Austerberry*, finding that any need for reform was a matter for Parliament. Finally, he considered and rejected the argument that the rule in *Austerberry* had been blunted by the benefit and burden principle. Hence, many of the same issues that are raised by the parties in this case were before the House of Lords in *Rhone v. Stephens*. It may be useful to set out the facts in *Rhone v. Stephens* before reviewing the court's analysis of the legal issues.

In 1960, the owner of a house and adjoining cottage, known as Walford House, sold the cottage, since known as Walford Cottage. Walford House and Walford Cottage were under the same roof. The vendor covenanted for himself and his successors in title as owners of Walford House to maintain that part of the roof which was above Walford Cottage in good condition to the reasonable satisfaction of the purchasers and their successors in title. The conveyance also had the effect of conferring and confirming on each property the right to be supported by the other. After 1960, both properties were sold: Walford Cottage to the plaintiffs and Walford House to the defendant.

In 1986 the plaintiffs brought an action against the defendant claiming that the roof above Walford Cottage was leaking and that the defendant was in breach of the covenant to repair the roof. The trial judge found the defendant liable both in nuisance and on the covenant. He based his finding of liability on the covenant on the principle of benefit and burden. On appeal by the defendant, the Court of Appeal reversed the trial judge's decision on both grounds. The Court of Appeal found that, contrary to the finding of the trial judge, the plaintiffs were in fact owners of the roof over Walford Cottage and therefore had no cause of action in nuisance against the defendant owner of Walford House. The Court of Appeal also rejected the plaintiffs' claim that the defendant was bound by the positive covenant to repair. On further appeal to the House of Lords by the plaintiffs, the appeal was dismissed. The reasons of the House of Lords, for the most part, are apposite to this case. Hence I will make extensive reference to the analysis in *Rhone v. Stephens*.

(3) The common law relating to covenants affecting land

The House of Lords reiterated the foundational principle underlying the law relating to covenants affecting land (at p. 67):

> At common law a person cannot be made liable upon a contract unless he was a party to it. In *Cox v. Bishop* (1857) 8 De GM & G 815, 44 ER 604 a lease was assigned to a man of straw and it was held that the covenants in the lease could not be enforced against an equitable assignee of the lease who had entered into possession. The covenants were not enforceable because there was no privity of contract or estate between the lessee and the assignee.

The House of Lords then noted that the rigours of the common law, which do not allow covenants to be enforced by and against successors in title, were relaxed, first by the doctrines laid down in *Spencer's Case* (1583), 5 Co. Rep. 16a, [1558-1774] All E.R. Rep. 68 (K.B.), and subsequently by statutory extensions of those doctrines, resulting in different treatment being afforded at law to leaseholds. As a result of this relaxation of the rule, as between landlord and tenant, both the burden and the benefit of a covenant, which touches or concerns the land demised and is not merely collateral, run at law with the reversion and the term of the lease whether the covenant be positive or restrictive. However, as between persons interested in land other than as landlord and tenant, the law remained as established in *Austerberry*. At law, the benefit of a covenant may run with the land, but not the burden. . . .

Hence, it would appear that the need for certainty in the ascertainment of title and its incidental rights served to maintain the traditional limits to the parties' contractual freedom in the case of freehold estates. I now return to the analysis in *Rhone v. Stephens*.

Despite this relaxation of the rigours of the common law with respect to leaseholds, Lord Templeman noted that the rule in *Austerberry* continued to apply with respect to freeholds. Hence, the rule had the following effect on the present owners of Walford House and Walford Cottage (at p. 68):

> Thus cl 3 of the 1960 conveyance [the positive covenant], despite its express terms, did not confer on the owner for the time being of Walford Cottage the right at common law to compel the owner for the time being of Walford House to repair the roof or to obtain damages for breach of the covenant to repair.

The plaintiffs in *Rhone v. Stephens* argued nonetheless that equity, if not the common law, compelled the owner of Walford House to comply with the covenant to repair the roof or to pay damages instead. This argument was rejected. Lord Templeman reiterated the principle that "equity supplements but does not contradict the common law" (at p. 68). He explained how this principle led to the enforcement of *restrictive* covenants in equity, in the seminal case of *Tulk v. Moxhay* (1848), 2 Ph. 774, [1843-60] All E.R. Rep. 9 (Ch.), and why the equitable rule established in that case cannot be extended so as to enforce *positive* covenants (at pp. 68-69):

> My Lords, equity supplements but does not contradict the common law. When freehold land is conveyed without restriction, the conveyance confers on the purchaser the right to do with the land as he pleases provided that he does not interfere with the rights of others or infringe statutory restrictions. The conveyance may however impose restrictions which, in favour of the covenantee, deprive the purchaser of some of the rights inherent in the ownership of unrestricted land. In *Tulk v. Moxhay* (1848) 2 Ph 774, [1843-60] All ER Rep 9 a purchaser of land covenanted that no buildings would be erected on Leicester Square. A subsequent purchaser of Leicester Square was restrained from building. The conveyance to the original purchaser deprived him and every subsequent purchaser taking with notice of the covenant of the right, otherwise part and parcel of the freehold, to develop the square by the construction of buildings. Equity does not contradict the common law by enforcing a restrictive covenant against a successor in title of the covenantor but prevents the successor from exercising a right which he never acquired. Equity did not allow the owner of Leicester Square to build because the owner never acquired the right to build without the consent of the persons (if any) from time to time entitled to the benefit of the covenant against building. In *Tulk v. Moxhay* 2 Ph 774 at 777-778, [1843-60] All ER Rep 9 at 11 the judgment of Lord Cottenham LC contained the following passage:
>
>> It is said, that the covenant being one which does not run with the land, this Court cannot enforce it; but the question is, not whether the covenant runs with the land, but whether a party shall be permitted to use the land in a manner inconsistent with the contract entered into by his vendor, and with notice of which he purchased.
>
> Equity can thus prevent or punish the breach of a negative covenant which restricts the user of land or the exercise of other rights in connection with land. Restrictive covenants deprive an owner of a right which he could otherwise exercise. Equity cannot compel an owner to comply with a positive covenant entered into by his predecessors in title without flatly contradicting the common law rule that a person cannot be made liable upon a contract unless he was a party to it. *Enforcement of a positive covenant lies in contract; a positive covenant compels an owner to exercise his rights. Enforcement of a negative covenant lies in property; a negative covenant deprives the owner of a right over property.* [Emphasis added.]

Hence, it was reasoned that the enforcement of a negative covenant in equity did not contravene the common law rule of privity of contract because, in essence, equity was simply giving effect to a legal right whose scope was restricted by the covenant. As Lord Templeman noted in *Rhone v. Stephens*, there was some suggestion in the jurisprudence following *Tulk v. Moxhay* that any covenant affecting land was likewise enforceable in equity provided that the owner of the land had notice of the covenant prior to his purchase. However, this extension of the principle did not survive the decision of the Court of Appeal in *Haywood v. Brunswick Permanent Benefit Building Society* (1881), 8 Q.B.D. 403 (C.A.). The Court of Appeal in *Haywood* decided that, in the absence of privity of contract, it would not extend the doctrine of *Tulk v. Moxhay* to affirmative covenants compelling a man to lay out money or do any other act of an active character. Equity will intervene only where there is a negative covenant, expressed or implied.

Lord Templeman concluded his review of the existing state of the law as follows (at p. 71):

> For over 100 years it has been clear and accepted law that equity will enforce negative covenants against freehold land but has no power to enforce positive covenants against successors in title of the land. To enforce a positive covenant would be to enforce a personal obligation against a person who has not covenanted. To enforce negative covenants is only to treat the land as subject to a restriction.

It is common ground between the parties that this is also the settled law in Ontario. Positive covenants do not run with freehold land, either at law or in equity. Hence, consonant with the result in *Rhone v. Stephens*, Amberwood is not bound to pay the interim expenses contained in the Reciprocal Agreement simply by reason of having acquired the land with notice of the covenant.

(4) The call for reform

The need for reform in this area of the law, and the different approaches that should be adopted to effect it, informed much of the argument advanced by the parties on this appeal. The determinative issues on this appeal were framed by the parties in terms of the English "exceptions" to the rule in *Austerberry* and their potential application to this case. DCC 123 took the position that the English exceptions were well established and it urged this court to adopt these principles as an incremental and much needed change in the law. Amberwood, on the other hand, took the position that the existence and scope of each exception was a matter of much controversy in England and in other common law jurisdictions and that, even if either exception was found to apply to the facts of this case, any reform in this area of the law was a matter for the Legislature and not the courts.

Hence, before dealing with the particular issues raised by the parties, it may be useful to briefly describe the need for reform in this area of the law, as identified by the OLRC and like bodies in some other common law jurisdictions.

In its 1989 *Report on Covenants Affecting Freehold Land*, the OLRC dealt with both positive and restrictive covenants affecting land, other than those between landlord and tenant. It defined a positive covenant as "one that requires a person to do something on his or her land." (p. 1 Executive Summary).

In an attempt to determine the rationale behind the rule that positive covenants do not run with the land, the OLRC made reference to the decision in *Keppell v. Bailey* [(1834), 2 My. & K. 517, 39 E.R. 1042], referred to earlier, and deduced from this decision that there were two related rationales. First, "such covenants would tend to render land inalienable" and second, "persons dealing subsequently with the land would have great difficulty in ascertaining the existence of such covenants, because they do not normally have a physical manifestation" (at p. 21).

The OLRC rejected both rationales as inapplicable to the reality of conveyancing in Ontario. With respect to the concern for inalienability, the OLRC observed that "it has now been generally recognized . . . that [positive covenants] do not tend to render land inalienable. On the contrary, positive and negative covenants tend to enhance alienability since they operate to protect the amenities of neighbourhoods and the competitiveness of businesses" (at pp. 100-01). With respect to the concern for the difficulty in ascertaining the existence of such covenants, the OLRC stated that it "is not now, and was not then, an obstacle in Ontario" (at p. 22) given Ontario's land registration system, a system that did not generally exist in England at the time of the *Keppell* decision. . . .

In light of the absence of any applicable rationale for the rule and of the difficulties it posed, the OLRC was of the view that the law required reform (at pp. 101-02):

> We have reached the conclusion that the present law, which prohibits the running of the burden of positive covenants upon a transfer of freehold land, operates to defeat the legitimate expectations of the parties. In our view, there can be no principled rationale for a rule that would preclude neighbours from agreeing, for example, to maintain a boundary fence, or, to keep certain drains clear, such that the covenant would run with the land. Nor is it justifiable, in our view, that, in a property development providing for parks, open spaces, and other amenities, obligations to pay for the maintenance of these amenities cannot be enforced against the successors of the original contracting parties. In addition, to the extent that a variety of methods have been developed to circumvent the undesirable effect of the present law, it has been productive of much uncertainty and confusion. For the foregoing reasons, the Commission recommends that the law should be reformed to permit the burden of affirmative obligations to run upon a transfer of freehold land.

The OLRC further concluded that the present law of restrictive covenants was also in need of reform because it is unduly complex and uncertain. Hence, the OLRC was of the view that the need for reform arose both from the uncertain and complex state of the law with respect to restrictive covenants, and the existing gap with respect to positive covenants. . . .

It may be useful at this point to return to the analysis in *Rhone v. Stephens* because the House of Lords made reference to a similar call for reform in England. Lord Templeman made reference to the Reports submitted to Parliament by the Law Commission, and noted that nothing had been done in response to them. In these circumstances, the court was invited to overrule the decision in *Austerberry*. Lord Templeman rejected this suggestion (at p. 72):

> To do so would destroy the distinction between law and equity and to convert the rule of equity into a rule of notice. It is plain from the articles, reports and papers to which we were referred that judicial legislation to overrule the *Austerberry* case would create a number of difficulties, anomalies and uncertainties and affect the rights and liabilities of people who have for over 100 years bought and sold land in the knowledge, imparted at an elementary stage to every student of the law of real property, that positive covenants affecting freehold land are not directly enforceable except against the original covenan-

tor. Parliamentary legislation to deal with the decision in the *Austerberry* case would require careful consideration of the consequences. Moreover, experience with leasehold tenure where positive covenants are enforceable by virtue of privity of estate has demonstrated that social injustice can be caused by logic. Parliament was obliged to intervene to prevent tenants losing their homes and being saddled with the costs of restoring to their original glory buildings which had languished through wars and economic depression for exactly 99 years.

In my view, the wisdom of these observations is unassailable. Similar words of judicial restraint were echoed in *R. v. York Twp., Ex Parte 125 Varsity Rd. Ltd*, [1960] O.R. 238 . . . (C.A.) where this court was urged to extend the doctrine on restrictive covenants in *Tulk v. Moxhay* to covenants in gross, that is, to covenants existing independently of a dominant tenement. Morden J.A. stated as follows (at pp. 243-44):

. . . it is, not only undesirable but in my opinion, too late now for this Court to return to the position as it was in 1848 and give countenance to a development of the doctrine along such substantially different lines; we ought, I think, to adhere to the greatly restricted scope of the doctrine in *Tulk v. Moxhay* as evidenced by the numerous decisions subsequent to that case. A restrictive covenant enforceable between persons other than the original parties is, in effect, an equitable interest in property. It is well recognized that decisions affecting real property upon the basis of which titles are passed and accepted should not lightly be disturbed; this is one branch of law which requires stability. As Middleton J.A., said in *Re Hazell* (1925), 57 O.L.R. 290, at p. 294:

> It is a well-established principle of real property law that questions such as this one, placed at rest, should not be again agitated, even if it should be shewn that the earlier decisions are not in all respects satisfactory.

These principles of judicial restraint were also reiterated in *Friedmann Equity Developments Inc. v. Final Note Ltd.* (2000), 188 D.L.R. (4th) 269 (S.C.C.) where the Supreme Court of Canada considered whether the sealed contract rule should be abolished. . . .

I therefore conclude that any modification to the rule that positive covenants do not run with the land should be made by the Legislature, and not by this court. Hence, Amberwood is not bound by the positive covenant to pay the interim expenses under the Reciprocal Agreement solely by virtue of having acquired the Phase 2 lands with notice of its terms. The question remains whether Amberwood is liable to pay the expenses under some other recognized legal principle.

(5) Statutory exceptions to the rule

Although the Ontario Legislature has not adopted a comprehensive scheme to deal with covenants affecting freehold land, there are a number of statutory exceptions to the rule that positive covenants do not bind freehold successors in title. For example, the burden of certain positive covenants made in favour of public bodies can run with the land under the provisions of the *Planning Act*, R.S.O. 1990, c. P.13. Similarly, the *Condominium Act*, 1998, S.O. 1998, c. 19 permits the enforcement of such covenants for condominiums governed by the statute. For various examples of other specific statutory exceptions to the rule see the following: *Agricultural Research Institute of Ontario Act*, R.S.O. 1990, c. A.13, ss. 3(*f*)(i), 4.1 and 4.2; . . .

The statutory exceptions to the rule do alleviate some of the difficulties that could otherwise arise from a strict application of the common law rule. However, it is common ground between the parties that no statutory exception applies to this case so as to allow the positive covenant to run with the land.

(6) Non-statutory methods to circumvent the rule

The inconvenience of the rule that the burden of a positive covenant cannot run with the land has resulted in the development of a number of methods by which its effect can be circumvented so as to obtain enforcement at law. The OLRC noted some of these methods in its 1989 Report and they are further described in Megarry and Wade, *The Law of Real Property*, 6th ed. (London: Sweet and Maxwell, 2000) at pp. 1006–1010.

The simplest and most obvious way of avoiding the rule altogether is to use a chain of covenants so as to maintain privity of contract. Indeed, if the chain had not been broken in this case by WHDC's financial difficulties, resulting in power of sale proceedings, in all likelihood the terms of the Reciprocal Agreement would have been included in any sale of the Phase 2 lands to a subsequent purchaser. Other devices, not relevant to this case, include use of a right of entry annexed to rentcharge, rights of re-entry generally, and an enlarged long lease (a long lease which can be enlarged into a fee simple under statutory power).

As stated earlier, DCC 123 relies on two exceptions or methods in this case: the principle of benefit and burden, referred to as the doctrine in *Halsall v. Brizell*, and the conditional grant. DCC 123 maintains that these two exceptions have been recognized by English courts, that they should be adopted in this province, and that Amberwood, as present owner of the Phase 2 lands, should be held liable on the covenant to pay the interim expenses under either or both of these exceptions. I will deal with each exception in turn.

(a) The doctrine in *Halsall v. Brizell*

The applications judge described the doctrine in *Halsall v. Brizell* in terms of the general underlying principle that "a person who claims the benefit of a deed must also take it subject to its burdens" (at para. 23, p. 676). He held that this doctrine "has been clearly adopted by the English courts" (at para. 24, p. 676). In support of this conclusion, he relied on the decision of the English Court of Appeal in *E.R. Ives Investment Ltd. v. High*, [1967] 1 All E.R. 504, [1967] 2 Q.B. 379, and on the decision of the Chancery Division in *Tito v. Waddell (No. 2)*, [1977] 3 All E.R. 129, [1977] Ch. 106. He then noted that while the principle of benefit and burden had not been applied in Canadian law, *Halsall v. Brizell* had been mentioned by the Supreme Court of Canada in *Parkinson v. Reid*. . . .

It is important to determine with more precision the nature and scope of the doctrine in *Halsall v. Brizell* and to examine the extent to which it has been adopted in English law before deciding whether it should be imported into Ontario law and, if so, whether it applies to the facts of this case.

In *Halsall v. Brizell*, purchasers of plots on a building estate were entitled under a trust deed to use private roads and other amenities, including sewers placed under the roads, and each, on purchasing a lot, covenanted to pay a just proportion of the cost of their maintenance. A question arose whether the purchasers' successors were liable for their due contribution while they made use of the roads.

Upjohn J. of the Chancery Division stated first, that a covenant in the terms of the covenant to pay the maintenance cost does not run with the land. Second, he noted that the particular provisions infringed the rule against perpetuities. Notwithstanding these difficulties, he held as follows (at p. 377):

> It is, however, conceded to be ancient law that a man cannot take benefit under a deed without subscribing to the obligations thereunder. If authority is required for that proposition, I refer to one sentence during the argument in *Elliston v. Reacher (1)* ([1908] 2 Ch. 665), where Sir Herbert Cozens-Hardy M. R., said (*ibid.*, at p. 669):
>
>> It is laid down in Coke on *Littleton*, 230b, that a man who takes the benefit of a deed is bound by a conditon contained in it though he does not execute it.

Upjohn J. concluded that if the defendants did not desire to take the benefit of the deed, they could not be liable to contribute to the maintenance cost. However since they did desire to use the roads of the park and the other benefits created by the trust deed, they were liable to contribute to the maintenance cost pursuant to the covenant. . . .

I note from the outset what will become clear from a review of the relevant jurisprudence that the doctrine in *Halsall v. Brizell* cannot simply be defined by reference to the underlying general principle "that a person who claims the benefit of a deed must also take it subject to the burdens". Indeed, if the doctrine were so wide as to obligate a successor in title to all the burdens contained in the deed simply by reason of his acceptance of the benefit of the deed, it would swallow the rule. Positive covenants *would* run with the land. Hence, while this general principle may have informed the reasoning underlying the concession of counsel in *Halsall v. Brizell*, reference must be made to later applications of the doctrine to further refine it.

Before referring to the subsequent jurisprudence, it is noteworthy that the decision in *Halsall v. Brizell* has been the subject of much debate and criticism. A frequently published commentator on English property law, F.R. Crane, has pointed out some of the weaknesses of the decision in a case comment at 21 [1957] The Conveyancer & Property Lawyer 160. He noted that the court in *Halsall v. Brizell* effectively by-passed both the decision in *Austerberry* and the rule against perpetuities, citing as only authority for doing so a brief remark by Lord Cozens-Hardy

M.R. during argument in *Elliston v. Reacher*, [1908] 2 Ch. 665 (C.A.) which did not form part of the judgment. R. E. Megarry (as he then was) also pointed out the frail underpinnings of *Halsall* in a 1957 case comment (1957), 73 L.Q.R. 154 at 155-56. He noted that the observation of Lord Cozens-Hardy M.R. in *Elliston v. Reacher*, relied upon by Upjohn J., provided doubtful authority for the proposition since it was simply made during the address by counsel and did not form part of the judgment. Further, the passage relied upon from Coke on *Littleton* confined the operation of the benefit and burden rule to a party who is specifically named in a deed but who does not execute it.

The subsequent case of *Tito v. Waddell (No. 2)* ("*Tito's case*"), that has applied the doctrine in *Halsall v. Brizell*, is of particular relevance to DCC 123's position. Indeed, the distinction sought to be made by DCC 123 between the benefit and burden principle on the one hand, and the conditional grant on the other, stems from the judgment of Vice-Chancellor Megarry in *Tito's* case.

Tito's case was lengthy and complex, involving a multitude of issues. However, it is not necessary for the purpose of this appeal to discuss it in any detail. The only part of the decision that is relevant to this case is Megarry V-C's discussion of the doctrine in *Halsall v. Brizell*. Ironically, the frailty of *Halsall v. Brizell* was the subject of substantial analysis in the judgment. However, of particular relevance to the appellant's position is Megarry V-C's identification of two aspects (amongst others) of the doctrine in *Halsall v. Brizell*—the conditional grant, and what Megarry V-C called the "pure principle of benefit and burden". He described the first as a function of the creating instrument that in effect attaches conditions to the exercise of a right and thereby restricts the scope of the benefit itself, and the second as a general category where the benefit and burden, although arising under the same instrument, are independent of each other. He stated as follows (at p. 281):

> *(a) Conditional benefits and independent obligations.* One of the most important distinctions is between what for brevity may be called conditional benefits, on the one hand, and on the other hand independent obligations. An instrument may be framed so that it confers only a conditional or qualified right, the condition or qualification being that certain restrictions shall be observed or certain burdens assumed, such as an obligation to make certain payments. Such restrictions or qualifications are an intrinsic part of the right; you take the right as it stands, and you cannot pick out the good and reject the bad. In such cases it is not only the original grantee who is bound by the burden; his successors in title are unable to take the right without also assuming the burden. The benefit and the burden have been annexed to each other *ab initio*, and so the benefit is only a conditional benefit. In the other class of case the right and the burden, although arising under the same instrument, are independent of each other: X grants a right to Y, and by the same instrument Y independently covenants with X to do some act. In such cases, although Y is of course bound by his covenant, questions may arise whether successors in title to Y's right can take it free from the obligations of Y's covenant, or whether they are bound by them under what for want of a better name I shall call the pure principle of benefit and burden.

The two aspects of the doctrine identified by Megarry V-C in *Tito's* case must be read in the light of the subsequent decision by the House of Lords in *Rhone v.*

Stephens. While the House of Lords accepted that conditions could be attached to the exercise of a power or a right, thereby rendering the conditions enforceable upon the exercise of the power or right, it rejected any notion of a "pure principle of benefit and burden" that would bind successors to burdens that stood independently of the right. Lord Templeman stated as follows (at p.73):

> Mr. Munby also sought to persuade your Lordships that the effect of the decision in the *Austerberry* case had been blunted by the "pure principle of benefit and burden" distilled by Megarry V-C from the authorities in *Tito v. Waddell (No 2)*, [1977] 3 All E.R. 129 at 291-292, [1977] Ch 106 at 301–303. I am not prepared to recognise the "pure principle" that any party deriving any benefit from a conveyance must accept any burden in the same conveyance. Megarry V-C relied on the decision of Upjohn J. in *Halsall v. Brizell*, [1957] 1 All E.R. 371, [1957] Ch. 169. In that case the defendant's predecessor in title had been granted the right to use the estate roads and sewers and had covenanted to pay a due proportion for the maintenance of these facilities. It was held that the defendant could not exercise the rights without paying his costs of ensuring that they could be exercised. Conditions can be attached to the exercise of a power in express terms or by implication. *Halsall v. Brizell* was just such a case and I have no difficulty in wholeheartedly agreeing with the decision. It does not follow that any condition can be rendered enforceable by attaching it to a right nor does it follow that every burden imposed by a conveyance may be enforced by depriving the covenantor's successor in title of every benefit which he enjoyed thereunder. The condition must be relevant to the exercise of the right. In *Halsall v. Brizell* there were reciprocal benefits and burdens enjoyed by the users of the roads and sewers. In the present case cl 2 of the 1960 conveyance imposes reciprocal benefits and burdens of support but cl 3 which imposed an obligation to repair the roof is an independent provision. In *Halsall v. Brizell* the defendant could, at least in theory, choose between enjoying the right and paying his proportion of the cost or alternatively giving up the right and saving his money. In the present case the owners of Walford House could not in theory or in practice be deprived of the benefit of the mutual rights of support if they failed to repair the roof.

Megarry and Wade, in their text on *The Law of Real Property*, at pp. 1008–1010, reviewed some of the relevant jurisprudence, including the decision of the English Court of Appeal in *E.R. Ives Investment Ltd.* relied upon by the applications judge and *Tito*'s case, and concluded that there must now be some doubt as to their correctness and as to the precise extent of the benefit and burden principle given the subsequent decision of the House of Lords in *Rhone v. Stephens*. The authors comment as follows (at pp. 1009-1010):

> The House of Lords has rejected any "pure" principle of benefit and burden, by which "any party deriving any benefit from a conveyance must accept any burden in the same conveyance". Although the House accepted that conditions could be attached expressly or impliedly to the exercise of a power, this was so only where the condition was "relevant to the exercise of the right". The party must, "at least in theory", be able to elect between enjoying the right and performing his obligation or renouncing the right and freeing himself of the burden. On that basis, the House held that the fact that A's roof was supported by B's property did not mean that B could enforce against A a positive covenant made by A's predecessor in title with B's to repair the roof. This approach provides little guidance as to when a party will be regarded as having a genuine choice whether or not to renounce the benefits in order to be relieved of the burdens. . . .

> The policy underlying the decision of the House seems to be to restrict the ambit of the doctrine of benefit and burden as a means of circumventing the rule that the burden of positive covenants does not run. The intention would seem to be to prompt the abolition of the rule by legislation that had been drafted with careful regard to the consequences.

In the subsequent case of *Thamesmead (Town) v. Allotey* (1998), 37 E.G. 161 (C.A.), Gibson L.J., writing for the unanimous English Court of Appeal, noted several difficulties with the reasoning in *Rhone v. Stephens* and concluded his judgment by expressing agreement with Professor Gravells' view expressed in an article on *Rhone v. Stephens* at (1994), 110 L.Q.R. 346, at p. 350, that since the House of Lords has "clearly ruled out a judicial solution, it is for Parliament to provide a legislative solution."

In my view, the case law does not support the applications judge's finding that the benefit and burden principle has been clearly adopted by the English courts as an exception to the rule that positive covenants do not run with the land. Indeed, had *Rhone v. Stephens* been brought to his attention, the applications judge undoubtedly would have held that the "pure" principle of benefit and burden, relied upon by DCC 123 in this case and identified as an aspect of the doctrine in *Halsall v. Brizell* by Megarry V-C in *Tito'* s case, was later expressly rejected by the English courts.

Further, the applications judge's conclusion that the benefit and burden principle would apply to the facts of this case is not consonant with the English jurisprudence. He concluded that Amberwood was bound by the burden of the covenant because it had received the following benefits: part ownership of the recreational and utility units in the Phase 1 building; payment by DCC 123 for the maintenance of, and security over, those units; and easements over the Phase 1 lands. However, the simple fact that Amberwood received certain benefits upon obtaining title to the Phase 2 lands is clearly not sufficient, without more, under the English common law to render it liable under the positive covenant contained in the same instrument. In so far as the easements over the Phase 1 lands are concerned, DCC 123 has not established *any* correlation between those benefits and the burden of the positive covenant, so as to justify the application of the English doctrine. In so far as the benefits related to the recreational facilities are concerned, DCC 123 has not shown any user or enjoyment of the benefit by Amberwood. While DCC 123 recognizes in its supplementary *factum* that those requirements cause difficulties in this case, it purports to resolve the issue by submitting that an "all or nothing" principle should be adopted in Ontario so as to bind Amberwood to all the terms of the Reciprocal Agreement, whether or not there is any direct link or any *de facto* use or enjoyment of the intended benefits. In my view, the adoption of such a wide exception would be tantamount to abolishing the rule itself. Any successor in title would be bound by the positive covenant by reason solely of its acceptance of the deed to the land.

I note further, with respect to the findings of the applications judge, that whatever rights or obligations may flow from the fact that the parties are presently co-owners of the recreational facilities to which the costs are related are irrelevant to, and beyond the scope of, the present application. The co-ownership, created not by the Reciprocal Agreement but by a later conveyance between DCC 123 and one of

Amberwood's predecessors in title, may well give rise to other issues that relate to the same interim costs, but it has no bearing on the question whether Amberwood is liable on the covenant contained in the Reciprocal Agreement.

Therefore, I conclude that, on proper consideration of the scope of the English doctrine in *Halsall v. Brizell*, Amberwood would not be liable to pay the interim expenses on that basis if the exception were adopted in Ontario law. In any event, it is my view that, having regard to the uncertainties and the many frailties of the existing common law in England in this area of the law, it would be inadvisable to adopt these principles in Ontario. Indeed, a review of the English experience with the doctrine of *Halsall v. Brizell*, lends further support to the conclusion that any reform to the rule in *Austerberry* is best left to the Legislature. It would appear from many of the commentaries that the English adoption of the benefit and burden exception may have created more problems than it has solved.

Quite apart from the uncertainties that the adoption of the exception could create in other existing commercial relationships, it is my view that the application of the benefit and burden principle in this case could give rise to a multitude of other issues, particularly in the event of non-compliance. I pose but a few hypothetical questions by way of example. What benefits would Amberwood lose if it failed to pay the interim costs? Would it simply lose any right to use the shared facilities? Or would all the easements be extinguished? Could any or all of these benefits be revived upon paying the arrears? Could the benefits be revived at any time by payment of the arrears whether it be by Amberwood or a subsequent purchaser? Or would payment have to be made within a reasonable time? Would Amberwood be liable to lose the benefit of the land itself because it did not pay the interim costs? Are these interim costs to be paid indefinitely, even if no second tower is ever built on the Phase 2 lands?

While issues of this kind are not at all remarkable in the context of a contractual dispute between parties, they do create much uncertainty when they arise by reason of a covenant that runs with the land because they affect the certainty of title. Indeed, in this case, Amberwood has sold the Phase 2 lands. How then would the subsequent purchaser's title to the lands be affected by the answer to these hypothetical questions? These questions exemplify some of the issues identified by the OLRC in its 1989 Report as matters that would need to be addressed by the Legislature under any scheme allowing for positive covenants to run with the land.

For these reasons, I would not give effect to this ground of appeal.

(b) The conditional grant

The applications judge also considered whether the rule that positive covenants do not run with the land was subject to the conditional grant exception in English law and whether this exception would apply to this case. He described the exception by reference to *Halsbury's Laws of England* as follows (at para. 32, p. 678):

> If the facts establish that the granting of a benefit or easement was conditional on assuming the positive obligation, then the obligation is binding. Where the obligation is framed so as to constitute a continuing obligation upon which the grant of the easement was conditional, the obligation can be imposed as an incident of the easement itself, and not merely a liability purporting to run with the land: *Halsbury's Laws of England* 4th ed., Vol. 14 at 79.
>
> . . .

The applications judge . . . concluded that this exception would apply to this case on the basis of article 13.1(b) of the Reciprocal Agreement. I again reproduce this general provision for convenience:

> *Section 13.1 — Provisions Run with the Land*
>
> . . .
>
> (b) The parties hereto hereby acknowledge and agree that the Easements, rights and provisions as set forth in this Agreement establish a basis for mutual and reciprocal use and enjoyment of such Easements, rights and provisions and as an integral and material consideration for the continuing right to such use and enjoyment each party hereto does hereby accept, agree to assume the burden of, and to be bound by each and every of the covenants entered into by them in this Agreement. . . .

In my view, the applications judge's observation that the "conditional grant" exception "is essentially a form of the benefit/burden doctrine" accurately describes the position taken by DCC 123 in this case and, in turn, leads me to the conclusion that this second argument must fail, essentially for the same reasons that I have rejected the first exception.

I note at the outset that the principle from *Halsbury's Laws of England* relied upon by the applications judge seems to me to be consonant with the rule in *Austerberry*. I repeat it here for convenience:

> If the facts establish that the granting of a benefit or easement was conditional on assuming the positive obligation, then the obligation is binding. Where the obligation is framed so as to constitute a continuing obligation upon which the grant of the easement was conditional, *the obligation can be imposed as an incident of the easement itself, and not merely a liability purporting to run with the land.* [Emphasis added.]

Hence, as a matter of construction of the creating instrument itself, if a grant of benefit or easement is framed as conditional upon the continuing performance of a positive obligation, the positive obligation may well be enforceable, not because it would run with the land, but because the condition would serve to limit the scope of the grant itself. In effect, the law would simply be giving effect to the grant. Indeed, as discussed earlier in this judgment at paragraphs 30 and 31, much the same reasoning underlies the law of restrictive covenants.

However, none of the grants of benefit or easement contained in the Reciprocal Agreement are framed in this way. Neither section 2.3 nor Article 3 of the Reciprocal

Agreement is expressed to be conditional or dependant upon performance of all obligations under section 2.9. Further, it is my view that section 13.1(b) is far too general to create a conditional grant within the meaning of the principle stated in *Halsbury's Laws of England.* At its highest, it can be said that the parties to the Reciprocal Agreement have attempted to write in, as a term of their agreement, essentially the same general benefit and burden principle, the adoption of which was urged upon this court as a first exception to the rule. In my view, section 13.1(b) achieves no more, and its application would give rise to the same difficulties that I have discussed earlier. The attempt to create a contractual exception to the rule in *Austerberry*, while binding on the original parties to the Reciprocal Agreement, cannot displace the rule that positive covenants do not bind successors-in-title. It is undisputed in English and Canadian law that the rule that positive covenants do not run with the land governs despite any express intention to the contrary contained in the agreement. Indeed, if the applications judge was correct in his conclusion that section 13.1(b) effectively created an exception to the rule, it would be open to anyone to simply abolish the rule at the stroke of a pen. All that would be required would be a general statement of intent that the continuing right to the use and enjoyment of all the benefits in an agreement was conditional upon the acceptance of the burden contained in any of the covenants. The recognition of such a wide exception would constitute a profound change in the law.

Hence, in the circumstances of this case, I would not give effect to this second ground of appeal. I would conclude that Amberwood is not bound to pay the interim expenses on the basis of the positive covenant contained in the Reciprocal Agreement.

DISPOSITION

For these reasons, I would conclude that the applications judge was correct in granting Amberwood's application and I would dismiss the appeal with costs. In order to comply with the rule that now requires this court to fix costs, Amberwood is to file a bill of costs and written submissions with the court within 10 days from the release of this court's decision, DCC 123 is to respond in writing within a further 10 days after filing, and a reply may be submitted within 5 days thereafter.

MacPherson J.A. (dissenting):

(1) Introduction

I have had the benefit of reading the reasons of my colleague, Charron J.A. I agree with her that it would be inappropriate for this court to abolish the rule in *Austerberry v. Corporation of Oldham* (1885), 29 Ch. D. 750 (Eng. C.A.) ("*Austerberry*"). I also agree with her that the application judge, Stinson J., erred in holding that the doctrine of *stare decisis* precluded him from adopting the English "exceptions" to the rule in *Austerberry.*

However, with respect, I do not agree with my colleague's analysis or conclusions relating to the benefit-burden and conditional grant exceptions to the rule in *Austerberry*. In my view, both exceptions should be adopted into the law of Ontario. Their application in this case would result in the appeal being allowed. . . .

Turning to the fundamental question, I can state my view that the benefit-burden exception to the rule in *Austerberry* should be adopted. . . . I also find persuasive the strong academic and professional support for the exception, extending from Professor Wade and Mr. Megarry in 1957 to Professor Aughterson in Australia, Professor Davis in the United Kingdom and Professor Ziff in Canada in recent years.

The final question then becomes: is the exception applicable in this case? I begin my answer to this question by noting that all of the judges and academics who favour the exception admit that there are problems with it. In *Tito*, Megarry V.-C. was particularly candid on this point. He began the summary of his conclusions with this sentence: "I emerge from a consideration of the authorities put before me with a number of conclusions and a number of uncertainties" (p. 302).

In spite of problems and uncertainties, in my view it is possible, based on the case authorities and the academic commentary, to state the components of the benefit-burden exception with a reasonable degree of clarity.

First, the assignee of a positive covenant must have notice of it. The burden of such a covenant cannot attach to a person who was not aware of it. That will rarely be an issue in Ontario where a wide variety of documents relating to land can be registered and are thus accessible.

Second, a positive covenant which imposes a burden on an assignee must be accompanied by a benefit. The burden will not run in isolation.

Third, it may be that there is some type of qualitative threshold in the benefit and burden analysis. Megarry V.-C. seemed to envisage one because in *Tito* he said, at p. 305:

> I do not think that the pure benefit and burden principle is a technical doctrine, to be satisfied by what is technical and minimal. I regard it as being a broad principle of justice, to be satisfied by what is real and substantial. . . .

Fourth, there need not be a direct relationship or linkage between the benefit and the burden. They are, as Megarry V.-C. said in *Tito*, "independent" (p. 290), which distinguishes them from conditional benefits (discussed below).

Fifth, the assignee must be able to exercise a choice about assuming the benefits and burdens. This was one of the fundamental components of the exception described by Upjohn J. in *Halsall* (p. 377). It should be recalled that *Halsall* was specifically approved in *Rhone*, although the approval is surprising and confusing in light of the House of Lords' rejection of *Tito*; on the issue of choice or election, Lord Templeman said: "In *Halsall v. Brizell* the defendant could, at least in theory, choose between enjoying the right and paying his proportion of the cost or alternatively giving up the right and saving his money" (p. 73).

Turning to the application of these factors in the present case, it is clear that they line up in favour of the appellant.

Amberwood had clear notice of the burdens which it would be required to assume. Indeed, before the litigation was commenced, there were extensive negotiations about the burdens and, at one point, Amberwood's counsel informed DCC's counsel, in a letter dated October 1, 1999, "I have advised my clients and they have agreed with me to accept that they are bound by the terms of the agreement".

In addition, there can be little question that Amberwood derived benefits from the agreement and that, on any standard, the benefits are "real and substantial". The recreational and utility units in DCC's building, which are partly owned by Amberwood, are maintained by DCC. There is 24 hour security for that building. Amberwood also has the benefit of 10 valuable easements provided for in section 3.1 of the agreement.

Finally, Amberwood exercised a clear choice when it accepted the benefits under the agreement. It has never disclaimed its entitlement to the benefits; indeed it has openly asserted that entitlement and an intention to use the benefits, including "for [Amberwood's] future marketing program" (Price-Kilgour letter, September 24, 1999).

In summary, I would apply the benefit-burden exception to the rule in *Austerberry* in the present case. Since Amberwood had notice of the burdens, since the benefits are "real and substantial", and since Amberwood elected to accept them, it must also accept the burden of paying its share of the interim costs.

Before leaving this issue, which I acknowledge is a difficult one, I want to make two final observations.

First, I do not think there is an inconsistency between the introduction of the benefit-burden exception into the law of Ontario and the continuation of the general rule that positive covenants do not run with the land. Put another way, I do not think that the exception swallows the rule. Professor Davis, in her article "The Principle of Benefit and Burden", stated that with respect to the "pure principle of benefit and burden . . . [e]nforcement is only possible in certain circumstances, not generally" (p. 552). The Ontario Law Reform Commission, in its *Report on Covenants Affecting Land* (1989), said that the usefulness of the exception in *Halsall* "is somewhat limited. It will operate only if there is a benefit to be claimed under the deed, and further, it will operate only so long as the assignee of the covenantor continues to claim that benefit" (p. 23). Professor Eileen Gillese, in her text *Property Law* (2nd. ed., 1990), made a similar observation: "The doctrine in *Halsall v. Brizell* . . . is of limited application, however, since it only applies if the assignees claim or use the benefit" (p. 20:10).

I agree with these comments. The exception will *not* apply if there is no notice of the burden or if there is no benefit for the assignee to receive or if the assignee elects not to accept the benefit. These are important factors; their presence will allow the general rule to continue to be applied in many appropriate cases.

Second, I do not think that the benefit-burden exception will hinder the alienability of land. Market forces will deal with the exception, just as they deal with all other relevant factors in a purchase and sale context. As explained by Professor Ziff in "Positive Covenants", [(1989) 27 Alberta Law Review 354] "market forces will take account of, and respond to, the effect of positive covenants on alienation: if a covenant renders a property less desirable, its price will fall until it again becomes attractive to purchasers" (p. 369). Moreover, in many situations, especially large scale development projects, the exception will be viewed by the contracting parties as highly desirable because it will *promote* alienability: see Ontario Law Reform Commission, *Report on Covenants Affecting Freehold Land*, at p. 100, and Gray, *Elements of Land Law*, at pp. 1133-34.

(4) The conditional grant exception

The conditional grant exception to the rule in *Austerberry* was succinctly explained by Megarry V.-C. in *Tito*, at p. 290. For ease of reference, I set out this passage again:

> An instrument may be framed so that it confers only a conditional or qualified right, the condition or qualification being that certain restrictions shall be observed or certain burdens assumed, such as an obligation to make certain payments. Such restrictions or qualifications are an intrinsic part of the right: you take the right as it stands, and you cannot pick out the good and reject the bad. In such cases it is not only the original grantee who is bound by the burden: his successors in title are unable to take the right without assuming the burden. The benefit and the burden have been annexed to each other ab initio, and so the benefit is only a conditional benefit.

I begin by observing that I think the case for importing this exception into Ontario law is even stronger than the case for importing the benefit-burden exception. I acknowledge that there is uncertainty about the existence of the benefit-burden exception in English law in light of the House of Lords' terse disapproval of it in *Rhone*. Nevertheless, I would import it into Ontario law because I think it will make the law of real property more just.

As for the conditional grant exception, on my reading of the cases, it is accepted in English law. There is no uncertainty concerning its existence. The reason for the certainty on this point is that in *Rhone* the law lords expressly approved of the result in *Halsall* and, perhaps surprisingly, explained *Halsall* as an example of the conditional grant category. Accordingly, the question in this aspect of the appeal is whether an accepted principle in English law should become part of the law of Ontario? For the reasons in the previous section, I would answer this question in the affirmative.

It remains to determine whether the conditional grant exception applies in the present case. In my view, it does apply.

I begin by noting the title of the governing document, the *Reciprocal Easement and Cost Sharing Agreement*. This title suggests, in my view, a direct linkage between the benefits of the easements and the burden of cost sharing.

The preamble to the agreement also explicitly links easements and cost sharing:

> AND WHEREAS the [owners] are entering into this Agreement to provide, without limitation, for . . . the sharing of responsibilities and costs for mutual services . . . and . . . the Easements required by each of the parties. . . .

Sections 3.1 and 3.2 of the agreement then set out an extensive list of highly valuable easements — 10 in favour of Amberwood's predecessor and 4 in favour of DCC. Amberwood's easements include rights of access to permit construction of Phase 2, rights of access for purposes of maintenance, repair, installation and vehicular and pedestrian movement, and rights to tap into existing facilities in the Phase 1 building.

Crucially, s. 13.1(b) of the agreement provides:

> *Section 13.1 — Provisions Run with the Land*
>
> . . .
>
> (b) The parties hereto hereby acknowledge and agree that the Easements, rights and provisions as set forth in this Agreement establish a basis for mutual and reciprocal use and enjoyment of such Easements, rights and provisions and as an integral and material consideration for the continuing right to such use and enjoyment each party hereto does hereby accept, agree to assume the burden of and to be bound by each and every of the covenants entered into by them in this Agreement.

The application judge interpreted s. 13.1(b) in this fashion:

> In my view, the language of that section makes it clear that the payment of interim costs, as one of the covenants in the reciprocal agreement, was intended to be a condition upon which the other easements were conveyed. The provision does not support Amberwood's submission that the cost-sharing obligations should be viewed as distinct from the scheme for mutual easements. To the contrary, paragraph 13.1(b) seems to envision a building project in which the owners would share costs in exchange for shared access and ownership. To undermine this clear intention by severing the cost obligations from the overall deal would amount to dismantling part of an intricate, complex, and well-planned scheme, and defeating legitimate party expectations.

I agree with this analysis. In my view, it is clear from a reading of the entire agreement — its title, preamble and substantive provisions — that there is a direct and intentional linkage or reciprocity between the benefits of the easements, which are numerous and valuable, and the burden of the interim costs that are in issue in this appeal. Accordingly, since Amberwood had notice of the burdens and elected to accept the benefits (even though their full value will not be realized until Amberwood either builds Phase 2 or sells the land, presumably for a price that would reflect the benefits of the easements), it must also accept the linked burden of paying its share of the interim costs.

(5) Conclusions and Disposition

This is a difficult case, in terms of both the proper role of the courts in changing the common law and the substantive law of real property. . . .

As to whether the courts can introduce the exceptions into the law of Ontario, I recall again what Justice Cardozo said about the role of the common law in *The Nature of the Judicial Process*: "There are gaps to be filled. There are doubts and ambiguities to be cleared. There are hardships and wrongs to be mitigated if not avoided" (p. 14).

In a similar vein, Bastarache J. recently discussed judicial reform of the common law in *Friedmann Equity Developments Inc. v. Final Note Ltd.* (2000), 188 D.L.R. (4th) 269 at 290-91 ("Friedmann Equity"):

> [I]t is necessary to understand the principles which govern judicial reform of the common law. In the past, this Court has considered the conditions which must be present to effect a change in the common law in several cases: [names and citations omitted]. From these cases, some general principles have emerged. *A change in the common law must be necessary to keep the common law in step with the evolution of society* . . . to clarify a legal principle . . . or to resolve an inconsistency. In addition, *the change should be incremental, and its consequences must be capable of assessment.* [Emphasis added.]

Canadian society and the patterns of property ownership in 2002 are very different from English society and land ownership in 1885 when *Austerberry* was decided. The Ontario legislature has recognized the differences and enacted laws mitigating the rigours of the rule in *Austerberry* — on 12 occasions.

In my view, the benefit-burden and conditional grant exceptions to the rule in *Austerberry* can perform a similar role if introduced into the common law of Ontario. As I have tried to explain the exceptions, their adoption would, as required by Bastarache J. in *Friedmann Equity*, result in incremental change with consequences capable of assessment. They would also meet Justice Cardozo's important objective of mitigating hardships or wrongs in appropriate cases. This is one of those cases. The intentions of the original contracting parties and the wording in the agreement they signed are both crystal clear: a regime of reciprocal easements and other benefits and cost sharing was established. Amberwood, a successor in title to one of the contracting parties, chose, with full knowledge of the clear terms of the original agreement, to accept and utilize the benefits of the agreement. In my view, it would be unjust to permit Amberwood to ignore the reciprocal burdens which the agreement so clearly imposes on it.

For these reasons, I would allow the appeal with costs.

NOTE

An application for leave to appeal to the Supreme Court of Canada was launched by Durham C.C. No. 123. However, before the hearing of the motion the dispute was settled out-of-court.

QUESTIONS

1. What are the policy justifications for denying the enforceability of positive covenants against new owners of the burdened lands? What are the reasons advanced by the majority in *Amberwood* for resisting judicial activism in reforming the law of positive covenants?

2. Review the provisions of the Ontario *Conservation Act*, reproduced above. How, if at all, do these provisions deal with the problems associated with the reform of the law of positive covenants?

3. Are the following covenants positive or negative in substance:

(a) "all buildings must be constructed with brick."

(b) "the owner shall not cause or permit the dilapidation of the buildings on the property."

(c) "the owner must maintain the property as a park".

4. The majority of the Court of Appeal identify an array of devices that are used to circumvent the rule prohibiting the running of the burden of positive covenants. What are those exceptions? Do they overwhelm the general rule?

5. Using the analysis in *Amberwood*, how can one distinguish between the doctrine in *Halsall v. Brizell* (which the majority of the Court concluded should not form part of Ontario law) and the doctrine of condition grants (which was said to be consonant with the *Austerberry* rule and which is regarded by the majority as good law)?

6. Assume that you have been retained to draft an agreement under which A is to pay for the cost of repairing an easement to be enjoyed over the land of B. How would you draft such an agreement so as to ensure that it was within the terms of the majority holding in *Amberwood*?

7. In *Weinblatt v. Kitchener (City)* (1968) 1 D.L.R. (3d) 241, 1968 CarswellOnt 92 (S.C.C.), property was sold by the city to Robert Hart for $33,000. The agreement provided, in part, that Hart or his assigns would commence construction on the land within one year. The document also provided that,

> failing commencement of construction pursuant to this covenant by the Purchaser (Hart) or his assigns within the time limit specified herein, the Vendor (City) may repurchase

> the land for the sum of THIRTY-THREE THOUSAND DOLLARS ($33,000.00) provided the Vendor (City) has fulfilled all covenants made by it herein.

The agreement was registered on title and the burdened land was shortly afterwards transferred to Weinblatt. The condition as to construction not having been met, the City sought a reconveyance in accordance with this clause. Among other things, Weinblatt argued that the covenant was a personal contract between the original parties and hence could not be enforced against a subsequent purchaser because it did not fall within the class of negative covenants that bind subsequent purchasers of the burdened land. Judson J., for the Supreme Court of Canada, curtly and obscurely replied (at 244) that "[t]his defence does not arise on the facts of this case." Why not?

8. In *Thamesmead Town Ltd. v. Allotey* [1998] 3 E.G.L.R. 97 (C.A.), referred to in passing in *Amberwood*, a claim to enforce the burden of maintenance charges against new owners of the putative burdened lands failed. The obligation was to contribute to the upkeep of certain common areas. The Court of Appeal applied and explained the approach in *Rhone*, holding that there must be a nexus between the benefit and the burden, and also that the new owner must have an opportunity to reject the burden by foregoing the benefit. Moreover — and here is a refinement — the Court held that for the doctrine to apply the relevant benefit must be one that the owner of the burdened land could demand as of right. In *Thamesmead*, the alleged benefit, the right to use the communal areas, was not in fact granted to the owners of the burdened land. It was also true — and perhaps highly significant — that the party seeking compensation for the outlays incurred was not under an obligation under the document to incur those expenses. For the Court, Peter Gibson L.J. said this (at 100):

> In my judgment, it cannot be sufficient that the taking of an incidental benefit should enable the enforcement of a burden against a person who has not . . . covenanted to undertake the particular burden. . . . [N]ot only is there no right conferred on the defendant [the new owner of the burdened land] by the 1988 transfer [the initial source of the covenants] to use the communal areas, but also the plaintiff has no obligation to maintain those areas.

How, if at all, would the *Thamesmead* refinement affect the analysis of the promises at issue in *Amberwood*?

9. In *Thameswood*, Peter Gibson L.J. said this (at 99):

> It is apparent therefore that the House of Lords [in *Rhone v. Stephens*] considered *Halsall v. Brizell* not to be an example of the pure principle of benefit and burden, which principle was rejected, but one falling into the . . . category of conditional benefit.

Is this point of view consistent with the language used in *Rhone v. Stephens* (referred to extensively in *Amberwood)?* Is the analysis found in *Amberwood* preferable?

10. One device that can be used to avoid the operation of the *Austerberry* rule is the incorporeal hereditament known as a "rentcharge". As alluded to earlier, a rentcharge

is a periodic payment annexed to a freehold, and is enforceable against the freeholder currently in possession (termed the *terre tenant*). In other words, a rentcharge will bind subsequent purchasers of the land even though it imposes a positive obligation, and despite the absence of privity of contract or estate. Moreover, it is thought that the amount of that obligation can be variable, so long as it is capable of being ascertained. For example, a rentcharge based on a percentage of the "rateable value of the property" from time to time is treated as being sufficiently certain: see *Beachway Management Ltd. v. Wisewell* [1971] Ch. 610. A failure to pay gives rise to an action in debt for the monies owing, and a right to levy distress.

The use of rentcharges to enforce positive obligations is not new. In the 1885 English decision of *Austerberry v. Corp. of Oldham* (1885) 29 Ch. D. 750 (C.A.), in which it was definitively established that positive covenants do not run, Lindley L.J. noted (at 783) that,

> If the parties had intended to charge this land for ever, into whosesoever hands it came, with the burden of repairing the roads, there are ways and means known to conveyancers by which it could be done with comparative ease; all that would have been necessary would have been to create a rent-charge and charge it on the tolls, and the thing would have been done.

In England, the rentcharge is used in another way to enforce positive obligations. This rather more elaborate technique involves attaching a right of entry to the rentcharge, so as to allow the holder of the charge to enter onto the servient lands in the event of a failure to perform whatever positive covenants are associated with that land. The right of entry can include the power to undertake the work required under the covenant, and charge the costs against the land. One should be cautious however: even though English statutory reforms seem to endorse the validity of this contrivance, it has apparently never been subjected to serious judicial scrutiny.

Susan Bright has observed that in England "[w]hat is often not appreciated by practitioners is that by using certain rentcharges it is possible to make positive covenants bind land for all time": S. Bright, "Estate Rentcharges and the Enforcement of Positive Covenants" [1988] Conv. 99, at 101. Likewise, in Canada the value of the rentcharge mechanism in this setting has been overlooked to date. The rentcharge is a rare bird in Canada, but there is no reason to believe that it does not form part of the received common law. Would a rentcharge have been of use in *Durham C.C. No. 123 v. Amberwood*? Can the rights contained in the agreement in that case be treated as, in substance, a rentcharge?

11. Compare and assess these two views of the *Amberwood* ruling:

    (a) J. Lem, "Annotation" (2002) 50 R.P.R. (3d) 4, at 7:

> There is no doubt that the decision in *Amberwood* leaves the property development bar woefully unsatisfied. In almost any multiple-use development of any size whatsoever, there are increasing incidences of reciprocal cost sharing agreements allocating responsibility for joint infrastructure works necessary for the success of the project. A finding

by the Ontario Court of Appeal to the effect that a covenant to pay a proportionate share of ongoing infrastructure maintenance costs runs with the land, and can be enforced against downstream owners, would have been a great practical relief for the bar. As is, practitioners are left with the awkward "cascading contractual privity" or "chain of covenants" approach to drafting, requiring successors in title to assume expressly the covenant, and to covenant to obtain further assumption covenants from their respective downstream successors, and so on. Perhaps even more disappointing for the real estate development bar, however, is the fact that *Amberwood* is not being appealed to the Supreme Court and the matter will not likely achieve any degree of legislative priority for some time to come.

(b) P.M. Perell, "A Commentary on *Amberwood Investments Ltd. v. Durham Condominium Corp. No. 123*" (2002) 50 R.P.R. (3d) 52, at 61-2:

> [I]t is this writer's view that Charron J.A. has the better side of the debate because of the problem of appropriate remedies for the breach of a positive covenant and because, with respect, MacPherson J.A. was too sanguine in his view that positive covenants do not affect the alienability of land. In other words, even if he is correct in arguing that the exceptions to the rule in *Austerberry v. Oldham Corp.* can be articulated with adequate certainty, the serious problems of the appropriate remedy fora breach of a positive covenant, which are highlighted by the report and recommendations of the Ontario Law Reform Commission, remain. Arguably, the work of the Commission also reveals that the changes to the law even for the more modest reform of adding exceptions would be fundamental and not incremental.
>
> One way of testing the merits of this criticism of the minority judgment is to observe that had MacPherson J.A.'s opinion formed the majority, then DCC would have been entitled to foreclose or sell the Phase II lands. In contrast, the Law Reform Commission would have limited DCC's remedies to damages with numerous limiting features, and it is not clear what material and prejudicial damages, if any, DCC suffered. Further, the Law Reform Commission recommended against any right of re-entry, and thus foreclosure of power for sale would not have been available under the Commission's proposal for change in the law. On the issue of alienability, to say that market forces would respond to the presence of a positive covenant is to concede that potential purchasers under the power of sale might find the burden of the positive cotenant burdensome and pay considerably less for the Phase II lands or not buy it. This is probably why the Commission recommended against a right of re-entry and, interestingly, if DCC foreclosed, then it would be free to release itself from the positive covenant. It then could sell the lands free of the positive covenant. All these thoughts seem better to support Charron J.A.'s conclusion for the majority.
>
> By way of a conclusion, several practical observations may be made that are relevant to the arguments of both the minority and the majority and also of the Ontario Law Reform Commission about the need for reform of the law. One observation is that the call for reform is, in part, based on the inconvenience of the current law. Reflection, however, reveal as that this complaint is relatively modest. Neither the Law Reform Commission nor the courts say that it is impossible for the parties to avoid the current rule; rather, they say that the inconvenience of the current rule has resulted in the development of a number of sometimes difficult methods by which the effect of the rule may be circumvented. Charron J.A. notes in her judgment that the rule may be avoided by a chain of covenants to maintain privity of contract, by the use of a right of re-entry annexed to rentcharge, by rights of re-entry generally, and by a long lease. Further, in many cases,

positive covenants will be enforceable quite simply as a matter of privity of contract because the dispute arises between the original contracting parties. Therefore, the final practical observation is that if the court cannot reform the law about the enforcement of positive covenants and if the legislature will not reform it, lawyers can and will just have to do it.

12. Below are the facts in *4348037 Manitoba Ltd. v. 2804809 Manitoba Ltd.* 2003 CarswellMan 247 (Q.B.). Assess the position of the applicant.

> The applicant and the respondent own two adjacent properties known respectively as 179 and 177 McDermot Avenue in the City of Winnipeg. The properties were originally heated by a steam plant operated by the City of Winnipeg. When the City discontinued the operation of their steam plant, these two properties were owned by the same person. That owner installed a boiler ("the furnace") in the basement of 179 McDermot to heat both buildings. The respondent purchased 177 McDermot from the joint owner in 1996. At that time it entered into an agreement with the joint owner, equally sharing the use, operation and expense of the furnace located at 179 McDermot. On May 10, 2001, the joint owner of 179 McDermot decided that he no longer wished to use or maintain the furnace. Consequently, he negotiated a new agreement ("the agreement") with the respondent whereby the respondent agreed to assume all future responsibility for operating and maintaining the furnace.
>
> In consideration of this new agreement, the respondent was given the right in perpetuity to use that portion of the basement in 179 McDermot in which the furnace was located as a furnace room. The new agreement was styled as a licensing agreement. However, it was registered and attached to a caveat in the land titles office as against the title of 179 McDermot.
>
> On July 1, 2001, the applicant purchased 179 McDermot with full notice and knowledge of the existence and terms of the agreement. From an equitable perspective there is no doubt that the applicant purchased the building in circumstances where it knew that its use of a portion of the basement was restricted. The applicant took possession of the building on July 1, 2001.

10. INVALIDITY AND TERMINATION

B. Ziff, "Restrictive Covenants: The Basic Ingredients" in *Special Lectures of the Law Society of Upper Canada 2002, Real Property Law: Conquering the Complexities* (Toronto: Irwin Law, 2003) 293 at 328–31 [footnotes omitted]

Even when the requirements for the running of covenants have been met, validity may be affected by extraneous principles. For example, a covenant may be void for uncertainty because it imposes an unacceptable restraint on alienation, or because it is contrary to statute. Under Ontario law, for example, a covenant that discriminates on the grounds of "race, creed, colour, nationality, ancestry or place of origin" is void. This specific prohibition does not preclude the possibility that a covenant might otherwise contravene public policy or the *Human Rights Code.*

Even though many covenants are created to control commercial dealings, the doctrines regulating agreements in restraint of trade have a very limited application to restrictive covenants. This is the case, it has been reasoned, because a party acquiring a property that is subject to a restriction on land use is not relinquishing a right that he or she already held. A person buying or leasing that land had no previous right to be there at all, and of course no pre-existing right to carry on a specific business on that property. However, the rules governing restraint of trade will apply in the (uncommon) case of a party with a present right to carry on a business who later surrenders that right under a restrictive covenant. Such a restriction will be unenforceable if it is unreasonable.

In theory, restrictive covenant may last forever. All else being equal, the rights obtained are treated as vested, and so a covenant is not *per se* subject to the rule against perpetuities. Even so, there are a number of ways in which a valid restrictive covenant may come to an end. All the parties involved may agree to a termination. Or, the covenant may have been intended to last for a specified time. For land governed by the Ontario *Land Titles Act*, a condition, restriction or covenant that has no period or fixed date of expiry is deemed to have expired forty years after registration. If a time for expiration is fixed, the covenant may be removed by the registrar no sooner than ten years from the time of the covenant's stated expiration date. When the benefited and burdened lands have come into the hands of a single party, it appears that the covenant is thereby extinguished, though in the case of building schemes it has been held that the covenants are merely suspended and can be revived at a later time.

It was noted above that when enforcement of a covenant is sought in equity, the general principles affecting equitable relief apply. Accordingly, a court of equity may refuse to enforce a covenant where the plaintiff has been guilty of delay or acquiescence. With regard to the later, the basic position is that a party will be estopped from enforcing a restriction owing to acquiescence if past breaches are so significant as to "deprive the covenants of their purpose". Likewise, when there has been a dramatic change in the locale, so much so that it would be fruitless to enforce the terms of a covenant, a remedy may be denied. This is a reflection of the maxim that equity will not act in vain.

In addition, statute may provide additional grounds for termination. For instance, in Ontario two provisions confer a judicial power to alter or discharge a restrictive covenant. The first of these, section 61 of the *Conveyancing and Law of Property Act*, provides that "a condition or covenant that the land or a specified part of it is not to be built on or is to be or not to be used in a particular manner, or any other condition or covenant running with or capable of being legally annexed to land . . . may be modified or discharged" by court order.

That language could not be broader. Understandably, the case law has endeavoured to provide guidance as to how this otherwise sweeping discretion should be exercised. It has been said that the function of the provision is to enable a court to remove a condition or restriction that is either spent or so unsuitable as to be of no value, such that it would be "clearly vexatious" to allow it to be enforced. Likewise, it has been maintained that this judicial power should be invoked only if the impact of the order on those holding the benefit would be negligible. Stated another way, the benefits of a court order should greatly exceed any resulting detriment. Often what is considered is whether discharging the covenant will significantly decrease the market value of the benefited lands, but I doubt whether monetary loss should be treated as the sole criterion. In any event, these guidelines reveal that the discretion has been given quite a narrow ambit, a reading that has been influenced by the fact that a court has no power to order compensation if a modification or termination is granted.

The second provision, found in the *Land Titles Act*, states that condition or covenant may be modified or discharged by a court on proof that such action *will be beneficial to the persons principally interested in the enforcement of the condition or covenant*. This qualification appears to set it apart from section 61. Indeed, a similar phrase was once contained in the predecessor of section 61 (from 1922 until 1927), and one might think that its deletion implies that a different test is to be applied. However, Ontario courts, cognizant of these developments, have nevertheless treated the two sections as functional equivalents.

QUESTIONS

1. You will notice that the British Columbia provision applicable to the termination of easements also applies to covenants. It is reproduced in Part 4, above. How do these compare with their Ontario counterparts?

2. Compare also the provisions concerning modification and termination found in subsection 48(4) of the *Land Titles Act*, R.S.A. 2000, c. L-4:

> The first owner, and every transferee, and every other person deriving title from the first owner or through tax sale proceedings, is deemed to be affected with notice of the condition or covenant, and to be bound by it if it is of such nature as to run with the land, but any such condition or covenant may be modified or discharged by order of the court, on proof to the satisfaction of the court that the modification will be beneficial to the persons principally interested in the enforcement of the condition or covenant or that the condition or covenant conflicts with the provisions of a land use bylaw or statutory plan under Part 17 of the *Municipal Government Act*, and the modification or discharge is in the public interest.

North Vancouver (District) v. Lunde
(1998) 162 D.L.R. (4th) 402, 1998 CarswellBC 1438 (C.A.)

[A residential apartment complex was constructed on the north shore of Vancouver. A restrictive covenant was placed on title restricting occupation to persons over the age of nineteen living with at least one older citizen. In 1990 a developer received permission from the local district authority to convert the rental units into condominiums. The developers also applied to have the restrictive covenant eliminated. The district did not approve that change.

The units were sold to some families who did not comply with the restrictive covenant and the district brought an action against the non-conforming owner/ occupiers.

In this case, the British Columbia Court of Appeal was asked to determine (a) if the restrictive covenant was discriminatory and thus contravened s. 5 of British Columbia's *Human Rights Act*, (b) if the district had the power to impose the covenant, and (c) if the covenant was obsolete and should be modified by court order.]

Lambert J.A.: . . .

The Covenant and the *Human Rights Act*

The *Human Rights Act* that was in effect when the Restrictive Covenant was created and registered was the Act as it was re-enacted in 1984. In that version there was no provision preventing differentiation between prospective purchasers of property or between prospective tenants of property on the basis of age. But in 1992 the Act was amended to change the definition of "age" and to include "age" in the section which prohibited differentiation between prospective tenants. No change was made with respect to "age" in relation to prospective purchasers. The definition. of "age" and the relevant part of s. 5 (now s. 10), read in this way after 1992:

Interpretation

1. In this Act

"age" means an age of 19 years or more and less than 65 years; . . .

Discrimination in tenancy premises

5.(1) *No person shall*

(a) *deny to a person or class of persons the right to occupy, as a tenant, space that is represented as being available for occupancy by a tenant*, or

(b) *discriminate against a person or class of persons with respect to a term or condition of the tenancy of the space,*

because of the race, colour, ancestry, place of origin, religion, marital status, family status, physical or mental disability, sex, sexual orientation or *age of that person or class of persons, or of any other person or class of persons.*

(2) *Subsection (1) does not apply . . .*

(b) *as it relates to family status or age,*

(i) *if the space is a rental unit in residential premises in which every rental unit is reserved for rental to a person 55 years of age or older or to 2 or more persons, at least one of whom is 55 years of age or older*, or

(ii) [to] a rental unit in a prescribed class of residential premises, . . .

[My emphasis; I have added the [to] at the beginning of (ii) where either [to] or some equivalent is missing.]

The *Human Rights Act* has since been replaced by the *Human Rights Code*, R.S.B.C. 1996, c. 210, but the changes do not affect the issues in this appeal.

It is important to note that the Restrictive Covenant relates to *occupation simpliciter*, whereas s. 5 of the *Human Rights Act* relates to *occupation as a tenant*. Under ss. 5(1), denial of a right of occupancy as a tenant, of space that is represented as being available for occupancy by a tenant, on the grounds of age, is prohibited, unless one of the two excepting conditions in para. 5(2)(*b*) makes ss. 5(1) inapplicable.

The prohibition in ss. 5(1) relates to a denial of a right to occupy "space", as a tenant. Sub-para. 5(2)(*b*)(i) refers to the circumstance where the "space" is a "rental unit" in "residential premises" in which every "rental unit" is reserved for rental to a person 55 years of age or older. The words and phrases that I have placed in quotation marks are not defined. But I think that the way those words and phrases are used in s. 5 of the *Human Rights Act* makes their meaning plain. In their application to this case, a strata lot becomes the "space" that is a "rental unit" when the strata lot is committed by the owner to availability for occupancy by a tenant. So owner-occupied strata lots are not rental units until they are committed by the owner to availability for occupancy by a tenant. The entire condominium project comprising all the strata lots and the common areas constitutes the "residential premises".

I turn now to whether either excepting condition in para. 5(2)(*b*) makes ss. 5(1) inapplicable in this case. The first one, in sub-para. (i) does not, because under the Restrictive Covenant each rental unit is reserved for a person 50 years of age or older and not for a person 55 years of age or older as the Act requires. The second one, in sub-para. (ii) does not, because no class of residential premises has been "prescribed". ("Prescribed" means prescribed by regulation. See the definition of "prescribed" in s. 29 of the *Interpretation Act*, R.S.B.C. 1996, c. 238. There is no relevant regulation.)

Since neither excepting condition in para. 5(2)(b) makes ss. 5(1) inapplicable in this case, ss. 5(1) applies when the owner of a strata lot commits the strata lot to availability for occupancy by a tenant. The owner can not deny occupation to a person, or discriminate against a person with respect to a term of the tenancy, on the grounds of age. And, of course, "age" is defined in the *Human Rights Act* as an age between 19 and 64 inclusive.

That brings me back to the question: "Whether the age restriction in the Covenant is discriminatory and contravenes s. 5 of the *Human Rights Act*." The age restriction in the Covenant does not require any strata lot owner to commit the strata lot to occupancy by a tenant. The *Human Rights Act* does not apply to owner-occupiers with respect to age. As Madam Justice Allan said, an owner-occupier who is contemplating committing his or her strata lot to occupancy by a tenant must comply with both the Restrictive Covenant and the *Human Rights Act*. That can be done by either not renting out the strata lot at all or by renting it only to someone over 64. That restriction on renting out a strata lot does not involve any conclusion that the age restriction in the Covenant is discriminatory in any relevant sense, nor any conclusion that it contravenes s. 5 of the *Human Rights Act*. The Restrictive Covenant does not require or compel an owner to rent out that owner's strata lot to someone over 50, or at all. So I would answer the first question in the same way as Madam Justice Allan: "It is not discriminatory and not in contravention of s. 5 of the *Human Rights Act*." . . .

[The Court of Appeal also held that the district had the power to impose such a restriction, and that the covenant was not obsolete even though it could contravene the *Human Rights Act*. The operation of the covenant was simply modified by the *Human Rights Act*. Lambert J.A. said this (at 411):

> . . . [T]he charge is not obsolete. It continues to have its full effect in relation to occupancy by an owner. And the modification of its applicability in relation to occupancy by a tenant under the combined effect of the Covenant and the Act, so that all rentals are prohibited other than those to a person over 64, does not make the covenant obsolete. What happens is that the *Human Rights Act* modifies the application of the covenant in relation to occupancy by a tenant.]

QUESTIONS

1. Do you see any problem with the following covenant (assume that the dominant land is adequately identified and is capable of being benefited by a covenant of this type)?

> "[N]o logging shall be carried out and no vegetation or plant life shall be disturbed or removed or interfered with on that part of the Servient Tenement comprised of the watershed for the community water utility presently known as Wilderness Mountain Water Corporation."

See *Mt. Matheson Conservation Society v. 573132 B.C. Ltd.* 2002 CarswellBC 1994, 3 R.P.R. (4th) 146 (S.C.).

2. Looking back on the foundation principles of private property, what is gained and what is lost by allowing restrictive covenants to run with land?

11. COVENANTS OVER PERSONALTY

Dominion Coal Co. v. Lord Strathcona Steamship Co. 1925 CarswellNS 55, [1926] A.C. 108 (Canada P.C.)

Lord Shaw:

This is an appeal from a judgment and order of the Supreme Court in Appeal of Nova Scotia (*en banc*), dated March 1, 1924 (57 N.S.R. 113), which affirmed a judgment and order of Mr. Justice Mellish in the Supreme Court of Nova Scotia, dated May 18, 1922.

The questions involved in the case depend upon a consideration of the charter-party about to be mentioned and of the [actions] of parties under and in reference to that contract.

The charter was dated April 20, 1914, corrected to July 24, 1914. It was made between the Lord Curzon Steamship Company, Limited, as the owners of the steamship "Lord Strathcona," and the respondents as charterers thereof. The charter was a long-term charter, namely, for 10 consecutive St. Lawrence seasons, commencing with the year 1915, with the option to the respondents of continuing the charter for a further period of five more seasons and a still further option of three more seasons thereafter. Should these options be exercised by the respondents as charterers the period of the contract thus extended to 18 years. The St. Lawrence season referred to was to commence, except as to the first season 1915, five days prior to the opening of navigation to Montreal and not later than May 15, in each year. The re-delivery to the owners of the steamship was to be between November 15 and December 15 in each year.

The ship went into the service of the respondent in 1916. She was delivered, or commenced service, on July 10, and she continued during the St. Lawrence season, namely, until December 14, 1916, being used by the respondents for their trade purposes under the charter-party. The British government, which had previously intimated that the vessel would be required for the purposes of war in 1915, when she was ready for the year, abandoned this position and allowed the use of the vessel under the charter for the season 1916 as stated.

They made, however, an effective requisition of the vessel at the close of the 1916 season, and the vessel remained under requisition for 1917 and 1918 by the British government. She came on service again by the withdrawal of the government requisition on July 2, 1919, and remained on service till the end of the season, namely, December, 1919. Shortly put, the vessel was thus under requisition for some two and a half years, namely, from the end of the 1916 season until early in July, 1919. During the course of these years various changes, to be afterwards referred to, were made in the ownership of the vessel. . . .

So far as the knowledge of the existence of the charter-party was concerned their Lordships are clearly of opinion that all these successive owners were well aware of it, and this knowledge was, by notice, passed very clearly and properly on from each owner to the successor. It was only very late in the day when any flaw on this point was attempted to be taken. An important document in the case is that of September 1, 1919, namely, a memorandum of agreement by which the Lathom Company agreed with the Strathcona Company about to be formed, which contained the following clause:

> The steamer is chartered to the Dominion Coal Company as per charter party dated New York, 20th April, 1914, corrected to 24th July, 1914, which charter the buyers undertake to perform and accept all responsibilities thereunder as from date of delivery in consideration of which the buyers shall receive from date of delivery all benefits arising from the said charter. All liabilities up to date of delivery to buyers to be for account of sellers.

In the opinion of the Board the appellants thoroughly understood that the charter-party and its responsibilities and obligations thereunder were to be respected. This is not a mere case of notice of the existence of a covenant affecting the use of the property sold, but it is the case of the acceptance of their property expressly *sub conditione*.

The position of the case accordingly is that the appellants are possessed of a ship with regard to which a long-running charter-party is current, the existence of which was fully disclosed, together, indeed, with an obligation which the appellants appear to have accepted to respect and carry out that charter-party. The proposal of the appellants and the argument submitted by them is to the effect that they are not bound to respect and carry forward this charter-party either in law or in equity, but that, upon the contrary, they can, in defiance of its terms, of which they had knowledge, use the vessel at their will in any other way. It is accordingly, when the true facts are shown, a very simple case raising the question of whether an obligation affecting the user of the subject of sale, namely, a ship, can be ignored by the purchaser so as to enable that purchaser, who has bought a ship, notified to be not a free ship but under charter, to wipe out the condition of purchase and use the ship as a free ship. It was not bought or paid for as a free ship, but it is maintained that the buyer can thus extinguish the charterer's rights in the vessel, of which he had notice, and that the charterer has no means, legal or equitable, of preventing this in law.

In the opinion of the Board the case is ruled by *De Mattos v. Gibson* (1858) 4 De G. & J. 276, at p. 282, 28 L.J. Ch. 165, 498 (45 E.R. 108) also a shipping case, the case of the user of a piece of property by a third person (*e.g.*, the respondent company in this case) of "the property for a particular purpose in a specified manner." Their Lordships think that the judgment of Knight Bruce L.J., plainly applies to the present case:

> Reason and justice seem to prescribe that, at least as a general rule, where a man, by gift or purchase, acquires property from another, with knowledge of a previous contract, lawfully and for valuable consideration made by him with a third person, to use and

employ the property for a particular purpose in a specified manner, the acquirer shall not, to the material damage of the third person, in opposition to the contract and inconsistently with it, use and employ the property in a manner not allowable to the giver or seller.

A principle, not without analogy, had previously been laid down in reference to the user of land.

In the opinion of their Lordships the case of *De Mattos v. Gibson*, *supra*, still remains, notwithstanding many observations and much criticism of it in subsequent cases, of outstanding authority.

The general character of the principle on which a Court of Equity acts was explained in *Tulk v. Moxhay*, 2 Ph. 774, 18 L.J. Ch. 83. . . .

The cases on this branch of the law are legion. But following the leading authorities just cited there may be specially mentioned that of *Catt v. Tourle*, L.R. 4 Ch. 655, 38 L.J. Ch. 665, in which Selwyn L.J., affirms, with precision, the principles of *Tulk v. Moxhay*, *supra*, and *De Mattos v. Gibson*, *supra*. . . .

In the opinion of the Board these views, much expressive of the justice and good faith of the situation, are still part of English equity jurisprudence, and an injunction can still be granted thereunder to compel, as in a Court of conscience, one who obtains a conveyance or grant *sub conditione* from violating the condition of his purchase to the prejudice of the original contractor. Honesty forbids this; and a Court of Equity will grant an injunction against it. . . .

A perusal of the numerous decisions on this branch of the law shows that much difficulty has been caused by the attempt to extend these principles to cases to which they could not, by the nature of the case, have been meant to apply. It has been forgotten that — to put the point very simply — the person seeking to enforce such a restriction must, of course, have and continue to have, an interest in the subject-matter of the contract. For instance, in the case of land he must continue to hold the land in whose favour the restrictive covenant was meant to apply. That was clearly the state of matters in the case of *Tulk v. Moxhay*, *supra*, applicable to the possession of real estate in Leicester Square. It was also clearly the case in *De Mattos v. Gibson*, *supra*, in which the person seeking to enforce the injunction had an interest in the user of the ship. In short, in regard to the user of land or of any chattel, an interest must remain in the subject-matter of the covenant before a right can be conceded to an injunction against the violation by another of the covenant in question. This proposition seems so elementary as not to require to be stated. And it is only mentioned because in numerous decisions, as is clearly brought out in the judgment of Lord Wrenbury, then Lord Justice Buckley, in *London County Council v. Allen*, [1914] 3 K.B. 642, at pp. 656–658, 83 L.J.K.B. 1695, it was necessary to shear away this misapplication or improper extension of the equitable principle. As Romer L.J., said in *Formby v. Barker*, [1903] 2 Ch. 539, at p. 554, 72 L.J. Ch. 716:

> If restrictive covenants are entered into with a covenantee, not in respect of or concerning any ascertainable property belonging to him, or in which he is interested, then the covenant must be regarded, so far as he is concerned, as a personal covenant — that is as one obtained by him for some personal purpose or object.

Applying that to the case of land and referring to numerous cases upon the subject, Lord Wrenbury says in *London County Council v. Allen, supra*, (at p. 658):

> Inasmuch as at the date when the covenant was taken the covenantee had no land to which the benefit of the covenant could be attached, it was held that the benefit of the restrictive covenant could not enure against a derivative owner even where he took with notice.

The Board notes the observations made by Lord Justice Scrutton in the case of *London County Council v. Allen, supra*, in which, alluding to various decisions, the learned Judge puts this point as to the possible inconvenience, not only private but public, which may result from a strict adhesion to the principle that the enforcement of a restrictive covenant must be confined to those having patrimonial interests in the subject matter. His Lordship takes the not unfamiliar case of restrictive covenants imposed by an owner of a large block of land in the terms of conveyance of the various fractions in which it may be split up for private use, and he observes (at p. 673):

> I regard it as very regrettable that a public body should be prevented from enforcing a restriction on the use of property imposed for the public benefit against persons who bought the property knowing of the restriction, by the apparently immaterial circumstance that the public body does not own any land in the immediate neighbourhood. But, after a careful consideration of the authorities, I am forced to the view that the later decisions of this Court compel me so to hold.

The question here alluded to may subsequently arise, and their Lordships are unwilling, because it is unnecessary in the present case, to make any pronouncement upon it; for the present is, as has been seen, a case as to the user of a ship, with regard to the subject-matter of which, namely, the vessel, the respondent has, and will have during the continuance of the period covered by the charter-party, a plain interest so long as she is fit to go to sea. Again, to adopt the language of Knight Bruce L.J., in the *De Mattos v. Gibson* case, *supra*:

> Why should it [the Court] not prevent the commission or continuance of a breach of such a contract, when, its subject being valuable, as for instance a trading ship or some costly machine, the original owner and possessor, or a person claiming under him, with notice and standing in his right, having the physical control of the chattel, is diverting it from the agreed object, that object being of importance to the other? A system of laws in which such a power does not exist must surely be very defective. I repeat that, in my opinion, the power does exist here.

In considering the character of the doctrines of equity in a case like the present it is essential to remember that these doctrines are of several kinds and fall partly, though not exclusively, under different heads. If this is not borne in mind uncertainty and confusion are apt to arise. *Dicta* of eminent Judges which apply under one principle get to be regarded as though they illustrated a principle which is in reality different.

Equity has, in addition to the concurrent jurisdiction, auxiliary and exclusive jurisdiction. The enforcement of trusts is in the main an illustration of the exclusive jurisdiction. The scope of the trusts recognized in equity is unlimited. There can be a trust of a chattel or of a chose in action, or of a right or obligation under an ordinary legal contract, just as much as a trust of land. A shipowner might declare himself a trustee of his obligations under a charter-party, and if there were such a trust an assignee, although he could not enforce specific performance of the obligation would fail to do so only on the broad ground that the Court of Equity had no machinery by means of which to enforce the contract. Subject to this an assignee of the charterer could enforce his title to the chose in action in equity, even though he could not have done so at law.

There are cases of a different type in which equity is proceeding, not on the footing of trust, but of following, by the exercise of concurrent and auxiliary jurisdiction, the analogy of the common law. Such are the cases of so-called equitable easements. This was explained by the Court of Appeal in *London County Council v. Allen, supra.* There it was held that an owner of land, deriving title under a person who had entered into a restrictive covenant concerning the land, which covenant did not run with the land at law, was not bound by the covenant although he took the land with notice of it, if the covenantee were not in possession of or interested in land for the benefit of which the covenant was entered into. In the judgments it was pointed out that such a covenant did not run with the land at law, and that there was a series of authorities which showed that in the case of land mere purchase with notice was not sufficient. The reason was that under this head of its jurisdiction equity had followed law except to the extent of recognizing a negative covenant as capable of operating for the benefit of a dominant tenement. The principle proceeded on the analogy of a covenant running with the land or of an easement, as explained by Jessel M.R., in *L. & S. W. Ry. v. Gomm* [20 Ch. D. 562, 51 L.J. Ch. 530]. This restriction of the principle on the analogy of easements at law rendered mere notice insufficient, and cut down the jurisdiction from the wider principle stated by Knight Bruce L.J., in *De Mattos v. Gibson, supra,* to the narrower head established in order to accord with the legal analogy in the case of land.

But in no other regard does this or any other decision of commanding importance seem to affect the general principle which Knight Bruce L.J., laid down. If a man acquires from another rights in a ship which is already under charter, with notice of rights which required the ship to be used for a particular purpose and not inconsistently with it, then he appears to be plainly in the position of a constructive trustee with obligations which a Court of Equity will not permit him to violate. It does not matter that this Court cannot enforce specific performance. It can proceed, if there is expressed or clearly implied a negative stipulation. The judgment of Lord Chancellor St. Leonards in *Lumley v. Wagner*, 1 DeG. M. & G. 604, 21 L.J. Ch. 898 (42 E.R. 687) appears to be conclusive of the principle.

> Wherever [says that very eminent Judge, at p. 619] this Court has not proper jurisdiction to enforce specific performance, it operates to bind men's consciences, as far as they can be bound, to a true and literal performance of their agreements; and it will not suffer them to depart from their contracts at their pleasure, leaving the party with whom they have contracted to the mere chance of any damages which a jury may give.

For the reasons already fully set forth the Board is of opinion that the injunction granted by Mr. Justice Mellish in the seventh head of his order of June 20, 1922, was correct, and was properly affirmed by the Supreme Court for the reasons set forth by Mr. Justice Chisholm. The fundamental point indicated is thus determined. . . .

The cause should be remitted to the Court below to deal with the question of damages. There will be no costs of this appeal, the order as to costs in the Court below to stand.

QUESTIONS AND COMMENTS

1. Generally speaking, the rule in *De Mattos v. Gibson* has not been well-received in England or Canada. It has had very little impact: but see *Paxton v. Spira et al.* 1965 CarswellBC 105, 54 D.L.R. (2d) 627 (S.C.). Typical is the critique found in G.H.L. Fridman, *The Law of Contract*, 4th ed. (Toronto: Carswell, 1999) at 215:

> [W]hile one may have great sympathy for this approach, it does not seem to have any proper or logical basis. A charter-party creates no proprietary interest in the ship being chartered: the charterer's rights are contractual. Hence, the *Tulk v. Moxhay* doctrine hardly seems appropriate in the context of a contract concerning the use or the restrictive use of a *chattel*.

See also the references cited at 214–7.

2. What legal consequences would flow from a broad application of the rule in *De Mattos v. Gibson*, assuming that what is required is actual knowledge of the third-party right affecting a chattel?

3. In *Lord Strathcona Steamship*, did Lord Shaw need to rely on the rule in *De Mattos v. Gibson* to support the ultimate holding? What other doctrines support the same outcome?

REVIEW QUESTION

In 1965, the Town of Red Moose entered into an agreement with Canton Industries. One purpose of the agreement was to allow for the Town to use a canal owned by Canton for run off for drainage. The town's drainage system ran near the canal and surrounding lands, but there was about a 100-metre gap between the town's land and the canal. Canton owned the land separating the canal from the Town's land. That portion was referred to by the parties as the Corridor Lands.

The agreement describes the Corridor and Canal lands but makes no reference to freehold lands owned by the Town. The agreement also provides, in part, as follows:

Covenants and Terms

> **1.** Canton Industries [hereinafter Canton] grants to the Town of Red Moose [hereinafter the Town], the right, liberty, power and licence to share use of the property described fully herein as "the Canal" for the purpose of storm drainage disposal, for a period of 40 years, or such shorter period should the Town acquire another means of disposal.
>
> **2.** Canton allows the Town the right to use and enjoy the property fully described herein as "the Corridor Lands", for a period of 40 years, for the placement of sewer pipelines and such other uses as the Town from time to time may require.
>
> **3.** At the expiration of the said terms, the right contained in clause 1, and/or the right contained in clause 2, may be renewed at the election of the Town for an additional term of not more than 21 years under the same terms and conditions as herein set out.
>
> **4.** Canton undertakes and hereby covenants not to enter or to allow or permit any persons to enter onto the Corridor Lands except with the permission and consent of the Town. . . .
>
> **8.** As a condition of the rights granted over the Canal, the Town hereby covenants to repair such damage as may be occasioned to the Canal so long as it shall be used under this agreement. . . .
>
> **10.** The Town hereby undertakes not to use the rights hereby granted for the drainage or storage of toxic materials.
>
> **11.** Canton will loan the Town a portable shed, garbage disposal unit, or other unaffixed construction suitable for use by the Town for the storage of non-toxic substances on the Corridor Lands for so long as this agreement subsists.
>
> **12.** The rights contained herein run with the land and may be assigned by either party to this agreement.

In 2003, Canton sold its freehold interest in the above lands to Exsmith. The Canal walls are cracking. Some toxic materials have been found stored on the Corridor Lands. The portable dumpster placed on the land by Canton, in fulfilment of clause 11, has apparently been stolen.

Can Exsmith enforce Clause 8 against the Town? Can Exsmith now terminate the Town's right to remain on the Corridor Lands? Assuming that the Town's right to the Corridor Lands cannot now be terminated, is Exsmith bound by the terms described in Clause 3?

CHAPTER 11
MORTGAGES AND OTHER SECURITY INTERESTS

1. INTRODUCTION

The point of this chapter is to provide a general introduction to security interests in property. The term "security" has a number of meanings in law: "security of the person" *à la* the *Charter*, investment "securities", "security of tenure', and so on. Here it is used to denote a form of property right designed to serve as a financial protection in the event that some primary obligation is not met.

The chief example is a mortgage of land consequent on a loan from a lender to a borrower. Where, for example, a lender (L) provides a loan to a borrower (B), B will promise to repay the loan on specified terms. B of course may fail to live up to this commitment. As one means of minimizing that risk, L may ask that property of B be provided as security for the loan. In short, should default occur, L may then seek compensation from the so-called secured property.

The mortgage of land will be used in this chapter to illustrate the issues that can arise when such loan transactions occur. The outline will concentrate on fundamental principles. In this area of property, more so than those discussed elsewhere in this casebook, provincial diversity is significant. Indeed, as Justice Baynton has observed:

> [I]t is essential to keep in mind that mortgages are now creatures of statute. Substantive mortgage law is no longer found primarily in the common law, but in the provisions of the legislation that has been enacted in each separate jurisdiction. This is true not only for the current mortgage law in England, but as well for the current mortgage law in Canada. As property and civil rights in Canada are a provincial matter, each province has enacted its own substantive law respecting mortgages, and each has its own land titles and registration system. Because of this legislative diversity, a court decision in one jurisdiction is not necessarily an authority respecting a mortgage issue in another jurisdiction.
>
> Even the basic legal principles of common law mortgages apply to a lesser extent to some jurisdictions than to others. The concepts and principles respecting land and mortgages that had been developed over centuries through the common law in England, had a significant impact on the statutes that were subsequently enacted in the 19th century to govern land registration and mortgage transactions. Many of these common law concepts and principles inherent in the early English legislation were incorporated in varying degrees into the legislation of several Canadian provinces. For example, both Ontario and British Columbia "imported" into their legislation the concept (albeit a notional one) that a mortgage involved the conveyance of the land and a redemption involved the reconveyance of the land.

Not all provinces followed the English statutory scheme of land registration enacted in the late 19th century and substantially reformed in 1925. As will be seen later, some adopted versions of the Torrens system of Australia, some a Deed or Registration system, and some a combination of both. Due to subsequent statutory reforms in each province, including a melding of the features of Torrens (land titles) systems, and Deed (registration) systems, it is difficult, if not impossible, to properly categorize what "system" is in effect in each province. For this reason it is futile to attempt to distinguish the mortgage laws in each province on the basis of the "system" that is utilized. The provisions of the legislation itself must be considered. . . .

Farm Credit Corp. v. Nelson 1993 CarswellSask 331 (Q.B.) at paras. 20–2.

The history of the law of mortgages reflects the enduring tension between the common law and equity. Equity's role as a moderating force on the common law is never more evident than in relation to the rights conferred on borrowers (mortgagors) and lenders (mortgagees).

2. THE ORIGINS OF THE MORTGAGE

W.S. Holdsworth, *An Historical Introduction to the Land Law* (Oxford: Clarendon Pr., 1927) at 70-1 [footnotes omitted]

The giving of land as the security for a debt was well known in early law — we can see instances of it in Domesday Book. But the machinery by which this purpose was effected has varied. At the end of the twelfth century, when Glanvil wrote, the estate of the mortgagee was an estate which had special features of its own. But, by the end of the thirteenth century, this species of estate had become obsolete, and a mortgage was effected by giving to the mortgagee one of the recognized estates or interests in the land — a fee simple, a life estate or a term of years.

From the thirteenth to the fifteenth century we can distinguish three different methods of effecting a mortgage. (1) The debtor might give the creditor a lease at a nominal rent. The rents and profits of the land paid off the debt and provided interest for the creditor without giving rise to the suspicion that the creditor was committing the sin of usury. (2) The debtor might convey the land to the creditor for a term of years, with a *proviso* that, if the debt be not paid at the end of the term, the creditor shall keep the land in fee. (3) The debtor might convey the land to the creditor in fee, with a *proviso* that, if the debt was paid by a fixed date, the land should be reconveyed; and this condition was strictly construed. Britton distinctly denies that there can be any equity of redemption. It is this third form which ultimately prevailed. The mortgagee took an estate in fee, defeasible upon the condition that the money was paid by the fixed date. It was recognized that his estate was merely a security for money lent. But the strictness with which the condition of payment on the day fixed was construed by the courts of common law obscured this fact; and it was not fully recognized till the court of Chancery began to relieve mortgagors whose property had been forfeited at law for the non-fulfilment of this condition. The elaborate rules evolved by the court of Chancery, on the basis of the narrow rules of the common law, constitute the main part of the rules of the modern law of mortgage.

D. Sugarman & R. Warrington, "Land law, citizenship, and the invention of 'Englishness': The strange world of the equity of redemption" in J. Brewer & S. Staves, eds., *Early Modern Conceptions of Property* (London: Routledge, 1995) 111, at 113–5, 119–21, 123–5 [footnotes omitted]

I The rise and persistence of the equity of redemption

1 Mortgages and the equity of redemption: an introduction and overview

Historically, a mortgage arose where an owner of property (usually land) required money and arranged to transfer the property to a lender as security in return for a loan. The loan agreement would generally provide for a reconveyance of the property to the borrower at a specific date on repayment of the money borrowed and the interest due. If the loan was not repaid, the property became forfeited to the lender. At common law, the date for repayment had to be strictly adhered to. A single day's delay in tendering repayment could result in the borrower losing the entire property to the lender, even though the amount of the loan might be far less than the value of the land.

Now the interpretive stance adopted by the common law courts was challenged by the courts of equity. Dating from at least the turn of the seventeenth century, the courts of equity determined that the strict date for repayment was somewhat irrelevant. Accordingly, the lender's claim to the property became subject

> to a right called the equity of redemption, which arose from the court's consideration that the real object of the transaction was the creation of a security for the debt. This entitled the [borrower] to redeem (or recover the property), even though he had failed to repay by the appointed time.

Time was not to be the essence of the agreement. Although the mortgagor's legal right to redeem the property was lost after the expiration of the time specified in the contract, in equity the mortgagor had an equitable right to redeem on payment within a reasonable period of the principal, interest and costs. A reasonable period could in some cases span many years.

The rights of the mortgagor were further enhanced by the rules governing foreclosure. Equity developed the decree of foreclosure, an order of court, made on application by the mortgagee, declaring the equity of redemption at an end and thus leaving the mortgagee with the fee simple absolute. But if the property was worth more than the amount owed by the mortgagor, the court would order a sale of property, the mortgagee taking the money owed to her/him, the remainder going to the mortgagor.

The discretion to allow the borrower to get back property notwithstanding the contractual term soon hardened into a right. In addition to this right (the fully fledged equity of redemption), the courts developed various analogous protections for borrowers. Partly under the umbrella of that seemingly tautological maxim of equity, "once a mortgage always a mortgage," the courts also laid down that the borrower's right to get property back could not be rendered ineffective either by postponing the right for some unacceptable period or by making the right subject to some penalty, such as the borrower being deprived of some or all of the property mortgaged on exercising the right to redeem. What became known as a "collateral advantage," that is, the lender asserting a claim to some or all of the borrower's property irrespective of repayment of the loan was outlawed.

2 *The establishment of the equity of redemption*

It is generally agreed that the exact origin of the equity of redemption in its modern form is probably lost. A.W.B. Simpson suggested that the Chancery courts were prepared to relieve mortgagors from strict forfeiture conditions from the fifteenth century. But although there are examples to support this, these probably relate to what Simpson calls "peculiarly scandalous cases." The most common example of this would be where the mortgagee was repaid entirely from the rents and profits of the property and still refused to reconvey the property to the mortgagor. Richard Turner, the leading historian of the equity of redemption, concluded that the equity of redemption arose during the reign of Elizabeth I. While the Court of Chancery did grant relief to mortgagors during this period, there are only two reported decisions where relief was given after a forfeiture. It was probably not until the start of the seventeenth century that courts began to grant relief to borrowers as a matter of course, without looking for the special circumstances that would have previously been necessary to activate equity's conscience. The courts gradually extended the list of circumstances that they regarded as causing the special hardship necessary for them to give protection. Thus, the jurisdiction to intervene which had originally operated only in exceptional circumstances became the rule; and the cases where no relief was granted became the exception. . . .

3 *The jurisdiction consolidated*

The courts quickly established that the mortgagor (the borrower) could not be prevented from redeeming, either before or after the contractual redemption date. Put simply, the date was fully effective against the lender, but rather less than effective against the borrower. Although later courts stressed that in certain circumstances the mortgagor might be prevented from redeeming early, the vital principle that a mortgagor cannot be prevented from seeking the return of the mortgaged property has been taken to be established in the seventeenth century by Lord Nottingham.

Lord Nottingham was instrumental in starting the shift of the equity of redemption from a "thing" to an "estate" in equity, that is, in conceptualizing the equity of redemption as a kind of real property rather than as a kind of chattel property. . . .

4 Little short of ideal

As we have seen, the equity of redemption was a highly interventionist jurisdiction. Why was this jurisdiction fair; and how was it justified? Judges and jurists tended to adopt two intersecting rationales for this special jurisdiction. First, one distinctive strand of equity's broad and highly discretionary jurisdiction in fraud concerned the protection of young heirs. In these cases it would be argued that landed heirs should be relieved from their bargains to borrow money, convey land, buy horses, jewellery, *etc.*, because these bargains were unconscionable and fraudulent. They were fraudulent and unconscionable because the young heirs concerned were in "necessitous circumstances," often shorthand for meaning that they had more money than sense! Because they felt impelled to undertake the sort of bargains that others would scorn, they were the obvious targets of what were characterized as "unscrupulous moneylenders" or "rogues" selling goods at a high price. There were other similar cases in which lenders to young heirs attempted to avoid the statutes of usury. It was coextensive with these developments that equity developed and consolidated the equity of redemption.

Thus, judges and jurists alike often asserted that when landowners pledged their property they did so "out of necessity" and were subject to all sorts of pressures from "crafty" lenders. The equity of redemption was intended to protect the landowner from the money-hungry activity of commercial interests. According to Lord Hardwicke in *Toomes v. Conset* (1745), to enforce the original agreement strictly would be to put "the borrower too much in the power of the lender who, being distressed at the time, is too inclined to submit to any terms proposed on the part of the lender." The borrower here was by definition a landowner, something Lord Macnaghten recognized over 150 years later in 1904 when he too was faced with the claim that the borrower ought to be protected automatically. Speaking of the jurisdiction he said: "It seems to have had its origin in the desire of the Court of Chancery to protect embarrassed landowners from imposition and oppression." But by then Lord Macnaghten was beginning to have doubts as to the justice of the doctrine. No such scruples had troubled Lord Henley, who was satisfied that the rule was based on the highest principles. "And there is great reason and justice in this rule for necessitous men are not, truly speaking, free men, but to answer a present exigency, will submit to any terms the crafty may impose upon them." The anomalous character of this protection for the "necessitous" is evident when one considers the many other instances in which starker necessitousness did not postpone debts due. In other words, the equity of redemption was the product of a jurisdiction which in important respects turned on the status of a party before the court, by reason of infancy, lunacy or the fact that a party was a married woman or landowner.

Secondly, it was emphasized that the court's function was to ensure that ultimately land was returned to its "rightful" (often meaning historical or traditional) owner. Even when the terms of the contract unequivocally pointed to an agreement to transfer the ownership of the land in exchange for money, goods or services, the courts were seemingly loath to accept it at face value. It was as if it were inconceivable that an English gentleman would give up his land, save in wholly exceptional circumstances. Thus the courts conceived the mortgagee's right as a right to money rather than land. From this perspective, for Englishmen to bargain away their land in these circumstances, and for "moneylenders" and "rogues" to acquire significant landholdings, was suspect, if not downright un-English. . . .

II Another way of seeing: the economic, cultural and political dimensions of the equity of redemption

Land gives so much more than the rent. It gives position and influence and political power, to say nothing of the game.

1 England's patrician polity, the law of real property and mythmaking

What were the particular circumstances that sustained the construction and expansion of the equity of redemption, and enabled the landed elite to exploit it? First and foremost was the fact that until the 1870s England was a "patrician polity". While comparative work is problematic, most commentators are agreed England's landed elite were collectively more wealthy, powerful and exclusive relative to their continental counterparts; and that the correlation between the property, position and power of the landed elite was probably more intense in England than elsewhere in Europe. On the Continent, each time land was inherited by a new generation it tended to be subdivided into smaller and more numerous units. Continental estates were therefore smaller in size, while the landed establishment tended to be somewhat larger in number. The ranks of the titled were further swollen as honours were bestowed on other groups, notably that service class which lacked a landed base but played a crucial role in the administration of the state. In these circumstances it was relatively more difficult to maintain the elite status of the landed. England's landed oligarchy was small in number compared with the landed elites of other European countries, and it seems to have exercised a more tenacious hold on power, wealth and status. Until the 1870s, the landed establishment owned about four-fifths of the land in the British Isles. Their political, economic and cultural hegemony is exemplified by their pre-eminence in government, Parliament, the law, the Church, the civil service and the armed forces. Despite Britain's unique status as the "first industrial nation," it was only from the last quarter of the nineteenth century onwards that the hitherto superior position of the landed establishment was gradually eroded. . . .

In myriad ways the law constituted and symbolized the elevated position of the landed establishment. In peacetime, at least until the end of the eighteenth century, the taxes levied on land were significantly less than those borne by trade. Significant spheres of public and private law were also feudal in character, such as the law governing crime, punishment, master-servant relations and the constitution, until well into the nineteenth century. Of major importance to the landed oligarchy was the fabrication of a system of equity alongside the common law from the fifteenth century onwards, that is, a jurisdiction based on the prerogative, discretion and civil law. The Court of Chancery was the great conduit of this equitable jurisdiction, a jurisdiction which tended to moderate the rigidities and formalism of the common law, particularly as it affected the landed. Thus equity mitigated "excessive contractual penalties, which the medieval business practice of insuring contracts at much more than their real value by written obligation engendered" when the common law stood aloof. And in the area of mortgages, equity developed technical rules to ensure that contracts were not penal or usurious. . . .

The Chancery refinements of mortgage law encouraged many landowners to borrow to the limits of their security and beyond, but they did not apparently discourage the lending of money. Mortgages were increasingly treated as a safe and popular form of investment. In his pioneering study of capital formation in Lancashire, B. L. Anderson concluded that the practice of borrowing and lending on mortgages "had taken deep root amongst all classes from the beginning of the [eighteenth] century." So also in Bath; R. S. Neale argued that the opulent development of Bath in the eighteenth century was possible partly because a wide, local, national and even international credit market was easily available to the owners of landed property. The increasing sophistication of land law encouraged lenders, and most of Bath's building architects and landowners relied heavily on mortgage finance. In short, the eighteenth-century development of mortgage law, the decline in the rate of interest, the growth of specialized lending institutions and the expansion of the mortgage market outside London all helped encourage borrowing, and none more so than aristocratic borrowing.

Most large landowners were therefore familiar with mortgages. As Powell put it: "There are few men possessed of either real or personal estate, who are not more or less concerned in that species of property called a mortgage." Although a series of law lectures delivered in the early nineteenth century, presumably to the sons of men who possessed either real or personal estate, discussed mortgages only in relation to the distinction between real and personal property, it is significant perhaps that the one substantive point of mortgage law that the lecturer thought fit to mention was that the mortgaged estate "was merely a pledge and not to be meddled with." If nothing else, sons of gentlemen were reminded that land was not just any form of wealth. Mortgagees were the servants of the landowner, not the other way round.

The attitude that it was the landowners' natural privilege to take loans on security and then be relieved from the terms of the bargain, persisted until well into the nineteenth century. . . .

3. THE CONTRIBUTIONS OF LAW AND EQUITY

Athabasca Realty Ltd. v. Lee
(1976) 67 D.L.R. (3d) 272 (Alta. S.C.)

[This case involved an agreement between the plaintiff company, as vendor, and three purchasers. The properties were built by Great Canadian Oil Sands Ltd. to provide accommodations for their employees in Fort McMurray, Alberta. The plaintiff was a wholly owned subsidiary of Great Canadian.

The agreements contained the following clause:

IF AT ANY TIME during the ten (10) years next following the date hereof:

(a) the Purchaser . . . ceases to be an employee of either the Vendor, Great Canadian Oil Sands Limited or any other employer approved in writing by the Vendor; or

(b) if the Purchaser ceases to remain in continuous possession of the said lands and premises; or

(c) if the Purchaser assigns his interest in or under this agreement or his interest in and to the said lands and premises;

then in any of such events the Purchaser agrees to sell to the Vendor and the Vendor agrees to purchase from the Purchaser the said lands and premises at and for the price or sum equal to the total of:

(a) the amount theretofore paid by the Purchaser on or on account of the principal portion of the purchase price; and

(b) the value of any building or improvement theretofore constructed by the Purchaser on the said lands and premises with the written approval of and in compliance with specifications approved by the Vendor;

less the cost of repairing any damage to any buildings or improvements on the said lands and premises, reasonable wear and tear only excepted. The said purchase price computed as aforesaid payable by the Vendor to the Purchaser shall be payable by the Vendor in cash or by depositing the same to the credit of the Purchaser in a chartered bank in Fort McMurray, in the Province of Alberta, and upon such payment or deposit the Purchaser shall execute and deliver to the Vendor a good and sufficient transfer or assignment of all of the interest of the Purchaser in and to the said lands and premises. If the parties cannot agree as to the value of any buildings or improvements erected or created by the Purchaser or as to the cost of repair of any damages as aforesaid, the matter in dispute shall be submitted to the decision of two arbitrators, one to be appointed by the Vendor and one to be appointed by the Purchaser, and the arbitrators so chosen to choose a third arbitrator, and otherwise the provisions of The Arbitration Act of the Province of Alberta shall apply to such arbitration.

The company claimed to be entitled on the facts to exercise its rights under this clause in relation to three properties.]

D.C. McDonald J.: . . .

[A]s the plaintiff seeks declaratory relief, an equitable remedy, Mr. Simons says on behalf of the defendants that equity ought to deny that relief because the clause constitutes a clog on the defendants' equity of redemption.

Mr. Mayson for the plaintiff says that the equitable doctrine that refuses to enforce covenants which constitute a clog on the equity of redemption has no application to an agreement for sale when the relationship is genuinely that of vendor and purchaser and not that of mortgagee and mortgagor.

The equitable doctrine was explained, historically and in terms of its policy, by Lord Macnaghten in *Samuel v. Jarrah Timber &. Wood Paving Corp.*, [1904] A.C. 323 at pp. 326-7, as follows:

> . . . the question here depends rather upon the rule that a mortgagee is not allowed at the time of the loan to enter into a contract for the purchase of the mortgaged property.
>
> This latter rule, I think, is founded on sentiment rather than on principle. It seems to have had its origin in the desire of the Court of Chancery to protect embarrassed landowners from imposition and oppression. And it was invented, I should suppose, in order to obviate the necessity of inquiry and investigation in cases where suspicion may be probable and proof difficult. I gather from some general observations made by Lord Hardwicke in *Mellor v. Lees* (1742) 2 Atk. 494, that he would have been disposed to confine the rule to cases in which the Court finds or suspects "a design to wrest the estate fraudulently out of the hands of the mortgagor," and to cases of "common mortgage" — that is, as I understand it, mortgage of land by deed. It will be observed that in the later case of *Toomes v. Conset* (1745) 3 Atk. 261, which is often referred to for a statement of the rule, his Lordship speaks only of "a deed of mortgage"; an instrument which perhaps rather lends itself to imposition for no one, I am sure, by the light of nature ever understood an English mortgage of real estate.
>
> In *Vernon v. Bethell* (1761) 2 Eden, 113, however, Northington L.C. (then Lord Henley) laid down the law broadly in the following terms: "This Court, as a Court of conscience, is very jealous of persons taking securities for a loan and converting such securities into purchases. And therefore I take it to be an established rule that a mortgagee can never provide at the time of making the loan for any event or condition on which the equity of redemption shall be discharged and the conveyance absolute. And there is great reason and justice in this rule, for necessitous men are not, truly speaking, free men, but to answer a present exigency will submit to any terms that the crafty may impose upon them."
>
> This doctrine, described by Lord Henley as an established rule nearly 150 years ago, has never, so far as I can discover, been departed from since or questioned in any reported case. It is, I believe, universally accepted by text-writers of authority. Speaking for myself, I should not be sorry if your Lordships could see your way to modify it so as to prevent its being used as a means of evading a fair bargain come to between persons dealing at arms' length and negotiating on equal terms. The directors of a trading company in search of financial assistance are certainly in a very different position from that of an impecunious landowner in the toils of a crafty moneylender.

Can this doctrine be applied other than to mortgages? In *Best v. Dussessoye* (1920), 52 D.L.R. 249, [1920] 2 W.W.R. 275, 30 Man. R. 270, the Manitoba Court of Appeal held that it does not apply to agreements for the sale of land of the kind that were common in Manitoba (and, like those in the present cases, are common in Alberta). At p. 256 D.L.R., p. 281 W.W.R., Perdue C.J.M. said: "An equity of redemption is not involved in the case." At p. 258 D.L.R., p. 284 W.W.R., Cameron J.A. said:

> Some of the extraordinary characteristics that have been imposed upon a mortgage security are set forth in the judgment of Lord Bramwell in *Salt v. Marquess of Northampton*, [1892] A.C. 1, at p. 18, 61 L.J. Ch. 49, cited in Galt J.'s judgment, 50 D.L.R. 640, at page 646. I quote the following further sentence from Lord Bramwell's decision at page 19: "It seems that a borrower was such a favourite with Courts of Equity that they would let him break his contract, and, perhaps, disabling him from binding himself, disable him from contracting on the most advantageous terms to himself."
>
> But the purchaser under the agreement in this case was not a borrower. He was not giving a security for payment of a debt. He entered into a contract with the vendor for the purchase of certain lands on certain terms of payment and otherwise on the performance of which the vendor agreed to convey and time was made the essence of the contract. Nothing has been paid on the agreement since November 2, 1916.
>
> There is no reason and no authority to justify the imposition on such an agreement as that before us of a right to re-open the first order made by the referee in the circumstances. To do so might, as in this case, be nothing short of judicial legislation.

Although the referee's order in that case had used the language of "foreclosure", Cameron J.A. denied that that language was appropriate or that it in any way altered what the real nature of the remedy was [at pp. 258-9 D.L.R., p. 284 W.W.R.]

> The practice followed in this case of securing a rescission of the agreement through an action for specific performance has been well established in this Province. There is no particular virtue in calling the order made pursuant to the judgment a final order of foreclosure. That is a term which is usually confined to a final order in an action for foreclosure of mortgage. But as applied to the first order of the referee in this case it is merely descriptive and cannot affect its meaning and substance and to call it such has no legal effect. It might just as well be called an "order" or "final order" or "order pursuant to judgment" or "order for rescission."

At p. 264 D.L.R., p. 289 W.W.R., Dennistoun J.A. said:

> Under similar circumstances had this been a mortgage contract there can be no doubt relief would have been given to the mortgagor and the time for redemption extended, notwithstanding the fact that a new purchaser had intervened, for there is authority for holding that a purchaser who contracts with a mortgagee in possession even after final order of foreclosure has notice that his vendor may be redeemed by order of a Court of Equity and that the order for redemption will prevail over his agreement to purchase if the Court thinks fits to so direct: *Campbell v. Holyland*, 7 Ch.D. 166, 47 L.J. Ch. 145; *Johnston v. Johnston* (1882), 9 P.R. (Ont.) 259; *Independent Order of Foresters v. Pegg* (1900), 19 P.R. (Ont.) 254.
>
> The contract in question is not a mortgage contract but one for the sale and purchase of land, and the rights of the parties are not the same. The Courts have in recent years consistently refused to regard a defaulting purchaser as entitled to the rights and remedies which have become associated with a defaulting mortgagor "that spoiled child of equity."
>
> A purchaser who is in default, time being of the essence of the agreement, has no right to specific performance, and so soon as the contract has been determined, he has no

> further right to the land and the Court has no jurisdiction to restore him to his former position . . .

That case was decided shortly after the case of *Davidson v. Sharpe* (1920), 52 D.L.R. 186, 60 S.C.R. 72, [1920] 1 W.W.R. 888, was decided in the Supreme Court of Canada. In one of the majority judgments, Anglin J. reviewed the doctrine as it applied to mortgages. At pp. 193-4 D.L.R., pp. 82-3 S.C.R., he said:

> The relations of mortgagor and mortgagee in English Courts of Equity are anomalous. *Platt v. Ashbridge* (1865), 12 Gr. 105, at 106. "Once a mortgage always a mortgage," is a doctrine so deeply rooted in our system of equity that after the period for redemption fixed by an ordinary judgment for foreclosure has expired the mortgagor's right to redeem *de plano* still subsists until a further and final order of foreclosure has been obtained. Even after such final order has been made our Courts of Equity regard the mortgage as still unextinguished and unsatisfied so long as the mortgagee retains the land. He may at any time enforce the personal obligation of the mortgagor on his covenant, thereby opening the foreclosure and revesting in the mortgagor his right to redemption as it was before the judgment; and the Courts maintain a corresponding jurisdiction to allow the mortgagor after final order, under exceptional circumstances raising an equity in his favour, to redeem on proper terms.

However, at p. 195 D.L.R., pp. 84-5 S.C.R., he made it clear that in his view his choice of the word "anomalous" was careful:

> The anomalies introduced by Courts of Equity in regard to the relations between mortgagor and mortgagee do not exist in regard to vendor and purchaser. A judgment or order declaring that on the happening of a certain event an agreement for sale shall be cancelled and at an end means precisely what it says and not merely that the plaintiff shall thereupon be entitled to have it cancelled and put an end to. When the purchaser under the order of the learned Chief Justice of British Columbia made default the agreement ceased to exist and the foundation for any right of personal recovery from the purchaser (except for costs) was gone. The purchaser had no further right to the land and the Court has no jurisdiction to restore him to his former position.

The authorities which distinguish between the effect upon the purchaser of an order for rescission of an agreement for sale, and an order for foreclosure under a mortgage, in terms of whether after the making of the order for rescission the purchaser has any right of "redemption", were reviewed by Hyndman Master in *Halskov v. Shandruk et ux.*, [1972] 4 W.W.R. 360.

Mr. Simons submits that the cases I have referred to so far concerned situations in which the purchaser had defaulted in making payments due even after having the time extended by the Court to a certain date, and explained the effect of an order determining an agreement for sale. He says that, according to those decisions, once there is such an order, the purchaser has lost all his rights, unlike the case of a mortgage when the mortgagor retains an equity of redemption even after the final foreclosure order is made. In the present cases, however, he says no such order has been made and the purchaser does retain an interest which is similar to the equity of redemption which a mortgagor has even after he has defaulted in making the payments required by the mortgage. He relies on the following passage from the learned work by the late C. C. McCaul, *Notes on Remedies of Vendors and Purchasers of Real Estate* (1910), at pp. 94-5:

> In *Pomeroy's Equity Jurisprudence* (vol. 6, par. 816), which is quoted with approval by Beck J. in *Great West Lumber Co. v. Wilkins* [(1908) 1 Alta. L.R. 155, 166], the rule is thus stated: "Equity in relieving against a forfeiture in a contract of sale, and thus declining to acknowledge the express terms of a contract, points to the *analogy of the mortgage.* It does not regard the forfeiture clause as of the substance of the contract. *Neither will it on a sale of land.* It assumes that the real intention of the parties was to create a security and not a forfeiture, and equity relieves against any forfeiture or penalty inserted for the purpose of enforcing the contract."
>
> Without multiplying authorities and quotations, can a closer analogy to a mortgage be found than such an instalment plan agreement as we are discussing? Apart from the form is not the effect of the transaction almost the same as if the vendor had conveyed, and taken a mortgage back? Especially is this the case where, as is perhaps usual, the purchaser is let into possession. The vendor retains his legal estate but holds it only as security for payment of the purchase-money; while the position of the purchaser resembles that of a mortgagor in possession.
>
> If this be so, surely a *method* analogous to that in which equity relieves against forfeiture in a mortgage action is the *method* applicable to a contract of sale. This was essentially the method of relief adopted *Re Dagenham (Thames) Dock Co.* [(1872) L.R. 8 Ch. 1022].
>
> *Cornwall v. Henson* (1900, 2 Ch. 298), so often, curiously enough, quoted as an authority for the *restitution* of instalments of purchase-money to the vendor, expressly approves *Re Dagenham.* Collins A.J. says: "If the contract had contained an express stipulation that on non-payment of any instalment, the purchaser should forfeit all the instalments which he had previously paid, I think the Court would have regarded that provision as a penalty, and would have relieved him from it, *as was done in Re Dagenham (Thames) Dock Co.*"
>
> This case, which merely granted an extension of time to the purchaser to remedy his default, a *locus pre nitentice*, was followed and applied in *H.B. Co. v. Macdonald* (1887, Man. L.R. 237, 480), in respect of which Beck J. (*Great West Lumber Co. v. Wilkins* 1 Alta. L.R. at p. 166) says: "It must not be supposed that, if the view I take of the law is correct, a vendor has no remedy against a defaulting purchaser, other than a proceeding in Court corresponding to proceedings by a mortgagee for foreclosure, *a right which he undoubtedly has.*"

The context of the passage must be examined. Mr. McCaul was discussing whether, after default by a purchaser in making a payment required of him by an agreement for sale, the Court might *at that stage* relieve against forfeiture. At the time Mr. McCaul wrote, it appears that the practice had not become as clearly to that effect as it subsequently became. There is in any event in Alberta no doubt that the *Judicature Act* (now R.S.A. 1970, c. 193, s. 32(*h*), first enacted in similar form by 1942 (Alta.), c. 37) has equated actions by mortgages for foreclosure with actions by vendors for specific performance of an agreement for sale in the sense that the Court shall, upon the making of the order *nisi*, give the mortgagor or purchaser a certain time for "redemption", *i.e.*, within which the mortgagor or purchaser may pay the balance owing if he is to prevent the Court granting a final order of foreclosure of the mortgage, or a final order that the agreement for sale is cancelled and determined. (In so stating the matter, I omit reference to details of the Alberta practice by which the order *nisi* is combined with an order for sale, tenders are advertised for, and the mortgagee or vendor then applies for either an order confirming sale or an order vesting title of the mortgaged property in the mortgagee or finally cancelling the agreement for sale.)

To the extent that as a result there is what may seem like an equity of redemption in the case of agreements for sale, that result has been achieved not by the operation of an equitable doctrine but by practice and by statute. In the case of agreements for sale the period of "redemption" of which the statute speaks is not an equity of redemption of the kind that has been recognized for four centuries in the case of mortgages, but rather a way of describing the practice which had been developed by the Courts in jurisdictions where agreements for the sale of land were a common phenomenon, of requiring the vendor upon default by the purchaser to obtain first an order *nisi* and then a final order.

What Mr. McCaul argued for was thus achieved by practice and statute. . . .

[I]n my view there is no "equity of redemption" available in these cases to the purchasers.

Mr. Simons says that, if that conclusion should be reached on the basis that the transactions were by agreement for sale, that basis is itself lacking for, he says, in reality the transaction was a loan and the agreement for sale is a security and really a mortgage. If so, he says, then the equity of redemption is available as in the case of all mortgages.

I recognize that it is the reality and substance of the transaction which is to be looked at, and not the form, in order to determine whether a transaction is a contract of sale or a mortgage.

However, there is a presumption that the agreement truly stated the transaction as an agreement of sale. To hold otherwise, I must be satisfied by collateral evidence that, notwithstanding the plain terms of the agreement, the relationship between the parties is that of mortgagee and mortgagors: *Barton v. Bank of New South Wales* (1890), 15 App. Cas. 379 (P.C.). In that case, at pp. 380-1, Lord Watson said:

> Now, undoubtedly, the terms of the conveyance may be qualified by collateral evidence; but in order to set aside the arrangement which the parties have assented to by executing and receiving the deed, very cogent evidence is required in a case like the present.
>
> When there is simply a conveyance and nothing more, the terms upon which the conveyance is made not being apparent from the deed itself, collateral evidence may easily be admitted to supply the considerations for which the parties interchanged such a deed; but where in the deed itself the reasons for making it, and the considerations for which it is granted, are fully and clearly expressed, the collateral evidence must be strong

enough to overcome the presumption that the parties in making the deed had truly set forth the causes which led to its execution.

In *Herron v. Mayland*, [1928] 2 D.L.R. 858 at p. 861, [1928] S.C.R. 225 at p. 231, Anglin C.J.C. said:

As to the claim that, notwithstanding the inconsistency of the form in which it was deliberately put, the transaction was in reality one of loan or mortgage, it would require most convincing evidence to justify such a conclusion.

At p. 862 D.L.R., pp. 232-3 S.C.R., Duff J. said:

The rule is well established. The principle upon which it rests is stated by that eminent Judge, Turner L.J., in *Lincoln v. Wright* (1859), 4 De G. & J. 16, at p. 22, 45 E.R. 6. Where the real agreement is that the transaction shall be a mortgage transaction, "it is, in the eye of this Court, a fraud to insist on the conveyance as being absolute, and parol evidence must be admissible to prove the fraud." Such being the principle, the rule excluding extrinsic parol evidence offered, in order to contradict, qualify or supplement a document which the parties have made the record of their transaction, was, in equity, displaced, in cases in which the principle came into play; and since the Judicature Act, this rule in equity is, of course, the rule in all the Courts. On the other hand, it is quite open to two parties of competent years and understanding, to enter into an agreement for the sale by one to the other of a property, and for the repurchase within a given nominated period, of the same property at the same price, with or without interest, at the option of the seller. The law recognizes such dealings, and gives effect to them according to their terms, where that is the true description of the dealing into which the parties have deliberately entered. *Williams v. Owen* (1840), 5 My. & Cr. 303, at pp. 306-7, 41 E.R. 386. And where, in the documents they have executed, the parties have clearly explained that such is the character of their transaction, it requires powerful collateral evidence to overcome the presumption that the record is a faithful one. *Barton v. Bk. N.S.W.* (1890), 15 App. Cas. 379, at pp. 380-1.

See also the judgment of Duff J. in *Wilson v. Ward*, [1930] 2 D.L.R. 433 at pp. 436-7, [1930] S.C.R. 212 at pp. 216-7, to the same effect. Then, at p. 440 D.L.R., p. 220 S.C.R., of that case, Duff J. said:

It is quite true that, *prima facie*, a sale, expressed in an instrument containing nothing to show the relation of debtor and creditor is to exist between the parties, does not cease to be a sale, and become a security for money, merely because the instrument contains a stipulation that the vendor shall have a right of repurchase . . .

At p. 441 D.L.R., p. 221 S.C.R., Duff J. referred to the refusal of equity to countenance a clog on the equity of redemption of the mortgagor, but ascribes its source to a different historical origin than that already noted. Having held that in the case before him "the express arrangement was that the document was to be used as security", he continued:

Such being the substance of the transaction, the law, as already observed, would disregard the stipulations professing to confer upon the respondent the right of purchase, even if the parties, between themselves, had intended that these should be binding. Such stipu-

> lations are repugnant to the equitable right of redemption; they would have the effect of converting what was intended to be a security into something entirely different. It has long been settled that equity will not allow a mortgagee to enter into a contract with the mortgagor, at the time of the loan, for the absolute purchase of the subject of the mortgage for a specific sum in case of default in payment of the mortgage money at the appointed time. The rule had its origin in the Ecclesiastical Courts. In the Court of Chancery, it was a rule of policy based upon a recognition of the disposition of money lenders to use their power of dictating the form of a security transaction, in order to shape it in such a way as to make it possible to "wrest the estate out of the hands of the mortgagor." *Mellor v. Lees* (1742), 2 Atk. 494, at p. 495, 26 E.R. 698; *Price v. Perrie* (1702), 2 Freem. 258, 22 E.R. 1195; *Willett v. Winnell* (1687), 1 Vern. 488, 23 E.R. 611; *Bowen v. Edwards* (1662), 1 Rep. Ch. 221, 21 E.R. 555; *Re Edwards* (1861), 11 Ir. Ch. R. 367. And it applies, not merely to mortgages, strictly so called, or to mortgages containing a contractual *proviso* for redemption, but, as well, to mortgages containing no such express *proviso*, and to agreements creating only an equitable charge. If it is clear that the transaction is a transaction of loan, and that the interest in the property affected is vested in the lender by way of security only, then such stipulations are void as repugnant to the equitable right of redemption. As Lord Parker said in *Kreglinger v. New Patagonia Meat & Cold Storage Co.*, [1914] A.C. at p. 52, in such a case "the right to redeem is from the very outset a right in equity only, and it is merely the right to have the property freed from the charge on payment of the moneys charged thereon. If the charge is for payment of a specific sum on a specific day, payment on that day will set the property free, and if the day passes without payment there will still be an equity to have the property so freed notwithstanding any provision in the nature of a penalty, such penal provision being a clog on the equity."

With respect, it is not at all clear that the cases cited by Duff J. provide authority for the historical origin for the rule as given by him. Reference may be made to Holdsworth, *History of English Law*, vol. 8, pp. 1045, where the learned author says that by the latter part of the fifteenth century the church did not regard the conveyance of land in mortgage as usurious so long as the debtor retained the right to redeem. Holdsworth allows that "It is perhaps possible that this last condition may have had some influence upon the growth of the doctrine as to redemption which, in the sixteenth century, the Court of Chancery was beginning to make an essential part of all mortgage transactions." However, having conceded the possibility, Holdsworth notes (p. 106n) that "this condition seems to be much more closely connected with the equitable prohibition of clogging the equity of redemption than the general law of usury". As for the prohibition against clogging the equity of redemption, Holdsworth at vol. 6, p. 664n, repudiates the opinion expressed by Lord Parker of Waddington in *G. & C. Kreglinger v. New Patagonia Meat & Cold Storage Co., Ltd.*, [1914] A.C. 25 at pp. 54-5, that the rule preventing a mortgagee, who takes a mortgage as security for a loan of money, from stipulating for a collateral advantage, "depended on the existence of the statutes against usury". Holdsworth's opinion was that "there is little or no authority for this view". In his opinion, the prohibition against clogs on the equity of redemption

> originated in the equitable idea that the mortgagor was the owner in equity of the land subject to the mortgage. Mortgagors were then, and often still are, needy persons; and to maintain their equitable ownership, they must be prevented from making bargains which would, in effect, have destroyed that ownership. In other words, without the rule,

mortgagors would, in so many cases, have directly or indirectly contracted themselves out of their equities of redemption, that such equities would have been either of rare occurrence or of little value. . . .

Kreick v. Wansbrough (1973), 35 D.L.R. (3d) 275, [1973] S.C.R. 588, [1973] 4 W.W.R. 350, was an example of an attempt, rejected by the Supreme Court of Canada, to translate what on the face of the documents was an agreement of sale with an option to repurchase into a mortgage transaction. (That intention having been rejected, Laskin J. said, at p. 278 D.L.R., p. 3.53 W.W.R., "the question of fetter or clog does not arise".)

In that case the purchaser had lent money to the vendor, and it was clear that the purchaser wanted to be secured for his loans by taking title to the vendor's lands. The lawsuit arose when the vendor failed to exercise his option to repurchase within the time specified. The trial Judge and Saskatchewan Court of Appeal held that the agreement was really a mortgage by virtue of which the vendor-debtor had a right of redemption. This position was rejected by the Supreme Court. Delivering the judgment of that Court, Laskin J., at pp. 278-9 D.L.R., p. 354 W.W.R., emphasized the following facts:

[1] The obligation of the purchaser to pay a fixed balance of the purchase price beyond the date of permitted exercise of the vendor's option . . .

[2] . . . the provision for continued occupancy by the vendor of his house rent free . . .

10-67 D.L.R. (3d)

[3] . . . the purchaser's written instructions to the solicitor at the time that the document was drawn up [and] the vendor's understanding as manifested by [a memorandum were consistent with a sale transaction].

[4] . . . the price fixed for the acquisition of the vendor's lands by the purchaser was not shown nor even alleged to be inadequate at the time that the agreement . . . was executed. . . .

The opposite result was arrived at in *Fleming et al. v. Watts*, [1944] 4 D.L.R. 353, [1944] S.C.R. 360, when the Supreme Court of Canada disagreed with both lower Courts and concluded that although the agreement in form was an agreement of sale, nevertheless its true nature and effect were that it was a mortgage from the purchaser to the vendor, and there was a right to redeem. The judgments of both Hudson and Rand JJ. found on the facts that, in Hudson J's. words at p. 356 D.L.R., p. 364 S.C.R.: "It was in essence a borrowing transaction." Both judgments emphasized that there was in the agreement nothing which "directly surrendered" or "released or surrendered" the equity which the purchaser had built up during the earlier years when he had been purchasing under earlier agreements of sale which were replaced by the last agreement when the vendor made a further "advance" to the purchaser. The purpose of that advance, as Hudson J. noted, was "to enable the purchaser to clear off his debts and make a new start in life". Rand J. placed emphasis on the agreement's language which spoke of "money advanced" by the vendor, which was to bear interest (at p. 361 D.L.R., p. 370 S.C.R.):

> A vendor does net stipulate for interest on money advanced. That language unconsciously reveals the mind of [the vendor] and it confirms the inference from the documents and the underlying facts that the money had not the character of sale price.

Hudson J. also stressed that the purchaser "had been in possession of the land directly or through a tenant for many years" and that "substantial improvements had been added by him and the value of the property at this time was placed at from $20,000 to $25,000, as against $12,000 named as the purchase price in the agreement" (p. 355 D.L.R., p. 364 S.C.R.).

In the cases at bar, there is no evidence that the vendor lent money to the purchasers. It is true, as Mr. Simons points out, that the agreement for sale provides for instalment payments, the compounding of interest in the event of default, the payment of taxes by the purchaser, the privilege of prepayment of the balance owing and a covenant against waste, all of which are features of the standard contemporary residential mortgage. Mr. Simons places much emphasis on the agreements themselves as indicating that the transaction in each case was a borrowing and the giving of security, and not a sale. He says it is not a question in this case of looking at evidence but merely of examining the documents. However, in my view an examination of the agreements of sale does not support his contention. The documents are agreements of sale. The similarity of the features just mentioned to features of mortgages does not translate the transaction in each case into one of a mortgage. Unlike the case of *Fleming v. Watts*, there is no language in the agreements which suggests that the parties considered that the balance of the expressed purchase price was being "advanced" by the vendor or "borrowed" by the purchaser. Moreover, although not invited by Mr. Simons to look at the evidence beyond the documents themselves, if I do so I still find no indication that the parties regarded the transaction as one of a borrowing by the purchasers.

It is true that, whether due to inflation or the shortage of housing in Fort McMurray or other causes, in each case the exercise by the vendor of its right to repurchase deprives the purchasers of the potential of substantial capital gain should they sell their respective houses. However, if that were to be regarded as sufficient to convert an agreement for sale into a borrowing secured by mortgage, it is difficult to conceive of an agreement for sale today which would not for that reason be so converted in contemporary conditions. The argument lacks the persuasive value which entitles me to reach a conclusion which, it seems to me, would have such a sweeping effect. . . .

Judgment for plaintiff.

QUESTIONS AND COMMENTS

1. In what way, if at all, do the two arguments raised by counsel for the purchasers differ?

2. Why would it be important to determine whether or not the agreement for sale was, in substance, a mortgage?

3. As noted in *Athabasca Realty Ltd. v. Lee*, in cases such as *Fleming et al. v. Watts* [1944] S.C.R. 360, 1944 CarswellOnt 79, a mortgage disguised as a sales transaction was found. Such a mortgage is effective as an *equitable* mortgage. Do you see why?

4. Equity will also find that a mortgage exists in other circumstances, such as where there is a deposit of title documents under circumstances that demonstrate that this action denotes that the land has been provided as security for a loan: see further *North West Trust Co. v. West* 1989 CarswellAlta 167 (C.A.), leave to appeal refused: (1990) 104 A.R. 160 (note) (S.C.C.). What is the effect of an agreement to create a legal mortgage? Under what circumstances can a defective legal mortgage create enforceable rights? See, *e.g.*, *Bank of Montreal v. Chedore* (1986) 34 D.L.R. (4th) 177, 1986 CarswellNB 379 (C.A.); *Humboldt Credit Union Ltd. v. Empire Shoe Store Ltd.* (1986) 56 Sask. R. 253, 1986 CarswellSask 109 (C.A.).

5. So far in this chapter the common law mortgage has been described as one under which legal title is placed in the name of the mortgagee, with the mortgagor retaining an equity of redemption. That construct is no longer used in many jurisdictions. For example, in Saskatchewan, *The Land Titles Act, 2000*, S.S. 2000, c. L-5.1, s. 123, states: "A mortgage has effect as security but does not operate as a transfer of the land charged."

In other words, pursuant to this provision the creation of the security interest is not accomplished by a transfer of title to the land to the lender; that title remains with the borrower. Instead, the security interest encumbers the title of the borrower. It is no longer the case that the pirates climb aboard the deck; it is rather more like the charge is a tenacious barnacle on the hull of title.

What difference, if any, does this make? That question can be answered only on a jurisdiction-specific basis. Ontario law now provides as follows:

> 1. . . . "charge" means a charge on land given for the purpose of securing the payment of a debt or the performance of an obligation, and includes a charge under the *Land Titles Act* and a mortgage, but does not include a rent charge; . . .
>
> "chargee" means a person in whose favour a charge is given . . .
>
> "chargor" means a person who gives a charge . . .
>
> 6. (1) A charge does not operate as a transfer of the legal estate in the land to the chargee. . . .
>
> (3) Despite subsection (1), a chargor and chargee are entitled to all the legal and equitable rights and remedies that would be available to them if the chargor had transferred the land to the chargee by way of mortgage, subject to a proviso for redemption. . . .

Land Registration Reform Act, R.S.O. 1990, c. L.4.

Given these provisions, the changes in Ontario seem to be largely cosmetic. (But see the discussion of severance in Chapter 9.)

6. As to the Saskatchewan provision quoted above, consider the explanation found in *Farm Credit Corp. v. Nelson* 1993 CarswellSask 331 (Q.B.) at paras. 24-5, 42–4 (*per* Baynton J.):

> Under common law, the first mortgage was known as the legal mortgage and it involved a conveyance of the land itself to the first mortgagee. The mortgagor, on redemption of the legal mortgage, was not entitled to a discharge of mortgage as such, but to a reconveyance to him of the land he had previously conveyed to the mortgagee.Subsequent mortgages could not be legal mortgages, but they were considered to be equitable mortgages. As the mortgagor had conveyed his land to the first mortgagee, he had no title to convey to a subsequent mortgagee. All he could give in effect was his right of redemption of the legal mortgage and the concurrent right to a reconveyance of the land. Once he had granted a subsequent mortgage, it was that subsequent mortgagee who became entitled to the right to redeem and to the reconveyance of the land. . . .
>
> The land titles legislation of Alberta and Saskatchewan originated as provincial re-enactments of *The Land Titles Act* of the North-West Territories. Back in 1920, they were similar to *The Real Property Act* of New South Wales, one version of the Australian Torrens system. The Manitoba land titles legislation was similar to another version of the Australian Torrens system in effect in Victoria. Harold Spencer, *Some Principles of the Real Property (Land Titles) Acts of Western Canada*, 1920. . . .
>
> A statutory mortgage under the Torrens system should be viewed not as a common law mortgage in statutory clothing, but as a new statutory instrument created by the legislation. Victor DiCastri, *Thom's Canadian Torrens System* (2nd ed.), at p. 491 puts it this way in referring to the Manitoba case of *Smith v. National Trust Co.* (1912), 1 W.W.R. 1122:
>
>> The rights and powers of a mortgagee under the Torrens system were reviewed in detail by the Supreme Court of Canada in *Smith v. National Trust Co.* . . . The majority opinion viewed the statutory mortgage not as a common-law mortgage in statutory clothing but as a new statutory instrument created by and primarily interpreted by *The Real Property Act*; in approaching the question of whether or not any particular right or power is enforceable or exercisable under such a statutory mortgage *the rule of interpretation is not first to consider the same right or power under a common-law mortgage*, and then to see if it is effected or forbidden by the Act as suggested in the dissenting judgment of Anglin J. [at p. 665], *but rather to look at the Act to see whether the right or power is given* either by express words or by implication, *paying particular attention to the "essential difference" between the common law and statutory mortgage*. If the statute does not expressly or by implication give the right or power then it does not exist. [Emphasis added; footnotes omitted.]
>
> Duff J. (as he then was) at p. 641 [45 S.C.R. 618] sums it up in this fashion:
>
>> . . . it is a question to be determined upon an examination of the statute as a whole, how far the rights of the parties are to be governed by the rules of law which, apart from the statute, are applicable as between mortgagor and mortgagee.

The comment of McGuire C.J. in *Colonial Investment & Loan Co. v. King* (1902), 5 Terr. L.R. 371 at 379-80, is germane as well to this issue:

> But under our Land Titles Act the mortgage does not operate as a transfer of title, but only as security. The mortgagor remains the owner of the legal estate. The mortgagee merely has a lien until payment, and in case of default he can proceed to get an order either to sell the land or to have the title thereto vested in himself. Upon getting a final order vesting the title in him he can obtain from the registrar of land titles a certificate which gives him an absolute title freed from all claim by the mortgagor. Under these circumstances *one must be careful when endeavouring to apply to mortgages here the rules and principles laid down, say in England or Ontario, as governing the rights of parties to a mortgage there*. [Emphasis added.]

In short, many — though not necessarily all — of the principles applicable at common law and in equity are rendered applicable to the charge as found in jurisdictions such as Saskatchewan. Indeed, even though under such a charge, the borrower retains legal title, it is commonplace to say that the mortgagor holds an equity of redemption. This usage serves as a reminder that equitable principles still largely inform the rights of property-holders taking subject to a charge: see further *Windella (N.S.W.) Pty. Ltd. v. Hughes* (1999) 49 N.S.W.L.R. 158 (Eq. Div.).

7. What is a clog or fetter on the equity of redemption, a term used in *Athasbasca Realty v. Lee*? What is the function of the relevant doctrines associated with that concept? See *Dical Investments Ltd. v. Morrison*, immediately below.

Dical Investments Ltd. v. Morrison
1990 CarswellOnt 563, 75 D.L.R. (4th) 497 (C.A.)

Lacourcière J.A.:

This appeal raises for the first time in this Court, in a commercial context, the applicability of the equitable doctrine prohibiting "clogs" on a mortgagor's equity of redemption. . . .

On February 23, 1984, Thomas agreed to advance to Dical Investments and its associates mortgage money in the amount of $225,000. Dical and its associates, who controlled 225 acres of raw land in the Town of Aurora, had planned to develop a 37-lot subdivision, South Aurora Estates, on a portion of the land. The officers of Dical had approached an Aurora law firm to assist them in obtaining financing for the subdivision project. It was for this purpose that Mr. Stabile, a principal in that law firm, contacted the respondent Thomas. Subsequent negotiations resulted in a letter of commitment for the principal sum of $225,000, to be advanced as a second mortgage loan bearing interest at the rate of 15 per cent per annum, repayable in 2 years.

It should be noted that the original mortgagee in this arrangement was not Thomas but Julsta Investments Ltd. Shortly after the agreement was finalized, however, Julsta assigned to Thomas all its rights under the mortgage. The original letter of commitment contained the following clause:

> Upon registration of the said mortgage, the Mortgagor shall provide the Mortgagee with an option to purchase from the Mortgagor Lots 27 to 31 inclusive, serviced lots, contemplated by a plan of subdivision, for the sum of $60,000.00 per lot to be payable in cash or certified cheque. The said option to expire upon payment in full of principal and interest accrued under the said mortgage.

In a letter to Thomas dated January 31, 1984, Mr. Stabile reported that these were "the best and only terms that I could extract." It is quite clear from the evidence that the respondent Thomas would not advance any mortgage money without the option because the respondent Thomas felt at some risk in making the advance.

Ultimately, by written agreement dated March 1, 1984, Thomas obtained an irrevocable option to purchase any five lots, except Lots 1 to 7 inclusive, shown on a proposed plan of subdivision, a copy of which was attached to the option agreement. According to the agreement, the option could be exercised "at any time after the date hereof," subject to certain conditions. Unlike the commitment letter, the agreement did not stipulate that the option was to expire upon payment of moneys owed under the mortgage. The option could be exercised by notice in writing, delivered to Dical at a given address. The agreement contained the following clause:

> 4. The Grantor covenants that the aforesaid building lots shall be serviced in accordance with the plans and specifications required by the Municipality and as set out in the draft plan attached hereto and that all municipal and government requirements shall be fulfilled and that the title to the lots available to the Grantee shall be good and free from all encumbrances, except as to any registered restrictive covenants and municipal by-laws or other governmental enactments.

It is clear that the second mortgage was conditional upon the signing of the option on the above terms, although no reference to the option is made in the mortgage document, and no reference to the mortgage is made in the option.

As found by the learned trial Judge, the mortgage was redeemed in October 1988, prior to the registration of the plan of subdivision in March 1989. The redemption included payment of the full amount of principal, interest and, in addition, a bonus equivalent to 3 months' interest.

In 1987, Dical sued Morrison, Thomas and the numbered Ontario company, seeking a declaration that the option to purchase any five lots in the subdivision was void and unenforceable because the option could be exercised after redemption of the mortgage, and therefore constituted a clog on the equity of redemption. Dical also claimed that the option agreement was void because it did not contain an express condition that the agreement was to be effective only if the provisions of s. 49 of the *Planning Act* were complied with.

The learned trial Judge reviewed the case law, with particular emphasis on *Kreglinger v. New Patagonia Meat & Cold Storage Co.*, [1914] A.C. 25 (H.L.), and concluded that the option did not constitute a clog on the equity of redemption. In his view, the option was a collateral undertaking independent of the mortgage, and part of a fair commercial arrangement between businessmen who fully understood the implications of the transaction.

The difficult and contentious issue in this case is whether the learned trial Judge erred in refusing to apply strictly to this transaction the doctrine against clogging. The appellant argues that, even if the option constitutes a collateral advantage which was to endure beyond the redemption date, it should be held void as being inconsistent with or repugnant to both the contractual and equitable right of redemption.

The doctrine which prohibits clogs on the mortgagor's equity of redemption was designed to preserve the inviolability of the mortgagor's right to redeem. The mortgagor is entitled to recover his security completely, and unimpaired by the terms of the mortgage. The doctrine was designed to protect necessitous landowners from oppressive agreements. Equity has always sought to protect the mortgagor from lenders who would take advantage of his vulnerability at the time of the loan. Subject to the power of sale under the mortgage, the mortgagor cannot be deprived of his property except through foreclosure, which tests the value of the property and preserves the mortgagor's inviolable right to redeem. See *Noakes & Co. v. Rice*, [1902] A.C. 24, [1900-3] All E.R. 34 (H.L.); *Samuel v. Jarrah Timber & Wood Paving Corp.*, [1904] A.C. 323 (H.L.), and *Lewis v. Frank Love Ltd.*, [1961] 1 W.L.R. 261, [1961] 1 All E.R. 446, 105 Sol. Jo. 155 (Ch. D.). . . .

The only Supreme Court of Canada decision to rely on the doctrine prohibiting clogs on the equity of redemption is *Wilson v. Ward*, [1930] S.C.R. 212, [1930] 2 D.L.R. 433. At issue in that case was a written agreement between the respondent and one Pellon, who subsequently sold his interest in the agreement to the appellant. The agreement recited that Pellon was the owner of certain land, that he wished to obtain a loan on such land, and that the respondent was willing to advance him a loan on certain "conditions", one being that Pellon agreed to sell the land to the respondent. Pellon was given an option to repurchase, exercisable within 90 days.

The Court held that the transaction was in substance a loan upon security, and that the respondent's right to purchase the property was therefore void as being repugnant to the equity of redemption. The Court relied on the principle that equity will not allow a mortgagee to enter into a contract with the mortgagor at the time of the loan for the absolute purchase of the subject of the mortgage. Such an agreement would have the effect of "converting what was intended to be a security into something entirely different" (at p. 221), and therefore violate the maxim "once a mortgage, always a mortgage".

The respondents argue that the rigid application of the doctrine to a contemporary commercial transaction, freely negotiated between equal parties, would produce an unreasonable and inequitable result. They rely on the House of Lords decision in *Kreglinger, supra*, and on academic criticism of the rule exemplified by G.C. Cheshire and E.H. Burn, *Modern Law of Real Property*, 14th ed. (London: Butterworths, 1988) at p. 638; R.E. Megarry and W.R. Wade, *The Law of Real Property*, 5th ed.

(London: Sweet & Maxwell, 1984), at p. 971; and Grant S. Nelson and Dale A. Whitman, *Real Estate Finance Law*, 2d ed. (St. Paul, Minn.: West Publishing Co., 1985), at pp. 35–37. Nelson and Whitman, for example, argue that an option's enforceability should depend not on an abstract principle, but on the nature of the parties, the terms of the option, and the circumstances under which the mortgagee is seeking to enforce it.

It was held in *Kreglinger*, *supra*, that a collateral stipulation is valid, provided that it is not "(1) unfair and unconscionable, or (2) in the nature of a penalty clogging the equity of redemption, or (3) inconsistent with or repugnant to the contractual and equitable right to redeem" (at p. 61).

In determining whether the transaction contravened the mortgagor's right to redeem, the Court must look at the substance of the transaction, the "real bargain" intended by the parties [*Kreglinger*, *supra*, at p. 61, per Lord Parker].

We are inclined to accept the view of Montgomery J. that the impugned transaction was intended to create a severable commercial bargain, freely and fairly negotiated. However, it is unnecessary and undesirable to say anything that would undermine the anti-clogging doctrine which is so firmly entrenched in the common law. It is sufficient, for the resolution of this appeal, to conclude that the option agreement offends s. 49(21) of the *Planning Act* and is unenforceable, as it does not create any interest in land. . . .

NOTES

1. McKinlay J.A. wrote a dissenting opinion, although he agreed with the trial judge that the agreement did not constitute a clog on the equity of redemption.

2. Leave to appeal to the Supreme Court of Canada was refused: (1991) 7 M.P.L.R. (2d) 258n (S.C.C.).

QUESTION

A obtained a loan from B in 1994 secured against a large property. The plan was to develop the land as a nursing home. Prior to the loan, A signed an undertaking providing that in return for the loan, A would provide B with a 50% interest in the enterprise to be set up in the future (none was set up) to run the home.

In the three years that followed, no interest was paid under the loan. Moreover, the plan to build a nursing home was abandoned and another development plan was created by A. In 1997, A sold a small portion of the mortgaged lands to C. B consented to the sale under an agreement that called for (i) the release of the lands from the debt; (ii) the proceeds of the sale to be applied to the unpaid debt; and (iii) B to acquire 50% of A's interest in the remaining lands. (The proceeds of sale were far from sufficient to pay off the debt in its entirety, which continued as a charge on the remaining lands.) Did term (iii) count as an invalid clog on the equity of redemption?

See *Jones v. Morgan* [2001] E.W.C.A. Civ. 995. See also M.P. Thompson, "Do We Really Need Clogs?" [2001] Conv. 502.

Canada Permanent Trust Co. v. King's Bridge Apartments Ltd. 1983 CarswellNfld 109, 8 D.L.R. (4th) 152 (C.A.)

Morgan J.A.:

This appeal is taken from the Order of Noel J. dated May 7, 1982, wherein he dismissed the application of Canada Permanent Trust Company, ("the appellant"), for an account to be taken as to what monies were due and owing the appellant as Trustee under a certain Debenture and for an order of foreclosure or sale of the mortgaged premises or for such other remedy as the Court might deem fit.

The relevant facts are that King's Bridge Apartments Limited, the first respondent, as mortgagor, and Thomas Collingwood and Seamus O'Regan, the third respondents, as guarantors, executed a mortgage of certain lands and premises to King's Bridge Realty Company Limited, the second respondent, as mortgagee. The mortgage was subsequently assigned and transferred by the mortgagee to the appellant under a deed of trust. Subsequently the mortgagor transferred its interest in the mortgaged property to King's Bridge Limited, the fourth respondent, without the consent of the appellant, as required by the mortgage deed. The appellant contended that the transfer by the mortgagor, without the appellant's consent, constituted a default under the mortgage and claimed foreclosure or sale. The relevant provision in the mortgage on which the appellant relied reads:

> *AND* the Mortgagor hereby covenants and agrees with the Mortgagee that it, the Mortgagor, shall not, without the written consent of the Mortgagee, sell, assign, convey, transfer, mortgage or encumber in any manner whatsoever the mortgaged premises, in whole or in part the mortgaged premises during the term of this mortgage;

There were other covenants respecting the use of the mortgaged premises, the payment of taxes, rates and assessments, the liability of the mortgagor for waste as well as covenants respecting insurance. The mortgage also contains the following *proviso*:

> *PROVIDED* that in default of the payment of any instalment of interest hereby secured or on breach of any covenant or *proviso* herein contained or if waste be committed or suffered on the mortgaged premises the whole of the principal sum and other monies, if any, hereby secured, remaining unpaid shall become, without notice or demand, immediately due and payable but the Mortgagee may waive its right to call in the principal sum and shall not be therefore debarred from subsequently asserting and exercising its right to call in the principal sum by reason of such waiver or by reason of any future default.

The learned trial judge held that the covenant by the mortgagor not to sell, assign or convey the mortgaged premises during the currency of the mortgage, without the mortgagee's consent, was an invalid restraint on alienation of property. He concluded:

> The covenant upon which the plaintiff relies is an unlawful restraint on the mortgagor's right to alienate its estate in the subject land and is void.

> The learned trial judge referred to *Re Bahnson and Hazelwood* [1960] 23 D.L.R. (2nd) 76, as supportive of his conclusion. With respect, that case did not deal with the issue before him. In that case the mortgage contained the following provision and I quote: "In the event of sale before the herein mortgage has been discharged the said mortgagor must pay an amount agreeable to both parties of the existing mortgage and the new purchaser must be approved by the mortgagee herein."

The mortgagor had assigned his equity of redemption and at issue was the validity of the purchaser's title. In the court below the trial judge held the condition void. On appeal, the Court of Appeal dealt only with the mortgagee's prior approval as affecting the purchaser's title and the right of the mortgagor to convey. Aylesworth J.A. speaking for the Court, stated at pp. 77-78:

> We, therefore, are in agreement with the Court of first instance with respect to the fact that that provision in the agreement cannot affect either the right of the vendor in this application to convey good title to the purchaser or the right of the purchaser to receive such title unaffected by the stipulation to which I have referred.
>
> It is further contended that the order goes beyond that which is required and with this we agree. Sufficient has been said to indicate to the parties the proper length to which the order should go to satisfy the needs in this transaction of the purchaser and the vendor. If the parties cannot agree upon the provision of the order in that respect a member of the Court may be spoken to. Save as to the direction to restrict the scope of the order so as to indicate that the vendor is at liberty to convey to the purchaser, his heirs, successors and assigns, a title completely free and clear from any effect of the said restriction and that the purchaser likewise is entitled to receive such a conveyance, the appeal is dismissed.

In that case the Court restricted the scope of its order to indicate that the *proviso* in question did not constitute a flaw on the purchaser's title to the equity of redemption. It refrained from commenting on the mortgagee's right to additional payment by reason of the sale.

I agree with the trial judge that a mortgagor's equity of redemption is an interest in land which he may convey, devise, lease or mortgage like any other interest in land and neither the common law nor equity allows restraints on the alienation of that interest. However that was not determinative of the issue before him.

It is not disputed here that the mortgagor effectively alienated its ownership of the mortgaged premises nor is it disputed that the purchaser, the fourth respondent, obtained a good title to the property, subject to the mortgage. The basis of the appellant's claim is that, when the mortgagor assigned its equity of redemption without the consent of the mortgagee, or its assigns, first had and obtained, the principal sum and interest, then due and owing, became payable at the option of the mortgagee and the mortgagee was then free to pursue its remedies at law if it so desired. The question for determination was the right of the mortgagee to demand accelerated payment of the principal sum and interest due under the mortgage upon the mortgagor's default under the covenant in question.

In my opinion the covenant on the part of the mortgagor not to alienate the property without the consent of the mortgagee should not be read in isolation, but in conjunction with the *proviso* that in the event of a breach of any of the covenants contained in the mortgage deed the principal sum and other monies then remaining unpaid would become payable. Undoubtedly a mortgagee's ultimate security is the mortgaged property but he is understandably interested in the financial position of the person or persons liable under the covenant to repay the principal sum and to meet the other financial obligation of taxes, insurance, repairs, etc.

The appellant cited *Briar Building Holdings Limited v. Bow West Holdings Limited et al*, [1981] 16 Alta. L.R. (2d) 42, as supporting his contention that a "due on sale" clause in a mortgage does not constitute a restraint on alienation of land.

In that case the Court of Queen's Bench of Alberta held valid a clause in a mortgage deed requiring that in the event the land was sold voluntarily or by operation of law, all monies owing under the mortgage immediately became due and payable. MacDonald J. before whom the matter was heard referred to *Royal Bank v. Freeborn*, [1975] W.W.D. 84, a decision of the same Court, in which the mortgage in question provided that the monies secured became due if the mortgagor sold the mortgaged property to a purchaser not approved by the mortgagee. In *Royal Bank v. Freeborn* the trial judge stated:

> It is, therefore, possible for a mortgagee to declare the whole amount of the mortgage due and payable when a transferee of land subject to mortgage is not acceptable to the mortgagee.

I agree with that statement and am of the opinion that, while the covenant not to alienate the mortgaged premises without the mortgagee's consent cannot, in any way, restrict the mortgagor's right to sell or otherwise part with possession of the mortgaged premises and to give the purchaser and/or assignee a good title, subject to the mortgage, nonetheless a *proviso* permitting an acceleration of the repayment of the principal sum and other monies payable under the indenture of mortgage is valid and is enforceable at the option of the mortgagee.

In the result the appeal is allowed and the order of the trial judge is set aside with costs.

QUESTION

What arguments for and against the validity of the clause at issue in *Canada Permanent Trust Co. v. King's Bridge Apartments Ltd.* can be marshalled? See Alberta Law Reform Institute, *Mortgage Remedies in Alberta*, Report No. 70 (Edmonton: A.L.R.I., 1994) at 85*ff.*

4. REMEDIES AND RELATED MATTERS

(a) introduction

A mortgagee will often have an array of remedies built into the mortgage deal. Some are common. Included in this category are an action on the personal covenant(s), the assumption of possession, the appointment of a receiver, foreclosure, and sale of the mortgaged property. Some are supplementary, such as where a guarantor signs the loan agreement.

(b) the personal covenant

Under all the layers of paper, a mortgage is no more than a secured loan, which the mortgagor promises to repay. Hence, as a general matter, a lender may sue in debt on this personal covenant when there is a default in repayment. In some jurisdictions, Alberta is a prime example, restrictions are placed on the ability to sue on certain covenants to repay, leaving the lender with recourse solely to the land under the other available remedies: see *Law of Property Act*, R.S.A. 2000, c. L-7, s. 44. The protections were introduced in the province during the Depression as a means of alleviating the crushing financial burdens that the collapse of the economy and the drought imposed on farmers and ranchers. However, other promises in the mortgages agreement, such as the personal covenant not to commit waste, are enforceable: see *Parisian Fashions Ltd. v. Petrus* (1996) 6 R.P.R. (3d) 219, 1996 CarswellAlta 1000 (Q.B.), and also sub. 44(1).

L lends money to B on the strength of a mortgage security. The mortgage is duly registered on title. B then sells the land to B'. The mortgage binds the land and encumbers the title acquired by B'. But can B' be sued by L under the personal covenant? See *384846 Ontario Ltd. v. 705464 Ontario Inc.*, below.

384846 Ontario Ltd. v. 705464 Ontario Inc.
1997 CarswellOnt 1319, 12 R.P.R. (3d) 42 (Gen. Div.)

J. deP. Wright J.:

This is an action for money owing on a mortgage. The mortgagee of land, using Section 20(2) of the *Mortgages Act*, sues a subsequent transferee of an interest in the equity of redemption for the amount outstanding on its mortgage.

In September 1988 the numbered defendant agreed to buy the land in question from the plaintiff. In November 1988 the numbered defendant executed a declaration of trust whereby the numbered defendant declared that it held its interest in the land in question in trust for itself and the defendant Michon Holdings Inc. as tenants in common, each having a 50% interest. The transaction closed on June 6, 1989. The plaintiff/vendor took back a second mortgage for $200,000. In August 1989 the numbered defendant conveyed the equity of redemption to itself and the defendant Michon Holdings Limited. That conveyance was said to be a conveyance from trustee to beneficiaries.

The mortgage went into default. The plaintiff/mortgagee now pursues the defendant Michon Holdings Limited as a transferee of the equity of redemption, utilizing Section 20(2) of the *Mortgages Act*.

Section 20(2) reads as follows:

> (2) Despite any stipulation to the contrary in a mortgage, where a mortgagor has conveyed and transferred the equity of redemption to a grantee under such circumstances that the grantee is by express covenant or otherwise obligated to indemnify the mortgagor with respect to the mortgage, the mortgagee has the right to recover from the grantee the amount of the mortgage debt in respect of which the grantee is obligated to indemnify the mortgagor; . . .

Section 20(2) is procedural only. It provides a mechanism in law whereby a mortgagee may pursue a subsequent transferee of the equity of redemption. At common law a mortgagee was a third party beneficiary to any agreement by a transferee of land to indemnify a transferor who was bound by a covenant to pay any mortgage. While the transferor could sue the transferee on this indemnity agreement, the mortgagee could not do so directly. The mortgagee could do so indirectly by taking an assignment of the transferor's right of indemnification. The mortgagee could then sue the transferee in the name of the transferor.

Section 20(2) provides a mechanism whereby the mortgagee may sue a transferee directly notwithstanding the absence of privity of contract between them. Such an action will only lie where the transfer:

> Is under such circumstances that the grantee is by express covenant or otherwise obligated to indemnify the mortgagor with respect to the mortgage . . .

In this case there exists no express covenant by the defendant Michon Holdings Limited to indemnify the numbered defendant with respect to this mortgage.

Is Michon "otherwise obligated to indemnify the numbered defendant with respect to this mortgage?"

The plaintiff says that Michon is so obligated.

The plaintiff says:

(1) That there is a presumption, enforceable in equity, that the transferee of the equity of redemption will, independent of an express contract of indemnity, indemnify the vendor against its personal obligation to pay under the mortgage.

(2) That inherent in the trustee/beneficiary relationship is an obligation on the part of the beneficiary to indemnify the trustee for liabilities incurred with respect to the trust property.

(3) That there was in effect a partnership between the transferor and the transferee and that inherent in the partnership relationship is a duty of contribution and indemnity.

I accept that the presumptions in paragraphs (1) to (3) above exist. I also accept that these presumptions must give way to any agreement to the contrary.

Was there an agreement to the contrary?

The plaintiff says that there could not have been. The plaintiff says that the parties were only entitled to claim land transfer tax exemption if the trustee was indemnified by the beneficial owners. The plaintiff argues that by taking the land transfer tax exemption, the defendant is precluded from arguing a contrary position.

The plaintiff points to the expectation of the defendant. The defendant expected to share in profits after mortgage payments had been met. The defendant expected to share in capital gains after the mortgage had been paid off. The plaintiff submits that this is conclusive evidence that the defendant accepted responsibility for this mortgage, which responsibility included an indemnification of the numbered defendant, which was personally liable upon the covenant.

With respect to the former point I observe:

(1) It is by no means clear that such an indemnity had to exist for land transfer tax purposes in this case. Here we did not have a simple transfer from a trustee to a beneficiary. Here we had a transfer from a trustee/beneficiary to itself and the other beneficiary.

(2) Even if the plaintiff is correct and the parties filed an affidavit stating that such an indemnity existed between them, that affidavit would be evidence on the issue but not conclusive evidence.

With respect to the latter point, I observe that there is a distinction between a recognition of the existence of a mortgage and the fact that one will be entitled to profits only after the satisfaction of that obligation and the assumption of responsibility for that obligation.

Could the numbered defendant have claimed contribution and indemnity against the defendant in law or in equity?

I have considered the previous dealings between the parties. I have considered their dealings in this transaction. I have considered the method of operation of both transferor and transferee. I have considered the purpose of the transfer and I have considered the evidence of the witnesses. I have absolutely no doubt that there was no intention between the transferor and transferee that the transferee (defendant) would be called upon to assume responsibility for this mortgage debt other than out of profits from the income of the land or on the sale of the land. Quite the contrary!

Both transferor and transferee accepted that the responsibility for this mortgage otherwise rested upon the numbered defendant. The numbered defendant would not and could not have sought indemnification from this defendant with respect to this mortgage.

Under the circumstances the action must be dismissed.

QUESTION

Compare the *Land Titles Act*, R.S.A. 2000, c. L-4. In what way, if at all, do these provisions differ from the Ontario law discussed above?

> 58(1) In every instrument transferring land for which a certificate of title has been granted, subject to mortgage or encumbrance, there shall be implied the following covenant by the transferee both with the transferor and the mortgagee: That the transferee will pay the principal money, interest, annuity or rent charge secured by the mortgage or encumbrance, after the rate and at the time specified in the instrument creating it, and will indemnify and keep harmless the transferor from and against the principal sum or other money secured by the instrument and from and against the liability in respect of any of the covenants contained in the instrument or under this Act implied on the part of the transferor. . . .

> 59(1) Every covenant and power declared to be implied in any instrument by virtue of this Act may be negatived or modified by express declaration in the instrument.

Langley Lo-Cost Builders Ltd. v. 474835 B.C. Ltd.
2000 CarswellBC 1229, [2000] 7 W.W.R. 46 (C.A.)

McEachern C.J.B.C.: . . .

The learned trial judge ruled that the interest provision in Langley's mortgage was invalid because it offended s. 8 of the *Interest Act*, R.S.C. 1985, c. I-15 (the "*Act*"). This provision of the mortgage stated that there would be no interest payable during the currency of the mortgage from December 8, 1994, to January 24, 1995. Interest would then run at the rate of prime plus three percent until the maturity date three days later on January 27, 1995, and after that, at prime plus three percent on any amounts in arrears on the mortgage.

Section 8 of the *Act* provides:

> 8(1) No fine, penalty or rate of interest shall be stipulated for, taken, reserved or exacted on any arrears of principal or interest secured by mortgage on real property that has the

effect of increasing the charge on the arrears beyond the rate of interest payable on principal money not in arrears.

(2) Nothing in this section has the effect of prohibiting a contract for the payment of interest on arrears of interest or principal at any rate not greater than the rate payable on principal money not in arrears.

The facts giving rise to this interest provision are important. Under the original arrangement, Langley was to sell the land to a company called MHI for cash with the deal closing on January 24, 1995. By an assignment agreement, MHI transferred its interest in the sale contract to a numbered company on November 17, 1994, *i.e.*, prior to the closing date. As already mentioned, the numbered company was the General Partner of the Panorama limited partnership.

By an amendment agreement dated November 25, 1994, the closing date for the sale of the land was moved forward to December 5, 1994. The agreement as first drafted provided that Langley would take back a first mortgage for $3 million payable on or before January 24, 1995. It was further provided that interest would be paid at the rate of prime plus three percent, but that Langley would waive this interest if the principle were paid before January 24, 1995.

The lawyers documenting the transaction recognized that the above interest provision might contravene s. 8 of the *Act*. Accordingly, they agreed that no interest would run until three days before the original closing date of January 24, 1995; and that interest would be payable at prime plus three percent from that date until the closing date; and at the same rate on arrears accruing after the closing date.

The reason for these changes, effected on December 1, 1994, was simply that it had been the parties' original agreement that no interest would be payable prior to closing. Under the amended agreement, Langley received a substantial pre-payment and for that reason it was willing to waive interest until the closing, but not beyond. When counsel identified a problem with the Act, they changed the agreement to provide for interest at the same rate for three days before and after maturity.

Conveyancing counsel in the matter were aware of and relied on the decision of Ryan J. (as she then was) in *Raintree Financial Ltd. v. Bell* (1993), 82 B.C.L.R. (2d) 28 (B.C. Master). They reasonably, and correctly, believed this arrangement did not offend against the *Act* as the law then stood.

In *Raintree*, the interest payable under a mortgage provided that the rate would increase from 18% to 24% one week before the maturity date. A Master of the Court ruled that this provision offended against s. 8 of the *Act*. Ryan J. ruled otherwise. At page 2, she reviewed the arguments of counsel and held that there was no increase in the interest rate triggered by a default or arrears. In other words, Ryan J. held that a contractual change in the interest rate immediately before the maturity date, and before any arrears accrued, did not offend s. 8 of the *Act*. Implicitly, she held that parties are entitled to craft their instrument in order to avoid offending against the *Act*.

In the subsequent case of *TD Trust Co. v. Guinness* (1995), 12 B.C.L.R. (3d) 102 (B.C. S.C. [In Chambers]), however, Tysoe J. did not follow the decision in *Raintree*. In the case he was considering, there was a one-year mortgage maturing on March 2, 1995. The interest rate under the mortgage was 16.5% until February 22, 1995 (one week before the maturity date) and 24% thereafter. No reason was offered in the instrument or at trial for this change in the interest rate.

Tysoe J. decided he was not bound to follow *Raintree* because of four authorities that had not been referred to Ryan J. In the first case, *Vancouver City Savings Credit Union v. National Holdings Ltd.* (1975), 59 D.L.R. (3d) 753 (B.C. S.C.), the mortgage provided for an extra payment of three months interest in the event of default. This was found to be an unenforceable penalty. With respect, I see no difficulty with that case, which appears to me to be correctly decided; but I do not think it affects the case at bar where the interest payable after maturity did not exceed the amount payable upon default. Perhaps the case is cited because of the dictum of Bouck J. that, "The law looks at the substance and not the form when deciding what is or is not a penalty."

In the second case, *Weirdale Investments Ltd. v. Canadian Imperial Bank of Commerce* (1981), 121 D.L.R. (3d) 150 (Ont. H.C.), the mortgage provided for interest at 10%, but provided that interest was to be waived if the mortgage was paid on or before the due date. In other words, the mortgage exhibited the "super-subtle" distinction mentioned, by Bouck J., between a penal and non- penal device. In one class of cases, the mortgagee is required to pay more after default; in the other class, the mortgagor loses the advantage of the interest waiver, and therefore pays more on default. It was held that the law, looking at the substance rather than the form, does not recognize such subtle distinctions.

In the third case, *Chu v. Columbia River Ranches Ltd.* (1986), 10 B.C.L.R. (2d) 72 (B.C. S.C.), the interest provision of an Agreement for Sale provided that interest would be payable both before and after maturity, but it would be forgiven annually if all payments were made on time. Although it was held that the *Act* did not apply to Agreements for Sale, Spencer J. commented favourably upon the decision in *Weirdale*, which was a mortgage case, but he held it did not apply to Agreements for Sale. Interest was therefore payable on the arrears.

In the last of these four cases, *Vohra Enterprises Ltd. v. Creative Industrial Corp.* (1988), 23 B.C.L.R. (2d) 120 (B.C. S.C.), there was an interest rate of 12% but the mortgage included a provision that no interest would be charged if the mortgagor complied with all the terms and conditions of the mortgage. It was asserted that the mortgagor defaulted on one minor term of the mortgage and a dispute arose over whether this triggered the interest obligation. Callaghan J. held that the provision requiring the payment of interest offended against the *Act*. In reaching this conclusion, he relied upon some of the cases cited above.

When this Court decided *North West Life Assurance Co. of Canada v. Kings Mount Holdings Ltd.* (1987), 15 B.C.L.R. (2d) 376 (B.C. C.A.), it expressed doubt about, but did not expressly overrule, *Weirdale*, *supra*, upon which Callaghan J. had relied. As a result, further submissions were made, and Callaghan J. delivered Supplementary Reasons for Judgment. He concluded that the *North West* case was decided on a consideration of a modification agreement, and that the decision of this Court on that question did not affect the conclusions he had previously reached concerning the provision requiring the payment of interest.

Thus, it appears to me that *Vohra* stands for the proposition that the loss of an interest abatement because of a minor and technical failure to pay property taxes on time is a penalty that equity will not tolerate. The result was that the interest abatement was restored.

In summary, these cases, each one decided on its particular facts, are authority for the view that a change in interest rate upon default, or some other arrangement such as a waiver of interest upon due payment may not offend against the *Act*. This raises the question of when the freedom of the parties to structure their bargain is restricted by the *Act*. Recognizing this difficulty, Tysoe J. in *TD Trust Co. v. Guinness* said this at 109-10:

> The authorities establish that in considering s. 8 the Court should not restrict itself to the form of the provision in the mortgage and should look to its substance. In this case the substance of the provision is clearly to extract a higher rate of interest if the mortgage was not repaid by its maturity date. It is apparent on the face that the wording of the provision was an attempt to avoid s. 8 and *no other explanation to justify the provision was offered*. Section 8 cannot be avoided by clever devices if the substance of the provision has the effect of increasing the interest rate in the case of default. In this case, the substance of the interest provision violates s. 8 and is unenforceable. . . .
>
> In her decision in the *Raintree* case Ryan J. placed some weight on the wording of s. 8(2). I think that all Parliament intended to accomplish with s. 8(2) was to clarify that interest can be charged on arrears as long as, in substance, the rate of interest is not greater than the rate payable prior to default.
>
> Where does one draw the line in deciding whether an interest provision contravenes s. 8? This is an obvious question and it was asked in the hearing before Master Bolton in the Raintree case. He said that he did not have to decide the point because he was satisfied that the provision before him was on the wrong side of the line. *In my view, the line should be drawn between interest provisions which are intended to extract a higher rate of interest in the event of default and interest provisions which have a legitimate commercial purpose. The true intent may be obfuscated by clever devices designed by ingenuous lawyers and it will be the function of the Court to determine the true intent.* (Emphasis added.)

The facts in this case disclose a sensible commercial explanation for the interest provision, arising out of the early payment of a large part of the principal. This makes understandable the non-accrual of interest until the original closing date, when the parties expected that interest would begin to be payable. I shall return to this question in a moment.

In addition to the above, it appears from Langley's *Factum* that there are a number of authorities that may not have been cited, and which were not mentioned by Tysoe J. These cases make it clear that s. 8 of the *Act* was intended to protect borrowers against penalties and oppression at the hands of a ruthless lender. They stress that the thrust of the section is to avoid, as the section says, any "fine" or "penalty". In *Dillingham Construction Ltd. v. Patrician Land Corp.*, [1985] 4 W.W.R. 468 (Alta. C.A.), a mortgage made no mention of interest before maturity, but provided for a rate of 14% after default. Stevenson J.A., writing for the Court, said this:

> In my opinion the section is directed towards implementing the equitable principle against penalties for non-performance. *A stipulation for an increased rate of interest is,* prima facie, *such a penalty*. It is something which, on the face of it, is held *in terrorem* over a defaulting debtor. So an increase from any stipulated amount of interest falls foul of the principle and the statute. Here, in a transaction which is not a commercial lending transaction, common sense dictates not that the transaction has a nil interest rate, but that it has made unspecified provisions for interest. *I say this because it is inconceivable that in entering into this transaction the parties did not appreciate, and make some allowance for, the cost of money in arriving at the terms*. It is possible, for example, that the mortgagee, as vendor, made a precise calculation based on the amount payable at maturity. I cannot say that the stipulation for interest at maturity has the effect of increasing the interest component. I am unable to conclude that the particular provision is penal and cannot, therefore, say that it comes within the principle which the section embodies.
>
> I am inclined to agree with Master Hyndman that, on the face of it, the application of s. 8 works an unreasonable hardship on the mortgagee rather than relieving against any penalty which he had exacted. The mortgage does not come within the literal prohibition of s. 8. The interest stipulation is not shown to be a penalty for non-performance. If it were a penalty the effect of the section, or the application of equitable principles, would be to remove only the additional interest payable under the mortgage and, as with Master Hyndman, the judicial implementation of an interest-free loan gives me considerable pause. I finally look to s. 2 of the Act:
>
>> 2. Except as otherwise provided by this or by any other Act of the Parliament of Canada, any person may stipulate for, allow and exact, on any contract or agreement whatever, any rate of interest or discount that is agreed upon. (Emphasis added.)

In another case, *Annis v. Annis* (September 10, 1984), Doc. 4467/82 (Ont. H.C.), no interest prior to default was stipulated, but 5% was payable after default. It was held that such a provision was ". . . surely very far from the evil intended to be combatted by s. 8 . . ." and it was directed that interest on arrears be paid as damages at the legal rate which was the same rate of 5% reserved in the mortgage.

The cases recognize that *prima facie*, a rate of interest which becomes payable at default, or which is increased in that event will offend s. 8 of the *Act*. But a business arrangement, not being a commercial lending transaction, may be analyzed to determine whether there is a business reason for the stipulation that does not amount to a penalty or to economic coercion or unfairness, and if so, it will not always be construed as offending against the *Act*.

This case falls somewhere between the two sets of cases just discussed. Because of the substantial pre-payment, no interest was charged until just before what would have been the closing date, when one would normally expect interest to be paid. To avoid the literal application of s. 8, the parties stipulated for an interest rate prior to the closing date with no express waiver of interest on due payment. It should also be noted that in this case, because the land was being transferred prior to the originally anticipated closing date, it was necessary to secure Langley's unpaid interest by a mortgage; the arrangement was entirely fair and carried none of the stench of coercion, intimidation or penalty. As such, it cannot fairly be characterized as a "clever device" not authorized by the law as it then stood.

Viewed that way, with respect, there was no reason to distinguish *Raintree*. I conclude the parties were entitled in the circumstances to fashion their agreement as they did in accordance with the existing law. I would therefore allow the appeal regarding the disallowance of interest, and direct that interest be payable under the mortgage according to its terms.

I would allow the appeal on both the validity of the agreement and on the question of interest.

QUESTIONS AND COMMENTS

1. Which view of section 8 do you prefer?

2. Comment on the validity of the following mortgage terms:

(a) A mortgage was agreed to under the following terms contained in a commitment letter:

> For a period of 36 months following the initial advance, the whole of the outstanding balance under the loan will only be due and payable in the event the member should default under the provisions of the commitment letter or the mortgage or any other security for the loan. Thereafter, and in the absence of default, outstanding advances under the loan and interest thereon and costs will be repayable on demand. In the absence of demand, outstanding advances under the loan are due in full not later than six months following the date the loan first becomes repayable on demand.
>
> The rate of interest payable on the outstanding balance of the loan shall be:
>
> i) For a period of 36 months following the initial advance a rate of interest 1% *per annum* in excess of Van City's prime lending rate in effect from time to time, calculated monthly, not in advance; and
>
> ii) Thereafter, if the loan is not renewed, a rate of interest 5% *per annum* in excess of Van City's prime lending rate in effect from time to time, calculated monthly, not in advance.

The subsequent mortgage document read:

> Prime as defined in the Filed Standard Mortgage Terms plus 1% *per annum* to 2000/11/1; prime plus 5% *per annum* thereafter.

[Due date]: On demand after November 1, 2000 without demand on May 1, 2001.

For greater certainty, the borrower hereby acknowledges and agrees that the Interest Rate payable under This Mortgage shall equal Prime plus 1% *per annum* calculated monthly, from the Date of Advance to and including November 1, 2000 and thereafter the Interest Rate payable under This Mortgage shall equal Prime plus 5% *per annum*, calculated monthly. The Borrower further acknowledges and agrees that from and after November 1, 2000 the Principal Amount together with all accrued Interest and Other Money due hereunder shall be payable on demand and in any event without demand on May 1, 2001.

The Borrower covenants and agrees that all representations and warranties of the Borrower contained in any loan application, commitment letter or similar application for This Mortgage loan (the "Application") shall be deemed incorporated and part of This Mortgage as if the same representations and warranties of the Borrower were fully repeated in This Mortgage and in the event of any breach by the Borrower of any of the representations and warranties contained in the Application, all of which shall survive throughout the term of This Mortgage, the breach shall be deemed to be a default under This Mortgage and shall entitled (sic) the Lender to exercise all of the rights and remedies of the Lender including, but without limiting the generality of the foregoing, the right to demand payment of the monies hereby secured. The commitment letter dated September 10, 1997 as signed by the Borrower and Lender shall not be merged with This Mortgage and shall continue in full force and effect.

"Maturity Date" means the earlier of the "Balance Due Date" specified in the Mortgage Form or such date on which the Lender lawfully requires payment of the Principal Amount and Other Money.

See *Vancouver City Savings Credit Union v. 535401 B.C. Ltd.* 2001 CarswellBC 2286, 44 R.P.R. (3d) 274 (S.C.).

(b) A mortgage was granted with a maturity date of May, 1997. The mortgage interest rate was 7.00% *per annum* calculated semi-yearly, not in advance. The mortgage also contained "additional or modified terms" contained in a schedule. One of those terms provided:

1.1(l) "Mortgage Rate" means the annual rate described as the "Interest Rate" in item 5(b) of the Mortgage Form calculated at the end of each Interest Calculation Period, not in advance, provided that the Mortgage Rate shall be adjusted seven (7) days prior to the Balance Due Date to become the Toronto-Dominion Bank Prime Rate plus five (5%) percent *per annum* compounded monthly not in advance. This adjusted rate shall continue in effect until such time as the Principal and all other amounts outstanding hereunder are paid in full or, alternatively, until the Mortgage is renewed pursuant to Clause 7.1.48 in this Mortgage . . .

See *Citizens Bank of Canada v. Babich* 2000 CarswellBC 1314 (Master).

3. Section 8 of the *Interest Act* contains just one of several measures designed to regulate the cost of credit. See also (i) the other provisions of that Act; and (ii) s. 347 of the *Criminal Code*, R.S.C. 1985, c. C-46, which creates an offence to charge

interest in excess of 60% *per annum* on a loan: see further *Degelder Construction Co. v. Dancorp Developments Ltd.* [1998] 3 S.C.R. 90, 1998 CarswellBC 2246, 1998 CarswellBC 2247. See also *Transport North American Express Inc. v. New Solutions Financial Corp.* 2004 CarswellOnt 512 (S.C.C.). In some jurisdictions, legislation mandates the articulate disclosure of the cost of credit to consumers: see, *e.g.*, *Cost of Credit Disclosure Act*, S.N.B. 1997, c. C-28, especially s. 15.

4. Mortgages typically provide that if the borrower misses a payment, or breaches any other obligations, or has lied in the mortgage application, or has committed some other specified wrong relating to the mortgage, the entire balance of the loan becomes due. In such an eventuality, what can the mortgagor do? One possibility is to pay off the mortgage, perhaps by obtaining refinancing from another source. If mortgage interest rates plunge, borrowers may be tempted to default, invite acceleration and refinancing. (See further *Shankman v. Mutual Life Assurance Co. of Canada*, below, where this game of financial cat-and-mouse is in evidence.)

5. However, a mortgagor may not, in fact, be in a position to pay off the entire balance. In such a case, a court may be prepared to grant relief to reverse the acceleration. For example, *The Mortgage Act*, C.C.S.M., c. M200, s. 14, provides:

> Where default has occurred in making any payment due under any mortgage or in the observance of any covenant contained therein and, under the terms of the mortgage, by reason of the default, the whole principal and interest secured thereby has become due and payable, the mortgagor may, notwithstanding any provisions to the contrary, and at any time prior to sale or foreclosure under a mortgage, perform the covenant or pay such arrears as may be in default under the mortgage, together with costs, and he is thereupon relieved from the consequences of non-payment of so much of the mortgage money as may not then have become payable by reason of lapse of time.

See, *e.g.*, *Island Savings Credit Union v. Durand* 2002 CarswellBC 1494 (Master).

(c) taking possession or appointing a receiver

Capsule Investments Ltd. v. Heck
1993 CarswellOnt 3810, 103 D.L.R. (4th) 556 (C.A.)

Carthy J.A.:

The appellants are joint second mortgagees appealing from the order of Henry J. confirming the report of Master Linton on a reference to take accounts in a mortgage action. The dispute is over the sharing of the proceeds of a sale of the property. The appellants claim a deficiency under their mortgage against the respondent in his position as the original mortgagor. As third mortgagee the respondent claims that on a proper accounting there is a surplus over the amount due on the second mortgage, and that the surplus is more than sufficient to pay out the indebtedness under his mortgage. The master found in favour of the respondent and awarded him $76,243, including prejudgment interest on his counterclaim.

The very full judgment of Henry J. is reported at (1990), 10 R.P.R.(2d) 281; 72 O.R.(2d) 481 (H.C.), and I will limit the recitation of facts to those that are necessary to deal with the issues on the appeal.

The second mortgagees went into possession of the mortgaged premises in July of 1981. At that time the first mortgage, in the principal amount of $435,000, had matured and was in default. It provided for interest at 12% *per annum* prior to maturity. The second mortgage, in the principal amount of $100,000, provided for interest at 14.5% or 4.25% above prime from time to time, whichever was the greater. At the time of taking possession the current prime rate was about 22.5% and the current market rate was about 24%. Rather than paying out the first mortgage, the second mortgagees negotiated extensions in six month periods, and paid interest to the first mortgagee at rates which were competitive from time to time. This arrangement continued until April of 1983 when the second mortgagees borrowed funds from the bank, paid out the first mortgagee and took an assignment of the first mortgage which was lodged at the bank as security for the loan.

Under the terms of the second mortgage, if the mortgagees redeemed a prior encumbrance, they were entitled to credit the payment to their own mortgage and charge interest at the rate set out in that mortgage.

Immediately upon taking possession the second mortgagees listed the property for sale at the appraised value, which was modestly above the total indebtedness of the mortgages against the property. No buyers were forthcoming until May of 1984, when the property sold for $725,000. The respondent, as third mortgagee, felt there should be a surplus for payment of his mortgage and asked for an accounting. The appellants responded by instituting this action for recovery of a deficiency on their mortgage indebtedness against the respondent as the original mortgagor. The respondent counter-claimed as a third mortgagee, and his position throughout has been that: the appellants' accounts on the second mortgage are excessively high because they charged the full interest paid to the first mortgagee prior to redemption of that mortgage in 1983; they committed waste and should not be entitled to credit the cost of refurbishing the buildings; and they failed to collect rents that could have been collected, or their agents absconded with rents.

An appeal from a judge's confirmation of a report on a reference may be the only instance in which this court is asked to conduct a second review without an intervening order granting leave to appeal. Thus, the question arises as to what standard of review is to be applied. It is in the nature of a reference that detailed accounting matters may be considered on a list of subjects and perhaps a myriad of items within those subjects. The reason for the reference is in large part that the subject matter does not lend itself to resolution within the general court trial system. That puts the confirming judge in an unusual position, because it is not in the strict sense an appeal, and the issues have returned to the general system where the niceties of detailed accounting cannot be appropriately resolved. Anderson J. dealt with this concern in *Jordan v. McKenzie* (1987), 26 C.P.C.(2d) 193 (Ont. H.C.), where he set down limits to the extent of review appropriate at the confirming stage. Since there is only one judgment, that given by the confirming judge, the appeal to this court is as of right. Thus, what standard of review is appropriate at this second level of review?

In answering this question, one must consider that while the parties to litigation should be entitled to an opportunity to complain of error, justice requires finality within a reasonable time. The statement of claim in this action was filed in February of 1985 and, depending upon our disposition of this appeal, may be concluded in 1993 or continue indefinitely if issues are remitted back to the master. With these factors in mind, there is an accentuated need to identify palpable and overriding error in factual matters before interfering at this second level of review.

I would add an observation as to the conduct of reference hearings. This reference was conducted on the basis of what was called the "English model" dealing with issues *seriatim*. The master made a decision after each issue was addressed, with a computer calculating the accumulated result and applying it to the accounts with appropriate rests. When the computer indicated that the third mortgagee had been fully compensated by the then established entitlement, the reference was suspended. This left outstanding claims by the third mortgagee that were treated as redundant at that point. This procedure ignored the potential of a confirmation motion and an appeal as of right thereafter, and that the second mortgagee might succeed on an issue, necessitating a return to the reference to deal with untouched subjects. That continuation, and its conclusion, would then be subject to another process of appellate review. If the reference had been completed, the confirming judge or an appellate court could correct any error and bring the proceedings to a conclusion.

Returning to the merits, the master found that the appellants entered into possession of the premises through an agent in July of 1981. By virtue of their own wilful neglect or default, they permitted a series of agents to abscond with rentals which were not credited to the mortgage account. The appellants did not take issue before us with the finding that they should be accountable for the full amount of rents that should have been collected less a vacancy allowance, but did contest the finding that the first agent attorned on their behalf. This was a concurrent finding of fact which we should not disturb, and for that reason the respondent was not called upon on that issue.

Another reason for the master's adjustment of the second mortgagees' accounts was that he refused to credit the second mortgagees with the full amount of interest paid to the first mortgagee between September 1981 and April 1983. As stated earlier, during that time there were a series of negotiated extensions at market rates, always keeping the mortgage open so that it could be paid on a sale. The master permitted a credit at the 12% rate of the first mortgage prior to maturity. This is a relatively substantial difference, because the market rates ranged in that period between 24% and 19.25%. The appellants argued that the master and confirming judge erred in law in making this deduction, because the second mortgagee has an entitlement and obligation to protect the property. Also, having listed the property for sale without success, there was no reasonable alternative to renegotiating the first mortgage and keeping it open so that it could be redeemed on a sale. It was pointed out that, if the appellants had redeemed the first mortgage in 1981 in the fashion in which it did in 1983, they would have been entitled to add the redemption amount to their own mortgage debt and charge interest under the terms of their own mortgage at prime plus 4%, which would in 1981 have totalled over 26%. Thus, the owner did not suffer and if credit is not given, then the second mortgagees are being penalized by putting form before substance.

While it may appear as form over substance, I agree with the respondent that in a settling of accounts the court is looking at what happened and not at what might have happened. There is no specific right in the mortgage to renegotiate a prior encumbrance without consent of subsequent encumbrancers and the owner. The consent is significant, because the owner has the protection of s. 8 of the *Interest Act*, R.S.C. 1985, c. I-15, prohibiting a higher interest rate after maturity than is stipulated for prior to maturity. See *Coupland Acceptance Limited v. Walsh et al.*, [1954] S.C.R. 90, [1954] 2 D.L.R. 129, at pp. 131-132 (D.L.R.), where a similar adjustment was made in a mortgagee's accounts. It is worth noting that the owner walked away from this property because the mortgages were maturing and he could not justify refinancing at the high interest rates of 1981. This alternative was also available to the second mortgagees. They could have walked away and left the property to the first mortgagee who, as an institutional investor, might have had a longer range view of the prospects of interest rates falling, and may have held the property for eventual sale. In that event, the interest on the first mortgage would have continued at 12% and, potentially, all secured parties may have been protected. The second mortgagees clearly chose not to expose themselves to a primary obligation to their own bankers of 22%, and waited until they could do so more comfortably at the lower rates in 1983. They should not in this fashion be enabled to effectively charge the owner more interest after maturity than before on the first mortgage. I would therefore affirm the allowance at the first mortgage rate of 12% for the period through to April of 1983.

The master found that the appellants failed to effect repairs during the first nine months, leading to serious water damage and the subsequent advice from consultants that substantial amounts must be spent to put the buildings in saleable condition. The master assessed the amount attributable to this neglect and deducted it from the accounts. The proper amount of that deduction will be discussed later in these reasons.

The appellants do not contest the allocation to them of the full amount of the rents that should have been collected less a 5% vacancy allowance. However, they do say that they had no obligation to repair the premises, because if there is a credit of the attributed rents and a credit of the 12% interest due to the first mortgagee while a further allowance is made for a 5% management fee, there would not have been sufficient funds after paying the interest on the second mortgage to pay for any repairs. It is argued that there is no obligation to repair before paying interest on your own mortgage.

This argument is premised on the figures put before us in argument and is against the findings in the courts below. This is the very type of accounting exercise that we should not engage in at an appellate level. One could never be confident of a deficit or a surplus without going into every constituent number that was included in the overall accounting. I would not interfere with these concurrent findings.

Henry J. reached this stage in his reasoning and then proceeded in obiter to deal with the legal obligation to repair before paying interest to the mortgagee in possession. He concluded that the statement in *Falconbridge on Mortgages* (4th Ed. 1977), at p. 656, is in error in concluding:

> A mortgagee is liable for neglect to repair only if there is a surplus of rents after payment of interest on the mortgage; he is not bound to expend his own money on repairs.

Since the law which roots that statement is some 200 years old, I do not think I should pass by the point even though it was obiter to Henry J. and is obiter to these reasons. I will not seek to duplicate the extensive analysis of the cases undertaken by Henry J. The passage from *Falconbridge* cites as authority *Richards v. Morgan* (1793), 4 Y. & C. Ex. 570, which notes the Lord Chancellor as saying:

> . . . that a mortgagee in possession ought to do such repairs as he can repay by the rents of the estate after his interest paid, but he need not rebuild or lay out large sums beyond the rent for that would be to lend more principal money, upon, perhaps, a deficient security.

Other text writers have reached the same conclusion as *Falconbridge*. See, Fisher and Lightwood's *Law of Mortgages* (10th Ed. 1988), at p. 370; Marriott and Dunn's *Practice In Mortgage Actions in Ontario* (5th Ed.), at p. 10-10 and Cousins, Edward F., and Ross, Sidney, *The Law of Mortgages* (1989), at p. 219.

My review of the English and Canadian authorities cited by Henry J. indicates that not one of them deals specifically with the situation where the rents are not sufficient to effect the repairs. They all speak of a duty to effect repairs and the entitlement to add the cost to the accounts.

Looking at the matter afresh and without the benefit of precedent, the basic rule is that a mortgagee in possession must act as a prudent owner and protect the equity of redemption. An owner with sufficient money to pay the interest on the second mortgage or, alternatively, to effect repairs, might well decide that the interest should be paid and the repairs put over to another day; otherwise there is a risk of loss of possession of the property. From the mortgagee's vantage point, there is an increased exposure to loss if the debt is increased by adding interest on unpaid interest. There may be a benefit by allocating the money to repairs, but it seems reasonable that the choice should be that of the mortgagee in possession. As a practical matter, if there is a deficiency of rent, the owner is unlikely to have any real equity. The mortgagee will be the one with the true exposure to loss.

Therefore, it is my view that Henry J. reached the wrong conclusion and the textbooks need not be rewritten.

The final point raised by the appellant concerns the amount of $61,254.22, which was deducted by the master from the appellants' accounts as being costs related to the deterioration of the building through the appellants' neglect in 1981-1982. The appellants say that the master failed to recognize that many of the items going to make up the amount that he disallowed would have been ordinary repairs or overlapped ordinary repairs, and thus a deduction should have been made on that account. Reading the description of the items from the exhibit there would appear to be merit in this submission. However, the respondent assured us that the appellants were pressed to present a list of items referable to waste. When this exhibit was eventually presented by the appellants listing the items totalling $61,254.22, the master made a decision and then permitted further argument, followed by a confirmation of his original decision. The first time any attempt has been made to separate items that belong in a different category has been before this court. We were also assured by the respondent that there are other repair accounts for the same period that represent the other category of ordinary repairs. Counsel for the appellants was unable to confirm or refute what we were told by counsel for the respondent.

This is obviously a factual area that we should not delve into at this second level of review. The evidence indicates that the buildings had deteriorated to the point where advisers said they could not be sold without refurbishing and the amount is not a surprising one in that context.

For these reasons it is my view that the appeal should be dismissed with costs.

NOTE

Leave to appeal to the Supreme Court of Canada was refused: (1993) 103 D.L.R. (4th) vi (S.C.C.).

North American Trust Co. v. Consumers' Gas Co.
1997 CarswellOnt 1827, 147 D.L.R. (4th) 645 (C.A.)

Finlayson J.A.:

The appellant North American Trust Company, formerly known as First City Trust Company, appeals in part the judgment of the Honourable Mr. Justice O'Driscoll of the Ontario Court (General Division) wherein he dismissed an application for an injunction restraining the respondent Consumers' Gas Company ("Consumers") from turning off or otherwise refusing to supply gas to certain premises in the City of Toronto upon which the appellant held mortgages that had gone into default. He granted the injunction with respect to premises referred to by the parties as the Balliol properties.

The distinction in the judgment below and the issues in this appeal relate to the difference as between the position of a mortgagee that has exercised a power under its mortgage and appointed a receiver and manager to assume control over the mortgaged property and the position of a mortgagee that has gone into possession of the property. In the case of a receiver and manager that is appointed as agent of the mortgagor, the mortgagor's occupation of the mortgaged property is deemed to continue. As a consequence, any outstanding debts to utility companies such as the respondent Consumers' Gas are also deemed to continue. If the arrears are not paid, the utility can discontinue service on the authority of s. 59 of the *Public Utilities Act*, R.S.O. 1990, c. P.52. On the other hand, a mortgagee in possession is deemed to be a new entity unburdened by prior commitments of the mortgagor and it is entitled to insist upon a new contract with the utility under the provisions of s. 55 of the *Public Utilities Act.*

The appellant submits that the appointment of a receiver is a separate remedy available to a mortgagee in possession. The remedies are not mutually exclusive and therefore, the appellant submits that, as mortgagee in possession, it is entitled to require Consumers' Gas to continue to supply gas to the properties in question.

Overview

The appellant was one of a number of lending institutions holding mortgages on an assortment of buildings containing residential apartment units, townhouse units, and/or commercial rental space. The owners and mortgagors were either one Kurt Pieckenhagen or corporations managed and controlled by him. The municipal addresses of the various buildings are 221 and 265 Balliol (the "Balliol properties"), 4000 and 4010 Lawrence Avenue (the "Lawrence Avenue properties"), 50, 100 and 150 Graydon Hall (the "Graydon Hall properties"), 10, 20, 30 and 40 Tuxedo Court (the "Tuxedo Hall properties") and 1436–1494 Avenue Road (the "Avenue Road properties"). All of the appellant's mortgages went into default and on April 28, 1993, the appellant took direct enforcement proceedings with respect to each of the above properties.

With the exception of the Balliol properties, the mortgages provided that the appellant as chargee was entitled at any time and from time to time where there was default under the provisions of the charge, and with or without entering into possession of the said lands, to appoint in writing a receiver, or a receiver and manager, or a receiver-manager, or a trustee (hereinafter "receiver"). These mortgage provisions granted sweeping powers to the receiver, including, without limitation, the power to manage, charge, lease and/or sell the lands, completely or partially, complete any construction thereon and receive advances of monies pursuant to security placed thereon. Each receiver and manager so appointed was given the further power to operate, repair, alter or extend the lands or any part thereof, and to execute or do all acts and things necessary to be done in respect of the lands and to commence, institute and prosecute all actions and other proceedings which may be necessary in respect of the lands.

The language in the mortgage documents containing a power to appoint a receiver differed in some respects from property to property, but all made clear (a) that in making the appointment of the receiver, the chargee was deemed to be acting as the agent or attorney of the chargor; (b) that the receiver was deemed to be the agent or attorney of the chargor in all instances relevant to this appeal; and (c) the appointment of the receiver did not have the effect of constituting the chargee as chargee in possession in respect of the lands or any part thereof.

The appellant appointed receivers under its mortgages where it was entitled to do so. The appointments contained no limiting language. At the same time, the appellant sent out direct notices to the tenants of the premises advising them that the appellant's mortgage was in default and instructing the tenant to make all rental payments to the named receiver "in trust for the North American Trust Company". In the same notice, the appellant also advised the tenant that the named trustee aforesaid was appointed "Receiver-Manager" of the premises in question.

In an affidavit of the Vice President of the Realty Financial Advisory Services Group of the appellant that was filed in support of the application before O'Driscoll J., the affiant asserted that the appellant was a mortgagee in possession with respect to all of the properties and as such was not responsible to the respondent Consumers' Gas for arrears of utility bills incurred by the owner/mortgagor of the various premises. The affiant further stated that the appellant decided to appoint the various receivers, where it was possible to do so, in addition to becoming a mortgagee in possession, in order to allow it to have certain additional rights that were not available solely to a mortgagee in possession. The purpose, therefore, in having the receivers was to allow the appellant to increase its powers and rights. The affiant recited the following examples of the practical issues a receiver could deal with which could not be dealt with solely by the appellant as mortgagee in possession.

> 1. Under the recent amendments to the Bankruptcy Act [sic], North American Trust Company, in taking over management of these properties would be considered a "receiver" for the purpose of notice and reporting provisions of that legislation. North American Trust is not directly equipped to provide the reports on an in-house basis and wished to employ the services of a receiver manager so that the reports would be issued in the name of the receiver manager.
>
> 2. A mortgagee in possession does not have the direct power to make improvements or modifications to any of the properties. In order to maximize the cash flow generated in each of these buildings, North American Trust required the additional power to be able to spend money by means of improvements.
>
> 3. North American Trust wanted the ability to enforce contracts, judgments and other benefits which were held on behalf of the mortgagor.

It was the position of the appellant that it became a mortgagee in possession of the subject properties and as such, was not liable to pay the arrears accumulated by the registered owners of the properties for the supply of gas from the respondent. It further asserted that it was entitled to open a new account with the respondent and pay for the supply of gas from the date upon which it became the mortgagee in possession. O'Driscoll J. held that with respect to the properties other than the Balliol properties, the mortgage documents contained a deemed agency clause constituting the receiver as the agent of the mortgagor or chargor that prevented the appellant from being a mortgagee in possession. Accordingly, the receiver was liable to the respondent Consumers' Gas for arrears of gas utility bills and the appellant was not entitled to an injunction restraining Consumers' Gas from discontinuing the supply of the utility.

With respect to the Balliol properties, the mortgage documents did not contain provisions permitting the appointment of a receiver and manager. The appellant entered into a property management agreement addressing issues relating to the control and management of the Balliol properties. O'Driscoll J. held that the manager was not deemed to be the manager of the mortgagor and the appellant was correct in its assertion that it was a mortgagee in possession. As a result, O'Driscoll J. prevented the respondent Consumers' Gas from terminating the supply of gas in respect of the Balliol properties. This portion of the judgment of O'Driscoll J. is not under appeal.

Analysis

As previously indicated, it is the position of the appellant that it was a mortgagee in possession by reason of its actions following default by the respective mortgagors. As a mortgagee in possession, it was not responsible for prior accounts of the mortgagor with the respondent Consumers' Gas. Counsel relies upon *Syncap Credit Corp. v. Consumers' Gas Co.* (1978), 18 O.R. (2d) 633 (H.C.) for the proposition that a mortgagee in possession is entitled to the supply of public utilities, including gas, electricity and water despite unpaid arrears owing by the owner of the premises. The mortgagee occupies the premises in its own right. It is there to protect its security and cannot be compelled directly or indirectly to pay the debts of the owner. The affirmative obligation to supply the utility is contained in the *Public Utilities Act*, R.S.O. 1970, c. 390; identical in its terms to the present Act for all purposes of this appeal.

The appellant also relied upon a precedent of its own making. In 1992, its predecessor, First City Trust Company, was involved in a similar situation with Consumers' Gas: see *First City Trust Co. v. Consumers' Gas Co.* (1992), 14 C.B.R. (3d) 275 (Ont. Gen. Div.). Austin J. held that the liability of the trust company depended upon whether it was a mortgagee in possession or was in control through a receiver and manager. He held that the trust company was not a mortgagee in possession because the receiver and manager was the occupant as agent of the mortgagor. In the circumstances, Consumers' Gas was entitled to discontinue service unless its arrears for gas service were paid. The appellant contends in this court that it has circumvented this judgment by becoming the mortgagee in possession. This analysis is directed to determining if that is so.

It is conceded that the charge, in each case, authorized the appellant "with or without entering into possession of the said lands" to appoint in writing a receiver of the "said lands". Additionally, there was no limitation in the appointment of the named receivers. It is also conceded as a matter of law, and under the terms of the mortgages that contained the power to appoint a receiver, that the receiver is deemed to be acting as the agent or attorney for the mortgagor. As such, it is responsible for the payment of all arrears of utility charges by the mortgagee to Consumers' Gas: see *Peat Marwick Ltd. v. Consumers' Gas Co.* (1980), 29 O.R. (2d) 336 (C.A.).

In my view, the appellant's position that it can invoke both its power to go into possession and at the same time appoint a receiver with very broad and overlapping powers is untenable. In asserting that it is the mortgagee in possession for some purposes and that the receiver is managing the properties for other purposes, the appellant is attempting to maintain a control over the activities of the receivers that is inconsistent with the duties that the receiver has to both the mortgagee and the mortgagor.

These duties were discussed by Houlden J.A. in *Peat Marwick*, *supra*, at p. 344. There the creditor bank under a floating charge debenture appointed Peat Marwick as receiver and manager of the debtor company called Rigidflex and instructed it to take possession of the debtor company's premises and proceed to liquidate its assets covered by the bank's security. The clause listing the powers of the receiver stated that it "shall for all purposes be deemed to be the agent of the Company and not of the Bank, and the Company shall be solely responsible for his acts or defaults and for his remuneration".

Once again, a problem arose with respect to the arrears of gas utility bills owed to Consumers' Gas. The argument on behalf of the receiver was that it was in reality the agent of the bank. The purpose of the clause quoted above was to enable the receiver to bring proceedings in the name of the debtor to realize upon its assets covered by the debenture. It was in this connection that Houlden J.A. stated at p. 344:

> It seems to me that the receiver and manager in a situation, like the present, is wearing two hats. When wearing one hat, he is the agent of the debtor company; when wearing the other, the agent of the debenture holder. In occupying the premises of the debtor and in carrying on the business, the receiver and manager acts as the agent of the debtor company. In realizing the security of the debenture holder, notwithstanding the language of the debenture, he acts as the agent of the debenture holder, and thus is able to confer title on a purchaser free of encumbrance.

In the case in appeal, the appellant as mortgagee was not obliged to appoint a receiver. It was only one avenue of relief available to it upon default by the mortgagee. However, as was stated by Houlden J.A. in *Peat Marwick*, *supra*, at p. 346:

> If the Court were to hold, as Mr. Thomson [counsel for the receiver] has submitted, that the receiver and manager was the agent of the bank, and hence not liable for the amount owing for gas supplied prior to the appointment of the receiver and manager, then it would, as I see it, give the bank the best of both worlds. If the receiver and manager became involved in some difficulty, the bank, to avoid liability, could claim that the receiver and manager was the agent of the debtor company: see Fraser and Stewart, [*Company Law of Canada*, 5th ed. (1962)]. If, however, there were amounts owing for public utilities supplied prior to the appointment of the receiver and manager, the bank, to avoid liability, could claim that the receiver and manager was its agent.

> If the bank chooses to provide in its debenture that the receiver and manager shall be deemed to be the agent of the debtor company, then it must not only take the benefits, but it must also accept the detriments which flow from such a provision. The gas was supplied to Rigidflex. The bank took possession of the premises as the agent of Rigidflex and did not pay the arrears owing for gas supplied to Rigidflex. Consumers' Gas was, therefore, entitled to exercise the powers given to it by s. 59 of the *Public Utilities Act* and to terminate the supply of gas.

I think that it is evident that the appellant is professing to proceed as mortgagee in possession, despite the language of the security instrument upon which it relies, for the sole purpose of avoiding past debts of creditors such as Consumers' Gas. At the same time, it acknowledges that it requires the appointment of a receiver to take advantage of beneficial contracts of the mortgagors, to make improvements or modifications to the mortgaged premises, and to provide certain reporting services as a deemed "receiver" under the *Bankruptcy and Insolvency Act*, R.S.C. 1985, c. B-3, which it was not in a position to provide itself. I do not think it can play such a game. Intention alone is not sufficient to constitute a mortgagee as a mortgagee in possession. Taking possession is not a question of intention but of fact and collecting rents is not conclusive on this issue: see *Noyes v. Pollock* (1886), 32 Ch. D. 53 (Eng. C.A.). The reality of this factual situation is that the receivers have taken possession of the mortgaged premises as agents of the mortgagor in order to take full advantage of the larger powers of a receiver in possession as opposed to a mortgagee in possession. They may still have obligations to the mortgagee that appointed them, but they are agents of the mortgagors so far as Consumers' Gas is concerned.

In my opinion, the trial judge was correct in his disposition of this case. I would dismiss the appeal with costs.

NOTE

For more on the duties of a receiver, see *Medforth v. Blake*, below.

(d) foreclosure (and redemption)

> In *Campbell v. Holyland*, 7 Ch. D. 166, at p. 171, Jessel M.R. says: "The principle in a Court of equity has always been that, though a mortgage is in form an absolute conveyance when the condition is broken, in equity it is always security; and it must be remembered that the doctrine arose at the time when mortgages were made in the form of conditional conveyance, the condition being that, if the money was not paid at the day, the estate should become the estate of the mortgagee; that was the contract between the parties; yet Courts of equity interfered with actual contract to this extent, by saying there was a paramount intention that the estate should be security, and that the mortgage-money should be debt; and they gave relief in the shape of redemption on that principle. Of course, that would lead, and did lead, to this inconvenience, that, even when the mortgagor was not willing to redeem, the mortgagee could not sell or deal with the estate as his own; and, to remedy that inconvenience, the practice of bringing a foreclosure suit was adopted, by which a mortgagee was entitled to call on the mortgagor to redeem within a certain time, under penalty of losing the right of redemption. In that foreclosure

> suit the Court made various orders — interim orders fixing a time for payment of the money — and at last there came the final order, which was called foreclosure absolute; that is, in form, that the mortgagor should not be allowed to redeem at all; but it was form only, just as the original deed was form only; for the Courts of equity soon decided that, notwithstanding the form of that order, they would after that order allow the mortgagor to redeem. That is, although the order of foreclosure absolute appeared to be a final order of the Court, it was not so, but the mortgagee still remained liable to be treated as mortgagee, and the mortgagor still retained a claim to be treated as mortgagor, subject to the discretion of the Court. Therefore, everybody who took an order for foreclosure absolute knew that there was still a discretion in the Court to allow the mortgagor to redeem.

Quoted in *Noble v. Campbell* 1911 CarswellMan 114 (K.B.) at para. 9.

Just as equity gave birth to the right of redemption even after the "law day" for payment of the debt had come and gone, so too did it devise a means of bringing the equity of redemption to an end. After all, the mortgagee could not be expected to wait forever to be repaid. If the law day was not the end of the matter, the point of no return, then what was? The answer is this: proceedings could be launched with a view to foreclosing off the equity of redemption; that is, extinguishing it. Procedures now exist in all Canadian common law jurisdictions to do just that, all of which can be traced to the protocols initially created in the Chancery to bring the right to redeem to an end. These processes are designed to give the mortgagor every possible chance to stave off final foreclosure. Moreover, as we will see, even a final order of foreclosure is not necessarily final!

The results of obtaining and maintaining a final order of foreclosure are drastic. Not only is the equity of redemption extinguished, but all interests built on that equity will also die. Assume, for example, that there are two mortgages on Blackacre. Default occurs on the first, and the first mortgagee elects to commence foreclosure proceedings. If the action is brought to completion the first mortgagee will wind up with Blackacre free and clear: free even from the second mortgage. It was, in effect, a mortgage of the equity of redemption only, and so dies once that equity is destroyed.

If the second mortgagee wishes to preserve its position it may choose to pay off the first mortgagee, redeeming the land. It can then seek reimbursement for those payments from the mortgagor. In short, one can foreclose down against all subordinate interests. Those subordinate interest holders may redeem up, if they choose to do so.

It can be seen that foreclosure and redemption go hand in hand. One is entitled to redeem (a) when the agreement allows; (b) when, due to the invocation of an acceleration clause, the full payment is demanded; or (c) whenever the mortgagee "resorts to the security", i.e., seeks to take action to draw on the land as security. The contours of this latter situation are considered in *Shankman v. Mutual Life Assurance Co. of Canada*, immediately below.

Shankman v. Mutual Life Assurance Co. of Canada 1985 CarswellOnt 719, 21 D.L.R. (4th) 131 (C.A.)

Cory J.A.:

High and fluctuating interest rates have created instability in mortgage transactions. Mortgagors who at one time were happy to obtain mortgage loans no matter how high the interest rates have become disenchanted with their lot as interest rates fall. Mortgagors are now endeavouring to extricate themselves from their commitments while mortgagees struggle to hold the bargain. The manoeuvring of mortgagors and mortgagees has been reflected in recent decisions of the Courts dealing with the legal ramifications of mortgage contracts. This appeal is concerned with just such an issue.

Factual background

On December 18, 1981, the Cadillac Fairview Corporation Limited ("Cadillac Fairview") charged the lands and premises, with which the parties are concerned, in favour of the respondent, The Mutual Life Assurance Company of Canada ("Mutual Life"). There was no provision in the charge for early redemption. The appellant, Shankman, then purchased the lands from Cadillac Fairview.

Mutual Life alleges that Shankman defaulted on all the payments that were due commencing August 1, 1983. As a result of Shankman's default, Mutual Life commenced an action in County Court claiming payment of the arrears due in the amount of $7,136 and also claimed possession of the lands which were the subject of the charge. Mutual Life made no attempt to accelerate the payment of the principal amount secured by the charge.

On December 21, 1983, Shankman tendered a cheque upon Mutual Life for $107,956.75, the amount he calculated was required for the payment of the principal, interest and taxes owing on the charge. At the same time, he asked Mutual Life to deliver a cessation of charge.

The cheque was returned by the solicitors for Mutual Life who stated that a bonus of interest for early redemption would be required.

Decision of the Motions Court Judge

Shankman brought an application for a declaration that he was entitled to pay the entire balance due on the charge without bonus or penalty. The Motions Court Judge refused to grant the application [reported at 33 R.P.R. 194]. His conclusion was set out in this way [p. 198]:

> I have come to the conclusion that this application differs from the cases wherein the mortgagee is exercising its rights under power of sale or its right to foreclose and, in my

view, the claim for possession is not taken against the security and thus the equitable right to redeem is not triggered. I base this conclusion on the fact that the phrase "resort to the security" to me means doing something which prevents the mortgagor thereafter from exercising the right to redeem. All of this learning, of course, started with the well-known decision of Mr. Justice Kekewich in *Bovill v. Endle*, [1896] 1 Ch. 648. It is the decision which leads us into the decisions to which reference has earlier been made. The fact that *Ex parte Wickens*, [1898] 1 Q.B. 543 (C.A.), and *Ex parte Ellis*, [1898] 2 Q.B. 79 (C.A.), both involved refinements of the basic principle set forth in *Bovill v. Endle* and were chattel mortgage cases does not, in my respectful submission, cause them to be disregarded so far as the present proceedings are concerned.

The appellant's position

Shankman contends that so soon as the mortgagee commenced an action for possession pending payment of the arrears, it resorted to the security of the mortgage. It is submitted that once a mortgagee "resorts to the security", then the equitable right to redemption is triggered and a mortgagor has the right to tender the full amount of the principal and interest owing on the mortgage, and the mortgagee must accept the payment in full satisfaction of the mortgage without any additional moneys being payable by way of notice or bonus.

Applicable principles upon which the parties are in agreement

Both parties agree upon the validity of the principles set out below.

(1) A charge registered under the *Land Titles Act*, R.S.O. 1980, c. 230, like a mortgage, grants a security interest in the land charged to the extent of the moneys advanced.

(2) The principal right of the mortgagee in such a situation is to repayment of the money advanced on the security of the mortgage together with the interest payable.

(3) The right of the mortgagor to redeem is inherent in the nature of a mortgage or charge. The Courts have always attached great importance to this right. They have given effect to it by enforcing the contractual right of redemption contained in the mortgage, and, as well, by giving recognition to the equitable right of redemption which will often relieve the mortgagor of some of the strict and rigorous terms of the mortgage document itself. See, for example, *Re Bank of Montreal and Sam Richman Invts. (London) Ltd.* (1973), 3 O.R. (2d) 191, 45 D.L.R. (3d) 24 (H.C.).

(4) The mortgagor cannot by contract waive or set aside his equitable right of redemption. See *Mun. Savings & Loan Corp. v. Wilson* (1981), 20 R.P.R. 188, 127 D.L.R. (3d) 127 (Ont. C.A.).

(5) A mortgagee cannot resort to the security of the mortgage and, at the same time, assert his option to prevent redemption. This is so, for when the mortgagee resorts to the security, he triggers the mortgagor's equitable right to redeem, notwithstanding the existence of any contractual provision in the mortgage providing for the acceleration of the principal at the option of the mortgagee. *See Ex parte Wickens*, [1898] 1 Q.B. 543 (C.A.), and *Mun. Savings & Loan Corp. v. Wilson, supra.*

For the purposes of this case, it was conceded that an action seeking possession of the premises was tantamount to the mortgagee taking physical possession of them.

From this point, the views of the litigants diverge. It remains to be determined what constitutes "resort to security" and whether, on the facts of this case, the mortgagee resorted to its security.

Examples of actions by mortgagees which have been held to constitute a resort to the security

It is useful, as a point of commencement, to consider cases where the Courts have determined that the mortgagee did in fact resort to the security.

In *Bovill v. Endle*, [1896] 1 Ch. 648, Kekewich J. considered the effect of a mortgagee taking possession of the mortgaged property. He first observed that when a mortgagee takes proceedings in Court to recover his mortgage money from the mortgagor, he cannot refuse tender of the principal and interest on the grounds that he is entitled to six months' notice or interest. He quoted the rule to be (at p. 651):

> If the mortgagee has himself demanded payment of the debt, or has taken any steps to compel payment of it, no notice by the mortgagor, and no payment of interest in lieu of notice, is required.

and then posed the question, "Is entering into possession taking proceedings with a view to compelling payment of the debt?" He answered the question affirmatively and stated (at p. 651):

> The mortgagee, in taking possession, exercises his legal right, but does not directly ask for payment. He says: "The houses will not be completed within the time or in a satisfactory manner except by my taking possession: I will run all risk in order to assert my legal rights" It appears to me that, although the case is not actually covered by authority, yet it is by principle; and that a mortgagee cannot enter into possession for his own benefit and then say he is entitled to remain in the position of a mortgagee out of possession, and to ask for six months' notice or interest. The two positions are inconsistent. In my opinion, by entering into possession the mortgagee says he requires payment, and payment in the way in which the law gives it to him.

It is to be noted that the mortgagee in the *Bovill* case physically took possession of two houses and expended funds to complete them and, upon completion, rented the premises. There can be no doubt that the mortgagee took possession of the premises not just to collect the arrears owing but to secure payment of the entire amount of the principal, interest and costs owing on the mortgage. It was this entire amount which was tendered by the mortgagor in satisfaction of the mortgage and which Kekewich J. deemed to be sufficient.

In *Ex parte Wickens*, *supra*, the English Court of Appeal considered a similar problem and came to the same conclusion. Once again, it should be observed that the bill of sale holder, (who was determined to be in a position analogous to that of a mortgagee), demanded payment of the entire principal sum with interest. The bailiff in possession advised that he would remain in possession until the full amount claimed was paid. These actions were found to constitute resorting to the security by the mortgagee.

These cases have both been cited with approval by this Court in *Mun. Savings & Loan v. Wilson, supra.* It can then be seen that if a mortgagee takes possession of the mortgaged property in order to obtain payment of his entire mortgage debt, such an action constitutes a "resort to the security".

What is the consequence of a mortgagee serving a notice of sale on the mortgagor pursuant to the power of sale provisions contained in the mortgage? This question was considered in the *Mun. Savings & Loan* case, *supra.* There, the mortgage provided for monthly payments of interest only until maturity. The mortgage contained no right to prepay principal. The mortgagor defaulted on several monthly interest payments. The mortgagee served notice of sale pursuant to the power of sale provisions contained in the mortgage. The mortgagor then tendered the entire balance due on the mortgage for principal, interest and costs and applied for an order discharging the mortgage. The Judge of first instance refused the order. This decision was reversed by the Court of Appeal.

Counsel for Shankman relied heavily upon this decision. However, it is evident that the case turned primarily on the effect of exercising the power of sale by service of notice. It was stressed that the mortgage could not survive the exercise of the power of sale. That is so, for what is to be sold is the mortgaged land itself. Once the sale is completed, the mortgagor's interest is foreclosed unless equity steps in to prevent the sale. Wilson J.A., in the reasons of the Court, expressed the principle in this way at pp. 193-94 [R.P.R.]:

> The real problem lies in the effect of the power of sale. Can a mortgagee exercise a power of sale without giving the mortgagor an opportunity to redeem? . . .
>
> The mortgage cannot therefore survive the exercise of such a power for what is authorized to be sold is the mortgaged land itself, the security for the debt. All the mortgagor is entitled to is the surplus proceeds of the sale. His interest in the land is gone. The mortgagee cannot convey the land subject to the mortgagor's interest because the very act of selling forecloses that interest unless equity steps in to prevent the sale and indeed, this is why equity steps in to prevent the sale.

The decision is not applicable to the facts of this case.

The foregoing authorities indicate two situations where the actions of the mortgagee constitute resorting to the security. First, when a mortgagee gives a notice of sale pursuant to the power of sale provisions contained in the mortgage, he takes a step that constitutes resorting to the security. Secondly, a mortgagee who takes possession in the course of seeking to collect the entire amount of the principal and interest owing on the mortgage is also taking a step that constitutes resorting to the security.

The question remains whether taking possession to recover payment of the arrears only and not the entire amount of the debt secured by the mortgage also constitutes resorting to the security. I think it does not.

Examples of actions by mortgagees which have been held not to constitute a resort to security

It is useful to start with *Ex parte Ellis*, [1898] 2 Q.B. 79, an English Court of Appeal decision that was also cited with approval by this Court in the *Mun. Savings & Loan* case, *supra.* Ellis dealt with a bill of sale. The Court specifically held that the situation was, once again, analogous to that of a mortgagor/mortgagee relationship. The bill of sale provided that the principal sum secured was payable at the end of two years with monthly payments to be made on account of interest. When a monthly payment of interest was in arrears, the grantee of the bill of sale took possession of the goods assigned as security for the purpose of holding them until the payment of interest due was made but not for the purpose of realizing the principal sum secured. The Court determined that in these circumstances the mortgagee had not resorted to the security. *Ex parte Wickens, supra,* was considered and distinguished. It was pointed out that the grantee (mortgagee) was doing no more than protecting his security when he took possession of the goods. Smith L.J. put it in this way at pp. 81-82:

> *Ex parte Wickens* [[1898] 1 Q.B. 543] is no authority as to the present case. It was there held that, where the holder of a bill of sale took possession of the goods, not for the purpose of maintaining his security, but for the purpose of realizing it by the sale of the goods, the rule of equity applicable to the case of a mortgagee seeking to realize his security applied, and the judge had jurisdiction to order that the security should be given up on payment of the principal with interest up to date and costs. The present case is not within that decision. I do not think that an order can be made that the bill of sale shall be given up where the grantee has seized for the purpose of maintaining and not of realizing his security. It would be a great hardship on him if it were otherwise. He has a contract whereby, in consideration of his lending a sum of money for a certain time, the grantor agrees to pay interest at a certain rate for that period. If the law were as contended for by the grantor the grantee could take no step to maintain his security or enforce payment of interest in arrear without running the risk of being paid off and having the contract to pay interest during the rest of the period vacated. On the other hand, if the grantee seizes the goods for the purpose of realizing the security by sale of them, it is no hardship on him that on payment of the principal, interest up to date, and costs, he should be ordered to give up the security. For these reasons I think the appeal should be allowed.

Vaughan Williams L.J. concurred in the result and expressed his reasons in this manner at p. 82:

> Chitty L.J., in dealing with the equitable doctrine applicable to such cases, said: "It may be a question whether, upon a demand for production of the last receipt for rent and upon failure without reasonable excuse to comply with that demand, and an entry into possession in consequence, the grantee may not maintain that he entered for the purpose of protecting his security. But I have no hesitation in saying that the seizure in this case was for the purpose of realizing the security — in other words, for the purpose of enforcing payment. It is clear beyond doubt in equity that, if a mortgagee takes proceed-

ings to enforce his security, the mortgagor can at once tender the principal, interest, and costs, and is absolved from the obligation of giving six months' notice to pay off the mortgage, or of paying six months' interest in lieu of notice." I gather from that passage in his judgment that, according to his view, if the seizure had been for the purpose of merely protecting the security, the equitable doctrine would not have applied, by which the mortgagor is entitled upon the mortgagee's taking steps to realize his security to have the security given up on payment of principal, interest due, and costs. I draw the same inference from the judgments delivered by my brothers A.L. Smith and Collins.

This case is authority for the proposition that if the mortgagee seizes the mortgaged property not to realize on the *entire* mortgage but rather to protect his security by enforcing the payment of the arrears only, then his action will not be deemed to be a resort to the security. The facts in the Ellis case bear a very close resemblance to those presented in the case at Bar.

Two recent decisions of the Court of Appeal of British Columbia lend support to the conclusion I have reached. The first is *Cameo Devs. Ltd. v. Nat. Life Assur. Co. of Can.* (1984), 56 B.C.L.R. 363. In that case, the mortgagor stopped making the monthly mortgage payments on April 1, 1983. Pursuant to a mortgage provision, the mortgagee appointed a receiver in June of 1983 to recover the income from the lessee of the mortgaged premises. The mortgagor then took the position that the mortgagee, through its agent the receiver, had gone into possession. As a result of the mortgagee going into possession, the mortgagor claimed to be entitled to equitable redemption upon payment of the full amount of principal outstanding together with the interest owing. The Judge of first instance gave effect to the mortgagor's position.

The Court of Appeal reversed that finding. The earlier cases of *Bovill v. Endle* and *Re Bank of Montreal and Sam Richman Investments*, *supra*, were considered but, nonetheless, it was decided that before the equitable right to redemption arose, the onus lay upon the mortgagor to show that the mortgagee had gone into possession for the purpose of realizing upon the security with an aim to recovering all the principal outstanding, together with interest. The Court determined that this onus had not been satisfied. The following appears in the reasons of Carrothers J.A., speaking for the Court at p. 368:

In either event, the agency of the receiver is not determinative of the matter of the mortgagor's equitable right of redemption. In order to trigger an equitable right of redemption in the mortgagor as a result of the mortgagee going into possession, the onus is upon the mortgagor to establish that a mortgagee has gone into possession for the purpose of realizing upon the security of the mortgaged premises *in order to recover the principal outstanding under the mortgage together with interest*. Here, in my view, this onus has not been satisfied.

The nature of that obligation is discussed in the cases of *Noyes v. Pollock* (1886), 32 Ch. D. 53 (C.A.); *Bovill v. Endle*, [1896] 1 Ch. D. 648; *Beckstead v. Ball*, [1961] O.R. 127, 26 D.L.R. (2d) 374 (H.C.); and *Re Bank of Montreal and Sam Richman Invt. (London) Ltd.* (1973), 3 O.R. (2d) 191, 45 D.L.R. (3d) 24 (H.C.).

> The mortgagee has taken no steps whatever by way of demand, or otherwise, to foreclose upon its mortgage and clearly has not gone into possession in the manner necessary to give rise to the right of the mortgagor of equitable redemption of the mortgaged premises.
>
> In passing, I would observe, this being an equitable remedy, the mortgagor seeking equity must come to court with clean hands. Those hands appear to be blemished by the deliberate and wanton stoppage of monthly mortgage payments and the further assignment of rents in an attempt to precipitate foreclosure proceedings by the mortgagee against its own interest. (Emphasis added.)

The second decision of the same Court which is of significance is *Prudential Ins. Co. of Amer. v. Hollyburn Properties (Alta.) Ltd.*, [1985] 1 W.W.R. 500, 58 B.C.L.R. 211, 15 D.L.R. (4th) 124. In that case, the mortgagor failed to pay a percentage of the rental income as required by the mortgage document. The mortgagee brought an action claiming, *inter alia*, the rental income for 1983 and an order appointing a receiver. The mortgagors alleged that as a result of the action brought by the mortgagee, the mortgage could be redeemed upon payment of all amounts found to be due and owing under the mortgage.

The Judge of first instance held that the mortgagors did not have the right to redeem unless the mortgagee had taken steps to compel payment of the *whole* amount of the mortgage debt. He found that the mortgagee had not taken such steps. He based his decision upon the following passage from *Falconbridge on Mortgages* (4th ed., 1977), at pp. 442-43, § 23.6:

> Where the principal has become due by virtue of the mortgage contract, on default in payment of interest, the mortgagee is not bound to claim the whole accelerated sum. He may if he chooses seek to recover only the amount that has matured by lapse of time. If, however, a mortgagee takes proceedings to enforce his security, he is not entitled to refuse to accept payment of the whole amount of principal and interest, even though part of it has not matured, but if his proceedings are confined to protecting his security, as, for example, if he takes possession, he cannot be compelled to accept payment of money not yet due, as the right to accelerate payment for default is at the option of the mortgagee.

The Court of Appeal upheld the decision of the Judge of first instance. Craig J.A., giving the reasons for the Court, found that the steps taken by the mortgagee did not amount to an enforcement of its security but, rather, indicated an intention to simply protect that security.

These recent cases of the British Columbia Court of Appeal indicate that an action instituted by a mortgagee claiming arrears which are due under the mortgage and seeking the appointment of a receiver to collect those arrears does not amount to a resorting to the security. That reasoning is applicable to the case at Bar.

Conclusion

There can be no difference between a mortgagee who is seeking no more than the payment of arrears through the appointment of a receiver and a mortgagee seeking the same relief by taking possession personally. It should not and cannot make any difference in the result whether the mortgagee acts directly and personally to take possession to collect the arrears or does so by or through his agent, the receiver. So long as the claim of the mortgagee is limited to the arrears owing on the mortgage, then taking possession of the mortgaged property for that limited purpose amounts to no more than protecting the security. It does not constitute a resort to that security.

In my view, the Motions Court Judge was correct in his conclusion. Accordingly, I would dismiss the appeal with costs.

Appeal dismissed.

QUESTIONS AND COMMENTS

1. What is the effect of foreclosure on leases of the mortgaged land? See *1420111 Ontario Ltd. v. Paramount Pictures (Canada) Inc.* 2001 CarswellOnt 4067, 56 O.R. (3d) 447 (S.C.J.) at paras. 9-11 (*per* Mesbur J.):

> The applicant's position is simple. It relies on the distinction between leases entered into before and after a mortgage. Here, the offer to lease was entered into before the mortgage. Since Famous Players went into possession, its offer to lease was no longer executory, but became a binding tenancy. The offer contains sufficient particularity to make it a binding lease. There was thus a binding lease in existence prior to the mortgage to Imperial Life. *Falconbridge* [W.B. Rayner & R.H. McLaren, *Falconbridge on Mortgages*, 4 th ed. (Agincourt: Canada Law Book, 1977)] discusses the distinction between leases entered into before and after a mortgage. At page 320, the text states:
>
> > If the owner of land free from encumbrance grants a lease of the land, and afterwards mortgages it, the mortgage affects merely the reversion retained by the mortgagor. The right of the lessee to possession in such case is paramount, and the rights of the mortgagee to possession and to have recourse to the land for recovery of the mortgage money are subject to the right of the lessee. A legal mortgagee becomes, however, the owner of the reversion subject to the mortgagor's right to redeem, and when the mortgagee becomes entitled to possession as against the mortgagor he may compel the tenant to pay rent to him instead of the mortgagor.
>
> *Falconbridge* goes on to say the effect of a mortgage granted after a lease is to convey the reversion to the mortgagee, and no attornment of the part of the tenant is necessary in order to create the relation of landlord and tenant.
>
> However, if a lease is granted after a mortgage, without the mortgagee's authority, the lease is merely a partial transfer of the equity of redemption. The mortgagee's rights are paramount, and the tenant's right to possession is subject to the mortgagee's right to take possession, and to have recourse to the land for recovery of the mortgage money. As the Court of Appeal held in *Goodyear Canada Inc. v. Burnhamthorpe Square Inc.*, [[1998] O.J. No. 4426 (Ont. C.A.)] the leasehold interest created after the date of the mortgage was terminated when the mortgagee took possession of the premises.

2. Absent statutory protection, a post-mortgage lease of residential premises is subject to the same rule of priority. To bolster a residential tenant's security of tenure, Ontario law now provides as follows:

> 47.(1) A person who becomes the mortgagee in possession of a mortgaged residential complex which is the subject of a tenancy agreement between the mortgagor and a tenant or who obtains title to the residential complex by foreclosure or power of sale shall be deemed to be the landlord under the tenancy agreement. . . .
>
> 48.(1) No person exercising rights under a mortgage may obtain possession of a rental unit from the mortgagor's tenant except in accordance with the *Tenant Protection Act*, 1997. (1997, c. 24, s. 215 (9))

Mortgages Act, R.S.O. 1990, c. M.40.

3. Can a tenant of mortgaged lands redeem? See *Martin v. Miles* (1883) 5 O.R. 404 (C.A.).

355498 B.C. Ltd. v. Namu Properties Ltd. 1998 CarswellBC 2815 (S.C.)

Scarth J.:

On June 15, 1998 I pronounced the following order:

> [1] The application of the respondent Namu Properties Ltd. for an order reopening the Order Absolute of Foreclosure granted in these proceedings on November 27, 1997 and reconveying the lands and premises the subject of these proceedings to the said respondent, all as set out in the notice of motion filed on March 16, 1998, is granted on the terms set out in the proposed form of order attached to the amended memorandum of argument of the respondent Namu Properties Ltd. with liberty to counsel to speak to said terms.

On June 24th counsel for the petitioner and respondents spoke to the terms of the order.

The reasons which follow are the reasons for the order made on June 15, 1998.

. . .

. . . *Pacific Savings & Mortgage Corp. v. Can-Corp Development Ltd.*, [1982] 4 W.W.R. 239 (B.C. C.A.) stands as authority for the proposition that a mortgagor can apply to reopen a final order of foreclosure as long as a certificate of title has not been issued to a *bona fide* purchaser for value. That is the situation which obtains here.

I turn then to a consideration of the grounds upon which a final order of foreclosure may be reopened by the Court. These are set out in the reasons for judgment of Mr. Justice Macfarlane, who delivered the judgment of the Court of Appeal, in *Ricard v. Richards* (January 27, 1986), Doc. Vancouver CA004441 (B.C. C.A.).

To succeed on an application to reopen a final order of foreclose the applicant must show that:

> 1. the application was made with reasonable promptness having regard to all the circumstances of the case;
>
> 2. there must be a reasonable prospect of payment at once or within a short period of time;
>
> 3. the applicant has been active in endeavouring to raise the money necessary and that by reason of some unforseen circumstances he was not able to redeem within the time appointed;
>
> 4. the applicant has a substantial interest in the mortgaged premises or the property has some special intrinsic value so far as he is concerned;
>
> 5. special circumstances exist which Justify the reopening of the foreclosure or, to paraphrase the language used in some of the older authorities, the equities in favour of reopening the order absolute strongly outweigh the equities against reopening the order.

Applying those factors to the present case it is plain that three months elapsed between the time the order absolute was filed on December 11, 1997 and the application to reopen that order was filed on March 16, 1998. It is apparent from the material that Namu, during the month of October, 1997, anticipated that it would be able to borrow funds from related companies and pay out the balance of the mortgage in full by November 30, 1997. Namu's expectation in that regard is corroborated by the fact that on October 31st it made the $100,000 payment on account of principal. One source of the anticipated funds was Sonora Logging Ltd. which, through a related company, had loaned Namu the funds required in order to make the $100,000 payment. In his affidavit sworn to May 13, 1998, Mr. Milne deposes that he:

> . . . anticipated borrowing additional funds to satisfy the balance of the indebtedness owing to the Petitioner and to settle the lien claim with Mr. Kornelson from additional funds from Sonora.

An anticipated sale of property which Sonora relied upon for the funds did not complete on December 5th. Other attempts by Namu to raise funds through a mortgage broker were unsuccessful. The sale by Sonora completed at the end of February, 1998 and, by March 13th, Namu's present solicitors held in trust $235,000. By the time this application was heard Namu's solicitors had sufficient funds in trust to pay the balance owing under the mortgage together with interest and taxable costs, an additional $53,000 to cover expenses incurred by the petitioner since the order absolute was granted, and the further sum of $160,000 to obtain reinstatement of the foreshore leases.

Namu's interest in the property prior to the foreclosure was substantial. It had paid $350,000 in cash at the time it purchased the property in 1995. It subsequently made two payments of principal in the amount of $100,000 each as well as payments on account of interest. Thus, by the time application was made for the order absolute, of the original $750,000 purchase price approximately $208,000 remained unpaid.

Namu is required to show that the equities in favour of reopening the order absolute undoubtedly outweigh all that are against it.

The petitioner has valid grounds of complaint. Namu allowed the foreshore leases to be cancelled with the result the principals of 355498 B.C. Ltd. are exposed to liability on their guarantees to the extent of $100,000 and the value of the property diminished. Namu also allowed a water licence, waste management permit and grant of mineral rights to expire. Prior to foreclosure occurring Namu not only failed to make the payments when due under the mortgage, it failed to comply with orders of the Court in that regard. Namu has also allowed waste to occur on the property with respect to the water system, buildings and boardwalks.

In my judgement, however, the equities in favour of reopening the foreclosure undoubtedly outweigh those against it. First of all, Namu's equity in the property represents approximately 75 percent of the value of the property based on the sale price of $750,000. Insofar as its investment in the property was concerned the petitioner was never at risk.

Second of all Namu continued to make payments on account of the mortgage, including a payment of principal in the amount of $100,000, after the order *nisi* was granted on November 12, 1996, all of which were accepted by the petitioner.

Thirdly, Namu's solicitors hold sufficient funds in trust to satisfy the balance owing under the mortgage including interest and petitioner's costs. Arrangements have been made to satisfy the builders lien although, in practical terms, it did not pose a threat to the petitioner particularly given the fact that the claim only amounted to about $16,000 and was subordinate to the mortgage.

Fourthly, any expense incurred by the petitioner in relation to the property after it obtained title under the order of foreclosure can be determined. Namu is prepared to pay those expenses after they have been determined, if necessary by the Court.

Fifthly, the material in essence establishes that the petitioner seeks only to sell the property. On such a sale the petitioner would take the benefit not only of any improvements made by Namu over the last three years but also the benefit of the large payments of principal it has made, in effect "reaping the benefit of a windfall". In the words of Mr. Justice Meredith in *Caromar Sales Ltd. v. Konzepta Real Estate Ltd.* (July 25, 1991), Doc. Vancouver H900710 (B.C. S.C.):

> To allow the final order to stand would bestow on the petitioner a double recovery of some principal: that is to say, the portion of the payments already made by the respondents

in reduction of principal will be received again when the petitioner disposes of the property.

In my judgment the equities on the side of Namu far outweigh those on the side of 355498 B.C. Ltd.

Accordingly the order will go as indicated above. My decision with respect to the form of order will follow.

Application granted.

NOTE

The order of Scarth J. was affirmed on appeal: *355498 B.C. Ltd. v. Namu Properties Ltd.* 1999 CarswellBC 472 (C.A.). Hall J.A., at para. 17, concluded:

> I consider that the decision of the learned chambers judge to permit the re-opening of the foreclosure was appropriate. As the chambers judge pointed out, the interest of the respondent in the property was substantial, it having paid $550,000 plus interest on the original mortgage debt of $750,000. The learned chambers judge observed that although the appellant had grounds for complaint about delay and non-performance on the part of the respondent, yet when all the equities were considered, it was a case in which it was appropriate to order that the foreclosure be opened and that the respondent be permitted to redeem. The chambers judge found, correctly in my view, that the appellant could be fully compensated and indemnified for any expenses it had been or might in future be put to and observed that if the order absolute was allowed to stand, the appellant would in effect would be reaping a "windfall". I am not disposed to differ from the comprehensive analysis and conclusion of the chambers judge. In my opinion, it was appropriate for the chambers judge to exercise the jurisdiction he undoubtedly possessed to allow the respondent to re-open the foreclosure and redeem on the terms he ordered. In those circumstances, I would therefore dismiss this appeal.

(e) sale

A sale of the mortgaged property is a remedy often considered of greatest practical value to a lender because it involves fewer complications than that associated with taking possession, receivership, foreclosure and action on the covenant. The ability to liquidate the security to recover the amounts owing is, in reality, the reason why that security was sought by the lender in the first place.

There are two main types of mortgage sales: judicial and contractual. In the former case, the conduct of the sale is subject to ongoing judicial supervision. In some jurisdictions, such as Alberta, this is the predominant mechanism used. Moreover, when foreclosure proceedings are commenced, they may be short-circuited by any of the parties to that proceeding, by seeking instead a judicial sale of the property. Do you see why that might often be viewed as advantageous?

A contractual power of sale is not conducted in accordance with ongoing judicial scrutiny. Yet, this is not to say that the mortgagee has free reign as to how to conduct the sale. Indeed, the following cases demonstrate some of the principles that inform the rights of those parties affected by exercise of the power of sale.

Logozzo v. Toronto Dominion Bank 1999 CarswellOnt 3477, 181 D.L.R. (4th) 221 (C.A.)

[Grann agreed to purchase a 500-acre property from the Toronto Dominion Bank (T.D.), under a power of sale contained in a mortgage between Logozzo and T.D. Prior to the closing of the sale, Logozzo attempted to redeem the property. He had arranged to sell the land to Purnell; that deal had been made subject to financing. Was Logozzo too late?

The *Mortgages Act*, R.S.O. 1990, c. M.40, sub. 22(1) states:

Despite any agreement to the contrary, where default has occurred in making any payment of principal or interest due under a mortgage or in the observance of any covenant in a mortgage and under the terms of the mortgage, by reason of such default, the whole principal and interest secured thereby has become due and payable,

(a) at any time before sale under the mortgage; or

(b) before the commencement of an action for the enforcement of the rights of the mortgagee or of any person claiming through or under the mortgagee,

the mortgagor may perform such covenant or pay the amount due under the mortgage, exclusive of the money not payable by reason merely of lapse of time, and pay any expenses necessarily incurred by the mortgagee, and thereupon the mortgagor is relieved from the consequences of such default.

The agreement of purchase and sale between Grann and TD contained the following terms, referred to below as "paragraph 2 of Schedule A":

2. It is further understood that on the date of acceptance of this offer there is default under the terms of the mortgage which entitles the Vendor to exercise the Power of Sale. The only evidence of the default, which the Purchaser may require, shall be a statutory declaration by the Vendor setting forth the facts entitling the Vendor to sell under the Power of Sale, including the particulars of the notice of exercising the Power of Sale, the names of the persons upon whom service of the notice has been effected, and declaring that default under the mortgage entitling the Vendor to exercise the Power of Sale has continued up to and including the date of acceptance of this offer and to the time of closing. *The Purchaser understands and agrees that the mortgagor has the right to redeem the property up to the time of waiver or expiration of all rights of termination or fulfillment of all conditions, and this Agreement is subject to that right. In the event of redemption, by the mortgagor, this agreement shall be null and void and only deposit monies paid will be refunded without interest.* [Emphasis added.]

At first instance Wright J. permitted Logozzo to redeem. Grann appealed.]

Borins J.A.: . . .

Analysis

In my view . . . there are a number of reasons why [Logozzo] was not entitled to redeem the land secured by the mortgage.

I

The first reason raises the issue of whether, under s. 22(1)(a) of the *Mortgages Act*, Logozzo was entitled to redeem the property after TD had entered into a binding agreement of purchase and sale with Grann.

It is common ground that absent paragraph 2 of the schedule, s. 22(1)(a) permitted Logozzo to redeem the property "at any time before sale under the mortgage". The effect of this provision is to extend the time to redeem from the time in the notice of sale — May 25, 1998 — to the time of the sale of the property pursuant to the power of sale in the Logozzo — TD mortgage. . . .

. . . The purpose of s. 21(1), of the 1970 Act, and its application, are outlined in Rayner & McLaren, *Falconbridge on Mortgages*, 4th ed., (1977) at 721-22:

> . . . [I]t permits the mortgagor to put the mortgage in good standing at any time before sale upon payment of any money due, "exclusive of the money not payable by reason merely of lapse of time" together with payments of costs. Payment must, however, be made or tendered *before an agreement for sale has been entered into by the mortgagee with a third party even where the agreement is said to be subject to the right of the mortgagor to redeem or put the mortgage into good standing. Before a mortgagor can obtain the benefit of s. 21 he must pay all arrears for such payment is a condition precedent to relief.* A vague hope of the mortgagor to find further financing, even where the security is ample is not sufficient reason to stay the sale proceedings. [Emphasis added.] . . .

Almost 90 years ago, before there was legislation on the subject, the court considered whether a mortgagor could redeem the property after the mortgagee had accepted an offer to purchase the property which was being sold under power of sale: *Standard Realty Co. v. Nicholson* (1911), 24 O.L.R. 46 (H.C.). In this case, the mortgagor presented the mortgagee with a certified cheque for the sum due on the mortgage, which the mortgagee rejected as the land was subject to an agreement of purchase and sale, which was later completed.

Riddell J. allowed the purchaser's action against the mortgagor, Nicholson, for possession of the property. It was significant to him that the purchaser had acquired rights under the contract it had entered into with the mortgagee. At p. 55 he stated:

> A binding contract for sale being entered into by the mortgagee, before any notice of any intention to redeem, I think that Mrs. Nicholson lost any right she previously had so to redeem. . . .

In addition, Riddell J. discussed the distinction between a mortgagor's right to redeem after a final order of foreclosure, and the right to do so after a sale under power of sale. He pointed out, at pp. 55-6, that the authorities permit a final order of foreclosure to be opened up in appropriate circumstances to allow a mortgagor to redeem. This right, however, depends on the exercise of a discretion by the court depending upon the circumstances of each particular case. On the other hand, to permit a mortgagor to redeem after the property has been sold upon power of sale, as in this appeal, would require the court to interfere with rights accruing to the purchaser and the mortgagee under their contract of purchase and sale. In other words, it would interfere with the mortgagee's contractual right to sell under power of sale contained in the mortgage entered into with the mortgagor, as well as the contractual rights of the mortgagee and the purchaser arising from the contract of sale under power of sale.

A similar approach was taken by Crossman J. in *Waring v. London & Manchester Assurance Co.* (1934), [1935] Ch. 310 (Eng. Ch. Div.). In that case, a mortgagee, exercising a power of sale pursuant to s. 101 of the *Law of Property Act*, 15 Geo. 5, c. 20, had entered into a contract to sell the mortgaged property. Subsequently, the mortgagor tendered the monies due under the mortgage and sought an injunction to prevent the completion of the sale on the ground that it had not been completed.

In refusing to issue an injunction on this ground, Crossman J. had this to say at pp. 317-18:

> The contract is an absolute contract, not conditional in any way, and the sale is expressed to be made by the company as mortgagee. If, before the date of the contract, the plaintiff had tendered the principal with interest and costs, or had paid it into Court in proceedings, then, if the company had continued to take steps to enter into a contract for sale, or had purported to do so, the plaintiff would, in my opinion, have been entitled to an injunction restraining it from doing so. After a contract has been entered into, however, it is, in my judgment, perfectly clear (subject to what has been said to me to-day) *that the mortgagee (in the present case, the company) can be restrained from completing only on the ground that he has not acted in good faith and that the sale is therefore liable to be set aside.* . . . In my judgment, s. 101 of that Act, which gives to a mortgagee power to sell the mortgaged property, is perfectly clear, and means that the mortgagee has power to sell out and out, by private contract or by auction, and subsequently to complete by conveyance; *and the power to sell is, I think, a power by selling to bind the mortgagor. If that were not so, the extraordinary result would follow that every purchaser from a mortgagee would, in effect, be getting a conditional contract liable at any time to be set aside by the mortgagor's coming in and paying the principal, interest, and costs. Such a result would make it impossible for a mortgagee, in the ordinary course of events, to sell unless he was in a position to promise that completion should take place immediately or on the day after the contract, and there would have to be a rush for completion in order to defeat a possible claim by the mortgagor.* [Emphasis added] . . .

. . . [A]t the time Logozzo commenced his application to prevent Grann from completing the purchase of the property, it was too late for him to redeem the property. Within the meaning of s. 22(1)(a), TD had already sold the property to Grann. Moreover, Logozzo had not fulfilled the necessary condition precedent to engage s. 22(1)(a) as he had failed to pay, or tender, the amount due to discharge the mortgage. At best, it can be said that he hoped to acquire the funds required to repay the mortgage debt by selling the property to Purnell.

II

Therefore, it comes down to whether paragraph 2 of the schedule to the Grann-TD agreement of purchase and sale makes any difference. . . .

[Borins J.A. then reviewed the authorities relevant to such terms, and in particular, whether an agreement of purchase and sale made conditional on the purchaser obtaining suitable financing fell within para. 22(1)(a) of the *Mortgages Act*.]

. . . It appears to have been the opinion of the judges deciding those cases that a conditional agreement of purchase and sale entered into under power of sale does not constitute a "sale under the mortgage" within the meaning of s. 22(1)(a) of the *Mortgages Act*. The correctness of this proposition need not be decided on this appeal.

Moreover, in my view, the provision of paragraph 2 of the schedule to the Grann-TD agreement of purchase and sale does not render it a conditional agreement. Once again, I repeat it for convenience:

> The purchaser understands and agrees that the mortgagor has the right to redeem the property *up to the time of waiver or expiration of all rights of termination or fulfilment of all conditions* and this agreement is subject to that right. In the event of redemption by the mortgagor, this agreement shall be null and void and any deposit monies will be refunded in full without interest. [Emphasis added.]

On its face, this clause represents an understanding and agreement between Grann and TD that there are circumstances in which TD may permit the mortgagor to redeem the property. As such, it has a similar effect to the similar clause in *Mission Construction* [*Mission Construction Ltd. v. Seel Investments Ltd.*, [1973] 2 O.R 190, 33 D.L.R. (3d) 286 (H.C.)]. However, this cannot serve to confer on Logozzo a right to redeem beyond the time permitted by s. 22(1)(a). This provision is likely for the benefit of TD. It gives TD the opportunity to make the best deal possible in realizing on its security notwithstanding the effect of s. 22(1)(a), and without incurring any liability to the purchaser. For example, if the amount for which it sold the property to Grann was insufficient to retire the mortgage debt, it reserved for TD the right to permit Logozzo to redeem on the payment, or tender, of a sufficient amount "up to the time of waiver or expiration of all rights of termination or fulfilment of all conditions". However, as between Logozzo and TD, it created no rights, nor did it provide Logozzo the foundation to prevent the completion of the Grann-TD transaction. As I have pointed out, in any event, at the time he brought his application, Logozzo had not effected a redemption as he had neither paid, nor tendered, the amount due on the mortgage.

In my view, although paragraph 2 permits Logozzo to redeem if certain circumstances are met, he could not enforce this benefit against Grann or TD for the reason that he was not a party to the agreement of purchase and sale. As a general rule, the doctrine of privity of contract provides that a contract can neither confer rights, nor impose obligations, on third parties. Paragraph 2 may permit the mortgagee to allow the mortgagor to redeem subsequent to the time of a binding agreement of purchase and sale. Indeed, as I stated earlier, TD has no objection to the court permitting Logozzo to redeem provided the court protects it from liability should Grann decide to enforce its contractual rights, as paragraph 2, in effect, provides. However, it is primarily the mortgagor, whose right to redeem is governed by s. 22(1)(a), who is seeking to enforce a term in a contract to which he is not a party.

As for the purchaser, if he or she is content to enter into an agreement of purchase and sale that contains such a provision, he or she is taken to have assumed the risk that the transaction may not close. The provision leaves the vendor free to accept a proper redemption within the time frame contained in the provision and return the purchaser's deposit, without incurring liability to the purchaser. Thus, although it is apparent that Grann acted in good faith in submitting his offer, he did so knowing that TD could terminate the agreement by permitting Logozzo to redeem the property within the time frame contained in the provision, in which event the agreement becomes null and void and TD must return his deposit. Grann is not prepared to relinquish the rights which he acquired under the agreement of purchase and sale and to go along with TD's willingness to permit Logozzo to redeem. TD's willingness to do so, as stated earlier, is conditional upon the court protecting it from any liability it may have to Grann if the court declares the agreement of purchase and sale null and void. However, had Logozzo effected a proper redemption in compliance with the provision in paragraph 2, Grann's rights under the agreement of purchase and sale would have been at an end.

It is helpful to examine the language of paragraph 2 which, in my view, is needlessly convoluted. As I read the penultimate sentence of that paragraph, it is similar, in effect, to the provision in the agreement of purchase and sale in *Mission Construction*, which Leiff J. found did not preserve the mortgagor's right to redeem. The clause in that case provided that the mortgagee's acceptance of the offer was "subject to the rights" of the mortgagor to redeem the property or to put the mortgage in good standing. In this appeal, the agreement of purchase and sale is "subject to [the] right" of the mortgagor to redeem the property "*up to the time* of waiver or expiration of all rights of termination or fulfilment of all conditions". The only difference between the two clauses is that in this appeal the mortgagor's right to redeem terminates on the occurrence of certain events, while in *Mission Construction* the right to redeem is not subject to termination.

As I have indicated, the clause in paragraph 2 does not render the TD-Grann agreement of purchase and sale a conditional agreement. It does not make the right of Grann to complete the purchase of the property dependent on the happening of a future event, such as the purchaser obtaining the funds to complete the purchase, as in *Saad* [*National Trust Co. v. Saad* (1997), 10 R.P.R. (3d) 145 (Ont. Gen. Div.)], or the mortgage not being redeemed prior to closing, as in *Miranda* [*Miranda v.*

Wong (April 4, 1986), Doc. RE 821/86, Steel J. (Ont. H.C.)]. The clause simply contains an acknowledgement that the mortgagor has the right to redeem the property up to a particular time. There are no conditions in the agreement to be fulfilled. . . .

As I stated earlier, it is TD's position that it remains open to the court to permit Logozzo to redeem as the time had not been reached for Grann to complete his examination of title when Logozzo commenced his application. TD submitted, therefore, that it could agree to a redemption of the property as the time for the "waiver or expiration of all rights of termination" of the agreement, as contained in paragraph 2, had not expired.

In making this submission, TD relied on the following language in paragraph 10 of the agreement of purchase and sale: "If within the specified times referred to in paragraph 8 any valid objection to title . . . is made in writing to Vendor and which Vendor is unable or unwilling to remove, remedy or satisfy and which purchaser will not waive this agreement . . . shall be at an end . . .". In my view, this language does not create a right of termination. In any event, as the period in which Grann was permitted to examine the title had not expired when the application was commenced, it was premature for TD, or Logozzo, to place any reliance on this aspect of the clause in paragraph 2.

My interpretation of paragraph 10 is based on the reasons for judgment of Danckwerts L.J. in *Property & Bloodstock Ltd. v. Emerton* (1967), [1968] Ch. 94 (Eng. C.A.), a power of sale and redemption case, in which it was held that conditions respecting title in the usual agreement of purchase and sale are just that — a mere matter of title and, therefore, one of the usual terms found in an agreement of purchase and sale — with the result that the agreement is an unconditional contract of sale. It is also noteworthy that the Court of Appeal in *Emerton* approved Crossman J.'s decision in *Waring* [*Waring v. London & Manchester Assurance Co.*, [1935] Ch. 310 (Eng. Ch. Div.)], observing, at p. 115, that it "was plainly correct".

In summary, notwithstanding that the doctrine of privity of contract precluded Logozzo from enforcing the apparent benefit which was conferred on him by the language of paragraph 2, as between Grann and TD, paragraph 2 entitled TD to accept a proper redemption by Logozzo "up to the time of waiver or expiration of all rights of termination or fulfilment of all conditions" contained in their agreement, and to walk away from the agreement without incurring any liability to Grann. However, as I have explained, in the circumstances of this appeal TD cannot rely on, and enforce, paragraph 2 for three reasons. Logozzo had not effected a proper redemption at the time his application was brought, as he had neither paid, nor tendered, the appropriate amount of money owing on the mortgage. Paragraphs 8 and 10 of the agreement did not, as TD contended, give Grann a right to terminate it which he had not waived and which had not expired. Finally, the agreement was not conditional.

Before leaving this analysis, it should be acknowledged that in certain circumstances the courts have permitted a third party to enforce a benefit or right established in its favour pursuant to the terms of a contract. For example, in *London Drugs Ltd.*

v. Kuehne & Nagel International Ltd., [1992] 3 S.C.R. 299 (S.C.C.), the Supreme Court of Canada introduced what was intended as a principled exception to the doctrine of privity of contract in the context of a limitation of liability clause in a standard form contract for the storage of a transformer. See, also, *Fraser River Pile & Dredge Ltd. v. Can-Dive Services Ltd.*, a judgment of the Supreme Court of Canada, released September 10, 1999, [1999] 9 W.W.R. 380 (S.C.C.). It was not argued in this appeal that the principle established in *London Drugs* should be applied to permit Logozzo to enforce the right to redeem contained in paragraph 2. However, were I inclined to apply *London Drugs*, it is my view that Logozzo would have failed for the reasons which I have summarized in the preceding paragraph.

Conclusion

As stated earlier, TD and Grann both regard their agreement of purchase and sale to be in force awaiting the release of this judgment. For all of the above reasons, they may now proceed to complete their contract, freed from the unhappy interference by Logozzo at the eleventh hour. . . .

Goudge J.A. (dissenting): . . .

In my opinion, the resolution of this appeal depends on the contract between the Bank and Grann. The critical term of that contract is paragraph 2 of Schedule A which forms part of the contract of purchase and sale. . . .

This paragraph constitutes the agreement of these two parties that the Bank can permit Logozzo to redeem the property "up to the time of waiver or expiration of all rights of termination or fulfilment of all conditions" and further, that if that happens, Grann's agreement with the Bank is rendered null and void.

This paragraph is designed to preserve for the Bank its right to be repaid in full by the redeeming mortgagor right up to the point at which the purchaser to whom the Bank is selling no longer has a legal escape hatch from the transaction. That is the point at which the Bank can look with certainty to the sale to be repaid. The purchaser contracts with full knowledge that until that point the Bank is entitled to be repaid by permitting the mortgagor to redeem, thereby voiding the contract of purchase and sale.

The question then is whether as of November 12, 1998, the deadline had passed for the Bank to permit Logozzo to redeem. I do not think that it had.

Paragraph 10, together with paragraph 8 as amended of the agreement of purchase and sale, provides that the purchaser has until November 13, 1998 to make any valid objection to title or to any outstanding work order or to the unlawfulness of the present use or to the lack of fire insurance. If the vendor does not satisfy the objection the purchaser may waive it. Otherwise the agreement is terminated. This provision gives Grann the right to terminate the contract up to November 13, 1998 if he refuses to waive an unsatisfied and valid requisition. Since Grann had not waived this right, until it expired on November 13, the Bank could not be certain that Grann was lawfully obliged to complete the transaction. Until then the Bank could not look with certainty to the sale to be repaid.

This, I think, is precisely the kind of provision contemplated by paragraph 2 of Schedule A. As I have said, its purpose is to entitle the Bank to be repaid by a redeeming mortgagor up to the point at which the purchaser under power of sale ceased to have a legal escape route from the transaction. At that point, the Bank can look with certainty to the sale as the basis for repayment and the justification for permitting redemption vanishes.

As of November 12, 1998, Grann's right under paragraph 10 had neither been waived, nor had it expired. The Bank could not yet be certain that it could look to the sale to Grann as the basis upon which it would be repaid. Hence, as of that date the contract of purchase and sale entitled the Bank to allow Logozzo to redeem. It could do so with no infringement of Grann's rights since the redemption would render the contract between Grann and the Bank null and void.

In summary, therefore, I conclude that as of the crucial date, November 12, 1998, Logozzo was able to redeem the property because the Bank has a contractual right to let him do so and it is willing to exercise that right. . . .

The conclusion I have reached is contractually founded. It does not depend at all on s. 22(1)(a) of the *Mortgages Act*. . . .

Appeal allowed.

Manufacturers Life Insurance Co. v. Huang & Danczkay Properties 2003 CarswellOnt 2990 (S.C.J.)

Garton J.: . . .

The duties of a mortgagee in a power of sale

The general rule with regard to the nature and extent of the duty upon a mortgagee in a power of sale was set out by Eberle J. in *Wood v. Bank of Nova Scotia et al.*, [1979] O.J. No. 3146 (H.C.J.), aff'd (1980), 29 O.R. (2d) 35 (C.A.), at para. 116:

> While it seems quite clear that a mortgagee is not a trustee for sale for the benefit of the mortgagor, the mortgagee is responsible for taking reasonable care to see that a proper value for the property is obtained.

The determination of whether this duty has been met is highly contextual and dependent upon the facts of the particular case. [See *Filion v. 689543 Ontario Ltd. (c.o.b. IMC Holdings)*, [1994] O.J. No. 189 (Div. Ct.) at para. 33]

The particular obligations of a mortgagee acting on a power of sale were reviewed in *Manufacturers Life Insurance Co. v. Granada Investments Ltd.*, [2001]

O.J. No. 3932 (C.A.). Osborne A.C.J.O., in speaking for the Court, referred to the case of *Oak Orchard Developments Ltd. v. Iseman*, [1987] O.J. No. 361 (Ont. H.C.J.), aff'd, [1989] O.J. No. 2394 (C.A.). At paragraph 67 he stated:

> In *Oak Orchard, supra*, a case in which the mortgagor contended that the mortgagee sold the mortgaged property for an insufficient price, Saunders J. extracted six propositions from the decided cases:
>
>> 1. *A mortgagee selling under a power of sale is under a duty to take reasonable precautions to obtain the true market value of the mortgaged property at the date on which he decides to sell it.* This does not mean that the mortgagee must, in fact, obtain the true value.
>>
>> 2. The duty of the mortgagee is only to take reasonable precautions. Perfection is not required. Some latitude is allowed to a mortgagee.
>>
>> 3. In deciding whether a mortgagee has fallen short of his duty, the facts must be looked at broadly and he will not be adjudged to be in default of his duties unless he is plainly on the wrong side of the line.
>>
>> 4. *The mortgagee is entitled to exercise an accrued power of sale for his own purposes whenever he chooses to do so. It matters not that the moment may be unpropitious and that by waiting, a higher price could be obtained.*
>>
>> 5. The mortgagee can accept the best price he can obtain in an adverse market provided that none of the adverse factors are due to fault on his part.
>>
>> 6. Even if the duty to take reasonable precautions is breached, the mortgagor must show that a higher price would have been obtained but for the breach in order to be compensated in damages. [Emphasis added.]

In terms of the timing of the mortgagee's exercise of its power of sale, Osborne A.C.J.O. stated at paragraph 68:

> The issue when a mortgagee must exercise its power of sale rights was considered by Anderson J. in *Hausman v. O'Grady* (1986), 61 O.R. (2d) 96 (Ont. H.C.J.), aff'd (1989), 67 O.R. (2d) 735 (C.A.). In *Hausman*, the mortgagor contended that the mortgagee sold too quickly and for too low a price. Anderson J. referred to and adopted Salmon L.J.'s statement in *Cuckmere Brick Co. Ltd. et. al. v. Mutual Finance Ltd.*, [1971] Ch. 949 at 965:
>
>> Once the power [the power of sale] has accrued, *the mortgagee is entitled to exercise it for his own purposes whenever he chooses to do so. It matters not that the moment may be unpropitious and that by waiting a higher price could be obtained. He has the right to realize his security by turning it into money when he likes.* Nor, in my view, is there anything to prevent a mortgagee from accepting the best bid he can get at an auction, even though the auction is badly at ended [sic] and the bidding exceptionally low. Providing none of those adverse factors is due to any fault of the mortgagee, he can do as he likes. [Emphasis added.]

It appears from the case law that as far as timing is concerned, the general rule is that mortgagees can act on a matured power of sale at their leisure, as long as the sale is reasonable at the time that it occurs. Timing itself is not indicative of a lack of reasonableness.

According to the Court of Appeal in the *Granada* case, the principle of mitigation has no application to a mortgagee's claim for repayment of a loan. . . .

Medforth v. Blake
[2000] Ch. 86 (C.A.)

[The plaintiff/respondent owned a large pig-farming operation. Financing for its operations was arranged through Midland Bank Plc., and involved two charges. Both of these instruments allowed for the bank to appoint a receiver in the event of default. Among other things, the receiver had the power: to take possession, carry on manage or concur in carrying on and managing the business of the farmer, to raise or borrow any money that may be required upon the security of the whole or any part of the property, to sell or concur in selling the property, and to do any such other acts and things as may be considered to be incidental or conducive to any of these powers as could be accomplished as agent for the farmer. Moreover, the receivers were "deemed to be the agent of the farmer and the farmer shall be solely responsible for his or their acts or defaults and for his or their remuneration."

Default occurred, and receivers were appointed as agents for the farmer, who carried on the farming operation. In time, a new financing arrangement was entered into, and the receivers were discharged. However, the plaintiff was dissatisfied with the manner in which the receivers had conducted operations. One chief complaint concerned the costs of obtaining feed supplies for the livestock. In particular, it was complained that the receivers had failed to obtain discounted feed prices from suppliers. Not only was a discount for large-scale orders a normal commercial practice, but also that the plaintiff/respondent had frequently advised the receivers of the importance of this practice.]

Sir Richard Scott V.C.:

The issue on this appeal is whether a receiver and manager of a pig farm, appointed by a mortgagee, owes any duty to the mortgagor, over and above a duty of good faith, as to the manner in which he conducts the pig-farming business. . . .

The trial of the action was due to start in September 1998 but the parties asked for the issue whether the receivers owed the plaintiff a duty of care or simply a duty of good faith in their conduct of the pig-farming business to be dealt with as a preliminary issue. They asked that the trial date be vacated and that the trial be relisted after the court had dealt with the appeal from the judge's decision on the preliminary issue. An appeal on the issue was apparently regarded as inevitable. The judge agreed to the request and expedited the hearing of the preliminary issue.

The formulation of the preliminary issue was as follows:

> Assuming that the plaintiff can prove the facts pleaded in the amended statement of claim and reply: (1) did the defendants in the course of the receivership of the plaintiff's farm owe to the plaintiff only a duty of good faith when (a) exercising their powers of sale; and/or (b) exercising their powers of managing the business; and/or (c) otherwise acting (if there is such a case) in the factual circumstances alleged in the amended statement of claim and reply? (2) If the defendants owed only a duty of good faith in cases (a) and/or (b) above (and (c) if appropriate), what is the nature and meaning of good faith in those cases? (3) If the defendants' duties in cases (a) and/or (b) (and (c) if appropriate) are not limited to good faith, did the defendants owe to the plaintiff in those cases where it is not so limited a duty of care (whether in equity or at common law) and what is the standard and scope of such duty in the factual circumstances alleged in the amended statement of claim and reply?

In a judgment running to some 60 pages and containing a careful analysis of the relevant cases, the judge expressed the following conclusions on the preliminary issue: (1) that the receivers, when exercising their power of sale, owed the plaintiff, over and above a duty of good faith, an equitable duty of care; (2) that the standard of that duty of care was the standard of a reasonably competent receiver; (3) that no sensible distinction could be drawn between the exercise of a power of sale and the exercise of a power to manage a business, that the power to manage was ancillary to the power of sale and that the equitable duty of care was applicable to both.

These conclusions answered paragraphs (1) and (3) of the preliminary issue and made paragraph (2) irrelevant. But the judge dealt with paragraph (2) none the less. He held that if the evidence showed that the receivers acted in a wholly unreasonable way in failing to seek discounts, the failure would be a breach of their duty of good faith.

In their notice of appeal the receivers contend that the answers that ought to be given to the questions posed by the preliminary issues are as follows:

> (1) The defendants ... owed to the plaintiff the following duties: (a) a duty when exercising their power of sale to take reasonable steps to obtain a reasonable price for the property to be sold; (b) a duty when exercising their powers of managing the business to act only in good faith; (c) a duty when otherwise acting (if there is such a case) only to act in good faith in the factual circumstances alleged in the amended statement of claim and reply. (2) The nature or meaning of good faith in the context of the defendants' duties to the plaintiff means that fraud or deliberate or wilful misconduct is required to constitute a breach of the duty. (3) The standard and scope of the duty at (a) above ... is irrelevant because the defendants were not exercising their power of sale. ...

The proposition that, in managing and carrying on the mortgaged business, the receiver owes the mortgagor no duty other than that of good faith offends, in my opinion, commercial sense. The receiver is not obliged to carry on the business. He can decide not to do so. He can decide to close it down. In taking these decisions he is entitled, and perhaps bound, to have regard to the interests of the mortgagee in obtaining repayment of the secured debt. Provided he acts in good faith, he is entitled to sacrifice the interests of the mortgagor in pursuit of that end. But if he does decide to carry on the business why should he not be expected to do so with reasonable competence? The present case, if the pleaded facts are established, involves the failure of the receivers to obtain discounts that were freely available. Other glaring examples of managerial incompetence can be imagined. Suppose the receivers had decided to carry on the business but had decided, through incompetence and not for any dishonest reason, that the pigs need not be fed or watered more than once a week, and as a result a number of pigs had died. The receivers would, I suppose, be in trouble with the R.S.P.C.A. but, if Mr. Smith [counsel for the receivers] is right, although they might be liable to the mortgagee, they would have no liability to the mortgagor. Or suppose that, as may well be the case, it is common practice to inoculate weaners against diseases to which pigs are prone but the receivers decided to save money by dispensing with inoculations, with the result that a number of the weaners contracted disease and died and that the rest had to be slaughtered. If Mr. Smith is right, the receivers would have no liability to the mortgagor whose business they had, by incompetence, ruined. It is accepted that, if the mortgagee had gone into possession and carried on the business similarly incompetently, the mortgagee would have been accountable to the mortgagor for the loss caused to the mortgagor by the incompetence. But, it is submitted, not so the receivers. . . .

Mr. Smith pointed out that the main reason for the development of the system under which the receiver is appointed by the mortgagee but is treated nonetheless as the agent of the mortgagor, is to enable the mortgagee to avoid becoming a mortgagee in possession while enjoying the advantages of his nominee, the receiver, displacing the mortgagor from control of the mortgaged property and from the receipt of the income derived from it. He argued that if the receiver is held to owe obligations to the mortgagor that go beyond duties of good faith, the advantages intended to be derived by mortgages from the receivership system will be undermined. They will be undermined, he said, because if the receiver is held to owe the mortgagor the same sort of obligations as a mortgagee in possession would owe, there will be no advantage to the mortgagee in avoiding being a mortgagee in possession. I am unable to accept these arguments.

If receivers who decide to carry on a mortgaged business do owe a duty to the mortgagor to do so with reasonable competence, I do not follow how that could adversely affect the mortgagee. If the receivers are in breach of that duty they will be answerable to the mortgagor. Mr. Smith suggested that the mortgagee would then have to indemnify the receivers. Why should they do so? If a mortgagee, on appointing a receiver, has undertaken to indemnify the receiver against any claims for default made against the receiver by the mortgagor, that undertaking might have to be honoured. But, if mortgagees choose to give indemnities to guard receivers against the consequences of the receivers' defaults, that is their affair. It is no reason at all for contending that the system of receivership is being undermined. In any event, Mr. Smith accepted that a failure on the part of a receiver to show reasonable competence in his management of the mortgaged property would probably constitute a breach of a duty owed by the receiver to the mortgagee who had appointed him. A mortgagee would hardly be likely to give a contractual undertaking to indemnify a receiver against the consequences of conduct which constituted a breach of the receiver's duty to the mortgagee.

Mr. Smith argued that the mortgagee might have given instructions to the receiver as to the manner in which the receiver should manage the business that was to be carried on. He argued that an action by the mortgagor based upon a complaint that the receiver had been managing the business in that manner would entitle the receiver to look to the mortgagee for an indemnity. It is difficult to deal with a submission of this sort otherwise than by reference to particular facts. A mortgagee who has appointed a receiver has no general right to instruct the receiver as to how or when to exercise the powers that have been conferred on the receiver. The mortgagee retains his own powers as mortgagee. He does not, for example, lose his power to sell by appointing a receiver with a power of sale. The receiver, on appointment, exercises his powers as agent for the mortgagor. Paragraphs 3(g) and (h) of the agricultural charges in the present case so provide. So does section 109(2) of the Law of Property Act 1925. If a mortgagee establishes a relationship with the receiver he has appointed under which the receiver exercises his powers in accordance with instructions given by the mortgagee, I can see the force of an argument that if the receiver is liable to the mortgagor then so will the mortgagee be liable. But this begs the question whether or not it is right that the receiver should be liable to the mortgagor. Take the present case as an example. Suppose that the reason why the receivers had done nothing to obtain the freely available discounts was that the bank, the mortgagee, had instructed them not to do so. The proposition that the law should refrain from holding the receivers liable to the mortgagor because to do so would lead to liability being imposed also on the mortgagee and that that would, in effect, be treating the mortgagee as a mortgagee in possession does not seem to me to make any sense. I agree that, on the supposed facts, if the receivers were liable to the mortgagor, the mortgagee would be liable too. And why not? If the mortgagee chooses to instruct the receivers to carry on the business in a manner that is a breach of the receivers' duty to the mortgagor, it seems to me quite right that the mortgagee, as well as the receivers, should incur liability. This conclusion does not in the least undermine the receivership system. What it might do is to promote caution on the part of mortgagees in seeking to direct receivers as to the manner in which they (the receivers) should exercise their powers. I would regard that as salutary.

For these reasons, Mr. Smith's reliance on the history of receiverships as justifying the exoneration of receivers from any duty to mortgagors other than that of good faith, falls, so far as I am concerned, on stony ground.

Let me now turn to the three authorities on which Mr. Smith particularly relied. They were *In re B. Johnson & Co. (Builders) Ltd.* [1955] Ch. 634, *Downsview Nominees Ltd. v. First City Corporation* [1993] A.C. 295 and *Yorkshire Bank Plc. v. Hall* [1999] 1 W.L.R. 1713.

In re B. Johnson & Co (Builders) Ltd. was a decision of the Court of Appeal. The issue was whether a receiver and manager, who had been appointed under a debenture, was an "officer" of the company for the purposes of section 333(1) of the Companies Act 1948. A second issue, assuming that the receiver/manager was an "officer," was whether a case of misfeasance had been disclosed. On the first issue the court held that the receiver/manager was not an "officer" for section 333 purposes. The court dealt also with the second issue, although its finding on the first issue had made that unnecessary.

In dealing with the first issue, Sir Raymond Evershed M.R. emphasised, at p. 646, that the receiver/manager, "is not managing on the company's behalf but is managing in order to facilitate the exercise by him, for the mortgagees, of the mortgagees' power to enforce the security." It is, I think, important, whenever considering the exercise by receivers of their powers, to bear in mind the point made by Sir Raymond Evershed M.R. The receivers' main function is to assist the mortgagee in obtaining payment of the secured debt. The Master of the Rolls commented also, at p. 647:

> it is elementary that a mortgagee seeking to realise his security has no duty of care to see that there is as much as possible left over for those who are interested in what is called the "equity."

This statement of principle has been qualified, but not invalidated, by *Cuckmere Brick Co. Ltd. v. Mutual Finance Ltd.* [1971] Ch. 949, a case to which I will return. On the second point in *In re B. Johnson & Co. (Builders) Ltd.* [1955] Ch. 634, 652, Sir Raymond Evershed M.R. analysed the pleaded complaints against the receiver/manager as constituting no more than "charges of mere negligence." A case of mere negligence could not, he held, be prosecuted under section 333.

Both Jenkins and Parker L.JJ. agreed with Sir Raymond Evershed M.R. that the receiver/manager was not an "officer" for section 333 purposes. Jenkins L.J., in doing so, made remarks about the nature of a receiver/manager's duty on which Mr. Smith relies. After stating that "The primary duty of the receiver is to the debenture holders and not to the company," Jenkins L.J. continued, at pp. 662-663:

> But the whole purpose of the receiver and manager's appointment would obviously be stultified if the company could claim that a receiver and manager owes it any duty comparable to the duty owed to a company by its own directors or managers . . . He is under no obligation to carry on the company's business at the expense of the debenture holders. Therefore he commits no breach of duty to the company by refusing to do so, even though his discontinuance of the business may be detrimental from the company's point of view. Again, his power of sale is, in effect, that of a mortgagee, and he therefore commits no breach of duty to the company by a *bona fide* sale, even though he might have obtained a higher price and even though, from the point of view of the company, as distinct from the debenture holders, the terms might be regarded as disadvantageous. In a word, in the absence of fraud or *mala fides* (of which there is not the faintest suggestion here), the company cannot complain of any act or omission of the receiver and manager, provided that he does nothing that he is not empowered to do, and omits nothing that he is enjoined to do by the terms of his appointment. If the company conceives that it has any claim against the receiver and manager for breach of some duty owed by him to the company, the issue is not whether the receiver and manager has done or omitted to do anything which it would be wrongful in a manager of a company to do or omit, but whether he has exceeded or abused or wrongfully omitted to use the special

> powers and discretions vested in him pursuant to the contract of loan constituted by the debenture for the special purpose of enabling the assets comprised in the debenture holders' security to be preserved and realized. That seems to me to be an issue wholly outside the scope of section 333.

This was not a reserved judgment and it is important to be clear about the object of Jenkins L.J.'s remarks. He was distinguishing the duties of a receiver/manager from those of a director/manager in order to explain why section 333 applied only to the latter. Mr. Smith is, however, entitled to point to the sentence commencing "In a word, in the absence of fraud or *mala fides*" as supporting his submissions.

Downsview Nominees Ltd. v. First City Corporation [1993] A.C. 295 was a Privy Council decision on an appeal from the Court of Appeal of New Zealand. The judgment of the board was given by Lord Templeman. He made clear his view that such duty as a receiver/manager owed to the mortgagor was, like the duty owed by the mortgagee, a duty imposed by equity. It was not a duty in tort. It was not attributable to the application of the "neighbour" principle of *Donoghue v. Stevenson* [1932] A.C. 562. This was important because the first instance judge, Gault J., had held [1989] 3 N.Z.L.R. 710, 742, 744:

> the proposition that a receiver will not be liable in negligence so long as he acts honestly and in good faith no longer represents the law of New Zealand . . . a receiver owes a duty to the debenture-holders to take reasonable care in dealing with the assets of the company.

and the Court of Appeal [1990] 3 N.Z.L.R. 265, 272 had held, that

> if there were any duties on the part of the . . . receiver to a subsequent debenture-holder, they would have to be based in negligence.

Lord Templeman did not disagree that the receiver owed duties to the subsequent debenture-holder but insisted that they were duties arising in equity and were not common law duties of care. In the result, Gault J.'s monetary award against the receiver and in favour of the subsequent debenture-holder was upheld, but placed on a different jurisprudential basis.

Lord Templeman cited with approval the passage from Jenkins L.J.'s judgment in *In re B. Johnson & Co. (Builders) Ltd.* that I have cited and said [1993] A.C. 297, 315:

> The general duty of care said to be owed by a mortgagee to subsequent encumbrancers and the mortgagor in negligence is inconsistent with the right of the mortgagee and the duties which the courts applying equitable principles have imposed on the mortgagee. If a mortgagee enters into possession he is liable to account for rent on the basis of wilful default; he must keep mortgage premises in repair; he is liable for waste. Those duties were imposed to ensure that a mortgagee is diligent in discharging his mortgage and returning the property to the mortgagor. If a mortgagee exercises his power of sale in good faith for the purpose of protecting his security, he is not liable to the mortgagor even though he might have obtained a higher price and even though the terms might be

> regarded as disadvantageous to the mortgagor. *Cuckmere Brick Co. Ltd. v. Mutual Finance Ltd.* [1971] Ch. 949 is Court of Appeal authority for the proposition that, if the mortgagee decides to sell, he must take reasonable care to obtain a proper price but is no authority for any wider proposition. A receiver exercising his power of sale also owes the same specific duties as the mortgagee. But that apart, the general duty of a receiver and manager appointed by a debenture holder, as defined by Jenkins L.J. in *In re B. Johnson & Co (Builders) Ltd.* [1955] Ch. 634, 661, leaves no room for the imposition of a general duty to use reasonable care in dealing with the assets of the company. The duties imposed by equity on a mortgagee and on a receiver and manager would be quite unnecessary if there existed a general duty in negligence to take reasonable care in the exercise of powers and to take reasonable care in dealing with the assets of the mortgagor company.

As a Privy Council case, the *Downsview Nominees* case is not binding but, as Mr. Smith submitted, is a persuasive authority of great weight. But what did it decide as to the duties owed by a receiver/manager to a mortgagor? It decided that the duty lies in equity, not in tort. It decided that there is no general duty of care in negligence. It held that the receiver/manager owes the same specific duties when exercising the power of sale as are owed by a mortgagee when exercising the power of sale. Lord Templeman cited with approval the *Cuckmere Brick* case test, namely, that the mortgagee must take reasonable care to obtain a proper price. So, a receiver/manager when selling must take reasonable care to obtain a proper price. In so deciding, Lord Templeman departed from the proposition to be found in Jenkins L.J.'s judgment in *In re Johnson & Co. (Builders) Ltd.*

In *Yorkshire Bank Plc. v. Hall* [1999] 1 W.L.R. 1713, Robert Walker L.J. reviewed a mortgagee's duty to his mortgagor. He referred to *China and South Sea Bank Ltd. v. Tan Soon Gin (alias George Tan)* [1990] 1 A.C. 536, *National Bank of Greece S.A. v. Pinios Shipping Co. No. 1* [1990] 1 A.C. 637 and the *Downsview Nominees* case [1993] A.C. 297 and then said [1999] 1 W.L.R. 1713, 1728:

> Those cases together establish or reaffirm that a mortgagee's duty to the mortgagor or to a surety depend partly on the express terms on which the transaction was agreed and partly on duties (some general and some particular) which equity imposes for the protection of the mortgagor and the surety. The mortgagee's duty is not a duty imposed under the tort of negligence, nor are contractual duties to be implied. The general duty (owed both to subsequent incumbrancers and to the mortgagor) is for the mortgagee to use his powers only for proper purposes, and to act in good faith . . . The specific duties arise if the mortgagee exercises his express or statutory powers . . . If he exercises his power to take possession, he becomes liable to account on a strict basis (which is why mortgagees and debenture holders operate by appointing receivers whenever they can). If he exercises his power of sale, he must take reasonable care to obtain a proper price.

These remarks apply, in my view, equally to the exercise by a receiver of a receiver's powers.

The *Cuckmere Brick* case test can impose liability on a mortgagee notwithstanding the absence of fraud or *mala fides*. It follows from the *Downsview Nominees* case and *Yorkshire Bank Plc. v. Hall* that a receiver/manager who sells but fails to take reasonable care to obtain a proper price may incur liability notwithstanding the absence of fraud of *mala fides*. Why should the approach be any different if what is under review is not the conduct of a sale but conduct in carrying on a business? If a receiver exercises this power, why does not a specific duty, corresponding to the duty to take reasonable steps to obtain a proper price, arise? If the business is being carried on by a mortgagee, the mortgagee will be liable, as a mortgagee in possession, for loss caused by his failure to do so with due diligence. Why should not the receiver/manager, who, as Lord Templeman held, owes the same specific duties as the mortgagee when selling, owe comparable specific duties when conducting the mortgaged business? It may be that the particularly onerous duties constructed by courts of equity for mortgagees in possession would not be appropriate to apply to a receiver. But, no duties at all save a duty of good faith? That does not seem to me to make commercial sense nor, more importantly, to correspond with the principles expressed in the bulk of the authorities.

In the *Cuckmere Brick* case [1971] Ch. 949, 968-969, the Court of Appeal held that a mortgagee when exercising his power of sale owed a duty to the mortgagor "to take reasonable precautions to obtain the true market value of the mortgaged property at the date on which he decides to sell it." This is firmly established now as a duty in equity. . . .

Mr. Smith has submitted that to hold a receiver liable to the mortgagor for anything more than a breach of a duty of good faith would require a number of established authorities on the law of mortgages to be torn up and thrown away. He instanced *Kennedy v. De Trafford* [1897] A.C. 180. This was a case where the mortgagors were two tenants in common. The mortgagees, in exercise of their power of sale, sold to one of the two. The trustee in bankruptcy of the other tenant in common applied to the court to have the sale set aside. He claimed, alternatively, damages against the mortgagees for negligence in the exercise of the power of sale. The report of the case in the House of Lords shows that the trustee's main complaint was that the purchaser from the mortgagees had been one of the two mortgagor tenants in common. It was argued that this individual stood in a fiduciary relationship to his co-tenant and was disqualified from purchasing. It was argued, also, that the sale had been at an undervalue. The House of Lords dealt with the case peremptorily. Counsel for the respondents was not called on. Judgment was delivered at once. Lord Herschell, in rejecting the argument based on sale at an undervalue, said at p. 185:

> if a mortgagee in exercising his power of sale exercises it in good faith, without any intention of dealing unfairly by his mortgagor, it would be very difficult indeed, if not impossible, to establish that he had been guilty of any breach of duty towards the mortgagor. Lindley L.J., in the court below, says that "it is not right or proper or legal for him either fraudulently or wilfully or recklessly to sacrifice the property of the mortgagor." Well, I think that is all covered really by his exercising the power committed to him in good faith. It is very difficult to define exhaustively all that would be included in the words "good faith," but I think it would be unreasonable to require the mortgagee to do more than exercise his power of sale in that fashion. Of course, if he wilfully and recklessly deals with the property in such a manner that the interests of the mortgagor are sacrificed, I should say that he had not been exercising his power of sale in good faith. My Lords, it is not necessary in this case to give an exhaustive definition of the

> duties of a mortgagee to a mortgagor, because it appears to me that, if you were to accept the definition of them for which the appellant contends, namely, that the mortgagee is bound to take reasonable precautions in the exercise of his power of sale, as well as to act in good faith, still in this case he did take reasonable precautions.

The other members of the House agreed.

Mr. Smith submits that the *Cuckmere Brick* case [1971] Ch. 949 is inconsistent with Lord Herschell's statements of principle in *Kennedy v. De Trafford* [1897] A.C. 180. He reserves the right to contend in a higher court that the *Cuckmere Brick* case was wrongly decided. In my judgment, *Kennedy v. De Trafford* did not lay down as an inflexible principle that the only duty owed by a mortgagee when selling was a duty of good faith. Lord Herschell's remarks about the difficulty of proving any breach of duty in a case where no want of good faith could be alleged show that he was leaving open the possibility of a case where, on the facts, that difficulty could be overcome.

Moreover, in my view, it is inappropriate to treat expressions of principle delivered *ex tempore* by no matter how august a judge as if they were of statutory effect. One of the great virtues of the common law duty of care is its inherent flexibility and its scope for development and adjustment in order to meet the changing requirements of society. Principles of equity, we were all taught, were introduced by Lord Chancellors and their deputies, the Vice-Chancellors sitting in the Chancery Courts, in order to provide relief from the inflexibility of common law rules. The equity of redemption was a Chancery invention, introduced in order to ensure that a conveyance by way of mortgage remained a security for the repayment of money whether or not the date fixed for repayment and reconveyance had passed. The duties imposed on a mortgagee in possession, and on a mortgagee exercising his powers whether or not in possession, were introduced in order to ensure that a mortgagee dealt fairly and equitably with the mortgagor. The duties of a receiver towards the mortgagor have the same origin. They are duties in equity imposed in order to ensure that a receiver, while discharging his duties to manage the property with a view to repayment of the secured debt, nonetheless in doing so takes account of the interests of the mortgagor and others interested in the mortgaged property. These duties are not inflexible. What a mortgagee or a receiver must do to discharge them depends upon the particular facts of the particular case. A want of good faith or the exercise of powers for an improper motive will always suffice to establish a breach of duty. What else may suffice will depend upon the facts. . . . The fact that the mortgagee had an interest in the purchasing company placed the mortgagee under an obligation to show that a proper price had been obtained. This was an obligation more onerous than would otherwise have been required. It is true that Lord Herschell in *Kennedy v. De Trafford* [1897] A.C. 180 expressed the duty on the mortgagee in terms much less onerous than the terms in which Salmon L.J. expressed the duty in the *Cuckmere Brick* case. That does not make the two cases inconsistent with one another. The facts that constituted the mortgagors'complaints were different. And the duty in equity appropriate to have been owed by a mortgagee selling in 1888 is not necessarily of the same weight as the duty appropriate to have been owed by a mortgagee selling in 1967. Equity is at least as flexible as the common law in adjusting the duties owed so as to make them fit the requirements of the time.

I do not accept that there is any difference between the answer that would be given by the common law to the question what duties are owed by a receiver managing a mortgaged property to those interested in the equity of redemption and the answer that would be given by equity to that question. I do not, for my part, think it matters one jot whether the duty is expressed as a common law duty or as a duty in equity. The result is the same. The origin of the receiver's duty, like the mortgagee's duty, lies, however, in equity and we might as well continue to refer to it as a duty in equity.

In my judgment, in principle and on the authorities, the following propositions can be stated. (1) A receiver managing mortgaged property owes duties to the mortgagor and anyone else with an interest in the equity of redemption. (2) The duties include, but are not necessarily confined to, a duty of good faith. (3) The extent and scope of any duty additional to that of good faith will depend on the facts and circumstances of the particular case. (4) In exercising his powers of management the primary duty of the receiver is to try and bring about a situation in which interest on the secured debt can be paid and the debt itself repaid. (5) Subject to that primary duty, the receiver owes a duty to manage the property with due diligence. (6) Due diligence does not oblige the receiver to continue to carry on a business on the mortgaged premises previously carried on by the mortgagor. (7) If the receiver does carry on a business on the mortgaged premises, due diligence requires reasonable steps to be taken in order to try to do so profitably.

In my judgment, Judge McGonigal's answers to the preliminary issue were, with one or two minor qualifications, in accordance with principle and correct. The minor qualifications are these. (1) The judge held that a receiver's power to manage a business was ancillary to the power of sale. I do not think it is. I would agree that in many cases, a receiver will manage a business in order to bring the mortgaged property to a state in which the business can then be sold as a going concern. But the power to manage is, in my view, independent of the power to sell. A receiver can manage a business for the purpose of generating profits from which the secured debt can be discharged. The management of the business does not have to be ancillary to an intended eventual sale. But I agree that in the management of the business an equitable duty of care is owed. (2) I do not think that the concept of good faith should be diluted by treating it as capable of being breached by conduct that is not dishonest or otherwise tainted by bad faith. It is sometimes said that recklessness is equivalent to intent. Shutting one's eyes deliberately to the consequences of what one is doing may make it impossible to deny an intention to bring about those consequences. Thereapart, however, the concepts of negligence on the one hand and fraud or bad faith on the other ought, in my view, to be kept strictly apart. Equity has not always done so. The equitable doctrine of "fraud on a power" has little, if anything, to do with fraud. Lord Herschell in *Kennedy v. De Trafford* [1897] A.C. 180 gave an explanation of a lack of good faith that would have allowed conduct that was grossly negligent to have qualified notwithstanding that the consequences of the conduct were not intended. In my judgment, the breach of a duty of good faith should, in this area as in all others, require some dishonesty or improper motive, some element of bad faith, to be established.

Finally, although I am not sure that it is strictly an answer to a question posed by the preliminary issue, in my judgment the facts pleaded in the amended statement of claim and reply would, if proved, and in the absence of any answer pleaded in the amended defence other than denial, constitute a breach by the receivers of the duty they owed in equity to the plaintiff.

I would dismiss this appeal.

QUESTIONS AND COMMENTS

1. Compare and contrast the duties owed by a mortgagor in assuming possession, acting as a receiver or selling under a contractual power of sale.

2. Apart from alterations made by statute, a mortgagee is entitled to pursue all the remedies contemplated under the mortgage arrangement. An action can be taken on the money under the personal covenant of the debtor; or one can go after the secured property. Of course, if part of the monies owing is recovered by action on the debt, the charge can only be enforced to recover the balance remaining due (and attendant costs). And if the land is sold under a power of sale, an action can be brought for any deficiency. If, however, foreclosure is first sought and obtained, then an action cannot then be maintained for a residual unpaid amount, unless the mortgagor is given the opportunity to redeem the land. Hence once the mortgagee has sold the land following foreclosure, the right to enforce the personal debt is gone. See *Gordon Grant & Co. v. Boos* [1926] A.C. 781, 1926 CarswellFor 3 (West Indies P.C.).

3. Some jurisdictions prohibit actions for deficiency following a final order of foreclosure: see, *e.g*, *Law of Property Act*, R.S.A. 2000, sub. 48(1). Should that right be available?

5. OTHER SECURITY INTERESTS: AN OVERVIEW

B. Ziff, *Principles of Property Law* 3rd ed. (Toronto: Carswell, 2000) at 407–10 [footnotes omitted]

(a) pledges, charges, liens

The term "security" refers to an arrangement under which a creditor can obtain a right over an object of property that is exercisable in some way in the event that an obligation is not fulfilled by the debtor. The mortgage of land is the best example. However, the brief outline of the history of the mortgage showed that there are other security forms that can be created. One is the *pledge* which, generally, involves a loan secured by the lender taking possession of an object, such as when goods are left with a pawnbroker. Another is the *charge*, which imposes an encumbrance on the property but which does not otherwise involve a transfer of title to the holder of the security. As we have seen, in Alberta a registered mortgage of land is regarded as a charge.

Another commonly found type of security is the *lien*, which is an embracing concept with legal, equitable, contractual and statutory forms. The common law recognized that it was often appropriate to allow creditors to retain possession of an object as a way of providing security for the payment of money owing. For example, innkeepers, common carriers, sea carriers and salvors are afforded such liens by the common law. Further, an artificer who improves the goods (other than by mere repair or maintenance) enjoys a lien for the authorized work that has been performed. Liens can also arise as a matter of trade usage, through an express contractual term or under statute.

The liens recognized by the common law are "particular", relating to the very goods for which a service has been rendered. "General" liens, which can arise under contract, trade usage or statute, permit a lien to be imposed over other property of the debtor. Normally, a lien over personalty arises when the creditor takes possession, and as a general rule, it survives only as long as that possession is retained. The possessory lien arising by operation of the common law allows the debtor to hold the goods hostage until the amount owing is paid. But there is no inherent right to sell the items. A power of sale can be inserted to bolster a contractual lien; is implicit in some liens arising through trade usage; or may be conferred by statute.

Equity can impose both liens and charges as part of its available stock of remedies. For example, on the sale of real property an equitable *vendor's lien* will be implied for the outstanding indebtedness of the full purchase price, and the existence of this security right is not dependent on the vendor retaining possession. A purchaser of real estate holds a lien to protect money that has been laid down as a deposit. Under statute, a *builder's lien* (sometimes called a *mechanic's lien*) is available to secure payments for improvements or repairs made to land. The rationale here is, quite simply, that "the land which receives the benefit [should] bear the burden." Like the vendor's lien, a person holding a builder's lien does not need to assume possession.

(b) other forms of personal property security

There are a host of other ways in which commercial and consumer transactions concerning personal property can involve a secured element. A *chattel mortgage* can be given under which legal title is held by the lender as security (as in a land mortgage). Property may be sold by means of a *conditional sales agreement*: here, title does not pass until the full purchase price is paid. This is similar to a device popular in England (but much less so here), the *hire-purchase agreement*. Under that type of agreement goods are hired by a lessee who is given an option to purchase the goods (usually for a nominal amount) at the end of the hiring term. If the rental payments are not made the lessor can repossess the goods.

A creditor may hold a security known as a *floating charge*. This instrument does not immediately attach to specific assets. Rather it hovers over designated goods until default or some other event occurs (such as the debtor ceasing to carry on business), at which time the charge crystallizes and fixes on the available assets. The floating charge is an ideal device to use to obtain security interests over goods that form part of a borrower's inventory. Another commonly used form of security involves the lender taking an *assignment of book debts* from the borrower. Under this method the lender obtains a right to enforce the accounts receivable of the person to whom funds have been advanced by that lender.

(c) modern personal property security law

The general law governing secured interests in personalty has been described as "conceptually inconsistent, administratively inefficient and unnecessarily complex." The devices listed above generate discrete legal issues and may be governed by different registration requirements and enforcement rules. The modern approach, now the predominant one in Canada, is to collect these diverse forms of security within a single system, one designed to provide a generic form of security interest to be governed by a uniform code.

For example, the Alberta *Personal Property Security Act* applies:

> (a) to every transaction that in substance creates a security interest, without regard to its form and without regard to the person who has title to the collateral, and
>
> (b) without limiting the generality of clause (a), [the Act also applies] to a chattel mortgage, conditional sale, floating charge, pledge, trust indenture, trust receipt, assignment, consignment, lease, trust and transfer of chattel paper where they secure payment or performance of an obligation.

For transactions caught within this wide net there is a common mode of registration. The new laws endeavour to respond to current commercial reality, abolishing the obsolete trappings of nineteenth century English commercial practice, and replacing these with a system that is supposed to meet the contemporary needs of consumers and lenders in this country. The purpose of the reforms is to promote efficiency by reducing the costs inherent in an uncertain system. However, it has to be said that the Canadian developments do not (yet) fully reach this goal: certain security transactions under federal law are not covered; some provinces have not opted for these reforms; and there is not complete symmetry among the P.P.S.A. statutes presently in force in Canada.

QUESTION

What effect do the protections afforded to mortgagors have on the economics of mortgage law? One plausible result is that loans are more costly. After all, if enforcement is arduous and protracted, this will increase the associated costs. The plenary protections discussed above explains Dennistoun J.A.'s description of the mortgagor as "that spoiled child of equity": *Best v. Dussessoye* (1920) 52 D.L.R. 249, 1920 CarswellMan 26 (C.A.) at 264. If all such costs cannot be recouped against the defaulting mortgagee or the secured land, they must be borne in the first instance by lenders.

Michael Schill's economic analysis of mortgage protection laws doubts that reasoning. The results of his empirical analysis suggest that:

> Given the small magnitude of the costs associated with these laws, at least relative to the estimates of most lawyers and economists, it is plausible that mortgage protection laws promote the objective of economic efficiency by functioning as a form of insurance against the adverse effects of mortgage default and foreclosure. . . . Government intervention in mortgage markets to mandate protection, in the form of deficiency judgment prohibitions, statutory rights of redemption, or a compulsory mortgage foreclosure insurance program, may be necessary to correct market failures attributable to imperfect information.

M. H. Schill, "An Economic Analysis of Mortgagor Protection Laws," 77 Va.L.Rev. 489 (1991) at 515, 538.

CHAPTER 12
PRIORITIES AND REGISTRATION

1. INTRODUCTION

Several foundational principles considered above resurface as key in this chapter. In Chapter 1 the divisibility of property rights was introduced. There, and in the chapters that followed, it was repeatedly shown that property rights are divisible, from top to bottom. Hence, rights associated with a single, modest parcel of land can be fractured an disseminated to a huge class of "owners", for on that parcel may be found easements, mortgages, covenants, life estates, leases, dower rights, co-owners and so forth. Likewise, it was shown that title under Canadian law is a relative term. What matters is that B can show a right superior to C in a conflict between those two, even if both must yield to the superior rights of A. That point was most evident in the analysis of the possessory rights of squatters and finders, covered in Chapter 4, but it arises throughout the law of property.

Because property rights are divisible and manifold, and because title is relative, doctrines are necessary to order such competing claims. In general, the common law adopted a simple approach: first in time is first in right. Notice, however, that sometimes latecomers are preferred over prior ones: that is one lesson to be gleaned from the law of adverse possession. Equity often — but not always — adheres to the importance of temporal priority in ranking claims.

For land (especially) these legal and equitable principles have been supplemented by statutory measures for the registration of land claims. These regimes provide procedures for recording and, in some instances validating (certifying) property claims. Although procedural in nature, it is vital to appreciate that these systems can affect priority ranking, and hence, like all procedures, can work to alter substantive rights. For example, the failure to register a property right correctly can result in the subordination of that right, sometimes to the point of rendering it valueless.

2. PRIORITIES AT COMMON LAW AND IN EQUITY

S. Levmore, "Variety and Uniformity in the Treatment of the Good-Faith Purchaser"
16 J. Legal Stud. 43 (1987) at 45–9 [footnotes omitted]

When a thief (T) steals an owner's (O) property and sells it to a buyer (B), the legal rule as to title is not very important if T is available and has in his possession either the proceeds of the sale to B or some other funds. Either O will be allowed to retrieve the property from B, in which case B will collect from T, or O will be left to sue T. There is at least one legal system in which, surprisingly, T may have been allowed to keep that which he had stolen, but we ought normally to expect the law to try to deter T and to permit the innocents, O and B, to be made whole. Any other rule would unnecessarily discourage both O and B from assisting in the capture of T, discourage investment in acquiring and improving property, and fail to deter T as much as is socially feasible.

Where T is judgment proof, however, the legal rule must allocate the loss between O and B. Fairness arguments will be of little help in guiding this allocation because T, not O or B, is the known wrongdoer. Other arguments might support a variety of rules. One the one hand, the more an owner is unable to recover his stolen goods, the more he may guard against theft. In computing the utility of extra locks and guards, the owner might be made to internalize all costs of theft from him by a rule that does not allow the owner to place some of the burden on another party (the innocent purchaser), who is surely unable to influence the level of care taken by the owner. A legal system thus might understandably disallow O's claim against B.

On the other hand, it is arguable that between the two relatively innocent parties B's behavior is most sensibly influenced at the margin. B decides with whom to do business, and perhaps a combination of the price, location, appearance and reputation of the party (whether it was T or some intermediary) from whom B is able to purchase O's stolen property should arouse B's suspicions. This argument builds on the notion that a party can be innocent and yet might not have been entirely unable to help the cause of law enforcement. Although a few buyers can be expected to notice all the circumstances of their purchases and to relay all their suspicions to law-enforcement authorities, it is surely true that a legal rule that threatens the repossession of some stolen property from B would influence the behavior of some B's and ultimately the profitability of thievery. A legal system thus might sensibly allow O to retrieve his property from B and attempt in this way to encourage B to monitor his sellers.

It is also possible to favour O or B because of their different abilities to absorb, diversify, or insure against the risk of loss. O may be a better insurer not only because theft insurance is more readily available for different kinds of property than is title insurance but also because it is less susceptible to a moral hazard problem. On the other hand, O will find it difficult for similar moral hazard reasons to insure any idiosyncratic value he places on his property. If instead we focus on the parties' capabilities to self-insure or to spread risks, then it may be sensible to allocate the loss in a way that depends on who deals more regularly in the sort of property that is at issue. If B, for example, purchases many such items, then he would seem to be in the better risk-bearing position. Indeed when additional transactions have taken place, as when B buys from an intermediary who innocently bought from T, then in some settings it may be this intermediary rather than O or B who can best predict, pass on the average cost of and therefore bear, the losses. It is clear, however, that the identification of the superior insurer in a case-by-case way would often require a good deal of fact-finding.

The conflict between O and B can also be approached from a behavioral perspective that focuses not on their relative ability to take extra precautions but rather on their likely postconviction behavior. O may have already replaced the stolen property, so that in a sense it is efficient to leave this property in the hands of B, who may, after all, have become quite attached to his new goods. This argument is unlikely to influence dispositively one's preference for a rule favoring an innocent O or B, however, because a legal system can easily decree that B is entitled to keep the stolen property but must pay O precisely what B paid T for the goods in question. For the most part, then, O would prevail, but B would be able to keep his new acquisition. No legal system seems to adopt such a rule, although O and B can clearly bargain in the shadow of any rule for B to keep the property.

In thinking about the many factors that may influence the law's preference for O or B, it is useful to note that this allocation of liability, as it were, is unlike that carried out by tort law in dealing with otherwise analogous multiple casual agents. Here it will often be the case that O had the best security system that money could buy or that B had every reason to think that he was dealing with a most reputable vendor. The system, in short, anticipates that occasionally O or B may make a positive contribution to the deterrence of thievery if encouraged by the risk of losing the right to identifiable stolen property. Unlike tort law, which takes a (remarkably) case-by-case approach to the problem of multiple casual agents, "property law" — perhaps because certainty of title is regarded as more important than is certainty of potential tort liability — looks for a general rule (as between O and B) and only infrequently allows particular circumstances to alter the rule.

In asking what this general rule might look like, the discussion in this paper assumes that different intuitions about O's and B's relative abilities to take extra precautions lie at the heart of the variety that different legal systems display. The relevant incentives that the different rules can place on the owner and the purchaser are of uncertain magnitude and cut in opposite directions. There is little reason to expect that lawmakers would make similar estimates of the advantages and disadvantages of various rules. Variety, or diversity in outcomes, is explained by the difficulty of the problem.

Finally, note that one should not expect any legal system to try simultaneously to influence both B's and O's conduct by decreeing that the stolen property (that B and O claim) belongs to a third party such as the state. B and O are vital links in nabbing the thief. Without O's identifying his property and describing the thief, and without B's noticing shady behavior and allowing his possessions to be inspected (more likely if the rule favors him), the probability of catching and convicting the thief must be fairly close to zero. This must surely have been so in primitive societies, which had little public law enforcement, but also seems true in modern societies, where public prosecution of property offenses remains heavily dependent on the cooperation of interested private properties.

The core of the theoretical argument suggesting variety in treatments is thus straightforward. Reasonable people can easily disagree over whether O or B is the second-best target of the law-enforcement system. Some legal systems may always allow the owner's claim to prevail, while others may do the opposite and look to owners to take better precautions against thieves. Still other legal systems may allow the owner to reclaim his property only in certain circumstances (where his precaution-taking ability is believed to be outweighed by a potential purchaser's ability to depress the market for stolen property). Moreover, empirical evidence is likely to be difficult enough to gather, so that rules can be expected to vary in reflection of the different judgments made by different people at different times.

COMMENTS

As can be seen from Professor Levmore's analysis, where a defective transaction has occurred, and where the original owner and the purchaser can be regarded as being without fault, the law must determine who should be entitled to what remedy. So, in the case of a deed forged by a rogue, one may prefer the *bona fide* purchaser over the original owner, leaving the latter with a cause of action against the rogue. Or, the original owner might be able to retain title, thereby leaving the duped purchaser to seek monetary recompense.

Prior to the introduction of registration systems, such conflicts were resolved though the combined effect of legal and equitable principles. Given that property rights can be legal and/or equitable, four conflict permutations can arise. One might have:

1. A legal interest followed by another legal interest (L v. L)

2. A legal interest followed by an equitable interest (L v. E)

3. An equitable interest followed by a legal interest (E v. L)

4. An equitable interest followed by a second equitable interest (E v. E)

As to permutation #1, imagine that A is the owner of Blackacre in fee simple absolute. A grants a legal lease of the land to B for a period of 10 years. Later, A sells the freehold to C. Assume C is unaware of the existence of the lease. One can even assume that a careful inspection of the premises might not have revealed that the land was subject to that leasehold interest. C is, let us conclude for the sake of argument, a *bona fide* purchaser for value without notice. Even so, C will be bound by B's pre-existing lease. Here, the common law rule is as straightforward as can be. Timing is everything, and first in time is first in right. Two latin phrases capture the principles at play. One is *nemo dat quod non habet* (one cannot give that which one does not have). The second is *caveat emptor* (buyer beware).

The *nemo dat* principle is clearly invoked in a second example. Here A purports to sell Blackacre to C. C obtains a deed and takes possession of the premises, all the while oblivious to any defect in title. As it turns out, A had earlier transferred the land to B. B acquires title; the transaction to C, valid on its face, is a complete nullity. (Nonetheless, you might consider the effect that the law of adverse possession might have on qualifying that basic rule).

The last three permutations each implicate equitable interests, and so engage equitable principles. In the cases that follow, ascertain which of the four contests has occurred, and identify the governing principles used in determining priority. And assess the ways in which the rules allocate the *risk* that a transaction might be defective.

North Counties of England Fire Insurance v. Whipp (1884) 26 Ch. D. 482 (C.A.)

On January 11, 1878, Crabtree, the manager of the plaintiff company, executed a legal mortgage of freehold property in favour of the company and handed over the title deeds to them. On May 24, 1878, Crabtree made a legal mortgage to the company of certain other freehold property and delivered the title deeds to them. The deeds of the mortgaged properties were placed in a safe of the company and were seen there on the occasion of an audit in May 1878. The safe had only one lock but there were duplicate keys, one of which was entrusted to Crabtree. In November 1878, Crabtree removed the deeds, except the mortgages, from the safe and handed them to the defendant, Mrs. Whipp, in whose favour he executed a mortgage for money advanced to him by her. The defendant was entirely ignorant of the mortgages which had been made in favour of the company. In November 1879, Crabtree went bankrupt and in the following month an order was made for winding up the company. In 1880, the liquidator, in the name of the company, brought this action for foreclosure against Mrs. Whipp and Crabtree's trustee in bankruptcy. Mrs. Whipp put in a defence and a counterclaim by which she asked that the securities be declared fraudulent and void as against her, or in the alternative that they might be postponed to her security and that the company might be ordered to convey the property to her, subject only to such equity of redemption as it was subject to under her mortgage. The Vice-Chancellor of the County Palatine of Lancaster held that the company ought to be postponed to Mrs. Whipp. The company appealed.

Fry L.J.: . . .

The question which has thus to be investigated is: What conduct in relation to the title deeds on the part of a mortgagee who has the legal estate, is sufficient to postpone such mortgagee in favour of a subsequent equitable mortgagee who has obtained the title deeds without knowledge of the legal mortgage? The question is not what circumstances may as between two equities give priority to the one over the other, but what circumstances justify the court in depriving a legal mortgagee of the benefit of the legal estate. It has been contended on the part of the plaintiffs that nothing short of fraud will justify the court in postponing the legal estate. It has been contended by the defendant that gross negligence is enough.

The cases which assist in answering the question thus raised will be found to fall into two categories: (1) those which relate to the conduct of the legal mortgagee in not obtaining possession of the title deeds; (2) those which relate to the conduct of the legal mortgagee in giving up or not retaining the possession of the title deeds after he has obtained them. The two classes of cases will not be found to differ in the principles by which they are to be governed, but they do differ much in the kind of fraud which is to be most naturally looked for.

In the case of a person taking the legal estate, and not seeking for or obtaining the title deeds from the mortgagor, the question may arise between the legal mortgagee and either a prior or a subsequent incumbrancer or purchaser. But in such a transaction the fraud about which the courts are most solicitous is that which is practised when a man takes the legal estate with knowledge of a prior equitable sale or incumbrance, and yet strives to place himself in a position to show that he took without notice — that kind of fraud which Lord Hardwicke explained in *Le Neve v. Le Neve* when he said: "The taking of a legal estate after notice of a prior right, makes a person a *mala fide* purchaser. . . . This is a species of fraud, and *dolus malus* itself; for he knew the first purchaser had the clear right of the estate, and after knowing that, he takes away the right of another person by getting the legal estate."

On the other hand, when the legal mortgagee has obtained the possession of the title deeds, and subsequently gives them up, no question can arise between him and a prior equitable owner, and no suspicion of the particular fraud which we have referred to can arise; the estate of the legal mortgagee can never be improved by any subsequent dealings with the deeds, and therefore, before the court can find a fraudulent intent in the legal mortgagee, it must be shown that he concurred in some project to enable the mortgagor to defraud a subsequent mortgagee, or that he was a party or privy to some other fraud in fact. The kind of fraud most to be looked for in this class of cases is such as was described by Lord Chancellor, Lord Cowper, in the case of the *Thatched House* when he said: "If a man makes a mortgage and afterwards mortgages the same estate to another, and the first mortgagee is in combination to induce the second mortgagee to lend his money, this fraud will without doubt in equity postpone his own mortgage. So if such mortgagee stands by and sees another lending money on the same estate without giving him notice of his first mortgage, this is such a misprision as shall forfeit his priority." . . .

The authorities which we have reviewed appear to us to justify the following conclusions:

(1) That the court will postpone the prior legal estate to a subsequent equitable estate: (a) where the owner of the legal estate has assisted or connived at the fraud which has led to the creation of a subsequent equitable estate, without notice of the prior legal estate; of which assistance or connivance the omission to use ordinary care in inquiry after or keeping title deeds may be, and in some cases has been, held to be sufficient evidence, where such conduct cannot otherwise be explained; (b) where the owner of the legal estate has constituted the mortgagor, his agent with authority to raise money, and the estate thus created has by the fraud or misconduct of the agent been represented as being the first estate.

But (2) that the court will not postpone the prior legal estate to the subsequent equitable estate on the ground of any mere carelessness or want of prudence on the part of the legal owner.

Now to apply the conclusions thus arrived at to the facts of the present case. That there was great carelessness in the manner in which the plaintiff company through its directors dealt with their securities seems to us to admit of no doubt. But is that carelessness evidence of any fraud? We think that it is not. Of what fraud is it evidence? The plaintiffs never combined with Crabtree to induce the defendant to lend her money. They never knew that she was lending it, and stood by. They can have had no motive to desire that their deed should be abstracted and their own title clouded. Their carelessness may be called gross, but in our judgment it was carelessness likely to injure and not to benefit the plaintiff company, and accordingly has no tendency to convict them of fraud.

Then comes the inquiry whether the plaintiff company constituted Crabtree heir agent to raise money, in which case the defendant might be entitled to priority. The circumstance most favourable to this contention was, in our opinion, the possession by Crabtree of the key. But the defendant has not proved the circumstances attending this fact, or the duties for the performance of which the key may have been essential, with sufficient distinctness to enable us to conclude from the possession of the key that it implied an authority to deal with the securities of the plaintiff company. The cases in which Crabtree did so deal with the securities, when carefully considered, appear to us insufficient to support the authority claimed; and the fact that Crabtree, in dealing with the defendant, suppressed his mortgage to the company and dealt with her, not as agent of the company having an authority to pledge its securities, but as the unencumbered owner of the property, goes, we think, far to negative the suggested authority. On this point, therefore, we agree with the Vice-Chancellor. . . .

Differing as we do from the learned Vice-Chancellor on the one point on which he decided against the plaintiffs, we conclude that his judgment must be discharged, and that instead of it the court must declare the plaintiffs entitled to priority and give the usual consequent relief. The plaintiffs must add to their security so much of the costs of the action in the court below as would have been incurred if the action had been a simple action for foreclosure and no question of priority had been raised, and the defendant must pay to the plaintiffs the residue of the plaintiffs' costs in the court below and the whole of the costs in the appeal.

Appeal allowed.

QUESTIONS AND COMMENTS

1. Which of the four contest permutations occurred in this case?

2. The Court in *Whipp* noted that the directors exhibited "great carelessness," yet failed to treat this as postponing conduct. The current view is that gross negligence by the prior holder can suffice: see *Tyrell v. Mills* [1924] 3 W.W.R. 387, 1924 CarswellBC 74 (Co. Ct.). Moreover, there are other circumstance in where the prior (legal) holder may be estopped by virtue of representations made, or appearances given, from asserting priority against the second claimant: see further P. Butt, *Land Law*, 4th ed. (Sydney: Law Book Co., 2001) at 596.

Australian Guarantee Corp. (N.Z.) Ltd. v. C.F.C. Commercial Finance Ltd. [1995] 1 N.Z.L.R. 129 (C.A.)

Tompkins J.:

This appeal concerns priorities between unregistered mortgages over land. On 14 September 1987, the appellant, Australian Guarantee Corporation (NZ) Ltd (AGC) entered into a hire purchase agreement with Dante Holdings Ltd (Dante) as borrower, and Richard Dante Mitri and Adrian Christopher Mitri (the principal shareholders in Dante) as covenantors, whereby AGC advanced to Dante $100,320 for the purchase of a Mercedes-Benz motor vehicle. On the same day AGC and Dante executed a deed of mortgage over property owned by Dante at Penny Road, Rotorua as a collateral security for the advance.

Four days later, on 18 September 1987 the respondent, CFC Commercial Finance Ltd (CFC) lent Dante $125,000, the advance being secured by a mortgage given by Dante as mortgagor to CFC as mortgagee over the same property at Penny Road, Rotorua. Neither mortgage was registered. CFC as plaintiff commenced proceedings in the High Court at Auckland against AGC as defendant, seeking a declaration that it was entitled to a first charge over the Rotorua property. In its statement of defence AGC denied the allegations upon which CFC relied. It claimed a declaration that it was entitled to a first charge over the property and any proceeds of it.

This action came before Hillyer J. on 18 June 1992, and 23 and 25 February 1993. In an oral judgment delivered on 25 February 1993, Hillyer J. made a declaration that CFC was entitled to priority and a first charge over the Rotorua property. From that decision AGC has appealed. CFC has cross-appealed, challenging certain of the findings that Hillyer J. had made against CFC.

The sequence of events

Most of the events crucial to this appeal occurred during September 1987. The sequence is significant.

On Wednesday 2 September 1987 a financial brokering firm acting for Dante sent to CFC an application for finance of $125,000, offering as security a first mortgage over the Rotorua property. The purpose of the advance was to assist in the finance of a property development in Wellington.

On Monday 7 September Mr Richard Mitri, a director of Dante, approached AGC for a loan to enable Dante to purchase a Mercedes-Benz car. Dante had $22,000 but wished to borrow a further $100,320 to complete the purchase. Dante offered as security a hire-purchase agreement over the car and a mortgage over the Rotorua property. Mr Mitri told AGC that the property was unencumbered and that AGC's charge would be a first ranking security.

On Friday 11 September CFC sent to Dante's brokers an offer for a loan of $125,000 for 12 months at an effective interest rate of 23.41 per cent. The interest, some $25,000, was payable at the commencement of the term of the loan. Dante would receive $99,534 net. The security was to be a registered first mortgage over the Rotorua property.

Three days later, on Monday 14 September, the transaction with AGC was complete. Dante executed a hire-purchase agreement over the Mercedes-Benz car. It also executed a collateral deed of mortgage over the Rotorua property. Messrs Mitri signed both as guarantors. It was a term of the mortgage that the property was not subject to any encumbrances and that Dante would not further encumber the property without the consent of AGC. The mortgage was not in registrable form. But the deed of mortgage provided for Dante and the guarantors to execute a registrable mortgage when called upon, and appointed AGC their attorney to execute a mortgage on their behalf. AGC did not require the title to the Rotorua property to be handed over.

Two days later, on Wednesday 16 September, in preparation for the making of its advance, CFC obtained a search of the title to the Rotorua property. The search showed it was unencumbered.

On Friday 18 September, Dante executed a registrable memorandum of mortgage over the Rotorua property to secure the CFC advance of $125,000. Richard Mitri also signed as covenantor. On settlement of the advance, the title to the Rotorua property was handed over to the solicitors acting for CFC along with the signed memorandum of mortgage.

On the same day, Friday 18 September, AGC wrote to its Hamilton solicitors enclosing a copy of the collateral deed of mortgage, the title search and a cheque with instructions to register a caveat against the title to the Rotorua property.

On the following Wednesday, 23 September, the *caveat* was lodged by AGC in the land registry office at Hamilton, claiming an estate or interest in the Rotorua property by virtue of "a certain collateral deed of mortgage bearing date the 14 September 1987" between AGC as lender and Dante and Messrs Mitri as borrowers.

On 5 October, CFC registered its mortgage at the Companies Office in the Register of Charges.

It was not until some two months after the charges were created, namely on 24 November 1987, that AGC and CFC became aware of each other's charge. On 24 November there appears to have been a telephone conversation between Mr Partridge of AGC and Mr Ross of Kensington Swan, the solicitors for CFC. Neither of these persons gave evidence but the telephone conversation is referred to in a letter from Kensington Swan to AGC of 25 November. After referring to the telephone conversation, the relevant part of the letter reads:

> Our client wishes to register a first mortgage over the land in Certificate of Title 22A/786 to CFC Commercial Finance Ltd. The principal sum of the mortgage is $125,000.00 and is to be repaid on 18 September 1988.
>
> In anticipation of your consenting to the above registration *we enclose* a consent to be executed by you. We would appreciate it if you would treat this matter as one of urgency.

There is no evidence of any reply to that letter.

There is no evidence of CFC taking any further steps at that stage to obtain registration of its mortgage in the Land Registry Office. But on or about 15 December, CFC lodged a caveat against the title to the Rotorua property, based on its mortgage. However, in April 1988 Kensington Swan, on behalf of CFC, apparently made a further inquiry of AGC in a letter of 14 April 1988 which has not been produced. AGC relied on 22 April 1988 by letter which included:

> We have still not received a recent valuation, addressed to AGC (NZ) Ltd, of the 1982 Mercedes-Benz 500 registration LX5794.
>
> On receipt of this valuation we will consider annexing our consent as Caveator.

At about this time in early 1988, Dante was regularly in default in payment of the hire purchase instalments due to AGC. On 14 September 1988 the final instalment of $103,430.83 was not paid. A default notice was issued on 16 September 1988.

On 16 December 1988 Rudd Watts & Stone, who by that time were acting for CFC, wrote to AGC as follows:

> We note your company has a Caveat No. H.752295 over the property comprised in Certificate of Title 22A/786 (South Auckland Registry).
>
> Pursuant to Section 92 of the Property Law Act 1952, we enclose a copy of the Section 92 Notice, which we have served on Dante Holdings Ltd in an attempt to bring the default by them under an unregistered mortgage dated 18 September 1987 to their attention. We also enclose a copy of a Section 92(6) Notice served on the Covenantor of the Mortgage. If compliance is not made with this, our client will be proceeding to a mortgagee sale of the property.
>
> We would be obliged if you could notify us of what is required to satisfy your caveat.
>
> We look forward to hearing from you.

AGC replied by letter dated 29 December that the amount required to satisfy its caveat was $111,738.01.

On 18 April 1989, on an application by CFC, Dante was wound up by order of the Court. It was also in that month — the date is not stated — that AGC was advised for the first time by CFC that its caveat was being challenged.

On 20 May 1989 CFC submitted its mortgage for registration. This caused the Registrar to give notice to AGC that its caveat would lapse pursuant to s 145 of the Land Transfer Act 1952. The result was an application by AGC for an order that its caveat should not lapse. That application came before Master Towle on 3 July 1989. In a reserved judgment delivered on 24 July 1989 he ordered that the caveat should not lapse. The principal issue argued before the Master was that, by virtue of ss 102 and 103 of the Companies Act 1955, the deed of mortgage was void against Dante's liquidator and against any creditor. That contention was not accepted by the Master. A similar submission was also rejected by Hillyer J. It was not pursued in this Court.

On 22 May 1989 the Mercedes-Benz car was sold by AGC for $65,005. As at 29 May 1989 the balance owing to AGC, which included penal interest up to that date, was $54,917.87. On 9 September 1990 Richard Mitri was adjudged a bankrupt.

A valuation from a registered valuer dated 21 September 1987 valued the Rotorua property at $225,000. On 10 October 1988 a Rotorua real estate agent expressed the opinion that the fair market value of the property was $185,000. It was sold, by agreement between AGC and CFC, on 15 February 1991 for $160,000. The proceeds of sale have been held pending a decision on which charge has priority. As at 18 March 1991, the amount due to CFC, including penal interest to that date, was $215,226.49, with interest accruing at $159.20 per day.

Judgment in the High Court

Hillyer J., after outlining the facts, approached the issue on the basis of the statement by Griffith C.J. in *Butler v. Fairclough* (1917) 23 C.L.R. 78, 91 approved by the Privy Council in *Abigail v. Lapin* [1934] A.C. 491, 502:

> In the case of a contest between two equitable claimants the first in time, all other things being equal, is entitled to priority. But all other things must be equal, and the claimant who is first in time may lose his priority by any act or omission which had, or might have had, the effect of inducing a claimant later in time to act to his prejudice.

CFC contended that AGC should lose its priority for two reasons. First, because of AGC's delay in caveating the title between Friday 18 September 1987, when Dante executed the AGC mortgage, until registration of the caveat on 23 September and secondly, because of AGC's failure to take possession of the title when the advance was made. Hillyer J. concluded that the delay in registering the caveat need not require the postponement of the prior equitable interest of AGC. But on the second ground, he found in favour of CFC. He concluded that AGC, by permitting Dante to retain the certificate of title, enabled Dante to obtain the CFC advance which it would not have been able to do had the title been in the possession of AGC. For that reason AGC's prior equitable interest should be postponed to that of CFC.

AGC further submitted that the subsequent conduct of CFC, in failing promptly to assert its rights, was a reason against reversing the priorities. The Judge did not accept this submission. He considered that if any criticism could be levelled at CFC for failing to take immediate action, the same criticism can be levelled at AGC. The matters advanced on behalf of AGC were not, in his view, of sufficient substance to overcome what he described as the fundamental flaw that AGC failed to obtain the certificate of title.

The priority of equitable interests

A general rule is that equitable interests take priority in order of date, other things being equal. . . .

In *Heid v. Reliance Finance Corporation Pty Ltd.* (1983) 154 C.L.R. 326 at p. 333 Gibbs C.J. expressed the general approach in these terms:

> If the merits are equal, priority in time of creation is considered to give the better equity. This is the true meaning of the maxim *qui prior est tempore potior est jure*: *Rice v. Rice* [(1853) 2 Drew 73 at p. 78 [61 E.R. 646, at p. 648]]. But where the merits are unequal, as for instance where conduct on the part of the owner of the earlier interest has led the other to acquire his interest on the supposition that the earlier did not exist, the maxim may be displaced and priority accorded to the later interest.

A particularly helpful statement of the proper approach, cited with approval in this Court in *Green v. Meltzer* (1993) 6 N.Z.C.L.C. 68, 393 by Casey J. at p. 68, 396 and Thomas J. at p. 68, 409, is in the joint judgment of Mason and Deane JJ. in *Heid* at p. 341:

> For our part we consider it preferable to avoid the contortions and convolutions associated with basing the postponement of the first to the second equity exclusively on the doctrine of estoppel and to accept a more general and flexible principle that preference should be given to what is the better equity in an examination of the relevant circumstances. It will always be necessary to characterize the conduct of the holder of the earlier interest in order to determine whether, in all the circumstances, that conduct is such that, in fairness and in justice, the earlier interest should be postponed to the later interest. Thus in *Latec Investments* (1965) 113 C.L.R. at p. 276 Kitto J. said that the case where the conduct of the prior owner leads the later owner to acquire his interest on the supposition that the earlier interest does not exist — the test stated by Dixon J. in *Lapin v. Abigail* (1930) 44 C.L.R. at p. 204 — was just one "instance" of a case when the merits are unequal: see also *Lapin v. Abigail* (1930) 44 C.L.R. at pp. 185-186 *per* Isaacs J.; *General Finance Agency, etc.; Co. (In liq.) v. Perpetual Executors and Trustees Association etc.* (1902) 27 V.L.R. 739 at pp. 742–744. To say that the question involves general considerations of fairness and justice acknowledges that, in whatever form the relevant test be stated, the overriding question is ". . . whose is the better equity, bearing in mind the conduct of both parties, the question of any negligence on the part of the prior claimant, the effect of any representation as possibly raising an estoppel and whether it can be said that the conduct of the first or prior owner has enabled such a representation to be made . . .": Sykes, *Law of Securities*, 3rd ed. (1978), p. 366; see also *Dixon v. Muckleston* (1872) L.R. 8 Ch. App. at p. 160; *Latec Investments* (1965) 113 C.L.R. at p. 276. Thus elements of both negligence and estoppel will often be found in the statements of general principle: see, for example, *Lapin v. Abigail* (1930) 44 C.L.R. at p. 204 *per* Dixon J.

An issue that arose in this appeal is the nature of the conduct to which the Court should have regard in determining priorities. Mr Liew for CFC submitted that in considering which of two conflicting equities should have priority, it is the conduct of the first equity holder that should be considered. The conduct of the second equity holder is not relevant. We do not accept that submission. Certainly the conduct of the first equity holder will be significant, particularly where it can be contended that that conduct may have led the second equity holder to believe that no prior charge existed. But there is ample authority for the proposition that the Court's consideration should not be restricted solely to the conduct of the first equity holder. In *Rice v. Rice* (1853) Drew 73 Kindersley V.C. said that in examining the relative merits or equities of two parties, the Court must direct its attention to "the whole conduct of each party". In *Abigail*, in the second passage to which we have referred, Lord Wright stated the test to be whether *either* has been guilty of an act or default that prejudices this claim. In *Heid*, in the passage from Sykes, *Law of Securities* (3rd ed., 1978), p. 336 adopted by Mason and Deane JJ., reference is made to bearing in mind "the conduct of both parties". The passage in *Heid* referring to the conduct of both parties was adopted by Brooking J. in *Cash Resources Australia Pty. Ltd. v. B.T. Securities Ltd.* [1990] V.R. 576 at p. 586.

A second issue is whether, in considering where the equities lay, the Court can have regard to conduct of the parties subsequent to the creation of the second interest. Mr Liew submitted that subsequent conduct is irrelevant and should be disregarded. Again we do not accept that submission. There is little authority on the point. The fact that in many of the decided cases there is no reference to subsequent conduct may simply reflect the absence of any material subsequent conduct. Of course, subsequent registration converting an equitable interest into a legal interest can be relevant, indeed determinative, but that is because of the priority accorded to a legal interest over an equitable one and does not bear on the issue of competing equitable interests. The only authority where this issue has been directly addressed of which we are aware is *Clark v. Raymor (Brisbane) Pty. Ltd. [No. 2]* 1982 Qd. R. 790, a decision of the Full Court of Queensland. Andrews S.P.J., with whom Campbell C.J. agreed, said at p. 791:

> It is my further view that subsequent events may alter the character of an equitable interest in land so as to make relevant the continuing expansion of relevant circumstances, that is to say, relevant to the question of the whole conduct of the parties.

To a similar effect is the statement by Thomas J., with whom the Chief Justice also agreed at p. 797:

> In my opinion the Court is not required to limit its examination to the events which have occurred up to the time of acquisition of the later equitable right. All acts or omissions of either party and the effect of those acts or omissions upon the other party may be relevant, irrespective of the time when they occurred.

This approach is, in our view, consistent with the principles applicable to determining priorities. If the Court is to determine the issue by deciding whose is the better equity, bearing in mind the conduct of both parties and all other relevant circumstances, it is difficult to see why the conduct of the holder of the later interest should not be taken into account. It may well be that greater emphasis will be placed on the conduct of the holder of the earlier interest, since that is the conduct that may have induced the holder of the later interest to take the interest in the first place. But if the holder of the later interest subsequently acts in a way that causes the holder of the earlier interest to act contrary to its interests, we see no reason why that conduct should not be placed in the scales when determining where the equities lay. The Court is, after all, concerned with the demands of fairness and justice. The preferable approach, where there is subsequent conduct of a kind that equity will regard as significant, will be to consider the whole picture at the time of decision and to fix priorities according to which party then is perceived as having the better equity.

The onus rests on the second equity holder as the party seeking to reverse the order of temporal priority. If, contrary to the normal rule, the later claimant is to be preferred, the onus lies on that claimant to demonstrate why: *General Finance Agency and Guarantee Co of Australia Ltd. (In Liquidation) v. Perpetual Executors and Trustees Association of Australia Ltd.* (1902) 27 V.L.R. 739 Holroyd J. at p. 743.

Authorities from other jurisdictions are to be treated carefully. Older English cases which place heavy emphasis on possession of title deeds are not necessarily directly applicable to circumstances in which caveat protection is taken. Similarly, the practice relating to and the effects of caveats are not the same in all countries. . . .

The task should therefore be approached by considering whether the secondary equity holder has established, at the time of decision, that there has been conduct sufficient to discharge the first equity holder's prima facie priority. It will be if the conduct is of such significance that the merits are no longer equal. That will be so if the conduct of the first equity holder has led the second equity holder to believe that there was no prior equity, by clothing another party with the means to confer an interest apparently not subject to the prior interest. But that is not the only test. In deciding whether it is fair and just that the equities be reversed, and if so whether any reversal should be on any conditions, the Court should have regard to all relevant conduct of both parties before and after the creation of the equities.

The factors relevant to priority

Three factors were raised relevant to whether there should be a change in the order of temporal priority. They were, first, AGC's delay in registering its caveat, secondly, AGC's action in not requiring the title to the Rotorua property to be handed over on settlement and, thirdly, CFC's delay in challenging AGC's priority. We consider each in turn, although in the end it is the combination of all these factors that will need to be considered.

Registration of the caveat

Failure to register the caveat promptly can, but not necessarily will, be conduct that may justify a reversal of priorities of equitable charges over land. In *Butler v. Fairclough* Griffith C.J., at p. 92, declined to draw any line prescribing the time within which a caveat should be lodged. But he observed that "The person who does not act promptly loses the advantage which he would have gained by promptitude." In *J & H Just (Holdings) Pty. Ltd. v. Bank of New South Wales*, Barwick C.J. at p. 554 declined to hold that a failure to lodge a caveat must necessarily involve the loss of priority. But there may be situations in which such a failure may combine with other circumstances to justify that conclusion. As Mason and Deane JJ. said in *Heid v. Reliance Finance Corporation Pty. Ltd.* at p. 342, the failure to lodge a caveat is "just one of the circumstances to be considered in determining whether it is inequitable that the prior equitable owner should retain his priority."

The AGC transaction was completed on Monday 14 September by the execution of the hire-purchase agreement and the collateral deed of mortgage. It was always AGC's intention to protect the interest created by the deed of mortgage by a caveat. But it was not until four days later on Friday 18 September that AGC wrote to its Hamilton solicitors with instructions to lodge the caveat. It was lodged five days after that, namely on Wednesday 23 September. No explanation was given for the delay in instructing its Hamilton solicitors. The evidence does not establish at what time on Monday 14 September the transaction was completed. But there was ample evidence to show that AGC could have had the caveat lodged by Tuesday 15 September.

In considering the significance of this delay, regard must be had to its causative effect. It was on Wednesday 16 September, two days after the AGC transaction was complete, that CFC obtained a search of the title. It did not obtain any further search prior to the settlement of the CFC transaction two days later on Friday 18 September. So for the lodging of the caveat to have been effective notice to CFC of the existence of the prior charge, it would have had to be lodged at the latest by the morning of Wednesday 16 September, two days after AGC transaction was settled. To have achieved this result AGC would certainly have had to move with considerable promptitude. However Mr Morpeth, on behalf of AGC, acknowledged that he considered, and discussed with Mr Mitri, the possibility that Dante might be approaching further lenders offering security over the Rotorua property. Mr Morpeth told Mr Mitri that any further security would require the consent of AGC.

The title to the Rotorua property

A prior equity holder can lose priority by allowing evidence of title, such as title deeds to land, share certificates and the like, to remain in the possession of the borrower, thus enabling the borrower to lead a second equity holder to believe that a charge he obtains will be a first priority. See for example *Waldron v. Sloper* (1852) 1 Drew 193 and *Farrand v. Yorkshire Banking Co.* (1888) 40 Ch. D. 182. By failing to obtain the evidence of title, the holder of the prior equitable interest has, as Lord

Selborne L.C. put it in *Dixon v. Muckleston* (1872) L.R. 8 Ch. App. 155 at p. 160, "armed another person with the power of going into the world under false colours."

There was evidence that both AGC and CFC knew of and adopted the practice of lending on unregistered mortgages which they protected by lodging a caveat but not by obtaining the certificate of title. In our view, that these two commercial lenders were apparently willing to take the risk of making advances secure by unregistered mortgages without insisting on possession of the evidence of title is certainly not conclusive. In considering where lie the equities, the Court should consider the likely actions of a prudent lender. We agree with the observations of Brooking J. in *Cash Resources Australia Pty. Ltd. v. B. T. Securities Ltd.* at p. 586:

> I should have thought that the first concern of any prudent man, lending money on the security of property, would be to obtain written evidence of the loan and to possess himself of the documents of title to the property offered as security. Possession of the documents of title is important for two reasons: to prevent the borrower from fraudulently disposing of or encumbering the property on the footing that it is unencumbered and to facilitate realisation of the security in the event of default. The first of these reasons is at least as important as the second. I should have thought that preservation of the security interest against subsequent fraudulent dispositions was a more fundamental consideration than the mechanics of realisation.

Cash Resources was a share certificate case but the same reasoning applies, if anything with more force, to certificates of title to land.

There is little doubt that the failure of AGC to acquire the title to be held by it was causative. We accept that possession of the title is not conclusive evidence that there may not be some unregistered mortgage interest. We also accept it would have been possible for Dante to have obtained a duplicate of the title, but this could not have occurred until well after AGC's caveat had been registered. As Mrs Hinton submitted, Dante was the registered proprietor of the land before the AGC transaction and it remained the registered proprietor afterwards. But it is clear from the evidence on behalf of CFC that it would not have made its advance had the title not been available, which it would not have been had AGC insisted on the registered proprietor's copy of the title being handed over on settlement.

The two factors of not registering the caveat quickly and not obtaining the title need to be considered together. The delay in registering the caveat becomes less significant had AGC obtained the title. Conversely, not obtaining the title may be less significant if CFC had moved quickly to register the caveat. The combination of the delay in registering the caveat and the failure to obtain the title justify the conclusion that, viewing the position shortly after the creation of the two interests, it is just and fair that the priorities should be reversed.

CFC's delay in challenging AGC's priority

It remains to consider whether, and if so to what extent, CFC's apparent acquiescence and delay in challenging AGC's priority should affect this conclusion.

The delay was considerable. CFC was apparently aware of the existence of the caveat when its solicitors, Kensington Swan, wrote to AGC on 25 November. It is reasonable to assume that it had searched the caveat. That would have disclosed that the caveat was claimed by virtue of a collateral deed of mortgage dated 14 September 1987, that is, prior in time to CFC's mortgage. Yet Kensington Swan's letter of 25 November did not state the date of CFC's mortgage. CFC ought then to have realised that AGC must have allowed Dante to retain possession of the title since it had been handed over to CFC. Not only did CFC not indicate an intention to challenge AGC's apparent priority, it simply sought consent to the registration of its mortgage, and when it received no reply to that request, it took no action until six months later in April 1988 when Kensington Swan made a further inquiry of AGC, receiving the response set out above. Eight months later, in December 1988, CFC's then solicitors again wrote to AGC asking what it required to satisfy the caveat, from which AGC reasonably could have assumed that CFC accepted AGC's priority. It was not until April 1989, one year and five months after it became aware of the caveat, that CFC notified AGC of its intention to challenge AGC's priority.

Mrs Hinton strongly urged that CFC is estopped from denying AGC's priority because this delay led AGC to believe that it had priority and that that belief caused AGC to act to its detriment by failing to realise its securities at a stage when not only it, but probably both lenders, could have been satisfied. She submitted that AGC was therefore lulled by CFC into a false sense of security. AGC took no steps to secure its position when in all probability, had it known its priority was challenged, it would have acted to secure its position against Dante. From early 1988 AGC could have realised its security over the car for breach of the hire purchase agreement and could have executed a registerable mortgage over the land, registered it and exercised the power of sale which (even after first paying out CFC) would have yielded enough to meet the balance of the indebtedness to AGC. If CFC is now accorded priority, its delay will have effectively destroyed the value of the AGC equitable interest in the land.

But there are other considerations. AGC learned as early as Kensington Swan's letter of 25 November 1987 that Dante had given another mortgage over the land, and that it must have done so, contrary to the discussions that Mr Morpeth had with Mr Mitri, without the consent of AGC. It should have assumed that Dante did so using the title to the land that AGC had allowed it to retain. It should also have realised that the existence of two unregistered charges created the possibility of problems arising, more so as time went by and the interest charges mounted.

Further, that AGC was prepared to consider consenting to the registration of the CFC mortgage after ascertaining the value of its security in the car, may suggest some recognition that CFC may have a greater claim than as a subsequent mortgagee. The correspondence in its full context, rather than requiring a finding of acquiescence or estoppel, might merely reflect attempts to achieve an amicable compromise between commercial financiers.

The relief to be granted

In the circumstances we would not go so far as to conclude that because of its delay CFC must forfeit the priority to which it otherwise is entitled. That does not, however, conclude the matter. CFC is seeking equity in the form of a declaration that its interest be accorded priority over another equitable interest earlier in time. . . .

CFC, as a condition of the declaration that its interest has priority, is to ameliorate the disadvantage AGC suffered from CFC's acquiescence and delay in challenging AGC's priority. Even a year after CFC learnt of AGC's interest, there was adequate security for full recovery by both parties. The same position likely prevailed almost until CFC eventually did challenge AGC's priority in April 1989. The deterioration thereafter resulted partly from a fall in the value of the land but more as a result of the high penal interest accruing to both lenders.

In May 1989, after realising its security over the car, AGC was owed $54,917.87. At that time the amount owing to CFC would have been less than $150,000. The total would probably have exceeded the market value of the land by only a relatively small amount.

While is it not possible or necessary to be exact, AGC will be put in the position it would probably have achieved but for the delay by requiring CFC, as a condition of the declaration of priority in its favour, to pay $54,917.87 to AGC out of the proceeds of the sale of the land. AGC should also receive its proportionate share of the interest earned from the time of the sale of the land on the net proceeds of sale.

To that limited extent, the appeal is allowed. In all other respects it is dismissed. Since CFC has retained its priority as declared in the High Court but subject to its making the payment to AGC, both parties have succeeded to some extent. There will be no order as to costs.

Appeal allowed in part.

QUESTIONS AND COMMENTS

1. In the end, the Court concluded that postponement of AGC's interest was warranted. However, it was added that "CFC, as a condition of the declaration that its interest has priority, is to ameliorate the disadvantage suffered form CFC's acquiescence and delay in challenging AGC's priority". Accordingly, CFC, while purportedly being given priority, was required to pay $54,917.87 to AGC. If so, in what way did CFC achieve priority?

2. As is apparent from the judgment, New Zealand operates under a land titles system of registration. Yet, equitable rules for priority determined the outcome of the case. The interplay between those rules and statutory regimes forms part of the analysis to follow.

Chippewas of Sarnia Band v. Canada (A.G.) (2000) 41 R.P.R. (3d) 1, 2000 CarswellOnt 4836 (C.A.)

[In 1839, Aboriginal leaders purported to sell lands to Malcolm Cameron. The Crown had been advised of the negotiations for the sale, and the agreement for sale was approved by an order in council. Title to the lands did not pass until 1853, at which time letters patent for the lands were issued to Cameron. It will be recalled that under the common law rules governing Aboriginal title, land is inalienable except to the Crown, and the mode of transfer to the Crown is by surrender. The order in council was consistent with the idea that there would be a formal surrendering of the lands, and the letters patent were apparently issued under the mistaken belief that a valid surrender had occurred.

It was not until about 150 years after these events that the Band disputed title to the patented lands. In the intervening period, the lands had been subdivided, sold and re-sold on numerous occasions to a string of private owners, all of whom were thoroughly unaware of the irregularities mentioned above.

Applications were brought by the government of Canada and the affected landowners seeking a summary judgment rejecting the land claim. The Government of Ontario supported these applications. The Chippewas of Sarnia also sought summary judgment. At first instance, it was held *inter alia* the application by the landowners succeeded, the motions judge holding that their entitlements were not encumbered by Aboriginal title.

The motions judge also held that the land had never been lawfully surrendered to the Crown. That conclusion was affirmed by the Ontario Court of Appeal. It was also held that the claim was not barred by virtue of a fixed limitation period. That being so, what was the correct state of title?]

Per Curiam: . . .

Remedies and Equitable Defences

A. Introduction

As we have concluded that there was no proper surrender and that the Chippewas' actions are not barred by any statutory limitation periods, the issue becomes whether, on the facts of this case, the Chippewas are entitled to the remedies they seek, namely, a declaration that the Cameron patent is void and a declaration that they are entitled to possession of the disputed lands. In particular, the issue is whether it is appropriate, in deciding whether or not to accord the Chippewas a remedy, for the court to consider that no claim was asserted for 150 years, and that innocent third parties may have relied on the apparent validity of the Cameron patent.

The issue of remedies and equitable defences, like the other issues in this case, has both public and private law dimensions. The aboriginal right asserted by the

Chippewas has been described as *sui generis* in nature. The *sui generis* nature of aboriginal title reflects the interaction between traditional aboriginal values and those of European settlers and consequently, aboriginal title is not readily classified in the conventional categories of the English common law tradition. In some respects, aboriginal title draws upon the concepts of public law. The rights it embraces are communal in nature and can only be understood in the context of the unique relationship between the Crown and the aboriginal community asserting the right. At the same time, aboriginal title has been held on the highest authority to be a right of property and it cannot be described or understood except in relation to the concepts of traditional common law private property rights.

The remedies claimed by the Chippewas reflect the dual public and private law dimensions of aboriginal title. As against the Crown, the Chippewas impugn the validity of the exercise of the Crown prerogative, invoking the principles of public law and the remedies available to challenge the legality of governmental action. At the same time, the Chippewas assert a claim to a property right against the private citizens who are the present occupiers of the property, invoking the legal principles governing the reconciliation of competing claims to private property. It follows that defences bearing upon the availability of remedies in both the public and private law settings must be considered.

As we have already noted, the issue of the Chippewas' right to damages against the Crown for breach of its aboriginal rights is not before us. The damages claim was not the subject of the motions for summary judgment and it was common ground that it would proceed to trial. Accordingly, we confine our attention to the Chippewas' claim for a remedy related to the return of the lands themselves and we do so on the basis that the Chippewas have a right of action against the Crown for damages. . . .

[The Court of Appeal then reviewed and rejected the Chippewas' arguments that public law remedies were appropriate in the circumstances of this case. In the course of doing so, the Court described the effect of the granting of defective letters patent.]

Apparently valid acts of public officials are relied upon by the members of the public at large in planning their affairs. Official documents are taken at face value. The purported exercise of a statutory or prerogative power creates legitimate expectations that the law will protect. The administration of government is a human act and errors are inevitable. The rights of a party aggrieved by the error must be reconciled with the interests of third parties and the interests of orderly administration. Accordingly, . . . a remedy may be refused where delay by the aggrieved party in asserting the claim would result in hardship or prejudice to the public interest or to third parties who have acted in good faith upon the impugned act or decision.

A Crown patent, apparently granting the fee simple in land, provides a classic example of an official act that will be relied on by innocent third parties. A Crown patent is accepted by all as the basis for rights to real property and no purchaser would consider it necessary to go behind the patent to determine whether or not it had been validly granted. It is for this reason that the courts have for long hesitated to invalidate patents that have created third party reliance. See, for example, *Bailey v. Du Cailland* (1905), 6 O.W.R. 506 (Div. Ct.), at 508 *per* Falconbridge J.:

> It was held in *McIntyre v. Attorney-General*, 14 Gr. 86, that where a bill is filed by a private individual to repeal letters patent on the ground of error, the onus of proof is on the plaintiff, although it may to some extent involve proof of a negative. "Patents are not to be lightly disturbed. They lie at the foundation of every man's title to his property."

To a similar effect is the following statement from *Fitzpatrick v. R.* (1926), 59 O.L.R. 331 (C.A.), at 342 quoting from *Boulton v. Jeffrey* (1845), 1 E. & A. 111 (U.C. Q.B.):

> It is difficult indeed to conceive a more prolific source of litigation than would be opened in this Province, if the patentees of the Crown were exposed to be attacked upon supposed equities acquired by other parties, while the estate was vested in the Crown, when no fraud, misrepresentation or concealment is imputed to the patentee, and when the Crown, at the time of making the grant, has exercised its discretion on a view of all the circumstances. Just such a patent as this lies at the root of every man's title.

The motions judge analyzed this aspect of the case in terms of whether the Cameron patent was "void". He held that the Cameron patent was "void". A "void" patent is said to be one that has no legal effect whatsoever, while a "voidable" patent is one that does have effect unless and until it is set aside. Whatever its merits for other purposes, the language of "void" and "voidable" seems to us to be not a particularly apt or helpful analytic tool in the present context. From a remedial perspective, the inherent discretion of the court is always in play. As Wade has explained, [Wade and Forsyth, *Administrative Law* 7th ed. (Oxford: Clarenden Press, 1980)] at 343-4, the term "void" is "meaningless in any absolute sense. Its meaning is relative, depending upon the court's willingness to grant relief in any particular situation." Wade adds, at 718, in relation to the discretionary nature of judicial review, "a void act is in effect a valid act if the court will not grant relief against it." See also Jones and de Villars, [*Principles of Administrative Law* 3rd ed. (Scarborough, Ont.: Carswell, 1999)] at 404. Accordingly, for practical purposes, a patent that suffers from a defect that renders it subject to attack will continue to exist and to have legal effect unless and until a court decides to set it aside. In our view, the issue is more clearly put and understood in terms of the discretion to grant or withhold a remedy and the factors that must be considered in relation to the exercise of that discretion. In fairness to the motions judge, it should be mentioned here that the arguments regarding the discretionary nature of public law remedies do not appear to have been presented to him with the same force and clarity as they were in this Court. . . .

Private Law Remedies

From the perspective of the private law of property, discretionary factors are traditionally associated with the determination of equitable claims and the availability of equitable remedies. Until the fusion of law and equity in the mid-19th century, a rigid line was drawn between law and equity, and discretion was associated with claims arising from equity as distinct from purely legal claims. That rigid dichotomy has since broken down, but historical factors continue to influence the applicability of equitable principles to claims traditionally associated with the common law. The issue to be addressed here is whether, from the private law perspective, the remedies claimed by the Chippewas are subject to the discretion traditionally associated with equity.

The Chippewas submit that a finding that there was no surrender of the lands covered by the Cameron patent must inevitably lead to the conclusion that their aboriginal title to the lands remains unextinguished and that they have a present entitlement to possession of the lands. The Chippewas rely on the *nemo dat quod non habet* principle — no one gives what he does not have. The Chippewas submit that as there was no surrender, the Crown had nothing to grant and that the Cameron patent did not and could not convey the fee simple to the lands unencumbered by the aboriginal title. The Chippewas contend that given the nature of aboriginal title, it is not subject to the discretionary factors governing the availability of equitable relief. There are two aspects to this submission. First, the Chippewas submit that aboriginal title is strictly legal rather than equitable in nature. Second, it is submitted that application of equitable doctrines to preclude the Chippewas' claim to the lands would constitute an unauthorized extinguishment of aboriginal title in favour of private interests, contrary to the fundamental rule that aboriginal title can only be surrendered to the Crown.

1. Equitable Nature of Remedies Sought

In our view, the Chippewas' position that equitable principles have no bearing upon their claim cannot be accepted. To the extent that the Chippewas claim the lands as distinct from damages, they assert a claim for an equitable remedy. Before the motions judge, the Chippewas asserted a claim for declaratory relief. In the factum filed on this appeal, the Chippewas reiterated that claim and sought as well an order requiring the Crown in right of both Canada and Ontario to enter negotiations with a view to resolving the Chippewas' claim. In oral argument before this court, Mr. Cherniak on behalf of the Chippewas maintained the position that the primary relief sought by the appellants was for a declaratory judgment, accompanied by a claim for an order directing the negotiations. However, Mr. Cherniak also pointed out that the statement of claim contained a claim for an immediate vesting order, and on behalf of his clients, he asserted that claim should this court consider that a declaratory order should not be granted on discretionary grounds.

It is well established, and not disputed before us, that the remedy of a declaratory judgment is equitable in origin and that its award is subject to the discretion of the court . . .

The power to grant a vesting order is conferred by the *Courts of Justice Act*, R.S.O. 1990, c. C.43, s. 100 which provides as follows:

> 100. A court *may* by order vest in any person an interest in real or personal property that the court has authority to order be disposed of, encumbered or conveyed. (Emphasis added.)

Vesting orders are equitable in origin and discretionary in nature. The Court of Chancery made *in personam* orders, directing parties to deal with property in accordance with the judgment of the court. Judgments of the Court of Chancery were enforced on proceedings for contempt, followed by imprisonment or sequestration. The statutory power to make a vesting order supplemented the contempt power by allowing the Court to effect the change of title directly: see McGhee, *Snell's Equity* 30th ed., (London: Sweet and Maxwell, 2000) at 41-42. As explained by Proudfoot V.C. in *Robertson, Re* (1875), 22 Gr. 449 (Ont. Ch.), at 456, the statute gives the court the power "to make a vesting order whenever it might have ordered a conveyance to be executed". Quite apart from its equitable origins, by the very terms of s. 100, the power to grant a vesting order lies in the discretion of the court. Cases decided under s. 100 explicitly refer to the power to grant a vesting order in discretionary terms: see *Ontario Housing Corp. v. Ong* (1988), 63 O.R. (2d) 799 (C.A.); *Holmsten v. Karson Kartage Konstruction Ltd.* (1997), 33 O.R. (3d) 54 (Gen. Div.).

Assuming, without deciding, that such an order could be made, an order requiring the Crown to enter negotiations with the Chippewas would be a novel remedy, not readily classified in conventional terms. Such an order would have a mandatory aspect and would require the ongoing involvement and supervision of the court. An order having these features plainly could not be available as of right. However such a remedy should be classified in the traditional terms of law and equity; its award must therefore necessarily be subject to the discretion of the court.

In our view, the Chippewas cannot escape the fact that, from a private law perspective, they are claiming remedies that are discretionary in nature and subject to equitable defences.

2. Aboriginal Title and Equitable Principles

Nor do we accept the submission that a claim to aboriginal title is strictly legal in nature and immune from the overriding principles of equity, particularly where equitable remedies are being claimed.

The Chippewas rely on recent decisions of the Supreme Court of Canada elaborating the nature of aboriginal title as a *sui generis* legal property right: see for example *Guerin* [*Guerin v. R.*, [1984] 2 S.C.R. 335 (S.C.C.)] at 382; *Delgamuukw* [*Delgamuukw v. British Columbia*, [1997] 3 S.C.R. 1010 (S.C.C.)] at 1081–97. These statements must not be taken out of context. They reflect the repudiation by the Supreme Court of Canada of the view that aboriginal title is a mere interest, held by grace and at the pleasure of the Crown. The important recognition of the legally enforceable nature of aboriginal title does not, however, reflect a rigid classification of aboriginal title as strictly legal in nature, immune from the principles of equity. Rights of equitable origin are every bit as legally enforceable as rights of a common law origin. By insisting that aboriginal title is legally enforceable, the Supreme Court of Canada did not, in our view, intend to classify aboriginal title in terms more relevant to the 19th century, pre-*Judicature Act*, pre-fusion of law and equity phase of our legal development.

The submission that aboriginal title is a strictly legal interest, untouched and untouchable by equitable considerations, ignores several important factors. As stated above, the Supreme Court of Canada has insisted that aboriginal title must not be considered in the strictly formal and traditional terms of the common law tradition, but rather that it must be seen as *sui generis* in nature. The Supreme Court has also held that in aboriginal title cases there is a "necessity for getting rid of the assumption that the ownership of land naturally breaks itself up into estates, conceived as creatures of inherent legal principle" (*Guerin*, *supra*, at 380). The court has also stated that "native land rights are in a category of their own, and as such, traditional real property rules do not aid" and that courts "do not approach [a case involving assertion of aboriginal title] as would an ordinary common law judge, by strict reference to intractable real property rules" (*St. Mary's Indian Band v. Cranbrook (City)*, [1997] 2 S.C.R. 657 (S.C.C.), at 667). Moreover, in this area, courts "must ensure that form not trump substance" (*Delgamuukw*, *supra*, at 1090).

There can be no doubt that the juridical character of aboriginal title has been influenced and shaped by equitable principles. The very nature of aboriginal title, in particular the core concept that aboriginal lands are inalienable except to the Crown, gives rise to a fiduciary duty. The fiduciary relationship imposed upon the Crown to deal with surrendered Indian lands for the benefit of the Indians is a central and fundamental aspect of aboriginal title. In *Guerin*, the case that identified and imposed the fiduciary duty upon the Crown, Dickson J. stated at 376 that "[t]he fiduciary relationship between the Crown and the Indians has its roots in the concept of aboriginal, native or Indian title".

It is difficult to see why a right having these characteristics and drawing so heavily upon the principles of equity for its shape and definition should be entirely immune from the principles of equity from a remedial perspective. Surely, a *sui generis* right should draw freely upon all otherwise relevant principles of our law, whatever their historic origin. An analogy may be drawn from *Cadbury Schweppes Inc. v. FBI Foods Ltd.*, [1999] 1 S.C.R. 142 (S.C.C.), at 179 where the sui generis nature of breach of confidence was found to support the argument for modifying the remedial strictures of the categories of common law and equity. Referring to the line of authority, discussed in the next paragraph, to the effect that "[e]quity, like the common law, is capable of ongoing growth and development," Binnie J. held that the authority to award damages is "inherent in the exercise of general equitable jurisdiction" and is no longer dependent upon the "niceties" of specific statutory authority to award damages in lieu of an injunction. He added, at 179-80:

> This conclusion is fed, as well, by the *sui generis* nature of the action. The objective in a breach of confidence case is to put the confider in as good a position as it would have been in but for the breach. To that end, the Court has ample jurisdiction to fashion

appropriate relief out of the full gamut of available remedies, including appropriate financial compensation.

To hold that aboriginal rights are immune from the principles of equity would be inconsistent with the repudiation of the traditional dichotomy between law and equity by this Court, the Supreme Court of Canada and by the House of Lords, particularly in relation to remedial issues. As Grange J.A. stated in *LeMesurier v. Andrus* (1986), 54 O.R. (2d) 1 (C.A.), at 9 with reference to the legislative direction that the courts "shall administer concurrently all rules of equity and the common law" (now found in the Courts of Justice Act, s. 96(1)), "the fusion of law and equity is now real and total". In *Canson Enterprises Ltd. v. Boughton & Co.*, [1991] 3 S.C.R. 534 (S.C.C.), at 582 La Forest J. adopted Lord Diplock's assertion in *United Scientific Holdings Ltd. v. Burnley Borough Council* (1977), [1978] A.C. 904 (U.K. H.L.), at 924-5 that the merger of law and equity is complete and that "the waters of the confluent streams of law and equity have surely mingled now."

While no doubt the categories that were shaped by the historical influences of common law and equity of law remain relevant for certain purposes, the spirit of the fusion of the two streams is the dominant theme and influence in the modern era. In our view, the modern conception of our private law as a fusion of equitable and legal principles provides added weight to the argument that the discretionary factors associated with equitable remedies may be considered in the present case. For these reasons, we reject the contention that the *sui generis* right of aboriginal title should be rigidly classified as falling exclusively into one of the historic streams of our legal history, completely immune from the influence of the other. Accordingly, as the Chippewas seek remedies that are discretionary in nature to vindicate a *sui generis* right that draws upon both common law and equitable sources, we conclude that it is appropriate to consider the effect of the Chippewas' 150-year delay in asserting a remedy and the consequent impact upon third parties of granting the Chippewas the remedies they seek.

On the facts of this case, we do not accept the submission that holding the Chippewas bound by the rules that govern the availability of equitable remedies constitutes an unauthorized extinguishment of aboriginal title. First of all, it is the Chippewas who invoke the principles of equity by their claim for the remedies described above. It is difficult to see a case for granting those remedies other than on the well-established principles governing their availability. Second, as indicated in our analysis of public law remedies, we are satisfied that although formal surrender procedures were not followed, the purpose of the surrender procedure — to protect the aboriginal interest — was fully met by the interposition of the Crown in the Cameron transaction.

3. The *Nemo Dat* Principle

The Chippewas submit that as there was no surrender of aboriginal title to the Crown, the Crown had nothing it could grant to Cameron by way of patent. It follows, in the submission of the Chippewas, that the Cameron patent was void and that nothing was conveyed. We have already dealt with the submission that the patent was "void" and concluded that established legal principles require the court to take into account the interests of innocent third parties before declaring a patent "void". In our view, the *nemo dat* principle, as it was applied to Crown patents, is entirely consistent with that view.

An early Canadian case, *Doe d. Malloch v. Principal Officers of Her Majesty's Ordinance* (1847), 3 U.C.Q.B. 387 at 394 dealt with a patent of land already set aside for another purpose. The judgment of Robinson C.J. was to the effect that at common law, the question whether such a patent was void or voidable was unsettled, although he was inclined to the view that it was merely voidable.

Other cases show that the *nemo dat* principle did not render void all Crown patents of lands to which the Crown lacked title. *Alcock v. Cooke* (1829), 5 Bing. 340 (Eng. C.P.) states that in the case of the Crown, the *nemo dat* rule was based on the notion that in making a subsequent grant of lands the Crown had already conveyed to another, the Crown must have been deceived. As Crown grants were "enrolled", in other words, officially recorded, the subject had the means of determining what grants had been made and was under a duty to inform the King of the existence of the prior grant before accepting a subsequent grant. It followed that the recipient of the grant previously made to another could assert no claim under the subsequent grant. However, where the Crown granted lands that were not subject to an "enrolled" grant, the court stated that the doctrine had no application. The following example was given by Best C.J. at 349:

> The attention of the court has been called to the circumstance of this being a lease from the king, which must be enrolled; and the doctrine which I am now laying down is applicable only to grants so enrolled: because, if an individual grants a lease, and the estate of which that individual grants a lease afterwards comes to the king, if the king regrants that, as the subject could not know with certainty that there was a previously existing lease, the position I have been laying down would not apply. The doctrine that I am delivering is applicable to a case where the subject cannot be deceived, and he must be deceiving the king; for if the king's prior lease be enrolled, the subject has the means of knowing of the existence of that lease, and it is his duty to inform the king of its existence.

These authorities show that competing claims between subjects were reconciled according to concepts akin to modern registry systems and equitable doctrines of constructive notice. The *nemo dat* principle did not automatically invalidate Crown patents. As we have already explained, where the validity of a patent is impugned, established legal principles require that the interests of innocent third parties must be considered.

4. Nature of Discretion to be Exercised

Accordingly, it is our view that whether the case is considered from the perspective of public law principles or from the perspective of private law, the discretion of the court is engaged. The discretionary factors bearing upon the availability of public law remedies is closely parallelled by equitable considerations applicable as between private parties in respect of proprietary claims. As with public law remedies, the discretion to grant or withhold an equitable remedy is constrained and is closely defined by established principles. Although the tradition of equity requires that the decision-making process be described as discretionary, upon analysis, it is apparent that there are well-defined rules and doctrines that shape the decision and control the result. Discretion is, as Lord Mansfield explained in *R. v. Wilkes* (1770), 4 Burr. 2527 (Eng. K.B.), at 2539, a "sound discretion guided by law. It must be governed by rule not by humour; it must not be arbitrary, vague and fanciful but legal and regular." Birks, "Rights, Wrongs and Remedies" (2000), 20 *Oxford Journal of Legal Studies* 1 at 16 aptly describes the orders rooted in the Court of Chancery as "weakly discretionary" in that the court acts upon firm discretionary rules that have "been settled over the centuries".

5. Laches and Acquiescence

Delay in asserting a right gives rise to the equitable doctrines of laches and acquiescence. The test for these defences was explained in the following terms by La Forest J. in *M. (K.) v. M. (H.)*, [1992] 3 S.C.R. 6 (S.C.C.), at 77-8:

> A good discussion of the rule and of laches in general is found in Meagher, Gummow and Lehane, [*Equitable Doctrines and Remedies*, (1984)] at pp. 755–65, where the authors distill the doctrine in this manner, at p. 755:
>
> > It is a defence which requires that a defendant can successfully resist an equitable (although not a legal) claim made against him if he can demonstrate that the plaintiff, by delaying the institution or prosecution of his case, has either (a) acquiesced in the defendant's conduct or (b) caused the defendant to alter his position in reasonable reliance on the plaintiff's acceptance of the *status quo*, or otherwise permitted a situation to arise which it would be unjust to disturb. . . .
>
> Thus there are two distinct branches to the laches doctrine, and either will suffice as a defence to a claim in equity. What is immediately obvious from all of the authorities is that mere delay is insufficient to trigger laches under either of its two branches. Rather, the doctrine considers whether the delay of the plaintiff constitutes acquiescence or results in circumstances that make the prosecution of the action unreasonable. Ultimately, laches must be resolved as a matter of justice as between the parties, as in the case with any equitable doctrine.

The doctrine of laches has been applied to bar the claims of an Indian band asserting aboriginal land rights: *Ontario (Attorney General) v. Bear Island Foundation* (1984), 49 O.R. (2d) 353 (H.C.), at 447 (aff'd on other grounds (1989), 68 O.R. (2d) 394 (C.A.); [1991] 2 S.C.R. 570 (S.C.C.)); *Roberts v. R.* (1995), 99 F.T.R. 1 (Fed. T.D.), at 77 and 79. There are also *dicta* in two decisions of the Supreme Court of Canada considering, without rejecting, arguments that laches may bar claims to aboriginal title: *R. v. Smith*, [1983] 1 S.C.R. 554 (S.C.C.), at 570; *Guerin*, *supra*, at 390.

The facts relevant to the defences of laches and acquiescence have already been discussed with respect to the consideration of delay in relation to public law remedies and it is unnecessary to repeat them here. In our view, those facts bring this case squarely within the principles governing laches set out in *M. (K.) v. M. (H.), supra.* The Chippewas accepted the transfer of their lands and acquiesced in the Cameron transaction. The landowners altered their position by investing in and improving the lands in reasonable reliance on the Chippewas' acquiescence in the *status quo*. This is a situation that would be unjust to disturb.

The motions judge refused to apply the defence of laches on the ground that there was no evidence that the Chippewas had knowledge of the actual terms of the Cameron transaction and that "[i]t is clear from *Guerin* that laches cannot bar an aboriginal claim unless the claimant has knowledge of the actual terms of the disputed transaction." The relevant passage from Dickson J.'s judgment in *Guerin* appears at 390:

> Little need be said about the Crown's alternative contention that the Band's claim is barred by laches. Since the conduct of the Indian Affairs Branch personnel amounted to equitable fraud; since the Band did not have actual or constructive knowledge of the actual terms of the golf club lease until March 1970; and since the Crown was not prejudiced by reason of the delay between March 1970 until suit was filed in December 1975, there is no ground for application of the equitable doctrine of laches.

On the facts of *Guerin*, the terms of the transaction were essential elements of the claim and without knowing the specific terms, which had been concealed by the Crown, the Band would not know it had a claim. The specific terms of the Cameron transaction are not an integral element of the Chippewas' claim in the present case. The claim is not based on the terms of the transaction, but on the assertion that the lands were transferred without a proper surrender. At para. 653, the motions judge found that the Chippewas had full knowledge of the facts essential to their claim in the 1850s:

> The Chippewas knew by 1851 that their unsurrendered land was occupied openly and notoriously by disagreeable settlers. They confirmed this knowledge, and more, in 1855 by their inquiries about the price and terms of payment. About the actual loss of their land, as opposed to the particulars of the Cameron transaction, there was nothing hidden or unknown. By January 9, 1851 at the latest their loss was clear and obvious. They knew with certainty that the disputed lands had been taken from them without a surrender. There is no evidence as to the point in time that this knowledge was lost to the plaintiffs.

In our view, this amounts to a finding that the Chippewas had knowledge of the facts necessary to assert a claim, and in view of that knowledge, *Guerin* is distinguishable. As we have already noted in the discussion of delay in relation to public law remedies, we are of the view that the Chippewas not only knew that the lands had been given up but actively acquiesced in the transfer by seeking and receiving payment of the proceeds. On these facts, we can see no reason why the equitable defences of laches and acquiescence should not apply.

6. Good Faith Purchaser for Value

The second equitable doctrine that bears upon the claim advanced by the Chippewas is the protection accorded a good faith purchaser for value. As the motions judge held: "the defence of good faith purchaser for value without notice is a fundamental aspect of our real property regime designed to protect the truly innocent purchaser who buys land without any notice of a potential claim by a previous owner." The motions judge described the defence in the following way (at paras 686-7):

> The defence of good faith purchaser for value without notice has been a fundamental element of our law for centuries. It protects the security of title to land acquired without notice of claim. It reflects a basic social value that protects the rights of innocent parties. Based in simple fairness, it provides a strong defence for the truly innocent purchaser. As Lord Justice James said over a hundred years ago in the case of *Pilcher v. Rawlins* [(1872), L.R. 7 Ch. App. 259 *per* Sir W. M. James, L.J. at p. 268]:
>
>> . . . according to my view of the established law of this Court, such a purchaser's plea of purchase for valuable consideration without notice is an absolute, unqualified, unanswerable defence, and an unanswerable plea to the jurisdiction of this Court. Such a purchaser, when he has once put in his plea, may be interrogated and tested to any extent as to the valuable consideration which he has given in order to show the *bona fides* or *mala fides* of his purchase, and also the presence of the absence of notice; but when once he has gone through that ordeal, and has satisfied the terms of the plea of purchase for valuable consideration without notice then, according to my judgment, this Court has no jurisdiction whatever to do anything more than to let him depart in possession of that legal estate, that legal right, that legal advantage which he has obtained, whatever it may be. In such a case a purchaser is entitled to hold that which, without breach of duty, he has had conveyed to him.
>
> Mellish L.J. in the same case said [at 273]:
>
> The general rule seems to be laid down in the clearest terms by all the great authorities in equity, and has been acted on for a great number of years, namely that this Court will not take an estate from a purchaser who has bought for valuable consideration without notice. . . .

The motions judge found that while it was arguable that Cameron had knowledge of the failure of the Crown to secure a proper surrender of the lands, there was no evidence to suggest that any subsequent owner knew or ought to have known that the Cameron lands were unsurrendered Indian lands. Moreover, the motions judge found that there was no evidence of equitable fraud on the part of Cameron that would defeat the operation of the defence in favour of those who acquired title from Cameron. He found that a prudent purchaser and conveyancer would consider that the Cameron patent, regular on its face, was a good root of title and would make no further inquiry.

The good faith purchaser defence is an equitable doctrine and the Chippewas assert that their interest in the lands is a purely legal one not caught by purely equitable defences. For reasons already given, we do not accept this argument. To the extent that the Chippewas assert a claim for the return of the lands, they assert a claim to an equitable remedy that is subject to equitable defences.

The good faith purchaser for value defence applies to the benefit of any purchaser who satisfies its requirements. On the findings of the motions judge, all purchasers from Cameron, the last of whom acquired lands in 1861, were good faith purchasers for value. However, the motions judge held that a rigid and unqualified application of the defence to cut off the Chippewas' claims in 1861 was too drastic given the nature of the aboriginal claim that was being asserted. He concluded that the need to reconcile the aboriginal and treaty rights with the rights of the landowners precluded the immediate application of the defence as of 1861, and, relying on *M. (K.) v. M. (H.)*, *supra*, he imposed an "equitable limitation period" of sixty years, during which the aboriginal right would survive. The practical implication of this finding was that the Chippewas' damages claim against the Crown would have crystallized in 1921 rather than in 1861.

In our view, the imposition of a strict sixty-year "equitable limitation period", extending the time within which the Chippewas could assert their claim to the lands unaffected by the operation of the good faith purchaser for value defence, is not supportable in law. A limitation period prescribes the time within which a claim must be brought. *M. (K.) v. M. (H.)* goes no further than affirming that, in some circumstances, to prescribe a claim that was concurrently legal and equitable, a court of equity would apply by analogy a legal limitation period. Properly understood, the sixty-year period created by the motions judge is not a limitation period at all. On the findings of the motions judge, the good-faith-purchaser defence would have defeated the Chippewas' claim in 1861. The sixty-year period he imposed was an "extension period", suspending the operation of a valid defence, and allowing a claim to be asserted after the point at which, by operation of ordinary legal principles, it would have been defeated. There is nothing in *M. (K.) v. M. (H.)*, *supra*, that would support this.

On the other hand, we accept that the factors that motivated the creation of the sixty-year "equitable limitation period", namely the need to reconcile aboriginal title and treaty claims with the rights of innocent purchasers, are factors that should be considered on a case-by-case basis. It may well be that where the denial of the aboriginal right is substantial or egregious, a rigid application of the good faith purchaser for value defence would constitute an unwarranted denial of a fundamental right. It is unnecessary to consider that possibility on the facts of the case before us. As we have concluded that the Chippewas accepted the terms of the Cameron transaction at the time it was entered, we can see no reason why the good faith purchaser for value defence should not be applied to preclude the Chippewas from asserting their claim against the landowners.

D. Conclusion on Remedies

For these reasons, we conclude that established rules governing the availability of public and private law remedies require the court to take into consideration the Chippewas' delay in asserting its claim and the reliance of innocent third parties on the apparent validity of the Cameron patent. On the facts of this case, it is our view that the Chippewas' delay, combined with the reliance of the landowners, is fatal to the claims asserted by the Chippewas. . . .

NOTE

Leave to appeal to the Supreme Court of Canada was refused: 2001 CarswellOnt 3952, [2001] 4 C.N.L.R. iv (note), 2001 CarswellOnt 3953 (S.C.C.) and a motion to rehear the leave application was likewise dismissed: 2002 CarswellOnt 1903, [2002] 3 C.N.L.R. iv (note), 2002 CarswellOnt 1904 (S.C.C.).

QUESTIONS AND COMMENTS

1. When the contest is between a prior equitable interest and a subsequent legal one, equity will accord priority to the latter, provided that the legal estate is acquired by a *bona fide* purchaser for value without notice of the equitable interest. This is the "good-faith-purchaser rule" referred to in the *Chippewas of Sarnia* case. Some fundamental elements of the good-faith-purchaser defence are set out in P.A. O'Connor, "Security of Property Rights and Land Title Registration Systems" Ph.D. Thesis, Monash University (2003) at 92–4:

> An equitable interest is not enforced against a *bona fide* purchaser of a legal estate who has given valuable consideration and had no notice of the prior interest. The historical origins of this "*bona fide* purchaser" rule lie in principles developed by the Court of Chancery for the enforcement of uses (the forerunner of the modem trust). The Court would enforce a use against persons whom it considered conscientiously bound by it. Holdsworth records that the doctrine of notice originated as a solution to the problem of proving the mental element of fraud. Its function was to define objectively verifiable circumstances from which fraudulent intent could be inferred. A person who took with notice of a use was deemed fraudulent, in the extended equitable sense of acting contrary to good conscience. The question of notice became an important question in many areas where equity was asked to enforce a right against a third party.
>
> From the 17th century, equity developed rules relating to constructive notice. This was prompted by a perceived need to give purchasers an incentive to seek out information about prior interests. The rationale for constructive notice is that if purchasers are affected by notice only of matters which have actually been brought to their (or their "agents") attention, they will take care to avoid acquiring such information. Purchasers were expected to show due diligence in searching for prior interests. If they failed to do so, they would be deemed to have constructive notice of prior interests that they should have discovered. The corollary was that if they made the inquiries that a reasonably prudent purchaser would make in the circumstances, they were protected against any prior interest

that they failed to find. The onus of proof lay on the purchasers to show that they did not have notice of the interest.

Questions of conscience apart, there is a practical justification for setting a limit to purchasers' search costs. Because of their mode of creation, some equitable interests may be exceedingly difficult for purchasers to discover. Equitable interests are less likely to be evidenced in documentary form or by possession than legal interests. Equity gives proprietary effect to certain transactions before the legal formalities have been completed. Wholly oral transactions can give rise to equitable interests in land under doctrines such as part-performance, estoppel and constructive trust. Informally created interests often leave no paper trail for a purchaser to follow.

Posner has sought to explain the *bona fide* purchaser rule consistently with his theory that many judge-made rules actually promote the efficient use of resources. He argues that the original owner is the "lower cost avoider" of mistake. The "mistake" is the acquisition of a later interest in the belief that it conflicts with no earlier interest. The cause of the mistake is a deficiency of information about the earlier interest. The theory of wealth-maximisation holds that resources should be allocated to those who value them most, and social costs allocated to those who can prevent them with the least expenditure of resources. Posner appears to be saying that the *bona fide* purchaser rule creates an incentive for the earlier owner to take steps to avoid the mistake because she can do so more cheaply than the purchaser.

It is difficult to see why this should be so. In the absence of land registration, an interest-holder has few means of alerting third parties to her rights, unless she is in possession of the land or the title deeds. Many interests in land give no immediate right to possession, nor an entitlement to hold the chain of title deeds. If a grantor is about to create an interest inconsistent with hers, the earlier owner is unlikely to know about it unless notified by someone. In these circumstances, it is the purchaser ho can avoid the mistake more cheaply, by making the usual inquiries. Posner's theory assumes that the *bona fide* purchase rule allocates the information cost to the earlier owner. It would be more accurate to say that the costs are split between the earlier owner and the purchaser, with the purchaser bearing the lion's share. The earlier owner bears the risk of loss only if her equitable interest is one that would not be revealed by the usual inquiries.

2. Was the contest at issue in the case between a prior equitable and a subsequent legal interest? If so, describe the equitable nature of the prior right and the subsequent legal claim. If not, is the *bona fide* purchaser for value test applicable?

3. What priority contest was argued for by counsel for the Chippewas of Sarnia?

4. Is it possible to characterize the contest as one involving a prior legal interest and a subsequent equitable one?

5. Is the Court of Appeal decision in the *Chippewas of Sarnia* case consistent with the law governing the extinguishment of Aboriginal title?

6. The Chippewas of Sarnia sought not only a declaration and a vesting order, but also possession against three companies holding land in the disputed area (C.N.R., Dow Chemical Canada and Imperial Oil). This is a legal action for the recovery of

land. Is it amenable to the same analysis as that used in relation to the granting of declaratory and vesting orders? See K. McNeil, "Extinguishment of Aboriginal Titles in Canada: Treaties, Legislation, and Judicial Discretion" (2001-2) 33 Ottawa L. Rev. 301.

7. What role does the Crown's fiduciary duty play in the resolution of this case?

T.G. Youdan, "The Length of a Title Search in Ontario" (1986) 64 Can. Bar Rev. 507, at 509–11 [footnotes omitted]

At common law, title to land is not absolute. It is based on possession and it is relative to the rights of others. We say that a person owns land when he has a better right to possession of it than others. Moreover, a vendor can only prove his title by showing "that he got it lawfully from someone else, and that someone else from someone else, and so on." Obviously, routine methods for demonstration of the required proof of title are necessary and, in England at least (where ordinarily there would be no evidence of the starting point of a title), there had to be some limit on how far back the vendor was required to show the antecedents of his title.

The practice for proof of title in England was generally established during the course of the eighteenth century, and it was rationalized and formulated by text writers in about the first half of the nineteenth century. It was essentially a private system. There was no registry for title documents affecting land in most of the country, and the relevant documents were ordinarily held by the current owner of the land.

Proof of title was facilitated by the use of an abstract. This consisted of a summary of documents and events relevant to the vendor's title. In the developed practice it was prepared by the vendor at his own expense and it was delivered to the purchaser who could "insist upon an abstract, and [was] not bound to wade through the deeds". The purchaser then had a period (which was usually fixed by the contract) in which to examine the vendor's title and to make objections and requisitions. There were two main parts to this process. First, the vendor (usually by his solicitor) "verified" the abstract by,

> . . . producing for examination by the purchaser or his solicitor the original deeds or documents abstracted, and the probates or office copies of the wills and other documents, of which the originals cannot be produced; also by furnishing proper evidence of every fact material to title.

The purpose of this was to enable the purchaser (or, usually, his solicitor) to check that the matters dealt with in the abstract were what they purported to be. The second part of the process was the examination of the abstract and this was ordinarily done by conveyancing counsel, instructed by the purchaser's solicitor, who would also put forward objections and requisitions arising out of the abstract.

Because proof of title to land depended on showing previous dealings with the land and because generally there was no obvious point at which the proof would commence, some conventional rule was necessary. The rule eventually established was that, in the absence of contractual provision to the contrary, the vendor was required to show a chain of title back to a good root of title at least sixty years old. A frequently cited definition of what was a good root of title is that of T. Cyprian Williams:

> . . . [It] must be an instrument of disposition dealing with or proving on the face of it (without the aid of extrinsic evidence) the ownership of the whole legal and equitable estate in the property sold, containing a description by which the property can be identified, and showing nothing to cast any doubt on the title of the disposing parties.

This conventional rule had the effect of limiting the vendor's obligation to prove his title; and consequently, it provided a starting-point for the abstract. Its effect was limited in three important and closely related ways. First it only applied in the absence of contrary contractual provision. The parties were free to bargain for a longer or (and this was more typical) a shorter period. Secondly, the title proof period did not generally affect the claims of third parties. There is one important qualification to this which is well expressed by Marcia Neave:

> The fixing of the period of commencement of title did not, of itself, extinguish the interest of a third party in the land. If the interest was legal it was enforceable against the purchaser regardless of his lack of notice. The terms of the bargain between the vendor and the purchaser could not affect an outstanding legal interest in a third person. If the interest was equitable it was not enforceable against a *bona fide* purchaser of the legal estate for value without notice. Of course notice included constructive notice (the case where a purchaser should have discovered the existence of an interest) as well as actual notice. The fact that the equitable interest arose before the period of commencement of title generally enabled the purchaser to argue that he had not omitted to make reasonable and proper searches. Thus he did not have constructive notice and took free from the interest.

The third important limitation on the effect of the proof of title period is that it did not determine the quality of the title to which the purchaser was entitled; it was only concerned with the length of the affirmative proof of the vendor's title. Consequently, the purchaser could make an objection to the vendor's title based on a defect arising from a document or event that preceded the commencement of the title proof period. Moreover, it seems that in the process of verifying the abstract, the vendor could be required to produce all the title documents — not just those comprised in the abstract. In addition, on completion the purchaser's entitlement to the title documents was not restricted to those within the title proof period.

3. THE ADVENT OF REGISTRATION

In early Canadian law no system of land registration existed. The priority rules outlined above governed. The purchaser was responsible for determining who else held interests in the property (such as mortgages, leases, *etc.*). The purchaser had to make sure that the person selling the property was actually the owner, and that the documents of transfer were not forgeries. In fact, even if the current seller was acting honestly, a previous owner might emerge and claim to be the rightful owner of the property.

From the eighteenth century onwards various registration systems emerged. All were designed to minimize the purchaser's risk in land transactions. The first-generation statutes established what are now called deeds registration systems. These are discussed in this Part. Title registration systems for land were introduced in the common law jurisdictions in the 19th century. These are described in Part 4.

In general, deeds registration systems encourage the owners of property interests to register their rights. The title deeds are noted in the government records and normally the documents are stored in a state-operated registry office. Speaking in general terms, a purchaser can rely on the registry to ascertain what interests currently exist in the property. The register and the documents can then be inspected by a prospective purchaser to see who owns what.

Deeds registration systems provide no guarantee that the seller has a valid title. The fact that a document is registered does not mean that it is authentic. Therefore, as under the old law, the purchaser is still required to conduct a search of the chain of title. And if it is later shown that some defect in that chain existed, a prior owner could reclaim the property and oust the purchaser. As under the prior law, this result can occur even if the purchaser had acted in good faith and was totally unaware of any defect, fraud or forgery. The value of a deeds system is that it encourages the registration of interests, and makes the process of searching title easier than it had been in the past.

Within the deeds registry family, three main variations can be found. Under one, priority is based on which interest was registered (as opposed to created) first. This is referred to as a race system, since the first to register is accorded priority. Under a second approach, the key effect of registration is to afford notice of a prior right. The function of this "notice system" is, therefore, to make it easier to provide notice and hence easier to detect prior interests.

A third approach, which is, for reasons to be explained shortly, the most common deeds system in Canada, is composed of a hybrid of the two, and so is called "race-notice". Under a common form of this system, priority is accorded to an otherwise valid subsequent interest if two circumstance exist: the second interest must be acquired without notice of the first (usually constructive notice is considered insufficient), and that subsequent interest must registered first.

Some systems seem to create a rather strict race system. For example, Nova Scotia's registration statute once provided that

> Deeds or mortgages of lands duly executed but not registered, shall be void against any subsequent purchaser or mortgagee for valuable consideration who shall first register his deed or mortgage of such land (R.S.N.S. 4 Series, c. 79, s. 19).

This system can be characterized as strict because it appears to render irrelevant the chance that a subsequent purchaser is actually aware of a prior unregistered interest. Under a true race system, that subsequent purchaser gains priority even when it is known by that person that a prior interest has been granted. Mindful of the unfairness that this might prompt, courts in Canada and elsewhere have held that actual notice of an existing interest by a subsequent party will mean that the prior interest will retain priority, despite the fact that the prior interest lost the race to the register. In other words, the courts have added a gloss to race statutes, transforming them into race-notice rules. For instance, in *Ross v. Hunter* (1882) 7 S.C.R. 289, Strong J., in construing the quoted Nova Scotia provision, stated (at 321) that "[i]t is well settled that nothing short of actual notice, such notice as makes it a fraud on the part of a purchaser to insist on the registry laws, is sufficient to disentitle a party to insist in equity on a legal priority acquired under the statute." In so holding reliance was placed, in part, on Sir William Grant's analysis of English law in *Wyatt v. Barwell* (1815) 19 Ves. 435, 34 E.R. 578, where it was said that:

> It has been much doubted whether courts ought ever to have suffered the question of notice to be agitated as against a party who has duly registered his conveyance . . . but they have said, "we cannot permit fraud to prevail; and it shall only be in cases, where the notice is so clearly proved as to make it fraudulent in the purchaser to take and register a conveyance in prejudice to the known title of another, that we will suffer the registered Deed to be affected."

Under all systems, whether deeds or title in nature, one question must always be addressed, and the appropriate answers are often not obvious. The question is this: to what extent do the rules supplant or merely supplement the judge-made priority doctrines? As a general matter it is undoubtedly the case that the title systems sweep away more of the older doctrines than do the deeds registry rules. But in each case remnants exist. For instance under most systems, subordinate status is accorded to those acquiring interests by virtue of a gratuitous transfer. Where that is so, donees can be held bound by unrecorded or registered prior interests.

C.I.B.C. Mortgage Corp. v. Quassa
1996 CarswellNWT 19 (S.C.)

Vertes J.:

This is an application to determine priorities as between a mortgagee and a subsequent purchaser who claims to be a *bona fide* purchaser for value without notice of the mortgagee's interest.

The defendants, Paul Quassa and Elisapee Quassa, have been noted in default and did not appear on this application. They are the lessees of a certain property described as "Lot 39 in the Town of Iqaluit, in the Northwest Territories, according to a plan of survey filed in the land Titles Office for the Northwest Territories under number 674". The lessor is the Commissioner of the Northwest Territories. The property is unpatented Crown land administered by the territorial government under the *Commissioner's Land Act*, R.S.N.W.T. 1988, c. C-11. No certificate of title has been issued so the property is not "registered" in any manner under the Land Titles registry system established by the *Land Titles Act*, R.S.N.W.T. 1988, c. 8 (Supp.).

The Quassas' leasehold interest was noted, however, in an *ad hoc* registry system maintained by the territorial Department of Municipal and Community Affairs. A number was assigned to the lease and anyone could attend at the department's office in Yellowknife to review the file. This *ad hoc* registry system is not based on any statutory provisions but is one that has been used by the government and others, such as solicitors undertaking conveyance work for clients respecting leases of Commissioner's lands, for many years. A similar practice is in place for unpatented Crown lands held by the Government of Canada. The informal registry procedure for such lands administered by the federal government received judicial recognition in *Pitts v. Steen et al.*, [1981] 3 W.W.R. 289 (N.W.T.S.C.).

On July 22, 1993, the Quassas executed a mortgage of their leasehold interest in favour of the CIBC Mortgage Corporation (the "applicant" herein). The amount was $256,250.00. This mortgage was consented to by the Commissioner as lessor and a copy of the mortgage was deposited at the department office in Yellowknife. It was marked as registered on July 28, 1993, as instrument number 1680. The original lease document in the file was marked with a notation that the lease was subject to a mortgage. Hence anyone attending at the office to do a search of the lease file would have seen the notation and the filed copy of the mortgage itself.

On July 21, 1994, the Quassas made an agreement to sell their interest in the property to the defendant Gerrasimus Logothetis (the "respondent" herein). The agreement was a hand-written document reciting a total purchase price of $230,000.00 payable by a down payment of $35,000.00 and monthly instalments of $4,000.00. The respondent made the down payment and took possession of the property. The mortgage was already in default by the date of the agreement. In March of 1995 the applicant commenced foreclosure proceedings. The mortgage debt is now in excess of $268,000.00.

The lease is still in the name of the Quassas. No steps were taken by them to transfer the lease to the respondent. It is also acknowledged that the respondent took no steps to ascertain the state of the Quassas' interest. He made no independent inquiries as to the state of the title but instead relied on assurances from the vendors. The respondent gave the following recitation of events in his affidavit filed on this application:

> 3. On or about July 21, 1994, I entered into a written agreement (the "agreement") for the purchase of the leasehold interest in the land of Paul Quassa and Elisapee Quassa (called "the Quassas"). Some time before I signed the agreement, Paul Quassa told me, in response to my inquiry, that the leasehold interest of the Quassas in the land was not subject to any encumbrances. He told me that there had been a mortgage against the Quassas' leasehold interest in the lands but that it had been paid out . . .

4. When I persisted in making inquiries, Paul Quassa told me that as far as he knew the Quassas' leasehold interest in the land was not encumbered in any way, but that as it was possible his wife, Elisapee Quassa might have encumbered their interest, he would double-check and let me know. He also said that if there was any encumbrance against the Quassas' interest in the land, it would be for a minimal amount of money, and that in any case, the Quassas would pay the amount owing on any such encumbrance and have it discharged before assigning the leasehold interest to me in accordance with the agreement. Paul Quassa did not, at any time thereafter or before I entered into possession, advise me that there were any encumbrances against the leasehold interest in the land. I therefore believed that there were no such encumbrances . . .

7. It was agreed between the parties that the Quassas' leasehold interest in the lands would be assigned to me, free and clear of all encumbrances, upon the payment by myself of $35,000.00 to the Quassas. Paul Quassa told me, at the time that I paid the balance of the $35,000.00, that that the assignment of lease was in the hands of his lawyers, and that it would be registered within a short period of time.

The parties are agreed that, in the absence of statutory registration provisions as in this situation, the common law applies. The respondent also concedes that the applicant holds an equitable mortgage. He claims, however, that he is a *bona fide* purchaser for value without notice of the mortgage and therefore is not bound by the applicant's prior charge on the leasehold.

It is settled law that the defence of purchase for value without notice is a defence which must be pleaded and proved affirmatively. It is a defence in respect of which the onus in the strict sense is on the party claiming the benefit of it. The respondent must affirmatively establish absence of notice: *Union Bank of Halifax v. Indian & General Investment Trust*, [1908] 40 S.C.R. 510. In my opinion, there are a number of reasons why the defence fails in this case.

The respondent has paid approximately $40,000.00 to date pursuant to his agreement with the Quassas. That agreement, while stipulating that ownership will transfer on payment of the initial downpayment, also reserves the right to the Quassas to cancel the agreement should the respondent miss any of the monthly instalments. In this situation the most that can be said is that the respondent also has only an equitable interest in the leasehold as purchaser. And, since the equitable mortgage was created a year before the respondent's equitable interest arose, then at common law the earlier interest has priority. This rule is known as "first in time is first in right": see J. E. Roach, *The Canadian Law of Mortgages of Land* (1993), pages 356-357.

The respondent, while acknowledging the rule, submits that the rule should be displaced due to negligence on the part of the applicant and/or its solicitors in not "adequately" securing the mortgage loan. Cases have refused to recognize a priority under this rule where there is evidence of fraud or negligence on the part of the mortgagee claiming a prior interest. The emphasis, however, is always on doing what is fair in the overall circumstances of the particular case. As stated by Anglin J. in *McDougall v. MacKay*, [1922] 64 S.C.R. 1 (at page 12):

> I fully recognize that a court of equity will not prefer one equity to another on the mere ground of priority of time until it has found by examination of their relative merits that there is no other sufficient ground of preference between them; that such examination must cover the conduct of the parties and all the circumstances; and that the test of preference is the broad principle of right and justice which courts of equity apply universally.

The respondent argues that, having regard to the relatively large amount of the mortgage loan, the applicant should have taken steps to better secure its position by having title raised pursuant to the *Land Titles Act* so that registration could be effected under that statute. The irony in this argument of course is that in this case the respondent admits that he made no search of title whatsoever but if there had been registration under the *Land Titles Act* he would have nevertheless been deemed by the statute to have notice of the mortgage.

I reject this argument for three reasons. First, as already noted, the respondent admits that he made no search of title, not at the government office where the lease was filed and not at the Land Titles Office. So any submission as to what may have happened if registration had taken place in the Land Titles Office is purely speculative. Second, also as previously noted, the *ad hoc* registry system maintained by the territorial government is one that has been in place for many years and familiar to solicitors in this jurisdiction. In the circumstances of this case I cannot say that it is negligence to not take steps to raise title. Finally, there is no evidence that title could be raised. It is a mere possibility contingent on factors that are wholly unrelated to the mortgage loan. For these reasons I do not find any act on the part of the applicant to displace the "first in time" rule. But there are other grounds favouring the applicant's position beside simply this rule of equity.

Applicant's counsel submits that the respondent does not meet the test of being a purchaser for value. He has not paid the full purchase price. He now has notice of the mortgage. The law is that a purchaser must pay the full amount of the purchase before receiving notice of the prior charge to claim priority as a purchaser for value: see Megarry & Wade, *Law of Real Property* (5th ed., 1984), page 143.

Applicant's counsel also submits that at a minimum the respondent had, if not actual notice of the mortgage, then constructive notice of it. Constructive notice is found where the purchaser has, either deliberately or carelessly, abstained from making those inquiries that a prudent purchaser would have made. Did the purchaser have some knowledge which ought to have put him on inquiry? Would he have acquired the necessary information but for his own gross negligence? The standard was explained by Roach, *supra*, at page 358:

> Gross negligence is more than mere carelessness; it is aggravated carelessness by someone who, on the one hand, disregards the standards of care of the reasonable person and, on the other hand, indicates a lack of concern for consequences of one's conduct, though the risks are obvious.

In this case, the respondent acknowledges that he made inquiries of the vendors as to the state of title and he received assurances that there were no encumbrances but, if there were, they were minor and would be cleared off. He admits that he made no independent inquiries or searches. The respondent did not retain a solicitor. He was content to rely on the vendors. To my mind, especially having regard to the amount of money at stake, these actions, or lack of action, on the part of the respondent reveal a lack of prudence and care. It amounts to gross negligence in the handling of his affairs. The respondent had a complete disregard for the care that a prudent purchaser would take in such a transaction. It is not as if the respondent was totally oblivious to the risks. After all, he says he asked the vendors about any encumbrances. In these circumstances it was unreasonable for him to rely on the vendors' assurances. This is in no way diminished by the fact that he only paid a small portion of the purchase price up front.

There are well-established authorities for the proposition that the purchaser bears the obligation to make reasonable inquiries into the state of title. And, in this regard, the purchaser cannot, in answer to a competing claim, simply rely on the vendor's representations or assurances: *Patman v. Harland* (1881), 17 Ch. 353 (M.R.); *Oliver v. Hinton*, [1899] 2 Ch. 264 (C.A.). In my opinion, in this day and age, it is unreasonable to think that a person would enter into a transaction such as this without at least making some independent inquiries if not, as in most cases, retaining the services of a solicitor to make sure that one got what one paid for. I therefore find that the respondent had constructive notice of the mortgage.

For these reasons, the respondent's claim to be a *bona fide* purchaser for value without notice fails. A declaration will issue that the applicant's mortgage is valid and has priority over the respondent's interest as purchaser.

Respondent's counsel suggested that the respondent should at least retain priority as to the approximate sum of $40,000.00 paid by him to the Quassas. While there may be some superficial appeal to this argument out of sympathy for the respondent, I find no evidence to support such a disposition. The respondent has apparently commenced separate proceedings against the Quassas so he will have to pursue that claim to recover what he has paid them. . . .

Application allowed.

QUESTIONS

1. What type of registration system was in use in *Quassa*?

2. In *Quassa* it was said that "a purchaser must pay the full amount before receiving notice of the prior charge to claim priority as a purchaser for value." Why should that be so?

Mayer v. Brüning
(2001) 38 R.P.R. (3d) 310, 2001 CarswellNS 95 (S.C.)

Boudreau J.:

Introduction:

Johann Georg Mayer, a resident of Germany, purchased a property in Nova Scotia from a Claudia Leipold without retaining a lawyer on his behalf and without conducting a title search. It turns out the property was encumbered by a $130,000.00 mortgage in favour of Heinrich Brüning, another resident of Germany. It also turns out the mortgage in favour of Mr. Brüning was registered out of the chain of title, but before the deed to Mr. Mayer. Is there a duty on the purchaser of property in Nova Scotia to conduct a title search and what is the effect of a mortgage registered out of the chain of title but before the deed to a subsequent purchaser?

Facts:

This case proceeded on an Agreed Statement of Facts which has been entered into evidence as Exhibit #2. It was also agreed that Exhibit #1, the Joint Exhibit Book, forms part of the evidence in this trial. It contains Tabs 1–8 and 10-11 inclusive, Tab 9 having been omitted by agreement. Most of the evidence contained in Exhibit #1 is referred to in the Agreed Statement of Facts which reads as follows:

Agreed Statement of Facts

1. The Plaintiff is a German National who currently resides in Altusried, Germany. He is in the trucking business. The defendant is a businessman residing in Rathmannsdorf, Germany. The Plaintiff is the owner in fee simple of certain real property at 2728 Long Point Road, Berwick, Nova Scotia. The Defendant is allegedly the holder of a mortgage over said property.

2. In December, 1996, the Plaintiff read an advertisement about certain property for sale in Berwick, Nova Scotia, in a local newspaper, the Kreisboten (Tab 11 of Exhibit 1). Consequently, he contacted the named owner, Claudia Leipold, with a view to purchasing the property. The Plaintiff did not know Ms. Leipold, but subsequently met with her in Oberammergau, Germany. After certain negotiations, the Plaintiff entered into an agreement with Ms. Leipold to purchase the property for the sum of 380,000.00 DM. While the agreement was oral, it is evidenced in part by a written document dated December 27, 1996 (Tab 5 of Exhibit 1).

3. Pursuant to this agreement, the Plaintiff paid Ms. Leipold a deposit of 30,000 DM on December 27, 1996. At no time during the negotiations with Ms. Leipold, nor in the written document, was there any mention of or reference to a mortgage or any other interest encumbering the property which would either affect the Plaintiff's title to the property or that he would be asked to assume on closing.

4. On February 17, 1997, before the transaction was concluded, the Plaintiff and his associate, Martin Karmann, travelled to Nova Scotia to meet Ms. Leipold and her associate, Wolfgang Kirchhoff, to view the property. During a car drive with Mr. Karmann, Ms. Leipold and Mr. Kirchhoff, the Plaintiff asked if there was a publicly accessible place in Nova Scotia where a prospective purchaser could search for mortgages and the like. In asking this, the Plaintiff used the word “”Grundbuchamt”, the German word for a land titles registry accessible to notaries, which word was known to Ms. Leipold and Mr. Kirchhoff. Both Ms. Leipold and Mr. Kirchhoff indicated that such a place did not exist.

5. At all material times, the Plaintiff assumed property conveyance in Nova Scotia was similar to that in Germany, where one notary or lawyer acts for both parties and attends at the Registry and a certified title document showing all encumbrances on its face is delivered to the purchaser upon closing. The Plaintiff made no further inquiries as to the validity of this assumption in advance of the closing of the transaction. The Plaintiff neither sought nor obtained legal advice prior to October, 1997, in part because of his reliance on Ms. Leipold and Mr. Kirchhoff and in part because of his limited English. The entire conversations which took place between Ms. Leipold, Mr. Kirchhoff and the Plaintiff were in German because of the Plaintiff's poor English skills.

6. Following this visit to the property and the Plaintiff's return to Germany, Ms. Leipold and Mr. Kirchhoff called upon the Plaintiff at his house in Altusried on February 24, 1997. At that time and in furtherance of the agreement with Ms. Leipold, the Plaintiff paid the balance of the agreed upon purchase price of 350,000 DM to Ms. Leipold in the presence of the Plaintiff's mother, Theresia Mayer, Ms. Leipold and Mr. Kirchhoff. In return, Ms. Leipold presented to the Plaintiff an original Trustee's Deed dated February 14, 1997, executed by Christopher K. Parker as Trustee and conveying the property to the Plaintiff (Tab 8 of Exhibit 1). This Deed had been recorded on February 19, 1997 at the Registry of Deeds for the County of Kings (Book 1095, page 75). Ms. Leipold told the Plaintiff that the Trustee's Deed had been drawn up by her lawyer, Christopher Parker

7. The Plaintiff took possession of the property after this transaction and had the use and enjoyment of it subject to a rental agreement with Mr. Kirchhoff.

8. At no time prior to receipt of the recorded Trustee's Deed from Ms. Leipold did the Plaintiff personally conduct a search of the records and indices maintained at the registry of Deeds for Kings County, nor did he cause anyone to conduct such a search on his behalf. At all material times, the Plaintiff was unaware of the details of Nova Scotia's system of property recording. Further, he relied upon Ms. Leipold to provide good and marketable title to the property. The Plaintiff accepted and assumed that the Trustee's Deed bearing a stamp with registration particulars and the signature of the Registrar of Deeds as presented by her to him conveyed the property free and clear of encumbrances as no such encumbrances were noted on the face of the Deed or on the legal description of the property.

9. On October 5, 1997, the Defendant contacted the Plaintiff and indicated that he held a mortgage of $130,000 Canadian over the property. This was the first time the Plaintiff had heard of or had any contact with the Defendant. The Defendant proceeded to demand full payment of the mortgage by the Plaintiff in instalments and sought immediate confirmation from the Plaintiff of his agreement to retire the mortgage in full. The Plaintiff refused.

10. Subsequently, the Plaintiff and Defendant met at the Defendant's request at his home in Rathmannsdorf on October 7, 1997. The Defendant provided to the Plaintiff a copy of a mortgage given by Ms. Leipold to Mr. Brüning on August 22, 1994 (Tab 3 of Exhibit 1). It was recorded on October 28, 1994 (Book 997, page 774). This was the first time the Plaintiff had ever seen a copy of the mortgage or had any knowledge of its terms. Present at the meeting in Rathmannsdorf were the Plaintiff, the Defendant, Mr. Karmann, his wife Josefine Karmann and the Defendant's secretary. The Defendant again made a demand for full payment of the mortgage and advised the Plaintiff that the full principal amount was outstanding as no payments on account of the mortgage had ever been made in the previous three years.

11. Following this meeting, the Plaintiff sought legal advice for the first time with respect to his purchase of the property and the subsequent claim by the Defendant relating to the mortgage.

12. The Plaintiff rejected any and all demands for payment of the mortgage made by the Defendant. No payments on account of the mortgage have been made by the Plaintiff since he obtained the fee simple in the property.

13. At the December 27, 1996 meeting with Claudia Leipold, Mr. Mayer asked her whether there were any claims or liens against the land. She replied that there were none.

14. The contract at Tab 5 of Exhibit 1 was reviewed by Mr. Mayer on December 27, 1996 and he was satisfied upon reading it that there was no mortgage or other claim against the land.

15. Mr. Mayer did not advert to the word "Grundbuch" in the contract at Tab 5 of Exhibit 1 when he reviewed it in December of 1996.

16. Mr. Mayer believed that Chris Parker, as Claudia Leipold's lawyer or notary, would handle the issuing of title and was the only person who could access the Registry, as is the case in Germany.

17. Mr. Mayer did not at any time link the German word "Grundbuch" in the German contract at Tab 5 of Exhibit 1 to a Nova Scotia Registry of Deeds or the like.

18. The words at the end of Claudia Leipold's signature on the contract at Tab 5 of Exhibit 1 suggest she is the sole owner and seller of the land.

19. Any examination of the facts must start with a review of the abstract of title in this matter as recorded at the Registry of Deeds at Kentville, Nova Scotia as follows:

1. Warranty Deed 990/29	Heinrich Brüning
22 August 1994	To
29 August 1994	Claudia Leipold
$1.00	
Lands Under Search	
2. Warranty Deed 997/449	Claudia Leipold
28 October 1994	To
25 October 1994	Christopher Parker in trust
$1.00	
Lands under search	
3. Mortgage 997/774	Claudia Leipold
22 August 1994	To
28 October, 1994	Heinrich Brüning
$130,000.00	
Lands under search	
4. Trustee's Deed 1095/75	Christopher Parker, Trustee
14 February. 1997	To
19 February. 1997	Johann George Mayer
Lands under search	

20. The mortgage in question was dated the same day as the deed from Brüning to Leipold as witnessed in item 1 and item 3 above.

21. The deed from Leipold to Christopher Parker in trust was dated and recorded on the same date October 25, 1994. The mortgage was registered three days later October 28, 1994,

22. Christopher Parker was the lawyer acting for Leipold and practising in the Greenwood area. Ron Richter was acting for Brüning throughout and practised in the Middleton area.

23. Richter acted for both Brüning and Leipold in the preparation of the deed and mortgage in item 1 and 3 above.

24. There was a dispute over the amount of the mortgage which delayed the late registration of this mortgage.

25. Christopher Parker did not know of the existence of the mortgage at Item 3 prior to the execution and registration of the deed in Item 2.

26. Richter was advised to register the mortgager (sic) on the 20th of October, 1994 and he mailed the mortgage to the Registry Office in Kentville for registration. It took 8 days to arrive at the registry office and was registered on the 28th day of October, 1994.

27. On or about the 14th day of February, 1997 Christopher Parker signed a deed over to the Plaintiff Johann G. Mayer. This deed was registered on the 19th day of February, 1997.

28. The plaintiff seeks the remedy of a declaration that he is a *bona fide* purchaser for value of the property without notice and alleges protection under Section 18 of the *Registry Act*, S.N.S. 1989 as amended.

Issues:

(1) What is the effect on the legal title to property of a prior instrument (in this case a mortgage) registered outside of the "recorded chain of title"; *i.e.*, registered after the legal title had already been conveyed to a third party and recorded, but before a subsequent purchaser for value without actual notice acquired title from the third party?

(2)(a) Is a purchaser of land in Nova Scotia under a legal duty to conduct a title search?

(b) If there is such a duty, would a title search necessarily have provided actual notice of the mortgage registered outside the chain of title?

(3) Is the doctrine of equitable mortgages applicable?

The Law:

Section 18 of the *Registry Act* reads as follows:

Every instrument shall, as against any person claiming for valuable consideration, and without notice under any subsequent instrument affecting title to the same land, *be ineffective unless the instrument is registered in the manner provided by this Act* before the registering of such subsequent instrument. [Emphasis added.]

The plaintiff relies on the case of *Ross v. Hunter* (1882), 7 S.C.R. 289 (S.C.C.), at 328 and *McDonald v. McDonald* (1905), 38 N.S.R. 261 (N.S. C.A.), for the proposition that an instrument registered "outside of the chain of title" but before the instrument under which title is claimed does not amount to constructive notice under the Registry Act and that there must therefore be actual notice. This argument is predicated on the Registry Act of Nova Scotia being a first in time/first in priority of title statute, but only within the chain of title

It appears clear that case authorities support the plaintiff's view of the *Registry Act*. Graham E.J., on behalf of Townshend J. and Fraser and Russell JJ., had the following to say in *McDonald, supra*, at page 267:

It is contended that Logan and Sutherland and McMullen are affected with notice of Nancy McKenzie's prior unregistered deed to Hugh D.B. McKenzie, because, at the time they purchased the land, that deed had in the meantime been registered. That means that registry of a deed, at any time and in any order, although not in the chain of title which they are searching, constitutes constructive notice of its existence. That they are obliged to search not only the title through which their proposed grantor holds, but also to search to see if anyone in the chain has given a prior deed, registered subsequently to the subsequent deed in the chain. I may say we have not, as they have in Ontario, a provision expressly making registry notice. In my opinion, the registry of that deed out of the order is not constructive notice to them of its existence and, besides that, there must be actual notice. And I rely for that upon the decision of *Ross v. Hunter*, 7 S.C.C. 289, and the English authorities to establish that position.

I also rely upon the case of *Ross v. Hunter* to establish what is perhaps preliminary to what I have just stated, that it is not material whether Hood, the first person, or Thomas A. McDonald, the last person in the chain, were purchasers for value, or had notice of the prior unregistered deed of Nancy McKenzie, provided Logan and Sutherland and McMullen were purchasers for value and had not notice.

It goes without saying that instruments registered in the chain of title or the subsequent purchaser having knowledge of an unregistered claim or turning a "blind eye" to facts which point to the existence of such claims may also be deemed to amount to actual notice. Cowan C.J.T.D. commented as follows in *Fort Garry Trust Co. v. Sutherland* (1980), 59 N.S.R. (2d) 298 (N.S. T.D.) at page 307:

The question as to what is "actual notice" is discussed at Falconbridge op. Cit., p. 133-4. The effect of the cases discussed and summarized there is that actual notice means knowledge not presumed, as in the case of constructive notice, but shown to be actually brought home to the party to be charged with it, either by proof of his own admission or by the evidence of witnesses who are able to establish that the very fact of which notice is to be established, not merely something which would have led to the discovery of the fact if an enquiry had been pursued, had been brought to his knowledge.

What is required is actual notice of the other person's adverse claim. There must be actual notice of the legal right claimed, though not necessarily actual notice of the instrument, if any, creating the right. "Taking with actual notice" means taking with such knowledge of another person's prior right that the attempt to take in defeasance of that right would amount to fraud. The onus of proof is upon the person alleging that he is a purchaser or mortgagee for valuable consideration, without actual notice.

It would seem from the above quote that only actual knowledge of a charge registered outside the chain, or of an equitable charge for that matter, by the present title holder, Mr. Mayer, can defeat his title within the registered chain. This appears to have been the view held by MacLellan J., as summarized in the head note of *Cunningham v. Nova Scotia (Attorney General)* (1996), 6 R.P.R. (3d) 71 (N.S. S.C.) as follows:

What is important to understand about the Cunningham decision, and the concept of the doctrine of actual notice generally, is that it is only the actual notice of the acquiring claimant that is important. That is, if a purchaser relies on a registered title without actual notice of an unregistered claim, then that purchaser takes free and clear of the equitable claim. It matters not that predecessors in title of the vendor knew that their title was subject to unregistered estates and that the principal of "*nemo dat qui non habet*" should have precluded them from affecting the transfer. Only the actual notice of the purchaser is at test. If one reads Cunningham too quickly, one might be tempted to conclude that because a vendor upstream in the chain of title knew of an unregistered deed covering the same lands, it follows that nobody, including the current purchaser, could ever take from that vendor. This is simply not the holding. Indeed, Mr. Justice MacLellan expressly recognizes that the previous generation's full knowledge of the beneficial title was irrelevant if the purchaser himself was an innocent.

Equitable mortgages and the priority of the Nova Scotia registry systems were also commented on by Hallett J.A. in *Scotia Mortgage Corp. v. Tucker* (1991), 107 N.S.R. (2d) 157 (N.S. C.A.), at paragraphs 6 and 7:

> The appellant further submits:
>
> > . . . that the case at Bar is one in which an equitable mortgage existed. Clearly the mortgage instructions and the documentation initially registered on behalf of Scotia Mortgage corporation referenced the incorrect name of the party. The appellant further submits that Mr. Pirie, holder of the Central Trust Self-Directed R.R.S.P. Plan No. 86333, had, at all material times, full knowledge of the intention for his mortgage to be a second charge against the Tucker property.
>
> With respect there isn't an equitable mortgage in existence on the facts of this case. There were two legal mortgages, one executed in favour of the Bank of Nova Scotia which was released, and a subsequent mortgage in favour of Scotia Mortgage Corporation which was executed and registered subsequent to the mortgage held by Mr. Pirie. Even if one were to consider that the mortgage made in favour of the Bank of Nova Scotia was an equitable mortgage in favour of the Scotia Mortgage Corporation, it was released and the release was registered in the registry of Deeds. *The equities simply do not favour the appellant, Mr. Markus. One cannot say that Mr. Pirie is guilty of any form of fraud. He is merely the beneficiary of Mr. Markus's failure to follow the instructions of Scotia Mortgage Corporation.* The underlying purpose of the Registry Act is to provide a system of registration of documents affecting title to real property so that persons can search the record and ascertain the true state of the title. Section 198 is intended to grant a degree of protection to persons who register documents, *provided of course they do not have actual notice of a prior unregistered instrument affecting title.* [Emphasis added.]

Is Justice Hallett concluding in the emphasized passage of the above quote that Section 18 of the *Registry Act* does not afford protection to a *bona fide* purchaser for value without actual notice of a prior instrument if that instrument is registered prior to the purchaser's instrument but outside of the chain of title? I do not believe that he is. To come to such a conclusion would mean that title searches would then be a matter of "chance" as opposed to a "registered chain". But what about the fact the purchaser, Mr. Mayer, did not conduct a title search before acquiring title to the property? Can he still rely on the registered chain of title? Is there a legal duty or obligation on him to conduct a search of the registered title?

While there can be no question that it is prudent to conduct a title search before purchasing a property in Nova Scotia, I find there is no legal duty to do so. Mr. Brüning argued the plaintiff cannot blindly turn his head and quotes the following passage from *Falconbridge On Mortgages* (4th ed.) at page 154:

> The principle of the statute is that a person acquiring land ought to ascertain whether there is anything registered against the land and that he is assumed to search the registry for that purpose . . .
>
> In the case of a person who acquires any interest in the land subsequent to the registration of an instrument against the land it would seem clear that he is affected with notice to the same extent as if he had received express notice of the instrument. [Emphasis added.]

In my view, the above noted quote does not indicate that there is a legal duty on purchasers to conduct title searches, but that persons who do not conduct searches, or conduct incomplete or faulty searches, are deemed to have notice of prior instruments registered in the chain of title.

Mr. Brüning further argues that Mr. Mayer should be affected with constructive notice because he did not conduct a title search and he quotes the following passage from *Falconbridge*, *supra*, at pages 115-116 in support of that proposition:

> Constructive notice means that the circumstances surrounding the taking of a mortgage are such as to induce the court to treat the mortgagee who in fact has no actual notice of an earlier charge as if in fact he had actual notice. He cannot raise the plea of purchase for value without notice. The circumstances which will affect a mortgagee with constructive notice are:
>
> > (a) His knowledge of facts which would naturally suggest the existence of the earlier charge.
> >
> > (b) His failure to make the enquiries which ought reasonably to have been made by him where, if he had made such enquiries, the existence of an earlier charge would have been disclosed to him.

The above quote is in the context of equitable mortgages, but if one applied it to legal instruments, I do not find that it raises the advisability of conducting title searches to a legal duty such that failure to do so can necessarily impart legal fault or ensuing liability on the part of a purchaser.

Analysis:

In the present case it cannot be said that Mr. Mayer owed a duty to Mr. Brüning to search the title in case it would turn up any charges against the property. On the basis of the Agreed Statement of Facts, I find that Mr. Mayer made reasonable enquiries in the circumstances. He believed, albeit erroneously, that his legal rights were being protected. He made enquiries and believed that the property was being conveyed to him free and clear of any encumbrances. He knew of no reason to make other enquiries. On the contrary, he was reassured that everything was as he believed.

There appears to be no question that Ms. Leipold was fully aware of the continued existence of the mortgage to Brüning. She appears to be the proverbial "rogue" as such parties were often referred to in earlier common law cases, although she may have been mistaken as to whom she was "duping". One also has to wonder why a mortgage which was apparently three years and some $75,000.00 in arrears had never been acted upon by Mr. Brüning prior to Mr. Mayer acquiring title. Certainly, if one were to apply equitable principles, as suggested by both parties, the equities alone would seem to favour Mr. Mayer.

Conclusion:

In the final analysis, I find that Mr. Mayer is a *bona fide* purchaser for value without notice of the Leipold mortgage to Mr. Brüning. I also find that this mortgage registered outside of the chain of title does not provide constructive notice to Mr. Mayer and is ineffective to encumber his fee simple title. There is no question that Mr. Mayer can consider himself fortunate, as was Mr. Pirie in *Scotia Mortgage Corp.*, *supra*, but to rule otherwise would make property conveyances and many title searches games of chance. That cannot be the objective of the *Registry Act* and the case authorities do not support the interpretation and application proposed by Mr. Brüning.

Christopher Parker acquired the legal title from Ms. Leipold, albeit as trustee. Mr. Brüning contends the chain of title argument does not hold if one of the predecessors in title under which the present owner claims was not a *bona fide* purchaser for value without notice. He argues that Christopher Parker who took title to the property in question as a trustee is not such a *bona fide* purchaser because he could not obtain a better title than Ms. Leipold had; *i.e.*, subject to the unregistered Brüning mortgage. At first glance this argument has some appeal; however, it is clearly rejected by the authorities quoted earlier. I find that Mr. Parker did have and he did convey the legal title to Mr. Mayer and there was no legal duty on Mr. Mayer to inquire into the terms of that trust. In any event it would in all probability have been of little avail because Ms. Leipold was, to all appearances, the beneficiary of that trust.

I also find that the principles of equitable mortgages have no application to this case. What we have here is a legal mortgage which was not registered in the chain of title.

In the result, Mr. Mayer shall have an order declaring that the mortgage dated August 22, 1994, from Ms. Leipold to Mr. Brüning in the amount of $130,000.00 recorded on October 28, 1994 in the Registry of Deeds office at Kentville, in the County of Kings, Nova Scotia, in Book # 997 at pages 774–779 is ineffective against Mr. Mayer and his successors in title.

I will entertain written submissions on the question of costs if the parties cannot agree. If the parties agree on the issue of costs I will issue an order consented as to form and costs by counsel for the parties.

Action dismissed.

QUESTIONS

1. Should Mayer and Parker be regarded as *bona fide* purchasers for value without notice? See B. Ziff, "Registering Disagreement: A Comment on *Mayer v. Brüning*" (2001) 39 R.P.R. (3d) 184.

2. Would the outcome have changed had Mayer searched the title?

3. In the face of this ruling, how can someone in the position of Brüning protect their interest once it is established that it has not been recorded in chronological order?

4. TITLE REGISTRATION

Under a title registration system, the state plays a more active role in the process of land transfer than is the case under deeds registration. First and foremost, under a pure-form land titles system, title is not merely recognised, but issued by the state. In other words, registration is the final step in the formal closing of a land transaction, and at that stage — not before — title is formally transferred into the hands of the new owner. Hence, sub. 66(4) of *The Real Property Act*, C.C.S.M., c. R30 states that:

> No instrument is effectual to pass an interest in land under the new system or to render the land liable as security for the payment of money as against a *bona fide* transferee thereof, until the instrument is registered in accordance with this Act.

Does this provision mean that prior to registration the purchaser acquires no interest in the property? See *Church v. Hill* [1923] S.C.R. 642, 1923 CarswellAlta 152.

There are three central features of titles systems. First, the state certifies the title of the existing owner. This means that an historic search of title is not required; one can rely on the "top title". So, it is said that a *curtain* is drawn on past dealings, and even if the title of the vendor is seriously flawed, a purchaser need not be concerned, provided that he/she is not guilty of fraud.

Second, under a titles registration system the register is supposed to serve as a *mirror* (or a *photograph*) of all interests relating to a given plot of land. The failure to register can have serious consequences: the unregistered interest may not be binding on interests acquired subsequently. (See the following three cases for more on this issue.)

One can see that both of these features work to lighten the load of purchasers. The number of searches and inquiries that a purchaser must perform before a property is bought are reduced, and the system provides the purchaser with protection against some defects in title. A purchaser who acquires a right under the system that is not vulnerable to attack on the basis of some antecedent event or defect is said to hold an indefeasible title to that interest.

Notice that the risk of error or misconduct is shifted from that which applies at law and under the deeds approach. But the risk does not — and indeed cannot — be completely obliterated from land transfers. Under a title system, it is original owner who now runs a heightened risk of losing the property in favour of a *bona fide* purchaser. Accordingly, title systems conventionally provide for monetary compensation for owners who are deprived of title by reason of the operation of the curtain principle. This is the insurance (or *net*) principle, the third pillar of land titles registration. It is applicable where errors in administration or wrongful conduct lead to the loss of, or an encumbrance on, an owner's interest.

Most of the title registration statutes found in Canada are derived from the ground-breaking work of Sir Robert Torrens, who spearheaded the introduction of land registration reforms in South Australia. By contrast, the origins of Ontario's *Land Titles Act*, R.S.O 1990, c. L.5. can be traced to the English *Land Transfer Act, 1875*, c. 87. (Ontario's first land titles statute was enacted in 1885.) While it is possible to overstate the differences between the Australian and English models, the cases that follow suggest that at least one important distinction exists in relation to their Canadian versions. Also, remember this: no title registration system implements the three basal principles perfectly. Some significant qualifications on the paradigm will become apparent throughout the following exposition.

United Trust Co. v. Dominion Stores Ltd. (1976) [1977] 2 S.C.R. 915, 1976 CarswellOnt 383, 1976 CarswellOnt 404

[United Trust entered into negotiations with the Geller and Granatstein, the owners of a commercial property, then occupied by a tenant, Dominion Stores. An agreement was reached under which the closing was conditional on United Trust obtaining a surrender of the lease from Dominion. Following unsuccessful attempts to obtain the surrender, United Trust agreed to waive this condition. It was also agreed that the interest on a mortgage to be paid to the vendor by United Trust would be reduced from 9% *per annum* to 8%.

Once the sale closed, United Trust changed the locks on the property and excluded Dominion. The lease had not been registered, and hence United Trust asserted that it did not bind its title.]

Spence J.: . . .

The title to the premises at 418 Spadina Road, Toronto, is under the provisions of *The Land Titles Act*, R.S.O. 1970, c. 234 as amended . . .

The appellant United Trust Company admits it had full actual notice of the lease which the respondent Dominion Stores Limited held on the premises and indeed it could not say otherwise as its officers had engaged in long negotiations with the officers of Dominion Stores Limited in an attempt to obtain a surrender of that lease and the offer to purchase made by the appellant United Trust Company to the respondents Geller and Granatstein was originally subject to the condition that such surrender of lease could be obtained from the respondent Dominion Stores Limited. It is the contention, however, of the appellant that under the provisions of *The Land Titles Act* the lease to Dominion Stores Limited never having been registered on the title in accordance with the provisions of that Act the purchaser took free of any encumbrances created by that lease. Put baldly, this contention is that under the Ontario *Land Titles Act*, apart from fraud, actual notice of a non-registered instrument is ineffective to put the burden of the encumbrance resulting therefrom upon a purchaser for value. . . .

It is the appellant's argument that the enactment of the Torrens land titles system in the Province of Ontario made applicable in that province the main theory of a Torrens title registration system, to wit, the absolute authority of the register, and that it is the effect of such a principle that actual notice, no matter how clearly proved so long as encumbrances do not appear on the register, does not affect the clear title of the purchaser for value. I am ready to agree that this is a prime principle of the Torrens system and that it had been referred to as such by various text writers which I need not cite in support thereof.

The Torrens Registration System was the brainchild of a Mr. Robert Torrens of South Australia and, due to his perseverance, a statute embodying the principles of his land titles system was enacted in South Australia in 1857. Similar statutes based on the same principles and using the same technique were enacted in rapid succession in Queensland in 1861, in Tasmania, Victoria and New South Wales in 1862, in New Zealand in 1870 and in Western Australia in 1874. Use of the system spread to Canada and a like statute was enacted in the Colony of Vancouver Island in 1861, and then in the Province of British Columbia in 1869. *The Land Titles Act* was enacted in Ontario in 1885. At that time, the Legislature in Ontario had before it as models all these previous enactments which I have listed. In every case, those enactments contained an express provision making actual notice ineffective to encumber the registered title.

The subsequent enactment of Land Titles Acts in Alberta, Saskatchewan and Manitoba contained a like provision. In Ontario, no such provision appeared. The respondent Dominion Stores Limited submits that this omission is crucial and certainly could not be considered to be an accident.

Counsel for the respondent Dominion Stores Limited submits, and I agree with him, that the many cases cited by counsel for the appellant for the proposition that actual notice is ineffective, including some cases which bear an almost exact resemblance to the present, are cases which depend upon the statutory provisions in the various jurisdictions containing such an express provision and, therefore, are irrelevant in considering the situation in Ontario which lacks such a provision. I have read the authorities cited by the appellant and I do find that in each of those cases there is express reference to such a section. As an example may be cited the provisions of s. 203 of *The Land Titles Act of Alberta*, R.S.A. 1970, c. 198, which I quote:

203. Except in the case of fraud, no person contracting or dealing with or taking or proposing to take a transfer, mortgage, encumbrance or lease from the owner of any land in whose name a certificate of title has been granted shall be bound or concerned to inquire into or ascertain the circumstances in or the consideration for which the owner or any previous owner of the land is or was registered or to see to the application of the purchase money or of any part thereof, nor is he affected by notice direct, implied, or constructive, of any trust or unregistered interest in the land, any rule of law or equity to the contrary notwithstanding, and the knowledge that any trust or unregistered interest is in existence shall not of itself be imputed as fraud.

There is no doubt that when such a term appears in the governing statute, the result is that unregistered encumbrances fail in any way to affect the title of the purchaser for value. . . .

However, in Ontario, only a few years after the enactment of *The Land Titles Act*, the Courts have expressed a disinclination to imply such an extinction of the doctrine of actual notice. There is no doubt that such doctrine as to all contractual relations and particularly the law of real property has been firmly based in our law since the beginning of equity. It was the view of those Courts, and it is my view, that such a cardinal principle of property law cannot be considered to have been abrogated unless the legislative enactment is in the clearest and most unequivocal of terms. Such a provision, as I have said, does appear in all the other statutes cited by the appellant.

[Spence J. then reviewed the decisions in *Re Skill and Thompson* (1908) 17 O.L.R. 186 (C.A.) and *John Macdonald & Co. v. Tew* (1914) 32 O.L.R. 262 (C.A.) and then continued.]

The next decision in Ontario to which I wish to refer is *Re Jung and Montgomery*, [[1955] O.W.N. 931, [1955] 5 D.L.R. 287, affirmed [1955] O.W.N. 935 [1955] 5 D.L.R. at 292 (C.A.)]. There, Duranceau D.C.J. had considered a landlord's application for possession. The landlord and a tenant had both been the tenants of adjoining parcels of land held under *The Land Titles Act*. The landlord purchased the parcel which he had previously leased and the parcel leased by Montgomery. Montgomery's lease, including the option to renew, ran for more than three years. Jung, the new registered owner, had full knowledge of Montgomery's tenancy at the time he purchased from the previous owner. After having closed the transaction, Jung continued to accept rental from Montgomery but later made application for possession. This latter fact, in my view, could have determined the case simply on the basis that Jung had accepted Montgomery as his tenant and was saddled with Montgomery's lease. The learned District Court Judge, however, mentioned this point only at the close of his reasons and devoted the main portion thereof to a consideration of the question of whether Jung's actual notice of Montgomery's lease prior to his having closed the transaction of purchase resulted in him having to take title subject to Montgomery's lease and held that it did so relying particularly on *Skill and Thompson* and *Macdonald v. Tew* which I have cited above. Jung appealed to the Court of Appeal and the disposition there is set out in the report in these words:

> The Court dismissed the appeal at the conclusion of the appellant's argument and orally expressed its agreement with the judgment appealed from.

In [1955] O.W.N. at p. 936, a similar notation appears.

Shortly thereafter, in 1960, *The Land Titles Act* was amended by the addition of s. 54(5). That amendment now appears as s. 85(5) of *The Land Titles Act*. . . .

[Subsection 85(5) reads:

> Subject to any entry to the contrary in the register and subject to this Act, instruments registered in respect of or affecting the same estate or interest in the same parcel of registered land as between themselves rank according to the order in which they are entered in the register and not according to the order in which they were created, and, notwithstanding any express, implied or constructive notice, are entitled to priority according to the time of registration . . .]

In the present case, both Jessup J.A. and Arnup J.A. considered s. 85(5) in giving the reasons for the Court of Appeal, as had Grant J. upon the hearing of the application. Jessup J.A. was of the opinion that by the enactment of s. 85(5) the Legislature had disclosed the intent of the statute and that it was the intent found in the decision of *Re Jung and Montgomery*, noting [6 O.R. (2d) at p. 201]:

> . . . The subsection does not purport to repeal generally the law is laid down in *Re Jung* and therefore was not enacted simply for the purpose of such repeal.

As an alternative reason for the conclusion, Jessup J.A. pointed out that s. 85(5) dealt with ". . . registered intruments in respect of or affecting the same estate or interest in the same parcel of registered land" while the issue considered was a freehold estate in the purchaser United Trust Company and a leasehold estate in Dominion Stores Limited.

Arnup J.A., in his reasons, dealt with the argument in this term [6 O.R. (2d) at p. 202]:

> The appeal narrows down to the question whether the enactment of s. 80(5) in R.S.O. 1960, c. 204 (now s. 85(5), R.S.O. 1970, c. 234), changed the law by abolishing the "doctrine of actual notice". If this is what the Legislature intended, the amendment was put in a very peculiar place, having regard to the context of ss. (1) to (4) of s. 85.

With respect, I am in complete agreement with that comment. It is difficult to understand why the Legislature, faced with a decision approved in the Court of Appeal that actual notice was still in Ontario effective to encumber the registered titleholder's estate, should have attempted to eliminate such a conclusion by the enactment of a subsection in a section dealing with details of registration when an appropriate amendment in plain words of s. 52 as to first registration or s. 91 as to subsequent transfers would have been appropriate. The form was available as it already appeared in many other provincial *Land Titles Acts*. Again, I agree with Arnup J.A. when he said that the law of real property should not be found to have been altered by the Legislature except where such alteration had been made by clear or appropriate words.

Arnup J.A. was of the view that s. 85(5) would have applied between registered instruments even if one were a transfer of the freehold and the other a lease, being of the opinion that the latter affected the former but found it unnecessary to so determine. In view of his opinion, with which, with respect, I agree, s. 85(5) did not affect the law as enunciated in *Re Jung and Montgomery*. . . .

Laskin C.J.C. (dissenting):

This appeal raises a question of first instance in this Court in respect of *The Land Titles Act*, R.S.O. 1970, c. 234, as amended. The question is whether an unregistered interest in land governed by the Act, and not being an overriding interest thereunder, may be asserted against a purchaser for value of the freehold of the land who obtains a transfer from the owner on the land titles register with actual notice of the unregistered interest. Grant J. held that the purchaser's title was subject to the unregistered interest, and this decision was affirmed by the Ontario Court of Appeal. I take a different view. In my opinion, notice, actual or constructive, of unregistered interests cannot qualify the title of a purchaser for value as shown on the register. . . .

Why the respondent lessee, a large food chain, which had first become lessee of the land in 1935, did not register notice of its leasehold interest is unfathomable. It had access to competent legal advice no less than did the appellant. On the argument of the appeal, its counsel contended that, in the circumstances of the case, the admitted notice and knowledge by the appellant of the respondent's outstanding leasehold interest before purchasing the freehold made its purchase through a land titles transfer fraudulent when it sought, on the strength of the transfer, to dispossess the respondent. The basis of this contention by the respondent, a contention which was not raised in its original application to Grant J. for relief from forfeiture and reinstatement of its lease, lies in the course of negotiations between solicitors for the respective parties when the appellant was seeking to obtain a surrender of possession by the respondent concurrently with the carrying out of its intended purchase of the freehold. I would not be justified, on the record in this case, in coming to a conclusion that there had been a deliberate misleading of the respondent. The latter knew of the agreement for purchase of the freehold by the appellant and had ample opportunity to protect its interest. The respondent cannot improve its position by labelling actual notice as fraud. If its position is maintainable, it must be on the ground that *The Land Titles Act* does not defeat unregistered interests of which a subsequent purchaser for value has actual notice. . . .

We face here another instance of a temptation to construe a statute in the light of the common law, to qualify a statute by an equitable doctrine alien to the purpose (a clear purpose in the circumstances underlying its enactment) which the statute sought to achieve. Because notice of unregistered interests was not expressly excluded as a qualifying consideration, the integrity of the land titles register is shaken by the judgment in appeal, although the scheme and language of *The Land Titles*

Act are, in my opinion, adequate enough to show the irrelevancy of such notice. A system of registration of title is treated, in respect of the effect of notice of unregistered interests, as if it were a system of registration of documents, such as exists under *The Registry Act*, R.S.O. 1970, c. 409, as amended, an Act now qualified by *The Certification of Titles Act*, R.S.O. 1970, c. 59, as amended.

If fairness from a common law standpoint was the dominant consideration, irrespective of legislative policy, irrespective of the circumstances which brought title registration systems into being, there could be less quarrel with the decision of the Courts below. We are not, however, concerned with the common law, but rather with a complete break from it through a choice of legislative policy reflected in some countries and in some Canadian Provinces by adoption of the Torrens system, and in England and Ontario by the adoption of a related system of title registration. . . .

A good deal of argument was addressed by counsel for the parties to Torrens system case law. The main value of the cited cases for the present case is the dissociation of notice and fraud, the rejection of the notion that a person with notice of an unregistered interest can be charged with fraud: see, for example, the Australian case of *Friedman v. Barrett*, [1962] Qd. R. 498. The importance of the distinction is underlined in Torrens system legislation by the express exclusion of notice and by making fraud an exception to the integrity of the register. In some jurisdictions, the legislature has gone further by providing that knowledge of an unregistered interest was not itself to be imputed as fraud. . . .

We are dealing with different, albeit related, systems of title registration, and I do not think that the presence of an express provision in Torrens system legislation is evidence of a gap in the Ontario Act or, indeed, in the comparable English legislation of 1875. Especially is this so when the consequence is said to be the importing of a doctrine which denies the central policy of the Ontario Act. Of course, an express exclusion of notice as a qualifying consideration in respect of title as shown on the register might have obviated this litigation, but so too would registration of notice of its lease by the respondent pursuant to s. 115 [am. 1972, c. 132, s. 24] of The Ontario *Land Titles Act*. . . .

The logic of *The Land Titles Act* is perfectly plain. If, as its terms stipulate, it is the register that determines where title resides, then actual notice becomes immaterial unless it is preserved, as fraud is preserved and as certain other interests called overriding interests, are preserved. To say that because notice is not expressly excluded (as it is excluded *ex abundanti cautela* in Torrens systems legislation) it is deemed to be preserved, is no less a pronouncement of policy than that which I espouse. The question then becomes one of determining which policy is more consistent with the Act, with its spirit as well as its letter. A succinct statement of the policy will be found in the Ontario Law Reform Commission's Report on Land Registration, issued in 1971, in which it summarizes the land titles system as follows (at p. 14):

> The land titles system was established in Ontario in 1885. It is essentially an affirmation by the province of the ownership of interests in land. Local offices have again been

> established — at present there are 30 — and a separate record is kept in these offices for each parcel governed by the system. The record includes an affirmation of the existence and ownership of interests — the fee simple and charges, and some leases and easements. Interests about which affirmations of existence and ownership are not made may be protected against loss of priority by registration of notices and cautions.
>
> A search is essentially an examination of the record and, usually, of some documents referred to in the record. The system imposes a larger degree of administrative supervision of conveyancing than the registry system does, and forms that must be used are specified for many transactions. If an interest is extinguished as a consequence of the making of an affirmation, the owner of the interest is entitled to compensation from a fund established for this purpose. A claim that does not appear in the record is of no effect against a purchaser unless the purchser has acted fraudulently.

When *The Land Titles Act* was first introduced in Ontario, there was already experience in the province with a system of registration of deeds, and the policy thereunder of priority of registration subject to actual notice was clearly expressed: see *The Registry Act*, R.S.O. 1877, c. 111, ss. 74, 78 and 80. To import actual notice in a title registration system without its express preservation is to change the basic character of the system. It is impossible, in my view, to adhere to the principle of the primacy of the register and at the same time to make it yield to a doctrine of notice.

I come now to s. 85(5), referred to in the reasons of the Court of Appeal in this case as a governing consideration in its decision. This provision reads as follows:

> (5) Subject to any entry to the contrary in the register and subject to this Act, instruments registered in respect of or affecting the same estate or interest in the same parcel of registered land as between themselves rank according to the order in which they are entered in the register and not according to the order in which they were created, and, notwithstanding any express, implied or constructive notice, are entitled to priority according to the time of registration.

I do not agree with the view expressed in the Court of Appeal that this provision is, in effect, an affirmation of the survival of notice as a qualification of the absolute character of the register (fraud, of course, apart). The Court dwells on the words in s. 85(5) "notwithstanding any express, implied or constructive notice" for its view, but I am unable to appreciate how the express inclusion of these words supports the conclusion that actual notice of an unregistered interest is still effective against title shown on the register.

If it is a provision that operates at large, it obviously excludes notice of an unregistered interest as a limitation of the title shown on the register. Treating s. 85(5) as operating at large, I cannot see how it can be construed to exclude the effect of notice where the notice is of a claim to the same interest as that purchased by another for value on the faith of the register, but not to exclude it where the notice is of a claim to a subordinate interest, as is the case here. Arnup J.A. in his concurring reasons in the Court of Appeal conceded the illogicality of a situation where a person would be better off claiming against a registered transferee through notice than by registering his interest, but he concluded that the Legislature must take responsibility for such a result. I think rather that the Courts must take responsibility, since it would be their interpretation, by no means a compelled one, which produces it.

In my view, if s. 85(5) be taken in the context of the whole of s. 85 it is capable of explanation without treating it as applicable at large, but yet reinforcing the indefeasibility of the register and of title according to the register, subject only to overriding interests and to fraud.

Section 85 deals with the procedure for registration and with the effectuation of registration. It begins with a provision requiring that the day, hour and minute of the receipt of instruments presented for registration must be noted by the attending officer or clerk. Then follow subsections (2) and (3) which I reproduce here in full:

> (2) Subject to the rules, an instrument received for registration shall be registered in the order of time in which it is so received, unless before registration is completed it is withdrawn or the proper master of titles decides that it contains a material error, omission or deficiency or that there is evidence lacking that he considers requisite or declines registration for any other reason, and notifies the parties or their solicitors accordingly within twenty-one days after being so received and allows a period of time not less than seven and not more than thirty days from the date of such notification for correction of the error, omission or deficiency or for furnishing evidence and, when the error, omission or deficiency is corrected or evidence furnished within the time allowed, the instrument has priority as if it had been correct in the first instance, but, if the error, omission or deficiency is not corrected or if evidence is not furnished within the time allowed or if the person desiring registration fails to appeal successfully from the decision, the proper master of titles may proceed with other registrations affecting the land as if the instrument had not been presented for registration, and the proper master of titles shall be deemed not to be affected with notice of the contents of the instrument.
>
> (3) Registration of an instrument is complete when the entry in the proper register and particulars of registration thereof on the instrument are signed by the proper master of titles, his deputy or a signing officer, and the time of receipt of the instrument shall be deemed to be the time of its registration.

What these provisions show is that entry on the register in fact may take place some time after receipt of an instrument tendered for registration but, nonetheless, the registration will be effective as of the time of receipt of the instrument. As s. 85(2) shows, entry may be held up pending correction of errors or deficiencies in the tendered instrument and yet may be accorded priority as against an intervening tender of another competing instrument which appears to be in correct form. When s. 85(5) speaks of priority "in respect of or affecting the same estate or interests in the same parcel of registered land" according to the order of entry in the register, it is dealing with competing instruments in the light of the provisions of s. 85(2) and (3). It appears to me to be an unnecessary punctuation of the obvious, but it could be said to emphasize the import of s. 85(2) that where an error or deficiency is corrected (as contrasted with the case where it is not) the intervening instrument is not entitled to priority merely because there is notice of it before the error or deficiency in the other one is corrected even if the intervening instrument was created first. . . .

I would allow the appeal, set aside the judgments below and dismiss the application of the respondent Dominion Stores Limited, with costs to the appellant throughout.

Appeal dismissed.

QUESTION

A and B purchase property as co-owners. B is unavailable for the signing of the closing documents, so title is issued in the name of A "in trust", and registered in that manner. The land is then mortgaged by A to C, and the mortgage is registered in the name of C. No mention is made in those documents to the trust. Is C bound by B's interest? See *Walshe v. Citizen's Bank of Canada* (2003) 8 R.P.R. (4th) 273, 2003 CarswellOnt 922 (S.C.J.).

Holt Renfrew & Co. v. Henry Singer Ltd. [1982] 4 W.W.R. 481, 1982 CarswellAlta 92 (C.A.)

McDermid J.A.:

In these appeals there are two questions to be decided: the first concerns the proper interpretation of s. 203 . . . of the Land Titles Act , R.S.A. 1970, c. 198 . . .; the second is as to the validity of the caveat filed by D. U. Pekarsky, barrister and solicitor, claiming "an interest as agent for an undisclosed principal".

Although I am in agreement with the facts as found by the trial judge [[1981] 3 W.W.R. 9, 20 R.P.R. 51, 118 D.L.R. (3d) 645, 30 A.R. 254 (Q.B.)], I have drawn different inferences from some of them.

Thompson & Dynes were the owners of a building located on Jasper Avenue in the city of Edmonton in which they conducted a business. In 1950 the business was sold to Holt Renfrew & Co. Ltd. and the property was leased to it. I shall refer to Thompson & Dynes as the owner vendor and to Holt Renfrew as the tenant. The trial judge found [p. 12]:

> The lease in question was for a term of 10 years from 30th March 1950, with an option to renew the said term for a further period of 10 years. The plaintiff's [the tenant's] interest under the lease was protected by way of a caveat registered at the land titles office on 15th April 1950 as 4384HM.
>
> In 1957 the lease was extended to 30th March 1973. In 1969 Holt Renfrew, in order to protect a planned expenditure of $200,000 to $300,000 for leasehold improvements, sought to obtain a new lease which would commence on 30th March 1973 and extend for 17 years to 30th March 1990.

The lease was drawn by the solicitor for the owner vendor, Mr. Archibald Dickson. It was sent by the local office of the tenant to its Montreal office and apparently the person who dealt with it there, being unaware of the provisions of the Alberta *Land Titles Act*, did not file the lease or a caveat to protect it. A caveat to protect the lease was filed by the tenant only after the property had been sold and the agent for the purchaser, the appellant Henry Singer Limited, had filed a caveat. Both *caveats* were filed before a transfer from the owner vendor to the purchaser Henry Singer Limited had been registered.

In May 1978 one of the appellants herein, Mr. Daniel U. Pekarsky, a lawyer in the city of Edmonton, telephoned the said Dickson and told him he might have a client interested in purchasing the property. The trial judge said [pp. 12-13]:

> Dickson told Pekarsky to send a letter to that effect and told Pekarsky that there was a long lease in favour of Holt Renfrew. The word "long" was not defined by Dickson. On 4th May 1978 Pekarsky wrote Dickson to confirm that he had a client that was sincerely interested in acquiring the Thompson & Dynes property. This letter was made Ex. 10 at the trial and includes the following:
>
>> At this moment in time our client has no preconceptions as to the manner in which the property might be acquired. We indicated to you that if, for example, the real property's relationship to the assets of Thompson & Dynes Limited was such that a purchase of the shares of the company was feasible, then our client could well be interested in something along those lines.
>>
>> In order to initiate meaningful discussion, we would like to obtain, if possible, a current income and expense statement for the operation of the property as well as an indication of the owner's price for the same. If there is interest in dealing on the basis of the entire company, then obviously we would require current financial statements.
>>
>> With respect to the matter of the existing tenant of the property, we do not believe that situation would be a deterrent to our client's interest.

As I will later explain, it is this letter which entitles the tenant to succeed in its lawsuit on the question concerning s. 203.

Upon receipt of the letter, after obtaining instructions from his client, Dickson wrote to Pekarsky advising that his client was prepared to receive offers for the sale of the land or for the shares of the company and asked what further information was required. On 28th August 1978 Pekarsky asked for financial information and a copy of the lease. Dickson sent Pekarsky financial statements and a copy of the lease. Pekarsky then advised Dickson that his client was not interested in buying the shares but was interested in purchasing the property. The trial judge found that Pekarsky had examined this lease and concluded that his client was not interested in buying the real estate subject to the lease. He did not advise Dickson of this conclusion, although he had advised Dickson that his client was not interested in purchasing the shares of the owner vendor. Both of these matters were referred to in his letter above quoted.

On 11th September 1978 Pekarsky made a written offer of $800,000. To this offer was attached a photocopy of the certificate of title. The offer to purchase was made "subject only to the encumbrances endorsed upon the said annexed photocopy of the certificate of title". The only encumbrance disclosed on the photocopy was the 1950 caveat filed by the tenant. This offer was rejected and no further negotiation took place until March 1979. Further offers and counter-offers were made. The trial judge stated [p. 15]:

> On 7th March 1979 Pekarsky forwarded a letter to Dickson including a revised offer in that amount ($1,320,000) and substantially in the same form as the offer of 11th September 1978. A trust cheque in the amount of $50,000 was enclosed. Attached to the offer again was a photocopy of the certificate of title to the property in question. The letter, the offer and the photocopy of the certificate of title were entered as Ex. 16.
>
> Again the only encumbrance shown on the photocopy of the certificate of title was the 1950 Holt Renfrew caveat as previously described.

The offer was accepted by Dickson on behalf of his client on 7th March 1979. The next day Pekarsky filed a caveat in the land titles office which I will subsequently set out when I consider its validity. Snowdon, a lawyer in Pekarsky's office, by letter dated 22nd March 1979, requested transfer documents in the name of the defendant Singer, the purchaser, and also forwarded a statement of adjustments, and in the letter enclosing the statement requested that his client be reimbursed for one-half of the April 1979 rentals which had been collected by the owner vendor from the tenant.

The trial judge found that it was common ground that the owner vendor acted openly and honestly throughout and kept the tenant advised of its negotiations. He also found that the tenant was content to remain as lessee and was not anxious about its legal position until after it learned that a sale had been made and a caveat filed on behalf of the purchaser, whereupon it took legal advice and then filed a caveat to protect its lease.

Dickson sent a transfer of the property to Pekarsky with a statement of adjustments prepared by him which included an adjustment for the April rental. The leasehold estate was not excepted out of the fee simple that was transferred, nor was any assignment of it forwarded to Pekarsky. The learned trial judge specifically found that after the copy of the lease was forwarded to Pekarsky on 5th September 1978 no further mention was ever made of the lease between the solicitors for the parties.

It was decided by the solicitors for the purchaser that the caveat filed by the tenant subsequent to the caveat filed by Pekarsky was ineffective, and they then filed the transfer and paid the vendor owner the purchase price for the property.

After reviewing the evidence in some detail, the learned trial judge said [pp. 19–21]:

> I am satisfied that throughout the transaction Thompson & Dynes intended to convey to Singer the property including the Holt Renfrew lease. I am also satisfied that after

> Pekarsky examined the 15th December 1972 lease between Holt Renfrew and Dynes, he then realized that he might be able to purchase the property for his client without the lease and proceeded to negotiate with that in mind. Pekarsky's evidence is that after seeing the 1972 lease he "perceived the opportunity" that presented itself from the fact that the lease was not protected by caveat. His evidence is to the effect that he was not entirely sure if Dickson was aware that the lease was not protected by caveat. He states that he was careful not to mislead Dickson.
>
> Fred Singer, an officer of the defendant Singer, testified that at all material times Pekarsky acted within the scope of his authority and further Singer adopted Pekarsky's actions as its own . . .
>
> Pekarsky certainly knew of Holt Renfrew's unregistered interest and that Holt Renfrew's interest could be defeated by concluding the transaction by registering his caveat. While he may have suspected that Thompson & Dynes might not sell the property unless the sale was subject to the Holt Renfrew lease, he did nothing after his letter of inquiry dated 4th May 1978 to lead Dickson or anyone else to believe that it was understood that Singer would be assuming the Holt Renfrew lease. I accept Pekarsky's evidence that he believed that he was quite within his rights to act as he did and I am further satisfied that he held this belief honestly. I am satisfied that he did not attempt to mislead or deceive Dickson or anyone else. I reject the suggestion that Pekarsky's offers of 11th September 1978 and 7th March 1979 were cleverly drafted in a deliberate attempt to lull Dickson into thinking that Pekarsky was accepting the Holt Renfrew lease executed in 1972.

The first question to be decided in this lawsuit is whether the conduct of Pekarsky constituted fraud within s. 203 of the Act which provides:

> 203. Except in the case of fraud, no person contracting or dealing with or taking or proposing to take a transfer, mortgage, encumbrance or lease from the owner of any land in whose name a certificate of title has been granted shall be bound or concerned to inquire into or ascertain the circumstances in or the consideration for which the owner or any previous owner of the land is or was registered or to see to the application of the purchase money or of any part thereof, nor is he affected by notice direct, implied or constructive, of any trust or unregistered interest in the land, any rule of law or equity to the contrary notwithstanding, and the knowledge that any trust or unregistered interest is in existence shall not of itself be imputed as fraud.

The trial judge then posed this question [p. 21]:

> The question then arises: Is knowledge of the existence of an unregistered interest coupled with knowledge that the unregistered interest will be defeated by concluding the transaction sufficient to constitute fraud under s. 203 of the *Land Titles Act*?

He concluded it was and gave judgment for the tenant. I am in agreement that there was fraud within the meaning of s. 203 but not for the reasons given by the trial judge. To constitute fraud under s. 203, more is required than knowledge of the unregistered interest and the registration of a transfer which defeats the unregistered interest. . . .

In my opinion [the] cases . . . do not support the proposition that knowledge of the existence of an unregistered interest, coupled with knowledge that the unregistered interest will be defeated by concluding the transaction, is sufficient to constitute fraud. There must be an additional element. . . .

The questions that . . . must be answered are:

(a) Was the representation made by Pekarsky, the lawyer for the purchaser of the property, that the lease was not a deterrent to the purchase of the property and his subsequent failure to correct it, a fraudulent misrepresentation within the meaning of fraud in s. 203 so that the protection of that section cannot be claimed;

(b) Did Dickson representing the vendors rely on it; and

(c) Was Dickson misled by it?

In *Ross v. Stovall*, 14 Alta. L.R., [1919] 1 W.W.R. 673 at 676, 45 D.L.R. 397, Harvey C.J.A., giving the judgment of the Appellate Division of the Supreme Court of Alberta, commenting on the precursor to s. 203 [the *Land Titles Act, 1906* (Alta.), c. 24, s. 135] stated:

> Sec. 135 [replaced by s. 203] provides that except in case of fraud a person dealing with a registered owner need not enquire as to other interests and that "knowledge that any trust or unregistered interest is in existence shall not of itself be imputed as fraud."
>
> In *Assets Co. v. Mere Roihi*, [1905] A.C. 176, the Judicial Committee had to determine the nature of the right of a registered owner under the New Zealand Act on a claim to set aside his certificate of title. That Act is in general tenor and effect similar to ours though the details and arrangements differ. In the judgment at p. 202 ([1905] A.C.), it is stated, "The sections making registered certificates conclusive evidence of title are too clear to be got over." Then again at p. 210 ([1905] A.C.), "Passing now to the question of fraud . . . ss. 55, 56, 189 and 190 appear to their Lordships to show that by fraud in these Acts is meant actual fraud, *i.e.*, dishonesty of some sort, not what is called constructive or equitable fraud . . . Further, it appears to their Lordships that the fraud which must be proved in order to invalidate the title of a registered purchaser for value . . . must be brought home to the person whose registered title is impeached or to his agents."

In the original conversation of Pekarsky with Dickson, Pekarsky was told that there was a long lease on the property. He then wrote to Dickson suggesting that his clients might be interested in purchasing the shares of Thompson & Dynes. If such was done and the property acquired in this manner, the purchasers would of necessity be bound by the terms of the lease. But, in addition, in his letter of May 1978 to Dickson he stated, "With respect to the matter of the existing tenant of the property, we do not believe that situation would be a deterrent to our client's interest". In addition to the letter in September, Pekarsky obtained financial statements and a copy of the lease from Dickson. He never subsequently advised Dickson that his client was not interested in buying the property subject to the lease. The trial judge found [p. 19]: "I am satisfied that throughout the transaction Thompson & Dynes intended to convey to Singer [the purchaser] the property including the Holt Renfrew lease". Although the trial judge says of Pekarsky [p. 21]:

> While he may have suspected that Thompson & Dynes might not sell the property unless the sale was subject to the Holt Renfrew lease, he did nothing after his letter of inquiry dated 4th May 1978 to lead Dickson or anyone else to believe that it was understood that Singer would be assuming the Holt Renfrew lease.

The evidence of Pekarsky himself to my mind makes it quite clear that he knew Thompson & Dynes would not sell except subject to the lease. This of course accords with the moral position and the common business sense of their position. Why would Thompson & Dynes subject themselves to a possible action by Holt Renfrew, which in fact was brought by Holt Renfrew, for damages? I think it clear that Pekarsky knew that Thompson & Dynes would not sell except subject to the lease.

What was Pekarsky's duty to Dickson; once he had led Dickson to believe that the lease was not a deterrent to the purchase, was he under an obligation to correct this representation when he knew his client would not honour the lease?

That this transaction took place between solicitors does not impose any higher obligation on them than that between average businessmen concluding a property contract. It does not fall into the realm of undertakings between solicitors which are considered *uberrima fide* transactions. (See R. 18 of Pt. I of the Professional Conduct Handbook of the Law Society of Alberta.)

It is the ordinary laws of contract that we must consider, and what constitutes fraud in such a property transaction.

The principle that it is necessary to correct a representation which is believed to be true at the time it is made or which subsequently becomes untrue was enunciated by Fry J. in *Davies v. London & Prov. Marine Ins. Co.* (1878), 8 Ch. D. 469 at 475:

> Again, in ordinary contracts the duty may arise from circumstances which occur during the negotiation. Thus, for instance, if one of the negotiating parties has made a statement which is false in fact, but which he believes to be true and which is material to the contract, and during the course of the negotiation he discovers the falsity of that statement, he is under an obligation to correct his erroneous statement; although if he had said nothing he very likely might have been entitled to hold his tongue throughout. So, again, if a statement has been made which is true at the time, but which during the course of the negotiations became untrue, then the person who knows it has become untrue is under an obligation to disclose to the other the change of circumstances. . . .

I am at a loss to understand why the failure of a party to understand that he has a duty to correct the false representation makes it any less a fraud. Surely such a mistake of law does not excuse him. It is still fraud although Pekarsky thought his duty to his client was to conceal the fact. He may have honestly thought he had no duty to reveal to Dickson that the position of his client had changed when he found out the length of the lease. The fact that he thought he had no such duty is not relevant. With respect to intention, it is not his view of the law which is relevant but it is his knowledge of his client's intention and whether that knowledge accorded or not with what he represented his client's intention to be.

The evidence clearly shows that some time after he wrote the letter of May 1978 he became aware that his client no longer intended to accept the lease in favour of Holt Renfrew, and he failed to correct the now false representation which he had made to Dickson in that letter. . . .

Pekarsky was under a duty to correct what he had written to Dickson when he discovered the fact that the lease was a deterrent to his client's interest. If he had not written his letter of 4th May 1978 he was under no duty to Dickson to advise him that the lease was not protected by a caveat. He could have remained silent; but once he had led Dickson to believe the lease was not a deterrent, he was under a duty to correct that representation. Not to do so constituted actual fraud even although he mistakenly thought he had an overriding duty to his client. I accept the trial judge's finding that Pekarsky, the solicitor for the purchaser, believed that he was quite within his right to act as he did and that he honestly held such belief and that he did not attempt to mislead or deceive Dickson or anyone else. It matters not that Pekarsky thought he was justified in his conduct and was only fulfilling his obligation to his client.

The difference between the result in the case at bar and *Union Bank of Can. v. Boulter Waugh* [58 S.C.R. 385, [1919] 1 W.W.R. 1046, 46 D.L.R. 41 (S.C.C.)], is that in that case Anglin J., in referring to the words in the Saskatchewan Act, which were the same as the last words of our s. 203, said: "here there was knowledge but nothing more". In the present case we have something more than knowledge of the unregistered interest. We have the representation made by Pekarsky that his clients were prepared to acquire the land subject to the lease and he never corrected that representation, even when he knew that the vendors believed and acted upon the belief that the sale of the land was subject to the lease. His reason for not withdrawing that earlier representation was his mistaken belief that his duty to his client would make it improper for him to do so. This in my view constitutes fraud within s. 203.

The next question that arises is, was Dickson misled by the representation made in the letter of 4th May 1978 that the lease was not a deterrent? I do not think that the representation which the trial judge said was contained in a letter of inquiry makes it any the less a representation. It was a representation and Dickson expressly said he interpreted this last paragraph of the letter, "Well I considered that his client would accept the lease in favour of Holt Renfrew". This was followed by a request for financial statements. As I have said, if the shares were purchased then of necessity the purchaser of the shares would have to accept the lease. In addition to the request for financial statements a copy of the lease was required. Following this Pekarsky advised Dickson that his client was not interested in buying the shares but he makes no mention of the lease. There are many reasons why a purchaser of property would not, in order to obtain a property, wish to purchase shares of the company that owned the property — this would not alert Dickson to the fact that the Pekarsky position was changed. The trial judge found that Pekarsky had examined the lease and concluded that his client was not interested in buying the real estate subject to the lease. He did not advise Dickson of this conclusion but dealt with only the question of the purchase of the shares. The owner vendor transferred to the purchaser a fee simple title which it did not have to transfer; out of the fee simple had been carved a leasehold estate. The liability of the owner vendor for selling something it did not have and of its solicitor does not have to be decided. However, taking all these matters into consideration, I can only conclude that Dickson's statement is supported, that he considered the purchaser accepted the lease and it was reasonable for him to do so. In fact, except for the statement of Pekarsky in his letter, there is no other reason for him to expect the lease would be accepted.

I conclude that there was fraud within the meaning of s. 203 and Dickson, representing the owner vendor, relied on the misrepresentation constituting the fraud and was misled by it. The purchaser is not entitled to rely on s. 203 to protect its title from the lease. . . .

Moir J.A.:

I have had the advantage of reading the reasons of my brother McDermid. I agree with him that, in order to avoid the protection given by the *Land Titles Act*, R.S.A. 1970, c. 198 [now R.S.A. 1980, c. L-5], actual fraud, dishonesty of some sort, must be shown. Mere knowledge of an equitable interest and knowledge that will be defeated by registration is not fraud. The trial judgment cannot stand for this reason.

My brother McDermid goes on to find actual fraud. He does so on the basis that, once Pekarsky had made a statement that the long term lease of Holt Renfrew might not be a deterrent to his client's interest, when he discovered that it was a deterrent he was bound to correct it. In my view that is a correct statement of the law but it is only true if the party to whom the representation was made relied upon that presentation. . . .

Here it is alleged that Pekarsky was guilty of actual fraud against Dickson and Dickson's client Thompson & Dynes Limited. First of all, we turn to who makes this allegation. It is not Dickson. It is plain that there were no transactions, dealings or conversation between Pekarsky and Holt Renfrew. It must be Pekarsky dealing with Dickson. Dickson does not say that he recalled the letter of 4th May and entered into the contract because of that representation. Dickson says when he saw the letter he thought that Pekarsky's client would accept the lease with Holt Renfrew. He never mentioned the letter again. Indeed, he could have done so but he did not.

Dickson then received an offer to purchase. It is said that it is a most peculiar offer and that at least some members of the court never heard of an offer in these terms. That may be because of the change in the Land Titles Act. No longer do we have certificates of title bound into books which must be searched. Searches now come from a photostatic copy of the certificate of title. This is a recent change and is reflected in many interim agreements produced in mass by large corporations who act as real estate agents. To my mind no assistance can be obtained from the form of the offer which was crystal clear. The offer was to buy the property listed in the agreement subject to, and only subject to, those things shown on the title. Further, it is contrary to the finding of the learned trial judge who said [[1981] 3 W.W.R. 9 at 21, 20 R.P.R. 51, 118 D.L.R. (3d) 645, 30 A.R. 254 (Q.B.)]:

> I reject the suggestion that Pekarsky's offers of 11th September 1978 and 7th March 1979 were cleverly drafted in a deliberate attempt to lull Dickson into thinking that Pekarsky was accepting the Holt Renfrew lease executed in 1972.

Dickson received the offer. He saw the title. He thought that Holt Renfrew filed a caveat to protect their leasehold interest. He no longer relied upon any representation of Pekarsky. He relied upon the certificate of title in the offer. He specifically says so. . . .

Nowhere in the evidence am I able to find that Dickson said that he recalled the letter of 4th May and that he relied upon it when he was determining what to do with the offer. Surely that is the test. The court, in the absence of evidence, should not find that Dickson was misled.

Another way of examining Dickson's evidence is to see what he said and did when he found that Holt Renfrew had not protected their lease. Firstly he searched the title. He then sought legal advice. His adviser, and later counsel at the trial, phoned Pekarsky. He told Pekarsky to go ahead and register. Next, all allegations of fraud were withdrawn against Dickson and Dickson was called as a witness for Holt Renfrew. He gave the evidence in chief that I have earlier quoted. Nowhere did he say he was misled. Surely he was the only person who could have been misled. Pekarsky says Mr. Dickson did not say he had misled him and indeed Pekarsky says he did not mislead anyone.

It is true that Mr. Dickson and John McClary discussed the transaction between themselves. They agreed to offer the Thompson & Dynes Limited property to Pekarsky's undisclosed principal for $1,400,000 with the purchaser assuming the lease. Mr. McClary made the offer to Pekarsky but did not mention the lease. A meeting attended by Mr. McClary, Mr. Dickson, Mr. Laird and Mr. Pekarsky followed. There was a counter-offer and another counter-offer which ultimately became the contract. At all times Thompson & Dynes Limited agreed to sell subject to the encumbrances shown on the photostat of the certificate of title. That was the contract. It was common ground that the lease was never mentioned in the joint discussion. Indeed, except for the initial letter of 4th May and the discussion that preceded it, the lease was not mentioned at all. Of course Pekarsky asked and wrote for a copy of the lease which was sent to Pekarsky by Mr. Dickson.

Perhaps I should not leave the summary of the facts without mentioning that McClary never said he was misled by the letter of 4th May. He was to make an offer in definite terms but failed to do so. Clearly neither John McClary nor Mrs. Ryan were misled. Mr. McClary was to make the offer subject to the lease. He failed to do so.

The way I understand the law, for the representation of 4th May to amount to fraud it must have been relied upon and induced the contract. There is simply no evidence that the letter had this effect. The learned trial judge specifically found that Mrs. Ryan and Mr. McClary looked upon the letter of 4th May 1978 as a letter of inquiry and nothing more. He further found that they were not deceived by Pekarsky.

In summary the learned trial judge found that the letter of 4th May was never treated as more than an inquiry by Mr. McClary or Mrs. Ryan. He also found in all of the evidence that Pekarsky did not attempt to mislead or deceive Dickson or anyone else. Further, the learned trial judge rejected the allegation that the offer was cleverly drafted to lull Dickson into the belief that Pekarsky's clients were accepting the Holt Renfrew lease. The learned trial judge heard the evidence and his finding on the question of fraud cannot be disturbed. It appears to me to be entirely correct on the evidence.

It is clear that Mrs. Ryan, Mr. McClary and Mr. Dickson thought that the purchase was subject to the Holt Renfrew lease. They signed their acceptance of the offer and delivered the title subject to a crystal clear offer. Holt Renfrew had filed a caveat. They did not discharge it. That led Dickson to believe that they had protected their leasehold interest. To find, in the absence of any evidence to support the finding, that the letter of inquiry constituted actual fraud, dishonesty of some sort, would result in an objective finding by the court on its own motion of fraud. Fraud must be specifically pleaded and proved. This case fails for the lack of proof thereof, even on the general and unsatisfactory pleading that existed in this case. . . .

NOTES

1. A five-member panel of the Alberta Court of Appeal heard the *Holt Renfrew* case. All members of the Court agreed that the trial judge's definition of Torrens fraud was incorrect. Stevenson and Kearns JJ.A. wrote reasons that accorded with those of Moir J.A.. Prowse J.A. concurred with McDermid J.A. Hence, Henry Singer prevailed on the fraud issue (i.e., there was no Torrens fraud).

2. However, all did not end well for Henry Singer. All members of the Court of Appeal found that the caveat filed by Pekarsky was fatally flawed because Henry Singer was not explicitly identified. Owing to this defect the caveat conferred no priority to Henry Singer's agreement to purchase the freehold. (Caveats are discussed again below.)

3. Leave to appeal to the Supreme Court of Canada was refused: [1982] 2 S.C.R. xi.

Alberta (Ministry of Forestry, Lands and Wildlife) v. McCulloch 1991 CarswellAlta 29, [1991] 3 W.W.R. 662 (Q.B.)

Sinclair J.:

This is an application by which the plaintiff seeks to maintain its interests in a parcel of land which was sold by the department to the defendant McCulloch and subsequently transferred by him to a numbered limited company which he now controls. The principal issue to be decided is whether the transfer by Mr. McCulloch to the numbered company eliminated his obligations to the department. I will refer to the minister and his predecessors as the department.

I should mention that the Alberta Treasury Branches, which were also named as a defendant, were not represented at the trial. By a letter to the Attorney General which was entered as Ex. 26 this defendant said it was prepared to abide by the outcome of any settlement or trial.

The facts are as follows:

1. By a written agreement of March 1, 1978 (Ex. 1) (to which I will refer as the original agreement) the department sold some land located along the McLeod River near Edson to Svedberg Lumber Co. Ltd. ("Svedberg"). Although included in one title, the land basically consisted of two parcels. The first, which I will call the residential parcel, is located west of a surveyed roadway. The second, which I will call the millsite parcel, is located east of the roadway.

2. The master agreement included these provisions: . . .

3. The Purchaser hereby covenants for himself, his heirs, executors, administrators, successors and assigns that the said land will be utilized only for the purposes set forth herein, namely:

a) millsite and operations incidental thereto,

b) accommodate existing residences (no new residences will be permitted).

4. It is hereby further mutually agreed that the Minister has and will continue to have a vested interest in the said land and that as a covenant running with the land and not offending the rule against perpetuities.

5. With the written consent of the Minister, the Purchaser may convey to or allow a third party to use a part or all of the aforesaid land provided that at the Minister's request the third party enters into an agreement in writing with the Minister, similar to this agreement.

6. Whenever the Purchaser discontinues the use of the said land for a period of one year for the specified purpose or any other use subsequently permitted by the Minister, the Purchaser shall thereupon in writing notify the Minister of the discontinuance of use within thirty days after the expiration of the said one-year period.

7. For one year after receiving the notice from the Purchaser, as provided by paragraph 6, the Minister shall have the option to buy back from the Purchaser the said land for the sum of $26,888.40 and at the Minister's request the Purchaser shall deliver to the Minister a properly executed transfer of the said land and surrender possession of the said land restored to as close to the original condition as may be reasonably possible to do, subject only to such rights of third parties as the Minister had expressly agreed to in writing.

8. In the event that the Minister does not exercise the option to buy back the land, the Minister will discharge his Caveat and thereby release and discharge the Purchaser from all his obligations under this agreement.

3. Pursuant to this agreement certificate of title 782241571 was issued to Svedberg. I will call this document the original certificate of title. A caveat against this title was filed by the department to protect its interest under the original agreement. I will refer to this caveat as the original caveat.

4. Svedberg later went into receivership. Ernst & Whinney Inc. was appointed receiver.

5. The original certificate of title was cancelled on March 7, 1986 and replaced by two new certificates — one covering the residential parcel and the other covering the millsite parcel. The new certificates were both subject to the original caveat. It would appear that the two new titles were created as a result of the registration of a plan of survey for the road which divides the two parcels.

6. Later in the spring of 1986 the receiver offered the millsite parcel for sale by tender free and clear except for certain encumbrances, one of which was the original caveat.

7. The millsite parcel was eventually sold by the receiver to Mr. McCulloch for $62,500. The documentary evidence makes it clear that he was aware of the department's interest in the land. I need only mention two documents. This first is Ex. 12, a letter to Mr. McCulloch from the receiver accepting his offer to purchase. Among other things, the letter said the acceptance was subject to: . . .

> b) the prior approval of "the Minister" referred to in the subject Sell-back Agreement, the obtaining of which approval may require you to enter into a new Sell-back Agreement . . .

The second such document is a letter from Mr. McCulloch to the department written September 12, 1986:

> Further to our telephone conversation today, I, as purchaser of the above property, agree to use the above lands:
>
> (a) as a millsite and operations incidental thereto;
>
> (b) to accommodate existing residences (no new residences).

8. On December 16, 1986 an order of the Court of Queen's Bench of Alberta approving this sale was granted. One of the terms of the order directed the registrar of land titles to issue a new certificate of title for the millsite parcel to Mr. McCulloch subject, among other things, to the original caveat. The new certificate of title in Mr. McCulloch's name was issued December 29, 1986 and the original caveat was among the memorials endorsed on it.

9. Toward the end of the following year, 1987, arrangements were made by the department to sell all or part of the residential parcel to the Svedbergs. As part of that transaction the department executed a discharge of the original caveat as to the

residential parcel. The discharge was registered March 14, 1988. However, because of a mistake made by the land titles office, the original caveat was also discharged from Mr. McCulloch's title. Neither Mr. McCulloch nor the department was initially aware that this mistake had been made.

10. Mr. McCulloch learned of this development before the department did. It was as the result of a telephone call from Mr. McCulloch that an official of the department discovered that the original caveat was no longer on Mr. McCulloch's certificate of title.

11. On April 12, 1988 Mr. McCulloch executed a transfer of his title to a numbered company 335522 Alberta Ltd. Mr. McCulloch was and is a shareholder, director and officer of the company.

12. A new certificate of title was issued in the name of the numbered company on April 15, 1988. The original caveat was not endorsed on this title.

13. On May 25, 1988 the department filed a caveat (the new caveat) against this new title, claiming the first right to repurchase the land by virtue of the original master agreement dated March 1, 1978.

I will later deal in more detail with the circumstances surrounding the events outlined in paras. 10 to 13. . . .

It is submitted that the transfer of the millsite parcel from Mr. McCulloch to the numbered company was not tainted with fraud. This is the main issue with which the litigation is concerned.

The key section in the Act dealing with fraud is s. 195:

> 195. Except in the case of fraud, no person contracting or dealing with or taking or proposing to take a transfer, mortgage, encumbrance or lease from the owner of any land in whose name a certificate of title has been granted shall be bound or concerned to inquire into or ascertain the circumstances in or the consideration for which the owner or any previous owner of the land is or was registered or to see to the application of the purchase money or of any part thereof, nor is he affected by notice direct, implied or constructive, of any trust or unregistered interest in the land, any rule of law or equity to the contrary notwithstanding, and the knowledge that any trust or unregistered interest is in existence shall not of itself be imputed as fraud.

Many authorities have considered the meaning of these words. I think it sufficient to reproduce what was said many years ago by Mr. Justice Anglin of the Supreme Court of Canada in the case of *Union Bank of Can. v. Boulter Waugh Ltd.*, 58 S.C.R. 385, (sub nom. *Boulter-Waugh Co. v. Union Bank of Can.*) [1919] 1 W.W.R. 1046, 46 D.L.R. 41 [Sask.]. Considering the effect of a similar section in the Saskatchewan Act, Mr. Justice Anglin said at pp. 395-96:

> Here there was knowledge, but nothing more. Knowledge, of course, could not of itself constitute fraud. Fraud must always have consisted in the doing of something which that

> knowledge made it unjust or inequitable to do. The meaning of the statute must, therefore, be that the doing of that which mere knowledge of "any trust or unregistered interest" would make it inequitable to do shall nevertheless not be imputed as fraud, within the meaning of that term as used in sub-sec. 1 of sec. 194. That which equity deems fraud, therefore, is by this enactment of a competent legislature declared not to be imputable as fraud.

At this stage it is necessary to examine in detail the events which led to the transfer of the millsite parcel by Mr. McCulloch to the numbered company. This private company was incorporated on September 3, 1985. Its original shareholders were Mr. McCulloch (25 per cent), his wife (25 per cent) and his mother (50 per cent). Mr. McCulloch's mother died in 1988 and he testified that he had acquired her interest. I note, however, that the income tax return filed by the company for its taxation year ending November 30, 1988 shows Mr. McCulloch and his wife as each holding 50 per cent of the voting shares. Mr. McCulloch is a director and president of the company as well as its authorized signing officer for the purposes of income tax returns.

In the spring of 1988 Mr. McCulloch learned the original caveat had been discharged. He got this information through discussions with Alberta Opportunity Company ("A.O.C.") and Mr. D.L. Kennedy of the Parlee McLaws law firm. Mr. Kennedy was acting for A.O.C. and the receiver of Svedberg. These discussions must have taken place after March 14 because that was the date the discharge was registered.

Mr. McCulloch searched the title to the millsite property, which was of course still in his name. The search confirmed the caveat had in fact been removed. Mr. McCulloch said that from his conversations with A.O.C. and Mr. Kennedy he understood the original caveat would eventually be removed from both the residential parcel and the millsite parcel because the department would be unable to realize on the rights covered by the caveat.

Mr. McCulloch says he telephoned an official of the department to see if it would be interested in buying the millsite property back from him to be used as a campsite. I am satisfied it was Mr. R.F. Raitz, director of the land administration branch, who was contacted by Mr. McCulloch, that the call was made during the first week of April 1988, and that during the conversation Mr. McCulloch asked Mr. Raitz why the caveat had been discharged. Mr. Raitz was surprised to learn the original caveat had been discharged. He told Mr. McCulloch that this should not have happened as the department did not intend to discharge the caveat. Mr. Raitz informed Mr. McCulloch that he wanted to investigate the situation.

As earlier mentioned, on April 12, 1988 Mr. McCulloch executed a transfer of his title to the millsite to the numbered company. He also took the affidavit of transferee as agent of the company. Mr. McCulloch did not advise the department that he was transferring the land. When he had acquired the title to the millsite parcel in 1986 for $62,500 Mr. McCulloch had put up $20,000 in cash. The balance of $42,500 came from the Treasury Branch at Edson. Half of the $20,000 cash had been loaned to Mr. McCulloch by his mother. He said that title to the parcel was transferred from his name to that of the numbered company essentially for income tax reasons, and to repay the $10,000 to his mother.

Since the Treasury Branch in Edson held the duplicate certificate of title as security for its loan to Mr. McCulloch, he made arrangements for new security to be provided to the Treasury Branch by the numbered company. The documents were signed April 14, 1988.

Mr. McCulloch called Mr. Raitz in late May 1988 to ask if the department was interested in buying the millsite parcel. He told Mr. Raitz the land had been transferred to a company, essentially for tax reasons. Mr. Raitz said he would have to consult with another branch of the department.

In July 1988 Mr. Raitz called Mr. McCulloch to inform him the department was interested in buying back the parcel, but only at a price which was based on that set out in the original agreement between the government and Svedberg. On a *pro rata* acreage basis the price suggested by Mr. Raitz was $18,800. Mr. McCulloch said this figure was unacceptable. During the course of this conversation Mr. Raitz told Mr. McCulloch the department had filed a new caveat.

The question to be considered is whether title to the millsite parcel was acquired by the numbered company from Mr. McCulloch in circumstances amounting to fraud as that term is used in the *Land Titles Act*. Common sense tells us that when the company acquired the title it knew the department had an unregistered interest in the land. Mr. McCulloch knew of this interest. The company must be deemed to have acquired this knowledge because Mr. McCulloch was one of its directors and its president.

As earlier mentioned, s. 195 provides, and the cases have held, that knowledge of the unregistered interest, by itself, does not constitute fraud. For there to be fraud, the knowledge must be used for an unjust or inequitable purpose.

There is, of course, evidence that a purpose of the transfer from Mr. McCulloch to the company was to repay a loan from his mother and to lessen the consequences of income tax. One cannot help but note, however, that a transfer for these purposes could have been effected while Mr. McCulloch's title was still subject to the original caveat or, later, after the new caveat was filed by the department. I have mentioned that the company's year end was November 30. It seems more than a coincidence that the transfer, including the new arrangements with the Treasury Branch, was carried out within a few days after Mr. McCulloch learned that the caveat had been discharged. I believe the transfer to the limited company was also made for the purpose of defeating the department's interests and of relieving Mr. McCulloch from his obligations to the department.

In all circumstances I am of the opinion that title to the millsite parcel was acquired by the numbered company in circumstances that amounted to fraud as that term is used in the *Land Titles Act*. . . .

In the result, the plaintiff will have judgment for the relief sought in its statement of claim.

Judgment for plaintiff.

QUESTIONS AND COMMENTS

1. An appeal to the Court of Appeal was dismissed: *Alberta (Ministry of Forestry, Lands and Wildlife) v. McCulloch* 1991 CarswellAlta 185, [1992] 1 W.W.R. 747 (C.A.). In a brief oral memorandum of judgment, Côté J.A. stated:

> We agree with the reasons of the trial judge. We only have this to add. In cases of this sort usually the transferor and transferee dealt at arm's length, and so the intent of the transferor is then irrelevant. Here, the transferor controlled the transferee numbered company and both filed a joint statement of defence and appeared by the same counsel. We have no doubt that the acts of the transferor were fraud in the narrow and strict sense and that the two parties shared that intent. This is therefore a case where the transferee had far more than mere knowledge. We find the trial judge made a clear credibility finding as well.

2. Neither judgment in *McCulloch* makes reference to *Holt Renfrew*. However, that case is thoroughly discussed in the factums filed in *McCulloch*. How, if at all, can one distinguish *Holt Renfrew* and *McCulloch*?

3. Assume that B, a rogue, enters into an agreement to sell Blackacre to C. In fact, B has no title and the transfer that is tendered is a forgery. Unaware of this fact, and otherwise acting *bona fide*, C accepts the transfer, obtains registration without ado, and receives a certificate of title. The forgery is then uncovered. A, the true owner, seeks to recover title. C seeks to retain title, arguing that A is left with a claim for compensation against the assurance fund. Who is correct?

For decades the prevailing view was that A should succeed, and that an indefeasible title would not exist until a subsequent transaction occurs, as when C sells to D (assuming that both remain unaware of the forgery). *Dictum* from the Privy Council decision of *Gibbs v. Messer* [1891] A.C. 248 (Victoria P.C.) supports this view, often referred to as the "deferred" indefeasibility theory.

A different approach emerged out of the Privy Council decision in *Frazer v. Walker* (1966) [1967] 1 A.C. 569 (New Zealand P.C.). The opinion in that case supports the view that indefeasibility arises *immediately* on the acquisition of title by a *bona fide* purchaser. If so, C would succeed on the above facts.

As critical as this aspect of the law is, title registration statutes do not always spell out which rule governs leaving room for both judicial activism, and of course, differences of opinion as to the appropriate rule. Immediate indefeasibility is now the dominant view in Australia. In Canada, that position was adopted in the Saskatchewan case of *Hermanson v. Martin* 1986 CarswellSask 262, [1987] 1 W.W.R. 439 (C.A.). *Cf.* the *obiter* comments in *Beneficial Realty Ltd. v. Bae* 1996

CarswellAlta 125, 182 A.R. 356 (Master). In British Columbia, however, the legislation points fairly clearly to the deferred rule: see *Land Title Act*, R.S.B.C. 1996, c. 250, sub. 297(3).

4. Are immediate and deferred indefeasibility the only possibilities? Consider subsection 57(13) of the *Land Titles Act*, R.S.O. 1990, c. L.5:

> Where a registered disposition would be absolutely void if unregistered or where the effect of the error would be to deprive a person of land of which the person is in possession or in receipt of the rents and profits, the Director of Titles may, in the first instance or after a reference to the court, direct the rectification of the register and, in the case of rectification, the person suffering by the rectification is entitled to the compensation provided for by this section.

5. Along the same lines, the *Land Registration Act*, S.N.S. 2001, c. 6, s. 35 provides that, as a general rule, deferred indefeasibility applies. If so, the deprived new owner (C, above) would be entitled to compensation. Moreover, the court would be given jurisdiction to confirm C's title and compensate A where it would be just and equitable to do so. In resolving that question, the court would be required to taken account of these considerations:

> (a) the nature of the ownership and the use of the property by the parties;
>
> (b) the circumstances of the unauthorized revision;
>
> (c) the special characteristics of the property and their significance to the parties;
>
> (d) the willingness of any of the parties to receive compensation in lieu of an interest in the property;
>
> (e) the ease with which the amount of compensation for a loss may be determined; and
>
> (f) any other circumstances that, in the opinion of the court, are relevant to its determination.

(See also Joint Land titles Committee, *Renovating the Foundation: Proposal for a Model Land Recording and Registration Act for the Provinces and Territories of Canada* (1990) at 109 (article 5.6(5)).

How, if at all, does the Nova Scotia approach differ from the current law in Ontario (quoted above)? Which approach, among those currently in place or proposed, is preferable?

6. In *Frazer v. Walker,* mentioned above, Lord Wilberforce (at 585) cautioned that this principle "in no way denies the right of a plaintiff to bring against a registered proprietor a claim *in personam*, founded in law or in equity, for such relief as a court acting in personam may grant." What counts as an *in personam* claim?

When, for example, the transfer and subsequent certificate of title are in error, so that the transferor can obtain an order of rectification against her registered transferee, an *in personam* claim can result in an alteration of the certificate of title. More generally, any cause of action tenable by a party — directly against the registered owner — should fall within the *in personam* exception. See further P. Butt, *Land Law*, 4th ed. (Sydney: Law Book Co., 2001) at 676*ff*. But see *Horvath v. Commonwealth Bank of Australia* [1999] 1 V.R. (C.A.).

Consider these facts: B agrees to sell Blackacre to C. The documents of transfer are forged, and had C made even the most modest inquiries, the illegality would have been uncovered. Yet, C was in fact unaware of the true facts. On discovering the fraudulent transfer, A sues C, seeking the recovery of the land based on equitable principles of unjust enrichment. Assume that immediate indefeasibility is the correct rule. Should A succeed? See the analysis in R. Chambers, "Indefeasible Title as a Bar to a Claim for Restitution" (1998) 6 Restitution L. Rev. 126. See also *Conlan v. Registrar of Titles* (2001) 24 W.A.R. 299 (S.C.).

7. In some Torrens jurisdictions, parties receiving gratuitous transfers (volunteers) are accorded fewer protections than purchasers for value. In general, what that means is this: a donee can acquire no greater interest than that held by the donor. Put another way: the curtain will not fall for a volunteer. This principle is enshrined in Ontario's *Land Titles Act*, R.S.O. 1990, L.5, s. 90:

> A transfer of registered land, made without valuable consideration, is subject, so far as the transferee is concerned, to any unregistered estates, rights, interests or equities subject to which the transferor held the same, but otherwise, when registered, in all respects, and in particular as respects any registered dealings on the part of the transferee, has the same effect as a transfer of the same land for valuable consideration.

Imagine, for instance, that A grants a lease to B, who fails to register the document. A then passes away, devising her interest in the subject property to C, who becomes the registered owner. C, a volunteer, cannot acquire title free from B's leasehold. What other rights, outside of the Torrens regime, can assist a volunteer in this context?

As just mentioned, not all Torrens jurisdictions treat volunteers in this subordinate way (see, *e.g*, *Conlan v. Registrar of Titles* (2001) 24 W.A.R. 299 (S.C.); *Land Title Act, 1994* (Qld.), s. 165.

8. As a rule, Canadian land titles statutes do not certify that the boundaries described in a certificate of title are correct. For example, *The Land Titles Act, 2000*, S.S. 2000, c. L-5.1, sub 13(4) provides as follows:

> No title defines or is proof of:
>
> (a) the boundaries of a parcel;
>
> (b) the extent or area determined by the boundaries of a parcel;

(c) the boundaries of a condominium unit or the common property included in a condominium plan; or

(d) the extent or area determined by the boundaries of a condominium unit or the common property included in a condominium plan.

See also *Turta v. Canadian Pacific Railway* 1954 CarswellAlta 24, [1954] S.C.R. 427.

9. *The Land Titles Act* of Saskatchewan also provides:

21(1) After the issuance of first title pursuant to a Crown grant:

(a) no person acquires by way of possession any right, title or interest adverse to or in derogation of the registered owner's title or right to possess the land for which the title has issued; and

(b) the right of the registered owner to enter or to bring an action to recover the land for which the title has issued is not impaired or affected by the possession of the land by any other person.

Can the law of adverse possession play a useful role under a land titles system?

10. Not all interests in land are amenable to registration. For example, an agreement for sale, although it can give rise to an equitable interest in land (see Chapter 6), cannot be registered under the Alberta *Land Titles Act*, R.S.A. 2000, c. L-4. Likewise, under that Act, the equitable interest of property held under a trust cannot be registered. Where a trust has been set up, the Act provides that the trustees named in the instrument are "deemed to be the absolute and beneficial owners of the land for the purposes of this Act": s. 47.

Interests that can not be, or are not, registered are, of course, vulnerable to being defeated by a transfer from the registered owner to a third party. To protect against such a turn of events, all land titles systems allow for the filing of a document that serves as notice to the world of such interests. Sometimes called a "notice" or a "caution", in Alberta the more common label "caveat" is used. The filing of a caveat or its functional equivalent provides notice and no more. It does not work to validate the interest being claimed. That property right must stand and fall on its own merits.

As with the issues relating to registration proper, the ancillary rules governing these notices vary among land titles jurisdictions. Important among these is the effect of a caveat on priorities. Some jurisdictions adopt a straightforward rule: as with a registered interest, the timing of *registration* is determinative. Moreover, notice outside the register is not equated with fraud. See *White Resource Management Ltd. v. Durish* [1995] 1 S.C.R. 633, 1995 CarswellAlta 4, 1995 CarswellAlta 407, and ss. 135, 147, and 203 of the *Land Titles Act*, R.S.A. 2000, c. L-4.

Given that the filing of a caveat does not validate the interest claimed, and the rule that priority is determined by the timing of registration, one can see that the caveat system used in Alberta resembles a deeds race system. Compare the approach taken in the New Zealand case of *Australian Guarantee Corp. (N.Z.) Ltd. v. C.F.C. Commercial Finance Ltd.* [1995] 1 N.Z.L.R. 129 (C.A.). How would one characterize the approach taken in that case as to the priority rules for caveated claims?

11. Some interests will bind subsequent purchasers even though they have not been registered. Such entitlements are, therefore, lingering invisible clouds on title. They stand as exceptions to the mirror/photograph principle of land titles registration. It is conventional to refer to such rights as "overriding interests". For example, The *Land Titles Act*, 2000, S.S. 2000, c. L-5.1 (s. 18 as am. by S.S. 2001, c. 20, s. 7) provides:

> 18(1) Subject to subsection (2), every title and the land for which the title has issued, is, by implication and without any special mention in the title, deemed to be subject to the following exceptions, reservations and interests:
>
> > (a) any subsisting reservations or exceptions, including royalties, expressly contained in the original Crown grant or reserved in or excepted from the Crown grant pursuant to any Act or law contained in any other grant or disposition from the Crown;
> >
> > (b) any right or interest granted by or pursuant to an Act or an Act of the Parliament of Canada that does not have to be registered: (i) to enter, go across or do things on land, including an easement or right of way, for the purposes specified in the enactment; (ii) to recover taxes, duties, liens, charges, rates or assessments by proceedings with respect to land; (iii) to expropriate land; (iv) to restrict the use of land; or (v) to control, regulate or restrict the subdivision of land;
> >
> > (c) any public highway or right of way or other public easement, however created, on, over or with respect to the land included in the title;
> >
> > (d) any subsisting lease or agreement for lease for a term not exceeding three years where there is actual occupation of the land for which title has issued pursuant to the lease or agreement;
> >
> > (e) any subsisting tenancy agreement within the meaning of *The Residential Tenancies Act*;
> >
> > (f) any claim, right, estate or interest set out in section 21; [*i.e.*, claims by persons who are "adversely in actual occupation and rightly entitled to the land . . . at the time first title to the land is issued.": sub. 21(2).]
> >
> > (g) the reservation of any minerals that become vested in the Crown pursuant to any *Mineral Taxation Act*, and the rights of the Crown with respect to those minerals;
> >
> > (h) any consent, right of way or easement, however acquired, whether before or after the coming into force of this clause, with respect to land situated outside the corporate limits of an urban municipality, to construct and maintain a pipeline on or under that land pursuant to a program established for the purpose of supplying natural or manufactured gas to one or more persons residing in that area, by: (i)

Saskatchewan Energy Corporation . . . (ii) Provincial Gas Limited . . .; or (iii) SaskEnergy.

(2) The exceptions, reservations and interests that are implied against a title pursuant to subsection (1) do not apply if the title expressly states that they do not apply.

(3) The exceptions, reservations and interests that are implied against a title pursuant to subsection (1) do not apply if an Act, an Act of the Parliament of Canada or any other law expressly states or implies that they do not apply.

See also ss. 19 and 20.

How, if at all, can one justify the presence of these overriding interests? What implications flow from the recognition of such unregistered interests for the conduct of real estate transactions?

12. Alberta's *Land Titles Act*, R.S.A. 2000, c. L-4, as with that found in Saskatchewan, allows public easements to exist as overriding interests. In addition, section 61(1)(f) of the Alberta statute confers that status on "any right of way or other easement granted or acquired under any Act or law in force in Alberta." In *Petro-Canada Inc. v. Shaganappi Village Shopping Centre Ltd.* (1990) [1991] 1 W.W.R. 169, 1990 CarswellAlta 153 (C.A.) it was held that this provision did not apply to express grants of easement. In so holding, Kearans J.A. (At 171-2) alluded to the types of rights that could be embraced by the phrase protecting easements that were "granted or acquired under any Act *or law*" [emphasis added]:

> The language of [s. 61(1)(f)] can reasonably bear an interpretation that excludes from its ambit private easements created by express contract unconnected to any statutory or common law rules creating easements. I say that because, first, the twinning of "law" with "Act" usually indicates that "law" is being used in the sense of the common law. Second, one does not usually speak of rights acquired by contract as "granted or acquired under common law", although to be sure the law of contract is part of the common law. Third, the common law can and does create a right of entry or easement in the absence of express contract. For example, the common law ceded to the holder of the mineral title a right, even in the absence of an express agreement, to enter on the surface to exploit the minerals. . . . Another example is easement by necessity. . . . Therefore, a more limited view of the ambit of the words "under any law" has meaning.

Looking back on the modes of creation for easements discussed in Chapter 10, what other types of easements would be covered under section 61(1)(f)? Why should those rights be exempt from registration? See *Petro-Canada Inc. v. Shaganappi Village Shopping Centre Ltd.*, *supra*.

Compare the wording of *The Real Property Act*, C.C.S.M., c.R.30, para. 58(1)(c), which provides that "any right-of-way or other easement, howsoever created, upon, over or in respect of, the land" is to be treated as an overriding interest. Is this language amenable to the same limited interpretation described above?

13. The list of overriding interests found in land titles legislation is not exhaustive. Provincial legislation may provide for others. Moreover, a right granted under federal law may not be affected by the operation of the principle of indefeasibility under a provincial land titles regime. Can the failure to register or record a claim to Aboriginal title under land titles legislation affect the legal viability of that claim? Consider the general principles governing land claims studied in Chapter 5.

14. An Aboriginal band launches a land claim. The claimants seek to file a caveat claiming that interest. Is such a caveat tenable? See *Skeetchestn Band v. British Columbia (Registrar of Land Titles)* 2000 CarswellBC 1853, [2000] 10 W.W.R. 222 (C.A.); *Lac La Ronge Indian Band v. Beckman* 1990 CarswellSask 153, [1990] 4 W.W.R. 190 (C.A.); *James Smith Indian Band v. Saskatchewan (Master of Titles)* 1995 CarswellSask 60, 123 D.L.R. (4th) 280 (C.A.).

15. In jurisdictions in which easements are not overriding interests, is registration of an easement on the title of the dominant lands sufficient to bind purchasers of the servient lands? Logic suggests that the answer should be no. However, in the context of the *Registry Act*, R.S.O. 1990, c. R.20, see *Jacuniak v. Tamburro* (2002) 4 R.P.R. (4th) 1, 2002 CarswellOnt 1088 (S.C.J.). See also the biting — and thoroughly convincing — critique of that ruling in J. Lem, "Annotation" (2002) 4 R.P.R. (4th) 3.

16. W acquired a right-of-way easement over Lot 1, then owned by D. The easement was supposed to include a turnaround area for cars, but that was not properly delineated in the easement document, which was registered in the land title office. D sold Lot 1 to K; that lot was later sold to B. B was under the mistaken impression that the turnaround area was included as part of the location of the easement until a survey was conducted in 2000, which revealed that such was not the case. W now sought rectification so that the turnaround area would be included, as B believed it had been when B purchased Lot 1. Should the order be granted? See *White v. Fisher-Banville* (2003) 9 R.P.R. (4th) 119, 2003 CarswellBC 1096 (S.C.).

5. TITLE INSURANCE

B. Ziff, "Title Insurance: The Big Print Giveth, But Does the Small Print Taketh Away?" [revised; footnotes omitted]

. . . Title insurance does two main things. First, it protects against defects in title leading to loss. It is commonly asserted that title insurance is not a *guaranty* of title, but rather a source of *indemnity*. This difference is not a semantic one. It means, in essence, that payments under the policy are not available merely because the assured state of title proves to be wrong, but only when an actual loss occurs. Second, challenges to a policy holder's title can trigger a duty on the insurer to defend the title on the insured's behalf. The protection against title losses is normally subject to a monetary limit; the duty to defend is typically not.

Generally speaking, title insurance differs from other kinds of coverage in three main ways. First, a title insurance premium is structured as a one-time payment for an indefinite (but ascertainable) term: policies are often stated to terminate on the sale of the property by the policy holder, or at some other designated point in time. For other types of coverage, such as casualty insurance, periodic billing and set terms are the norm. Second, the risks covered by title insurance are predominantly retrospective. That is, coverage is obtained against defects in title that exist at the date the policy comes into force. Most other forms of coverage are directed at future risks. Third, title insurance is premised on risk elimination. By undertaking appropriate searches, the title insurer seeks to locate risks that might trigger coverage. Other forms of coverage rely more heavily on actuarial evidence to assess risk, and premiums are more finely adjusted to match the degree of risk assumption.

There are also some fundamental points of convergence between title insurance and other forms of coverage. In every Canadian jurisdiction there is a body of legislative regulation much of designed to provide consumer protection against insurance providers of all kinds. In addition, courts have conventionally interpreted insurance policies to protect policy holders. Contracts are construed strictly against the insurer; an insured's reasonable expectations will be respected in matters of interpretation; the policy will be construed as a whole and will not be interpreted so as to give the insurer an unconscionable advantage. These principles apply to title coverage.

American Antecedents

Title insurance is indigenous to the United States. The first underwriter is reputed to be the Real Estate Title Insurance Company of Philadelphia, which was established in 1876. The instigating event is often said to be the Pennsylvania case of *Watson v. Muirhead*. There, an action was launched against a conveyancer based on the negligent preparation of an abstract of title. The claim failed, and it created the impression that the existing protections against defects in title were inadequate. Other factors may also have been key: an anticipated land boom; the deplorable state of the government land records; and the opportunistic actions of a cadre of "Philadelphia lawyers" (I suppose in both literature and figurative senses) might well also account for the genesis of title insurance.

The dominance of title insurance is inversely proportional to the impact of Torrens title in the United States. Torrens has never achieved a secure foothold there, the predominant view among commentators being that it is preferable to the American recording regimes. Illinois adopted a Torrens system in 1895 and in the early part of the twentieth century there were 19 states with some form of Torrens. That number has dwindled to just nine, and in none of these states is title registration the sole system in use. It may be, as some claim, that Torrens has been repeatedly thwarted by the existing vested interests, such as title insurers. Another view is that inertia, coupled with the up-front costs of bringing land into the system, and the ongoing administrative expenses that must be incurred, serve to explain the failure of Torrens in America. Moreover, the Torrens systems that are in place in the United States have not served as exemplars of title registration.

In the 1930s it could be said that title insurance business operations were still local commercial endeavours. Today nothing could be further from the truth. The industry grew dramatically after the Second World War, especially in the western American states. As a western migration occurred (especially to California), there was a call for capital that the local state banks could not supply. National life insurance companies entered the field, using title insurance as a means of protecting their investments against the spectre of faulty titles. The mortgage industry also precipitated a second major spurt, which has been ongoing for about 20 years. Owing to changes in fiscal policy introduced in the 1980s, a large secondary market in mortgages has flourished throughout the country. In other words, lending institutions have been engaged in the business of buying and selling existing mortgages (*i.e.*, receivables). In the course of so doing, it has become standard business practice to seek title insurance. The secondary mortgage market is substantial: it is estimated that about 65% to 70% of new mortgages are sold on the secondary market each year. In brief, title insurance in America is now a multi-billion dollar sector of the American economy. A handful of large firms provide the lion's share of the coverage in the United States. . . .

Robin Paul Malloy and Mark Klapow maintain that in the United States there is "virtually compete agreement among major players in the modern real estate market that the benefits associated with obtaining title insurance — no-fault protection from loss — far outweigh the relative costs of the product". For all intents and purposes, the purchase of title coverage is mandatory in commercial transactions and within the secondary mortgage market. As for residential properties, Malloy and Klapow found that adoption patterns varied across the country and even within a given state. For example, in New York State use of title insurance was found to be routine in New York City, whereas in upstate centres (such as Buffalo, Syracuse and Rochester) resort to title insurance was far less common. The authors are highly critical of upstate practice: in their view, the failure to obtain title insurance in home purchases amounts to malpractice. Only where a client declines coverage in the clearest of ways after full disclosure should a lawyer be relieved of liability if an insurable loss has occurred.

The rise of title insurance in America has been marked with conflict. It is a leitmotif in the history of title insurance that the legal profession has been wary, worried and at times openly antagonistic to the intrusion of title insurance into the field of real estate conveyancing. One response to this posture has been the co-optation of lawyers into the industry by the major underwriters. Another has been the development of rival insurance providers established by the legal profession. Since 1947, a number of bar-related companies have entered the title insurance business. They operate more or less as private insurance providers, and indeed commonly employ industry-standard policies. Most underwrite their own policies; some take the form of insurance agencies, relying on the stand-alone insurance companies to underwrite the policies. . . .

Much of what has occurred in the United States holds lessons for other jurisdictions. At the very least, there is a benefit to be derived from delving into the bountiful American jurisprudence relating to the meaning and effect of policy clauses. I am not aware of a single Canadian decision that can cast light on the meaning of the terms found in the title policies now extant. Moreover, English and Canadian authorities have said that where insurance policies are derived from American sources, as is certainly the case here, resort to American authority in the name of promoting uniformity is appropriate.

However, it is not just that the policies used in Canada so closely resemble their American counterparts that courts should look to American case law for guidance. The clashes over market share, the reaction of the legal profession, issues around professional ethics and the unlawful practice of law (by title insurance companies), even anti-trust problem, seem likely to recur wherever title insurance seeks to make inroads. This view is borne out by the Canadian experience, to which attention now turns.

The Emergence of Title Insurance in Canada

The presence of title insurance on the Canadian real estate scene is thought to be a recent occurrence. In fact, the first registered provider appears to be the Title Insurance Company of Canada, which was created by private act of Parliament in 1914. The fate of this company is not known. However, a renewed interest in the idea began in Ontario in the 1950s. American investors, involved in both commercial and vacation properties in Canada, wanted to obtain the types of title protections with which they were familiar. In the late 1980s, the trickle of interest became a rising tide. Ontario, the most populous province, with a strong economy and a red-hot real estate market, especially in Toronto, seemed to offer tremendous business opportunities to the title insurance industry.

Almost at once, the legal community was on guard. The progress of title insurance was being monitored closely, and there were initial concerns that this development posed a threat to the bread and butter of many Ontario solicitors. Moreover, some insurance firms moved to develop so-called "closing centres", which were designed to provide comprehensive, inexpensive and, in other ways, consumer-friendly real estate services.

As we have seen, this kind of apprehension was not new; nor was the response adopted by the Ontario bar. In 1997, after a study of the available options, the Law Society of Upper Canada . . . decided to embrace the title insurance concept. In that year it established a title insurance company, TitlePlus, owned by the Law Society's professional liability company, now known as LawPro. TitlePlus is modelled on the American bar-affiliate approach. Its basic policies are underwritten by Chicago Title (Canada), and TitlePlus also offers real estate software packages as well as coverage to purchasers and lenders for errors and omissions committed by one's lawyer in the conveyancing process.

The creation of a for-profit insurance company owned by the governing body of the profession raises ethical concerns. How might the existence of a bar-affiliated insurer affect a lawyer's duty to advise clients? Here again the American experience is instructive. In 1972 the American Bar Association (A.B.A.) issued a formal opinion on the conflict of interest ramifications of bar-affiliated insurance programs. The A.B.A. concluded that it was not necessarily unethical for an attorney to act for a client and serve as an examiner for the title insurer. Drawing on the general rules governing multiple representations, it was advised that a lawyer should make full disclosure of the relationship between the attorney and the bar program. The lawyer must also become apprised of competing policy alternatives, and provide advice in a totally disinterested way. Moreover, any commission received from an insurer must not result in a fee to the client that is excessive.

The A.B.A. standard has been decried as being too lax, and when Ontario amended its ethics rules to take account of the formation of TitlePlus, somewhat more stringent protections were put in place. Under Ontario's Code of Professional Conduct, a lawyer must assess all reasonable options to assure title, and is required to advise a client that title insurance is not mandatory and provides only one means of protecting a client's interests. A lawyer is not entitled to a fee for recommending a specific title insurance policy, and must disclose that no commission or fee is being provided to the lawyer by an insurer or agent. And if the lawyer chooses to discuss TitlePlus, the lawyer must fully disclose the relationship between the legal profession, the Law Society and LawPro. Again, the Law Society of Upper Canada owns LawPro, which owns TitlePlus. Members of the Ontario bar do not own shares in these companies; nor of course do they own shares in the Law Society. . . .

The response of the Law Society of Upper Canada is not entirely surprising. The concern that title insurance might erode real estate practise is tempered significantly by a regulatory provision that was introduced in 1957, just as title insurance was surfacing in the province. Under Regulation 666 of the Insurance Act, a licence issued to offer title insurance is "subject to the limitations and conditions that no policy of title insurance shall be issued unless the insurer has first obtained a concurrent certificate of title to the property to be insured from a solicitor then entitled to practise in Ontario and who is not at that time in the employ of the insurer. Therefore, while the major American underwriters do business in Ontario alongside TitlePlus, Ontario lawyers remain part of *every* title insurance transaction.

Some tensions remain. As mentioned above, quite early on concerns were voiced within the profession that the introduction of closing centres would marginalise lawyers. In this regard, First Canadian Title was singled out as the *bete noir* of the industry. When First Canadian began operations in Ontario in the late-1980s, it seemed content to live with the regulation mandating the participation of a lawyer who is not employed by a title insurance company. However, in time it made a bid to have that provision repealed. In August 2000, with these events still fresh in the minds of some, the Canadian Bar Association (C.B.A.) voted by a margin of about 2 to 1 that First Canadian Title and its American parent company would no longer be allowed to advertize in C.B.A. publications or to sponsor association events.

The movement west to the Prairie provinces and British Columbia has given rise to a very different response from that taken in Ontario. As interest in the idea was gaining support in Ontario, the Law Society of Alberta established a Title Insurance Working Group to examine the issue. Was title insurance "a tool or a threat?" asked Jack Dunphy, chair of the Group. The President of the Law Society of Alberta regarded it as axiomatic that "[m]ost solicitors are concerned that the growing involvement of U.S. title insurance companies in Canada could seriously erode their real estate legal practices". Likewise, when the resolution concerning First Canadian/American was endorsed by the Canadian Bar Association, John Jones, president of the Manitoba Bar Association applauded the stand. He described title insurance as:

> the most serious attack on the financial viability of my practice in my career. . . . It's not just my lunch money. It's my kids' college fund, my retirement fund, my vacation money. Multiply that by a dozen times within 50 miles of me and multiply that by thousands of lawyers across the country.

In due course, the law societies in the four Western provinces — all of which have entrenched Torrens systems — banded together to undertake what was termed a Western Torrens Project. Its mandate was to review the procedures used in conveyancing in order that these might be modified to compete within the contemporary marketplace. This was a thinly disguised "code" for responding to the title insurance alternative.

As we have just seen, the Law Society of Upper Canada adopted the adage "if you can't beat them, join them". In the West, by contrast, the law societies have tried to "build a better mousetrap". In 2001, a Western Torrens Protocol was established, with each of the four provinces crafting minor variations on the basic theme. Stripped to essentials, the protocol contains two main elements. First, basic conveyancing procedures have been streamlined, especially in client reporting, and in relation to the completion of financing arrangements. For example, in appropriate circumstances the need for an up-to-date survey has been dispensed with in most financing deals. Plus, when the protocol is invoked, money can be dispersed by a lender prior to formal registration of the security documents. There is, of course, a chance that in this interval a competing interest might be registered, and if such an event does occur, the second main element of the protocol can come into play. When a loss occurs as a result of action taken in conformity with the protocol, a claim can be made against the solicitor's errors and omissions coverage; moreover, the normal deductibles are waived in such cases.

This is *not* bar-affiliated title insurance, the approach adopted by the Law Society in Ontario. The insured in Alberta under the protocol is the solicitor. The Torrens protocol seeks to reduce costs of lawyer-driven services, and to provide clients with a greater source of recovery when errors and omissions arise. Moreover, unlike title insurance, there is no duty to defend under the protocol.

It is difficult to measure the relative success of these different tacks. And so far the protocol has not been widely used in Edmonton or Calgary, though it has found some favour in the smaller communities in the province. One development may prove to be telling. Some of the major companies are already doing business in the West, though far less than in Ontario. Now TitlePlus, bolstered by its successes in Ontario, has branched out to other regions of the country. The logical starting point for this roll-out was Atlantic Canada; the four Atlantic provinces have deed recording systems. In February, 2003, TitlePlus announced its western initiative. Coverage is now available in Manitoba and Alberta. TitlePlus believes that even in the face of the Western Torrens Protocol, that there is a viable market in Western Canada. . . .

The growth of title insurance in Canada has been swift. By the end of 1997, title insurance was not yet a major factor in real estate transactions. That is no longer the case. In 2001, First Canadian Title, which holds the largest market share, issued 260,000 polices, a 46% increase over the previous year. Likewise, TitlePlus enjoyed a 50% increase in policy underwriting in 2000; its sales grew by as much again in 2001. The most recent estimates suggest that more than 50% of residential real estate purchases, and 80% to 90% of refinancing arrangements in Ontario, now involve the use of title insurance.

As with Torrens, these developments may not have the calamitous impact on the profession that some lawyers foresee. Patricia Wilson has recently described the relationship between legal practice and title insurance as being symbiotic. She notes that in the United States attorneys continue to serve in any number of capacities in the title insurance business, including as:

> (1) title insurance agent, where the attorney's role is like that of any other title insurance agent with respect to issuing policies in the name of the insurer, consistent with the underwriting policies of the insurer;
>
> (2) examining counsel, where the lawyer has various responsibilities related to writing the title policy, including examining the title, attending the closing, and remitting the title insurance premium;
>
> (3) attorney/agent, wherein the lawyer has a dual capacity as both the legal representative of a party to the transaction — either the buyer, the seller or the lender — and also represents the title insurer as its agent;
>
> (4) abstract company owner, through which title searching services are provided and through which the attorney may also serve as an agent for one or more title insurance underwriters;
>
> (5) participant in a bar-related title insurance company, *i.e.*, a title insurance company, sometimes referred to as a "bar fund," that provides a means of ownership of a title insurance company by the attorneys who are members or shareholders of the company;
>
> (6) outside counsel, representing either or both the insured and the insurer in suits involving third parties; and
>
> (7) in-house staff attorney for a title insurer, representing either or both the insured and the insurer in suits involving third parties.

Even so, there seems little doubt that title insurance has reduced the involvement of lawyers in real estate transactions in the United States. In a study published in 1997, Braunstein reported that in only 8 of the 40 responding states was it found to be conventional for lawyers to prepare transactions for closing. In the other 32 states, "the preparation of the closing documentation and the closing itself are handled by the real estate agent, the title insurance company, a corporate closing company, an escrow agency, or some combination of them." He concluded:

> Lawyers have tended to become marginalized in the residential real estate transaction, and it is very unlikely that this tendency will be reversed. The cause of marginalization is not hard to identify. The concept of title and the process by which the real estate purchaser is assured good title is the most difficult part of the residential conveyance. Once title insurance companies took over this part of the residential real estate transaction, it was inevitable that the simpler and more routine parts of the transaction would be handled by others as well. If a lawyer was not needed for the hard part, it would not take the buyers and sellers of real property long to realize that the lawyer was probably not needed for the easier parts of the transaction either.

Title insurance will probably thrive and the legal profession will likely adjust to the new order, somehow. Of course, none of this means that title insurance is actually worthwhile. In the end, that is largely a question of cost-benefit, for it is one thing to identify the theoretical place of insurance within, say, a Torrens system, but it is another to know how often it comes to the aid of the insured. Here the American experience is not fully helpful because in many states the recording systems are poorly maintained. The data from Canada, however, might shed light on the issue of the efficacy of title insurance.

First Canadian Title publishes information on the types of claims that have been successfully made under its policies. In 2001 about $2 million in claims were paid out. The kinds of claims, and the percentage of payout dollars for each type, are as follows:

municipal issues (work orders, building permit violations, and tax arrears)	37%
title/legal description defects	24
fraud/forgery	19
Survey issues	6
Liens and encumbrances	6
Transactional and Conveyancing errors	5
Executions	3

This chart describes the relative frequency of certain payouts, but it does not purport to describe the overall frequency of claims. To gain an understanding of that one must turn to the financial information available on the title insurance industry in Canada.

In 2001, First American received $35.65 million dollars in revenue from premiums. It paid claims and incurred adjustment expenses totalling just under $4.5

million. After taking into account other forms of income (mainly investment) and expenses (mainly salaries and physical plant), its net income was just under $2.5 million. As at the end of the third quarter of 2002, the figures were already comparable: premiums written — $38.64; net claims and adjustment expenses — $3.67 million; net income — $2.425 million. Some underwriters have also been quite successful. Stewart Title earned a net income of nearly $3.7 million in 2001, and $3.3 million in the first three-quarters of 2002. (However, Chicago Title has not fared well. In 2001, it reported a net loss of over $300,000. Its net income by the third quarter of 2002 was a very modest $67,000.)

Consider now the First American/Canadian figures within the context of other insurance industry benchmarks. In 2001, the ratio of premiums acquired to net claims and adjustment expenses was, to be precise, $35,632,000:$4,456,000, or approximately 8 to1. This means that for every $8 received in premiums, $1 is paid out in claims and adjustment expenses. Put another way, for every $1 received, 12.5 cents is paid out. In Alberta, in 2000, First American collected $2,242,000 in premiums, and paid out $146,000 in claims and expenses. Therefore, for every $1 received, only 6.5 cents were expended on claims and related expenses.

Compare these figures with the overall foreign property and casualty insurance data reported for 2001. Total underwriting revenue was just above $5 billion; net claims and adjustment expenses were $4.4 billion. The premium/claim ratio was therefore about 1.14 to 1 (or a cost of 88 cents on the dollar). These firms tend to have significant investment income ($778 million in 2001), but nevertheless the net income for the ENTIRE property and casualty foreign insurance sector in Canada in 2001 was just slightly more than $18.5 million. And this figure includes the net incomes of the title insurance companies.

One might be tempted to conclude that because the risks protected by title insurance rarely materialize, seeking coverage is a waste of money. However, the question is not whether title insurance is a more or less protective measure when compared to others kinds of insurance, but rather whether the benefits conferred are better and more economical than the *conveyancing* alternatives. And here the contest is not between, say, Torrens and title insurance; rather, it is between title insurance and the other means available for closing off the risks that remain within any given registration or recording regime. This is a harder computation to make, and it awaits further study. However, one thing seems clear: Whatever its intrinsic merit, the emergence of title insurance has rocked the conventions of real estate practice in Canada. The presence of this alternative mode of risk prevention has affected the costs and styles of conveyancing dramatically.

REVIEW QUESTIONS

1. Jeremy Watson and his wife, Miriam Cole, owned a house as joint tenants. The couple had recently separated. Miriam went to live with her mother in Wisconsin to think about her future. She did not want a divorce. She was planning to spend the spring and summer at the family cottage to think things over.

While Miriam was away, John decided that the marriage was finished. He had been having an affair for the past twelve months with Meg Vailler, with whom he planned to live. However, he was deeply in debt.

Watson was angling to arrange a loan from Robin Edelstein, a business acquaintance, whom Watson had once described as having "more money than brains". Although he wanted to borrow money from Edelstein, all of his properties were already subject to substantial mortgages. The house was subject to a large mortgage in favour of his brother-in-law, Wendel Cole. Watson decided to forge a discharge of mortgage form for the Wendel Cole mortgage which Watson presented for registration. The mortgage was discharged off the title.

A few weeks later, Watson went to see Edelstein, and did arrange for a mortgage. Watson claimed that the transaction was a matter of some urgency. No formal mortgage was drawn up. Instead, Edelstein filed a caveat (or caution) in which he claimed "a legal mortgage in the amount of $140,000". The loan was, in fact, for $40,000; the wrong amount had been inadvertently typed in.

Watson soon realized that he needed more money. So, several days later, Watson entered into an agreement to sell the house at a price below market value. He tendered an agreement for sale purporting to have his wife's signature. The property was purchased by Paul Durack. It was Durack's intention that the property be a gift to his wife, Susan Durack. "I will pay everything", Durack said. The Edelstein mortgage was to be assumed.

When the Duracks reviewed the relevant transfer documents, they both thought it strange that Miriam's signature on the agreement was dated March 4th, and was purportedly signed locally. They had heard through the grapevine that Miriam Cole was in Wisconsin. Nevertheless, they said nothing. Title was taken in the name of Susan Durack, and a certificate of title was issued in the name of Susan Durack.

Watson was not finished. He held title to two investment properties. One had been purchased in his name, although all of the money had been provided by his wife. It was in Jeremy's name purely as a matter of convenience, and it was their understanding that he was merely holding title in trust for her. That property was sold to Amster Properties Ltd. Watson also transferred a small investment property on Pinto St. into the name of his nephew, Eric Sandusky. No money changed hands at the time of that transfer.

Only now have these events come to light. Miriam Cole's signature had been forged throughout. Wendel Cole has now placed a caveat on the property to protect the mortgage that was purportedly discharged by Watson. Sandusky, who has made two payments on a mortgage on the Pinto St. property, has now decided not to make any further payments until his rights are determined. The validity of the Edelstein caveat has been called into question. Everything is in turmoil, but Watson is nowhere to be found. He and Vailler have absconded.

Using the law of your home jurisdiction, who is entitled to what?

2. Assess the four main approaches discussed in this chapter: (i) common law/ equitable priority rules; (ii) deeds registrations; (iii) title registration; and (iv) title insurance, with reference to their ability to advance the fundamental goals and values of Canadian property law, as discussed throughout this casebook. What empirical information would assist in such an assessment?

INDEX

- A -

- B -

- C -

- E -

- F -

- G -

- H -

- I -

- J -

- K -

- L -

- M -

- N -

- O -

- P -

- Q -

- R -

- S -

- T -

- U -

- V -

- W -

- X, Y, Z -